DRAMA
CRITICISM

Guide to Gale Literary Criticism Series

For criticism on	Consult these Gale series
Authors now living or who died after December 31, 1999	*CONTEMPORARY LITERARY CRITICISM (CLC)*
Authors who died between 1900 and 1999	*TWENTIETH-CENTURY LITERARY CRITICISM (TCLC)*
Authors who died between 1800 and 1899	*NINETEENTH-CENTURY LITERATURE CRITICISM (NCLC)*
Authors who died between 1400 and 1799	*LITERATURE CRITICISM FROM 1400 TO 1800 (LC)* *SHAKESPEAREAN CRITICISM (SC)*
Authors who died before 1400	*CLASSICAL AND MEDIEVAL LITERATURE CRITICISM (CMLC)*
Authors of books for children and young adults	*CHILDREN'S LITERATURE REVIEW (CLR)*
Dramatists	*DRAMA CRITICISM (DC)*
Poets	*POETRY CRITICISM (PC)*
Short story writers	*SHORT STORY CRITICISM (SSC)*
Black writers of the past two hundred years	*BLACK LITERATURE CRITICISM (BLC)* *BLACK LITERATURE CRITICISM SUPPLEMENT (BLCS)*
Hispanic writers of the late nineteenth and twentieth centuries	*HISPANIC LITERATURE CRITICISM (HLC)* *HISPANIC LITERATURE CRITICISM SUPPLEMENT (HLCS)*
Native North American writers and orators of the eighteenth, nineteenth, and twentieth centuries	*NATIVE NORTH AMERICAN LITERATURE (NNAL)*
Major authors from the Renaissance to the present	*WORLD LITERATURE CRITICISM, 1500 TO THE PRESENT (WLC)* *WORLD LITERATURE CRITICISM SUPPLEMENT (WLCS)*

ISSN 1056-4349

DRAMA
CRITICISM

Criticism of the Most Significant and Widely Studied
Dramatic Works from All the World's Literatures

VOLUME 18

Janet Witalec
Project Editor

GALE®

THOMSON
™
GALE

Detroit • New York • San Diego • San Francisco • Cleveland • New Haven, Conn. • Waterville, Maine • London • Munich

THOMSON ™
GALE

Drama Criticism, Vol. 18

Project Editor
Janet Witalec

Editorial
Scott Darga, Kathy D. Darrow, Julie Keppen, Ellen McGeagh

Research
Nicodemus Ford, Sarah Genik, Tamara C. Nott, Tracie A. Richardson

Permissions
Lori Hines

Imaging and Multimedia
Lezlie Light, Kelly A. Quin, Luke Rademacher

Product Design
Michael Logusz

Composition and Electronic Capture
Carolyn Roney

Manufacturing
Stacy L. Melson

LIBRARY OF CONGRESS CATALOG CARD NUMBER 76-46132

ISBN 0-7876-5947-9
ISSN 1056-4349

Printed in the United States of America
10 9 8 7 6 5 4 3 2 1

Contents

Preface vii

Acknowledgments xi

Preface

*D*rama Criticism (DC) is principally intended for beginning students of literature and theater as well as the average playgoer. The series is therefore designed to introduce readers to the most frequently studied playwrights of all time periods and nationalities and to present discerning commentary on dramatic works of enduring interest. Furthermore, DC seeks to acquaint the reader with the uses and functions of criticism itself. Selected from a diverse body of commentary, the essays in DC offer insights into the authors and their works but do not require that the reader possess a wide background in literary studies. Where appropriate, reviews of important productions of the plays discussed are also included to give students a heightened awareness of drama as a dynamic art form, one that many claim is fully realized only in performance.

DC was created in response to suggestions by the staffs of high school, college, and public libraries. These librarians observed a need for a series that assembles critical commentary on the world's most renowned dramatists in the same manner as Gale's *Short Story Criticism* (SSC) and *Poetry Criticism* (PC), which present material on writers of short fiction and poetry. Although playwrights are covered in such Gale literary criticism series as *Contemporary Literary Criticism* (CLC), *Twentieth-Century Literary Criticism* (TCLC), *Nineteenth-Century Literature Criticism* (NCLC), *Literature Criticism from 1400 to 1800* (LC), and *Classical and Medieval Literature Criticism* (CMLC), DC directs more concentrated attention on individual dramatists than is possible in the broader, survey-oriented entries in these Gale series. Commentary on the works of William Shakespeare may be found in *Shakespearean Criticism* (SC).

Scope of the Series

By collecting and organizing commentary on dramatists, DC assists students in their efforts to gain insight into literature, achieve better understanding of the texts, and formulate ideas for papers and assignments. A variety of interpretations and assessments is offered, allowing students to pursue their own interests and promoting awareness that literature is dynamic and responsive to many different opinions.

Approximately five to ten authors are included in each volume, and each entry presents a historical survey of the critical response to that playwright's work. The length of an entry is intended to reflect the amount of critical attention the author has received from critics writing in English and from foreign critics in translation. Every attempt has been made to identify and include the most significant essays on each author's work. In order to provide these important critical pieces, the editors sometimes reprint essays that have appeared elsewhere in Gale's literary criticism series. Such duplication, however, never exceeds twenty percent of a DC volume.

Organization of the Book

A DC entry consists of the following elements:

- The **Author Heading** consists of the playwright's most commonly used name, followed by birth and death dates. If an author consistently wrote under a pseudonym, the pseudonym is listed in the author heading and the real name given in parentheses on the first line of the introduction. Also located at the beginning of the introduction are any name variations under which the dramatist wrote, including transliterated forms of the names of authors whose languages use nonroman alphabets.

- The **Introduction** contains background information that introduces the reader to the author and the critical debates surrounding his or her work.

- A **Portrait of the Author** is included when available.

- The list of **Principal Works** is divided into two sections. The first section contains the author's dramatic pieces and is organized chronologically by date of first performance. If this has not been conclusively determined, the composition or publication date is used. The second section provides information on the author's major works in other genres.

- Essays offering **overviews and general studies of the dramatist's entire literary career** give the student broad perspectives on the writer's artistic development, themes, and concerns that recur in several of his or her works, the author's place in literary history, and other wide-ranging topics.

- **Criticism** of individual plays offers the reader in-depth discussions of a select number of the author's most important works. In some cases, the criticism is divided into two sections, each arranged chronologically. When a significant performance of a play can be identified (typically, the premier of a twentieth-century work), the first section of criticism will feature **production reviews** of this staging. Most entries include sections devoted to **critical commentary** that assesses the literary merit of the selected plays. When necessary, essays are carefully excerpted to focus on the work under consideration; often, however, essays and reviews are reprinted in their entirety. Footnotes are reprinted at the end of each essay or excerpt. In the case of excerpted criticism, only those footnotes that pertain to the excerpted texts are included.

- Critical essays are prefaced by brief **Annotations** explicating each piece.

- A complete **Bibliographic Citation,** designed to help the interested reader locate the original essay or book, precedes each piece of criticism.

- An annotated bibliography of **Further Reading** appears at the end of each entry and suggests resources for additional study. In some cases, significant essays for which the editors could not obtain reprint rights are included here. Boxed material following the further reading list provides references to other biographical and critical sources on the author in series published by Gale.

Cumulative Indexes

A **Cumulative Author Index** lists all of the authors that appear in a wide variety of reference sources published by the Gale Group, including *DC*. A complete list of these sources is found facing the first page of the Author Index. The index also includes birth and death dates and cross references between pseudonyms and actual names.

A **Cumulative Nationality Index** lists all authors featured in *DC* by nationality, followed by the number of the *DC* volume in which their entry appears.

A **Cumulative Title Index** lists in alphabetical order the individual plays discussed in the criticism contained in *DC*. Each title is followed by the author's last name and corresponding volume and page numbers where commentary on the work is located. English-language translations of original foreign-language titles are cross-referenced to the foreign titles so that all references to discussion of a work are combined in one listing.

Citing *Drama Criticism*

When writing papers, students who quote directly from any volume in *Drama Criticism* may use the following general formats to footnote reprinted criticism. The first example pertains to material drawn from periodicals, the second to materials reprinted from books.

Susan Sontag, "Going to the Theater, Etc.," *Partisan Review* XXXI, no. 3 (Summer 1964), 389-94; excerpted and reprinted in *Drama Criticism,* vol. 1, ed. Lawrence J. Trudeau (Detroit: Gale Research, 1991), 17-20.

Eugene M. Waith, *The Herculean Hero in Marlowe, Chapman, Shakespeare and Dryden* (Chatto & Windus, 1962); excerpted and reprinted in *Drama Criticism,* vol. 1, ed. Lawrence J. Trudeau (Detroit: Gale Research, 1991), 237-47.

Suggestions are Welcome

Readers who wish to suggest new features, topics, or authors to appear in future volumes, or who have other suggestions or comments are cordially invited to call, write, or fax the Project Editor:

Project Editor, Literary Criticism Series
The Gale Group
27500 Drake Road
Farmington Hills, MI 48331-3535
1-800-347-4253 (GALE)
Fax: 248-699-8054

Acknowledgments

The editors wish to thank the copyright holders of the excerpted criticism included in this volume and the permissions managers of many book and magazine publishing companies for assisting us in securing reproduction rights. We are also grateful to the staffs of the Detroit Public Library, the Library of Congress, the University of Detroit Mercy Library, Wayne State University Purdy/Kresge Library Complex, and the University of Michigan Libraries for making their resources available to us. Following is a list of the copyright holders who have granted us permission to reproduce material in this volume of *DC*. Every effort has been made to trace copyright, but if omissions have been made, please let us know.

COPYRIGHTED MATERIAL IN *DC*, VOLUME 18, WAS REPRODUCED FROM THE FOLLOWING PERIODICALS:

The Christian Science Monitor, November 4, 1980. Reproduced by permission.—*The Daily Telegraph,* January 15, 1993; July 8, 1993; June 20, 1994; March 8, 1995; March 2, 2000; November 21, 2001. © Telegraph Group Limited 2002. Reproduced by permission. —*French Studies Bulletin,* v. 41, Winter, 1991-1992. Reproduced by permission.—*Hispanic Review,* v. 41, Spring, 1973. Reproduced by permission. —*Hispanofila,* v. 39, May, 1970. Reproduced by permission.—*Manchester Guardian Weekly,* January 24, 1993 for "Rattigan Triumphant" by Michael Billington. © The Guardian. Reproduced by permission.—*Modern Drama,* v. XX, June, 1977; v. XXII, December, 1979; v. XXIV, March, 1981; v. XXVI, September, 1983; v. 29, June, 1986; v. 29, December, 1986; v. 30, March, 1987; v. XXXIII, September, 1990; v. 15, 1997; v. 40, 1997. Copyright © 1977, 1979, 1981, 1983, 1986, 1987, 1990, 1997, University of Toronto, Graduate Centre for Study of Drama. Reproduced by permission.—*Mosaic: A Journal for the Comparative Study of Literature and Ideas,* v. 4, Winter, 1970. © Mosaic 1970. Acknowledgment of previous publication is herewith made. Reproduced by permission.—*Neophilologus,* v. LXXVII, April, 1994 for "Projections of the Unconscious Self in Buero's Theatre: *El Concierto de San Ovidio, La Fundacion, Dialogo Secreto*" by John P. Gabriel. Reproduced by permission of Kluwer Academic Publishers; v. LXXVII, October, 1993. Reproduced by permission of the author.—*The New Criterion,* v. 19, November, 2000. Reproduced by permission.—*The New York Times,* December 29, 1989; June 17, 2001; October 12, 2001; October 21, 2001; March 15, 2002. Reproduced by permission.—*Renascence: Essays on Values in Literature,* v. 35, Spring, 1983. Reproduced by permission.—*Revista Canadiense de Estudios Hispanicos,* v. XVII, Spring, 1994. Reproduced by permission.—*Revista de Estudios Hispanicos,* v. II, April, 1969; v. VIII, May, 1974; v. XII, May, 1978. Reproduced by permission.—*Revista Hispanica Moderna,* v. XXV, April, 1969. Reproduced by permission.—*Romance Notes,* v. VII, Autumn, 1965; v. XXI, Fall, 1980; v. XXVI, Fall, 1985 v. XXXIV, Winter, 1993. Reproduced by permission.—*Scandinavian Studies,* v. 62, Winter, 1990; v. 65, Fall, 1993; v. 66, Summer, 1994; v. 68, Summer, 1996; v. 71, Fall, 1999. Reproduced by permission.—*South Atlantic Review,* v. 51, May, 1986. Reproduced by permission.—*Sunday Times,* February 15, 1998. © Times Newspapers Limited, 1998. Reproduced by permission.—*Symposium,* v. XX, Summer, 1966; v. XXIX, Spring-Summer, 1975; v. XXXIX, Summer, 1985; v. XL, Summer, 1986. Reproduced by permission.—*Theatre Research International,* v. 18, Supplementary Issue, 1993. Reproduced by permission of Cambridge University Press.—*The Times,* June 29, 1994; March 8, 1995; April 26, 1995; December 3, 1996; June 18, 2001; February 23, 2002. © Times Newspapers Limited, 1994, 1995, 1996, 2001, 2002. Reproduced by permission.

COPYRIGHTED MATERIAL IN *DC*, VOLUME 18, WAS REPRODUCED FROM THE FOLLOWING BOOKS:

—Bark, Richard. From "Strindberg's Dream Play Technique," in *Strindberg's Dramaturgy.* University of Minnesota Press, 1988. Copyright © 1988 by University of Minnesota Press. All rights reserved. Reproduced by permission. —Carlson, Harry G. From "Collecting the Corpse in the Cargo," in *Strindberg and the Poetry of Myth.* University of California Press, 1982. Copyright © 1982 by The Regents of the University of California. All rights reserved. Reproduced by permission.— Carlson, Harry G. From "Easter: Persephone's Return," in *Strindberg and the Poetry of Myth.* University of California Press, 1982. Copyright © 1982 by University of California Press. All rights reserved. Reproduced by permission.—Ekman, Hans-Goran. From "*Abu Casems tofflor*: Strindberg's Worst Play?" in *Strindberg and Genre.* Norvik Press, 1991. Copyright © 1991 by Norvik Press. All rights reserved. Reproduced by permission.—Innes, Christopher. From "Terence Rattigan: The Voice of the 1950s," in *British Theatre in the 1950s.* Sheffield Academic Press, 2000. Copyright © 2000 by Sheffield Academic Press. All rights reserved. Reproduced by permission of The Continuum Publishing Group.—Jacobs, Barry. From "Strindberg's *Advent* and *Brott och brott*: Sagospel and Comedy in a Higher Court," in *Strindberg and Genre.*

Norvik Press, 1991. Copyright © 1991 by Norvik Press. All rights reserved. Reproduced by permission.—Lide, Barbara. From "Perspectives on a Genre: Strindberg's *comédies rosses*," in **Strindberg and Genre.** Norvik Press, 1991. Copyright © 1991 by Norvik Press. All rights reserved. Reproduced by permission.—Rokem, Freddie. From "The Camera and the Aesthetics of Repetition: Strindberg's Use of Space and Scenography in *Miss Julie, A Dream Play,* and *The Ghost Sonata,*" in **Strindberg's Dramaturgy.** University of Minnesota Press, 1988. Copyright © 1988 by University of Minnesota Press. All rights reserved. Reproduced by permission.—Rusinko, Susan. From "Morality Plays for Mid-Century or Man, God, and the Devil," in **Terence Rattigan.** Twayne Publishers, 1983. Copyright © 1983 by Twayne Publishers. All rights reserved. Reproduced by permission.—Walsh, Paul. "Textual Clues to Performance Strategies in *The Pelican,*" in **Stindberg's Dramaturgy.** University of Minnesota Press, 1988. Copyright © 1988 by University of Minnesota Press. All rights reserved. Reproduced by permission.—Wansell, Geoffrey. From "A One-Hit Wonder?" in **Terence Rattigan.** Fourth Estate, 1995. Copyright © 1995 by Geoffrey Wansell. All rights reserved. Reproduced by permission of HarperCollins Publishers Ltd.—Wirmark, Margareta. From "Strindberg's History Plays: Some Reflections," in **Strindberg and Genre.** Norvik Press, 1991. Copyright © 1991 by Norvik Press. All rights reserved. Reproduced by permission.

PHOTOGRAPHS APPEARING IN *DC,* VOLUME 18, WERE RECEIVED FROM THE FOLLOWING SOURCES:

Buero Vallejo, Madrid, Spain, 1986, photograph. AP/Wide World Photos. Reproduced by permission.— Rattigan, Sir Terence, 1971, photograph. AP/Wide World Photos. Reproduced by permission.—Strindberg, August, photograph. The Bettmann Archive. Reproduced by permission.

Literary Criticism Series Advisory Board

The members of the Gale Group Literary Criticism Series Advisory Board—reference librarians and subject specialists from public, academic, and school library systems—represent a cross-section of our customer base and offer a variety of informed perspectives on both the presentation and content of our literature criticism products. Advisory board members assess and define such quality issues as the relevance, currency, and usefulness of the author coverage, critical content, and literary topics included in our series; evaluate the layout, presentation, and general quality of our printed volumes; provide feedback on the criteria used for selecting authors and topics covered in our series; provide suggestions for potential enhancements to our series; identify any gaps in our coverage of authors or literary topics, recommending authors or topics for inclusion; analyze the appropriateness of our content and presentation for various user audiences, such as high school students, undergraduates, graduate students, librarians, and educators; and offer feedback on any proposed changes/enhancements to our series. We wish to thank the following advisors for their advice throughout the year.

Antonio Buero Vallejo
1916-2000

Spanish playwright, poet, essayist, and translator.

INTRODUCTION

One of Spain's leading dramatists, Buero Vallejo has contributed significantly to the revitalization of postwar Spanish theater. Eschewing the frivolous plots and comforting sentimentality of much early twentieth-century Spanish drama, Buero Vallejo wrote deeply serious, moralistic plays that frequently depicted characters consumed by despair and frustration. He is commonly regarded as a tragedian and advanced a conception of drama characterized by the redeeming presence of hope. Buero Vallejo suggested that by inviting people to confront reality without self-deception, the writer of tragedies raises issues fundamental to human existence and the improvement of society.

BIOGRAPHICAL INFORMATION

Buero Vallejo was born in Guadalajara, Spain, in 1916 to Francisco Buero, a military engineer, and Cruz Vallejo. From 1934 to 1936 he studied painting at the San Fernando School of Fine Arts in Madrid. Buero Vallejo was a medical assistant in the Loyalist army during the Spanish Civil War; for his involvement in the war he was imprisoned for six years by the regime of Generalissimo Francisco Franco. When he was released from prison in 1949, Buero Vallejo introduced his play *Historia de una escalera,* which presents a brutal picture of postwar Spain. The play won the Premio Lope de Vega prize and gained Buero Vallejo a position of prominence in Spanish drama. Many artists chose to flee the repressive censorship of Franco's government, but Buero Vallejo decided to stay and vent his frustrations in thinly veiled metaphorical and symbolic dramas criticizing government policies. In 1972 he was elected to the Real Academia Española. He was awarded both the Medalla de Oro al Merite en las Bellas Artes and the Medalla de Oro de la Sociedad General de Autores de España in 1994. He died on April 29, 2000, in Madrid, Spain.

MAJOR WORKS

In his plays, Buero Vallejo presents many of the problems of Francoist and post-Francoist Spain, but the dramas always suggest the hope that problems can be overcome.

Buero Vallejo uses a series of author surrogates to infuse his political ideology into his work. He commonly creates sensory experiences through music, art, and set design, termed "immersion effects" by critics, to cause the audience to feel the same sensations as the protagonist and thereby identify more closely with him. In *En la ardiente oscuridad* (1950; *In The Burning Darkness*) Buero Vallejo uses the mental and physical impairment of his protagonist to symbolize the condition of Spanish society. The play is about a conflict between two students at a blind school, one of whom refuses to accept his blindness. One of Buero Vallejo's stage effects in this play is the darkening of the theater to simulate for the audience the experience of blindness. The play is seen as a metaphor for the Spanish people's passive acceptance of totalitarian rule. *La doble historia del doctor Valmy* (1968) covers the themes of torture, guilt, cowardice, isolation, and loss of communication. While the drama is an indictment of police torture, it unfolds from the point of view of a security police officer in the fictional nation of Surelia. *El sueño de la razón* (1970; *The Sleep of Reason*) is based upon Spanish artist Francisco de Goya's resistance to the tyranny of King Ferdinand VII. To dramatize Goya's deafness, Buero Vallejo's characters engage in incoherent dialogue and use sign language or notes to communicate with the protagonist. He projects Goya's infamous Black Paintings at the rear of the stage to reflect the cruelty and terror Goya experienced at this time. In *La fundación* (1974; *The Foundation*), Buero Vallejo's first drama about life in Spain as the Francoist regime is ending, he proposes that to achieve true freedom one must pass through a series of prisons, and that each small step toward freedom is important. In this work he employs an immersion effect that causes the audience to share the main character's hallucinations. *Jueces en la noche* (1979; *Judges in the Night*), *Caimán* (1981), and *Diálogo secreto* (1984) all delve into the problems of building a democracy after years of authoritarian rule.

CRITICAL RECEPTION

Reviewers note Buero Vallejo's innovative dramatic techniques, including his use of immersion effects to fully involve the audience's senses and create a psychological bond with the protagonist. Some reviewers complain that, later in Buero Vallejo's career, his symbolism and imagery became overwhelming and too disparate. A few commentators, however, hold that his imagery is well-researched and demonstrates a calculated use of certain songs and artwork. Critical discussion of Buero Vallejo's work often centers on his relationship with censorship in Francoist Spain rather than his dramatic technique. Some critics disagree with his decision to continue to write under the restraints of censorship, but many praise what they consider his courageous attempt to voice his criticism of the political and social climate. In retrospect, many reviewers are surprised that Buero Vallejo was able to slip as much past the censors as he did. Many commentators praise Buero Vallejo for his insistence on facing the reality of political and social tragedies that many prefer to ignore. Reviewers generally agree that the overwhelming concern of Buero Vallejo's work is to inspire action to fight against political and social ills.

PRINCIPAL WORKS

Plays

Historia de una escalera 1949

Las palabras en la arena 1949

En la ardiente oscuridad [*In the Burning Darkness*] 1950

La señal que se espera 1952

La tejedora de sueños [*The Dreamweaver*] 1952

Casi un cuento de hadas: Una glosa de Perrault 1953

Madrugada 1953

Aventura en lo gris 1954

Irene o el tesoro 1954

El terror inmovil: Fragmentos de una tragedia irrepresentable 1954

Hoy es fiesta 1956

Las cartas boca abajo 1957

Un soñador para un pueblo [*A Dreamer for the People*] 1958

Teatro. 2 vols. 1959-1962

Las meninas: Fantasia velazquena en dos partes [*Las meninas: A Fantasy*] 1960

El concierto de San Ovidio [*The Concert of Saint Ovide*] 1962

Buero Vallejo: Antologia teatral 1966

Teatro selecto 1966

El tragaluz [*The Basement Window*] 1967

La doble historia del doctor Valmy 1968

El sueño de la razón [*The Sleep of Reason*] 1970

Llegada de los dioses 1971

La fundación [*The Foundation*] 1974

La detonación [*The Shot*] 1977

Jueces en la noche [*Judges in the Night*] 1979

Caimán 1981

Diálogo secreto 1984

Lázaro en la laberinto [*Lazarus in the Labyrinth*] 1986

Música cerana [*The Music Window*] 1989

Obra completa. 2 vols. 1994

Las trampas del azar 1994

GENERAL COMMENTARY

Robert E. Lott (essay date autumn 1965)

SOURCE: Lott, Robert E. "Scandinavian Reminiscences in Antonio Buero Vallejo's Theater." *Romance Notes* VII, no. 1 (autumn 1965): 113-16.

[*In the following essay, Lott finds similarities between Buero Vallejo's and Henrik Ibsen's treatment of family tension and bickering in their work.*]

When Antonio Buero Vallejo's ***Las cartas boca abajo*** was first performed in Madrid in 1957, Felipe Bernardos correctly pointed out that the most obvious precedent for the role of Anita, the supposedly mute sister of Adela, was Miss Y (Amelie) of Strindberg's *The Stronger.*[1] Both Miss Y and Anita are silent throughout, relying solely on action and gesture, and at dramatic moments both seem to be on the verge of breaking their silence. Miss Y chooses not to talk, and thus conceals her spitefulness and viciousness behind the appearance of strength and disdain. Anita's case is ambiguous: one is never certain that she is truly mute, though it does become clear that she wishes her sister ill.[2]

It is no doubt true that reminiscences of Strindberg are seen here and in Buero Vallejo's frequent treatment of family bickerings and hatred.[3] Buero, like Lorca, has been able to adapt Strindberg's "war between the sexes" to Spanish themes and situations. The struggle in *The Father* between the Captain and his wife Laura, and their disagreement about keeping their daughter Bertha at home have their parallels in *Las cartas boca abajo*. Also there is resemblance between the ending of *The Father* and the removal of Dimas to an insane asylum in Buero's *Irene, o el tesoro*. One might also compare the dream sequences in *The Dream Play* and in the Spaniard's *Aventura en lo gris*.

However, Buero's dramaturgy is particularly reminiscent of Ibsen's.[4] Both often use a rebellious, visionary protagonist struggling through the obstacles imposed by society and self toward understanding and the hope of reconciliation. The vehicle for each is usually a carefully constructed play, with a slow-moving symbolic action and an artistic utilization of the dramatic values inherent in every scene, every speech, every gesture. In Ibsen, as well as in Strindberg (not to mention O'Neill, Williams, and Miller), Buero found ample treatment of the warring family and of the failure as protagonist. And his occasional use of symbolism and fantasy are more in keeping with Ibsen's.

Besides general similarities of theme and tone between the two writers, several specific affinities are recognizable, though frequently with shifts in meaning. In Ibsen's *Rosmersholm* suicide is a test of faith and love. In Buero's *La señal que se espera* a husband's weak faith and understanding are put to the test by an unsuccessful suicide attempt. In both *The Lady from the Sea* and *Irene, o el tesoro* the woman protagonist living in an unsatisfactory home environment is forced to make a momentous decision in the face of impending insanity. In *The Master Builder* as in *Irene, o el tesoro,* a final death-fall can be interpreted with equal validity as a victory in defeat. The end of *Irene . . .* is meant to suggest simultaneously her suicide and her supernatural ascent to Heaven. Solness of *The Master Builder* held himself morally responsible (because of his desire to use a fire as the first step up the ladder of success) for the death of his twin babies, even though the fire was not caused by the cracked chimney he refrained from repairing. Silverio of *Hoy es fiesta* feels responsible because he secretly wished the death of his wife's illegitimate daughter. In both these plays and *Irene . . .* dead children weigh heavily on the characters. There is considerable ambiguity about the insanity and suicide of Beata in *Rosmersholm* and of Irene in Buero's play. Rebec-

ca's unholy scheming and concealment of the past in *Rosmersholm* are echoed in Adela of *Las cartas boca abajo.* Both women's schemes backfire.

The closest parallel is probably seen between *Las cartas boca abajo* and Ibsen's *John Gabriel Borkman.*[5] In *Las cartas . . .* two sisters, Anita and Adela, had first been rivals for their father's preference when their mother died, then for the love of Ferrer, who has since become a famous scholar, and now for the affection of Adela's and Juan's grown son. Adela had stolen Anita's sweetheart, Ferrer, and then had married Juan to spite Ferrer. This shock apparently brought on Anita's muteness. Adela's marriage has turned sour, and she actually conspires to have her husband, a would-be professor, fail in his efforts to win a professorship. Anita symbolically gives the sweater she had been knitting not to the son, but to the boy's father, thus again becoming a rival of her sister. At the end Juan wins his son over to his side and Adela loses her last illusions.

Though the two plays are quite different in many respects, the basic situation in *John Gabriel Borkman* is rather similar to that of *Las cartas . . .* Ella believed that her twin sister Gunhild had robbed her of Borkman, though he finally discloses that he had married Gunhild for her money. During the haughty swindler's long imprisonment and subsequent voluntary confinement, Ella has lived on her hatred of Gunhild and her desire to seek revenge by attaining the love of Borkman's and Gunhild's son Erhard. Borkman and Gunhild have lived in constant misunderstanding and hate, completely isolated from each other in the same house. The previous struggle over Borkman has continued unabated for the love of the selfish, unworthy son. In both works the characters' secret, selfish, and malevolent motives—the "cards turned face down," to use Buero's metaphor—have created a paralyzing atmosphere of malicious rancor. As the motives are gradually revealed the air is cleared and there is hope for love and understanding, but things have progressed too far to save Borkman, who dies, and Adela, who will be left to suffer her anguish in a solitude not unlike that endured by Borkman.

A close analysis of all the plays would reveal other similarities between Buero Vallejo and Ibsen, but these are the main ones. The most important thing is that the Spanish playwright has so successfully applied the Norwegian's symbolic-realistic dramatic method to the socio-moral problems of contemporary Spain.

Notes

1. "Sin remontarnos al *Hamlet,* sin recordar las estatuas mortuorias del *Convidado de piedra, Don Juan,* etc., quizá sea la amiga silenciosa que Strindberg colocó de oyente en *La más fuerte,* junto con el criado viejo de *El malentendido,* de Camus, los casos más característicos de personajes acusadores del teatro moderno." Quoted from *Teatro español 1957-1958,* ed. F. C. Sainz de Robles (Madrid, 1959), p. 8.

2. Cf. Pilar's equally ambiguous and crucial deafness in *Hoy es fiesta.*

3. Readers unfamiliar with Buero Vallejo will find additional information and bibliography in my article, "Functional Flexibility and Ambiguity in Buero Vallejo's Plays," *Symposium* (Summer, 1966).

4. That is, among the Scandinavians. I hope to show in a future study Buero's even closer affinities with Arthur Miller.

5. In both *John Gabriel Borkman* and Buero's *Madrugada* chronological and stage time are perfectly synchronized.

Robert E. Lott (essay date summer 1966)

SOURCE: Lott, Robert E. "Functional Flexibility and Ambiguity in Buero Vallejo's Plays." *Symposium* XX, no. 2 (summer 1966): 150-62.

[*In the following essay, Lott defines Buero Vallejo's term "functional flexibility" in relation to his work and attempts to classify the playwright's dramatic oeuvre.*]

Antonio Buero Vallejo has rightly decried attempts to classify his plays according to the direct and realistic method represented by *Historia de una escalera* and, presumably, *Hoy es fiesta,* or the speculative, symbolic, or imaginative manner of most of his other works.[1] He says that *En la ardiente oscuridad* is different from both tendencies, and that *Hoy es fiesta* is as close to it as to *Historia de una escalera,* despite the similarity of settings in these two plays. Yet, useful distinctions and parallels can be made, but only with full awareness of the complex interrelations and multiple functions of his diverse works, concepts, and characters. A serious classification should consider all fourteen of his plays, explain the titles and subtitles, include his own perceptive comments, and analyze his concept of tragedy. In this paper I shall treat briefly several of these matters, all of which deserve thorough study.

Buero Vallejo uses the term "flexibilización funcional" to cover the multiple and tragic aspects of victory and defeat in *La tejedora de sueños.*[2] These aspects, though only one manifestation of his very appropriately named "functional flexibility," also appear in other plays, as we shall see. *La tejedora de sueños* is an original treatment of the Penelope myth. In it the publicly triumphant Ulysses suffers the loss of Penelope's love and the destruction of normal family relations and his self-esteem. Penelope loses the idealistic Anfino as a possible husband, but is consoled by the idea that she will be a youthful, loved image of goodness and beauty, locked forever in his noble soul. This is more important to her than the false public opinion of her prudence and faithfulness which Ulysses will propagate.

She is flattered that because of her the suitors have waged a "little Trojan War" and have died. Rising above this meaner side of her nature, she applies the hollow words of the chorus to drive home the moral of the play and to express her greatest victory: the firm belief in future, better men, like the pre-Christian Anfino, who will neither be cold, crafty "reasoners" like Ulysses nor go away to needless wars, abandoning their homes and wives and thus ultimately causing the kind of crimes which befell Agamemnon and Clytemnestra.

Buero poses unanswered questions about the events and characters, especially Penelope. Is her vanity a form of tragic pride which leads to rebelliousness and errors in judgment and yet, through suffering, to unique insight into the condition of man and of the cosmos? Is her suffering just or unjust? Or does she fall short of truly tragic proportions because of her pettiness and the lateness of both her decision to bear her burden of private grief and her awareness of being a prototype of woman's suffering? As in all tragedy, the answers, however uncertain, must be searched for in the work itself. But Buero is not simply relativistic, for he definitely prefers Penelope's victories, even while recognizing her defects and Ulysses' understandable concern.

In *En la ardiente oscuridad* the concepts of victory and defeat vary, and not merely according to the literal and symbolic meanings, although in Buero these two meanings nearly always form part of the intricacy of functions and interpretations.[3] The arrival of Ignacio at a school for the blind and his bitter, questioning attitudes shock the students out of their delusions of normalcy. Now cognizant of shadows and darkness, they join his search for acceptance of their sad plight and for the light of understanding. His positivistic rival, Carlos, kills him, apparently winning the struggle. But when the body is brought into the room, Carlos sees how short-lived Ignacio's influence was and realizes in his irremediable loneliness how much like Ignacio he really is. He will continue the prophetic, visionary work of Ignacio, who is victorious in death.

As one commentator says of this very profound play, in my opinion the best Spanish tragedy since Lorca:

> *En la ardiente oscuridad* is symbolic of human nature. Human beings long continually to reach out, to see beyond the limits which their very physical nature and their society impose on them. The symbol of blindness represents the obscurity which surrounds man, his uncertainty, his continual fear of the unknown. Ignacio, the proud rebel, symbolizes the dreamer of things unknown, the iconoclast who rejects and yet longs passionately for something beyond his possession, who cannot be content existing with blindness in his heart.[4]

Neither a saint nor martyr nor Messiah, Ignacio is an imperfect human being, sometimes needlessly cruel to others.[5] His higher ideals and metaphysical aspirations unfold gradually and blend with his human desires for love, understanding, and companionship, in spite of his attempt to repress them. His seemingly destructive effect would eventually be constructive, since the blind students would probably come to reject the institution's superficial optimism and therapeutic pragmatism, and struggle for happiness within their limitations.[6] Buero tells us that such a change would be significant but not definitive. After Carlos' work is accomplished, another Ignacio will appear; then perhaps the first Ignacio's vague dream of some remedy for their blindness could become a reality. Perhaps, too, as Ignacio suggests, death is the sole remedy and only death brings true vision.

The central meaning of **Hoy es fiesta** must be sought among the complexities of hope and despair, guilt and forgiveness, and lack of communication, especially in their relations to Silverio's quandary. On a paradoxical feast day the bickering inhabitants of a poor apartment building learn that, instead of winning considerable sums of money, they have been duped into buying from Doña Balbina the previous week's worthless lottery tickets. Their anger soon turns to violence. Against this background Silverio struggles to surmount his ingrained egoism and cowardice in order to confess his secret guilt to his deaf, ailing wife Pilar. He holds himself responsible for the death of her child, the fruit of a soldier's brutal attack on Pilar before their marriage.[7] Silverio cannot help others until he overcomes his weaknesses, first by an act of bravery, and then by his altruistic assumption of leadership to hold off the vengeful mob. He achieves atonement by saving Daniela, Balbina's daughter, and with his recently acquired courage and moral strength plans to confess in writing to Pilar. The supreme irony of the play, one which gives it an open ending full of tragic ambiguities, is that Pilar dies before Silverio makes his confession. But the words of the fortuneteller point beyond their superficial banality and irony to a true spiritual message: "Hay que esperar . . . Esperar siempre . . . La esperana nunca termina . . . La esperanza es infinita. . . ."[8]

Apparently condemned to eternal suffering without Pilar's pardon, Silverio may still hope for it to be disclosed in some way. Or a closer analysis of the day's events may persuade him that it was unnecessary or, as is hinted, that she already knew of his guilt and had tacitly forgiven him. As Silverio had assured Daniela, "Obras son amores," and he has discovered through compassion and altruism strange, new feelings of strength, peace, and oneness with his fellow creatures. Buero accepts neither hope nor despair as the unique meaning of the dénouement, saying that the two concepts complete each other, and adds: "Esto carece de lógica. Pero el arte, y la vida que refleja, están por encima del principio de contradicción. La vida y el arte ofrecen de hecho una simultánea multiplicidad de significados dispares" (page 101). Each spectator may interpret the final words as conveying irony or a profound spiritual truth, or both. The same applies to Silverio:

el autor *no sabe* si le conmueve la esperanza que pueda latir para él en esa invocación final o si le duele desesperadamente el sarcasmo que encierra. Es posible que sienta ambas cosas a un tiempo. La obra se desenvuelve y se cierra en esa viva ambivalencia, para la que sólo cabe una definición unitaria: la interrogante.

(p. 103)

Ambiguities of victory and defeat figure so prominently in the three plays discussed so far because they come the closest to tragedy. Tragic overtones and situations with several possible interpretations of victory and defeat and the concept of victory in defeat are found in other plays too. In **Aventura en lo gris** Silvano overcomes his habitual selfishness and cynicism and becomes the visionary leader of a group of refugees. Between the play's two acts is an "Intermedio," a symbolic, prophetic dream, common to all except the political leader Gólver, too much of an activist to dream. In this quasi-surrealistic dream—characterized by special effects of lighting, music, and costume, stylized dialogue, and panomime—the repressed desires of the characters, their lasciviousness, egoism, and hatred become manifest and unconscious urges and obsession are acted out. Isabel, mother of an infant sired by an enemy soldier, relives the bestial attack and Albo, the supposedly ascetic follower of Gólver's party and protector of Isabel, acts out his ill-controlled desire for her. Gólver's embittered mistress, Ana, is fascinated by Silvano's goodness and ecstatically exclaims: "Gracias, Silvano. ¡Tú me haces soñar la aventura de tus palabras de luz en el gris de mi vida!"[9] Near the end of the dream Isabel is found dead. In the stark reality of dawn Isabel is in fact found strangled. Silvano proves that it could have been done only by Gólver, whom Albo then kills. The refugees, now more humane because of their common dream, escape, leaving the baby with Silvano and Ana. After Ana persuades the enemy soldiers to care for the child, she and Silvano calmly await their execution, having gained a moral victory. The nameless child for whom they sacrifice themselves is the hope for the future.

Silvano's and Ana's joint adventure of Light, achieved by means of charity and abnegation, dispels the depressing gray shadows of human imperfections at the moment the rising sun breaks through the shadows of night. Thus this drama, like the one-act play, **Las palabras en la arena,** aims to be what Buero has called "teatro evangélico."[10] It is especially significant in Buero's dramatic development because its early date shows that the unreal, even fantastic elements seen in later works should not be considered regrettable aberrations from an earlier, superior dramatic method (of social realism), but rather another indication of the author's complexity, dramatic range, and exploratory spirit.

Juan, the weak protagonist of **Las cartas boca abajo,** gains self-esteem and a personal victory, while again failing to win a university chair, partly because of his obsessive envy of Ferrer, a former friend and now famous intellectual, and the stubborn pride which prevents him from asking for two of Ferrer's books which might have enabled him to win the competition. A greater reason is that his shabby home is a nest of envy, frustration, and rancor. His wife Adela had married him only to spite Ferrer, after having maliciously taken Ferrer away from her older sister Anita. The latter act had supposedly caused Anita to become mute. Adela clings to childish illusions of becoming free and happy like the birds she hears singing, and of winning back Ferrer, with the help of her son Juanito. She has insisted on keeping all the "cards face down," and even sent her brother to seek Ferrer's intervention in Juan's behalf. Her wish was to negate Juan's own merits if he won, and to revile him still more if he lost. Juan, however, tricks her into betraying her design by letting her believe that he has won. After turning up his own "card" (the destructive envy of Ferrer for which he has paid the price of failure), Juan also discloses her other "cards" (concealed motives and attitudes), including her unholy reasons for marrying him and the deliberate alienation of his son's love and respect. Juanito overhears his father's insistence on sending him away to school where he will be free from the malignant influence of their home, and realizes his father's merits and his mother's selfish malice. Adela is told that the birds' singing at night actually reflects disillusionment and terror of death. Anita's inexorable silence and hatred are the only answers to her frantic pleas for forgiveness. Adela's pernicious victory has left her in utter desolation and despair, whereas Juan's reactions to his external defeat have ennobled him and earned his son's love and understanding.

The background of the historical drama, *Un soñador para un pueblo,* is this: the reforms of Carlos III's minister, the aging Marqués de Esquilache, lead conservative nobles to instigate a rebellion. At the same time, Esquilache's unhappy family life is brightened only by his virtuous servant, Fernandita. She is persecuted by the brutal coach driver, Bernardo, to whom she is unwillingly attracted. Later Esquilache, virtually imprisoned, is horrified to learn that Fernandita has submitted to Bernardo's attack. The king presents Esquilache the difficult choice of either yielding to the mob's demands, or punishing the rebels, thus risking more bloodshed. Tempted to save his pride and seek revenge, Esquilache decides to sacrifice himself. He will be exiled to his native Italy, but for him the greater loss is that of Fernandita's affection and companionship. In a confrontation with the cynical Marqués de Ensenada, Esquilache concedes that he has only followed Ensenada's earlier work, but replies that he, like Fernandita and unlike Ensenada, is of plebeian origin and believes in the people. Unless a ruler is a dreamer of and for a people, like himself, he can achieve nothing. Esquilache watches Fernandita, in whom he has placed his hopes for the future of the Spanish people, as she definitively rejects Bernardo, the symbol of stupidity and brutality. So notwithstanding his personal defeats, Esquilache gains an intimate victory

through self-denial, Fernandita's victory over her instincts, and the aid of some poor people during a moment of peril. These facts indicate to him the people's basic goodness and eventual acceptance of his and subsequent reforms.

The famous painter Velázquez is the protagonist of *Las Meninas.* He suffers no defeat, but loses his only friend, the beggar Pedro, who had earlier posed for his painting of Aesop. Velázquez' family and associates are led by envy and lack of understanding to have him brought before a hearing of the Inquisition, presided over by King Philip IV and witnessed by the Infanta María Teresa. Velázquez refutes the charge of having violated the law against lasciviousness in his nude Venus and proves that his current painting, "Las Meninas," is not trivial and inappropriate. He is also accused of giving refuge to Pedro, who had committed youthful acts of rebellion because of deplorable conditions. On learning of Pedro's death, Velázquez confesses his own profound rebelliousness and unwillingness to lie. María Teresa calls upon her father to open his eyes to the truth, and to correct the errors and injustices of his regime, beginning with his own moral waywardness. But the tired and ineffectual king absolves Velázquez and punishes no one. Velázquez is pathetically alone in his victory, having lost the opportunity to enjoy Pedro's and María Teresa's understanding friendship, incomprehensible in the corrupt court.

The main significance, however, is found in the central ambiguity of what the painting was about and its relations to Buero's play. Pedro interpreted the work as "un cuadro sereno: pero con toda la tristeza de España dentro. Quien vea a estos seres comprenderá lo irremediablemente condenados al dolor que están. Son fantasmas vivos de personas cuya verdad es la muerte." Velázquez called it "un cuadro de pobres seres salvados por la luz . . . ," and Pedro thus explained Velázquez' almost mystical feeling of peace at seeing and painting the truth: "Sólo quien ve la belleza del mundo puede comprender lo intolerable de su dolor."[11] Velázquez becomes aware that he had symbolized the beautiful but sad truth of Spain in his earlier painting of Pedro. Guillermo Díaz-Plaja has called Pedro "the key figure of the play" and has described the painting "Esopo" as follows: "He appears in the painting erect, enveloped in a large and wrinkled cloak and with a book in his hand. His head is noble, his hair grey with a strange mark of defeated dignity."[12] Pedro, who was born poor and wanted to be a painter in his youth, is Velázquez' alter ego, and what happened to him could have happened to Velázquez. Just as in the painting the ugliness and trivialities of the court are counterbalanced by the radiant beauty of the Infanta Margarita and by the insight into suffering and weakness, so in the play do the strength, compassionate understanding, and virtue of María Teresa, Pedro, and Velázquez stand out like beacons of light amidst the corruption, slander, and intrigue of the court. And in both the painting and the play there is the justifiable glorification of the individual, creative artist and the creative act. Buero, who rightly gave his play the subtitle of "Fantasía ve-lazqueña," has shifted the emphasis from the *meninas* back to the artist at work, as Velázquez perhaps originally intended.[13]

Whether or not Buero was guilty of misinterpreting Velázquez, as Díaz-Plaja has charged, he was artistically correct in making him somewhat visionary and inwardly rebellious. His Velázquez is not the ideal courtier of history, but a "conjunción única de arrogancia y sencillez" (page 18), a compound of noble sentiments (despite his humble origin) and ironic cleverness, a man impassioned by truth. Here and throughout his plays Buero shows his fondness for multi-faceted themes, and protagonists capable of suggesting various interpretations, with apparently contradictory traits joined in a strong character. This is true of Velázquez, Esquilache, Silverio, and others, but Velázquez is morally the greatest and noblest of his creations.

Buero's latest play, *El concierto de San Ovidio,*[14] uses the historically accurate exploitation of blind beggars during the festival of St. Ovidio in 1771 as a vehicle for indignant protest. The only talented musician among them, David, becomes rebellious because their villainous impresario, Valindin, plans to present them as grotesque players. David had hoped to help his companions by teaching them to be real musicians. One day Valindin surprises his mistress Adriana with David's adolescent protégé, Donato, and begins to beat them. When David intervenes, Valindin easily subdues him. David follows Valindin to the closed café-theater, where, in his native element, darkness, he defeats and kills him. Jealous because Adriana loves David, Donato betrays him to the police. Valentín Haüy (a historical figure who worked to help the blind) tells the audience that he suspects that one of those poor men he saw abused in Valindin's café twenty-nine years before is an old blind man (Donato) who always plays a musical piece by Corelli (as David had done). But who, he asks, will assume the responsibility for David's unjust execution? Perhaps "music" is the only possible answer for some questions.

This play takes up some of the author's basic preoccupations and deepens his first treatment of the blind. The contrast between the *videntes* and *invidentes* ("seers" and "non-seers") and the symbolism are obvious: music, illusion, dreams of a better world versus the almost overwhelming odds of despotic exploitation and collective indifference. Not a tragedy in the strictest sense, it has qualities that are tragic and "evangelical"—it is rightly subtitled a parable. It opens with the paternoster (which contrasts ironically with Valindin's evil designs) and David's faith in a better life, and, because of Haüy's charitable commitment, ends on a strong note of hope. The blind characters' personal loss results in a long-range victory for all blind, oppressed people. It would be useful to compare David with Buero's other dreamer-protagonists,

as well as this play with *En la ardiente oscuridad.* Like Ignacio, David is a visionary nonconformist who serves as a catalyst to his lethargic companions, and the David-Donato relationship is similar to that of Ignacio and Carlos. But David's death is more pathetic and more gratuitous than Ignacio's, since Haüy's reforms occurred independently of it.

A second feature of Buero's functional flexibility is ambiguity, which occasionally results in perspectivism and relativism. *La señal que se espera* is a study of the ambiguities of faith and doubt or, as Buero says, of "el problema de las relaciones mágicas, los milagros y los providencialismos. El problema, en suma, de las posibilidades activas de la fe."[15] Enrique has brought Luis, a young composer and former sweetheart of his wife Susana, to spend the summer with them in Galicia in order to clear up his doubts about his wife and Luis. Rejected by Susana for Enrique and his money, Luis had become so disturbed that the forgetting of one of his melodies had caused him to lose his musical talent. He has formed the illogical belief that the wind will play his lost melody on an aeolian harp, as a sign of God's grace. Other characters share this belief, but for each it will be a sign of something different. Susana feels guilty about Luis's infirmity and asserts that her and Enrique's great fault has been the selfishness of not wanting children. One evening Luis's melody is played on the harp, and he recovers his talent. The next morning letters arrive bringing solutions to the others' problems. One informs Enrique that he has lost his fortune. Susana tells him that she played the melody, but that it was not wrong to do so because through faith these people's lives were straightened out. Even for her there is a sign: she is at last going to have a child. The once skeptical Enrique now has faith and believes that the harmony of the spheres is audible in this moment of perfect love and understanding.

For Buero the miracle of this "comedia feérica" consists not of the playing of the melody, which has a natural explanation, nor of the apparent coincidences, which he ascribes to a sort of distributive justice, but of the marvelous moment of harmony that envelops his characters.[16] Enrique, having overcome his selfishness and skepticism, will be happier with Susana in the future. Thus the play's theme, reminiscent of Pirandello, is that faith in some illusion, although it cannot resist rational analysis, can serve powerfully to sustain or transform human beings.

Casi un cuento de hadas is set in the eighteenth century. The older of twin princesses, Leticia, beautiful but stupid, is constantly ridiculed and belittled. An old prediction is fulfilled when the kindness and love of a grotesque suitor, Prince Riquet, awaken her latent intelligence and love. This makes her see him as the handsome, dashing Riquet *el hermoso.* After a three-months' absence, Riquet thinks that Leticia now loves the handsome but vain Prince Armando instead of him because she manages only momentarily to see Riquet *el hermoso*. The two suffering Riquets are left alone and Riquet *el feo* voices the play's central metaphysical question: "¡Oh, Dios, Dios! ¿Cómo somos? ¿Qué somos en realidad? Cada uno nos ve a su manera. ¿Cómo nos ves tú? ¿Cómo me ves? ¿Qué soy para ti?"[17] He despairingly answers his own question: "Me ves como me has hecho. Horrible." And he says to Riquet *el hermoso*: "Despertemos del sueño mentiroso de la belleza . . ." The ugly twin, Laura, scorned by Riquet, provokes a quarrel between the two suitors, but is horrified at the ensuing duel. She now sees Riquet *el hermoso,* as does Armando, who is killed by Riquet. Only love and death work this transformation. Leticia's claim that for her Riquet is handsome again is untrue. Nevertheless, they will marry and try to love each other, while Riquet *el hermoso* waits for them "desde algún mundo sin dolor."

This study of the tragic interrelations of beauty and ugliness, intelligence and stupidity, is based on Perrault's fairy tale, "Riquet," and, to a lesser extent, on nineteenth-century treatments of the same theme. About these Buero has said:

> Pero el tema de *La bella y la bestia* . . . no es . . . el verdadero tema de "Riquet," . . . como tampoco es el tema verdadero de mi comedia. Más que una cuestión sentimental en torno a la belleza y la fealdad, se trata en el fondo de la cuestión general, que engloba a aquélla, de la esencia de la personalidad humana. O, dicho de otro modo: la duda de lo que esencialmente podemos ser, a la vista de lo que circunstancialmente parecemos.[18]

The ambiguity of having two quite different Riquets is heightened by the characterizations of Laura and Armando and especially by the varying, perspectivistic concepts of Leticia. Changes in Leticia depend on others' attitudes toward her. Yet, motivated in part by the sad example of her parents' married life and Armando's disillusioning selfishness and emptiness, she chooses to marry Riquet, the only one capable of appreciating her as a person. But her earlier rejection of ideal beauty for physical beauty has compromised her and Riquet's prospects for happiness and a typical fairy-tale ending. Thus Buero made explicit Perrault's implicit "almost," and thus is explained the note of tragic hope for love within nostalgic yearning for a lost ideal.

While *Madrugada,* a quest for self-esteem, is ambiguous only in that the audience knows more about the situation than most of the characters, *Irene, o el tesoro* is Buero's most "perspectivistic" play. The usurer Dimas tyrannizes his family, especially his orphaned and widowed daughter-in-law, Irene. She is obsessed with the memory of her dead son and confuses him with Juanito (an elf-child visible only to the audience and Irene), who seeks a hidden treasure according to the instructions of a supernatural Voice. Dimas and his family believe that Irene is losing her mind. But a psychiatrist claims that Dimas, who wants

to get rid of Irene and who behaves strangely because of Juanito's tricks, is really the insane person and that Irene will improve if Dimas is put away. This is done. The play ends ambiguously: the Voice tells Juanito to bring Irene to him and the audience sees her walk away from the balcony on a marvelous pathway of light, singing a cradle song to Juanito. The other characters look out the balcony and see her dead body on the street below, amid shouts also heard by the audience.

The author explains that the whole play, a "tragedia matizada con perfiles costumbristas y facetas 'fabulosas,'" is based on *equívocos.*[19] The title is at once double, equivalent (Irene *is* the treasure), and disjunctive (since Juanito thinks he must choose one or the other). The subtitle, "Fábula," is equivocal because the word and the play comprise both the fantastic and the ethical. Juanito, he says, may be interpreted as the materialization of Irene's frustrated maternal instinct, and as such, a hallucination, just as the Voice may be a projection of Irene's unconscious. Both the Voice and Juanito may be said to be living the tragedy of their existence and their struggle to exist in Irene's mind,[20] but the Voice is superior to Juanito, whose faith is being tested. Deep in Irene's unconscious the Voice may signify her indestructible faith, which has been manifested throughout in her belief in fairy tales and in the possibility of regaining her son.

Buero's remarks about the multiple ambiguities of this play also constitute a major statement of his dramatic method:

> Es para el autor esencial el mantenimiento en el ánimo del espectador de toda clase de preguntas. Adicto al teatro de problemas, pretende inquietar y hacer pensar a su público, además de entretenerlo. Las preguntas por las que se manifiestan los equívocos de la obra pueden multiplicarse: ¿Ficción o verdad? ¿Obra realista o de evasión? ¿Locura, o bondad en Irene? ¿Locura, o maldad en Dimas? ¿Quiénes los locos? ¿Quiénes los cuerdos? ¿Qué son locura y cordura? La primera contestación a cada una de ellas puede ser . . . "¿Quién sabe?" También pueden contestarse de manera menos lógica, pero acaso más cierta: Ficción y verdad. Las dos cosas a un tiempo. Realidad, y también fantasía. El duende y la Voz no existen, pero existen. Todo, todo, depende de la perspectiva con que lo miremos. El autor quiere mostrar que las cosas del mundo nunca tienen una sola perspectiva, sino varias.

> (Pp. 122-123)

But not all perspectives are of equal value. For instance, the conclusion seen by the spectators is superior to the one seen by the characters. It affirms the reality of mystery and its profound relationship with everyday reality. As the Voice told Juanito: "Para la loca sabiduría de los hombres, tú y yo somos un engaño. Pero el mundo tiene dos caras . . . Y desde la nuestra, que engloba a la otra, ¡ésta es la realidad! ¡Esta es la verdadera realidad!" (p. 110).

I have used the term "functional flexibility" to embrace a wide range of the essential characteristics of Buero Vallejo's dramatic art: perspectivism and relativism, the ambiguities of victory and defeat as well as of life itself, the various levels of meaning, and the complexities of actions, concepts, and characterizations, which vary according to the viewpoints adopted. Because of these complexities and ambiguities, the usual distinctions of literal and symbolic meanings,[21] or of visionary and socially oriented perspectives,[22] though useful as first steps, do not adequately treat the variety of meanings the works present. However, the term does not include important aspects of his work, such as his strong ethical basis, which is manifested in the criticism of moral defects—especially selfishness, hypocrisy, and lack of understanding—and in the praise of hope, faith, charity, honesty, compassion, and understanding. Neither is it applicable to **Historia de una escalera, Las palabras en la arena,** and **Madrugada.** Another term he has used to describe his view of art and life is "viva ambivalencia," and he repeatedly stresses how much the interpretation of things depends on the standpoint from which they are seen or evaluated.

Although it was impossible in this exploratory essay to investigate Buero Vallejo's sources and his affinities with better-known playwrights, I believe that many of his worthwhile innovations stem from his resumption of the modern, often symbolic realism of such writers as Ibsen, Chekhov, and Galdós,[23] but with a broader concept of reality than these writers usually had. For him whatever is real and significant to individual human beings, though scientifically unprovable, must be considered. His growing interest in treating historical themes which, like parables, can be related to ethical problems of modern Spain and the world, has brought increasing attention to his similarities with Bertolt Brecht's plays and Arthur Miller's *The Crucible.* Also, more than any other contemporary Spanish dramatist and with greater success, he strives for the creation of a tragic form, the necessary vehicle for his tragic and empathic insights into the problems confronted by modern man.[24]

Notes

1. *Hoy es fiesta* (Madrid: Alfil, 1957), "Comentario," pp. 106-108. Unless otherwise indicated, I have used the editions of Buero Vallejo's plays published in the "Colección Teatro" by Ediciones Alfil. They usually include his commentaries, but not in all editions and printings.

2. *La tejedora de sueños* (Madrid: Alfil, 1952), "Comentario," pp. 99-100.

3. Cf. Isabel Magaña de Schevill, "Lo trágico en el teatro de Buero Vallejo," *Hispanófila,* No. 7 (Sept. 1959), 51-58. On the tragic aspects, see also Fr. Rosendo Roig, S. J., "Talante trágico del teatro de Buero Vallejo," *Razón y Fe,* Tomo 156, Núm. 718 (Nov. 1957), 363-367.

4. Juan R.-Castellano, "Introduction," *En la ardiente oscuridad,* ed. S. A. Wofsy (New York, 1954), p. xvii. For bibliography, see pp. xix-xxi.

5. See *En la ardiente oscuridad,* 2nd ed. (Madrid: Alfil, 1954), "Comentario," pp. 85-94.

6. This is valid on both the literal and symbolic planes: blindness—ignorance, delusions, wishful attitudes—is the incomprehensible evil that God or nature has inflicted on man. The nature of tragedy is to be caught up in a dilemma of suffering, but man attains true dignity by facing up to the tragic human condition.

7. Cf. the similar situations of Isabel in *Aventura en lo gris* and Fernandita in *Un soñador para un pueblo.* The early but only recently performed *Aventura en lo gris* treats several of the problems taken up in *Hoy es fiesta,* and there are close parallels between Silverio and Silvano.

8. *Hoy es fiesta,* p. 98.

9. *Aventura en lo gris* (Madrid: Ediciones "Puerta del Sol," 1955), p. 60.

10. In the commentary on *Las palabras en la arena,* published with *Historia de una escalera,* 3rd ed. (Madrid: Alfil, 1958), p. 104. Other aspects of Buero's dramaturgy, especially his frequent treatment of faith, hope, and charity, also partake of evangelical qualities. Cf. above, n. 3, Fr. Roig's study.

11. *Las Meninas* (Madrid: Alfil, 1961), pp. 71-73.

12. "Theater in Spain (1960-61): The Artist Velázquez in the Theater," *Modern Drama,* IV (1961), 179-183. See J. R.-Castellano's introduction to the Scribner's ed. of this play (New York, 1963).

13. Bernardino de Pantorba [pseud. of José López Jiménez] says that the painting's title, first used in 1843, was not especially appropriate (*La vida y la obra de Velázquez* [Madrid, 1955], p. 197). See also pp. 197-198 for queries concerning María Teresa's absence from the painting.

14. Published in *Primer Acto. Revista del Teatro* (Madrid), No. 38 (Dic. 1962), 18-54. In the same number are articles by Carlos Muñiz (8-10) and Gonzalo Torrente Ballester (11-14) and reviews by Ricardo Domenech (14-17) and José Monleón (58-59). Major points made about Buero are: his Sartrian commitment; the primarily ethical, rather than social nature of his dramaturgy; and the Brechtian "distanciamiento" of his historical situations, with ever clearer parallels with modern Spanish problems.

See, now, the recent school edition, prepared by Pedro N. Trakas, with an introduction by Juan R.-Castellano (New York: Scribner's, 1965), and the Madrid, Alfil edition (1963).

15. *La señal que se espera* (Madrid: Alfil, 1952), "Comentario," p. 68.

16. Silverio has similar feelings of unusual understanding and fellowship in *Hoy es fiesta* (pp. 54 and 97).

17. *Casi un cuento de hadas* (Madrid: Alfil, 1953), p. 59.

18. *Ibid.*, p. 76. As Buero adds, this problem has been treated often; Cervantes, Unamuno, and Pirandello come immediately to mind.

19. These and following comments by Buero are from the "Comentario" on *Irene, o el tesoro* (Madrid: Alfil, 1955), pp. 117-125.

20. For their Unamunian doubts about their existence, see pp. 75-76, 91-93, and 110. Very important in this connection are the conclusion to Irene's song (p. 113) and the play's epigraph, taken from one of Unamuno's poems:

    "El secreto del alma redimida:/vivir los sueños al soñar la vida."

21. Such as those made by Magaña y Schevill and by G. Torrente Ballester.

22. See M. Manzanares de Cirre, "El realismo social de Antonio Buero Vallejo," *Revista Hispánica Moderna*, XXVII, Núms. 3-4 (Junio-Octubre, 1961), 320-324. He adds that these two viewpoints are complementary.

23. Francis Fergusson has described some of the possibilities and limitations of modern realism in ch. V of his *The Idea of a Theater* (Garden City, N.Y., 1949), pp. 159-190.

24. Since this was written, I have seen a new study on Buero Vallejo, Jean-Paul Borel's "Buero Vallejo ou l'impossible concret et historique," ch. V of his *Théâtre de l'impossible: Essai sur une des dimensions fondamentales du théâtre espagnol au XXe siècle* (Neuchâtel, Suisse: Éditions de la Baconnière, 1963), pp. 153-191. This is an interesting, existentially oriented book, though with very little critical apparatus and no tie-in with European and American drama of the 20th century.

    First we are shown how Buero Vallejo treats the themes found in the previous four chapters: (1) impossible love (in Lorca); (2) impossible truth (in Benavente); (3) the impossibility of living (in Unamuno); (4) the passion of the impossible (in Valle-Inclán). Respective examples in Buero Vallejo are: (1) *Historia de una escalera*; (2) *Palabras en la arena* and *Las cartas boca abajo*; (3) *En la ardiente oscuridad* and *La tejedora de sueños*; (4) *Casi un cuento de hadas* and *Irene, o el tesoro*. Then the "concrete and historical possibility" is treated, in three basic dimensions: community life (*Hoy es fiesta*), the socio-political dimension (*Un soñador para un pueblo*), and that of war (*Aventura en lo gris*).

Robert L. Nicholas (essay date April 1969)

SOURCE: Nicholas, Robert L. "The History Plays: Buero Vallejo's Experiment in Dramatic Expression." *Revista de Estudios Hispánicos* II, no. 1 (April 1969): 281-93.

[*In the following essay, Nicholas considers the intrinsic artistic merit of* Un soñador para un pueblo *and* Las Meninas, *asserting that Buero Vallejo was "attempting to approximate, in the plays' structures, the spirit of the historical moment depicted in each play."*]

Un soñador para un pueblo (1958) and *Las Meninas* (1960) constitute something of a digression in the career of Antonio Buero Vallejo. They are preceded by ten years of largely realistic playwriting and followed by what appears to be a renewal of that realistic current.[1] The central characters in these plays are not middle class figures, but intellectuals and artists cast in a heroic mold. Buero is more interested in having them make statements of artistic and political truths than in engaging them in psychological involvements. The settings, of course, do not reflect a contemporary, middle class environment. Both character and scene are historical in nature, but this does not diminish the contemporary relevance of the problems treated by the playwright. Indeed, his main reason for selecting such an era is to criticize the present through the perspective of the past.

The occasional distortion of historical incidents and figures has provoked censure on the part of critics. Their inability to suspend disbelief has generally hampered serious criticism of these plays, limiting it to discussions of historicity, the author's intent, his similarity to Brecht, etc.[2] These are valid topics for critical endeavors, but unfortunately their frequent treatment has obscured something more significant, the intrinsic artistic merit of these plays.

My purpose is to examine the inner dramatic forces around which Buero has structured the action of these two works. That action involves an ideological dispute which centers around the protagonist. In *Un soñador para un pueblo* Esquilache's political reforms are debated and in *Las Meninas* Velázquez's innovations in the pictorial art are argued. The protagonists' theories, political and artistic, are important thematically, but, more significantly, they are reflected in the very structure of their respective dramas. The symmetrical presentation of characters and ideologies in *Un soñador para un pueblo* creates a tripartite structure reminiscent of the classic manner. In *Las Meninas* the confused, chaotic life of the court of Philip IV, suggested visually in the multiple staging and simultaneous actions on stage, is portrayed in a manner that recalls the impressionistic technique of painting which Velázquez anticipated.[3]

By developing the action of these plays according to the requirements of artistic philosophies and forms, the playwright is, I suggest, attempting to approximate, in the plays' structures, the spirit of the historical moment depicted in each play. The systematic juxtaposition of characters and attitudes in *Un soñador para un pueblo* facilitates the contrasting of political ideologies and, therefore, is an evocation of the atmosphere of eighteenth-century Spain, an epoch characterized by ideological struggles. The impressionistic manner of *Las Meninas,* with its movement and shifting focus, is meant to reflect the suspicion, disloyalty, vested interests and fear of Inquisitional Spain of the seventeenth century.

Un soñador para un pueblo is a dramatization of the famous revolt of 1766 by segments of the Spanish nobility and peasantry against the Marqués de Esquilache, the Italian prime minister who tried to introduce into Spain the reforms of the Enlightenment. The play is divided into two parts. Part I depicts the rising opposition to Esquilache's regime by continually contrasting the street, the world of the governed (the lower classes), with the palace, the world of those who govern (the upper classes). This section begins with a street scene involving the peasantry followed by three interior scenes dealing with the prime minister and his colleagues. After another scene in the street the focus shifts back to Esquilache's mansion for three more scenes. Another street scene follows and, after that, three more interior scenes. Part I concludes with a final scene in the street, thereby completing the symmetrical design of this section.

Part II portrays Esquilache's final defeat. This section, however, lacks any sequential organization. This

> while Buero invokes an art form (music) as a moral force and uses it to heighten his dramatic expression, he does not structure the play's action according to any discernible musical pattern.

is probably due to the fact that it portrays the consummation of the ideological and personal conflicts initiated in Part I. That initial presentation remains the most striking structural aspect of the play. Its symmetrical arrangement reveals with great clarity the political and personal forces present in eighteenth-century Spanish society. Each series of interior scenes is characterized by a downward progression from the highest to the lowest social class. The aristocrats, Villasanta, Ensenada and the king, precede Pastora, embodiment of the "nouveaux riches," who in turn comes before the peasant Fernandita. The good element of the lower class (Fernandita) is followed by and contrasted with the evil segment of the lower class (in the street scenes). And the cycle begins again.

A closer look at Part I reveals the symmetry we have been talking about. The first scene of each interior series presents a political viewpoint. Esquilache first meets with his predecessor, the Marqués de Ensenada, whose philosophy "'Todo para el pueblo, pero sin el pueblo.' El pueblo es siempre menor de edad." lacks the idealism of Esqui-

lache's position: ". . . [el pueblo] *todavía* es menor de edad."[4] The second political stance emerges when Esquilache encounters the Duque de Villasanta. When Esquilache says that nations must change if they do not want to die, Villasanta replies: "¿Hacia dónde? ¿Hacia la Enciclopedia? ¿Hacia la 'Ilustración'? ¿Hacia todo eso que sus señorías llaman 'las luces'? Nosotros lo llamamos, simplemente, herejía."[5] The third political position is that of the current regime. The king himself explains its essence to Esquilache: "¿Sabes por qué eres mi predilecto, Leopoldo? Porque eres un soñador. Los demás . . . sólo esconden mezquindad y egoísmo. Tú . . . eres un soñador ingenuo, capaz de los más finos escrúpulos de conciencia . . . España necesita soñadores que sepan de números como tú . . . Hace tiempo que yo sueño también con una reforma moral, y no sólo con reformas externas."[6]

Esquilache's high moral character is emphasized in the second and third scenes of the three series of interior sequences. In their first scene together the deviousness and possible unfaithfulness of Essquilache's wife Pastora are contrasted with her husband's honesty. In their second confrontation he informs her of his plan to request the king's approval for their separation and for their sons' dismissal from government jobs obtained through her connivance.[7]

The servant Fernandita talks with Esquilache in the third scene of each set of three. In the first two her humility and sympathy contrast with the vanity and cruelty of Pastora who, in each instance, just precedes her on stage. In her third appearance Fernandita warns Esquilache of the bands of "embozados" in the streets. Part I concludes with a street scene in which a band of rebels breaks the symbols of reform and enlightenment, new street lamps that Esquilache has had installed.

The play is not an indictment of the society's class structure. It shows, rather, in its structural arrangement, the good and evil elements present in every social class. Buero's presentation of Esquilache in each interior scene of Part I does seem, however, to encourage a fluid social structure, one which would allow change and progression for the individual. Born a peasant, he has been able to rise. In a sense, he fits into every class: he is an idealist like the king, ambitious, at least in part, like his wife, and honest and sincere like Fernandita. He is basically identified with the upper classes, however. His failure is perhaps due to his inability to rid himself of the evil elements within his social class: the personal ambition of his wife and the political ambition of Ensenada.

The play's structural development further encourages social advancement and responsibility for the lower classes by giving each social class a temporal designation. Ensenada and Villasanta represent egoistic, myopic ideas of the past. Esquilache and Pastora typify the unfulfilled present and Fernandita is the symbol of the idealistic future. Again Esquilache provides the synthesis: he calls himself a "niño envejecido,"[8] indicating that his initial idealism has been thwarted. The youthful Fernandita is the hope of the future because she does not let her integrity be tainted by the evil element in her social class.

As we have seen, Buero's evocation of an eighteenth-century atmosphere is markedly enhanced by the clear, orderly arrangement of the action of the play's first part. I submit that the playwright has attempted to reflect the spirit of classicism, the dominant artistic mode of the epoch, in the symmetrical ordering of the action of his play.

The second history play, *Las Meninas,* is a dramatization of Diego Velázquez's famous painting. Most of the characters in the play are the historical figures immortalized in his masterpiece. The painter himself is portrayed as the lonely intellectual who attacks all that is false and unjust in seventeenth-century Spanish society.

This play is also divided into two parts. Character development in Part I is not structured in an orderly, sequential pattern; here Buero emphasizes the spatial rather than the linear. Action shifts to various areas of the stage within the same scene. This section is an impressionistic "painting"—a dramatic *Las Meninas*—which offers an overwhelming impression of intrigue and subversion in everyday court life. Buero converts Velázquez's pictorial technique into a dramatic medium through the use of multiple scene changes, simultaneous actions and different degrees of illumination. Significantly, the principal plot motivation in this first part of the play is Velázquez's efforts to obtain permission to do this painting.

An examination of the first few scenes of Part I illustrates the constantly changing focus of the action. The first scene is a conversation between Martín and Pedro, former models for Velázquez who have returned to seek refuge in his home. While they speak at the left, two serving girls of the royal family appear at the right and are soon joined by doña Marcela. Attention flits between these two groups, one on the street and the other on a side balcony, until the presence of a soldier forces the two beggars to move on. Then the center curtains are drawn, revealing doña Juana and Mazo, Velázquez's wife and son-in-law. For a brief time the spectators' attention alternates between them and doña Marcela and the *menina* Isabel at the right. Shortly, however, the focus moves to the left where Velázquez appears on a balcony. He speaks with his ex-slave Pareja while the others observe them carefully. This complex aligning of scenes and shifting of focus continue throughout the very long Part I.

By the end of the first part the characters and their attitudes toward the main figure have been presented, but in a deliberately chaotic fashion. V. Fernández de Asís, who has not seen this deliberateness, criticized the length of Part I, its many scenes, changes, extemporaneous entrances and exits.[9] Gonzalo Torrente Ballester refers to its "indudable lentitud" in his critique.[10] The reason for the confusion of Part I in contrast to the well ordered structure of Part II is due, I suggest, to Buero's aesthetic approach.

The play is about a painter and his new theory of painting. Early in the drama Velázquez reveals to Pedro the essence of that theory: "Ahora sé que los colores dialogan entre sí . . . ."[11] Later he describes this intimate relationship between colors, this "dialogar" of which he spoke:

> VELÁZQUEZ. He advertido, señor, una tenue neblina verdosa que rodea al sayo verde de su San Jerónimo . . .
>
> NARDI. Exageráis. Sólo es un modo de dar blandura a las gradaciones.
>
> VELÁZQUEZ. ¿Con una neblina verdosa alrededor del sayo?
>
> . . . . .
>
> NARDI. *(Ríe.)* ¿Tendré que recordaros cierta nubecilla verdosa que rodea las calzas de vuestro "Don Juan de Austria"?
>
> VELÁZQUEZ. Olvidáis que las calzas de mi bufón son carmesíes . . . No pinté la nubecilla verdosa porque me ha parecido advertir que las tintas carmesíes suscitan a su alrededor un velo verdoso.[12]

Earlier in this same scene Velázquez explains to Nardi how he creates this effect:

> VELÁZQUEZ. Respondedme como pintor a una pregunta, maestro. Cuando miráis a los ojos de una cabeza, ¿cómo veis los contornos de esa cabeza?
>
> NARDI. *(Lo piensa.)* Imprecisos.
>
> VELÁZQUEZ. Esa es la razón de la manera abreviada que a vos os parece un capricho.
>
> NARDI. Es que para pintar esos contornos, hay que dejar de mirar a los ojos de la cabeza y mirarlos a ellos.
>
> VELÁZQUEZ. Es vuestra opinión. Vos creéis que hay que pintar las cosas. Yo pinto el ver.[13]

Velázquez's theory of art, according to Buero, rests on the following points: it is the eye that receives an impression, an impression created by the relationship of disparate colors and by the distance between the object and the beholder.

But *Las Meninas* is more than a play about painting or artistic theory; it *is* a painting. The impressionistic technique which Velázquez expounds is the dramatic technique Buero employs in the first part of this drama. In the first place, the playwright only presents hints of the characters' ambitions, failures, jealousies, etc. Many things are suggested but none explained or justified. Attention moves quickly from one character to another, from one place on stage to another, from one action to another. The result is an enigmatic kaleidoscope of purposeful confusion and suspicion. Secondly, the characters are developed according to the way they see each other and in their very efforts to see or to conceal: leaning from balconies, spying continually, locking doors, hiding paintings, etc. Princess María Teresa's method of perceiving life illustrates this point. She states:

> Sabéis que ando sola a menudo por palacio. Mi padre me riñe, pero algo me dice que debo hacerlo. La verdad de la vida no puede estar en el protocolo . . . A veces, creo entreverla en la ternura sencilla de una lavandera, o en el aire cansado de un centinela. Sorprendo unas palabras que hablan de que el niño está con calentura, o de que este año la cosecha vendrá buena, y se me abre un mundo . . . que no es el mío. Pero me ven, y callan.[14]

She learns truth from details that are usually concealed by protocol. The importance she gives to these nuances is a reflection of Velázquez's approach to painting. Life is seen as snatches of overheard remarks and sighs just as colors can be seen as snatches of hues and tones in an impressionistic painting.

In Part II Buero interprets, through trial procedure with its systematic appearances of witnesses, the impressionistic details of the first part. The characters' secret motives are brought into the open, into sharp focus. This is symbolized by the suspension of action in the play's final scene. There the characters take the places of their namesakes in the painting *Las Meninas*. The work for which Velázquez sought approval in Part I is now finished.

In his painting Velázquez tries to give a true picture of court life by the action of freezing people at work rather than having them assume poses. This "candid-camera" dimension is the painter's greatest achievement, according to Ortega y Gasset:

> . . . ha sido menester esperar a la pasmosa invención mecánica de la fotografía instantánea para . . . revelarnos la audaz intuición artística de Velázquez . . . pinta el tiempo mismo que es el instante, que es el ser en cuanto que está condenado a dejar de ser, a transcurrir, a corromperse. Eso es lo que eterniza y ésa es, según él, la misión de la pintura: dar eternidad precisamente al instante . . .[15]

Buero, in his *Las Meninas,* has brought to life the frozen expressions and postures of Velázquez's masterpiece. With regard to technique, the play is pictorial just as the painting is dramatic.[16]

The interaction between drama (life) and painting is also reflected in the thematic development of the play. If the portrayal of servants and artist at work is the true representation of court life, then the reflection of the posed figures of the king and queen in the mirror at the back of

the painting symbolizes the falseness of that life. In the play the king has a dream in which he is naked but his mirrored image is clothed in the royal robes and crown.

During his trial in Part II Velázquez refuses to conceal to the king the injustice and poverty rampant in the country, just as he refuses to destroy his nude *Venus*. This painting becomes symbolic of truth. Velázquez's defense of it before an Inquisitional review board is the action in Part II which provokes and facilitates the unveiling of the shrouded motives of Part I. In a symbolic sense, therefore, this second section of the play is itself a kind of nude *Venus*.

In the painting *Las Meninas* the artist is identified with the lower social classes. In the play this bond is crystallized in Velázquez's relationship with the beggar Pedro. Through this relationship Buero seems to be saying that only he who appreciates artistic beauty can comprehend how intolerable is the suffering of the world. Conversely, only he who is cognizant of human suffering can comprehend the beautiful in art. The nearly blind Pedro is the only one to sense the real significance of Velázquez's new painting. He summarizes that significance thus:

> Un cuadro sereno: pero con toda la tristeza de España dentro. Quien vea a estos seres comprenderá lo irremedia-blemente condenados al dolor que están. Son fantasmas vivos de personas cuya verdad es la muerte. Quien los mire mañana, lo advertirá con espanto . . . pues llegará un momento . . . en que ya no sabrá si es él el fantasma ante las miradas de estas figuras. Y querrá salvarse con ellas . . . puesto que ellas lo miran. Y tal vez mientras busca su propia cara en el espejo del fondo, se salve por un momento de morir.[17]

It is difficult to objectify life because it always continues. Art and the lessons it offers can, however, be contemplated with detachment. Individuals may save themselves from a living death by sensing the cry for social justice that is *Las Meninas*.

Buero's play is a similar plea for justice. More than that, it is a call to responsibility for the intelligentsia. Buero has pictorially revived a moment of history in order to address his contemporaries. In both its technical and thematic aspects the aesthetic process through which he conveys his message is complex indeed. Buero himself suggests the complexity of that aesthetic approach when he writes: "Probablemente, el más antiguo motivo que determina el nacimiento de mi obra *Las Meninas* es mi inicial y fallida vocación de pintor. Es difícil resignarse a su abandono, y se intenta pintar de otra manera."[18]

These two history plays together represent, I think, the greatest technical achievement of Antonio Buero Vallejo. The innovation distinguishing them from his realistic dramas is not so much their historical settings as it is the fact that they fuse other art forms with the dramatic. This fusion causes the magnifying of the role of one or more of the traditional dimensions of a dramatic presentation, the visual, the auditory and action itself. The presentation thereby acquires an affective intensity calculated to engulf the spectator with an overwhelming emotional impression.

Both the merging of art forms to enhance emotion and the emphasis on knowing through feeling recall Richard Wagner's concept of theater. Wagner preferred drama to poetry because drama is a dynamic art and appeals to several of man's senses. I suspect that Buero left painting to become a dramatist because he was attracted by the multiple possibilities of expression which drama offers.

One might well ask why Buero is so concerned with the emotional effect of these dramas. The answer can be found, I think, in his desire to write tragedies. He wants to trigger an emotional reaction in the audience in spite of the historical distance of these plays. The supreme function of tragedy, according to Buero, is revelation and its resultant provocation to action. And this provocation to action—the desire to help one's fellow man—must come through catharsis, "no por explícitas consideraciones ni moralejas . . . sino por la fuerza ejemplar del argumento y sus pasiones," that is "por directa impresión estética y no discursión." He goes on to add that "la belleza estética es un hallazgo . . . supremo del hombre que, con su sola presencia, puede expresarlo todo sin decir nada."[19]

A solution whose basis is pathos rather than dialectics not only permits the playwright to express what he cannot say directly, but also permits, in the case of these dramas, an expression that reveals the range, the brilliance, the delicacy of nuance, the power and poetry of Buero Vallejo's dramaturgy.

Notes

1. In his critique of *El tragaluz,* Buero's latest play, José María de Quinto writes: "Así es que regresa Buero Vallejo. Y vuelve, a mi modo de ver, por sus propios fueros, los que le dieron crédito y renombre en . . . [los] dramas que cabría englobar bajo la denominación general de 'tragedias de la vida vulgar . . .' Bajo este epígrafe habría que reunir todo ese teatro de Buero, que arranca con *Historia de una escalera* y parece culminar con *El tragaluz.* Salvo las piezas históricas y otras entre las que habría que situar *En la ardiente oscuridad,* todo el teatro de Buero Vallejo viene confirmado por una fundamental preocupación: retratar, con perfiles trágicos, hondamente psicológicos, la vida y los sueños de la clase media española." "*El tragaluz,* de Buero Vallejo," *Insula,* No. 252 (November 1967), p. 15.

2. Included in this category are critics like Rodríguez Méndez, Gonzalo Fernández de la Mora, Rafael María de Hornedo and V. Fernández de Asis. Some ideological enemies go so far as to point to the influ-

ence of Brecht's theory of alienation in these works as proof of Buero's communism. Ironically, certain admirers attribute the plays' dramatic defects to Buero's failure to align himself completely with Brecht's theories.

3. I am not including *El Concierto de San Ovidio* (1962) in this study. It also depicts an epoch of history in order to draw analogies with the present, but its central character is not an important historical figure like Esquilache or Velázquez. And

4. Antonio Buero Vallejo, *Un soñador para un pueblo* in *Teatro Español: 1958-1959* (Madrid, 1960), p. 216 (underlining mine).

5. *Ibid.,* p. 233.

6. *Ibid.,* p. 244.

7. The only exception in the elaborate structural plan which Buero follows is Pastora's failure to appear a third time. Instead, Ensenada appears again.

8. *Un soñador para un pueblo, op. cit.,* p. 224.

9. "Español: *Las Meninas* de Antonio Buero Vallejo," *Pueblo* (December 13, 1960), p. 17.

10. Torrente attributes this slowness to the expository nature of the first part. He praises Part II, however, noting its sobriety, unity, timing and "garbo escénico." "Estreno de *Las Meninas* en el Español," *Arriba* (December 10, 1960), p. 25.

11. Antonio Buero Vallejo, *Las Meninas* in *Teatro Español: 1960-1961* (Madrid, 1962), p. 121.

12. *Ibid.,* pp. 169, 170.

13. *Ibid.,* p. 168.

14. *Ibid.,* pp. 112, 113.

15. José Ortega y Gasset, *Velázquez: Obras Completas,* VIII (Madrid, 1962), 487.

16. Ortega sensed the dramatic quality of *Las Meninas.* He said: "Está, pues, obtenido el espacio en profundidad mediante una serie de bastidores como en el escenario de un teatro." *Obras Completas,* p. 653.

17. *Las Meninas* in *Teatro Español: 1960-1961, op. cit.,* p. 135.

18. "*Las Meninas* es una obra necesaria?" *La Carreta,* No. 2 (January 1962), p. 9.

19. Antonio Buero Vallejo, "La tragedia," *El teatro: enciclopedia del arte escéncio,* ed. Guillermo Díaz-Plaja (Barcelona, 1958), pp. 66, 67.

William Giuliano (essay date May 1970)

SOURCE: Giuliano, William. "The Role of Man and of Woman in Buero Vallejo's Plays." *Hispanofila* 39 (May 1970): 21-8.

[In the following essay, Giuliano discusses how Buero Vallejo's male and female characters exemplify the underlying thematic concerns of his plays.]

The underlying theme of Buero Vallejo's plays is unquestionably man's efforts to realize his full capacities against the internal and external forces that restrain him. These efforts are directed toward the search for truth, the essence of reality, the creation of social justice, the attempt to establish personal, political, and artistic freedom, and other aspects of the human condition.[1] Hope is eternally present, but the nature of man and of things is such that life is inherently tragic and happiness and self-fulfillment is achieved only through great effort. "En el fondo es una tragedia [*Historia de una escalera*] porque la vida entera y verdadera es siempre, a mi juicio, trágica."[2]

The object of this article is to examine to what extent Buero's characters have exemplified the author's underlying theme, and the reasons for their success or failure. In his dramas man succumbs to circumstance primarily because his inability to face reality and his inclination to delude himself leads to procrastination which in turn paralyzes the will and shackles him to inaction and subsequent defeat.

Urbano and Fernando (*Historia de una escalera*) are complete failures because they talked and dreamed about what they were going to do, but did nothing to further their dreams. Some critics have blamed their failure on their environment, symbolized by the unchanging stairway, yet others in the play did manage to raise their standard of living, namely Elvira's father, and the "Joven" and "Señor" who appear briefly at the beginning of Act. III. The latter three seemed well satisfied with their economic achievements. Urbano, however, placed all his hopes in his industrial union while Fernando considered himself a superior intellectual above menial work. Neither faced the hard fact of concentrated individual effort and struggle to inch ahead and break the chain that bound them to "*la escalera.*" Jean Borel attributes their failure to their being untrue to love—Fernando for marrying a girl he did not love, and Urbano for marrying a girl who did not love him.[3] In Act I, however, before declaring his love to Carmina and while still indifferent to Elvira, Fernando already showed signs of his lack of ambition. Paca says of him, "Además, que le descuentan muchos días de sueldo. Y puede que le echen de la papelería . . . porque no va nunca." The odds were against success in their environment, but neither Fernando nor Urbano made an effort to achieve it.

Silverio (*Hoy es fiesta*) also suffers from inertia. Feeling that he was the cause of the death of his wife Pilar's daughter he abandoned his painting and life in general, spending much time helping others in order to forget what he thought was his crime. Buero tells us that Silverio finally decided to face up to reality and unburden himself by confessing his negligence to his wife, but just before he did so, she passed away, thus bringing into focus the tragedy of his procrastination.[4] Had he told her his story from the outset, Silverio, a very capable man, would have developed his talents to his utmost, but instead, he spent years brooding, trying to make up his mind to speak frankly to his wife.

Another character defeated because of his inability to face reality is Juan (*Las cartas boca abajo*). He refused to admit openly the merit of Carlos Ferrer, and failed to win a professorship because he was unable to answer questions concerning Ferrer's authorative books. He finally admits his weakness, saying, "Le he envidiado [a Ferrer] toda mi vida . . . Le envidio aún. No he sabido sobreponerme a ese sentimiento destructor . . . No me ayudaba nada en mi propia casa para conseguirlo, pero eso cuenta poco ahora. Yo era inteligente, pero la obsesión de sus éxitos me ha anulado. Y el pago es el fracaso." (segunda parte, cuadro II)

Many critics blame Adela for the ills that befell the family, among them Ricardo Domenech who says, "*En las cartas boca abajo* se ventila el problema de la culpabilidad. Adela es culpable de haber impedido la felicidad de los demás, y, a la postre, la suya propia."[5] This is not fair to Adela, as Juan was also at fault. Referring to the lack of communication between his wife and him, he says, "Los dos mantenemos nuestras cartas boca abajo, en vez de enseñarlas." (primera parte, cuadro II) This weakness of character and his inability to accept the intellectual superiority of Ferrer rendered Juan inactive and his failure should not be attributed to Adela.

Mario of *El tragaluz* may also be considered unsuccessful, even though at the end he is hopeful of a better future. His brother Vicente showed greater strength of character but unfortunately was selfish in his actions. Mario, on the other hand, although morally upright, was afraid of life and preferred to know the world only through the window of his basement apartment which he rarely left. Buero himself alluded to the weakness of Mario when he stated, "No me complace la idea de defender a ultranza a un paralítico voluntario [Mario] . . . me quedaría con el menor [Mario] si me obligan a escoger entre los dos hermanos . . . pero . . . en el desarrollo de la tragedia él también tuvo su lado negativo, y el tipo ideal para una conducta equilibrada hubiera sido un hombre intermediario entre los dos hermanos, un simbiosis de ambos, un setenta por ciento del menor y un treinta del mayor."[6]

Not all of Buero's characters are overcome by life's circumstances. Some of them, although they meet death, are not tragic in Buero's ideology since they have realized their capacities to the fullest and have contributed something to the future of mankind. Such a character, to some degree, is Ignacio (*En la ardiente oscuridad*). Although he met a violent death when still young, in the brief time he had lived in the institution for the blind, he had shaken the other students who, before he came, had deluded themselves into thinking they were normal and perfectly happy. Even Carlos, who murdered him, retained some of the powerful drive to face reality, to seek knowledge, and to improve himself that had been characteristic of Ignacio.

Buero himself speaks of Ignacio's heroic qualities while comparing him with another blind protagonist, David (*El concierto de San Ovidio*). In an article entitled "La ceguera en mi teatro," Buero explains that "La ceguera en mi teatro es una limitación del hombre o sea, algo que se opone a su libertad, a su libre desarrollo."[7] He goes on to say that both Ignacio and David sought to surmont the limitations of their handicaps. David, being older and more experienced, was better able to understand the world and had greater success. "En ambas [las dos obras] se plantea la misma cuestión, la de una sana rebeldía contra nuestras limitaciones . . . se plantea la posibilidad de superarlas."[8]

David met death, but his life was an outstanding success. He had shown the other blind beggars and the world that they (the blind) were capable of playing as an orchestra, something never attempted before; he had killed the tyrannical and greedy Valindin who had tried to divest them of their dignity; he had inspired Valentín Haüy to devote his life to the blind, teaching them to read and to play music in harmony. David died, but his life's efforts were a permanent contribution to the development of normal living and social respectability for the unfortunate blind who up to that time had been considered utterly useless.

Among other relatively successful characters we might add Silvano (*Aventura en lo gris*) and Luis (*La señal que se espera*)—Silvano for having aided in bringing the dictator Goldmann to his death and giving up his life to save that of a child, and Luis for finding himself and renewing his musical activities.

Perhaps the most outstanding protagonists of Buero's plays are Esquilache (*Un soñador para un pueblo*) and Velázquez (*Las meninas*) for having realized their abilities to their greatest extent. Both were men of humble birth who rose to positions of importance. Esquilache was forced to leave Spain because of the machinations of selfish nobles and the lack of understanding by the common people. Charles III offered to retain him as minister even at the risk of civil war, but Esquilache, wishing to preserve the advances he had brought about in education, public lighting, street paving, relaxation of the Holy Inquisition, and lessening of crime through the prohibition of *el embozo*, elected to leave the Spain he loved to return quietly to Italy. Esquilache did more than any other character in Buero's plays to raise the level of Spain in many aspects. His forced departure might be considered a tragedy, but he was really triumphant as his reforms, having been won against bitter opposition, were preserved for future generations.

Velázquez is one of the few protagonists who lived to enjoy his success. He fought for personal and artistic freedom, and social justice against the opposition of the

most powerful nobles of the court, and even dared to disobey the key. At the end he was the victor, having earned the whole-hearted support of the king.

Up to this point discussion has been restricted to male characters because the underlying theme as stated in the first paragraph of this article refers almost exclusively to men. In keeping with Spanish tradition, however, the activities in which the above-mentioned protagonists engaged are reserved for men. Women are concerned, in Buero's plays, primarily with love and the begetting of children. "Por y para amar vive la mujer si es plenamente femenina,"[9] the dramatist tells us. The desire to love and be loved is the greatest motivating force in the behavior of the women in Buero's dramas, and if we study this aspect of his works, it becomes evident that their degree of happiness or unhappiness and fulfillment of self is directly proportionate to the depth of the love they feel for a particular man and the intensity of the response inspired.

The character who achieves the greatest heights in the realization of her role as a woman is Amalia (*Madrugada*), the central figure of one of Buero's most tense dramas. Amalia, who felt a coldness developing in her husband Mauricio's attitude toward her, was unable to find out the reason for it before his death. Feeling that it was the result of gossip spread by one of his relatives before his death, she called them to her home minutes after his demise, pretending that he was still alive but liable to pass away at any moment. She attempts to extract the truth, promising that she will not permit her husband to leave her his wealth, but to leave it to them instead. By playing on their lust for money she finally discovers that her conjecture was correct, and, moreover, that her husband had loved her deeply to the end.

Amalia had been the mistress of a painter before becoming the mistress, and later, wife, of Mauricio. His death meant wealth for her, but, this was of no importance. She was tortured by the thought that he had married and left her his fortune merely as payment for services rendered. She loved him profoundly and had to find out if he had still loved her up to the time of his death. Her bold plan was successful, and the knowledge that she was still united to Mauricio even in death, gave her the strength to continue living. Her supreme effort, and the depth of their mutual love made Amalia, in Buero's ideology, reach the zenith of feminine accomplishment.

Vying with Amalia for success in carrying out a woman's function in life to its greatest heights and as a richly developed dramatic character is Penelope, protagonist of *La tejedora de sueños*. Buero destroys Homer's characterization of Penelope as the perpetually faithful loving wife, and substitutes for it a Penelope who, true to her womanly instincts, cannot wait indefinitely for a husband who has abandoned her to fight a war over another woman. She falls in love with Anfino, one of her many suitors, who loves her sincerely. Their love, however, remains platonic. When Ulysses returns and slays the suitors, including Anfino, Penelope reproaches him for his long absence and his cowardliness in disguising himself, and declares her undying love for the deceased Anfino. Both Amalia and Penelope, therefore, give meaning to their lives only through fulfillment in a love which transcends mortal existence.

Two other characters who have lesser roles in their plays, Adriana (*El concierto de San Ovidio*) and Ana (*Aventura en lo gris*), the former mistress of the cruel Valindin and the latter mistress of the tyrant Goldmann, abandon their lovers to find true requited love in the blind David and in the intellectual Silvano respectively. Both pairs of lovers find their unions short-lived as death soon claims three of them.

The four female characters discussed are not virtuous women by normal standards. We see, therefore, that for Buero, the spiritual union of a man and a woman transcends conventional morality as well as mortal existence.

Irene (*Irene o el tesoro*) differs from the aforementioned heroines in that she achieves fulfillment in an abnormal manner. After the death of her husband and loss of her child in childbirth, Irene rejects love with another man, and creates in her mind *el duende Juanito* who replaces the child she had lost. She too goes to her death, happily, led by Juanito.

Although the women herein described have had their love relations interrupted by death, their lives have been, in a real sense, not tragic, since death is only a natural phenomenon that alters physical contacts but does not change the spiritual union. The survivors find an inner tranquillity from the knownledge that they have completed their missions as women.

Both the positive and negative aspects of Buero's concept of the role of love in the happiness of a woman is seen in his *Casi un cuento de hadas,* based on Charles Perrault's *Riquet à la houppe.* The unhappy Princess Leticia, beautiful but considered stupid, is made to feel intelligent by the ugly Prince Riquet whom she sees as a handsome man. They are happy for a while. Riquet, however, is obliged to leave for a time, and in his absence Leticia falls in love with the handsome Armando. The latter agrees to marry her only for reasons of state. Leticia is not happy with this unrequited love. Riquet returns, and is rejected by Leticia. Later he kills Armando, in a quarrel generated by the latter. Leticia now seeks Riquet for her husband even though her love for him has died. She begs him to marry her, realizing that her only possibility for happiness lies in him. She pleads, "¡No te marches! ¡Sólo tú tienes el poder de abrir mis ojos. Aunque sea en el dolor, busquemos el sortilegio de nuevo!" (Acto III).

Thus, while she and Riquet were deeply in love, Leticia was sublimely happy and even saw him as the handsomest of men. Her betrothal to Armando, however, negated the concept of "love and be loved" and therefore led only to frustration and despair. In her final reunion with Riquet it was she who lacked love, hence a state of unhappiness prevails although the play ends on a note of hope as she strives to recapture the spirit of her first, uplifting love for Riquet.

The tragic consequences in the lives of women who fail to follow the formula of "love and be loved" is seen clearly in other female characters of Buero's plays. In *Historia de una escalera* both Carmina and Elvira, though married, have not found happines. Both betrayed the formula—Carmina for having accepted Urbano with whom she was not in love, and Elvira for having pursued Fernando who was not in love with her. The depths of the tragedy is expressed in the final scene when Carmina, who had been in love with Fernando, accuses Elvira of having stolen him from her when they were young. In the presence of both husbands, Elvira angrily replies, "¿Cree Vd. que se lo quité? Se lo regalaría de buena gana!" (Acto III).

When all were young and unmarried, Carmina and Fernando were in love with each other. Their union probably would have brought happiness, but the marriages consummated were lacking in mutual love, and subsequent bitterness, recriminations, and unhappiness were the inevitable results. The children Carmina and Fernando pledge their love, but their future is left in doubt.

The character who reaps the most tragic consequences of the failure to be true to her womanly role in life is Adela (*Las cartas boca abajo*). Most critics view her as a woman who destroys the life of others. F. C. Sainz de Robles calls this play "el problema de una familia deschecha, acobardaba, por el egoísmo feroz de uno de sus miembros."[10] Domingo Pérez Minik calls Adela a Hedda Gabler, a Bernarda Alba, "Adela ejerce una matriarcada feroz, que recuerda al de *La Casa de Bernarda Alba* . . . , se asemeja a la Hedda Gabler ibseniana . . . Es otra comedia de víctimas de un despotismo político familiar ejercido a la fuerza por Adela."[11]

While it is true that Adela was a destructive force in the lives of those close to her, in the end, she was the most abject victim of all, having lost the affections of sweetheart, sister, husband, and son, and was condemned to a life of spiritual loneliness.

The basic reason for the action which led Adela to make others, and eventually herself, unhappy, was rooted in her failure to remain true to her role as a woman, to "love and be loved."

Adela, when young, wooed Carlos Ferrer away from her sister even though she was not in love with him. Carlos later abandoned her when he realized she did not love him. When it was as too late Adela did fall in love with Carlos. She married Juan merely to spite Carlos, and hoped to show him that her inspiration would make Juan more successful in life, but fate ruled otherwise, and it was Juan who was the failure. Though never mentioned, Carlos created a wall between Adela and Juan. She had married the man she did not love, and the spirit of the one she loved wrecked her life and that of her family.

Adela was the most active of Buero's female characters in betraying her role as a woman. To lure a man she did not love from another woman, and later to marry a man she did not love, were grievous sins in the eyes of Buero Vallejo, and for these she received a severe punishment—the loss of even her son's love and respect. At the end she was a tragic figure, more to be pitied than to be condemned.

This article has been limited to a discussion of the *underlying* role of man and woman in Buero's plays. The references to action in the plays has been restricted to the bare minimum required to substantiate the observations made. Frequently the characters and action symbolize situations which are far different from their surface appearance, but space does not permit a deeper interpretative study.

In spite of the repeated criticism that Buero's plays are entirely pessimistic and devoid of hope, by using the criteria of the author it can be said that there is much optimism and achievement in the actions of Buero's heroes and heroines. The fact that many of them die does not make them tragic figures, "Tragedia no es necesariamente catástrofe final, sino una especial manera de entender el final, sea feliz o amargo."[12] Upon considering the vicissitudes of Buero's characters, we may conclude that individual deaths are irrevelant and not necessarily tragic, that a man's success in life is to be measured by the importance of the contribution he has made to the betterment of society, and a woman's success by the depth of a requited love and her role as a mother.

Notes

1. For a full discussion of Buero's dramatic theory read Kessel Schwartz's "Buero Vallejo and the Concept of Tragedy, *Hispania,* (December 1968), pp. 817-824.

2. Antonio Buero Vallejo, *Historia de una escalera,* (Barcelona: Janes, 1950), p. 155.

3. Théatre de l'Impossible, (Neuchâtel: La Bacconière, 1963); Spanish translation *El teatro de lo imposible,* (Madrid: Guadarrama, 1966).

4. Comentario de Antonio Buero Vallejo, *Hoy es fiesta.* Colección teatro no. 176 (Madrid: Escelier, 1957), pp. 99-109. (Subsequent editions have omitted the *comentario.)*

5. "Reflexiones sobre el teatro de Buero Vallejo," *Primer Acto,* no. 11 (noviembre-diciembre 1959), p. 6.

6. Angel Fernández Santos, "Una entrevista con Buero Vallejo," *Primer Acto,* no. 90, (noviembre 1967), p. 12.

7. *La carreta* (septiembre 1963), p. 5.

8. *Ibid.*

9. Comentario de Buero Vallejo, *Madrugada,* Colección teatro no. 96, (Madrid: Escelier, 1954), p. 91. (Subsequent editions have omitted the comentario.)

10. *Teatro español, 1957-58,* (Madrid: Aguilar, 1959), p. VII.

11. *Teatro europeo contemporáneo,* (Madrid: Guadarrama, 1961), p. 389.

12. Comentario de Buero Vallejo, *Irene o el tesoro,* Colección teatro, no. 12, (Madrid: Escelier, 1955), pp. 122-23. (Subsequent editions have omitted the *comentario*).

Kenneth Brown (essay date May 1974)

SOURCE: Brown, Kenneth. "The Significance of Insanity in Four Plays by Antonio Buero Vallejo." *Revista de Estudios Hispánicos* VIII, no. 2 (May 1974): 247-60.

[*In the following essay, Brown explores the function of mentally ill characters in four of Buero Vallejo's plays.*]

Eloy, in *Mito*; Goya, in *El sueño de la razón*; Irene, in *Irene o el tesoro*; and the Father, in *El tragaluz* are all characterized as mentally unsound. In *Mito,* Eloy is "El pobre [que] sueña en fantasmas."[1] He readily admits to being in contact with Martians in flying saucers, and these so-called hallucinations earn for him the title of "iluso." In *El sueño,* Goya is considered "¡Un estafermo sin juicio!"[2] by Calomarde, the King's minister; "un viejo demente" by his mistress, Leocadia; and an old man suffering from "locura senil" and "miedo" by Arrieta, Goya's physician and friend. The artist, another Eloy, admits to seeing *hombres voladores* on the mountain behind his villa. In *Irene,* the protagonist is deemed "esquizofrénica"[3] by Campoy, her psychiatrist, and "loca" by Aurelia, er sister-in-law. Even Irene's hallucination, Juanito, the little ghost, himself realizes that Irene is mentally unbalanced:

> JUANITO. Está loca [referring to Irene], ¿verdad? Voz. Por lo menos, es muy desgraciada.
>
> (147)

Finally, the Father, in *El tragaluz,* shares a similar nomenclature. This old man cuts out figures of paper dolls, forgets the names of his immediate relatives, and thinks that his home is a railway station and that the *tragaluz,* a type of skylight, is the window of the "train."[4] Consequently, he is considered "loco" by his wife and by his son Mario, and a victim of arteriosclerosis by his son Vicente.

The Father, Irene, Goya and Eloy are judged insane in their respective environments. Taking into account these environments, the moments of lucid dialogue of the insane ones, and hope, *la esperanza,* as a direct result of their insanities, we shall see, however, that the requisites of insane actions—that they be "mad, idiotic, utterly senseless, and irrational"—[5] are not at all fulfilled. Buero's insane characters are much more than mere victims of mental disease. One Buero critic states, ". . . nevertheless, madness, in literature, is often a vehicle to express truths which cannot be conveyed by normality."[6] Eloy, Goya, Irene and the Father do express truth and hope under the guise of insanity. This is to be expected of a Buero Vallejo, who titles and subtitles his plays "Myth" *(Mito),* "a fantasy" (subtitle of *El sueño*), "a fable" (subt. of *Irene*) and "an experiment" (subt. of *El tragaluz*): the denial of reality—the titles and subtitles play down the actuality of the events in the play—gives vent to an affirmation of unreality; the factuality of sanity is denied while the truth of insanity is affirmed.

Psychopathologically or contextually, Eloy, Goya, Irene and the Father, nevertheless, are schizophrenics. They fit the following definition: "As a complex of pathological conditions the term schizophrenic includes a wide variety of bizarre and disturbing behavioral experiences, including *hallucinations,* delusions, extreme apathy, *personalized* and *illogical speech,* and the whole gamut of phenomena once classified as madness. The schizophrenic . . . is literally *alienated* and divorced from reality, living in a world of uncanny, overpowering terrors and unable to make contact with those around him."[7] Eloy sees men from Mars and lives in his own world; he almost always remains apart from the other characters, who are members of the cast of the play *Don Quijote.* Goya sees flying men, hears divers and diverse animal and human sounds continually throughout *El sueño,* converses with the subjects in his paintings, and lives secluded in his villa and in his deafness; he rarely speaks to his mistress, Leocadia, and only addresses his friends, Duaso and Arrieta, occasionally. In *Irene,* the protagonist sees her *duendecito* and lives retired, absorbed in a dream state. And the Father, of *El tragaluz,* lives in his railway station cutting out paper figures of people from pictures, and asking the seemingly moronic question "¿Quién es ése?", when referring to the paper people. The four characters live in their subconscious subworlds[8] in order to escape from their oppressive environments. Yet, as we shall see, they do this in order to truthfully and objectively reflect on and try to save this very environment. On the elementary, contextual level of analysis, the four characters are lunatics. This achieves verisimilar theatrical situations. Insanity on the elementary, mental level, however, and that on the symbolic level are diametrically opposed.

Eloy wants to escape the bomb threats, the atomic bomb drills with their authentic explosions attributed to *la pedagogía,* the workers' strikes, the rotten, foul city in which he lives, and the phony sense of security that his cohorts accept. In this city in which the cast of *Don Quijote* praise their "President" with cheers of "¡Viva el Señor Presidente!," life is a continual retreat into the *foso,* the fallout shelter, reality. Eloy's leader is a despot who has shackled liberty. For example, we see that the stagehands openly demonstrate their hatred for the police by resisting being searched, and that the inspector of police places a gun on Eloy's corpse at the end of the play in order to avoid public consternation. Eloy's insanity is a dissociative device by which he can enter the world of the Martians and leave the reality of oppression behind; he communicates with the Martians by means of Don Quijote's *yelmo de Mambrino,* a transmitter and receiver. As with Don Quijote, only from a conscious (he remains apart) and subconscious (he dreams) distancement from meaningless reality can Eloy objectively criticize and aid his environment. This is insanity. In an article concerning *El tragaluz,* Buero states that ". . . muchas veces no logramos tener una visión justa de la realidad y de las personas, tal vez por un exceso de racionalización previa sobre ellas."[9] In Eloy's case, this a priori reasoning is the programming fed his race by the despot, and only by transcending this "reality" can he rationally judge his *circunstancia.*

Goya is another Quixotic schizophrenic; he is less active physically than Eloy, for he lives almost totally secluded in his villa, yet his influence to create a better environment is equally as potent. Goya's insanity or reason produces monsters; the animalesque hallucinations of his "insanity" signify the ability to truthfully depict, by means of his impressionistic "pinturas negras" and "caprichos," the despotism of Fernando VII, a despotism infamous for its heinous persecutions of political liberals (masons, *comuneros* and those known as "negros") opposing the tyrannical regime. The artist explains the caption (and the title of the play) "El sueño de la razón produce monstruos" by adding, "La fantasía abandonada de la razón, produce monstruos imposibles: unida con ella, es madre de las artes y origen de sus maravillas."[10] When Goya explains his "Asmodea" to Arrieta, he states, "Eso sí es imaginación. Un pobre solitario como yo puede soñar que una bella mujer . . . de la raza misteriosa . . . le llevaría a su montaña. A descansar de la miseria humana." (32) This artistic imagination, however, combines aesthetic "fantasy" with reason. The painting itself—a beautiful woman and a man flying over a battlefield—is fantasy, yet the intent of the flight—to flee from human misery to a better life "on the mountain"—are Goya's Quixotic ideals graphically represented. This "reason" is also verbally represented by Arrieta, who, when discussing Goya's future with Duaso, says that the artist must "huir de este pozo, donde respira emanaciones de pantano." (50) Tis "pozo" is the "foso" in *Mito*; it is the reality of a hell. Speaking to his paintings and hearing animal noises are justifiable manifestations of Goya's fear; the fear is alive and haunting.

As for the *hombres voladores,* these are Goya's subconscious and conscious desires to envision the liberators of mankind graphically made manifest. This is the same case as in "Asmodea." Goya does say, "Yo he visto estos hombres voladores . . . ¡Le digo que los he visto!" He adds, however, his greatest wish: "que un día . . . bajen. ¡A acabar con Fernando VII y con todas las crueldades del mundo!" (32-33) This statement parallels several by Eloy. For example, Eloy, speaking about his Martians, informs us that "Ellos nos visitaban ya hace siglos con sus raudos platillos voladores y ahora aterrizarán para salvarnos de nuestra propia insania." (28) The two previous endeavors are by no means moronic verbal concatenations, but rather conscious and subconscious Quixotic, heroic expressions of both men's desire to save humanity represented in a dimension absent in Buero's theatrical sanity. The subconscious and conscious hallucinatory minds of both men, desirous of "unwronging wrongs," provide them with graphic interpretations of their hope.

Insanity in these heroes, far from being "utterly senseless," is of paramount significance; it signifies the only "sane" prognosis and cure for an infectious environment. Goya's opposition to despotism—his refusal to touch up a painting of the royal family, and his letter to Zapater openly denouncing Fernando VII—and Eloy's verbal manifestations of opposition to his society are examples.

The protagonist of *Irene,* humillated in the position of maid in her in-laws' home, when her husband dies shortly after their marriage, escapes to her dream world of cradlesongs and fairy tales recited to an imaginary child that she never had. Whereas Goya is precariously balanced on a tightrope of fear-ridden nerves, attributable to his impending persecution by Fernando VII, and to the pathetic realization that he is old and impotent, Irene is in a worse situation: she is on the brink of self-destruction. "No puedo más," Irene cries, as she once again feels the brunt of her father-in-law's wretchedness. He, Dimas, incessantly uses her as a victim of his own psychopathic nature.[11] For example, the "insidious," miserly Dimas refused to buy medicine for his son, Irene's husband, when the latter was dying, even though, as Dimas proudly admits, "¡Yo era el que más le quería de todos." (179) This traumatic experience coupled with the miser's insistent harping on Irene's economic worthlessness—she sews and cleans house, "but does not bring in money"—makes the poor woman feel that life is hell.[12]

Buero also gives Irene Quixotic symbolism. Campoy decribes her hallucinations as follows: "Don Quijote era hombre y veía gigantes con quienes combatir. Ella es mujer y puede ver un duendecito, o un niño, a quien besar." (163) Her subconscious wishes come true, the lovable Juanito helps Irene combat Dimas and all he represents by magically providing her with a world of "awe-inspiring spectral visions" or "caminos de luces," which bring her happiness. The Unamunian epitaph of the play, "Vivir los sueños al soñar la vida," is the epitaph of Irene's life. She can never stop dreaming, for Juanito, her subconscience personified, would die; Irene's soul would die. Being physically weak and in an extreme state of mental depression, Irene is not as heroically portrayed by Buero as are Eloy and Goya. Nevertheless, her insanity, her conscience of goodness, the "treasure" of the title of the play, is as viable in providing an effective contrast to her environment as are the more active attempts to do similarly by Goya and Eloy. She, unlike these two, passively displays her "bondad," and only Juanito can find, appreciate and happily gratify her. This insanity, seemingly more of a personal and lightly egocentric one, is contextually attributable to the advanced stage of Irene's psychopathological withdrawal.

Thus we see that Eloy, the iconoclast, attempts to break the false idols of security and contentment, and that Goya, the liberal, and Irene, "the self-absorbed dreamer," all rebel against sanity by adopting what is deemed insanity.

It would seem that the Father, in *El tragaluz,* is totally mentally lost. At least Irene has several extremely lucid dialogues. When she says, for example, "todo está oscuro . . . Huérfana cuando me casé con él . . . Huérfana ahora . . . Huérfana de mi hijo" and when she tells Daniel, after he unsuccessfully proposes marriage to her, that what he had proposed to her was truly "beautiful," she has demonstrated her ability to realistically evaluate her condition: everything is dark, reason is obscured, in a house whose owner refuses to let the lights burn in order to save money. The Father, on the other hand, hardly says anything lucid from a contextual point of view of the play. The major exception comes at the end of the play when he and his son Vicente are "speaking" to each other:

> V. Pero, ¿quién puede terminar con las canalladas en un mundo canalla?
>
> F. Yo.
>
> 　　　　　. . . . .
>
> V. Pero no se puede volver a la niñez.
>
> F. No.

The rest of the dialogue appears to be a regression to the senility or insanity state:

> F. No subas al tren
>
> 　　　　　. . . . .
>
> Tú no subirás al tren.
>
> 　　　　　　　　　　　　　　　　　　(98)

Even when the Father and his son Mario are "speaking," the "dialogue" can be considered in one of two ways: nonsensical, or as a Socratic dialogue in which the Father elicits general truths from Mario and molds them to win the argument and consequently save his son:

F. Y tú, ¿quién eres?

M. Mario.

F. Tú te llamas, ¿como mi hijo?

M. Soy tu hijo.

F. Mario era más pequeño.

M. He crecido.

F. Entonces subirá mejor.

M. ¿A dónde?

F. Al tren.

(18)

Since the unfortunate Vicente, long since corrupted by a "dog-eat-dog" world, cannot be convinced by his Father's "reason," he must suffer the consequences: the Father kills him.

Everything the nameless Father says in "the experiment" is actually reasonable and lucid. The Father, Mother, El and Ella all function as allegorical and universal or collective characters. The Father is the vindicator, the *desagraviador* symbol. The Mother symbolizes collective acquiescence to the reality of the base, despicable acts of society. El and Ella, humans supposedly from the future who present this play as if it were history, the experimenters, are the collective conscience of man at a distanced view, from a view outside the context of the play (several centuries later). The Father, however, is this conscience at a distanced view—busy at his "insane" trivialities—from inside the context of the play. When the Father declares, "Claro. Yo soy Vicentito" and "¡Si Vicente soy yo!," he expresses the truth. Ella seemingly answers the question "¿Quién es ése?" when she says "Yo soy tú, y tú eres yo. Todos hemos vivido, y viviremos, todas las vidas" (83), but one cannot forget that the Father has been saying this all along by stating that he indeed is Vicente; he is a part of humanity's collective conscience. The Father is his "son," and for this reason he is trying to save Vicente, for in the process he is saving himself; he is saving Man. The Father, therefore, is as lucid as is the audience that "judges" him and his family.

The Father, too, joins the ranks of the Quixotic schizophrenics—Eloy, Goya and Irene. Vicente attributes Quixotism to his senile father and to his dreamy brother, Mario, who is equally eager to find an answer to "¿Quién es ése?," when he says the following to Encarna, his mistress: "Porque tú no tienes nada que reprocharme . . . Eso queda para los ilusos que miran por los tragaluces y ven gigantes donde deberían ver molinos." (77) A seemingly passive Father is, in the reality of his insanity, actually an extremely active Quixotic character. By saving paper dolls of people whom he does not know, the Father demonstrates his "insane" desire to save souls. As in the other three plays, insanity on the contextual, elementary level of analysis is the tragic poet's artifice for creating verisimilar human situations. On the symbolic level, however, as we shall see, the Father, Irene, Goya and Eloy generate a very sane hope.

Eloy dies attempting to save his friend, Ismael, the union leader, from a typical despotic government plot. This sacrifice, however, serves a hopeful purpose: it proves to the hard-line union leader, who had once said "Eloy, la acción es impura" (43), though captured by police, that non-remunerative Quixotic actions are not in vain. Ismael's followers will hopefully combine their zealous quest for liberty with an equally zealous, Quixotic human charity, and thus create a better world. To the dying Eloy, Ismael regrets, "Yo moriré también. Somos dos locos." Eloy replies, "No es todo inútil . . . Aunque no le entiendes . . . Los actos son semillas . . . que germinan . . . Germinará tu acción . . . También la mía." (109) A second indication of hope lies in the cast's uneasiness after Eloy dies. The show can never be the same.

Eloy's insanity, his ability to soundly judge, criticize and rectify his environment, is noble. It reflects "his integrity and refusal to compromise"[13] an ideal, and for this reason his Martians, his ideal, will never die. Even after being tricked by the cast, who dress up as spacemen and try to convince Eloy that they, men from Jupiter, have defeated the Martians and have now come to subject the world to their tyranny, Eloy knows that his hallucinations were and are real: "Tal vez mi flaco juicio no distingue / lo real de lo soñado. Quizá nunca / descendieron platillos a la Tierra. / Acaso nos desprecien y permitan / nuestra extinción en el apocalipsis / que estamos entre todos acercando. / Pero tal vez jamás hubo marcianos / y entonces soy un viejo demente." (85) Martians do exist because one named Eloy dies at the end of the play. Others have existed, and hopefully more will exist. In the seventeenth century they came on Rocinantes, in the nineteenth they came by mechanical wings, and in the twentieth they came by flying saucers. The "vehicle" of madness changes with the times.

Unamuno writes in his *Quijotismo y Cervantismo* about a type of insane heroism: "Predicar la cordura suele ser predicar la muerte, combatir la locura del sueño de la vida es zapar el heroísmo."[14] Arrieta, in *El sueño,* echoes similarly: "Para que viva Goya, acaso destruyamos a Goya . . . No querré que un gigante se vuelva pigmeo porque soy un pigmeo." (84) Goya, the "giant," must continue to paint his hallucinations; he must continue to protest Fernando VII's regime by painting its façade if he is to spiritually survive. Unfortunately, spiritually destroyed by fear at the end of the play, he leaves for France. He has, however, managed to leave his mark, for Fernando VII has been and still is afraid of Goya and the liberals. This is shown when the artist states that "Me han vencido. Pero él ya estaba vencido." (105) Moreover, Goya's paintings will remain to reveal his impressions of a country plagued by despotism. The paintings also reveal hope, for as Goya's subconscience, represented by Mariquita, the little girl who is sitting on the right side in the "Aquelarre," states, ". . . soy yo. Una niña sin miedo a las brujas. ¡La mayor bruja de todas!" (67) This symbolic "demon" is Fernando VII and what he represents, who can no longer effectively wield fear against Goya and those who support similar ideals of political liberty.

Speaking about the tragic hero in Buero's plays, one critic states that ". . . his outward defeat implies the survival of his inner ideals and hopes."[15] Although Goya and Eloy have been "outwardly defeated (Goya is self-exiled and Eloy dead), their ideals or hallucinations remain.

Unamuno continues his essay *Quijotismo y Cervantismo*: "Penétrate de que el mundo eres tú, y esfuérzate en salvarlo, para salvarte. El mundo es tu mundo, tu mundo eres tú, pero no el yo egoísta, sino el hombre. Dentro del mundo, de mi mundo, que soy yo, yo soy uno de tantos prójimos."[16] This might as well be Ella, in *El tragaluz,* answering the ontological question[17] "¿Quién es ése?" This is Don Quijote's credo as well as the Father's. Vicente had either to be saved or removed; although the Father kills him, hope exists. Taken away to a mental institution and deprived of his scissors, the surgeon's scalpel, the Father's function in the drama has ceased. It is hoped that the Father, Mother and Mario will now be able to "live." The great lie that burdened them psychologically is now gone. Mario, for example, can now evaluate his brother, and in the process evaluate himself. He admits: "Yo lo maté . . . Mi hermano no era malo, por eso volvió. A su modo, quiso pagar. El quería engañarme . . . y ver claro; yo quería salvarlo . . . y matarlo." (101) Mario finally begins to answer the question "¿Quién es ése?"; the audience, too, can now try to evaluate themselves and their brothers, the victims of Civil War and despotism.

The end result of Irene's insanity is her death. The denouement, an ambivalent one, is typically Buerista.[18] Irene physically dies as she leaps from the balcony, yet she spiritually finds contentment in the "camino de luz" that her subconscious mind has erected for her. Juanito, asleep in her arms, although this act is strictly forbidden him by the Voz that directs his actions, symbolizes Irene's oneness with her dream. Irene has saved herself from a world of evil with potential goodness *(la bondad)*. Her immediate subconscious needs, however, provide her with a death or new life of dreams. Hope results from her "sacrifice": Daniel, the professor without a profession, will have to voluntarily transcend his mediocrity, and Dimas' family, the miser having been institutionalized instead of Irene, is saved. The ambivalence rings true as Aurelia continues in her father's image and rebels against them all. The characters will all have to earn and find *bondad*.

Insanity in *Mito, El sueño de la razón, Irene o el tesoro* and *El tragaluz* is, as Campoy, Irene's psychiatrist, admits, contagious. Its potency affects others around it, and the result is hope in a better future for mankind starting now. Insanity, in Buero's theater, is "sanity" plus. It signifies man's conscious and subconscious desire to eliminate despotism and wretchedness and his ability to at least start the process. Insanity signifies the ability for self-knowledge, and a broader, collective knowledge among mankind's brothers. Sanity, on the other hand, in Buero's theater, signifies: Dimas' pathological tendencies, and the household's subservience to the tyrant, in *Irene*; the President's gestapo-like tactics, and the cast's acquiescence to oppression, in *Mito*; the pathetic embroidery bordering Fernando VII and his regime, and the greed of Goya's family, especially of Gumersinda, his daughter-in-law, who only wants the artist's inheritance, in *El sueño*; and Vicente's life of "deceit, trickery and compromise," in *El tragaluz.*

Notes

1. Antonio Buero Vallejo, *Mito* (Madrid: Escelicer, 1968), p. 23.

2. Antonio Buero Vallejo, *El sueño de la razón* (Madrid: Escelicer, 1970), p. 12.

3. Antonio Buero Vallejo, *Irene o el tesoro,* in *Teatro* (Buenos Aires: Editorial Losada, 1962), p. 163.

4. Antonio Buero Vallejo, *El tragaluz* (Madrid: Escelicer, 1968), p. 21.

5. *The Oxford English Dictionary,* Vol. V (Oxford: Oxford University Press, 1933), p. 327.

6. Martha T. Halsey, "The Dreamer in the Tragic Theater of Buero Vallejo," in *Revista de Estudios Hispánicos,* Vol. II, No. 2 (Alabama, Nov. 1968), p. 271.

7. Leslie A. Rabkin, *Psychopathology and Literature* (San Francisco: Chandler Publishing Co., 1966), p. 93. (The italics are mine.)

8. See, for example, Angel Fernández-Santos, "El enigma de *El tragaluz,*" in *Primer Acto* (Madrid, setiembre 1967), p. 6: "Nuestros submundos son el producto de una esclerosis histórica y, por lo tanto, de una persistencia de la catástrofe."

9. Angel Fernández-Santos, "Una entrevista con Buero Vallejo," in *Primer Acto* (Madrid, setiembre 1967), p. 12.

10. F. D. Klingender, *Goya in the Democratic Tradition* (New York: Schocken Books, 1968), p. 92.

11. Rabkin, *Psychopathology,* p. 219. "The psychopath or antisocial individual is an enigmatic case. He displays none of the anxiety or symptomology of the neurotic or psychotic; *he may not commit any overt acts of criminality*; he can make a good impression, charm those around him, and display a lively intelligence. At first blush he may appear a model citizen.

Yet closer examination of these individuals shows an *insidious* side to their personalities . . . they are typically *without morals or a sense of guilt.* They are constantly self-defeating and irresponsible, *living on the surface of life and unable to create a meaningful world of relationships.* The swindler, the con-man, the pathological liar are examples of antisocial personalities." Dimas fits many of these descriptions perfectly. (The italics are mine.)

12. Buero, *Irene,* p. 143. Daniel says, "Te quiero salvar de este infierno."

13. Halsey, "The Dreamer," p. 285.

14. Miguel de Unamuno y Jugo, *Obras Completas, Quijotismo y Cervantismo,* tomo V (Madrid: Afrodisio Aguado, 1958), p. 710.

15. Halsey, "The Dreamer," p. 285.

16. Unamuno, *Quijotismo,* loc. cit.

17. Fernández-Santos, "Una entrevista con Buero," p. 13. Buero compares the problem of identification in *El tragaluz* with "el enigma ontológico como en Segismundo."

18. Cf. *En la ardiente oscuridad,* in which Carlos, having murdered the dreamer Ignacio, generates hope by verbally repeating and hopefully adopting Ignacio's desire to transcend physical and spiritual blindness.

William Giuliano (essay date June 1977)

SOURCE: Giuliano, William. "The Defense of Buero Vallejo." *Modern Drama* XX, no. 2 (June 1977): 223-33.

[*In the following essay, Giuliano traces the critical reaction to Buero Vallejo's career and attempts to revive the dramatist's reputation.*]

Today's heroes are sometimes tomorrow's villains, and unfortunately, to a limited extent, that is the unhappy lot of Antonio Buero Vallejo,[1] whose play *Historia de una escalera* (*Story of a Staircase*) in 1949 injected new life into the stagnant Spanish theater and inspired many young dramatists to write serious plays, directly or indirectly criticizing the political, social, and economic policies of Spain. A prisoner for six and a half years, under sentence of death for eight months, Buero was released in 1946 and soon after won the Lope de Vega prize for *Historia de una escalera,* which became an instant hit. Within several years, he and another outstanding young dramatist, Alfonso Sastre, became symbols of liberal opposition to the Franco regime. liberal opposition to the Franco regime.

Unfortunately, the two playwrights became involved in a polemic which severed their friendship and paved the way for a gradual undermining of the reputation of Buero as a

sincere exponent of Spanish liberalism. In 1960, Sastre accused Buero of "posibilismo," that is, of compromising his principles by disguising his liberal views so that his plays would be approved by the censors for performance.[2] Buero replied that he opposed the "imposibilismo" suggested by Sastre, since this would render production impossible in Spain. He advocated boldness but rejected undue rashness, and he continued to write as before. Sastre had great difficulty in having his plays approved for performance and eventually stopped writing for the stage. In 1973 he was jailed as an accomplice in a bomb explosion but later was released on bail, probably because of international pressure brought to bear on the Franco government. Buero, on the other hand, although he had difficulty in securing licenses for his plays, was able to see all his plays but two (approved years later) passed by the censors.

The youth of Spain in Buero's early years as a dramatist rallied behind him and Sastre as bulwarks of courageous resistance against a repressive political environment. The youth of twenty years later, however, began to lose faith in Buero, thinking, as Sastre had earlier, that he had capitulated to government censorship. He encountered disfavor not only ideologically but also esthetically. He was severely criticized for persisting to use a technique which gave him, as author, full control of the text, instead of permitting greater audience participation in the manner of the Living Theater.

Although he had deliberately sought to involve the audience in his plays (as early as 1950 in *En la ardiente oscuridad* [*In the Burning Darkness*], the theater lights were completely extinguished for a moment to make the audience feel the darkness of the blind protagonist), Buero refused to involve the audience actively. On seeing *Orlando Furioso,* directed by Luca Ronconi, Buero[3] expressed his ideas on the performance. Ronconi inspired much action, he observed, but this was purely physical. Unless the spectator is spiritually as well as physically involved, such participation is purely illusive. In an interview two years later,[4] Buero restated his opinion on spontaneous audience participation, declaring it sometimes counterproductive. He did not, however, object to the collective writing of a text. A text, he conceived, was necessary for the permanent preservation of artistic achievement. His own technique represented a striving for psycho-physical participation emphasizing the spiritual, with elements of Brecht on one hand and Beckett on the other (Brechtian *Verfremdungseffekt* and Beckett's Theater of the Absurd).

In 1970, after not having produced a play for three years, Buero presented the theater public with a drama that embodied the principles of audience participation as he had evolved them. The play, entitled *El sueño de la razón* (*The Sleep of Reason*)[5], which was not approved by the censors for five and a half months, is based on the life of Francisco de Goya at the age of seventy-six, when, refusing to accept the tyranny of Ferdinand VII, he retired to his country home and created the famous Black Paintings. Goya was deaf at this time, and Buero skilfully makes the audience see and feel everything through his eyes. When Goya is on the stage, the other characters communicate with him by writing, gesturing or using sign language. They move their lips, but the audience does not hear them. Goya, of course, does speak. There are voices which the painter and the audience hear, but the other characters do not. Among other sounds Goya hears laughter, the howling of cats, the screeching of owls, the braying of donkeys, and the cackling of hens. Dozing off, he sees grotesque figures which attack him. Through these dramatic means, the audience feels intimately the solitude of deafness and the terrible fear which slowly grips Goya, who refuses to submit to Ferdinand by begging forgiveness for derogatory remarks made about him. Later, however, threatened by the king and his soldiers, the aged Goya finally breaks down in terror and asks father Duaso, his friend, to beg the king's forgiveness and permission to leave the country.

Buero, who had previously become more Brechtian in his estrangement technique, now identifies the spectator completely with his main character, a procedure which he declared did not necessarily prevent *Verfremdungseffekt.*[6] Obviously Ferdinand represents the twentieth-century dictator and Goya, the liberal resister. There are references to censorship, the Holy Inquisition, and religious and political oppression. In this play, however, Buero is more pessimistic than he has ever been. The Black Paintings, which are flashed on the back of the stage, and the action of the play reflect the malice, hypocrisy, greed, cruelty, and terror which overwhelm man with only a faint ray of hope to offset their devastating effects. Goya is defeated, and the play consequently would seem to reveal the triumph of tyranny, but there is one saving grace. Father Duaso, Ferdinand's official censor, and doctor Arrieta, an avowed liberal, are hostile to each other in the beginning, but later both men forget their differences to help Goya avoid the wrath of the king, both realizing that they must mitigate the undue violence that is an integral part of both factions. These two characters may symbolize the opposing sides of the Spanish Civil War, both of which must suppress extreme elements to effect a peaceful synthesis.

This play has been one of Buero's most widely acclaimed. It was performed in Italy, Russia, East and West Germany, Czechoslovakia, Hungary, Rumania, and other countries, and although it was a triumph at home as well as abroad, the youth who had criticized Buero before continued to do so.

Undoubtedly a desire to answer his youthful critics motivated the writing of the next play, *Llegada de los dioses* (*Arrival of the gods*),[7] produced in 1971. In it Julio, a young painter, suddenly becomes blind for one of two reasons which the author deliberately leaves open to question: the first, Julio learns that his father, years before, had been a member of the military and tortured prisoners; the

second, several days later, immediately after Julio's exhibition has met heartbreaking failure, his father, who is an amateur painter, informs him of the great success of his own exhibition.

The young painter visits his father with Veronica, his mistress, and denounces him for having taken part in torturing prisoners. Felipe, the father, says he was obliged to do so to obtain vital information during the war, but that all that was forgotten and he had helped to develop his country with distinction economically. In spite of his diatribe against his father and those of his class, Julio decides to remain with him even when Veronica warns him that he is being contaminated. Felipe at first resents Veronica's influence on Julio, and tells her: "Your revolution ends up in psychodelic dances, in drugs . . . even in senseless crime." "Your revolution will resort to torture when it begins to fight or seize power" (Part I). Later, however, he realizes Veronica's depth of understanding and asks her to take care of his son. Soon after he dies of a heart attack, when he learns that Nuria, his illegitimate child by Matilde, has been killed by accidentally jumping on a bomb left unnoticed since the war.

As in *El sueño de la razón,* the action is seen through the eyes of the protagonist, Julio. When Julio enters the stage for the first time, the stage becomes totally dark. A spotlight is focused on him, then on Artemio, his father's best friend. Artemio has horns protruding from his head: the sign of the cuckold, since his wife, Matilde, who appears with the head of a fox, has been deceiving him with Felipe, who appears with smoked glasses. These and many other stage effects are used to make the audience see everything from Julio's point of view.

Julio represents the young well-to-do Spanish radical who likes to talk about revolution but does nothing concrete while he still enjoys the benefits of what he considers his father's ill-gotten wealth. Veronica, ten years older than Julio, is more realistic and sincerely revolutionary. She chides Julio for adopting a pose that has become fashionable—that of looking scornfully upon bourgeois society as if it were composed of insignificant insects—while in reality being fearful of its power, unable to confront it as if it were a pack of dangerous wolves. When his father dies, Julio recognizes his own shortcomings. He had considered himself a "god" come to right wrongs, but now he realizes that he is merely a sick person in a sick world, and other gods (other young people) more sincerely dedicated must come to purify society.

Angel Fernández Santos, in his review of the play, finds the stage effects unnaturally superimposed on the action in contrast to the brilliant integration of effects and action in *El sueño de la razón,* and he declares that *Llegada de los dioses* "has justified his [Buero's] many detractors."[8] He also criticizes the structure of the play, declaring that Buero merely poses questions without coherent development. In an interview with the same Angel Fernández Santos,[9] Buero clarifies the significance of the role of Julio by repeating essentially what Veronica said to Julio, then going on to say:

> I know that expressing myself in this manner now and on the stage I may alienate some of my young friends. Nowadays the thing to do is to flatter youth, but this is an irresponsible game which I will not play, for this is to be disloyal to them and render them ill service. . . . Perhaps one might say that whatever discourages youth is ill-advised and destructive, but I would answer that to give young people a 'deified' concept of themselves is far more destructive. The best means of showing confidence in them is precisely to speak to them truthfully.[10]

Buero explains that Julio represents only a segment of Spanish youth, and Veronica is a little more experienced and understands the real situation better. Both, however, are still tainted by the bourgeois world in which they live, and Julio's rebellion may be caused more by his failure as a painter than by his horror at his father's black deeds. Finally, Buero affirms that his play is a condemnation of the bourgeois society of Spain and concludes: "I do not attempt, therefore, to bring out the deficiencies of an apparently rebellious young man in order to justify the actions of his parents but I do try to study his deficiencies in confrontation with his parents who are not all in the right and who, in part, are the cause of these deficiencies."[11]

Obviously *Llegada de los dioses* did not endear Buero to the hearts of the younger generation, nor did his inauguration into the Real Academia Española (Royal Spanish Academy) in May 1972 (he had been elected early in 1971). This acceptance of an honor closely related to the Establishment put Buero on the defensive from another quarter. Some labeled it a surrender to the forces of conservatism, but Buero's friends of long standing did not desert him. Francisco García Pavón, the noted critic and novelist, defended him in an article[12] approving Buero's decision to accept the honor. He excoriates those who remain in Spain but maintain silence and those who fled the country. Buero, he says, has had the courage to stay in Spain and speak his mind, using symbols imposed by circumstance (obviously censorship), but nevertheless speaking out. Emilio Gascó Contell also supported Buero, declaring that this unexpected honor was totally unforeseen but clearly earned. He states: "Everyone is acquainted . . . with his calm rebelliousness—direct, tenacious and uncorruptible. . . . What annoys many are Buero Vallejo's ethics, his thoughts, the tension of his 'engagé' works, reflecting the ideas of an author anxious to awaken dormant consciences and not afraid to call a spade a spade."[13]

In a long interview with Armando Carlos Isasi Angulo,[14] Buero defends his reasons for accepting the seat in the Academy. He notes that his action has elicited many adverse comments and even been called a capitulation. He goes on to explain his reasons for the acceptance, observing that as early as 1957 he had been cautiously approached for possible membership but had displayed no interest. He declares that the Academy is an independent body whose prestige not only affords him protection from his enemies, but also makes it easier for him to obtain permission from the censors to present his plays. When the interviewer asks him if he considers himself a leftist writer and why, Buero replies: "Man! What a question! I have been clearly under a definite political banner all my life. I was on the point of losing my life for being a leftist."[15]

As usual, Buero delayed a long time in preparing his next play, *La fundación* (*The Foundation*),[16] for performance in Madrid in 1974. The action of this play takes place in the jail where Tomás and other political prisoners await sentence. Again we have audience participation in the Buerian sense. The spectators see the cell as Tomás sees it, with nice beds, fine glassware, a good bar with drinks, a telephone, et cetera. The other prisoners do not see these things. They are all a dream world created by Tomás to escape reality—the reality of having betrayed his fellow revolutionaries. Ascl, the eldest of the prisoners, slowly brings Tomás back to reality. The luxuries imagined by Tomás disappear one by one until he finally realizes his true situation. Asel has been trying to get them transferred to a punishment cell by behaving improperly, but they are not removed. When Max is called out, Asel tells Tomás and Lino of a plan to escape from the punishment cell to the outside. They suspect that Max has told the authorities of their wish to be transferred. Their suspicions are confirmed. Asel is called for execution, and while the door is open, Lino, in retaliation, hurls Max over a railing to his death. Tomás and Lino are ordered to pack their belongings. They know that they are going to be executed or taken to the punishment cell. Tomás, who had opposed Asel's plan to escape, is now inspired by Asel's words and actions to declare that he will try to escape if taken to the cell.

Asel summarizes the main theme of the play when he tells the others that they live in a violent world in which men are killed for fighting injustice, for belonging to a particular race or religious creed, a world in which even children are killed and maimed by napalm bombs (reference to Vietnam?). Even they, the oppressed, may become the oppressor. He tells Tomás: "This time we are the victims, my poor Tomás, but I tell you something . . . I prefer it so. If I should save my life perhaps someday I would be the hangman." In spite of this, Asel continues, they must keep fighting in order to stop all atrocities and oppression. They should, however, try to distinguish between justifiable cruelty and unjustified violence, a difficult procedure because the enemy makes no distinction (Part I).

In his review of the play, Miguel Bilbatúa criticizes Buero for being unspecific about the political society he is portraying and for being ambiguous: "Some will say it [the play] is a marvel in being able to avoid the obstacles of censorship, others will say it is a fine example of how to swim and keep your clothes dry."[17] According to Bilbatúa, Buero is evidently telling us that violence will always exist and the oppressed will be the oppressors when they come to power. This interpretation, however, would seem to be based on the speech of Asel quoted above without reference to the limitations he added immediately after. Angel Fernández Santos[18] also finds that the play is subject to varying, even diametrically opposed, interpretations, but calls it one of Buero's most daring works in which the author is playing with fire.

The apparent paradox—the resort to oppression by the oppressed come to power—is the inevitable result of a world steeped in hatred, evil, and cruelty, and even though a revolutionary must also have recourse to cruelty, he must seek to control his natural inclination to violence, continue the fight for freedom, and strive to establish the rights of man. This is the lesson taught Tomás by Asel. Tomás, who had sought to escape reality, is inspired to escape prison; the killing of Max was unnecessary: "If we do not succeed in separating violence from cruelty, we will be crushed" (Part II). Perhaps Buero may be referring to the many acts of terrorism committed in the cause of freedom which have cost many innocent lives and accomplished little in furthering the cause.

In an interview with José Monleón[19], in which Buero answers the critics who contended that his play was not explicit, the author replies that a play should pose problems, not solve them, and goes on to differentiate between unrestrained violence and effective, premeditated cruelty, the latter unfortunately being necessary to achieve a humane and just world. This universal immorality is not peculiar to Spain but prevalent throughout the world. Criticized also for allegedly inaccurate details regarding prison life, Buero replies that he described them from firsthand knowledge. When Buero speaks of cruelty, Monleón reminds him that certain sectors seem to feel the desire to be cruel with him (Buero). Monleón speaks of those who, overlooking the years Buero spent in prison, concentrate on condemning his plays instead of trying to understand them, and reproach him for having joined the Academy. They accuse him of having compromised with the Establishment, because his plays are produced on television and conservative critics accept them readily. Buero replies that many liberal foreign authors who should definitely have been rejected also have their plays performed and are applauded by the conservative critics. He points out that he has been well received by both the conservative and the liberal critics. Sometimes the Establishment approves critical writers, involving them with itself so that they seem to be ideologically associated with it. The authors, however, can always show through their works that they are not captives of the Establishment.

To add to Buero's troubles, he has become involved in a dispute with Fernando Arrabal. In the first issue of *Estreno*,[20] John Dowling, in passing, mentioned that Arrabal had received the support of Buero in the production of one of his plays. Arrabal, in a letter published in *Estreno*,[21] maintains that neither he nor any other exiled or muzzled author has ever read a line of Buero in his support, and that Alfonso Sastre is in jail while Buero accepts the highest prizes of Franco Spain, including membership in the Royal Academy. Arrabal also refers to the "posibilismo" polemic mentioned earlier and asserts that the jailing of Sastre proves that he was right.

In the same issue of *Estreno*,[22] Buero answers Arrabal (apparently he had been told of the scheduled publication of Arrabal's letter), deploring the fact that Arrabal had recently mentioned the Sastre polemic to the Italian press. He cites his support of Arrabal in *Triunfo* January 1959 and in *Ya* September 17, 1967, and his defense in numerous periodicals of other young writers who were having difficulties with censorship. Buero justifies the writers who have remained in Spain and have published and produced their works under censorship. He rejects Arrabal's contention that the only worthwhile theater after the Civil War has been produced by exiled or muzzled dramatists (those who did not submit their plays to censorship), the latter having lost the right of having their plays officially licensed. (Arrabal also mentions in his letter that his plays are clandestinely performed and copied for distribution.)

It is clear that Buero has lost favor with many of those with whom he wished to be associated, and in particular with the younger generation. We ask ourselves why this has come about; and this writer finds a number of reasons for it. The young who have not known the horrors of the Civil War resent the lack of political freedom and feel the urge to act—hence the constant student demonstrations that have closed the universities so many times for so long. They do not understand that an author cannot do individually what they do collectively. To write exactly what he thinks is impossible—a rigid censorship determines every single work to be published, every line an actor can speak. The censors sometimes license plays that are very critical of the regime, but performances are limited to one night stands and university functions, or they are otherwise restricted. Thus, this type of play is usually seen only by those who are already in sympathy with the author's views. In order to receive a license for the commercial theater which will give him the widest audience, an author must resort to subterfuge if he wishes to be critical of conditions in Spain. Buero usually does this by choosing a well-known story or a well-known figure from the past as the basis for a play in which the discerning spectator easily perceives an analogy to conditions in the present. He does this so effectively that even the members of the society he is attacking find his plays so different, so artistically superior to run-of-the-mill commercial drama, that they welcome and praise each new one. This technique accounts for the approval of the conservative press, which accepts the play at the level of its superficial stage action; and for the approval of the liberal press, which, aware of a second level, sees the underlying themes and problems applicable to Spain and to the world in general, the questions which Buero leaves open because he believes his function as a dramatist is to awaken an interest in man's problems with a view to inciting him to action.

This open interpretation often leads to misinterpretation, particularly inasmuch as in the more recent plays Buero has become more skeptical of man's ability to rise above himself and finds even the most idealistic of purposes tainted with an inevitable propensity toward immoral behavior. These later plays also suggest that a head-on clash could be averted if restraint and understanding brought about a meeting of the minds. It is true that Buero's earlier plays are more direct and more critical of dictatorship and tyranny as the present youth of Spain would prefer, but the plays discussed here are a far cry from favoring dictatorship or tyranny.

The younger generation tends to be limited in its criteria: entirely unreasonable in insisting that Buero's technique follow a definite pattern, especially in the light of his dramatic successes; and, as far as content is concerned, failing to realize that, given the strict censorship imposed, a writer in Spain must either stop writing or, as Domingo Pérez Minik phrases it, "find his mask."[23] Buero's *Aventura en lo gris* (*Adventure in Gray*), written in 1949, was not licensed for performance until 1963 in a modified version, and *La doble historia del doctor Valmy* (*The Double Case History of Doctor Valmy*), written in 1964, presented in the Farris Anderson translation at Chester, England, November 22, 1968, has just been approved for its first performance in Spanish.[24]

La doble historia del doctor Valmy should silence many of Buero's detractors. The granting of a license by the censors astonishes this writer, for this play is unquestionably Buero's most virulent, direct attack on the police state. In it Daniel Barnes, a member of the Special Police, is engaged in torturing prisoners. One day he is forced to assist in making a prisoner permanently impotent. From then on he cannot fulfill his sexual obligations with his wife. He consults Doctor Valmy, who narrates the story to the audience. The doctor informs Barnes that he feels guilty for having deprived the prisoner of his virility and consequently has annihilated his own desires in punishment. Daniel's wife, Mary, who had not known of his torture activities, is horrified. Daniel tries to resign, but he is not permitted to do so. Mary believes he does not wish to resign, and one day she seizes his pistol and tells him not to come near her. He does approach her, and she kills him. The other case history is that of The Gentleman and The Lady, neighbors of the Barneses, who occasionally interrupt the action to tell the audience that the Barnes

story is false. They represent the guilty who refuse to see repression and consequently do nothing about it.

This brief outline is enough to reveal the play as a powerful indictment of dictatorship. Intensely dramatic, it moves rapidly and smoothly from one scene to another without the interruption of a curtain. It is Brechtian in technique and one of Buero's best plays. Certainly if Buero has compromised his principles, he would not permit the performance of this play. It will be interesting to assess the reaction to it. If nothing else, *La doble historia del doctor Valmy* should inspire respect for a man who has suffered much to play his part in restoring the dignity of man and who has steadfastly and courageously been true to himself.

Notes

1. For a full discussion of Buero's plays, see: Ricardo Doménech, *El teatro de Buero Vallejo* (Madrid, 1973); William Giuliano, *Buero, Sastre y el teatro de su tiempo* (New York, 1971); Martha Halsey, *Antonio Buero Vallejo* (New York, 1973), in English; a short review by William Giuliano, "The Theater of Buero Vallejo, 1949-1969," in *Modern Drama* 13 (February 1971), 366-73.

2. *Primer Acto*, 14 (June 1960), 1-2; Buero replied in the following number, 15 (July-August, 1960), 1-6. For a discussion, see: Kessel Schwartz, "'Posibilismo' and 'imposibilismo,'" *Revista Hispánica Moderna* 34 (January-April 1968), 436-45.

3. "Illusión de participación," *Primer Acto* 126-27 (Nov.-Dec. 1970), 60-61.

4. Armando Carlos Isasi Angulo, "El teatro de Antonio Buero Vallejo," *Papeles de Son Armadans* 67 (December 1972), 281-320.

5. Published in Carlos Sáinz de Robles, ed., *Teatro español, 1969-70* (Madrid, 1971), 147-237; and in *Primer Acto* 117 (February 1970), 28-63.

6. "A propósito de Brecht," *Insula* 200-201 (July-August, 1963), 1, 14.

7. Published in Carlos Sáinz de Robles, ed., *Teatro español, 1971-72* (Madrid, 1973), 95-169; and in *Primer Acto* 138 (November 1971), 39-73.

8. "Ibsen, Buero y Valle-Inclán," *Insula* 300-301 (Nov.-Dec. 1971), 39-73.

9. "Sobre *Llegada de los dioses*, una entrevista con Antonio Buero Vallejo," *Primer Acto* 138 (November 1971), 27-38.

10. *Ibid.*, 32-33.

11. *Ibid.*, 33.

12. "Antonio Buero Vallejo, sus trabajos y sus días," *Destino*, February 20, 1972, 22-23.

13. "Antonio Buero Vallejo, o el inconformismo en la Academia." *El libro español* 170 (February 1972), 66.

14. "El teatro de Antonio Buero Vallejo," *op. cit.*

15. *Ibid.,* 294.

16. Published in Carlos Sáinz de Robles, ed., *Teatro español, 1973-74* (Madrid, 1975). 223-318; and in *Primer Acto* 167 (April 1974), 18-56.

17. *"La fundación," Destino,* February 19, 1974.

18. *"La fundación* de Antonio Buero Vallejo," *Insula* 328 (March 1974), 15.

19. "Buero: de la repugnante y necesaria violencia a la repugnante e inutil crueldad," *Primer Acto* 167 (April 1974), 4-13.

20. Número extraordinario, 1, 1975, published by the Univ. of Cincinnati: the relevant paragraph was reproduced in issue no. 3, Autumn 1975, 6.

21. *Ibid.,* 5.

22. "Desde España," *Estreno,* Autumn 1975, 13-17.

23. *Teatro europeo contemporáneo* (Madrid, 1961), 386.

24. Published bilingually with translation by Farris Anderson, *Artes Hispánicas, Hispanic Arts,* I, 2, Autumn 1967, 85-169; ed., Alfonso M. Gil, *La doble historia del doctor Valmy* (Chicago, 1970).

Ida Molina (essay date May 1978)

SOURCE: Molina, Ida. "Truth and Compassion: *Aventura en lo gris* and *La maison de la nuit.*" *Revista de Estudios Hispánicos* XII, no. 2 (May 1978): 217-25.

[*In the following essay, Molina compares the relationship of truth and compassion in* Aventura en lo gris *and Thierry Maulnier's* La maison de la nuit.]

The central theme of both Buero Vallejo's **Aventura en lo gris** and Thierry Maulnier's *La maison de la nuit* deals with the question of the relative value of truth.[1] Of the many possible aspects of this theme, the authors concentrate on the general relationship between truth and compassion. A fanatical pursuit of truth at all cost, personified by Maulnier's Krauss, can be as pitiless as the opportunistic use of truth as an instrument of achieving personal power by Buero's Alejandro. Maulnier's major protagonist, Krauss, is a dogmatist who hopes to create a "pitiless world" in which there will be no need for pity. Buero's dictator Goldman (Alejandro), the opportunist, uses other people and ideas to attain control over human beings for personal gratification.

In Buero's play, the pragmatic doer, Alejandro, is contrasted with Professor Silvano, a thinker and idealist who sets high value on the pursuit of truth. Silvano is also a compassionate man, capable of sacrifice in the name of his convictions. Krauss, the young fanatic in *La maison,* finds himself in conflict with his companion, Hagen, who, though serving the same ideology as Krauss, does not become a victim of the limitless fanaticism leading to Krauss' boundless cruelty.

The central themes of both plays are complementary and, taken together, throw significant light on the problem of the relationship between compassion and truth.[2] Buero takes the position of condemning the use of truth solely as a means for attaining personal goals of aggrandizement. Alejandro embodies this concept and commits numerous crimes motivated by his insatiable passion and lust for power. For him the concept of truth is meaningless. He twists and distorts it to satisfy his hunger for power.

However, no less cruelty results from the blind acceptance of a ruthless ideology claiming a monopoly on truth. In the name of such a truth, Krauss condemns to death several innocent people, among them his best friend and the woman who loves him. At this point Buero's and Maulnier's themes seem to converge. Both, fanatical absolutism—setting infinite value on a particular brand of truth—and extreme pragmatism—making truth subservient to power—are in some fundamental way incompatible with compassion. Thus, the purely instrumental use of truth by Alejandro and the pitiless sacrifice of human values on the altar of dogmatic ideology by Krauss lead to similar consequences.

In his fearless pursuit of truth, Professor Silvano, Buero's idealistic protagonist, had denounced Goldman whose dishonest manipulation of national interests endangered the well-being of his native land. In response, the dictator, using slander, attempted to destroy his reputation. After the fall of the dictator, Silvano met him at the railway station near the frontier of the country to which Alejandro hoped to escape. Even in such desperate circumstances, Goldman managed to rape Isabel, a young girl who was fleeing with her baby fathered by an enemy soldier, and murders her to cover his guilt. Though all circumstantial evidence pointed to Carlos, the partially deranged protector of Isabel, Silvano insists on finding the assassin. His search results in irrefutable proof of the dictator's guilt and his subsequent "execution" by Carlos. The boundless cruelty of the opportunist is laid bare by Silvano, "un aprovechado que muerde por última vez en la carne de la patria vencida antes de marcharse."[3]

As the enemy troops approached, Silvano and Ana, the dictator's loyal mistress, reject the opportunity to save their lives either by fleeing or by claiming credit for killing Goldman. Instead, they choose to remain behind to save the life of Isabel's child. The enemy soldiers, convinced by Silvano that one among them could be the father of the baby, shot Silvano and Ana, but spared the child. The professor could have saved his life if he did not have compassion and if he were capable of distorting the truth. He refused to flee because the baby could not survive the ordeal. He forfeited a second opportunity to save his life when he refused to claim credit for the elimination of the dictator. At every point, Silvano was thinking and weighing the moral impact of his actions. While deciding to sacrifice himself for the baby, he said, "salvemos el mañana,"[4] indicating his deep awareness of the existence of a transcendental moral order and relating it to his immediate actions. Similarly, when arguing with Ana against lying, the professor acts in the same vein and stresses the need of a person to overcome the fear of death in the name of truth: "Ana, has empezado muy tarde a aprender. Aún no sabes . . . lo que es vencerse."[5]

The fanatic, Krauss, of *La maison* believes that his ideology represents the ultimate truth. He believes that it is his duty to sacrifice all human values and feelings, including pity, for the sake of the promised millennium. For him pity is a "dirty word"—"Votre sale pitié que se gagne comme une maladie"[6]—and can neither solve nor eliminate social problems and injustices. According to Krauss, it might ameliorate some evils, but a merciless, cruel revolution is necessary to drastically change the world and to remove the exploitation and sufferings of mankind in the future.

A climactic expression of his convictions came at a crucial moment in the play when Krauss communicated to Hagen the party's order to shoot all persons possessing any knowledge or information on Werner, a prominent escapee from an Eastern state. Among the prospective victims was Lydia, a young girl in love with Krauss. Hagen is outraged, "L'ordre est juste. Lydia t'aime. Tuons Lydia." Krauss replies, "Crois-tu être le seul a sentir que cela est abominable? Nous marchons dans le sang. Hagen, nous marcheron dans le sang pendant années encore. Nous pietinons toute la douleur de histoire humanine. Nous devons tuer parce que nous devons vaincre."[7]

Krauss is convinced that he possesses the truth and that it is his duty to spread it at all costs. He sacrifices the lives of innocent people, his friend, and even the woman whose love he seems to reciprocate, all in the name of *his* truth.[8] His sacrifice is both heroic and tragic. If it were not for his supreme dedication to the cause, Krauss would appear to be an extremely cruel and heartless individual. However, in his way of thinking, a lofty end justifies the means. Thus, the execution of Lydia and the others is justified in these terms: "Pourquoi épargnerait-il Lydia? Parce qu'elle est innocente? Il ne s'agit pas de punir des coulpables mais de garder un secret d'État . . ."[9] No pity should be permitted in the pursuit of his truth. The ultimate goal is to create a "pitiless world" in which there will be no need for pity.

The action of Krauss strikes the reader as a manifestation of extreme cruelty. But he attempts to justify his negation of pity as a *conditio sine qua non* for a successful revolution leading to a millennium in which all sufferings will be abolished. Moreover, his own suffering and sacrifice contain elements of grandeur. In Maulnier's words, "Il y a dans ce sacrifice de Lydia, auquel Krauss consent par discipline et que lui coute si cher, une atroce abnégation qui est une des formes authentique de la grandeur."[10] Maulnier feels that Krauss can "trouver un réconfort dans la certitude qu'en tuant ce qu'il aime, ou qu'il est près d'aimer, dans cette douleur et cet arrachement qui ne le feront pas faiblir c'est luimême qu'il torture."[11]

Krauss sacrifices such values as friendship and love for the sake of a value he cherishes most—dedication to the cause. Paraphrasing Brutus, Krauss might have said, "not that I loved my friend less, but that I loved my ideology more." His figure is truly a tragic one. One can hardly say the same about Goldman. While the reader can sympathize with the agony of Krauss, it is difficult to imagine feeling sorry for the dictator, who only serves himself.

One can hardly sympathize with an ideology which not only permits, but requires the use of cruel means to reach its goals. However, Krauss' sincerity and devotion to his cause, no matter how erroneous, has elements of nobility. Goldman ruthlessly sacrifices the lives of other people. Krauss, blinded by his fanatism does the same, but in the name of a higher ideal. There is no compassion in Goldman, whereas compassion in Krauss is distorted in a paradoxical manner. In the name of pity he acts without pity to create a world which will need no pity.

Hagen shares the same ideology as Krauss, but he cannot reconcile the paradox which Krauss accepts. He does not follow the ideology as blindly nor as unconditionally as Krauss. Compassion for Lydia, Lise and other innocent victims to be offered on the altar of revolution, overwhelms him and leads him to sacrifice his own life. Throughout his life, Hagen was dedicated to his revolutionary cause, but the senseless cruelty which he encountered in the Party's orders destroyed his allegiance. Compassion reigned over fanaticism.

In contrast with the other protagonists, compassion was a dominant trait in Silvano's character. Like Hagen, he sacrificed his life because of it. But unlike Hagen, compassion did not come as the result of a violent break with the past, but rather, it grew in an ascending sequence of incidents until reaching the point of supreme negation.

Traditionally, the central theme of Buero's *Aventura en lo gris* is expressed in terms of thinkers versus doers, and this is correct. And though the focus of this study is on the relationship between compassion and truth, the parallelism between *Aventura* and *La maison,* in respect to the thinker-doer theme, is striking. Both Goldman and Krauss are doers. The dictator is a pragmatic man who uses ideas as instruments, i.e. a doer *par excellence.* Krauss is primarily a doer because of his blind acceptance of an ideology. He never analyzes the basic premises, goals or methods prescribed by the ideology he follows. Only when challenged by Hagen does he attempt to rationalize and justify his *credo.* Like Carlos, who, after killing Ignacio in Buero's **En la ardiente oscuridad,** finds in himself the seeds of Ignacio's ideas, Krauss, close to the end of the play, seems to reappraise his own position.

Hagen is both, a thinker and a doer. The shocking experience of the fateful night near the frontier shook most of his previously accepted beliefs and forced him to reevaluate the basic tenets of the ideology to which he was so devoted. The logic Hagen uses against Krauss is compelling, "L'ordre est juste. Lydia t'aime. Tuons Lydia."[12] Thus, he lays bare all the inherent cruelty and brutality of the system which he had supported all his life.

Professor Silvano is predominantly a thinker. He neither engaged in a struggle for power nor in any political activity which would stop Goldman. The only weapon he used was his word, a typical weapon of a thinker who is dedicated to the pursuit of truth. Under the most adverse circumstances, at the climax of the play, he acts decisively and courageously. Characteristically, he thinks and justifies his actions by logical arguments. He is clearly aware of *why* and for *what purpose* he gives his life. In contrast to his previous behavior, at the most dramatic moment of the play, Silvano accomplishes a perfect merging of act and thought.

Of all the protagonists in the plays compared, Krauss is the only one who takes the extreme position of placing the highest value on truth itself. Obviously, Goldman, in his actions, is not guided by the pursuit of truth. Hagen, at first, accepts Krauss' ideology as his truth, but later rejects it in the name of compassion. On the surface, Professor Silvano seems to place supreme value on the truth, but in the ultimate analysis his pursuit of truth was really in the name of the well-being of society which cannot exist without compassion. At the moment of his supreme sacrifice, truth and *pieté* seem to merge into a sublime act of negation.

Notes

1. The term *truth,* as used in both plays by the protagonists, is not defined. The writer of the paper assigns to the term the same meaning as the protagonists. It seems that their implied definition of the truth is a close approximation to the Aristotelian concept of "moral truth," i.e. conformity between statement and thought. However, any attempt to define truth would lead to an infinite and fruitless discussion and is outside the scope of this paper.

2. The terms *compassion* and *pity* will be used interchangeably to convey the meaning of the French word *pieté* used by Maulnier in *La maison de la nuit.*

Pity here means compassion and carries no derogatory connotations frequently associated with this English word.

3. Antonio Buero Vallejo, *Aventura en lo gris* (Madrid: Ediciones Alfil, 1964), p. 91.

4. *Ibid.,* p. 98.

5. *Ibid.,* p. 105.

6. "Your dirty pity which is transmitted as a disease." Thierry Maulnier, *La maison de la nuit* (París: Gallimard, 1954), p. 58.

7. "The order is just. Lydia loves you. Let's kill Lydia." Krauss replies, "Do you think you are the only one who finds it abominable? We are marching in blood. Hage, we will march in blood for many years to come. We will trample over all the sufferings of the history of mankind. We must kill because we must conquer." *Ibid.,* p. 182.

8. "Krauss raporte l'ordre de tuer tout le monde. Tout le monde. Lydia aussi. Lydia qui l'a sauve, Lydia qui l'a ému par son admiration d'enfant." Krauss brings back the order to kill everyone. Lydia too. Lydia who saved him, who loved him with childish admiration . . . Lydia whom he is about to love. *Ibid.,* p. 35.

9. "Why spare Lydia? Because she is innocent? It is not a question of punishing the guilty, but of protecting a secret of state." *Ibid.,* p. 36.

10. "There is in the sacrifice of Lydia, to which Krauss agrees because of discipline which he values so highly, a cruel abnegation which is one of the authentic forms of grandeur." *Ibid.,* pp. 36-37.

11. ". . . find consolation in the certainty that by killing the one whom he loves, or whom he is about to love, and in this grief and anguish, which did not weaken him, he is the one who is tortured." *Ibid.,* p. 182.

12. "The order is just. Lydia loves you. Let's kill Lydia." *Ibid.,* p. 18.

John A. Moore (essay date fall 1980)

SOURCE: Moore, John A. "Buero Vallejo—Good Mistresses and Bad Wives." *Romance Notes* XXI, no. 1 (fall 1980): 10-15.

[*In the following essay, Moore examines the portrayal of mistresses and wives in several Buero Vallejo plays.*]

Anyone acquainted with Antonio Buero Vallejo as man or dramatist knows that he is a highly moral writer, but a peculiar turn of circumstances has caused him to write a series of plays with mistresses who uphold standards of conduct which command respect or sympathy from the audience while other plays picture wives who are presented as shallow selfish women. In this article I would like to develop this anomaly and seek a plausible explanation.

In *Aventura en lo gris* Ana is the mistress of the fallen dictator, Goldmann. She gradually falls under the influence of the pacifist, Silvano, since she can see the contrast between the stoic idealism of Silvano and the selfishness and pragmatism of Goldmann. She does not abandon her man except in a dream scene between acts but does what she can to keep peace between him and the others at the refuge hostel where all the characters are staying. After Goldmann is killed, and when the group decides to try to reach the frontier, Ana decides to stay at the hostel along with Silvano to face certain death because she believes that the baby of the dead Isabel can thus be saved.

In *El concierto de San Ovidio* Adriana is the mistress of the entrepreneur Valindin, having been promoted from singer and dancer at the fairs. The distinctive stamp of Valindin, like that of Goldmann, is the exploitation of humanity. He conceives the idea of dressing blind musicians in ridiculous costume to play cacophonous music at the fair of San Ovidio. David, the only blind musician with musical ability and ambition, soon discovers that it is farce, not music, that Valindin wants. Adriana is torn between her loyalty to Valindin as his long-term mistress and her growing sympathy for David's ambition. She cannot prevail against Valindin's will, however. Finally David kills Valindin and Adriana tries in vain to protect him from being executed.

In *El tragaluz,* Encarna is the mistress and secretary of Vicente. She is pregnant with Vicente's child, but for a long time, does not acknowledge it for fear of his reaction. She also is sympathetic toward Vicente's brother, Mario, who is a dreamer and idealist, and becomes inevitably a part of the quarrel between them. Amidst all this activity her role is completely passive. Eventually Vicente is killed by his insane father and Mario asks Encarna to marry him, by that proposal consciously accepting his brother's child.

In *El sueño de la razón,* Leocadia, mistress of Goya, is essentially the same type of person as the mistresses described above although the circumstances vary slightly Leocadia had been married but her husband has left her and does not figure in the plot. In contrast to the lot of other mistresses, Leocadia's situation is that her man is the hero of the tragedy, but her life is no easier for that reason. Goya's deafness, senility, and his adversities combine to make him a difficult consort. He calls her *ramera* and *buscona,* is suspicious of her and acts in many ways to make her life unpleasant. She tells the audience—for Goya cannot hear her—"Mi pobre Francho, te he querido—sin entenderte. . . . Tú vivías tras una muralla y, sin embargo, seguí a tu lado . . . velando por ti, sufriendo mi temor, que no es el tuyo. . . . Las noches de soledad, el lecho frío. . . . Escucho los gruñidos de tu desvelo desde mi alcoba, sabiendo que ya no vendrás."[1]

Leocadia admits being somewhat promiscuous. "Estoy perdida. Pensaba en otros cuando me entregaba a ti, pensaré en ti cuando me entregue a otros."[2]

In *La llegada de los dioses,* Verónica is the mistress of the protagonist, Julio, and, based upon the title of the play, might be considered the co-star. The play was premiered in 1971 and her characterization seemed to be based upon what was *de rigueur* around that time; that is, the moral sincerity of the mistress was contrasted to the hypocrisy of the older generation. Before the time of the play's action, Julio had become psychosomatically blind, and he and Verónica had gone to visit his father at a resort archipelago. Of course Verónica now served as guide as well as *amante.* Her character is contrasted to that of Felipe, Julio's father, rather than to Julio himself. Verónica is the only mistress who enjoys equality with her man.

Buero characterizes all these mistresses realistically but sympathetically and without opprobrium. For contrast we will now picture some of the wives. In *Un soñador para un pueblo* Esquilache is the enlightened minister of Charles III of Spain. He heads a reform government which tries to give a better life to the common people while trying to restore honest government and guarantee merit as the criterion for high position. His wife, having utter scorn for his ideals, uses her influence to gain for her sons positions of authority for which they are not qualified, spends her money on extravagances, and associates with other selfish people. She even chides him for being old. When Esquilache falls, she suffers more than he since he preserves an inner satisfaction, knowing that his efforts were appreciated by the King and by Fernanda as a representative of the people, while her future promises to be utterly empty.

In *Las Meninas* Buero has Velázquez represent the strong man defending truth and serving as the conscience of the King, Phillip IV. The painter's wife, Juana, daughter of Velázquez's tutor, Pacheco, is not wicked in the same way as Esquilache's wife, but her weaknesses threaten his undoing. She is jealous of her husband because in Italy he had a model pose nude for his *Venus.* She suspects that this model may have been his mistress, a charge that he denies. Velázquez kept this painting secret and locked for fear that it would be considered lascivious if displayed, but Juana reveals its presence to Velázquez's cousin, Nieto, and so Velázquez is denounced to the Inquisition by the envious cousin. While Juana is not a villainess, she is depicted as weak and somewhat resentful.

In *Las cartas boca abajo,* Adela, the wife, is far from being an admirable person. Her choice for a man was the distinguished professor Carlos Ferrer, a man who, had showed some interest in her sister, but when Adela eventually lost him, she married his friend, Juan, hoping to drive him to success. As might be expected, her efforts confirm his failure in his profession and contribute to the failure of a loveless marriage. Eventually Juan confesses his own weakness and envy and exposes hers, thereby making their cards face upward. He succeeds in recovering the affection of his son, who previously had scorned him, but Adela is mired in self-pity, alienated from her husband, son, brother and sister.

In most of the plays mentioned thus far, the woman, whether wife or mistress, is given a secondary role, and it is obvious that she is presented in order to contrast with the hero or villain in bringing out the man's salient qualities.[3] There are two plays by Buero in which the woman is the protagonist and in which the question as to whether her role is that of wife or mistress is in some doubt.

In *Madrugada* Amalia is introduced as the mistress of a dying painter, Mauricio. Amalia, however, is concealing two data which one would have expected her to flaunt. She is no longer the mistress but the wife of Mauricio, who has already died, having left her the bulk of his considerable fortune. Because of her long time status as Mauricio's mistress and the short period of her being secretly his wife, Amalia wants to learn whether it was love or gratitude that prompted him to marry her and will her his fortune as he was dying. The key to her reassurance is the explanation of certain enigmatic words that Mauricio uttered just before his death. By letting the relatives believe that Mauricio is in a coma but can still awake long enough to sign a will, which she implies is written but not signed, she eventually gets her reassurance from statements by Mauricio's brother and nephew which show that Mauricio loved and trusted her completely.

In *La tejedora de sueños* Buero stays amazingly close to the outer trappings of ancient legend and epic to bring a radically new slant to Penelope's fabled fidelity and to characterize what is probably Buero's best female character so far. With Ulysses gone for twenty years, Penelope has been putting off her suitors by promising to make a decision about marriage as soon as she finishes a shroud which she weaves by day and unravels by night. Four fatuous people and one charismatic person represent the suitors. Each of the unworthies is supported by an army, but Amphion, the desired one, is by himself. Buero's Penelope is in love with Amphion but will not choose him for fear that the other suitors will turn upon him when her choice is revealed. Ulysses returns, looking old, but still strong and disguised as a beggar. He suggests the drawing of Ulysses' bow as a test for the suitors. All fail. He then uses the same bow to kill the suitors, including Amphion.

Penelope then turns on him, not just for killing the suitors, but for a series of things: his staying away for twenty years, returning in disguise, killing the suitors without giving them a chance to defend themselves (Amphion was given the chance), and fearing that Penelope had aged. She tells him that Amphion had showed her what true love is although she has been faithful to Ulysses in the physical

sense. She will guard Amphion's memory and at the same time preserve the hollow shell of her marriage. Ulysses seems to accept this position provided that his reputation in history is intact.

Penelope reveals further her human characteristics by showing her envy of Helen and suggests that there is a parallel between her game of holding her suitors at bay with Helen's game with Menelaus and Paris which started the Trojan War. Ulysses suggests another parallel in that he knew of Clytemnestra's murder of Agamemnon and Orestes' vengeance as a lesson to him to return home in disguise.

William Giuliano considers the role of women in Buero (wife mistress) as primarily that of loving and being loved.[4] If a female places something other than love first in her life, she betrays herself and suffers tragic consequences. He cites Adela of *Las cartas boca abajo* as the most convincing example, contrasted with Amalia of *Madrugada.* According to this criterion the mistresses in Buero's plays recognize their role and try to conform though they are at times torn by sympathy for more innocent males instead of their tyrant lovers and have trouble becoming complete rebels. The wives would be responsible for the tragic turn in their lives, and to some extent in their husbands' for placing other considerations ahead of love.

Buero offers no attack upon the institution of marriage; in fact, he clearly shows it to be a preferred status for women. There is no mention of the sacramental character of marriage, however, and certainly he holds that the basic character of a woman is more important than her marital status. Where the relationship consists of man and mistress, the woman tries to be faithful to a man who is a pragmatist, unworthy of her. She almost instinctively shows protectiveness toward another man, one full of dreams and ideals, but she cannot help this man except in an ineffective or symbolic way. There is no suggestion that liberation from the tyrant can be her salvation. Even in the plays in which the woman is the protagonist, her role is that of dependence upon her man. If he is worthy, e.g. Velázquez or Esquilache, the woman is usually a weak or unworthy wife. If the man is essentially selfish and incapable of love, e.g. Valindin or Goldmann, the woman is mistress, not wife, but is worthy of the audience's sympathy. In *La tejedora de sueños,* Buero, with the same basic ideas about the man-woman relationship, breaks out of this mold, and the result is his creation of a more complete and much more interesting woman—Penelope, faithful wife and loving mistress.

Notes

1. Antonio Buero Vallejo, *El sueño de la razón* (Colección Teatro, No. 655. Madrid: Escelicer, 1970), p. 99.

2. *Ibid.,* p. 100.

3. One Buero play, *La señal que se espera,* does not fit the scenario; in fact, it seems to contradict my thesis.

4. William Giuliano, "The Role of Man and Woman in the Plays of Buero Vallejo," *Hispanófila,* No. 39, pp. 21-28.

Peter L. Podol (essay date March 1981)

SOURCE: Podol, Peter L. "Reality Perception and Stage Setting in Griselda Gámbaro's *Las paredes* and Antonio Buero Vallejo's *La fundación.*" *Modern Drama* XXIV, no. 1 (March 1981): 44-53.

[*In the following essay, Podol considers the relationship between the stage settings and the portrayal of reality in* La fundación *and Griselda Gámbaro's* Las paredes.]

In his introduction to the book *Encounter with Reality,* John Horrocks makes the following observation: "To a large degree, man can control reality—even as he can create, he can destroy, and sometimes he is defenseless, and reality can be imposed upon him. But of all man's activities, the struggle to come to terms with reality is at the apex of his experience."[1] Human nature is such that the confrontation of reality, under any conditions, is never an exact replication of the environment, but rather an individual process of rearrangement and modulation.[2] And in Griselda Gámbaro's *Las paredes* and Antonio Buero Vallejo's *La fundación,* both of which present a dramatic milieu permeated with imprisoning totalitarian forces, the need on the part of the protagonists to seek refuge in a subjective, inner reality becomes paramount. The implementation of the process of modifying reality is manifested through the stage settings of the plays. This technique involves the audience in a direct and immediate manner in the task of defining and dealing with the nature of man's existence, while posing the Pirandellian question of the interrelationship between life and form, between illusion and reality.[3]

Las paredes (1963), Griselda Gámbaro's first published play, was written in her native Argentina. The play has a metaphysical and universal dimension, but also dramatizes the political situation in her strife-torn country. The opening description of the apartment where the Youth finds himself imprisoned communicates immediately the essential role of self-deceit and illusion in the work; the heavy curtains on the wall "ocultan lo que parece ser una ventana."[4] In fact, as the Official demonstrates, there is only a blank wall behind those curtains. And hanging on that same wall is a painting which "representa a un joven lánguido mirando a través de una ventana" (p. 9).[5] The adjective "lánguido" serves to foreshadow the Youth's complete loss of spirit and of the will to survive that we witness at the play's conclusion. The window that is in the painting but not in the actual room adds another level of reality to the drama, undermining both the protagonist's and the audience's confidence in the range and veracity of their perceptions. The Official adds further to this doubt and insecurity by explaining: "¿Observó Vd. el cuadro? Pintura de primera calidad. Usted creyó que había una ventana detrás de los cortinados, yo creí que había aquí una ventana (señala la ventana en el cuadro). Aquí en estos vidrios que reflejan el sol, que se ensucian como los reales. Optimismo, joven. Mejor que la ventana no esté en ningún lado. Prefiero enriquecer los símbolos. Fraguar ventanas sobre un muro, un cuaderno, un ojo. En todos lados, menos en las ventanas" (p. 19).[6] The Official, then, who controls the perceptions, thoughts, and ultimately the very existence of the Youth, communicates early in the play the deceitful nature of a world which conspires to thwart all of our attempts to perceive and comprehend its essence.

The threatening, irrational nature of life is underscored further by contradictory forces in the drama; the clash between the Custodian's "barba despareja y de varios días" and "el aseo del uniforme" (p. 9)[7] helps to explain his role in the work which consists of aiding the Official in his quest to disorient and ultimately destroy the Youth. And the Official's superficial concern for the Youth and dignified, decorous manner conflict with the reality of his sadistic perversity. The most powerful symbol of the destructive force inherent in Gámbaro's dramatic ambience, however, is the room itself. Throughout *Las paredes* it becomes smaller and less comfortably furnished. As Sandra Cypess has noted, "The mental transformation of the Youth is reflected in a parallel diminution of the physical surroundings."[8] Through the visible stage setting, the audience participates actively in this transformation. At the beginning of the second and final act, the picture is no longer hanging on the wall. The different levels of reality are being sorted out, leaving only the inescapable destruction of the protagonist. The oppressive nature of this impending reality is heightened in the stage directions at the beginning of the final scene: "El ambiente se verá luego notablemente reducido al cuadro anterior. Como únicos muebles, un cate y una silla ocupan casi todo el espacio" (p. 47).[9] The furniture itself has become a threatening component of the Youth's environment, limiting his movement and impinging on his freedom on both a physical and a symbolic plane.

The visual elements that communicate the Youth's predicament are reinforced by the Official's psychological torture of his prisoner. When the Youth, who never does learn why he has been brought to the site of his ultimate destruction, admits to the Official that he expected to encounter a prison cell and not an elegant apartment, the latter responds knowingly: "¡Qué lejos de la realidad vive Vd!" (p. 14).[10] This ironic statement is true precisely because the apartment *is* a prison cell and the Youth's defense mechanisms do not allow him to recognize and accept the true nature of his "circunstancia dramática." The Youth is even told his fate, first implicitly, then explicitly, yet he still blocks it out. Several times during the play, terrifying cries are heard. When the Youth questions the nature and significance of those screams, the Official, laughing, responds: "Los otros, Están como usted, alojados confortablemente y gritan. ¿Se les cae la pared encima?" (p. 17).[11] Although we do not actually witness the horrifying death of the Youth that the Official has alluded to so deviously (a death worthy of the creative imagination of an Edgar Allan Poe or Horacio Quiroga), we are equally disturbed by the former's spiritual annihilation.

At the end of the drama, the Official and the Custodian abandon the Youth to his fate. But now they leave the door open, telling him not to move, just to wait. And "el joven mira hacia la puerta, luego con obediente determinación, muy rígido, la muñeca entre los brazos, los ojos increíble y estúpidamente abiertos, espera" (p. 60).[12] The life-sized doll that he holds had been brought to him from his apartment. It is an object that he has always despised and did not destroy only because it belonged to his landlady, another representative of authoritarian force in his life. By accepting the existence of ugliness and passivity, embodied by the doll, the Youth has helped to bring about his own demise. He has become as docile, rigid, and inhuman as the doll he holds on his lap as he waits for the walls to crush him. The grotesque nature of his existence is made manifest through this human-like creature[13] that symbolizes the dehumanization of the Youth.

Props and stage setting are active components of Gámbaro's dramatic ambience. They play essential roles in communicating her themes and in contributing to the efficacy of the drama as a staged work in the theater. They also help to underscore the circularity inherent in both the structure and the theme of the drama. The picture of the languid youth staring out of the window is removed from the room, and the Official informs us that it is now hanging in a different room (or prison cell). Thus, the dehumanization of man, effected in part through the undermining of his reality perceptions, is shown to be an ongoing process. This circularity manifests itself in a number of ways in the work. As Cypess has observed: "Its structure is circular in that it begins and ends with the anguished cries of unknown origin. There is also a sense of circularity in the progress of the Youth's knowledge, for despite his questions, he knows no more than when he was first detained."[14]

Just as the audience participates, through the changes in stage setting, in the Youth's psychological and physical destruction, we also share the guilt of allowing totalitarian forces in Argentina and throughout the world to govern our behavior. Gámbaro has continued to explore in subsequent plays the machinations of social and political pressures that deprive man of his basic human dignity. Those very forces obliged her to leave her native land and emigrate to Spain, where she could continue to pursue her career in her native language, free from external restraints.[15] Until just a few years ago, of course, the political ambience in Spain also precluded such artistic freedom. In response to the totalitarian forces present in his country and inspired in part by his own memories of the inside of a Spanish prison, Buero Vallejo authored a play that parallels *Las paredes* in its utilization of stage setting to reflect the inner states of consciousness of its protagonist and ultimately of the audience as well.

La fundación (1974), like *Las paredes,* begins with a detailed description of a well-appointed room; in the case of the Buero play the lovely landscape visable through the window is also included. This description contains an allusion to the clash resulting from the juxtaposition of several of the components of the setting; this clash as well as the prescribed lighting introduces an element of uncertainty that is central to the theme of the work. The opening stage directions conclude as follows: "con su *contradictoria* mezcla de modernidad y estrechez, la habitación sugiere una instalación urgente y provisional el servicio de alguna actividad valiosa y en marcha. La risueña luz de la primavera inunda el paisaje; cernida e irisada claridad, un tanto *irreal,* en el aposento."[16] Both of these works, then, deceive the audience by presenting a stage design which proves to be a falsification of the true nature of the drama's setting.

To an even greater degree than in *Las paredes,* the progressive changes in the set of *La fundación* mirror the evolution of the psychological state of the play's protagonist, Tomás. Buero Vallejo himself has emphasized the importance of Tomás's gradual emergence from the protective cloud of insanity into the reality of his betrayal of his fellow prisoners, his incarceration, and his impending death. Buero's statement, extracted from a letter written to a critic, reads as follows: "El *cambio* de Tomás en la obra es la esencia de la obra—y con él, el posible cambio de los espectadores igualmente alienados—. Es la madurez, precipitada por el zarpazo de la realidad; es la desalienación progresiva que también quisiéramos para el público. Estéticamente, se articula mediante esos efectos míos de 'participación', que creo legítimos dramáticamente y que Domenech ha llamado en su libro 'efectos de la inmersión'."[17]

In *La fundación,* the exposition, which is traditionally presented in the opening scenes of a play, is delayed and purposely obfuscated. The gradual clarification of the characters' true situation becomes an essential component of the central conflict in the drama. This clarification is effected primarily through the evolution of the stage setting; it initially appears to represent a large, comfortable room ideally suited to the work conducted there by young, talented researchers, but is finally shown to be a stark prison cell whose inhabitants all await death. Tomás and the audience experience mutually the painful realization that the ineluctable reality of the play and of life is both grim and absolute. As in Luigi Pirandello's *Henry IV,* the other characters attempt to help Tomás regain his sanity and come to grips with the truth by pretending that his fantasy is an accurate representation of their situation. Accordingly, they feign actions that might occur in a "Foundation," but are impossible in their prison cell. And we, the audience, are forced to question our own perceptions. When Tulio, a fellow inmate, gathers imaginary glasses and takes them to the sink, Tomás and the spectators become perplexed; but the other characters, who are all seeking to assist Tomás by accepting *his* perceptions, act as if nothing were wrong. And when Tulio obligingly snaps a photograph—utilizing, of necessity, a glass instead of a camera—Tomás is infuriated; he does not yet comprehend what is occurring, but on some level senses that Tulio's action is a threat to his subjective vision of life. The strength of his feelings is explainable by the fact that reality construction is a fundamental feature of our instinct for self-preservation. As Murphy and Spohn explain, "the decisive criterion of the adequacy, completeness, or appropriateness of reality construction is a pragmatic one; namely the survival of the individual organism, of species, and ultimately, of culture."[18]

As in *Las paredes,* the importance of visual perceptions is reinforced through the motif of painting. Tomás avidly examines an art book, describing some of the paintings to his companions. But it is Tulio, the photographer, who knows the exact details of each painting, even though he is not looking at them. Seeing, then, transcends the physiological function of the eyes, acquiring a more profound, metaphysical dimension. The only painting that Tulio does not know is also significant to the meaning of the play; it is described by Tomás as follows: "Ratones en una jaula. Un tema sórdido. Hay algo repelente en las expresiones de estos animales. Tom Murray. No sé quién es" (p. 170).[19] The grotesque image of the rat alludes to Tomás himself; this identification is reinforced by the name of the artist and by Tomás's girlfriend, Berta. In Tomás's fantasy, she is also at the Foundation, conducting research with rats. She has made a pet of one of the creatures and named it "Tomasito." In an important scene, Tomás, speaking to Berta, says of these laboratory animals and their fate: "Un martirio dulce: ellos ignoran que lo sufren y hasta el final se les trata bien. ¿Qué mayor destino? Si yo fuera un ratoncito lo aceptaría." But Berta admonishes him: "No. Tú eres un ratoncito y no lo aceptas" (p. 140).[20] When we come to realize that this scene has transpired in Tomás's imagination, it acquires a whole new meaning. Tomás is wrestling with himself to recognize and accept the reality of his situation: that of a prisoner who will be slaughtered like an animal. And central to that internal struggle is the component of his subconscious represented by Berta that is urging him on toward that acceptance. Tomás, like the Youth in *Las paredes,* has not yet recognized the symbolic value of what is depicted in the painting. But while the Youth affirms the passive role the painting assigns to him, Tomás, who is both the creator (Tom Murray) and the

interpreter of his destiny, does employ his evolving insights to assert his existential freedom.

Tulio plays an important role in Tomás's gradual emergence into the reality of life as a prison. He is the only character whose supposed research mission at the Foundation corresponds to his work in real life; hence, symbolically, he serves as a bridge between the two realms that give shape to Tomás's existence. As a photographer, Tulio has become interested in holography—the projection of illusory images in the air. He tells of a humorous episode in which his girlfriend and assistant got him to kiss her hologram, thinking it was really she in the flesh. The hologram becomes the central metaphor of the play; reinforced by the progressive changes in stage setting, it helps to create the different levels in the work. Asel, the oldest of the prisoners, and a principal spokesman for Buero, affirms the importance of the metaphor in the following words addressed to Tomás: "Todo, dentro y fuera, como un gigantesco holograma desplegado ante nuestras conciencias, que no sabemos si son nuestras, ni lo que son. Y tú un holograma para mí, y yo, para ti, otro . . ." (p. 239).[21]

Life, then, is a hologram. And if the ultimate reality seems to be imprisonment, that too may be yet another illusion. As Tomás emerges from the sanctuary of his subjective vision, he sees the prison as it is; but he also sees beyond that level of reality, recognizing that all of life is a series of illusions. This important concept is strikingly reminiscent of a central theme in the dramas of Jean Genet. The following observation about Genet's theater also elucidates, indirectly, *La fundación*: "What we call reality is only illusion piled on illusion. When all the layers of illusion are stripped away, what is left is emptiness."[22] Tomás's keenest perceptions transcend the level of reality contained in the final stage setting, calling into question the possibility of man's knowing the form of his existence. His words, filled with existential import, are as follows: "Ya sé que no era real. Pero me pregunto si el resto del mundo lo es más . . . También a los de afuera se les esfuma de pronto el televisor, o el vaso que querían beber, o el dinero que tenían en la mano . . . O un ser querido . . . Y siguen creyendo, sin embargo, en su confortable fundación . . . Y alguna vez, desde lejos, verán este edificio y no se dirán: es una cárcel. Dirán: parece una fundación . . . ¿No será entonces igualmente ilusorio el presidio?" (p. 239).[23]

Buero Vallejo's principal theme in *La fundación* appears to be the need to face reality, no matter how painful it may be. As Francisco Ruiz Ramón states in his excellent study of the Spanish contemporary theater: "La única condición es mantener los ojos abiertos a la verdad, negarnos a soñar Fundaciones que nos hagan felices, pero enajenados."[24] Yet the need to dream is also affirmed. Although Tulio, when he is led off to his death, tells Tomás not to dream, it is difficult to dismiss the authenticity and the merit of his hopes as expressed in his earlier defense of fantasizing, directed to Asel: "¡Déjanos soñar un poco, Asel! ¡El se reunirá con su novia y yo con la mía! La vida no tendría sentido si eso no sucediera. Yo te comprendo muy bien, Tomás. ¡Un día las abrazaremos! Y no serán ilusiones, no serán hologramas" (p. 204).[25] And Asel himself, as he in turn is led off to his death, tells Tomás, "Tu paisaje es verdadero" (p. 241).[26]

This need to hope, to fantasize, is also encountered in Genet's work. In her analysis of *The Balcony,* Bettina Knapp notes, "Man cannot live within the framework of reality (rational approach); he must be spurred on by some symbol-image or fantasy to realize his dream."[27] Although her statement is equally valid with respect to *La fundación,* Buero's theater departs from Genet's both in technique (the Artaudian component of Genet's drama is absent in Buero—it is far more evident in Gámbaro's *Las paredes* and becomes increasingly important in her subsequent works) and in the incorporation into the conclusion of a definite element of hope.[28] Just before Tomás himself is removed from the cell to face an uncertain end, which is probably death, but still contains the possibility of escape and freedom, he finds the strength to confront his dramatic situation honestly and to state: "Yo no enloqueceré ya por esa ilusión, ni por ninguna otra. Si hay que morir, no temblaré . . . ¡ Pero mientras viva, esperaré! . . . Esperaré ante las bocas de los fusiles y sonreiré al caer, porque todo habrá sido un holograma" (p. 255).[29] Hope, in one respect, resides in the possibility that the cruelty and horror inherent in life may also be illusions. But in a more profound sense, hope emerges from human empathy, from Tulio and Asel's willingness to assist Tomás, despite his betrayal, under torture, of his companions; and there is hope in the resilence of youth, the renewed energy and desire that Tomás finds at the end of the play which enable him to accept his fate but also to continue to fantasize the existence of a better world, of a higher reality.

La fundación, like *Las paredes,* projects a central view of life as a prison and of man as the victim of totalitarian forces. Both plays coincide in their utilization of a prison official and his assitant as insidious representatives of political oppression, all the more terrifying because of their superficial politeness and hypocritical concern for their "guests." As Asel states in *La fundación,* the worst prisons are those which actually are as lush as Tomás's Foundation, because "a sus inquilinos les parecerá la libertad misma. Habra que ser entonces muy inteligente para no olvidar que se es un prisionero" (p. 241).[30] And as has been noted, both plays employ stage setting to involve the audience actively in the process of discovering and recognizing the truth: in Spain, in Argentina, and in much of the modern world, man is, in many respects, a prisoner. Both works further underscore the tragic finality of the human condition through the circularity of their structures. This feature of *Las paredes* has already been considered; in *La fundación,* at the very end of the play, the stage setting is restored to its original form and the *Encargado,*

with sardonic politeness, invites the new occupants (and indirectly the audience) to enter the Foundation. As the curtain falls, the audience is obliged once again to reassess or edit reality. Murphy and Spohn affirm the fundamental role of this process in human existence in the following manner: "It is this editing of the real, this calling into existence of that which was only potentially there, and of turning back again into the potential that which a minute ago was real, that is the process of facing the real and of creating the real."[31]

In the totalitarian world that these two playwrights place on the stage, reality is almost too horrifying to face. Yet the process of editing that reality and coming to terms with it on a personal, subjective level, can be in itself a therapeutic and ultimately hopeful venture. In that respect Buero's and Gámbaro's plays are diametrically opposed. Her play ends on a note of total despair because the protagonist loses the will to affirm life and to deal with reality; but Buero's work concludes hopefully precisely because Tomás finally does confront fully his situation in life and finds the strength to persevere. However, the two dramatists' depiction of totalitarianism, choice of metaphors, and use of stage setting to oblige the audience to participate in the process of examining and identifying reality, coincide to a remarkable degree. Both owe a debt to Pirandello and Genet in their treatment of illusion and reality, yet both manage to create unique works that have their own individuality and that diverge in technique and theme from their predecessors. That both playwrights now live and write in a Spain which at the present moment affords the greatest degree of artistic freedom to Spanish-speaking dramatists is but another example of the mutability of reality, the theme that Gámbaro and Buero have so innovatively and movingly examined in their respective works.

Notes

1. Gardner Murphy and Herbert E. Spohn, *Encounter with Reality* (Boston, 1968), p. viii.

2. Ibid., p. 29.

3. Richard Gilman, in his discussion of Pirandello's theater in *The Making of Modern Drama* (New York, 1974), makes the following pertinent statement about this theme: "Things are not either illusion or reality, but both, and to make this truth present on the stage is one driving purpose of Pirandello's complex dramatic art" (p. 159). There is a Pirandellian component in these plays, although the Italian dramatist's exploration of the autonomy of character and of the levels of illusion inherent in theater is of limited importance, particularly in the case of *Las paredes.* A more complete comparison of Pirandello's theater and these works is beyond the scope of this comparative study.

4. Gámbaro, *Las paredes,* in *Teatro: Las paredes, El desatino, Los siameses* (Barcelona, 1979), p. 9. All

references to *Las paredes* will be taken from this edition of the work and all of the English translations of quotations are my own. The English equivalent of this quotation is as follows: "hide what appears to be a window."

5. "represents a languid young man looking out of a window."

6. "Did you observe the painting? A work of high quality. You thought that there was a window behind the curtains, and I believed that there was one here (he points to the window in the painting). Here on these panes of glass that get dirty just like real ones. Optimism, my young man. It is better that the window not be anywhere. I prefer to enrich symbols. To forge windows on a wall, a notebook, an eye. Everywhere except on windows."

7. "his unkempt beard that has been neglected for several days" and "neatness of his uniform."

8. Sandra Messinger Cypess, "The Plays of Griselda Gámbaro," in *Dramatists in Revolt: The New Latin American Theater,* ed. Leon F. Lyday and George W. Woodyard (Austin, Tex., 1976), p. 96.

9. "The atmosphere has become noticeably constricted in comparison with the previous scene. As the only furniture, a bed and a chair occupy the entire space."

10. "How far from reality you live!"

11. "The others. They are comfortably lodged, like you, and yet they scream. Are the walls falling in on them?"

12. "the young man looks at the door, then with obedient determination, very rigid, like the doll between his arms, his eyes incredibly and stupidly opened wide, he waits."

13. The puppet and doll are often used as grotesque objects because of their resemblance to the human form and ability to assume awkard, ludicrous positions and to mimic human emotions in a manner that is both disturbing and amusing. See any of the standard studies of the grotesque (e.g., Wolfgang J. Kayser, *The Grotesque in Art and Literature,* Bloomington, Ind., 1963).

14. Cypess, p. 97.

15. Since the completion of this study I have been informed that Gámbaro has decided to abandon her career as a playwright and to return to Argentina because her husband, a sculptor, was unable to adjust to life in Spain and to continue to create art there.

16. Buero Vallejo, *La fundación* (Madrid, 1974), p. 137. The italics, which draw attention to several significant words, are my own. All subsequent references to this play will be taken from this edition. The translation

of the quotation is as follows: "with its *contradictory* combination of modernity and intimacy, the room suggests a provisional installation designed for an important activity that is well under way. The smiling light of spring floods the landscape; sifting, rainbow-hued brightness, somewhat *unreal,* in the room."

17. Buero Vallejo, letter of 4 June 1975, quoted in Emilio F. Bejel, "El proceso dialéctico en *la fundación* de Buero Vallejo," *Cuadernos americanos,* 219 (julio-agosto, 1978), 239. "The change in Tomás is the essence of the work—and with it, the possible change in the equally alienated spectators—. It is the maturity, precipitated by the resounding blow of reality; it is the progressive disalignment which we also wish to effect in the public. Esthetically, it is expressed by those 'participatory' effects of mine, which I believe to be dramatically legitimate, and which Domenech has called in his book 'effects of immersion'."

18. Murphy and Spohn, p. 4.

19. "Rats in a cage. A sordid theme. There is something repellent in the expressions of these animals. Tom Murray. I don't know who he is."

20. "What greater destiny? If I were a little rat I would accept it." "No. You are a little rat and you will not accept it."

21. "Everything, within and without, like a gigantic hologram unfolded before our consciences, which we cannot be certain are ours, nor can we know what they are. And you a hologram for me, and I, for you, another. . . ."

22. George Wellwarth, *The Theater of Protest and Paradox* (New York, 1964), p. 114.

23. "I know now that it was not real. But I ask myself if the rest of the world is more so . . . Also those on the outside may suddenly have their television set vanish, or the glass of water that they wanted to drink, or the money that they had in their hand . . . Or a beloved one . . . And they continue believing, nevertheless, in their comfortable foundation . . . And some day, from afar, they will see this building and they will not say: it is a prison. They will say: it appears to be a foundation . . . Will the prison then not be equally illusionary?"

24. Francisco Ruiz Ramón, *Historia del teatro español,* 3rd edition (Madrid, 1977), II, 114. "The only condition is to maintain one's eyes open to the truth, to refuse to dream Foundations that make us happy, but alienated."

25. "Let us dream a little. Asel! He will be reunited with his sweetheart and I with mine. Life would not make any sense if that didn't happen. I understand you

very well, Tomás. One day we will kiss them! And they will not be illusions, they will not be holograms."

26. "Your landscape is genuine."

27. Bettina L. Knapp, *Jean Genet* (New York, 1968), p. 127.

28. See Martha T. Halsey's "Buero Vallejo and the Significance of Hope," *Hispania,* 51 (1968), 57-66, for a consideration of this theme in Buero's theater. Halsey has also examined the reality-illusion theme in an early play of Buero's in her study "Reality versus Illusion: Ibsen's *The Wild Duck* and Buero Vallejo's *En la ardiente oscuridad,*" *Contemporary Literature,* 11 (1970), 48-57.

29. "I will no longer go mad because of that illusion nor any other. If it is necessary to die, I will not tremble with fear . . . But while I live, I will hope! . . . I will hope in front of the mouths of the guns and I will smile when I fall, because everything will have been a hologram."

30. "they will seem like freedom itself to their inmates. One will have to be very clever not to forget that one is a prisoner."

31. Op. cit., p. 137.

Elizabeth S. Rogers (essay date September 1983)

SOURCE: Rogers, Elizabeth S. "Role Constraints versus Self-Identity in *La tejedora de sueños* and *Anillos para una dama.*" *Modern Drama* XXVI, no. 3 (September 1983): 310-19.

[*In the following essay, Rogers finds parallels between the female protagonists of* La tejedora de sueños *and Antonio Gala's* Anillos para una dama, *asserting that both women "experience the dual conflict of coping with both the external demands of their roles and the personal needs for self-identity, freedom, and self-fulfillment as human beings and as women."*]

"I was attracted to Penelope as an image because I had always believed her situation as the wife of Ulysses to be one of the most challenging of Greek mythology." This statement by Naomi E. S. Griffiths elucidates the source of the title of her work *Penelope's Web: Some Perceptions of Women in European and Canadian Society.* She further explains her use of Penelope as a symbol of woman by stating that, she "was a woman trying desperately to achieve a balance between what she wanted, what she could obtain, and what the immediate circumstances permitted her to obtain."[1]

In this study I would like to elaborate on this dilemma of role demands versus personal desires as it relates to two twentieth-century Spanish dramas.[2] While both of these dramas are based on the mythic stories of legendary heroes, Ulysses and the Cid, the focus is nevertheless not on the heroes themselves, but rather on their wives, Penelope and Jimena. Both women have come to be prototype figures who represent the loyal, faithful, passive but supportive wife whose love for her husband is exemplary and unquestioned.

In *La tejedora de sueños* (*The Weaver of Dreams*) (1952), Antonio Buero Vallejo asks what life might have been like for Penelope during Ulysses' twenty-year absence, whereas Antonio Gala in *Anillos para una dama* (*Rings for a Lady*) (1973) speculates on Jimena's life after the Cid's death.[3] Buero and Gala, while not altering the epic and mythic content, delve into a neglected inner component of the stories, and show how each woman might have suffered and dreamed, and how each might have sought fulfillment in love. The women are thus presented in a human dimension which is in conflict with their stereotyped obeisant roles, and as a result they become victims of their particular status as "the wife of a hero." They experience the dual conflict of coping with both the external demands of their roles and the personal needs for self-identity, freedom, and self-fulfillment as human beings and as women.

Both dramas humanize and at the same time demythologize the legends, since Buero Vallejo and Gala call into question the totality of the truth of the myths. The Homeric myth of Ulysses, the epic poem of the Cid, and the subsequent re-creations of both works are products of the artistic mind and belong to the realm of mythic thinking. As is typical of such products of a patriarchal mode, the masculine aspect is glorified at the expense of the feminine—a device termed by Freud, with reference to the manifest content of dreams, "displacement of the accent."[4] Commenting on this emphasis on the masculine, Joseph Campbell has noted that throughout all patriarchal mythologies:

> The function of the female has been systematically devalued, not only in a symbolical cosmological sense, but also in a personal, psychological. Just as her role is cut down, or even out, in myths of the origin of the universe, so also in hero legends. It is, in fact, amazing to what extent the female figures of epic, drama, and romance have been reduced to the status of mere objects; or, when functioning as subjects, initiating action of their own, have been depicted either as incarnate demons or as mere allies of the masculine will.[5]

Buero Vallejo and Gala effectively unmask the hidden face of the myths by penetrating beyond the exterior, official version of History which supports the patriarchal traditions and maintains mythic thinking. Both demythologize what is accepted as "historical" by offering a new point of view and pursuing it to its very logical and human conclusion. Reminiscent of Unamuno and his *intrahistoria,* the dramatists present official History as incomplete, inaccurate, and lacking in a human dimension. Jimena captures this discrepancy between truth and History when she notes that the actors who represent a story (*historia*) without costumes, props or the appropriate dialogue which corresponds to the story may be perceived as crazy. But they are madder who believe that they are acting out true History (*la Historia*). Jimena has always felt lost in her role in History, which has submerged her on all sides.[6]

Yet it is this official version of History (with its capital H) which sets the standards of behavior and thus becomes the basis of role definition in society, as much in the past as in the present. Through tradition and repetition it determines what is expected of a woman: what limits are placed on the woman in assuming the role; how the roles are determined by political, economic, and social motives; and to what extent a woman may deviate from the assigned role. Eva Figes notes that women's roles, standards, and images have been designed by men with the result that:

> for the great majority of women the obvious course of events is to subside meekly or gracefully into the tradition role assigned to them, whilst for the really determined woman, for whom that role is inadequate, unsatisfactory or simply unavailable, there is an uphill struggle to compete in a game where all the rules have been laid down by the other party without her having been consulted, and where all the vital moves were probably made before she arrived on the scene.[7]

When a woman attempts to reject her given role, such as that of Penelope or Jimena, she discovers that her way is fraught with pain, suffering, and ultimate defeat.[8] The role of the wife of a hero comprises total loyalty, respect, purity and high morality, obedience, undaunting support, admiration, service, passivity, and the security of *his* honor and *his* image as a loving husband, a responsible father, and a heroic warrior and just ruler.[9] Should the wife not adjust her personal needs to this role, and should she refuse to lose her self-identity in assuming this role, she condemns herself to a futile struggle for self-fulfillment.

In *La tejedora de sueños* Penelope is depicted first and foremost as a woman and a multidimensional human being who is not without flaws or imperfections. She suffers from pride and jealousy when Ulysses abandons her to fight for Helen of Troy; her initial reaction is to compete with Helen and to avenge the hurt she has suffered by attracting her own retinue of suitors. As the years pass, however, she discovers true love for Anfino, the one suitor who, while lacking position, wealth, and armies, offers her love which is without demands, sincere love in which she will be ever beautiful. Penelope's weaving and unweaving of Laertes' shroud as a stratagem to postpone the selection of a husband thus acquires a new dimension. Believing Ulysses dead, she designs this delaying tactic to exhaust the kingdom of its wealth and thereby the suitors' interest in her, until Anfino remains her only choice. Thus, her weaving is a silent and secret expression of the dreams of her impossible love for him, not for Ulysses.

Penelope indeed fights to create a situation in which she can, without fear of reprisal, obtain self-fulfillment in ultimate marriage with Anfino. It is a struggle which resides completely within her, and she does not dare admit her objectives publicly. Anfino represents hope for a future when the world would be governed by superior men of ideals and love, rather than by the cold reasoners, such as Ulysses, who depend on violence, pride and cowardly acts to assert and maintain power. Needless to say, Penelope's dreams are shattered by the return of her husband. Disguised as a beggar, he learns the truth and quickly regains control of his kingdom by slaying all the suitors, including Anfino. Penelope condemns his disguise as cowardly, since it means that Ulysses knows he has aged and has feared his wife's rejection. It is not his wrinkles and gray hair, however, but his fear and cowardice which cause Penelope's negative reaction. As a result she now detests her husband, blaming him for everything, and praises Anfino's death as a superior heroic act, since even in death *he* never was afraid.

In truth, Penelope has won an internal victory, for she has only to await her reunion with Anfino in the world beyond. But in spite of this symbolic victory, outwardly Penelope has been defeated. The drama concludes with Ulysses insisting that, "Our name must remain clean and resplendent for the future. No one will know anything about this. . . . We must save face!"[10], and he commands the chorus to intone the rhapsody he himself has composed:

> Penelope was alone and surrounded
> by dangers and fears.
> But only for Ulysses does she live.
> She embroidered her dreams on the cloth.
> Her desires and dreams are: Ulysses!
> Glory smiled on the prudent queen
> who never loved a man other than her husband.
> Penelope is the name of the queen.
> She is an everlasting example of a wife.[11]

Thus the traditional version of the myth is reaffirmed, and the life remaining to Penelope is filled with barren silence and devoid of love, allowing only a faint hope of eternal union with Anfino in her dreams.

In Gala's drama *Anillos para una dama,* Jimena, after having spent two years in mourning for her hero husband, the Cid, now desires her freedom to remarry, this time out of love and to the man of *her* choosing. She longs for the true expression of love and personal fulfillment which had been denied her in her previous marriage; not unreasonably, she wishes to satisfy her own needs as a human being and a woman. King Alfonso is willing to arrange a politically sound marriage for her, but refuses "the Cid's widow" a publicly sanctioned marriage based on love, for such a marriage would be a betrayal of the Cid's memory, as well as politically disadvantageous to Alfonso. He points out that for the people the Cid is irreplaceable: no one can ever occupy his place, least of all with Jimena. The king clearly understands the value of myths, and how they must be carefully maintained and even embellished.

Jimena, however, staunchly refuses to continue her role and declares her desire to marry Minaya, the Cid's faithful companion and the man whom she has always loved. She points out that she lost *her* life when she married the Cid, whom she never loved, and refuses now to be "sold" again in marriage.[12] All she wants is to be a woman and to escape from her predestined historical role. She yearns to escape from History, and asks only to be left alone and given an opportunity to be herself. Jimena is tired of her role as a model for the other women of the kingdom.[13]

Minaya, in spite of his own personal feelings and mutual love for Jimena, is quick to point out the impossibility of their relationship. He knows only too well that Jimena, even now as a widow, is still the Cid's wife, and that their love can never be fulfilled. They have been like two parallel wheels, always close but never coinciding, while the Cid has been the axle which both unites and separates them. For Minaya and Jimena to realize their love would mean the undoing of everything, since without an axle there would be no wheels, no Jimena nor Minaya. He accepts that their destiny is the Cid and that destiny can not be changed.

A resigned Minaya therefore withdraws and is subsequently sent off to battle by Alfonso, while Jimena is left no choice but to accept the defeat of her dreams to remarry on her own terms. Attendant upon this defeat is the threat that Valencia, the supreme conquest of the Cid, is on the verge of attack by the Moors. When Alfonso, aware that he can not save the city, decides to destroy it by fire upon his departure, Jimena is again caught in a dilemma. She realizes that without her support, the Cid's dream of Valencia will cease to exist in History, and without the Cid's reputation as conqueror and hero, she too will perish. She therefore agrees to accompany the Cid's coffin to a monastery, to remain there for the rest of her life, and thus to perpetuate the unblemished legend of the Cid's greatness. Tearfully, Jimena admits that she has become a heroine, since she now must go on so that the Cid can survive. Without Jimena there is no Cid: she is his proof that all was true, and she is fated to preserve that which remains—"his rotting corpse and the wedding bands" which she now will wear forever.[14]

The worlds of Penelope and Jimena are thus totally dominated and defined by the traditional forces of society (the Church, the State, and the family), and maintained by History.[15] The individual who does not support the system and willingly accept his assigned role is quickly victimized and sacrificed. Any outward expression of interior desires meets with defeat and a curtailment of personal freedom. To suggest that truth is something other than the official version is equivalent to treachery and betrayal. Consequently, to imply that Ulysses was a coward, or that the Cid was a timorous hero and an unwilling lover, is to shatter the image of that hero, an image which must be maintained at all costs.

What is left to the victims of History, such as Penelope and Jimena, is merely the freedom to dream of the realization of their desires for love in the world beyond. As Minaya tells Jimena: "When you truly awaken, we will be together. . . . you will see me again . . . From then on, forever."[16] But Penelope is able to sustain her internal struggle only through the weaving of her dreams of Anfino, and after his death her survival depends on the dream of future happiness in the hereafter. To dream is the only recourse, and it is a tragic note that only in death can the dreams be realized, as indeed Anfino makes explicit: "Death is our great dream. To die in life is worse."[17]

Thus the dreamers, the truth-seekers, are suppressed, and the official lies of History remain intact. Both women learn that Historical figures are not real people, since History strips the individual of his emotions and personal identity. Jimena observes that the world is divided into two basic groups, the heroes and the resigned. For the heroes everything is great, bloody, dangerous, but happy, for their experience has to do with the war which they invented and where they blindly lead us, totally unaware of the price to be paid. In contrast, the resigned, while good, know their places and obey. Like cowards, they resign themselves to renounce beforehand that which is useless to desire.[18]

Although Minaya and Anfino represent a higher standard and a better world, the marriage of a hero's wife is nevertheless an impossible dream for them. The resigned can not effectively take charge of their own destinies, and in the end Penelope and Jimena are forced to join this group of the resigned. Katharine M. Rogers quite astutely has observed: "Finally, the patriarchal tradition has always maintained—has had to maintain, in order to justify itself—that woman is a creature weak in mind and morals who must be kept in check if society is to survive and man to progress."[19]

Machiavellian politics, designed to benefit the powerful and those seeking power, is what governs the resolution of the dramatic action in both plays, just as it does in real life. The slave Dione, jealous of Anfino's love for Penelope, orchestrates the discovery of Penelope's secret and causes her downfall. She originally had hoped to gain Anfino's love and then rule through him, once he had married Penelope. Equally motivated by policy, Jimena's daughter María dismisses love as nonessential and bases her life on this premise. She chastises her mother for allowing love to take precedence over matters of state, and maintains that it is much easier to administer a household, be a wife and mother, and raise an heir when love is absent. It is only when Jimena in defeat accepts her role as the grievous widow that María embraces her. King Alfonso, continually motivated by political designs, denies

Jimena remarriage, since it would not be practical to destroy the image of the Cid: the hero must live on in the person of his widow. The priest Jerónimo as the representative of the Church completes the composite picture of society's value system by supporting Alfonso and denying Jimena any modicum of Christian charity or understanding. Ulysses too places a higher value on his political image and power than on the value of human emotions. With the exception of the defeated and resigned, Anfino and Minaya, all are incapable of a vision beyond the practical needs of power; all are incapable of dreams. In both dramas order and authority must be reestablished and maintained. The appearance of truth is more important than truth itself.

In essence, the two women are alone is trying to solve their problems. By virtue of their different sets of values and their refusals to continue to bear false images, they are isolated individuals. Penelope alone has to stave off the advances of the suitors, and locks herself up in order to weave her dreams. Alfonso places Jimena under house arrest until she recants her wish to remarry for love.

In the end the wives become victims who are successfully silenced and made to conform to their assigned roles. The symbol of the rings effectively reinforces the permanence of their positions.[20] As a widow, Jimena now wears both her wedding band and that of the Cid, binding them together not only in life but also in death to an eternal commitment which is inescapable. Her only recourse is to await the arrival of death and an explanation from God for her suffering. Resignation and pointless suffering, tempered by a needed dream of love, are all that remain for the futures of the wives.

For reasons of the State, both women must remain as their husbands' wives until their deaths, and even beyond, in the account of History. They are victims of a role and society's obligation to that role, and ultimately both are psychologically and emotionally destroyed. The individual continues to be defeated by History, for not even in History is the individual's suffering recorded. Instead, the truth is obscured, and the myth is retained and reinforced through its repetition. Penelope and Jimena will live on as the faithful wives who loved and served their husbands as an example to all women. Their human qualities and emotional sufferings are passed over to sustain the image of the glorious ideal hero who must be eternally admired. At the end of the drama Jimena observes that History will record the beautiful scene: "the sobbing widow, the king who recognizes the power of a vassal, the bishop who blesses and offers good advice, and the daughter who kisses her mother's hand."[21] But she quickly adds in confidence that someday someone will tell *her* painful little story (*historia*), of how Jimena, stripped of everything, accompanied the coffin of the Cid and cried for her own death.

Buero Vallejo and Gala transform Penelope and Jimena, women of the past, into universal and contemporary figures through a humanization process. The women's roles have been assigned them by virtue of their marriages, and these roles have become permanent and inescapable. While their social positions set them apart from the ordinary woman and their prominence is legendary, they nonetheless—as perceived by the dramatists—share the human dilemma of all women. They reach a point when they wish to be individuals: breaking from the molds society has designed for them; having a say in their futures; fulfilling their inner desires and goals; in short—finding personal happiness.

Both dramatists have created new figures out of the fabric of the traditional epic narratives by investigating the inner reality of the human psyche. Each points up a universal element common to humanity, regardless of the historical context, and in doing so each designs a modern work applicable to the problems of the twentieth century.[22] Perhaps both Buero Vallejo and Gala look forward to a time when men, and more especially women, will not be forced to compromise their dreams and individualities, and when society will not be so structured as to sacrifice the individual to the dictates of prescribed roles, societal norms, and the achievement and maintenance of political power.

Notes

All translations from the Spanish are mine.

1. Naomi E. S. Griffiths, *Penelope's Web: Some Perceptions of Women in European and Canadian Society* (Toronto, 1976), p. 8.

2. The presentation of the social problems confronting women is not new to twentieth-century Spanish theatre. One has only to remember Federico García Lorca's dramatic works (e.g., *Yerma, La casa de Bernarda Alba*) which focus on the multifaceted and tragic consequences facing women in traditional Spanish society.

3. Antonio Buero Vallejo (1916-) is Spain's most celebrated and prolific living dramatist. His first work, *Historia de una escalera* (1949), signifies the turning point for contemporary Spanish theatre and represents the shift to a more realistic, artistic, and intellectual focus. Antonio Gala (1936-) produced his first dramatic work, *Los verdes campos del Edén,* in 1963, and has since become a well-established and respected playwright in the Spanish theatre. Both of these prize-winning dramatists treat the problems of contemporary man, his need for both love and awareness of self.

4. Sigmund Freud, *A General Introduction to Psychoanalysis* (New York, 1935), p. 125.

5. Joseph Campbell, *The Masks of God: Occidental Mythology* (New York, 1964), p. 158.

6. Antonio Gala, *Anillos para una dama,* in *Teatro español, 1973-1974* (Madrid, 1975), pp. 176-177.

7. Eva Figes, *Patriarchal Attitudes: Women in Society* (London, 1970), p. 19. The inferior status of women and their entrapment by male-created roles have been perceptively discussed by Lynda M. Glennon, *Women and Dualism* (New York, 1979), p. 39. She explains how sociologists have helped to maintain dualism by applying sexual labels: "Sociological pronouncements about the 'universality' of, and 'necessity' for, sexual dualism have legitimated the status quo. Such pronouncements have established a 'social scientific' rationale for a linkage existing in the modern world between gender and behavior orientations. Thus, as females have begun to behave more instrumentally by becoming more assertive or independent, their behavior can be labeled an act of defiance against nature, society, and True Masculinity." See also Sheila Rowbotham, *Woman's Consciousness, Man's World* (Harmondsworth, 1973).

8. Elizabeth Janeway, *Man's World, Woman's Place: A Study in Social Mythology* (New York, 1971), discusses the effects of the mythic (not rational) thinking which maintains that woman's place is in the home.

9. Jimena in the *Cantar de Mio Cid* is portrayed as the ideal of womanhood: she is always obedient and humble; views the Cid as her lord; defers to his opinions and judgments; inspires his masculine pride; and basks in his reflected honor and glory. María del Pilar Oñate, *El feminismo en la literatura española* (Madrid, 1938), pp. 7-8, describes Jimena as "the self-denying wife, faithful administrator of the domestic household and titular guardian of the home. Busy with the overseeing of the household chores, the singular mission of the woman at that time, she does not sense the humiliation of her situation, which on the other hand her love for her husband and affection for her children ease." Lucy A. Sponsler, *Women in the Medieval Spanish Epic & Lyric Traditions* (Lexington, Ky., 1975), p. 8, notes how the Spanish epic stresses the role women and family play in creating and maintaining a man's honor and masculinity. She states, "there can be no doubt that the main aim of the poem is the glorification of a masculine hero, and in achieving this, woman, from a modern standpoint, is viewed in a subordinate and submissive role." Carolyn Bluestine, "The Role of Women in the *Poema de Mío Cid*," *Romance Notes,* 18 (Spring 1978), 409, demonstrates how the passive resignation of the woman accents the valor and virility of the hero: "What is clear, however, is that the women were depicted as the pale incarnations of virtue, submission and martyrdom by a skilled craftsman who deliberately chose to represent them in that way."

10. Antonio Buero Vallejo, in *La tejedora de sueños*; *Llegada de los dioses,* ed. Luis Iglesias Feijoo (Madrid, 1976), p. 204. Moses I. Finley, *The World of Odysseus,* 2nd rev. ed. (New York, 1978), p. 28, referring to Homeric heroes states: "For the latter everything pivoted on a single element of honour and virtue: strength, bravery, physical courage, prowess. Conversely, there was no weakness. no unheroic trait, but one, and that was cowardice and the consequent failure to pursue heroic goals."

11. Buero Vallejo, pp. 205-207.

12. Sponsler, p. 3, points out that this was a time of prearranged marriages and absentee husbands: "Rarely did a woman have a choice of mate, for marriages were arranged primarily with political, social, or economic considerations in mind." It is not surprising that love might be absent in such marriages and that marriage itself did not inherently offer a picture of nuptial bliss. See Sponsler, and also Health Dillard, "Women in Reconquest Castile," in *Women in Medieval Society,* ed. Susan Mosher Stuard (Philadelphia, 1976), pp. 71-94, for a discussion of the rights of and legal restrictions on women in Spain during the Middle Ages.

13. I disagree with Angel Fernández Santos, Rev. of *Anillos para una dama* by Antonio Gala, *Insula,* No. 325 (December 1973), p. 15, when he faults Jimena for desiring remarriage on her own terms and concludes that she does not really love Minaya. He feels that her actions are caused by her awareness of aging, and that she simply uses Minaya as a protest and as a means to gain freedom.

14. Gala, pp. 207, 210.

15. Winston Weathers, *The Archetype and the Psyche* (Tulsa, 1968), p. 17, sees the *Odyssey* "as a handbook on . . . morals and manners" in which the ethical and moral system of a society is articulated. Finley, pp. 128-129, observes that in this context woman was the second sex in an unequal partnership, and man should receive more affection than he gives: "And that is precisely what we find in Homer. While Odysseus was absent the loss to Penelope, emotionally, psychologically, affectively, was incomparably greater than the loss to her husband."

16. Gala, p. 209.

17. Buero Vallejo, p. 194.

18. Gala, pp. 180-181.

19. Katharine M. Rogers, *The Troublesome Helpmate: A History of Misogyny in Literature* (Seattle, 1966), p. 276. Victoria Ocampo, *La mujer y su expresión* (Buenos Aires, 1936), p. 13, reinforces this idea when she comments: "For centuries, having wisely realized that the right of the strong is always the best (though

it ought not to be so), woman has resigned herself to repeat, in general, the scraps of the masculine monologue, hiding at times among those scraps something of her own harvest. But in spite of her qualities as a faithful dog who seeks refuge at the feet of the master who punishes it, woman has ended up by discovering that the task is tiring and useless."

20. Janeway, p. 73, in discussing the conflict between public and private roles, states that, "any society . . . is capable of forcing private, feeling individuals to play public roles that are grindingly unsympathetic, overdemanding and dehumanizing."

21. Gala, p. 211.

22. There is no doubt that each of these dramas, written during the time of the Franco regime, can be given a political reading. The conflicts of Spain are buried in the web of public pronouncements and censorship. Penelope and Jimena may well symbolize Spain, its tragic hope and tentative dreams for a better future when the individual will be allowed to achieve dignity and self-identity. See Joelyn Ruple, *Antonio Buero Vallejo (The First Fifteen Years)* (New York, 1971), pp. 36-37, and Hazel Cazorla, "Antonio Gala y la desmitificación de España: Los valores alegóricos de *Anillos para una dama*," *Estreno*, 4 (Fall 1978), 13-15.

John P. Gabriel (essay date April 1994)

SOURCE: Gabriel, John P. "Projections of the Unconscious Self in Buero's Theatre: *El Concierto de San Ovidio, La Fundación, Dialogo Secreto*." *Neophilologus* LXXVIII, no. 2 (April 1994): 351-61.

[*In the following essay, Gabriel investigates psychological aspects of* El concierto de San Ovidio, La Fundación, *and* Diálogo secreto *and explores the implication of these elements for Buero Vallejo's work.*]

In their symbolic journey from darkness to light, the protagonists of Antonio Buero Vallejo's theatre take part in a dynamic evolution of self that underscores their unyielding desire to rebel against and overcome limitations thrust upon them by fate. Their rebellion has very definite psychological implications. They become engaged in a deep inner struggle that leads ultimately to a reassertion of self. Over the years, we have come to appreciate Buero's frequent and varied use of symbols as an effective means for conveying dramatic tension and representing on the stage the complex interaction between his characters' inner reality and the external world. Worthy of mention are the ubiquitous stairway in *Historia de una escalera* (1949), the "duende" in *Irene o el tesoro* (1954), the omnipresent basement window in *El tragaluz* (1967), Ro-

sa's marvelous garden in *Caimán* (1981), and Alfredo's maniacal obsession with videotaping his life for posterior viewing in *Música cercana* (1989). Equally important in this regard is the playwright's repeated use of light and dark, blindness, deafness, painting and music.

Buero's concern for the intuitive side of his protagonists has not gone unnoticed and is, in the opinion of many critics, most evident in his later works. Robert Nicholas, for example, in viewing the development of Buero's theatre, remarks that "individual works tend to exhibit a more or less chronological evolution in dramatic attitude from an initial view of the stage as a vehicle for portraying real life to an acceptance of theatricality as a means for exploring the total person . . . this involves a deepening inner view, an increasingly subjective interpretation of reality" ("Antonio Buero-Vallejo: Stages" 25-26). Jean Cross Newman also recognizes this facet of Buero's more recent work when she remarks that Buero "bucea reiteradamente cuestiones de conciencia" (18). In spite of the general agreement among critics regarding this aspect of the Spanish playwright's work, no one has persuasively explored the psychic dimension of his protagonists.

Critics who have written about *El concierto de San Ovidio* (1962), *La Fundación* (1974) and *Diálogo secreto* (1984) have suggested that they are well suited for revealing the psychological disposition of Buero's characters. José Ramón Cortina, for example, writes that *El concierto de San Ovidio* dramatizes "la lucha del hombre por encontrar un sentido a la vida a pesar de que tiene ante sí un obstáculo que parece imposible de vencer. De encontrarlo," concludes Cortina, "el hombre ha logrado con ello la realización de su personalidad" (30). Regarding *La Fundación,* Martha Halsey speaks of Tomás's "inward journey of the soul" and Buero's prominent use of the techniques of "psychic participation" and "interiorization" ("Reality" 49). Similarly, for Margaret Jones, the association of visual elements and action in *Diálogo secreto* supports a "psychological depth" that she considers a "major concern of this drama" (34).[1] If the three plays in question are indeed introspective in nature, precisely what psychological elements are portrayed, and what are the possible implications of these elements for Buero's art and a greater appreciation of his craft?

David's personal drama, in *El concierto de San Ovidio,* has to do with his compelling desire to overcome the physical limitations thrust upon him by his blindness. Fully aware of his handicap, he has struggled to rebel against the limitations of his blindness since childhood. He tells us that he learned to use his cane with unusual dexterity "porque se me rieron de mozo, cuando quise defenderme a palos de las burlas de unos truhanes! Me empeñé en que mi garrote llegaría a ser para mí como un ojo. Y lo he logrado" (28). The situation he faces now is altogether analogous to the one he faced as a youth. While the conviction that he and his comrades can become skilled musicians is the result of his desire to avoid the humiliation that is sure to ensue from their performance dressed as clowns at the Concert of Saint Ovide ("¡Nosotros no seremos payasos!" 72), his actions also reflect a strong determination to achieve his full potential.

David's rebellion is only minimally evident at first in lines such as "Y si no lo queréis, resignaos como mujerzuelas a esta muerte en vida que nos aplasta" (29), but becomes more obvious as the play progresses: "Los ciegos no somos hombres: ése es nuestro más triste secreto. Somos como mujeres medrosas. Sonreímos sin ganas, adulamos a quien manda, nos convertimos en payasos . . ." (89). Despite the obstacles before him and in spite of the efforts of others to convince him otherwise, David believes that he and the other musicians can learn to play in harmony in the short time before the concert takes place. His conviction is conveyed in the image of a sightless French noblewoman, Melania de Salignac, of whom he has heard and dreams about and who, in David's own words "sabe lenguas, ciencias, música . . . Lee. ¡Y escribe! ¡Ella, ella sola! No sé cómo lo hace, pero lee . . . ¡en libros! ¡Es ciega! (27).

Indeed, Melania represents what is possible for a blind person—the Davids of the world—to accomplish. David's growing obsession with Melania ("¡Para ella hablo y para ella toco! Y a ella es a quien busco . . . A esa ciega . . ." [92]) is an expression of his visionary outlook, as several critics have noted (Halsey, "The Dreamer" 275; Holt 120). If we view David's rebellion as a journey with a specific goal, that of overcoming the limitations of his blindness, then his perception of Melania and the action that follows take on a distinctly archetypal quality with regard to his psychological maturation. Before proceeding in light of this hypothesis, a brief exposition of the psyche's development according to C. G. Jung, M.-L. von Franz and Edward C. Whitmont, will be helpful in realizing the present analysis of Buero's work.

Jung tells us that self-awareness comes about as a result of self-realization or "individuation", as he calls it; which is a crucial and ongoing process that allows persons to establish a meaningful balance between the different levels of their psyche. According to Jung, through individuation we are able to integrate the conscious and unconscious and become aware of qualities about ourselves that may otherwise go unnoticed. Ultimately, what one seeks through this process is selfhood, to become an individual and develop a personality that is purposeful (*The Development of Personality* 167-68; "The Relations Between" (103-11). The process is a contentious one. The confrontation between the conscious and the unconscious is very often conflictive and unpleasant because the encounter challenges how we perceive ourselves by revealing qualities within us that we are hesitant to acknowledge and accept (Whitmont 220). As Whitmont would put it, the meeting of the conscious and unconscious elements of the

psyche is a crucial step in the process of psychological maturation (169). For an individual to accept and understand fully his or her particular reality, a confrontation with the shadow is required (220). The shadow, in the words of M.-L. von Franz, represents the "unknown or little-known attributes and qualities of the ego" (174). It is further understood that individuals may experience such encounters periodically.

Given this psychological premise, as long as David's ego resists assimilation of the shadow, he will never fully comprehend his situation nor will he be able to achieve his goals in a realistic manner. I do not mean to imply that David denies his handicap. This is clearly not the case. Yet I do wish to suggest that what we see effectuated in the development of David's character are aspects of the ongoing process of individuation or psychological maturation.

It is a commonplace that the confrontation with one's own shadow is initiated by persons other than the individual himself (Whitmont 163). In David's case, it is Adriana who initiates the abandonment of false hope and precipitates a reevaluation of the former's limitations. A crucial moment in the process comes in the third act of the play when Adriana strikes at the core of David's idealistic vision. Referring to Melania, she tells him that "Te engañas. No dudo de que exista . . . Pero supongo que será rica. Sólo así habrá podido aprender lo que sabe. Figúrate, una ciega . . . Es rica y por eso no es de los tuyos. Ella nunca habrá padecido miedo, o hambre . . . , como nosotros" (92). Adriana symbolizes general skepticism but also represents residual doubts that David himself has. Melania is an appropriate model for David's determination yet an unrealistic one in the present situation. It is highly unlikely that he and the others can become accomplished musicians in the short amount of time that remains before the concert. Thus David's evocation of Melania constitutes an attempt on his part to rationalize an undertaking founded in the subjective rather than objective world.

It is shortly after this encounter with Adriana, that we witness the progress David has made toward a more realistic sense of awareness regarding the situation. First, he asks Lefranc, "¿Verdad que noestro espectáculo es indigno?", to which the latter answers "¡Es intolerable!" (100). This is followed by an admission of his delusion that he directs to the other musicians: "Os decía que yo antes soñaba para olvidar mi miedo. Soñaba con la música, y que amaba a una mujer a quien ni siquiera conozco . . . Y también soñé que nadie me causaría ningún mal, ni yo a nadie . . . ¡Qué iluso!" (113). Ultimately, he reaffirms that "¡Estoy ciego y soy un mendigo!" (118) thereby suggesting a reconciliation with his condition from a realistic point of view.

In *El concierto de San Ovidio*, David moves from the subjective to the objective. His personality parallels that of individuals that Jung classifies as an "introverted thinking types" for however clear to David "the inner structure of his thoughts may be, he is not in the least clear where or how they link up with the world of reality" ("Psychological Types" 243). According to Jung, these types rationalize "as a result of a psychic disposition often existing from early youth" and their judgment is rational, "only in that it is oriented more by the subjective factor." ("Psychological Types" 250, 251). By the play's end, the real supplants the ideal as the earmark of David's vision, a shift in his perspective that is appropriately personified by Valentín Haüy whose presence points to a distant future when the Davids of the world will be able to fulfill their potential. By the same token, David's murder of Valindin—an otherwise reproachable act of violence—is not without its positive effect. It puts an end to the humiliation of the blind musicians.

Tomás, the protagonist of *La Fundación,* also displays a rebellious nature although his behavior might be classified more appropriately as denial. A political prisoner, unable to accept the responsibility for the capture and incarceration of his comrades, Tomás fantasizes that the prison is a research center for artists and scientists. Aside from interacting with the other prisoners, he converses with Berta, an imaginary figure. It is important to note that in performance there is physical interaction between Tomás and Berta. Only later do we learn that Tomás imagined the encounters with her. In the play, he progresses from a period of mental illness to a state of lucidity, an evolution that appropriates certain aspects of the process of individuation. A closer look at the psychological significance of the action in *La Fundación* provides greater insight into Tomás's attitudinal development.

The first indication that Tomás denies objective reality is his delusion that he believes himself to be confined to an elegant research center instead of a prison. While critics have not spoken of Tomás's character in terms of self-denial and individuation, they have on numerous occasions underscored the unmistakable introverted nature of his character. Robert Nicholas has done so in terms of the play's setting by declaring that "changes in the stage décor" are used to depict the protagonist's "recovery and acceptance of reality . . . until the Foundation can be seen for what it really is, a sordid prison cell" ("Illusions and Hallucinations" 63). More recently, Jean Cross Newman has illustrated that Berta represents Tomás's *alter ego,* concluding that his conversations with her are in actuality, "diálogos consigo mismo" that "dan expresión a dudas que Tomás . . . admitir en su pensar consciente" (16).

The resistance to knowing painful aspects about ourselves is altogether common. The ego actively keeps motives and actions from consciousness in the interest of selfprotection, itself a form of rebellion. As indicated earlier, "before the ego can triumph, it must master and assimilate the shadow" (Henderson 112). For Tomás, this means accepting the responsibility for the situation he and his comrades now face in prison. In *La Fundación,* this supposition is conveyed in the Elysian-like scenery and Bertás character, both projections of Tomás's perspective on reality. Elaborating further on Newman's insightful interpretation of the play, a closer look at Berta reveals that her character incarnates at once Tomás detachment from the objective world of reason and the crucial link that is necessary to establish the dynamic psychic rapprochement of the conscious and unconscious. When the relationship between Tomás and Berta and the idyllic setting are viewed in conjunction, the intricate psychic orientation of their relationship is further established.

When we are first introduced to Berta, her redemptive mission and her subliminal identification with Tomás are made clear immediately. She wears a blouse bearing the same identification number as that of Tomás, A-72, and she enters carrying a little white mouse that symbolizes the protagonist. Referring to the mouse, Berta makes her wishes known: "Me gustaria rescaterle de lo que le espera" (139). The prison cell is filled with "la risueña luz de la primavera" and a "cernida e irisada claridad." Through the window is projected a "dilatada vista de un maravilloso puisaje" (137). If the relationship between Berta, Tomás and the scenery represents, as I suggested earlier, a symbolic meeting of the external world and the protagonist's inner reality, then the evolution of the relationship of these three elements will be helpful in mapping out the latter's psychic development. To see this, one need only compare what Tomás divulges as the play progresses with the changes in the scenery and Berta's character.

As part one of the play draws to a close, both the scenery and Tomás's words indicate that a significant change has occurred. Whereas at the beginning of the play he talks of the brilliant and lush colors of the field and of "un día tan luminoso" (138), at the end of the first part, Tomás painfully acknowledges that "la escoba que teníamos se ha transformado en una escoba vieja . . . ni el televisor ni el altavoz funcionan . . ." (179). Almost simultaneously, we sense through Tomás's own admission a growing sense of awareness when he tells Max and Asel that "vosotros sabéis algo que yo ignoro" (179). When the second part of the play opens, the cell's interior reflects the change in Tomás's mental state while his words reflect an element of doubt previously absent ("No puedo creer que fueran imaginaciones" [92]). As the stage directions indicate, the illuminated scenery outside the window now stands in contrast to the transformed decor of the cell's interior: "Tomás gira la cabeza y contempla la radiante luz del paisaje. La del aposento está bajando muy lentamente" (190). Shortly after, the ilusion disappears altogether as Tomás himself notes: "No puedo creerlo. Cuando han abierto la puerta . . . no se veía el campo" (195).

Berta's next appearance is prefaced by Tomás's heightened awareness which reveals itself further in their second encounter. In comparison to the affirmative attitude that

Tomás displayed in his initial meeting with Berta, in their second encounter he comes across as doubtful and suspicious. In a scene reminiscent of one between therapist and patient, Tomás remains on his cot as Berta approaches him and sits by him as he proceeds to ask her a series of probing questions: "¿Cómo has podido entrar?", "¿Por qué la Fundación es tan inhóspita?", "¿Tú lo sabes?", "¿No quieres contestarme?", "¿Has venido a burlarte?", "¿Por qué lloraste en el locutorio?" (213-14). After Berta exits, Tomás concludes that "Ella no ha venido" (217) and acknowledges that "Estamos en . . . la cárcel." Buero writes that "durante un segundo," Tomás "mira el paisaje, ahora oscuro y borroso" (218). Once he externalizes what was internally intolerable, reality is immediately de-idealized.

For Tomás, Berta's imagined presence serves to justify his personal fantasy. In theory, the evolution of their relationship is similar to that of David and his vision of Melania. Here the psychoanalytic evaluation comes in the words of Asel who has throughout the play functioned in the same capacity as Adriana in *El concierto de San Ovidio*. Having initiated Tomás's contact with his shadow, Asel offers his diagnosis: "La desaparición de Berta es la realidad que le invade a su pesar . . ." "Esa cita ha sido quizá la última tentativa de refugiarse en sus delirios y la crisis definitiva" (217). With the onslaught of objective reality, Berta loses her purpose. Ultimately, the admission of guilt, denunciation of the unreal and evidence of an altered psychic disposition comes in Tomás's own words: "¡Yo os denuncié!" (226) and "Ya sé que [la Fundación] no era real" (239).

Tomás's inability to accept responsibility for his actions leads to a denial of reality, which in turn causes him to restructure reality in relationship to what he feels. What he experiences is symptomatic of "introverted intuitive types," according to Jung. For these individuals, who may be called "mystical dreamers or seers," perception is the main problem. Moreover, Jung points out that these types "rely predominantly on their vision" and adapt themselves according to their inner reality not the objective world ("Psychological Types" 261, 263). In short, Tomás eludes objective reality by creating his own reality. On a subconscious level, he recognizes that his actions have led to the incarceration of his friends. Yet there is no conscious recognition or acknowledgement of his actions. We might say that Tomás's conscious rebels against his unconscious and resists assimilation. Thus in the play the scenery symbolizes the externalization of Tomás's inability to accept the truth. Berta in turn represents the crucial link between the conflict that arises between Tomás's internal reality and the external world. It follows then that when Tomás's conscious side ceases to resist an encounter with unconscious elements of his psyche, he progresses to a realistic appraisal of the immediate situation and Berta disappears.

Of the protagonists under consideration here, it is Fabio of *Diálogo secreto* who provides the most complex character from a psychoanalytic standpoint. In a fascinating confluence of past and present, self and other, real and unreal, Buero creates an exquisite vehicle of psychic tension. Essentially, Fabio's character combines David's compulsion for self-preservation and Tomás's compunction for self-justification. Criticism has already shown that Fabio's imagined conversations with his father Braulio are in essence a dialogue with himself that externalizes "Fabio's constant fear of being discredited" as an art critic and reflect "the truth that he refuses to acknowledge publicly" (Halsey, "Dictatorship to Democracy" 13). Further analysis shows that Braulio and Aurora—Aurorín when she appears in Fabio's recollection of the past—play a more pivotal role in the dramatization of Fabio's lifelong internal struggle than previously thought.

Aurora brings about one of the play's most suspenseful and tenseridden moments when she threatens to expose her father's color blindness. Her role in Fabio's psychic evolution is no less critical. This is first evident during the second of Fabio's imagined conversations in which Braulio, Fabio and Aurorín debate the capability of persons to distinguish colors. At a cerain juncture in the discussion, Aurorín turns to Braulio, closes her eyes and claims that "Si yo ahora cierro los ojos . . . y quiero ver tu cara verde . . ." Then suddenly opening her eyes she declares, "¡Te veo verde!" The action sparks an irrational display of aggression by Fabio toward his daughter. Threatening to strike her, he chastises her, calling her a "¡Mentirosa!" and "¡Embustera!" (58). His recollection ends and we are abruptly transposed to the present where we hear immediately of the suicide of Samuel Cosme, Aurora's artist boyfriend. Much in the vein of the concert performance in *El concierto de San Ovidio* and the state of imprisonment in *La Fundación* with regard to David and Tomás respectively, the event of Cosme's death triggers Fabio's need to reexamine his condition from a realistic standpoint. Consequently, subsequent imagined conversations with Braulio and Aurora do reveal a heightened anxiety on the part of Fabio to address once again the nature of his handicap. At the end of the first part of the play, for example, we find out that Braulio could not bring himself to tell his son of his color blindness. The following interchange illustrates that Fabio blames his father for concealing the truth. Yet Braulio insists that Fabio is as much to blame for not fully acknowledging the facts about his condition as he grew older.

> Fabio.—¡Para darme una vida auténtica y no este simulacro asqueroso, debiste explicarme a tiempo lo que me pasaba!
>
> Braulio.—Ya te he dicho . . .
>
> Fabio.—¡El culpable eres tú!
>
> Braulio.—Tú, por cobarde.

Fabio.—¡Tú has sido el cobarde! ¡Yo era un niño!

Braulio.—¡Pero llegaste a hombre! ¡Un hombre cobarde e hipócrita!

(86)

Shortly after this encounter, we are displaced in time once again. We witness a rapid shift between the images of a probative young Aurora and an obstinate grown woman who "reenacts" her face painting. Aurorín reappears, insisting that "los niños no inventan cuando pintan. Si cierro los ojos . . . quiero ver tu cara verde. ¡Te veo verde!" (94). Abruptly, the scene shifts to the present and a grown Aurora paints her face green, challenges her father to look her in the face and asks "¿Y qué ves?" "He answers "¡No hay nada más que ver!" to which Aurora responds "Tu hija se ha vuelto una ranita verde. ¡Cro, cro! Y tú no lo has visto" (100). Fabio has always fought to overcome the limitations of his handicap. Now as a result of Cosme's death, he is forced to reaffirm his struggle if he is to continue to fulfill his potential.

During the ongoing process of individuation, M.-L. von Franz reminds us that the ego can feel "hampered in its will or desire" as it progresses toward awareness and will accuse some other outside force of being responsible for the situation that it is unable to accept (169). The resentment Fabio harbors for his father may very well be explained in light of von Franz's claim. What is more, the same may be said of the contentious relationship between Fabio and his daughter. Jung's findings also corroborate this view of Fabio's behavior. It follows that Cosme's suicide serves to wound Fabio's ego, resurrecting old fears and apprehensions and setting off one of the many confrontations between the conscious and unconscious that Fabio is sure to have experienced throughout his lifetime. Here Jung might say that the unconscious has risen up in opposition to Fabio in the persons of Braulio and Aurora (*The Symbols of Transformation* 294).

Like David and Tomás before him, Fabio is a complex individual whose idealized vision must be defined or redefined in realistic terms. In his particular case, the past plays a crucial role. Characteristic of "introverted sensation types," whom Jung tells us are most often alienated from present reality and oriented toward the past ("Psychological Types" 257), Fabio is trapped in a dynamic confluence of past and present. His situation is less a case of delusion or denial than one of maintaining a hopeful outlook. Fabio has been involved in a long-term struggle to keep others from finding out about his color blindness. In order to maintain the lie and continue to embrace the hope of a better future he must face and understand his handicap completely. To do so he must acknowledge anew certain aspects of his past, as Fabio himself tells his wife: "Ahora mismo estoy intentando distinguir matices en la maravilla cromática que tú ves ahi y que a mí se me ha negado . . . Y vuelvo a acariciar la il-

usión infantil de que un día se descubran remedios que curen mis ojos . . . No podré renunciar a ese mundo que persigo. Tendré que mentir . . . o desaparecer" (131).

In her study, "Buero's Women: Structural Agents and Moral Guides," Linda Sollish Sikka makes a valid argument for the structural importance of women characters in Buero's theatre. She illustrates convincingly that the playwright's female characters are integral, if not essential, to the development of plot, theme and action in his work. It is no less the case in the plays discussed here that the female character is essential to Buero in his exploration of his protagonists' psyche. From Melania, who is a real person but void of physical presence on the stage, to Berta, likewise imagined but present on the stage in performance, to Aurora, who is both real and imagined, appearing in different stages of her life, Buero displays a growing concern to explore the intuitive side of his protagonists.[2] Each of these female characters assumes deeply subconscious roles rooted in the archetypal "collective unconscious," which Jung describes in terms of the *animus*—the subconscious masculine side of the feminine nature—and the *anima*—the feminine personification of the man's unconscious. As noted by von Franz, the *anima* "embodies," among other "psychological tendencies in a man's psyche, his relationship to his unconscious" (186). She then adds, "whenever a man's logical mind is incapable of discerning facts that are hidden in his unconscious, the *anima* helps him dig them out" (193).

Knowledge of self is crucial to any understanding of the objective world and how we function in it. More importantly, as exemplified by David, Tomás and Fabio, knowing oneself is neither a prescriptive nor a definitive process but one that is incidental and ongoing. Moreover, it requires that we persevere and continually reassert ourselves in our effort to become purposeful. For Buero's characters, it is their propensity toward rebellion that leads them to explore the full potential of their existence. Rebellion, according to Buero, dispels false hope and serves to authenticate personal aspirations. Given the playwright's own definition of the human condition, it is positive, constructive and, above all, indispensable for survival:

> La vida humana auténtica es, a mi juicio, siempre trágica. En definitiva, el que la vida humana sea en fondo siempre trágica lo único que afirma es la realidad de nuestra limitación frente a nuestra sed de ilimitación. Eso es un hecho trágico y, por consiguiente, el último sentido de cualquier vida humana es un sentido trágico. Sin embargo, identificar al ciento por ciento ese sentido de lo trágico con el sentido fatalista y falta de salidas que tantas veces se ha aplicado al concepto de lo trágico eso es en lo que yo nunca he estado de acuerdo y que siempre he rebatido en la medida de mis posibilidades

(Gabriele 21).

For one whose theatre has displayed historically a unique interplay of action, signs, words, images, and other elements to convey a message of hope, it comes as no surprise that the personification of the unconscious serves an equally transcendental purpose in Buero's moral and social work. Throughout his career, Buero has perfected his craft while concentrating on the human elements of his art. It is altogether logical that one so concerned with human nature should occupy himself with the latent and manifest meanings of the self. Exploring this protagonists from a psychological standpoint intensifies dramatic tension and gives profound meaning to the process of interiorization and catharsis that so uniquely characterizes Buerian Tragedy. Ultimately, the technique lends greater validity to the context of Buero's work by allowing his audience to connect motives to actions and purpose to aspirations.

Notes

1. The plays chosen for discussion here occupy pivotal places in the evolution of Buero's theatre. *El concierto de San Ovidio* was the third in a cycle of three historical dramas, the first two being *Un soñador para un pueblo* (1958) and *Las Meninas* (1960), and was considered at the time of publication Buero's most refined attempt at total theatre. According to Iglesias Feijoo, "con el *El concierto de San Ovidio* Buero aprovecha y profundiza todo lo anterior para construir, probablemente su mejor obra hasta el momento" (294). *La Fundación* was the last of Buero's play written under the Franco Regime and one in which the themes of truth and freedom, both on a personal and national level, are of paramount importance, an Martha Halsey has indicated: "the dialectical struggle between tranquil blindness and painful awareness, that occurs on both the socio-political and metaphysical levels characterizes all of Buero's dramas. However, it is in *La Fundación* that this struggle is seen in all its complexity and where ideas presented in earlier dramas are presented most skillfully" ("Reality" 47). *Diálogo secreto* was the first of Buero's plays to be written and staged in Socialist Spain and is, according to Margaret Jones, unique among Buero's repertoire in that the play signals "a reordering of priorities." In the critic's own words, "we find an increased emphasis on man's inner struggle . . . accompanied by a diminished interest in circumstantial, social, or other exterior factors of reality" (35).

2. Those who have written about these three plays have suggested that Melania, Berta and Aurora are integral to the development of David's, Tomás's and Fabio's personal drama yet these comments constitute little more than a passing acknowledgement of the fact. Typical, for example, is Luis Iglesias Feijoo's observation that Melania is an "elements decisivo en la evolución de David" (311). In her discussion of the relationship between Tomás and Berta, in *La Fundación,* Magda Ruggieri Marchetti writes that "si nota como es scontro tra i due personaggi rappre-

senta la lotta tra il subconscio e la pazzia di Tomás" (33) Regarding Aurora, Margaret Jones remarks, "Fabio's outraged denial is shown to be a lie when Aurora appears with her face painted apple-green" (33).

Works Cited

Buero Vallejo, Antonio. *Diálogo secreto.* Madrid: Espasa-Calpe, 1985.

———. *El concierto de San Ovidio. La Fundación.* 7ª ed. Madrid: Espasa-Calpe, 1986.

Cortina, José Ramón. *El arte dramático de Buero Vallejo.* Gredos, 1969.

Gabriele, John P. "Entrevista a Antonio Buero Vallejo." *Estreno* 17.2 (1991): 20-24.

Halsey, Martha T. "The Dreamer in the Tragic Theater of Buero Vallejo." *Revista de Estudios Hispánicos* 2 (1968): 265-85.

———. "Dictatorship to Democracy in the Recent Theater of Buero Vallejo (*La Fundación* to *Diálogo secreto*)." *Estreno* 13.2 (1987): 9-15.

———. "Reality, Illusion and Alienation: Buero Vallejo's *La Fundación.*" *Hispanófila* 90 (1987): 47-62.

Henderson, Joseph L. "Ancient Myths and Modern Man." *Man and His Symbols.* Ed. Carl G. Jung. New York: Dell, 1964. 95-156.

Holt, Marion. *The Contemporary Spanish Theater (1949-1972).* Boston: Twayne, 1975.

Iglesias Feijoo, Luis. *La trayectoria dramática de Antonio Buero Valleje.* Santiago de Compostela: Universidad de Santiago de Compostela, 1982.

Jones, Margaret E. W. "Psychological and Visual Planes in Buero Vallejo's *Diálogo secreto.*" *Estreno* 12.1 (1986): 33-35.

Jung, C. G. *The Development of Personality.* Princeton: Princeton UP, 1954. Vol. 17 of *The Collected Works of C. G. Jung.* Eds. Herbert Read et al. 20 vols 1953-79.

———. "Psychological Types." *The Portable Jung.* Ed. Joseph Campbell. New York: Viking Press, 1971, 178-269.

———. "The Relations Between the Ego and the Unconscious." *The Portable Jung.* Ed. Joseph Campbell. New York: Viking Press, 1971. 70-138.

———. *The Symbols of Transformation.* Princeton: Princeton UP, 1956. Vol. 5 of *The Collected Works of C. G. Jung.* Eds. Herbert Read et al. 20 vols. 1953-79.

Nicholas, Robert L. "Illusions and Hallucinations (Antonio Buero Vallejo: Three Recent Plays)." *Estreno* 12.2 (1986): 63-63.

————. "Antonio Buero-Vallejo: Stages, Illusions and Hallucinations." *The Contemporary Spanish Theater. A Collection of Critical Essays,* Eds. Martha T. Halsey and Phyllis Zatlin. Lanham, MD: University Press of America. 1988. 25-43.

Newman, Jean Cross. "Traumas de conciencia en el teatro de Buero Vallejo." *Estreno* 17.2 (1991): 15-19.

Ruggieri Marchetti, Magda. "*La Fundación*: sintesi tematica del teatro di Buero Vallejo." *Rivista di Letterature Moderne Comparate* 32 (1970): 1-28.

Sollish Sikka, Linda. "Buero's Women: Structural Agents and Moral Guides." *Estreno* 16.1 (1990): 18-22; 31.

Franz, M.-L. "The Process of Individuation." *Man and His Symbols.* Ed. Carl G. Jung. New York: Dell, 1964. 157-254.

Whitman, Edward C. *The Symbolic Quest: Basic Concepts of Analytical Psychology.* New York: Harper & Row, 1969.

EN LA ARDIENTE OSCURIDAD (IN THE BURNING DARKNESS)

CRITICAL COMMENTARY

Reed Anderson (essay date spring-summer 1975)

SOURCE: Anderson, Reed. "Tragic Conflict and Progressive Synthesis in Buero Vallejo's *En la ardiente oscuridad.*" *Symposium* XXIX, nos. 1-2 (spring-summer 1975): 1-12.

[*In the following essay, Anderson considers Buero Vallejo's ideas about tragedy and applies them to* En la ardiente oscuridad.]

En la ardiente oscuridad first reached the stage in 1950, though it was written in 1946, a year before the prize-winning *Historia de una escalera* which had launched Buero Vallejo's career as a dramatist.[1] *En la ardiente oscuridad* is a tragedy in the purest sense, and its treatment of conflict is uncompromising. The dramatic action moves compellingly and resolutely toward catastrophe, and the ending suggests the synthetic and affirmative reconciliation of the conflictive principles whose clash is the drama's primary motive force. While it is not my purpose in this article to discuss the concept of tragedy as such, I believe that it is only from the perspective of certain ideas—both Buero Vallejo's and others'—as to what tragedy is about that *En la ardiente oscuridad* can be most thoroughly understood.

To begin with, Buero Vallejo regards the functional qualities of tragedy as supremely important. He alludes to the dynamic relationship between the spectator and the drama in Aristotle's concept of catharsis. Fundamental to the idea of catharsis is the conviction that human character can be morally refined and perfected through aesthetic experience, and that a profoundly integrated and serene outlook may be cultivated through the formal dramatization of the most fearfully catastrophic events. According to Aristotle, the terror and pity aroused in the spectator as he witnesses the dramatic conflict and catastrophe are subsequently purged and altered by the final vision that is projected through the tragedy.

In order to explain the sources of these emotions attributed to the tragic experience by Aristotle, Nietzsche metaphorically characterized the tragic vision by suggesting that the world of tragedy is ruled by the opposed principles of Dionysus and Apollo: the realm of spontaneous and primitive emotion and of victimizing and terrifying chaos, opposed to the sublimely controlled, civilizing principle of formal order, harmony and restraint. The dramatic suggestion of eternal conflict between these two principles is, for Nietzsche, at the heart of tragedy's appeal to the spectator's mind and emotions, and its most significant discovery of truth. The cathartic process, however, refers more accurately to the prevailing emotional mood at the end of the tragic spectacle, and to the final suggestion of what man's understanding of these opposing principles must be. The cathartic effect is achieved through the conciliatory and harmonizing tendency inherent in the formal qualities of classical tragedy. Having experienced the terror of the boundless Dionysiac world of chaos which threatens to return man to an undifferentiated, instinctive level of will-less being, "here, when the danger to his will is greatest, art (the Apollonian) approaches as a saving sorceress, expert at healing."[2] The final reassertion of the Apollonian world of formal and harmonious order as the universal principle that is to prevail purges the strong emotions of terror and pity experienced as the tragic drama unfolds. But these emotions are in no way annulled, weakened or repressed through the cathartic experience of tragedy. Rather, they are sublimated, given an ethical dimension, a human dimension which restores the integrated and tonic will to live, but without ever entirely displacing the annihilating and darkly seductive level of Dionysian insight into the dangerous world of chaos and terror.

This ethical side of the function of tragic catharsis is for Buero Vallejo supremely important; as he sees it, terror and pity, "por obra de los significados del relato trágico adquieren la calidad ética y humana que acaso inicialmente no tenían en el ánimo del espectador. Con lo cual, naturalmente, se desprenden de su cualidad instintiva y casi animal. Se serenan. Mas no porque pierdan fuerza, sino porque ganan nobleza. La catarsis no es ya descarga, sino mejora. La piedad y el terror, dignificados por el asunto trágico, se purifican."[3]

It is through the dramatic struggle of the tragic hero that the spectator is led to perceive the fearful dimensions of the tragic experience. The deeply disruptive and dangerous quality of the hero's vision consists in its suggestion that the world of laws and conventions, held by society to be universally valid, is merely an elaborate formal façade which protects man from perceiving the dreadful and amoral nature of the universe which lies beyond the veil of his illusory ethics. Classical tragedy allows the hero's vision to burst forth in all its terrifying and seductive strength, but subsequently (often over the course of a trilogy of plays) shows that tragic vision yielding to the reassertion of the formal social order which it has so seriously threatened to destroy: "it is this final inhibition of tragic vision, this imposition of formal and moral order upon that which threatens it, that allows these dramas to be properly called classical in the best sense."[4] The defeat of the hero in classical tragedy does not prove his vision false; it does, however, prompt the spectator to investigate the reasons for that defeat.

Neither the hero nor the ethical order of society he seems to threaten can make claims to exclusive authority or truth, then. Buero Vallejo observes that, "la limitación del hombre posibilita que dos verdades parciales puedan oponerse y luchar entre sí, pues en su misma parcialidad reside su fallo."[5] The spectator may be inclined to attribute the hero's downfall to unintelligible and capricious blows of fate, extrapolating from such a vision an absurd and amoral universe. But as Buero Vallejo suggests, tragedy, when properly understood, compels us to examine the tragic hero's weakness, and not to see his defeat as the product of forces external to his character or to the nature of his ideas. The function of tragedy, as Buero Vallejo so eloquently defines it, is to strip back the illusion of blind fate and to bring us to confront the true and objective reasons for the hero's fall: "La tragedia intenta explorar de qué modo las torpezas humanas se disfrazan de destino."[6] This leads Buero Vallejo to the conclusion that, "El absurdo del mundo tiene poco que ver con la tragedia como último contenido a deducir, aunque tenga mucho que ver con ella como aparencia a investigar."[7]

As Nietzsche implies, then, what we see at the end of the tragic drama does not suggest a return to a state of "unendangered comfort"; having experienced the relentless vitality and the compelling truth of the tragic visionary, such a return is impossible. The force of the tragic hero's vision (Nietzsche's Dionysian principle) continues to reverberate, even when submitted to the cold and conservative light of reason and order (the Apollonian). A final synthesis of the two conflictive principles is thereby suggested, wherein the vision of the tragic hero may serve to carry the ethical order beyond its former narrow and severe dedication to pragmatic stability and toward a more profound and inclusive sense of the truth.

Now we must ask how this sense of truth is conveyed in Buero Vallejo's *En la ardiente oscuridad.*

The scene of the drama is restricted to the interior of a school for the blind. In setting the stage, Buero is careful to specify in his directions that, "la ilusión de normalidad es, con frecuencia, completa."[8] The opening scenes depict the society of blind students as stable and positive; they are adjusted perfectly to their surroundings, and their surroundings are unchanging. They move unhesitatingly from one place to another without the aid of canes. In such a stable atmosphere the students have developed a high level of confidence and self-reliance. Even the school's language has been adjusted in order to encourage this sense of normalcy: the word "ciego" is prohibited, and has been replaced by the more neutral, "invidente" (literally, 'nonsighted').

Appearing in abrupt contrast to this secure and positive social order is Ignacio. His arrival as a new student in the school is marked by the sound of his cane. This cane, which Ignacio refuses to relinquish throughout the play, symbolizes his repudiation of the secure and practical norms imposed on the students by the school, and, in a broader sense, the cane is emblematic of his skepticism concerning the immutably ordered but dangerously hermetic world in which the students live. Ignacio, like the others, is blind; but unlike the other members of the school's society, he refuses to nurture in any way the illusion that he is normal.

Faced with the problem of Ignacio's intransigence, the Director, as representative and defender of the school's social and moral order, offers a facile diagnosis of Ignacio's nonconformity: "Es lo de siempre. Falta de moral . . . los muchachos de este tipo están hambrientos de cariño y alegría . . ." (p. 23). He proposes a therapy designed to ensure his happiness by bringing him into conformity with the school's norms of ethics and conduct: "hay que convencerle de que es un ser útil y de que tiene abiertos todos los caminos, si se atreve"; the other students must see to "la creación de una camaradería verdadera, que le alegre el corazón" (p. 23). It is added that Ignacio must be infused with, "nuestra famosa moral de acero" (p. 24). The terminology itself has the fraudulent ring of moral propaganda dedicated to the cultivation of a shared and very particular state of mind and spirit.

Ignacio attacks outright the superficiality of the students' cheerful optimism and accuses them of fleeing from confrontation with the truth of their tragic condition. He tells Juana that her companions are too complacent, insincere and cold, and he declares that he feels himself burning inside, "ardiendo con un fuego terrible, que no me deja vivir y que puede haceros arder a todos . . . Ardiendo en esto que los videntes llaman oscuridad, y que es horroroso . . . porque no sabemos lo que es" (p. 30). When Juana cannot comprehend what it is that Ignacio is suffering and searching for, he answers that he is searching for the ability to see. Refusing to adapt himself to the Center's norms, he warns Juana that it is strife that he brings into their midst, and not peace: "tu optimismo y tu ceguera son iguales . . . la guerra que me consume os consumirá" (p. 30).

The Center's functional illusion of normalcy only obscures certain fundamental truths concerning the material and spiritual condition of the blind; truths which, for Ignacio, are more important than the narrow practical lessons and superficial temper fostered by the school. Behind Ignacio's relentless probing is the notion that man cannot and should not rest until he has become fully aware of his human capacities and until he has discovered his true place in the universal scheme of human society. According to this, until the blind recognize the truth of their inferiority to the sighted, and all the implications of this inferiority, they will be incapable of reaching beyond the condition of shallow and complacent optimism which is the norm that the Center is dedicated to creating and maintaining. The sighted are superior in two basic ways, as Ignacio points out: first, they have power—they can confidently perceive the world which surrounds them with a glance and even at great distances, whereas the blind only know what they can touch and sometimes hear or smell; second, the sighted are the privileged possessors of an aesthetic world of light and color and the sensual visual presence of other people, phenomena which the blind cannot even begin to imagine.

The demoralizing and disruptive effect Ignacio's ideas have on the school are manifested in the second act of the play where it is observed that the students are falling behind in their studies and showing little enthusiasm for their normal learning activities. They no longer abide by the school's code of proper dress; rejection of that norm, indicated all along by Ignacio's comparatively unkempt appearance, is now shared by most of the Center's students. Erosion of the will which Nietzsche perceived as a product of the Dionysian vision achieves concrete expression here. As though hypnotized by the horrowing experience of truth that Ignacio has opened up to them, the students fall into passivity, cease to observe the school's regimen or to struggle for their own individual improvement; they seem to abandon themselves with Ignacio to the seductive and chilling realm of speculation concerning their true nature as blind members of a sighted universe. The formerly stable social order of the Center thus begins to deteriorate.

The extreme position in defense of the Center's traditional moral and social order is led by the Director, and articulated among the students by Carlos. Carlos begins by attempting to defeat Ignacio, "por fuerza del razonamiento," and expresses absolute certainty concerning the correctness of his position. His concern is with the disintegration of will and morale that he observes in his fellow students; the ethical purpose of his attack on Ignacio is stated directly to his antagonist:

> Mis palabras pueden servir para que nuestros compañeros consigan una vida relativamente feliz. Las tu-

yas no lograrán más que destruir; llevarlos a la desesperación, hacerles abandonar sus estudios.

(p. 47)

tu influencia está pesando demasiado sobre esta casa. Y tu influencia es destructora. Si no te vas, esta casa se hundirá.

(p. 60)

Finally, the struggle is defined by Carlos in terms of the principle of life—the positive social order which allows the blind to live "normally"—against the principle of death—Ignacio's demoralizing insistence on the inferiority of the world of the blind:

> ¡Yo defiendo la vida! ¡La vida de todos nosotros, que tú amenazas! Porque quiero vivirla a fondo, cumplirla; aunque no sea pacífica ni feliz. Aunque sea dura y amarga. ¡Pero la vida sabe a algo, nos pide algo, nos reclama! . . . Todos luchábamos por la vida aquí . . . hasta que tú veniste . . .

(p. 62)

Carlos' claim to the principle of life is compelling on the surface, and it is his most eloquent expression of the position he intends to defend.

But tragedy consists of the clash between two necessities, and Ignacio upholds the intrinsic truth of his own vision with equal strength. Carlos' contention that the blind can be as capable and secure as the sighted is quickly demolished, as Ignacio submits him to a test of his ability to move about without fear when a single piece of furniture, without Carlos' knowing it, has been moved out of its customary place in the room. Carlos' confidence breaks, and he fails the test. The illusion of security is possible only insofar as the physical world is arranged according to a pattern which the entire community accepts and learns. Ignacio not only refuses to conform to the illusion of normalcy which prevails, but he is dedicated to the open challenge and destruction of that illusion in the name of a higher truth; Ignacio declares that, "La región del optimismo donde Carlos sueña no le deja apreciar la realidad" (p. 44). "Este Centro está fundado sobre una mentira . . . La de que somos seres normales" (p. 47).

The illusion obscures the realities of the blind person's condition, and until those realities are admitted and understood, the positive aspects of Ignacio's idealism cannot be appreciated. Out of the confessed horror and mutilation of his condition as a blind man, Ignacio attempts to project himself through imagination into an understanding of what sight is, what it really means to see. The passion to understand the world of sight transforms itself for Ignacio into a faith that he himself might someday see. For Ignacio, then, Carlos' fanatic dedication to stability and order prevents him from knowing the urgent and passionate desire to understand his own condition: "Y esa es tu desgracia," he tells Carlos, "no sentir la esperanza que yo os he traído. . . . La esperanza de la luz. . . . De algo que anhelas comprender . . . , aunque lo niegues" (p. 61).

As Buero Vallejo develops the tragic conflict, the two principles which are set against one another seem irreconcilable so long as they are upheld by two antagonists who defend them with equal passion as moral absolutes. Each individual's claims to ultimate authority amounts to a personal blindness, an egotism which precludes any possibility for compromise or accommodation, and therefore, the catastrophe seems inevitable.

But Buero Vallejo does not carry the conflict through exclusively on the level of two opposing ideal principles. Ignacio is the first to expose the fact that much of Carlos' desperate attempt to expel him from the Center is motivated by his fear that Juana has fallen under Ignacio's influence and that he has consequently lost her affection. Moreover, Ignacio's own egotistical need for Juana's understanding and love is likewise a central motivating force behind his struggle against Carlos' attempts to drive him out. Buero Vallejo's protagonists, in other words, suffer the human flaw of egotism, and it therefore becomes evident that the two conflicting principles are not irreconcilable in and of themselves, but that they are irreconcilable insofar as they are upheld in this particular context wherein there is also a conflict of wills between two all-too-human protagonists.

The dramatic catastrophe, then, arises, out of a social order which finds itself threatened with progressive disintegration due to the powerful presence in its midst of a visionary who refuses to compromise his vision, even in the interest of preserving certain traditional and stable social values. Threatened with chaos, the social order—represented here by Carlos, who, as we have seen, is egotistically motivated as well—wields its inherent power to achieve the violent elimination of the subversive visionary.

As he witnesses this conflict of opposing principles, where are the spectator's sympathies directed? In creating his tragic hero, Prometheus, Shelley was careful to show that the rebellious Olympian was without flaw, that his motives were pure, and that the order he was opposing was blatantly tyrannical and violently unjust.[9] Shelley's tragedy, then, depicts the suffering of a totally blameless hero at the hands of an unreasonable and blind order of authority. Prometheus is the revolutionary hero of mankind, while Zeus represents the rigid order which is to be overthrown. In this case, our allegiance as spectators lies unequivocally with the cause of revolution; we are terrified at the violence with which that revolutionary impulse is punished, and we stand in awe of the hero's transcendent message of uncompromising struggle for the ideal, even as he suffers for his deed.

Buero Vallejo, of course, has set his play among ordinary people. Their physical blindness is paralleled by the blindness of their social order and its ethic; the message of light which Ignacio brings among them reveals the Promethian metaphor lying behind the drama as a whole. But the situation in *En la ardiente oscuridad* is far less imminently revolutionary than in Shelley's *Prometheus Unbound,* and for that reason, more complex. In spite of the catastrophe which results in the death of the rebellious figure, Ignacio, the play's conclusion forcefully suggests the possibility for reconciliation and synthesis of the two conflictive principles. The spectator's sympathies, therefore, are claimed to some degree at various moments in the drama by both sides of the conflict, and it is precisely this refusal on the part of the dramatist to yield to the categories of romance or melodrama that makes for the authentic complexity of the tragic clash of character and ideals.

Nevertheless, even granting the complexity of the claims made on the spectator's moral allegiance, the play's hero is, without question, Ignacio; it is not Carlos, nor is it the social order which he represents and violently defends. And the principles which Ignacio represents are heroic by comparison; they are daring, they risk the truth which lies beyond conventional forms, and they enable Ignacio to summon the faith to carry his vision beyond the limits of formal reason as well. These are the admirable weapons with which Ignacio combats the vain practicality, the illusions upon which a society's order is founded. The spectator's sympathies are thus lured into the province of the rebellious visionary, and arrayed against the universal order that cannot accommodate his disturbing and dangerous vision of truth. From this perspective, the spectator is led to share the hero's judgment of the universal moral and social order as both shallow and artificial.

Buero Vallejo takes the situation even farther. Over the course of the repeated confrontations between Carlos and Ignacio, it becomes increasingly apparent that Carlos himself understands quite clearly the force, the attractiveness, and even the fundamental truth of Ignacio's tragic vision. Carlos as an individual is far more capable of accommodating Ignacio's vision than would be indicated by the attacks he directs against Ignacio both out of his egotism and in the name of the Center. After Ignacio's eloquent and moving speech in which he describes the vastness of his longing for vision and for an understanding of light,[10] Carlos is described as having brusquely to shake off "la involuntaria influencia sufrida a causa de las palabras de Ignacio" (p. 62), before confessing to Ignacio that he has understood perfectly: "Te comprendo, sí; te comprendo, pero no te puedo disculpar" (p. 62). And it is with disdainful irony that Carlos observes the superficiality and frivolity of his fellow students who had flocked to Ignacio, fascinated with the poetry of his words, but without ever experiencing their profound and terrifying truth. Only Carlos, who we may believe has experienced that terror, is convinced sufficiently of its moral danger to social order to be willing to take the drastic steps necessary to eliminate the threat from their midst. Once Carlos has acted to remove Ignacio and his seductive and demoralizing vision, the other students quickly express their relief that this disruptive force has been eliminated and that life can return to its normal channels. Carlos, now become a murderer, remarks ironically and bitterly, using the word "ciegos" in the same deprecatory way as Ignacio had:

> Muerto Ignacio, sus mejores amigos le abandonan: murmuran sobre su cadáver. ¡Ah, los ciegos, los ciegos! ¡Se creen con derecho a compadecerle, ellos, que son pequeños y vulgares! Miguelín y Elisa se reconcilian. Los demás respiran como si les hubiesen librado de un gran peso. ¡Vuelve la alegría a la casa! ¡Todo se arregla!
>
> (p. 73)

While on a formal social level the moral order of the past is restored with the elimination of the visionary from the community, the play's final scene symbolically achieves the synthesis of opposing principles that had been impossible so long as they were upheld and espoused by two individuals with the egotistical failings of individual human beings.

Through conflict and the ensuing catastrophe, Carlos has come to acknowledge to himself the terrifying truth of Ignacio's ideal vision. His murder of Ignacio has been witnessed by the only sighted member of the Center's community, the Director's wife. Carlos, whose self-inflicted blindness compounds his physical handicap, failed to consider the superior power implicit in this woman's ability to see. Her sight has given her possession of a devastating secret, and regardless of how viciously Carlos attempts to negate the fact, the truth that her sight has afforded her ultimate power over him remains irrefutable, thereby confirming in fact Ignacio's abstract assertion that the sighted hold an arbitrarily vested power over the blind.

Finally, alone with Ignacio's corpse on the dimly lit stage, Carlos is once again only an insecure blind man, as he gropes about and sends the chess board crashing to the floor. And as he delivers his final soliloquy to the stars, after having run his hands over Ignacio's dead face, "en la suprema amargura de su soledad irremediable . . . [y] con la desesperanza de quien toca a un dormido que ya no podrá despertar" (p. 76)—as Carlos speaks, the final words we hear on stage are not Carlos' alone, but Ignacio's. The tragic vision formerly embodied in the dead hero has come now to inhabit the body and the spirit of his executioner.

It is Carlos, in *En la ardiente oscuridad,* who has suffered the cathartic experience, and not the society as a whole. Carlos is the only individual in Buero Vallejo's play who is capable of grasping both extremes of this dialectical conflict at once—indeed, his anguish at the end indicates the awesomeness of these extremes when they both take root in a single mind, and when seemingly irreconcilable

truths make their claims to authority. Carlos' sense of the final truth about man's tragic nature is made more complex and more profound by the cathartic process of experiencing and acknowledging the validity of Ignacio's tragic vision, while recognizing as well the imperatives of the Center's ethical order for the survival of its society, and for the progress of its legitimate function of enhancing the positive will to live in its members. Murray Krieger has admirably summed up the fundamentals of the process we have seen at work in Buero Vallejo's play:

> It is as if the security of the older order wanted to test the profundity of its assurances, its capacity to account for the whole of human experience, and thus bred within itself the tragic vision as its *agent provocateur.* And by having the rebellion incarnate in the tragic visionary finally succumb to a higher "destructive element", by purifying itself through the cathartic principle, tragedy is asserting the argument *a fortiori* for the affirmation of its humanistic and yet superhuman values.
>
> (p. 7)

The play's final hopeful vision is that of a progressive raising of consciousness which increasingly expands the range of human possibility by incorporating more and more synthetically the extremes of human experience and vision.

It is tempting to speculate on the "political" (in the broadest sense of the term) vision that Buero Vallejo implies through his play, *En la ardiente oscuridad.* His emergence from prison into a culture still paralyzed by a relatively primitive stage of fascist control and whose ethical self-justification was couched in a rhetoric of moral righteousness and a crusading sense of mission—his emergence into such a society must have suggested the metaphor of physical as well as spiritual blindness that is the core of *En la ardiente oscuridad.*

The spiritually crippling effects of an imposed political and moral order with absolute claims to universal authority must have been immediately apparent to any sensitive intellectual in such times. The genius of Buero Vallejo's vision, however, lies in his literary formulation of the problem, and the deeply humanistic resolution he suggests in this work. The unrelenting opposition of ideals produces the extraordinary emotional pitch of conflict necessary for the catharsis. But Buero Vallejo does not yield to the temptation of replacing the old moral tyranny with another tyranny whose newness and heroic dimensions could, were we confronting a more facile and less complex view of reality, lend this new order the spectacular and daring appeal of revolutionary progress and thereby inspire the liberal and discriminating spectator's wholehearted support. But Buero Vallejo avoids simplistic political categories; rather, in extremely complex times, he perceives the function of his theater as one of effecting a higher level of consciousness in his public. He is thereby able to encourage his public to struggle beyond the political contradictions of the hour toward an ultimately progressive and humane synthesis of the seemingly irreconcilable oppositions which characterized the historical time of the play's creation.

Notes

1. Martha T. Halsey, *Antonio Buero Vallejo* (New York: Twayne, 1973), p. 17.

2. Friedrich Nietzsche, *The Birth of Tragedy,* trans. Walter Kaufmann (New York: Random House, 1967), p. 60.

3. Antonio Buero Vallejo, "La tragedia," *El teatro. Enciclopedia del arte escénico,* ed. Guillermo Díaz-Plaja (Barcelona: Noguer, 1958), pp. 66-67.

4. Murray Krieger, *The Tragic Vision* (Baltimore: Johns Hopkins University Press, 1973), p. 6.

5. Buero Vallejo, "La tragedia," pp. 70-71.

6. Antonio Buero Vallejo, "Sobre teatro," *Hoy es fiesta, Las meninas, El tragaluz* (Madrid: Taurus, 1963), p. 62.

7. Buero Vallejo, "La tragedia," p. 71.

8. Antonio Buero Vallejo, *En la ardiente oscuridad,* Colección teatro, núm. 3 (Madrid: Escelicer, 1970), p. 3.

9. As Shelley explains in his prologue, Prometheus is, "exempt from the taints of ambition, envy, revenge, and a desire for personal aggrandizement . . . [he is] the type of the highest perfection of moral and intellectual nature, impelled by the purest and the truest motives to the best and noblest ends." Percy B. Shelley, *Shelley's 'Prometheus Unbound': The Text and the Drafts,* ed. Lawrence John Zillman (New Haven: Yale University Press, 1968), p. 37.

10. There are actually three long speeches by Ignacio in this scene of confrontation with Carlos. The second and third of these speeches (pp. 61-62) have all the dramatic majesty of soliloquy. The fact that in this scene with Carlos, Ignacio gradually abandons his polemic tone in favor of the exalted lyricism of soliloquy is the first strong indication of the profound mutual understanding that implicitly links these two protagonists. Ignacio speaks with Carlos present as though he were speaking to himself, and, at the end of the play, Carlos speaks Ignacio's words in soliloquy as though they were his own; as indeed they are, now that we have come to understand the synthesis of the antagonistic principles at work within Carlos.

EL CONCIERTO DE SAN OVIDIO (THE CONCERT OF SAINT OVIDE)

CRITICAL COMMENTARY

Eric Pennington (essay date fall 1985)

SOURCE: Pennington, Eric. "The Role of Music in *El concierto de San Ovidio.*" *Romance Notes* XXVI, no. 1 (fall 1985): 18-21.

[*In the following essay, Pennington investigates the significance of music in* El concierto de San Ovidio.]

As *El concierto de San Ovidio* concludes, an actor playing the role of Valentín Haüy appears before the audience and relates the historical veracity of the events dramatized in the play. He mentions how the degrading spectacle of blind musicians being ridiculed for profit spurred him in his life's work to better the fate of the blind,[1] but as he comtemplates the death of the blind violinist David (the protagonist of the work), and the sorry circumstances surrounding his demise, Haüy rhetorically asks, "¿Quién asume ya esa muerte? ¿Quién la rescata?"[2] He then pauses to listen to the music which Donato, a former companion of David, plays in the background. With the violin melody accompanying his words, Haüy subsequently suggests that perhaps the only answer to such questions resides in ". . . la música . . . la única respuesta posible para algunas preguntas . . ." (p. 113). The curtain falls, leaving the spectators to ponder this thesis while Donato's music gradually fades.

To appreciate fully the meaning of Haüy's last words, the music which prompted such ideas must be analyzed.[3] Donato was playing the *Adagio* (from the third movement) of Arcangelo Corelli's *Concerto Grosso in G Minor, Opus 6, No. 8.* Throughout the play David consoles himself often with this piece, and Donato apparently also turns to this music for consolation, after betraying his friend to death. In interpreting the function of this music in the work, Martha Halsey suggests that the melody expresses David's longing to be like Melanía de Salignac, his idealized concept of what blind people may become.[4] While this observation bears validity, it does not completely explain the role of the music in the play. Why, for example, does Buero choose this particular piece? How does this composition perhaps provide "la única respuesta posible" to Haüy's anguished queries?

The opus in question is a *concerto grosso,* a musical form interpreted by two groups of instruments: a small group of usually two or three (*concertino*), and a much larger one (*tutti* or *ripieno*). These two ensembles are essentially musical adversaries and compete with each other throughout the piece. One group may perform alone for a number of measures, only to have the other respond in a similar manner, constantly presenting dynamic and textual contrasts to that which has preceded. Without fail *concerti grossi* end with all instruments playing in concert. In other words, the larger ensemble absorbs the less powerful *concertino*.[5] The similarity between David and his group of social underdogs struggling against a larger and more dominant force (the impresario Valindin and society in general) becomes immediately evident.

The most intriguing clue to Buero's motivation in choosing this music for *El concierto de San Ovidio* lies in the phrase which follows the title of the composition: "Fatto per la notte di Natale." English translations of this subtitle refer to the work as "Christmas Concerto," since the Italian master-composer specifically designated the piece for performance on Christmas Eve. Its source of inspiration was the medieval shepherds who descended from the hills of Italy during the holiday season. These humble peasants would play their simple tunes in commemoration of that night before the first Christmas, when other shepherds gathered at Bethlehem from the plains of Judea.

Referring to Corelli's skill in communicating the mood and meaning of the shepherds' music, the musicologist Harry Halbreich remarks:

> Not only does Corelli capture the universal meaning of the fervent and naive art of the *pifferari*, but in ending the work in C *major*, the dark nocturnes of the previous sections seem suddenly illuminated as though the great hope symbolized by the birth of Christ has come to fulfill man's long expectation.[6]

As the quote above suggests, this music convincingly conveys a feeling of hope.[7] The biblical shepherds hoped for the birth of *Messiah*, who would usher in a reign of peace and love. Buero subtly endeavors to resurrect the essence of this hope by including Corelli's music in the play. This musical reference to Jesus' birth should probably not be regarded as Buero inferring that salvation is through Christ. Though Buero's attraction to Jesus' teachings cannot be ignored, in matters of religion his comments are frequently termed "open-end."[8] To what extent the hope of the shepherds was fulfilled in the following centuries is not at all germane to Buero's message. The music captures the feeling of anticipation or "great hope" which existed the night *before* Jesus was born. It is, then, a celebration of the hope surrounding that birth, not an exhortation to consider the historical results of the event.

Thus while on one hand the artistic execution of Corelli's music communicates David's yearning to better his lot in life, on another, universal, level this particular piece symbolizes mankind's hope that someday deliverance, or social change, will come.[9] If "la única respuesta posible" lies in this composition by Corelli, the reply coincides with the admonition proffered in virtually all of Buero's plays (particularly *Hoy es fiesta* and *El tragaluz*): "Hay que esperar." One must eternally hope that one day conditions will improve and that "el hombre nuevo" will evolve. To this end the playwright employs Corelli's music: to rekindle a conviction in the people of the present comparable to the expectation of the Judean shepherds on that especial night; to evoke the memory of hope and perhaps engender a resolution to continue hoping.

Notes

1. Haüy, history confirms, worked out a rudimentary system by which the blind could read. One of his students, Louis Braille, later perfected the system.

2. Antonio Buero Vallejo, *El concierto de San Ovidio,* Colección Teatro, No. 370 (Madrid: Escelicer, 1972), p. 113. Subsequent references are to this edition.

3. A study similar to this present essay was written prior to the existence of *El concierto de San Ovidio,* investigating the role of music in some of Buero's earliest plays. See Beth W. Noble, "Sound in the Plays of Buero Vallejo," *Hispania,* 41, No. 1 (March 1958), 56-59.

4. Martha T. Halsey, *Antonio Buero Vallejo* (New York: Twayne Publishers, Inc., 1973), p. 100.

5. "The chief distinguishing feature of the form is the contrast of the *concertino* and *tutti,* which are constantly pitted against one another." See Christine Ammer, *Harper's Dictionary of Music* (New York: Harper and Row, Publishers, 1972), p. 79, and "Concerto grosso," *The Concise Encyclopedia of Music and Musicians,* ed., Martin Cooper (New York: Hawthorn Books., 1968), pp. 115-16.

6. Harry Halbreich, Jacket Notes, *Celebrated Christmas Concerti,* by Arcangelo Corelli, et al., cond. Claudio Scimone, The Musical Heritage Society Inc., MHS 1234, n.d.

7. Merely listening to the piece under discussion does much to sustain the thesis of this essay. It is quiet, fervent and resolute. The most popular of Corelli's *concerti grossi* (he wrote only twelve), it is easily obtained at any music library.

8. For a conversation with Buero on this subject, see Eric Pennington, "Entrevista con Antonio Buero Vallejo," *Hispania,* 64, No. 1 (March 1981), p. 137.

9. The importance of this music in connection with David should not go unmentioned, though this essay primarily focuses on the role of the music at the conclusion of the play. Corelli's composition serves to underscore the similarity between Buero's David and his biblical namesake. David, King of Israel, ac-

companying himself with his harp, sang of a Deliverer who would not "leave my soul in hell" (Psalms 16:10), and looked forward to his coming. This scripture is generally regarded as referring to *Messiah.* The blind David of *El concierto de San Ovidio,* plays a melody on his violin which, to those familiar with its origin (and I understand that the piece is still quite well known), represents the same hope. Thus one can see how understanding this piece of music strenghthens the observation made by one critic regarding the similarities of the two Davids. See Joelyn Ruple, *Antonio Buero Vallejo: The First Fifteen Years* (New York: Eliseo Torres and Sons, 1971), pp. 163-64.

EL TRAGALUZ (*THE BASEMENT WINDOW*)

CRITICAL COMMENTARY

Frank P. Casa (essay date April 1969)

SOURCE: Casa, Frank P. "The Problem of National Reconciliation in Buero Vallejo's *El Tragaluz.*" *Revista Hispánica Moderna* XXXV, no. 3 (April 1969): 285-94.

[*In the following essay, Casa analyzes the sociopolitical significance of* El tragaluz, *contending that it was the first Spanish play to explore the moral consequences of the Spanish Civil War.*]

Buero Vallejo's **El tragaluz** is one of the most important works of Spanish post-war literature. That its importance is due to political-cultural circumstances rather than to its literary merit does not, in any way, diminish the significance of the play.[1] The peculiar distinction of the drama resides in the fact that for the first time inside Spain a theatrical work discusses the moral consequences of the Civil War.

The victory of the insurgent forces was historically anomalous in that it represented a return to an oligarchic type of government not in consonance with the West's movement toward more democratic and socially responsive political systems. However, this is perhaps less important for the present cultural climate of Spain than the decision of the government to impose strict and crippling censorship after its victory.[2] The effects of the War are known to anyone barely acquainted with Spanish history. The long struggle, its viciousness, the climatic nature of the century-old contest between traditionalists and progressives

traumatized the national psyche. For the Spaniards who lived through the War and suffered through the bitter years of its aftermath, separated from the rest of the Western World, immersed in searing memories, suffering hunger, the post-war was a period of anguish. Exhausted physically and spiritually, the Spaniard sought to isolate himself from the tyranny of past events. This interiorization was a necessary reaction to insure survival; time was needed to placate enmities, sooth angers, and heal wounds. Only the most extreme of partisan had the strength to continue to fight. In these first years of the post-war period, silence, forgetfulness, were needed much more than violent reactions. When Benavente was accused of writing inconsequential little plays, the old playwright remarked that there was enough real tragedy abroad without adding to it artificially.[3]

It was the exiles who, after finding new homes in the New World, first begans to look back to try to explain what had happened. The exercise was cathartic. Anguished, embittered, nostalgic, they slowly recovered their bearings and gradually integrated themselves into the lives of their new countries.[4] But for those who stayed behind, their suffering was physical as well as mental. Hunger stalked the land while the Allied victors, undecided as to the political desirability of replacing the regime, temporized by keeping Spain isolated and helpless. The natural withdrawal of the people, caused by the experience of the War, could not continue forever. Sooner or later the trauma had to be healed and it could only be healed by coming to terms with its causes,—this time not to fight the same struggle but to explain its origin, its development, its consequences. It was necessary to criticize, analyze, fix moral and physical responsibility, seek new directions. But this great retracing which was to lead to a cleansing of the air and an eventual softening of feelings never took place. The rigidity of the system could not allow for such an open discussion of the events. The regime, in a real way, willfully accepted the festering of the wounds rather than risk the consequences of the discussion. The passing of the years although muting differences never quite removed from the consciousness of the Spaniards the trauma of the Civil War. Those who think that the great number of years have lessened the Spaniards' fascination with the War, are ignoring the passionate interest that the public shows in every work on the War that is published in the country.[5]

However, in spite of the fact that several playwrights have dramatized their preoccupation with socio-economic matters and in spite of Sastre's revolutionary plays, the Civil War and its consequences have had no major dramatic treatment. The plays of Olmo or Muñiz, the first in a more traditional social theater, the other, more expressionistic, deal rather with the oppression of the individual within the economic system than with a particular set of historic events and its influence on the nature of present-day Spanish society. Some plays, like Calvo Sotelo's *La muralla,* use the conflict to create a personal, moral problem deprived of its political context. Ruiz de Iriarte's comedy, *Primavera en la plaza de París,* changes the antagonists into either defeated or irascible old men fighting old battles. Jaime Salom in *La casa de las Chivas* neutralizes the issues by converting them into a religious question.[6]

Buero Vallejo was the first to abandon the tired themes that dominated the Spanish theater of the forties. He gauged correctly the nation's need for a dramatic expression more in keeping with the conditions of the times. Benavente's reluctance to tackle the harsh reality no longer made sense. There comes a time when it no longer benefits a country to ignore or cover its conflicts, just as there is a time when insistence on them is more harmful than useful. Years later, in *El tragaluz,* Buero was to allude to this situation when one of his investigators says: "Durante siglos tuvimos que olvidar, para que el pasado no nos paralizase; ahora debemos recordar incesantemente, para que el pasado no nos envenene."[7] Thus, inspite of his well-known position on *posibilismo*[8] or perhaps because of it, by 1967 he felt that political circumstances in Spain allowed for a forthright, if not completely open, discussion on the effects of the Civil War.

The Spanish theater of the present is admittedly behind the times.[9] In general, it still makes use of over-realistic stage settings, unimaginative direction, and themes that harken to times and social customs long since ignored by other theaters because they represent settled issues. This insistence on themes, such as the equal importance between a woman's emotional commitment and her physical actions,[10] which remind one of Ibsen, should not, however, be dismissed as another proof of the *atraso* of Spanish literature. It is perhaps useful to repeat once again that the drama, more than any other literary genre, is directed toward a specific audience, influenced by definite circumstances, and possessing particular reactions. While the spectator need not dictate what the playwright presents, the fact remains that unless writer and audience can communicate with each other, the exercise is futile. The dramatist should be ahead of his audience but should base himself on it; the audience in turn should be capable of receiving the author's advanced ideas and assimilate them. If one forgets the essential nature of this mutual nourishment, one risks being ignored. Whatever the moral correctness of Sastre with respect to the responsibility of the writer, it cannot be forgotten that Sastre himself has turned out to be a writer for a minority (a circumstance which he considers fatal for any writer)[11] precisely because of his steadfast insistence on treating subjects without any concessions to political or social realities. The other response to the problem of incommunication can be represented by Arrabal's decision. Arrabal felt that he could not, either because of the political situation or the cultural conditions of Spain, continue to write in his country. His move to France is therefore another proof that writer and audience must be able to understand each other

to make theater possible. On the other end of the spectrum, one finds dramatists of the Paso, Ruiz Iriarte, Calvo Sotelo, José María Pemán, Luca de Tena kind who not only fail to lead their audiences into new awareness but often indulge them in their prejudices.[12]

Buero Vallejo, to an exemplary degree, is able to fulfill the dramatic requisites I have outlined. He is ahead of his audiences in his perception of the moral and cultural problems that beset the country and, at the same time, he is able to maintain intact his ability to reach them. For this reason and for the relevance of his themes, Buero is considered the most important living Spanish dramatist.

Twenty years after he revealed to Spain the need to deal with subjects more directly concerned with the problems of the people, he achieved the same kind of success by uncovering the deep scars left by the War.[13] When one considers the great body of literature concerning the Civil War that the last thirty years have produced, one might be tempted to view the statement as to the importance of the play as exaggerated. The significance of *El tragaluz* resides not in the novelty of the themes treated[14] but in the fact that the themes were treated within Spain, in a dramatic form, and for a general audience.[15] I attach great importance to the fact that it was a theatrical presentation because of the more immediate impact that the theater has on the public. It is for this reason that censorship of the theater has traditionally been more severe than of other literary forms.[16] The capacity of the theatrical performance to affect the public is due precisely to its representational quality. As far as I know, this is the first play dealing with the still sensitive subject of the Civil War to bring to the attention of so many people a problem so close to the hearts of the country and one which the official authorities deem best forgotten.[17]

It is central to Buero's vision of the Spanish condition that the antagonists in his play are not drawn along political lines. While this may be due to a realistic assessment of what is politically feasible, it should not be seen as the primary motivation for the disposition of the characters. The play would have gained very little from a rigid confrontation of Falangists and Republicans. Rather it would have lost considerably because it would have limited it to a political play with its doubtful quality of propaganda and equivocal ideological defense. Moreover, it would not have responded to Buero's perception of the problem as one of national rather than factional character. The fact that both winners and losers, victims and tormentors are of the same family stresses the intimate nature of the tragedy. The Civil War was a family tragedy with its characteristics of unreasonable bitterness and ferocity. Yet there is something positive in viewing the conflict in this way, because rather than continuing to see Spain as hopelessly divided into two camps, it implies an essential unity and an eventual reconciliation, for family feuds hold within themselves the seeds of reunion.[18]

This particular vision, moreover, points toward a common suffering, a shared experience of pain in which both sides agonized. It underscores the destructive nature of the War and prevents ideological differences from clouding what should be, and is for Buero, our constant and incessant preoccupation, a concern for human, individual suffering.

It is in connection with this sentiment that the relevance of the investigators comes to light. In an interview with Fernández Santos, Buero rejected the criticism that his futuristic investigators were a clumsy Brechtian device or an unfortunate idea and insisted on their indispensability: "Para mi, *El tragaluz,* sería inconcebible sin estos personajes. No entiendo esta obra, me resulta literalmente incomprensible despojada de los 'investigadores'."[19] The investigators are the physical representation of a moral principle. Their existence assures us that our actions do not occur only to be forgotten. It warns us that the universe itself keeps alive our thoughts and our actions, and that these phenomena can be recalled now or in the distant future as witnesses against us. The moral principle that informs Buero's theater finds then a cosmic manifestation in *El tragaluz.* The frequent interventions as well as the final frankly moralizing remarks keep constant in the minds of the audience the concept of future generations able to recall our very thoughts and to judge us accordingly. Buero refuses once again to apply the judgement of a particular epoch upon the events. By extending the time intervals between action and judgement, he reduces the historical impact and increases the moral important of the actions. I say reduce and not eliminate because he forces the audience to play a dual role, that of the judge and of the judged. The spectators operate on a double time slot: as individuals living within the same period as the protagonists of the drama, they share with them the events narrated; as contemporaries of the investigators, they are visualizing by mechanical recreation the events that have occurred centuries before. The audience is made to feel contemporaneous to both the twentieth and the twenty-second century.

It is evident from Buero's words that he considers the existence of individuals capable of judging our actions more important than the events narrated. After all, he says, there are other stories that one could dramatize, but the investigators cannot be replaced.[20] In spite of this observation, the action itself has capital importance because through it a moral man, sensitive to the realities of his country, aware of the historical import of the events, reflects on the major experience of the lives of all living Spaniards.

For the first time in the theatrical experience of post-war Spain, the spectators are made to relive their suffering and face the moral consequences of the conflict.[21] By rejecting the idea of separating victors and vanquished along political lines, he underscores the lamentable consequences of the war. If the victorious side has gained a solid economic

and social position, it has, at the same time, lost its spiritual balance. What Buero seems to insist upon is that there should be no illusion that what has been gained in the War is simply a re-establishment of one's rightful position. In an internecine struggle such as the Civil War, one side can only gain at the expense of the other. Thus, one's well-being can only come as a result of another's suffering. It is important to insist on this imbalance because it is basic to Buero's conception of the Spanish situation. The struggle itself was a calamitous event in which all sides lost; the victory was not a political victory but the survival of those who placed their own lives above those of the others. Unfortunate and cruel as the effort at survival was, what is brutal and intolerable is the continuation of the mentality and behavior that made that survival possible. Buero is willing, although reluctantly and painfully, to accept the errors of the past, but he cannot countenance the existence of those same conditions years after the end of the circumstances that called them forth. In the climatic scene of the play, Mario, that ambivalent personality, says to Vicente: "No te culpo del todo; sólo eras un muchacho hambriento y asustado. Nos tocó crecer en años difíciles . . . ¡Pero ahora, hombre ya, sí eres culpable!" (p. 231).

The War is over, the choices made during it were difficult and not always morally sound, but now, without the pressure of death or even hunger, any persistence in the same pattern is intentionally evil. The evil that hovers over Spanish society is the indifference to those who lost and these are not simply those whose political programs were checked by their defeat. The vanquished are the great number of Spaniards who participate in none of the meager economic progress, those who never "caught the train," to use the play's phrase. Buero is more afflected by the cruelty of present indifference than by the brutality of events long past. Not that he is willing to forget everything; he simply draws an order of priorities. In this, he shows his sense of practicality that does not degenerate into callousness. Buero is never willing to forget moral insensitivity; the long memory of mankind, exemplified by the recreation we witness, is an indication of that. At the same time he has no inclination toward vengeance. He is willing to forgive but not to forget. He will tolerate human frailty but not useless cruelty.

Vicente, like all the victors, is guilty not only because of what he did but because of what he continues to do. His unprincipled use of Encarna, the scandalous abandonment of the writer Beltrán, his willingness to reach an accomodation with the new management are all evidences of indifference to suffering. His action as a child which in its selfishness caused the death of his younger sister, is thus not left as an isolated, although grave, sign of weakness but as a foreshadowing of his future egoism. The past foretells the future and the future reinforces the past. So the actions done in the heat of battle become significant and representative rather than circumstantial.

It is clear then that Buero, far from forgetting or excusing the cruelty visited upon the people in the War, renders a harsh judgement upon it. Buero cannot accept that this moral error can be borne with indifference; Vicente, like all those who have built their lives upon the suffering of others, is made to feel keenly his guilt. The playwright does not abandon the victors to moral unconsciousness. He has too much optimism both in the essential worth of man and in his country's redemptive qualities. Vicente's sense of guilt and his yearning for expiation exemplify this. The device of having both victims and conquerors in the same family becomes more visibly integrated in the theme. The struggle was a truly fraternal one in which the bitterness of the circumstances led to unbearably savagery. But since the pain was inflicted upon one's own flesh, the victor cannot forget his sin nor his responsibility. The War, like all family quarrels, cannot be forgotten but must eventually be faced, come to terms with, and finally put to rest.

This process of returning to the original point in order to undergo the same experience, not in passion but in contemplation, to purify oneself before emerging cleansed, is what Vicente and the nation need. Vicente's voyage is then return to his starting point, a return to the very center whence he fled. Dramatically, the voyage backwards is expressed in the ever-increasing visits that Vicente pays his family. The initial physical abandonment is followed by occasional monetary help which then becomes a fixed monthly allowance, first sent by mail and then delivered personally. Mario exclaims: "Pero vienes. Estás volviendo al pozo, cada vez con más frecuencia . . . , y eso es lo que prefiero de tí" (p. 197). Vicente's return to his origin is accompaniend by a series of signs that indicate such a movement. He refers to himself as a *niño*; the father in his obsession refuses to recognize the adult Vicente and returns to a state of infantilism, as if wishing to replace the lost son.[22] The reference to the basement as a well into which the family has sunk and to which Vicente returns has a double significance. Socially speaking, it is a reference to the condition of the people. The metaphor is developed more explicitly in his next play, *El sueño de la razón*, when Goya's two friends have the following exchange:

> Duaso. ¿Pensó en algún remedio?
>
> Arrieta. Por lo pronto huir de este pozo, donde respira emanaciones de pantano.
>
> Duaso. ¿De esta casa, quiere decir?
>
> Arrieta. Quiero decir de este país, padre Duaso.[23]

From the dramatic point of view, the *pozo,* is a clear archetypal symbol of the womb.[24] The process of Vicente's purification needs, as a first requirement, a return to his original state of lost innocence; that is, a willful rejection of the present circumstances so that another start can be made, not by forgetting the past, but by seeking it out and facing it. Buero is inviting the nation to undergo a *toma de consciencia,* to free itself of the trauma under which it has been living. The value of the play resides, among others, in the symbolic process of purification that the theater with its ritual power can impose upon its audience. Victors and vanquished, judges and accused are made one so that a truly cathartic experience can be undergone.

But this voyage of redemption has to be undertaken jointly, for without this fusion there cannot be any solution. The drawing together of the two sides must be an indispensable first step. Vicente must come to terms with the people he has abused. He has to reconcile himself with his father, with his brother, and with Encarna. The play is in essence a metaphor for the process of national reconciliation. The movement toward this desirable goal is not without obstacles. How can Vicente achieve this reconciliation when he has ruined his father mentally, has been instrumental in the distortion of Mario's personality, and has badly abused a poor, ignorant country girl whose main preoccupation was to be able to make a living without becoming a street walker. The sense of guilt felt by Vicente is then not sufficient to bring about a reunification of the family. Those terrible moments in which concern for one's survival or selfish positioning at the expense of others dominated, cannot be forgotten.

The immense responsibility that weighs upon Vicente is in itself a source of danger. The victims, broken in spirit, twisted in mind, do not seem to have within them the power to forget. The very situations in which the characters find themselves point to this inability. The father, the major victim, has lost control over his capacity to reason, and Mario is torn between a desire for union and his own inflexibility. The situation is further complicated by the love relationship. Mario and Encarna are in love with each other and desperately need each other in order to survive, but her involvement with Vicente and her state of pregnancy seem to preclude any possibility of accomodation. Given the cultural context, no amount of love on Mario's part can overcome the difficulty inherent in the triangle. This same near-physical impossibility to see a way out is reflected in the father's madness. All possible roads to a solution seem barred. Each character is suspended between desire and fear. The father is frantically looking for his son but cannot recognize him because of his madness; Vicente is looking for forgiveness but cannot let go of the pretense that has allowed him to live; Mario is looking for union but cannot overcome his bitterness.

Mario becomes aware of the explosive nature of the situation when he retells Encarna the dream he has had: "Escucha lo que he soñado esta noche. Había un precipicio . . . Yo estaba en uno de los lados, sentado ante mis pruebas . . . Por la otra ladera corría un desconocido, con una cuerda atada a la cintura. Y la cuerda pasaba sobre el abismo, y llegaba hasta mi muñeca. Sin dejar de trabajar, yo daba tironcitos . . . y le iba acercando al borde. Cuando corría ya junto al borde mismo, di un tirón repentino y le despeñé" (p. 184). Vicente's sins are so great that not even the gentle nature of his brother can find room for forgiveness. Mario instead finds himself feeling more hostile toward his older brother. Is it because of his own personality which has been distorted by years of impotence and resentment or is it because of the magnitude of the transgression? The question of the forgiveness is complicated because it must come from two sources: the father and the brother. I have already remarked that in the case of the father, there is no possibility of a rational decision. The poor man has been locked in his obsession, in his search for what the investigators call "la tremenda pregunta," the recognition of the sacredness of each individual. This is indeed the central point of the drama and all the protagonists are involved in the quest: the investigators who are trying to relive the precious moments of a long-gone period because the individuals who lived them are important; the father who cuts out people from post-cards with a pair of scissors because they too were once people and their individuality must be preserved; Mario whose quiet hate for his brother stems from Vicente's total disregard for the value of the individual; and even Vicente whose search for forgiveness implies a rejection of his selfishness and a new awareness that human life has an individual value.

Their unity of purpose does not cloud the fact that the father and the brother represent two critical moments in the life of Vicente and the nation. The father has been frozen in a long-gone moment that he keeps agonizingly present; the brother, while aware of that old transgression is more concerned with the present infractions. Thus the past and the present stand in judgement of "those who caught the train." It is very difficult to affirm with any authority the meaning of this duality, especially since a neat ideological explanation would impose on the natural theatricality of the play. Yet we are faced with this doubling off: the father locked in the past and physically unable to forgive; the brother preoccupied with the present and spiritually unable to forgive. The past can no longer forgive while the present is unwilling to betray the legacy. Buero seems to be unsatisfied with this impasse while recognizing its inevitability. But a solution has to be found, and Vicente returns to those whom he has betrayed, to ask for forgiveness, recognizing thus his guilt as well as his need for reconciliation with his family. In the critical moment of the play, that is, in the moment of judgement, the past, made painfully present by the leitmotif of the train's whistle overtakes the present and reveals clearly the betrayal of the young Vicente. Vicente's transgression and what it symbolizes cannot be forgiven. The scissors, the instrument used by the father to affirm the individual worth of everyone of us, are now transformed into the tool of punishment and the mad father stabs Vicente to death.

It has been impossible for the father to forgive his son, but Vicente's death brings for Mario a realization of his own part in the events. Mario recognizes his own inflexibility as well as Vicente's desire to make amends: "Él quería engañarse . . . y ver claro; yo quería salvarle . . . y matarle. ¿Qué queríamos en realidad? ¿Qué quería yo? ¿Cómo soy? ¿Quién soy? ¿Quién ha sido víctima de quién? (p. 235). Mario accepts his own fault and in the process becomes one with his brother. The transmutation of roles from victim to tormentor takes place and the theme of mutual suffering with its implication of spiritual unity and of a new start is sounded.

Thus the play ends ambiguously. Vicente is punished and forgiven at the same time. He is made to pay by the past for past actions but is pardoned by the present for his willingness to recognize his guilt. The forgiveness, however, comes only after the punishment. Buero seems to imply that what has gone on, what is still going on, must be faced by the transgressors, must be punished and then forgotten. The present can only come to grips with the fixing of responsibility; the unification will come in the future. As in *Un soñador para un pueblo,* the future Spain must come out of the union of antagonists. In *El tragaluz,* Buero returns to this fervent hope as the only solution to his country's tragedy.[25]

Notes

1. I am indebted to several friends and colleagues for some important suggestions and emendations.

2. For a discussion on censorship as relates to the post-war period, see Henry F. Schulte, *The Spanish Press, 1470-1966* (Urbana, Illinois, 1968), particularly Chapters Two and Three.

3. "Bastantes angustias sufre ya el mundo para entenebrecerlo con tragedias de invención a las que da ciento y raya la realidad. Por eso prefiero divertir y distraer al público con comedias ligeras y comedietas que, como me reprochan mis detractores, son deliberadamente frívolas y triviales." See José Monleón's "Una actitud crítica," in *Carlos Muñiz* (Madrid, 1963), p. 15.

4. See Juan Marichal's essay in *El nuevo pensamiento político español* (México, 1966), pp. 65-77 for a discussion on the exiles' effort to find a cultural role for themselves and their contribution to a new understanding of Spain.

5. I am thinking of the strong interest aroused by the memoires of Gil Robles and books such as *Tres días en julio, Las últimas banderas, El otro árbol de Guernica* (all published around the same time as Buero's play) not unmindful of the government's ambivalent attitude toward their success.

6. The last play, performed the same year as Buero's, is typical of Spanish plays dealing with the Civil War. It uses the War as a backdrop for a theme that has

nothing to do with the causes or consequences of the War. There is no explanation for this continuous skirting of the issue other than unwillingness to deal with it. In connection with this conscious avoidance, it is instructive to read an unsigned article in *España, hoy,* no. 6 (1970), pp. 37-42, an official propaganda organ for overseas consumption, in which a consideration of Buero's theater is concentrated on his very first play, *Historia de una escalera,* and where *El tragaluz* is only alluded to. Equally revealing is the fact that in this short article, the author feels compelled to deny the political nature of Buero's theater three times (pp. 38, 39, 40). On the other hand, Ricardo Doménech's "*El tragaluz,* una tragedia de nuestro tiempo," *Cuadernos Hispanoamericanos,* LXXIII (1968), 124-36, is interesting for the allusive nature of its language. The reader, in spite of the title, only gets as close as "tragedia social" to the problem Doménech would like to discuss.

7. For the sake of availability, I am using Carlos Sainz de Robles' edition for *Teatro español, 1967-68* (Madrid: Aguilar, 1969), p. 220. All further quotations will refer to this edition and will be included in the text.

8. For a full discussion of the Buero-Sastre controversy over the position of the playwright with respect to censorship, see Kessel Schwartz, "Posibilismo and imposibilismo," *Revista Hispánica Moderna,* XXXIV (1968), 336-45. See also Anthony M. Pasquariello, "Censorship in the Spanish Theater and Alfonso Sastre's *The Condemned Squad,*" *Theater Annual,* XIX (1962), 19-26.

9. On this point see, for example, Marcial Suárez, "La 'apertura' teatral y la necesidad de su aprovechamiento," *Revista de Occidente,* VI (1968) 313-30.

10. I am referring to Joaquín Calvo Sotelo's *La amante* which was performed the same season as Buero's play.

11. See Sastre's discussion on this point in his *Drama y sociedad* (Madrid, 1956), p. 126.

12. Both José María Pemán and Juan Ignacio Luca de Tena have written plays with Civil War themes. In *Callados como muertos,* Pemán presents exiled Republicans as wild-eyed extremists whose motivating force is personal rancor. He also includes a rejection of "free love" and a conversion to Catholicism. Luca de Tena's *El cóndor sin alas* develops the theme of sacrifice by a noble son for the socialist extravagances of his father.

13. The plot of *El tragaluz* is as follows: Two investigators of a future century are reproducing, by means at their disposal, moments in the lives of people who lived in the 20th century. Vicente a successful editor lives estranged from his parents and brother. His ac-

tions reveal a callous disregard for others and a pronounced sense of selfishness. He is attracted more and more to his family and during his visits, incidents that occurred during and after the Civil War are recalled. Specifically, those incidents relating to his responsibility for the death of his young sister. This responsibility has always been, unsuccessfully, ignored by the family. His demented father refuses to recognize in Vicente his lost son until the final confrontation. Vicente comes to recognize his guilt and begs his father's pardon. However, the mad old man, whose madness had taken the form of cutting figures out of postcards so that their worth as individual might be retained, stabs the son with a pair of scissors.

14. There is an intriguing note from a column written by Miguel Delibes in *Destino,* no. 1759 (June, 1971), p. 7. Delibes notes that in the same year that Buero wrote *El tragaluz,* he was writing a novel around the same theme with characters possessing the very same names.

15. As early as 1944, Max Aub had written plays with a Civil War theme. Naturally, being so close to the events, the mood is combative rather than contemplative. His point in *Morir por cerrar los ojos,* as the title indicates, is the blindness of those who seek to protect themselves by separating themselves from those who are threatened. As it always happens, when the collapse comes, all are affected.

16. Some information on this can be gleaned from Patricia O'Connor's two articles, "Censorship in the Contemporary Spanish Theater and Antonio Buero Vallejo," *Hispania,* LII (1969), 282-88; "Government Censorship in the Contemporary Spanish Theatre," *Education Theater Journal,* XVIII (Dec., 1966), 443-49.

17. Actually, the government's attitude is more complex than the statement indicates. The government's official policy is to affirm that the problems of the Civil War are no longer relevant to modern Spain. But since problems still exist, all official propaganda is directed toward reminding the nation of the disorder and violence of the Republican years. This is to discourage any interest in politics and democracy since these activities bring disorder. Thus national television frequently shows disorders in other countries while national propaganda stresses the uninterrupted years of peace enjoyed by Spain.

18. The fraternal nature of the conflict is recognized and developed by both defenders and antagonists of the government.

19. See, "Una entrevista con Buero Vallejo," *Primer Acto,* no. 90 (1967), p. 10.

20. "Quiero decir que, a efectos de lo que en realidad es *El tragaluz,* los investigadores son insustituibles y la

historia investigada no lo es, ya que pueden encontrarse otras historias de significado semejante al de ésta," Ibid.

21. The importance of this fact can be appreciated only if one realizes what I have outlined in note 17. Thus the attention of the reader is always directed toward the moral and personal conflicts of man. Adolfo Prego, for example, in his review of the play for *Blanco y Negro* states: "Porque no se trata de una obra política, sino social," quoted in *Teatro español,* op. cit., p. 154. In direct opposition to this, one finds the regime's antagonists. Isaac Montero in a Socialist journal emphasizes that, "a través de la historia individualizada por Buero, la sociedad española se nos muestra tal y como es hoy por causa de un hecho aún omnipresente: la guerra civil," *Nuevos horizontes,* nos. 3/4 (1968), p. 33.

22. References to this backward journey of the protagonists can be found on pp. 173, 174, 176, 180, 199.

23. See the edition of the play in Colección Teatro, no. 655, p. 50.

24. The play can, of course, be seen on a purely dramatic level as a play of repentance, purification and rebirth. There is something of the guilt-ridden wanderer in Vicente. We feel from the very beginning the existence of a basic and unforgivable transgression about him. While his present actions stress his capacity for evil, the long-gone act is what constitutes the first or core offense. When, slowly, the infraction is revealed, we are surprised both by the triviality of the act itself and the seriousness of its meaning. This inherent ambiguity of the action has allowed the characters to mask their emotions and to give Vicente a feasible cover. Vicente, and to some extent his mother, have focused their attention on the physical action of his getting on the train (see the beginning of the second part of the play). The father and the brother have not forgotten the consequences of that action, the death of the little sister and the sinister implications with respect to Vicente's personality. But what affects the spectators is not so much the death of a child, one of thousands that were visited upon a nation in conflict, but what they come to consider an unforgivable rejection of human solidarity. There is in Vicente an irrevocable affirmation of the self that denies the communal bond. Indeed, some have seen this tension between the affirmation of the self and the responsibility toward the social group as the essential characteristic of the tragic form. The audience reliving the anguish of past suffering views Vicente's selfish preservation as an unspeakable betrayal of them all. Vicente's journey backward is symbolically the journey that every Spaniard must undertake to achieve the purification necessary to begin a new life. For a thorough analysis of this recurrent pattern in literature see Maud Bodkin's *Archetypal Patterns in Poetry* (London, 1934), pp. 60-89.

25. On the theme of hope in Buero, see Martha Halsey Taliaferro, "Buero Vallejo and the Significance of Hope," *Hispania,* LI (1968), 57-66. It is important to point out that the customary note of optimism sounded by Buero at the end of each play, is missing in his last play, *El sueño de la razón.* It is as if Buero, like his protagonist, had gotten tired of waiting for something to happen. Buero who for thirty years has been hoping for a new Spain, seems to be less sure of ever achieving it. These words reveal the depth of his doubt: "Hay un tumor tremendo en nuestro país y todos queremos ser cirujanos implacables La sangre ha corrido y tornará a correr, pero el tumor no cura. . . . *Op. cit.,* p. 83.

John W. Kronik (essay date spring 1973)

SOURCE: Kronik, John W. "Buero Vallejo's *El Tragaluz* and Man's Existence in History." *Hispanic Review* 41 (spring 1973): 371-96.

[*In the following essay, Kronik provides a thematic and stylistic analysis of* El tragaluz *and views the play as the culmination of Buero Vallejo's dramatic work.*]

In *El tragaluz,* Buero Vallejo addresses himself to a problem of existence that pervades his entire dramatic output of the past twenty years: the interrelationship between man and his circumstance, between his inner and outer realities. The play, which began a highly successful run in Madrid on October 7, 1967, is neither a novelty nor a departure in Buero's line of development as a dramatist. Rather, it is a culmination, and as such is a gateway to his art. A probe of its contents gives answers to the questions that Buero has posed across the years through a variety of characters and situations. At the same time, a scrutiny of its formal elements shows that, rather than mere novelties of staging, these are integrally related to the exposition of his theme.

Though the subject of war is not new to Buero's theater, *El tragaluz* is his first play to treat openly the experience of the Spanish Civil War, or more precisely, its aftermath. In the retrospective examination of a classical myth that he undertook in *La tejedora de sueños,* Buero noted that war—any war—sunders and perverts the most intimate human relationships. In *Aventura en lo gris,* he dramatized the physical, moral, and spiritual destruction in the imaginary (but easily imagined) land of Surelia and by extension everywhere. More specifically, the Spaniards' recent war, even where left entirely unmentioned, surely marked those people in Buero's plays that lived it. The spent and crumpled aspect of Paca and the sorrowful expressions that disappointment and suffering had etched on the faces of Rosa and Trini in Act III of *Historia de una escalera,* the first of Buero's plays to be produced, reflected the spirit of post-Civil War Spain. That war passed through the play between its second and third acts. The economic plight and the social paralysis of the group of neighbors in *Hoy es fiesta* are also related implicitly to the Civil War. Phase two of the war—the police state's tyranny and autocracy—made its way into *El concierto de San Ovidio* and *La doble historia del doctor Valmy.*[1] Buero's plays are so very much plays of their historical time that the time's chief historical event in his country can hardly be expected to have left him or his creations unaffected. But if the war and post-war experience entered his earlier work only in veiled and indirect fashion, either as a latent force or as an abstract consideration, Spain's special political conditions must be held to account. *El tragaluz,* in the company of several other novels and plays, stems from a moment of lessening official restraint on artistic expression.[2] Though by no means an overridingly political work (it is as wrong to label Buero a political dramatist as it is to reproach him for being apolitical), this play confronts the fact of the Civil War and draws its consequences starkly. Simply stated: but for the war, the mental and economic states and the interpersonal relations of the father, mother, and two sons portrayed in *El tragaluz* would have been different—different surely in the sense of better. The lives of these people thus are sketched in a historical context.[3] Yet, the inevitable question remains: is war the result of man's character or man's character the result of war? In broader terms, this question resolves itself into another: is man's circumstance the fruit of historical determinism or of individual choice? It is precisely to this problem that Buero turns his attention in *El tragaluz* and to which, accordingly, we are invited to turn ours.

I

Experimento en dos partes is the descriptive subtitle that Buero gives to *El tragaluz.* Those who know Buero imperfectly might see in this tag a "commedia dell'arte" echo or the presaging of a Pirandellian game. Not so, however: Buero is not given to facetiousness. Neither is this, despite surface similarities, the cue for a distancing process in the manner of Brecht.[4] And it is certainly more than a practical measure taken to assuage the censors. *El tragaluz* is, in fact, an experiment because it contains an experiment. It is a play within a play, temporally and spatially rather than in terms of dramatic action. That is, the inner play constitutes the core of the action, which the outer play nuances (in contrast to the *Hamlet*-like case of the inner play at the service of the outer play). The nuancing results in the action of the inner play being converted into history. The manipulators of the experiment, the characters in the outer play or frame, are two researchers of a distant future century, Él and Ella. They appear eight times in the work—at the beginning and at the end of each

part and twice within each—in order to present to the audience the action of *El tragaluz* as a projection of the past. These two characters evidently troubled many spectators and reviewers, who failed to grasp them as more than the dispensable artifice that at first sight they appear to be. The penchant for seeing the content of the work of art as separable from its form provides the quickest path to the destruction of *El tragaluz.* Without the experimenters, *El tragaluz* is an ordinary play, not an "experiment." Without the formal framing device, the drama of Mario and Vicente is another story of our times, another of those movingly human tales that Buero likes to recount. Without Él and Ella, the play is divested of the history-as-theme element that gives it its special import.

The complicated temporal structure of *El tragaluz* hinges on these two characters, who embody the thought with which T. S. Eliot opens his *Four Quartets*: "Time present and time past / Are both perhaps present in time future, / And time future contained in time past." The time of the play's main action is now, mid-twentieth century, the 1960's. The time of the researchers is many centuries hence. Within the play, the past is made present: that is the experimenters' experiment. The play as such by making the future present makes the present past and the past subsistent in the future: that is Buero's experiment. The audience, for its part, finds its present made past in the future as well as that future made its present. It consequently assumes a dual temporal identity: its consciously lived time is today; but when directly addressed by the researchers as their contemporaries, it experiences the illusion of tomorrow. In other words, the audience that witnesses the experiment within *El tragaluz* is the same one that witnesses the experiment that *El tragaluz* itself is. It is subject and object of the story. With its discrete roles fused, it becomes party and key to the stuff of this play: the removal of today's circumstance in time and space, the replaying of today's historical moment.[5]

El tragaluz thus is not an Orwellian sally into the unknown, nor are its science-fiction trappings more than a point of departure.[6] As a result of the frame, *El tragaluz* becomes on the one hand the recreation of a concrete historical reality (present) so transmuted by time as to be rendered a curiosity to the new historical reality (imagined future). On the other hand, it is Buero's conjecture of a future—a future which, however, he does not examine in itself, for its fact corresponds to his ideal, but which he uses to examine the present. This present that Buero studies through Él and Ella acquires a perspective *in the present* that allows it to be absorbed without what is regarded as the necessary lapse of time. The spectator gains the illusion of being able to contemplate his own time—his real time—with the historian's inevitable sense of detachment. In fact, since the present always stands in a position of superiority vis-à-vis the past, and by extension the future vis-à-vis the present, the spectator, drawn into this historical abstraction of the present, develops towards the figures of the play a feeling of condescension that, rather than resulting in their belittlement, leads to an understanding of their plight. Buero knows as well as Eliot that time is unredeemable, but the experience of the past need not be lost upon the present. In Buero's play, our specific moment in human existence is seen in reference to the totality of human existence, whereby the absurdity of our present circumstance is readily portrayed. In the fictionalized context of *El tragaluz*'s experimental recreation, the blinding seriousness of the lived experience is recast in the light of a more reasoned retrospective view. This is a procedure entirely different from that of Buero's historical plays. In *Un soñador para un pueblo, Las Meninas, El concierto de San Ovidio,* and *El sueño de la razaón,* Buero stepped into the past in order to project by implication a known present from that vantage point. Where in these works he could launch a dream for the future of whose realization or failure we of the twentieth century can have full historical awareness, in *El tragaluz* the dream for the future is projected fictionally as realized, thereby remaining a dream—a dream whose historical realization in the twentieth century can only be a matter of faith and responsibility. *El tragaluz* places us in a time machine (or computer) that gives us a sense of our own circumstance in historical perspective. Thanks to the experiment, today can see today and judge today and shudder.[7]

If the manipulation of time through the characters of Él and Ella enables us, as spectators, to reflect on ourselves, of even greater importance is the fact that such a process lies within the realm of conception. As the researchers tell us: "La acción más oculta o insignificante puede ser descubierta un día. [. . .] El misterioso espacio todo lo preserva. [. . .] Cada suceso puede ser percibido desde algún lugar. [. . .] Y a veces, sin aparatos, desde alguna mente lúcida" (p. 34). This thought, implying as it does a threat, should give finite man pause about his comportment, for he exists in a historical sequence of time that is infinite. If he does not stop to question himself today, others shall judge him tomorrow. *El tragaluz* reproduces as a play this process of history and becomes part of it. Precisely as the contemporary film does, Buero manipulates the time-space continuum, moving time simultaneously forward and back. Modern artist that he is, he goes one step beyond the ideological-scientific concern with time: he stands in full mastery of motion. Given the form that he chose for it, *El tragaluz* is Buero's most direct and lucid examination of the subject of man and history. The inner play, the action of Mario and Vicente, examines their individual relationship to the specific and limited historical circumstance of the war and post-war years in Spain. The outer play then functions in such a fashion that the inner play becomes history. Finally, expanding in space and time to our situation as spectators of ourselves, *El tragaluz* as a whole addresses the over-all problem of man in historical context. It thus contains both history and the myth of history; and to the extent that it becomes an agent of change, it is in itself a force of history.

II

"La literatura es faena difícil [. . .] Hay que pintar la vida, pero sin su trivialidad." So says Vicente in *El tragaluz* (p. 24). A creature of his moment, the serious artist reflects the national circumstance in which he lives and at the same time participates in the universal *Zeitgeist.* Buero can be taken at his word when he says of this play that it transcends the Spanish scenario from which it springs: "no se trata de un problema específicamente español, pese a las connotaciones típicamente españolas que mi obra tenga. Es al público de nuestro tiempo, de los años oscuros que vivimos, al que trato de sobrecoger." And he goes on: "no puedo disgregar la cara externa, la del individuo en cuanto ser situado en unas coordenadas históricas y sociales determinadas, de la cara interior, la del individuo en cuanto enigma ontológico."[8] Fitting into the post-war Spanish literary current of a realism that is at once social and existential, *El tragaluz* deals as much with life as it does with Spanish life. The impact of the Civil War is intertwined with fundamental questions of human behavior. Into the commentary on history that the very form of *El tragaluz* submits, Buero has wrapped an etiological study of personality and a symbolic representation of man's existence as it balances between the opposing forces of socio-historical reality and inner reality.[9] It is the second of these realities in the face of the first—the ontological enigma, as he calls it—that Buero investigates through the contrasting personalities of the brothers Mario and Vicente.

The present situation finds three members of a former family of five living in a modest basement apartment in Madrid. The Father, a government employee before the war, now mentally disturbed or senile (depending on whether one adopts Mario's or Vicente's point of view), lives in a world far removed, recreating moments of the past and seemingly without recognizing his family. For warmth and protection he looks to his wife as his mother, and to paper dolls as companions. The Mother tries to sustain herself through the illusion of a tolerable present and seeks affection by giving it, but for various reasons she is unable to reach any member of her disintegrated family. Mario lives with his parents, in the shadow of his father. He is an idealist on whom society would look as a misfit, a failure. Vicente, the only one to have prospered, holds a purely material connection to the family. He is the purveyor of their monthly check and at special times of a refrigerator or television set. He is the dutiful occasional visitor, never there long enough to commit himself emotionally. Elvirita, the third child, died some twenty-five years earlier at the age of two.

The Civil War literally forced the family underground—not as political activists, but as victims of its aftermath. "Hombres arrojados," their sort has been called. The Father, evidently on the side of the vanquished, was purged from his post in one of the Ministries and then was too proud and too defeated to reclaim it when that became possible. Mario, ten years old when the hostilities ceased, had his education thwarted. Destitute as a result of the political situation, Mario and his parents never managed to rise from their cheap basement quarters. The family's inability to regain its strength was due to a combination of factors: the interruption of its life pattern, a structure of political and social injustice, and the elements of financial need, personal pride, and spiritual exhaustion. But there occurred a specific incident that is key to the action of *El tragaluz* and whose impact on the persons involved has not been lessened by the passing of a quarter-century. In the immediate post-war days of hunger, illness, and confusion in the country, of people—soldiers and civilians— desperate to get back to their homes, little Elvirita died. She died of starvation because the rest of the family was unable to get on the train to Madrid that Vicente did manage to mount through a lavatory window. The family's provisions and the child's milk were in a bag that Vicente had hung around him. The Father's state of mind and the family relationships stem from that incident. According to Vicente, he was unable to obey the Father's orders to get off the train because several soldiers, squeezed into any available space on the train, were holding him back. In reality, he was struggling to stay on in a furious, and successful, attempt to save himself. Subsequently he also saved himself from the family's lot in that cellar.

Vicente alone made his escape, while Mario was left behind, on that day of flight and ever since. Why? Five years older than his brother and stronger, Vicente was able to push his way onto the train. But that fact is no more than a metaphor on the physical level, for once on the train to Madrid, Vicente never again got off to rejoin his family. Mario tells him accusingly: "el tren arrancó . . . y se te llevó para siempre" (p. 56). Indeed, Vicente, from that moment on, has gone ever forward, machine-like, carried on by the mechanical structure, by the system, in directions set by it, not by him, with nothing obstructing his way, distancing himself more and more from his family and from emotional ties. Like some and unlike others, he has been able to do this because he is a pragmatist rather than an idealist, because he is an unrelenting egoist by nature, because he lives by material values and not by principles, because he is willing to compromise and bend to the wind, because his self-respect is a commodity for sale, because (unlike Mario or Beltrán) he forges ahead, unconcerned about sullying himself. Understanding and compassion have no place in his world. He sees only the surface of people, if he sees them at all, and those whose behavior he fails to comprehend (to wit, his brother), he classifies as queer.

The tragedy of Vicente's way is that it leaves no room for his fellows (the train was overcrowded), that his success sacrifices and victimizes others. His little sister was his first victim. Now it is Encarna, the country girl whom he takes on as his secretary and mistress, and the novelist Eu-

genio Beltrán. Through the person of Beltrán, Buero strikes out against censorship, against the systematic strangulation of the artist for political reasons, and against the whimsical manipulation of the artist's impact on society by elements ("el grupo") unrelated to art. (Buero's personal involvement in this kind of situation is well known, as are his feelings on the matter.) The fact that he never appears on stage lends Beltrán his special importance. He is a symbol. He does not exist. Yet he has a name. Therefore, he has been made not to exist. Not only is he tied off economically, he is eradicated through silence. An identifiable person pushed into non-existence by an order stronger than he, Beltrán is a Mario poetized. And Vicente, an admirer of Beltrán's work, prostitutes his tastes, his convictions, and his allegiance when, for his own protection, he becomes a willing agent in the annihilation of Beltrán.

There is no doubt that Vicente's way is dirty: one recalls that he reached salvation through a lavatory; and he chose, even fought, to remain in that lavatory. However, Vicente is not so blind to the implications of his choice as the spectator initially suspects. Vicente knows that his actions are base, that he exists in a world where business bargains replace love and friendship, and that the discomfiture he feels in the very surroundings which were once his comes from his substitution of material success for deeper satisfactions. He knows all that, and he is troubled. The train that symbolizes the path of cruel and selfish competition that is his also symbolizes the rumblings of his conscience.[10] Vicente's increasingly frequent visits to his family's cellar home reflect his awareness of the dastardliness of his actions on the train and thereafter. They are his attempt to cleanse himself, to seek pardon, a growing *crise de conscience* that culminates in his final confession to his father—to God, as it were.

If one questions why Vicente never veered from his callous ways, one must again remember the lavatory scene, where the soldiers into whose midst the fifteen-year-old Vicente squeezed himself tried to push him back out. He was a burden to them just as his family was to him. Struggling, he won. He had made a decision, instinctively perhaps, and the lesson to him was clear. He admits to his father: "Es cierto [. . .] Les abandoné, y la niña murió por mi culpa. Yo también era un niño y la vida humana no valía nada entonces . . . En la guerra habían muerto cientos de miles de personas . . . Y muchos niños y niñas también . . . , de hambre o por las bombas . . . Cuando me enteré de su muerte pensé: un niño más. Una niña que ni siquiera había empezado a vivir . . ." (p. 57). While for the Father the paper dolls he cuts out have as much life as his daughter had (perhaps more, for they live now and in her place), to Vicente his baby sister meant no more than these figures. No matter how profound his recognition of his own moral evil, in his comportment Vicente remains consistent to the last moment, for his behavior is his response to his view of life. (He cannot enjoy, we must remind ourselves, the benefit of El and Ella's distant perspective.) He sees fear and bad faith as facts of existence, one the consequence of the other and the two inevitably acquired as man grows out of childhood. He says: "El otro loco, mi hermano, me diría: hay remedio. Pero ¿quién puede terminar con las canalladas en un mundo canalla? [. . .] Ahora hay que volver ahí arriba . . . y seguir pisoteando a los demás" (p. 58). He is convinced that survival is possible under no other mode of existence. His code of life, then, is the fruit of his individual reaction to experiences shared with others. Ironically, Vicente is engulfed in a system that requires him to be as he is to succeed in its terms. His material success shows ever so clearly how man's inner nature is goodness' worst enemy. The system sets certain paths before Vicente, and he willingly follows them, though others are open to him. He chooses a way—activism, opportunism, and imposition of himself on circumstance—that, given the tenor of today's society, enables him to conquer daily life, even if not himself.

Mario, on the other hand, by all appearances and by his own confession, has been broken by the war. He has been living in the depths since then, both physically and spiritually. Prevented by circumstance from taking the train on that one particular occasion, he has been unable because of his nature and unwilling because of his moral stance to board it subsequently. Tangible satisfactions have been passing him by, for which he is certainly to blame in part. He is not a fighter; he is an idealist who cerebralizes and suffers, an echo of Dostoievsky's underground man. Offered the opportunity to battle from their midst against the forces that oppress him (a post with the publishing firm for which his brother works), he rejects it: for personal reasons and out of pride and misguided humility; but also on principle; and furthermore because he is passive, because it is not his way to grapple with contrary elements directly. Mario rejects both the animalistic way of life that commands: "¡devora antes de que te devoren!" and the ideologies that have been invented to support it. Not merely a man of weakness in flight from the aggressivity of others, Mario adopts a position which, described positively, calls for no devouring at all. In fact, just as Buero sets up this play as an experiment, so does Mario set up his existence as an experiment: can anyone survive who does not fight for his life? Is "live and let live" a workable standard? While not devouring his fellow man, can he keep from being devoured himself? Vicente and Mario coincide in their view of the order of things. If one appears to succeed where the other fails, it is the result of their respective personalities and faiths, which do not coincide. Within the historical moment that has torn families apart, Mario and Vicente live according to their private ethic, the very privacy of which, to say nothing of its nature, makes inevitable the disjunction that Buero here dramatizes. "Los de arriba, arriba. Los de abajo, abajo," says a character in a similar situation in a play by Antonio Gala (see n. 20). In defense of his father and himself

against Vicente's accusations, Mario insists: "Me doy plena cuenta de lo extraños que somos. Pero yo elijo esa extrañeza" (p. 48).[11] For Vicente this way of life is inconceivable, frightening. So it is a fact that both Vicente and Mario, the one as much as the other, each being what he is, have opted for a code of behavior and a mode of existence. From a common point of departure, they have gone in opposite directions; for the same question, they have found opposing answers. Which of the two is right remains the problem.

Buero himself prefers Mario, but he recognizes Mario's weaknesses, his paralysis, his stubborn nature, and his resentments. In Buero's own words to this effect, "el tipo ideal para una conducta equilibrada hubiera sido un hombre intermedio entre los dos hermanos, un [sic] simbiosis de ambos, un setenta por ciento del menor y un treinta del mayor."[12] Neither of the two men is right; the path of neither is fully satisfactory. Explanations for Mario's character, both circumstantial and psychological, are easy to come by, but to understand his behavior is not to condone it. His moral superiority over his brother and over so many others who have succeeded is unquestionable, but his very failure and his isolation in the nether regions of life attest to the insufficiency of his path, and the insufficiency constitutes an irony that makes his personal plight and the nature of man appear all the more tragic. Those who function best in life are not necessarily those richly endowed with the worthiest human qualities. This conviction Buero already dramatized, generally through three-sided relationships, in earlier plays: Carlos-Juana-Ignacio in **En la ardiente oscuridad,** Ulises-Penélope-Anfino in **La tejedora de sueños,** Valindin-Adriana-David in **El concierto de San Ovidio,** Alejandro-Ana-Silvano in **Aventura en lo gris.** One of the researchers in **El tragaluz** defines the moral dilemma in its historical perspective: "El mundo estaba lleno de injusticia, guerras y miedo. Los activos olvidaban la contemplación; quienes contemplaban no sabían actuar" (p. 58). Besides, the notion that Vicente-Mario represent the activism-passivity dichotomy, while basically true, is an oversimplification, as is the conclusion that the one is all bad and the other good. Vicente is as passive as Mario insofar as he follows obediently the rules of "the system," and his recognition of the shortcomings of his own mode of existence mitigates its reprehensibility. By the same token, to the extent that Vicente's fate is the materialization of Mario's nightmare of having dragged a man into an abyss, Mario is active and not without guilt, victimizer at the same time as victim. The situation of Mario and Vicente is remarkably similar to that of the brothers Victor and Walter Franz in Arthur Miller's *The Price.*[13] In each case the individual in given circumstances is faced with an existential choice that he makes according to his abilities, his experience, his convictions, and his ethic. Certain modes—those of Mario and Victor—seem more indicated than others, more noble and compassionate. Yet, a clear victory belongs to no one, and whatever the individual's choice, there is a price that he must pay for it.

The implications of the Vicente-Mario confrontation in *El tragaluz* are political, ontological, and ethical. As we have pointed out, Buero in this play is as explicit as artistic bounds permit in regard to the Civil War, its effects, and the social order under the Franco regime. The times— times of war, persecution, separation, hunger, fear—have helped to mold man's nature. If man carries within himself the seeds of both selfishness and altruism, the Civil War and its aftermath in Spain, the World War more broadly, have operated to stimulate the negative side of his character, to structure in such critical fashion his image of survival, that there is no room in it for anyone but himself nor time for any activity but existence. Love, charity, abnegation are luxuries that man cannot afford in such times. Or if he practices them, he goes under. The war is thus the single concrete factor that incited Vicente to elbow his way through life and that threw Mario into the "pozo" in which he lives. This is only a partial truth, however. Mario points out to Vicente: "La guerra había sido atroz para todos, el futuro era incierto y, de pronto, comprendiste que el saco era tu primer botín. No te culpo del todo; sólo eras un muchacho hambriento y asustado. Nos tocó crecer en años difíciles . . .[14] ¡Pero ahora, hombre ya, sí cres culpable! Has hecho pocas víctimas, desde luego; hay innumerables canallas que las han hecho por miles, por millones. ¡Pero tú eres como ellos! Dale tiempo al tiempo y verás crecer el número de la tuyas . . . Y tu botín" (p. 57).

The suggestion is that in reacting to events as they did, all the Vicentes helped to establish an order that has come to be *the* order of the day. Mario again points to this in talking about his father: "Este pobre demente era un hombre recto [. . .] Y nos inculcó la religión de la rectitud. Una enseñanza peligrosa, porque luego, cuando te enfrentas con el mundo, comprendes que es tu peor enemiga. [. . .] No se vive de la rectitud en nuestro tiempo. ¡Se vive del engaño, de la zancadilla, de la componenda . . . ! Se vive pisoteando a los demás. ¿Qué hacer, entonces? O aceptas ese juego siniestro . . . y sales de este pozo . . . , o te quedas en el pozo" (p. 39). By way of Mario, Buero imprecates an order that subjugates the honest person and elevates the ruthless, self-interested opportunist. Mario becomes the victim (not innocent) of an idealistic education that centered on man's moral stance and his spirit, an education that operated from a base of optimism and did not prepare him to cope with a hostile, aggressive social pattern.

But the downtrodden cannot convincingly explain away their situation by blaming either historical circumstance or the established order. Every man has powers of discretion, a conscience, and the ability to exercise his will. If he is a puppet in the hands of history, history alone is not the culprit. Buero casts the blame in three directions: on the system that forces the opposition of attitudes to which we are witness in *El tragaluz*; on the strong who act immorally; on the weak who succumb. Mario, so inclined, elects the path of self-sacrifice and poverty, the frantic avoidance of which is the key to Vicente's behavior. One suffers for refusing to compromise; the other lives and succeeds by compromising himself. Prostitution pays under this system, but there are still those, like Mario, incapable of prostituting their principles and their ways. Yet Mario's nobility, admirable as it is, is rendered absurd in the clash of the two elements that, wrapped up in one, constitute his stand: the consistent maintenance of personal integrity and the uselessness of inaction. (This self-annihilating dichotomy is maddening to all concerned: to Mario, to Vicente, to Buero, to us.) In his cellar, Mario may feel secure, but he is not awake to the totality of man. While he recognizes in an abstract way the lucidity in his father's frantic desire to learn the identity of the people on the postcards he collects, he himself can only see legs and feet through the cellar window. Upright as his dreamer's position is, it is a frustrating course. In other words, voluntary alienation cannot lead to an approximation towards man. The Mario-like individual chooses it for its antisepsis, but sacrifices in the process the possibility of knowledge and reform, of imposing his own superior character on the character of man. He condemns himself to live alone and to die unfelt. The vacuum he creates is then filled by those like Vicente. The depressing situation thus is that those who are aware of man's needs and his predicament hide and screen themselves behind bars that protect them but at the same time isolate them from a course of positive action, while those that are immersed in the active world are blind to the needs of anyone but themselves. Just as Buero does not condemn Vicente unequivocally for having taken the train, he strongly implies that Mario, too, could and should have caught a train—not the same one as Vicente, but a later one, in some fashion or other. It is neither to his benefit nor to his credit that he preferred to sink into a subterranean existence, staying behind forever and letting life go by without him. *El tragaluz* affirms the need to live consciously and actively, but this answer to existence is given in a moral context.[15] Man must ponder how he is to board the train, how he is to lead his life. Only before he can arrive at the proper answer to the question of his own existence, there is another question he must ask, as we shall see later.

For the moment, we can point to Buero's conviction that man bears a responsibility and that it is up to each individual to define and exercise that responsibility. When in *Las palabras en la arena* Christ labels Asaf a murderer before the act is accomplished, he is not predestining him as such, but describing the violence in Asaf's nature. Forgiveness was as open to Asaf as vengeance against his wife. The evil in the world is never imposed on man; he rejects or embraces it. One critic has spoken of Buero's characters as beings "trágicamente arrastrados a su fin por fuerzas vitales incontrolables."[16] To be sure, the characters in *El tragaluz* had no control over the Civil War and had to share Spain's destiny of living in its wake; but within that larger context, they shaped their own lives. If they ended as victims of the choice they did or did not make, one cannot speak unqualifiedly of uncontrollable forces.[17] The very change that Buero foresees for the future presupposes a man whose volition is not hamstrung. True, we are little, we sin, we commit errors. But neither the individual nor mankind is predestined. A composer of tragedy in the modern vein, Buero at no moment conceives of man as a puppet in the hands of immutable forces of destiny.[18] The lesson that El and Ella show their audience is clear: if the individual seemingly cannot control the tides of history, he can at least in his minute kingdom exercise the moral responsibility with which he has been fit. And miraculously, this latter course of behavior is tantamount to shaping history! We are thus now in a position to answer the questions that Buero poses in *El tragaluz.* War affects man, but it is he who causes and wages it. It is not a catastrophe of nature. Man lives by an order, but it is he who establishes it. Historically, man is influenced but not determined; ontologically, man is free to choose; ethically, some choices are better than others.

III

Will in time those better choices be made? Outside the confines of the play, who can tell? Within *El tragaluz,* however, where the future state is concretely recorded, the answer is an unequivocal yes. The nightmares of war and the selfishness of man are depicted as matters of the past, horrifying curiosities of a bygone age that this future society looks on in the way we regard the practice of human sacrifice in past societies. It is for the spectators of *El tragaluz* and their heirs to take heed and to shape the faith that Buero expresses. Buero has given time dimensionality so that history can take on that educative potential which it is said to contain and which man is said to ignore all too often. By fancying man beyond the twenty-second century to have learned from events in the twentieth, Buero projects him as a potential controller and molder of history. Since he is an artist, not a prophet, he may be right or wrong, and his experiment, like any, may succeed or founder. Thus, the ambiguity of resolution that critics have frequently pointed to as typical of Buero's dramaturgy,[19] in the case of *El tragaluz* lies outside the play to the extent that our own future comportment is unpredictable. But as Buero traces the path of history within the play, there is no doubt or ambiguity about the outcome or about its positive nature. Furthermore, Buero sketches the steps that will (or can) lead to this outcome. This he does through the symbolic structure of his play, specifically through three central elements: the physical nature of the family's abode; the figure of the Father; and a question that is much repeated.

The quarters in which Mario and his parents reside have two salient features: an enclosed subterranean space; and at sidewalk level the window that gives title to the play. Confinement, determined not by stage necessity but of a symbolic nature, is a strong element in several of Buero's plays: *Historia de una escalera, La tejedora de sueños, Hoy es fiesta,* and especially *Aventura en lo gris.* Modern dramatists have frequently displayed a taste for speaking through enclosed spaces filled with significant emptiness. Sartre's *Huis clos* has become the classic example. Sastre uses the device in *Escuadra hacia la muerte* and *En la red,* Pinter in *The Dumb Waiter.* Arrabal's *El laberinto* is perhaps the most frightening and despairing such case, and Ionesco fills his spaces with multiplying objects that crowd man out. The stage lends itself temptingly to this metaphor of man trapped in his surroundings. In *El tragaluz,* written by one well qualified to talk about life in a cell, the distancing of present time is an initial confinement: the play's temporal perspective—the present seen from centuries beyond—is a reduction of the time circumstance, the 1960's, that parallels the spatial reduction. Further, the geometric image of enclosure is here cut by a linear image: the cell is in a cellar. The cubicle and the vertical line pointing down together define the family's fate. Most importantly, of course—and we are dealing now with Mario alone—this symbol of isolation leads to the interrelated questions of who wills the isolation and what, if any, is its value.[20]

Mario's habitat represents, to be sure, the confinement that man suffers, the imposition upon him of forces—social, historical, or other—that leave him imprisoned and unable to interact with those very forces. But we must recall that matter of choice. Mario's exile is self-willed. He has isolated himself from a pattern alien to him and substituted a hermetic world exclusively his own. Axiologically, the division is between a concept of authenticity in human behavior on the one hand and pure existence, survival without meaning, on the other. Mario feels that encased and uncorrupted he can live in greater depth. On a psychological level, this sentiment can be described as a conflict between outer and inner reality. A room or apartment—a confined space—is an extension of the self. The outer world cannot be that. Therefore, the artifice of withdrawal into a created private world serves as a palliative for the individual in search of an antidote to historical circumstance. But is isolation by choice a position of weakness (flight from outer reality) or of strength (willful implantation of inner reality)? It is both, for the process is cyclical, but being both, it cannot be the perfect answer. The romantic notion that the subjective process can override outer reality is the illusion of a very private stance. As laudable or heroic as this solipsistic attitude may be at its most positive, it represents a denial of the objective fact of a reality existing outside man, a reality that inevitably shapes and influences and even victimizes him and therefore invites, or rather, demands, confrontation. Mario's psychic confrontation is not enough. The basement dwelling signals his condition and also the insufficiency of his way.

There is, however, a breach in the hermetism of Mario's inner world, a nascent solution for the schism. The setting of *Huis clos* would not have suited Buero's play, for in Mario's gloomy living room there is a window. This "tragaluz" that lights the "semisótano" is many things to the play, as it is different things to the different characters.

The cellar window divides symbolically the inner and outer reality (the room and the street) that exist on either side of it. But it is a passageway between two worlds at the same time as it is part of a barrier. Its nature as a window, its transparency, which differentiates it from a solid building wall that would block communication and even cross-consciousness between the two, allows the two worlds to see each other. Only through it is the drama of their coexistence possible. Particularly the members living in confinement may descry existence outside themselves and either reach out to it or remold their inner consciousness in response to what they discover. However, a cellar window is small, the angle of view is awkward, the picture is cut. The world outside is seen imperfectly. By the same token, while for those in the enclosure the window is their path to light and light's path to them—without it they would live in total darkness—its very presence indicates that light is meager, that light has been literally swallowed up. Again, vision is imperfect, full clarity is not achieved, and the distinction between outside and inside remains. Now, given the emphasized existence of outer reality combined with the reduction and blurring of its image, it is natural that those within, whether occupants or visitors, should find themselves acted upon to supply, through the imaginative projection of themselves and their experiences, elements that are not there. Accordingly, the "tragaluz" is yet another stage on which dramatic scenes are enacted. (In this sense it is a mirror of Buero's own artistic process.) That these scenes are mental projections, based on fancy or experience like any artist's creations, is emphasized by the device of not having the window visible on stage; only the shadows of its grating can be seen when it is open. The "tragaluz" thus becomes a window onto the world of the mind. Through it Vicente's conscience is aroused; on three occasions he is shaken by his interpretation of what he hears or sees through the bars. For the Father, the "tragaluz" is not a cellar window but a train window, the one that Vicente squeezed through to gain freedom and through which little Elvirita could have been saved too. In this way the old man relives the pain of a shattering memory (and on the diminute stage recreates time as Buero does on the large one). Finally, through the bars of the window Mario concretizes his own inner world

as he sees fit. Illusion and reality, event and invention, meaning and interpretation cease to have set frontiers when viewed through the "tragaluz"—or through time or through art.

In the context of our discussion, Mario's indulgences at the window, though not separable from Vicente's and the Father's actions, are the most significant. One can interpret Mario's perspectivistic games negatively as one more manifestation of his withdrawal syndrome. Faces, not limbs, are our clues to recognition. If we focus on limbs, we construe identities, we do not capture them. In effect, Mario prefers to create people imaginatively rather than going out to meet them, to see them whole, and to confront them as they are. Focusing on a leg, a shoe, a snatch of conversation, Mario in his dream world restructures the disembodied creatures of the outside world to his own satisfaction. Naturally, he cannot be assured of the truth of his hypothetical explanations. He knows that. Nevertheless, he has been able to capture the wholeness of one detail or another as it flashes by. He has done what Vicente, living on the outside, never does: stop to look, to question. Immersion in the inner world is no way to conquer life, Buero tells us, but neither is a headlong, unquestioning rush into the outside a satisfactory solution. The "tragaluz" is not a symbol of escape because embracing outside reality at the cost of inner reality is not desirable. If it were, the apartment's doors could, after all, have been used freely. That is why Buero chose a window, not a door, for his symbolic structure in this play. Although it is no gateway to heaven, through this small barred opening Buero can announce the possibility of eventual harmony between the worlds that exist on either side— that is, eventual communion between man and himself. At one moment in the action of Part I (p. 42), a shadowy figure looks into the basement. Just as Mario's questioning game sets him apart from all the Vicentes, rare is the passer-by who stops to take a crouching glance inward. Rare, but he exists, and he and Mario are one. The view into the semi-darkness inside is no more whole than the view of legs walking by: the answers are not clear. But what matters is the act of stopping, looking, and wondering.

For the Father, wondering is a constant occupation, so much so that it is taken as one of his several fetishistic aberrations. This enigmatic character—artifice as much as character—has in relation to the past fled from history, and in regard to the future he shapes it. Past and future split his roles as vulnerable mortal and superhuman entity that coalesce in the complex present of *El tragaluz.* Seen now in relation to the past, he emerges in no uncertain terms as a casualty of the Civil War. More than anyone else in the play, he has been broken by the force of historical circumstance as it touched him personally.[21] The Father's answer to a tragedy he could not bear—the death of his daughter—has been to withdraw into an inner world narrower yet than Mario's, for he does not even recognize the reality of his own family in the basement apartment. He is one of Buero's several characters (Irene in *Irene o el tesoro,* Anita in *Las cartas boca abajo,* Goya in *El sueño de la razón*) who live in an inner world so closed to others that they are judged deranged. The brothers' argument as to whether their father is mad or suffering from arteriosclerosis is irrelevant. Whatever the physiological explanation and even if his condition is a self-imposed veil over lucidity, his invention of a childish world is a disorder. If he can cut out a paper doll and give it life, make it be a child, create it and preserve it as he could not preserve his flesh-and-blood daughter, it is because he has found in his *Lebenslüge* a security that the other characters, still tied to outer reality, can only strive for. In Freudian terms, the Father is suffering from a psychic trauma (not dating to childhood, however). Buero correctly portrays the typical time lag or "latency period" between the initial trauma and the later neurosis that is the reaction to it (as Freud describes the phenomenon in *Moses and Monotheism,* Pt. III, Sec. I, Ch. ii). He also records the Father's fixation on the trauma, the so-called "repetition-compulsion," which explains the Father's taking the cellar window for a train window, his constant references to a waiting room, and his confusion of Encarna with Elvirita (Elvirita reincarnated). The accompanying defensive reaction of forgetting is likewise a result of fixation on the trauma. The apparently opposing but actually complementary reactions to the trauma result in a displacement of normal associations by a series of seemingly absurd ones. The latter are substituted for the more profound associations that have been suppressed by the psychic mechanism or, as Freud puts it, under the pressure of the censor (ibid., Ch. iii,[22] and *The Interpretation of Dreams,* Ch. vii). As in a dream state, the Father engages in hallucinatory occupations for the sake of self-gratification; but since these inventions cannot lead to full gratification, they are accompanied by the elaboration of a barrier between meaning and perception that causes a change in the outer world. The illusion of joy substituted for the reality of sorrow becomes the only remaining reality. Psychology dissolves history by making the past into a present defined and valued as the individual wills it. Mario and the Father have both, under differing impulses, turned their backs on an unendurable reality and spring into action only when, subconsciously recognizing the limitations of dream, each one in his own way avenges himself on Vicente. Without himself realizing the implications of his words, Vicente sees this partnership earlier when he says to his brother: "Estás en peligro: actúas como si fueses el profeta de un dios ridículo . . . De una religión que tiene ya sus ritos: las postales, el tragaluz, los monigotes de papel . . ." (p. 48).

Vicente's comment suggests that this old man who in terms of human psychology has been driven mad by the force of circumstance is a shaper of circumstance, a God-figure. There can be no doubt that this is the case.[23] The very elements that constitute the outward signs of the Father's aberrations reveal him endowed with a power to give life and to take it. In the initial scene between Vicente and Encarna, it is established that he likes postcards that show people walking about. A postcard and a basement window: two rectangles in which are framed lifeless scenes of the outer world. The paper people on the cards are parallel in their inanimateness to the faceless bodies whose legs are seen parading by the cellar window. The people so framed are separated in space from the world to which the Father belongs, and he can give them identity and meaning as he sees fit. What results, as in Mario's imaginative sallies, he has created. But having reached a state far more critical than Mario's, he is also more powerful. He cuts the figures from the postcards and puts them on an imagined train, saying: "al que puedo, lo salvo" (p. 27). If this behavior is interpreted as pathetic, Buero's skillful manipulation of irony and point of view is diluted. On the psychological level of the subconscious, this act has a specific and personal meaning for the Father. Beyond that, however, the symbolic value is evident. The Father watches over his flock. To the figures imprisoned on the cards in a state of inanimation he gives life. They escape from their confinement, they take flight. In assuming the role of creator, the Father has, so to speak, usurped history.

Having created, the Father has the power to destroy. That is the lesson of the murder scene, in which he stabs Vicente, his son and namesake, with the very instrument—the scissors—with which he gave life to the paper figures.[24] Again the Father's motives in performing this deed are distinguishable from its implications, for the murder is a therapeutic gesture. Humanity is cleansed when a violator of the moral order is struck down. The murder is not, except in legal terms, an act of madness, but an act of justice. The transgressor is punished, a sentence is carried out. In retrospective light, the Father fancies he will prevent Vicente from mounting the train so that Elvirita will not die. In terms of the present, he punishes him for having done so. Prospectively, he keeps Vicente from getting back on the train from which in this moment of contrition and confession he had descended for the very first time. Vicente will not go on to victimize others. Whether punitive or interdictory, the act is God-like: God can help man to purge himself of selfishness and evil and to mold history in a new form.

Since the Father is a God-figure, it is natural that the ethical demands placed on man should, in the context of *El tragaluz,* emanate from him. Unsure of the identity of even his wife and children, he is haunted by the desire to identify his paper creatures. He punctuates the entire play with the question, "¿Quién es ése?" This question, which is another way of his to create, to give life and meaning, eventually comes to haunt all those about him. "¿Quién es ése?" is the play's basic question, the need to ask it its overriding implication, and the fact that only few make this inquiry—"hombres oscuros, habitantes más o menos alucinados de semisotanos o de otros lugares parecidos" (p. 51)—its elemental truth.[25]

If it is a fact, as Buero has his researcher say, that "siempre es mejor saber, aunque sea doloroso" (p. 51), then the Father's obsessive query is a sign of lucidity, even of superiority. It is not the great or the powerful who stop to ask "¿Quién es ése?" Rather, the asking of the question endows the person who asks it with moral preeminence. Moreover, one need not voice the question; to feel it is enough. But why is it so important to pose this child-like question? Simply because he who asks it recognizes the existence of individuality outside himself and distinguishes the individual from the mass. The researcher reveals the Father's "method" as a touchstone of ethical ideals when he says: "Compadecer, uno por uno, a cuantos vivieron, es una tarea imposible, loca. Pero esa locura es nuestro orgullo," which Ella phrases thus as the result of the inquiry: "Ese eres tú, y tú, y tú. Yo soy tú, y tú eres yo. Todos hemos vivido, y viviremos, todas las vidas" (p. 52). The question is a metaphor of man's concern for humanity, a concern that Mario, the dreamer, evinces, though not the activist Vicente, who not only lacks the time for it but cannot conceive of it.[26] The nameless individual caught unknowingly by the camera as it focused on the Place de l'Opéra in Paris or on a crowded street in Vienna—that is, on the place, the thing—that individual yet has an identity. He is not dead, merely stopped in time, as the characters in this play have been stopped in time. And his significance (if we prefer, we can call it his immortality, as Unamuno would have) depends on others' recognition of his uniqueness. The thinking man's answer to his own identity rests on the question "¿Quién es ése?" as he asks it about others and as others ask it about him.

Man's well-being, then, depends on the *asking* of the question, not on any concrete response to it, for the asking constitutes an act of creation, while the answer is unascertainable and irrelevant. The answer to the question would imply a solution to identity, whereas all that is possible or even desirable is a consciousness of identity. Consciousness of others, a collective consciousness, is the key to solidarity and the most satisfactory path to self-knowledge at the same time. To ask "¿Quién es ése?" is a restatement of the golden rule. Consequently, the riddle of the Father's question implies an ethical solution to an ontological dilemma. Buero defines *El tragaluz* as "una investigación sobre el individuo en cuanto enigma ontológico," and so it is, as we have seen. But the problem of man's being ultimately dissolves into one of ethical postures precisely because the ontological angle, the answer to the question, is obscure, while the ethical solution, the asking of the question, is within reach.

In the question "¿Quién es ése?" the historical and individual levels of the play coalesce. The trick accomplished by Buero's refraction of time is that with the

promise or the threat of future generations probing into us, we are led to inquire about those who stand at our side. What the postcards are to the Father and the cellar window to Mario, the play is to us. Given the perspective in *El tragaluz*—the view from a distant post-cataclysmic century—the historical situation is parallel to the Father's personal one. In the twenty-second century all men finally begin to ask "¿Quién es ése?" after the destruction wrought earlier, just as the Father asks it after the incident of his daughter. He has, so to speak, suffered a historical shock. So, too, according to Buero's artistic intuition of the future, did mankind. Buero suggests that a historical cataclysm, such as the Spanish Civil War, can and should discharge a collective moral reassessment and catapult man into a position where he begins to remold his nature. Since the moment for self-interest is always propitious and the opportunist, the exploiter, and the little dictator have manipulated the world since time immemorial, only a thorough self-renovation can save a putrid civilization. It is within every man's power to initiate that renovation, and unless he exercises that power, there will always be Vicentes and history will be an infinite projection of its bankrupt past. That is why Mario's final word is so significant: "Ellos." It is the solution to the play as it is the solution to the problem. "Ellos" is the question "¿Quién es ése?" restated declaratively. It is the sum of Él and Ella, the people of the future. It is Mario and Encarna fusing into that future through their own reconciliation. When the shift from "yo" to "ellos" takes place, Él and Ella can have nothing to say. The experiment is over. Man has initiated his conquest of history.

Notes

1. The plays mentioned in the text are readily accessible in various editions. *La doble historia,* to date performed only in England, has been published in *Artes Hispánicas / Hispanic Arts,* 1, No. 2 (1967), 85-167. Later textual references to *El tragaluz* are to its first printing in *Primer Acto,* No. 90 (Nov. 1967), 20-60. The play has been reprinted in the *Colección Teatro,* No. 572 (Madrid, 1968), with *Hoy es fiesta* and *Las Meninas* in Taurus' "Mirlo Blanco" series (Madrid, 1968), and with *El concierto de San Ovidio* in the Clásicos Castalia series (Madrid, 1971). It is also in F. C. Sainz de Robles, *Teatro español 1967-1968* (Madrid, 1969), pp. 161-236. Since submission of this essay for publication, two articles have appeared that in some respects bear upon our interpretation: Gottlieb Blumenstock, "Antonio Buero Vallejo: *Das Kellerfenster (El tragaluz).* Eine Interpretation," *Die Neueren Sprachen,* 70 (1971), 602-12; and Martha T. Halsey, "*El tragaluz*: A Tragedy of Contemporary Spain," *RR,* 63 (1972), 284-92.

2. I am grateful to Antonio Buero Vallejo for his own stimulating opinions on this particular subject. Quite possibly, Ildefonso Manuel Gil uttered a prophecy when he recently wrote: "La guerra civil, como tema

de nuestros escritos, apenas ha empezado su camino" ("Sobre la Generación de 1936," *Symposium,* 22 [1968], 111).

3. In answer to a question about the mission of the theater in contemporary society, Buero asserted that the theater must reveal "lo que el hombre tiene de humano y de inhumano; y lo que tiene de ser histórico" (*Primer Acto,* Nos. 29-30 [1961-62], 6).

4. Though an admirer and translator of Brecht, Buero does not share his concept of *Verfremdung.* See "A propósito de Brecht," *Insula,* Nos. 200-201 (1963), 1, 14.

5. The division is enhanced by the use of light. Él and Ella, living in the play's present, are brightly illuminated with the clear light of the visible present. The other scenes, which are in the play's past, are performed with pale, unreal lighting, the vague, suffused light of history. (The contrast could be seen on a symbolic-spiritual level as the split between the search for knowledge and the flight into ignorance that Buero frequently has dramatized and that his critics never tire of commenting on, most recently Martha T. Halsey, "'Light' and 'Darkness' as Dramatic Symbols in Two Tragedies of Buero Vallejo," *Hispania,* 50 [1967] 63-68, and Norma L. Hutman, "Todo es querer," *PSA,* 49 [1968], 37-54.)

6. Moreover, the experimenting and juggling with time does not diminish the reality of the events or of the characters in our contemporary terms. On the contrary, the Él-Ella device opens to Buero a path of psychological analysis generally not available to the dramatist. The "experiment" can recreate not only past physical action but past mental action as well, so that the mind, rather than merely unfolding itself, becomes, as in the novel, an object of direct study.

7. In one of the most sensible reviews of Buero's theater, José Monleón writes: "Buero es de los que sitúan siempre el presente dentro de una línea histórica; quiero decir que el presente se explica por el pasado, lo que no significa que los jóvenes personajes del desenlace de *Historia de una escalera* hayan de repetir, necesariamente, la historia de sus padres. En otras palabras, y con talante noventayochista, Buero sabe que la historia puede ser la gran enemiga de la intrahistoria, el gran obstáculo. Lo que empuja a examinar la historia para encontrar en ella la clave de las falsificaciones, los malentendidos, las deformaciones" ("Un teatro abierto," in A. B. V., *Teatro: Hoy es fiesta. Las Meninas. El tragaluz* [Madrid, 1968], p. 28).

8. Ángel Fernández-Santos, "Una entrevista con Buero Vallejo sobre *El tragaluz*," *Primer Acto,* No. 90 (1967), 10, 14 (reprinted in A. B. V., *Teatro,* pp. 64-78).

9. José María de Quinto (*Insula,* No. 252 [1967], 15-16), misled by its middle-class characters, classifies *El tragaluz* as "neogaldosiano" and as one of Buero's "tragedias de la vida vulgar." This is not only a deformation of the force and nature of Buero's theater as a whole, but reflects a truncated understanding of the play.

10. In fact, the train, central to the retrospective action of *El tragaluz,* is also a basic and multifaceted element of the play's symbolic structure (not simply the symbol of modern civilization that it often is elsewhere, as in Alas' "¡Adiós, Cordera!," Azorín's "Una lucecita roja," or Delibes' *El camino,* or the instrument of destruction it is in Sánchez Ferlosio's *El Jarama* and Muñiz's *El tintero*). Literally and figuratively, it is the vehicle to freedom and escape from death that only some—the strongest and most willful—manage to board. (Cf. *Aventura en lo gris,* where this last hope of escape from circumstance never comes.) Beyond that, it is the way of life that the individual molds for himself according to his will and which he subsequently can neither guide nor halt. For that very reason, along with the specific reminders it holds for him, is the train related to Vicente's conscience. On several occasions in the drama, the noise of a railway is heard in symbolic accompaniment to Vicente's thoughts, reaching an unbearable stridence at the climactic moment when he pays with his life for his transgressions and coming to an end with his last breath. Of like significance is Vicente's hiding from his father a post-card picturing an old train. For the Father the train is a gnawing memory and a part of his illusion. Leaving in its wake painful reminders of the past and pressing forward implacably to an unsure future, the train, symbol of this life, is itself swallowed up in the framework of Buero's historical projection.

11. This stance can be labeled quixotic. It was inevitable that a writer with the taste and concerns of Buero would ultimately examine the figure and the myth of Don Quijote, which in fact he does, though not so much here with Mario as through the character of Eloy in his opera libretto *Mito.*

12. Fernández-Santos, "Una entrevista . . . ," p. 12.

13. *The Price* had its Broadway première on February 7, 1968; the two productions are thus virtually concurrent. The plays constitute one of those instances in which two artists were thinking independently along strikingly similar lines. (The Spanish version opened in Madrid in early 1970.)

14. Before submission to the censors, this last phrase read: "Nos tocó crecer en tiempo de asesinos y nos hemos hecho hombres en un tiempo de ladrones." See Patricia W. O'Connor, "Censorship in the Contemporary Spanish Theater and Antonio Buero

Vallejo," *Hispania,* 52 (1969), 286. (O'Connor's use of "vivir" for "crecer" in the final version is an error.)

15. In a "Production Note" to *The Price,* Arthur Miller says about the brothers he created: "As the world now operates, the qualities of both brothers are necessary to it" ([New York, 1968], p. 117).

16. M. Manzanares de Cirre, "El realismo social de Buero Vallejo," *RHM,* 27 (1961), 323.

17. Ricardo Doménech, in "'El tragaluz,' una tragedia de nuestro tiempo," *CHA,* No. 217 (1968), 130, says of Vicente: "Las conmociones sociales e históricas son propicias para la erupción social de este tipo humano [. . .] Una subversión de valores en las relaciones humanas [. . .] puede desviar las mejores energías de un individuo en contra de los demás y de sí mismo. El 'activo' Vicente, en un mundo ajeno a la disyuntiva de devorar o ser devorado, probablemente habría encauzado sus energías hacia un fin positivo, habría hecho su vida de otra forma." But Doménech is wise to add: "Ahora bien, sea cual sea el tiempo o el lugar en que se vive, hay siempre una íntima, intransferible libertad individual para elegir lo que somos, lo que vamos a ser. Vicente es víctima de su sociedad y de su tiempo, pero él ha elegido serlo. Es víctima y es culpable: todo a la vez. Cuanto más culpable, más víctima; cuanto más víctima, más culpable."

18. Kessel Schwartz, without offering further comment, summarizes this conviction of Buero's in his "Buero Vallejo and the Concept of Tragedy," *Hispania,* 51 (1968), 817-24. Earlier, Jean-Paul Borel, in *Théâtre de l'impossible* (Neuchâtel, 1963), p. 190, made the following lucid statement in regard to *Aventura en lo gris*: "L'humain semble ainsi constitué par un problème impossible, mais auquel chacun, dans le combat personnel qui lui incombe, peut pourtant apporter sa solution. Et c'est en perdant par rapport à notre monde impossible que chacun gagnera par rapport à ce qu'il pouvait faire, lui, en tant qu'homme socialement et historiquement défini. C'est précisément à cause des dimensions historiques et sociales de l'homme que le problème se pose toujours de façon absolument concrète, au niveau de l'individu. Ni la faiblesse, ni l'égoïsme, ni le destin, ni la vérité, ni la politique, ni la guerre ne sont l'affaire 'des autres'. C'est toujours *mon* problème [. . .]"

19. E.g., Robert E. Lott, "Functional Flexibility and Ambiguity in Buero Vallejo's Plays," *Symposium,* 20 (1966), 150-62.

20. *El tragaluz* invites comparison, in theme and setting, with a more directly political play by Antonio Gala, *Noviembre y un poco de yerba,* which opened less than two months after Buero's play and deals with a Civil War "vencido" who lives as a recluse in the cellar of a railway station (published in *Primer Acto,* No. 94 [1968], 19-45).

21. Of course, the Mother's gaiety is parallel to the Father's madness: each one has invented a system to block out the bitterness of memory. The Mother's refrain is "Hay que olvidar aquello," something she naturally cannot do, for within herself the tragedy of "aquellos días tremendos" (p. 37) lives on. But hers is the solution of the more stable individual who veils sterile thought in a flurry of activity, laughs for the sake of others, and, in the only way she knows, makes a futile attempt to generate peace in her own sphere.

22. Note especially the applicability of these words to the Father: "All these phenomena, the symptoms as well as the restrictions of personality and the lasting changes in character, display the characteristic of compulsiveness; that is to say, they possess great psychical intensity, they show a far-reaching independence of psychical processes that are adapted to the demands of the real world and obey the laws of logical thinking. They are not influenced by outer reality, or not normally [. . .] They are as a state within a state, an inaccessible party, useless for the common weal; yet they can succeed in overcoming the other, the so-called normal, component and in forcing it into their service. If this happens, then the sovereignty of an inner psychical reality has been established over the reality of the outer world; the way to insanity is open."

23. Doménech writes (p. 133): "Ninguno de los rasgos observados nos permitiría decir resueltamente que es un símbolo de Dios; mas, ante ellos, tampoco nos atreveríamos resueltamente a afirmar lo contrario." The reasons for this wavering are incomprehensible. Naturally, one cannot go so far as to say that the Father *is* God, for that would divest him of his human dimension and lead to ludicrous conclusions (e.g., God is psychotic); but neither he as a character nor the action of the play are fully intelligible unless he is seen as a God-figure. Moreover, the textual evidence (some of which Doménech cites) points with all clarity to this inference.

24. Note the Mother's prophetic warning to the Father near the beginning of the play: "¡Y cuidado con las tijeras, que hacen pupa!" (p. 28).

25. As would any critic dealing with this play, Fernández-Santos touches on this question in "El enigma de *El tragaluz,*" *Primer Acto,* No. 90 (1967), 4-6.

26. Ironically, when Mario finds out the truth about Encarna's liaison with his brother, that is, when the question "¿Quién es ése?" has been answered in this case, he rejects her, saying: "¡Pero tú ya no eres Encarna . . . !" (p. 51).

Ronald J. Friis (essay date winter 1993)

SOURCE: Friis, Ronald J. "'Hoy ya no cameos en aquellos errores': Mimetic Violence and Transcendence in Buero Vallejo's *El Tragaluz.*" *Romance Notes* XXXIV, no. 2 (winter 1993): 203-10.

[*In the following essay, Friis offers a stylistic and thematic analysis of* El tragaluz, *focusing on Buero Vallejo's use of mimesis in the play.*]

The Platonic conception of mimesis as the depiction of reality has received a new interpretation in the writings of René Girard. For Girard, imitation and similarity are the keys to understanding many of the puzzles of human nature, especially desire and violence. Antonio Buero Vallejo's *El tragaluz* (1967) features a dual representation of mimesis, providing at once a social message on the effects of the Spanish Civil War[1] and an exploration of the psychology of violence. The interplay of these interior and exterior themes is structured by the *Investigadores,* the narrators from a future century who present the play's action to the audience in the form of flashbacks. This study examines the convergence of opposing forces that leads to the violent conclusion of the play-within-a-play.

In the opening chapter of *Violence and the Sacred,* René Girard claims that each society carries a certain amount of violence that will, if not placed in check, form a contagious, destructive cycle of action and reaction, violence and revenge. When society enters a crisis of this nature on a large scale, chaos reigns over order. Ironically, the only way out of this sequence is through more violence, a "pure" cleansing sacrifice sanctioned by society as a whole. In order for this "purifying" act of justice not to mirror the initial crime and simply deteriorate into revenge, it must be enacted upon a third party, a scapegoat. Girard writes: "To make a victim out of the guilty party is to play vengeance's role, to submit to the demands of violence. By killing, not the murderer himself, but someone close to him, an act of perfect reciprocity is avoided and the necessity for revenge by-passed" (26).

Girard emphasizes that peace and order depend, not upon cultural similarities, but upon society's differences. A cycle of violent reciprocity eliminates these necessary distinctions. Drawing on mythological and literary examples such as Cain and Abel and Romulus and Remus, Girard demonstrates that the presence of two figures who share more similarities than differences often brings war and violence into society. Freud, Lacan and Levi-Strauss have all, at one time or another, explored this fear of resemblance in the context of the incest taboo.[2] Brothers have a particularly strong potential for violence due to their many similarities: they share the same mother and father, nationality, language and religion. Twins are a perfect example of lack of differentiation because of their identical age and appearance. The disintegration of fundamental differences in society or a text acts as a contagion, creating an overall crisis of identity and consequently begetting violence.

The fraternal quality of the Spanish Civil War has often been described, as in Unamuno, in the context of the Cain and Abel myth. In *El tragaluz,* we are faced with a similar structure of brother fighting brother in a time of crisis. In the immediate aftermath of the War, the family of the drama attempt to return to Madrid by boarding a train laden with other refugees and soldiers returning from battle. Up to this point, the Mother, Father, their two sons Mario and Vicente, and their daughter Elvirita had sidestepped the War's path and avoided bloodshed. As they push through the crowd toward the overfilled train, only Vicente, who holds the family's food supply in his backpack, manages to board through a lavatory window. As a result, the family is stranded without food and the infant Elvirita dies of hunger. "Boarding the train" thus becomes a metaphor for ruthless and violent egoism throughout the rest of the play and sets the rhythm by which Vicente is to live the rest of his life: social climbing and the pursuit of material gains by means of victimization. John W. Kronik writes: "There is no doubt that Vicente's way is dirty: one recalls that he reached salvation through a lavatory; and he chose, even fought, to remain in the lavatory" (379). Although the train's bathroom is a viable metaphor for Vicente's attitude, one must not overlook the presence of the soldiers who supposedly took him in. It is here that Vicente comes directly in contact with the carriers of what before was an external crisis. Girard writes that "A special sort of impurity clings to the warrior returning to his homeland, still tainted with the slaughter of war" (41). Vicente's contact with this "impure" violence effectively internalizes the outside crisis of the war, bringing the pain of loss and the blind rage of violence into his family.

Toward the end of the first act, Vicente's contagion with violence is illustrated in a particularly graphic scene. His mad father is waving a pair of scissors near his fingers, threatening to cut off two. As Vicente runs to the old man wanting to help, Mario pushes him away, saying afterward: "Si tú te precipitas, quizá se habría cortado" (60). Vicente is seen by his brother as the embodiment of violence, containing a malevolent force that might push his Father into drawing his own blood.

The consequences of Vicente's selfishness affect each character in a unique way. After his brother moves away from home, Mario seeks refuge from the painful past by caring for his parents and hiding in the family's meager basement home. His father falls into a state of insanity, regressing into an enigmatic, child-like recluse who shuffles from one room to another, his sole interest being faces in old magazines, photographs and postcards. This madness comes as result of the internalized violence of the Civil War and parallels precisely the War's violent lack of differentiation. War, like death, acts in a democratic manner, unpredictably claiming victims without regard to their personal identity. Just as sickness passes from an infected organism to a pure one, so do violence and its symptoms; they are contracted and reproduced, always keeping their original form. In the Father's world, strangers become friends while family members become strangers; inanimate paper dolls are transformed into living human souls. He alternates between a world without differences and occasional cognizance where we glimpse his deep internal struggle and complexity.

The Father's search for identification, like all of the play's techniques, reflects Vicente's actions and their repercussions. When the eldest son left his family at the train's platform, he treated them like any of the other victims of the War. Looking back upon his sister's death, Vicente thought of her as "un niño más" (103), just another anonymous casualty of the surrounding battles. The Father on the other hand, searches through the unknown multitudes of his photographs and randomly assigns identities. These two conflicting points of view are united by one thread: lack of differentiation. In a time of crisis, Vicente overlooked the sacred bonds and unique obligations that link him to his family and differentiate between this unit and society at large. Conversely, his father acts in a compensating role that also fails to provide an accurate vision of different aspects of reality such as life and death, knowledge and the unknown, and presence and absence. The fact that the Father's insanity begins with a fit of violence (smashing his cane) the very night that Vicente boarded the train shows the speed and means by which violence spreads.

Mario and Vicente's childhood game of looking out the basement window and inventing personalities for passersby represents another search for identification. The game mirrors the Father's struggle against anonymity by nature of the importance it places on the individual. The brothers attempt to play the game as adults, but only Mario is able to piece together the passing limbs into unique individuals. Vicente, on the other hand, becomes callous, uninterested in the subtleties of the different people and calls them "no sé qués" (62). At this point Mario's words "tú ya no juegas a eso" (59) are obvious to all; Vicente is a ruined man and this game illustrates how far he has strayed from his childhood innocence.

Twenty years pass between Elvira's death and the play's conclusion. Girard notes that: "The more a tragic conflict is prolonged, the more likely it is to culminate in a violent mimesis; the resemblance between the combatants grows ever stronger until each presents a mirror image of the other" (47). This convergence of opposing forces is evident in Mario and Vicente, and although they do not entirely exchange roles, the process of double formation will eventually bring about Vicente's downfall. Although the classic duality of action versus passivity applies validly to

the brothers, a Girardian reading of their roles reveals a more complex interplay. In the crisis of *El tragaluz,* Mario and Vicente slowly begin to adopt the same means of fulfilling their desires; Mario becomes more active and Vicente more passive. When the brothers share the same desire, as in the case of Encarnación, their differences are further eliminated and their desires become truly mimetic.

Encarnación represents the fulcrum of the brothers' conflict. She is Vicente's obliged lover and Mario's girlfriend. In her capacity as Vicente's secretary, she assists Mario in trying to save the writer Beltrán, a process that intentionally crosses Vicente. When Mario finds out about her relations with his brother, he laments: "Pero tú ya no eres Encarna" (87). The disappointment and disillusionment that Mario feels ruins his image of Encarna and, ironically, forces him into changing her identity. For Mario, this relationship is one step closer to "Vicente's way": he cannot save Beltrán or Encarna without stepping on his brother.

The younger brother's shift from an initial state of passivity towards action is further revealed through the medium by which he is often labeled: dreams. In the dream Mario recounts to Encarna, he is seated on one side of a deep gorge holding a string connected to an unknown person on the opposite side. While casually doing paperwork, he tugs on the cord, bringing the victim closer to and finally over the edge of the cliff. Not only does the dream suggest Vicente's victimization of others, it is a reflection of Mario's losing battle against victimization. The "desconocido," the anonymous victim on the other side, can clearly be read as Vicente and the gorge as judgment in the *semi-sótano* where the family lives. This desymbolization of Vicente by Mario is a mirror image of his brother's original disregard for the individual.[3] By dreaming away his brother's identity, Mario has converted Vicente into just another person, "un niño más." Through the years and with mixed intentions, he slowly brings his brother closer and closer to home, to judgment. At one point, he tells Vicente: "Estás volviendo al pozo, cada vez con más frecuencia . . . y eso es lo que más me gusta de ti" (58). This statement, like the dream and the Father's words, is laden with ambiguity and underscored with semi-conscious double intent.

What Mario detests most about his brother is the fact that he does not change the attitude that created his first victim and that he continues "pisoteando a los demás." Quoting Jules Henry's *Jungle People,* Girard comments on the same kill-or-be-killed attitude espoused by Vicente: "'With a single murder the murderer enters a locked system. He must kill and kill again, he must plan whole massacres lest a single survivor remain to avenge his kin'" (54). While Vicente's "massacres" are more figurative than those in Henry, there is little doubt of the violence inherent in his process of victimization. The elder brother is responsible for his father's madness, his brother's isolation, the compromised life of his secretary Encarnación and the extinction of the writer, Beltrán. Through all of this, he continues to treat individuals as passing, disconnected limbs or faces in a crowd, not as unique souls. When Mario confronts his brother about "pisoteando a los demás," he outlines the exchange of roles taking place between them. Mario complains of a world full of 'activos dormidos' (58) like Vicente who act without regard to consequence. Still, as the dream shows, Mario in his own way is also an *activo dormido* whose internal impulses are beginning to surface. Although Vicente's indifference is well established, he still returns often to visit his home and help his family's finances. Be it from kindness or from years of guilt, he does visit. His interior battle, like Mario's and the Father's, is dynamic in its oscillation from insensibility to caring.

As Mario becomes a violent double, another convergence is forming in the play: that of Vicente and his father. While Vicente and Mario share the same desires and begin to use the same means of fulfillment, the similarities between Vicente and his father are present in a more literal sense. As the old man slips further into a world without differences, his utterances become more ambiguous and rich with double meaning. "Luego te daré una sorpresa, señorito," (57) he tells Vicente ominously in the first act. The coincidence of names between father and son becomes a repeated and intentional play on words ("Yo soy Vicentito" [73]). This textual punning is farther complicated when the Father falls into an almost infantile state and addresses his unnamed wife as "Madre." Moreover, he often expresses mental reenactments of the train scene verbally, taking the role of his son: "¡Tengo que volver con mis padres!" (32). The confusion caused by this fragmented double identity, like the other examples of convergence, all point in the same direction. The tension of these similarities insures a violent outcome; there are too many doubles and too few differences. The only question remaining is: who will pull Vicente into the abyss?

Judging from the violent nature of the Father's illness and Mario's characteristic inactivity, the former is the likely candidate. His scene in the train station and later destruction of the television set are clearly projections of anger against his son. Girard writes that: "The more men strive to curb their violent impulses, the more these impulses seem to prosper. The very weapons used to combat violence are turned against their users" (31). In the end, this is exactly the case. As Kronik suggests, the Father's life-giving scissors become the means of execution (393-4). Up until this point, Mario has acted as a cohort to this crime by slowly, at times unknowingly, feeding the fire of violence in his father and bringing Vicente closer to judgment. But when his brother is at the edge of the cliff, Mario falls back into his characteristic passivity, leaving his father to take the final action.

The Father tries, as Kronik points out, to usurp history, but he cannot (393). He is too caught up in the web of violence to escape mimesis. The murder of his son is a mirror image of Vicente's original violence against his own family. In the context of this reading, the only way out of a violent crisis is through society's sanctioned and non-corrupt justice system or the scapegoat mechanism, not through eye-for-an-eye style revenge. In Girardian terms, this infanticide only feeds the fire of reciprocal violence. Although Vicente might have some qualities of a scapegoat, he does not fit the criteria of the substitute victim. Firstly, his absence will not cleanse the family or society entirely from violence. Secondly, the violence that his actions provoked was mimetic and was not carried out upon an other. Thirdly, one must not forget that Encarna's child was not fathered by Mario, but by Vicente, so the potential of perpetuation or possibly even revenge is still present. Although the Father is a God-like figure, this murder is not the ethical goal of the drama. It does not reflect the lesson of "la pregunta tremenda," but rather contradicts it by breaking down the special individual differences that lend a sacred quality to the father and son relationship. In a sense, Vicente's death can be seen as a reflection of the society in which he lived. The War had ended, but the violence continued. *El tragaluz* portrays the end of a violent crisis by means of the same "impure" violence that began it.

The denouement of *El tragaluz* relies on a mixture of convention and innovation. Reading the play-within-a-play as a cycle of violence leads us to a fairly pessimistic conclusion uncharacteristic of Buero's tragedies. The playwright uses the innovative technique of the *Investigadores* to transcend Mario and Encarnación's difficult circumstances. The researchers from the future pull the lesson out of the context of the twentieth century and have the last word, confirming that peace and order are possible through a historical conscience. They look back upon Vicente, Mario and their Father and say "Hoy ya no caemos en aquellos errores" (105). This transcendence is essential to the impact of the play; it is the final goal of the "immersion" techniques and identification with the characters. Él and Ella speak directly to the spectators allowing what Casa calls "the symbolic process of purification that the theater with its ritual power can impose upon its audience" (292).

The function of the inner action of *El tragaluz* is cathartic, but cannot stand without the transcendent role of the Investigators. The story of the family is one of violence from beginning to end; a violence that overlooks necessary differences and eliminates "la importancia infinita del caso singular" (14): the infinite importance of individual differences, the crux of Buero's experiment.

Notes

1. For a thorough explanation of this point see Frank P. Casa.

2. Girard addresses the theories of Levi-Strauss in chapter nine and Freud in chapters three, seven and eight of *Violence and the Sacred*.

3. Kronik writes: "By the same token, to the extent that Vicente's fate is the materialization of Mario's nightmare of having dragged a man into an abyss, Mario is active and not without guilt, victimizer at the same time as victim" (383).

Works Cited

Buero Vallejo, Antonio. *El tragaluz. El sueño de la razón.* Madrid: Espasa Calpe, 1989.

Casa, Frank P., "The Problem of National Reconciliation in Buero Vallejo's *El tragaluz.*" *RHM* 35 (1969): 285-94.

Girard, René. Trans. Patrick Gregory. *Violence and the Sacred.* Baltimore: Johns Hopkins UP, 1972.

Kronik, John W., "*El tragaluz* and Man's Existence in History." *HR* 41 (1973): 371-96.

F. Komla Aggor (essay date spring 1994)

SOURCE: Aggor, F. Komla. "Derealizing the Present: Evasion and Madness in *El tragaluz.*" *Revista Canadiense de Estudios Hispánicos* XVIII, no. 2 (spring 1994): 141-50.

[*In the following essay, Aggor provides a psychoanalytic interpretation of* El tragaluz.]

Michel Foucault, in *Maladie mentale et psychologie,* makes an important contribution to the understanding of mental illness by illuminating some inner dynamics which were previously overlooked. According to Foucault, mental illness is much more than regression (when the patient attempts to relive the past through fantasies) because, if this were the case, madness would be an innate tendency in each of us by the very movement of our evolution.[1] "Regression is not a natural falling back into the past; it is an intentional flight from the present. A recourse rather than a return" (Foucault 33). He points out that the past is invoked only as a substitute for the present situation, and that process is realized only to the extent that it involves what he calls "a derealization of the present" (33). Derealizing the present in illness means reliving the past, and that implies a need for the patient to defend himself or herself against the present (Foucault 35). It is a defense mechanism.

Josef Breuer and Sigmund Freud, in their studies on hysteria, show that the psychical trauma that produces hysterical phenomena is not the kind whereby the trauma "merely acts like an 'agent provocateur' in releasing the symptom, which thereafter leads an independent existence" (7). On the contrary, the memory of the shock acts like "a foreign body which long after its entry must continue to be regarded as an agent that is still at work" (7). Breuer and Freud indicate that the origin of the

pathological condition needs to be brought into consciousness if the patient is to be cured. Thus, they propose catharsis as psychotherapy for hysteria. They claim that the abnormality usually stays because it has been denied "normal wearing-away processes" by means of vital reactions related to the precipitating cause: reactions such as tears, speaking (confession, utterances), revenge, etc. They caution that if the reaction is suppressed, the emotion remains attached to the memory and the condition persists (8).

The complex problems raised by El Padre's madness in *El tragaluz* (1967). Antonio Buero Vallejo's famous play, can be better understood in light of these psychoanalytic ideas. In this article, I focus on the causal relationship between the lack of an effective reaction on the part of El Padre to his trauma and the collective evasion of the facts surrounding that trauma, on the one hand, and, on the other, his madness. I will also argue that El Padre's lunatic regression is an attempt to "derealize" the present as a cathartic antidote to his disorder.[2]

One question that needs to be addressed is whether El Padre's madness is pathological, that is, if he is truly mad, in the modern, clinical connotation of the term. As one evaluates the lunacy of mad characters, it becomes essential to determine what kind of abnormality they suffer, since madness is often employed in literature for different purposes. El Padre is a man who cannot recognize his own sons, thinks his wife is his mother, tries to eat through his eyes instead of through his mouth and therefore has to be fed by his wife, likes to go out through the wardrobe instead of through the doorway, asks a priest if the parishioner in his company is his spouse, etc. Kenneth Brown contends that everything the father says in *El tragaluz* is actually reasonable and meaningful (255), but it is not far-fetched to realize that what the madman says at times is wrapped in complete absurdity. The instances of incoherence and delusions cited above are indications of an ailment bordering on severe psychosis. It is important to understand this fact because only then can we fully appreciate El Padre's persistent struggle to free himself from mental captivity.[3]

Mario, who best seems to identify the family's problems, explains to Encarna the incident leading to his father's lunacy, by concluding this way.

> La nena murió unos días después. De hambre . . . Nunca más habló él de aquello. Nunca. Prefirió enloquecer.
>
> (101)[4]

As Newman says, the reason for El Padre's silence is that he probably wants to avoid an outburst of violence on his part against Vicente (71). The crucial point Mario makes is that El Padre's condition is directly connected with the lack of an effective means of "energetic reaction" on his part. As Foucault reminds us, even language—a verbal complaint of some sort—is a powerful tool under such circumstances in wearing away the shock (8). By internalizing the stress caused by the loss and by refusing to discuss the blow, to ventilate his pain, El Padre paves the way for his own tragedy.[5]

He is not alone, however, in promoting the silence. There is a collective effort that sustains his derangement by evading direct confrontation with the fact of its origin. Let us begin with Vicente. He intentionally misrepresents the facts by maintaining, without any clear foundation, that his father's delusions are a result of arteriosclerosis, an effect of old age; but the audience cannot accept his reasoning. For if Vicente truly believed that his father's problem is old age, we would consider Vicente to be foolish, yet his cleverness at outwitting others and the way he readily takes advantage of circumstances show that he is astute. When his mother asks him why he remembers the incident, he emphatically replies with a rhetorical question: "Pero ¿cómo iba yo a olvidar aquello?" (72). The answer suggests that he has been feigning ignorance of any possible link between the train incident and his father's constant reference to the train. He has simply chosen to dodge the problem and pretend that his father's aberration is entertaining, until he finally gets caught. If Vicente can be forgiven for deliberately running away with the family's provisions, he deserves no pardon for lying about it.

The mother's role in contributing to El Padre's state is even more significant. Not only does she endorse Vicente's misinformation about the death of Elvirita, she also supports his claim that El Padre's troubles are a mark of old age: "Son cosas de la vejez, Mario . . ." (94), she insists. And yet at the same time, she bans from the household any mention of Elvirita and of the word "tren." When Vicente finally comes to talk about the episode with Mario, she fiercely intervenes, forbidding any reference to it:

> La Madre.—¡No, hijos!
>
> Vicente.—¿Por qué no?
>
> La Madre.—Hay que *olvidar aquello.*
>
> (99; my emphasis)

To Mario's question as to whether she thinks much of Elvirita, she whispers: "Todos los días" (52). Like the madman, she prefers silence over the whole case: "Y tú [Mario] no le hables a tu padre de ningún tren. No hay que complicar las cosas . . . ¡y hay que vivir!" (54), she whispers. For the mother, silence is an expedient remedy for the family's worries because it offers the only guarantee, even if temporary, against a revival of distressing memories. Silence, however, is an uncertain flight from the past, since that past continues to invade the present and to make life increasingly complicated and unbearable for everyone in the household. As Felman recalls, "Our past is not what is past. It is something that never stops coming to pass, and to pass us by; it is what never ceases to be repeated as a vanished Present" (69).

Mario is the only one who attempts to pursue the truth about the event. But even he is prepared to do so only in the absence of his father. This is why when El Padre appears during the dispute and asks, "¿Pasa algo en la sala de espera?," he lies to him: "Nada, padre. Todos duermen tranquilos" (100). As for Encarna, all she says on hearing the story told her by Mario is: "Hay que *olvidar,* Mario" (45; my emphasis).

All these references to evasion and denials go directly against the commentaries of the narrators: "Durante siglos tuvimos que olvidar, para que el pasado no nos paralizase; ahora debemos recordar incesantemente, para que el pasado no nos envenene" (88). Since the entire family has chosen the path of pretext and has failed to probe the source of its discontent for years, it is able to survive, but in a hopeless and miserable way. The family must now consciously recollect its painful history in order to ensure peace. In Buero Vallejo's quest for a rediscovery of the past, what becomes imperative is a search for the truth, a turn-around from evasion and fear, no matter how bitter the reality may be: ". . . siempre es mejor saber, aunque sea doloroso" (87). So indispensable and so pertinent has the message been to post-war Spain that it was echoed in a statement made in 1968 by Ildefonso-Manuel Gil:

> Hacer imposible que algo semejante vuelva a repetirse es la mejor justificación de nuestras vidas y eso no se logra desde el olvido, sino desde el recuerdo obsesionante. Hay que volver una y otra vez sobre el examen de aquellos hechos, detalle sobre detalle y hasta lo más hondo, porque es necesario dar a conocer aquello cuya repetición es necesario evitar.
>
> (108)

The latent paradox in this statement—to expose the fearful—is central to Buero Vallejo's purpose in creating the dementia of El Padre. It constitutes the cathartic cure that Breuer and Freud propose as a formula for correcting mental pathology, although obviously El Padre's case is acute. El Padre's attachment to the past through the skylight is a painful return to a horrible episode; and yet it is a vital means by which he is able to "derealize" a present of psychological agony. Unfortunately, the failure of those around him to open a dialogue with him frustrates the process of regression and prompts him to enter into monologue with himself. Consequently, his apparently lunatic question, "¿Quién es ése?," signifies a yearning for a historical bond with the past, a past full of mystery, lies and catastrophe that need to be revealed:

> Él.—Hemos aprendido de niños la causa: las mentiras y catástrofes de los siglos precedentes la impusieron como una pregunta ineludible.
>
> (87)

There are several ways in which El Padre concretely dere-alizes the present. The principal one is the special relation-ship he maintains with the *tragaluz,* the skylight. He is completely obsessed with it because, through it, he perceives the presence of the train, symbol of the journey back to Elvirita. As the narrators tell us, the train is a state of mind; its sound serves to evoke events of a traumatic past, to open up old wounds: "Lo utilizamos para expresar escondidas inquietudes que, a nuestro juicio, debían destac-arse. Oiréis, pues, un tren; o sea un pensamiento" (15). It is clear, then, that the madman's fascination with the skylight is, in part, a burning desire to uncover hidden grievances that he was unable to communicate while sane.

The "escondidas inquietudes" may be interpreted in two ways. Firstly, they refer to the gamut of social and ontological problems being faced by a society. When Vice-nte at last agrees to observe the skylight with Mario, this is what they discover: a group of run-away children smok-ing cigarettes; a man hurrying to the pharmacy, apparently in response to an emergency situation; an old house-maid with varicose veins carrying left-overs; a dejected, common-looking lady carrying a suitcase made of cardboard boxes; and finally, Beltrán. The appearance of Beltrán in particular is of high dramatic consequence, since in the play he is presented as an absent character. He does not appear on stage, but thanks to the "tragaluz" one is reminded of the need to broadcast the injustice perpetrated against him.[6] The very basement experience is created by the dramatist to disclose what Pennington calls a "self-destructive force" (1980-1981: 150) in a society unwilling to admit its existence. Thus, along with seeing the "semisótano" life (darkness) as a self-imposed evasion from the truth (external light), as Martha T. Halsey sug-gests (1972: 285), one can also consider it as a manifesta-tion of the hypocrisy of a society that spurns and shuts out its problems—such as madness—and buries them from public awareness.

Secondly, by "escondidas inquietudes" the playwright points specifically to El Padre's personal problems, whose remote causes are rooted in the past. In this case, the madman's fixation on the "tragaluz" symbolizes the criti-cal necessity to expose a concealed, yet indelible, past in order to challenge and rectify a disturbing present. In other words, El Padre's obsession represents Buero Vallejo's resolve to draw attention to a dark history that needs to be re-examined in light of the present. That resolve, accord-ing to Luis Iglesias Feijoo, restores to the theatre a tragic tone that cost Buero Vallejo "no pocas acusaciones de pe-simismo y amargura" (3). But Iglesias Feijoo also shows that the tragic tone reflects Buero Vallejo's desire to distance himself from the theatre of evasion amidst "un panorama escénico como el español de posguerra, en el que se rehuía cualquier aspecto conflictivo en beneficio de una imagen sin problemas de la realidad" (3). What distinguishes Buero Vallejo is precisely this competence to revive a tragedy evaded by others as an instrument to

question and judge history and thereby awaken conscious-ness to a precarious social reality.

From another angle, El Padre carries out the process of rediscovery through Encarna. Ricardo Doménech com-ments on El Padre's failure to distinguish between En-carna and Elvirita: "no es casualidad que El Padre la con-funda con la hija muerta," for "desde su lúcida demencia, reconoce en ella una nueva víctima inocente" (35). One can say that, besides considering Encarna as an addition to Vicente's victims, the mistaken identity is perhaps studiedly created by the playwright to establish a special connection, through the madman's eyes, between the past and the present. El Padre can by means of Encarna—a concrete reality of the present—reach out to his desires for peace and tranquility. Like the imagined sound of the train, Encarna's presence becomes a cathartic medium (because she recalls Elvirita) by means of which El Padre is able to transcend the present in order to attain a level of sanity impossible in that present. Seeing Encarna as an offshoot of Elvirita is further grounded on the prospects a future child could bring by filling the gap left by Elvirita. La Ma-dre seems assured when she stresses this fact before Mario: "Vendrá [Encarna] . . . y traerá alegría a la casa, y niños . . ." (54), though as Kessel Schwartz warns, "the chance for a better world creates a tragic possibility for man [because it is] based on a future hope which may not provide a solution" (818); no one can predict when El padre's situation will be normalized.

There are also two symbolic acts by El Padre that need elucidation. The first is related to his destroying the televi-sion set brought home by Vicente; the second to his murder of Vicente. It is worth noting that El Padre destroys the television set not because he dislikes it in general, but because of the commercials that interfere with the pro-grammes. The act is symbolic, firstly, because it signals a rejection of Vicente's world of corruption and exploitation, a world that is associated with commercialism (the audi-ence knows well that the money used in buying the televi-sion set is, in the first place, not "clean"). Secondly, it prepares the way for the eventual violent murder. The almost instinctive manner in which the destruction is car-ried out is shocking. On close observation, however, El Padre's violent behaviour can be taken as an expression of self-liberation from a perturbed state. In a way, his action is therapeutic. For the first time, he is able to display the inner contradictions that rack his existence. The "private world" of his fantasies is all too familiar (paper dolls, trains, etc.); the other, the "real world" of doom and constraints in which he lives (the world of the supposedly sane), is unveiled.[7]

El Padre kills Vicente because in spite of the latter's confession, he remains adamant about the need to continue his exploitation of others: "Pero ¿quién puede terminar con las canalladas en un mundo canalla?" he asks. And his father surprisingly responds: "Yo" (103). To prove his determination, Vicente is resolved to leave, that is, symbolically to climb onto the train, which, in turn, means maintaining the status quo. As Vicente is eliminated, Mario is allowed to triumph, and in that way, the drama glorifies the principles of Beltrán: honesty, morality, justice.[8] Still, the lunatic murder presents no assurance that the father will regain sanity. It is not clear whether he is aware of the atrocity he has committed by murdering his own son.[9] In fact, by killing Vicente, he complicates the crisis of his family, for another member is dead; the sole bread-winner is gone. But even if the father does not recover, his act is momentous for two reasons: it successfully converts tragedy into hope by enforcing justice;[10] but, even more importantly, it represents an "energetic reaction" on El Padre's part to displace effectively the psychical trauma suppressed for three decades.

Susan Sontag, in *Illness as Metaphor,* shows that madness:

> reflects in the most vehement way the contemporary prestige of irrational or rude (spontaneous) behaviour (acting-out), and of that very passionateness whose repression was once imagined to cause TB, and is now thought to cause cancer.

(36)

What Sontag implies is that irrational acts of madness can be explained as evidence of liberation from repressed conditions. In a sense, El Padre's act of murder, like his crazy destruction of the television, voices his longing to free himself not only from the chains of mental upset but also from the burden of wretched existence in general. There is a common element that unites all of El Padre's specific reactions (his obsession with the skylight, his identifying Encarna with Elvirita, his destroying the television, and his killing Vicente): they all involve the experience of some form of stressful test to confront adversity. But, in Freudian terms, that paradoxical process is imperative for El Padre's recovery.

It can be affirmed that El Padre's madness stems primarily from his futile attempt to block out of his memory anxiety-provoking situations related to a traumatic event, as well as from a deliberate effort, on the part of his family, to evade any debate over that tragedy. As Breuer and Freud have pointed out, the trauma that produces the psychological problem remains effectively attached to the memory of the patient. This means that a blockade of thoughts or a lack of active reaction to the shock leads the patient to suffer an internal conflict between silence (the failure to discuss the blow) and turmoil (the reality of the pain). In effect, El Padre and his family's insincerity about the Elvirita incident shut out any meaningful avenues by which he could react in order to purge himself. As the bitter memory remains vivid, however, El Padre must necessarily regress to relive the trauma as protection against his present predicament. Thus, in Foucaultian terms, the regression by way of the "tragaluz" can be viewed as a

process in which El Padre attempts to "derealize" the present of insanity to attain a room for coherence. As the precipitating sociological factors involved in his condition are taken into account, it becomes apparent that the lunatic, personal process of derealization is also a collective call to the rest of the characters to probe their past. As a result, an investigation into the origins of El Padre's madness becomes a medium for exposing a society's ills. If the sound of the train is what sparks that journey, then it is a harsh but indispensable healing mechanism for El Padre; and for the rest of the players too, because it represents an invitation to open a dialogue on history so that legitimate identity with the present can be attained.

Notes

1. It should be noted that, strictly speaking, Foucault uses the term "regression" meaning a recourse to childhood. However, the idea is perfectly applicable to any such resort to the past to recapture the hidden origins of an illness.

2. In 1973, John W. Kronik made a brief reference to Freud's "repetition-compulsion" theory in explaining El Padre's condition (391-92). Eric Pennington, in his excellent study of 1980, applied psychoanalysis in explaining Vicente's psyche, especially his rationalizations. However, the most extensive study on Buero Vallejo dealing with psychoanalysis is Jean Cross Newman's *Conciencia, culpa y trauma en el teatro de Antonio Buero Vallejo* (1992).

3. It must be stated that there is debate surrounding the criteria used in determining what constitutes mental illness. Thomas S. Szasz, for example, argues that there is no such thing as mental illness. In *The Myth of Mental Illness,* Szasz maintains that the term "mental illness" is a myth aimed at disguising what he calls "the problems of living" (the stresses and strains of existence). For Szasz, only a disease of the brain qualifies to be called "mental illness." However, the American psychologist, David P. Ausubel, challenges Szasz's ideas and reaffirms the psychopathological basis of abnormal behaviour by proving that "personality disorder 'is' disease" (69-74). From a philosophical perspective, Shoshana Felman recalls that it is not easy to determine where "reason stops and madness begins, since both involve the pursuit of some form of reason" (39). According to Felman, what characterizes madness is "a blindness 'blind to itself,' to the point of necessarily entertaining an illusion of reason" (36).

4. All references to the play are to Editorial Espasa-Calpe's 1987 edition of and are given in parentheses in the text.

5. Newman cites other possible causes of El Padre's madness: "la traición moral implícita en la conducta de Vicente" (that is, Vicente's failure to live accord-

ing to the "religión de la rectitud" so strictly upheld by his father); El Padre's "falta total de satisfacciones en la vida profesional, sufrida como consecuencia de contarse entre los vencidos de la guerra"; and El Padre's personal guilt for failing, as a parent, to save Elvirita (69-74).

6. Eugenio Beltrán is a writer whose works used to be published by the press that Vicente works for, until the latter is asked to stop publication of the former's work. Vicente collaborates with the publishing house to sabotage Beltrán, for no plausible reason other than that Beltrán is known to stand firmly for justice and high moral standards amidst a societal proliferation of ethical degeneration.

7. So vital is the sociological element in mental illness for Foucault that he sees schizophrenia, for example, as a product of the existential conditions under which we live:

. . . when man remains alienated from what takes place in his language, when he cannot recognize any human, living signification in the productions of his activity, when economic and social determinations place constraints upon him and he is unable to feel at home in this world, he lives in a culture that makes a pathological form like schizophrenia possible; a stranger in a real world, he is thrown back upon a "private world" that can no longer be assured of objectivity; subjected, however, to the constraints of this real world, he experiences the world in which he is fleeing as his fate. (84)

What Foucault proposes here is simple: it is society that makes the mad. Naturally, he is led to conclude that it is wrong to call the sick person schizophrenic, because schizophrenia is the only outlet open for the victim to escape from constraints in our world. In *El tragaluz,* the social conditions of a brutal war already prepared a high propensity to lunacy, and in the case of El Padre, the train episode, and the resulting evasions, simply exacerbate that state of fragility.

8. Gerard R. Weiss has amply demonstrated that Vicente epitomizes a reality where "man is caught up in his environmental struggle and becomes a victim of the system of which he is part," whereas Mario exemplifies a reality where "man freely chooses to go on fighting honourably, even though a life of suffering and privation may be the result" (155).

9. Kronik seems more certain when he says that the murder "is not, except in legal terms, an act of madness, but an act of justice. The transgressor is punished, a sentence is carried out" (394). Pennington rejects the view that El Padre's act is vengeance for the past (Elvirita's death), proposing instead that the murder is in direct response to Vicente's refusal to keep and take care of the doll entrusted to him by his father (1986: 117-124).

10. One of the cornerstones of the drama of Buero Vallejo is the celebration of hope as the indispensable product of tragedy; that is, tragedy should not be viewed as an end in itself, but should serve as a catharsis for the betterment of humanity. In that respect, his theatre is anti-romantic and hardly existentialist, in the sense that it celebrates life instead of equating it with death. Kessel Schwartz discusses this point in full detail (817-24). For a comprehensive study on the theme of hope in Buero Vallejo's theatre, see Halsey (1968: 57-66).

Works Cited

Ausubel, David P. "Personality Disorder 'is' Disease." *American Psychologist* 16, 1961: 69-74.

Breuer, Josef, and Sigmund Freud. *Studies on Hysteria.* Trans. James Strachey. New York: Basic Books, 1957.

Brown, Kenneth. "The Significance of Insanity in Four Plays by Antonio Buero Vallejo." *Revista de Estudios Hispánicos* 8.2 (1974): 247-60.

Buero Vallejo, Antonio. *El tragaluz. El sueño de la razón.* Madrid: Espasa-Calpe, 1987.

Doménech, Ricardo, ed. *El concierto de San Ovidio. El tragaluz.* By Antonio Buero Vallejo. Tercera edición. Madrid: Castalia, 1987.

Felman, Shoshana. *Writing and Madness.* Trans. Martha Noel Evans and the author. Ithaca: Cornell UP, 1985.

Foucault, Michel. *Mental Illness and Psychology.* Trans. Alan Sheridan. New York: Harper Colophon Books, 1976.

Gil, Ildefonso-Manuel. "Sobre la Generación de 1936." *Symposium* 22.2 (1968): 107-11.

Halsey, Martha T. "Buero Vallejo and the Significance of Hope." *Hispania* 51.1 (1968): 57-66.

———. "*El tragaluz*: A Tragedy of Contemporary Spain." *The Romanic Review* 63.4 (1972): 284-92.

Iglesias Feijoo, Luis. *La trayectoria dramática de Antonio Buero Vallejo.* Santiago de Compostela: Universidad de Santiago de Compostela, 1982.

Kronik, John W. "Buero Vallejo's *El tragaluz* and Man's Existence in History." *Hispanic Review* 41 (1973): 371-96.

Newman, Jean Cross. *Conciencia, culpa y trauma en el teatro de Antonio Buero Vallejo.* Valencia: Albatros Hispanófila Ediciones, 1992.

Pennington, Eric. "The Forgotten *Muñeco* of *El tragaluz*." *Ulula* (Department of Romance Languages, University of Georgia) 2 (1986): 117-24.

———. "Psychology and Symbolism in the Death of Vicente in Buero Vallejo's *El tragaluz*." *Journal of the School of Languages* (Jawaharlal Nehru University, New Delhi) 7.1-2 (1980-1981): 141-56.

Schwartz, Kessel. "Buero Vallejo and the Concept of Tragedy." *Hispania* 51.4 (1968): 817-24.

Sontag, Susan. *Illness as Metaphor.* New York: Farrar, Straus and Giroux, 1978.

Szasz, Thomas S. *The Myth of Mental Illness.* New York: Dell, 1961.

Weiss, Gerard R. "Buero Vallejo's Theory of Tragedy in *El tragaluz." Revista de Estudios Hispánicos* 5 (1971): 147-60.

LA DOBLE HISTORIA DEL DOCTOR VALMY

CRITICAL COMMENTARY

Eric Pennington (essay date summer 1986)

SOURCE: Pennington, Eric. "*La doble historia del Doctor Valmy*: A View from the Feminine." *Symposium* XL, no. 2 (summer 1986): 131-39.

[*In the following essay, Pennington provides an interpretation of* La doble historia del Doctor Valmy *from a feminist perspective, perceiving the play as a scathing indictment of a repressive patriarchy.*]

Antonio Buero Vallejo's *La doble historia del doctor Valmy* (1964) brings to the stage the difficult issue of political torture. Daniel Barnes, the protagonist, works as a member of a security police force in the fictional country Surelia, and as part of his profession regularly utilizes physical torture as a means of obtaining confessions from his prisoners. He does not relish his work, however, and much of the action of the play charts his efforts to win permission to leave his employment. By focusing on the predicament of the torturer instead of the fate of the victim, the playwright prevents the play from slipping into melodrama, and the spectator from losing focus of its central issue: the global issue of torture itself and society's reactions to it.[1] The question, how potent a denunciation of torture the play sounds, can be answered partially by way of a review of the censorship problems the author experienced in having the play approved and performed.[2] Further confirmation of the work's forcefulness can be found in literary critics' evaluations of its caliber, and in the more than six hundred consecutive performances following its Spanish premiere.[3] I suggest that *La doble historia del doctor Valmy* communicates more than an outcry against inhuman political practices, that it is not just the story of Daniel, but perhaps more a tale of his wife Mary. By observing the world in which she must move, as well as focusing on her character and behavior, one may interpret the drama as a resounding indictment of a savage, insensitive patriarchy, as stifling to women as to political prisoners.

The initial point of tension in the play occurs as Daniel discovers he can no longer perform sexually. His condition results from his involvement in emasculating a prisoner, Aníbal Marty. Though the problem resides in Daniel, his wife suffers equally, and naturally shares his desire for a solution. In this respect one could safely designate her a coprotagonist, as Doctor Valmy, in effect, does at one point in his narration.[4] In an engaging article, Frank Dauster argues the existence of more than one protagonist should not be termed unusual and sides with Clifford Leech, who offers, "We have to recognize that the tragic burden can be shared."[5] Not only does Mary share her husband's tragic condition. In the end, her burden is heavier. She must learn the previously hidden truth about the nature of Daniel's profession and decide how to act upon this knowledge. Thus critics perceive in Mary more psychological change and certainly a rounder character than is the case with Daniel. González-Cobos Dávila views her as the best drawn character of the play and the only one "que asume la verdad de una manera total y valiente, al afrontar los sufrimientos y decepciones que ello le pueda acarrear."[6] Iglesias Feijóo adds she "es la única que evoluciona ante la verdad" (p. 332). Doménech regards her as perhaps the most interesting character and, with the possible exception of the narrator, "el personaje a cuyo através el espectador puede—es invitado a—hacer la experiencia del problema trágico planteado."[7]

In light of such comments it seems appropriate to examine the play from a feminine perspective, particularly Mary's. Such an approach reveals a woman dependent upon man for fulfillment, a victim of man's wars and torture machines, a person treated insignificantly, who must endure verbal humiliation and physical threats, while being limited in her creative expression. Mary's final destructive act of killing her husband then can be interpreted not so much as a move of desperation, but as one of liberation and hope. Her deed will be seen to symbolize not only a rebellion against what man (generic) does to man, but what man (specific) inflicts upon women.

If a reader, spectator, or critic approaches the drama sensitive to the feminine point of view, he or she rapidly concludes that the words, attitudes, and actions of the men of the play reflect disregard for the dignity of women. The female characters are treated either negatively and with condescension, or as simply inferior human beings. This attitude surfaces early in the play, as the spectator witnesses Daniel's patronizing remark to his wife, implying that her previous nervous problems were cured by marrying him: "A ti te alivió el matrimonio, pitusa" (p. 36).

Daniel's conclusion is false, however, for Doctor Valmy clarifies that, despite her marriage, "En el fondo seguía siendo una persona nerviosa" (p. 29). We note that Mary's initial mental or emotional problems were not produced by the absence of man, but because war, man's doing, had taken her loved one from her: "Me habían matado a mi novio en la guerra" (p. 57). Rather than the cure, man is, then, the cause of Mary's problems. Only after she has irreversibly distanced herself emotionally from her husband, at the conclusion of the play, does Daniel realize that his wife, "Mi paciente, mi abnegada mujercita" (p. 109), has suffered at his hands rather than received a cure: "No he logrado enjugar aquellas lágrimas; todo ha sido una gran mentira" (p. 99).

Daniel's affection for Mary appears suspect when we scrutinize the curious description she gives of his first attraction to her: "Era muy afortunado con las mujeres; yo creo que se casó conmigo por compasión" (p. 58). One is not surprised to learn, then, that Daniel's concern for his sexual relations with his wife reached the point that he attempted sex with another woman in order to determine if their problem was specifically his: "Y me fui, tan confiado, con otra mujer que también me gustaba" (p. 42). While such regard for his marital relationship is not convincing, this passage subtly reveals the basic inequalities between man and woman. Daniel's account of this episode raises not the slightest rebuke or censure from Doctor Valmy for his patient, neither in his office consultation nor in his narrative commentary. There is nothing objectionable in that Daniel has another woman who "también me gustaba."

Upon analyzing further Mary's relationship with Daniel one can determine that she suffers from the ingrained expectations of a patriarchal society: a woman should marry young and bear children or suffer subsequent humiliation for not having done so. When Lucila, one of Mary's former students and the wife of the imprisoned Marty, visits her teacher, Mary recounts her prior embarrassment at being an old maid while teaching school and marrying late in life: "es que a mí sí me dio vergüenza, Lucila. Ante vosotras . . . me creía una vieja" (p. 57). As she continues she reveals the pain and fear at being left alone, unmarried: "os veía y pensaba: ellas crecerán, se casarán . . . y yo seguiré siendo la señora maestra. Tú nunca sabrás lo que es eso, Trencitas . . ." (p. 57). It is possible to decipher from such words the power of socialization that prompts many women to feel they can only be fulfilled through marriage: "Women have internalized the norms prescribing marriage so completely that the role of wife seems the acceptable one. And since marriage is set up as the *summum bonum* of life for women, they interpret their marriage as happiness, no matter how unhappy the marriage itself may be."[8] Such an attitude or outward appearance is evident in Mary. Her unhappiness is denied, but seeps through her gushing description of her marriage to Daniel: "Tenemos nuestros problemillas, pero también

pasarán" (p. 58). Doctor Valmy notices, as they chat some time after her marriage, that she is uncomfortable talking about her husband: "Él . . . siempre anda tan ocupado" (p. 29). Furthermore, he mentions how her promised invitation to dinner never arrived, raising the implication that their "problemillas" are more than Daniel's impotence, and that the term expresses a fundamental discomfort in the marriage.

To trace some of this marital friction, attention should be drawn to what Mary relinquished when she married: her teaching position, or in Simone de Beauvoir's term, "gainful employment." In *The Second Sex* Beauvoir concludes that, in accepting the economic support of man, a woman remains "dependent, she lives through another, for childbreeding and domestic chores are not transcendent activities or projects but mere continuation of life."[9] To become an authentic human being, woman must work in the wholehearted and total way that men do—for money, Beauvoir suggests. Mary eventually offers to return to teaching so that Daniel may quit his job outright but, in a significant revelation of his sexist stance, her husband refuses to address the issue and changes the subject of their conversation (p. 75). Additional irony in the imbalance between their creative or transcendent activities can be seen when we recall that, while Daniel writes articles for a magazine, likes to read, and admits, "Me gusta la cultura" (p. 43), he expresses incredulity that a book sent to their house could be for his wife (p. 71). Claude Levi-Strauss observes, "The invention of writing meant a new source of power in the development of patriarchy permitting men to exclude women," and this exclusion is represented in this passage of Buero's play.[10]

Mary's dealings with her mother-in-law demonstrate another burden of women in traditional society. Daniel's mother lives with the couple, her jealousy scarcely veiled. A recent study on women in Spain provides an objective report of the factors which come into play in such situations:

> The tension between a mother and her son's wife . . . centers on the son, and the right and responsibility to think out his daily needs and to meet them and extends from there to the organization of the lives of the other household members and of the house itself. A mother and her daughter-in-law are competing for the same niche. In effect, when a son marries, he brings his mother's replacement into the house, another woman who threatens to deprive the mother of part of herself.[11]

This tension and competition for territory can be seen as Mary and the grandmother practically argue or debate over who is to change the diapers of the child (p. 31), prepare the *biberón* (p. 32), and fix the *puchero* (p. 32). Mary is good-natured about their relationship and recognizes the rivalry: "Le gustaría quedarse sola con su hijo y su nieto, ¿eh, abuela? Pero no te guardo rencor" (p. 32). But she speaks these words knowing that the near-deaf woman cannot hear, and she quietly explains to Daniel: "Está ce-losilla" (p. 34). The psychological burden is indeed great and volatile, the conflict between a mother and her son's wife being described by Harding as "one of the most serious confrontations that women experience in their lives," and it is a by-product of marriage (p. 167).

Venturing outside Mary's relationship with Daniel, we see women treated more negatively by Daniel's co-workers. Rather than patronizing or superior attitudes, it becomes a more severe question of verbal abuse, ridicule, and ultimately physical torture. The first clear example appears as Marsán telephones inquiring about Daniel, and Mary, who has answered the phone, must endure the flirtatious remarks she hears (p. 37). Though such a scene might be interpreted as serving no other purpose than demonstrating the torpidity of Daniel's companions, it is pertinent to note that such ridicule and humor have been termed "the psychic counterpart of violence to blacks."[12] Later, when Marsán stops by their house to investigate Daniel's absence, Mary is subjected to an extremely degrading instance of coquetry, dramatizing again the social disadvantage which she suffers because of the traditional restraints imposed on women's language:

Mary (fría): El caso es que yo iba a salir ahora mismo.

Marsán (se levanta): ¡Magnífico! ¿Me permite que la acompañe?

Mary (contrariada): ¿Cree que estaría bien?

Marsán (se acerca): ¿Por qué no? Yo no tengo prejuicios.

Mary: Yo sí.

Marsán: ¿Y . . . son muy fuertes, señora Barnes?

Mary: ¿Qué quiere decir?

Marsán (se acerca algo más): No puede imaginar cuánto me gustaría que no lo fuesen.

Mary (se aparta un paso): No le entiendo.

Marsán: Sí que me entiende. Me entiende desde la primera vez que vine a esta casa.

Mary: Señor Marsán, haga el favor de salir.

Marsán (le tiembla la voz): La vida ofrece pocas cosas agradables, Mary. No me diga que es feliz con su marido: eso nunca es cierto. (Avanza).

Mary (retrocede): ¡Salga!

Marsán: Hay algo en usted . . . irresistible. Algo que no tienen las demás.

Mary: Es intolerable que en mi propia casa se atreva usted a . . .

Marsán (fuerte): ¡Yo soy muy terco, Mary! Usted lo pensará.

Mary: ¡Váyase ahora mismo!

(p. 66)

This scene presents an example of a female holding to the tentative and nonassertive language which Robin Lakoff has shown to be a manifestation of women's role-related difficulties.[13] Only after enduring numerous insulting remarks does Mary mount a firm command, one that she doubtlessly felt like voicing upon first hearing Marsán speak.

Another manifestation of the verbal barriers women in the play encounter appears in Lucila's frustrated endeavors to address the authorities concerning her husband's unlawful torture. She knows it useless to attempt to bring his case before a judge (p. 59). Talking with a lawyer has only left her with advice that she do nothing, lest matters become worse (p. 58). For this reason she is left to address Mary, who would then request that Daniel intercede.

Lucila's visit also underscores the insignificant position of Mary in her relationship with her husband. She is the classic inessential Other, denied knowledge of the specifics of her husband's employment. Though an accurate description of his work would be an unpleasant revelation for most people, in shutting his wife out of the professional aspects of his life Daniel demonstrates again his faithfulness to traditional male behavior. The phrase "trained incapacity to share" reflects such a posture and is produced by the ideal of masculinity that "To gripe about the job carries the connotation of weakness."[14] Thus Daniel remains silent for fear of his wife's incomprehension and disapproval as well as for ingrained fear of appearing unmasculine. As Kamarovsky puts it, "A strong man bears his troubles in silence and does not dump his load on the family" (p. 189).

Nowhere does one observe a total disdain for women symbolized more explicitly than in the rape of Lucila. In an attempt to force Marty to confess, a few days before his castration his wife is brought before him, and he must watch the physical abuse she suffers. As ugly a vision as the act conjures, it merits special attention. For it discloses that, in the eyes of these men, women serve the same function as tools or objects used to achieve desired results. The scene reflects what Susan Brownmiller terms "a male ideology of rape": "It is nothing more or less than a conscious process of intimidation by which all men keep all women in a state of fear."[15] Such fear is felt by Mary as she listens, at first in disbelief, to her former student's account of the horrors inflicted where Daniel works. She lives in relative ignorance and bliss until Lucila shatters her world with her accusations. Like Campbell's hero experiencing the unexpected call to adventure, she is roused from a state of psychic inactivity and thrust upon a journey for the truth of Lucila's words. Her quest toward enlightenment impresses because of the high stakes involved: the only happiness she knows; her traditional roles as wife, mother, and female.

As she discovers the particulars of Daniel's daily actions and realizes his genuine lack of resolve in dissociating himself from his work, Mary begins to experience increasing repugnance and fear of the world such men have created. She suffers nightmares wherein she sees Daniel trying to mutilate their son (pp. 91-93); regrets bringing a child into the world (p. 94); wholly refuses the idea of additional children (p. 90); wishes she had never met her husband (p. 110); and feels "una infinita desgana, una gran indiferencia" (p. 94) toward everything except her son, "¡Pobre hijo mío!" (p. 94). Prompted by this concern for her son, coupled with the disgust she feels for such a perverted world, Mary takes Daniel's pistol and uses his own weapon against him. By usurping the act of giving death, historically reserved for men, she symbolizes her rejection of the deviant patriarchy and signals how far she has evolved from her initial passive stance.[16] So Mary's action acquires political symbolism. Since the torture described in the play can be interpreted readily as a reference to the Franco regime (hence the censorship the work encountered), Mary's change of attitude and final action can also symbolize total rejection of the existing political situation. Janet Pérez has observed and discussed such techniques of literary dissent in Franco's post-war Spain, and notes that the "slaughter of sacred cows" is a common form of attack. Authors would sometimes consciously undertake to express a subtle rejection of "myths and stereotypes promulgated by the regime via the creation of counter-myths."[17] In a passage which corresponds to what Buero accomplishes in *La doble historia del doctor Valmy* she explains:

> The Madonna/mother stereotype—a chaste, long-suffering woman, self-sacrificing, faithful to husband, and god and country, a model of virtue and abnegation, domesticity and altruism—a character inhuman and angelical, was rejected by liberal writers as being on the one hand limited and unrealistic and on the other, an embodiment of Falangist ideology. Thus women characters who did not conform to the stereotype constitute a rejection, symbolic or real, of traditional programs and values.
>
> (p. 224)

As her name indicates, Mary clearly stands as a Madonna archetype. But much of the play's power derives from her conscious rejection of this role as she lashes out against a world become vicious, inhuman to *all* weaker human beings.

Such an act of rebellion is inherently positive and not lessened by the fact that Mary is insane as the play concludes. It would seem that Buero has deliberately played on the sanity/insanity concept he develops more perfectly in *El tragaluz*.[18] Mary had emotional problems before she met Daniel and the latter jokes throughout the play of curing her. Yet Daniel is the one who is sick, and Doctor Valmy and Daniel himself voice this diagnosis (pp. 84, 112). Mary's movement towards "insanity" parallels her distancing from Daniel and his infirm environment,

and reminds one of *el padre* retreating from Vicente's world of "devorar o ser devorado." In the end, Mary's act of shooting Daniel makes as much sense as the Father's stabbing of Vicente.

A confluence of images occurs as the play closes to support the thesis that the conclusion is more positive than pessimistic. As the *abuela* recites the fable to Daniel's son which opened the series of flashbacks, Brahms's *Lullaby* is also heard again in the background. It is noteworthy that the fable and lullaby, as well as nursery rhymes and folktales, are regarded as feminine genres of creative expression. Commenting on the factors which lead to the "silences" which prevent creative expression, Tillie Olsen remarks, "Very close to this last grouping are the silences where the lives never came to writing. Among these the mute inglorious Miltons: those whose waking hours are all struggle for existence; the barely educated; the illiterate; woman. Their silence the silence of centuries as to how life was, is, for most humanity. Traces of their making, of course, in folk song, lullaby, tales. . . ."[19] Coincidentally, Brahms's *Lullaby* was taken from a folk tune, embellished by the composer, and dedicated to celebrate the birth of a female friend's son.[20] Finally, the grandmother's second rendition of the fable does not faithfully duplicate the version recited by her earlier. She omits one line which referred to Daniel: "Y todas las nenas se volverán locas por él" (p. 30). As *La doble historia del doctor Valmy* graphically depicts, this passage also referred literally and tragically to Mary. The grandmother's failure to repeat the line may represent her comprehension of the tragedy she has seen unfold, or symbolize a resolution. The omission perhaps represents the hope that Danielito will not repeat the errors of his father in dealing with his fellow man . . . and woman.

Notes

1. Juan Mollá, "Doce años después," *El Ciervo*, 227 (February 1976), 31.

2. One of the best summaries of such censorship issues is to be found in Luis Iglesias Feijóo, *La trayectoria dramática de Antonio Buero Vallejo* (Universidad de Santiago de Compostela, 1982), pp. 319-20. For a comment on the specific issues raised by censors see Patricia W. O'Connor, "Censorship in the Contemporary Spanish Theater and Antonio Buero Vallejo," *Hisp,* 52 (1969), 282-88, particularly p. 286.

3. William Giuliano states flatly, "*La doble historia del doctor Valmy* es uno de los mejores dramas de Buero." See his *Buero Vallejo, Sastre y el teatro de su tiempo* (New York: Las Américas, 1971), p. 140. Iglesias Feijóo reports that "la acogida de la crítica fue esta vez unánimemente favorable, así como la del público (se sobrepasaron las 600 representaciones), lo que prueba el permanente interés de la obra" (p. 320).

4. Throughout this study the following edition of the play is cited: Antonio Buero Vallejo, *La doble historia del doctor Valmy. Relato escénico en dos partes,* edición, prólogo y notas por Alfonso M. Gil (Chicago: Rand McNally, The Center for Curriculum Development, 1970). Doctor Valmy's allusion to Mary as protagonist occurs as he reflects on Daniel's case: "Ella vino días después a contarme otras cosas. El caso es más frecuente de lo que el profano cree: un enfermo nos confía algo y luego vemos en nuestra consulta al otro protagonista de la obra" (p. 84).

5. From Clifford Leech, *Tragedy* (London: Methuen, 1964), pp. 45-46, quoted in Frank Dauster, "Toward a Definition of Tragedy," *Revista Canadiense de Estudios Hispánicos,* 7, 1 (October 1982), 9.

6. Carmen González-Cobos Dávila, *Antonio Buero Vallejo. El hombre y su obra* (Ediciones Universidad de Salamanca, 1979), p. 162.

7. Ricardo Doménech, *El teatro de Buero Vallejo. Una meditación española* (Madrid: Gredos, la Reimpresión, 1979), p. 237.

8. Jessie Bernard, "The Wife's Marriage," in Mary Evans, ed., *The Woman Question. Readings on the Subordination of Women* (Oxford: Fontana, 1982), pp. 115-16.

9. Jean Leighton, *Simone de Beauvoir on Women* (Cranbury, NJ: Associated University Presses, 1975), p. 35.

10. This quotation is from Marielouise Janssen-Jurreit who paraphrases Levi-Strauss in her *Sexism: The Male Monopoly on History and Thought,* trans. Verne Moberg (New York: Ferrar Straus Giroux, 1982), p. 284.

11. Susan Harding, "Women and Words in a Spanish Village," in Dorothy G. McGuigan, ed., *New Research on Women and Sex Roles* (Ann Arbor, MI.: The University of Michigan Center for Continuing Education of Women, 1976), p. 166.

12. See Wendy Martyna, "Beyond the 'He/Man' Approach: The Case for Nonsexist Language," in Evans, *The Woman Question,* p. 422, where she quotes Pauli Murray, testimony, United States Congress, House, Special Committee on Education and Welfare, *Discrimination against Women,* 91st Congress, Second Session, 1970, on section 805 of HR 16098.

13. Robin Lakoff, *Language and Woman's Place* (New York: Harper and Row, 1975), particularly p. 61.

14. Mirra Komarovsky, "The Quality of Domestic Life," in Evans, *The Woman Question,* p. 189.

15. Susan Brownmiller, *Against Our Will: Men, Women and Rape* (New York: Simon and Schuster, 1975), p. 14.

16. Concerning the role-related significance of killing, Simone de Beauvoir suggests "superiority has been accorded in humanity not to the sex that brings forth but to that which kills," see her *The Second Sex,* trans., H. M. Parshley (New York: Wiley, 1968), p. 64.

17. Janet Pérez, "Techniques in the Rhetoric of Literary Dissent," in Harry L. Kirby, Jr., ed., *Selected Proceedings of the Third Louisiana Conference on Hispanic Languages and Literatures 1982* (Baton Rouge: Louisiana State University, 1984), p. 224.

18. For a broader discussion on Buero's use of insanity see Kenneth Brown, "The Significance of Insanity in Four Plays by Antonio Buero Vallejo," *Revista de Estudios Hispánicos,* 7 (1974), 247-60.

19. Tillie Olsen, "Silences: When Writer's Don't Write," in Susan Koppelman Cornillon, ed., *Images of Women in Fiction: Feminist Perspectives* (Bowling Green, Ohio: Bowling Green State University Popular Press, 1972), p. 100 (first published in 1965).

20. Peter Latham, *Brahms* (London: Dent [1948], 1951), pp. 34-35.

EL SUEÑO DE LA RAZÓN (THE SLEEP OF REASON)

CRITICAL COMMENTARY

David K. Herzberger (essay date summer 1985)

SOURCE: Herzberger, David K. "The Painterly Vision of Buero Vallejo's *El sueño de la razón.*" *Symposium* XXXIX, no. 2 (summer 1985): 93-103.

[*In the following essay, Herzberger maintains that the artistic metaphor in* El sueño de la razón *is the key to fully understanding the structural and thematic unity of the play.*]

Francisco de Goya first appears in *El sueño de la razón* in the second scene of Act One, a scene repeated early in Act Two: the artist at work, painting. It is not a fortuitous configuration of events that advances this view of the protagonist near the beginning of each act. For painting (and the nature of art) inheres in the basic structure of *Sueño* and provides the frame within which it unfolds. As a number of critics have pointed out, most of *Sueño* develops with Goya as the center of consciousness.[1] His deafness functions as one of the principal dramatic determinants of the play, and when Goya is present on stage, the audience is permitted to hear only what he hears and to perceive reality as he perceives it. The use of gestures and mime thus becomes crucial to communication: the characters are compelled to converse with Goya in a way that focuses always on his perspective of things. However, it is not merely his inability to hear that shapes Goya's perceptions (and therefore our own) but also his view of art and artistic creation. Above all in *Sueño,* Goya is portrayed as a painter. Even as a political dissident, or in his moments of personal anguish with Leocadia, Goya's essential being is defined always within the painterly metaphor. Hence it is to this metaphor that we must attend in order to grasp fully the underlying structural and thematic unity of the play.[2]

In addition to the systematic representation of Goya-as-artist, the commingling of several correlative elements in *Sueño* enhances the centrality of the artistic metaphor. For example, Goya's *pinturas negras* are projected on the stage throughout the play, reminding us always of his imaginative power to create the world as he sees it. In addition, titles of several of the *Caprichos* and *Desastres de la guerra* inform the dialogue of the violent attack on Goya's home, thus combining art and life in the structuring of plot. Other principal characters (Arrieta, Duaso, Leocadia) play an equally important part in expanding the artistic metaphor. They interpret Goya's paintings in several dialogues during the course of the play, and their commentary casts art as an undisguised device for shaping the reality made available to the audience. Clearly, Buero has sought to integrate the artistic metaphor into the very fabric of his work, and, as it develops, the paintings function less as props outside the central drama than as essential *dramatis personae.* Unlike in a picture book, where illustrations often serve an augmentative function, safely paralleling what has been conveyed in language, Buero's incorporation of painting into *Sueño* creates an iconicity that defines the nature of the entire aesthetic enterprise. It not only reveals the deep meaning of the play, but also structures and mediates its constituent elements.

To a greater or lesser degree, all art is about itself and its own creation. Goya himself admits that this principle impels his painting by offering an interpretive inroad to his artistic imagination: "El sueño de la razón produce monstruos." That is to say, Goya's etching of his creative process turns his art back on itself as its own referent. His art in effect becomes his imagination incarnate. The self-consciousness of the undertaking thus creates a system of meaning in which the work's own artistry serves as both point of departure and destination.[3] Since Buero co-opts the title of Goya's *capricho,* the artistic substance of the drama is immediately laid bare. As icons, the paintings projected on the screen during the drama contain their own referent. Their very nature intimates a desire in the artist to be free of the world, to be suspended in the rarefied reality of the artistic condition. Hence the peculiarly Goyesque vision is firmly established from the outset of the play and the forms and strategies of artistic self-sufficiency move to the fore. Goya in fact suggests the self-reflexive aspect of his art in *Sueño* when he makes the verb "to paint" intransitive: "No es fácil pintar, pero yo pintaré" (p. 130); "Tengo que pintar aquí" (p. 139).[4] Goya does not proclaim the need to paint *something,* but rather the urgency *to paint.* Artistic composition thus becomes for Goya an ekphrastic enterprise whose meaning lies in creation as an expression of the human will and in the sovereignty of the imagination.

The implied autonomy of Goya's work is also linked to one of the principal sub-themes of the play: isolation and solitude. Goya lives in both physical and spiritual isolation in the *guinta del sordo* and endures an inner exile that segregates him from direct contact with contemporary society.[5] He has rarely left his house in two years and is mindful that he exists "en el desierto" (p. 165). Furthermore, he affirms that he spends his days "sin que se acuerden de mí y pintando lo que me dé la gana" (p. 130). This idea is reiterated throughout the play and underscores his impotence in the face of political challenges from the king. More importantly, however, the stark portrayal of Goya's seclusion facilitates the elaboration of an artistic norm that is at once affirmed and transgressed by the whole of the play. That is to say, since Goya's solitude subjugates all other aspects of his existence, it inspires him to unleash the mystery and terror of pure imagination. Cut off from the outer world, his art comes to embody the inner patterns of the mind rather than convey the observable flow of social reality. The dominion of the *pinturas negras* hints at this process, and at first glance they appear to preclude the desired continuity between political and artistic commitment.

Yet isolation does not suggest insulation for Goya, just as the autonomy of his imagination never engenders art that is singularly self-reflexive. At the core of Buero's vision of Goya (and at the center of Buero's writing as a whole) lies refusal to admit the romantic disenchantment that art has no obvious function. Buero denies that art's unique position as aesthetic object bestows upon it what Terry Eagleton terms "the status of a solitary fetish."[6] Despite the systematic affirmation of Goya's isolation in *Sueño,* and the concurrent authority invested in the autonomous imagination, there is nonetheless a generative energy in the play that vivifies what Charles Morris called the "double semantic thrust" of art, and what Paul Ricœur more recently has termed "split referentiality."[7]

In essence, both Morris and Ricœur recognize that art is not one thing and life another, but rather that the two are conjoined on a single plane of being. In order to grasp the full measure of this interfusion, it is necessary to account for the creative imagination, the artifact produced, and the interpretive function of the reader (viewer). Buero seems to be supremely aware of the conjunctive nature of this process, for its constituent elements are threaded throughout his play, affording thematic and structural unity within the artistic frame. I have already suggested that, at least in part, Goya turns the artistic process back on itself, and that *Sueño* lays bare this process by portraying the painter isolated from society and his art nourished by pure imagination. Yet art for Goya (Buero) is also able to represent the world about him, and is projected into that world through a type of referential reciprocity derived less from mimesis than from avoidance of the prevailing artistic norms of correspondence. If we view mimetic art not as a mirror of reality but as a correspondence to rules, conventions, and forms structuring reality within art, it becomes evident how Goya turns convention on its head. Despite his isolation, social reality indeed imposes itself on his art. But the nature of this imposition in *Sueño* grows from a bi-modal sequential process. On the one hand, we witness the manner in which his paintings depart from current artistic canons, while on the other we observe how the characters (including Goya) become the principal interpreters of the artist's work.

Goya's aesthetic deviation assumes thematic significance from the outset of the play. Early in Act One Calomarde (the king's adivsor) dismisses the worth of Goya as court painter: "¡No es el gran pintor que dicen, señor! Dibujo incorrecto, colores agrios . . . Retratos reales sin nobleza ni belleza" (p. 17). For Calomarde, Goya transgresses the norms of mimetic tradition and therefore is to be scorned and ridiculed. In contrast, the painter Vicente López adheres to established conventions and merits recognition and praise: "Un gran pintor es Vicente López. . . . [él] es también un pintor virtuoso. Sus retratos dan justa idea de los altos méritos de sus modelos. Cuando pasen los siglos, Vuestra Majestad verá, desde el cielo, seguir brillando la fama de López y olvidados los chafarrinones de ese fatuo" (p. 118). Although Calomarde's judgment is infused with an irony he fails to perceive, the aesthetic posture he assumes locates Goya on the margins of mimesis and, therefore, on the fringe of artistic value.

Calomarde's interpretation of Goya's work shapes the action of *Sueño* in a practical sense, since his influence over the king ensures Goya's continued exclusion from the court. More importantly, however, it establishes from the outset of the play the central role afforded interpretation. The artistic position enunciated by the characters, as well as their evaluation of Goya himself, in large part turns upon their view of the *pinturas negras*. Furthermore, Goya's character is also developed most fully through recurrent reflection on his own work and his desire for exegetic completeness. This interpretive enthusiasm enables the painterly metaphor to be cultivated not parenthetical to the action as a contrived literary device, but rather as an essential component of the work's dramatic center.

The judgment of Goya's aesthetics by the other characters of the play in large part duplicates Calomarde's stance. Each of the characters speaks to the nature of Goya's art and denounces it as an affront to artistic tradition. Arrieta asserts, for example, that "[Goya] ya no es un gran pintor, sino un viejo que emborrona paredes" (p. 191). Father Duaso concludes concerning Goya's paintings that "bellas no son" (p. 156), and explains to the king that Goya "decora las paredes con feas y torpes pinturas" (p. 170). For her part, Leocadia simply judges Goya's works to be "espantosas" (p. 124). In each of these instances, the paintings clash with the expectations of the viewer and are therefore dismissed as inartistic. As a result, the confluence of two essential aspects of *Sueño* is confirmed. The refusal to embrace Goya's painting complements on an artistic plane the isolation he already suffers as a political exile. At the same time, it focuses the attention of the audience on art and aesthetics, thus validating the centrality of the artistic vision that gives shape to the play.

Buero has complicated the problem here, however, by implicitly incorporating the spectator of the play into the interpretive process. The audience—of the play—observes the characters observing the paintings of Goya. While the internal spectators (the characters) reject Goya's new art, Buero clearly demands more sympathy from his external audience. Of course, the larger frame of reference for the play is defined by the assumed artistic knowledge of the external audience. The projection of the black paintings on the backdrop of the stage represents for this audience a kind of artistic symbiosis (of literature and painting) in which it is invited to evaluate the works at the same moment they are discussed on stage by Buero's personages. In this sense, the play stands as a literary adumbration of Goya's aesthetics and their sustained vitality over time. The contemporary spectator is expected to affirm this proposition, even as the internal interpreters scorn Goya's work as "ugly and stupid."

Despite their derogation of Goya's art, the characters nonetheless draw upon it in order to understand and explain the world around them. And it is precisely by means of their frequent discussions of the paintings that Buero affords Goya's art a referential role in the play over and above their presence as artistic objects. For example, in one fashion or another, each of the characters attempts to interpret Goya's mental state through the concretized product of his imagination. Leocadia finds firm evidence of Goya's insanity in the paintings:

> Leocadia: Estas [pinturas] son horribles pinturas de viejo. . . . De viejo demente.
>
> Arrieta: ¿Estás insinuando que ha enloquecido? (*ella cierra los ojos y asiente*).
>
> (p. 124)

Arrieta, on the other hand, encounters both anguish and mental instability in Goya's painting on a personal as well as political level:

Arrieta: Ahora, bajo el gran silencio, el pintor se consume y grita desde el fondo de esta tumba, para que no le oigan.

Duaso: ¿Por miedo?

Arrieta: O por locura. Tal vez las dos cosas.

(p. 156)

For his part, Dr. Duaso, who dismissed the artistic validity of Goya's work, agrees with Arrieta's conclusions and reports to the king that Goya's condition "podría ser indicio de locura senil" (p. 170).

The characters' search for a determinate meaning in Goya's paintings suggests a fundamental question that intrudes upon all exegetic inquiry: is the specific interpretation, the giving of meaning, correct? Is Goya indeed a madman whose delusions and terror are embodied in the stroke of his brush? Is Goya himself identifiable and available to the characters within his art? In short, do the paintings function as a kind of diaphanous synechdoche of the artistic personality that stands behind them? These questions call forth a wide range of complex issues, of course, and raise theoretical problems that lie outside the scope of this study. Nonetheless, within the play Buero suggests an answer that allows for the precarious centering of the author within his work at the same time that he discounts the interpretations offered by the other characters. In order to grasp this intrinsic proposition of the play we must again turn to the role of painting, but in this instance, to Goya's understanding of his own artistic process.

What first distinguishes Goya from the other interpreters of his art is the absence of aesthetic shock at his divergence from artistic norms. Although Goya recognizes that his black paintings controvert tradition, and he even suspects their value as art—"Yo gocé pintando formas bellas, y éstas son larvas. Me bebí todos los colores del mundo y en estos muros las tinieblas se beben el color" (p. 184)—he is less concerned with value than with the process of creation and the relationship between art and life. Through much of the play Goya evinces an almost obsessive need to tell others what his art *means,* thus affirming his desire to express a view of the world by means of the painterly metaphor. Rather than offer a determinate or restrictive meaning, however, Goya seeks to illustrate to his friends (i.e., the interpreters of his art) the nature of his entire creative process.

In the first place, Goya is aware that an undefined and even uncontrolled imagination impels the course of his painting. Hence he is able to construct a new, virtual reality that supplants what is concrete and specific. His discussion with Arrieta of the "hombres voladores," for example, must be seen as evidentiary rather than symbolic: "No estoy soñando con ángeles . . . ¿Imaginar el futuro? ¡Le digo que los he visto! (*Arrieta traza signos y señala a Asmodea.*) Eso sí es imaginación. Un pobre solitario como yo puede soñar que una bella mujer . . . de la raza misteriosa . . . le llevaría a su montaña" (p. 137). What is important in this instance is that imagination not only allows Goya to dream, but to paint. Imagination for Goya is not merely the rearranging of what already exists into newly configured patterns, but rather an enabling energy that permits him to emancipate his art from the limiting confines of reality and the ordering control of aesthetic doctrine.

Buero portrays Goya's imagination as splendidly autonomous, but never remote. Hence despite the sense of pure creation suggested above, the imagined coalesces with the real in Goya's art in a way that precludes the dichotomy between mimesis and self-reflexivity. If on the one hand Goya has imagined the flying men, on the other he has painted the violence of the world "porque la he visto" (p. 162). His portrayal of the priests in *El Santo Oficio* is similarly inspired: "Igual que cuando me denunciaron a la Santa Inquisición. Me miraban como a un bicho con sus ojos de bichos, por haber pintado una hembra en puras carnes . . . Son insectos que se creen personas. Hormigas en torno a la reina gorda. . . . Les parece que el día es hermoso, pero yo veo que está sombrío. . . . Sí, al fondo brilla el sol. Y allá está la montaña, pero ellos no la ven. . . . Una montaña que yo sé que hay" (p. 131). Goya clearly imposes here his vision on the world around him and makes it available to others through the images of his canvas. Art never mirrors life for Goya, but rather appropriates and trans-figures it, with the imagination as catalyst.

In contrast, however, life may imitate art. Buero writes in one of his stage directions, for example, that Goya is transformed into "uno de los penitenciados que él grabó y pintó tantas veces" (p. 202). Goya likewise perceives his circumstances as linked to the painting that stands before him: "Mire *Las Parcas*. Y un gran brujo que ríe entre ellas. Pues alguien se ríe. Es demasiado espantoso para que haya una gran risa. . . . Este muñeco que sostiene una de ellas soy yo" (p. 185). Art works similarly upon the painter's imagination. A woman's voice in one of his reveries declares, "Imita este pobre imbécil de tu pintura" (p. 175); while later, in the long dream sequence that parallels the etching, "El sueño de la razón," Goya again evokes an image from his art that depicts the political terror of the moment: "Los voladores están llamando a todas las puertas de Madrid" (p. 199). Hence Goya invests reality with the creative authority of art, and by doing so reaffirms the eminence of the play's painterly vision.

Two additional examples help define the importance of imagination for Goya, both in the creation of his art and in its intrusion into the world. The first has to do with his recurrent evocation of Mariquita and the central role afforded the painting, *Asmodea*. Mariquita does not appear directly on stage, but rather inhabits Goya's private world of imagination. He "hears" her voice throughout the play and even orders Leocadia to bring her to the house. At the same time, Goya's imaginative powers are placed in the service of art most explicitly in his creation of *Asmodea*. He not only breaks with the concrete reality of everyday existence in the painting, but projects the newly created reality into the future and links it with a reverie of hope (p. 184). The eventual conjoining of Mariquita and *Asmodea* thus speaks to the nature of split referentiality that Buero envisions as the essence of Goya's art. This becomes evident near the end of Act One: Goya speaks with Mariquita as *Asmodea* is projected on the stage. Mariquita first evokes the painting ("¿Cómo no va a oir a su Asmodea?" [p. 165]), then relates it to her own existence: "Quita, quita, quita . . . Mariquita, Mar, Marasmodea, dea, dea, dea, . . . Marasmo" (p. 165). The interfusion of the two occurs entirely within Goya's imagination, of course, and it underscores the way in which all reality in the play is channeled through his artistic vision. Mariquita indeed exists, as does the painting: both are objects *in* reality. However, both are metamorphosed by Goya's imagination and their contextual association, and come to be identified with hope.

A number of critics have suggested that *Sueño* embodies the darkest vision of Buero's theater, and that the hope associated with his earlier tragedies has been replaced by despair.[8] Goya's defeat by the king and exile to France humiliate the artist, and the *pinturas negras* he leaves behind are portrayed as the work of a madman. In contrast, others have encountered a vision of optimism in the play. William Giuliano, for example, points to the friendship of Duaso and Arrieta as an attempt at reconciliation between liberals and conservatives, while John Dowling finds a small note of hope present in *Asmodea*. Martha Halsey underscores the ambivalence at the end of the play, though she cites the final utterance ("Si amanece, nos vamos" [p. 213]) as a clear sign of optimism.[9] It must be remembered, however, that since Goya's artistic vision stands behind much of what occurs in the play, any suggestion of hope is best understood as a product of the painterly image. *Asmodea* indeed offers a reprieve from despair, but its message remains ambiguous amid the cluttered ruins of Fernando's Spain and its link to Mariquita and fear. The authentic hope of *Sueño,* therefore, lies not in the specificity of a single work, but in the broader proposition of painting and imagination.

Goya's imaginative freedom, in marked opposition to his political repression, enables him to challenge the limits of the possible. His dreams and paintings, as well as the social and historical circumstances in which he lives, coalesce to blur the distinctions between art and life. Buero's portrait of the artist as an old man near death, rather than as a young man on the verge of life, in no way mitigates the power of his artistic vision to represent and shape the world as he perceives it. This, then, is the hope that finally obtains in the play—a hope based not on the

symbolic implications of a single painting, or on the potential resolution of political turmoil, but on the whole of painting as an existential and political act that liberates the painter from the imposed patterns of reality. Significantly, Goya never turns from reality to pretend it does not exist, but rather reshapes it with the creative vision of his art. Even when it appears that he may be locked into what James Joyce calls a "black adiaphane" (a material darkness), he is able to project himself into future and different worlds through the constant play of his imagination, which is concretized and affirmed by his painting. This is suggested by the stage directions as Goya leaves his house for the final time: "[Goya] gira y lanza una ojeada circular de despedida a las pinturas. Contemplándolas, una extraña sonrisa le calma el rostro" (p. 213).[10] To be sure, the *pinturas negras* may be inspired by fear or madness, but the tranquility of Goya's demeanor at the end of the play reflects the liberating authority of art and imagination, which enables him to transcend the finitude of life.

The marriage of artistic imagination and reality is most explicitly rendered in *Sueño* during the violent scene in which Goya is beaten and Leocadia raped. Several critics have pointed to the juxtaposition of this segment to Goya's dream, and have shown how the grotesque figures of the latter are mirrored by the equally grotesque *voluntarios realistas* participating in the attack on Goya's home. That is to say, critics have underscored the way in which Goya's dream has prefigured reality. Of greater significance, however, is the role of Goya's art in these segments. As the attack grows in intensity, unseen men and women voice titles from *Desastres de la guerra* and the *Caprichos*. On one level, of course, the titles complement the specific action taking place on the stage: the violence of the attackers and the horror of Goya's response are captured in titles such as "Para eso habéis nacido" (p. 200); "Murió la verdad" (p. 204); "No se puede mirar" (p. 204), etc. More importantly, however, the voices function as narrators who use art to establish a concrete reality and to reveal the way in which Goya, as artist, defines the nature of that reality. Hence it is less Goya's dream that prefigures the attack on his home than the way in which Buero foregrounds the commingling of art and imagination to convey the protagonist's personal and political anguish.

The painterly metaphor also shapes a number of other scenes in *Sueño.* For example, Goya's art is cast into the social world of the play from the very beginning. When Calomarde describes the execution of General Riego to Fernando, the king interrupts him and proposes a visual metaphor: "Se diría un grabado de Goya" (p. 116). The king in effect proclaims Goya's art a more dramatic and concise representation of the particular reality at hand, thus the painterly image supplants language as mediator of his perception. Fernando is also linked to the artistic metaphor through his embroidery. In both scenes in which he appears, the king embroiders throughout his dialogue with other characters. Calomarde, however, elevates the king's handicraft to the level of art: "Bordar también es pintar . . . ¡Vuestra Majestad pinta mejor que ese carcamal [Goya]!" (p. 118). The implied meaning of Fernando's "art," of course, is the weaving of a plot in which to ensnare Goya. This is confirmed at the end of the play by one of the narrative voices and by Goya himself:

> Voz Masculina: Yo sé que un hombre termina ahora un bordado . . .
>
> Goya: Y dice . . . Me ha salido perfecto.
>
> (p. 212)

Again here, life conforms to art, and Goya perceives the parallel even as he laments the outcome.

The artistic metaphor also prevails in the scene where the *realistas* break Goya's window with a stone. The message attached conveys a threat not with words, but with a drawing. As Goya notes, "Un consejo pictórico. También son pintores. Escuchen: ¿Cuál es la diferencia entre un masón y un lacayo de los masones? Pinta una horca con un sapo viejo colgando y pone debajo: aunque no me apunté, el son bailaba" (p. 164). As with Goya's own drawing for the king, art takes the place of language here and Goya articulates clearly the power of the artistic image.

Near the end of the play Goya utilizes a metaphor analogous to painting that further affirms his artistic perception of the world. When Leocadia confesses her fears and desires after being raped by the sargeant, Goya draws upon the theater to illustrate his feelings: "Nunca sabré qué has dicho. Pero quizá te he comprendido. . . . Y a mí también me he comprendido. ¡Qué risa! ¡Comedia de cristobitas! Pasen, damas y caballeros. Deléitense con los celos del cornudo Matusalén y las mañas del arrogante militar . . . El viejo carcamal amenaza a su joven amante porque no se atreve a disparar contra otros. ¡Así es! ¡Cuando ellos entraron yo no llegué a tiempo a la escopeta porque no quise! Porque no me atreví a llegar a tiempo. ¡Pura comedia!" (p. 208). A few minutes later, following an eruption of anger and despair, Goya reiterates the comparison: "Otra vez la comedia" (p. 210). What is important here, of course, is not Goya's awareness that he is playing a dramatic role (this is not metatheater), but rather his self-definition using an image that suggests life follows the patterns of art.

There is in Buero's portrait of Goya a nourishing reciprocity between the real and the imaginary. The *pinturas negras* do not merely echo at ever-intensifying levels the anguish of the painter as it is represented on stage, but rather share in the actual creation of reality. Goya's artistic imagination, therefore, begets not only a painting, but also a world that is shaped by painting. His work represents, in short, an aestheticizing of history and an artistic autobiography.

Buero is supremely aware of this process, since his recurrent use of the painterly metaphor promotes a consistent *weltanschauung* grounded in the dominion of art. To understand Buero's portrayal of Goya, therefore, is to acknowledge that art reveals, as Paul Ricœur writes, "the deep structures of reality to which we are related as mortals who are born into this world and who dwell in it for a while."[11] Goya's paintings enrich the world because they enable us to see it anew. This capacity to shape reality, and the process through which it is represented in *Sueño* (creation-artifact-interpretation), stand as both the medium and message of the whole of Buero's play.

Notes

1. See, for example, Martha Halsey, "Goya in the Theater: Buero Vallejo's *El sueño de la razón*," *KRQ*, 18 (1971), 207-21; John Dowling, "Buero Vallejo's Interpretation of Goya's 'Black Paintings'," *Hispania*, 56 (1973), 449-57; John Kronik, "Buero Vallejo y su sueño de la razón," *El Urogallo*, 5-6 (1970), 151-56; Ricardo Domenech, *El teatro de Buero Vallejo: Una meditación española* (Madrid: Gredos, 1973); Luis Iglesias Feijoo, *La trayectoria dramática de Antonio Buero Vallejo* (Santiago: Universidad de Santiago de Compostela, 1982), pp. 397-421.

2. My essay therefore takes the opposite approach of Dowling, whose purpose is to show how the play enhances our understanding of the paintings rather than the way in which the paintings inform and structure the play. I am aware that the term "metaphor" is complex and often confusing. (See, for example, Sheldon Sacks, ed., *On Metaphor* [Chicago: University of Chicago Press, 1979] for an excellent and diverse commentary on the subject.) I employ the term "metaphor" here, however, in its broad usage as a fundamental form for the artistic conceiving of reality. For an excellent discussion of this and other problems in the relationship between art and literature, see Wendy Steiner, *The Colors of Rhetoric: Problems in the Relation Between Literature and Painting* (Chicago: University of Chicago Press, 1982).

3. Within the play Dr. Arrieta and Father Duaso comment on the process of understanding art and affirm that the etching is indeed about Goya's own work and the way in which to interpret it. Antonio Buero Vallejo, *El sueño de la razón* (Madrid: Espasa Calpe, 7th ed., 1981), p. 193. Parenthetical page references to *Sueño* are to this edition.

4. It has become commonplace today to use the verb "to paint" intransitively, in the same way as the verb "to write." For a discussion of the ramifications of the latter (and through analogy, of the former), see Roland Barthes, "To Write: An Intransitive Verb?,"

in R. Mackey and E. Donata, eds., *The Structuralist Controversy* (Baltimore: The Johns Hopkins Press, 1970), pp. 134-45.

5. For a discussion of inner exile and its relation to artistic creation see Paul Ilie, *Literature and Inner Exile* (Baltimore: The Johns Hopkins Press, 1982).

6. Terry Eagleton, *Literary Theory* (Minneapolis: University of Minnesota Press, 1983), p. 21.

7. Charles Morris, "Esthetics and the Theory of Signs," *Journal of Unified Science,* 8 (1939), 131-50; and Paul Ricœur, "The Metaphorical Process as Cognition, Imagination, and Feeling," in *On Metaphor,* pp. 141-57.

8. See Frank Casa, "The Darkening Vision: the Latter Plays of Buero Vallejo," *Estreno,* 5, 1 (1979), 30-31; and John Dowling, op. cit.

9. See respectively, William Giuliano, "The Defense of Buero Vallejo," *MD,* 20 (1977), 223-33; John Dowling and Martha Halsey.

10. In *La trayectoria dramática de Antonio Buero Vallejo* Luis Iglesias Feijoo discusses the importance of Goya's final gesture, but links it to the idea of achieving immortality through painting (p. 420).

11. Paul Ricœur, p. 151.

LA FUNDACIÓN (THE FOUNDATION)

PRODUCTION REVIEW

Stephen Holden (review date 29 December 1989)

SOURCE: Holden, Stephen. "*Foundation*: A Spaniard's Political Metaphor." *New York Times* (29 December 1989): C6.

[*In the following review, Holden provides a mixed assessment of the 1989 New York City production of* The Foundation.]

In the opening scene of Antonio Buero-Vallejo's play **The Foundation,** Thomas (Thomas Nahrwold), an aspiring young novelist, paces before the picture window in the lounge of what appears to be a luxurious Alpine spa and exults in the ecstatic music of Rossini wafting through the room he occupies with five other men.

It is Thomas's fantasy that they are all guests of a cultural foundation at an intellectual conference where their every whim will be gratified. He remains obstinately oblivious to the setting's discordant features. One of the conferees is ill and bedridden on a cot in the corner. The other four seem strangely depressed and taciturn. All of them, including Thomas, wear badges that identify them by number rather than name. When one of the men complains about the stench from a backed-up toilet, Thomas says the management has assured him it will be fixed momentarily. When a meal is served, it is a single minuscule portion of steak with mushroom sauce. As the drama, which is receiving a low-key, Spartan production at Theater for the New City, unfolds, the amenities are gradually withdrawn. The supply of beer, wine and cigarettes runs out, and the telephone disappears. Finally the picture-postcard view of misty mountaintops vanishes, replaced by window bars. When the hotel attendants return they have become prison guards. The man who seemed under the weather has been dead for six days. Instead of distinguished intellectuals, Thomas learns that his companions are ordinary citizens with everyday jobs who were arrested, as he was, for political dissent. They also tell Thomas that he informed on them while under torture. They have been waiting for days for him to regain his senses.

In Thomas's awakening, the eminent Spanish playwright, who was jailed for five years at the end of the Spanish Civil War, has created a powerful, resounding metaphor for the shaking off of political slumber. But he carries the fable farther and to richer depths, suggesting that imprisonment is a basic condition of life itself, and in a final paradoxical stroke, embraces to a degree the sort of fantasy that the play had seemed to deplore.

As the prisoners are taken from their cell for interrogation and possible execution, only one slim possibility for survival is held out—the digging of a tunnel from a different, much less well-appointed cell in the basement of the prison. Each prisoner's actions will depend on his readiness to cling to a faint hope that may be as illusory as Thomas's delusion of the foundation. Without such a hope, there is no future at all. Political and social improvement, the playwright implies, may depend on dreams as unreal as Thomas's possibly schizophrenic delusion.

If **The Foundation** is a drama teeming with ideas, its production, directed by James Houghton, is not especially gripping. The director has wisely avoided treating the fable as a prison melodrama, yet the tone of the production is so distanced that the characters of Thomas and his fellow prisoners never come into very precise focus. While Mr. Nahrworld and John Woodson, Peter G. Morse, Sean O'Sullivan and Scott Sowers succeed in suggesting their characters' personalities, the performances lack an emotional cohesion that would give the production a dramatic core of suspense and apprehension.

JUECES EN LA NOCHE (JUDGES IN THE NIGHT)

CRITICAL COMMENTARY

J. J. Macklin (essay date October 1993)

SOURCE: Macklin, J. J. "Tragedy and Politics in *Jueces en la noche.*" *Neophilologus* LXXVII, no. 4 (October 1993): 587-600.

[*In the following essay, Macklin considers the political nature of* Jueces en la noche, *contending that "the play's exploration of problems confronting the collectivity is firmly rooted in the portrayal of the individual and his tragic dilemma."*]

Jueces en la noche (1979)[1] may not be one of Buero Vallejo's best plays, but it is the one which most directly engages with the issues of the day, namely, the political dangers besetting the Spanish state in the immediate post-Franco era.[2] On one level, then, it is an overtly political play, dealing with the transition from the old to the new order and with the difficult accommodations which established politicians have to make in order to survive. This fundamental theme is set in the context of the rise of the Left, the continued power of the Right and, above all, the threat of terrorist violence to the stability of the new democratic institutions. This engagement with actuality on Buero's part has attracted both criticism and praise; criticism, because it is felt that the theatre is not the place for political statements, praise, because it is an act of moral courage to deal with such issues on the contemporary stage. At the same time it is important to recognise that, as in all of Buero's work, the play's exploration of problems confronting the collectivity is firmly rooted in the portrayal of the individual and his tragic dilemma. In *Jueces en la noche* private and public interact in conformity with the dramatist's assertion, in a phrase with unmistakeable Unamunian resonances, that in all his artistic endeavour "lo social nos interesa por cómo repercute en seres concretos de carne y hueso".[3]

Jueces en la noche was written in 1978 and 1979 and received its first performance in the Teatro Lara in Madrid on 2nd October 1979. The immediate reaction was not favourable. Alberto Fernández Torres and Moisés Pérez Coterillo described the play as "una incómoda y patética confesión de impotencia teatral",[4] and Fernández Torres, writing alone, claims that Buero has put himself into "un claro callejón sin salida" and that the play is flawed technically.[5] For this critic the language is careless, the staging conventional, the use of dream sequences excessive and clumsy, and all the characters save the protagonist are portrayed with a rigidity and coldness which deprive them of all authenticity and vitality. Fernández Torres' real concern, however, is that *Jueces en la noche* aims to be a political play but has no statement to make on politics. The issue is rather "la de un conflicto ético entre un hombre agobiado por sus muchas contradicciones y su mala conciencia", with the result that we are faced with "un texto agarrotado, que intenta impotentemente decir algo sobre la *política,* cuando lo único que puede decir es algo sobre la *moral*". Moreover, the play says precisely the opposite of what it intends to say: a political reading will lay the blame for the failure of democracy on the centre, whereas the theatrical reading shows an individual struggling with his conscience and being justified, indeed being absolved, "ante la Historia". This is a curious commentary upon the play, to say the least. For one thing, it is difficult to see how a political and a theatrical reading can be separated, or even defined, and, for another, how a man's conscience and the "presente histórico-político" can be conflated. One might be forgiven for thinking that Fernández Torres is attempting to be over-subtle. Nevertheless, one has no difficulty in accepting the notion of the play's moral dimension, although one would want to argue that this is a strength, not a weakness. Buero Vallejo is not making an original political statement in the sense of a commentary on contemporary events—major writers rarely do—but he is drawing on an immediate set of political circumstances in order to dramatise a clash of values and to explore the interrelated questions of guilt, responsibility and punishment. What one might concede is that the political references are a little too intrusive in a play which purports to be the artistic representation of an acute personal dilemma. At the same time, questions of guilt and responsibility lie at the heart of Buero's analysis of post-Franco society, and the crucial point of convergence between the theatre and politics is their mutual concern with role-playing, with the mask. In Buero's previous play, *La detonación,* the protagonist Larra, as he puts the pistol to his head, looks at his own image and asks himself who he is: "Ahora comprendo que también es una máscara. Dentro de un minuto la arrancaré . . . y moriré sin conocer el rostro que esconde . . . , si es que hay algún rostro. Quizá no hay ninguno. Quizá sólo hay máscaras".[6] The role that one is called upon to play in life is, of course, corrosive of authenticity and it is the falseness at the root of human affairs, and hence their fundamental unreality, which forms the theme of *Jueces en la noche,* and nowhere is it more clearly seen than in the political sphere.

While *Jueces en la noche* is far from being a political tract, the political positions portrayed in it are relatively straightforward. Juan Luis Palacios, a former minister under the *Régimen,* is now a centrist deputy whose main aim is to hold on to his political position, but is unable to free himself from the phantoms of his past, a past in which his private life and public role, as a result of an unscrupulous, though hidden, deceit, are inextricably intertwined. The main action of the play concerns the slow and painful revelation of this secret, namely, that Juan Luis had used his dubious right-wing associations to trick his wife into marrying him by alienating her from her boyfriend, a left-wing activist. This act of deception returns to destroy his present life, although it is clear that his marriage, conceived in falsehood, was vitiated from the outset. Here we find a classic Buerian theme, that in the moral order acts of wrong-doing will inevitably haunt their perpetrator and that relationships can only prosper if they are genuine and authentic. The return of the agent of his deception, Ginés Pardo, apparently planning an act of political assassination, offers Juan Luis the opportunity to act honourably and restore the moral order, but he is prevented by the fear that his wife will leave him if the truth of their marriage is revealed. This dilemma is thus explored in the context of a very real political situation, the early years of Spain's tentative emergence from dictatorship to democracy. The fragility of the new order and the reality of Buero's fears about the survival of the new institutions were confirmed in less that than two years in the attempted coup of 23-F. The forces that characterised Spanish society of the late 1970s are represented emblematically in a number of characters: Padre Anselmo (the Church), D. Jorge (capitalism, the business world), Un General (the Army), Cristina (the Left), Ginés Pardo (the militant Right), Julia (the apolitical middle class) and, as we have seen, Juan Luis himself (the politically opportunist centre).

The symbolic nature of the characters is made manifest from an early stage (and, if early reviews of the play are to be believed, the nature of the acting tended to emphasise this) when Anselmo calls the general and says "La Iglesia tiene que decirle algo a la Milicia" (p. 39), thereby reminding the audience of the alliance of Church and Army in Franco's Spain as well as of the power of the Church and the idea of Spain as a unified Catholic State. Indeed, the general recalls the ideal of the Christian soldier ("fiel cristiano y velando las armas"). The General, in fact, plays no major role in the play other than to be assassinated (or perhaps more accurately to signify the assassinated general). The priest, on the other hand, plays a major role in the second act. As we have seen, Juan Luis suspects strongly that Ginés Pardo is in Madrid to organise an assassination in order to destabilise the country and provoke a right-wing coup, but is afraid to go to the authorities lest his wife learn, through Pardo's confession, the truth about the past. This crisis of conscience leads him to consult Padre Anselmo. Juan Luis's Catholicism is rooted in his upbringing and naturally forms part of his fundamental conservatism. It is embodied in the presence of the large crucifix in his room, but it is a Catholicism which is outward and conventional and Julia casts serious doubts on its sincerity: "No cree en nada, salvo en Dios . . . si es que en realidad cree en Él" (p. 83). If this is so, then religion is part of the social fabric and hence Juan Luis goes to the priest to seek confirmation or justification of the course of action he wishes to take. The Church can find justification for all kinds of actions depending on the

circumstances. As an illustration, it is evident that Juan Luis once shared the attitudes of Ginés Pardo: "La agresividad nos parecía un deber, una defensa de España contra la subversión", a position which Anselmo can qualify as "fanatismo, a veces bien intencionado" (pp. 106-07). The priest speaks using the typical formulae of the Church, which signifies unoriginal thinking and narrowmindedness, but he can still recognise Juan Luis's sophistry and point it out to him, despite Juan Luis's desire to keep the whole issue on an abstract level. Nevertheless, the Church's capacity for prevarication is apparent, as is its desire to preserve the social order of which the family is the cornerstone. Political circumstances may change, but "la integridad de la familia cristiana debe defenderse a toda costa, en bien de nuestra fe y de la estabilidad social" (p. 109). Juan Luis can read this as an indication that he should do nothing. At the very least, Anselmo's advice is ambiguous and the interview serves to underline the moral impotence of the Church. Anselmo himself is aware of this when he contacts Juan Luis after the assassination and both seek justification. To Anselmo's question "¿se decidió dar algún aviso?" Juan Luis replies "Usted no me lo recomendó", to which the priest further replies "¡Tampoco se lo desaconsejé! . . . ¡Yo le remití a su conciencia!" (p. 140)

The telephone conversation also raises a point about terrorism which is a recurrent theme in the play. Anselmo accepts the conventional view that terrorism is the weapon of the left, but the ensuing dialogue expounds the thesis that the right have a vested interest in creating this scenario:

> P. ANSELMO: (*Distante*) Rece mucho, hijo. Todos tenemos que rezar para que la extrema izquierda no nos lleve al caos.
>
> J. LUIS: No olvide que la extrema insania no es exclusiva de ese campo. No olvide a los militantes de izquierda asesinados últimamente . . . y años atrás.
>
> P. ANSELMO: No lo olvido. Pero hechos como el de hoy imponen la evidencia: terroristas de la izquierda. No lo dude.
>
> J. LUIS: Aunque así sea, puede haber alguien detrás.
>
> (p. 140)

This is merely a repetition of what he had said earlier to Ginés Pardo: "Algo que parezca ejecutado por revolucionarios, y que acaso lo lleven a cabo verdaderos fanáticos de la extrema izquierda . . . , porque en sus organizaciones hayan sabido infiltrarse hábiles agentes como tú" (p. 74). This is indeed the role played by Ginés Pardo, a former policeman and agent provocateur, who appears in the first dream sequence in the play. Present, though initially passive, he re-enacts, in a flashback, his role in the destruction of Julia's relationship with Fermín Soria. This scene reveals the sinister relations of power under the dictatorship in which Juan Luis's right-wing allegiances are made clear, firstly through his father ("Medalla individual en la Cruzada y miembro de la Casa Militar de su Excelencia"), then through his employer ("Sanz Moles. Ya sabe, fundador del partido"), and finally through the fraternal solidarity of the victors of the Civil War (p. 48). Ginés Pardo's presence suggests the secret police, detention, interrogation and torture, all employed to "defender la paz de España" (p. 50), and is intended to indicate the continued existence and clandestine power of right-wing elements: "Organizaciones de ultraderecha, policías paralelas del exterior . . ." (p. 72), with whom some sectors of the police are in sympathy, if not connivance: "Nunca son tan eficientes mis antiguos compañeros, entre otras razones porque algunos no quieren serlo" (p. 74). In a moment of candour, Juan Luis admits his real political beliefs, which continue to be rooted in a non-democratic past and from which even Ginés Pardo, in a spirit of "Hay que adaptarse a la nueva situación" (p. 72), has evolved: "Ahora todos tenemos que jugar esta partida miserable de la democracia, pero con la esperanza de recobrar un día la España verdadera. Y si para ello hay que llegar a la violencia, Dios nos perdonará" (p. 72). Ultimately Ginés Pardo, although involved in political activity for mercenary ends, comes to recognise the emptiness of political ideals and accept that all sides fundamentally are self-seeking and that personal motive and ambition always take precedence over professed beliefs:

> Yo tuve mis ideales, que eran los tuyos. ¿Y qué he visto durante años y años? Que todos los traicionabais. Por dinero, por ambición o por subsistir. En toda esa gentuza de la izquierda no se podía creer; pero resultaba que tampoco se podía creer en los nuestros. (*Baja la voz*) El mejor de todos, un farsante.
>
> (p. 142)

From a different perspective Julia is equally cynical about politics, as her initial dialogue with Cristina makes clear: "Toda la política es una engañifa" (p. 54). Cristina, however, is the voice of radicalism and revolt in the play and makes the most potent political intervention in the play when she says: "No vale dar la espalda a los problemas que nos acosan" (p. 56).[7] For her, Julia has the luxury of despising politics and hers is essentially the argument of the Right and one which permits the status quo to continue. To be cynical or devoid of interest implies acquiescence. Cristina sees this in part as a legacy of the regime, which cultivated apathy among the population, but also led to political immaturity among the committed, who are victims of "impaciencia, oportunismo, sectarismo" (p. 56). But Cristina still believes in the possibility of change and is conscious of the need to guard against the forces standing against it, those who are aided by terrorism. Democracy can be blamed for instability when there is still "mucho nostálgico de la dictadura" (p. 80) on the part of those who wish to "asustar el país con el coco rojo" (p. 56). Julia's disillusionment is of course largely due to the circumstances of her life which is characterised by empti-

ness ("años vacíos", "insustancial") and lack of idealism caused by her conviction that Fermín betrayed both her and his colleagues: "Desde entonces no he podido creer en nadie ni en nada" (p. 85). In other words, the personal and the political are entwined in her relationship with Juan Luis Palacios.

Juan Luis is the classic politician of the "transición", the former minister trying to find a role and hold on to his position. What he most fears is obscurity and in the first dream sequence he sees his guests make their excuses and depart since they recognise that "Está hundido" (p. 44). It is an insecurity which is inherent in politics but is even more acute in Palacios' case because of his past, revealed in the reconstructed scene involving himself, Ginés Pardo and Julia. In a sense, Juan Luis is a prisoner of his time, his allegiances formed in "la atmósfera de triunfalismo y de privilegios en que crecí" (p. 153), the ambivalence of his new position seen in his unwitting use of "procuradores" instead of "diputados", and in his uncertainty as to which political grouping to belong. His rumoured intention of joining the Socialists cannot be separated from Cristina's revelation of the electoral gains being made by the Left. Indeed, Juan Luis's desire to be all things to all men is evident in his appropriation of historically incompatible affiliations: "Católico, liberal y socialista" (p. 59). His new socialist leanings have also to be seen in relation to his associations with the business world and also in his hard-headed and prophetic observation in the context of Spanish socialism that "las decisiones de la alta política no se pueden tomar ignorando los grandes poderes económicos" (p. 62). In fact, it is to Don Jorge that he confides his thoughts about a change of party not in order to "abandonar la moderación" but to "ocupar áreas que no debemos dejar escapar" (p. 87) and to dilute the worst tendencies of socialism by making it come to terms with "la economía del mercado y el incentivo de beneficios legítimos" (p. 88). Curiously, Don Jorge in the dream sequences is given the role of Fermín's father in which he represents the voice of the vanquished of the Civil War and of the oppressed under the dictatorship. His son and Eladio González, to whose execution Juan Luis had agreed, represent the militant opposition and their strength resides in their capacity to resist and oppose. This is their victory: "decir 'no' es vencer" (p. 98). Their victory is a personal one and in it lies the hope for a more humane future against the dark impersonal forces which seem to intervene anonymously in human affairs. The argument that the system is too complex to identify personal responsibility is Don Jorge's justification. The idealist seems naive to the sophisticated man of the world:

> Ni usted ni yo somos niños. Los dos sabemos que en el mundo actúan intereses poderosos y que a veces no vacilan en recurrir a métodos reprobables . . . Cumplamos honestamente nuestro trabajo sin especular dema-

siado acerca de esas oscuras fuerzas, con las que quizá estemos condenados sin saberlo a fatales conexiones, dada la intricada estructura de la economía moderna.

(p. 137)

There is a fundamental divide, however unreal, between the two sides and in the ideology of the right the battle against the left is a war against evil which threatens all the traditional values. As the violinist points out to Juan Luis, he has created his own undoing: "Y eres tú quien sigue enarbolando como un garrote el fantasma de las Españas" (p. 163). So whereas Don Jorge expresses the view that Juan Luis' time has come ("la patria te va a necesitar" (p. 159)) while his personal life is ruined, the violinist sees clearly that "no creo que tú puedas ayudar a nuestra patria . . . Tu pasado te lo impide" (p. 163).

While *Jueces en la noche* may ultimately concern the personal tragedy of a man who is destroyed by his own ambition, it nonetheless makes a coherent statement on political conditions in contemporary Spain which, while in no sense original, correctly identifies the forces at work and the vital issues at stake to the extent of being, in a sense, prophetic. To that extent we can agree with Carlos Muñiz's assessment of Buero as a committed writer: "El escritor está comprometido en la medida en que se pone en contacto con los problemas de su tiempo y adopta, frente a ellos, actitudes radicalmente críticas. En este sentido no se puede negar a Buero su condición de autor comprometido".[8] Drama, however, is not made of political statements alone and it is now necessary to see how this context underpins and indeed embodies a characteristically Buerian modern tragic vision. In fact, Buero views the tragic dimension of his work as a safeguard against its falling into pure propaganda or, for that matter, merely committed literature. If it is excessively affirmative a work "se saldría del marco de la tragedia para entrar en el de la propaganda doctrinal".[9] Even on the level of politics, *Jueces en la noche* transcends its immediate historical context to embody more universal concerns—the nature of democracy, the interaction of private and public, freedom and historical inevitability, the workings of power. Thus, while Buero wishes his audience to see in his work a reflection of their own times, he also wishes them to consider individual, as well as national, destinies, and to recognise the inevitability of suffering in human affairs.

While it is undeniable that the contemporary political and social dimension of *Jueces en la noche* forms part of its impact, no play by Buero has ever limited itself to a specific time or restricted its relevance to a call for a specific kind of social action. He makes this clear in his essay on the nature of tragedy: "si ante una obra de tema social de nuestros días el espectador sólo experimenta deseos de actuación inmediata y no se plantea—o siente—con renovada viveza el problema del hombre y de su destino, no es una tragedia lo que está viendo" (*T*, 67-8). If, up until now, we have seen Juan Luis simply as the

embodiment of the unscrupulous politician, it is important to recognise that that he is not a unidimensional creation devised simply to carry the weight of an ideology which is the object of the playwright's critical focus. In fact, in the case of Juan Luis it is probably inappropriate to speak of an ideology at all. Juan Luis is disembodied of conviction, "no tiene nada dentro" (p. 83), in Julia's words. But he is a complex individual whose identity has disintegrated into the roles he is called upon to perform and who seeks a core of being in an authentic relationship with another being, although he himself has condemned that relationship to inauthenticity from the start. Juan Luis is essentially divided between his inner self and his public projection, not only in the sense of the external image of the politician, but also in the sense of the pathetic reality of his life which is hidden behind the façade of his public success. In the words of Luis Iglesias Feijóo, he is "un personaje complejo, dubitativo por debajo de su aparente seguridad y contradictorio",[10] and this makes the play ultimately more compelling in terms of its dramatic conflict. If Juan Luis's public self is located in history, his intimate self is revealed in the manifestation of his agony. Buero dramatises the inner torment of his protagonist as he wrestles with his past, his conscience and his unshakeable feelings of guilt. The judges who come to interrogate him in the dream sequences are his own creation and the interplay of dream and reality is also the persistence of the past in the present. We could in fact say that the reality of the political world is unreal whereas the dream scenes are those which are most real. This technique, as well as Juan Luis's monologues, objectifies the inner forces to which he is subject and provides the dynamics of the dramatic action. On the structure of the play, Gregorio Torres Nebrera writes: "*Jueces en la noche* se construye mediante sucesivos enfrentamientos dialécticos, en varios planos y en diversas direcciones, que van delimitando las responsabilidades de un pasado—el de Juan Luis y Julia—cuando se enfrentan con un presente crítico que exige actitudes de diverso signo moral".[11]

The moral dimension is of course a constant in Buero's theatre and he himself has written: "La belleza estética no es una categoría divorciada por fuerza de la ética . . . Lo estético lleva implícitos con gran frecuencia valores éticos" (*T*, 68-9). The form of *Jueces en la noche* is carefully structured and crafted in order to provide a series of perspectives on the question of responsibility for one's actions and for the consequences of those actions.

That the consequences of Juan Luis's actions are tragic in the broad sense is undeniable, for death and suffering, essential ingredients of any tragic work, are integral parts of it. What we are concerned with, however, is not any rigid formal notion of tragedy, but a combination of elements which may be said to constitute a tragic vision. These may be seen to be fate, guilt, death, suffering and recognition, and must operate in a sufficiently complex and awe-inspiring way to produce in the spectator the appropriate tragic emotions of pity and terror. For this to occur, it is important that the tragic hero should stand above ordinary man, that his fall should in some way be momentous. It is not easy to concede the title of hero to Juan Luis Palacios, though his eminence as a public figure makes his plight more dramatic. What does border on the tragic is that curious interaction of character and circumstance which is essential to tragedy in the idea that the tragic figure in some measure contributes to his own downfall. While Juan Luis is a prisoner of the society into which he is born, he also makes the choices which eventually shape his destiny. Tragedy implies a view of human existence where the threat of suffering is always present, and this suffering is neither willed nor totally unmotivated. This paradoxical quality is central to the tragic vision, which is founded on tensions and ambiguities. Characters are forced to make decisions and choices upon which their future happiness depends, but these choices involve of necessity either sacrifice or conflict with the desires of other people. Such situations are the seed-bed of tragedy and for them to occur it is necessary for the tragic hero to be in some way divided within himself. To undergo the truly tragic experience, he must attain a growth of self-knowledge, a state of recognition. Arguably, this recognition is to be found only in Julia, for Juan Luis is always aware of his dilemma and seeks merely a way out of it. By making Juan Luis so manifestly guilty, Buero robs him of the potential to be great tragic figure. Recognition can of course be transferred from the characters to the audience or spectator, and it is in this sphere that Buero Vallejo makes his particular contribution to a concept of modern tragedy.

Buero's views on tragedy are relatively straightforward and he has expounded them in several of his essays, most notably in "La tragedia", to which I have already made reference, published in 1958. His fundamental idea that tragedy and hope are not incompatible underscores his thinking to such an extent that David Johnston can write: "The phrase 'tragedia esperanzada' has become emblematic of his theatre as a whole".[12] His essay "La tragedia" is an extended justification of this notion of "tragedia esperanzada", drawing on Greek tragedy both in its formal characteristics and also on what he sees as its essential spirit, the recognition of suffering leading to a greater humanity and dignity. In many of his plays, this vision is made explicit, but in *Jueces en la noche,* concerned as it is with the inauthenticity of contemporary politics, it is revealed more obliquely. Arguably, the recognition is on the part of the spectator rather than of the characters themselves. This is the special meaning Buero gives to dramatic catharsis: "La catarsis no es ya descarga, sino mejora" (*T,* 67). The awakening of pity and terror, and their sublimation, lead us to "actitudes humanas de valor permanente", and is therefore an ennobling experience. Morality, as we have implied already, is inseparable from Buero's tragic vision and in his essay he in fact writes of "la moral trágica" (*T,* 68). He accepts the Greek idea of error followed by punishment, *hubris* leading to *nemesis,*

and therefore acknowledges man's complicity in his own downfall. While there may be at work some inscrutable fate, a set of unavoidable circumstances, this is only part of the pattern for, in Buero's words, "el destino no es ciego ni arbitrario, y . . . no sólo es en gran parte creación del hombre mismo, sino . . . a veces, éste lo domeña"(*T,* 69). To violate the moral order is to court suffering. In this way, Buero does not conceive freedom and fate as opposites, but as existing in a dialectical relationship. It is not a simple pattern of cause and effect, for often man's actions are ambivalent and their consequences can be similarly ambivalent. Tragedy is born in this imprecise area of the conflict and interaction of partial truths and so when he describes tragedy as "el género más moral" (*T,* 71), he is not advocating moralistic or didactic writing in a narrow sense, but rather seeks through drama "una aproximación positiva a la intuición del complicadísimo orden moral del mundo" (*T,* 71). If the protagonist is brought to this kind of awareness, it is possible to speak of a happy ending to tragedy: "El protagonista sabe, o llega a aprender por la fecunda lección del dolor, la fuerza desencadenante de la reflexión" (*T,* 73). In this way, Buero denies the existence of a pessimistic vision in tragedy and, as Derek Gagen shows, he has been immersed in the debate between optimism and pessimism which goes back to the early nineteenth century.[13] The dramatist's view is quite simple: if the vision presented in a play is irredeemably bleak, then there is no stimulus for struggle and change; if it is too positive, it will not engage the audience. True tragedy is built upon the tension between these two poles, it is engendered by "la fe que duda" (*T,* 77). This dialectic is inherent in both the political sphere, and also in the realm of individual self-affirmation, and is thus doubly applicable to *Jueces en la noche.* One of the ways in which Buero distinguishes tragedy from pessimism is his belief that it can contribute to an improvement in the human situation rather than be a simple exposition of life's suffering: "la tragedia representa en el terreno del arte un heroico acto por el que el hombre trata de comprender el dolor y se plantea la posibilidad de superarlo sin rendirse a la idea de que el dolor y el mundo que lo partean sean hechos arbitrarios. No hay pesimismo más radical que el de dar por segura la falta de sentido del mundo" (*T,* 75). In fact, Buero firmly believes in an underlying moral order which can be perceived in the enactment of the dramatic work through the behaviour and interaction of individuals in moments of extreme tension and conflict. In the case of *Jueces en la noche* death itself is seen as a kind of triumph and a re-establishment of the moral order in that, as we shall see, it functions both as a kind of poetic justice wrought against the guilty and as a liberation offered as a kind of hope to the victim. Such an order can pertain only to the ideal world of art but it holds out to the audience the prospect of a more human set of values by which life can be organised. In this way Buero sets out to show that man's complicity with human destiny can be organised for his good and that fate is not an abstract force but is created by man's own actions. "La tragedia", he writes, "intenta explorar de qué modo las torpezas humanas se disfrazan de destino."[14]

Although she is not the prime mover of the action, Julia is perhaps the most tragic figure in the play. Her willingness to believe in the charade enacted by Juan Luis and Ginés Pardo undermines her faith in Fermín and leaves her completely disillusioned. Her dignity resides in the fact that she is prepared to face this reality without evasion: "Prefiero la tristeza a la mentira" (p. 56), and thus immediately emerges as morally superior to her husband. The irony is that her sadness is based upon a lie, and therefore her present is founded upon an unreal past. Her whole life is past-directed, as she herself recognises both in her words: "Sé que no tengo futuro porque veo sólo el pasado" (p. 91), and in her actions: she seeks out Cristina, returns to the student café, refuses to move on. Julia's belief in Fermín's betrayal led to her death to the world. Her remark "Y ahora estoy tan muerta como tú" (p. 67) is a recognition of this and also a premonition of her actual death at the end of the play. When the play opens, it is as if the intervening twenty years have not occurred and now the significance of the original events is being unravelled. Part of Cristina's function in the play is to bring Julia to a new awareness.

Julia, however, has become so identified with her error that there is no other reality for her. Despite Cristina's assurance that "atreverse a cambiar es empezar a curar" (p. 92), to change would be to destroy the role she has created for herself. From this point on the past becomes ever more present in Julia's life, though it is progressively reconstructed. The key point in her transformation is after the assassination of the general and the visit of Ginés Pardo to Juan Luis, when she does realise that her husband had deceived her. A recurrent theme is the melodramatic nature of the deceit: "una historia de tebeo", "mi tragedia de veintiún años ha sido un folletín" (p. 152), and this recognition puts the wider tragedy in perspective. What is known as "la tragedia española" was converted, through official propaganda, into a "retórica y topiquera película de buenos y malos" and in this climate it was easy to adopt the same device "para hacer de mi pobre tragedia de señorita burguesa otro folletín" (p. 153). In this frame of mind, devoid of self-pity, Julia is brought to a recognition of her own guilt. If Juan Luis's deceit led to the destruction of all three of them, Julia herself had not enough strength or faith to resist. Her fear of Fermín's way of life and her passive acceptance of Juan Luis's version are the two main elements of her complicity: "Los dos lo matamos" (p. 154). She had fallen into guilt by doing the apparently guiltless thing. Julia reaches her moment of tragic recognition: "Ya me he iluminado", "Lo veo todo tan claro" (p. 133), and her acceptance of her own error, her own guilt, leads to her death through suicide and to the final scene of the play where, in the poetic world of the theatre, a proper order is restored. Julia finally recovers her true identity.

Juan Luis too has a false identity. On one level this is part of his protean nature as a politician, taken to an extreme in the telling phrase: "Cuando la libertad es mayor hay que ser más hipócritas" (p. 72), and in different situations he adopts a series of *personae*. But the play itself opens with a false identity for Juan Luis, portraying him as a doctor, happily married with two children. In the opening dream sequence, he appears to appropriate the identity of Fermín Soria, just as he had usurped his role as Julia's partner. The theme of identity is further developed in the mystery surrounding the two musicians and in the absence of the third member of the trio. The sense of unease and strangeness which characterises the opening sequence is paralleled by the sense of order and harmony when the scene is re-enacted at the end of the play. In between, the gradual revelation of both the secret and of the relationships between the various identities provides the means of unravelling the mystery of the play. In fact, Buero gave his play the subtitle "Misterio profano", which naturally evokes the medieval mystery tradition, although without religion in the sense of a specifically Christian dimension. Given Buero's views on the ethical nature of drama, it is difficult not to think also of the morality plays and of the notion of theatre as being in some way corrective and recuperative. Nevertheless, the underlying belief in meaning, as opposed to pure chance and contingency, is fundamental, even if this can be only dimly apprehended, and here we shade into the other more obvious meaning of mystery. The tragic writer, observes Buero, "plantea una y otra vez el enigma del mundo y de su dolor precisamente porque lo cree enigma—cifra poseedora de significado—y no amargo azar. Si sus convicciones religiosas, filosóficas o sociales son concretas y positivas, el enigma poseerá sus claves y de simple enigma pasará a ser misterio" (*T,* 77). One way in which Buero conveys this sense of mystery and meaning is through the use of music, the March of Beethoven's Trio Serenata, which is used to begin and end the play, though with a different effect on each occasion. The trio of musicians performs the role of a Greek chorus, but they do not stand apart from the action and simply comment on it, for they are intimately involved in the action. In Buero's thinking on tragedy, the chorus, though different from the protagonists, is part of the action: "Nada, pues, de 'espectador ideal', sino actor. Pero, eso sí: actor colectivo" (*T.* 80). The chorus provides the link between the individual and the community.

The trio of course provides the title of the play, for they are the judges who appear in the night to haunt Juan Luis, and it is only at the end of the play that the identity of the third judge is made known. One way in which Buero interconnects the various identities is by giving Don Jorge a dual role, as a father-figure to Juan Luis and, in the dream sequences, as the father of Fermín. In this guise, he appears towards the end of the first part of the play as Juan Luis, in his altered state, approaches madness and, in another dream, is made aware of his responsibility for the death of the general. This is part of the symmetry of the play's treatment of the theme of revelation and concealment: both Fermín and Juan Luis kept silent but whereas Fermín's silence was an act of heroism and solidarity, Juan Luis's was based on fear and self-centredness. Cristina explains the destructive nature of Juan Luis's passion for Julia:

> CRISTINA: . . . No me parece que puedas enorgullecerte de tu pasión por ella.
>
> JUAN LUIS: Es lo más noble de mi vida.
>
> CRISTINA: Tal vez. Pero es, sobre todo, tu fracaso . . . La quieres . . . porque, muy adentro, sientes que nunca la has conseguido. En tu cariño no hay abnegación, sino vanidad contrariada.
>
> (pp. 120-21)

At this point, Juan Luis's judges reappear and it is clear that it is he who calls them, that he is in fact his own judge. In the final scene, which takes place in some unreal world, the cellist implies that Palacios's constant seeking out of these judges, his constant visits to the place of the dead, means he is seeking his own escape through death. It is death in fact which provides the solution to this private and political tragedy. Buero wrote in "La tragedia" that "El último y mayor efecto moral de la tragedia es un acto de fe. Consiste en llevarnos a creer que la catástrofe está justificada y tiene un sentido" (*T,* 71), and earlier in the same essay, he wrote "La tragedia no sólo es temor, sino amor. Y no sólo catástrofe, sino victoria" (*T,* 69). The spectacle of human suffering offered in *Jueces en la noche* is far from being an edifying one. The moral cowardice of Juan Luis is heightened by its being located firmly within the world of opportunist politics, but the paradoxical convergence and divergence of his "yo íntimo" and his "yo público" underscores man's uncertain struggle between freedom and destiny as well as the audience's ambivalent reaction to the competing claims of "fe" and "duda". If tragedy is to have the element of hope, the sense of underlying purpose which Buero perceives as being essential to its very nature, then death cannot be the sole outcome. That death must be set in some context suggesting a wider purpose or transcendence. In *Jueces en la noche* the dream element is made to provide this kind of denouement, for the same dreams that had been the substance of Juan Luis's tortured conscience become the scenario, in theatrical or artistic terms, for a positive reversal of the disruption of the moral order. The emptiness of Julia's life, which had been symbolised in the empty box containing no anniversary present, is filled in the other world. It is filled by the present of the viola which reveals Julia to be Juan Luis's third victim and final judge. This act completes the trio, thereby restoring the disrupted order, and also reunites Julia with her rightful partner as Juan Luis is enveloped in the obscurity he had feared all his political life. The pattern of tragic inevitability adumbrated in the opening stages of the play is allowed to work itself out but, in keeping with the fundamental tenets of Buerian tragedy, the vision of human suffering is firmly contained within a humanist ethic of purpose and perfectability. Underlying it is an almost religious view of the interconnectedness of all things, "aquella intuición, muchas veces inefable, por la que el hombre advierte su dependencia de una grandiosa Unidad sin fronteras y que determina las más diversas actitudes religadoras con el mundo o con sus semejantes" (*T,* 83). Seen in this light, *Jueces en la noche,* as so many of Buero's works, stands as a powerful warning against the dangers, in both public and private affairs, of excessive awareness of the self and against the tragic consequences of its concomitant, the denial of selfhood to others. In true tragic fashion, Buero traces patterns of death in life but, as always, a spirit of affirmation pervades his work so that even in death life is made to triumph and tragedy, like la Marcha del Trío Serenata, asserts itself as "un himno a la vida, a la esperanza en el futuro" (p. 114).

Notes

1. All references are to *Jueces en la noche,* edited by Luis Iglesias Feijóo (Madrid: Espasa-Calpe, 1981), and are incorporated in the body of the text in the form of page references.

2. This is of course not surprising for the abolition of censorship led to increasing engagement with contemporary issues on Buero's part in successive plays, culminating in the rider, more typical of the cinema, attached to *Música cercana* (1989): "Los personajes y el argumento de esta obra son ficticios. Cualquier posible semejanza con personas y acontecimientos reales será casual y no debe entenderse como alusión a ellos". Significantly, the writer's relation to censorship is the source of the dramatic conflict in *La detonación* (1977), Buero's first 'democracy' play.

3. "De mi teatro", in *Romanistisches Jahrbuch,* 30 (1979), 222.

4. *Pipirijaina,* 11 (November-December, 1979), 30.

5. *Insula,* 396-97 (November-December, 1979), 31.

6. *La detonación,* edited by David Johnston (Warminster: Aris and Phillips, 1989), 238.

7. This attitude is very reminiscent of that of Verónica in *La llegada de los dioses* (1978), whose words "Moriremos caminando" end the play in an exhortation not to despair but to hope in the face of apparently impossible odds.

8. Carlos Muñiz, "Antonio Buero Vallejo, ese hombre comprometido", in *Estudios sobre Buero Vallejo,* edited by Mariano de Paco, Los trabajos de la Cátedra de Teatro de Murcia, 2 (Murcia: Universidad de Murcia, 1984), p. 17.

9. "La tragedia", in *El teatro, Enciclopedia del arte escénico,* edited by Guillermo Díaz-Plaja (Barcelona: Noguer, 1958), pp. 63-87 (p. 86). All subsequent references to this work will be incorporated in the text in the form *T,* followed by page reference.

10. Luis Iglesias Feijóo, *La trayectoria dramática de Antonio Buero Vallejo* (Santiago de Compostela: La Universidad de Santiago de Compostela, 1982), p. 505.

11. Gregorio Torres Nebrera, "Construcción y sentido de *Jueces en la noche* de Antonio Buero Vallejo", in *Estudios sobre Buero Vallejo,* p. 336.

12. David Johnston, *Antonio Buero Vallejo, El concierto de San Ovidio,* Critical Guides to Spanish Texts, 48 (London: Grant and Cutler, 1990), p. 91.

13. Derek Gagen, "The Germ of Tragedy: The Genesis and Structure of Buero Vallejo's *El concierto de San Ovidio*", *Quinquireme,* 8 (1985), 37-52.

14. "Sobre teatro", *Cuadernos de Agora,* 79-82 (May-August, 1963), 14.

FURTHER READING

Criticism

Dowling, John. "Buero Vallejo's Interpretation of Goya's 'Black Paintings.'" *Hispania* 56, no. 2 (May 1973): 449-57.
  Investigates Buero Vallejo's insights on Goya's "black paintings" in *El sueño de la razón.*

Geldrich-Leffman, Hanna. "Vision and Blindness in Dürrenmatt, Buero Vallejo and Lenz." *MLN* 97, no. 3 (April 1982): 671-93.
  Examines the role of blindness in the works of Friedrich Dürrenmatt, Siegfried Lenz, and Buero Vallejo.

Halsey, Martha T. "Buero's *Mito*: A Contemporary Vision of Don Quijote." *Revista de Estudios Hispánicos* VI, no. 2 (May 1972): 225-35.
  Considers the protagonist of *Mito* as heavily influenced by the character of Don Quixote.

———. *Antonio Buero Vallejo.* New York: Twayne Publishers, 1973, 178 p.
  Full-length critical study.

———. "Dramatic Patterns in Three History Plays of Contemporary Spain." *Hispania* 71, no. 1 (March 1988): 20-30.

Explores the role of history in the dramas of Buero Vallejo, Martín Recuerda, and Rodríguez Méndez.

Irizarry, Estelle. "Some Approaches to Computer Analysis of Dialogue in Theater? Buero Vallejo's *En la ardiente oscuridad." Computers and the Humanities* 25 (1991): 15-25.
  Presents computer-aided analysis of Buero Vallejo's dialogue in *En la ardiente oscuridad.*

Johnston, David. Introduction to *The Shot,* by Antonio Buero Vallejo. Warminster, Eng.: Aris & Phillips, 1989, 248 p.
  Provides a stylistic and thematic study of *La detonación.*

Jordan, Barry. "Patriarchy, Sexuality, and Oedipal Conflict in Buero Vallejo's *El concierto de San Ovidio." Modern Drama* XXVIII, no. 3 (November 1985): 431-50.
  Views the struggle against patriarchy and sexism as a major thematic concern in *El concierto de San Ovidio.*

Molina, Ida. "Dreamers and Power: Buero Vallejo's *Un Soñador ara un Pueblo* and Ibsen's *An Enemy of the People." Revista de Estudios Hispánicos* IX, no. 2 (May 1975): 241-58.
  Finds parallels between the dreamer protagonists of *Un soñador para un Pueblo* and Henrik Ibsen's *An Enemy of the People.*

———. "Vita Activa and Vita Contemplativa: Buero Vallejo's *El tragaluz* and Hermann Hesse's *Magister Ludi." Hispanofila* 53 (1975): 41-8.
  Delineates the thematic similarities between *El tragaluz* and Hermann Hesse's novel *Magister Ludi.*

Moreno, Antonio. "The Theater of Antonio Buero Vallejo: A Cry in the Dark." *Topic: 29* XV (1975): 21-31.
  Discusses the defining characteristics of Buero Vallejo's plays.

Nicholas, Robert L. *The Tragic Stages of Antonio Buero Vallejo.* Chapel Hill: University of North Carolina, 1972, 128 p.
  Thematic and stylistic overview of Buero Vallejo's work.

Weiss, Gerard R., F. M. S. "Buero Vallejo's Theory of Tragedy in *El tragaluz." Revista de Estudios Hispánicos* V, no. 2 (May 1971): 147-60.
  Places *El tragaluz* within the context of Buero Vallejo's work.

Additional coverage of Buero Vallejo's life and career is contained in the following sources published by the Gale Group: *Contemporary Authors,* **Vols. 106, 189;** *Contemporary Authors New Revision Series,* **Vols. 24, 49, 75;** *Contemporary Literary Criticism,* **Vols. 15, 46, 139;** *Drama for Students,* **Vol. 11;** *Hispanic Writers,* **Ed. 1;** *Literature Resource Center,* **and** *Major 20th-Century Writers,* **Eds. 1, 2.**

Terence Rattigan
1911-1977

(Full name Terence Mervyn Rattigan) English playwright and screenwriter.

INTRODUCTION

Regarded as one of the most important British playwrights of his generation, Rattigan is renowned for his well-crafted plays that explore the vicissitudes of love, family, friendship, and sexual relationships. A prolific author, he wrote twenty-four plays during his long career and was praised for the diversity of his oeuvre, which features comedies, farces, romances, and historical dramas. At one point overshadowed by the work of British playwrights such as John Osborne and Harold Pinter, Rattigan's plays have enjoyed a revival in recent years.

BIOGRAPHICAL INFORMATION

Rattigan was born June 10, 1911, in London to an upper-class family. His father, Frank, was a diplomat, serving as acting high commissioner in Turkey and British minister in Rumania. Rattigan was educated at Sandroyd School and at the Harrow School. As a youngster, he became enamored with the stage and resolved to become a playwright. He was influenced by the work of Anton Chekhov, Bernard Shaw, and John Galsworthy. In 1930 he attended Oxford's Trinity College as a history scholar, earning his B.A. in 1933. He began to write plays, and his first work, *First Episode,* was produced in London in 1933. The play had brief and poorly received runs in London and New York City. A few years later, *French without Tears* (1936) became a smash hit in London and cemented Rattigan's reputation as a successful playwright. He served in the Coastal Command of the Royal Air Force during World War II, yet continued to write plays. In 1948 he was awarded a New York Drama Critics Circle award, and the title of Commander of the British Empire in 1958. In his later years, Rattigan adapted many of his plays to the screen and wrote several radio and television scripts. He was knighted in 1971. He died November 30, 1977, in Hamilton, Bermuda.

MAJOR WORKS

Rattigan's plays are noted for their widespread appeal as well as their emphasis on craftsmanship. In his work he explored thematic concerns such as the relationship

between father and son, marital incompatibility, repressed emotion, and sexual hypocrisy. In his early work, he wrote several plays about schoolboys and university students. *French without Tears* is a farcical look at a group of schoolboys in a summer language school on the Riviera. A major critical and commercial success, *The Winslow Boy* (1946), was based on the Archer-Shee case, in which a young naval cadet was accused of stealing a five-shilling postal order. At much risk to his financial and physical well-being, the cadet's father fights to clear his son's name. In the one-act play, *The Browning Version* (1948), a retiring schoolmaster confronts his failure as a teacher and a husband after being given a copy of Browning's translation of Aeschylus's *Agamemnon* by a student. Rattigan's later works have been characterized as complex and poignant character studies that focus on the psychological problems of flawed, upper-class characters. In *The Deep Blue Sea* (1952), a desperately unhappy woman becomes embroiled in an adulterous affair with a much younger RAF pilot. *A Bequest to the Nation* (1970) chronicles the tempestuous love affair between Lord Nelson and Lady Hamilton. Based on the relationship of Rex Harrison and his wife, Kay Kendall, *In Praise of Love* (1973) explores the ways in which an insensitive husband and his devoted wife deal with her terminal illness: he tries to keep the dire prognosis from her; she knows and tries to hide it from him as well as their son. After the arrival of an American novelist, the truth is revealed and long-repressed emotions come to the surface.

CRITICAL RECEPTION

Rattigan's initial success with such plays as *French without Tears* and *The Winslow Boy* earned him a reputation as an author of economical and well-crafted plays. Yet with the overwhelming success of a group of British playwrights known as the "Angry Young Men" in the 1950s, Rattigan's work was overshadowed. These young playwrights— Joe Orton, Harold Pinter, and John Osborne—garnered commercial and critical success for their raw, innovative plays. In contrast, Rattigan's work was suddenly viewed as dated and fell out of favor. Several critics derided Rattigan's attempt to appeal to every segment of his audience, contending that it resulted in bland and boring theater. In recent years, however, commentators have urged a reassessment of Rattigan's work. Many critics now assert that Rattigan's plays reflect England's changing social, political, and cultural consciousness in the postwar years. Several of his plays have enjoyed successful recent revivals in London and New York.

PRINCIPAL WORKS

Plays

First Episode 1933
French without Tears 1936
After the Dance 1939
Follow My Leader 1940
Flare Path 1942
While the Sun Shines 1943
Love in Idleness 1944
The Winslow Boy 1946
Playbill: The Browning Version and Harlequinade 1948
Adventure Story 1949
Who Is Sylvia? 1950
The Deep Blue Sea 1952
The Sleeping Prince 1953
Separate Tables 1954
Variation on a Theme 1958
Ross 1960
Man and Boy 1963

A Bequest to the Nation 1970
In Praise of Love 1973
Cause Célèbre 1977

Other Major Works

French without Tears [with Anatole de Grunwald and Anthony Asquith] (screenplay) 1939
The Day Will Dawn [with Anatole de Grunwald and Patrick Kirwin] (screenplay) 1940
The Way to the Stars (screenplay) 1946
Bond Street [with Anatole de Grunwald and Rodney Ackland] (screenplay) 1948
The Winslow Boy [with Anatole de Grunwald] (screenplay) 1950
The Browning Version (screenplay) 1952
The Sound Barrier (screenplay) 1952
The Deep Blue Sea (screenplay) 1955
The Prince and the Showgirl (screenplay) 1957
The Yellow Rolls Royce (screenplay) 1965

GENERAL COMMENTARY

Richard Foulkes (essay date December 1979)

SOURCE: Foulkes, Richard. "Terence Rattigan's Variations on a Theme." *Modern Drama* XXII, no. 4 (December 1979): 375-82.

[*In the following essay, Foulkes explores Rattigan's recurring theme of the love triangle and its influence on his work.*]

In the preface to the second volume of his **Collected Plays,** Terence Rattigan recalls an early attempt at play-writing as a fourteen-year-old in a junior form at Harrow. The playlet was in French, and for it he was awarded two marks out of ten and the comment: "French execrable: theatre sense first class." The youthful Rattigan's flair for dramatic effect is clear from the scenario which he recalled in later life: "I . . . plunged straight into the climactic scene of some plainly very turgid tragedy. The Comte de Boulogne, driven mad by his wife's passion for a handsome young *gendarme,* rushes in to the Comtesse's boudoir where she sits at her dressing-table having her hair done by three maids (in those days I was less economical in my use of small parts than I have since become). . . ."[1]

In retrospect, the subject matter of this adolescent piece is noteworthy not so much for its precocity as for its prescience, for it embodies the theme to which Rattigan was to return time and again throughout his creative life.

In play after play, Rattigan explores the triangular situation of a character torn between the rival claims of two potential partners. In *Flare Path, The Browning Version, The Deep Blue Sea, Variation on a Theme, Cause Célèbre,* and the film *The Yellow Rolls-Royce,* it is a woman torn between an older man and a younger; in *Who Is Sylvia?, While the Sun Shines, Love in Idleness* and *A Bequest to the Nation,* it is a man who is similarly torn between two women; and, just occasionally, Rattigan runs the gamut of conformity by presenting a character torn between the attractions of two rivals of different sexes, as in *First Encounter* and *Variation on a Theme.*

The eternal triangle is, of course, a time-honoured theme, and like most dramatic situations, it has been used for both tawdry sensationalism and sensitive exploration of character. Thus, it is for his handling of this recurring theme rather than for the theme itself that Rattigan must be judged. Of the various triangular situations enumerated above, it is the first that has proved most fertile for Rattigan—the woman married to an older man finding herself possessed by a deep and apparently uncontrollable passion for a younger man. This is the situation in three of his most accomplished works: *The Browning Version, The Deep Blue Sea,* and *Cause Célèbre.* In each of these, Rattigan uses the triangular situation to explore the nature of those emotions defined by that "portmanteau word" *love,* contrasting the passion which the woman feels for her young lover with the much more restrained, inhibited feelings which she has, or had, for her husband.

It is significant that for his first major exploration of this theme, Rattigan should create a drama which depends for its full effect upon powerful classical reverberations, for such is the case with *The Browning Version.* The "version" referred to is, of course, Robert Browning's version of *The Agamemnon* of Aeschylus, through which the public schoolmaster, Andrew Crocker-Harris, is guiding his enthusiastic but not very accurate pupil Taplow (a shade of Rattigan himself). As Taplow enthuses over *The Agamemnon*—"it's rather a good plot, really, a wife murdering her husband and having a lover and all that"[2]—we become aware of the parallels between Crocker-Harris, his wife, Millie, her lover, Frank Hunter, and their counterparts in the classical drama. Not that Millie adopts the crude physical weapons of Clytemnestra; instead, she uses the no less deadening battery of psychological warfare as she relentlessly humiliates and degrades her husband. In terms of exploration of character and motive, *The Browning Version* is closer to Euripides and his treatment of that other archetypal triangle (Theseus, Phaedra and Hippolytus) in *Hippolytus* than to Aeschylus's bloody chain of murder and revenge.

By making the husband in his drama a classical scholar of considerable, albeit unrealised, distinction, Rattigan has created a character who might plausibly be expected to analyse his situation and articulate it. This is what Crocker-Harris does in a key speech at the end of the play:

> You see, my dear Hunter, she is really quite as much to be pitied as I. We are both of us interesting subjects for your microscope. Both of us needing from the other something that would make life supportable for us, and neither of us able to give it. Two kinds of love. Hers and mine. Worlds apart, as I know now, though when I married her I didn't think they were incompatible. In those days I hadn't thought that her kind of love—the love she requires and which I was unable to give her—was so important that its absence would drive out the other kind of love—the kind of love that I require and which I thought, in my folly, was by far the greater part of love. I may have been, you see, Hunter, a brilliant classical scholar, but I was woefully ignorant of the facts of life. I know better now, of course. I know that in both of us, the love that we should have borne each other has turned to bitter hatred. That's all the problem is. Not a very unusual one, I venture to think—not nearly as tragic as you seem to imagine. Merely the problem of an unsatisfied wife and a henpecked husband. You'll find it all over the world. It is usually, I believe, a subject for farce.[3]

"Brilliant classical scholar" that he was, Crocker-Harris must have been aware of the serious thought given to this problem of the "two kinds of love" by the writers of antiquity, not only by the dramatists, but more especially by philosophers, particularly Plato; and indeed, the scholar's whole speech is nothing less than an exposition of the view of love put forward by Pausanias in *The Symposium:*

> If there were a single Aphrodite there would be a single Love, but as there are two Aphrodites, it follows that there must be two Loves as well. Now what are the two Aphrodites? One is the elder and is the daughter of Uranus and had no mother; her we call Heavenly Aphrodite. The other is younger, the child of Zeus and Dione, and is called Common Aphrodite. It follows that the Love which is the partner of the latter should be called Common Love and the other Heavenly Love.[4]

Thus, in his marriage Crocker-Harris has seen his own aspiration to "Heavenly Aphrodite" stymied by his wife's increasing absorption in "Common Aphrodite." Of the "two sorts of ruling or guiding principle . . ." expressed by Socrates in *Phaedrus,* Crocker-Harris might be said to represent "an acquired judgment that . . . guides us rationally towards what is best . . ."; his wife, "an innate desire for pleasure[;] . . . the name given to that rule is wantonness."[5]

The situation in *The Deep Blue Sea* is closely analogous to that in *The Browning Version,* and though the classical foundations are not as self-evident as in the earlier play, they still inform its whole texture. Like Crocker-Harris, Sir William Collyer—a judge—has failed to satisfy the other kind of love for which his younger wife, Hester, feels need, and she, like Millie, has sought comfort elsewhere in the former R.A.F. pilot Freddie Page. Again, it is the problem of the two kinds of love that has afflicted Hester with her husband: "Oh, I'm not denying you married for love—for your idea of love. And so did I—for my idea of love. The trouble seems to be they weren't the same ideas. You see, Bill—I had more to give you—far more—than you ever wanted from me."[6] Collyer dismisses his wife's feelings for Freddie as "lust" and exhorts her to "exert every effort of will you're capable of in order to return to sanity at once,"[7] in other words, to return to the principle of judgement and self-discipline advocated by Socrates in *Phaedrus* and embodied, as befits his professional calling, by Collyer himself. But, as Hester movingly testifies, she, like Phaedra before her, has gone to elaborate lengths in order to suppress her feelings for her lover and to avoid meeting him. Furthermore, she denounces the notion that because her relationship with Freddie is founded on sexual attraction, it should be denied that "portmanteau word" *love*. On her side, at least; for, in the classic tradition, her young lover does not reciprocate her feelings in like manner, and in a speech to his R.A.F. crony Jackie Jackson, shows himself to be a victim of the same dilemma as Crocker-Harris, and indeed, Hester's estranged husband: "But look at it this way, Jackie. Take two people—'A' and 'B'—'B' doesn't love 'A', or at least not in the same way. He wants to, but he just can't. It's not his nature. Now 'B' hasn't asked to be loved. He may be a perfectly ordinary bloke, kind, well-meaning, good friend, perhaps even a good husband if he's allowed to be. But he's not allowed to be—that's my point. Demands are made on him which he just can't fulfil. If he tries, he's cheating, and cheating doesn't help anyone."[8]

The destructive effect of Hester's, and Millie's, "Common Love," and its apparent incompatibility with the "Heavenly Love" sought by Crocker-Harris and Collyer, emerge clearly from these two plays. In his last completed play, *Cause Célèbre,* Rattigan returns with renewed insight and imagination to the two loves and achieves arguably his most accomplished exploration of the theme which had preoccupied him for so long. In *Cause Célèbre,* Rattigan takes as his source a famous trial of the 1930s in which Alma Victoria Rattenbury, thirty-eight, was tried with her lover, George Percy Stoner (Rattigan changed his name to Wood), for the murder of her sixty-eight-year-old husband. Alongside this part of the play, which, as we shall see, follows the facts of the case very closely, Rattigan creates the character of Edith Davenport, chairman of the jury at the trial, her estranged husband, and her son, Tony, about the same age as Wood. The play was first written for radio and later rewritten for the stage, and although the revisions in the later version were occasioned partly by the change in medium, some indicate a further refining of the central theme of the play.

The amazing appropriateness of Alma Victoria Rattenbury for the role in which Rattigan casts her extends even to her name, of which he occasions her to say: "Do you know what Alma means in Latin? A professor told me once, it means life-giving, bountiful. In olden times they used it about goddesses, like Venus. (*Sipping her drink.*) Well I'm not Venus, God knows—but apparently it also means kind and comforting, and that I am, George, though I say it who shouldn't. . . ."[9]

Alma Rattenbury also wrote love songs of striking suitability to the play, such as "Dark-Haired Marie" and "Night Brings You to Me." Indeed, scarcely ever can a character drawn from life have served her author's purposes so appositely, for as F. Tennyson Jesse writes in her introduction to the transcript of the trial: "That worst of all Anglo-Saxon attitudes, a contemptuous condemnation of the man and woman, but more particularly the woman, unfortunate enough to be found out in sexual delinquency, never had finer scope than was provided by the Rattenbury case."[10] Tennyson Jesse further highlights the appropriateness of the case for Rattigan's exploration of the nature of love: "The expression 'falling in love' is an attempt to define something which escapes definition. Mankind has a natural weakness for labels, for they simplify life, and though this particular label is one of the most pernicious which has been evolved, it must be remembered that it covers not only a multitude of sins, but of virtues. Perhaps no two people would give quite the same definition of its meaning."[11]

In her introduction, Tennyson Jesse goes so far as to apply to Alma's passion for Stoner a label from which Rattigan had shrunk in the cases of Millie and Hester, though it denotes something which is probably latent in them: "Mrs. Rattenbury was a highly sexed woman, and six years of being deprived of sexual satisfaction had combined with the tuberculosis from which she suffered, to bring her to the verge of nymphomania." She goes on to point out that: "She was fond of her husband in a friendly fashion, and he was devoted to her, very interested in her song-writing and anxious for her to succeed."[12] The couple therefore enjoyed a degree of companionship and affection even though their relationship had ceased to operate on a personal level. Tennyson Jesse also confronts the question of who holds the balance of domination between an older woman and a younger man: "The actual truth is that there is no woman so under the dominion of her lover as the elderly mistress of a very much younger man."[13] Thus, Alma expresses from the dock a view with which her dramatic predecessors Millie and Hester would heartily concur: "Ever since this case began the one thing I've heard is how I must have dominated this—boy. Well I can only say that if anyone dominated anyone else, it was George who dominated me. . . ."[14]

Tailor-made though the Rattenbury case was for Rattigan's purpose, some changes became necessary. In *The Winslow Boy,* Rattigan wrote a court-room drama which took place entirely outside the court, and to a certain extent he was obliged to do the same in *Cause Célèbre,* a play in which he shows himself master of a much freer form of dramatic construction. Stoner was not called to give evidence in court, so Rattigan constructs scenes between Wood and his lawyer in which Wood's assertion—the basis of his defence—that he was a cocaine, addict is shown to be untrue. Another crucial scene between Alma and her elder son, Christopher, takes place outside the courtroom but determines Alma's behaviour in court when, reluctantly, she ceases to shield Wood. However, it is in Wood and Alma's avowal of their love for each other (not merely "lust," as Collyer would argue), their attempts to shield each other, and the play's predetermined climax, that Rattigan is best served by his source. Kenneth Tynan roundly criticised Rattigan for denying Hester her suicide in *The Deep Blue Sea,* a decision which Rattigan stoutly defended.[15] In *Cause Célèbre,* Alma's suicide is foreknown, and the fact that it takes place shortly before Stoner receives his reprieve endows it with its own inbuilt dramatic irony. Furthermore, Alma Rattenbury's own letters written just before she killed herself have a lyricism which Rattigan, the earnest upholder of everyday speech, had eschewed hitherto. Indeed, in the following passage, reproduced with some varying omissions by Rattigan, it is life that transcends art:

> Eight o'clock. After so much walking I have got here. Oh to see the swans and spring flowers and just smell them. And how singular I should have chosen the spot Stoner said he nearly jumped out of the train once at. It was not intentional my coming here. I tossed a coin, like Stoner always did, and it came down Christchurch. It is beautiful here. What a lovely world we are in! It must be easier to be hanged than to have to do the job oneself, especially in these circumstances of being watched all the while. Pray God nothing stops me to-night. Am within five minutes of Christchurch now. God bless my children and look after them.[16]

In the section of the play dealing with Edith Davenport, Rattigan was free to create characters unfettered by considerations of historical accuracy, and the scenes in which she and her family take part were most extensively revised between the radio and stage versions. In the radio play, Mrs. Davenport does not appear until the Rattenbury ménage has been well-established, and she plays no part in the climax. In the stage version, she and Alma are immediately juxtaposed in the opening sequence, and Alma's suicide is punctuated by Mrs. Davenport's reactions to it. In both versions, Mrs. Davenport embodies repressive attitudes towards sex; in her marriage, it is she who is unable to accommodate the "Common Love," the sexual drive of which her husband is possessed, and she is suing him for divorce. It is no accident that Rattigan makes her the daughter of a judge, symbol of the qualities of judgement and restraint embodied by Collyer, in stark contrast to Alma Rattenbury's indulgence.

Collyer and Crocker-Harris are products of an educational system, of which the latter is still an agent, which has as its moral foundation the tenets of self-discipline and fel-

lowship drawn from antiquity and inculcated by a classically based curriculum. Until he wrote *Cause Célèbre,* Rattigan had concerned himself principally with the products of such an educational system (of which he was an example). But in the creation of Mrs. Davenport's son, Tony, he explores the effects of that system on a boy whose age is the same as Wood's, but whose class singles him out for a very different upbringing. In the radio version, he is at school near Bournemouth (where the Rattenburys lived), and a brief scene shows the excitement generated by the case among the boys, who contrast Wood's sexual indulgence with their own limited opportunities. Tony Davenport is the object of admiration by a younger Siamese schoolfellow, and to his avowal "Purely platonic," another boy ripostes: "If you were in the classical sixth you'd learn what Platonic really meant."[17] Mrs. Davenport seems to regard such a relationship as less dangerous than one with a member of the opposite sex, and so embraces the Platonic distinction between Heavenly Love and Common Love in its sexual exclusivism far more purely than any other Rattigan character. The outcome of his mother's attitudes for Tony is a fruitless visit to a prostitute and a golfing holiday in Scotland with the Siamese princeling.

In the stage version, some of Rattigan's changes were clearly determined by practical considerations (the scene at the school, the visit to the prostitute were omitted). But more significantly, he heightens the drama of Tony's visit to a prostitute by making the visit a "successful" one and dwelling on the results as the boy reluctantly discloses to his mother the disease from which he is suffering as a result of his visit, itself a result of her sexual repression. The destructive effect of sexual repression is emphasised when we learn that Tony has attempted suicide, and during a visit to Mrs. Davenport, her husband contrasts her attitudes with those of the woman whose case she is trying: "I don't give much for her chances with you judging her. I don't know anything about Mrs. Rattenbury, except what I've read in the papers, but that's enough to tell me that her vices, which I am sure are deplorable, do add up to some kind of affirmation. Your virtues, Edie, which I know are admirable, add up to precisely nothing. Goodbye!"[18]

In the event, of course, Mrs. Davenport does find Alma innocent of murder, and the stage play ends with her drunken exclamation: "I gave you life." Thus, at the end of his career, and, as he realised, near the end of his life, Rattigan found characters and a narrative which were supremely suited to the further exploration of a theme which had absorbed him for so long. Through his creation of the complementary character of Edith Davenport, he was able to present concurrently the two kinds of love, the "heavenly" and the "common," in the Platonic definition. It may well be that in Mrs. Davenport's final verdict in favour of Alma is to be found Rattigan's personal resolution of this time-honoured conflict. Whether or not *Cause Célèbre* proves to be the masterpiece to which Rattigan aspired, only time will tell, but it indubitably constitutes a fitting summation to the exploration of a theme which haunted Rattigan throughout his career as a dramatist and which gives to his work a cogency and consistency unmatched amongst his peers in the English theatre.

Notes

1. Terence Rattigan, *Collected Plays* (London, 1953), II, p. vii.

2. Terence Rattigan, *The Browning Version,* in *Collected Plays,* II, p. 7.

3. *Ibid.,* pp. 44-45.

4. W. Hamilton, trans., *The Symposium* (Harmondsworth, 1951), pp. 45-46.

5. R. Hackforth, trans., *Plato's Phaedrus* (Cambridge, 1952), pp. 38-39.

6. Terence Rattigan, *The Deep Blue Sea,* in *Collected Plays,* II, p. 354.

7. *Ibid.,* p. 338.

8. *Ibid.,* p. 329.

9. Terence Rattigan, *Cause Célèbre* (London, 1978), p. 10.

   I am indebted to Dr. Jan van Loewen for the loan of typescripts of both the radio and stage scripts of *Cause Célèbre.* References to the radio script are to the typed manuscript; those to the stage version, to the published edition.

10. F. Tennyson Jesse, ed., *The Trial of Alma Victoria Rattenbury and George Percy Stoner* (London, 1935), p. 4.

11. *Ibid.,* p. 7.

12. *Ibid.,* p. 5.

13. *Ibid.,* p. 13.

14. *Cause Célèbre,* stage version, p. 68.

15. See Kenneth Tynan, *Tynan on Theatre* (Harmondsworth, 1964), pp. 20-21; and Terence Rattigan, *Collected Plays,* II, p. xvii.

16. F. Tennyson Jesse, p. 295. Rattigan used this letter as the basis for Alma's suicide speech in both versions, but varied his editing of it.

17. Terence Rattigan, *Cause Célèbre,* radio script, p. 19.

18. Terence Rattigan, *Cause Célèbre,* stage script, p. 49.

Susan Rusinko (essay date 1983)

SOURCE: Rusinko, Susan. "Morality Plays for Mid-Century or Man, God, and the Devil." In *Terence Rattigan,* pp. 96-113. Boston: Twayne Publishers, 1983.

[In the following essay, Rusinko analyzes how Rattigan's plays matured after the transformation of British drama in 1956, and contrasts Rattigan's work with other British playwrights of the time.]

A NEW HERO: JIMMY PORTER

During the long two-year West End run of **Separate Tables,** the inevitable occurred. The long-awaited stage revolution finally erupted on 8 May 1956. Its force unleashed repressions of the economic-cultural anger in post-World War II England and disrupted prevailing stage conventions. Writers, actors, directors—indeed the entire theatrical community—felt the impact of the history-making *Look Back in Anger* by John Osborne. Its leading character is the angry young Jimmy Porter, trapped in a dead-end existence in the midlands of England and also trapped in his marriage. For him there are no more great causes, and so he turns his frustrations and anger on his wife, genteel Alison Porter, and on their long-suffering friend, Cliff Lewis, with whom Jimmy operates a sweets stall. The people he loves most are the only means by which he can exorcise his anger. In a world of no exits, he makes them his only exit. In spite of the cruel treatment he receives, Cliff serves as a buffer between the volatile Jimmy and the passive Alison. In doing so, he becomes with Alison the object of Jimmy's frustrated passions. Bitter in his verbal and physical expression of anger, Jimmy vents his feelings on whoever and whatever are in his path. Even as one emotional upheaval subsides another is already forming, allowing its victim little or no time to recover from the previous one. Alison reels from Jimmy's love-hate actions until she can bear no more. Discovering she is pregnant, she leaves him without revealing her pregnancy. Meantime, Helena, an old actress-friend of Alison's, moves in and assumes Alison's place. At the conclusion of the play she leaves and Alison returns, having lost her child. Both she and Jimmy are exhausted from their journeys back to families and friends who love them, and they resume their life with all the illusions gone and the emotion having taken its toll on them. Both accept the truth of their cultural and psychological incompatibilities, yet realize their obsessive need for each other and that each is all the other has. They seem very close indeed to the characters of Hester Collyer and Freddie Page, Anne Shankland and John Malcolm, and other variations of these characters in Rattigan's dramas.

Yet it is Jimmy Porter who has become the legendary antihero of modern British drama. The generation of the 1930s, highly idealistic, channeled its idealism into the Spanish Civil War. The succeeding generation found similar outlet and purpose in World War II, a struggle that developed into one of sheer survival for England. In the 1950s, however, no such outlet existed for the lower-class, university-educated, intelligent, sensitive person. Jimmy can look forward to nothing beyond the running of a sweets stall in a midlands town and living in an oppressively dreary flat, *ménage à trois* fashion, where frustrated emotions constantly rise to the boiling point. Values seem not to exist, or they exist in a vacuum. They tend, such as they are, to be highly personal, having no connection with the existing societal structure and social consciousness.

Consequently, there is not even anything to rebel against except one's self and those most intimately related. The Strindbergian torture which Jimmy imposes on Alison is his self-flagellation. For him and for her as well, the concluding reconciliation is one of exhaustion, their futures seeming not less bleak than at the beginning of the play.

Ironically, the structure and style of Osborne's play are at best conventional, and it remained for Harold Pinter, at the same time as the emergence of Osborne's antihero, to introduce the first real and certainly influential experimentation in these respects. Osborne's surfaces and dramatic narrative are naturalistic, as are Ibsen's and Strindberg's and Rattigan's. In conventional modern dramatic fashion, he takes his characters into their pasts, where the roots of the present are to be found. Like Norah of Ibsen's *A Doll's House,* Alison is partly revealed by her association with an animal—a squirrel, Jimmy by a bear. The secret on which the plot turns, so important to the Scribean well-made play, is Alison's pregnancy, withheld from Jimmy until late in the action. The domestic triangle of Jimmy, Alison, and Cliff (later Helena) is a 1956 version of similar marital problems in Ibsen's or Strindberg's or Rattigan's plays. The teeter-totter action of the psychological, sometimes physical, struggle contains the tensions of the well-made problem play, including the big scene, the *scène à faire.*

Traditional though its structure and style are, its importance lies in the no-holds-barred honesty, the sheer brutal force, and the animal magnetism that characterize the marriage of Jimmy and Alison. For the first time on the modern English stage uninhibited expression of complex passions, contradictory and violent feelings totally unleashed, with their paradoxical mixture of irrational impulses and reasoned attitudes, created a succession of emotional scenes which left the audience as drained as are the characters in the play.

The year of the play was 1956, and its stage home was the experimental Royal Court Theatre in Sloane Square, which became the residence not only for Osborne's plays but for other new writers whose plays could be given opportunities of production. In addition to providing such opportunities, the Royal Court enjoys historical importance in its launching of the stage revolution which was to stigmatize earlier playwrights and their work as "old-fashioned," "French-window," "well-made." Rattigan felt keenly the stigma of the label and never quite recovered from the injury.

In fact, he attended the opening of *Look Back in Anger,* after which he made his well-known, oft-repeated comment about the impact of Osborne's play. He said that the future basis for reaction to plays would be, "Look how unlike Rattigan I'm being." For a few critics such as Kenneth Tynan, Rattigan became the whipping boy as the embodiment of the old-fashioned play.

Yet Rattigan was not the old-fashioned playwright or the slick dramatist of public-school virtue and traditional English values, as his critics frequently accused him. For all his light-hearted comedies such as *French without Tears* and for all his concern with upper-middle-class characters, one can go as far back as his first play, *First Episode,* to begin tracing the disillusionment that would find such brutally honest expression in the lower-middle-class characters of Osborne in 1956. The disenchantment of Jimmy Porter hangs heavily in the post-World War I and pre-World War II generations in *After the Dance.* The common cause of World War II temporarily dissipated the emotional dissatisfactions and marital mismatches, although these were present in his war drama, *Flare Path.* Once more they became the subject of his dramas after the war and continued to become increasingly important with every play, reaching their highest intensity in the flawed and failed characters of Andrew Crocker-Harris, Hester Collyer, Anne Shankland and John Malcolm, Sibyl Railton-Bell and Major Pollock, Lydia and Sebastian Crutwell, and in the historical characters of Alexander, Ross, and Nelson.

The tension of Rattigan's plays essentially consists of the ambivalence created by the gap between deep-seated, complex emotional needs of the characters and their upper-middle-class sensibilities and composure which restrained them from satisfying or expressing those needs.

Consequently, the ambivalence created pain, failure, and social ostracism which forced them to find whatever means necessary to survive. However, unlike the fate of the alienated characters of the new drama, Rattigan's emphasis in resolving the problems of his characters was reintegration into the human community by means of their choice of a life in some segment of their society. Individuality and community are equally necessary forces in their lives. Isolation and alienation function only as a means toward the end of community, not as an end in themselves. The Hester Collyers and Alma Rattenburys are a means of integrating the Aunt Ednas and the Mrs. Davenports with social pariahs by the painfully slow process of increased tolerance of unconventional behavior and attitudes and by increased awareness of the emotional injury caused by ignorance, particularly in sexual and marital matters.

Curiously enough, Rattigan did not rely on the more obvious techniques of the Scribean well-made play, such as withheld secrets, to complicate his plots and create tension, frequently false and at best mechanical. What secrets may exist are openly handled and disclosed in plays such as *The Winslow Boy, The Browning Version, The Deep Blue Sea, Separate Tables,* etc. They certainly do not constitute the big scene or the climactic moment even in the comedies.

Osborne's *Look Back in Anger,* on the other hand, makes obvious use of the devices. In fact, both Osborne and Joe Orton have been described as old-fashioned in structure and techniques, shockingly frank as their subject matter and language were at the time. The importance of their work was recognized by Rattigan, much as he felt injured by the peremptory critical dismissal of his own. He invested financially in Joe Orton's plays; he admired Pinter's work and was a friend of the Pinter family; he admired Osborne's work, frequently calling attention to the well-made-play style of this former actor, who epitomized all that seemed to be new, even as Rattigan became the embodiment of the old.

Finally, differences between the English stage before and after 1956 seem to consist of two major changes. One of these changes is the admission onto the stage of characters from the lower classes as worthy of serious attention, rather than as secondary, frequently comic, figures or as victims of society to be pitied. The second is the total freedom to use whatever language and experience is appropriate to the expression of that character. After repeal of censorship laws in the late 1960s, distinction between the kind of play put on by theaters such as the Royal Court and that staged by West End theaters diminished.

The new freedoms of the English stage became obvious in Rattigan's remaining plays. In particular, the next three plays illustrate a remarkable shift in subject matter that was obliquely and discreetly handled, sometimes disguised, in his earlier work. Although basic themes have not changed, their increasing complexity and closeness to real-life situations from which they are derived are more frankly sexual. He said that he wanted to "blow up the establishment" by writing a confessional play about homosexuality. At the time, a report (Wolfendon) was being prepared to begin repeal of the law which made homosexuality a crime. In fact, the report is alluded to in *Variation on a Theme*. His next three plays, wedged between the 1956 debut of Jimmy Porter and Rattigan's 1963 self-exile from the England stage, are open in their treatments of homosexual characters: *Variation on a Theme, Ross,* and *Man and Boy.*

Variation on a Theme

Variation on a Theme (1958) appeared four years after *Separate Tables,* a significant fact in the light of the close succession of his plays during the 1940s and early 1950s. Certainly work on film versions of *Who Is Sylvia?, The Deep Blue Sea,* and *The Sleeping Prince* (as well as an unproduced script for *Lawrence of Arabia*) occupied much of his time. And although readjustments in personal affairs made claims on his time, it was the new turn of English stage history that had something to do with the four-year hiatus in his stage writing.

Whatever the reasons for the prolonged absence of a new play, *Variation on a Theme,* dedicated, "with deep gratitude and affection, to Margaret Leighton for whom this play was most eagerly written and by whom it was most brilliantly played" (direction by John Gielgud),

opened on 8 May 1958, during a time when Osborne and Pinter were commanding the lion's share of critical attention. Even with Margaret Leighton in the leading role, however, its run, as Rattigan runs go, was a short one, contrasting with the 513 performances of *The Deep Blue Sea* and the 726 of *Separate Tables.*

Set in a villa in Cannes, France, it is the story of Rose Fish, married four times to rich husbands and on the verge of still another marriage. This time the prospective husband is a German tycoon by the name of Kurt Mast, who has acquired his wealth on the black market of World War II. Their impending marriage, however, is thwarted as a result of Rose's meeting with a ballet dancer, Anton Valov, who turns out to be Ron Vale, from the same general Birmingham origins as Rose. After dropping the assumed name and accent at the beginning of the play, he develops a relationship with Rose because he needs her money and love and she needs to give both. At the time of their meeting, Ron is involved in a homosexual relationship with Sam Duveen, director-choreographer.

In his characterization of Ron, Rattigan develops the theme of the strong influence of the younger on the older person as the main idea of the play. Ron is twenty-six and Rose is in her mid-thirties. Inequalities are compounded by Fiona, Rose's teen-age daughter by her first husband and an aspiring actress who refuses to allow Rose to love her. Only Hettie, an impoverished noblewoman who serves as Rose's loyal, paid companion, seems to reciprocate genuine love. Inequality of love relationships, particularly those in which the recipient is less than worthy of love, is richly developed in the drama. Rattigan's is, indeed, a realistic version of the nineteenth-century Camille story.

The narrative lacks the tautness of *Separate Tables* and is more closely allied to the looser, Chekhovian "states of being" drama in which people talk and talk. After a series of duologues in which Rose discusses her emotional needs frankly and honestly and we discover the emotional states of the other characters, Rose finally decides to leave Kurt, knowing that her living with Ron does not contain even the element of a gamble. For she knows that her ignoring the doctor's advice to move to Switzerland—she has consumption—means her imminent death. In unmelodramatic fashion she states that she's "always imagined an end far more lurid and horrifying than a winter in Cannes with a man I love more than life. More than life? Silly phrase, that—isn't it? Just a woman's exaggeration." Her self-parody is Rattigan's way of deflating an emotionally poignant moment to avoid the possibility of mawkish sentimentality. The melodrama of this "Camille" is tempered by Rose's realistic assessment of her state and by the choice made in a responsible awareness of the consequences.

Perhaps the most revealing dialogue in the play is that between Rose and Sam as they talk about Ron, who has just left Sam for Rose. Confessing her need for loving someone even when that love cannot be returned, Rose hears Sam's explanation of Ron:

> You don't seem to understand that the Rons of this world always end by hating the people they need. They can't help it. It's compulsive. Of course it probably isn't plain hate. It's love-hate, or hate-love, or some other Freudian jargon—but it's still a pretty good imitation of the real thing. You see—when day after day, night after night—you're being kicked hard and steadily in the teeth, it's not all that important what the character who's doing it feels for you. You can leave that to the psychiatrist to work out. All you can do is to nurse a broken jaw and, in your own good time, get the hell out. I'll give you six months—from the honeymoon. Take a bet?

Without passion, Sam then describes Ron's staging a phony suicide scene because of his strong jealousy of another young ballet dancer. In response to Sam's characterization of Ron's professional mediocrity and his personal liaisons, Rose explains why she has decided to stay with Ron. "It's just because his needing me is—well—the best thing that's ever happened to me, and without it I wouldn't see much point in going on living. That's not a woman's exaggeration, Sam. It's the simple truth. I can't explain why it means so much. Hettie quoted Horace at my head the other day. Something about expelling Nature with a pitchfork, but it always comes back. Meaning, I suppose, that since Birmingham I've suppressed my natural instincts, and now Nature has taken a mean revenge—"

Sam brutally accuses Rose of turning the tables on Nature "by taking a boy nine years younger than you and turning him from a fairly good virtuoso dancer into a male Rose Fish." With conversations such as these constituting much of the play's content, Rattigan conducts an ongoing debate between nurture and nature without the lean, spare dialogue of earlier plays that leaves much of the meaning to the implicit or unspoken. Here the explicit dominates, and much of the emotional tension is dissipated. Reference to "a male Rose Fish" is a naked statement that makes awkward its disguise of a homosexual character. In *Separate Tables* the disguise became so natural that it could not be bent back. The very calm, rational debate—in fact, a long discussion—about Ron by Rose and Sam as a substitute for the dramatic tension in the less verbalized earlier plays results in something like self-parody on the part of the author.

Yet the *scène à faire* of the play, a card game between Ron and Kurt, does restore, although with theatricality, some of the lost tension. The game subtly develops into a classical morality duel in which each fights his battle for Rose. When he wins, Ron flings the money at Rose to express his rejection of his parasitic dependence on her money. However, she prevents a fist fight between the two

men by coming between them. Very deftly Rattigan builds up to this "big scene" and just as deftly deflates it of the conventional theatricality.

But the real conflict occurs within each of the two main characters, Rose and Ron. Their decisions are not made blindly, for she is aware of her impending death and he of his potentially mediocre ballet career. Their emotional inequality is dramatized with brilliance rather than in the poignantly moving manner of *Separate Tables.* Rattigan's laying out all his dramatic "cards on the table" did not "blow up the establishment," but his free working in a less disguised fashion was, indeed, a variation on a theme that carries its own impact.

The obsessive need to love, even when that love is unreturned or its object unworthy, and the need to express that love, are etched with sharper and more explicit naturalistic surfaces than in the earlier dramas and make the narrative a fascinating variation on earlier characters who could not articulate their needs and frustrations. The pain and humiliation, preferable at all costs to the repressions of the Camille-like love of Rose and Ron, are the result of rational choices made by both with existentially clear awareness of the consequences.

On another level, the psychological and autobiographical subject matter is intimately Rattigan's. "Chips" Channon, an American who had married into the British upper class, enjoyed a close relationship with Rattigan similar to that of Kurt and Rose. Early liaisons with older men and later ones with younger men are variously treated in the characters of Rose, Ron, Sam, and Kurt. But if the play draws on personal experiences, the truths of those experiences have freed themselves of the factual realities in which they originate.

In addition, Rattigan wrote the play for Margaret Leighton, who had become a close friend. Even though her unhappy marriage to Laurence Harvey was in part another source for the drama, it would be difficult to draw close parallels, as the fictional truths create their own characters and situations.

The cultural milieu of the times, especially the literary scene, receives its share of attention in the play in the person of Rose's young daughter, Fiona. For her, existentialism, the angry young men, and James Deanery are old-fashioned. She has a novelist friend who writes about "a lot of young people who have love affairs with each other and don't much enjoy it, but go on doing it because there isn't any point in doing anything else." Her attitude resembles the mood of the 1939 characters of *After the Dance,* the 1948 views on art in *Harlequinade,* and, in their fullest form, the state of the arts in their times by the characters in *In Praise of Love* in 1973. The views are expressed frequently as a conflict between fathers and sons or between old and new generations. There are few plays of Rattigan's in which a youthful character does not serve importantly in this capacity.

Variation on a Theme finds kinship with the type of drama Tennessee Williams wrote about rich, older American women in relationships with young men in Italy who needed above everything else to give love and/or sex by whatever means necessary. Rattigan's Rose is not so bizarre, certainly, but neither does she emerge in as sympathetic a role as his earlier heroines, and this fact may account in part for the mixed critical reception. In fact, Shelagh Delaney, incensed by Rattigan's treatment of a homosexual relationship, particularly with Margaret Leighton in the leading role, wrote *A Taste of Honey* to express her views of the subject in what she felt was a much more sensitive treatment.

Ross

If *Variation on a Theme* enjoyed neither the critical nor popular success of Rattigan's other plays of that decade, it was more than compensated for in his next play, *Ross* (1960), with whose performance he began his fourth decade of writing for the stage. Not since *French without Tears* in 1936 and *While the Sun Shines* in 1942, with their respective 1,030 and 1,154 runs, had a London production of his enjoyed such success.

What made its success stand out was that in that same London season Harold Pinter's *The Caretaker* and Arnold Wesker's *Roots* opened, and the English stage was luxuriating in Shakespearean productions at the Old Vic and the Aldwych. *Ross* more than held its own among the dramatic excitements of that year.

When it opened in New York with John Mills (in London Alec Guinness played the lead), its reception was equally strong. "Gripping Hit" (*Journal American*), "John Mills Triumphs" (*Daily News*), "*Ross* Magnificent Study of a Legend" (*New York Mirror*) read the tabloid headlines. In the *New York Times* Howard Taubman began his review by ranking it with Tennessee Williams's *The Night of the Iguana* as "two notable plays" that "pay the theatre the compliment of regarding it as a place where the sources of man's nature may be explored with boldness and wonder. They adorn the theatre by bringing to it disciplined craftsmanship, distinction of style and integrity of purpose. With these plays the tone of the Broadway season gains greatly in quality." In New York as well as in London *Ross* rivaled the best theater offerings of the season.

Recipient of such accolades, *Ross* was an auspicious revival of Rattigan from the blow dealt him by the New Wave critics and particularly from the mixed notices of *Variation on a Theme.*

Once more at the beginning of a new decade Rattigan returned to an historical theme. A dramatic portrait of the legendary T. E. Lawrence, *Ross* reflects Rattigan's lifelong interest in historical characters, beginning with the schoolboy play about Cesar Borgia and his reading of history at Oxford. Like the leading character in *After the Dance* (1939), who is a writer of history, Rattigan at times felt that he, too, should have chosen that career. His history plays are an artful wedding of two important interests.

Like *Adventure Story, Ross* is on its most obvious level concerned with the rise and fall of an historical hero whose actions in the drama turn on the question of identity. In the earlier play Alexander asks, "Where did I go wrong?" Now Lawrence of Arabia, who believes firmly at the outset in the Greek injunction to "Know Thyself," asks himself, "Oh Ross—how did I become you?" The episodic narrative of both historical plays leads to a question asked by each of the two heroes.

Lawrence knows that his strength lies in the strong will by which he controls and therefore directs himself and others. He exercises his will quietly in his influence over his Arab friends and very actively in the battles in which he engages the Turks. In the climactic moment of his life, Lawrence's will is broken by Turkish captors who violate him sexually, thereby destroying the will by which he was able to repress his own homosexuality, or to sublimate it in the Arabian dream. Having such a specific focus for his portrait of Lawrence, Rattigan was able to tighten the episodic narrative with eight very brief and equally taut scenes in each of the two acts by creating a tension lacking in *Variation on a Theme* and lacking also in *Adventure Story.* The concentration is so masterful that the play seems seamless even with its episodic style.

The framework for the narration of Lawrence's Arabian adventure is his enlistment in the Royal Air Force at Uxbridge under the assumed name of Ross. He hopes his new identity will provide him with the anonymity he has chosen as his means of survival. However, a fellow serviceman discovers his secret and reveals it to the newspapers, resulting in Ross's departure from the base at the end of the play, to continue his search for anonymity in still another identity as Shaw. Between arrival at and departure from Uxbridge there is the dream-reenactment of the English-Arab conflict with the Turks, in which Lawrence played a powerful and enigmatic role. The Uxbridge framework for the Arabian episodes provided Rattigan with an effective structure from real life. Like the provincial hotel in *Flare Path* and the Beauregard in *Separate Tables,* Uxbridge allowed past events as they gathered retrospective momentum to merge subtly into Ross's move into still another attempt at anonymity.

Lawrence's mystical political faith in the Arabs' right to govern themselves is the motivation for his rise from cartographer for the British military to Arab confidante who inspired in superiors and aides alike the fierce loyalty that is the special brand of Arabs. He worked with a quietness and unassuming force which his British and Turkish superiors or equals tended to see as arrogance but which the common run of military personnel and "the uncommon" superiors such as General Allenby and Auda Abu Tayi sensed to be a profound clarity, wisdom, and honesty.

The three parallel scenes, in which Lawrence earns the respect of Auda, Allenby and, with disastrously negative consequences, the Turkish general, illustrate Rattigan's mastery of scene construction, in which leanness and implicitness of dialogue are at their best.

In the first of the three, the theatrical irony is brilliant. After discussing the military realities of the Arabs, a Turkish captain arrives to negotiate with Auda, in the presence of Lawrence, the capture of this fanatic Englishman. His offer is a set of false teeth for Auda, just as in the opening scenes there is a price to be extracted by Dickinson from either the newspaper or Lawrence himself for the revelation or concealment of Ross's identity. Auda carries his joke so far as to ask Lawrence, dressed as an Arab, to escort the captain out of the tent. Both men laugh about the joke they have just played on the Turk, even as Auda looks longingly at the fragments his rifle has just made of the false teeth.

In a second equally forceful scene with General Allenby, Lawrence's ability to inspire respect is further dramatized. Allenby's fear of the intellectual superiority of Lawrence is quickly dismissed when the latter incorrectly identifies the date of an alabaster perfume jar which he had presented to the general. Lawrence smilingly receives Allenby's correction, and the tension breaks. The two find they have reading interests in common; in addition Lawrence had made it a point to learn of Allenby's interests in "Shakespeare, Chippendale, mobile warfare, Chopin and children." The tension of a first meeting relieved, both men proceed to discuss military strategy and, even more importantly, matters of self-knowledge, belief, and the ability to will one's self into a belief. The last point, in the form of a question to Lawrence, is significant as it is Lawrence's will that the Turks later break by their homosexual rape of him. With the breaking of that will came the loss of belief in his dream and the subsequent searches for peace under assumed identities of Ross and Shaw.

The third parallel occurs two scenes later. The audience is prepared for it by a short conversation between the Turkish general and captain in which the former discussed Lawrence as a man with two faiths: one in the Arabs' readiness for statehood, and the other, "more vulnerable— what I hear he calls his bodily integrity." Like Allenby they have done their homework well. But unable to get Lawrence to recant his first faith, they proceed by rape to destroy the second. After the sexual violation, the general explains to Lawrence the reason:

> I do pity you, you know. You won't ever believe it, but it's true. I know what was revealed to you tonight, and I know what that revelation will have done to you. You

can think I mean just a broken will, if you like. That might have destroyed you by itself. But I mean more than that. Far more. (*Angrily.*) But why did you leave yourself so vulnerable? What's the use of learning if it doesn't teach you to know yourself as you really are? . . . For you, killing wasn't enough.

The Turkish general's intelligence of Lawrence had gone beyond that of Auda and Allenby, and the Turk's violence on Lawrence ironically carried out the early conversations between Allenby and Lawrence on the matter of will. Even to Allenby and Auda, Lawrence's unwillingness to be touched and his talent for self-concealment were known, so that his rape by the Turks is subtly and credibly prepared for. Lawrence's flaw is self-concealment, and the Greek *hubris* (a word used in the play) is very much the theme of Rattigan's psychological portrait of Lawrence.

Lawrence's assumed identities were the means by which he sought the peace he talks about to his Uxbridge acquaintances. In the final scene of the play, the sympathetic efforts of his comrades to keep him in their company is a first step in that direction. When Parsons indignantly comments on the way Ross is being treated as the "most dirtiest, bleedingest trick that even those bastards have ever pulled on one of us," Lawrence quietly questions, "On one of us?" His earlier belief in himself and in the Arabian dream destroyed, he welcomes the simply human sympathy of the sergeant, who expresses the men's intentions to help Ross, because there's no one "in this world who can't be made to fit in somehow—" Both separateness and community are necessary for his survival. In the tradition of Rattigan's endings, Ross "looks round the hut for the last time and then shouldering his kitbag, he follows the Flight Sergeant out." Again there is the Chekhovian continuity of life. Ross's search for peace will continue under still another identity. The peace he searches for is community on an anonymous basis that would allow him a measure of separateness within that community.

Those early attempts of Rattigan in **French without Tears** to construct scenes in a Chekhovian manner have matured into the lean tautness of the episodes in **Ross** in which implicit truths about the characters are effectively drawn.

Most reviews of the play referred to the fact that Rattigan had completed a film script for *Lawrence of Arabia,* whose shooting was postponed and eventually canceled. Later a screen version by Robert Bolt was filmed, but Michael Darlow regards Rattigan's script as being superior to Bolt's. In any event, the screenplay was partly responsible for the dramatic polish to **Ross** which his other history plays may have lacked.

Like the plays it preceded and followed, **Ross** is a play about a homosexual subject, handled without the need for disguises or apology or even the need to shock the establishment. The specific sexual problem could just as easily have been of another sort, and its truths would have remained intact. Dealt with as an intensely human condition, without affectation, stereotypes, or propagandistic intent to increase public tolerance, the subject matter takes on natural rhythms of historical event and private experience. In *Ross* implicitness, focus, and seamless flow of dramatic narrative are at their best.

Finally, *Ross* is Rattigan's last successful stageplay before, under the impact of personal events and professional disappointment, he turned from the stage to films. The very question which Lawrence asks himself at the end of Act I, "Oh Ross—how did I become you?", is the question that Rattigan frequently asked himself from 1960 until 1970, when once more he returned to the London stage with *A Bequest to the Nation.*

MAN AND BOY

In the immediate post-1956 period, Rattigan wrote a third but less successful play, ***Man and Boy,*** in which homosexuality was openly handled, although not of primary interest in the narrative. This time one of the major confidence men of the twentieth century, Ivar Kreuger, is fictionalized in his relationship to a son who had disowned him and is now living in a small Greenwich Village, New York, apartment.

The thickly plotted play involves Gregor Antonescu, who uses his illegitimate son's apartment in the Village to extricate himself from the most catastrophic financial situation of his career. Having been involved in the shady financial schemes of his father, the disillusioned son had broken with him five years earlier and has seen nothing of him since. A struggling pianist, he lives in a cheap Greenwich Village apartment with an actress, Carol Penn. He knows nothing of his father's present scheme until suddenly Gregor shows up, revealing nothing of his real purpose but asking the use of the apartment. A parasitic aide, Sven, has now replaced Basil in his father's manipulations.

The current confidence game entails the softening of a public announcement of the failure of an Antonescu merger with the holdings of American Electric, whose executive head, Herries, is a homosexual. The weapons Gregor employs to achieve the softening are his knowledge of Herries's homosexual affair with Harter and the use of Basil Antonescu as homosexual bait for Herries. Both prove abortive when the newspaper headlines scream the news that the FBI, having been informed of forged collaterals in a recent Bank of London scandal, is looking for Antonescu. Basil, who had furiously left the apartment upon realizing what his father was up to, returns with the newspapers to inform Gregor and Sven. One by one wife and colleagues desert Gregor, who even helps Sven plan his own suicide. Only Basil refuses to leave him. As it began, the play ends with the radio blaring the latest news about the swindler.

On one level the play deals with the struggle within Antonescu to live without a conscience. Up to this time he has managed so successfully he did not need the love that boy could offer man. Now it is all he has left, and with the vanishing of his world, he acknowledges that the roles of man and boy are reversing. "Who is now the strong and who the weak?" Beyond disillusion himself, Gregor attempts to disillusion Basil by branding as sentimental lies the stories about his (Gregor's) boyhood. His attempt to discard the very idea of a conscience is rejected by Basil, and at one moving point they embrace in a scene reminiscent of the Willy Loman-Biff relationship in Arthur Miller's *Death of a Salesman.* It is the only emotion that Gregor has allowed himself in a long time, very much like the emotional release of Andrew Crocker-Harris in *The Browning Version.* It is indeed a refutation of Gregor's own contention that he has no conscience and an affirmation of the Rattiganesque need for belonging to humanity. Yet even this brief emotional moment cancels itself out in Gregor's last words to his son: "Whatever happens never, in the future, let the truth make you cry." Basil's response is "I won't—not any more." The strong hatred which the son had felt for the father has surfaced as love. The utter unscrupulousness and amorality have for a brief moment been transformed into feeling and, therefore, into humanity.

The ironic ambivalence is underscored in the final words of the play in the form of a radio announcement that the president of American Electric, Mr. Mark Herries, would make a guest appearance to discuss the widely hunted swindler. Herries's comment "that to be absolutely powerful a man must first corrupt *himself* absolutely" reflects Rattigan's skepticism about the possibility of any kind of redemption for the tycoon. In an interview Rattigan had said that *Ross* is about a man who wanted to be God and *Man and Boy* is about a man who wanted to be the devil.

Personal parallels obtrude on this modern morality play. Basil Anthony (like Ross of the previous drama, he has an assumed identity) is twenty-three years old and was born in 1911, the year of Rattigan's birth. At twenty-three Rattigan had made a break with his own father regarding a career choice. The time of the events in *Man and Boy* is 1934, two years before Rattigan's huge success with *French without Tears.* Nearly thirty years later, Rattigan dramatizes the old myth of selling one's soul to the devil, feeling keenly in his own financial successes at the time the aspiring, idealistic boy he once was and the successful man he now is. As his last play before giving up the stage for the film world for the next seven years, *Man and Boy* seems an ironically fitting expression of his own state at the time. Further, Antonescu is from Rumania, where Frank Rattigan had spent some years as diplomat and which is drawn upon for characters in *The Sleeping Prince.* The mistresses of Antonescu, whom the American tycoon Herries described as the "most highly publicized mistresses of any man in the world—also a beautiful young wife" suggest the women in Frank Rattigan's much-publicized affairs, already dramatized in *Who Is Sylvia?* Basil's financial problems as a struggling pianist were Rattigan's when he worked for Warner Brothers studio. The homosexual Herries and his young male friend who committed suicide are drawn from Rattigan's early experience. Autobiographical details are woven deftly into this play, which Michael Darlow sees as a parallel to Rattigan's possible reassessment of his own relationship to his father.

Man and Boy is Rattigan's most pessimistic play. Like Shaw's *Heartbreak House,* Ibsen's *Wild Duck,* and Chekhov's *The Cherry Orchard,* there is a void at the center of things left by the cancellation of idealism by realism, youth by age, optimism by pessimism. In no other play of Rattigan's is the void so pronounced as in *Man and Boy.*

In varying ways, all of Rattigan's plays deal with internal and external conflicts of conscience, whether in the small man taking on the highest court in the land or in legendary heroes such as T. E. Lawrence and Sir Horatio Nelson in conflict with themselves. The succession of leading characters in Rattigan's work presents a varied pattern of the forms that battles of conscience take. The battle ends with some measure of victory, even though minuscule in a few instances. The victory for right in the case of Ronnie Winslow affected an entire nation. In Hester Collyer, Crocker-Harris, and Major Pollock, some measure of private dignity has been achieved, and in Rose Fish the mere presence of conscience in her final, fatal choice of Ron over the Kurt Masts of her life is a victory, however slim, of the needs of the individual over prevailing social pressures. However, Gregor Antonescu's success in disillusioning Basil about the last "lie" on which the financial empire had been built seems a prelude to his rejecting the son's love after an intense but brief expression of that love. The lies and rejections are major components in relationships between Rose and her daughter Fiona, between Crocker-Harris and his wife, between Major Pollock and the outside world, but nowhere is their consequence so total as in *Man and Boy.* Even though the father has sold his soul to the devil, the son can love him. Yet there is his troubling promise to Antonescu never to let the truth make him (Basil) cry.

The possibility of redemption for the man seems minuscule indeed, as Gregor's truth is that of a man who has rejected conscience and knowingly continues to reject it. Basil's ability to love even a father who has tried to become the devil is the ultimate attempt to keep Gregor's connection with humanity. Love is offered and rejected. The moral and emotional wasteland of Gregor seems unrelieved. Yet in this moral desert Rattigan's narrative power, Bernard Levin wrote, fuses with his dramatic cunning and his "imaginative curiosity about the springs of human activity—hot and glowing into his finest work and a play that outdistances all but a handful of authors writing in England today."

Negative reactions to the play were strong, however. Because of the homosexual matter and the absence of psychological explanation for Gregor's actions, some criticism was quite harsh. Yet, one can argue, psychological explanations are not the terms of Rattigan's dramatic style. To expect the patterned motivations of Ibsenian or Strindbergian characters is to ignore those terms, which are the revelation of character through narrative means.

As Rattigan's wasteland play, *Man and Boy* lacks the questioning whose end is the self-knowledge of the previous plays. The question asked by a radio interviewer is put to Herries, himself of questionable moral cast. "Why did a man who, by 1929, had achieved every ambition that any great financier could hope for, a man who was already acclaimed. . . . Why did this man descend to . . . common swindling . . . and to total ruin—both for himself and for millions of those who trusted him?" The answer is clearly dramatized throughout the play by Gregor's actions and can be found in his two favorite words: liquidity and confidence.

The big confidence game, success, creates hero-worship, Gregor contends, "but to be loved and worshipped by one's own boy—and by this boy above all. . . . Oh, no. No. I will take almost any risk—you know that, Sven—but not the risk of being so close to the pure in heart. 'And virtue entered into him'—isn't that from the Bible?" Underneath the hatred, man and boy find that there is still love. But Gregor takes a step to the point of no moral return to disillusion the boy, and he does succeed. Neither man nor boy has any more questions, and it is left to the American tycoon Herries to provide the expected, hypocritical answer to the question of the radio announcer.

John Russell Taylor regards *Man and Boy,* along with Coward's *A Song at Twilight,* "as the first completely convincing, completely serious well-made play in the British theatre for more than half a century. . . ." Taylor's assessment that the play is a distinct advance on *The Deep Blue Sea,* however, many would dispute. He continues that *Man and Boy*

> for all its neatness as a piece of plotting . . . has the fascination of a tale that is told, not precisely explicable, seeming to imply much more than it says. For unlike *The Deep Blue Sea* it does not actually say anything: or what it has to say escapes all neat, pat formulation. It is the character-portrait of a man without qualities, and Rattigan seems in it for the first time to be moving outside the neat, clear-cut world of the well-made play, where there is always an explanation hidden somewhere in a secret drawer, and into the shifting, indeterminate world of contemporary drama, which might take as its motto Gertrude Stein's supposed last words "What is the answer . . . ? Very well then what is the question?" But still preserving the form of the well-made play: a curious and potentially explosive combination.

With its intentionally limited run and despite some harsh reviews, *Man and Boy* intrigues and fascinates with its conventional plotting of surface action, its articulate dialogue and its near Beckettian sense of the void at the center of things riding close to the surface features of the play. A modern-day *Faust,* it is the third of Rattigan's stage dramas after 1956 and the last stage production before his self-exile to the film world.

All three plays written after the Osborne explosion at the Royal Court Theatre deal openly with homosexual subject matter. All three deal with characters confronting the harsh realities of sex, confidence games, and political and financial power. The inevitable consequences are relentlessly natural, particularly in *Ross* and *Man and Boy,* in which man aspires to be God in one and the devil in the other. As modern morality plays, the comment on the arts, politics, and finances is intertwined with painfully intimate experiences. A godlike Ross, a satanic Antonescu, and a totally human Rose Fish (embodying both the romantic and disillusioned in her very name) are indeed both representative types and distinctive individuals whose failures have only affirmed their respective strengths. The fragility and disguises of the characters in earlier plays now give way to power and honesty. The effects are noticeable in the very construction of the scenes in which tension-building debates and ironical situations deepen characterizations of people in whom separateness, community, and conscience still battle with each other in a fascinating blend of human activity. This trilogy of post-1956 plays, impressive each in its own way, is Rattigan's response to the challenge of the new waves of drama. In that response he has developed a direction that took him into seven years of writing for films and then into seven more years of stage activity in which he wrote three final plays.

Robert F. Gross (essay date September 1990)

SOURCE: Gross, Robert F. "'Coming Down in the World': Motifs of Benign Descent in Three Plays by Terence Rattigan." *Modern Drama* XXXIII, no. 3 (September 1990): 394-408.

[*In the following essay, Gross asserts that Rattigan's three most successful plays*—The Deep Blue Sea, Separate Tables, *and* Ross—*reflect the changing identity of England in the post-World War II period.*]

Although Terence Rattigan first gained recognition for his commercially successful high comedies, *French without Tears* (1936), *While the Sun Shines* (1943) and *Love in Idleness* (1944), the postwar period showed him gaining critical and popular acclaim for realistic psychological dramas. His three greatest successes in the West End, racking up runs of over five hundred performances apiece, were *The Deep Blue Sea* (1952), *Separate Tables* (1954), and *Ross* (1960). All three reflect the changing identity of Great Britain in the postwar period, and address the anxieties of the Theatregoing public during that era.

The years immediately following World War II were ones of intense and rapid political change for Britain.[1] The 1945 electoral landslide for the Labour Party opened the way for the development of the Welfare State, with the nationalization of the Bank of England and key industries (including radio television, civil aviation, coal, gas and electricity), as well as the institution of the National Health. But these reforms brought little sense of greater well-being or prosperity to the people at large. Economic recovery from the War was slow, certain forms of rationing continued until 1954, and "austerity" was the word of the day. Abroad, Britain was busily divesting itself of its largest colonies: 1947 brought independence to India and Pakistan; 1948, to Sri Lanka and Burma. Straightened circumstances at home and diminished influence contributed to a collective sense of downward national mobility. Intellectuals, whether on the Right or the Left, found very little to say in favor of the age.[2] T. S. Eliot's gloomy pronouncement in *Notes Towards a Definition of Culture* found its supporters in a variety of ideological camps:

> We can assert with some confidence that our own period is one of decline; that the standards of culture are lower than they were fifty years ago; and that the evidence of this decline are visible in every department of human activity.[3]

In many areas of the arts and letters, the British seemed bested by competition from abroad. The popular West End stage found it hard to compete with such lucrative imports as *Arsenic and Old Lace, Oklahoma!,* and *Annie Get Your Gun,* and the works of such young American playwrights as Tennessee Williams and Arthur Miller exhibited a rough vitality that the British theatre was unable to match until the advent of John Osborne in mid-decade.[4]

It took British playwrights a number of years before their writing began to reflect the realities of postwar life.[5] Most playwrights, like Noel Coward, T. S. Eliot, and Christopher Fry, largely stuck to the social and political assumptions of the prewar period. Rattigan's first postwar efforts were similar to Coward's, Eliot's and Fry's. *The Winslow Boy* (1946) was Edwardian both in form and content, looking back to the aesthetic values and psychological types found in the plays of Arthur Wing Pinero. *Harlequinade* and *The Browning Version* (1948) were both well-made, realistic, one-act plays. The latter foreshadowed Rattigan's increased use of Freudian insights and psychosexual motivation in his plays of the 1950s, but there are relatively few references in the play to postwar life. With only minor editing (the memorable characterization of Crocker-Harris as the "Himmler of the Lower Fifth" the greatest loss), it could easily be set in the 1930s. A costume drama based on the life of Alexander the Great, *Adventure Story* (1949), seems more indebted to Bulwer-Lytton than any playwright of the twentieth century. It is only in the final act of his 1950 comedy, *Who Is Sylvia?,* that Rattigan even attempts a direct and detailed depiction of postwar life. Deft and amusing as the Mayfair models and old duffers of the diplomatic corps may be, however, it is clear that the jokes all revolve around the embarrassments of December/May liaisons, not any particular characteristics of the age. It is not until the 1952 premiere of *The Deep Blue Sea* that Rattigan presented a sustained dramatic depiction of postwar British life.[6]

By the time of this premiere, the heyday of the Labour Party had passed. The Conservatives had returned to power in October 1951, leaving most of the Labour controls intact, and bringing no increased affluence in the immediate wake of their victory. When the curtain rises on the setting of *The Deep Blue Sea,* we are shown a shabby and decayed environment, far removed from the posh drawing rooms of Coward and Eliot, or even that of Rattigan's *Who Is Sylvia?*:

> *The sitting-room of a furnished flat in the north-west of London. It is a big room for it is on the first floor of a large and gloomy Victorian mansion, converted to flats after World War I, but it has an air of dinginess, even of squalor, heightened by the fact that it has, like its immediate badly-blitzed neighbourhood, so obviously "come down in the world."*

(2:293)[7]

From mansion, to flats, to the squalor of a rooming house in a blitzed-out neighborhood, the set is an emblem of Britain's material decline in the modern world. But it is not only the sitting room that has "come down in the world"; it is occupied by Hester Collyer, daughter of a clergyman and wife of a judge, who has left her husband to live with an ex-RAF pilot, Freddie Page. As the play opens, Hester and Freddie are reaching the end of their affair. She feels an intense sexual desire for Freddie that humiliates and shames her, while he shrinks back from her in mingled fear and repulsion. Hester's social descent is depicted neither as a catastrophe nor a punishment. Her former social circle is depicted as vapid and stifling, smothering the little talent that she may have had as a painter. Its view of human nature, composed of the religious and civic notions of the genteel upper middle class, is completely unable to help her understand her current situation:

COLLYER:

> Hester, what's happened to you?

HESTER:

> Love, Bill, that's all—you know—that thing you read about in your beloved Jane Austen and Anthony Trollope. Love. "It droppeth as the gentle dew from heaven." No. That's wrong, isn't it? I know. "It comforteth like sunshine after rain . . ."

COLLYER:

> Rather an unfortunate quotation. Go on with it.

HESTER:

> I can't. I've forgotten.

COLLYER:

> "Love comforteth like sunshine after rain and Lust's effect is tempest after sun."

HESTER:

> "Tempest after sun?" That would be very apt, wouldn't it, if that were all I felt for Freddie.

(2:335-6)

The canon of English bourgeois literature, from Shakespeare to Austen and Trollope, is unable to give Hester a way of speaking about her intense sexual and emotional dependency on Freddie that is free of negative connotations. In the language of her father the minister it is "sin," in the language of her husband the judge it is "grounds for divorce," and the entire genteel tradition would label it "lust." Thus, the language she has inherited repeatedly reminds Hester of her own negative valuation of her feelings. If she is to survive, she must begin to discover a new set of values.

Hester's most immediate dramatic predecessors in British domestic drama are Pinero's Paula Tanqueray and Zoë Jenkins, women who become *declassé* through their fornication and adultery, and are driven to take their own lives. But Hester is different from these Edwardian heroines. Society does not demand her death; only she does. Her genteel upbringing has given her no way to view her passion but with revulsion and shame. At the opening of the play, she has attempted, like Paula and Zoë, to commit suicide, but her attempt is foiled by her unfamiliarity with the world in which she now lives. Having turned on the gas in her apartment to asphyxiate herself, she neglected to put enough money in the meter. Genteel gestures are undercut by simple realities, and Edwardian conventions are presented as outmoded and unenlightened.

Hester's lover has also "come down in the world," though not socially. He has declined from his days of wartime adventure to present unemployment and a decidedly unglamorous future. The RAF, with its mixture of classes, had provided the wartime public with most of its slang and jargon, and served as a popular model for the British serviceman. In time, its "breezy irreverence and relatively classless approach" had helped to establish a more egalitarian type of British masculinity for the Welfare State.[8] As such, Freddie's decline is not only that of an individual, but of a social ideal as well. The postwar period has found no satisfying place for him; "He's never been really happy since he left the RAF," Hester observes (2:337).

Hester and Freddie's romance, despite their mutual affection, has taken its toll on both of them. He drinks heavily, she attempts suicide. Their attempt at an amorous relation-

ship across class lines—a domestic variation on the
Welfare State ideal—has only led to mutual deterioration.
When Freddie realizes that the only hope for both of them
depends on a separation, Hester is left without money,
respectability, close companionship or self-respect. Once
again, suicide appears to Hester as an attractive possibility.

She is saved by a fellow lodger who has also "come down
in the world": Doctor Miller, a one-time physician and ex-
convict who acts as *raisonneur,* and articulates an ethical
vision different from both Hester's father-clergyman and
husband-judge. He explains:

> Listen to me. To see yourself as the world sees you
> may be very brave, but it can also be very foolish.
> Why should you accept the world's view of you as a
> weak-willed neurotic—better dead than alive? What
> right have they to judge? To judge you they must have
> the capacity to feel as you feel. And who has? One in a
> thousand. You alone know how you have felt. And you
> alone know how unequal the battle has always been
> that your will has had to fight.
>
> (2:263)

Miller presents an alternative to a hierarchy of judgements
internalized from the imagined expectations of others, the
leftover conventions from the plays of Pinero. He pleads
for a self-acceptance founded in compassionate self-
knowledge. Hester finds Miller's alternative difficult to accept:

HESTER:

> "I tried to be good and failed." Isn't that the excuse
> that all criminals make?

MILLER:

> When they make it justly, it's a just excuse.

HESTER:

> Does it let them escape the sentence?

MILLER:

> Yes, if the judge is fair—and not blind with hatred
> for the criminal—as you are for yourself.
>
> (2:363)

If Hester is to survive, we are told, she must learn to
refrain from judging herself responsible for her current
situation. The intensity of her passion is not something she
can master by acts of will; her volition can shape her life
to only a very limited extent. Her descent in the world
becomes an education in the limits of volition. Rattigan
evaluates Hester's movements from clergyman to judge to
ex-doctor, from wealth to poverty, from self-esteem to
disturbing self-knowledge, in unambiguously positive
terms. Hester's loss of social station, money, husband and
lover emerges, through the alchemy of Rattigan's *raison-*

neur, as painful moments in a process of personal growth.
It brings his protagonist to the point where she can begin
again, stripped of her genteel uselessness and conventional-
ity, understanding the intensity of her passions and the
limits of her will. Perhaps she will go back and nurse her
small talent as a painter; certainly, she will find a way to
survive as an independent woman.

The relationship established between Miller and Hester,
however tentative, is advanced as the model for a more
egalitarian, compassionate and comforting world than Hester has known before. Unlike the judge or the clergyman,
Miller stresses that he and Hester are equals—friends—
rather than physician and patient:

MILLER:

> (*Smiling.*)
> Surely I have a right to feel sad if I lose a new-
> found friend—especially one whom I so much
> like and respect.

HESTER:

> (*Bitterly.*)
> Respect?

MILLER:

> Yes, respect.

HESTER:

> Please, don't be too kind to me.
>
> (2:363)

The Deep Blue Sea is more traditionally structured than
either *Separate Tables* or *Ross.* It all transpires in a single
day in a single setting, has no subplots, and focuses un-
swervingly on Hester Collyer. As an exploration of social
relations, therefore, it is far more limited in scope than the
two later plays. Although Hester's descent is mirrored in
the stories of Miller, Freddie, and the surrounding
neighborhood, the priority Hester exercises in the dramatic
structure makes it appear that all of these other stories are
secondary variations on the principal theme that she
embodies. Hester's descent in the class system plays virtually no role in her crucial encounter with Miller; rather, it
is her recognition of the force and legitimacy of her
"lower" drives that is the issue. In *The Deep Blue Sea,*
contemporary social realities are used as secondary elements that underscore primary, psychological processes.

Social realities are explored more for their own sake in
Rattigan's 1954 triumph, *Separate Tables.* Here the focus
is not on an individual, but on a society in transition. The
play is composed of two related one-act plays, linked by
the common setting of the Beauregard Private Hotel, and
the appearance of the same cast of supporting characters.
Most of these characters are representatives of the old
middle class, which had been particularly hard hit by the

economic pressures of the postwar years.[9] Lady Matheson is the widow of a Civil Servant, who can no longer afford to have her radio repaired or attend the movies more than once a week. Mr. Fowler, an ex-public-school master, and Miss Meacham, an eccentric spinster living off a meagre inheritance, are other residents of the Beauregard who live in genteel poverty. "You're the unlucky victims of our revolution," John Malcolm, the socialist journalist, admits (3:123). Socialism, Malcolm tells us, is distinguished by its "passionate sympathy" for the poor (3:123). Only Mrs. Railton-Bell, the villainess of the piece, is not to be pitied for her economic station; she lives off her investments. *Separate Tables* does not contain any characters whose lots seem to have improved as a result of the Welfare State, but it never suggests that the Welfare State should be dismantled. In fact, Rattigan allows Malcolm's socialist analysis of the Beauregard Arms to go unchallenged.

No single character dominates *Separate Tables* the way Hester Collyer dominates *The Deep Blue Sea.* The leading actors (Eric Portman and Margaret Leighton in the original production) play a different pair of lodgers in each act. In the first play, *Table by the Window,* Leighton played Anne Shankland, the aging society beauty and drug addict, who has come to the Beauregard in hopes of effecting a reconciliation with her ex-husband, John Malcolm (played by Portman). Malcolm, a one-time rising star of the Labour Party, appointed a Junior Minister in the 1945 Labour government while still under thirty, has sunk into oblivion and alcoholism after having his career ruined by a trial for wife-beating that resulted in his conviction.

Like Hester and Freddie, the Malcolm-Shankland misalliance stems from the early days of the Welfare State. Both were initially attracted by what they thought was the other's strength. She had the social status; he had the ambition. She had the beauty; he had the force. In time, however, it became clear that both were deeply insecure and driven individuals, both of whom, not unlike Hester and Freddie, could only harm each other. On one level, this story is a continuation of *The Deep Blue Sea,* in which Hester and Freddie do even worse separated than they did together. It is only their desperation and mutual recognition that neither of them stands a chance alone that brings them together at the end. Cross-class alliances are stripped of any facile glamour, but are shown to offer the only possible hope for survival. Rattigan has grafted the Conservative/Labour division onto the model of heterosexual romance, thus implying that a coalition of these forces presents the only possible hope for either. *Table by the Window,* in its mixture of domestic romance and political argument, stands somewhere between the interior, psychological focus of *The Deep Blue Sea* and the social focus of *Separate Tables'* second play, *Table Number Seven.*

Inspired in part by the scandal occasioned by John Gielgud's arrest for an act of homosexual solicitation the previous year, a scandal that, many predicted, would ruin his career, *Table Number Seven* tells the story of Major Pollock (played again by Portman), a windy bore of a bogus military man, who is arrested for soliciting a woman in a movie theatre.[10] The transformation of the offense from a homosexual to a heterosexual one brings it more readily within the immediate sympathies of Rattigan's 1950s West End audience, helping to give this play the warmly sentimental tone that has rendered it so popular. Rattigan is neither out to shock his audience nor to widen its understanding of alternative sexual practices, but to lead it to congratulate itself on its sense of tolerance and fair play. Mrs. Railton-Bell spearheads a campaign to expel Pollock from the Beauregard Arms, and almost succeeds in marshalling the lodgers behind her and against Pollock. Only two lodgers oppose her: a young physician, a feistier version of Dr. Miller, who aptly notes, "Senator McCarthy could use your talents, Mrs. Railton-Bell" (3:176), thus explicitly relating the politics of the Beauregard Arms with the larger politics of Red hysteria in the Cold War era; and the delightfully idiosyncratic Miss Meacham, who gives a less clearly reasoned but no less energetic rejoinder to Mrs. Railton-Bell:

> my views on Major Pollock have always been that he's a crashing old bore, and a wicked old fraud. Now I hear he's a dirty old man, well, I'm not at all surprised, and quite between these four walls, I don't give a damn.
>
> (3:175)

Mrs. Railton-Bell's daughter Sybil (played by Margaret Leighton) is even more deeply disturbed by the news of Major Pollock's crime than her mother. Sybil is a hysterical and lonely spinster who had grown fond of the Major during their long walks together. Now she is horrified and disgusted by him. Miss Cooper, the play's *raisonneuse,* encourages a more compassionate point of view:

> the one thing I've learnt in five years is that the word normal, applied to any human being, is utterly meaningless. In a sort of a way it's an insult to our Maker, don't you think, to suppose that He could possibly work to any set pattern.
>
> (3:185)

Malcolm's "passionate sympathy" for the poor is here translated into a passionate sympathy for all human suffering, virtually identical with Miller's philosophy in *The Deep Blue Sea.* Like Miller, Miss Cooper talks to Major Pollock in the hopes of ministering to his sense of shame and self-loathing. She tells him that she has no intention of giving way to Mrs. Railton-Bell, and hopes he will stay at the Beauregard. Although he is terrified at the prospect of starting anew, he insists that he must leave; he cannot bear to face the lodgers after his public disgrace. Like Hester, he is the prisoner of his own shame, and he considers taking his own life.

In the final scene of *Separate Tables,* however, Major Pollock takes his dinner at his appointed table in the Hotel dining room. Though Mrs. Railton-Bell orders the other guests to cut him, little by little they begin to make him welcome, and Mrs. Railton-Bell's dominion is shattered when Sybil quietly defects to the more liberal position. The final stage direction celebrates the new social order in Rattigan's characteristically understated manner:

> *A decorous silence, broken only by the renewed murmur of "the casuals," reigns once more, and the dining-room of the Beauregard Private Hotel no longer gives any sign of the battle that has just been fought and won between its four, bare walls.*

(3:195)

Though much of **Separate Tables** is dramatic and pathetic in tone, the ending is triumphantly comic, showing the transfer of social power from the hierarchical order of the old and intolerant Mrs. Railton-Bell to the more egalitarian order of the younger and more tolerant Miss Cooper.[11] Despite economically straitened circumstances, the tenants come to prefer the democracy and social latitude her hotel provides. Sybil's quiet defiance of her mother climaxes the play, completing the transformation of a class society into a classless one.

In **Ross,** Rattigan taker his social exploration even further, making the loss of the British Empire the subject of investigation. In choosing the story of T. E. Lawrence as the vehicle for this exploration, he was able to integrate many of the themes from **The Deep Blue Sea** and **Separate Tables** within a larger political framework.

By 1960, it was far more appropriate to deal with the loss of the Empire as a sign of Britain's decline than economic austerity. The years 1957-1963, under Conservative Prime Minister Harold Macmillan, were the most prosperous the country had known in decades.[12] The exoticism and epic sweep of **Ross** are far removed from the more restrained expressions of **The Deep Blue Sea** and **Separate Tables**.

From early on, T. E. Lawrence's popularity had owed a good deal to the theatre. Reporter Lowell Thomas's multimedia presentation, entitled *With Allenby in Palestine,* opened to great popular and critical acclaim at London's Covent Garden Theatre on August 14, 1919.[13] The material on Lawrence proved to be the most successful, and was expanded upon in Thomas's successive revisions of the show. Capitalizing on the euphoria and patriotism of England in the wake of the armistice, Thomas's show appealed to a gaudy and popularized British Orientalism, as described and analyzed in Edward Said's influential study, *Orientalism.*[14] The evening opened with a band of the Welsh Guard playing as the audience entered the theatre. The curtain rose to reveal a scene on the banks of the Nile, with moonlight and pyramids. Dancing maidens entered and performed the *Dance of the Seven Veils,* and were followed by a tenor who sang a vaguely Arabic chant composed by Thomas's wife, Fran. Braziers of incense added to the exotic atmosphere. Finally, Lowell Thomas

appeared and narrated his experiences in the East, illustrated by documentary footage of "Allenby in Palestine," a story which climaxed at the end of the first act with Allenby's triumphal entry into Jerusalem. After the intermission, a cinematic trip down the Nile prefaced the story of Lawrence of Arabia, with stops at such landmarks as Mount Sinai and Petra. The climax of this half was, as the program announced:

> the capture of Aleppo and the downfall of the Ottoman Empire—Mesopotamia, Syria, Arabia and the Holy Land at last freed after four hundred years of oppression.[15]

With Allenby in Palestine was not only popular in England, moving from Covent Garden to the Royal Albert Hall, but was applauded in Philadelphia, Washington, D.C., Australia, New Zealand, South East Africa and India. It affirmed imperialistic values in the wake of the disastrous defeats and extensive loss of life suffered during the War.

Almost forty years after Lowell's show, the story of "Lawrence of Arabia" was still a potent draw at the box office. Rattigan's **Ross,** with Alec Guinness in the title role, provided the playwright with his longest West End run since his 1943 comedy, **While the Sun Shines.** Earlier conceived by Rattigan and Anatole de Grunwald as a film script for Dirk Bogarde, it was extensively revised by Rattigan for the stage when the financial instabilities of the British film industry rendered the project impossible.[16]

Like Hester Collyer, Anne Shankland, John Malcolm, and Major Pollock, Lawrence is presented as a man who is almost destroyed by the recognition of his own psychosexual forces. Rattigan follows Lawrence's own assertion that his torture and rape at the hands of Turkish soldiers was the key event in his life. Although later writers have tended to doubt the veracity of Lawrence's account of his ordeal at Deraa, Rattigan builds his play around it.[17] By doing so, Rattigan chooses once again, even in this, his most overtly political work, to emphasize the psychological over the political, and the personal over the public. **Ross,** in many ways the climax of this series of experiments in psychoanalytic realism, grafts the theme of Empire onto the sexual etiology of those earlier plays.

On the surface, Rattigan's Ross and Lowell Thomas's Lawrence appear to differ widely.[18] Thomas places his protagonist in a sensuous Orient of dancing maidens, incense, and views of the Nile. The Arabian desert and the Nile valley are collapsed to provide a luxuriant setting for the drama. Rattigan sets his hero in the heat and dryness of the desert. His world is exclusively male; the cast of twenty-three does not include a single woman. Thomas's Lawrence is a man of action; presented through silent film documentary and Thomas's account, he never speaks, let alone broods. Rattigan's Ross is introspective; the whole Arabian experience is seen through a flashback inside Airman Ross's head as he asks himself, "Oh Ross—how did I become you?" (3:363). He is constantly examining his motives and trying to understand his character; "I'm a Greek scholar," he explains, "I have a profound belief in the virtues of self-knowledge" (3:370). Thomas's spectacle has been replaced by psychological introspection.

On a deeper level, however, Thomas and Rattigan share a common belief in the Empire as a place of sensuality. Whether Egyptian maidens or Turkish soldiers, both see the Empire as a place where the veneer of repression cracks and reveals the truth of sexual desire. The Empire is reduced to serving as an appropriate setting for acts of Empire, both military and sexual.[19] Ross's antagonist, the Turkish Military Governor, is a character who makes little sense on the realistic level. As Stanley Weintraub has quite rightly noted, it is unconvincing that he would allow his most dangerous enemy to escape.[20] He functions rather as the agent and voice of Ross's own sexual awakening. The Governor explains:

> Yes, it's a strange relationship I have with Lawrence. He doesn't even know of my existence, while I probably already know more about him than he knows about himself. I wish all relationships were so pleasant and uncomplicated.
>
> (3:377)

Mysterious and omniscient, he knows from the first the truth about Ross. Perverse and epigrammatic, he sounds far more like a *fin de siècle* aesthete than a military governor. Pouring himself a glass of wine, he observes, "I'm so glad I'm not a Christian. In their religion this isn't a sin" (3:376). Later, when a soldier asks what Lawrence is sacrificing, the Governor, sipping burgundy and ruffling his subordinate's hair, replies, "Oh, . . . everything that makes life worth living" (3:378). Rattigan has not drawn this figure from the pages of *The Seven Pillars of Wisdom*, but from *The Picture of Dorian Gray*. Homosexuality is presented as an exotic attribute; there is no suggestion of it in the scenes at British headquarters or the RAF barracks. Lawrence, who styles himself an Arabian in dress, language and manners, and thus apes the behavior of the colonial "Other," is the only British character identified as homosexual. In *Ross*, the protagonist's sole defeat is founded in the forced recognition of his own sexuality. Despite all the historical and even epic trappings of the play, Ross's dilemma differs little from Hester Collyer's. Although he refuses to speak to his captors as they command, his own body betrays him and speaks his desire just the same. The Governor asks the Sergeant in charge of Ross's torture:

> Well? (The SERGEANT, *with a broad grin, nods slowly.*)
>
> He said yes? (The SERGEANT *shakes his head, still grinning. The* GENERAL *looks at him questioningly.*)
>
> SERGEANT (*at length*) He didn't need to say it.
>
> (3:385)

All of Ross's military atrocities and cruelties take place after this episode, and after his formal request to be released from his role in the Arab Revolt. These atrocities are only fleetingly described and never depicted, which minimizes Ross's responsibility, making them comprehensible as the result of his molestation.

So far, Rattigan and Thomas seem to be merely repeating a stale topos familiar to us from Conrad, Kipling and Maugham: the discovery of the libido in torrid climates. But Rattigan, writing at a time when Britain has lost much of its colonial power, uses Ross's failure to illuminate the failure of the imperialist project altogether. Ross learns at Deraa that he enjoys not mastery, but subjugation; not victory, but defeat; not will, but the breaking of that will. His later transformation of identity in the RAF to Ross and his even later transformation into Colonel Shaw become a penance for both his earlier desire for fame and his acts of cruelty.

Ross's flashback begins with a parody of the Lowell Thomas show. To the strains of "Land of Hope and Glory," a screen is lowered and we see a slide of Lawrence of Arabia.[21] The stage direction tells us:

> *He is lying on the ground, a rifle by his side, gazing thoughtfully into space. A camel squats sleepily behind him. The desert background looks decidedly unreal and the whole effect is phony and posed.*
>
> (3:333)

Empire is an exterior form that bears no correlation to the state of the souls who sustain it. Self-knowledge is not gained through activity, but passivity; not by giving pain, but by accepting it. The Empire represents a sphere of self-delusion that provides an escape from the demands of self-knowledge. "What's the use of learning," says the Military Governor, "if it doesn't teach you to know yourself as you really are?" (3:386). From the beginning of the play, Ross has known about the Sykes-Picot treaty, which determined that Arabia should be divided between France and England after the War. Rattigan simplifies the complexities of this treaty, presenting it only as an act of treachery. Lawrence is casual about the treaty, and seems to feel no guilt about using the Arabs for imperialist ends. Only after Deraa can he realize his perfidy: "I have come to believe that the Arab Revolt is a fake, founded on deceit and sustained by lies, and I want no further part in it" (3:394). This realization, however, does not succeed in releasing him from his treacherous position, but, ironically, leads him to play a role in a British propagandistic spectacle, as General Allenby enters into Jerusalem. Both Christ and the Crusaders are ironically suggested by this entry, and even soldiers involved view it cynically:

ALLENBY:

> What do they think I am? A Roman emperor?

STORRS:

> Brass bands, victory marches, beautiful girls hurling
> flowers at us. I'm looking forward to it.

(3:396)

This scene ends with Allenby sending Ross back to the Revolt, despite his entreaties. Expediency triumphs over morality, and Allenby, like Ross, is painfully aware of it:

> Am I supposed to care about what's right? It was necessary. That's all that concerns me. (*Unhappily*) All that ought to concern me [. . .] Oh God, Storrs, won't it be wonderful when this damn war's over.

(3:399)

The "damn war" is driven by a lust for power that gives pleasure to none. It is an imperialist war in disguise, since the British authorities are shown to have no intention of granting the Arab allies the independence for which they are fighting.

The moral ruthlessness of the Desert Campaign is later replaced by the comradeship of the RAF barracks. There, Ross's mates are concerned with his poor health and inability to keep up with the work. They support him when they learn he's about to be taken away from them. They sing together, and Aircraftman Parsons puts his arm around Ross's shoulder. The RAF barracks becomes, like the boarding house in *Separate Tables,* with its tolerant and sustaining landlady, or the apartment in *The Deep Blue Sea* with its kindly Dr. Miller, a place where those who suffer from self-knowledge can be ministered to. It also draws on the mythology of the RAF, which had appeared in far sketchier form in *The Deep Blue Sea.*[22] In *Ross,* the soulless expediency of British headquarters is replaced by the instinctive concern of the men toward each other. Small pockets of democratic souls provide a refuge for those who suffer. Ross, for all of his timidity and evasiveness, finds acceptance here. "For the first time in five years," he explains, "I'd remembered what it was to feel life worth living" (3:322). Egalitarian community becomes a possibility only for those who have "come down in the world."

Rattigan transforms the loss of imperial power for his audience by stressing its cost, not to the ruled, but to the rulers. For the rulers to come down from their positions of power is a recognition of common humanity and self-knowledge. Rattigan consoles his British post-imperialist audience by turning their loss of political power into a proof of moral superiority. After all, Ross does not merely become one of the "common people" and indistinguishable from everyone else in the play. His role is clearly that of the protagonist, and a protagonist in the commercial, star-oriented theatrical world of London's West End theatre. So, even when Ross makes his first entrance as a supposedly anonymous member of the RAF, the audience recognizes the star who is playing the title character, and immediately transfers the aura of the "star" to the purportedly "ordinary" figure he pretends to be on his entrance. Anonymity, humility and egalitarianism, having been transformed into aspects of moral superiority, serve to replace a hierarchy of rank with one of virtue. Margaret Leighton and Eric Portman were no less stars for playing the unglamorous spinster and Major in *Separate Tables.* Their dual performances, including ones in which they renounced their own glamour, stressed their virtuosity, range, and, by implication, their wealth of sympathy and understanding in playing these roles. Renunciation becomes a gesture that redounds to the credit of the exceptional person, rather than diminish its stature. Hence, Britain, by diminishing its stature, proves its superiority.

There is no way, then, for a star to become one of the crowd; even the renunciation of glamour enhances his status. It is this insight that makes the ending of *Ross* far less comic than that of *Separate Tables.* Ross is forced out of the all-male Eden of the RAF by Aircraftman Dickinson, who recognizes him and sells this information to the press. Ross is nothing but a conscious negation of Lawrence, and offers no real refuge from his previous identity. "Aren't you confusing Ross with Lawrence?" asks the protagonist. "Or is Ross a fake too? Perhaps you're right. It doesn't matter much anyway. Fake or not he's been a dreadful failure" (3:328). The movement down in the world cannot negate the past, nor can it render the individual invulnerable to alienation from the group. *Ross* points out the hidden limitations in the world of *Separate Tables.*

Yet Rattigan finds a new way to console his middle-class British audience. Since he can no longer maintain his belief in social consolations, he moves to religious ones, and makes T. E. Lawrence a saint. When Ross killed his beloved friend Hamed, rather than leave him wounded for the invading Turks, Hamed assured him, we are told, "God will give you peace" (3:408). This line is heard again twice, once spoken by the hero to himself as the final curtain falls. Grace is now the gift to those with self-knowledge, and that grace more than compensates for the loss of Empire, but the vision of social integration for those who have "come down in the world," held out to Hester Collyer in *The Deep Blue Sea,* and achieved in *Separate Tables,* no longer exists. The only consolations for Ross are spiritual, not social.

Notes

1. For political and social histories of Great Britain in the immediate postwar period, see Alfred Havighurst, *Britain in Transition: The Twentieth Century* (Chicago, 1979), pp. 368-491; Harry Hopkins, *The New Look: A Social History of the Forties and Fifties in Britain* (Boston, 1964); David Thomson, *England in the Twentieth Century (1914-1963)* (Hammondsworth, 1965), pp. 217-257.

2. For an analysis of the intellectual and artistic life of the period, Robert Hewison's *In Anger: British Culture in the Cold War, 1945-60* (New York, 1981) is invaluable. See particularly pp. 1-31.

3. T. S. Eliot, *Notes Towards the Definition of Culture* (London, 1948), p. 19.

4. Hopkins, pp. 107-109.

5. J. B. Priestley, always a writer with a keen topical sense, addressed the tensions of postwar austerity as early as 1947 in *The Linden Tree.* The play counseled a cautious but nonetheless genuine optimism for the future of the Welfare State. This play remains, however, an isolated case.

6. The best analysis of Rattigan's postwar plays is John Russell Taylor's excellent structural analysis in *The Rise and Fall of the Well-Made Play* (New York, 1967), pp. 150-160.

7. Terence Rattigan, *The Collected Plays,* 4 vols. (London, 1953-79). All citations from these volumes will be noted parenthetically in the text.

8. Hopkins, p. 19.

9. Hopkins, pp. 153-158.

10. Michael Darlow and Gillian Hodson, *Terence Rattigan: The Man & His Work* (London, 1979), pp. 227-228.

11. For the use of the term "comic" here, I refer the reader to Northrop Frye, *Anatomy of Criticism* (Princeton, 1971), pp. 169-171.

12. Thomson, pp. 258-263.

13. Michael Yardley, *Backing into the Limelight* (London, 1985), pp. 149-157.

14. Edward Said, *Orientalism* (New York, 1978), pp. 2-49. For Said on Lawrence, see pp. 229-243.

15. Quoted in Yardley, p. 155.

16. Darlow and Hodson, p. 250.

17. For various analyses of the Deraa episode and its veracity, see Yardley, pp. 110-13; Jeffrey Meyers, *Homosexuality & Literature 1890-1930* (Montreal, 1977), pp. 114-129; Thomas J. O'Donnell, *The Confessions of T. E. Lawrence: The Romantic Hero's Presentation of Self* (Athens, OH, 1979), pp. 108-130.

18. For the sake of clarity, I will refer throughout to Rattigan's protagonist as "Ross" and Thomas's as "Lawrence."

19. See Said, esp. pp. 188-190; also O'Donnell, pp. 88-95.

20. Stanley Weintraub, "Lawrence of Arabia: The Portraits from Imagination, 1922-1979," in *The T. E. Lawrence Puzzle,* ed. Stephen E. Tabachnick (Athens, GA, 1984), pp. 282-83.

21. See John Osborne's use of the same device in his play of homosexuality and empire, *A Patriot for Me* and the parody of it in Alan Bennett's *Forty Years On.*

22. It is worth noting, parenthetically, that Rattigan himself served in the RAF. See Darlow and Hodson, pp. 104-136.

Theodore Dalrymple (essay date November 2000)

SOURCE: Dalrymple, Theodore. "Reticence or Insincerity, Rattigan or Pinter." *New Criterion* 19, no. 3 (November 2000): 12-20.

[*In the following essay, Dalrymple compares the work of Rattigan and Harold Pinter in order to illuminate the significant cultural shift that took place in England in the 1950s.*]

History is a seamless robe, of course, but there are nevertheless discernible tears in its fabric. One of these occurred in the 1950s, in the small world of the British theater. No doubt unimportant in itself, this quasi-revolution heralded, and perhaps even contributed to, a profound change in our culture.

The year in which the change started was 1956: the year, not coincidentally, of the Suez crisis, when it was unmistakably clear as never before that Britain, after two centuries of world influence, was now reduced to the status of a third-rate power, a kind of larger Belgium, which could disappear from the face of the earth without anyone beyond its shores noticing that anything very much had happened. Such abrupt losses of status are apt to result in a reduction of cultural self-confidence, both individually and collectively, as well as in a change of sensibility amounting to a gestalt switch. What previously appeared self-evidently good now appeared self-evidently bad, and vice-versa: and in the process, babies were thrown out with bathwater.

It was in 1956 that John Osborne's play *Look Back in Anger* was produced at the Royal Court Theatre in London. The living playwright who until then had dominated the London stage, Terence Rattigan, recognized it at once as a threat not merely to his commercial supremacy, but to his whole conception of the drama. Having attended the first night, Rattigan was asked by a newspaper reporter what he thought of the play. He replied that he thought Osborne was trying to say, "Look, Ma, I'm not Terence Rattigan." Accustomed from the early age of twenty-five to theatrical success, his long night of critical disdain had begun. He died if not an embittered, at least a very much saddened, man.

Osborne was not by any means the only playwright at work transforming the London stage. A couple of years after his triumph, another playwright, a young actor named

Harold Pinter, had emerged. Within ten years his was perhaps the dominating presence in the English theater. And so distinctive was his work that, in a very short time, a new adjective came to describe the menacing atmosphere, heavily laden silences, and deep incomprehension between characters that were the hallmark of his plays: "Pinteresque." No doubt his name was admirably suited to the formation of adjectives, as Rattigan's name was not: for "Rattiganesque" or "Rattiganish" are clumsy, ugly locutions. But the remarkable fact is that, after the production of a mere handful of plays, many people who had never seen or read a work by Pinter knew precisely what the word "Pinteresque" meant. Such implicit recognition is given to very few authors, and is a sign of their cultural significance.

A comparison of Rattigan with Pinter might help us understand, or at least pinpoint, some of the enormous cultural changes that have occurred in England in the last half-century—and not only in England. It goes without saying that literary difference does not necessarily imply opposition: Chekhov is very different from Shakespeare, but in no sense opposed to him. And, despite their enormous differences, Rattigan and Pinter had a high regard for each other's work, which speaks well of them both. Among other things, they were united by a passion for cricket, that team sport so prolonged and subtle that there is little place for it in the modern world, except in India, where prolongation and subtlety remain in vogue.

Rattigan was the practitioner and advocate of "the well-made play," a phrase that came quite suddenly to bear precisely the opposite connotations from the ones a naive speaker of our language might have supposed. The opposite of a well-made play being a badly made play (something which no sensible person, surely, would wish to waste his time or money on), the naive speaker would conclude that the desirability of a play being well-made was unquestionable: but in fact, the phrase came to be code for trivial, facile, middlebrow entertainment, with a beginning, a middle, and an end, and with little that, in the words of Mr. Podsnap, could call a blush to the cheek of a young person. In short, the well-made play was a typical product of English bourgeois complacency, hypocrisy, moral cowardice, and intellectual laziness.

Unfortunately, Rattigan did not help his own case by his invention of Aunt Edna, the notional average playgoer for whom, in the preface to the second volume of his collected plays published in 1953, he said he wrote his plays. Aunt Edna, according to Rattigan, was the kind of person who predominated in theater audiences the world over, and always would predominate, and whom the playwright could therefore ill afford to ignore or offend. Mildly interested in the arts, but not excessively so, Aunt Edna knew what she liked and knew even better what she did not like: morbid concentration on the unpleasant aspects of life to the exclusion of all else, artistic experimentation, and cleverness for its own sake.

Rattigan could hardly have expressed himself worse. What he meant, of course, was that he saw no reason why serious drama should not also be entertaining and accessible to all those with a modicum of intelligence. Plays could and should have different levels of meaning, with moral or philosophical depth being embedded in a coherent narrative. It was of this layering that the playwright's skill consisted.

But just as Mrs. Thatcher was hated by millions for her strident enunciation of ideas that she never actually put into practice, so Rattigan was condemned for a compromise with shallowness and complacency that he never actually made. On the contrary, his best plays were subtle explorations of human dilemmas and of the tragically destructive power of passion. Capable of evoking the most visceral of emotions from the smallest of events, his vision was a tragic one. He would have laughed at the idea of the perfectibility of life or of man.

It is not difficult to find the biographical source of his tragic vision. He was born in 1911 into an upper-middle-class family of Irish origin, his father having been a charming but rakish diplomat and his grandfather the chief justice of the Punjab and a noted legal scholar and linguist. Rattigan received the traditional education of his class and time; handsome and talented, he seemed to have the world at his feet.

But he was homosexual, and, while homosexuality was scarcely unknown or unpracticed at that or any other time, it was still legally proscribed and socially unacceptable. Deeply desirous of social success, he was obliged to conceal his true nature from the world: public revelation, he thought, would have been the ruin of his career. Moreover, he never told his much loved mother, who lived on well into his middle age, about his homosexuality, which she would have been unable to accept. He was therefore forced to lead a double life; he never allowed his homosexual lovers to live with him in case the mask slipped. Externally, therefore, he was the debonair and elegant English gentleman; internally, he was a man of unfulfilled longing for love and companionship. What he saw as a social obligation—the need to present a decorous facade to the world—frustrated his innermost desires. It was this personal experience of conflict between two powerful imperatives that gave him such insight into, and sympathy with, the broken human heart.

More recently, there have been attempts to turn Rattigan into a homosexual icon, as if his work were simply a disguised plea for homosexual liberation. Such a view of him is a symptom of the extreme balkanization of the imagination that has taken place since he wrote: as if the left-handed could really only understand the left-handed, and the blue-eyed speak only to the blue-eyed, et cetera. But while Rattigan's predicament was the psychological source of his tragic vision, his work was not dominated by resentment. His sympathies were not entirely with himself: for being a victim of circumstances was not yet a full-time occupation or a justification for having lived.

If he wasn't campaigner for homosexual rights, exactly, Rattigan was made into a fierce social critic by an eminent British writer on the theater, Michael Billington, in his obituary of him in *The Guardian.* "His whole work," wrote Billington, "is a sustained assault on English middle class values: fear of emotional commitment, terror in the face of passion, apprehension about sex." This turns Rattigan into a theatrical advocate of sex education and a prophet of the Sixties sexual revolution, which is simply preposterous. The problem was that Billington, like most intellectuals, believed that all serious artistic work must, virtually by definition, assail middle-class values. (Could serious work assail proletarian values, for example, or uphold aristocratic ones?) Since Rattigan was, at his best, a serious artist, it followed therefore that he must have assailed middle-class values. But Rattigan was genuinely non-ideological: he believed that life was (or ought to be) too subtle and variable to be caught in the coarse-meshed net of theoretical principles.

Rattigan's plays do not lead to the conclusion that if only we could indulge in a little emotional incontinence everything would be all right. It is true that he once said, "Do you know what 'le vice anglais—the English vice— really is? Not flagellation, not pederasty—whatever the French believe it to be. It's our refusal to admit our emotions." But we have already seen that his declarative statements are not necessarily the best guide to his deepest thought; and his plays certainly do not suggest that he would have regarded our modern mania for emotional openness and explicitness either as a positive contribution to civilization or as conducive to happiness. Quite the contrary: he was the poet of insolubility, who saw passion as unavoidable, necessary, and destructive at the same time.

Rattigan was certainly not a believer in the kind of confessional frankness and literal-mindedness that has swept the English speaking world since his apogee, and which has exerted such a coarsening effect upon our sensibility. In *Separate Tables,* for example, he makes a quiet case for reticence as a precondition for true tolerance. This play takes place in the dining room of the Beauregard Private Hotel, one of those residential hotels for retired gentlefolk who have come down in the world financially, which were once so plentiful in market towns and on the South Coast of England, and which called forth an entire literature of their own, offering authors a ready-made metaphor for both personal and national decline.

The principal residents of the hotel are Mrs. Railton-Bell, Lady Matheson, Major Pollock, and Mr. Fowler. Mrs. Railton-Bell has a daughter, Sybil, a timid creature whom she dominates entirely, and is herself a woman of implacably conventional and rigid social views, which she assumes that Lady Matheson, who is too polite to contradict her, shares.

One day, through the pages of *The West Hampshire Weekly News,* Mrs. Railton-Bell discovers that Major Pollock is not a retired major at all, or a member of the upper middle class, but an impostor, a mere former lieutenant, and that he has appeared before the magistrates because he has indecently approached several women in a local cinema. It is clear that Mrs. Railton-Bell enjoys her righteous indignation as she makes her friend, Lady Matheson, read the item out loud:

LADY MATHESON:

> (*reading*)
> Ex-officer bound over. Offence in cinema. (Looking
>   up.) In cinema? Oh dear—do we really want to
>   hear this?

MRS. RAILTON-BELL:

> (*grimly*)
> Yes, we do. Go on.

Mrs. Railton-Bell says a little further on that she regards it as a stroke of luck that she had subscribed privately to The West Hampshire Weekly News.

LADY MATHESON:

> Luck, dear? Is it luck?

MRS. RAILTON-BELL:

> Of course it's luck. Otherwise we'd never have
>   known.

LADY MATHESON:

> Wouldn't that have been better?

Lady Matheson's deceptively simple question implies a sophisticated understanding that a tolerable and tolerant life cannot be lived entirely in the open, and that civilized human relations cannot long survive an unwillingness to remain uninformed about the discreditable little episodes that mar each and every human life.

Mrs. Railton-Bell, having publicly exposed the major, calls a meeting of the residents to demand that the manageress of the hotel, Miss Cooper, expel the Major forthwith. Mr. Fowler, a former teacher of classics, initially agrees with Mrs. Railton-Bell: "Tolerance is not necessarily good, you know. Tolerance of evil may itself be an evil." But he also later recognizes an uncomfortable truth. "The trouble about being on the side of right, as one sees it, is that one sometimes finds oneself in the company of such very questionable allies." In the event, however, the manageress of the Beauregard refuses to expel Major (now plain Mr.) Pollock, and all the residents—except Mrs.

Railton-Bell—accept him back into the fold. To the presumed satisfaction of the audience, Mrs. Railton-Bell's moral absolutism is defeated.

Rattigan is pleading for tolerance within a certain code of behavior. He is not suggesting that the standards by which the major was judged were in themselves wrong—that it is right for a man to manufacture a completely fake persona for himself, tell lies about his past, and touch up women in cinemas. But he is asking for the constant exercise of judgment rather than the mechanical application of rules, and his tolerance emerges not from abstract ideas, being neither ideological nor strident, but from genuine understanding of and sympathy for human weakness. The major explains himself to Sybil who—in her timid and inhibited way—has entertained an affection for him:

> I'm not trying to defend it his behavior. You wouldn't guess, I know, but ever since school I've always been scared to death of women. Of everyone, in a way, I suppose, but mainly of women. I had a bad time at school—which wasn't Wellington, of course—just a Council school. Boys hate other boys to be timid and shy, and they gave it me good and proper. My father despised me, too. He was a sergeant-major. He made me join the Army, but I was always a bitter disappointment to him. He died before I got my commission. I only got that by a wangle. It wasn't difficult at the beginning of the war. But it meant everything to me, all the same. Being saluted, being called sir—I thought I'm someone, now, a real person. Perhaps some woman might even—(He stops.) But it didn't work. It never has worked. I'm made a certain way, and I can't change it. It has to be the dark, you see, and strangers, because—.

Sybil asks him to stop: she cannot bear more of his raw-never confession. But what is quite clear is that the major is not talking modern psychobabble: that genuine confession requires painful self-knowledge and is not possible for people who talk about themselves incontinently, or only as an egotistical conversational gambit.

In Rattigan, the ability of his characters to respond to others with genuine and intense emotion is intimately connected with their reticence. Early in *Separate Tables,* Sybil asks the major, who is then still playing his part as a bluff former officer of an elite regiment, whether he will accompany her on her walk.

MAJOR POLLOCK:

> (*embarrassed*)
> Well, Miss R.B.—jolly nice suggestion and all
>   that—the only thing is I'm going to call on a
>   friend—you see—and—.

SIBYL:

> (*more embarrassed than he*)
> Oh yes, yes. Of course. I'm so sorry.

In this little speech there is, for those attuned to hear it, the longing, despair, and loneliness of a lifetime, all disciplined by the need to conduct oneself properly in a social world. And in all of Rattigan's best plays—*The Deep Blue Sea, The Browning Version, The Winslow Boy*—there are conflicts between passion and good sense, between what is good for the individual and what is good for the collectivity, between duty and inclination. These conflicts are presented both entertainingly and truthfully, so that one ends with an understanding that civilization depends upon an endless interplay of incompatible desiderata, and that even the good life cannot be lived without unhappiness.

It is not difficult, however, to see how and why, after Rattigan's world of gentility and polite understatement, Pinter's plays made such an immense impact. His characters (at least in the first few plays) were drawn mainly from a lower social stratum than Rattigan's: which was in tune with the nascent intellectual fashion for believing that the unpolished and the brutal were somehow more real and authentic than the refined and the civilized. Ugliness was also henceforth more real than beauty and impoverishment more real than wealth. Pinter's audiences—which were, after all, still overwhelmingly drawn from the supposedly inauthentic middle classes—were enabled to imagine that they were immersing themselves in the boue for which they apparently had such a nostalgia. This was both pleasurable and, in their own eyes, the fulfillment of a moral duty. They believed they were bravely facing life as it is.

It was assumed at once that Pinter's depiction of the lower orders, as totally inarticulate, uncomprehending and uncouth, was true to life. In fact, many in the old working classes of England shared the values of reticence, restraint, and good manners with their social superiors: values that still exist among the older folk. For example, recently in the hospital in which I work, I happened to see the husband of a working-class patient of mine in a waiting room. In his seventies, he had lost a lot of weight since I saw him last, and he was deeply jaundiced. I knew at once that he had secondaries in his liver. I greeted him, and, when I inquired after his health, he replied with the utmost lack of drama, "I'm here for tests. It might not be very good news, I'm afraid." I wished him well, and saw him again a few days later in the same place. "It's not very good news," he said, meaning that he would be (as in fact he was) dead in two weeks. I said that I was sorry to hear it. "Well, we must make the best of it," he replied. Our dialogue was straight out of Rattigan.

He understood that I felt for him all the sorrow it is possible and reasonable for a stranger to feel for a fellow being: it required nothing other than a few simple words to establish it. Moreover, I understood that he, even in his extremity, was trying to spare my feelings, by not making a fuss. To the very end of his life, he was a social being with social obligations, with a true humility that was part of a profound moral framework. It was this framework that once made the English, for all their many faults, an admirable and sometimes a noble people: and it is the destruction of this framework that has turned them into such savages.

Pinter recorded the turning point and perhaps contributed to the change. Because of his skill, his plays hold our attention in the theater; he creates an atmosphere with a minimum of words and stage effects, and his verbal skill gives to his dialogue the quality (sometimes) of poetry. But before long, a certain intellectual thinness is evident, and we come to the realization that not only is there no explicit meaning in Pinter's plays, but there is no implicit meaning either.

In Rattigan, people do not say all that they think for reasons of social inhibition, in Pinter, both because they lack the words and because communication is in any case impossible. There is no doubt, of course, that many people—more than there used to be, thanks to modern educational methods—are inarticulate or that many people cannot stick to the point. If you listen to barroom conversations, it becomes clear that they do not always progress like Socratic dialogues. Verbosity and incoherence are by no means opposites: and intelligent conversation is at least as much a matter of omission as of inclusion. But the characters in Pinter's plays are inarticulate for a deeper reason; life for them lacks meaning because one moment is unconnected with another and because lack of meaning is inherent in all existence. In other words, there is simply no possibility of meaning. His characters are creatures of desire but no intellect; and therefore if disputes arise among them, they are mere struggles for power. When there are events—for example, the arrival on the stage of two thugs in *The Birthday Party,* Pinter's first full-length play—they are completely arbitrary and without explanation. This arbitrariness is ontological; for Pinter admits that he has no explanation for the events he himself has put into his plays.

There is a celebrated passage in the early play entitled *The Dumb Waiter* that illustrates the Pinteresque view of disagreement as a mere struggle for supremacy between the people who disagree. *The Dumb Waiter* is a typical Pinter play in that it takes place in an impoverished environment with characters whose names are simple diminutives (Ben and Gus), who have no memorable distinguishing features (one never gives a damn what happens to any Pinter character), and who are plunged into an arbitrarily enigmatic situation. They are hired killers who have come to an unoccupied room to await their unknown victim, a room in which—as it happens—there is a dumb waiter that unexpectedly delivers orders to them for various dishes. Ben and Gus, while waiting for their victim, would like a cup of tea. Ben—the senior of the two men—orders Gus to make it.

BEN:

(*powerfully*)
If I say go and light the kettle I mean go and light the kettle.

GUS:

How can you light a kettle?

BEN:

It's a figure of speech! Light the kettle. It's a figure of speech!

GUS:

I've never heard it.

BEN:

Light the kettle! It's common usage.

GUS:

I think you've got it wrong.

BEN:

(*menacing*)
What do you mean?

GUS:

They say put on the kettle.

BEN:

(*taut*)
Who says?
(*They stare at each other, breathing hard.*)
(*deliberately*): I've never in all my life heard anyone say put on the kettle.

GUS:

I bet my mother used to say it.

BEN:

Your mother? When did you last see your mother?

GUS:

I don't know, about—.

BEN:

Well, what are you talking about your mother for?
(*They stare.*) Gus, I'm not trying to be unreasonable. I'm just trying to point something out to you.

GUS:

Yes, but—.

BEN:

Who's the senior partner here, you or me?

GUS:

You.

BEN:

I'm only looking after your interests, Gus. You've
got to learn, mate.

GUS:

Yes, but I've never heard—.

BEN:

(*vehemently*)
Nobody says light the gas! What does the gas light?

GUS:

What does the gas—.

BEN:

(*grabbing him with two hands by the throat, at
arms' length*)
THE KETTLE, YOU FOOL!

Clearly, the verbal disagreement—beautifully captured in
rhythmical dialogue—is about nothing substantive. Ben is
merely trying to crush Gus, to render him utterly subservient to him. This is a trick that Pinter often uses (one soon
learns to recognize his devices that empty the world of
meaning). In the first of his plays depicting educated
middle-class people, *A Slight Ache,* an unhappily married
couple argue over the question of whether a wasp bites or
stings. The critic Martin Esslin used this play to illustrate
Pinter's mastery not just of lower-class vernacular, but of
educated middle-class speech also. In fact, it illustrates the
opposite: his uncertain command at the time of middle-
class speech. No educated middle-class person would
maintain that wasps bite—to use such an expression would
immediately establish one as an uneducated member of the
lower classes. I checked that this was so with some friends,
one of them a judge of the sharpest intellect. He immediately said, with legal precision, "Now if Pinter had
used mosquitoes instead of wasps." The same kind of
verbal power struggle appears in his late work, though
suitably coarsened to appeal to the sensibility of the times:
for example, whether a man should properly be called a
cunt or a prick.

Obviously, verbal power struggles undoubtedly take place,
and there is no reason why a playwright should not depict
them. The problem with Pinter, however, is that this power
struggle—verbal or otherwise—is almost all there is. His
plays lack a moral dimension entirely. No situation poses a
moral dilemma for any of the characters; no one speaks of
any matter of principle. Everything in Pinter has the
concreteness of the arbitrary. Again, of course, there are
people—alas, an increasing number of them, if my experience in medical practice is anything to go by—for whom

life is like this. To take an example at random, I asked a
young man recently who had smashed a man's skull with
a fire extinguisher why he did it. "He was irritating me,"
he replied. "And how was he irritating you?," I asked. "He
just was," replied the skull-crusher. He displayed no awareness that some people might think he had a duty to contain
his irritation, and he likewise displayed no curiosity about
the reasons that his victim had provoked so intense a reaction in him. As far as he was concerned, everything was as
it was, and could have been no different from how it was.
The givenness of the world was absolute and incontest-
able.

The exploration of this disastrous state of mind, that turns
existence into a living hell, is a legitimate subject for
literature. And Pinter's characters live in precisely this
state. But there is something alarming about Pinter's use
of them; he does not stand outside them, or criticize their
brutally solipsistic world view. The lack of any other view
in his plays suggests, indeed, that theirs is the only view
possible.

Quite early on in his career, in 1962, Pinter gave a speech
at the National Student Drama Festival in Bristol in which
he explained the lack of moral content in his plays.

Warnings, sermons, admonitions, ideological exhortations,
moral judgements, defined problems with built-in solutions. The attitude behind this sort of thing might be
summed up in one phrase: "I'm telling you!" If I were to
state any moral precept it might be: beware of the writer
who puts forward his concern for you to embrace, who
leaves you in no doubt of his worthiness, his usefulness,
his altruism, who declares that his heart is in the right
place, and ensures it can be seen in full view, a pulsating
mass where his characters ought to be. What is presented,
so much of the time, as a body of active and positive
thought is in fact a body lost in a prison of empty definition and cliché. This is astonishingly crude, a mile away
from the subtlety of Rattigan's moral sensibility. For
Pinter, the choice is between Mr. Pecksniff and Elmer
Gantry on the one hand and the kind of moral nihilism
exhibited in his work on the other. But even if these were
the only two possibilities in the world—which is quite
clearly not the case—I would prefer Pecksniff to the nihilist; for if hypocrisy is the tribute that vice pays to virtue,
at least it recognizes that there is a difference between the
two.

There is something even more profoundly terrible in Pinter's work: a sustained attack on the power of the human
intellect to impose order on experience or to make sense
of existence. Although Pinter began his speech to the
drama festival by declaring baldly "I'm not a theorist," he
later said:

> Apart from any other consideration, we are faced with
> the immense difficulty, if not the impossibility, of
> verifying the past. I don't mean merely years ago, but

yesterday, this morning. What took place, what was the nature of what took place, what happened? If one can speak of the difficulty of knowing what in fact took place yesterday, one can I think treat the present in the same way. What's happening now? We won't know until tomorrow or in six months' time, and we won't know then, we'll have forgotten, or our imagination will have attributed quite false characteristics to today. A moment is sucked away and distorted, often even at the time of its birth.

Pinter is not a very good theorist perhaps, but he is a theorist nonetheless.

With this outlook, then, it is hardly surprising that his plays lack—indeed, deliberately eschew—a strong narrative line. And this cognitive nihilism is emphasized again and again in his work. Even in the dialogue quoted above, we can see it. Gus says not that his mother did say "Put the kettle on," but that he bets that she did, leaving open the distinct possibility that she did not. And if a son does not know his mother's verbal habits, who can know anything about anything?

In a world in which there is such radical uncertainty, such permanently shifting cognitive ground, such inescapable relativism, people behave psychopathically: they must do what they feel like at each successive instant not because it is right to do so, but because they could literally do not other. The question of right doesn't come into it. And there is little doubt that, during the period of Pinter's ascendance, our society has evolved according to such principles—if principles is quite the word I seek.

There is one further observation to make, however: on the complete dishonesty of it all. There is only one way to describe Pinter's philosophical outlook: that of a poseur. I refer not to the internal contradiction in his speech. (If we can't know the truth about any moment, how can we possibly say that any recollection of it is false?) Since we all commit errors of logic from time to time, Pinter may be forgiven on this count. What he cannot be forgiven for, in my opinion, is the brazenness of his insincerity. It is quite clear that he doesn't believe a word of what he says, and his reason for saying it must therefore be more concerned with self-advertisement and self-promotion that with a search for the truth. Pinter does not in the least believe it is impossible to know truths about the past. While many of his plays concern uncertainties about the events gone by—about the impossibility of knowing, for example, whether X really did commit adultery with Y—he exhibits no uncertainty about other aspects of the past. I doubt that he has ever been quite so sceptical about his royalty checks. And I now quote from an open letter by Pinter to Anthony Blair published in *The Guardian* on February 17, 1998.

The US has supported, subsidized and, in a number of cases, engendered every right-wing military dictatorship in the world since 1945. I refer to Guatemala, Indonesia, Chile, Greece, Uruguay, the Philippines, Brazil, Paraguay, Haiti, Turkey, El Salvador, for example. Hundreds of thousands of people have been murdered by these regimes but the money, the resources, the equipment (all kinds), the advice, the moral support, as it were, has come from successive US administrations.

The deaths really do mount up: 170,000 in Guatemala, 200,000 in East Timor, 80,000 in El Salvador, 30,000 in Nicaragua, 500,000 in Indonesia—and that's just to be going on with. They are, every single one of them, attributable to your ally's foreign policy.

The point here is not of course whether Pinter is right or wrong (though having lived for some time in Central America, I came to the conclusion that Guatemalan soldiers knew how to burn down straw huts with flame throwers without much in the way of American tuition, to say nothing of the opposing revolutionary intelligentsia's distinct lack of enthusiasm for intellectual, economic, or political liberty as conventionally conceived). The point is that Pinter's open letter does not suggest a man who has much difficulty deciphering the past or making moral judgments about it. If it is possible to know that precisely 170,000 people were killed in Guatemala, and that the American government was responsible for all those deaths, it is surely possible to discover whether X committed adultery with Y. It is also possible to make some reasonable moral assessment of the adultery, if it occurred.

The displacement of Rattigan by Pinter (notwithstanding their relative and distinct talents) as the dominant force in British theater therefore represented the following social trends, inter alia: a coarsening of sensibility, the triumph of irrationalism, a scepticism about the ability of the human mind to order experience, a loss of faith in the ability of language to deliver meaning, a belief that only relations of power are real and all else is illusion, a slide into intellectual dishonesty and attitudinizing, and a tolerance of psychopathy. To what extent Pinter merely recorded the trends, and to what extent he actually promoted them, I cannot say. I suspect the relationship is what our friends the Marxists (when there were any) used to call "dialectical."

Christopher Innes (essay date 2000)

SOURCE: Innes, Christopher. "Terence Rattigan: The Voice of the 1950s." In *British Theatre in the 1950s*, edited by Dominic Shellard, pp. 53-63. Sheffield, Eng.: Sheffield Academic Press, 2000.

[*In the following essay, Innes regards Rattigan's plays as embodying the social and cultural consciousness of the 1950s.*]

Rattigan has had an unusually, indeed undeservedly bad press. Ever since the 1950s his work has been treated with critical disdain. He is almost always represented as the potentially serious playwright who sold out to popularity; who substituted craftsmanship for vision, dealing (one critic as early as 1953 remarked) 'less in terms of observed life than in those of observed theatre'.[1] Undeniably, there's a certain truth in all that. However, on a quite different level, Rattigan's plays express the essential quality of English society as a whole in the 1950s. The deeper, conceptual structure of his drama can be seen as embodying dominant aspects in social consciousness of the time; and on this level even the obliquity and apparent refusal of challenging reality, for which he was attacked, have representative value.

Looking back on English theatre from the vantage-point of the end of the century, it might seem wilfully eccentric to call Terence Rattigan the 'voice of the 1950s'. After all, Bernard Shaw's death in 1950 effectively marked the end of a theatrical era. And in the mid-1950s came a revolution in British drama: one that Rattigan explicitly fought against. This radical shift was fuelled by the innovations of Sam Beckett and the belated influence of Brecht—both of which Rattigan attacked. The strident voice of this revolution, of course, was John Osborne—whose plays Rattigan disliked, however generous his public comments. However, it is all too easy for theatre-historians to mistake a change in the tone and subject-matter of drama for change in society at large. In fact there was a significant disjunction between events on the stage (particularly the stage of the Royal Court), and the state of affairs outside the theatre. The major changes that reshaped the political landscape of postwar Britain, and provided a social consensus that survived more or less intact right up to the Thatcher era, had already taken place in the 1940s. During the 1950s in particular English society stayed very much in a holding pattern—and Rattigan remained writing exactly the same kind of plays as he had in the previous decade. From one perspective it is precisely this that makes his drama representative of the period, even as it made his drama seem dated to critics who recognized, and promoted the new theatrical wave.

After *Look Back in Anger* in 1956, anger, youth, authenticity and working-class experience were the new critical touchstones—while Rattigan, as the most successful West End playwright of the time, was clearly on the wrong side: the self-declared representative of the discredited establishment to be strung up from the nearest lamppost. Indeed, to a large degree the new wave of English dramatists defined themselves in direct reaction against Rattigan. For instance, it was outraged disgust at seeing Margaret Leighton wasting her talents in Rattigan's *Variations on a Theme,* that moved Shelagh Delany (still a schoolgirl in 1958) to write her first play, *A Taste of Honey.* Ten years later Rattigan was just as much a target for John Arden and Margaretta D'Arcy, whose choice of Nelson as a symbol of oppression in their 1968 play, *The Hero Rises Up,* was in conscious opposition to Rattigan's 1966 television-drama, *Nelson: A Portrait in Miniature.* And Ken Tynan, the criti-

cal spokesman for the new wave, singled Rattigan out as 'the Formosa of the contemporary theatre, occupied by the old guard'.[2] Even though Tynan went on to say that Rattigan might also be 'geographically inclined towards the progressives', that implied he was not simply a reactionary, but a traitor to the cause.

It might even seem a gratuitous example of black humour to identify Rattigan with the 1950s—since Rattigan greeted the decade with a series of public statements, which set him graphically at odds with his contemporaries in the theatre, and handed his critics the ammunition that forced his work almost completely off the stage in the 1960s.

The first of these statements was an article he published in March 1950, attacking the 'Play of Ideas' and asserting that 'from Aeschylus to Tennessee Williams the only theatre that matters is the theatre of character and narrative'.[3] This provoked the immediate response that Rattigan's argument showed his own plays (supposedly solely 'about people')[4] as anything but non-politica: as one critic remarked, 'Equate Character with Right thinking and Idea with Subversive thinking, and you begin to appreciate what Mr Rattigan is trying to say'.[5] Then, when the first two volumes of his *Collected Plays* were published in 1953, Rattigan used the prefaces to defend his plays on the basis of their public success, as 'middlebrow entertainment', specifically written for a popular audience he characterized as 'Aunt Edna'—'a nice, respectable, middle-class, middle-aged, maiden lady'.[6] All too naturally, 'Aunt Edna' was read as a close relation of Mrs Grundy, the prurient Victorian embodiment of philistine morality. Inevitably 'Aunt Edna' became the perfect stick for beating Rattigan's work; even being adopted a decade later by Joe Orton—under the pseudonym of 'Edna Welthorpe'—as the primary target for the new drama to demolish. (In fact Rattigan clearly struck a chord here, since she is still with us in the form of Barry Humphrey's 'Dame Edna Everage'.) But the effect of Rattigan's stress on the commercial success of his plays intensified the critical suspicion that he was selling out his moral, even dramatic principles; and it was this that directly destroyed the very success by which he had justified his work.

Yet the 1950s were the chronological centre of Rattigan's career, his first play having been staged in 1933 and his last in 1977. Indeed, throughout the decade, in the face of continuing critical attack as well as the growing politicization of the theatre from 1956 on, Rattigan dominated the West End. There was hardly a month without at least one of his plays on the stage; while *Separate Tables* and *Ross* both ran for well over 700 performances, *The Deep Blue Sea* for more than 500, *Who Is Sylvia?* for 381. By contrast in the early 1960s, as he later recalled: 'I discovered that any play I wrote would get smashed. I just didn't have a chance with anything.'[7] Rattigan was not exaggerating. *Joie de Vivre* closed after just four performances in 1960; *Man and Boy* ran for only 69 performances in 1963; and for the next seven years Rattigan withdrew altogether from the stage.

Some 40 years down the road, Rattigan's plays are revived rather more often than Osborne's, or Arden's, and it becomes clear that the critical attack on his work throughout the 1950s had less to do with its actual dramatic quality, than its 'voice'—which Rattigan himself identified as being 'middle-class vernacular'.[8]

But this 'voice', in a rather wider sense, is precisely what makes his plays valuable as documents of the period. It is not so much in the explicit themes of his plays, but in the way these are expressed that Rattigan typifies the Fifties.

To return briefly to Rattigan's self-defeating attack on the 'Play of Ideas': the timing of that essay seems particularly odd since, when it was written in 1950, Osborne was still an obscure actor; Tynan had not yet started on his career; and it would be another three years before Beckett's first play reached the stage. In a sense what Rattigan's essay highlighted was actually the absence of 'ideas' or social commentary in British theatre at the time. The controversy that followed involved James Bridie, Sean O'Casey, Christopher Fry and even Bernard Shaw (in one of his last public utterances). All argued that ideas were inseparable from drama, and that—as when Shaw started writing in the 1890s—there was an urgent need for theatrical renewal. Achieving the opposite of what he apparently intended, Rattigan had created the climate for the founding of the English Stage Company and the emergence of the new playwrights like Osborne and Pinter.

Yet on another level Rattigan, whose essay specifically linked 'ideas' with 'ideology', was serving as a sensitive barometer of the period.[9] In the aftermath of the war against Fascism, this was the height of the Cold War—the Iron Curtain, Stalinism versus MacCarthyism, the outbreak of the Korean war, and the development of the hydrogen bomb: 'ideology', which had almost destroyed Europe in the 1940s, was now threatening the very survival of human society. And though (typically) all this remains an unexpressed subtext in the article, Rattigan can be seen as responding to a widespread fear of social polarization and potentially destructive idealism.

To understand the underlying significance of Rattigan's plays, it is necessary to look briefly at the state of English society in this period. The Labour government, which came to power as the war ended in 1945, is remembered for the most far-reaching programme of reform that had ever been known in England, in many ways even outdoing Oliver Cromwell. In the six years from 1945 they established the National Health Service and Universal State Welfare; nationalized 20 per cent of British industry and the Bank of England; and committed the economy to full employment through Keynsian techniques. By 1951 all this was in place. The system was set for the 1950s,

and beyond. At the same time they pursued the ideal of a classless society through punitive taxation. In this they were extending a process that had already begun under earlier Liberal and even Conservative regimes. Take income tax: in 1913 it had been 8 per cent, in 1919 it was raised to 51 per cent and in 1939 to 78 per cent. Now, from 1945 on, as statements in the House of Commons claimed with pride, the highest incomes were taxed at 94 per cent. Over the same period Death Duties were raised from 15 to 80 per cent.

What this meant in real terms was illustrated by the Labour Chancellor in answer to a parliamentary question in 1950. The very wealthiest citizens, earning £100,000 a year, who would have had £91,700 to spend in 1913, now had an after-tax income of just £2,097. A judge earning £5,000, who would have taken home £4,708 in 1913, was now reduced to £843. Of course, businessmen and professionals in 1950 were paid perhaps five times what their predecessors had earned in 1913; but their real income (not counting for inflation) was still less than a quarter of what it would have been then. As for the judge, whose salary had remained exactly the same over the years: his net earnings were less than 1/6 of his predecessors. The average after-tax pay of the once wealthy middle-classes was estimated to be only 1.8 to 2.6 times the take-home wages of the working class—certainly not enough to sustain their previous life-style.

To bring this down to a personal level, in 1946 Terence Rattigan, by far the highest paid author in Britain, who was stated to earn £600 per week (which works out to £31,200 a year), publicly claimed that he actually had no more than £12 a week to live on—adding up to a meagre £624 in the year.[10] That should be compared to the ceiling below which no tax was paid, which was £500 for a family with three children. Thus the childless Rattigan would have had just £2.1s.0d. more a week to spend than a family of workers on minimal wage.

As official figures show, this progressive redistribution of wealth had been taking place over much of the century. Yet it is hardly surprising that (at the time) the whole blame or credit—depending on your point of view—was attributed to the postwar Labour government. And news articles during the 1950s, particularly in American magazines, headlined 'The Destitution of the British Middle Class', or 'The Disappearance of the English Gentleman'.

Since West End audiences were largely middle-class, the public Rattigan aimed at might well be feeling threatened and insecure; and this was reinforced at least into the latter part of the 1950s by a general sense of impoverishment throughout the country. The withdrawal of Marshall Aid at the end of the war together with the sheer cost of the conflict, led to a grim and debilitating austerity, which affected every level of society. At the beginning of the 1950s food was still rationed; reconstruction of the bombed-out cities was slow; and industrial machinery remained unmodernized, unable to compete with a rebuilt Germany.

At the same time, as one commentator noted in 1952: 'the remarkable thing is that on the surface of life there is little visible evidence of the far-reaching levelling of incomes'.[11] Not only were appearances—and social pretensions—still kept up, class accents and attitudes were learnt by the upwardly mobile. So the old hegemony had the appearance, at least, of being completely unchanged. To cap it all, in 1951 the Conservatives were re-elected. Despite the very real social reforms—and the Conservatives, who left the Welfare State as it was, had little choice but to continue the same tax-policies—nothing seemed to have changed in the power-structure (which was indeed Osborne's complaint in *Look Back in Anger*).

In a sense, this sort of double vision was epitomized by the event that opened the decade: the Festival of Britain. Perhaps partly an electoral tool for the Labour government (the 'feel-good' factor), but publicly promoted to offset the climate of austerity and generate new national energy, this celebrated 'Great Britain's contribution to the Arts and Sciences'.[12] Rattigan himself was commissioned to write a television play for the Festival, *The Final Test,* which was characteristic in combining an innovative technical use of modern media with the most traditional of British sports: cricket. In London, futuristic temporary landmarks—the rocket-shaped Skylon and aluminum bubble of the Dome of Discovery—not only displayed space science and nuclear research, but were inhabited by Shire horses and British cheeses; miniature stages, each set with a scene from Shakespeare accompanied by a snatch of recorded dialogue; and even an 'Eccentricities Section'. Elsewhere (and the Festival was spread over 23 towns and the whole summer from May to the end of September) it was largely, as according to the brochure for Dunster: 'a pageant of knights-in-armour, medieval booths, hucksters, jugglers . . . monks chanting round the church, minstrels . . . Morris and country dances, exhibitions of local handicrafts . . . and a fireworks display'.[13]

In short, what the Festival demonstrated was an almost schizoid state: city-wide illumination at a time of frequent power-cuts; nostalgic illusion versus austerity; the 'Merrie England' of traditional society (as J. B. Priestley admiringly put it) 'at a time when the cost of living is rising steeply and we are bearing a burden of tax that is heavier . . . than any recorded in history'.[14] And it is precisely this sense of a double life—of an illusory surface disguising a very different, sometimes painful reality—that Rattigan's plays convey.

There are at least three, quite different levels on which we can read any of Rattigan's plays. Take *The Winslow Boy,* first performed in 1946, but revived successfully in 1958 which indicates its continuing relevance to our period. On the level of action it is a courtroom drama about historical injustice. The subtext, specifically relevant for middle-class feelings at the time, showed the triumph of the beleaguered individual in the face of a monolithic state bureaucracy. Such an antagonist could be easily transposed by the audience from the autocratic 1911 Admiralty to the Labour government 35 years later. And indeed that reading was emphasized by Rattigan's comments to the press in advance of the first night, outlining the parallels to the small man's fight for 'ancient freedoms' against 'the new despotism of Whitehall'.[15] However, the play can also be viewed contextually. From this perspective, it is a conscious period piece. Deliberately written in the style of Granville-Barker—the pre-eminent social playwright of the first decade of the century, whose productions of Shaw and Galsworthy were on the stage at the time of the actual events—*The Winslow Boy* was not only appealing stylistically to nostalgia. It indicated the continuance of tradition, with the theatrical form standing for the social attitudes that were becoming increasingly hollow. The imitation also pointed to Granville-Barker's focus on an inner or 'secret life' (the title of his last play), hidden beneath a surface of social issues.

Rattigan himself repeatedly emphasized the 'power of implication' and the 'weapons of understatement and suggestion' in his plays, claiming that 'drama is inference and inference is drama'.[16] Much of this obliqueness, of course, relates to the homosexual basis of his plays, which—particularly in the 1950s—had to be disguised. Quite apart from 'Aunt Edna's' unwillingness to accept any depiction of homosexuality, which would have led to box-office failure, official censorship was still very much in force. Even the most tacit reference to homosexual preferences would have been banned by the Lord Chamberlain: at least up until the Wolfenden Report in 1957 (which even rated a mention in Rattigan's *Variations on a Theme*). In addition, all homosexual acts, even between consenting adults in private, were illegal. Rattigan himself was living a double life, not only hinting at a possible marriage with Margaret Leighton in the press, but keeping his male lovers strictly segregated from his social life. So it is hardly surprising that both his major plays during the 1950s use heterosexual relationships as disguises for a homosexual original.

In *The Deep Blue Sea,* Hester (who has left her wealthy husband for younger lover and is now being abandoned in her turn) is found lying in front of an unlit gas fire, having tried to commit suicide: the money in the gas meter ran out after she lost consciousness. As Rattigan's biographers have noted, this directly repeats his own tragic experience with a young actor called Ken Morgan who, after living with Rattigan for some years, had walked out on him in 1949 for another man. He then gassed himself in his rented room when that relationship broke up, leaving Rattigan distraught.[17] In fact Rattigan's earliest version of the play had a young man in Hester's role and the lovers were explicitly homosexual.[18]

Similarly, in the first play of **Separate Tables** the histrionic tempestuousness of the alienated lovers echoes Rattigan's own relationships—and in order to get at an emotional reality, some casts have found it helpful to rehearse both characters as men—while in the second play Rattigan himself pointed out that the crime the seedy Major is trying to live down (a conviction for indecently exposing himself to a young woman in a cinema) was originally a homosexual act. In fact, the inspiration for this was Gielgud. Charged in 1953 with a homosexual offence, which was plastered across the pages of the Daily Express immediately before he was due to open in a new play, Gielgud literally faced down the publicity. To Rattigan's open admiration, Gielgud refused to withdraw from the production, appearing on the stage as usual.

But the point is not in fact that these plays, as well as **Variations on a Theme**, are disguised transpositions of a forbidden sexuality. Beneath all that, on the contextual level, it is the double nature of Rattigan's work as such—the surface appearance of normality, and the very different reality underneath—that is significant. It is this split-focus that expresses the experience of the 1950s so well: in theatrical terms, the glamour purveyed by Binkie Beaumont and Cecil Beaton versus the 'kitchen sink' drama of Osborne and Wesker. On one hand the new Welfare State, on the other the widespread sense (particularly on the part of its supposed beneficiaries in the working class) that the hierarchy of inequality was still intact. Conversely, there was the impoverishment of the middle-class versus the appearance of a traditional lifestyle that they still kept up. On the public plane, the glittering lights and traditionalism of the Festival of Britain, followed two years later by the rhetoric of a 'new Elizabethan age' and the pageantry of the Queen's Coronation—for which Rattigan wrote a 'Coronation play', **The Sleeping Prince** (showcasing the reigning couple of the theatre, Laurence Olivier and Vivian Leigh)—versus the bleak postwar austerity, which only began to fade during the 1950s.

Then, too, there was the disintegration of the Empire, the dramatic decline in Britain's global status. Throughout the 1950s, the country still clung to the illusions and trappings of imperial power—even after the Suez debacle had shown these to be empty posturing. And it is no accident that Rattigan frames the decade with two plays about Empire: **Adventure Story** in 1949, and **Ross** in 1960.

The first dealt with the one historical figure who could be seen to have conquered as far-flung an Empire as Britain in its heyday: Alexander the Great. In drawing a picture of this quintessential empire-builder as man who starts off with democratic ideals, only to end up a tyrant, Rattigan may have had Hitler and Stalin in mind, as his letters show. But being performed barely a year after the loss of India, the 'jewel in the crown', Alexander's key question 'Where did it first go wrong?'[19] echoes what must have been a common British response to the loss of global prestige—while the transience of Alexander's empire, which disintegrated with his death, was all too apt.

Ross, written right at the end of the decade, showed one of the last of the imperial heroes (T. E. Lawrence) as a man hollowed out by his victories, and destroyed by the revelation—under homosexual assault—that he had been driven by unrecognized urges he despised. As at least one of the reviews recognized, Rattigan was presenting 'the uneasy specular symbol of the conscience of the West in the twentieth century. After both the great wars of our time the victorious powers have been assailed by feelings of guilt'.[20] But the obvious analogy was far closer to home . . .

Osborne and Arden were writing explicitly against the society of their time, demanding a change in the apparent status quo, and in a sense preempting that change in the new tone or the stylistic experimentation of their plays. They might, as Ken Tynan claimed, have been speaking for all the young—but the impact of their plays was so powerful, precisely because they were not talking the 'official' language, or expressing normative assumptions.

Rather it is Rattigan who encapsulates the period. Not so much because he identified with 'the Establishment'—even though he certainly did so, writing plays for the Coronation, and at the request of the Duke of Edinburgh, and accepting a knighthood. Not even because he aimed his work specifically at middle-class audiences, and (although to a lesser degree than his critics assumed) pandered to their tastes. But because, beyond any political implications, the deeper structures of his drama voiced the dominant feelings of society as a whole. The doubleness, the split vision, the opposition between a sometimes cliched external experience and an inner, secret life—not just in terms of the characterization, but contextually—subliminally expresses a social consciousness unique to the period. It encapsulates the psychology of the 1950s.

Notes

1. George Jean Nathan, *Theatre Arts,* January 1953, p. 21.

2. Kenneth Tynan, 'The Lost Art of Bad Drama' (1955), reprinted in *idem, Curtains* (London: Longmans, 1961), p. 91.

3. Terence Rattigan, 'The Play of Ideas', *Theatre Arts,* August 1950, p. 16 (originally published in the *New Statesman and Nation,* 14 March 1950).

4. Rattigan, 'The Play of Ideas', p. 14

5. Robert Muller, *Theatre News Letter,* 25 March 1950.

6. *The Collected Plays of Terence Rattigan* (2 vols.; London: Hamish Hamilton, 1953), II, p. xii

7. Rattigan, interview in *Kaleidescope,* BBC Radio 4, July 1977.

8. *The Collected Plays of Terence Rattigan,* I, p. xix.

9. Cf. Rattigan, 'The Play of Ideas', p. 15: 'ideology equals intellect'.

10. This figure may not be quite honest, since Rattigan was renowned for a lavish life-style, although correspondence from his accountant shows that he was continually in debt. However, it was accepted in the Press without question as being in line with the norm.

11. J. H. Huizinga, 'The Bloodless Revolution', *Fortnightly,* April-May 1952, p. 258.

12. It is perhaps worth noting note this use of 'Great' that still characterized a Britain agonized over visible impoverishment and the very tangible loss of global power, which effectively sums up this double vision.

13. Advertising brochure, Dunster 1951, np.

14. J. B. Priestley, 'The Renewed Dream of a Merrie England', *New York Times Magazine,* 15 July 1951, p. 31.

15. Rattigan, 'The Play of Ideas', p. 15. Michael Darlow and Gillian Hodson, *Terence Rattigan: The Man and his Work* (London: Quartet Books, 1979), p. 141.

16. *The Collected Plays of Terence Rattigan,* I, p. xx; 'A Magnificent Pity for Camels', in John Sutro (ed.), *Diversion* (London: Max Parrish, 1950), p. 184

17. Cf. Darlow and Hodson, *Terrence Rattigan,* pp. 173-75.

18. This script is referred to by Gielgud and others, but does not seem to have survived—it is not with the papers acquired by the British Library.

19. *The Collected Plays of Terence Rattigan,* II, p. 107.

20. Harold Hobson, *Sunday Times,* 15 May 1960, p. 25.

FRENCH WITHOUT TEARS

CRITICAL COMMENTARY

David Steel (essay date winter 1991-1992)

SOURCE: Steel, David. "Ionesco and Rattigan . . . Or Watson at the Theatre Tonight?" *French Studies Bulletin* 41 (winter 1991-1992): 12-15.

[*In the following essay, Steel finds parallels between Rattigan's* French without Tears *and Eugene Ionesco's* La Canatrice chauve.]

Like the eponymous anti-protagonist of Ionesco's *La Cantatrice chauve,* the Bobby Watson of the first scene puts in no appearance in the play though he perhaps has more hair than her. Or does she? Or had they? For Bobby Watson, we remember, unlike the singular prima donna, is plural, indeed multitudinous. As the playwright himself confirmed: 'Les trois quarts des habitants de la ville, hommes, femmes, enfants, chats, idéologues, portaient le nom de Bobby Watson'.[1] Dead and buried but alive and kicking, married yet single, of variable gender and relationship, the Watpersons have, as sole common denominator, in addition to their name, their profession. No, not Bobbies on the beat, but *commis-voyageurs* to a man, or to a woman or to a cadaver.

Ionesco, in Rumanian, means Johnson. Whence, one might ask, the name Watson? Conan Doyle? Too elementary, my dear . . . Or the noted exponent of Behaviourism, J. B. of that ilk? B. for Bobby? Alas, no! (and yet like the *tropismes* of *Les Caves du Vatican* 'les automatismes du langage, du comportement' are one of the butts of the play's satire (*NCN,* 159)). Could our percipient playwright have had an inkling that a Watson, along with Crick and Wilkins (obviously pseudonyms for Smith and Martin) was about to discover the structure of D.N.A., that allows a Watson to beget a Watson to beget a Watson?

Or is the *Urwatson,* the *Watsonquelle,* as is known was the case for Smith and Martin, that 'manuel de conversation franco-anglaise à l'usage des débutants' which, when he bought it around 1948, inspired Ionesco to write his play (*NCN,* 155)? He first thought of entitling it not *La Cantatrice chauve* but *L'Anglais sans peine* with alternative titles being *Big Ben Folies* and *Une Heure d'anglais.* A much-performed one-act vaudeville of 1899 by Tristan Bernard, *L'Anglais tel qu'on le parle,* excluded that title as an option. It so happens that the 'Assimil' English-language-learner, published in 1930, was entitled precisely *L'Anglais sans peine.* A recent attempt to procure it from the shelves of the Bibliothèque Nationale, at *cote* 8x 18697 (i), produced a frustrating response of 'manque en place'— like the prima donna of the play! A copy of *L'Anglais sans peine* is not, it seems, available *sans peine.* Was Bobby Watson also a borrowing from 'Assimil'? Are all the staff rue de Richelieu called Bobby Watson and covering their tracks? Or did Ionesco not buy the book, as he alleged, but borrow . . . perish the thought!

Or could it just be that Ionesco's Watsons hailed from Terence Rattigan country? The expression *L'Anglais sans peine* is the cross-Channel equivalent of **French without Tears,** the title of Rattigan's first play, produced in November 1936. As the title indicates, it is a comedy set in an English-language-learning situation. The scene is the French Mediterranean coast, in the villa of Mons. Maingot, who takes in young English people wishing to learn French. Kenneth Lake and his sister Diana—an irrespressible teenage flirt—are spending a year with the Maingots in the company of a naval officer, two budding diplomats and a business-man-to-be. The comedy of character and situation revolves around the shifting relationships between Diana and the various unattached male 'pupils'.

In translation the play was considerably reshaped for its Parisian audience by Pierre Fresnay and Maurice Sachs. They transposed the French-learning scenario into an English-learning one, switched the Riviera to the Southampton area (!), made Maingot into Mr Watson and his daughter into Coco (*Chanel oblige?*), kept Lake and Diana, but altered the four young English boarders into three Frenchmen and a German naval officer, von Henck. All that remained to do was to find a title and Bob Watson's your uncle. Fresnay and Sachs eventually settled on . . . *L'Ecurie Watson*. 'Comédie en trois actes et cinq tableaux', the play had its first performance at the Théâtre Saint-Georges in Paris on 9 July 1937 and proved a success: 'Une pièce excellente (. . .) les critiques n'ont eu que des éloges', wrote *La Petite Illustration* which reproduced the text with photographs and an anthology of critical opinion.[2]

The chief affinity between Rattigan's and Ionesco's plays is the language-learning setting. In this context it is worth noting that *La Cantatrice* is not Ionesco's only dramatic piece inspired by language-learning. In 1966 appeared *Leçons de français pour Américains,* a *spectacle* composed of seven sketches drawn from the original twenty-eight dialogues he wrote for the Bénamou/Ionesco grammar book *Mise en Train*.[3] The title *Leçons de français pour Américains* evokes a combination of elements from *La Cantatrice chauve/L'Anglais sans peine* and *La Leçon*. No English-language text is used. Characters have French names. In part the dialogue, mostly set in teaching situations, is modelled on *La Cantatrice* practice, e.g. 'Le pupitre est dans le cahier. Le professeur est dans la poche du gilet de la montre' (p. 52), though there is an amusing nonsensical half-page *Leçon Phonétique* offering practice in nasal sounds and another featuring repeated use of the future tense. These sketches contain no Watsons, though they do predate Robbe-Grillet's deliberate incorporation of graded vocabulary and syntax learning patterns into fiction in his *Djinn* (1981). Alongside *faction* a new genre was born—*flection*—the teaching of *Français-comme-Langue-Etrangere* via fiction.

However, whereas Rattigan uses a language-learning scenario as the main framework for his plot, Ionesco does not, choosing only to exploit the language patterns and the 'characters'—the Smiths and the Martins at least—presented in his learner's book. 'Le texte de *La Cantatrice chauve* ne fut une leçon (et un plagiat) qu'au départ (. . .) le texte se transforma sous mes yeux (. . .) les répliques (. . .) se déréglèrent' (*NCN,* 158). It would seem that the abandoned lesson structure was displaced to his next play, *La Leçon*. And in contradistinction to Rattigan's comedy which, like Tristan Bernard's vaudeville, makes use of

bilingual dialogue for comic purposes, Ionesco's does not. Proper names, 'darling', 'how do you do' and a line or two in scene 10 apart, there is little use of English as such in *La Cantatrice chauve*.

Ionesco's comedy in *La Cantatrice* partly derives from the device of adopting clichéd or inane 'inauthentic' phraseology, calqued on the grammatical or idiomatic example of the primers of the time, and of transplanting it into an 'authentic' (albeit here theatrical) communicative situation. One result of the dehumanizing of character through the automatization of language is to allow for cloning—hence Bobby Watsons galore. As elsewhere in Ionesco there is in scene 11 much dehumanizing play with subverted cliché, maxim and proverb to ludicrous effect, 'Mme Martin: J'aime mieux un oiseau dans un champ qu'une chaussette dans une brouette' etc. The same devices are used in the Rattigan play: 'MAX: Le matin, comme ça, de bonne heure, je ne suis pas encore en train. Mais, à partir de 10, 11 heures, si un Anglais me demande où est la plume de ma tante, du tac au tac je lui réponds qu'elle est dans la poche du jardinier' (p. 3); or 'KENNETH: Oh! Oui. Si Edouard le voulait, il serait reçu les mains dans les poches. MAX: On dit: il arriverait les doigts dans le nez' (p. 4).

Comic dehumanization can also be achieved by Bergsonian *raideur* stemming, for example, from the fixation of a national or a professional characteristic: 'le flegme britannique' in the case of the two plays under consideration (deliberately unleavened in the Ionesco by any *humour anglais* à la *Colonel Bramble*), or rigid military or para-military behaviour, backed up or not be the wearing of uniform. In this latter respect the Capitaine des Pompiers of *La Cantatrice* plays a similar role to that of the *lieutenant de vaisseau* Hans von Henck in *L'Ecurie Watson*.

Another affinity is in the undercutting of stereotyped expectations. The prima donna, whom we expect both to have hair and, given the title, to play a main role in the action, is bald (or is she?) and mentioned only once in scene 10. In *L'Ecurie Watson* our expectations are built up about the arrival of a new guest, the dashing, wealthy Duc de Luze whose appearance is delayed until the close of the play, when he turns out to be—'abominable tragédie'—a twelve-year-old boy.

Though there is little English in Ionesco's play, there is of course much Englishness, as there is also in the French version of Rattigan's. Both are French plays set in England—'les environs de Londres' on the one hand, of Southampton on the other. Each play has only one decor and they are remarkably similar.

For *L'Ecurie Watson*: 'le living-room d'une villa sur la côte anglaise de la Manche. Il est 9h. du matin au mois de juillet. Le living-room est meublé comme le sont tous ceux de ces cottages anglais. Le mobilier consiste essentiellement en une longue table entourée de cinq chaises et devant laquelle se trouve une banquette. Il faut en outre deux fauteuils et que le tout soit très anglais! (. . .). La table est mise pour le petit déjeuner avec une énorme théière au milieu et une quantité de toasts (. . .)' (p. 3). For *La Cantatrice chauve*: 'Intérieur bourgeois anglais, avec des fauteuils anglais. Soirée anglaise. M. Smith, Anglais, dans son fauteuil et ses pantoufles anglais, fume sa pipe anglaise et lit un journal anglais, près d'un feu anglais. Il a des lunettes anglaises (. . .)' etc.

One notes the common insistence, exaggerated by repetition in the Ionesco, on the absolute Englishness of the decor. Interesting too that it is 9 o'clock in the morning Rattigan-time, 9 o'clock in the evening Ionesco-time. The conspicuously copious English breakfast in the one parallels the opening conversation on the very English dinner in the other—'Comme c'est curieux et quelles coïncidences'!

In Rattigan's English play of 1936 there are no Watsons. In the French adaptation, first produced in 1937, thirteen years before *La Cantatrice* of 1950, there are two. The title however gives the impression that they are more numerous. Was Ionesco familiar with the French version? The answer is not elementary my dear . . . despite Mary the maid revealing in scene 5 of *La Cantatrice* that her real name is Sherlock Holmes (could Conan Doyle have been a source after all?). Ionesco certainly came to know of Rattigan's name and work, although at what date is uncertain. In *The Observer* of 22 June 1958 Kenneth Tynan, a propos of Ionesco, spoke of Rattigan's 'semi-vérité' in an article translated, reproduced and commented on in *Notes et Contre-Notes* (*NCN*, 70); and later Ionesco wrote dismissively of a Rattigan play he had watched on television in the early sixties (*NCN*, 247).

But, in whatever relationship *La Cantatrice chauve* of 1950 stands to the 1937 French version of **French without Tears**—or to the 'Assimil' *L'Anglais sans peine*—and Ionesco himself saw his play as a parody of the *théâtre de boulevard* that **French without Tears** almost is—the French author's novelty is paramount. The bland *marivaudage* of Rattigan's comedy wholly lacks the penetration of Ionesco's acid disclosure of the hollowness of relationships and of the comedy of meaning itself. The antics of monolingual innocents abroad may serve the comedy of a flaccid vaudeville such as *L'Anglais tel qu'on le parle*; the language-lesson may be a convenient dramatic framework for verbal humour; the *faux-ami* device may readily raise laughs. But Ionesco's originality, once he had been alerted by the language-learning scenario and its attendant imbroglios, was precisely to sidestep it, while adapting its jejune language-patterns to everyday relationships *hors classe* (in both senses of the term) and—the England of the play notwithstanding—*hors pays*. Oh! and I almost forgot. One of the best books on Ionesco (not co-authored

is still that by R. N. Coe and Ionesco's distinguished English-language translator is called . . . Watson! 'Comme c'est curieux, mon Dieu, comme c'est bizarre! et quelle coïncidence!'.

Notes

1. Ionesco, *Notes et Contre-Notes* (Gallimard, 1962), pp. 67-68, henceforth referred to in the text as *NCN* followed by the page reference—mainly to the articles 'La Cantatrice chauve—la tragédie du langage', 'A propos de *La Cantatrice chauve* (Journal)' and 'Naissance de *La Cantatrice*.'

2. *La Petite Illustration* No. 837, Théâtre No. 422; 4 sept. 1937, pp. 1-38.

3. *Cahiers Renaud-Barrault,* 54 (1966), 48-61; Michel Bénamou, *Mise en Train. Première Année de Français* (New York: Macmillan, 1969).

FLARE PATH

PRODUCTION REVIEWS

Kate Bassett (review date 26 April 1995)

SOURCE: Bassett, Kate. "Flying High, Falling Flat." *The Times* London (26 April 1995): 12.

[*In the following mixed review of the 1995 London revival, Bassett describes the circumstances surrounding the writing of* Flare Path.]

Terence Rattigan's drama depicting Air Force pilots and their anxious wives, where the chaps are sent on a dangerous raid the very night they had planned to catch up on their personal lives, has an adventurous history. Rattigan's own rough draft, I mean.

Advised by his psychiatrist to join the RAF to cure writer's block, Rattigan scribbled away between missions. Then, during a long flight to Africa, an engine failed Rattigan was about to throw his kit bag to the winds to lighten the load, when he remembered **Flare Path** was inside. Ripping out the pages of his exercise book, he stuffed them in his pocket, and put the finishing touches to the script in Freetown, surrounded by officers "going spectacularly to pieces in the White Man's Grave", armed with gin and tonic. **Flare Path,** set in the Falcon Hotel, Milchester, Lincolnshire, is more subtly dramatic. Its wartime couples put on brave faces when racked with fear, from Teddy, the flight lieutenant who suffers airborne panic attacks, to Doris, whose Polish husband does not return with the rest.

Rattigan is sensitive to the unsaid: the servicemen's chipper euphemisms and military secrets; others keeping mum about private passions, first out of moral cowardice, then self-sacrificingly in the case of Teddy's actress-wife Patricia and her true love, the film star Peter Kyle who has come to find her.

The twists of Rattigan's plot cleverly press home the poignancy. Suddenly facing life without Patricia, Kyle (a fine Nicky Henson with Clark Gable moustache) is asked by Doris to translate Skriczevinsky's painfully formal yet loving "goodbye" letter.

Unfortunately, director Andrew Hay's company seem to have squinted over the script during a blackout. Or at least, they have not read between the lines sharply enough. There is, for instance, little sign that Squadron Leader Swanson (Jack Hedley, groping for his words rather) has twigged Patricia's imminent domestic desertion and is steering her back to base.

Barbara Wilshere's Patricia, getting tight on gin, could be far more fraught. Amanda Harris's Doris accrues intensity, briskly polite as her pain grows, but does not consistently sound like a former barmaid. Helen Sheals's Mrs Miller is lovably dour. Terry Taplin is bemusedly Polish with panache. But elsewhere both the class tensions and the comedy get flattened.

The hotel architect appears to have roofed the Falcon with the top half of a charred hangar, which creates a ghostly effect as the characters kiss farewell beyond the gauze walls. Yet the thrill of racing clouds, projected between scenes, rapidly fades.

There is one moment of heart-shaking power when the house reverberates with the roar of engines as the squadron takes off and disappears into silence. What was worrying, though, was that the preceding hour of human interaction had touched no such nerve.

Jeremy Kingston (review date 23 February 2002)

SOURCE: Kingston, Jeremy. A review of *Flare Path. The Times,* London (23 February 2002): 10.

[*In the following review, Kingston offers a favorable assessment of the revival of* Flare Path.]

Cliches can attach themselves like the proverbial burrs to a playwright whose work dips out of fashion, and sometimes they continue to cling to him even when his

work is climbing back into popularity. Terence Rattigan's reputation is still firmly linked to the idea of the stiff upper lip, where tongue-tied upper-middle-class characters find themselves unable to express what grieves them to similarly tongue-tied upper-middle-class characters. There is the element of truth in this perception, but for his earlier plays it is unfair. *French Without Tears,* his first hit, was a famously long-running comedy, though the current revival at the Northcott, Exeter, seems to be the first in a long time.

Flare Path, his 1942 drama set in a Lincolnshire hotel within sight and sound of an airfield, was revived at the King's Head Theatre, Islington, North London, in 1990 and proved itself to be a winner. A new production by the Worcestershire-based Middle Ground Theatre Company is now on an extensive tour. Michael Lunney, the director, has assembled a strong cast, led by Colin Baker as Squadron Leader Swanson. His team of bomber pilots are a varied lot, and the hotel is the weekend home for the wives and girlfriends who share anxieties and hopes for a better life.

Watch out for the natural way in which Rattigan arranges for characters to remain on stage to have crucial confessions with those who mean most to them. Some of the men's jolly outbursts sound odd today, but at least none of them is tongue-tied.

CRITICAL COMMENTARY

Geoffrey Wansell (essay date 1995)

SOURCE: Wansell, Geoffrey. "A One-Hit Wonder?" In *Terence Rattigan,* pp. 120-31. London: Fourth Estate, 1995.

[*In the following essay, Wansell chronicles the successful staging of Rattigan's second British hit,* Flare Path.]

> Me—who am as a nerve o'er which do creep
>
> The else unfelt oppressions of this earth.
>
>   —Shelley, *A Lament*

The Lord Chamberlain's reader's report on '*Flare Path,* also known as *Next of Kin*', observed that the play was 'Mr Rattigan in a more serious mood', and added, 'I do not suppose there is anything secret in this play, but it should be vetted by the Air Ministry before a licence is granted.' By the end of April both the Air Adviser to the Ministry of Information and the Lord Chamberlain had agreed that the play could be produced, and asked for only minor changes. The Air Ministry wanted Margate changed to 'say, Littlehampton' and did not want any character to say how many air raids they had taken part in. The Lord Chamberlain's office—as ever—decided to niggle about the language. In their formal letter to H. M. Tennent they insisted 'bloody' be changed to 'damned' in several places, that they would not accept 'a pissy type', 'pissed', 'caught with our knickers down' or 'stone the bloody crows'. Neither Beaumont nor Rattigan objected. The cuts were accepted and the licence was granted on 8 June 1942.

By then, Rattigan was a bundle of nerves. He telephoned Peters endlessly, demanding to know every detail of what was happening; he pestered Puffin Asquith, whom Beaumont had accepted as director, badgered Beaumont himself, and consulted Newman both in person and on the telephone. To outsiders Rattigan may have appeared his usual languid self, sipping champagne, cutting a dash in a London just recovering from the Blitz, but his friends— Asquith especially—knew the truth, his genuine fear that he might turn out to be a 'one-hit wonder' if his new play failed to please. he resumed his sessions with Keith Newman, sometimes three in a week and always held in a darkened room.

Rattigan's anxiety increased even further when he learned that Beaumont was so unconfident about the play that he had declined to confirm the booking of a London theatre. He had in mind the Apollo, in spite of Rattigan's unhappy memories of **Follow My Leader** there, but was not prepared to confirm it until the provincial tour had got under way. 'He doesn't believe it is going to work, and certainly isn't going to waste his money on guaranteeing a London theatre,' whispered one friend. Worse still, Peters told Rattigan that Beaumont was not prepared to risk his own money, but had offered shares both to Linnit & Dunfee, who had invested in **French without Tears,** and to the bandleader and impresario Jack Hylton. It was even rumoured that he was putting the play on as a tax loss. Rattigan's response was to drink heavily. Asquith kept him company. Newman looked on impassively.

The urgent task of casting the play went ahead none the less. One young actor whom Rattigan and Asquith auditioned was Jack Watling, from Chingford in Essex, then just nineteen. Watling had just volunteered for the RAF himself, but had not yet been called up 'because there was a bottleneck of people who wanted to join air crew'. Watling, who had trained at stage school, was almost unknown in the theatre when he was invited to meet Rattigan and Asquith in the cocktail bar of the Savoy hotel, though he had appeared in two films. 'I'd never been in anything like the cocktail bar of the Savoy,' Watling recalls, 'and I was totally overawed. But there was Rattigan, and Anthony Asquith, and another bod, whom I didn't know.'

Asquith had worked with Watling once before, on his film *We Dive at Dawn*. It was one of the stars of that film, Eric Portman, a friend of Asquith's, who had suggested Watling as a candidate for the young pilot in Rattigan's new play. Asquith gave Watling the script and asked him to read 'the breakdown' scene in which the pilot, Teddy Graham,

admits to his wife Patricia how afraid he really is. It was the scene Rattigan had written after his experience with the Heinkel 115 on his way to Freetown, and the emotional centre of the play.

> You don't know what it's like to feel frightened. You get a beastly bitter taste in the mouth, and your tongue goes dry and you feel sick, and all the time you're saying—this isn't happening—it can't be happening—I'll wake up. But you know you won't wake up. You know it's happening and the sea's below you and you're responsible for the lives of six people. And you pretend you're not afraid, that's what's so awful . . .

'I read the scene,' Watling remembers, 'and they totally ignored me for a bit. Rattigan was at his most charming, and so was Puffin. The other fellow said nothing. Anyway, after a few minutes' discussion Rattigan said, "We'd like you to play the part—there's only one thing. Anthony Asquith's directing the play, and this gentleman will be directing you." The gentleman in question was Keith Newman. Watling was stunned.

'At that moment I'd never heard of such a thing, and I wish to God I hadn't to this day,' Watling says now. Newman was to all but wreck his life, and his career. During the run of **Flare Path** and for the next three years, Newman came to exercise as powerful an influence over Watling as he did over Asquith, Rattigan and Tony Goldschmidt. Newman insinuated himself into every aspect of the young actor's life, even insisting that Watling should live with him in his flat in Oxford. 'On the strength of *We Dive at Dawn* I'd been offered a contract by Gaumont British Pictures,' Watling recalls. 'I was a working-class lad, with no education to speak of, and all I wanted was to be a film star. But Newman told me, "Don't accept the contract. You are an actor."' The young Watling meekly agreed.

Phyllis Calvert had been signed to play Patricia, the young pilot's wife, and Martin Walker was to be Kyle, her American former lover. During rehearsals, which took place at the Apollo, Newman said nothing. 'He just sat there in the stalls, silent', according to Watling. 'But just before the play opened in Oxford, where I was to stay with him in his flat at Number 36 Holywell, he took me to the Lake District for three days of what he called intensive voice training.' The psychiatrist had devised a set of vocal exercises, which he insisted he practised for hours at a time. 'It was unbelievable,' Watling recalls. 'He took over my life completely.'

Watling was not aware that the author of **Flare Path** was homosexual, or that his taste was for handsome, fresh, round-faced young men, as Watling was at the time. 'I didn't discover any of that until much later,' he explains now. 'But I did find out that Newman was telling Rattigan not "to bother with me". Certainly Rattigan never made a pass at me, as he did at some actors.' At this stage Newman had not made a homosexual pass at Watling. That came later. Newman simply frightened him beyond words.

'I couldn't do anything without asking his permission. I was heterosexual then, and I am now, but Newman pretty much gave me a nervous breakdown. I couldn't cope with him.' Why Newman had this power, or why people submitted to him, Watling is just as unable to explain now as he was then.

The pre-London tour of **Flare Path** opened on 13 July 1942 at the New Theatre, Oxford, but with Rattigan called back to Coastal Command, only Newman and Asquith were on hand to witness its reception. Whatever Beaumont's reservations, the audience clearly liked it, and by the time it had finished its week, he had plucked up the courage to book the Apollo for the middle of August.

By coincidence, two of the films which Rattigan had co-scripted—*The Day Will Dawn* and *Uncensored*—were released about this time. *The Day Will Dawn,* which he had written with Tolly de Grunwald, had emerged in May to no more than lukewarm notices. 'It could have been, should have been, enormously exciting. But to my mind, it never gets beyond the inspired mediocre,' said the *Observer*'s C. A. Lejeune of this story by Frank Owen about the destruction of a U-boat base in Norway. 'Would have been a better film and no less popular if its climax had been subtly timed,' was the opinion of the *New Statesman.*

When *Uncensored,* which Rattigan had scripted with Rodney Ackland, was released in July, the critics were a little more enthusiastic, not least because Eric Portman was its star and Anthony Asquith its director. Dilys Powell in the *Sunday Times* complimented Puffin specifically, and called the screenplay 'a neat job'. William Whitebait in the *New Statesman* felt it 'a more finished piece of work than the same director's *Freedom Radio*'. Even so, none of the critics felt the film was as moving or as exciting as it could have been, though they thought Peter Glenville, Rattigan's friend and house-sharer from Oxford, deserved particular praise for his portrayal of the jealous partner who betrays the hero.

For once the reviews hardly interested Rattigan. His attention was focused on the fate of **Flare Path.** The Air Ministry not only approved of the play, but had also asked for seats for the opening night. Air Chief Marshal Sir Charles Portal, the Chief of the Air Staff, intended to be present. This cheered Binkie, who saw the publicity possibilities. So, on the warm evening of 13 August 1942, Rattigan established his parents in their box and went to stand with Asquith at the back of the circle as the first act unfolded. Inevitably Vera had brought the famous champagne cork in her handbag, and Rattigan had once again had his hair cut. As always, he observed the rituals and deferred to his superstitions. Now he was in the hands of Adrienne Allen and Phyllis Calvert, Martin Walker, Kathleen Harrison, Jack Watling, and a very young George Cole.

By the middle of the third act some women in the stalls were actually crying, and Rattigan risked whispering to Puffin, 'I think we've brought it off.' It certainly seemed

so. Then a strange thing happened. The curtain slowly began to fall. It stopped half-way down, and stayed there for what seemed like an eternity, until, just as inexplicably, it began to rise again. There was hesitant applause from the audience, which grew to a storm a few minutes later, when the play actually ended and the curtain fell as it was intended. It was the warmest reception Rattigan had received since **French without Tears.**

The Chief of the Air Staff sent a message to Flying Officer Rattigan, inviting him to his box to receive his congratulations. Newman summoned Jack Watling: but not to offer any praise. Sitting impassively in the stalls, he had been making notes on how his protégé could improve his performance. Rattigan and Asquith then retired to Puffin's house in Bloomsbury, to wait for the first editions. Applause was welcome, but what mattered to Rattigan were the reviews. He was worried, and rightly.

'Given technical competence,' *The Times* noted sniffily, 'a play on the subject of bomber pilots and of the women who wait for them to return from their raids can hardly fail to move a London audience today. But something more than mere competence is required if these semi-public figures are to reveal themselves and their problems.' Most of the rest of the dailies were equally cool, criticising particularly the 'unimaginative' characters, which the *Spectator* added at the weekend were never 'roundly drawn by the dramatist'.

By a strange irony only James Agate, scourge of **French without Tears,** correctly assessed the play's strengths. 'Considered as entertainment Mr Rattigan's piece is extraordinarily lively. A laugh every minute, a roar every five minutes, and a tear every ten,' he wrote in the *Sunday Times,* adding, 'At times it is a little better than this.' Paying tribute to its author's 'craftsmanship', he concluded, 'Notable acting by everybody makes the piece safe for a year.' In fact it was to be safe for eighteen months.

Most of the critics had totally failed to appreciate the public mood, just as Beaumont and Bronson Albery had done when the play was first offered to them. London's theatregoers already had their 'entertainments'. Noël Coward's *Blithe Spirit* was playing almost next door at the Globe, also presented by Beaumont, while Gielgud, Edith Evans and Peggy Ashcroft were at the Phoenix in *The Importance of Being Earnest*. But there were no other plays in London which accepted the facts of the war, and none that brought those realities home in as palatable and moving a form as **Flare Path.**

Rattigan's experience of writing propaganda films for Asquith, coupled with his own sympathy for the everyday life of the airmen he had lived and served with, gave his play a quality with which the audience immediately identified. Finished on the veranda of a former school in Africa, with his fellow officers looking over his shoulder offering suggestions, the play's affection for its characters shone through. It touched a nerve, even if the critics thought it too sentimental. And, above all, it was optimistic. It carried the message that those fighting the war might just survive, no matter how long the odds. In the months after the fall of Singapore and Tobruk, while the British army was still being forced back by Rommel in the Western Desert, that message was welcome. Agate and the other critics may have called for a tragic ending, but Rattigan was, instinctively, a better judge of the country's mood. 'To be successful,' he wrote seven years later, 'a playwright must take so many factors into consideration; the changing background of everyday life; changing tastes; changing fashions; changing manners.' *Flare Path* showed he could do so.

Terence Rattigan had written his second hit, and it brought back his confidence. 'I don't know whether you have heard the figures,' he wrote to his father shortly after the play opened, 'but they are extremely good. First full week £1,287, second £1,305 and this week up a little, so far, on last. This is a better start than *French without Tears.* I get a daily and eagerly awaited telegram telling me the returns.'

Flare Path also captured the public appetite for stories about the RAF. Air Chief Marshal Sir Arthur 'Bomber' Harris, head of Bomber Command, went to see the play shortly after it opened, and went backstage afterwards. 'Bloody disgraceful,' he bellowed at Jack Watling, 'showing cowardice in front of the enemy.' Harris knew that many of his own air crew would go to see the play and identify with the young pilot who was losing his nerve after so many missions. What he failed to understand was that the frank admission of fear could provide its own inspiration. Nevertheless he helped to speed up Watling's own admission to the RAF.

Even that, however, did not allow the young actor to escape Newman's clutches. By pulling strings the psychiatrist arranged for Watling to be posted to the Allied Squadron, where French and Polish officers were taught English at a base in London. This meant that Watling, even after his official call-up, could still perform. Newman meanwhile sat in the stalls for every single performance and watched his young charge in action. Though neither Rattigan nor Watling knew it, Newman was planning a book, which he would later publish himself, called *250 Times I Saw a Play.* When he sent a manuscript to George Bernard Shaw the playwright commented, 'I don't know what to say about this book. The experience on which it is founded is so extraordinary that an honest record of it should be preserved. But it would have driven me mad; and I am not sure that the author came out of it without a slight derangement.'

By the autumn of 1942, and in spite of Newman's brooding presence, *Flare Path* was established as the most popular new play in London. In late October Eleanor Roosevelt went to see it, writing afterwards in the *News Chronicle,* 'It was beautifully cast and acted, and I am glad it is going to the United States, because it is a true and moving picture of the RAF.' By then Gilbert Miller, together with the Theatre Guild, had bought an option on the play for Broadway, and were negotiating for Alec Guinness to make his Broadway début as the young airman. Meanwhile, with Rattigan's encouragement, A. D. Peters had turned down two offers for the film rights, £5,000 from Warner Brothers and £8,000 from Twentieth Century-Fox. Rattigan was determined they should get £15,000 at least, and he succeeded. Early in 1943 Fox bought the rights for £20,000—almost as much money as Rattigan had made from the entire run of *French without Tears*—and then failed to make the film.

Flare Path changed the course of Rattigan's life. Had it failed he might never have risked writing for the stage again, taking refuge instead in screenplays. Its success, and the remarkable impact it had on its audiences, had a cumulative effect on his confidence, which he was to draw on in the years to come. 'Each fresh success gives more confidence; more knowledge of the likes and dislikes of audiences; and, of course, more experience in stage technique,' he wrote later. Though his fear of failure was never quite to disappear, it was never again to be so intense.

When Winston Churchill went to see the play with his wife Clemmie and Margot Asquith in January 1943, shortly before leaving for the Casablanca conference with Roosevelt, he told the cast, 'I was very moved by this play. It is a masterpiece of understatement. But we are rather good at that, aren't we?' The Prime Minister's remark made up for the disappointment Rattigan had felt just a few days earlier, when the Broadway production closed after only fourteen performances at the Henry Miller Theatre. Though he had been in New York, arriving there on the *Queen Mary,* he missed the Broadway opening by one day. Under orders from the RAF, he had left to ferry Catalinas back from America to Prestwick in Scotland. He flew throughout Christmas Day 1942, his route via Bermuda, and took twenty hours to reach the Scottish coast, having got hopelessly lost. So it was some days before he discovered that the Broadway production had flopped. *Variety* prophesied:

> It is doubtful if the American reception of *Flare Path* will approximate the click being enjoyed currently by the original London offering. Perhaps one reason for this lies in the fact that the play is somewhat ahead of its time over here. Being concerned with air raids and life under the immediate war conditions of embattled Britain, it is obvious that a London audience would look upon the drama as an actual piece of their existence lifted bodily on to a stage.

The other New York reviews confirmed this judgement. 'The drama seems sentimental, slow and confused,' wrote Lewis Nichols in the *New York Times.* Once again Rattigan felt, as he was to feel many times in the future, that he would never succeed in the United States. It was all the more galling because he firmly believed that he had put far more than mere propaganda into the events in the residents' lounge of the Falcon Hotel in Lincolnshire.

As Rattigan had explained to his parents in a letter, there were echoes of his unproduced *Black Forest* in *Flare Path*. It too focused on the fact that lovers, husbands and wives were often unable to express their emotions, even in the most extreme situation. Even more significantly, the central triangle in *Flare Path,* the young bomber pilot, his wife and her former lover, a Hollywood star who has returned to claim her, also mirrored a crisis in the playwright's own life. Kenneth Morgan had left him and gone to live with another actor.

Morgan's decision that he was not going to remain faithful had come as a tremendous shock to Rattigan, who saw himself as someone whom no lover should ever leave. The shock was so great that it was to colour his view of love in the years to come. It was to recur time and again in different guises throughout his later work. But, in this first instance, it meant that Rattigan put a substantial part of himself into *Flare Path,* and in particular into the character of the glamorous Peter Kyle, the movie star who is unable to recapture the woman he loves once she has discovered that her husband, a young bomber pilot called Teddy Graham, needs her more. And though Kenneth Morgan was eventually to return to him, the experience of being deserted by someone he loved deeply left a wound that was to remain with him throughout his life.

Flare Path's two subplots, one involving a Polish count (Gerard Heinz), whose wife (Kathleen Harrison) was a barmaid until they married and is convinced that her aristocrat husband will leave her once the war is over; the other concerning a cockney Sergeant, Dusty Miller (played by Leslie Dwyer), whose wife has taken enormous trouble to come down to the hotel for the night, only to see her husband disappear on a sudden bombing raid, are extensions and reflections of the triangle between Kyle, and Patricia and Teddy Graham at the heart of the play. Both subplots are designed to underline the fact that love can conquer, no matter how strange its twists and turns may appear. In fact the Polish countess discovers that her husband will never leave her, when Peter Kyle translates a letter from him after he has gone missing, and the cockney wife reveals how much she cares about her husband, no matter how gloomy she may appear. *Flare Path* passed this optimistic message to its audience.

Rattigan revelled in the play's success. He had struck a chord in the hearts of the London theatre audience. It was what he wanted. In the introduction to the first volume of his collected plays, published a decade later, he was even to overlook the critics' original unenthusiastic reaction. He wrote: 'At long last I found myself commended, if not exactly as a professional playwright, at least as a promising apprentice who had definitely begun to learn the rudiments of the job.'

Not that he was to practise his craft again for some time. In the Air Force his next posting was as Gunnery Officer to 422 Squadron, where his job was to devise training programmes for the air crew while still flying missions himself. He wrote to his parents, apologising that he could not tell them exactly where he was stationed, but explaining, 'The camp is large and damp and Nissen hutted. There is nothing to do and nowhere to go after working hours. To quote from a sergeant friend of mine, "We are fourteen miles from f- all."' The period of isolation was soon to come to an end. *Flare Path*'s success brought his transfer from active duty to the RAF Film Unit. He would still wear uniform, but his days as a serving air gunner and wireless operator were over. He was no longer expected to fly. His transfer took place in March 1943.

The RAF wanted Rattigan to collaborate with the American novelist and screenwriter Richard Sherman on a film about an airfield, meant to illustrate the collaboration between British and American air forces. The idea had come from William Wyler, the Hollywood director, now mobilised with the rank of Major and working on a documentary in Britain. In the end Wyler returned to America without working on the story that Rattigan and Sherman had come up with. It had grown out of *Flare Path,* but it was to be almost two years before the screenplay would finally reach the screen with Asquith's help.

Another project the RAF had in mind for Rattigan was based on the work of Flying Training Command. Produced entirely within the Film Unit, the film was to be directed by another serving Flight Lieutenant on secondment to the unit, John Boulting. He had worked as a producer with his twin brother, Roy, in the years before the war on films like *Thunder Rock* and *Pastor Hall*. The film was to centre on the life of two young men from the start of their initial training to their final posting to a Lancaster and their participation in a bombing raid. Rattigan wrote the script himself, without the customary collaboration from either Asquith or Tolly de Grunwald, and called it *Journey Together.* Again it was to take almost two years before the film was finished.

In the meantime Rattigan and De Grunwald worked on a script for a film that Harold French and Two Cities had suggested. It was to be called *English without Tears,* and was planned as a sequel to his first great success. The project did not enthuse him. He could not see the point of bringing Diana back to life, but the fee was welcome, and he accepted de Grunwald's assurance that the job would not take long. This time he chose an English butler and manservant, Gilbey (another of his private jokes, this time on his friendship at Harrow), in the tradition of P. G. Wodehouse's Jeeves, to carry the comedy. Gilbey is the focus for the affections of the fickle but charming Joan Heseltine, who has launched an English class for Allied officers in her own contribution to the war effort. But, like Diana in *French without Tears,* Joan proceeds to fall in love with a number of the officers she is teaching, including a Pole and a Frenchman, and forgets Gilbey, because he is only a manservant. Nevertheless, when she volunteers herself, she is posted to work for her former butler, now promoted to the rank of Major, and finds that she loves him. Even the neat ending could not conceal the flimsy nature of the piece. It was escapist entertainment, a way of earning money. Privately Rattigan despised it.

On Easter Day, 25 April 1943, the brutal reality of the war intervened when Anthony Goldschmidt was killed in battle. Handsome, brilliant, and a loyal friend since Harrow, though never a lover, Goldschmidt had married after giving up his career as a stockbroker to become a writer. His loss devastated Rattigan, and everyone else who knew him. Newman's strange book on *Flare Path* is dedicated to Goldschmidt's memory, though it never once mentions the name of Terence Rattigan. For a time Rattigan was so distraught that he could not bring himself to work. He and Goldschmidt had been friends for nearly twenty years, used to laughing at each other's jokes, Rattigan mimicking everyone they knew and Goldschmidt collapsing in tears as a result. Rattigan was thirty-one, Goldschmidt a year younger.

Theirs was a friendship that Terence Rattigan was to recreate within a few months in his screenplay for John Boulting's film *Journey Together.* In his story, two young men share every experience, until finally they find themselves in a rubber dinghy lost in the North Sea after their Lancaster has ditched on its way back from a raid on Berlin. It was Rattigan's way of coping with his loss.

Flare Path continued to run successfully at the Apollo, surviving cast changes in January, February and June 1943. Leueen MacGrath replaced Phyllis Calvert and Griffith Jones Jack Watling. Inquiries for possible production rights were coming in from around the world, in spite of the play's failure on Broadway. The film rights money was safely lodged in Rattigan's bank, Coutts & Co. in the Strand. He was still paying for the upkeep of his parents' house at Pepsal End, including their grocery bills, and providing his father with an allowance for the usual undiscussed purposes, though he seldom went down to see them. Rattigan's affair with Kenneth Morgan had survived far less well. They had argued persistently until Morgan left. Rattigan had reproached him for his persistent unfaithfulness during his tours of duty with Coastal Command, but Morgan had responded by complaining that his famous partner would not let him live with him. Morgan would stump off in a huff, return, then stump off again.

Rattigan's brother Brian was another worry. Now drinking very heavily, he had finally managed to qualify as a solicitor but could not find a place in a London firm. The chip on his shoulder, which he had tried to conceal by his outrageous behaviour at Harrow, had never shifted. He relied on his parents for financial support. Though he did not realise it, indirectly it was Rattigan's generosity that sustained him while he completed his law exams. Like his younger brother, he also showed no inclination to marry, and Frank Rattigan had long since lost the little sympathy he had for his crippled elder son. The Major still had no time for him.

In spite of the financial burdens of his brother and his parents, which he bore without complaint, the success of *Flare Path* meant that Rattigan was considering taking an apartment again. The RAF had confirmed that he was to stay with the Film Unit rather than return to active service as aircrew. As always he favoured Mayfair, or somewhere as close to it as possible, and in June 1943 he took a small set of chambers in Albany, the elegant Georgian building just off Piccadilly that already housed his fellow playwright J. B. Priestley, another of A. D. Peters's clients. Byron had been one of its early inhabitants, as had Gladstone when he was prime minister, the historian Macaulay, and the novelist Compton Mackenzie. Built originally in 1771, and then called York House, it was one of London's most fashionable addresses. Applicants for sets were subject to discreet vetting. 'Mr Rattigan,' the trustees record, 'took a lease for two years in the set of apartments known as K5 from 24 June 1943 to 24 June 1945 at a rent of £250 per annum.'

WHILE THE SUN SHINES

PRODUCTION REVIEW

Alvin Klein (review date 21 October 2001)

SOURCE: Klein, Alvin. "An Esoteric Rattigan Play That Wants to Entertain." *New York Times* (21 October 2001): 10.

[*In the following positive review of* While the Sun Shines, *Klein asserts that "the production is charming, not unfunny and quaint enough to be endearing."*]

Presenting a play by the British playwright Terence Rattigan, whose glory days were from 1936 to 1956, is a long shot. This is because Rattigan's works are better known to American audiences as period pieces, the last vestige of British theater convention.

This is true even of his Broadway hits, like *The Winslow Boy* (1946). Even *The Deep Blue Sea,* his masterpiece by English critical consensus, was dismissed in its 1952 Broadway staging, as was a recent revival at the Roundabout Theater Company. But Centenary Stage Company in Hackettstown is opening its season with an obscure Rattigan play, *While the Sun Shines,* a comedy set during the London blitz. And the production is charming, not unfunny and quaint enough to be endearing.

The play seems to want only to entertain. It hardly seems representative of Rattigan, whose trademark theme was repression, the result of his life as a closeted homosexual, though he lived openly for over 20 years after the late 1950's. And yet here is one case where knowledge of a playwright's masked life unlocks the depth beneath trivia.

The piece is set in the apartment of Bobby, a sailor, who is the Earl of Harpenden. When the curtain rises, he is sharing his bedroom with Joe, an American officer whom he met in a club. Joe was drunk, but that is too crass a word for the titled English class, which uses synonyms like "very pickled." Bobby's fiancee, Lady Elisabeth Randall, is "rendered blotto" when after two Scotches, she falls into Joe's arms. Joe and Elisabeth fall in love, and Elisabeth decides not to marry Bobby. Bobby says, "Oh." Later, she decides she will marry Bobby. Bobby says, "Oh."

Don't ask why a French officer, also enamored of Lady Elisabeth, wanders in and winds up in Bobby's bed one night later. Or how, that same night, Joe marches right back to that same bed.

But that prompts Mabel, who cannot resist these military men, not to mention uniformed others, to point to the bedroom and announce, "All the Allies are in there."

The two female characters are stereotypes. Mabel, in a form-fitting dress and red high-heeled shoes, is the good-hearted tart with business instinct. Lady Elisabeth, virginal and uptight, settles for marriage, sealed by a handshake, not giving in to "a white-hot burning of the heart."

The plot is full of mistaken identities, darting in and out of doors, all following the classic dictates of farce, with flair. Under the deft direction of Carl Wallnau, Centenary's artistic director, the company gives—and from all appearances, has—a high time. There is more of an ensemble sense in this staging than is found in performances at many better-known regional theaters in the metropolitan area. Even seasoned theatergoers are not likely to discover a more enjoyable piece of theater esoterica.

THE WINSLOW BOY

PRODUCTION REVIEW

John Beaufort (review date 4 November 1980)

SOURCE: Beaufort, John. "One Man's Battle against Officialdom." *Christian Science Monitor* (4 November 1980): 18.

[*In the following review of the 1980 New York revival, Beaufort lauds the humor and compassion of* The Winslow Boy *and deems the play a "humanly appealing drama."*]

Inspired by the Archer-Shee case of 1908, this play stirringly dramatizes one man's fight against the weight of officialdom, in this case the British Admiralty. Retaining principal elements of the legal battle that once shook a nation, playwright Terence Rattigan tells how retired bank manager Arthur Winslow (Ralph Clanton) goes about clearing the name of his son Ronnie (David Haller). Winslow acts with courage and unswerving resolution when he becomes convinced that Ronnie is innocent of the petty theft for which he has been expelled from Osborne Naval College.

The Winslow Boy apparently has not been acted professionally in New York since its 1947 Broadway premiere. As if to make up for the prolonged neglect, the Roundabout Theater Company has mounted a stalwart production. Within the modest confines of the company's Stage Two basement arena, the performance directed by Douglas Seale seizes upon all the salient strengths of a humanly appealing drama about a wrenching family ordeal. This means responding to the light touch of comedy with which Rattigan skillfully leavens his perceptive study of the emotional conflicts that ensure when family and personal loyalties are placed under stress.

The Roundabout revival is strongest where it counts most. Mr. Clanton's portrait of the crusty, implacable, yet paternally compassionate Arthur Winslow, for instance. And Giulia Pagano's finely sensed Catherine Winslow, the feminist daughter who never falters in her support of what sometimes seems like a lost cause. Remark Ramsay as Sir Robert Morton, the barrister whose coldness and reserve mask a passionate dedication to the triumph of right, is also strong. It is a magnificent part and Mr. Ramsay plays it magnificently. *The Winslow Boy* is also helped by the performances of young Mr. Haller (Ronnie), Elizabeth Owens (Mrs. Winslow), Lee Toombs (brother Dickie), and others in the nine-member cast.

Save for the heavy but unseen hand of bureaucracy, there are no villains in *The Winslow Boy.* This is a play about honorable people, about civil rights and civil behavior. Some of the play's concerns have to an extent become unfashionable—as indeed Rattigan himself had seemed to for a while. There is more than a touch of Shavian moral passion to *The Winslow Boy* and the Roundabout deserves due credit for this high-minded production. Roger Mooney has designed the modest Kensington drawing room where the pre-1914 action takes place. The costumes are by A. Christina Giannini.

Jeremy Kingston (review date 18 June 2001)

SOURCE: Kingston, Jeremy. A review of *The Winslow Boy. The Times* London (18 June 2001): 12.

[*In the following favorable review of the 2001 production of* The Winslow Boy, *Kingston commends the play as well-crafted and thrilling.*]

Rattigan's finest full-length work has all the qualities that gave the well-made play a good name. Well-made plays went out of fashion, not least because few writers could do them as well as Rattigan, but also because their formal "completeness" came to seem unreal in a world where few experiences end neatly. But neat endings are the stuff of thrillers, and whatever else it is, *The Winslow Boy* is also a gripping thriller of a peculiarly rare kind: a courtroom drama without an on-stage courtroom. The story is based on the true struggle of Martin Archer-Shee to clear the name of his son, a 13-year-old cadet at Osborne Naval College, of the charge that he stole a postal order. Insisting on a proper inquiry, which the Admiralty refused, he pursued the case through the courts and then Parliament, until at last a high-handed government department was obliged to confess itself in the wrong. Archer-Shee's determination is a lesson for all time.

Rattigan had an eye for a great story but he also had the dramatic skill to animate the facts through the interrelating behaviour of credible characters. He creates a cheerfully idle elder brother, a suffragist sister, grittily persistent father, anguished mother, a neatly varied brace of suitors, and of course, the seemingly ice-cold barrister, Sir Robert Moreton, who takes on the case. Even the unseen cook is given her moment of reality when we hear that jubilant crowds have knocked her hat off.

The wider issues surrounding this seemingly minor injustice are hinted at at the very start of Christopher Morahan's production at the Festival Theatre when the Elgarian amplitude of Ilona Sekacz's music is interrupted by ominous jabs on the cello. The lights go up and Nicholas Deigman's Ronnie, still wearing his cadet's uniform, is seen in the family drawing-room awaiting his father's return.

Morahan's clever control of movement on the open stage allows good sightlines, even when up to six characters at a time are to be shown reacting to a crisis at the centre. During Sir Robert's interview with the boy, climaxing the first half, the shifts around the stage are both easy and logical.

The performances, too, vigorous and natural, present a similar ease. Edward Hardwicke's paterfamilias, at one moment stricken by doubt, and Osmund Bullock's stooping, lovelorn solicitor are notable. But the crucial roles are those of the Tory Sir Robert and the "New Woman" Kate. Elisabeth Dermot Walsh beautifully conveys qualities of certitude and shrewd perception allied with an inner grace, and David Rintoul is a charismatic political animal, his voice at one and the same time silk and steel, touching in his moment of triumph and relishing Rattigan's gift to him of the play's elegant last line.

THE BROWNING VERSION

PRODUCTION REVIEW

Charles Spencer (review date 29 June 1994)

SOURCE: Spencer, Charles. "Crying with Pain and Laughter." *Daily Telegraph* (20 June 1994): 19.

[*In the following review of the 1994 London revival of* The Browning Version, *Spencer contends that "Rattigan is a matchless chronicler of English reserve and deep-buried pain."*]

Terence Rattigan was discovered by his valet "weeping uncontrollably" as he wrote *The Browning Version* (1948), and it isn't hard to see why. In this marvellous one-act play, now receiving a deeply moving revival at the Greenwich Theatre, Rattigan conjures up a world of almost unbearable pain. It is a small masterpiece, which, like *The Deep Blue Sea,* makes the playwright's long years in the critical wilderness seem frankly inexplicable. Clive Merrison gives a magnificent performance as Andrew Crocker-Harris, a desiccated classics beak at an English public school who is taking early retirement because of ill health. In the course of 75 minutes, he is repeatedly humiliated—by his snobbish wife who openly cuckolds him, by the headmaster who denies him a pension, and by a new teacher who casually lets slip that "the Crock" is known as the "Himmler of the lower fifth". And then a small miracle happens. A boy comes to say farewell and gives him the Browning translation of Aeschylus's *Agamemnon,* touchingly inscribed. The floodgates open, and this painfully reserved man who believes himself to be dead inside, howls with emotion. Even this glimpse of redemption, however, is brutally destroyed by his wife, a Harrovian Clytemnestra, who suddenly seems not merely dislikable but evil. Philip Franks's production finds all the play's strengths. There isn't a moment or an emotion that rings false, and Merrison's mixture of dry dignity and naked grief is like a dagger plunged into the audience's heart. All the supporting roles are admirably played too—Diana Hardcastle even elicits a shudder of sympathy for the Crock's appalling wife. Rattigan is a matchless chronicler of English reserve and deep-buried pain, and I defy anyone to sit through the play without tears in their eyes.

Benedict Nightingale (review date 29 June 1994)

SOURCE: Nightingale, Benedict. "Full Marks for a Magisterial Performance." *The Times* London (29 June 1994): 22.

[*In the following review, Nightingale praises the casting and acting of the 1994 London revival of* The Browning Version.]

It was bold of Philip Franks to cast Clive Merrison as the failed schoolmaster at the centre of Terence Rattigan's **Browning Version.** The role was created with John Gielgud in mind, and not long ago was finely performed at the National by another of our warmer, gentler actors, Alec McCowen. But if memory serves me right, Merrison first came to public attention when he played an Enoch Powell clone in a fiercely radical play by Howard Barker. He is a tense, gritty actor with an acerbic manner and a long, wintry face. And recently the tip of his head seems to have got balder, adding to the impression of an inaccessible human Alp. The result is a Crocker-Harris who is more cold fish and less Mr Chips than any actor I have seen in the role. It is an austerely unsentimental approach and one that brings with it distinct gains. For one thing, Merrison is more credible as "the Himmler of the Lower Fifth" than McCowen's crusty but less-than-menacing Crocker-Harris. For another, it makes the character's eventual collapse into tears disturbing as well as moving.

What causes this transformation is the gift of a book. Crocker-Harris, it emerges, began his career as a respected classics scholar, evolved into a joke public-school beak, and now, as he prepares prematurely to retire, is a universal hate-object. Everyone dislikes him, from his colleagues to his pupils, from his frustrated wife to his own alienated self. But then a boy presents him with Browning's version of Aeschylus's *Agamemnon,* a play he loves and once translated but now teaches dully and by rote. For the few minutes before his wife destroys the gift's meaning by impugning the giver's motives, the dry-as-dust pedagogue is emotionally regalvanised.

Sounds of music from the school chapel combine with the period hair-cuts and clothes on Steven Brimson Lewis's living-room set to create the atmosphere of 1948; but, like Rattigan's **Deep Blue Sea,** this is a play that has not dated. The subjects are repression and humiliation, the difficulty we English have in dealing with emotion and the tendency of emotion to waylay and betray us. It is not only Crocker-Harris who suffers, but his wife, besotted as she is with a young master who cares little for her. The cruel inequalities of love always absorbed Rattigan; and not least here.

The result is an evening from which everybody emerges with credit: author, director, supporting cast, leading actors. As Crocker-Harris's wife, Diana Hardcastle achieves a nice blend of disappointment, grievance and rage, allowing us to see both why she feels badly used and how vindictive this has made her. But it is, as it should be, Merrison's evening. Nobody could be bleaker, yet few could exude as much regret, grief and forlorn childishness. It is as if a withered child were calling across the years to his mother: a devastating performance.

THE DEEP BLUE SEA

PRODUCTION REVIEW

Charles Spencer (review date 15 January 1993)

SOURCE: Spencer, Charles. "Mysteries of the Human Heart: Charles Spencer on an Outstanding Revival of a Rattigan Classic." *The Daily Telegraph* (15 January 1993): 17.

[*In the following review, Spencer notes the honesty and tenderness in* The Deep Blue Sea.]

In one of his last plays Terence Rattigan wrote: "Do you know what *le vice anglais* really is? Not flagellation, not pederasty. It's our refusal to admit to our emotions." But this English reserve, the determination to keep a stiff upper lip in the face of an unbearable depth of feeling, is what makes his masterpiece, **The Deep Blue Sea** (1952), such an overwhelming dramatic experience. It is a play about destructive sexual love in which the word sex isn't even mentioned. One of the characters, offering clumsy sympathy, speaks awkwardly of "the physical side" and that's as near as anyone gets to describing what people actually get up to in bed. There are those who accuse Rattigan of a similar evasiveness. His well-made plays, which once enjoyed invincible success in the West End, were the chief victims of the Royal Court "revolution" in the mid-Fifties. His determination not to offend "Aunt Edna", whom Rattigan described as the "universal and immortal middle-class playgoer", was seen as dishonest cowardice. His detractors would view it as typical of Rattigan that although **The Deep Blue Sea** was inspired by the suicide of a former male lover, the dramatist performed a speedy sex change and made his anguished leading character a woman, hopelessly in love with a younger man. Yet watching Karel Reisz's superb revival at the Almeida, Islington, it is the emotional truth and unsentimental compassion of the writing that again and again strike home. Hester Collyer, the daughter of a clergyman, has abandoned her respectable judge of a husband to live in a bleak Ladbroke Grove flat with a younger RAF hero and test pilot. At the start of the action, she is revived from a failed suicide attempt, and the play movingly uncovers the agony of an affair in which Hester knows that her absolute and unconditional love will never be satisfactorily returned. Almost every detail here is spot on, creating an atmosphere of drab post-war austerity you can almost smell. When someone bangs their hand on the ugly brown sofa in Hester's flat (a magnificently cheerless and claustrophobic design by William Dudley) you just know that a cloud of dust will fly out of it. The awkward class-consciousness between the tenants of the flats and their cockney landlady is beautifully observed, and even the smallest characters are brought to detailed life—the mixture of primness and prurience that Emma Amos brings to her tiny role as a curious neighbour is a masterclass in tellingly unobtrusive acting. Penelope Wilton, for too long consigned to TV sitcoms, is outstanding in Peggy Ashcroft's old role of Hester. Rarely can the phrase "putting a brave face on things" have been more affectingly enacted. Her brisk manner, self-defensive irony, above all her courageous, desperate smiles, are heart-breakingly true to life, and when her fiercely maintained dignity finally collapses in racking sobs and pitiful pleading it is almost unbearable to watch. But there are no villains in *The Deep Blue Sea*. Hester's beloved Freddie may be superficial and selfish but he is also a victim of what E. M. Forster called the undeveloped heart. Linus Roache captures all the petulant, child-like bluster of a man who arouses love but is incapable of returning it, a war hero ill at ease in time of peace, retreating into matey slang and boozy camaraderie as an escape from adult emotions he is incapable of experiencing, let alone handling. There's fine sympathetic support, too, from Nicholas Jones as Hester's kind, ineffectual husband, and from the Polish actor Wojtek Pszoniak as the enigmatic Mr Miller, who delivers the play's difficult lesson that life must go on without sounding remotely preachy. Despite its period setting and careful, old-fashioned construction, this is a work that still speaks with tenderness and truth about the mystery and misery of the human heart. The Almeida's outstanding production must surely transfer to the West End that was once Rattigan's natural home.

Michael Billington (review date 24 January 1993)

SOURCE: Billington, Michael. "Rattigan Triumphant." *Manchester Guardian Weekly* (24 January 1993): 26.

[*In the following positive review of the 1993 Almeida production, Billington examines Rattigan's portrayal of the inequity of passion in* The Deep Blue Sea.]

Forty years after its premiere Terence Rattigan's *The Deep Blue Sea* begins to look like a modern classic as timelessly true as Phaedre in its portrait of the inequality of passion. But the great irony, as Karel Reisz's meticulous new Almeida production proves, is that Rattigan, in attacking the undernourished English heart, fills the theatre with emotion.

Rattigan's mastery lies in showing the dilemma confronting his heroine, Hester Collyer, a judge's wife now living with a former test pilot in a dingy flat in Ladbroke Grove. Hester, a clergyman's daughter, has a sexual hunger that her husband clearly never satisfied and an emotional ardour that her current lover cannot return. As so often, Rattigan suggests that most relationships are founded on a

one-sided passion and that the average English male is crippled by an incapacity to feel. Hester is confronted, therefore, by the choice between suicide or an imperfect life. For a model piece of dramatic writing, one has only to look at the final confrontation of Hester and her absconding lover, Freddie. Here are two people facing the destruction of a relationship and she asks "Had any food?" to which he replies "Yes. I had a bit at the Belvedere". It is the ability to imply a wealth of unarticulated emotion bubbling away beneath the crust of English politeness that makes Rattigan such a superb dramatist.

Reisz and his designer, William Dudley, short-circuit the West End conventions in a number of ways. First, by placing the sitting room at an angle to the audience as if to suggest a life out of kilter. Secondly, by making the grey-green walls murkily transparent to convey the on-going life of the apartment block and to forewarn us of impending visitors.

But the play stands or falls by its Hester, and Penelope Wilton is much the best I have seen. Her flashes of smiling warmth towards her separated husband make you believe her natural habitat is an Eaton Square dinner table; yet her devouring kisses of Freddie, whom she artfully steers towards the bedroom, persuade you of her sensual hunger Wilton's great gift is for suggesting unexpressed emotion: I shall long remember the sight of her wan features, poised on the brink of tears, as the conscienceless Freddie breezes in after a weekend's golfing.

Linus Roache as Freddie is a shade youthful for an ex-fighter pilot whose life allegedly stopped in 1940. But here is first-rate support from Wojtek Pszoniak as the struck-off doctor who puts the case for life's continuance with wry matter-of-factness from Nicholas Jones as the well-meaning judge totally bemused by Hester's sexual zeal and from William Osborne as a preachy neighbour who tells Hester that life's physical side is "really awfully unimportant".

SEPARATE TABLES

PRODUCTION REVIEW

Charles Spencer (review date 8 July 1993)

SOURCE: Spencer, Charles. "Putting a Brave Face on Desperation." *Daily Telegraph* (8 July 1993): 17.

[*In the following favorable review of the 1993 production of* Separate Tables, *Spencer reflects on the critical neglect of Rattigan's work.*]

I suspect 1993 will be remembered as the year Terence Rattigan finally came in from the cold. In the Forties and early Fifties he was the most successful of West End playwrights, but with the arrival of the angry young men his stock fell disastrously. He was seen as a dishonest, even cowardly writer, pandering to the complacent morality of "Aunt Edna", whom Rattigan described as "the universal and immortal middle-class theatre-goer". But with the superb revival of *The Deep Blue Sea* earlier this year and now Peter Hall's excellent production of *Separate Tables* at the Albery, his neglect seems baffling and his detractors foolish. There is a spirit of charity and human understanding in both these works that is deeply moving. *Separate Tables* (1954) really consists of two one-act plays. The supporting cast remains constant, as does the setting, the shabbily genteel Beauregard Private Hotel near Bournemouth. But the two leading actors, in this production Peter Bowles and Patricia Hodge, each play two different characters, offering a chance for virtuosity of which they both take full advantage. But there is nothing remotely showy about these pieces. Rattigan, for all his glossy public success, is a chronicler of the lonely, the loveless and the dispossessed, of characters courageously trying to put a brave face on lives of quiet desperation. It has to be said that the first piece, *Table by the Window,* isn't a complete success. I never quite believed in the painful love between a disgraced junior Labour minister and his ageing fashion model of an ex-wife who has tracked him down to the South Coast hotel. But Peter Bowles powerfully captures masochistic passion and drink-slurred self-contempt, while Miss Hodge's progress from icy beauty to racking sobs as she contemplates a lonely old age sends shivers down the spine. In *Table Number Seven* it is Miss Hodge who is unrecognisable, all stooped shoulders, ugly glasses and mouse-like demeanour. I never thought this actress could look dowdy but she certainly does here in a most touching performance as a repressed spinster with a terror of sex. Her mother (surely Rattigan's revenge on Aunt Edna) is a vicious old trout who reacts with vindictive pleasure when it's discovered that their fellow guest, "Major" Pollock, has lied about his rank and been convicted of making "insulting" advances to women in the local cinema. This would have been an even more interesting play had Rattigan been able to stick to his original idea of making the major's offence a homosexual one, but Peter Bowles is again in superb form. The old soldier's jaunty blazered bogusness is right up Bowles's street, of course, but his pain and panic when he's found out, and his clear-eyed acknowledgment of his own cowardice to the sympathetic hotel manageress cut to the quick. Mrs Railton-Bell, played with splendidly malevolent relish by the marvellous Rosemary Leach, is robbed of victory when the other residents and even her own daughter rally round the "major". I suppose you could accuse this ending of being sentimental, but I found it both moving and generously funny, a gleeful routing of oppressive morality and meanness of spirit. Peter Hall's production, evocatively designed

by Carl Toms, gets to the heart of these decent and affecting plays, and there is a wealth of strong supporting performances. Miriam Karlin, Faith Flint and Rachel Gurney all offer excellent value, but it is Charlotte Cornwell as the manageress who movingly delivers the plucky, heart-breaking moral of these plays: "It's surprising how cheerful one can be when one gives up hope." Such fortitude is not to be despised. Rattigan is the poet of the stiff upper lip.

IN PRAISE OF LOVE

PRODUCTION REVIEW

Charles Spencer (review date 8 March 1995)

SOURCE: Spencer, Charles. "Rattigan with His Heart on His Sleeve." *Daily Telegraph* (8 March 1995): 15.

[*In the following review, Spencer provides a mixed assessment of the 1995 London production of* In Praise of Love.]

One of the most welcome theatrical trends of recent years has been the rediscovery of Terence Rattigan. Outstanding productions of *The Browning Version* and *The Deep Blue Sea* have revealed this once derided dramatist to be a writer of exceptional insight and sympathy, a poet of the British stiff upper lip. *In Praise of Love* features many of his humane strengths without achieving the overwhelming depth of emotion of his greatest work. It was a late piece, first seen in 1973, and apparently based on the relationship between Rex Harrison and his wife Kay Kendall, who was dying of leukaemia. Amazingly Harrison went on to play the character he had inspired on Broadway. The main problem is that you never quite believe in the central characters. Sebastian Cruttwell is a literary critic, a Marxist and the author of a brilliant novel the success of which he has never been able to repeat. His wife, Lydia, is an Estonian who suffered dreadfully in the war, as a refugee, resistance fighter and concentration camp victim, ending up in the Berlin red-light district. The couple married in order to provide Lydia with a British passport. Now almost 30 years later in Islington, Lydia is dying. She refuses to tell her selfish, dependent husband the news, because she doesn't want to be a "bore", but in the second half it emerges that Sebastian knows just how ill she is, believing his wife isn't aware of the fact. He is deeply in love with her, devastated by her fatal illness, but determined to keep the brutal truth from her. So he maintains his uncaring facade. Despite excellent performances from Peter Bowles and Lisa Harrow, all of this rings slightly false. Lydia is such a warm, strong character you never believe she would have become so subservient. Nor does it seem possible that Sebastian, who is clearly a sensitive man beneath his brusque manner, would only realise how much he loved his wife when he learnt she was dying. The characters seem to have been distorted to exemplify the play's moral, which is laboriously spelt out by Sebastian. "*Le vice ang-lais*," we are told, isn't flagellation or pederasty; "it's our refusal to admit to our emotions. We think they demean us, I suppose." This may have been true in the Forties. It seems less persuasive in the let-it-all-hang-out Seventies and among characters who have been through so much together. The play's development is schematic, its dramatic devices (tell-tale letters hidden in a hat-box) contrived. But Bowles is marvellous as Sebastian, infuriatingly off-hand and patronising in the earlier scenes while suggesting an intolerable burden of pent-up pain after the interval. His beautifully delivered account of Lydia's terrible experiences in the war reduces the audience to rapt silence. There is much more to this actor than the smoothie smartypants he always seems to play on television. Lisa Harrow has the difficult task of making a saintly character seem human, and she largely succeeds. Richard Olivier's absorbing production also features strong support from Ray Lonnen as the loyal family friend Mark and from Christian Anholt as the likeable son who infuriates his lefty father by working for the Liberals. *In Praise of Love* is a play with a heart; unfortunately it wears it a little too ostentatiously on its sleeve.

Benedict Nightingale (review date 8 March 1995)

SOURCE: Nightingale, Benedict. "Upper Lips Stiff and Wooden." *The Times* London (8 March 1995): 28.

[*In the following negative review, Nightingale finds the 1995 London revival of* In Praise of Love *dated yet poignant.*]

Terence Rattigan based this touching play [*In Praise of Love*] on his observation of Rex Harrison as Kay Kendall succumbed to leukaemia. Had so self-absorbed a husband started behaving in a considerate, outgoing way, Kendall would have guessed that her sickness was more serious than anybody admitted, so the rows continued as normal. After one ferocious bust-up, Harrison actually threw the terminally ill woman's clothes out of her hotel suite, then locked the door on her. "You wouldn't tell me I'm not dying if I were, would you?" she asked as she lay in hospital. "Of course not, you silly little fool. See you tomorrow," replied Harrison. That was their last conversation. She died a few hours later.

In his biography of Harrison, Alexander Walker adds a suggestive gloss to the tale. He has evidence that Kendall

knew how ill she was, but wanted Harrison neither to know nor to know she knew. Could there be a more English situation, in or out of Brief Encounter?

Certainly that seems to have been Rattigan's view when he penned his tale of the grumpy critic, Sebastian, and his wise, saintly wife, Lydia, each conspiring in the other's ignorance.

Back in 1973 not even Donald Sinden and Joan Greenwood were able to make a critical and commercial success of the first production of *In Praise of Love,* partly because Rattigan's reputation was itself still on the sick-list, partly because the play proper came with an idiot curtain-raiser, a burlesque of Tosca called *Before Dawn*. Thankfully, that has been dropped here.

What remains is a piece that seems simultaneously poignant and dated, worth reviving in itself but, thanks to Richard Olivier's less-than-tense production, dubiously worth its slot on Shaftesbury Avenue.

The main reason the play dates is Sebastian's political credo. He spends a lot of time spouting a sort of champagne Marxism and mocking his son, an aspiring playwright who is an active member of what at the time was a trendily subversive organisation, the Young Liberals. This produces little heat, less light, nothing but the odd distracting flicker. But that need not greatly affect our appreciation of what really matters in the play: the love the husband has for his wife, and she for him, all appearances to the contrary.

Peter Bowles's literary critic exudes a selfishness so blithely absolute you feel he really ought to be wearing a Garrick Club nappy. His performance is witty and intelligent, but lacking in the blackness of feeling the situation finally demands.

Similarly, Lisa Harrow's Lydia has a pluck and a warmth that hides little but more pluck and warmth. They are not helped by making their separate confessions to a confidant who, as played by Ray Lonnen, treats matters deeply pathetic and hideously ironic with all the feeling of a table loaded with crockery. It is a challenge, having continually to deliver lines like "How do you know?" and "What then?"; but emotional mahogany is not the answer.

Still, the play makes its point. Maybe the *vice anglais* is not pederasty but "our refusal to admit to our emotions". So Sebastian says, and so Rattigan thought and repeated in piece after piece. He was the bard of embarrassed repression and well-meant lies, and, whatever its fate here, *In Praise of Love* was one of his most articulate laments.

CAUSE CÉLÈBRE

CRITICAL COMMENTARY

John Peter (review date 15 February 1998)

SOURCE: Peter, John. "Cause for Celebration." *Sunday Times* London (15 February 1998): 14.

[*In the following mixed review of* Cause Célèbre, *Peter chronicles the renaissance of Rattigan's dramatic work and reputation.*]

Rattigan's last play is enjoying an emotional revival—with a 1990s slant on the British stiff upper lip.

When is a revival not a revival? People have been talking of a Shaw revival, on and off, for decades, but there has never been one for the simple reason that his best plays have never gone away. On the other hand, when James Roose-Evans staged a blistering production of *Private Lives* 35 years ago at Hampstead, he did initiate a Coward revival: people realised that his best plays were not merely pieces of drawing-room virtuosity but masterpieces of high comedy that put him at the peak, up there with Congreve and Wilde. Has there been a Terence Rattigan revival? Rattigan died just over 20 years ago, aged 66, less than five months after the premiere of *Cause Celebre,* which Neil Bartlett is directing at the Lyric, Hammersmith, with an affectionate but hard-edged accuracy. This tough and deeply felt production is part of an extraordinary renaissance. Rattigan was a near contemporary of Arthur Miller and Tennessee Williams, but towards the end of his life he seemed already to belong to the past, surrounded by volcanoes of subversive modern sensibility such as Osborne, Pinter and Arden. Rattigan was upper class. He was the 1940s and the 1950s. His dialogue needed to be spoken in good Rada accents: it was well-shaped, articulate, and politely sequential, in the sense that his people invariably replied to everything that was said to them. There were none of the unsettling evasions and sinister non sequiturs of modern dialogue; and I think it came to be assumed that Rattigan's seamlessness was simply a sign of blandness.

Then came Karel Reisz's production of *The Deep Blue Sea* at the Almeida five years ago. It was a revelation. Reisz burrowed under the West End sheen of Rattigan's middle-class melodrama and uncovered a subtext of desire, pain and shame played out by characters who were lonely, betrayed, frightened and painfully ordinary. Rattigan was revealed as an English Tennessee Williams: a cartographer of a private hell in which sexual desire and emotional fragility are at war with coldness, social propriety and the monolithic power of class.

Cause Celebre is another such play. Technically, it is about the famous 1935 Rattenbury murder case. Who killed the elderly Francis Rattenbury (John Quentin): his much younger, sexually voracious but neglected 38-year-old wife Alma (Amanda Harris), or her 17-year-old lover, here named George Wood, who was their servant and chauffeur? If it was Wood, did Alma egg him on? But the play is much more than a courtroom drama. There is a semidetached subplot, about Edith Davenport (Diane Fletcher), who is the foreman of the jury but wants to be excused because, she tells the judge, she feels a profound prejudice against Alma. "It is," she says, "as if I knew her."

The point about Edith, who is a few years older than Alma, is that she is her opposite: a strong, principled, placid woman who lost interest in sex when she was 40 and is, as a result, in the midst of a bitter divorce from her sexually still aggressive husband, John (Tim Preece). He is, incidentally, something very grand in the Home Office. Edith's sister, Stella (Delia Lindsay), is in the opposite situation again, staying in a marriage in the vain hope of reactivating her husband. Edith's adolescent son, Tony (Nitzan Sharron), is in the throes of sexual awakening; torn desperately between his parents, he is about to side with his more liberal-minded and less oppressive father.

I detect a sense of public-school male camaraderie in this last bit, which rings rather hollow, mostly because Tony's father carries more pompous gravity than flesh. But Rattigan's agenda emerges, quizzically and yet clearly. A society in which men and women of the same class are bound to one another in sexual incompatibility and frustration wants to take its revenge on a woman with a lower-class, younger lover. The prosecution, like the virtuous crowds outside, is more indignant about Alma's appetites than about her possible guilt. Handy-dandy, who is the justice, who is the voyeur?

This is not one of Rattigan's best plays. He was already gravely ill when he wrote it, and you can sense the absence of that iron control that makes *The Deep Blue Sea* and *Separate Tables* so relentless and yet so subtle. Some of the writing is strident or flaccid or both. Some of the characters sound as if they were making statements on life and morality on their author's behalf. Edith, John and Stella have not enough substance as characters: they illustrate Rattigan's argument rather than embody it and drive it forward. Laurence Mitchell makes a powerful stage debut as George Wood, grave and cocky, shy and dangerous all at once, but he cannot hide the fact that the role is thin and perfunctorily written.

Ultimately, the play is about Alma, and on her Rattigan bestowed all the psychological perception and cruel-kind imagination he had left. Harris gives a complex and beguiling performance, both waif and predator, both iridescent and a little coarse, unscrupulous but with a dark, stubborn moral core. She begins as a practised hunter, frivolous but desperate: her little seductive stratagems are so obvious as to be almost sad. She hies from the lower-middle class and has her sights fixed on the pleasures of the middle-middle—though Rattigan does not really explore the attraction such a woman feels for a lower-class boy who is more excited by being called "sir" than by sex. But then, as I say, George as a character does not give her much of a purchase.

The courtroom scenes have a harsh, sardonic expertise, just this side of melodrama. Neil Stacy and Terry Taplin lead magisterially for the defence and the crown; and they catch perfectly the atmosphere in which rituals, technicalities and personal vanity strut hand in hand with passions and beliefs.

Is there more of Rattigan to revive? The Bristol Old Vic did **Flare Path** extremely well recently (with Terry Taplin in it, as it happens): a much less dated play than I expected. Will someone now tackle **Separate Tables** with the brutal insight Reisz brought to **The Deep Blue Sea**? As Tennes-see Williams might have said, playwrights depend on the kindness, and courage, of strangers called directors.

FURTHER READING

Criticism

Clark, Mike. "Mamet's Way with *Winslow*." *USA Today* (April 30 1999): 6E.
> Favorable review of David Mamet's film adaptation of *The Winslow Boy*.

Wansell, Geoffrey. *Terence Rattigan*. London: Fourth Estate, 1995, 434 p.
> Provides a critical and biographical overview of Rattigan and his work.

Young, B. A. *The Rattigan Version: Sir Terence Rattigan and the Theatre of Character*. London: Hamish Hamilton, 1986, 228 p.
> Traces Rattigan's dramatic development.

Additional coverage of Rattigan's life and career is contained in the following sources published by the Gale Group: *British Writers Supplement*, **Vol. 7;** *Concise Dictionary of British Literary Biography,* **1945-1960;** *Contemporary Authors*, **Vols. 73-76, 85-88;** *Contemporary British Dramatists; Contemporary Literary Criticism*, **Vol. 7;** *Dictionary of Literary Biography*, **Vol. 13;** *DISCovering Authors Modules*: **Dramatists;** *Drama for Students*, **Vol. 8;** *International Dictionary of Films and Filmmakers: Writers and Production Artists*, **Eds. 3, 4;** *Literature Resource Center; Major 20th-Century Writers*, **Eds. 1, 2; and** *Reference Guide to English Literature* **Ed. 2.**

August Strindberg
1849-1912

(Also wrote under the pseudonym of Härved Ulf) Swedish playwright, novelist, short story writer, poet, essayist, and journalist.

INTRODUCTION

Strindberg is considered one of the most important and influential dramatists in modern literature. With the plays *Fadren* (1887; *The Father*) and *Fröken Julie* (1889; *Miss Julie*), he proved himself an innovative exponent of Naturalism, while the later plays *Ett drömspel* (1907; *A Dream Play*) and the trilogy *Till Damaskus* (1898-1904; *To Damascus*) are recognized as forerunners of Expressionism, Surrealism, and the Theater of the Absurd.

BIOGRAPHICAL INFORMATION

Strindberg was born in Stockholm. Although he portrayed himself in his autobiographical novel *Tjänstekvinnans son* (1886; *The Son of a Servant*) as the unwanted product of a union between an impoverished aristocrat and a former servant, recent biographers have constructed a more favorable picture of the circumstances of his birth. His father was involved in the shipping trade, and although his mother had worked as a maid for a short time, she was the daughter of a tailor. Life in the Strindberg home was by all objective accounts rather comfortable, but Strindberg was an extremely shy and sensitive child who held an excessively negative perception of his own circumstances. He was educated first at the local primary school, then at the Stockholm Lyceum, a progressive private school, where he was an average student. In 1867 Strindberg enrolled at the University of Uppsala. While at the university, he wrote his first play; the endeavor afforded him such satisfaction that he resolved to make playwriting his profession. During 1869 he wrote three more plays, two of which were accepted for production by the prestigious Royal Theater in Stockholm. However, these plays were not financially successful, and Strindberg was obliged to write stories and articles for periodicals in order to earn a living, a practice he considered degrading. It was not until the publication of his novel *Röda rummet* (*The Red Room*) in 1879 that Strindberg became a highly respected and nationally recognized author.

Essential material for Strindberg's subsequent works was provided by his three tempestuous marriages. The first and longest, to Sigrid von Essen, was the basis for a novel,

two collections of short stories, and several plays. The story collections, titled *Giftas* (1884-86; *Married, Parts I and II*) contained irreverent passages that caused Strindberg and his publisher to be charged with blasphemy. Following the breakup of his second marriage in 1891, Strindberg experienced a period of deep depression and hallucinations that he called his Inferno Crisis, because it occurred while he was writing the novel *Inferno* (1897; *The Inferno*). While his behavior had always been slightly bizarre, during this period he appears to have suffered a complete psychological break with reality. Severely paranoiac, he moved from lodging to lodging, convinced that his enemies were trying to murder him with electrical currents and lethal gases. Further manifestations of Strindberg's breakdown are observed in his abandonment of his literary career in order to devote himself to alchemical experiments and in the radical alteration of his religious thinking from agnostic to traditionally Christian. Believing that his affliction had been decreed by God as punishment for his sins, Strindberg sought a reconciliation with the deity as a possible cure, becoming fascinated with the work of Emmanuel Swedenborg, a Christian mystic. Strindberg's eventual recovery from his psychosis was accompanied by a surge of creative activity. He returned to the theater to transform the horrors of the Inferno Crisis and his new-found religious mysticism into dramatic images. Strindberg's final years were relatively peaceful and productive, and he was revered by the Swedish people, who staged an enormous celebration in honor of his sixtieth birthday. He continued to write until he became incapacitated by illness. He died in 1912.

MAJOR WORKS

Critics divide Strindberg's work into two phases, citing the Inferno Crisis as the fulcrum of the playwright's career. The historical drama *Mäster Olof* (1881; *Master Olof*) and the naturalistic plays *The Father* and *Miss Julie* are the most significant examples of his pre-Inferno writings. *Master Olof,* Strindberg's first theatrical success, is also first in a cycle of twelve chronicle plays concerning Swedish historical figures. As Shakespeare had done, Strindberg dramatized a series of historic events that embodied the social and political issues of his own day. Although *Master Olof* introduced Strindberg as an important playwright, *The Father* and *Miss Julie* established his reputation as a brilliant innovator of theatrical form. In these works Strindberg developed a new, intense form of Naturalism. Influenced by the French novelist Emile Zola, Strindberg depicted his characters and their lives with scientific objectivity. However, he furthered this concept by focusing solely on the "moment of struggle," the immediate conflict or crisis affecting his characters. Dialogue and incidents not pertaining to this moment were eliminated. Thematically, *The Father, Miss Julie,* and Strindberg's other Naturalist plays are rooted in Friedrich Nietzsche's conception of life as a succession of contests between stronger and weaker wills. Strindberg applied this theory to his recurring subject of the conflict between the sexes for psychological supremacy. The female characters of his Naturalist dramas are typically diabolic usurpers of the "naturally" dominant role of males in society: with infinite cunning and cruelty, they eventually shatter the male characters' "superior" psyches and drain their creative and intellectual powers.

The stylistic experiments of Strindberg's post-Inferno period proved a turning point in modern drama. From his studies, Strindberg concluded that earthly life is a hell which men and women are forced to endure, a nightmare in which they suffer for sins committed in a previous existence. *To Damascus, A Dream Play,* and *Spöksonaten* (1907; *The Ghost Sonata*) are based on this premise, presenting a fragmented and highly subjective view of reality. To achieve this effect, Strindberg employed symbolism and structure of dreams, creating a grotesque

and ludicrous world that is both believable and frighteningly unreal: individuals appear and disappear at random; scenes and images change at the slightest provocation; and characters encounter their worst fears and fantasies. With *To Damascus* and *A Dream Play* Strindberg prefigured the major dramatic movements of the twentieth century, and his influence can be seen in the work of playwrights such as Samuel Beckett, Eugene O'Neill, and Eugène Ionesco.

CRITICAL RECEPTION

Early reaction to Strindberg's plays was often highly mixed. Because Strindberg was an intensely autobiographical and self-analytical writer, some early critics dismissed his plays as self-absorbed and overly confessional. His early Naturalist plays, while successful, were often controversial, particularly for the anti-feminist and unorthodox religious views they presented. The plays from the period after the Inferno Crisis, with their highly subjective interpretations of experience and nightmarish effects, often confounded Strindberg's contemporaries, to whom the playwright appeared to have lost touch with reality. Modern critical evaluations, however, have been much more favorable. Harry G. Carlson, for example, while conceding that Strindberg was "a diligent journalist, plundering the details of his own life for copy," asserted that he was also "a developing author, restlessly experimenting with new forms of expression in drama and fiction" and "an eloquent mythopoeic artist, constantly searching for ways to anchor the present more firmly in the past." Modern commentators almost universally agree that Strindberg's later work initiated, in both content and form, the dramatic methods of modern theater. Pär Lagerkvist, a younger contemporary of Strindberg and himself an influential dramatic innovator, shortly after Strindberg's death praised the elder playwright's "distinctly new creative work in the drama": "If one wishes to understand the direction in which the modern theatre is actually striving and the line of development it will probably follow, it is certainly wise to turn to [Strindberg] first of all." Similarly, in a remark, cited approvingly by several critics, O'Neill declared that Strindberg "was the precursor of all modernity in our present theatre."

PRINCIPAL WORKS

Plays

Fritankaren 1869
En namnsdagsgåva 1869
I Rom [*In Rome*] 1870

Den Fredlöse [The Outlaw] 1871
Mäster Olof [Master Olof] 1881
Lycko-Pers resa [Lucky Pehr] 1883
Fadren [The Father] 1887
Fordringsägare [The Creditors] 1888
Fröken Julie [Miss Julie] 1889
Advent: Ett mysterium [Advent] 1898
Till Damaskus, första delen [To Damascus, I] 1898
Till Damaskus, andra delen [To Damascus, II] 1898
Brott och brott [Crimes and Crimes] 1899
Erik XIV 1899
Folkungasagan [The Saga of the Folkungs] 1899
Gustaf Vasa [Gustavus Vasa] 1899
Dödsdansen [The Dance of Death] 1901
Ett drömspel [A Dream Play] 1901
Kristina [Queen Christina] 1901
Påsk [Easter] 1901
Svanevit [Swanwhite] 1901
Carl XII [Charles XII] 1902
Gustav III 1902
Till Damaskus, tredje delen [To Damascus, III] 1904
*Brända tomten [The Burned House] 1907
*Oväder [Storm Weather] 1907
*Spöksonaten [The Ghost Sonata] 1907
*Pelikanen [The Pelican] 1907
Abu Casems tofflor [Abu Casem's Slippers] 1908
*Svarta handsken [The Black Glove] 1908
Stora landsvägen [The Great Highway] 1910

Other Major Works

Röda rummet [The Red Room] (novel) 1879
Sömngångarnätter på vakna dagar (poetry) 1884
Giftas. 2 vols. *[Married]* (short stories) 1884-86
Tjänstekvinnans son [The Son of a Servant] (memoir) 1886
Hemsöborna [The People of Hemsö] (novel) 1887
Inferno [The Inferno] (autobiographical novel) 1898
En blå bok. 4 vols. *[Zones of the Spirit]* (essays) 1907-12

*Known collectively as *The Chamber Plays*, these five works were written by Strindberg for his Intimate Theater, which he founded in 1907.

GENERAL COMMENTARY

Harry G. Carlson (essay date 1982)

SOURCE: Carlson, Harry G. "Collecting the Corpse in the Cargo." In *Strindberg and the Poetry of Myth*," pp. 78-91. Berkeley: University of California Press, 1982.

[In the following essay, Carlson examines the progress of Strindberg's naturalistic period, from The Father *through* Miss Julie *to* The Creditors.*]*

The sheer intense virtuosity of Strindberg's performance during his so-called naturalistic period was impressive. He was a diligent journalist, plundering the details of his own life for copy; a developing author, restlessly experimenting with new forms of expression in drama and fiction; and an eloquent mythopoeic artist, constantly searching for ways to anchor the present more firmly in the past.

In his plays there are two progressions apparent from **The Father** to **Creditors.** First, there is a process of distillation, Strindberg trying to present what is quintessentially dramatic and nothing more. He scraps the elaborate intrigue apparatus of the well-made play—with its numerous characters, complicated subplots, and heavy exposition—in favor of a minimum of characters presenting the heart of an action in the shortest time possible. In **The Father** there are nine speaking roles and three acts. In **Miss Julie** there are only three speaking roles and one act, but there is the complication of a time change: the stage directions call for the sun to rise. **Creditors,** as well, takes place in one act, but Strindberg took pride in the fact that it was leaner and more compact than **Miss Julie;** in a letter he boasted: "three persons, one table and two chairs, and no sunrise!"

The other progression involves experimentation in a range of styles that can be seen as representing different phases in the development of dramatic form from more primitive to more sophisticated. The three plays are alike in that they all approach the boundary line of drama and ritual, even to the inclusion of sacrificial victims: in each instance the tragic fate of the protagonist has about it the quality of an offering demanded by the inexorable movement of destiny. The plays differ in that while **Miss Julie** and **Creditors** have the superbly disciplined austerity of classical tragedy, drama stripped down to the archetypal confrontation of three actors—protagonist, deuteragonist, and tritagonist—**The Father** has a rough-hewn, primitive feel, like a chunk of archaic statuary. If **Miss Julie** and **Creditors** resemble classical Greek tragedy, **The Father** seems preclassical, a throwback to an earlier time when conflict was not between two or three characters, but antiphonal, between chorus and chorus leader. At the end it is the Captain versus everyone else, the sacrificial victim versus the followers and servants of the Great Mother.

Like certain Greek tragedies, **Miss Julie** has two choruses. The first is the group of offstage midsummer celebrants who are heard mocking Julie and Jean in song before they come on stage to dance and sing while the mistress of the manor and her father's valet are making love in his room. The second chorus is Kristin. In true classic spirit she is a reminder to Jean and Julie of the larger social consequences of their actions: she warns them of the price they will have to pay for their indiscretion.

In mood and tone, **Creditors** differs sharply from its predecessors. The almost formal symmetry of its scene structure, together with the cynical, often brutal, but nevertheless elegant and witty dialogue, make the play a gem of sophisticated black comedy. The streamlined plot involves a man who comes to take vengeance against his former wife by committing a psychic murder of her current husband. Returning incognito to the same resort hotel room he once shared with his wife, Gustav visits Adolph while Tekla is away on a trip and uses the power of suggestion to blacken her image and to produce a fatal attack of epilepsy in his hapless victim. The play's continuous action is separated into three scenes: in the first, Gustav undermines Adolph's faith in his marriage; in the second, Adolph confronts the returning Tekla with his suspicions while Gustav eavesdrops next door; and in the third, Gustav demonstrates Tekla's fickleness while Adolph now eavesdrops and presumably fumes with anger until he suffers the fatal attack.

As was true of his other naturalistic plays, much of the power of **Creditors** is due neither to its fidelity to an objective, scientific approach, nor its elegant construction; the power is generated by an evocation of mythic forces in conflict.

The mythic setting is the same as it was in **The Father** and the second half of **Miss Julie:** after the Fall. In **Miss Julie** Jean and Julie fearfully await the return of the Count, as Adam and Eve awaited inevitable retribution from Yahweh. In **Creditors** Yahweh has arrived in the person of Gustav. As we listen to him pretending to speculate to the unsuspecting Adolph about how Tekla and Adolph must have met behind his back, we can also hear the wrathful God of the Book of Genesis describing how he discovered that his laws had been disobeyed:

GUSTAV:

> [*cooly, almost jokingly*]

> The husband was on a research trip and she was alone. . . . Then *he* arrived and gradually the emptiness was filled. By comparison, the absent one began to fade, for the simple reason that he was at a distance—you know, fading in proportion to the distance. But when they felt passion stirring, they became uneasy—about themselves, their consciences, and about him. They sought refuge and shielded themselves behind fig leaves, played brother and sister, and the more carnal their feelings became, the more spiritual they pretended their relationship to be; . . . they found each other in a dark corner where they were certain no one could see them. [*with mock severity*] But they felt that there was *one* who saw them through the darkness and they became frightened; . . . he became a nightmare who disturbed their dreams of love, a creditor who knocked at the door; . . . they heard his disagreeable voice in the stillness of the night. . . .

> (*23,* 206-207)

There is a peculiar, omniscient quality in the speech, and this is not the only peculiar thing about Gustav: he is uncanny, and what makes the uncanniness particularly ef-

fective is that it is rendered subtly. As the play unfolds, the mood is that of a psychological thriller, and the focus of attention is primarily on Adolph, Tekla, or their marriage; we are never encouraged to question deeply Gustav's nature. His cynicism is entertaining and the fact that we do not completely understand at first what he is doing or why he is doing it only stimulates our curiosity and adds to the suspense. When we finally discover that he is Adolph's predecessor, was slandered by Tekla, and depicted as an idiot in one of her novels, we can accept tentatively that his behavior was provoked by revenge, despite the fact that he acts "cooly, almost jokingly" and is curiously devoid of passion. Carl Reinhold Smedmark has described Gustav as the least explained character in the play: "About him we know no more than what his actions reveal and that he helped to shape Tekla's personality." I think we know a good deal about him, but much of the information is mysterious.

Gustav is first presented as an unknown benefactor, whose visit has had a salutary effect on the precarious state of Adolph's health.

ADOLPH:

> In these last eight days you've given me the courage to face life again. It's as if your magnetism radiated over me. To me you've been a watchmaker, fixing the works in my head and rewinding the mainspring.

> (197)

The numinous powers ascribed to the visitor—restoring the "courage to face life," "magnetism," "watchmaker"—indicate that he might be a healer of some sort. But the healer's powers are frightening.

GUSTAV:

> Take my hand!

ADOLPH:

> What dreadful power you must have! It's like gripping an electrical machine.

> (217-218)

Adolph is constantly startled by how much the stranger knows about his life.

GUSTAV:

> What did you say to annoy her?

ADOLPH

> You *are* dreadful! I'm afraid of you! How can you know this?

GUSTAV:

> I know what it was. You said: "You ought to be ashamed of yourself. Flirting at your age, when it's too late for another lover."

ADOLPH:

Did I say that? I must have said it. But how could you know?

(219-220)

Tekla, too, is fascinated by Gustav's unusual powers— "You've said exactly what I was thinking," she admits to him, "you've understood me!" (251)—and she finds him disturbing, almost supernaturally so.

TEKLA:

Go away! I'm afraid of you!

GUSTAV:

Why?

TEKLA:

You take away my soul.

(259-260)

Gustav's personal life is only vaguely sketched, and what he says about it himself is sometimes deliberately misleading. He tells Tekla, for example, that he is going to remarry, then later admits he lied.

TEKLA:

And now you're going home to your fiancée!

GUSTAV:

I have none—and never want one! I'm not going home, because I have no home and don't want any.

(267)

The rootlessness Gustav admits to here adds to the uncanniness. When Tekla finally discovers the destructive purpose of his visit, she asks, "Are you absolutely void of feelings?" He replies, "Absolutely" (264-265). A frightening figure without feelings and without a home. Everything we learn about Gustav tends to abstract and dehumanize him. His resemblance to the unforgiving Yahweh, who catches up with Adam and Eve, is reinforced by his occupation: a teacher of dead languages (217). What a splendidly ambivalent image! On the one hand are implied ancient tongues and ancient truths; the languages of the Bible and of religious ritual. On the other hand, obsolescence: the languages are dead and, by implication, so is God. The character becomes an illustration of a paradox Strindberg long found fascinating, one which he would explore intensively after the Inferno. In the conscious mind of modern, skeptical man, God is dead, but in the unconscious mind a presence persists: it is we but also an Other—an awareness with awesome power. Gustav is Adolph's double and he is God, Adolph can no more escape this creditor than Adam could escape Yahweh.

As in **Miss Julie,** the aspect of the Fall theme stressed in **Creditors** is alienation. In the fear of the Count in the first play and Gustav in the second is mortal fear of alienation from the divine. A deeper implication is that, although Adam and Eve had to pay a penalty for having tasted the forbidden fruit, the punishment meted out was too severe: banishment from the harmony they shared with God.

The most eloquent expression of the alienation theme appears in the final moments of the play. Behind the dialogue between Tekla and Gustav runs another dialogue: between Eve and Yahweh, with Eve trying to fathom the meaning of alienation from the divine, and Yahweh insistent upon exercising such prerogatives as vengeance.

TEKLA:

How is it that you, who regard me as innocent since I was driven by my nature and the circumstances to behave as I did . . . how can you think you have the right to vengeance?

GUSTAV:

For that very reason. Because my nature and the circumstances drove me to seek vengeance!

Have you nothing to reproach yourself for?

TEKLA:

Nothing at all! . . . Christians say that Providence governs our actions, others call it fate. So, we're guiltless, aren't we?

GUSTAV:

. . . Guiltless, but responsible! Guiltless before Him, who no longer exists; responsible to yourself and to your fellow human beings.

I'm going to leave by the eight o'clock boat. . . .

TEKLA:

Without reconciliation?

GUSTAV:

Reconciliation? You use so many words that have lost their meaning.

(264-267)

Strindberg at one time thought of ending the play the moment Adolph reenters the room and collapses in the doorway. In the final version two additional speeches follow the collapse, resuming and concluding the sotto voce dialogue of Eve and Yahweh.

TEKLA:

[*throwing herself upon Adolph's body and caressing him*]

. . . No, God, he doesn't hear. He's dead! Oh, God in heaven, oh my God, help us, help us!

GUSTAV:

> She really does love him, too! . . . Poor creature!

> (269)

Something has happened to Gustav in this last speech. It is as if after disbelieving in human emotion he suddenly has cause to question the disbelief. But the gap between Tekla's cry for help and Gustav's continued detachment—between mortal aspiration and divine aloofness—is too great to bridge. Gustav resembles the God of Strindberg's creation play: the demiurge, who creates the world for his own amusement, like a game, and is oblivious to the meaning of human suffering. At the end of *Creditors* the game suddenly ends and only the gamemaster is ignorant of how high the stakes were.

Throughout the play the loss of Eden, the loss of harmony, implies a longing to restore it. This longing is what Adolph is talking about when he explains how and why he came to need Tekla: "She would be what God was for me before I became an atheist. . . . I cannot live without . . . a woman to respect and worship." Gustav replies in disgust, "Oh hell! You might as well take God back then, if you need to have something to genuflect to" (213). He is contemptuous of the lure of the eternal feminine and assumes the watchmaker role Adolph attributed to him earlier. Woman as a machine, Gustav asserts, is an inferior version of man:

GUSTAV:

> You see, something is wrong with the mechanism! The watchcase is that of an expensive lever-escapement, but the works are cheap cylinder-escapement.

> Have you ever seen a naked woman? Yes, of course! An adolescent male with teats, an immature man, a child that shot up but stopped developing, a chronic anemic who has regular hemorrhages thirteen times a year! Whatever can come of that?

> (214)

There is an outrageous objectivity in Gustav's tone, not only here but elsewhere in the play, an arrogant distancing; this is a manufacturer talking about an imperfect product, or the creator talking about an abortive creation. The effect produced is one of the secrets of the play's continuing popularity with theatre audiences: Gustav's outrageousness is amusing as well as shocking, witty as well as uncanny. "You have a way of saying rude things," Tekla tells him, "that makes it impossible to be angry with you" (260). Strindberg must have been aware that if the character came across as too portentously, too obviously God-like, the play would turn into leaden melodrama. Probably nothing is more responsible for production difficulties with his plays than the failure to understand how marvelously he could use humor both to mitigate and enrich the pessimism of his themes. "After the Fall" has

comic as well as tragic aspects. The archly amusing dialogue of *Creditors* works beautifully to mute without obscuring the uncanniness. When Edward Brandes wrote in a review of the published play that he found Gustav a moralizing avenger, Strindberg hastened to warn the actor who was to perform the role in the first production:

> Dear Hunderup, perform the whole role playfully good-natured . . . and . . . solely as psychological demolition work—so that there is truth to Tekla's words: that she finds Gustav "so free from morality and preaching."

> In other words: Gustav as the cat playing with the mouse before he bites him! Never angry, never moral, never preaching!

The most important clue to Gustav's mythic identity is in the last scene. While Adolph eavesdrops in the adjoining room, Tekla unknowingly allows her former husband to entice her into a compromising intimacy, and she is horrified when Gustav makes her realize the situation.

GUSTAV:

> Do you know where your husband is?

TEKLA:

> Now I think I know! . . . He's in your room next door! And he's heard everything! And seen everything! And he who sees his *fylgia* dies!

> (268)

A *fylgia* in Norse mythology is an attendant spirit, a kind of follower or second ego, capable of assuming human form. English-speaking translators of *Creditors* have rendered fylgia as "guardian spirit," "familiar spirit," and "ghost". In 1894, when a French production was being prepared at Lugné-Poe's Théâtre de l'Oeuvre and translator Georges Loiseau wrote the author for advice, Strindberg recommended that Tekla's line read: "*Celui qui a vu son ombre, va mourir,*" but *ombre* (ghost or shadow) did not quite satisfy him, for he added: "In our mythology to see oneself (*Sosie*?) [double, second self] was an omen of death." The playwright's efforts at clarification went for naught, however; the line was omitted in the published version.

Double, second self, shadow, ghost: each points up Gustav's uncanniness. But for what purpose? Was Strindberg simply adding a spooky quality to the play, or was he attempting to illuminate character relationships and theme? To answer this, we need to know more about Gustav's intentions: what has he really come for? At the opening of the play the one thing we know for certain is that he is interested in probing, searching, and digging. After learning that Adolph has a serious marital problem he asks,

GUSTAV:

> "Tell me, since you've already taken me so deeply into your confidence, have you no other secret wound that torments you? It's unusual to find only one cause for

disharmony, since life is positively gaudy with opportunities for things to go wrong. Have you no corpse in the cargo that you're keeping to yourself?"

(203)

For English-speaking readers the phrase "corpse in the cargo" ("*lik i lasten*") is more meaningfully translated as "skeleton in the closet," but what is lost thereby is an expressive nautical resonance. An old superstition among Scandinavian sailors holds that a ship with a corpse on board will sink. Ibsen is usually credited with adding a metaphoric meaning: in a letter to Georg Brandes he used a corpse in the cargo to indicate the ghosts of old ideas that must be dumped overboard so that new ideas can be heard. But the image has more poetic meaning than this. Peer Gynt, returning home to Norway as an old man after a wasted, unfulfilled life, is also a corpse in the cargo, and the ship he travels on goes down.

In *Creditors,* the corpse is a buried mystery that perhaps should remain buried. Gustav, after first trying to get Adolph to reveal the "secret wound," seems to change his mind and indicates that it would be better to leave well enough alone:

GUSTAV:

"You see, there are disharmonies in life that can never be resolved. So, you have to stuff wax in your ears and work! Work, grow old, and pile masses of new impressions on the cargo hatch—that way the corpse will remain quiet"

(204)

Piling "masses of new impressions on the cargo hatch" brings to mind the passage discussed earlier in connection with *Master Olof* about the organist in *The Romantic Organist on Rånö,* whose reluctance to remember the circumstances of his mother's death caused him to "pile masses of impressions" on "the black spot" (*21,* 245). Not surprisingly, perhaps, *Creditors* and the novella were written at about the same time and provide another example of Strindberg's ability to make similar or even identical images function well in different contexts.

Adolph, like the organist, has something to hide, and Gustav is only feigning disinterest in finding out what it is; he is deadly serious about collecting the corpse, and he ferrets for it until Adolph is destroyed. If Gustav is one of the "creditors" the play is about, it is not in an ordinary sense. His uncanniness, we can now see, is similar to the uncanniness of the character in fairy tales who reappears after a long absence to collect debts that have accumulated as promises unfulfilled. Adolph owes a debt, not so much to Gustav as to himself. He has failed to pursue the quest for the lost harmony properly; there are disharmonies still to be resolved within.

In seven years of marriage Adolph has done all the giving and Tekla all the taking. The consequence is that he has become hopelessly dependent on her. He sometimes

thought of being free of her, but no sooner had she gone for a time than he missed her dreadfully. He is an Adam whose undoing was the making of Eve:

ADOLPH:

[I] longed for her as if for my arms and legs! It's strange, but sometimes it seems to me as if she were not a separate person but a part of me, an intestine that carried away my will, my desire to live. It's as if I had deposited in her my very solar plexus that the anatomists talk about

(*23,* 194)

His longing for Tekla has its roots in the same problem suffered by the Captain in *The Father:* a difficulty in separating the need for maternal love from the need for sexual love. And Tekla, like Laura, no longer wants to play impossible roles:

TEKLA:

I've grown tired of being a nursemaid.

ADOLPH:

Do you hate me?

TEKLA:

No! I don't, and I don't think I can, either! But that's probably because you're a child.

(242-243)

Tekla is accused of having totally devoured Adolph—his courage, soul, knowledge, and faith—and Gustav characterizes the situation as an instance of "cannibalism." Yet, when Tekla appears, she turns out not to be the terribly evil person conjured up in the two men's conversation. The reason Adolph is so dependent on her and has allowed his marriage to deteriorate is that he had wanted Tekla to be his "better self," to which Gustav responds with advice Adolph might have profited from earlier: "Be your own better self" (209).

Gustav is not simply a bitter former husband seeking revenge, he is a force of destiny thrusting Adolph into a terrible self-confrontation, and his uncanniness serves the purpose Freud indicated in his essay "The Uncanny": "that class of the terrifying which leads back to something long known to us, once very familiar." As fylgia, Gustav is Adolph's double, and a double, says Freud, is a "ghastly harbinger of death." The terrifying and familiar thing that Adolph is led back to by Gustav's presence is a fatal psychic weakness, a lack of will.

When Adolph speaks of a loss of will, he resembles the protagonists in Strindberg's other naturalistic plays. The Captain says that he was an unwanted child, conceived against his parents' will and so was born "without a will" (66). Julie says that as far as she knows she came into the world against her mother's wishes, and when she wants Jean to give her the strength to commit suicide, she says to him: "You know what I *should* do, but lack the will to. . . . Will it, Jean, order me to carry it out!" (185).

Strindberg connects faith and will in an essay, "Mysticism—For the Present," written between the time he wrote *The Father* and *Miss Julie* and *Creditors:* "Faith is nothing other than a concentration of wish and desire heightened into conscious will, and the will is the greatest manifestation of nerve movement and therefore summons for its disposal the maximum possible energy" (*22,* 186-187). Faith and will become the instruments through which psychic energy flows; when they are absent, the individual lacks the means to cope with life's problems. In the context of Strindberg's naturalistic plays, lack of will represents the incapacity to battle and conquer the destructive aspects of the unconscious. The Captain cannot overcome the challenge of the Great Mother; Julie canot deal with the fear of Eros; and Adolph cannot resolve psychic disharmonies on his own, as an independent person, in order to become his own "better self."

Perhaps in the concept of a lack of will Strindberg was searching for a modern psychological mechanism equivalent to the tragic flaw of Greek tragedy. Both are like the concealed flaw in a piece of metal that is often invisible to the naked eye. The metal appears to be perfectly sound, until one day, under a certain kind of stress, it cracks. The concealed flaw is the corpse in the cargo Gustav is after. In this way he becomes, along with Laura in *The Father* or Jean in *Miss Julie,* not so much a villain as a catalyst who precipitates the moment of fatal stress. The Captain, Julie, and Adolph are not crucified by their adversaries; they impale themselves on their own weaknesses. The power of the unconscious arouses in them a feeling of dread, that paralyzing combination of fear and fascination. They feel a calling to fight against the power, but they are doomed soldiers in a futile war. They cannot win because of the ambivalent feelings they have about the enemy: their desire to win is undermined by a desire to surrender; the desire to live, to answer the challenge of Eros, is canceled by a stronger allegiance to Thanatos. Gustav is the herald who reminds Adolph of the calling that went unanswered, the self that was never realized.

Gustav and Laura belong to that tribe of dramatic figures—Iago is also a member—often described as pure evil. It is difficult to find a personal motivation in them strong enough to explain the terrible destruction they bring about. Hate might explain it, but Gustav especially is not really emotionally involved enough to hate. We can understand these characters better in terms of the concept so highly valued by programmatic naturalists: survival of the fittest. Rather than forces of pure evil, they are nature's instruments for finding and eliminating weakness. In a sense, they are no more evil than any predator who searches for the one lame animal in a herd and then tracks it endlessly

until it is brought down. Consequently, the sense of awe we feel in the tragic destiny of a figure like the Captain, or Othello, is not in the distance they fall but in the sovereign majesty of a nature constantly balancing the scales. "I can find the joy of life," Strindberg said in the preface to *Miss Julie,* "in its cruel and powerful battles, and my enjoyment comes from being able to know something, being able to learn something" (*23,* 101).

If Strindberg's so-called naturalistic plays survive as viable stage pieces that attract actors and audiences alike, while other specimens of the genre, even from eminences like Zola, are dead, it is because Strindberg knew how to stage the kind of confrontations that make for great drama. The intersection at which his characters meet is only incidentally the "scientifically" fixed point of historic time and place defined by late-nineteenth-century literature, where the laws of heredity and environment reign. His people obey higher laws than deterministic naturalism. "Human society," said Joyce, "is the embodiment of changeless laws which the whimsicalities and circumstances of men and women involve and overwrap. . . . Drama has to do with the underlying laws first, in all their nakedness and divine severity, and only secondarily with the motley agents who bear them out."

The real adversarial relationship between Strindberg's "motley agents" is not character versus character but the hero versus the Other. In *The Father* and *Miss Julie* the Other—Laura's mother in the first play, the Count in the second—is offstage, as if to indicate that its presence is so terrible that one dare not face it directly. In *Creditors* Strindberg brings the Other, Gustav, onstage, and the enemy proves as formidable as we had been led to anticipate. But whether offstage or on, the Other is both more and less than an external force; the enemy for the hero is within.

A paradox exists: because the enemy is an intimate, because the enemy is oneself, even as the Other throws down the gauntlet and challenges to mortal combat, it is a potential ally. Intimate enemy can also be intimate friend. But there is a big "if": enemy can become friend only if the hero can transcend the fear and respect that are so rightly due the Other as personification of the awesome powers of the unconscious, and learn trust. From *Master Olof* through *Creditors* we have seen that the heroes either perish, as the Captain, Julie, and Adolph do, or capitulate to a life of slavery, as do Olof and Jean. They could not learn that a calling involves the paradoxical obligation both to battle and to trust the Other.

Between 1893 and 1897 a crucial hiatus occurred in Strindberg's career as a dramatist. He not only abandoned drama but belles lettres generally. When he returned to playwriting in *To Damascus,* his hero's struggle for self-realization moved into a new phase. The hero and the Other continued to grapple, and the stakes were just as high, but the hero had a acquired a measure of confidence and the contest become less one-sided. A particular mythic image now appeared and reappeared in Strindberg's fiction and drama: Jacob wrestling with the angel. The Strindbergian hero had learned that like Jacob he could wrestle all night with the Other and not only survive but earn his opponent's respect and even support. Of course, a price must be paid: Jacob walked lame for the rest of his life. And before one exults in the victory it would be well to remember, as Jung observed, that the angel emerges from the fight without a scratch.

Richard Bark (essay date 1988)

SOURCE: Bark, Richard. "Strindberg's Dream Play Technique." In *Strindberg's Dramaturgy,* edited by Göran Stockenström, pp. 98-106. Minneapolis: University of Minnesota Press, 1988.

[*In the following essay, Bart explores Strindberg's use of the "dream play" technique.*]

When Strindberg wrote his preface to *A Dream Play,* he called *To Damascus* (**I**) "his former dream play." So in a sense the author has given his approval for us to call these two plays—and perhaps others, such as *The Ghost Sonata*—"dream plays," bearing in mind that although they are different in character and technique, there are more things that unite them than separate them—above all a basic view of reality.

When *To Damascus* (**I**), *A Dream Play,* and *The Ghost Sonata* were first published, the critics discovered their "dream atmosphere." Ever since then, scholars, professionals in the theater, readers, and spectators have tried to ascertain how Strindberg created this dream atmosphere in the text and how it could be portrayed on stage.

The term "dream play" already existed in Swedish (*drömspel*) as well as in German (*Traumspiel*) before Strindberg used it (although it did not exist in English and French), but in those days it meant only the presence of a dreamlike reality in a play. Strindberg seems to be the first one to have used it to designate a dramatic genre, and as such it is used in present-day English.

To experience reality as a dream is nothing unique for Strindberg. Human beings have done so throughout history. Even during his so-called naturalistic period, Strindberg could express such a concept. In a letter to the author Axel Lundegård, November 12, 1887, he wrote concerning *The Father:* "It seems to me as if I am walking in my sleep; as if fiction and life were blended. I do not know if *The Father* is fiction or if my life has been one; . . . Through much writing my life has become a life of shadows."[1] It is easy to find paraphrases of these state-

ments in *A Dream Play.* But the point here is that, when he wrote *The Father,* he did not depict reality as dreamlike. The fact that directors have tried to stage *The Father* and *Miss Julie* as dream plays is a different issue. It is after the Inferno crisis that the depiction of reality as dreamlike will become the dominant aspect of Strindberg's work.

A study of Strindberg's dream-play technique must start from an understanding of the author's experience of reality at the time of the Inferno crisis. In the books *Inferno* and *Legends,* it is obvious that he conceives reality as being like a dream. There is, of course, a basic level of fictional reality; he is walking on the street or sitting in a café when, suddenly or gradually, this reality is transformed into a dreamlike one. And all this is depicted with the same naturalistic means as before. In this way Strindberg remains a naturalist; the same view of reality that is expressed in *Inferno* and *Legends* is in his dream plays. Strindberg has never depicted a "real" sleeping dream in his plays (perhaps with the exception of the Alchemists' Banquet and the Inn scenes in *To Damascus* [**II**]). It is always reality that he depicts as dreamlike. And it is in this way that I use "dream play" in connection with plays, a term depicting a reality that is partly dreamlike, a reality that temporarily has the atmosphere of a dream.

It is true, however, that sleeping dreams have been staged from the very beginning of theatrical history—ever since the ghost of Clytemnestra appeared in front of the sleeping Furies in Aeschylus's *The Eumenedies*—not to mention dreams in the medieval mystery and miracle plays, in Shakespeare's dramas, in the baroque, the romantic, and the symbolistic theater.

There was a time when Strindberg was regarded as having been totally ignorant of the technical aspects of the theater. Nothing could be more wrong, as later research has proved. His writings about theater, his letters, and his discussions with directors and actors give the picture of a professional man of the theater. His plays themselves are the best proof of his theatrical knowledge, proof that he wrote them with the stage before his eyes.

When Strindberg was twenty years old, he tried to become an actor and was accepted as a pupil at The Royal Dramatic Theater in Stockholm. Even though he did not have great success in this endeavor, he did have the opportunity to work as an extra in many Royal Opera productions, including Bjørnson's *Maria Stuart i Skottland,* Halm's *Fäktaren från Ravenna* (The Swordsman from Ravenna), Birch-Pfeiffer's *Ladyn av Worsley-Hall,* and such operas as Hérold's *Zampa,* Halévy's *Judinnan* (The Jewess), Rossini's *Wilhelm Tell,* Verdi's *Ernani,* and Meyerbeer's *Afrikanskan* (The African Woman). Meyerbeer's opera featured one of the most magnificent shipwrecks that had ever been put on a Swedish stage. Strindberg, with his sharp powers of observation, of course registered everything concerning the techniques of the stage. The fact that the changes of scenery in *A Dream Play* could be a problem, did not deter a theater professional who had actually seen the most advanced machinery.

Strindberg wrote his dream plays for a stage that perhaps did not exist at the time but that *had* existed when he was young. It was something he knew as well as his own writing desk—a stage that had been destroyed by realism and naturalism, by what he called "byggandet på scenen" ("building on stage" [i.e., realistic scene construction]), which created endless intermissions and made fast scenery changes impossible. Strindberg wrote for the elegant machinery of the baroque theater with its potential for "changements à vue," which he himself had used in *Lucky Per's Journey* (written at the beginning of the 1880s).

It is misleading to say that it is the technique of the modern theater that has done full justice to Strindberg's later plays. They could have been produced in his time on a baroque stage with entertaining and astonishing effects. Of course, today such effects would seem old-fashioned and unsatisfying. But a production of *A Dream Play* at The Drottningholm Court Theater could, in the right hands, be a sensation in our time as well.

Many scholars have tried to explain how a dream atmosphere is created in Strindberg's dream plays—as literature and as stage productions. Most of them say the effect is created when something "dreamlike" is put into the text or staging. This is self-evident—if not a case of circular reasoning. Attempts have been made to characterize this dreamlike quality as distortion, immobility, slow motion, chiaroscuro, and soundlessness, and in addition as exaggerated rapidity, visual sharpness, and loudness— opposite characteristics! The dream effect, then, can be created through any means at all; it is the *context* that matters, the circumstances in which these techniques appear. With this in mind, the dreamlike effect could better be defined as a violation of time and space. Of course there must be some technique for creating dream atmosphere, but manipulating iconic elements—that is, elements that imitate an actual sleeping dream—may not be sufficient.

In Strindberg's dream plays there is always a sort of reality (fictitious, of course) established, but this reality is either suddenly or gradually transformed into a dreamlike one and then, in a permanent motion, returned to its original state. Sometimes "objective" reality and dreamlike reality appear simultaneously. The boundaries are impossible to draw. It is through special relationships, changes, and contrasts between these two levels, that the dream atmosphere is created, above all as it is expressed in the relation between the protagonist and his or her reality. Dream atmosphere is always created in contrast with the "reality" of the fictitious world of the play. I shall delineate these structures beginning with the protagonist, who may be confronted with a dreamlike reality as the spectator of a

play-within-a-play, or perhaps drawn into it, becoming a dream character.

Strindberg is often regarded as one of the forerunners of expressionism and this is of course correct. But we must stop examining Strindberg in the light of expressionism as if he had been an expressionist himself, and instead emphasize how he is different, in order to discover his uniqueness. We cannot be content with regarding *To Damascus* (I) as a "drama of the soul" (which is the most important aspect of expressionism), acting in a "landscape of the soul," a drama that takes place entirely inside the Stranger, who is the protagonist. In *To Damascus* (I) there is an objective reality and the presence of a higher power that intervenes and directs everything. (There is also a god in the background of *A Dream Play* and *The Ghost Sonata;* in *A Dream Play* it is the god Indra, but he has already created the world once and for all and no longer intervenes.)

To Damascus (I) starts entirely realistically, but after a while dreamlike things begin to happen that have the effect of abolishing time and space. The Stranger is a kind of representative of reality throughout the play, increasingly tortured by fear. He looks at all these things as would a spectator of a dreamlike play-within-a-play. He exists on two levels: the real and the dreamlike. What he sees has an objective existence within the fiction of the play, but since we see these things partly through the eyes of the Stranger, we have the impression that we are looking into his soul. He also has visions and hallucinations, but they are never made visual or audible in the scenic dimension. There is a great difference between what the Stranger *says* that he experiences and what he *is shown* to experience (consider, for example, the vision in the Lady's crochet work and the sound of the grinding mill).

Let me mention *some* of these dreamlike plays-within-a-play, to which the Stranger is a spectator and which thereby take on a dream atmosphere. When he wants to give the Lady a new name, he shouts, "Fanfares!" and makes a gesture toward offstage; but instead of fanfares a funeral march is played. The Beggar has a scar similar to that of the Stranger, and when he learns that the Beggar, like himself, has received it from a close relative, he says: "No, now I am becoming afraid. May I feel if you are real?" and he touches the Beggar's arm and confirms, "Yes, he is real!" But the Beggar is still a sort of double—an evident violation of time and space. Then the six brown-clad pallbearers enter and, when the Stranger asks why they are mourning in brown and not in black, they answer that it *is* black, "but if Your Grace so commands, it will be brown to you." At the Doctor's Home he is confronted with the so-called Werewolf (the Doctor, husband of the Lady); an arm and a leg of a corpse, which the Doctor pulls out of an icebox; and the Madman Caesar, who bears the name the Stranger had in school.

At the Hotel Room everything is quite different. Here the Stranger is no longer a spectator of a play-within-a-play. Both he and the Lady are trapped in a dreamlike situation—becoming, in a way, dream characters themselves.

In the Asylum scene the Stranger makes his most obvious appearance as a spectator of a dreamlike play-within-a-play. He is sitting at a table to the left, and at a table to the right there is a strange party:

> *The brown-clad pallbearers from the first act; the Beggar; a Woman in mourning with two children; a Woman, resembling the Lady but who is not the Lady, and who is crocheting instead of eating; a Man who resembles the Doctor but is not he; the Madman's double; the doubles of the Father and the Mother; the Brother's double; the Parents of the "Prodigal Son" and others. All are dressed in white but over their clothing is gauze in various colors. Their faces are waxen, deathly white; and their whole appearance and gestures are ghostlike.*

These people also have an objective existence (within the fictitious world of the play) although here they abolish time and space. The Stranger has only to ask the inevitable question: "Are they actually like that?" and the Abbess answers: "If you mean are they real, yes, they're terrifyingly real." In his next question he directly refers to the play-within-a-play: "Is it a play being performed?" Then the Confessor confuses everything even more—by introducing the doubles as actually *being* the characters they resemble.

After the Asylum, the scenes reappear in reversed order, and the dream atmosphere gradually disappears—as in an awakening.

In *To Damascus* **(II)** the structure is quite different—more similar to the one at the Hotel Room in part I. In part II the Stranger is outside the dream atmosphere only when he listens to the Doctor's speech while sitting on the bench of the accused; and when he sees his children, their new parents, the Doctor, and the Madman on the bridge. In all other cases he is drawn into a dreamlike situation and becomes a part of it, transformed into a dream character himself—for instance, at the Alchemist's Banquet and the Inn scenes, which he afterward refers to as a dream, an actual sleeping dream. It is obvious that here Strindberg is very close to expressionism, but it would be wrong to interpret all his dream plays on the basis of these scenes.

A Dream Play begins as pure baroque theater, when Indra's Daughter descends to earth in a cloud chariot. Although she comes from heaven, from a world of gods and myths, she functions as a representative of reality throughout the play—sometimes in company with the Officer, the Lawyer, or the Poet. She walks through the play as the spectator of many dreamlike plays-within-the-play, wherein time and space are abolished. The growing castle,

for example, is situated on another level of reality, a violation of time and space. The Daughter and the Officer "then stop, frozen in their gestures and mime" and watch a scene in the parents' home. She takes the Doorkeeper's place in the theater corridor to "sit here and look at the children of man," and she sees how the Officer is waiting for his beloved Victoria who never comes, and how he grows older and older—a dream character. She sees the world transform before her eyes: for example, a tree becomes a coat rack, which becomes a candelabra, while people on stage are frozen in their positions. In the Promotion scene in the church, the Lawyer enters a dreamlike situation and becomes a dream character when the Daughter, who actually remains outside, places the crown of thorns on his head. Although she is performing the crowning, she does not become a dream character. The levels are thus mixed.

In the room where a hellish marriage is enacted, the Daughter becomes a part of the dream level when she is nearly choked by Kristin's papering of the windows. We can also observe the people standing in the doorway as silent spectators of the scene.

At Foul Strand the Daughter again sees several strange people: a quarantine master, two patients exercising on some gym machinery, an old dandy in a wheelchair, an old coquette, her lover, a poet with a pail of mud, and a loving couple who have to go into quarantine. At Fair Haven she sees Ugly Edith, whom nobody wants to dance with but who achieves a moment of triumph by playing Bach on the piano. During the School scene, the Officer becomes a dream character when he cannot give the answer to two times two.

And after all this comes the Coal Heavers' scene—a totally realistic scene without any dream atmosphere, although the Daughter and the Lawyer are spectators during it. Here there is no violation of time and space (the shift to the Mediterranean is only mentioned in the stage directions) and the Coal Heavers are really not dream characters.

The drama concludes with a magnificent dreamlike play-within-a-play: the "defile," where all the people in the drama enter offering their attributes to the fire, with the Daughter and the Poet as spectators. Finally, at the end of the play, the Poet alone remains a spectator while the Daughter enters the burning castle, returning to her father in heaven.

In *The Ghost Sonata,* the Student's role as a spectator is not as clear as those of the Stranger and the Daughter. In the first act, Hummel is a kind of lecturer and the Student a spectator, when, for example, the former describes the strange people in the house just as they become visible in the windows (as on an inner stage) and in the street: the Colonel, the statue of the Mummy, the Fiancée, the Caretaker's Wife, the Woman in Black, the Aristocrat, the Young Lady, the Dead Man, the Beggars, the Milkmaid.

In the second act in the round drawing room, the Mummy is introduced by the two servants as a character in a play-within-a-play while she sits in her wardrobe as on an inner stage, chattering like a parrot. The "ghosts" in the ghost supper constitute by their immobility and silence the dreamlike violation of time and space. But from the moment the Mummy stops time by stopping the clock, several levels of a dreamlike reality are introduced: the Milkmaid enters—seen only by Hummel—and at last he goes into the closet to hang himself, with all the other characters functioning as spectators.

In the third act in the hyacinth room, the Cook belongs to a dreamlike level: she stands in the doorway like a character in a play-within-a-play, with the Student and the Young Lady as spectators. The Student loses his temper and reveals all the rottenness in the house. His speech kills the Young Lady, who escapes into another world. She is joining the other ghosts, becoming a dreamlike character, while the Student is a spectator of her death and of the transformation of the hyacinth room into the Isle of the Dead—the final abolition of time and space.

I have exposed the structure of some of the dream play scenes in these three plays. In the history of their productions, one can see how directors have attempted to realize their two-layered structures. In the first productions—during the period of symbolist theater—directors tried to make everything on stage as dreamlike as possible while the spectators themselves were designated as dreamers of the plays. For the 1900 production of *To Damascus* (I), Grandinson and Grabow erected an extra stage (three steps high) on the main stage and framed it with an additional proscenium in the shape of an arch. In only one scene—the Asylum—was the Stranger (played by August Palme) represented as the spectator of a play-within-a-play, watching the doubles who were placed on an inner stage within an additional arch. For their production of *A Dream Play* (1907), Castegren and Grabow also used an extra proscenium in the shape of a poppy-arch, but this time it was not possible to remind the spectators of their role as dreamers. In *The Ghost Sonata* at Strindberg's Intimate Theater (1908), everything on stage was made to look like a dream, and the Student (played by Helge Wahlgren) was represented in a totally realistic way—a failed concept in most respects. In the Bernauer-Gade production of *A Dream Play* (1916), the stage was given an extra proscenium as well: a huge oval with a transparent veil, behind which everything was enacted within a fairy-tale framework, giving the audience the function of dreamers. Moreover, Indra's Daughter (played by Irene Triesch) was made a spectator of several plays-within-a-play, in which the Officer (played by Ludwig Hartau) was part of the most dreamlike of these. In Reinhardt's production of *The Ghost Sonata* (1916), the Student (played by Paul Hartmann) was a spectator of many plays-within-a-play, in which Hummel (played by Paul Wegener) appeared in the most dreamlike sequences.

Molander and Skawonius succeeded in making the settings for *A Dream Play* (1935) transformations of each other. The Daughter (played by Tora Teje) was often a dream-play spectator to scenes in which the Officer (played by Lars Hanson) portrayed a memorable dream character. In Molander's *To Damascus* (I) (1937), Lars Hanson created a protagonist who was fearful, wondering always whether or not he was dreaming. In Molander's *The Ghost Sonata* (1942), both the Student (played by Frank Sundström) and Hummel (played by Lars Hanson) were represented as "real" people—that is, spectators of plays-within-a-play—one of which, the ghost supper, at last engulfed Hummel.

In Ingmar Bergman's production of *A Dream Play* (1970), the drama was shown as a theatrical event that the Poet was creating while it took place on stage. The Poet, his creation, and the audience were all on the same level—as in Brecht's theatrical Verfremdung. Bergman was at that time not interested in creating the illusion of a dream, nor in creating any illusion at all. For his 1973 production of *The Ghost Sonata,* he perceived the play as Strindberg's dream and wanted gradually to penetrate deeper and deeper into the consciousness of the author. However, there was no clear expression of this intention in the production, other than an increasingly intense acting style. In Bergman's *To Damascus* (I) and (II) (1974) the Stranger (played by Jan-Olof Strandberg) was a part of the dream level, a character in sleeping dreams—"a mental landscape" created through an intensified expressionism in stage design and acting.[2]

Why so much fuss about dream atmosphere? Is it that important? I think so. If we exclude this effect from Strindberg's plays, we exclude a view of life: life as a dream—which I think is the basic aspect of the dream plays. If we can create a dream atmosphere on the stage of our minds, and in our theaters, we will gain the impression of a much truer reality, as if we were seeing behind the surface of illusion and reality into inner reality.

I have tired to demystify Strindberg and to show that dream atmosphere has nothing to do with imitation of sleeping dreams but that it relies on a particular scenic structure that is simple and practicable. Dream atmosphere is not achieved through exterior means or theatrical tricks (although they can help). It can be created in daylight in any space if the audience is made aware of this structure through visual means.

It is very difficult—if not impossible—to create a dream atmosphere in the theater if the director wants to depict actual sleeping dreams, but it is quite possible if reality is to be depicted as a dream, which is Strindberg's method. His dream atmosphere seems to build on the contrast between two levels: the transformation of reality into dreamlike reality and the relation between the protagonist and his or her world, in which he or she sometimes becomes a dream character in his or her own dream but ultimately is a spectator of a dreamlike play-within-a-play.

It is impossible to create an absolute illusion of reality on stage, but through the dream-play technique it is possible to create an absolute illusion of a dreamlike reality. Nobody in theater can deny that what is shown on stage really *is* a dreamlike reality—and this is perhaps Strindberg's greatest contribution to the history of drama and theater.

Notes

1. Letter from August Strindberg to Axel Lundegård, Nov. 12, 1887, in *August Strindbergs Brev* (Stockholm: Albert Bonniers Förlag, 1958), 6:298. Unless otherwise indicated, all translations are my own.

2. For more detailed information about these productions, see Richard Bark, *Strindbergs drömspelsteknik—i drama och teater* (Lund: Studentlitteratur, 1981).

Freddie Rokem (essay date 1988)

SOURCE: Rokem, Freddie. "The Camera and the Aesthetics of Repetition: Strindberg's Use of Space and Scenography in *Miss Julie, A Dream Play,* and *The Ghost Sonata.*" In *Strindberg's Dramaturgy,* edited by Göran Stockenström, pp. 107-28. Minneapolis: University of Minnesota Press, 1988.

[*In the following essay, Roken spotlights Strindberg's presentation of visual information as an element of his narrative technique.*]

The question of how that which the writer-dramatist wants to communicate is passed on to the reader-spectator as experience of knowledge was one of Strindberg's primary concerns. In several of his plays, the actual process of passing on information and the issue of its authenticity are placed in the foreground, thus confronting us as spectators with problems that careful narratological and rhetorical analysis of fiction has taught us as readers to carefully sift and weigh for possible counterversions that are in some way embedded in the text itself.[1]

In this paper I investigate how the visual information, based primarily on our perception of the scenographic elements in some of Strindberg's major plays, is "narrated" by the dramatist through the manner and order of its presentation to us. The playwright's selection of *locus* and events are the key to the narratological scheme of the play. An examination of how the dramatist-narrator has visually "cut into" the fictional world of his characters with his selection of stage events will clarify how the rhetorical devices affect us. Watching a theatrical performance (and reading a script) implies that we are constantly adjusting visual and verbal information to make it coherent. By concentrating here on the visual aspects, I hope to fill a gap in the appreciation of Strindberg's genius.

In an interview about his art as a stage director, Ingmar Bergman made the following comparison between Ibsen and Strindberg:

> To me, the most fascinating thing about Strindberg is that enormous awareness that everything in life, at every moment, is completely amoral—completely open and simply rooted. . . . With Ibsen, you always have the feeling of limits—because Ibsen placed them there himself. He was an architect, and he built. He always built his plays, and he knew exactly: I want this and I want that. He points the audience in the direction he wants it to go, closing doors, leaving no other alternatives. With Strindberg—as with Shakespeare—you always have the feeling that there are no such limits.[2]

This statement is true in several respects, finally, because Strindberg has presented us with a very subjective view of the world, a view that not only changed several times during his own career as a writer but also took sudden and unexpected turns within the individual works themselves. I will show how this subjectivity operates in the theater.

In Strindberg's dramatic production, the stylistic developments that had been started by Ibsen's decision—after writing *Peer Gynt*—to place the dramatic action in the bourgeois drawing room, now came full circle: in Strindberg's expressionistic plays we again find ourselves in the vast landscapes that have to be understood and interpreted as metaphorical explorations of the vast inner landscapes of the subjective mind. In *Peer Gynt* there is an excursion into these inner landscapes when Peer visits the world of the trolls. It can take place, however, only after Peer hits his head on the rock and faints (act 2). It is thus motivated on the "realistic" level of plot in the progression of the play. In Strindberg's post-Inferno plays, the so-called expressionistic ones, the motivation for this exposure of the inner regions of the mind is, however, only "aesthetic." This means that it is based solely on an acceptance by the spectator of the literary and theatrical conventions through which the protagonist's mental life is presented.

These aesthetic intentions were given a rather negative interpretation during Strindberg's own lifetime when the post-Inferno plays were originally published and performed in Stockholm (the first decade of this century). Even in the recent study *Tragic Drama and Modern Society* by John Orr, these conventions are seen as a limitation that finally hinges on Strindberg's own madness. Orr claims.

> The limitation of Strindberg is seen more easily by comparison with the painting of Munch or Kokoschka. Here the expressionist method was used to enlarge the figurative dimensions of art and represented a step forward in the history of painting. But theatre invariably imposes a distance between the spectator and the hero which has to be overcome both technically and thematically by the actor's performance. It has no equivalent of the novelist's "point of view" which can lead us, through indirect speech, into the mind and

sensibility of the character. Strindberg's attempt at such direct exposure through dramatic speech can be compelling and equally disturbing, but the sense of distance is always there. The attachment of an expressionist method to the exploration of the human unconscious ultimately led him to a pathological vision of the world.[3]

If, on the other hand, we accept the aesthetic "limitations" or "givens" of the theater as an artistic medium, limits that involve the fundamental issue of how and to what extent the inner privacy of the mind can be presented to an audience during a live performance, then the methods of perception developed by Strindberg do not seem as disturbing as Orr implies. Strindberg is, rather, bringing the narrative techniques of the theater into areas of perception that had not been explored before. As Orr rightly observes, the questions of point of view and narrative technique lie at the center of Strindberg's communication with his audience. This shift of emphasis in the modes of theatrical communication and perception has determined the nature of Strindberg's plays on almost all levels, although I will concentrate primarily on the visual implications of the shift. The major change Strindberg effects is the gradual abandonment of the realistic stage convention wherein the proscenium arch is the aesthetic frame through which the dramatic action and the fictional world are statistically presented and perceived.

In the dramas of Ibsen and Chekhov, for instance, the proscenium arch is basically equivalent to the imaginary fourth wall that separates the stage action from the audience. It is a dividing line that places the dramatic action and the audience in a *static* relationship to each other. In Strindberg's plays, however, there is a constant manipulation of our vision and point of view, which in many respects resembles the function of the narrator in a novel or even the camera in a movie. Strindberg has elaborated a *dynamic* dramatic/theatrical method of presentation through which he shows us his heroes and their fictional world from several changing points of view during the progress of the action. This also leads to a different, and sometimes much closer, involvement of the reader-spectator in the fictional world Strindberg presents than in those of Ibsen and Chekhov.

Susan Sontag, in an article analyzing the differences between theater and film, quotes Panofsky's formal distinctions between seeing a play and seeing a movie:

> In the theatre (Panofsky argues) "space is static; that is, the space represented on the stage, as well as the spatial relation of the beholder to the spectacle is unalterably fixed," while in the cinema, "the spectator occupies a fixed seat, but only physically, not as the subject of an aesthetic experience. In the theatre, the spectator cannot change his angle of vision." In the cinema the spectator is "aesthetically in permanent motion as his eye identifies with the lens of the camera, which permanently shifts in distance and direction."[4]

Sontag subsequently argues against Panofsky's attempt to keep the two art forms separate. Sontag quotes from several movies and theater styles to show that only in the use of "a realistic living room as a blank stage"[5]—that is, in the plays of Ibsen—does the theater become as static as Panofsky claims. Here I will argue, in concurrence with Sontag's views, that Strindberg developed theatrical techniques in which the eye of the spectator actually "identifies with the lens of the camera, which permanently shifts in distance and direction," and that he has actually turned this lens into an invisible narrator in some of his plays. I will primarily focus on *Miss Julie, A Dream Play,* and *The Ghost Sonata.* These plays illustrate Strindberg's fundamental dramatic-theatrical devices that bridge the distinctions often made between the pre- and post-Inferno plays. These similarities do not of course completely erase the important differences between these two periods in Strindberg's creative life.

No matter what final meaning we ascribe to Ibsen's plays, his principal characters are usually involved in quests toward understanding and overcoming specific past events that have become overshadowed by guilt. When these past experiences resurface, there is usually some kind of catastrophe. By "closing doors," as Ingmar Bergman expresses it, Ibsen really leaves "no other alternatives" for his heroes. In Chekhov's plays, all the doors have been opened, but his main characters have no deep urges or possibilities to use them to change their lives or move on to new situations or places. His protagonists are caught somewhere between paralysis and despair, which, precisely because the doors have been opened, involves them in very painful struggles. In the context of Chekhov's major plays, these struggles are understood neither as failures nor as successes, just as phases of suffering and despair, mixed with varying degrees of irony.

These fundamental differences of presentation of the fictional world are also expressed on the level of scenographic presentation. In Ibsen's realistic plays, the setting very often focuses on a single physical point, which, in terms of the play's action and the main character's past, is a visual representation of the past catastrophe. Examples of this principle are the attic in *The Wild Duck* or the mill stream in *Rosmersholm.* Chekhov, on the other hand, presents a scene that leads in several different directions. His protagonist stumbles because he or she is not sure which choice to make, whereas Ibsen's fails because his or her choice is undermined by a sense of guilt from the past.

In Strindberg's plays, it is never clear what his main character's world looks like and whether it has one or many focal points. This obviously makes it much harder to interpret his plays and is probably one of the reasons why so much of the criticism and interpretation of his work had drawn correlations between Strindberg's own life as son, husband, father, and writer and his literary output.[6] There was for a long time no other direction to take. His poetry, novels, and dramas have in several cases even been treated as private documents or "diaries" of a struggling individual, who in his writing sought a final and public outlet for his personal suffering. Strindberg himself is largely responsible for directing his critics toward this kind of criticism by writing the confessional autobiographical novels *The Defense of a Madman* and *The Son of a Servant*.

Several of his plays, such as **Miss Julie, The Father, To Damascus (I),** and many more, have also been given biographical interpretations. In them he exposes not only the private lives of his characters but also his own private life in the public sphere of the theater. This of course is a further development of the dialectic between the private and the public, a very important aspect of theatrical communication, which in this case is realized in the form of open confession.

In analyzing the works of Ibsen and Chekhov it is possible to use the visual focal points in their fictional worlds as "keys" to interpreting the strivings and dreams of the characters. One of the salient features of these focal points, whether they are singular or multiple, seen or unseen, reachable or unattainable, is that apart from being physically present in the fictional world and in the consciousness of the characters, they are *static*. Once such a focal point has been established, in Ibsen's plays for example, there is a relatively high degree of certainty that it will remain in place until the characters have concluded their struggle at the end of the play. One of the primary guarantees and safeguards for this static quality is the steady frame of the proscenium arch through which the fictional world is perceived. And in Chekhov's plays, where there are several focal points or where the physical point of view changes in different acts, for example, in *The Cherry Orchard,* they still remain rather constant.

However, the assumptions that are part of the realistic tradition are drastically altered in Strindberg's plays. It is possible to identify two important features in several of his plays which, by being present in varying degrees, change the whole relationship between the presentation of the stage action and the perception of the audience. The first feature is a visual focal point that constantly changes or occasionally disappears or is very difficult to find; this feature is present in the proposed set for the play as well as in the consciousness of the characters in relation to the world they inhabit. The second important feature, which relates to the first, is the superimposition of some kind of "filter" or "camera" on the fictional world presented on stage. With the help of this "camera," Strindberg directs the audience's perception and vision of the stage world in a manner similar to the manipulations of the narrator in the novel and the camera in the movies. The camera has of course frequently been compared to the narrator.[7]

I am using the concept camera very deliberately here because Strindberg succeeded in arriving at theatrical effects that resemble the way a photograph "cuts out" a piece of reality: not a symmetrical joining of one wall to the other walls in the house—the basic fourth-wall technique of the realistic theater—but rather an asymmetrical cutting-out. Furthermore, Strindberg used cinematographic techniques resembling zoom, montage, and cut, which are highly significant from the strictly technical point of view and for the meaning of the plays. Historically, photography and movies were making great strides at the time and were art forms to which he himself—as photographer and as movie writer—gave considerable attention and interest. During Strindberg's lifetime, both **The Father** and **Miss Julie** were filmed as silent movies by the director Anna Hofman-Uddgren and her husband, Gustaf Uddgren, writer and friend of Strindberg, but only **The Father** has been preserved.[8]

Strindberg thus developed dramatic theatrical techniques that, like the movie camera, can bring the viewer very close to the depicted action and, at the same time, can quite easily change the point of view or direction of observing an event or succession of events. The disappearance or near disappearance of the static focal point is largely the result of the introduction of these different photographic and cinematographic techniques. When the characters, the action, and the fictional world are continuously presented, either from partial angles or from constantly changing ones, it is often impossible for the spectator to determine where the focal point is or what the central experiences are in the characters' world. This in turn is a reflection of the constant and usually fruitless search of the characters for such focal points in their own lives.

Whereas Hedda Gabler's lack of will to continue living was based on her refusal to bear offspring within the confines of married life, Miss Julie's despair primarily reflects her unwillingness merely to exist. Of course, there are external reasons for her suicide, and Strindberg has taken great care both in the play and in the preface almost to overdetermine her final act of despair. Nevertheless, as several critics have pointed out, there are no clear and obvious causal connections between her suicide and the motives presented. Instead, this final act of despair is triggered by an irrational leap into the complete unknown, as she herself says "ecstatically" (according to Strindberg's stage direction) in the final scene when she commands Jean, the servant, to command her, the mistress, to commit suicide: "I am already asleep—the whole room stands as if in smoke for me . . . and you look like an iron stove . . . that resembles a man dressed in black with a top hat—and your eyes glow like coal when the fire is extinguished—and your face is a white patch like the ashes."[9] These complex images within images resemble links in a chain, and they illustrate the constant movement or flux of the despairing speaker's mind. For Miss Julie there is no fixed point in reality, no focal point, except her will to die, to reach out for a nothingness.

In Strindberg's description of the set in the beginning of *Miss Julie,* he carefully specifies how the diagonal back wall cuts across the stage from left to right, opening up in the vaulted entry toward the garden. This vault however, is only partially visible. The oven and the table are also only partially visible because they are situated exactly on the borderline between the stage and the offstage areas. The side walls and the ceiling of the kitchen are marked by draperies and tormentors. Except for the garden entry, there are no doors or windows. As the play reveals, the kitchen is connected only to the private bedrooms of the servants Jean and Kristin; there is no direct access to the upper floor where the count and his daughter, Julie, live except through the pipe-telephone.

In his preface to the play, Strindberg explained: "I have borrowed from the impressionistic paintings the idea of the asymmetrical, the truncated, and I believe that thereby, the bringing forth of the illusion has been gained; since by not seeing the whole room and all the furnishings, there is room for imagination, i.e., fantasy is put in motion and it completes what is seen."[10] Here Strindberg describes the imaginative force of this basically metonymic set. But rather than following the custom in realistic theater of showing the *whole* room as part of a house that in turn is part of the fictional world of the play, Strindberg very consciously exposes only *part* of the room. He claims it should be completed in the imagination of the audience. As Evert Sprinchorn comments: "The incompleteness of the impressionist composition drew the artist and the viewer into closer personal contact, placing the viewer in the scene and compelling him to identify with the artist at a particular moment."[11]

The audience comes closer not only to the artist through this view of the kitchen from its interior but also, by force of the diagonal arrangements of the set, to the characters inside the kitchen. This is because the fourth wall, on which the realistic theater was originally based, has been moved to an undefined spot somewhere in the auditorium, the spectators are in the same room as the dramatic characters. It is also important to note that, to achieve this effect, Strindberg also removed the side walls from the stage, thus preventing the creation of any kind of symmetrical room that the spectator could comfortably watch from the outside. Furthermore, the audience is not guided regarding the symmetries, directions, or focal points in the set itself, which the traditional theater strongly emphasized. The only area that is separated from the kitchen is the garden, visible through the vaulted entry, with its fountain and, significantly enough, its statue of Eros. Thus, the physical point of view of the audience in relationship to the stage is ambiguous.

What is presented is a "photograph" of the kitchen taken from its interior, drawing the audience's attention to different points inside or outside as the play's action develops. The set of *Miss Julie* can, furthermore, be seen as a photograph because while the spectators get a close view from the inside of the kitchen, they also experience an objective perception of it and the events taking place there through the frame of the proscenium arch. The comparison between Strindberg's scenic technique in *Miss Julie* and the photograph is compelling because of the very strong tension between intimacy and closeness on the one hand and objectivity and distance on the other; this sort of tension has often been observed to be one of the major characteristics not only of the play but also of photography, as the practice of documenting and preserving large numbers of slices of reality. The photograph also "cuts" into a certain space from its inside, never showing walls as parallel (unless it is a very big space photographed from the outside), at the same time it freezes the attention of the viewer upon the specific moment. In photography the focus is on the present (tense), which is "perfected" into a "has been" through the small fraction of a second when the shutter is opened. Barthes even goes so far as to call this moment in photography an epiphany.[12]

This is also what happens in *Miss Julie* when the attention of the audience is continuously taken from one temporary focal point to the next by force of the gradual development of the action. Our eyes and attention move from the food Jean is smelling to the wine he is tasting, to Miss Julie's handkerchief, to Kristin's fond folding and smelling of the handkerchief when Jean and Miss Julie are at the dance and so on. In *Miss Julie* these material objects force the characters to confront one another and to interact. They are not objects primarily belonging to or binding the characters to the distant past toward which they try to reach out in their present sufferings—as are the visual focal points in Ibsen's plays or even the samovars and pieces of old furniture in Chekhov's plays. The objects in *Miss Julie* are first and foremost immersed in the present, forcing the characters to take a stance and their present struggles to be closely observed by the audience.

In *Miss Julie* the past and the future have been transformed into fantasy, so the only reality for the characters is the present. Because Jean and Miss Julie are forced to act solely on the basis of the immediate stimuli causing their interaction, and because the kitchen has been cut off diagonally leaving no visually defined borders on- or offstage, it is impossible to locate any constant focal points, either outside or inside the fictional world of the play and the subjective consciousness of the characters. This "narrative" technique achieves both a very close and subjective view of the characters and a seemingly objective and exact picture of them. The temporal retrospection has also been diminished because Jean and Miss Julie are not as disturbed by irrational factors belonging to a guilt-ridden past as, for example, the Ibsen heroes are. Strindberg's characters are motivated primarily by their present desires.

This of course does not mean that there are no expository references to the past in *Miss Julie;* on the contrary, there are a large number of references to specific events in the lives of the characters preceding the opening of the scenic action. The play, in fact, begins with a series of such references, all told by Jean to Kristin. Thus, we learn that Miss Julie is "mad again tonight" (inferring that it is not the first time this has happened), as represented by the way she is dancing with Jean. And to give her behavior some perspective (just before her entrance), Jean relates to Kristin how Miss Julie's fiancé broke their engagement because of the degradations he had to suffer, jumping over her whip as well as being beaten by it. These events are, however, never corroborated by other characters in the play. Miss Julie's subsequent behavior does to some extent affirm Jean's story, but we can never be completely sure.

What is specific to Strindberg's plays is not the omission of the past—which absurdist drama emphasizes—but rather a lack of certainty regarding the reliability of what the characters say about that past. And since in many of Strindberg's plays there is no source of verification other than the private memory of the character speaking, the past takes on a quite subjective quality. Miss Julie gives *her* version of *her* past and Jean relates *his,* and the possible unreliability of these memories is confirmed when Jean changes his story of how he as a child watched her in the garden. Unlike the past in most of Ibsen's plays, which is objectively verified through the independent affirmations of other characters. There are certain important events that cannot always be completely verified, such as the real identity of Hedvig's father in *The Wild Duck,* but the characters act on the assumption that they know. And there is enough evidence, given by several characters independently of one another, to grant that they are right.

The major outcome of past actions, guilt, is objectified in Ibsen's plays. That is the reason why it can be given a specific geographical location in the outside world, which becomes the "focus" (in all respects) for it. In Strindberg's fictional worlds there is definitely an awareness of past actions, that is of guilt, but it exists as a private limbo in the subjective consciousness of the individual characters and thus cannot be projected onto the objective outside world. That is why in Strindberg's plays there is either no visual focus or a constantly moving one.

In *Miss Julie* the two principal characters continuously try to turn their respective opponents into the focal point onto which their own guilt and related feelings of inadequacy and general frustration can be projected. That is one of the major reasons for their sexual union and the distrust and even hatred to which it leads. Just how fickle those focal points are, however, can also be seen as in Miss Julie's last desperate attempt to find some kind of support in Jean for her step into the unknown realm of death. Jean's face has become a white spot, resembling to Miss Julie the ashes of a fire because the light of the sun—which is rising at this point in the play—is illuminating him. Again the present situation becomes the point of departure for her wishes. And when Miss Julie wants to die, her wish is

thus focused on Jean's illuminated face. In *Ghosts* Ibsen used the same images (the fire and the sun) at the end of the last two acts as objective focal points. Strindberg has compressed these images into one speech in which they are projected onto Jean by the fantasy of Miss Julie's subjective consciousness. Ibsen gives a "scientific" explanation of Oswald's madness for which the sunset is a circumstantial parallel, whereas Strindberg lets the sunset motivate the outburst of Julie's death wish, as expressed from within. Thus the preparations for the introduction of expressionism, wherein everything is projection, had already been made in Strindberg's pre-Inferno plays.[13]

In *A Dream Play,* in which the subjective is much more emphatically central than it is in *Miss Julie,* Strindberg wished to integrate and develop the complex procedures of perception related to photography with an explicit moral vision of humanity. In *A Dream Play* there is not only a single lens photographing the stage of tragic events at one relatively fixed point in time and space as in *Miss Julie* but a complicated camera that zooms in and out on the events and juxtaposes different images in space and time through a dream filter, using a montage technique.

In his first expressionistic play, *To Damascus* (I), in which the protagonist quickly moves from one place to another, Strindberg used a variation of the "station drama,"[14] employing a mirror construction. This means that the scenes of part II, after the climax in the Asylum, are arranged in reverse order from part I and lead the hero gradually back to the place where he began. In a letter to a friend, the Swedish author Geijerstam, Strindberg described his use of this structure:

> The act lies in the composition, which symbolizes the repetition (Gentagelsen) Kierkegaard is talking about; the events roll up towards the asylum; there they reach the edge and are thrown back again; the pilgrimage, the homework to be done over again, the swallowings; and then things start anew, where the game ends it also started. You may not have noticed that the scenes roll up backwards from the Asylum, which is the backbone of the book which closes and encloses the plot. Or like a snake that bites its own tail.[15]

When Strindberg in his short preface to *A Dream Play* also refers to the "nonconnected but seemingly logical form"[16] of the dream used in this play (as well as in the earlier *To Damascus*), the assumption that the mirror construction has also been applied would not be farfetched. In *A Dream Play,* however, the realization of the mirror construction is only partial and very fragmentary. In its present form, the play contains the following scenes:

1. prologue in heaven

2. garden with growing castle

3. a room in the castle

4. another room in the castle with the dead parents

5. opera corridor

6. Lawyer's office

7. church

8. Fingal's Cave

9. living room behind Lawyer's office

10. Foul Strand (Fair Haven behind)

11. Fair Haven (Foul Strand behind)

12. classroom in yellow house in Fair Haven

13. by the Mediterranean

14. Fingal's Cave

15. opera corridor

16. outside the castle

Lamm claims that Strindberg had actually intended at some point to repeat the scheme of mirror construction from *To Damascus* (I) but that he later abandoned it. Ollén has called the structure of the play "Contrapuntal" in an attempt to reflect Strindberg's own use of musical terminology to describe his dramatic structure, as in the Chamber Plays. Sprinchorn has likewise argued that the repetition of certain scenes reinforces the cyclical structure for the purpose of what he sees as a Freudian "secondary elaboration."[17]

However, as can be easily seen in the preceding enumeration of scenes, Strindberg has actually repeated only three scenes in part II. Going backward, scene 16 repeats the location of scene 2, scene 15 returns to that of scene 5, and scene 14 to that of scene 8. It is worth noting that in the last three scenes of part II the locations of three different scenes from part I (2,5,8) are repeated, and that each time two scenes from part I (3-4 and 6-7) are skipped in the return. Scene 13, the scene with social pathos, which takes place by the Mediterranean, does not appear in part I and, as a matter of fact, Strindberg added it, along with the opening scene—the prologue in heaven—to the already finished play at a later time. In one sense the scenes of Foul Strand and Fair Haven are also repetitions because each time the other is shown in the background. The aesthetic technique Strindberg employed in the scenic depiction of the two beaches, which is where the so-called edge mentioned in his letter about *To Damascus* (I) is located, will be carefully analyzed below.

In the kind of artistic economy that Strindberg practiced in *A Dream Play,* the scenes missing in the mirror construction are not completely absent, however. Instead of visu-

ally repeating the scenic images from part I in reverse order in part II, Strindberg often repeats on the level of dialogue and appearance of representative characters. These repetitions become in effect reminders of the scenes that are missing. They also, interestingly enough, usually appear in the text in the exact reverse order from part I, so that we are at least reminded of the mirror construction. In part II the Lawyer's dwellings, the church, and the Lawyer's office are not presented as full scenes but are referred to textually; the journey of Indra is proceeding in reverse order. The Lawyer appears at the end of the schoolhouse scene (scene 12) asking his wife to return to their home (scene 9 in part I). At the end of his second appearance in Fingal's Cave (scene 14) the Poet has a vision of the church tower, which returns us to the church (scene 7 in part I), which then came before the cave (scene 8). At the end of the second opera corridor scene (scene 15) the Lawyer again appears, reminding his rebellious wife of her duties and thus repeating the scene in the Lawyer's office (scene 6 in part I). In this last example the strict order of the mirror construction is, however, somewhat upset.

One interesting instance of this verbal repetition of scenes is the description of the soldiers marching on the tower of the church (end of scene 14), an image Lamm refers to as "one of those places in *A Dream Play* where the reader is called upon to make fruitless interpretations."[18] In the framework of the scenic structure of the play, however, Strindberg actually makes us return to the church (scene 7 in part I) through the powerful image of death. This poetic description recalls the complex arrangement of image within image seen in *Miss Julie* when the fire in the oven is extinguished, when one image becomes involved in the next through a constant metamorphosis between light and shadow. The Poet in *A Dream Play* is describing soldiers marching on a field while the sun is shining on a church so that its shadow can be seen on the field. Through the juxtaposition of images on the field, they appear to be actually walking on the church tower:

> Now they are on the cross, but I perceive it as if the first one who is walking on the rooster must die . . . now they approach . . . the corporal is the first one . . . haha! A cloud is approaching, covering the sun of course . . . now they are all gone. . . . The water of the cloud extinguished the fire of the sun! The light of the sun created the dark image of the tower, but the dark image of a cloud muffled the dark image of the tower.[19]

What we see on the field is actually some kind of photographic image, a "dark image" (*mökerbild* in Swedish), a negative through which the movement of the cloud is transformed into another image. It is worth emphasizing that in both plays Strindberg superimposed images of light and shadow—a technique closely related to photography—to create the different images of death.

In addition to the complex metamorphosis on the level of imagery, the scenery onstage changes from Fingal's Cave to the corridor outside the opera while the poet is speaking (from scene 14 to 15), thus superimposing additional images upon the already rather complex visual images presented. This combination of verbal and visual images could without a doubt be termed theatrical montage, in analogy to Eisenstein's "film montage."

Before I analyze how and when the "edge" of *A Dream Play* is reached, I must make some general remarks about the technique of "zooming" in *A Dream Play*. What the audience actually *sees,* at least in the first part of *A Dream Play,* is a fictional dream world, a world with a "dream atmosphere" *(drömstämning),* to use Bark's terminology,[20] in which the walls of the castle and of other dwellings are peeled off, crumble, or simply go through various metamorphoses, gradually drawing the audience closer and closer toward the fictional offstage world, in the direction of some kind of center that remains elusive. This is, as a matter of fact, a visual version of Peer Gynt's famous onion, which leaves him with empty hands after it is completely peeled. Strindberg very carefully specifies in his stage directions that the transitions from scene 2 to 8, 9 to 13, and 14 to 16, respectively, stress the continuity of movement from scene to scene. Backdrops and screens are removed, replaced, or turned when the curtain is open, and objects that had a certain function in one scene are transformed through the dream to reappear with a different function in the next.

One of many such changes is the transformation of the organ in the church in scene 7 into Fingal's Cave near the ocean in scene 8, a shift effected primarily by lighting, as the stage directions indicate. The continuity between the different locations presented on stage is strongly stressed and represents Strindberg's theatrical expression of the connectedness of images in the dreamer's mind. Strindberg has introduced a theatrical, aesthetic continuity as a reflection of the dream, thereby underscoring its isolation from all kinds of everyday reality. As Harry Carlson has explained, the aesthetic principle behind these transformations is the revelation of "a critical continuity of identity between the two scenes. Objects have changed, but somehow remain the same. One implication is that no matter how the two locations may seem to differ from each other, underneath they are fundamentally alike: we are still in a world of illusion and pain."[21] I must stress, however, that this identity is not static because there is flux and movement from place to place effected by the zoom action of the "camera" through which we perceive Strindberg's fictional world.

The two outdoor scenes at Foul Strand and Fair Haven (10 and 11) are extremely important with regard to the visual aesthetics of *A Dream Play.* When we see the ugly landscape of Foul Strand in the foreground in the first of these two scenes, beautiful Fair Haven can be made out in the background on the other side of the bay that separates them. In the following scene, after the short blackout

prescribed in the stage directions, the relative positions of Foul Strand and Fair Haven have changed so that Fair Haven is now visible in the foreground, the bay again in the middle ground, and Foul Strand submerged in shadow in the background. This kind of visual technique, which can be termed a "turn-around," has been used by Strindberg several times. The "turn-around," or "edge," as Strindberg calls it in his letter to Geijerstam, is the place from which the scenes are rolled up backward again. The very important innovation in *A Dream Play,* however, is the interesting manipulation of the spectator's point of view. It can be described as a change of position on the part of the audience so that after the "turn-around," the fictional world is perceived from exactly the opposite standpoint: in each of these two scenes the other place is seen in the background. Through the change of angle or "camera" position, the audience is allowed to see the action from a vantage point behind the scene, thereby viewing from behind what was formerly seen from the front.

With the help of Strindberg's "camera lens" on the action, the audience can not only follow the heroine from one point in space to another as in picaresque "station drama" but also examine the fictional world by perceiving it through specific angles, perspectives, and sudden jumps from one point in space to another diametrically opposite point in space. In cinematographic terms, the camera has moved, and, from the audience's perspective, Indra's slow and gradual return to heaven is now seen from the completely opposite angle.

It is thus as a result of the "turn-around," or reversal of directions, that the backward movement in the scenic succession is actually precipitated. Now the camera that had been zooming in toward the open seaside landscape of the archipelago has been turned the opposite way. But instead of returning directly to the home of the Lawyer and his rebellious wife, we are given a look into the schoolhouse where the grown-up Officer is sent back to the school-bench and where normal everyday logic breaks down. At this point the Lawyer appears again to remind his wife of the duties that still remain: "Now, you have seen almost everything, but you have not seen the worst. . . . / Repetition. . . . Returns. . . . Going back! . . . Redoing the homework. . . . Come!"[22] Both Agnes and the Officer thus have to return in humiliation to a former traumatic situation of confinement. This is, however, not simply a return to a trite childhood or marital reality; in the larger structure of the play, the heroine is taking the route back to heaven, the place from where she originally came.

Strindberg has, as he explains in the letter to Geijerstam, employed the Kierkegaardian moral-psychological concept of *gentagelsen,* or repetition, in *A Dream Play.* In 1843 Søren Kierkegaard had published an introspective work called *Repetition: An Essay in Experimental Psychology,* which Strindberg clearly knew about or had read. Kierkegaard's work is a philosophical and autobiographical explication of the moral-psychological concept of repetition. He writes:

> When one does not possess the categories of recollection or of repetition the whole of life is resolved into a void and empty noise. Recollection is the pagan view of life, repetition is the modern view of life, repetition is the *interest* of metaphysics, and at the same time the interest upon which metaphysics founders; repetition is the solution contained in every ethical view, repetition is a *conditio sine qua non* of every dogmatic problem.[23]

In *A Dream Play* Kierkegaard's moral concept is also used as an aesthetic structuring principle in that the idea of return is the basis for development of the plot and for the succession of the dramatic locations. Strindberg also applied it on the moral level of the play in that the central lesson Indra learns about humankind is that everything in life is repetitious. This is true of the small and the large duties of everyday life, the fixed return to childhood and, of course, the constant suffering of all humankind, which is the central theme repeated over and over again in the play. One could even claim that Strindberg attempts to unify the ethical and aesthetic spheres, presented as irreconcilable opposites in Kierekegaard's *Either/Or,* by showing in *A Dream Play* that repetition is an aesthetic concept as well as a moral one. For Indra and the Poet, beauty is contained within the ethical law based on her return to heaven, which, in terms of the play's aesthetics, is structurally worked out as a formal repetition. The theme and concept of repetition is thus embedded in the play in multilevel fashion to interweave its aesthetic and moral dimensions.

It is also possible to compare Strindberg's methods of theatrical composition and perception with the perceptual modes developed at about the same time by Picasso in his cubist paintings.[24] In his attempt to depict a three-dimensional reality in a two-dimensional medium, Picasso gave a pictorial account of how he moved around the depicted objects in space by showing through paint on canvas what these men and women looked like from different angles simultaneously. Strindberg, working in the three-dimensional, temporal medium of theater, also depicted characters and objects from several angles and points of view. By repeating the events and locations from the first part of *A Dream Play* from *behind* the scene in the second part, the audience is visually drawn into the fictional world from two completely opposite points of view.

This multiple perspective technique is also comparable to the complex structure developed by Stoppard in *Rosencrantz and Guildenstern Are Dead,* in which a certain number of episodes in the backstage world of *Hamlet* are independently dramatized. We can even imagine two audiences—one watching Shakespeare's play and the other watching Stoppard's—sometimes seeing the same play

from diametrically opposed angles but usually watching different parts of one fictional world. The actor in Stoppard's play tells Rosencrantz and Guildenstern what they, as actors, are really doing in the theater: "We keep to our usual, more or less, only inside out. We do on stage the things that are supposed to happen off. Which is a kind of integrity, if you look on every exit being an entrance somewhere else."[25]

The aesthetics of repetition Strindberg in various ways developed has been extremely important for writers like Beckett, Pinter, Ionesco, and Genet and for modern theater and art in general.[26] Suffice it to mention here that when we are watching *Waiting for Godot* we have no idea how many times the ritual of waiting has been repeated before the play starts and between the two acts. This kind of repetition is very different from the probing of their own past in which Ibsen's protagonists are involved or the nostalgia in which Chekhov's are caught. Strindberg's protagonists are trapped in a condition that, once we accept the premises and the presentation, is a universal Sisyphean limbo, not just a psychological probing into the tragic past of an individual. One of the primary features of this Strindbergian *condition humaine* is the fact that the protagonists are caught and imprisoned in behavioral patterns and in a fictional world they are never sure they can leave or transcend, not even at the moment of death, unless of course the protagonist is a divinity, as is Indra's daughter in *A Dream Play.*

In *The Dance of Death* (I), for example, the central theme is that there is definitely no transcendence from the repetitive patterns Edgar and Alice have created in their marriage. The five opening lines of the play are extremely indicative of the kind of repetitive life the couple has led for almost twenty-five years:

THE CAPTAIN:

> Would you like to play something for me?

ALICE:

> What shall I play?

THE CAPTAIN:

> What you want!

ALICE:

> You don't like my repertoire!

THE CAPTAIN:

> And you don't like mine![27]

The Captain's request to hear his wife play something is not granted at all at this point; much later she plays the "Dance of the Bojar," during which he has his famous fainting spell, a symbolic death within a life that is very much like death. Alice does not answer but retorts with another question, which leaves it up to the Captain to decide what music he wants to hear. But he also refuses to make a decision and returns the initiative to Alice, who refrains once more by claiming that he does not like her repertoire, to which he in turn retorts that she does not like his.

This kind of procedure in which both partners refuse to gratify the other one is repeated over and over in *The Dance of Death* (I) until, ironically enough, they agree at the end of the play to seek reconciliation in the celebration of their twenty-fifth wedding anniversary. The repetitive patterns of behavior from which their marriage suffers are expressed implicitly on the level of the dialogue itself. The use of the word repertoire, ambiguously referring to Alice's playing the piano as well as to all the petty tricks of their married life, is the key to the motif of repetition in the play; this repertoire is constantly repeated.

The principle of repetition, as Strindberg developed it in his plays, was an attempt to artistically concretize something beyond the particular fate of the individual and to reach a dramatic formulation of a universal human condition. Strindberg's characters are not primarily motivated as individuals trying to find a solution to a personal problem, as are Ibsen's, but are representative types of human beings, caught in an existential dilemma in which there apparently is very little or no chance for redemption.

The spatial-scenographic metaphor most frequently used by Strindberg to express this universal condition is the presentation of different kinds of closed spaces from which the main characters cannot escape. The kitchen in *Miss Julie,* the Captain's hiding room in *The Father,* and the straitjacket into which he is tricked are motivated primarily on the realistic level, even though they achieve a more general social or spiritual significance. In *The Dance of Death* (I), however, the tower in which Edgar and Alice "live" is a metaphysical and spiritual prison that makes it impossible for them to escape from their "death in life." In *A Dream Play* this imprisonment is dramatized on a grand scale through the separation and opposition between the worlds of matter and spirit. There remains only one channel of communication between them through which the daughter of Indra but not the mortals can escape. The sufferings of this world are a universal condition for which there is no solution—except for death itself.

In my opinion the play by Strindberg that most forcefully presents death, not only as the accidental outcome of a situation where all other solutions have failed but as the one necessary escape from the confinement of the base repetitiveness of the material world, is *The Ghost Sonata.* Here the Young Lady gradually withers away into a death that is the logical result of the degraded and depraved spiritual condition of humanity. Not even the love of the Student can redeem her from this universal depravation.

I am particularly concerned with how the scenography expresses this separation from life and the growing awareness that ultimate truth lies beyond life in *The Ghost Sonata.*[28] The visual representation is in this case too, of course, parallel to the textual elaboration of the same theme: behind the façade of appearances and that which *seems* to be true about the lives of the characters in the play, a very different truth has been hidden. What we initially perceive is false. Hypocrisy and deception reside behind the walls of the modern well-to-do bourgeois house presented in the first act. As they are gradually exposed, they threaten to shatter the very foundations not only of the house but of society and the whole social order as well. The play's revolutionary message has, however, been immersed in an atmosphere of resignation and religious sentiments so that when *The Ghost Sonata* ends, the only future that seems to remain is one of eternal death. The three short acts of the play present a gradually intensified revelation of the rotten foundations of the house as well as of society itself. Visually this is presented by a gradual zooming in toward the center of the house.

The first act presents the exterior facade of the house, the street corner with a fountain, and a telephone booth; and through the windows on the facade, the so-called oval room is visible. In the second act, the Strindbergian camera has zoomed in on the oval room, which now opens up into two different directions in the background: to the right is the green room where the Colonel can be seen, and to the left is the hyacinth room where the Young Lady is visible from the beginning of this act and where the Student later joins her. The third act takes place in the orientally furnished hyacinth room, which was visible in the background during the second act. This succession accentuates the continuity of the fictional space throughout the three acts. But instead of zooming in on the scene in the hyacinth room from the oval room and thereby gradually drawing the audience into the fictional world in straight one-directional fashion, Strindberg has effected a "turn-around" with his camera, displaying (in act 3) the oval room—which was the setting for act 2—in the background with the Colonel and the Mummy visible through a door on the right. The kitchen, from which the destructive forces of this act appear in the form of the vampiric Cook, appears in the background on the left.

The effects this "turn-around" can have on an audience are quite stunning. At the end of the ghost supper in the second act, the mad Mummy who has been imprisoned in the closet for twenty years is finally released. The Mummy is actually the Young Lady's mother, who conceived her with Hummel, her former lover, outside of her marriage. It is mainly the guilt resulting from this union that has led the Mummy to a state of death and madness, and only through the mock reunion with Hummel (who, because he killed the Milkmaid, is even more guilt-ridden than she) can she be released. When Hummel takes over her place in the closet, it is a ceremonially structured revenge, which in a way is also a minor "turn-around," wherein the characters exchange points of view. Hummel, his sinful past now completely revealed, is, by taking the Mummy's place, thus "liberating" her, while one of the servants, Bengtsson, places a death screen in front of the door of the closet. After all the characters present have pronounced a ceremonial "amen" over the death of Hummel, Strindberg directs the audience's attention toward the hyacinth room—in the background behind the oval room—where the Student is singing a song of reconciliation and hope with the Young Lady accompanying him on the harp. The older generation has found no resolution to their conflicts and guilt except in hatred and revenge, so the audience is naturally guided to the only existing hope: the younger generation.

The setting of the third act confirms this hope because, as mentioned above, it takes place in the hyacinth room where the young couple has been seated throughout the second act. Thus our attention has gradually become focused on the young couple and the possibility of a happy future for them. Because of the "turn-around," the older generation—having definitely outplayed its role—has been placed in the background. The "turn-around" changes the audience's point of view in relation to action in space, since it is now viewing from "behind" what was formerly seen from the "front," as in *A Dream Play.* Moreover, the "turn-around" changes the audience's temporal points of reference: in act 2 the young couple in the background represent the future and its possibilities, in act 3 the characters in the background represent the lost past and its guilt and limitations.

Strindberg has also achieved another interesting effect in the passage from the second to the third act, an effect involving our perceptions and interpretation of time as well as space. The first words uttered in the third act are the Young Lady's exclamation "Sing now for my flowers!" They seem to refer directly to the song about the sun that the Student has just sung at the end of act 2, while he and the Young Lady were still in the background. Thus there seems to be a temporal continuity in the plot, as in Ibsen's *John Gabriel Borkmann* in which all the acts are consecutive. What at first seems to be temporal continuity is in fact underlined by the spatial continuity of the same two rooms in both acts. This sense of continuity is further reinforced by the continuing presence in act 3 of almost all the characters from act 2. The Student and the Young Lady are now in the foreground instead of the background, and the Colonel and the Mummy—"the parents"—remain in the oval room following the fatal ghost supper that has just ended.

After approximately five minutes of performance, however, the audience learns through the young couple's conversation that Hummel's funeral has already taken place; thus it is *not* seeing a scene directly subsequent in time to the death scene of Hummel that took place at the end of act 2.

This detail is one of the ever more numerous contradictions between what the audience *thinks* it sees and what is actually presented. Törnqvist affirms this interpretation of the play: "The fundamental theme or leitmotif of *The Ghost Sonata* is found in the conflict between illusion and reality, between *Sein* and *Schein.* In the antithesis between mask and face, façade and interior, word and deed, in the depiction of the dead—everywhere we are confronted with the fundamental idea that the world is not what it looks like and mankind not what it seems to be."[29] Strindberg has transformed not only the Student (who, as Törnqvist has pointed out, is the protagonist-observer in the play) but also every spectator into an active participant-observer in the revelation of deceptions and lies and the discovery of something that at least for the moment *seems* to be closer to the truth. The audience thus becomes involved in the actual process of discovery, Aristotelian *anagorisis,* not only through the mediation of the characters and their dialogue but through directly presented theatrical events. In this kind of direct presentation the spectators are no longer passive eavesdroppers who can sit back and pass moral judgments on what they see. Instead they have become active participants in the process of perception and interpretation itself, just as the protagonist perceives and interprets what to him *seems* to be the truth.

The "camera" Strindberg has introduced as a mediator between the fictional events and the audience does not necessarily bring the audience closer to the truth of the depicted reality in *The Ghost Sonata.* Rather, it brings it so close to the action, selecting the angles and points of view in such a narrow manner, that the moment new information is available, enabling the audience to make new connections and draw different conclusions—which the very limited "camera angle" has left unexplored or ambiguous—the fictional reality itself has to be reinterpreted and reevaluated. The problem is not that the "camera" lies; it just gives a very limited and selective slice of reality, one that can heavily distort the images projected, especially in their relationship to the fictional world as a whole. By presenting in *The Ghost Sonata* the possibility of distortions of fictional reality and by emphasizing the role of the spectators as participant-observers in such clear terms, Strindberg has in effect precisely identified the limitations in the methods of representation and perception that the realist theater thought it could solve unambiguously by tearing down the fourth wall of the drawing room, thereby opening it up for what was considered "objective" observation. Strindberg showed, however, that the closer the distance from which spectators observe an event, the more "subjective" their viewpoints.

The Ghost Sonata also contains an image of inversion that is related to the light-shadow images from *Miss Julie* and *A Dream Play.* In the latter plays, death is seen as a photographic image in which there is some kind of exchange between light and shadow. In *The Ghost Sonata,* this reversal is conceived in terms of language and silence. Hummel claims that languages are codes and that words actually hide the truth. It is only through silence that everything is revealed, he says. Furthermore, it is when the Student wants to tell the Young Lady "his" truth about her beauty that she gradually crumbles behind the death screen. When the screen makes its second appearance in the play, to separate the Young Lady from the world, the Student can only give her his blessings for having been able to escape from all the madness and suffering of this material world.

Just as what the audience sees is a clouded reality, what it hears is masked truth. Silence alone hovers over truth, as in Wittgenstein's enigmatic final statement in his *Tractatus Logico-Philosophicus:* "Wovon man nicht darüber, reden kann, muss man schweigen" (What we cannot speak about we must pass over in silence). In *The Ghost Sonata,* this silence is realized through that final exit behind the death screen where some kind of truth can supposedly be reached. But the living have no access to it. In its unattainability it resembles the frustrated attempts of Didi and Gogo to reach the world of Godot, who is situated beyond the place where they are now.

Strindberg leaves no road unexplored in his effort to materialize the grandeur of that beyond. The final gesture of the play, when *"the room disappears; Boecklin's* Toten-Insel *becomes the backdrop,"*[30] is Strindberg's desperate effort to make the immaterial perceivable. The movement of the "camera" in space thus becomes completely frozen, showing the barren landscape that cannot be further penetrated. If only because the audience's perceptions cannot stretch any farther.

Notes

1. See, e.g., Wayne Booth, *The Rhetoric of Fiction* (Chicago: University of Chicago Press, 1961).

2. Interview with Ingmar Bergman in Frederick J. Marker and Lise-Lone Marker, *Ingmar Bergman: Four Decades in the Theater* (New York and London: Cambridge University Press, 1982), 222.

3. John Orr, *Tragic Drama and Modern Society* (Totowa, NJ: Barnes and Noble, 1981), 52. Strindberg's contemporary critics, particularly in Sweden, considered him to be a pathological madman whose writing bore witness to the fragmentary nature of his mind. Only after Max Reinhardt presented his productions of the Chamber Plays in Sweden did the predominantly negative view of them change there too. See Kela Kvam, *Max Reinhardt og Strindbergs visionaere dramatik* (Copenhagen: Akademisk Forlag, 1974); Göran Stockenström, *Ismael i öknen: Strindberg som mystiker* (Uppsala: Almqvist and Wiksell, 1972), 483; and Freddie Rokem, *Tradition och förnyelse* (Stockholm: Akademilitteratur, 1977), 27-34.

4. Susan Sontag, "Theatre and Film," in *Styles of Radical Will* (New York: Farrar, Straus and Giroux, 1976), 103-4. See also, e.g., Nils Beyer, *Teater och film* (Stockholm: Bonniers, 1944); and Allardyce Nicoll, *Film and Theatre* (New York: Thomas Y. Crowell, 1936).

5. Sontag, "Theatre and Film," 104.

6. Martin Lamm's important study on Strindberg, originally published in 1918-20, made the correlation between Strindberg's private life and his art, and many later critics have followed suit. (See n. 17).

7. See, e.g., Peter Wollen, *Signs and Meaning in the Cinema* (Bloomington: Indiana University Press, 1972); William Luhr and Peter Lehman, *Authorship and Narrative in the Cinema* (New York: Putnam, 1977); and Christian Metz, *The Imaginary Signifier* (Bloomington: Indiana University Press, 1982).

8. Rune Waldekranz, "Fröken Julie i filmiska gestaltningar," in *Perspektiv på Fröken Julie,* ed. Ulla-Britta Lagerroth and Göran Lindström (Stockholm: Rabén and Sjögren, 1972), 135-52.

9. August Strindberg, *Samlade skrifter* (Stockholm: Bonniers, 1914-21), 23:186. All translations of citations from this source are my own.

10. Ibid., 111-12.

11. Evert Sprinchorn, *Strindberg as Dramatist* (New Haven and London: Yale University Press, 1982), 28.

12. Roland Barthes, *Camera Lucida,* trans. Richard Howard (New York: Hill and Wang, 1981).

13. See, e.g., C. E. W. L. Dahlström, *Strindberg's Dramatic Expressionism* (Ann Arbor: University of Michigan Press, 1930), for an interesting expressionistic interpretation of Strindberg's naturalistic plays.

14. See Peter Szondi, *Theorie des modernen Dramas* (Frankfurt am Main: Suhrkamp, 1956), 40-42, who calls this structure "station drama." (English trans: *Theory of the Modern Drama,* trans. Michael Hays [Minneapolis: University of Minnesota Press, 1987], 25-28.)

15. Strindberg, *Brev* (Stockholm: Bonniers, 1970), 12:279-80. Letter of Mar. 17, 1898. My translation.

16. Strindberg, *Samlade skrifter* 36:215.

17. Lamm, *Strindbergs dramer* (Stockholm: Bonniers, 1966), 217; Sprinchorn, *Strindberg as Dramatist,* 156-58.

18. Lamm, *Strindbergs dramer,* 331. My translation.

19. Strindberg, *Samlade skrifter* 36:309.

20. Richard Bark, *Strindbergs drömspelsteknik i drama och teater* (Lund: Studentlitteratur, 1981).

21. Harry Carlson, *Strindberg and the Poetry of Myth* (Berkeley: University of California Press, 1982), 165.

22. Strindberg, *Samlade skrifter* 36:282.

23. Søren Kierkegaard, *Repetition: An Essay in Experimental Psychology,* trans. W. Lowrie (New York: Harper and Row, 1941), 52-53. On Kierkegaard's importance for Strindberg see, e.g., E. Johanneson, *The Novels of August Strindberg* (Berkeley: University of California Press, 1968); and Gunnar Brandell, *Strindbergs Infernokris* (Stockholm: Bonniers, 1950).

24. Sprinchorn writes: "It is worth noting that Strindberg composed *The Ghost Sonata* and liberated drama from its long enslavement to character and motivation in the same year that Picasso painted *Les Demoiselles d'Avignon* and shattered the old concepts of the relationship of art to nature" (*Strindberg as Dramatist,* 276). Sprinchorn does not, however, elaborate the details of the pictorial similarities between the two artists. It is also important in this connection to stress Strindberg's own work as a painter. See Göran Söderström, *Strindberg och bildkonsten* (Stockholm: Forum, 1972).

25. Tom Stoppard, *Rosencrantz and Guildenstern Are Dead* (London: Faber and Faber, 1969), 20.

26. S. Rimon, "The Paradoxical Status of Repetition," *Poetics Today* 1, no. 4 (1980): 151-59, has, on the basis of Lacan's work, analyzed different categories of repetition that are applicable to modern literature. Metz, in his analysis of film (see n. 7), extends these to include the act of viewing itself as a constant repetitive return to the primal scene of the parents.

27. Strindberg, *Samlade skrifter* 34:7. See also Rokem, "Dödsdansens första tur," in *Tidskrift för litteraturvetenskap* 1 (1981), where I have indicated how Searle's speech-act theory (John R. Searle, *Speech Acts* [London, New York: Cambridge University Press, 1969]) can be applied to an analysis of the opening scene of *The Dance of Death* (I) in order to understand the dramatic tensions this kind of unresolved speech-act pattern generates. In the opening scenes of Ionesco's *Chairs,* it is clear that the old couple is involved in a "game" that has definitely been played a number of times before.

28. References are to Strindberg, *Samlade skrifter* 45.

29. Egil Törnqvist, *Strindbergian Drama: Themes and Structure* (Stockholm: Almqvist and Wiksell, and Atlantic Highlands, NJ: Humanities Press, 1982), 205. See also his more detailed analysis in *Bergman och Strindberg: Spöksonaten—drama och iscensättning Dramaten 1973* (Stockholm: Bonniers, 1973).

30. Strindberg, *Samlade skrifter* 45:211.

Barbro Ståhle Sjönell (essay date winter 1990)

SOURCE: Sjönell, Barbro Ståhle. "The Plans, Drafts, and Manuscripts of the Historical Plays in Strindberg's 'Green Bag.'" *Scandinavian Studies* 62, no. 1 (winter 1990): 69-75.

[*In the following essay, based on the notes in Strindberg's "green bag," Sjönell describes Strindberg's construction of the history plays and his plans to complete a history cycle.*]

During Strindberg's second long stay abroad (1890-98) he began to collect his drafts and manuscripts in a green cloth bag. The bag aroused great curiosity among all who met him, and it is mentioned in several of the memoirs written by friends he made during his time in Berlin. Dr. Carl Ludwig Schleich gives the following description of the repository:

> Alla sina planer, utkast, fragment, skisser stoppade han i en stor grön flanellsäck, som kunde tillsnöras och vilken han vaktade som en skatt. Hur månget av honom i samtal präglat bonmot samlades icke likt sädeskorn i denne "grön säck" till kommande utsäde och skörd!
>
> —[Schleich 30]

> (He puts all his plans, drafts, fragments and sketches into a green flannel bag, the opening of which is drawn together with a string, and he watches over it as if it were a treasure. What a number of bon mots coined in conversations he must have gathered in his "Green Bag" for future sowing and reaping!)

When Schleich later visited the aging Strindberg in the Blue Tower, he was allowed to go into the library to see how the contents of the Green Bag had grown, and it then filled a whole cupboard. Schleich compares the neatness and order he found there with "som i ett av kvinnohand vårdat linneskåp [Schleich 56]" ("that in a linen closet looked after by a woman").

In the beginning of the 1920s the collection was deposited with the Royal Library, where it was arranged and itemized by the head of the Manuscript Department, Oscar Wieselgren. Today the Green Bag consists of about 25,000 sheets, kept in over 70 cardboard boxes as well as in 60-odd folders and envelopes.

In connection with the ongoing publication of the National Edition of *Strindberg's Collected Works,* it is the task of the subeditors to register all extant drafts for Strindberg's works in a separate critical commentary. In 1982, I was entrusted with producing a detailed catalogue of the contents of the Green Bag, in which each sheet is to be registered, identified, and described. The catalogues will be published in their entirety in the Royal Library's Acta series.

Very little of the material in the collection is from the Berlin years; the bulk of it spans the time from the writing of *Inferno* (1897) to Strindberg's death in 1912. In other words, it does not contain any drafts of the six early historical dramas he wrote in the 1870s and 1880s. On the other hand, it does include the drafts of the eleven post-Inferno dramas with plots all taken from Swedish history and of the four plays on themes from world history. Most of this material is in three boxes, which also contain some plans for incomplete historical dramas.

In one of the boxes with early drafts and notes for plays with themes from world history there is also a number of sketches for a drama cycle with such ambitious titles as "Menniskans Saga" ("The Saga of Man"), "Verldshistoriska Dramer" ("Dramas of World History"), and "Jordens Saga" ("The Saga of the Earth"). The development of Strindberg's plans to dramatize the story of man from Antiquity up to the French Revolution can be traced back to the letters he wrote in the 1880s, while his attempts to realize those plans can be found in the notes and drafts to "Peter I," "Maria Stuart," "Karl den store" ("Charlemagne"), "År 1000" ("The Year 1000"), and "Domedagar" ("Days of Judgment"). A fragment of "Maria Stuart" has also been preserved. However, Strindberg's grand scheme gave birth to only four plays: *Näktergalen i Wittenberg* (*The Nightingale in Wittenberg*), *Genom öknar till arfland* (*Through Deserts to Ancestral Land*), *Hellas,* and *Lammet och vilddjuret* (*The Lamb and the Beast*), all written in 1903; and a collection of short stories, *Historiska miniatyrer (Historical Miniatures),* published in 1905.

Even where Swedish history was concerned, the number of plays Strindberg actually wrote proved to be far fewer than what he had originally planned. Among early incomplete drafts is a drama about Saint Birgitta, titled "Karl Ulfsson och hans Moder" ("Charles Ulfsson and His Mother"), which is a dramatized version of a short story in *Nya svenska öden och äventyr* (1906, *New Swedish Destinies and Adventures*), and also the drafts to "Johan III" ("John III"), "Karl IX" ("Charles IX") and "Karl XI" ("Charles XI").

There are many examples of how Strindberg used the same notes for more than one work, as well as indications that he continued to work on older drafts. In one draft to *Engelbrekt,* written in 1901, one can see how the author exhorts himself to read the notes he had made for *Svanevit* (1901; *Swanwhite*) and *Kronbruden* (1900-01; *The Crown Bride*). In *Ockulta dagboken* (1977, *The Occult Diary*) Strindberg writes that he examined the drafts to "Bosättningen" ("Setting Up House") and "Korridordramat" ("The Corridor Drama") when he began to work on *Ett drömspel* (1901; *A Dreamplay*), and if one looks at the drafts of the various historical dramas, it becomes clear that they have in common a similar structure, indicating their compositional interdependence.

If we examine the approximately 300 extant notes, plans, and sketches for the historical dramas on Swedish themes that Strindberg wrote between 1899 and 1908, a clearly distinguishable working pattern emerges.

One type of preparatory work, presumably the oldest, can be classed as part of Strindberg's groundwork. Belonging to this category is a list of the literature pertaining to the life and times of the monarch that Strindberg is focusing on, as well as the notes on historical items that directly reflect his studies on the subject. Frequently there are long investigations into the family relationships of the title figures and other characters, but most of the notes refer to historical events. Dates are carefully recorded. Occasionally excerpts from Strindberg's readings are included.

The next step in development of the plays can be observed in notes pertaining to dramatic motifs or themes and to character sketches, as well as lists of the dramatis personae and suggestions for act divisions. One outstanding characteristic of Strindberg's preparatory work is the beautifully produced headings. Here it seems that Strindberg attempted to create the right mood for the play that lay ahead of him. Thus the decorative title page for the drama about Gustav II Adolf, that is, a work dealing with a time in history when Sweden was a great political power, exhibits the Swedish blue and yellow colors, while the draft to *Engelbrekt* contains ornamentation reminiscent of the folk art of Dalecarlia, the setting of the play.

The final version of a given work was probably preceded by a draft in which the division into acts was marked. All eleven completed historical dramas have such drafts, which also include lists of characters and detailed descriptions of individual scenes.

Yet another category of material found in the Green Bag consists of corrections and additions, probably made after the actual writing had been completed. As a rule Strindberg used paper that he bough in whole, undivided sheets—the so-called Lessebo Bikupa, which has a watermark with the year of printing, thus, it can sometimes be used to decide the chronology of the preparatory work.

The origins of the three dramas *Carl XII* (1901), *Kristina* (1901; *Queen Christina*), and *Gustav III* (1902) have been investigated by several scholars. Thus Göran Stockenström has traced the nearly two-year period of gestation for *Carl XII* (Stockenström, "Kring Tillkomsten" 24). The preparatory work for *Carl XII* consists of 23 pages. There are unusually extensive notes for this historical drama, most of them dealing with the character of the king. The Green Bag material reveals some of the sources for the portrayal of the monarch. For instance, under the title "Carl XII" Strindberg has written in Greek letters the name of his brother-in-law, Hugo von Philp. Elsewhere, the King and Görtz are compared to Napoleon and Bernadotte. Strindberg apparently intended to give the King's sister,

Ulrika Eleonora, some of the traits he found in his own sister, Anna von Philp, who in one draft is referred to in Greek letters as "dum och fräck" ("stupid and insolent"), a clear reflection on Strindberg's part of the hostility that existed between him and his sister's family at the time.

In about half the drafts of the historical dramas on Swedish themes that Strindberg wrote in 1898 and later, he seems to have vacillated about the number of acts he had in mind, while he kept the remaining drafts to a fixed plan of five acts. There are ten fragmentary drafts of *Carl XII* in which the text is divided into acts, with their number varying between three and six. Strindberg's uncertainty in terms of the structural lay-out of *Carl XII* is also revealed in his hesitation about the setting for the opening scene of the play. In some drafts the *locus dramaticus* is the student quarter of Lund; in others it has become the coast of Skåne, which is also the setting in the final version. Strindberg also has difficulty deciding on the ending of *Carl XII*. In the drafts there are such variants as "Swedenborgs syner" ("Swedenborg's visions"), "Likvakan i Tistedalen" ("The wake in Tistedalen"; cf. the short story of that name in *Nya svenska öden och äventyr*), "I Tranchén" ("In the trenches"), and "Fredrikshall." Those drafts that are divided into acts contain eight different versions of the drama, but only two of them are in any detail, and one of them must be classified among the fragmentary drafts mentioned earlier. None of the versions corresponds completely to the drama in its completed form. The following characters however are found in all versions: the King, Görtz, Swedenborg, and members of the various classes of society who represent the dissatisfaction of the people with the monarch.

Carl XII shows less agreement between drafts and completed play than do either *Kristina* or *Gustav III*. Yet the 21 pages of preparatory work for *Kristina* give us a picture of the growth of the play that is very similar to that of *Carl XII*, despite the fact that it was written in a very short period of time in September 1901—approximately three weeks. In his recent dissertation on *Kristina*, Ola Kindstedt lists 36 source works, mostly historical, for the play, as well as novels and dramas (Kindstedt 60-65). This preparation might be compared to the 60 source works mentioned by Stockenström in his study of *Carl XII* (Stockenström, "Strindberg och historiens Karl XII" 30-36).

In the preparatory work for *Kristina* there are several lists of dramatis personae and historical data, as well as two closely written pages of notes on the Queen's character. None of the other Swedish historical dramas written after *Inferno* has such extensive notes on the personality of the monarch as do *Carl XII* and *Kristina*. The name "Aspasia" occurs several times in the drafts of *Kristina*, a reference to Dagny Juel, the bohemian woman who was erotically involved with Strindberg and several others in the artistic circle gathering at Ferkel's in Berlin in the beginning of the 1890s.

As for dramatic composition, only three drafts showing act divisions remain for *Kristina*, which is considerably fewer than for *Carl XII*. But, on the other hand, the most detailed of them are very close to the final version of the play. The two earliest drafts have five acts, and the last draft was changed by Strindberg from four to five acts, which is particularly interesting since the drama in its final form has only four acts. In fact, just two days before he finished *Kristina*, Strindberg wrote to his wife, Harriet Bosse, who had left him, and mentioned five acts. In the final manuscript version there is a note just before the scene between Kristina and Carl Gustav in Act Four, stating "Forts . . . sid 75 med maskinskriften" ("Cont . . . p. 75 on typewriter"). The lacuna consisted originally of a word that has been crossed out, probably "tryckandet" ("printing"). But no typewritten pages have been preserved. Kindstedt supposes that the changes were made after Harriet Bosse read the play. The drafts suggest that there might have been a scene in which the Queen was quite crushed by the criticism directed at her. But in the final version the Queen defends herself successfully against the accusations brought by Carl Gustav and Oxenstierna. Strindberg's letters to his wife, in which he repeatedly asks to be allowed to "resonera fram slutet med henne" ("reason out the end with her"), also indicate that he was not certain how to finish the play. The more positive ending might be a gesture of reconciliation toward his wife, for whom he wrote the part of Kristina (cf. Kindstedt 29).

Strangely enough, a similar situation is to be found in the manuscript of *Gustav III*. Half way through the last act, in the middle of a scene between the King and Armfelt, Strindberg has made a note "Fortsättes på nästa sida, 87 (med skrifmaskinen)" ("Continues on next page, 87 [typed]"). In this case there are in fact some typewritten pages preserved, but there is also an ending by hand. In Gunnar Ollén's critical commentaries to *Kristina* and *Gustav III* in the National Edition, he discusses the interrelationship between the typed and handwritten versions of the latter play.

Gustav III was probably begun in February 1902 and, according to *Ockulta dagboken* ("The Occult Diary"), was completed on 16 March in the same year. Strindberg had studied the subject since September 1901. In Ulla Wattman's paper on the play, she mentions five historical works and a couple of novels that were used as sources (335-38). If Strindberg's book collections, book loans, authored works, and letters were to be searched for source material to *Gustav III* as thoroughly as Stockenström and Kindstedt have searched through such material for *Carl XII* and *Kristina*, it is likely that a great many more sources would be found for the genesis of *Gustav III*.

The number of pages from the material in the Green Bag devoted to *Gustav III* is small—only 18 pages. As in the other two plays discussed here, the preparatory work reflects Strindberg's reading of historical works. Notes on them are often included in his listing of the characters. But, the preparatory work for **Gustav III** differs from that of the other plays in that there are no detailed notes on the King's character. His personality is dismissed in one line with the description "Upplyst despot—poet—dramatiker—skådespelare—kvinnlig—Voltairian" ("Enlightened despot—poet—dramatist—actor—effeminate—Voltairian"). On the other hand, there are several pages of suggestions for strikingly dramatic scenes, an indication of the play's Scribean structure.

For **Gustav III** there are only three drafts divided into acts; two of them have five acts, and both end at the Opera, where the historical king was shot in 1792. One incident occurs in all three versions: the fête at Drottningholm where the Dalecarlian regiment is in hiding. The first version opens in fact with the fête at the Drottningholm Palace, that is, with the event that forms the last act of the completed drama. The second version begins in Holmberg's bookstore, just as the finished play does. The third version is incomplete, containing only Acts 2, 3 and 4—which appears to be the last. This version is however very detailed; it fills several pages and is very close to the play in its final form.

The drafts of **Carl XII, Kristina** and **Gustav III** do very little to support the statement Strindberg made in his *Öppna brev till Intima teatern* (1908-09; "*Open Letters to the Intimate Theater*"), that when he was writing a drama, he always began with the last act. Quite possibly he did so until he put his plans down on paper. When he sat at his desk with a draft in front of him, he apparently felt his way forward by sorting his material and dividing it into a varying number of acts. Frequently only a few of the scenes or themes to be found in the first sketches have survived right up to the final product.

Furthermore, it is obvious that Strindberg felt unsure of how to conclude the plays discussed here. Indications of his uncertainty can be noticed even in the final manuscript stage. Ollén has found no less than five different variants of the final lines in **Gustav III,** both in the first handwritten manuscript and in the various revisions Strindberg made of the drama (Strindberg 327). The ending of **Karl XII** also shows traces of manuscript alterations made by the author. His hesitation about the final scene of **Kristina** has already been mentioned. However, the existence of more than one possible ending is not unique in Strindberg's production, as suggested by such well-known examples as his various experimental conclusions for *Röda rummet* (1879, *The Red Room*), and **Fröken Julie** (1888; **Miss Julie.**).

Works Cited

Kindstedt, Ola. *Strindbergs Kristina. Historiegestaltning och kärleksstrategier. Studier i dramats skapelseprocess.* Litteraturvetenskapliga institutionen vid Uppsala universitet 24. Stockholm: Almqvist & Wiksell International, 1988.

Ollén, Gunnar. "Textkritisk kommentar till *August Strindbergs Samlade verk.*" Vol. 48: *Gustav III. Kristina.*" See Strindberg.

Schleich, Carl Ludwig. *Hågkomster om Strindberg.* Stockholm: Björck & Börjesson, 1916.

Stockenström, Göran. "Kring tillkomsten av *Karl XII.*" *Meddelanden från Strindbergssällskapet* 45 (1970): 20-43.

———. "Strindberg och historiens *Karl XII.*" *Meddelanden från Strindbergssälskapet* 47-48 (1971): 15-37.

Strindberg, August. *Kristina. Gustav III.* Vol. 48 of *Samlade verk.* Ed. Gunnar Ollén. Stockholm: Norstedts, 1988.

———. *Strindbergs brev till Harriet Bosse.* Med kommentarer af Harriet Bosse. Stockholm: Natur och kultur, 1932.

Wattman, Ulla. "Strindbergs drama *Gustav III.*" Meddelande från Avd. För dramaforskning vid Litteraturhistoriska institutionen 13. Uppsala: Dramaforskning, 1968.

Barry Jacobs (essay date 1991)

SOURCE: Jacobs, Barry. "Strindberg's *Advent* and *Brott och brott*: *Sagospel* and Comedy in a Higher Court." In *Strindberg and Genre,* edited by Michael Robinson, pp. 167-87. Norvik Press, 1991.

[*In the following essay, Jacobs discusses Strindberg's comedy and fantasy plays.*]

In *Tjänstekvinnans son,* Strindberg dismisses **Lycko-Pers resa,** the *sagospel* (fairy-tale play) that had been his most popular theatre piece in Sweden, as 'en anakronism och en konjunktur på samma gång' (simultaneously an anachronism and a profitable enterprise—SS 19, p. 188). He seems always to have undervalued this work and to have been somewhat embarrassed by its success. In *Tal till svenska nationen,* he claims that because it lacks both artistic form and living characters, it is far inferior to Oehlenschläger's *Aladdin,* the work that inspired it (SV 68, p. 100). Therefore when Bernard Shaw tried that same year to persuade him to let Sir Herbert Beerbohm Tree produce **Lycko-Pers resa** at His Majesty's Theatre in London, Strindberg rejected the proposal out of hand. In his initial letter, Shaw explained that ever since 1904, when J. M. Barrie had made a stunning success with *Peter Pan,* every London manager's dream had been to find another play like it—for want of a more precise generic designation in English Shaw describes it as 'a sort of fairy-play for children'. In 1909 Maeterlinck's *The Blue Bird* had been acclaimed by the British public; now, Shaw implied, the pragmatic bourgeoisie of London had not only acquired a taste for make-believe, but also possessed a degree of generic recognition that would enable them to take **Lycko-Per** to their hearts. He apologized for this mild sort of pioneering by intimating that the production of Strind-berg's *A Midsummer Night's Dream* would make the London public intensely eager to see his *Hamlet*.[1] Strind-berg, who had by no means abandoned this rather frivolous genre, countered with the last of four fairy-tale plays that he had written since his Inferno crisis: a 'lyrical fantasy' entitled *Svarta handsken,* which to this day has never enjoyed much success, except as a radio play.[2] His continued interest in the *sagospel* and his tendency to overvalue plays like *Svarta handsken* raise some interest-ing questions about his later use of genre.

Genre, as Alastair Fowler observes, is 'a communication system, for the use of writers in writing, and readers in interpreting.'[3] Strindberg's use of generic and modal designations—and even of the more or less interchange-able words *genre* and *form*—often sends confusing mes-sages to his readers. Such is the case with **Gillets hem-lighet** and **Brott och brott** which he called comedies, with **Fordringsägare,** which he called a tragicomedy, and with **Advent,** which he called a mystery play (*ett mysterium*). 'Hjärnornas kamp' (The Battle of the Brains), the title of a short story he wrote in 1887, refers to a concept of conflict largely based on Hippolyte Bernheim's findings about psychic suggestion in the waking state that became the dominant theme of the works he wrote during the late 1880s. In January 1887 he proudly proclaimed that he had invented a new *genre,* 'hjärnornas kamp'. 'Denna genre (Edgar Poe),' he wrote to his publisher in 1888, 'blir de närmaste tio årens, och började med Bourget fortsättande i Maupassants Pierre et Jean, implanterades hos oss med Rosmersholm och Fadren' (This genre (Edgar Poe) will dominate the next decade, and began with Bourget, continuing in Maupassant's *Pierre et Jean,* was implanted here [in Scandinavia] by *Rosmersholm* and **The Father**'— VII, p. 212). This instructive misuse of the word *genre* shows how Strindberg conceived of the relation between theme and form. Years later (in *Öppna brev till Intima teatern*) he clarified this relationship in the famous dictum: 'Ingen bestämd form skall binda författaren, ty motivet betingar formen' (No predetermined form is to limit the author, because the theme (or motif) determines the form—SS 50, p. 12). Using 'form' here in its widely-accepted meaning of genre (or kind), he appears to be say-ing two things about the relationship between form and content: not only does literature—like genre painting—make its appeal primarily through content, but the content will determine the structure of the plot and the mode of the work.

In 1899—after his Inferno crisis had culminated in his conversion to a portmanteau belief in 'unseen', corrective powers—Strindberg invented yet another *genre* (in his sense of the word), that is to say, a literary form based on the theme he called 'Nemesis Providentia' in the notes he kept while **Advent** was beginning to take shape in his mind.[4] This genre, which one might call 'the nemesis play', achieves roughly the same prominence in his post-Inferno

production as 'The Battle of the Brains' does in the naturalistic works he wrote during the late 1880s. The plot structure determined by the nemesis theme (the content) can be accommodated by various literary kinds: the Strind-bergian 'commedia' (**Brott och brott**),[5] the historical play (**Carl XII**), and the *sagospel* (**Advent**). But the true progenitor of the nemesis play would appear to be the *sa-gospel*.

Shaw's uncertainty about the proper generic designation for *Peter Pan*—'a sort of fairy-play for children'—points to some of the problems one encounters in trying to define (and confine) the rather nebulous *sagospel*—what is called *Märchendrama* (or *Zauberstück*) in German, *féerie* in French, and *fairy-tale play* (or *extravaganza*) in English. Much as these national variants may differ from each other in emphasis, they are all based on fairy-tale, mythic, or biblical motifs. They usually depict a world in which the laws of time, space, and causality are suspended and where personifications of supernatural beings (gods, spirits, fair-ies, wizards, and the like) freely interfere in human affairs. Though works by Aristophanes (*The Birds*) and Shake-speare (*A Midsummer Night's Dream* and *The Tempest*) may be regarded as the antecedents of this literary kind, the immediate ancestors of the romantic *sagospel* are Carlo Gozzi (*Fiabe dramatiche*), Schikaneder (*Die Zauberflöte*), Goethe (*Faust*), and Tieck (*Der gestiefelte Kater*).[6] In stories and plays representing the interpenetration of the natural and the supernatural worlds, several Scandinavian writers produced some of their masterpieces: H. C. Ander-sen's collections of *Eventyr (Fairy Tales)*, Oehlen-schläger's *Aladdin* (1805), Atterbom's *Lycksalighetens ö* (*The Isle of Bliss,* 1824-7), and Ibsen's *Peer Gynt* (1867)— all of which helped inspire **Lycko-Pers resa.**

Somewhat surprisingly, Zola valued the *féerie* very highly, despite its contempt for *le vrai*—or rather because of it. For him, the charm of this fanciful genre is that it lets us escape briefly from earth and takes us into the world of the impossible.[7] The young naturalist Strindberg, on the other hand, clearly felt uncomfortable in the realm of fantasy at this point in his career; yet in 1882, when he got a commission to write a Christmas entertainment, he did not hesitate to employ an elf (*tomte*), a good fairy, a wishing ring, talking rats, a dancing broom, and other *sa-gospel* conventions to tell the story of Lucky Peter, who has all the characteristics of the typical fairy-tale hero: compassion, humility, and naïveté. The poor lad is cruelly treated by his cynical, misanthropic father, a Swedish Scrooge, whose heart has been hardened not by material-ism, but by matrimony. To spare his hapless son from the same fate, he has sequestered him in a church for the first fifteen years of his life. But the spirit of Peter's deceased mother is still very much alive as the protecting, loving fairy godmother who liberates him from his father and sends him out into the world to discover what life is really like and to become 'en människa och en mänsklig människa' (a human and a humane human—SS 9, p. 282).

Whereas the path of the fairy-tale hero generally begins in a drab world of everyday reality and moves through a magical realm in order to emerge in a shining new reality, Strindberg reverses this pattern.[8] Departing from a world where rats go into mourning for their lost babies, where a mysterious voice reprimands blasphemy, and where the picture of the madonna nods and speaks, Peter moves out into a more or less recognizable distortion of everyday reality. His mission is not only to search for *lycka* ('happiness', 'good fortune', or 'success'), but to divest that word of its ambiguities and to find its one essential meaning. To help him satisfy his hunger for life and happiness, the elf has provided him with a wishing ring; to help instruct him in the vanity of human wishes, his fairy godmother has given him a female companion, Lisa, a human avatar of herself. For most of the play Lisa remains a supernatural shape-shifter who regularly shows up to rescue him from serious difficulties and to see that he has learned his lesson; but she cannot really become a source of *lycka* herself until Peter overcomes his self-love.

The play ends, as it began, in a church where the fairy-tale realm is reestablished: a broom dances and religious statues speak. Peter sees his own shadow (*skugga*) from whom he learns that it is our failings, not our virtues, that make us human, and that self-knowledge is the only road to real manhood. As a result of his experience of the interpenetration of invisible, supernatural world with the visible world of everyday reality Peter has finally matured to the point at which he can renounce his youthful dreams. When the sexton (Peter's transfigured father) comes to expel Peter and Lisa from the church—from Paradise, Lisa says (SS 9, p. 380)—Peter realizes that the enchantment is broken and that they can now take paradise with them. From windows in the church the elf and the fairy godmother watch as the three now fully-human characters reenter the world divested of their dreams and their illusions.

The lasting technical lesson Strindberg learned from this first experiment with the *sagospel* derives from the stage practice of another of his mentors in this genre, the Viennese actor-playwright Ferdinand Raimund, who had made brilliant use of the *changement à vue* (i.e., change of scene without lowering the curtain). This theatrical convention lies well within the reader-spectator's horizon of expectations because the generic paradigm prepares us for the rapid alternation between the two interpenetrating worlds of the *sagospel*. Strindberg experimented with this technique in **Lycko-Pers resa** and later used it with startling effect in the changed context of such post-Inferno works as **Till Damaskus, Ett drömspel,** and **Stora landsvägen.** The real trouble with **Lycko-Pers resa**—and surely this is what embarrassed Strindberg about it—is that it deals with the interpenetration of two unreal worlds. In fact, it is easier to accept the talking rats and the wishing ring than it is to believe in Peter and his embittered father as human characters. With **Himmelrikets nycklar** in 1892

Strindberg made an unsuccessful attempt to resurrect this genre, but before he would be ready to reshape the *sagospel,* his world view would have to change.

'Genres survive,' as Harry Levin observes, 'by meeting the conditions that reshape them.'[9] The conditions that reshaped Strindberg's whole outlook on life arose during his Inferno crisis. Strindberg's efforts in youth and early manhood had been to liberate himself first from Pietism (his legacy from his mother), then to reject the ethically-based Unitarianism he had gained from reading Theodore Parker, and finally—in the late 1880s—to espouse a form of nihilistic humanism. This final view, which attempts to reconcile determinism with ethics, is perhaps best expressed by Gustaf in **Fordringsägare.** Arguing that everything happens by necessity, his unfaithful former wife, Tekla, declares herself innocent of any form of wrong-doing in her marriages. 'Oskyldig,' he replies, 'inför honom som icke finns mer; ansvarig inför sig själv och inför sina medmänniskor' (Innocent in the eyes of Him who no longer exists; responsible in one's own eyes and in the eyes of one's fellow man—SV 27, p. 270). The moralistic outlook that began to emerge in Strindberg's conscious mind during the last phase of the 'Inferno crisis' forced him to link his inescapable guilt feelings with past misdeeds. When he was at last able to find a connection between suffering and guilt, his anxiety was transformed into remorse.[10] This new sense of guilt and remorse eventually led Strindberg to conclude with Maurice, the hero of **Brott och brott,** that we are guilty of 'thought crimes', even when we are not responsible for committing them.

The Inferno crisis began as a period of intense, apparently innocent suffering for Strindberg. During its early stages he resorted to ideas of metempsychosis, Doppelgänger, or life as a penal colony in order to explain his own meaningless suffering. In 1896 he began to keep an 'occult' diary. This document—part intimate diary, part dreambook, part scrapbook full of Bible quotations, alchemical formulas, and curious facts gleaned from the newspapers—was an attempt to reduce the world to a text that could be read backwards and forwards in order to show purpose, meaning, and causality (or at least probable causality) in the world. On the first page of *Ockulta dagboken* he copied down a dictum from the Talmud: 'Om du vill lära känna det osynliga, då iakttag med öppen blick det synliga' (If you want to learn about the invisible [world], scrutinize the visible [one] with care). This phrase clearly indicates why Strindberg spent so many years (1896-1908) recording and collating his observations of the visible world in this diary: his study of the 'world text' he produced convinced him that the visible world really is interpenetrated by an invisible one peopled with good and evil spirits.[11]

During the Inferno years Strindberg devoted himself to alchemical experiments and became involved with the Paris Occultists (Eliphas Lévi, Stanislas de Guaita, and Dr

Papus), who opposed oriental (theosophical) mysticism with a brand of Western occultism based on the hermetic tradition stemming from Paracelsus and Saint-Martin. He also read some of Swedenborg's neo-platonic theological works, as well as Balzac's Swedenborgian novels, *Séraphîta* and *Louis Lambert*. As Swedenborg had done during the crisis that led to his religious conversion, Strindberg began to keep a record of his dreams. Moreover, he developed a strong interest in mystical dramatic works like Maeterlinck's *L'Intruse* and the works of Sâr Péladan. As a reader, he was very like a post-structuralist in that he tended to produce meanings that often had little to do with the intentions of the authors he read. As a diarist, he was a structuralist, hoping to lay bare the systems that underlay his chaotic life. All of his 'occult' interests point in the same direction: he was looking for the hidden narrative, the masterplot for his own life. What he found was a new kind of masterplot for 'nemesis plays', plays about a familiar, visible world in which the manifestations of the invisible world have a terrifying reality.

This masterplot is certainly evident in the first two parts of the *Till Damaskus* trilogy (1898) the so-called '*vandringsdramer*' (sometimes called 'station plays' or 'quest plays' in English) that signalled his return to literature.[12] In the next two plays, *Advent* and *Brott och brott,* one sees a change of direction. That these two plays (in quite different styles) were published together in one volume in 1899 with the overall title *Vid högre rätt* (*In a Higher Court*) points to their thematic similarity. Both plays deal with a man and woman who are unwilling (or unable) to confront their own culpability until they have gone through a hellish series of torments; both works begin in a place of burial and end when the erring characters genuinely repent for their sins and have some grounds for hope of salvation.

When he wrote these two plays, Strindberg was in the process of inventing a new *genre* (in his sense of the word), but he hardly knew what to call it. 'Mitt lif är sig likt,' he wrote to a friend on 10 November 1898, 'kryper, dag efter dag, i arbete och stundom får jag tankar med skön drägt. Skrifver en sagospelstragedi utan fé och tomte; endast de store outgrundlige Osynlige drifva sitt spel' (My life is the same as usual, creeps along, day by day, with work and at times my thoughts come to me beautifully dressed. Am writing a 'fairy-tale tragedy' without either good fairy or elf; only the great, inscrutable Invisible Powers are abroad—XIII, p. 35). In the manuscripts of the play he variously designated this work as 'Advent, En Barnpjes', 'Mausolén. Mysterium', and 'Advent. Ett mysterium' ('Advent, a Children's Play', 'The Mausoleum. A Mystery Play', and 'Advent. A Mystery Play'). In one letter (XIII, p. 50) he referred to it as his 'nya Swedenborgsdrama (Ett Mysterium) som blir en sagospelstragedi med mystik' (new Swedenborgian drama [a Mystery Play] that will be a fairy-tale tragedy with mysticism). In another (XIII, p. 54) he called it 'mitt Mysterium eller religiösa

Sagospel' (my Mystery Play or religious Fairy-Tale Play).[13] On 19 December he noted simply in *Ockulta dagboken,* 'slutade "Advent", sagospelet' (finished "Advent", the fairy-tale play). These Polonian combinations of generic and modal terms point to a combined genre.

Near the end of the 'Inferno crisis' Strindberg found comfort in some of the visionary works of Swedenborg, who was keenly aware of a dynamic tension between the visible world of human affairs and an invisible world of corrective spirits. Like *Den Andra* (The Other) in *Advent,* these Swedenborgian spirits are charged with the vastation and regeneration of erring man.[14] But if Swedenborg provided a good deal of the content in this new 'genre' of Strindberg's, two other writers gave him the literary matrix that helped him find suitable forms. Before starting *Advent* he had immersed himself in the novels of H. C. Andersen; later, while working on *Brott och brott* he became obsessed with the 'occult' tales of Rudyard Kipling. The conflict between imagination and reality is a major theme in Andersen's novels and the poetic atmosphere in which he develops this theme doubtless explains their immense appeal to Strindberg after the Inferno crisis. In a letter to his children in Finland (XIII, p. 59), Strindberg called attention to Andersen's influence on *Advent.* Kipling made an even more profound impression on Strindberg. In early February 1899 he wrote to a friend that [Kipling] 'är ju ett fullt uttryck af nutid. Han är "halfgalen" och alla hans hjeltar äro "galna". . . . Men Kipling är ockult, d. ä. tror på anden hos menniskan och rör lätt vid de Infernoproblem jag lagt ramarne på' (is indeed the complete expression of the moment. He is 'half-crazy' and all of his heroes are 'crazy' . . . But Kipling is occult, that is, he believes that man has a soul and [he] touches lightly upon the problems I got my paws onto in *Inferno*—XIII, p. 86). A few days later, he wrote to another friend (XIII, p. 92) that Kipling had dredged up all of the mysticism that was lurking in the depths of Strindberg's own being. In other words, reading volume after volume of Kipling's realistically presented stories, in which stolid, pragmatic English colonials are profoundly changed by their brushes with ghosts, gurus, or mysterious Indian divinities, helped corroborate Strindberg's passionate belief that unseen powers are guiding us toward peace in the Hereafter.

Writing about Lucky Peter's quest for self-discovery, as Strindberg said in a letter to Helena Nyblom (II, p. 363), was like playing hooky from the grim school of life. While writing *Advent,* on the other hand, he actually lived through some of the same mysterious and disquieting experiences that plague the wicked characters in that play.[15] Like Strindberg, these two characters, the Judge (*Lagmannen*) and his Wife (*Lagmanskan,* the wicked stepmother of the piece), are tormented by a dancing sunbeam (*solkatt*). In order to perpetuate their relations to the familiar elements of their earthly life, they have built themselves a mausoleum in the midst of their vineyard. Unwittingly, however, they have constructed this monument to their own goodness on what was formerly a place of execution. The newly-completed structure, intended to perpetuate their false, self-serving image of themselves, actually houses the ghosts of all the people who have suffered and died because of their evil. In this modified *sagospel,* familiar fairy-tale motifs are reshaped by being placed in a Swedenborgian context of protective and corrective spirits. Amalia and Adolf, the Judge's daughter and son-in-law, have been deeply wronged: Amalia has been reduced to the status of a servant, while Adolf has been cast out of the family circle altogether. Their innocent children, Erik and Thyra, whom the Judge's Wife has locked in the cellar, are protected by a mysterious, supernatural Playmate, who turns out to be the Christ Child. In this fairy-tale, moreover, it is the ogres, not their victims, who are sent out upon a quest of self-discovery.

The most startling transformation in this play, however, has little to do with the Swedenborgian context. It is the contrast between what the characters see and what is truly to be seen. When the curtain rises *we* see both the visible and the invisible worlds. Though we see the set as they see it (a vineyard, the new mausoleum, a peach tree), the Judge and the Wife look very different to us than they do to each other and to themselves: his costume, dating from the 1820s, links him with his double, the Unjust Judge, who was once executed on the spot where the mausoleum now stands; the Wife (with her kerchief, cane, glasses, and snuffbox) is identical with her double, the Witch, whose ballgown she later borrows. As if we were looking at X-rays of the Judge and the Wife, we see their inner corruption; looking at extremely flattering, retouched photographs of themselves (and each other), they see a Swedish Philemon and Baucis whom we can barely imagine.

The Judge and his wife feel that they have led exemplary lives. He attributes his incredible prosperity to the fact that he was born with a cowl (*segerhuva*). Though both husband and wife greatly fear the heat and light of the sun, the Judge uses sunshine to figure forth their serenity: 'Livets afton,' he observes to his wife, 'har slutligen skänkt oss det solsken som dess morgon lovade' (The evening of life has finally given us the sunshine its morning promised—p. 15). Basking in this metaphorical sunlight, the old couple can almost forgive their envious neighbours and their ungrateful children. The dancing sunbeam (*en solkatt,* literally a 'sun-cat') that suddenly shimmers on the wall of the mausoleum seems to the Wife to be a good omen: 'Det betyder att vi skola se solen lysa ännu en lång tid,' she says (That means we shall see the sun shining for a long time to come—p. 18). Following a familiar Strindbergian pattern, however, events in the rest of the scene soon make it clear that they have misread the omens. The Judge has illusions of probity, the Wife delusions of pulcritude. The vineyard was not, as the Judge has always believed, once a battlefield, but a place of execution; the new mausoleum stands where the gallows once stood.

Though each is still blind to his own faults, by the end of the first scene the dancing sunbeam has become a searing spotlight: the Judge now sees the Wife for the witch she is; his shameful, criminal nature is now fully revealed to her.

The prosperity of the Judge and the Wife is built on a career of misdeeds that has caused untold suffering to others. The Judge has robbed or cheated the living: he has misappropriated a silver coffee service from a poor family and stolen the legacy of an orphan whom he has apprenticed to a chimney sweep. The Wife has plundered the dead: she has stolen the money intended for funeral wreaths for her mother; from her step-daughter, Amalia, she has stolen the memory of her real mother. By substituting a monstrance of silver-gilt for the pure gold one she promised to the church, she has even cheated God. The mausoleum they have built in order to enshrine themselves really houses Death, a Fool mocking the Judge's cowl, the shades of all of the people who have suffered at the hands of the Judge and the Wife, as well as the ghost of the Judge's double, the Unjust Judge. The structure is, in other words, a metaphor for the hidden, inner lives of these two sinners: not a tribute to their goodness, but a barrier to their salvation. Near the end of the play this monument becomes (in the peep show the Judge squints into in Hell) a place of excrement. No hope of forgiveness is possible until it is destroyed.

The Judge and the Wife both have ghostly doubles whose physical defects correspond to the moral defects of their human counterparts: the Hanged Judge has a rope around his neck and is missing an index finger, because he once swore falsely on the Bible; the Wife encounters avatars of herself in her deceased bother, the hunchbacked Prince, whose deformity is obvious to everyone but himself, and in the Witch, who drives her out to wander alone until she freezes to death. The Judge and the Wife are haunted by spectral processions of their victims or of the Seven Deadly Sins. Whereas all of these spectres seem to be projections from within—'våra egna sjuka drömmar' (our own sick dreams—p. 41), the Wife suggests—other corrective spirits seem to have been sent by Providence to drive these sinners back onto the path of righteousness. Chief among these is The Other (*Den Andra*), a seedy, down-at-the-heel devil, who appears from time to time in the guise of a Schoolteacher, a Franciscan Monk, or of the Master of Ceremonies in Hell.[16] In life he was an evil person who fell because he touched the forbidden tree and then went around tempting others to do the same; his punishment in death is to serve the forces of Good: not to tempt with wealth and power, but to punish with whips and scorpions (p. 58). Immune to *apotropaia,* this penitent devil cannot be banished by the sign of the cross or by music.

The conflict between good and evil in this play is scenically reinforced by the interplay of darkness and light. Both the Judge and the Wife are extremely fearful of the heat and light of the sun. Not only does the Judge prefer darkness, he blackens everything he touches: the silver service he has stolen is so tarnished that no amount of polishing can brighten it; and the orphan he has plundered and pushed into the life of a chimney sweep seems permanently besmirched. But whereas the imagery of darkness in this play is quite conventional, the light imagery is strikingly original. The Wife first sees the dancing sunbeam ('sun-cat') just after she speaks of dissolving Amalia's marriage; its subsequent appearances always highlight their evil deeds, such as, the expulsion of Adolf and the revelation that the Wife has lied about the monstrance she presented to the church. The 'sun-cat', in short, begins to stalk them like a beast of prey, tormenting and exposing them mercilessly.

One of the theological peculiarities of Strindberg's post-Inferno religion is that though he continued to reject the notion that man could be redeemed by the vicarious suffering of Christ, he eagerly accepted the idea of the Incarnation—even in its highly developed Roman Catholic form. He apparently took quite literally Jesus's words 'Whosoever shall not receive the kingdom of God as a little child, he shall not enter therein' (Mark 10:15). Therefore in **Advent** the Christ Child becomes both the protector and the playmate of the innocent children, Erik and Thyra. The 'sun-cat', one of his attributes, becomes a helpful animal that leads the children directly into the land of enchantment. It literally becomes a cat:

LEK-KAMRATEN:

Kom barn! Ut i solen att fröjdas åt livet.

THYRA:

Få vi ta katten med oss; det ar så synd att han skall stanna har i mörkret?

LEK-KAMRATEN:

Ja, om han vill följa med er! Locka på honom!

ERIK OCH THYRA:

[gå mot dörren, sol-katten följer dem på golvet.]

ERIK:

Nej se så snäll han är! [Jollrar till sol-katten.] Kisse Misse Plurre Murre!

LEK-KAMRATEN:

Tag honom på armen nu Thrya för annars kommer han inte över tröskeln!

(PLAYMATE:

Come children—out into the sunlight to rejoice in life!

THYRA:

May we take the kitty with us? Such a pity to leave him here in the dark.

PLAYMATE:

Yes, if he'll come along! Coax him.

ERIK AND THYRA:

[approach the door; the sun-cat follows them.]

ERIK:

Oh, look how good he is! [Talks affectionately to the sun-cat.] Here Puss Puss! Come, Pusscat!

PLAYMATE:

Pick him up now, Thyra. Otherwise he won't cross the threshold!)

—pp. 65-6

The land of enchantment they enter (Act III, Sc. 2) is a garden full of flowers and topiary hedges in the centre of which is a healing spring (said to have been touched by an angel). Beside the spring stands a giant Fuchsia (called *Kristi Bloddroppar,* 'Christ's Blooddrops', in Swedish), the only forbidden tree in this Eden. Far away we see a field of ripe grain, cliffs, ruined castles, and a gothic archway framing a statue of the Madonna and Child. The only disquieting elements in this earthly paradise are a scarecrow and the sooty chimney-sweep, who enters and timidly watches the children at play. Before revealing himself as the Christ Child accompanied by a lamb, the Playmate allows Erik and Thyra to tear down the scarecrow so that the birds will come to sing to them; then he washes (baptizes) the chimney-sweep in the healing spring and restores him to his lost mother.

Though the Playmate can easily turn punishment to play for the innocent children, their mother, Amalia, finds it impossible to make light of her unjust suffering. What pains her even more than the heavy work she must do is the fact that she cannot love the Wife, the woman she has always taken to be her mother. Though she feels guilty about this unnatural lack of love, she still refuses to accept the idea of suffering as punishment. The wise Neighbour, who becomes the spokesman in this play for some of Strindberg's religious ideas, comforts her by explaining the meaning of suffering: 'Mitt goda barn: att lida rättvist, det göra straffångarne, och det är ingen ära, men att *få* lida orätt, det är en nåd och en prövning som den ståndaktige hämtar gyllene frukter av' (My good child, to suffer justly is what prisoners do—and there's no honour in that; but *to be allowed* to suffer unjustly, that is a gift and a test which bring golden fruits to the steadfast—p. 35). As soon as she has undergone the tests set for her, the Neighbour reveals the secret of her life: her real mother is dead and the Wife is her stepmother. After learning this, Amalia can rejoice that God has allowed her to retain an unblemished image of her true mother; now she can understand and accept the cruelty of the Wife.

The tribulations of the Judge and the Wife more than counterbalance the saccharinity of the scenes involving the children in this play. Once the 'sun-cat' has begun the unmasking, the Judge and the Wife are visited by all manner of occult manifestations. In an atmosphere of mounting terror, they begin to suspect each other of poisoning the food they eat and the water they drink. But though they soon think of fleeing from their haunted home, holding a big auction, and starting a new life somewhere else, they continue to find rational explanations for these supernatural warnings. In Act IV the unmasking process begun by the 'sun-cat' is completed. The Wife meets her double, the Witch, at a crossroads and is outfitted for a ball in what turns out to be the Waiting Room in Hell. She meets and dances with the (recently deceased) Prince. When she unmasks him by referring to his hunchback, he pulls off her wig and threatens to remove her false teeth. Thus stripped, they recognize one another as brother and sister. No longer able to conceal her baseness, the Wife finds herself back at the crossroads, where the Witch sends her out to wander until she freezes to death in a marsh. In the mean while the Judge, who still refuses to believe in supernatural powers, is judged by an invisible tribunal (p. 102). When he threatens to appeal to a higher court, The Other tells him that his case has been through all the courts except the very highest and that he has been sentenced to be stoned to death. Not until they are reunited in the Waiting Room of Hell on Christmas Eve do the deceased Judge and the Wife, now both fully penitent, become capable of seeing what is truly to be seen. Despite their realization that the wrongs they have done cannot be undone, they still have some grounds for hope: The Other tells them that though the sun never penetrates to this region, on this one night of the year a single star ascends so high in the heaven that it can even be seen in Hell (p. 125). The 'sun-cat' has now been transformed into the star of Bethlehem. The mausoleum, the symbol of death and vainglory, is replaced by the nativity scene symbolizing life and hope of salvation. A choir sings the *Gloria.*

Stockenström sees the ending of *Advent* as lapsing into cheap, sentimental theatricality and suggests that if Strindberg had carried out his original plan for the mausoleum motif, *Advent* would have become the first of his Chamber Plays.[17] Disconcerted by what he considers a highly unsuccessful blend of fairy-tale, mystery, nightmare, and stark realism in this play, Ollén too undervalues *Advent.*[18] Both critics appear to ignore the generic paradigm Strindberg was at such pains to provide. Medieval dramatic method presupposed an unsophisticated audience that could easily accept sharp contrasts between comic, often crassly realistic scenes and sacred history. Moreover, it frequently staged simultaneous action: the torments of the damned in Hell juxtaposed to Jerusalem and the Temple. *Advent,* subtitled 'Ett mysterium' ends with a diptych: a nativity scene and an angel chorus—as seen and heard from Hell. The contrast between the two worlds of the play is as naive, as startling, and potentially as effective as the final scene in the 15th century Wakefield Master's *Secunda pastorem:* the thieving Mak has stolen a sheep from his fellow shepherds and his wife Gill concealed it by wrapping it in swaddling clothes and pretending it is her newborn babe; no sooner are these culprits unmasked and punished at the end of this farcical parody of the nativity story, than an angel appears to the shepherds announcing the birth of the Saviour. As at the end of *Advent,* a chorus sings the *Gloria;* then the transposed shepherds go to Bethlehem with touchingly humble gifts for the Holy Infant: a bunch of cherries, a bird, and a ball. They receive the benediction of the Blessed Virgin, who promises to pray her son to keep them from woe. In his modern mystery play, *Advent,* Strindberg is experimenting with a kind of religious theatre that he felt could accommodate both everyday realism and providential contradiction (vastation) and regeneration.

Advent, Strindberg's first attempt to adapt the *sagospel* to religious drama, has proved far less successful in the theatre than *Brott och brott,* his first attempt to use realistic 'comedy' as a medium for dramatizing what he called Nemesis Providentia. In a very famous passage in the *Biographia Literaria,* where Coleridge describes the origin of the plan of the *Lyrical Ballads,* he says that while he directed his endeavours to 'characters supernatural, or at least romantic', Wordsworth sought to 'give the charm of novelty to things of every day, and to excite a feeling analogous to the supernatural' by removing 'the film of familiarity' that makes us blind to the 'wonders of the world before us'.[19] True poetry, he implies, results from the tension between the willing, if momentary 'suspension of disbelief' (poetic faith) and the mind's sudden awakening from 'the lethargy of custom'. Something very like this modal complementarity seems to be at work in Strindberg's 'nemesis plays', where we can see a similar tension between the Andersenian world of make-believe and the nightmarish Kiplingesque realities that make one believe.[20]

The generic subtitle of *Brott och brott* has caused readers problems from the very start. Some early reviewers (Levertin, Warburg, and Wirsén) found 'komedi' utterly inappropriate (SV 40, p. 266); when he produced the play in 1902, Max Reinhardt relabelled it 'tragicomedy'.[21] This sort of discomfort with the generic subtitle shows the play to be an early example of a new mixed genre that has been variously described as 'melodrama',[22] 'metacomedy',[23] 'commedia',[24] and as 'dark comedy', the modern umbrella mode defined by J. L. Styan.[25] Hans-Göran Ekman rightly suggests that Strindberg's use of the word 'comedy' is easier to understand if placed in a Dantean context, but one really need look no further than the kind of nineteenth-century well-made play in which conversion, a radical change of mental attitude, 'unties the knot and brings the curtain down'[26]—or to Kipling's short story 'The Conversion of Aurelian McGoggin'—to find the generic paradigms that underlie *Brott och brott.*[27]

Though *Brott och brott* is simply a further development of the material on which *Advent* was based,[28] the realistic demands of the genre Strindberg is using in his second 'nemesis play' occasion a shift in scenic effects: in **Advent** he used lighting to represent the impingement of the transcendent world on everyday reality; here he uses sound to demonstrate the interaction between the two. The play opens in the Montparnasse Cemetery in Paris, where Jeanne and her five-year-old daughter, Marion, have been waiting for two hours for Maurice, Jeanne's lover and Marion's father. In the background is a stone cross bearing the message of the play: *O crux! Ave spes unica!* Though a friendly Abbé translates the Latin words for her, Jeanne is not yet ready to understand the secret of suffering, which is the true meaning of the inscription. A mourning woman kneeling nearby at a flower-bedecked grave seems to be talking with the deceased, but her words are inaudible, and Jeanne, who no longer believes in life after death, rejects the notion that there can be any communication with the supermundane. The interaction between these two worlds gives us the plot of **Brott och brott**. The real hero, the intriguer, as Strindberg said in a letter to his friend Litt-mansson (XIII, p. 120), is 'The Invisible One', who—like Adolphe later in the play—reveals himself in veiled terms through *en halvkväden visa* (literally, 'a half-sung song'—SV 40, p. 236).

In the first scene of the play, Jeanne, a good-hearted working-class woman, fears that her long liaison with Maurice may soon end. After years of trying to make his mark as a playwright, Maurice believes that his new play will make him rich and famous, but he is too embarrassed by Jeanne's lack of sophistication to want her by his side on opening night. The only bond that still holds the couple together is their deep love for Marion. Sensing his discomfiture, Jeanne refuses the theatre ticket Maurice half-heartedly offers her, but gives him a package containing a scarf and a pair of gloves that she begs him to wear in her honour on the evening of his triumph. Shortly thereafter at Madame Catherine's Crémerie, the favourite haunt of Maurice and his artist friend, Adolphe, Maurice is transfixed at his first encounter with Adolpe's mistress, Henriette. Fearing that he might lose Henriette to Maurice, Adolphe has tried to prevent their meeting; now his worst fears come true. *Rus* (intoxication) was Strindberg's working title for the play; that word perfectly describes the passion that flares up in Maurice and Henriette, who eagerly accepts the theatre ticket Jeanne refused. Though she and Maurice insist that Adolphe join them at a café after the theatre, they already see him as superfluous.

Though Maurice fancies himself an amoral, bohemian artist, he is really—to an even greater extent than Tonio Kröger—'a bourgeois *manqué*'. His extremely idealistic play, as described by Adolphe, easily wins popular approval because it rehabilitates mankind and frees the public from lifelong nightmares (p. 184). Ironically, though Maurice convinces the public that man is a bit better than his reputation, he himself is attracted to the evil in Henriette. Waiting in vain for Adolphe, who is present only as an empty champagne glass, Maurice and Henriette become intoxicated with passion. Crowning him with laurel, Henriette tempts him to glory in his theatrical triumph, and he worships her as Astrate, the jealous incarnation of sexual pleasure who demands human sacrifice. His best friend, Adolphe, becomes the first sacrificial victim. Jeanne, whose tawdry gift of a scarf and a pair of gloves Henriette-Astrate ridicules and throws into the empty fireplace, is the next. But Maurice cannot betray his bourgeois values with impunity: 'half-sung songs' begin to reach him from the hidden world.

In the next room someone begins playing the allegretto movement of Beethoven's Piano Sonata No. 17—now softly, now wildly—ceaselessly repeating the transitional passage (measures 96-107) that Strindberg told his friend Littmansson affected him 'som en centrumborr i samvetet på mig' (like a centre-bit drilling into my conscience—XIII, p. 115). The unseen pianist starts playing just at the moment when Maurice begins to regret his failure to join his old friends, as promised, for a celebration at the Crémerie. Next the absent Adolf begins to speak through the mouth of Maurice, who imagines the speech he will make when and if he does show up: 'Ja, jag litar på dig Maurice, dels därför att du är min vän, dels därför att dina känslor äro bundna på annat håll!' (Yes, I trust you, Maurice, partly because you are my friend, partly because your feelings are anchored elsewhere!—p. 177). This epideictic exercise proves too much for Maurice, who begins to shudder with cold—or with terror. When Henriette covers him with her pelisse, he feels that he has received her skin, has been invested with a new soul and new thoughts—he even believes he is beginning to assume a female body. At this point Maurice's guilty conscience is fully articulate: the music becomes so obtrusive that it drives the hapless lovers to seek refuge at the pavilion in the Bois de Boulogne.

Henriette is almost entirely motivated by hatred for the bourgeois values that still have such a hold on Maurice. By helping her mother and her siblings wish the life out of her father, she early became guilty of a thought crime, a crime that cannot be punished by any court. Later her bungled attempt to perform an abortion on a friend made her guilty of an actionable crime, manslaughter. Killing both her friend and the unborn child placed Henriette outside society, and cut her off from reality. Since that moment, she tells Maurice, she has only lived a half-life, a dreamlife, in constant dread of discovery and the gallows (p. 175). Though Adolphe's goodness attracted her 'som ett vackert försvunnet barndomsminne' (like a beautiful, vanished childhood memory—p. 176), she is now too steeped in blood to regain her innocence. Hoping to find a Nietzschean superman in Maurice, she soon discovers that he is neither beyond good, nor truly capable of evil. Embarrassed by the generosity and resignation of Adolphe, whom she had arrogantly hoped to humiliate at the pavilion in the Bois, Henriette-Astarte craves the sacrifice of the child, Marion, and the intoxicated Maurice assents without protest and wishes the child dead. They plan to break old ties unceremoniously and flee south to a new life the very next day. At the moment of her triumph, however, Henriette recoils when she draws the five of diamonds from a pack of cards. This symbolic representation of the supports under the gallows at the Place Rouquette softens her. She sends Maurice to bid farewell to Marion one last time before their departure.

Adolphe does not emerge as a major character in this play until the third act. He too has experienced an artistic triumph: he has been awarded a gold medal for a painting that subsequently fetched a great price in London. But because he shuns success, he has returned the medal. Though he claims not to believe in God, events in his life have made him aware that some eternal power permeates existence and steers our lives; therefore he can easily forgive Maurice and Henriette, because he feels they are not acting of their own free will: they were simply driven into each other's arms by the intrigues of this invisible power. Only those who have needed forgiveness, that is, those who have committed an act for which they are truly penitent, are capable of forgiving others. The thought crime that has altered his life, as he tells Henriette in a 'half-sung song' about a fictional friend of his, was his wish that his father would die (pp. 211-12). When his father did suddenly die, Adolphe was so obsessed with the idea that he was a murderer that for a time he was confined in a mental institution. Cured there of all but his sense of guilt, he has continued to punish himself for his evil thoughts. Near the end of the play he advises Henriette to part with Maurice, abandon her artistic career, and return home to her mother. Above all, she must try to turn her hatred against herself, to lance, as it were, her own boils (p. 236).

Maurice's thought crime, his wish that little Marion were out of the way, is suddenly fulfilled when the child is found dead shortly after his last visit to her. The testimony of good, (invisible) waiters at the café and the pavilion cast suspicion on him. His play is cancelled, his reputation ruined, his former friends of two minds about his guilt or innocence. Worst of all, he and Henriette begin to suspect everyone else of vengeful acts and each other of murder—like the Judge and the Wife in *Advent,* they poison life for each other. Their lives become hellish: Henriette is mistakenly arrested as a common prostitute; Maurice is accused of being her pimp and is even forced to spend a night in jail, a night that permanently alters his character. Even the discovery that Marion has died of a rare disease—one that she may have contracted from the flowers she was playing with in the cemetery—cannot allay the consciousness of sin that has begun to drive Maurice to accept the Abbé's oft-expressed view that these uncanny events 'är icke människors verk' (pp. 198, 202, and 209—are not the work of man). After two excruciating days, Maurice feels ready to renounce hope of worldly success and to seek refuge in the bosom of the Church. Not only is Marion dead, but he has also lost both Jeanne and Henriette forever. His final dilemma arises when he must

choose between joining penitent prison inmates at a religious service or receiving the homage of his admirers at the theatre, where his play has been reinstated. At the banal conclusion of the play, he solves his problem by deciding to go to church that night and to the theatre the next.

'Mitt pjesslut är nog banalt' (My dénouement is certainly banal—XIII, p. 120, n.6), Strindberg admitted to his friend Littmansson, but this kind of ending is, after all, part of the generic paradigm for the comedy of conversion. The shocking peripety, the sudden death of little Marion, removes the 'film of familiarity' from Maurice's bourgeois world and leads him to the awareness that the intrigues of the Invisible One were intended for his moral edification. In other words, **Brott och brott,** no less than **Advent,** is a 'nemesis play', loosely based on Swedenborgian ideas of contradiction leading to regeneration. Sprinchorn makes a very convincing case for a Kierkegaardian-Swedenborgian reading of **Brott och brott.**[29] It is also possible to make a Kierkegaardian reading of the play's generic (or modal) subtitle. Following Aristotle, Kierkegaard saw the unity of the tragic and the comic in the fact that both arise from contradiction (*Modsigelse*). The tragic is a suffering contradiction, the comic a relatively painless one. This is not to say, however, that the comic does not involve suffering; in fact, Kierkegaard felt that suffering is the very source of our sense of the comic. One of his most striking examples of the relation between suffering and the comic occurs in the long fictional diary entitled 'Skyldig?'—'Ikke-Skyldig?' (Guilty?/Not Guilty?) in *Stadier paa Livets Vej* (Stages on Life's Way):

> The more one suffers, the more sense, I believe, one gains for the comic. Only by the most profound suffering does one gain real competence in the comic, which with a word magically transforms the rational creature called man into a *Fratze* [caricature]. This competence is like a policeman's self-assurance when he abruptly grips his club and does not tolerate any talk or blocking of traffic. The victim protests, he objects, he insists on being respected as a citizen, he demands a hearing—immediately there is a second rap from the club, and that means: Please move on! Don't stand there! In other words, to want to stand there to protest, to demand a hearing, is just a poor, pathetic wretch's attempt to really amount to something, but the comic turns the fellow around in a hurry and, by seeing him from behind, with the help of his club makes him comic.[30]

Seen objectively, the suffering of the indignant citizen is laughable; he is the 'fall guy', he who gets slapped, one of the mainstays of the comic tradition. Swedenborgian suffering (vastation), on the other hand, is a painful, totally subjective experience. Strindberg has a remarkable talent for making us experience both sides of the Kierkegaardian comic at virtually the same time, as when Henriette is picked up by the police as a common prostitute, or when

Maurice and Henriette identify themselves with Adam and Eve as they are being driven out of the Jardin de Luxembourg. We experience their suffering as both pathetic and comic, because we are able to see it both subjectively and objectively. In this sense, 'the comic' perfectly characterizes the mode of **Brott och brott,** where the protagonist is turned around in a hurry by his unrelenting, but invisible antagonist. We feel here the same peculiar *vis comica* that Dürrenmatt sensed coursing through **Dödsdansen,** which he reduced to a boxing match in his 'arrangement' of the play, *Play Strindberg.*[31] One critic describes Strindberg's Alice and Edgar as 'tragic characters in a comic situation.'[32] One might say the same about both the Judge and the Wife in **Advent** and Henriette and Maurice in **Brott och brott.**

Though the characteristic mutability of literary genres makes them very difficult to define, generic statements, as Fowler observes, are 'instrumentally critical'.[33] In other words, we cannot fully discover the meaning of a literary work until we have determined the generic matrix from which it issues. The multiplicity of generic and modal terms that have been applied to Strindberg's post-*Inferno* works indicates that his is a particularly difficult case. In creating the religious *sagospel* and the comedy of conversion—or what I have been calling 'the nemesis play'—Strindberg certainly modified two familiar genres. Reading **Advent** and **Brott och brott** together, however, invites us to see these two works not as complementary genres, but as unfused modal variants of the same hybrid genre, the *sagospel.* Both plays involve the interaction between two worlds. In **Advent,** the Coleridgean component, we wander in imaginary gardens with real toads in them, while **Brott och brott,** the Wordsworthian component, excites 'a feeling analogous to the supernatural' in us by placing us in real gardens full of imaginary toads. This kind of modal complementarity would seem to be a key to many of Strindberg's later works. In some of his 'nemesis plays'—like **Dödsdansen**—the Wordsworthian mode prevails; others—like **Spöksonaten**—are cast in a Coleridgean mode. 'A man of genius will create for his theatre a form which has not existed before him,' wrote Théodore de Banville, 'and which after him will suit no one else'.[34] The Strindbergian 'nemesis play' is the perfect example of that form.

Notes

1. Bernard Shaw, *Collected Letters: 1898-1910,* edited by Dan H. Laurence (New York, 1972), pp. 907-9. British audiences were, of course, already very familiar with the fairy extravaganzas of writers like J. R. Planché and W. S. Gilbert, whose works inspired the political and philosophical extravaganzas that Shaw wrote in the latter part of his career. See M. Meisel, *Shaw and the Nineteenth-Century Theater* (Princeton, N.J., 1963), pp. 380-428.

2. Gunnar Ollén, *Strindbergs dramatik* (Stockholm, 1982), p. 574. Strindberg's other four *sagospel* are *Himmelrikets nycklar* (1892), *Advent* (1898; publ.

1899), *Svanevit* (1901), and *Abu Casems tofflor* (1908). See G. Lindström, '*Sagospel*', in *Svenskt litteratur lexikon* (Lund, 1964), pp. 440-1.

3. Alastair Fowler, *Kinds of Literature: An Introduction to the Theory of Genres and Modes* (Cambridge, Mass., 1982), p. 256.

4. See G. Stockenström, *Ismael i öknen* (Uppsala, 1972), p. 426.

5. This generic designation was coined by Cyrus Hoy. See his *The Hyacinth Room* (London, 1964), pp. 292ff.

6. See Lindström, pp. 440-1.

7. See Émile Zola, *Le Naturalisme au théâtre,* ed. E. Fasquelle (Paris, 1928), pp. 285-293.

8. See Maria Tatar, *The Hard Facts of the Grimms' Fairy-Tales* (Princeton, N.J., 1987), p. 61.

9. Harry Levin, *Playboys and Killjoys: an Essay on the Theory and Practice of Comedy* (New York, 1987), p. 122.

10. See Gunnar Brandell, *Strindberg in Inferno,* translated by B. Jacobs (Cambridge, Mass., 1974), pp. 98-159.

11. The manuscript of *Ockulta dagboken* is preserved in the Royal Library in Stockholm. In 1977 Gidlund's Publishing Company brought out a facsimile edition of the handwritten manuscript, hereafter cited in parentheses after a quotation as OD.

12. Besides being the generic ancestor of Strindberg's four post-Inferno *sagospel, Lycko-Pers resa* also gave rise to a group of *vandringsdramer* based on the quest theme: *Himmelrikets nycklar, Till Damaskus I-III, Ett drömspel,* and *Stora landsvägen.* The protagonist in each of these works is involved in a metaphysical quest that brings him into conflict both with other people and with supernatural powers. See G. Ollén, p. 59 and Ruprecht Volz, *Strindbergs Wanderungsdramen* (Munich, 1982). Volz defines the Wandrungsdrama as '[ein] Schauspiel . . . in dessen Mittelpunkt ein wandernder Mensch steht, der im Verlauf der dramatischen Begebenheiten die Schauplätze wechselt,' p. 29. To confuse matters still further, in the brief preface to *Ett drömspel,* Strindberg refers to *Till Damaskus* as his 'former dreamplay'. This reference has given rise to widespread acceptance of yet another Strindbergian genre, 'the dreamplay'. See Richard Bark, *Strindbergs drömspelsteknik—i drama och teater* (Lund, 1981).

13. Hans-Göran Ekman (SV 40, p. 255) quotes Gustaf Uddgren's account of an interview with Strindberg, who said that he chose the generic subtitle of *Advent* to underscore the fact that an age of religious drama was in the offing—'liksom dessa mysterier, som in-

ledde Englands dramatiska storhetstid' (like those mystery plays that preceded the great period of English drama). English critics borrowed the distinction between 'mystery play' (a play based on a biblical subject) and 'miracle play' (a play concerned with legends of the saints) from French in the 18th century; see E. K. Chambers, *English Literature at the Close of the Middle Ages* (New York, 1947), p. 16. In Swedish, *ett mysterium* means both 'a medieval play based on biblical material' and 'a reality that cannot be understood, but is the object of belief'. Strindberg clearly wishes to activate both meanings in connection with *Advent.*

14. Whether or not one agrees with Karl Jaspers's diagnosis that Swedenborg and Strindberg were both suffering from schizophrenia, it is clear that both shared a poetic or mythic need for the supernatural, for a world where the question of reality does not arise. 'Enfin on peut prouver l'existence de ce monde surnaturel en lui donnant la plénitude sensible d'une chose vécue subjectivement, et c'est cette expérience qui précisément est valable pour Strindberg et Swedenborg,' Jaspers writes in *Strindberg et van Gogh, Hoelderlin et Swedenborg,* translated by H. Naef (Paris, 1953), p. 188.

15. On 13 December 1898 he made the following entry in his 'occult' diary: 'På morgonen när jag satt vid skrifbordet . . . syntes en sol-katt pa väggen framför mig så att jag vid en rörelse på hufvudet hade honom i nacken. Jfr. sol-katten bildades af rak-spegeln i sofrummet./ (Jfr. Solkatten i mitt drama som nu skrifves 'Mausolén' (This morning as I was sitting at my desk . . . a dancing sunbeam appeared on the opposite wall so that when I moved my head it reflected on the back of my neck—OD, p. 81). Cf. the reflection came from the shaving mirror in my bedroom./ Cf. the dancing sunbeam in the play I'm writing now, 'The Mausoleum').

16. *Den Andra*'s name is ambiguous. Though the primary meaning in this context would appear to be 'The Other' (i.e. 'The Devil'), this character also uses it to mean 'the second': 'Jag blev den Andre emedan jag ville vara den Förste' (I became the Second because I wanted to be the First—SV 40, p. 43).

17. Stockenström, p. 403.

18. Ollén, p. 268.

19. S. T. Coleridge, *Selected Poetry and Prose of Coleridge,* ed. D. Stauffer (New York, 1951), p. 264.

20. Whereas Strindberg apparently saw profound metaphysical implications in the sudden surprising turns of plot in many of Kipling's short stories, Fowler (p. 166) sees Kipling as a transitional figure who continued to use *peripeteias* in a way that had been rendered meaningless by the decay of the universe of belief: 'Kipling is a transitional instance: his stories still have plots, and plots still take odd turns (as in *Without Benefit of Clergy*), but the metaphysical implication seems too explicit for the device to hold much potential for future development'. Strindberg obviously felt that sudden turns of plot, such as the unexpected death of little Marion, do disclose the mysteries that are usually concealed from us.

21. See Ollén, p. 282.

22. See E. Sprinchorn, *Strindberg as Dramatist* (New Haven, Conn., 1982), p. 241, n., where Sprinchorn suggests that Strindberg uses setting to hint that this play is both 'a melodrama with deeper implications and a comedy about crime.' See also M. Valency, *The Flower and the Castle: An Introduction to Modern Drama* (New York, 1963), p. 311, where Valency says that 'by exaggerating the conventional effects of melodrama well past the point of credibility, [Strindberg] succeeded not only in giving to a banal action the fabulistic quality of a fairy-tale, but also the glaring realism of a nightmare.'

23. See Levin, pp. 123-132.

24. See Hoy, pp. 293-4, where he defines Strindberg's comic manner as 'laced with irony, but compassionate'.

25. See J. L. Styan, *The Dark Comedy* (Cambridge, 1962), who regards *Brott och brott* as a prime, early example of the unpopular, implicitly didactic 'drama of the split mind' (p. 281) that he designates 'the dark comedy'.

26. See William Archer, *Play-Making: A Manual of Craftsmanship* (New York, 1928), p. 339.

27. In a letter to his friend Axel Herrlin (XIII, p. 248), Strindberg claimed that the form of the play was inspired by the last movement of Beethoven's Piano Sonata No. 17 (Op. 31, No. 2). Because Beethoven told his friend Schindler that the explanation to this sonata could be found by reading Shakespeare's *The Tempest,* this work is now usually called 'The Tempest'. In the same letter Strindberg says that his friend Peterson-Berger told him that this piece is called 'die Gespenstersonate' (the 'ghost sonata'), which made the work seem even more relevant to his play that he had at first imagined. For a fascinating discussion of the structural parallels between the allegretto movement of the Beethoven sonata and *Brott och brott,* see Sprinchorn, pp. 240-5.

28. See Stockenström, p. 428.

29. Sprinchorn, pp. 238-9.

30. S. Kierkegaard, *Stages on Life's Way,* translated H. V. & E. H. Hong (Princeton, N.J., 1988), pp. 245-6.

31. Dürrenmatt himself claimed that through his efforts a bourgeois marriage tragedy ('eine bürgerliche Ehetragödie') had been transformed into a comedy about bourgeois marriage tragedies ('eine Komödie über die bürgerlichen Ehetragödien'). See F. Dürrenmatt, *Play Strindberg: Totentanz nach August Strindberg* (Zürich, 1969), p. 67. For an interesting discussion of the relation between tragedy and comedy in *Brott och brott* see Hans-Göran Ekman, 'Klädernas funktion i Strindbergs *Brott och brott*' in *Läskonst Skrivkonst Diktkonst: till Thure Stenström* (Uppsala, 1987), pp. 330-31.

32. K. S. Whitton, *The Theatre of Friedrich Dürrenmatt* (Atlantic Highlands, N.J., 1980), p. 205.

33. See Fowler, p. 38.

34. See 'How to Write a Play', translated D. Miles in *Papers on Playmaking,* ed. B. Matthews (New York, 1957), p. 83.

Barbara Lide (essay date 1991)

SOURCE: Lide, Barbara. "Perspectives on a Genre: Strindberg's *comédies rosses*." In *Strindberg and Genre,* edited by Michael Robinson, pp. 149-66. Norvik Press, 1991.

[*In the following essay, Lide looks at the body of Strindberg's work that can be classified as comedy.*]

In an article entitled 'Why We Can't Help Genre-alizing and How Not to Go About It', the American genre specialist Paul Hernadi proposes as one of two main theses that 'all knowledge is genre-bound in both senses of the word: it is tied up with and directed towards conceptual classification.' Hernadi quotes I. A. Richards's statements that 'perception takes whatever it perceives as a thing of a certain sort' and that 'thinking, from the lowest to the highest—whatever else it may be—is sorting.'[1] Or, as Jan Myrdal phrased it, 'it's the human aspect—you sort things out.'[2] As literary scholars, we consistently engage in such conceptual classification of the works we study in order to increase our knowledge of them. To use Hernadi's term, we 'genrealize.'

Hernadi's second thesis is equally pertinent to our classification of literary texts: 'The superabundance of potential knowledge and the corresponding generic overdetermination of all particulars demand polycentric rather than monolithic classifications.'[3] While this premise is more complex than the first, it certainly is clear enough to those of us who tend to categorize literary works according to our own perception of them, often in the face of opposing classifications. Because of a multiplicity of meanings inherent in all discourse, perhaps especially in literary discourse—meanings dependent upon the perception of

readers and spectators representing various cultures and historical periods—literary classification becomes a highly complex and often contradictory endeavour that in many cases not only demands, but also produces, polycentric classifications.

Thus we can read about Molière's contemporaries either applauding or rejecting Alceste, his misanthrope, as a comic figure; or about Rousseau's contemporaries perhaps seeing Alceste as 'the unduly ridiculed hero of a tearful comedy'; whereas Goethe's contemporaries might regard him as tragic,[4] an opinion echoed later by Brunetière, who saw both *Le Misanthrope* and *Tartuffe* as 'bourgeois tragedies that Molière had tried in vain to place in the ranks of comedy.'[5] Today we might 'align Alceste with such tragicomic misanthropes as Shakespeare's Timon, Lessing's Tellheim, and Ionesco's Béranger in *Rhinoceros.*'[6] Or we might see in Alceste nothing more than a ridiculous, pretentious, self-centred ass, without whom the members of his society—however small-minded they may be—are better off, in which case *Le Misanthrope* could be described as a comedy with a happy ending for most of the characters in the play, with Alceste's withdrawal representing the victory of comedy at the price of his defeat.[7] Could we not, however, interpret the play as a comedy with a happy ending for Alceste, since he is perhaps better off to be rid of Celimène and her circle of friends?

It is in the light of such contradictory 'genre-alizing' that I shall discuss perspectives on what have been called Strindberg's *comédies rosses*. In my discussion, which will be limited to the two plays *Första varningen* (*The First Warning*) and *Leka med elden* (*Playing with Fire*), I shall also engage in some of my own 'genre-alizing', the purpose of which will be threefold: to perform the kind of sorting out activity that, it is hoped, will help us to increase our knowledge of the plays discussed; to argue, even at the risk of appearing to present a monolithic classification, against opposing views considered by some to be equally tenable; and, finally, to make a plea for a growing, yet still minority, view that there are indeed lighter, comic aspects of Strindberg's *oeuvre* than most people, who know Strindberg primarily as the creator of unsettling psychological dramas and tragedies of sexual conflict, are aware of.

Several years ago American theatregoers were treated to a production of *Playing with Fire,* which enjoyed a six-month run on a double bill with *Miss Julie* at the Roundabout Theatre in New York. The play proved to be more than merely a second-rate curtain raiser on a bill of two one-act plays. Judging by comments of many in the audience, who 'never knew that Strindberg could be so funny—or so delightful',[8] people were pleased to be shown a side of Strindberg not often seen and not sufficiently appreciated, even in Sweden. In 1985, Eivor and Derek Martinus were involved in a London production of *The First Warning,* which prompted a good deal of laughter among the spectators. Like the audiences in New York who saw *Playing with Fire,* the London audiences who saw *The First Warning* showed their appreciation of Strindberg's comic spirit. As we shall see, however, reception of these two plays by academics has not always been as favourable.

First some background: *Leka med elden* and *Första varningen* belong to a group of six one-act plays—including also *Debet och kredit, Inför döden, Moderskärlek,* and *Bandet*—that Strindberg wrote in quick succession in 1892 and categorized under the heading 'Ur det cyniska livet' (From the Cynical Life—SS 19, p. 148). These plays are suitable for an experimental theatre with a small troop of actors and a limited budget, along the lines of André Antoine's famed Théâtre Libre in Paris, where Strindberg had at one time hoped to see productions of *Fadren, Fröken Julie,* and *Fordringsägare.*[9] Their form is that which Strindberg, in his frequently quoted essay 'Om modernt drama och modern teater' (On Modern Drama and Modern Theatre), calls 'den utförde enaktaren', or 'fully executed one-act play' (SS 17, pp. 281-303), a form that has its roots in the *proverbes* of Carmontelle, was further developed by Leclerq, Musset, and Feuillet, and continued to evolve in France. It was employed by Strindberg's contemporary Henry Becque, whose play *La Navette* Strindberg not only admired but also regarded as a work approaching the 'fully executed one-act play' that he suggests might become the formula for the drama of the future (SS 17, p. 301).[10]

With the exception of the commentary accompanying them in their various editions, relatively little has been written about these plays. Maurice Valency, for example, devotes almost half a book to some of Strindberg's major dramas, but only half a sentence to the six one-acters, writing that the 'short plays . . . [Strindberg] wrote in 1892 . . . do nothing to enhance his reputation.'[11] Birgitta Steene includes *Första varningen* among plays which she maintains—and, for the most part, rightly so—appear to be 'mere trifles . . . when compared to most other dramas in the Strindberg canon.'[12] Steene at least classifies *Leka med elden* as 'one of Strindberg's few comedies' (p. 64), in contrast to a statement made several years earlier by Atos Wirtanen, that one could question whether Strindberg 'någonsin skrev en enda genuin komedi' (ever wrote a single genuine comedy).[13] Walter Johnson, who customarily wrote lengthy introductory essays to accompany his translations of Strindberg's plays, provides his readers with only a short preface and a brief introduction to the volume *Plays from the Cynical Life,* which contains, with the exception of *Bandet,* the six one-act plays from 1892.[14] Johnson's main judgement of these plays appears to be that they all 'share the same gloomy view of human nature, human behaviour, and human society' (p. v), and that all of them 'are interpretations of human situations from a cynical point of view' (p. 3). Nevertheless, he writes that the plays 'should not be disregarded by any student of

drama seeking to understand Strindberg's contribution' (p. v). Johnson himself did at least grant *Första varningen* and *Leka med elden* more favourable criticism in another, previously written, context, in which he describes *Första varningen* as 'perhaps the most delightfully amusing of all his [Strindberg's] short plays', a play in which he sees 'such merits as excellent lines, amusing situations, and an interesting set of characters.' Concerning *Leka med elden,* Johnson claims that 'Strindberg never wrote a lighter play', adding that 'the roles are very good indeed, the lines excellent, and the solution amusing.'[15] Egil Törnqvist has made a careful and penetrating analysis of *Första varningen* in terms of its structure, plot, theme, character depiction, setting, and symbolism. Concerning the comic elements and the lighter aspects of the play, however, Törnqvist's remarks are limited. While he does quote Barry Jacobs's comment that the comedy is '"more witty and playful than anything Strindberg wrote in the preceding period," i.e. from 1886 to 1889', Törnqvist himself states merely that 'regarding genre', the play is 'what Strindberg himself . . . called a play "from the cynical life", a comedy of sorts.'[16] It was Børge Gedsø Madsen who linked both *Första varningen* and *Leka med elden* to the French *comédies rosses,* a genre that developed in France in the heyday of the Théâtre Libre (1887-1894). Gedsø Madsen presents brief analyses of the two plays; because he is interested in Strindberg's *comédies rosses* primarily as naturalistic dramas, however, he approaches them more as plays exemplary of the naturalistic tradition than as comedies.[17]

There has also been some decidedly negative criticism. Martin Lamm, for example, regards *Första varningen* as little more than an unsuccessful and 'especially distasteful' comic reworking of the jealousy motif in *En dåres försvarstal.*[18] *Leka med elden* does not fare much better under Lamm's scrutiny. After briefly discussing the play as a comedy in the French manner and comparing it to Sardou's farcical comedy of manners *Divorçons!,* he contrasts it with Sardou's play, a lighter and less cynical comedy, and criticizes Strindberg's play for being 'brutal and depressing.'[19] Lamm's reaction stands in marked contrast to that of audiences who saw the more recent New York and London productions of the plays.

One might suppose that such differing responses to the same works could be attributed to tastes changing throughout the years, allowing for audiences in our post-absurdist and post-theatre of cruelty age to be more receptive to Strindberg's so-called cynical comedies than they were when Lamm wrote his critical comments back around 1924. One must consider, however, that as early as 1910, Felix Salten, reviewing *Mit dem Feuer spielen* in Vienna, called the play 'ein kleines Jewel von einem Lustspiel.'[20] Perhaps Lamm's reaction, in contrast to Salten's, is based not on a response to a theatrical performance of the play that brings out its inherent comic qualities, but on an interpretation of the text determined by and corresponding to the *Erwartungshorizont* prevailing in Sweden in the 1920s, when Max Reinhardt's productions of Strindberg's plays, stressing their demonic, mystic, and chaotic elements, still dominated the stages of Sweden and Germany. In order to help us understand the situation at that time, we might consider a comment by the critic Sven Wetterdal, who observed that, as soon as an actor was given a role in one of Strindberg's plays, he drew down the corners of his mouth as far as he could, spoke with a deep bass voice, wrinkled his forehead, rolled his eyes, hissed, gnashed his teeth, and generally behaved like a lascivious murderer in an older opera. The women transformed themselves into poisonous vampires with long claws and sharp tongues. Such was the so-called 'strindbergstil' (Strindberg style) that had spread throughout Europe.[21] In short, in the 1920s, Strindberg was expected to be 'brutal and depressing.'

This *Erwartungshorizont* still prevails, however, in the minds of many involved in both producing and performing Strindberg's plays and in the study of dramatic literature. If we consider present-day Sweden, where Lars Norén's grim and brutal dramas of family conflict are performed frequently before consistently full houses, and not only receive wide critical acclaim for being some of the best dramas written in Sweden today, but are also praised for their rapier-like wit, we might think that Strindberg's little comedies about jealousy in the marital nest would appear, by comparison, to be mere bits of fluff—or in any case, certainly not as 'brutal and depressing' as Lamm found them to be. Yet it was not too long ago that Hans-Göran Ekman, in an essay on *Leka med elden,* presented an interpretation of the play in which he concentrates on its tragic aspects and seriously calls into question the use of 'comedy' as a proper genre designation.[22] This he does after citing Gunnar Ollén, Sven Rinman, and Gunnar Brandell, who agree that, with *Leka med elden,* Strindberg had indeed written a play that deserves to be called a comedy, and even after quoting Strindberg, who in a letter written in 1908 called the play 'komedi, och icke lustspel: och en mycket allvarlig komedi, der menskorna dölja sin tragedi under en viss cynism' (comedy, and not *lustspel:* and a very serious comedy, in which the characters hide their tragedy under a certain cynism—XVI, p. 167). Strindberg's letter shows that he was well aware of the differences between 'comedy' and 'lustspel', the latter of which is used to designate light comedy, while the former is applied 'to a more serious type of comedy, inclined to the satirical and the expression of human frailty and impotence.'[23] As the German scholar Otto Rommel explains, in a Komödie (as opposed to a Lustspiel), 'through all the merriment, one usually senses the sharpness of satirical anger or the bitterness of impotence.'[24]

Ekman's reading of *Leka med elden* as more tragic than comic recalls the conflicting interpretations of Molière's satirical comedy *Le Misanthrope,* for he regards the character of Axel to be the protagonist of the play, seeing him as an Alceste, an *honnête homme,* a truth-sayer in a corrupt world. Ekman cites a letter written by Strindberg in March 1892 (only about five months before he wrote *Leka med elden*), in which he shows his sympathy for Molière's suffering Alceste by expressing compassion for an acquaintance, Ivar Fock, whom he apparently regarded as an Alceste figure. Strindberg refers to Fock as 'den lidande Fock' (the suffering Fock) and adds, in parentheses, 'Alceste! min Vän!' (Alceste! my friend!—IX, p. 16). For further support, Ekman cites Strindberg, writing in 1908, that the play 'är ämnadt tragisk men får halft komisk utgång!' (is intended to be tragic, but has a half-comic ending—XVI, p. 172). For Ekman, the play is clearly Axel's tragedy.

Conversely, I regard Axel as a blocking character, whose departure allows re-establishment and reconfirmation of the society, such as it is, depicted in the play. One could also cite at least one letter by Strindberg to support this view. In March 1894, he wrote to his French translator Georges Loiseau, that *Leka med elden* 'n'a pas plû (sic) aux philstres parce que la tradition de la parterre exige à voir le mari ridiculisé et que dans cette comédie l'amant tient le dessous' (did not please the philistines because the tradition of the parterre demands to see the husband ridiculed, and in this comedy it is the lover who is left holding the bag—X, p. 29). According to this letter, Strindberg clearly regards Axel as the butt of his comedy, not his suffering protagonist. It appears that by 1908, when he wrote the letter cited by Ekman, Strindberg might have changed his own perspective on the play.

When reading Gunnar Ollén's accounts of critical responses to performances of both *Första varningen* and *Leka med elden,* one becomes acutely aware, especially in the case of the latter play, of the extent to which directors and actors—and critics as well—have, through their interpretations, 'genre-alized' the plays by accentuating, in some productions, the cynical and bitter aspects, and, in others, stressing the comedy.[25] Occasionally Strindberg himself changed his views on plays he had written, and in at least one case—that of *Fordringsägare*—he even altered his original genre designation. His 'genre-alizing' is illustrated by two letters concerning *Fordringsägare* that he wrote to the Danish actress Nathalie Larsen early in 1889, when she was both translating the play into Danish and rehearsing the role of Tekla for the première in Copenhagen. In the first letter, dated 9 January 1889, Strindberg informed Larsen that his tragedy *Fordringsägare* 'skall nu kallas: *Tragikomedi*' (will now be called: *Tragicomedy*—VII, p. 222 (Strindberg's italics)). This indicates perhaps not only a change in Strindberg's perspective on the play but also an awareness on his part that modern naturalistic drama was showing a tendency to move away from tragedy in the classic sense. In the second letter, dated 26 February 1889, which Strindberg sent to Larsen after having watched a rehearsal of the play, he wrote, 'Om Ni går åt tragedien (den gamla) eller komedien, vet jag ej. Möjligen gå vi alla—tragedien också—åt komedien och då är Ni med!' (Whether you are moving towards tragedy (the old) or comedy, I don't know. Perhaps all of us—including tragedy—are moving towards comedy, and then you're right in step!—VII, p. 254).

At this point, I should like to propose a meeting of minds between those who focus on the idea of 'tragedy hidden under a certain cynicism' in **Leka med elden,** and those, including myself, who prefer to regard the play as a comedy even less serious, especially for our time, than its author may have regarded it to be. Perhaps we can resolve our hermeneutic conflict by considering both **Leka med elden,** as well as its companion piece **Första varningen,** as *comédies rosses,* plays belonging to a genre that encompasses both the tragic and the comic and includes many examples which can indeed be called tragicomedies. Considering this possibility might free us from the limited hermeneutic circles we may be caught up in. There is no intent on my part to make any final pronouncement regarding genre on these or any other of Strindberg's plays, for I agree firmly with the American comparatist Herbert Lindenberger, that genre should not be approached 'as a category for which I seek out timeless rules', but 'as a term that opens up opportunities for both formal and historical analysis, that in fact allows the analyst to observe the interactions between the aesthetic order and the social order.'[26]

First, a brief definition of the genre *comédies rosses:* this is not a definition that derives from a theory to be imposed upon a given body of dramatic literature; it derives, rather, from the observations of that literature by André Antoine, director of the Théâtre Libre in Paris; by Jean Jullien, playwright and author of the *comédie rosse, La Sérénade;* and others involved with writing and producing the plays. In a list of plays he considered representative of the *comédies rosses,* Antoine included Henry Becque's *La Navette,* which Strindberg mentions favourably in his essay 'Om modernt drama och modern teater' (SS 17, p. 301), as well as another of Becque's plays, *La Parisienne,* with which Strindberg was familiar (X, p. 291). Some of the other plays on Antoine's list are Jullien's *Le Maître, La Mer,* and the above-mentioned *La Sérénade,* the latter of which Strindberg had in his library;[27] Oscar Méténier's *Monsieur Betsy,* as well as *En Famille,* a play that Strindberg had seen and commended highly (SS 17, p. 297); George Ancey's *L'École des veufs, L'Avenir,* and *La Dupe;* Edmond de Goncourt's dramatization of *Germinie Lacerteux,* the novel he wrote with his brother Jules in 1864; Jules Lemaître's *L'Age difficile;* and Georges Courteline's *Boubouroche*—all of which were written in the late 1880s and early 1890s.[28]

Because they are works by various authors, these plays differ considerably, yet most of them have in common a number of characteristics. To begin with, the main characters are usually amoral. Many of them are hypocritical, yet they are blithely unaware of their hypocrisy. A straightforward eroticism pervades many of the plays, and love is treated with sophisticated flippancy and regarded from a cynical viewpoint—rarely is it depicted as caritas. The passions that come to the fore in the *comédies rosses* are jealousy, which is often a stimulant to love, and anger, usually that of a deceived husband or lover. These passions are frequently expressed in strong, brutal language, with no attempt on the part of the playwright to shy away from *le mot juste.* Money is very important to the characters in the *comédies rosses,* and many of them devote their entire lives to pursuing it. Their pursuit leads to unhappy marriages and many an unhappy *ménage à trois.* In addition to the pessimistic view of life reflected in the *comédies rosses,* there is a cynical humour which is usually clothed in witty, flippant dialogue—dialogue which reflects what the French playwright and critic Jules Lemaitre describes as 'le pessimisme essentiellement jovial.'[29] Coupled with the witty dialogue are some comic situations that arise when the wives and mistresses in the plays deceive their husbands and lovers. A fitting, though relatively mild, example of a comic scene in a *comédie rosse* is the opening scene of Becque's *La Parisienne,* which takes place between two of the main characters, Lafont and Clotilde. The spectator does not know what their relationship is, but one might assume that they are married, for Lafont acts like a jealous husband who fears that his wife is about to be untrue to him. He shouts at Clotilde. He demands to see a letter that she is hiding from him. He then pleads with her to remain faithful to him and to maintain her dignity and her honour. Clotilde displays a markedly nonchalant attitude toward Lafont's jealous rantings. Finally, in the midst of his pleading, she calmly cuts him short, goes to the door, listens, and says, 'Prenez garde, voilà mon mari' (Look out, here comes my husband).[30]

Let us turn now to Strindberg's two cynical comedies **Första varningen** and **Leka med elden.** In the first and shorter of the two plays, **Första varningen,** Strindberg presents as his main characters a jealous husband and a wife who displays a flippant attitude toward her husband's jealousy. The primary motif of the play is related not so much to any of the *comédies rosses* as it is to an earlier French comedy, Octave Feuillet's one-act play *Le Cheveu blanc* (1856). In Feuillet's play, a wife has been looking forward to the day when her estranged husband will begin to show signs of ageing, for she hopes that he will no longer attract other women, and that she will then have him for herself. She is delighted when she sees the first white hair on his head, exclaiming, 'That poor white hair! I have waited for it as for a friend; it seems to me that it marks a happy day in my life.'[31] The single strand of grey hair does in fact bring about a happy reconciliation.

In Strindberg's play, it is the husband who has waited impatiently for his wife to grow older. He tells her:

Hur ofta har jag icke önskat att du redan vore gammal och ful, att du hade fått kopporna, förlorat tänderna, bara för att jag skulle få behålla dig för mig själv och se ett slut på denna oro, som aldrig överger mig!

(How often haven't I wished that you were already old and ugly, that you had become pock-marked and lost your teeth—just so that I could have you for myself and see an end to this anxiety that never leaves me!)

—SV 33, p. 123

The lines above from *Le Cheveu blanc* and *Första varningen* show that Strindberg's language is decidedly coarse when compared with that of Feuillet's little salon comedy. It is much more in line with the naturalistic, often crude dialogue of the *rosses* playwrights. The ending, too, of *Första varningen* indicates that the play is more closely related to the *comédies rosses* than it is to the more traditional nineteenth-century comedy with which it shares thematic similarities. At the end, the wife breaks a front tooth and, realizing that she is beginning to lose her beauty, fears that she might lose her husband as well. Although the broken tooth, like the white hair in *Le Cheveu blanc,* brings about the reconciliation of husband and wife, Strindberg's conciliatory ending is considerably less optimistic than Feuillet's, as the final exchange of words between the husband and wife suggests. When the wife asks, 'Och är du lugn nu?' (And are you content now?), the husband replies, 'Ja—i åtta dagar!' (Yes—for eight days!—p. 146). His answer indicates that after a short time, the bickering, the fighting, and the jealousy can flare up again.

The relationship between the husband and wife in *Första varningen*—characterized by the husband's unrestrained jealousy and the wife's unruffled attitude toward his jealousy—is typical of the relationships between men and their wives and/or mistresses in the *comédies rosses.* The example of Lafont and Clotilde in Becque's *La Parisienne,* cited above, is but one of many that could be mentioned. It should also be pointed out that, as in many *comédies rosses,* jealousy in *Första varningen*—first on the part of the husband, and at the end of the play on the part of the wife—acts as a stimulant to love, or as the glue that holds the love relationship together. As the wife points out to her husband, '. . . det har visat sig att din kärlek blir ganska kylslagen, så snart du icke har anledning att vara svartsjuk' (it is evident that your love becomes rather lukewarm, as soon as you have no reason to be jealous—p. 123).

Also in keeping with the nature of the *comédies rosses, Första varningen* displays a straightforward eroticism apparently unheard of in the Swedish theatre of Strindberg's day. Strindberg includes among his characters a fifteen year old girl, Rosa, who in her infatuation for the husband rips open the sleeve of her dress and then kisses him passionately. Her rash actions are accompanied by some decidedly spicy dialogue. She invites the husband to come up to the attic to read old love letters written to various women by her father, whom she describes as a man 'som kunde älska, och som vågade älska! Han darrade inte för en kyss och väntade inte tills han blev bjuden!' (who could make love and who dared to make love! He wasn't afraid of a kiss and didn't wait until he was invited!—p. 139) That Strindberg, like the *rosses* playwrights, did not shy away from *le mot naturel* is further illustrated by Rosa's lines:

Hahaha! Ni är rädd att jag skall förleda er, och ni ser förvånad ut. Förvånad över att jag, en flicka, som varit kvinna i tre år, har reda på att kärleken icke är oskyldig! Inbillar ni er att jag tror det barn föddas genom örat,——Nu föraktar ni mig, det ser jag, men det skall ni inte göra, för jag är icke sämre, och icke bättre heller än de andra . . . så är jag!

(Hahaha! You're afraid I'll seduce you, and you look surprised that I, a girl who has been a woman for three years, is aware that love is not innocent! Do you think I believe that children are born through the ears—— You despise me, I see that, but you shouldn't, because I'm no worse, nor am I any better, than the others . . . it's just the way I am!)

—p. 140

It is generally assumed, as Carl Reinhold Smedmark points out, that it was the frankness in sexual matters expressed in Rosa's lines that prompted the actors of the Royal Dramatic Theatre to refuse to perform the play in 1892 because they regarded it as immoral,[32] even after Strindberg had deleted what he thought were 'uttryck som kunde anses opassande' (expressions that could be regarded as unsuitable—IX, p. 29).

Rosa's lines, however, are not typical of the dialogue in *Första varningen.* More characteristic is the polished, quick repartee between the wife and the husband, Olga and Axel, especially in the opening scene, with most of the witty lines spoken by the flippant Olga. Secure in the knowledge that Axel loves her, she can allow herself to treat his jealousy lightly, as she does in the following exchange that takes place when Axel, in the midst of some lightly sarcastic conjugal bickering, begins to finger a bouquet of flowers that an admirer, a captain, has sent to her:

FRUN:

Låt bli och förstör mina blommor!

HERRN:

Har det varit kaptenens förut?

FRUN:

Ja, och sannolikt trädgårdsmästarns, innan det blev blomsterhandlarns. Men nu är det mina!

OLGA:

Stop destroying my flowers!

AXEL:

Weren't they the captain's before?

OLGA:

Yes, and probably the gardener's before they became the florist's. But now they're mine!)

—pp. 121-2

Axel continues to complain about the attention that the captain was paying to Olga at a party they attended on the previous evening. Finally, venting his anger by flinging the bouquet aside, he exclaims, 'Det är ett vackert bruk här i orten att sända blommor till andras fruar'! (It's a pretty custom they have here—sending flowers to other men's wives!—p. 122) His actions, however, scarcely make an impression on Olga, who remains completely unruffled and even assumes a haughty tone, as the following exchange illustrates:

FRUN:

Herrn skulle gått hem och lagt sig litet tidigare, tror jag.

HERRN:

Jag är fullständigt övertygad om att kaptenen önskat et-samma. Men som jag bara hade att välja på att stanna och vara löjlig, eller gå hem ensam och vara löjlig, så stannade jag . . .

FRUN:

Och var komisk!

OLGA:

The gentleman should have gone home and gone to bed a bit earlier, I think.

AXEL:

I am absolutely convinced that the captain wished the same. But since I had only the choice of staying and being ridiculous and going home alone and being ridiculous, I stayed . . .

OLGA:

And were comical!)

—p. 122

Olga's rejoinders are at times cutting. Consider the following exchange:

AXEL:

Kan du förklara huru du vill vara en komisk herres fru? Jag skulle inte vilja vara man åt en löjlig hustru!

OLGA:

Det är synd om dig!

AXEL:

Tycker du inte det! Jag tycker det själv rätt ofta. Men vet du var det tragiska i min löjlighet ligger?

OLGA:

Svara själv, så blir det kvickare än om jag gör det!

AXEL:

Därute . . . att jag är förälskad i min hustru efter fem-ton års äktenskap . . .

OLGA:

Femton år! Går du med stegräknare på dig?

(AXEL:

Can you explain why you'd want to be the wife of a comical man? I shouldn't want to be married to a ridiculous wife!

OLGA:

You are pitiable!

AXEL:

Don't you think so! I think so too—very often. But do you know where the tragical in my ludicrousness lies?

OLGA:

Answer that yourself—it will be wittier than if I do!

AXEL:

It lies in . . . my being in love with my wife after fifteen years of marriage . . .

OLGA:

Fifteen years! Do you go around with a pedometer?)

—pp. 122-3

Olga's witty incisiveness loses a good deal of its sting towards the end of the play, however, when she breaks her front tooth. Realizing that she is beginning to lose her youthful beauty, she becomes aware that she is no longer in a position where she can afford to be so flippant, and, consequently, is no longer as witty as she is earlier in the play. Also, since Axel's jealousy has subsided, he ceases to act like the ridiculous figure of a ranting, jealous husband, thereby depriving Olga of an appropriate target for her barbed wit. Still, Axel's final words to Olga, that he will be content for eight days, show promise that he will, after that short period, return to his jealous ways, and that the banter between the two will begin anew.

In *Leka med elden*—a somewhat longer and more complex play than *Första varningen*—both jealousy and a desire for forbidden fruit act as catalysts which set off erotic reactions on the part of several of the characters. These characters, who are listed simply as 'Fadern, Modern,

Sonen, Sonhustrun, Vännen, and Kusinen' (The Father, The Mother, The Son, The Daughter-in-Law, The Friend, and The Cousin—p. 215), are spending the summer on one of the islands in the Stockholm archipelago. In their summer paradise, they are bored to distraction, and one can perceive an erotic undercurrent ready to surface at any time. In this dull but charged atmosphere the characters begin to play with fire—that is, to play the game of love.

Precisely because it is a game, love is treated lightly, often with a scepticism characteristic of the *comédies rosses*. The friend, Axel, for example, just after declaring to Kerstin, the son's wife, 'Jag älskar dig, med kropp och själ' (I love you with body and soul—p. 265), answers her impassioned question, 'Ska vi fly?' (Shall we escape?) with the incisive, yet comic, remark, 'Nej! Men jag skall fly!' (No, but I shall escape!—p. 266) Finally, when Axel and Kerstin confess to Knut, the son, that they love each other, Knut appears to gain control of himself rather quickly after being, according to stage directions, 'något förkrossad' (somewhat crushed—p. 267) and lamenting, 'vi sökte genom en konstlad öppenhet förebygga faran, skämtade med den, men den har dragit närmare, och slagit ner över oss!' (we tried to prevent the danger by being open about it—artificially. We even joked about it, but it's drawn closer, and now it's come crashing down on us!—p. 268). He even appears to display a relatively jovial cynicism in the face of the problem. After asking Axel and Kerstin to help him, and themselves, come to a satisfactory solution, he says to Axel, 'Hör du min vän! Vi måste komma till ett hastigt avgörande, för det ringer till frukost om några minuter' (Listen, my friend! We have to come to a quick decision about this matter because the lunch bell is going to ring in a few minutes—p. 269). In a matter of seconds, Knut decides to solve the problem by agreeing to withdraw from the love triangle, but he states as a condition that Axel must marry his wife. It is not long before Axel is seen escaping through the garden 'som om han haft eld i bakfickorna' (as if his pants were on fire—p. 272), and the son and his wife are reconciled.

From the beginning of the play up until the *scene à faire* described briefly above, one can observe the motif of jealousy acting as a catalyst to love. Axel and Kerstin have been drawn to each other for some time, but it is not until Kerstin observes Axel talking to Knut's cousin Adèle that her feelings for Axel are aroused. Kerstin acknowledges the connection between her love and her jealousy when she answers Axel's question whether she has never felt as if she could love him by replying, 'Jo, när ni talar med Adèle!' (Yes, I have—when you are talking to Adèle!—p. 248). Axel observes that, whenever Knut sees him and Kerstin together, Knut's feelings for Kerstin also seem to flare up. He comments: 'Fröken Adèle och jag tyckas med ett ord ha till uppgift att vara braständare' (In a word, Adèle and I seem to have the same function: we light the fire—p. 249).

Another aspect that *Leka med elden* has in common with both the *comédies rosses* and, more generally, with the French comedy of manners, is an interest in money on the part of the main characters. Typical of many French comedies is an intrigue that revolves around marrying for money or inheriting money. Such an intrigue is unusual in Strindberg's plays. Although it is not central to *Leka med elden,* it is, nevertheless, present. Early in the play Knut and Kerstin discuss the possibility of arranging a marriage between Adèle and Axel, because they fear that Knut's father, who apparently is infatuated with Adèle, will leave his money to her and not to them. Their conversation takes on a distinct *comédie rosse* flavour when Kerstin asks, 'Har du tänkt dig den möjligheten att din mor skulle kunna dö?' (Have you thought about the possibility that your mother might die?), and Knut answers flippantly, 'Nå, än sedan?' (Well, so what?). Kerstin explains, 'Sedan kan din far gifta om sig!' (Then your father can remarry!—p. 228). Knut catches on and replies, 'Med Adèle? . . . Det måtte man väl kunna hindra för resten . . . Det vill säga att hon skulle bli styvmor och hennes barn dela arvet!' (To Adèle? . . . Well, we'll have to stop that, won't we . . . That means that she would become my stepmother, and her children would share the inheritance—p. 229). Characters in several of the *comédies rosses* display an attitude similar to Knut's. One thinks, for example, of Henri, the son in Ancey's *L'École des veufs,* who is cruelly indifferent towards his mother's death but exhibits a strong interest in inheriting his father's money.

Coupled with the cynical and somewhat decadent atmosphere of *Leka med elden* is some of Strindberg's lightest, most playful comic dialogue. In the discussion about where Axel will be staying on his visit to the island, for example, Knut tells Axel rather jovially:

> Du stannar bara här, helt enkelt! Låt dem prata! Bor du här, så är du naturligtvis min hustrus älskare; och bor du i byn, så har jag kört ut dig! Då tycker jag det är mer hedrande för dig att anses vara min hustrus älskare, eller hur?

> (You'll simply stay here! That's all there is to it! Let them talk! If you live here, of course, you're my wife's lover. And if you live in the village, then I've driven you out! I think it's more honourable for you to be regarded as my wife's lover, don't you?)

> —p. 236

The flippancy of these lines resembles that of *comédies rosses* dialogue. Also similar to such dialogue is the bantering that frequently has erotic or risqué overtones, as in the exchange between Knut and his mother early on in the play, when the mother returns from market with some ducklings in her shopping basket. When Knut, rummaging in the basket, finds the ducklings, and the mother complains, 'De kunde ha varit lite fetare . . . känn här under bröstet,' Knut answers, 'Jag tycker brösten äro vackra jag!' (They could have been a little plumper . . .

feel here under the breast.—Oh, I do think breasts are beautiful—p. 220). A few lines after he makes the pun on the word 'bröst', Knut answers his mother's question whether he and Kerstin slept well last night with the playful reply, 'Vi ha inte sovit alls!' (We didn't sleep at all!—p. 221).

While many similarities can be found between Strindberg's *Första varningen* and *Leka med elden* and the French *comédies rosses,* there are also striking dissimilarities. Unlike the characters portrayed in the *comédies rosses,* for example, the wives and husbands in Strindberg's plays do not deceive each other, nor do they lie to one another. Strindberg includes no secret meetings with lovers, as does Becque in *La Parisienne* and *La Navette,* or Ancey in *L'Avenir,* to name but a few examples, nor are there in Strindberg's plays lovers hidden in closets, as in Courteline's cynical comedy *Boubouroche.* Strindberg presents in neither of his comedies a *ménage à trois,* as in Jullien's *La Sérénade,* Ancey's *L'École des veufs,* and Becque's *La Parisienne.* In *Första varningen,* although there are two women who attempt to win the affection of the husband, it is clear that he is interested only in his wife. Nor does Strindberg give any hint that the wife's flirtations have extended beyond accepting flowers from admirers, and so an arrangement *à trois* does not enter into the equation. In *Leka med elden,* there is one point at which Knut almost gives the impression that a *ménage à trois* might be a possible arrangement. Referring to Axel, he tells Kerstin:

> . . . Denna man håller jag så mycket av, att jag icke skulle kunna neka honom någonting! Ingenting! . . . det är galet, brottsligt, lågt, men om han bad att få sova hos dig skulle han få! . . . vet du, jag förföljs ibland av en syn . . . jag tycker mig se er tillsammans; och jag lider inte av det, jag snarare njuter, såsom vid åsynen av något mycket skönt! . . . det är kanske ett ovanligt fall, men erkänn att der är djävligt intressant!
>
> (I am so fond of that man that I shouldn't be able to deny him anything! Nothing! . . . it's crazy, criminal, base, but if he asked to go to bed with you, I'd let him! . . . you know, sometimes I'm pursued by a vision . . . I imagine that I see the two of you together. And I'm not pained by it. I rather enjoy it, as if I were seeing something very beautiful! . . . it's perhaps an unusual case, but you must admit it's damned interesting!)
>
> —p. 255

The impression, however, is false, for, as Knut explains later:

> Att för mig fortsätta samliv med en kvinna, som älskar en annan, kan icke bli något helt, då jag alltid skall tycka mig leva i polyandri. Därför—avgår jag, men icke förr än jag har garantier för att du gifter dig med henne.
>
> (For me to continue to live intimately with a woman who loves another can never amount to anything complete, since I would always regard myself a living

in polyandry. And so—I'm withdrawing, but not until I have your word that you'll marry her)

—p. 269

Because of such basic differences in the relationships between the husbands and wives of Strindberg's comedies and those of the *comédies rosses,* Strindberg's characters are not hypocritical, as are so many of those portrayed in the French comedies. His plays, therefore, do not depict the kind of society represented in the *comédies rosses,* a society described by the French writer and critic Augustin Filon as one which has the decalogue as its code, but is governed by the seven deadly sins;[33] consequently, Strindberg's plays lack, for the most part, the ironic comedy that arises from the discrepancy between the opinions that the characters have of themselves and the picture that they present to the public. It is precisely in this discrepancy that the French author and literary critic Jules Lemaître believes that the essence of the comic in the *comédies rosses* lies.[34]

The main characteristics, then, that *Första varningen* and *Leka med elden* share with the *comédies rosses* are the theme of jealousy as a stimulant to love, a straightforward eroticism, and an essentially jovial pessimism. Strindberg's plays, like the *comédies rosses,* exhibit a decidedly sceptical attitude toward love and marriage, which—as is well known—many had regarded for some time before he wrote *Första varningen* and *Leka med elden* as a quintessentially Strindbergian attitude. Although the married couples are reconciled at the end of each play, in *Första varningen* the truce can only last 'i åtta dagar' (a week), and in *Leka med elden* there is no assurance that Knut and Kerstin will be happy; on the contrary, they have already hinted strongly that happiness is impossible for them in a typically Strindbergian exchange, in which they shout at each other, 'Du har aldrig älskat mig!' (You have never loved me!), and Knut declares, 'Ja, nu ha vi kommit in i det grälet som räcker till döddagar!' (Well, now we've begun the kind of fighting that will last until we die!—p. 258).

It should be remembered, however, that no matter how much unhappiness enters into the marriages depicted in Strindberg's two dramas, his plays end with the husbands and wives—who do love each other after a fashion—reunited, their marriages intact. Neither play ends with a *ménage à trois,* a lover or mistress, or thoughts of infidelity. Nor are the characters hypocritical. In a sense, Strindberg's endings are essentially happier—or at least a little more optimistic—than those of the *comédies rosses.* It is noteworthy that even in the comedies that he himself labelled 'ur det cyniska livet', Strindberg, whose reputation for brutality and cynicism is widespread, does not match the cynicism expressed by his Gallic contemporaries in their *comédies rosses.*

This, then, is my perspective on two of Strindberg's comedies, *Första varningen* and *Leka med elden*—the result of my 'genrealizing.' One of my stated purposes, to bring to light the comic aspects of Strindberg's *comédies rosses,* is partly in response to a largely unheeded plea that Eric Bentley made as long ago as 1946 that Strindberg's comedies 'need to be recovered from the blanket of ignorance and solemnity that hides their author and his work from view.'[35] Not only do Strindberg's comedies need to be recovered, but the comic aspects of his works, so long neglected, need to be brought forth. This is not a task to be appropriated exclusively by academics who gather at symposia to theorize over genre and other aspects of Strindberg's works. We need to cross boundaries, to go beyond the perimeters not only of the academy, but of the written text, to move beyond the word on the page to the word as performed, with all its nuances and accompanying non-verbal, visual aspects of interpretation and performance. The task must be shared by theatre workers, and also by audiences and critics.

In the last decade or so, there have been productions of some of Strindberg's plays that give strong evidence that efforts are being made to recover—perhaps 'uncover', or even 'discover', would be more appropriate—the comic side of Strindberg. Among these are the Fria Proteatern's production in Stockholm in 1984 and 1985 of *Fordringsägare,* directed by Stefan Böhm, with Keve Hjelm, Bibi Andersson, and Tomas Bolme, a production that did not ignore the comic aspects of Strindberg's tragicomedy; the Roundabout Theater's *Playing with Fire;* and Eivor and Derek Martinus's London productions of *Första varningen, Moderskärlek,* and other plays. At the Source Foundation in New York, Susan Flakes has directed performances of Strindberg's plays that gave their comic aspects the recognition they deserve. Included in her productions have been *Playing with Fire* and *The Dance of Death,* in translations by Flakes in collaboration with Barry Jacobs. The American actress Geraldine Page, who played in the Source Foundation's *The Dance of Death,* described the play as one with 'many laughs', and suggested that 'it would be good for people to know that and to get the doom and gloom lifted from the play.'[36] (Compare this with John Ward's criticism of the London National Theatre production of *The Dance of Death* in 1969, in which Ward accuses the actors of 'attempting to milk a dour text for laughs, with the result that what should have been demonic inconsistencies appeared as absentminded absurdities').[37]

If these productions are any indication of what might be brewing in the world of Strindbergian theatre, then I think we can expect that Strindberg's wonderfully incisive, cynical, comic spirit—which has been stifled for so many years—will be free at last to add another dimension, a comic dimension, to what many have come to agree is a disturbingly one-sided critical image of Strindberg. Strindberg was, after all, an observer and recorder of life, and those who approach his works must bear in mind that there is in almost all of them, as in life itself, an intermingling of the tragic and the comic, or, to use Strindberg's own words, 'tragiskt och komiskt, stort och smått omväxla såsom i livet' (the tragic and the comic, the great and the small, alternate, as they do in life—SS 19, p. 27).

Notes

1. Paul Hernadi, 'Why We Can't Help Genre-alizing and How Not to Go About It: Two Theses with Commentary', *Centrum,* 6:1 (1978), pp. 27-8.

2. Extemporaneous comment made at the Tenth International Strindberg Conference on 2 April 1990.

3. Hernadi, 'Why We Can't Help Genre-alizing', p. 27.

4. Paul Hernadi, *Beyond Genre: New Directions in Literary Classification* (Ithaca and London, 1972), p. 3.

5. Ferdinand Brunetière, *Études critiques,* Vol. 8, pp. 116-117. Cited in P.J. Yarrow, ed., *A Literary History of France,* Vol. II, The Seventeenth Century 1600-1715 (London, 1967), p. 215.

6. Hernadi, *Beyond Genre,* pp. 3-4.

7. Cf. Alfred Simon, 'From Alceste to Scapin', *Molière: A Collection of Critical Essays,* ed. Jacques Guicharnaud (Englewood Cliffs, N.J.), p. 145.

8. Barbara Lide, heard after performance of the play, 27 December 1981.

9. Letters to Karl Otto Bonnier, 21 August 1888 (VII, p. 105), and Joseph Seligmann, 16 October 1888 (VII, p. 144).

10. I have used Børge Gedsø Madsen's translation, 'the fully executed one-act play.' Børge Gedsø Madsen, *Strindberg's Naturalistic Theatre: Its Relation to French Naturalism* (Seattle, 1962), p. 129.

11. Maurice Valency, *The Flower and the Castle* (New York, 1966), p. 282.

12. Birgitta Steene, *The Greatest Fire: A Study of August Strindberg* (Carbondale, 1973), p. 64.

13. Atos Wirtanen, *August Strindberg: Liv och dikt* (Stockholm, 1962).

14. August Strindberg, *Plays from the Cynical Life,* translated by Walter Johnson (Seattle and London, 1983), pp. 3-6.

15. Walter Johnson, *August Strindberg* (Boston, 1976), pp. 150-51.

16. Egil Törnqvist, '*Första varningen*/The First Warning—an Effective Drama', *Strindbergian Drama: Themes and Structures* (Stockholm, 1982), pp. 37 and 19.

17. Gedsø Madsen, pp. 28-29 and pp. 128-137.

18. Martin Lamm, *Strindbergs dramer,* I (Stockholm, 1924), p. 393.

19. Lamm, p. 402.

20. Review in *Die Zeit,* 2 February 1910, of Josef Jarno's production at the Theater in der Josefstadt.

21. Quoted by Gunnar Ollén in his 1961 edition of *Strindbergs dramatik* (Stockholm, 1961), p. 29.

22. Hans-Göran Ekman, 'Sanningssägaren som komediförfattare: En Studie i Strindbergs komedi *Leka med elden*', *Samlaren* (1979), pp. 75-104.

23. Kenneth S. Whitton, *The Theatre of Friedrich Dürrenmatt: A Study in the Possibility of Freedom* (London, 1980), p. 20.

24. Otto Rommel, 'Komik- und Lustspieltheorie', *Deutsche Vierteljahresschrift,* XXI: 2 (1943), pp. 252-286, here p. 273. (Cited in Whitton, p. 21.)

25. Gunnar Ollén, *Strindbergs dramatik,* 4th ed. (Stockholm, 1982), pp. 204-209 and 218-227. See also Ollén's commentary in SV 33, p. 358-368.

26. Herbert Lindenberger, *Opera: The Extravagant Art* (Ithaca and London, 1984), p. 20.

27. *Förteckning öfver en Samling Böcker, hvilka försäljes på Stockholms Bokauktionskammare Onsdagen den 30 November 1892* (Stockholm, 1892), p. 24.

28. Antoine prepared his list for Heinrich Weber, who quotes it in his study, 'Die "comédie rosse" in Frankreich', *Archiv für das Studium der neueren Sprachen und Literaturen,* Jahrgang 54, 105 (N.S.V.), 1900, p. 345.

29. Jules Lemaître, *Impressions de Théâtre,* Troisième Série (Paris, 1889), p. 224.

30. Henry Becque, *Oeuvres complètes* (Paris, 1924), Vol. 3, pp. 3-9.

31. Octave Feuillet, *Théâtre complet* (Paris, 1897), Vol. 2, p. 24.

32. Carl Reinhold Smedmark, ed., *August Strindbergs dramer,* Vol. 4, p. 240.

33. Augustin Filon, *De Dumas à Rostand. Esquisse du Mouvement dramatique contemporain* (Paris, 1898), p. 70. See also Gedsø Madsen, p. 28.

34. Lemaître, p. 224.

35. Eric Bentley, *The Playwright as Thinker: A Study of Drama in Modern Times* (New York, 1945), p. 163.

36. Cited in *The New York Times,* 28 April 1986.

37. John Ward, 'The Neglected Dramas of August Strindberg', *Drama: The Quarterly Theatre Review,* No. 92 (1969), p. 32.

Margareta Wirmark (essay date 1991)

SOURCE: Wirmark, Margareta. "Strindberg's History Plays: Some Reflections." In *Strindberg and Genre,* edited by Michael Robinson, pp. 200-06. Norvik Press, 1991.

[*In the following essay, Wirmark discusses Strindberg's history plays.*]

At the turn of the year 1898-9 Strindberg entered upon an intense period of dramatic writing. 'Jag har nu lagt undan allt annat och ägnar mig uteslutande åt teaterförfatteri' (I have now put everything else aside and am devoting myself entirely to writing for the theatre—XIII, p. 59) he wrote, in a letter dated 26 December 1898. In January 1899 he was to celebrate his fiftieth birthday, which may have been one of the reasons for this new start. In the letter Strindberg refers to his youthful masterpiece **Måster Olof,** which was to be revived for the occasion.[1] The time has come to present Sweden with a dramatic art worthy of the name, Strindberg proclaims, and his intention is to fulfil the promise of his youth, at the same time recreating Swedish dramatic art.

The grandness of Strindberg's plans can be traced from his drafts. One of them, which Claes Rosenqvist dates to summer 1898, lists both written and unwritten dramas: 'Folkunga-Sagan, **Mäster Olof**, Gustav Vasa, **Erik XIV,** Karl IX, Gustaf Adolf, **Kristina,** Karl XI, Karl XII, Friedrich, **Gustav III**' (The Saga of the Folkungs, Master Olof, Gustav Vasa, Erik XIV, Charles IX, Gustav Adolf, Queen Christina, Charles XI, Charles XII, Friedrich, Gustav III).[2]

The title of this draft is 'Svenska Historiska Dramer' (Swedish Historical Plays). Strindberg thus identifies the history play as a category of its own, a tradition which has been upheld by scholars from Martin Lamm onwards. We must ask whether this tradition is a useful one. Does it in fact increase our ability to discern and describe what is unique to Strindbergian drama? It is a question to which I shall return in due course.

Walter Johnson's *Strindberg and the Historical Drama* is the most thorough study of this genre. The dramas treated, twenty-one in all, are those that deal with historical figures, usually a king. Johnson tries to distil what is common to this group and finds in all of them a drive towards cosmic order and a struggle for power. He also notes their 'remarkable variety of plots and the variety in the characterizations'.[3]

At first sight Johnson's study seems adequate. But he has neglected one thing: he does not prove that his characteristics are unique to the historical plays. The possibility remains that the same characteristics may, in the same combination, appear in all of Strindberg's dramas.

It is hard to find an acceptable criterion for the history play if the simple fact of its dealing with historical figures proves unsatisfactory. Yet it is even harder to discern the borderline with other types of drama. We may then abstain from a precise definition, and accept this common denominator, that a historical drama deals with a historical person, in order to continue to use the term. This is what I intend to do in what follows.

Most of Strindberg's history plays, including the best ones, were written around the turn of the century. He consciously set out to write history plays, and proclaimed himself the reviver of the genre before he had even started. It was a remarkable venture: he set out to dramatize nothing less than the whole of Swedish history. Today we know that he succeeded. He portrayed the kings in chronological order, covering five hundred years of Swedish history in only three, and devoting one drama apiece to seven kings and one popular hero. As Johnson remarks, only Sweden and Great Britain possess such a treasury of history plays.

When Strindberg embarked upon this scheme, he began with the Middle Ages and the Reformation, epochs he was familiar with from his earlier plays *Mäster Olof, Gillets hemlighet,* and *Herr Bengts hustru.* He followed the order of his draft and completed four plays in one year: *Folkungasagan, Gustav Vasa, Erik XIV,* and *Gustav Adolf.* Three of them were accepted at once by the theatre and *Gustav Vasa* especially was warmly received by the critics as well as the public.[4]

Strindberg then took a pause in writing history plays and switched to dramas with contemporary subjects. But a year later, in summer 1901, he began again. This time he completed a further four plays: *Carl XII, Engelbrekt, Kristina,* and *Gustav III.* But he no longer follows his original plan all that strictly. He jumps over some of the kings and alters the order: after *Carl XII,* for example, he returns to the fifteenth century and writes about Engelbrekt. Nor does he devote himself exclusively to the history play: *Ett drömspel* is written parallel with *Kristina.*

This second quartet of history plays was received quite differently. Some of them were refused, and those which were produced were not very successful. *Kristina* was considered unhistorical, even provocative, and was not performed at all. *Engelbrekt* was withdrawn after only two performances, and *Carl XII* was staged, but met with no success.[5]

In fact these two quartets of history plays, written in 1899 and 1901 respectively, have very little in common. As far as form and dramaturgy is concerned, the first group belongs to the nineteenth century. Strindberg follows the traditional method of constructing a drama. He employs the Freytag model, and it is easy to trace the dramatic curve, from exposition to climax and the denouement. The plot is easy to follow. The drama is based on a selection and concentration of events that cover several years in historical time and the regal protagonist, who is portrayed as powerful and treated as a positive hero even if tyrannical, meets with affliction in the course of the drama and is transformed into a better man. There is no doubt that the king is the centre and the subject of the drama.

The second quartet, written at the dawn of the new century, deviates in almost every aspect from this pattern. It is true that the Freytag model is also used here, but only its last stage. Strindberg focuses on the final period of each reign. *Kristina* deals with her abdication; *Gustav III* centres upon a plot to assassinate the king; and in *Carl XII* the king dies at Fredrikshald. Christina, Gustav III and Charles XII are all engaged in a war, but none of them is seen fighting. Their power is seldom stressed; they do not always know what decision they should reach, and it is hard to tell if the monarch is the subject of the play.

In Strindberg's later historical plays war is already lost and the defeated return to their native country. Both *Carl XII* and *Gustav III* begin with the king re-entering Swedish territory, to be tried by his people and have sentence passed upon him. Several of the plays deal with the king's death, which is never ordinary, though in the case of Gustav III the actual assassination is only anticipated and not portrayed while in *Kristina* another woman becomes a surrogate, stabbed in the street because she resembles the Queen.

Reference to specific historical events is rare in Strindberg's history plays. Sometimes the month or the day of the week may be mentioned, but never the precise year. The spectator has to determine for himself the exact period in which the play is set. In act four of *Gustav III* we learn that the Bastille has just fallen; every spectator familiar with history can deduce from this that the drama takes place in late summer 1789. From the stage directions we see that *Carl XII* begins in December 1715, but the information is never given in the dialogue. The spectator is ignorant of the exact date. There is only one reference to time: we are told that the last scene at Fredrikshald takes place on the first Sunday in Advent.

If one limits oneself to the information afforded by the dialogue, Strindberg's history plays are difficult if not impossible to date. In his *Öppna brev till Intima teatern* he states that this is intentional, and maintains that every dramatist is free to set historical chronology aside. His task is not to teach the audience history, nor is he obliged to give correct information: 'Den som fordrar den kronologiska ordningens iakttagande vid händelsers hopfogande i ett historiskt drama, den har ingen aning om ett drama och borde icke få yttra sig med anspråk på att bli hörd' (Anyone who insists on chronological order in the construction of a historical drama knows nothing whatsoever about drama, and should not be permitted to express himself with any claim to being heard—SS 50, p. 248).

In *Gustav Vasa* different events covering between five and ten years are compressed into only five days. Gustav Vasa reigned for almost forty years, from 1523 to 1560. Strindberg selects the years 1542-43 for his drama, the years of Nils Dacke's rebellion in Småland. However, no one in the play mentions the precise year. To locate it, the spectator has to apply his own knowledge of history. Anyone who fails to do so will nevertheless understand the action. In the *Öppna brev till Intima teatern* Strindberg explains why he chose to depict Gustav Vasa at a time when his power was placed in question: 'Denna förtvivlans tid ger bäst tillfälle skildra den stora människan Gustav Vasa med alla hans mänskliga svagheter' (That time of despair affords the best opportunity of depicting the great human being Gustav Vasa in all his human weakness—SS 50, p. 247).

But Strindberg is not content to describe only the Dacke rebellion. He also adds some further events which cannot be so easily placed at a particular time. The king is not only shown in conflict with his people, he also quarrels with his son, the future Erik XIV. This conflict between father and son no doubt covered several years but Strindberg abbreviates it to cover the same period as the Dacke rebellion. Furthermore, Vasa is not the only father in the play who is portrayed as fighting against his son; Strindberg augments it with the parallel action of the Hanseatic councillor Herman Israel, who is likewise in conflict with his son, Jacob, thus refining upon the material provided by history in a dramatically effective way.

Despite his afflictions, however, Gustav Vasa is depicted as a strong ruler. His absence from the stage during the first half of the play does not prevent the audience sensing his power, and when he finally appears, carrying Tor's hammer, his resemblance to a god is underlined. *Carl XII,* on the other hand, which may be described as a vacuum, an endless waiting, depicts a monarch who is devoid of Vasa's strength and power. The king's death is anticipated by everyone in the play, but is continually deferred, though he is perceived from the start as a loser.

This is underlined by the setting, which conveys everything to the spectator from the outset. The play opens with 'The Man' (at once a late Adam and a parallel to the king) returned from the war and strolling amidst the debris of his past. What remains of the Eden of his youth is a ghastly place from which all life has departed. His wife and children have succumbed to the plague and the apple tree of life in his ravaged garden bears a single, rotten apple. This use of setting differs from Strindberg's practice in *Gustav Vasa.* Here, everything has to be interpreted as a symbol. Sweden is a tree bereft of all its leaves, the king a rotten apple which refuses to fall.

Throughout the play the king is described with the help of negations. Not only is he a decayed fruit: he is also surrounded by darkness, stillness and silence. He moves little,

preferring to remain in bed, and says nothing at all for two acts. Indeed, he is offstage for half a play which contains little specific information about history but much about the terms of human life. It is an existential drama in which man is seen as suffering from guilt but unable to find a solution to his dilemmas.

Carl XII ends with the king's death at Fredrikshald, but Strindberg leaves even this unresolved in the spectator's mind, since no one is able to tell from where the bullet has come, whether from the Norwegians in the fortress that Charles is besieging or 'from above', from God himself. Strindberg leaves the question unanswered, or rather he ends with two evenly weighted and contrasting answers.

However, immediately following the King's death he appends an additional ending: 'Allt upplöses. MANNEN och MISSNÖJD kasta sig över Görtz och släpa ut honom. Alla rusa ut i villervalla; lägereldarne slockna; facklor och lyktor bäras ut. Det blir mörkt på scenen' (Everything dissolves. The Man and Malcontent throw themselves upon Görtz and drag him out. Everyone rushes out in chaos, the campfires go out, torches and lanterns are carried out. Darkness falls on the stage—SS 35, p. 223).

Thus, *Carl XII* has *two* endings. First, the king is shot down. Then follows an ending in which the dramatic fiction dissolves bit by bit. First of all the actors rush out in chaos, then the lights are extinguished and the stage remains in darkness ('Det blir mörkt på scenen'). At this point, all the instruments of the stage have stopped working.

But Strindberg is not content with this double ending. After a moment of silence a new light is activated. A lantern shines brightly at the same spot where the king was just now shot down. Strindberg's drama is an open one; he leaves the interpretation of this final sign to the spectator.

Gustav Vasa and *Carl XII* were written at almost the same time and they both belong to the same genre. But the two dramas have very little in common: in almost every respect they are the antithesis of each other. In the one people are seated on wooden benches in farms and wine-cellars, in the other The Man stands alone on the seashore, surrounded by darkness and cold. In one the king kills everyone who dares oppose his will, in the other for most of the time the king seems to be asleep. Gustav Vasa changes during his various struggles and learns something about himself whereas Charles XII is never seen fighting against anyone, and he does not change. The one is a hero, the other an antihero.

Is it reasonable to assign two so different dramas to the same genre? We may of course continue to do so if we remember that the term 'history play' is a vague one. One way of being more strict would be to make use of a double classification, to add another term, perhaps just as vague, to the first one. *Gustav Vasa* might be characterized as a historical play which is also a conflict drama, *Carl XII* is a historical play which is also a modern drama.

Although not very impressive, this way of classifying these dramas seems to me for the time being the best solution. To describe each drama more adequately, however, we require a new terminology. In order to trace the transformation of the logical drama of the last century into a modern one, we need to invent new tools. No such language is as yet available, and we have to stick to the old-fashioned way of characterizing plays, even though it is now some ninety years since Strindberg's experiments in dramatic form, when he used every possible genre, including the history play, as a melting pot for his explorations.

Not surprisingly, the portrait of the king in *Carl XII* met with little understanding from Strindberg's contemporaries. As a king he appeared odd and bizarre whereas Gustav Vasa was probably easier to comprehend because he accords with conventional notions of a king, being strong and powerful. Today our judgement differs. To us Gustav Vasa stands out as odd and rather bizarre while Charles XII is easier to comprehend. In many respects he can be interpreted as a symbol of Man, an Everyman from our own century. He is our contemporary, the ancestor of Beckett's Vladimir and Estragon in *Waiting for Godot,* for—though written in 1901—it is evident that Strindberg's history play has much in common with the drama of the absurd.[6]

Notes

1. Svenska teatern performed *Mäster Olof* from 22 to 30 January 1899. See Gunnar Ollén, *Strindbergs dramatik,* 4th ed. (Stockholm, 1982), p. 43.

2. Claes Rosenqvist, *Hem till historien. Strindberg, sekelskiftet och 'Gusaf Adolf'* (Umeå, 1984), p. 15.

3. Walter Johnson, *Strindberg and the Historical Drama* (Seattle, 1963), p. 286.

4. See Ollén, pp. 292, 302, 315.

5. Ollén, pp. 423, 411.

6. See Margareta Wirmark, '"Skaffa mig en spindel att leka med!" Strindbergs drama *Carl XII* som förabsurdistisk text', *Strindbergiana* VI (1991), pp. 61-94.

Lynn R. Wilkinson (essay date fall 1993)

SOURCE: Wilkinson, Lynn R. "The Politics of the Interior: Strindberg's *Chamber Plays.*" *Scaninavian Studies* 65, no. 4 (fall 1993): 33-50.

[*In the following essay, Wilkinson examines a group of five plays known as the Chamber Plays:* Oväder (Storm Weather), Brända temten (The Burned House), Spöksonaten (Ghost Sonata), Pelikanen (The Pelican), *and* Svarta handsken (The Black Glove).]

In 1907 and 1908, Strindberg composed five plays for performance at his own small theater in Stockholm, *Intima teatern* or The Intimate Theater. *Oväder* or *Storm Weather,* *Brända tomten* or *The Burned House,* *Spöksonaten* or *The Ghost Sonata,* and *Pelikanen* or *The Pelican* were written in 1907; *Svarta handsken* or *The Black Glove* followed a year later. Numbering the plays opus one to five, he called them *Kammarspel* or *Chamber Plays.* In his choice of names, *Chamber Plays* and The Intimate Theater, Strindberg harked back to innovative small theaters set up on the continent from the 1890s onward, especially Max Reinhardt's *Kammerspielhaus* in Berlin, which had opened in 1905. Nevertheless, as Reinhardt himself recognized, Strindberg's *Chamber Plays* represented the best of their kind, the most successful and suggestive attempts at creating a new kind of drama that might be called, like Strindberg's establishment in Stockholm, intimate theater.[1]

The notion of an intimate theater seems to represent a contradiction in terms. How, one might ask, can one combine intimacy or privacy, on the one hand, and theatricality, traditionally associated with the making public of gestures with far-reaching public consequences, on the other? At first, the idea of an intimate theater seems to imply a retreat from politics, a withdrawal into private worlds sealed off from the large-scale cocophonous conflicts of mass politics and industrialized or industrializing societies into the kind of spaces where chamber music might be performed. It may be difficult to imagine what kind of *theatrical* performance might take place within such settings.

Many turn-of-the-century dramatists or would-be dramatists did, in fact find this combination of privacy and theatricality a problem. In Germany, intimate theater was often aligned with the interests of a bourgeoisie anxious to escape from any kind of politics, especially the politics of the left and to focus on individual psychology rather than public life. Some authors took the apparent dissociation of public and private one step further, turning to the creation of unperformable dramas intended for reading only. Mallarmé is one such writer, but a focus on the mind as a little theater also characterizes the work of Freud, who drew heavily on dramatic tradition, including Ibsen as well as the Greeks. Unperformable dramas had proliferated in European literature in the nineteenth century, but the tendency reached its apogee at the turn of the century. As the studies of cultural historians such as Carl Schorske have suggested, European *fin-de-siècle* culture gave pride of place to psychology, and it was, in fact, overwhelmingly psychological in focus, often appearing to substitute psychology for politics. But attempts to separate the two were never entirely successful. Even Freud's theater of the mind, Schorske insists, grew out of and reflected developments in Viennese and European politics in the late nineteenth and early twentieth centuries.[2]

Strindberg's *Chamber Plays* draw on both earlier forms of intimate theater and the psychological culture of turn-of-the-century Europe. His interest in psychology—in mesmerism, hypnosis, and the theories of Charcot—dates back at least to the 1880s. In contrast to many European writers, however, Strindberg almost always ties his psychological interests explicitly to questions of power, domination, sexual difference, and politics. In this respect, the highly psychological *Chamber Plays* are no different from his earlier work. References in the plays to work and to the household as an entity that transcends private life and the nuclear family lend these plays a political dimension missing in many similar works produced on the continent.[3]

This is an aspect of these plays that is easily overlooked when they are read or performed in isolation. Even Reinhardt's brilliant productions tended to present them as intensely isolating versions of what the Germans call *Ich-Dramen*. In this country, the only play of the series often performed or read, *The Ghost Sonata,* is interpreted in a similar light, as evidence of Strindberg's absurdist and apolitical view of life in the decade preceding his death in 1912.[4]

Written with performance in a small theater in mind, Strindberg's *Chamber Plays* have an essentially dialogic dimension that is lost to interpretations that view them in isolation. As a sequence, however, the plays take on a very different meaning, forming part of a narrative that questions and redefines traditional notions of public and private and of the role of politics within individual psychology and the home.

I

The implications of Strindberg's interpretation of European intimate theater can best be seen against the background of two contemporary movements in turn-of-the-century culture that give pride of place to private and psychological themes: psychoanalysis and art nouveau. Strindberg's psychological interests often parallel those of Freud, and the staging of *The Chamber Plays* at The Intimate Theater conformed to a European style, art nouveau, that both drew significantly on late nineteenth-century psychology and, like the work of Freud, appeared to affirm the separateness of interior space. Recent work on both subjects, however, has emphasized the public and political dimensions of the most private aspects of both psychoanalysis and the art nouveau movement. These interpretations have important implications for our understanding of Strindberg's late work.

Critics such as Schorske have focused attention on a widespread tendency in turn-of-the-century Europe to attempt to substitute psychology for politics. The work of

Freud stands at the center of Schorske's study of Viennese culture at that time. For the intellectual historian, Freud's "discovery" of the unconscious is repeated in many forms in the aesthetic, cultural, and political life of the city. Arguing mostly on the basis of an interpretation of Freud's *Interpretation of Dreams* as an autobiographical work, Schorske suggests that Freud turned to the invention of a new branch of psychology, or even a new science, out of frustration because political careers were closed to Jews. He criticizes Freud, however, for his turning away from the public or political implications of his theories. The Greek Oedipus, Schorske notes, had also been a king (199).

Fin-de-siècle Vienna has far-reaching implications for the interpretation of turn-of-the-century Scandinavian culture, especially for the work of Strindberg. The Swedish writer's interests, many critics have remarked, parallel the work of Freud very closely. If, in the 1880s, he read Charcot and other pre-psychoanalytic psychologists, by the first decade of this century, he was writing plays that aimed to present on stage visionary sequences that followed a kind of dream logic. What has been noted far less often is the coincidence of Strindberg's psychological and political interests. Most often critics identify one or the other with rational or irrational, worldly or other-worldly, interests. Cultural histories such as Schorske's show that this is untenable. To an even greater extent than Freud's, Strindberg's psychological interests were inseparable from his political desires and beliefs. Indeed, works such as *The Chamber Plays* are about the impossibility of separating the two.[5]

The parallels between *The Chamber Plays* and psychoanalysis are striking. Ever the autobiographer, Strindberg recounts aspects of his life throughout these plays and in ways which suggest a therapeutic aim: the urge to confess is often tempered with a quest for absolution or relief from guilt or anxiety. Although the tendency is perhaps most pronounced in *The Ghost Sonata,* all of these plays follow Strindberg's *A Dream Play* in their reproduction of a kind of dream logic that diverges from the linear and apparently explicable progression of events associated with rational, waking experience. Moreover, in *The Chamber Plays,* as in Freud's studies of the first decade of this century, the focus is on an interior drama reflecting and repeating events which have taken place within a household and above all in the triangle: mother, father, child. Several of the plays refer to a child who should be saved. In two respects, however, the plays diverge from Freud's family narratives: in their emphasis on work and who does it and in the evocation of a radical change in the structure of the household. These themes tie Strindberg's late plays more closely than any of Freud's studies to politics and political change.

Because Strindberg was so prolific a writer, his opinions on political issues are well documented. But this wealth of information has both advantages and disadvantages, for it is easier to determine what he thought about specific issues than it is to discern coherent patterns in his politics: his commentators often point, for example, to his simultaneous espousal of the cause of the working classes and denigration of the women's movement, both liberal causes, in the 1880s. Some see no other mainstay in Strindberg's political thought than a constant sympathy for the underdog.[6] There have, however, been some notable attempts to make order out of this apparent chaos. Sven-Gustaf Edqvist, for example, has convincingly pointed to the affinity of Strindberg's writings in the 1880s to contemporary anarchism. More recently, Björn Meidal has attempted to show how Strindberg's theological interests informed his thinking about politics in the first decade of the twentieth century, above all in his history plays. Our understanding of Strindberg's politics during the last decade of his life has been further nuanced by the publication of the newspaper articles he wrote during the last years of his life, articles which made him the hero of the Social Democrats and the Labor Unions.[7] *The Chamber Plays,* however, have almost always been viewed in complete isolation from these aspects of Strindberg's writing.

In the context in which they were first produced, these works were intricately bound up with politics. Both the founding of The Intimate Theater and Strindberg's later reentry into Swedish journalism in a debate over the role of the Social Democrats represent attempts on his part to participate in the political culture of Stockholm, where he had been living in relative isolation since the beginning of the decade. But the degree to which politics and aesthetics are intertwined in *The Chamber Plays* is most strikingly indicated by their debt to a style which focused on domestic interiors to the apparent exclusion of politics and contemporary society.

Both in the design of his own Intimate Theater and in the settings of the individual Chamber Plays, Strindberg drew on art nouveau. A passage from *Öppna brev till Intima Teatern* or *Open Letters to The Intimate Theater* comments on the use of this style in August Falck's staging of *The Pelican* and, moreover, suggests the relation of the style of this setting to the action of the play:

> *Den första uppsättning jag såg på Intiman var **Pelikanens**. Jag överraskades av ett rum i l'art nouveau-stil, med möbel därefter. Det var både riktigt och vackert, men där fanns något mera i det rummet; det var stämning, en vit doft av sjukrum och barnkammare, med något grönt på en byrå ditsatt av en osynlig hand. "Jag ville bo i det rummet," yttrade jag, fastän man anade den tragedi son här skulle spela sin sista akt med den antika tragediens rysligaste motiv: oskyldigt lidande barn, och humbugsmodren, Medea.*
>
> (L, 291)[8]

(The first production I saw at the "Intimate Theater" was that of *The Pelican.* I was surprised by a room in art-nouveau style, with matching furniture. This was both appropriate and attractive, but there was something else in this room: this was atmosphere, a pale fragrance of the sickroom and nursery, with something green on the bureau that had been put there by an invisible hand. "I'd like to live in that room," I uttered to myself, although one could sense the tragedy that would come to play out its last act here with the most horrifying themes of classical tragedy: innocent, suffering children and the humbug-mother, Medea.)

[my translation]

The passage evokes Strindberg's intense ambivalence concerning the domestic interiors which were the central feature of art nouveau decoration: he wanted to live there, but could not, and saw them as the site for the most terrible conflicts, conflicts which had their origins both in the family and in the world outside the home.

The art nouveau interior marks the culmination and, to some extent, the disintegration of a style of interior decorating that had echoed and affirmed the bourgeois separation of home and workplace in nineteenth-century Europe.[9] Its emphasis on crafts and organic form pointed in two very different directions. If it suggested a radical separation of the home from any kind of industrialized labor by denying the world of the factory, it also brought work back into the home. In her path-breaking study of the style in France, Debora Silverman has shown how the radical dissociation between interior and workplace reflected transformations in the French labor market. She further points out how the art nouveau interior reflected changing views of the inside of the human body, above all in the pre-psychoanalytic theories of Charcot and other French psychologists. The art nouveau household, as she presents it, is an ideological construction which allows itself to be read in terms of the interests of its inhabitants.

There is, unfortunately, no correspondingly general study of art nouveau in Scandinavia, although the catalogue of Kirk Varnedoe's recent exhibition of turn-of-the-century Scandinavian art and Lara-Vinca Masini's overview of the international art nouveau movement suggest how important the style was there. One can, however, point to Strindberg's awareness of the speciousness of the separation of home and work and to his suspicion of the genuineness of the crafted furniture. On several occasions in the second Chamber Play, for example, characters remark on the "fake" qualities of the supposedly valuable furniture in the house: like the mother in Strindberg's remarks on the art nouveau setting of *The Pelican,* it is "humbug."[10] Further, as in the theoretical writings of Charcot and Freud, the interiors of *The Chamber Plays* are sites which are traversed by invisible currents: *stämning*—atmosphere—or desire. Strindberg's own essays on psychology suggest the extent to which he was aware of the coincidence of the two.[11]

Perhaps Strindberg's relation to art nouveau in Sweden is best understood from the point of view of his early friendship with the most famous practitioner of the style in that country, Carl Larsson, whose sketches of Strindberg in the 1880s point to a time when the Swedish writer believed that the idyll suggested in art nouveau representations of the interior was possible. Larsson's well-known paintings of households decorated in the best of the Scandinavian craft tradition and filled with happy children represent everything that *The Chamber Plays* do not: these plays suggest, if anything, a nightmarish reversal of the dream.[12]

But this reversal is not just a result of the fact that the families they represent are almost always very unhappy. If as Silverman has shown, how French art nouveau interiors betray the traces of work outside the home, the settings and plots of *The Chamber Plays* make the presence of work explicit: dissatisfied and vengeful servants wreak havoc in the most private areas of the household in one play; in another, a building razed by fire disgorges the people who have done all the work to maintain it. Moreover, along with the kinds of work traditionally performed outside the middle-class household, *The Chamber Plays* also bring into focus activities not traditionally viewed as work at all: housework. Issues related to work—its distribution, its reimbursement, its monotony or lack of productivity—make the inhabitants of the worlds of Strindberg's *Chamber Plays* as unhappy as more specifically biological or sexual problems.

In these plays, the representation of work transforms the home into a political space. The middle-class interior of the nineteenth century can be viewed as a late expression, perhaps even a caricature, of the Greek *oikos*, the private realm of necessity where the unfree, women and slaves, catered to the needs of the body, while male citizens discussed politics in the public squares. The term is at the root of the word economics and evokes the problematic relation of politics to economics in political thought since the Greeks. Some political theorists, notably Hannah Arendt, see the separation between public and private suggested by the *oikos* as a healthy one, arguing that the lack of separation between politics and economics in much political theory and practice since the French Revolution has corrupted politics. More recently, however, some theorists have reexamined the separation between household and politics implied by the *oikos* in the light of the political aspects of housework. Although the history of this debate is beyond the scope of this essay, juxtaposing Strindberg's interiors to the notion of the *oikos* emphasizes the distance between the two. Despite his misogyny, he is far closer to a feminist evaluation of housework than even a radical economic theorist like Marx. There is, moreover, no area in these interiors not traversed by politics, economics, or desire. The personal here *is* political.[13]

The Intimate Theater thus served to debunk a generally accepted distinction between public and private, political and domestic spheres. In the performances of *The Chamber Plays* there, this redefinition drew not only on the action of the plays, but also on their settings. Specta-

tors entered the "intimate" theater only to be brought face to face, more often than not, with a set showing a city street through which they had to pass in order to reach the interiors where the domestic dramas took place. Further, in case the audience forgot the relation of what they saw take place onstage to some kind of larger pattern or design, Strindberg had had the stage framed by large reproduction of Böcklin's paintings, *The Isle of Life* and *The Isle of the Dead*.[14]

In Strindberg's Intimate Theater, thus, politics, the interior, and theatricality entered into a new relationship with one another and one which could best be experienced by participating in a performance of one of the *Chamber Plays* there or in a similar theatrical space. If, then, the interiors represented in the individual chamber plays make sense in a larger political and institutional context, what about the relationship of the individual plays to one another? Can they, too, be seen as embedded within a larger social or cultural context? Does this change the way they should be read or performed? In order to address these issues, I turn first to a scene from *The Ghost Sonata* that critics have most often characterized as both jarring and enigmatic and then to a reading of *The Chamber Plays* as a whole.

II

In the final scene of *The Ghost Sonata*, a virginal young woman, the pampered daughter of an aristocratic household, expires, apparently at the mere thought of housework. "What," she asks the Student who has come into her room to ask for her hand in marriage, "is the wrong thing you know?" He is able to respond quite briefly: his most detested task is sorting the laundry. She, in contrast, has a whole list, comprising all the chores the maidservant refuses to perform or performs badly. The list makes for one of the odder monologues in dramatic history:

> *Att sopa efter henne, att damma efter henne, och att göra eld i kakelugnen efter henne, hon bara lägger in veden! Att passa spjällen, att torka glasen, duka om bordet, dra upp buteljerna, öppna fönstren och vädra, bädda om min säng, skölja vattkaraffin när han blir grön av alger, köpa tändstickor och tvål, som alltid saknas, torka lampglas och klippa vekar, för att lamporna icke skola röka, och för att lamporna icke skola slockna, när det är främmande måste jag fylla dem själv.*
>
> *(XLV, 203-04)*

(To sweep up after her, to dust after her, and to start the fire in the stove after her—all she does is throw on some wood! To adjust the damper, to dry the glasses, to set the table *over* and *over* again, to pull the corks out of the bottles, to open the windows and air the rooms, to make and remake my bed, to rinse the water bottle when it's green with sediment, to buy matches and soap, which we're always out of, to wipe the chimneys and trim the wicks to keep the lamps from smoking—and to keep the lamps from going out I have to fill them myself when we have company.)

[146][15]

And think, she goes on to add, what would happen if one had, as well, to take care of the children's room—and presumably its inhabitants. She can, she tells the student, never marry him. As if in response to her complaints, a third figure appears at the door, the Cook, who carries a Japanese bottle in her hand and whom we should probably imagine as a woman of gigantic proportions. This person, the Young Woman believes is responsible for the spiritual and physical ills of her employers. "Jo, vi få många rätter, men all kraft är borta" the Young Woman had complained,

> *How kokar ur köttet, ger oss trådarne och vatten, medan hon själv dricker ur buljongen; och när det är stek, kokar hon först ur musten, äter såsen, dricker spadet; allt vad hon vidrör förlorar sin saft, det är som om hon sög med ögonen; vi få sumpen, när hon druckit kaffet, hon dricker ur vinbuteljerna och fyller med vatten.*

(XLV, 200)

(We get course after course, but all the strength is gone from the food. She boils the beef until there's nothing left of it and serves us the sinews swimming in water while she herself drinks the stock. And when we have a roast, she cooks all the juice out of it and drinks it and eats the gravy. Everything she touches loses its flavor. It's as if she sucked it up with her very eyes. We get the grounds when she has finished her coffee. She drinks the wine and fills up the bottles with water.)

[144]

Like the monologue on housework, this list, too, evokes the tedium of everyday life, as well as the absolute dependence of even the most ethereal of human beings on the repeated performance of household tasks that make life possible. This passage also suggests—more clearly than the outburst on housework—that all is not right with the young woman, as well as the household as a whole. Would a sane person blame her weakness on the presence of a vampire-cook in the kitchen?

But if the Cook's appearance resembles a nightmare, her words affirm the validity of the young woman's fears. Further, this woman, who knows what it is to perform the kinds of tasks the Young Woman abhors, gives a political interpretation to her actions: "Ni suger musten ur oss," she tells the pair,

> *och vi ur er; vi tar blodet och ni får vattnet igen—med koloriten. Det är kolorit!—Nu går jag, men jag stannar ändå, så länge jag vill!*

(XLV, 205)

(You suck the sap from us and we from you. We take the blood and give you back water—with coloring added. This is the coloring! I'm leaving now, but that doesn't mean I haven't stayed as long as I wanted to.)

[147]

The exploited, the cook suggests, take their own back in any way they can.

Whereas the Cook's words imply that class conflict and exploitation lie at the root of the household's problems, the young man sees them as a sign of the universal rottenness of human beings, especially women who, like the one he has just proposed to, are especially dangerous because they look so beautiful. This insight evokes in him a memory from his childhood: how his father had been driven to madness by former friends who had, the son believes, been turned against the family after its head told the truth about them. The Student tells the story in the longest monologue of the play—some 600 words—aware, perhaps, but untroubled by the fact that the young woman is dying before his eyes. Her death is the occasion for him to invoke Buddha and chant a stanza of a translation of *Sólarljóð*. Finally, he blesses the spirit of the dead young woman and disappears. A gigantic reproduction of Böcklin's painting, *The Isle of the Dead,* takes the place of the student, the young woman, and the Hyacinth Room.

What to make of this scene? Does it explain, diagnose, or merely embroider upon the situation in the household as a whole? What is its relation to the other four plays in the collection? Does it make sense at all? And what about its literary value? Can a play which focuses on housework pass muster?

The consensus of Strindberg's critics has been that it does not. Most see this scene as representative of the failings of *The Chamber Plays* in general: a lonely and aging dramatist cannot resist "confessing" his aversion to the household tasks he is forced to perform after the departure of his third and last wife. The references to household tasks represent a discordant note in the "music," the dreamlike atmosphere, of the collection.[16]

Yet the scene makes perfect sense within the contexts of both *The Chamber Plays* and Strindberg's work as a whole. It represents the penetration or initiation of the Student, who in this work represents the role of the wandering observer, into what he has imagined as the innermost sanctum of the household he had previously admired from the street. Like his predecessors, the Stranger in *To Damascus* and Indra's Daughter in *A Dream Play,* the Student in *The Ghost Sonata* discovers that the interior, however sealed off or insular it may appear, is as rife with conflict and disharmony as the world outside. If he gives a psychological interpretation to the death he witnesses, the interaction of the three characters onstage suggests that the explanation for the event must also include political and social conflict. Significantly, the laboring body which dies is female, and that death is represented as tragic.

The scene marks a turning point in *The Chamber Plays* sequence, although Strindberg probably did not recognize this fact until he began work on the next Chamber Play which would take up where *A Dream Play* left off. This fragment, which he soon abandoned, is set within the frame of the painting which appears at the end of the third scene of *The Ghost Sonata* and which was reproduced at one side of the stage in Strindberg's Intimate Theater: Böcklin's *The Isle of the Dead*. In this fragment, also entitled "The Isle of the Dead" ("Toten-Insel"), a corpse comes to life in the afterworld, only to take up the young girl's lament about housework: he, too, has suffered from the apparently meaningless, repetitive tasks of everyday life. Even for Strindberg, however, the representation of housework in the afterworld seems to have been too much. The remaining two plays represent a reorientation towards the social world: housework, like labor in general, may be tragic, but it is very much a this-worldly and practical concern.

The final scene of *The Ghost Sonata* by no means represents the first depiction of repetitious and nonproductive work in Strindberg's dramatic production. Consider, for example, the striking parallels between this sequence and *Miss Julie,* which was written in 1888 but had recently been revived and which Strindberg had very much in mind when he composed *The Chamber Plays.* In the earlier work as well, three characters, a man and two women, confront one another. In the later play, however, the relation between gender and class has shifted considerably. Just as Julie, like the daughter of *The Ghost Sonata,* is aristocratic, both Jean and Kristin are servants, although he, like the student in the later play, is anxious to move up in the world. In the earlier play only one character is represented as working. Although Kristin is female, she lacks both the malevolent intelligence of the cook in *The Ghost Sonata* and the pathos of the daughter of the house: Kristin *is* what she does. The later play, on the other hand, psychologizes conflicts surrounding work and class status. The cook resents, rather than identifies with, her job, and the Young Woman has been psychologically and perhaps physically crippled by an upbringing which has rendered her incapable of taking on the least practical task. Julie's fall and probable death suggest that as an anachronistic class, the aristocracy is in the process of withering away and dying. Twenty years later, the demise of apparently anachronistic class systems no longer seemed so fated: the problem, it seems, lies not with the existence of specific classes, but rather with the tendency of human beings to repeat and relive the hierarchical patterns of the past even within the most intimate aspects of their lives. In *Miss Julie* the characters were to some extent psychologically bound to inherited social roles, but in *The Chamber Plays* it is impossible to tell where psychology leaves off and role-playing begins.

Both Strindberg and Freud would agree that the young man and woman in *The Ghost Sonata* fail to marry because of patterns established within their families in early childhood. Where the two differ, however, would be in the extent to which this explanation is viewed as complete. For the psychoanalyst, all later conflicts are experienced in terms of the individual's earliest experiences within the family; for Strindberg, on the other hand, both in *The Chamber Plays* and elsewhere, the family is an integral part of the social structures surrounding it, structures which are presented as in constant flux. Strindberg and Freud differ markedly in their representation of the relation between social and sexual difference. Nowhere is this difference more apparent than in their depiction of women servants. The nursemaids in Freud's case studies, for example, who often witness or participate in scenes of infantile seduction, are presented almost exclusively as surrogates for the mother.[17] For Strindberg, however, nursemaids and women servants are both women and servants, in *The Chamber Plays,* as well as elsewhere. The Cook in *The Ghost Sonata* is a caricature both of a nurturing mother and of a loyal servant. Certainly, gender and class, motherhood and servitude, overlap for Strindberg for very personal reasons: in the opening volumes of his autobiographical novel series, he had represented himself as *Tjänstekvinnans son* (*The Son of a Serving-Woman*). But if in his works of the 1880s, gender and class serve as markers denoting the inferiority of certain social groups as well as individuals, in *The Chamber Plays,* the very notion of a hierarchy that this implies seems to have come into question. Like Freud's work of the same decade, these plays seem to have a therapeutic purpose, but their implications are social and political as well as private and psychological. Curing the malaise evoked in plays such as *Miss Julie* and *The Ghost Sonata* will require more than rescuing a child, a motif which runs throughout the collection: it may very well entail burning down or at least reordering the entire household.

III

One of the reasons *The Chamber Plays* have so often been viewed as unacceptably enigmatic is that both directors and critics have insisted on approaching the plays separately. The metaphor most often used to describe their possible unity—a unity most often depicted as flawed—is musical: certain themes, leitmotifs, run throughout the works. Each play, for example, focuses on a single building, and in several, there is a question of a fire and a child to be rescued. And here, as in Strindberg's other "dream dramas," at least one character assumes the role of an observer who both participates in and stands outside of the situation represented in the play. Generally, too, there has been a tendency to view Opus 5, *The Black Glove,* which Strindberg composed in late 1908, apart from the others.

Unlike the first four plays, written entirely in prose, *The Black Glove* contains substantial passages in verse. Further, it ends happily with the restoration of a lost child to its mother and of order to a household, and its links to public ritual and festivities—the action takes place at Christmas and turns on the activities of a *jultomte* or Christmas elf—set it apart from the far more tortured and private worlds of the others. For many critics, *The Black Glove,* like Strindberg's other late verse dramas, such as *Abu Kassems tofflor (Abu Casem's Slippers)* and *Stora landsvägen (The Great Highway),* represents a decline in the powers of the aging dramatist. The play detracts from the accomplishment of the first four *Chamber Plays.*[18]

This view of *The Black Glove,* however, grows out of the reception of Strindberg's "dream dramas" in general, a reception which emphasizes the personal and idiosyncratic, almost to the total exclusion of public aspects of performance. First of all, only two of the plays have often been revived, Opus 3, *The Ghost Sonata,* and Opus 4, *The Pelican,* and performances of these two, perhaps taking their cue from Max Reinhardt, have emphasized the aspects of the plays which suggest private nightmares. Second, *The Chamber Plays* have become part of a myth that sees Strindberg as the precursor of the ego-dramas of German Expressionism.[19] What the expressionist interpretation of Strindberg fails to see, however, is that *The Black Glove* might very well represent a conclusion to *The Chamber Plays,* a conclusion which ties the unmasking of private anguish in the first four plays to the possibility of transformations in the social world at large.

In this play, the loss and recovery of the child take place within an interior that is shown to be an integral part of a larger community, a house in which injustices can be remedied. The resolution of the conflict, moreover, takes place both through economic redistribution—the servants are paid their just wages—and through a kind of personal transformation: the young wife learns the value of her relationships to other people. And the conclusion of the play suggests a redefinition of politics to include values often associated with the domestic interior: a healthy community will include, to some extent, at least, the kind of nurturance a mother offers her child.

Strindberg himself left the relationship among the five plays open to conjecture, for although he wrote copiously on *The Chamber Plays* and his Intimate Theater, nowhere does he explicitly address this question. The *Open Letters to the Intimate Theater* suggests certain common thematic concerns among the five plays, some underlying models, such as Shakespeare's *The Tempest* and locates Strindberg's own attempt to found an intimate theater in the context of similar enterprises on the continent, but it gives no explicit instructions for the performance of these plays. Nor were they produced as a cycle at The Intimate Theater. Originally, as well, Strindberg seems to have planned a series of twenty chamber plays—one of several vast projects he scaled back or abandoned during this decade.[20] As a cycle, *The Chamber Plays* may very well represent a fragment of a larger project, although, of course, this possible fragmentary nature does not preclude their forming a coherent whole. What is clear is that Strindberg intended to include *The Black Glove* among *The Chamber Plays* and that this play makes explicit a public and social dimen-sion of the dramas that may be hidden if the plays are read or performed separately.

IV

If, then, *The Black Glove* represents a kind of conclusion to *The Chamber Plays,* what story or stories do these plays tell? Charles Mauron's psychoanalytic interpretation of Racine's dramas suggests one way of reading the sequence as a whole. For the psychoanalytic critic, the secular plays of the seventeenth-century dramatist represent different stages in a replay of the Oedipal conflict, evoking a much earlier stage of male character development projected outwards onto history.

The Chamber Plays invite a similar reading. The resonances of the black glove in the play by that name, for example, are a good illustration. Lost by the young wife, it circulates throughout the building before the old man in the attic makes possible its return. The glove, which contains the woman's wedding ring, figures both desire and loss. The glove circulates as a fetish—a symbolic representation of the phallus—from one man to the next clearly suggesting that issues associated both with castration and the formation of male identity are important aspects of *The Chamber Plays.*

But such a reading may miss the extent to which Strindberg's evocation of an "unconscious" differs from that of Freud. Mothers, not fathers, predominate in *The Chamber Plays,* while their representation of a psychological interior is far more suggestive of social and political issues than is the case in Freud's work of the same decade. In a manner similar to the embedded structures of The Intimate Theater, the sequence of plays called *The Chamber Plays* evokes an interior which is at once unspeakable and penetrated by the world outside.

Like Freud, Strindberg often worked on the basis of self-analysis, and autobiographical references in *The Chamber Plays* suggest how he drew on aspects of his personal experience in his construction of dramatic interiors which, like Freud's account of dream processes, might be recognized as typical, rather than idiosyncratic.

Storm Weather is the most explicitly autobiographical of *The Chamber Plays.* Strindberg began this play shortly after he learned of his third wife's remarriage and in letters indicated that it was very much about this subject and was intended to hurt her.[21] In *Storm Weather,* an aging man, called simply "Herrn" or "The Gentleman," observes his former wife and his child after her remarriage: by the end of the play, he seems to have accepted her departure—although not without considerable bitterness—and his imminent death, evoked by the first lighting of the street lamps of the year and the approach of winter. Similar situations recur throughout the plays in the depiction of old age, motherhood, lost children, and outsiders who peer longingly into the interiors of apartments from the city street outside. In the final play of the sequence, however, *The Black Glove,* it is most perfectly echoed and in a manner which suggests that Strindberg was consciously attempting to work through both his personal loss and what he felt was a fundamental injustice in marriage. Here, too, the representation of the young woman is not without bitterness: the Christmas elf punishes her for her lack of concern for others—her failure to appreciate her marriage or to pay her servants adequately—by temporarily removing her child. The young woman's carelessness takes the concrete form of the lost glove containing her wedding ring. Only when she realizes the value of what she has lost does the young woman find both child and ring. The character who is above all responsible for making this possible is the old man in the attic, who presents himself as a philosopher emmeshed in the web of a lifeless system and as the young woman's father. His feelings towards her are more husbandly than paternal, and the young woman's husband is significantly absent throughout the play. The old man both returns the glove to her and appears to clear the way for the restoration of peace in her marriage and in the household as a whole: he does this not only by sacrificing his claim to her, but also by dying.

If *Storm Weather* and *The Black Glove* constitute a kind of narrative frame, the three middle plays form a cycle of their own: Opus 2, *The Burned House,* opens on the smoking ruins of the childhood home of the central character, while Opus 4, *The Pelican,* closes with the suicidal rush into a fire in the home by a brother and sister who attribute all of their present unhappiness to their upbringing by a cruel and stingy mother; Opus 3, *The Ghost Sonata,* it should be noted, also opens with a reference to the mysterious collapse of a building, from which the protagonist, the Student, has rescued a child who has since disappeared.

The action of *The Burned House* suggests what is at stake in this embedded structure. As the characters sift through the ashes, they attempt to determine, not only who was responsible for the fire, but also what really happened in the past. The fruit tree in the background, which has burst prematurely into blossom in the heat of the fire, suggests a renewal that can only come through a radical break with the past but stands in sharp contrast to the dialogue of the characters, who are incapable of forgiving, forgetting, or changing: like most of the characters in *The Chamber Plays,* they seem doomed endlessly to repeat their mistakes and those of others. *The Burned House* thus can be read as posing a question which the following two plays attempt to answer: What are the origins of the failure of the old men in *Storm Weather* and *The Black Glove* to live what might be considered a good life, a life which is not only productive but also includes other people?

As three stages of an investigation, *The Burned House, The Ghost Sonata,* and *The Pelican* take us backward in time towards the possible origins of the frame situation in an unhappy childhood. The returning stranger of *The Burned House* is middle-aged (the family nurse, fru Vesterlund, is still alive) and contemplates the smoking ruins of his childhood home as if from a great distance, while in *The Pelican* the protagonist still inhabits the rooms he grew up in and, in the final scene, believes that he has returned to his childhood. *The Ghost Sonata,* the middle play, also falls into this pattern, although this work is by far the most complex of the entire collection. Here the protagonist is a young man who has left the house of his childhood, a student who perhaps believes himself to be free. In this play, however, all ages are represented and the failure of the student to break away from the past might be characterized as overdetermined. There are nothing but unhappy, criminally inclined, and physically stunted characters in the household evoked here. How could the young man have chosen differently?

The situations evoked in the three middle plays of *The Chamber Plays* seem to call for a solution far more radical than that proposed in *The Black Glove,* which points to a renewal of traditional obligations and rituals. The juxtaposition of fire and nature, especially in *The Burned House* and *The Pelican,* suggests both the anarchist tendencies of Strindberg's writing of the 1880s and the more recent aesthetic theories and practice of French writers in Mallarmé's circle, in whose work the evocation of a kind of secret fire in things was often bound up with a belief that violence, particularly fiery violence, was the best way to bring about social change.[22] But if Strindberg's belief in the rottenness of social structures had not changed since the 1880s, except perhaps to become even more profound, he no longer seems to think that a simple tearing or burning down of traditional structures will improve things. After the fire, the characters of *The Burned House* reproach one another endlessly, able to see the tree, but unable to decide what to do about it.

The five plays thus can be read as presenting five moments in time or aspects of a single situation. As a group, they pose a central question: What is to be done? *The Black Glove* suggests one solution: the happiness of the mother and child and the peace in the house point to the possibility of the renewal of old bonds and obligations, a return to the family, as a means for reconciliation, both with the past and with other people. As a whole, however, *The Chamber Plays* are more enigmatic and open-ended than the final play might suggest. What comes to the fore here is a kind of dialogic process in which the events and structures of the past are unearthed, held up to the light, scrutinized, and discussed, perhaps even changed.

This narrative reconstruction of the unity of *The Chamber Plays* suggests how Strindberg transformed personal experience into an aesthetic artifact. He worked from the outside in, the most autobiographical aspects of the plays occurring in the first and last plays of the sequence, which function as a kind of frame. Within the embedded structure of the series, he moved backwards in time in order to evoke common patterns underlying the conflicts represented in *Storm Weather* and *The Black Glove*. The process here recalls the unearthing of childhood experiences in psychoanalysis, which also attempts to help the adult by "saving" the child, except that what is called for in *The Chamber Plays* is a kind of reciprocal working through of the past, on the part of both playwright and actors and their audiences.

The embedded structure of *The Chamber Plays* series echoes the interior of The Intimate Theater. Each apparent interior gives way to another, until one is no longer certain what is inside or out, and the process seems infinitely regressive, infinitely suggestive: What interiors, after all, lurk just beyond the periphery of our vision?

Both text and performance, then, invite us to imagine our way into an interior space that is both very private and common to all of us. One can, if one chooses, compare this space, never actually seen on the stage or put into words in the text, to psychoanalytic notions of an unconscious. If so, Strindberg succeeded in evoking an unconscious that is thoroughly political.[23]

V

If Strindberg's *Chamber Plays* are among his most progressive works, it would be a mistake to see his politics as unambiguous—even here. In a clear-sighted late essay, Raymond Williams singles out the work of the Swedish dramatist as the one of the most prominent examples of the uncertain political implications of European avant-garde art at the turn of the century. In Strindberg's writing, as in many modernist works of art, a call for political change exists side by side with blatant misogyny and other forms of contempt, as well as a dangerous admiration of violence. We need, Williams argues, to rethink the work of Strindberg and other modernist artists precisely in the light of the ambiguous political heritage of modernism. Such a reevaluation is obstructed by interpretations and performances which emphasize the dream-like and psychological aspects of the plays at the expense of their public and political dimensions; even Reinhardt's productions, which might be seen as the prototypes of later performances emphasizing the isolating dream-like qualities of *The Chamber Plays*, were not divorced from German politics in the first decades of this century. As Peter Jelavich has shown, the transformations of theatrical space implied by the invention of the carbaret and intimate theater, as well as more spectacular forms of entertainment, were closely bound up with the development of and reaction against mass culture and politics at this time of the period. Theatrical production in Germany at this time was dependent on the need to find—or create—a theatrical and political community, a problem which was also of crucial importance for Strindberg when he wrote *The Chamber Plays* for his Intimate Theater.

In contrast to productions at The Intimate Theater, Reinhardt's stagings of *The Chamber Plays* were commercially as well as aesthetically successful—even in Stockholm. While it is sometimes claimed that the German director compromised the political and aesthetic ideals of less profitable avant-garde ventures, his expressionist Strindberg productions were ground-breaking.[24] Moreover, Reinhardt is to my knowledge the only director to have staged all five *Chamber Plays,* although never in sequence.[25] One wishes he had taken the step, consistent with one important precedent for both his own and Strindberg's work, Wagner's *Ring,* of directing all five plays in sequence.

The one recent performance to emphasize the political dimension of Strindberg's late work, Ingmar Bergman's *The Ghost Sonata* of 1973, illustrates some of the problems confronting a director who stages one of these plays in isolation. If Bergman directed certain scenes, above all the confrontation between the cook and the young man and young woman, to bring out the element of class conflict in Strindberg's text, the political implications of these sequences are overshadowed by the play's ending, which, in Bergman's production, is even bleaker and more isolating than Strindberg's. For the final scene, he chose not to exhibit the Böcklin reproduction, but rather to let the stage gradually darken.[26]

Many directors and critics have found the appearance of *The Isle of the Dead* at the end of *The Ghost Sonata* time-bound and distracting. Bergman's decision, then, reflects a common desire to cut through those aspects of the play that have a period flavor to its aesthetic and existential core. This choice, however, removes a political and narrative dimension implied by the ending of Strindberg's text, where the painting points not only to another chamber play he never finished, but also other places, other communities, in this world as well as—possibly—the next, and to the implications of the student's actions.

Strindberg's *Chamber Plays* need to be read and seen in relation to one another, as part of a sequence that includes *The Black Glove.* Such performances might take as their model other cycles produced during the last 150 years, cycles intended, like *The Chamber Plays,* to bring into being a new theatrical and political community. Stagings might also reflect more closely early presentations at Strindberg's Intimate Theater. Most late twentieth-century versions of *The Ghost Sonata,* it is true, take place within a small theatrical space. Few, however, frame the stage with reproductions of Böcklin's painting, so that the final appearance of *The Isle of the Dead* also suggests the consequences of one possible choice at the end of the play. Allusions should be made to the political issues at stake in Strindberg's version of intimate theater: to the parallels between Strindberg's criticisms of the nuclear family and depiction of the larger community residing in a single house and the development in Sweden at this time of a notion of the state as a home for all its members.

Similarly, it should be made clear that Strindberg's very mixed representation of women in these plays, often attributed solely to the failure of his third marriage, reflects public debates on women's participation in any kind of state. And it would be helpful to tie the fires of *The Burned House* and *The Pelican* to more than a personal anarchism.

Further, it would be illuminating to emphasize the voyeuristic aspects of *The Chamber Plays,* which like many of Strindberg's dramatic works anticipate the development of the film close-up in their attempt to bring the spectator closer than ever before to the character onstage. The dissolution of traditional distinctions between public and private in these works has its dangerous or oppressive aspects. A good performance might make the spectator aware of his or her desire to *see* what under some circumstances might better be left unseen.

Such a performance of Strindberg's *Chamber Plays* would have more than an antiquarian value. It might bring us face to face with the ambiguous political heritage of modernism and our own participation in it.[27]

Notes

1. On the subject of Max Reinhardt and Strindberg, see Kvam; and Styan esp. 33-50.

2. On turn-of-the-century theater, see Gould; Szondi, *Das lyrische Drama;* and Jelavich esp. 39-85 and 236-46. For a suggestive discussion of the poetic or readerly aspects of *The Chamber Plays,* see Sprinchorn, Introduction.

3. Rokem discusses Strindberg's representation of public and private in the context of cinematic aspects of his plays.

4. Even those critics who do approach the collection as a whole emphasize the affinities of *The Chamber Plays* with music and poetry. See, for example, Hallberg; Sprinchorn, Introduction and Ward 239-68. An allegorical interpretation of the plays can be found in most commentaries on them; for a representative study, see Sprinchorn, *Strindberg* 246-75.

5. The best overview of Strindberg's intellectual development is still Lamm's *August Strindberg.* On Strindberg's attitudes towards women, see Boethius, although this study covers Strindberg's work only through the mid-1880s.

6. Most critics make this point. See, for example, Boethius and Steene.

7. The articles have been published by Järv. See Meidal for a discussion of the debate.

8. All references to Strindberg's works in the original Swedish come from *Samlade skrifter.* The new edition of the *Kammarspel,* volume 58 of *August Strind-*

bergs Samlade Verk (Stockholm: Norstedts, 1991), came into my hands as I was working on the final revision of this article. The same is true of Eivor Martinus's attractive translation of all of the *Chamber Plays.* Martinus also makes a case for the performance of the entire series, although her suggestions differ from my argument here that they should be presented in sequence: "In an ideal world, I would like to see these five plays performed in repertoire, using the same set, starting with the autumn play, Opus 1 where the action takes place both outside and inside the building, proceeding to Opus 5, *The Black Glove* which also uses the whole building and takes place at Christmas, then on to *The Pelican* which is confined to a claustrophobic flat that goes up in flames; this leads naturally on to the burnt house in *After the Fire* early in the spring, finishing in a surreal landscape in *The Ghost Sonata.* With a dozen actors, an imaginative set and trimmed versions of the plays it could be a riveting experience" (12).

9. For an overview of representations of the bourgeois interior and some common interpretations, see Perrot. See also Adorno, Benjamin, and Rybczynski.

10. See *Samlade skrifter* 40: 114; and Sprinchorn et al., *The Chamber Plays* 79.

11. See especially the essays, "Hjärnornas kamp" ("The Battle of the Brains"), "Nemesis divina," "Mystik—tills vidare" ("Mysticism—for Now"), and "Själamord" ("Soul Murder"), in *Samlade skrifter* 22: 123-157 and 163-201. There is, unfortunately, no overview of Strindberg's psychological theories. But on psychology in his work in the 1880s, see Lindström. See also Vogelweith.

12. On Strindberg's opinion of Carl Larsson at the time he wrote *The Chamber Plays,* see his essay in *En blå bok 2,* "Hopljugna karaktärer" ("Characters Composed of Lies"), in *Samlade Skrifter* 47: 780-88. See also Lagerkranz esp. 123-144, and 406-07.

13. See Arendt esp. 22-78. For a sympathetic but critical evaluation of her position, see Pitkin. For Arendt, as for many of the economic thinkers she criticizes, housework, like all repetitive labor, is intrinsically apolitical.

14. Few interpretations of *The Chamber Plays* call attention to the presence of reproductions of both paintings in The Intimate Theater. For a recent exception, see Fraser. See also Stockenström and Vowles.

15. Unless otherwise noted, translations from the first four chamber plays come from Sprinchorn et al., *The Chamber Plays*

16. See, for example, Ollén, *Strindbergs dramatik* 258; and Lamm, *Strindbergs Dramer* 2: 401.

17. See Swan, however, for a wide-ranging interpretation that emphasizes the political dimensions of Freud's representation of women servants. See also Grigg;

McGrath 213-17; and the essays collected in Bernheimer and Kahane for a consideration of Freud's representation of women from a mostly Lacanian perspective.

18. Meyer's appraisal of *The Black Glove* sums up the arguments for its omission: "*The Black Glove* is a Christmas piece, a slight morality play about a shrewish young woman who loses a ring and accuses her servant of stealing it; for this, she is punished by having her small daughter stolen from her, regaining her only when she herself has been chastised and purified. Strindberg wrote it, as he did *Abu Casem,* in humdrum verse and, like *Abu Casem,* it was rejected by the Stockholm theatres but performed by a touring company in the provinces, with his daughter Greta in the lead" (522). In the introduction to her very recent translation of all of the *Chamber Plays,* however, Eivor Martinus gives a far more positive interpretation of the play that emphasizes its links to the first four of the series.

19. Even Szondi fails to see beyond this myth. On the implications of this interpretation, see Sokel's very useful survey.

20. For an overview of the genesis of *The Chamber Plays,* see Paul 86-96.

21. On the autobiographical aspects of *Oväder,* see Ollén 241-47; and Meyer 476-77.

22. For an account of anarchist tendencies in Strindberg's work through 1890, see Edqvist. The theme of fire in *The Chamber Plays* also recalls the aesthetics of some French writers in Mallarmé's circle who not only espoused anarchist theories but also were activists. On this subject, see Halperin.

23. The notion of a political literary unconscious has been explored from a Lacanian perspective by Jameson.

24. For a balanced assessment of Reinhardt's work, see Styan esp. 1-16.

25. See Styan, 128-56, for a list of Reinhardt's productions. He staged Strindberg's *Black Glove* on February 26, 1918, at the Kammerspiele in Berlin.

26. See Törnqvist for a detailed account of this production.

27. I would like to thank Peter Jelavich and Linda Henderson for their comments on earlier versions of this essay.

Works Cited

Adorno, Theodor. *Kierkegaard: Zur Konstruktion des Aesthetischen.* Vol. 2 of *Gesammelte Schriften.* Frankfurt a.M.: Suhrkamp, 1979.

Arendt, Hannah. *The Human Condition.* Chicago: U of Chicago P, 1958.

Benjamin, Walter. *Das Passagen-Werk.* Ed. Rolf Tiedemann. 2 vols. Edition suhrkamp 1200/neue folge 2000. Frankfurt a.M.: Suhrkamp, 1983.

Bernheimer, Charles, and Claire Kahane, eds. *In Dora's Case: Freud—Hysteria—Feminism.* New York: Columbia UP, 1985.

Boethius, Ulf. *Strindberg och kvinnofrdgan till och med Giftas I.* Stockholm: Prisma, 1968.

Edqvist, Sven-Gustaf. *Samhällets fiende: En Strindbergsstudie.* Stockholm: Tidens, 1961.

Fraser, Catherine C. "Visual Clues to Interpreting *Spöksonaten.*" *Scandinavian Studies* 63 (1991): 281-92.

Gould, Evlyn. *Virtual Theater: From Diderot to Mallarmé.* Baltimore: Johns Hopkins UP, 1989.

Grigg, Kenneth A. "All Roads Lead to Rome: The Role of the Nursemaid in Freud's Dreams." *Journal of the American Psychoanalytic Association* 21 (1963): 108-26.

Hallberg, Peter. "Strindbergs Kammarspel." *Edda* 58 (1958): 1-21.

Halperin, Joan U. *Félix Fénéon, Aesthete and Anarchist in Fin-de-Siècle Paris.* New Haven: Yale UP, 1988.

Jameson, Fredric. *The Political Unconscious: Narrative as a Socially Symbolic Act.* Ithaca: Cornell UP, 1981.

Järv, Harry, ed. *Strindbergsfejden.* 2 vols. Staffanstorp: Cavefors, 1968.

Jelavich, Peter. *Munich and Theatrical Modernism: Politics, Playwriting, and Performance, 1890-1914.* Cambridge: Harvard UP, 1985.

Kvam, Kela. *Max Reinhardt og Strindbergs visionaere Dramatik.* Copenhagen: Akademisk, 1974.

Lagerkranz, Olof. *August Strindberg.* Stockholm: Wahlström och Widstrand, 1979.

Lamm, Martin. *Strindbergs Dramer.* 2 vols. Stockholm: Bonniers, 1924-26.

———. *August Strindberg.* 1949. Stockholm: Aldus/Bonniers, 1968.

Lindström, Hans. *Hjärnornas kamp: Psykologiska idéer och motiv i Strindbergs åttiotalsdiktning.* Uppsala: Appelberg, 1952.

Martinus, Eivor, trans. *The Chamber Plays.* By August Strindberg. Bath, England: Absolute, 1991.

———. Introduction. *The Chamber Plays.* By August Strindberg. Trans. Eivor Martinus. Bath, England: Absolute, 1991. 4-12.

Masini, Lara-Vinca. *Art Nouveau.* Trans. Linda Fairbairn. London: Thames and Hudson, 1984.

Mauron, Charles. *L'Inconscient dans l'oeuvre et la vie de Racine.* Gap: Ophrys, 1957.

McGrath, William J. *Freud's Discovery of Psychoanalysis: The Politics of Hysteria.* Ithaca: Cornell UP, 1986.

Meidal, Björn. *Från profet till folktribun: Strindberg och Strindbergsfejden, 1910-12.* Stockholm: Tidens, 1982.

Meyer, Michael. *Strindberg: A Biography.* Oxford: Oxford UP, 1987.

Ollén, Gunnar. *Strindbergs dramatik.* 1961. Stockholm: Prisma, 1966.

Paul, Fritz. *August Strindberg.* Stuttgart: Metzler, 1979.

Perrot, Michelle, ed. *From the Fires of the Revolution to the Great War.* Trans. Arthur Goldhammer. Vol. 4 of *A History of Private Life.* Ed. Philippe Ariès and Georges Duby. 4 vols. to date. Cambridge: Harvard/Belknap, 1990.

Pitkin, Hanna Fenichel. "Justice: On Relating Public and Private." *Political Theory* 9 (1981): 327-352.

Rokkum, Freddie. *Theatrical Space in Ibsen, Chekhov and Strindberg: Public Forms of Privacy.* Ann Arbor: U of Michigan P, 1986.

Rybczynski, Witold. *Home: A Short History of an Idea.* New York: Viking, 1986.

Schorske, Carl. *Fin-de-Siècle Vienna: Politics and Culture.* New York: Random House, 1981.

Silverman, Debora. *Art Nouveau in Fin-de-Siècle France.* Berkeley: U of California P, 1989.

Sokel, Walter. *The Writer in Extremis: Expressionism in Twentieth-Century German Literature.* Stanford: Stanford UP, 1959.

Sprinchorn, Evert, Seabury Quinn, Jr., and Kenneth Peterson, trans. *The Chamber Plays.* By August Strindberg. 2nd edition. U of Minnesota P, 1981.

———. Introduction. *The Chamber Plays.* By August Strindberg. Trans. Evert Sprinchorn, Seabury Quinn, Jr., and Kenneth Peterson. 2nd edition. Minneapolis: U of Minnesota P, 1981.

———. *Strindberg as Dramatist.* New Haven: Yale UP, 1982.

Steene, Birgitta. *The Greatest Fire: A Study of August Strindberg.* Carbondale: Southern Illinois UP, 1963.

Stockenström, Göran. "The Journey from the Isle of Life to the Isle of Death: The Idea of Reconciliation in *The Ghost Sonata.*" *Scandinavian Studies* 50 (1968): 133-49.

Strindberg, August. *Samlade skrifter.* Ed. John Landqvist. 55 vols. Stockholm: Bonniers, 1912-1919.

———. *Toten-Insel. Samlade otryckta skrifter.* 2 vols. Stockholm: Bonniers, 1918-19. 1: 295-310.

———. *The Chamber Plays.* Trans. Evert Sprinchorn, Seabury Quinn, Jr., and Kenneth Peterson. 2nd edition. Minneapolis: U of Minnesota P, 1981.

———. *The Chamber Plays.* Trans. Eivor Martinus. Bath, England: Absolute, 1991.

Styan, J. L. *Max Reinhardt.* Cambridge: Cambridge UP, 1982.

Swan, Jim. "*Mater* and Nannie: Freud's Two Mothers and the Discovery of the Oedipus Complex." *American Imago* 31 (1974): 1-64.

Szondi, Peter. *Das lyrische Drama des Fin de Siècle.* Ed. Henriette Beese. Vol. 4 of the Studienausgabe der Vorlesungen. Suhrkamp taschenbuch wissenschaft 90. Frankfurt a.M.: Suhrkamp, 1975.

———. *Theory of the Modern Drama.* Trans. Michael Hays. Minneapolis: U of Minnesota P, 1987.

Törnqvist, Egil. *Bergman och Strindberg. Spöksonaten— drama och iscensättning. Dramaten 1973.* Stockholm: Prisma, 1973.

Varnedoe, Kirk. *Northern Light: Nordic Art at the Turn of the Century.* New Haven: Yale UP, 1988.

Vogelweith, Guy. *Le Psychothéâtre de Strindberg (un auteur en quête de métamorphose).* Paris: Klinksieck, 1972.

Vowles, Richard. "Strindberg's *Isle of the Dead.*" *Modern Drama* 3 (1962): 366-78.

Ward, John. *The Social and Religious Plays of Strindberg.* London: Athlone, 1980.

Williams, Raymond. "The Politics of the Avant-Garde." *The Politics of Modernism: Against the New Conformists.* London: Verso, 1989. 49-63.

Egil Törnqvist (essay date summer 1996)

SOURCE: Törnqvist, Egil. "The Strindbergian One-Act Play." *Scandinavian Studies* 68, no. 3 (summer 1996): 356-69.

[*In the following essay, Törnqvist examines Strindberg's one-act plays.*]

Strindberg's international reputation as a dramatist is usually connected with two enterprises. Before the so-called Inferno Crisis in the mid-1890s, he was an eminent representative of naturalist drama. His famous preface to *Fröken Julie* [*Miss Julie*] is generally recognized along with Zola's *Le Naturalisme au théâtre* as its most important manifesto. After the Inferno Crisis, he penned his preexpressionist plays, in which the protagonists are more in conflict with themselves and with the Powers, as Strindberg termed them, than with each other. Both enterprises have been rather extensively researched.

Strindberg's two other notable contributions to modern drama have received considerably less attention and recognition. I refer to his cycle of plays about the Swedish royals—we would have to go to Shakespeare to find a counterpart—and to his commitment to the one-act play as a serious and independent form of drama, our concern at the moment.

One of the relatively few scholarly works devoted to the one-act play as a genre unequivocally states that "seit Strindbergs theoretischem Debüt von 1889 muss der Einakter als eigenständige Gattung gelten" (Schnetz, 24) [since Strindberg's theoretical debut in 1889, the one-act play must count as an independent genre].[1] Such a statement certainly invites more attention to Strindberg's one-act plays than has hitherto been bestowed on them.[2]

Schnetz speaks of the one-act play (*der Einakter*), not of the short play (*das Kurzdrama*). The distinction, although important, is rarely made. To qualify as a one-act play, I would suggest, a play must not contain any intermission, curtain, or black-out indicating a change of time and/or place. The "short play" or *Kurzdrama* is of another order. It is of course true that most one-act plays are fairly short, but their length, which is usually considered of great importance, is in fact irrelevant to the question of whether they are one-act plays. Thus Strindberg's **Fröken Julie** and **Fordringsägare** [**Creditors**], both plays that fill a whole evening, formally qualify as one-act plays, although **Fröken Julie,** with its intermediate "Ballet," is arguably a disguised two-act play. Strindberg's Chamber Plays, on the other hand, whose performance time is about the same, do not qualify as one-act plays; lacking a unity of time and to some extent of place, they are divided into different parts separated by, one must assume, a curtain or a black-out.

According to this single, intersubjective criterion, Strindberg penned fourteen one-act plays. Of these, two—the verse drama **I Rom** [**In Rome**] and the historical play **Den fredlöse** [**The Outlaw**]—belong to Strindberg's earliest period, while the puppet play **Kaspers fettisdag** [**Casper's Shrove Tuesday**] is relatively late. The remaining eleven were all written between 1888 and 1892 during the playwright's so-called naturalist period. In the following, I shall limit myself to these eleven one-act plays of the middle period and focus on two of them: **Den starkare** and **Inför döden** [**In the Face of Death**].

When Schnetz speaks of Strindberg's debut as a theoretician in 1889, she refers to the article "Om modernt drama och modern teater" ["On Modern Drama and Modern Theater"] published in the Danish journal *Ny jord*.[3] But Strindberg had, in fact, commented on the one-act form the year before. In his preface to **Fröken Julie,** he says:

Vad det tekniska i kompositionen angår, har jag på försök strukit aktindelningen. Detta emedan jag trott mig finna, att vår avtagande formåga av illusion möjli-

gen skulle störas av mellanakter, under vilka åskådaren får tid att reflektera och därigenom undandrages författaren-magnetisörens suggestiva inflytande. . . . Min mening vore framdeles få en publik så uppfostrad att den kunde sitta ut ett helaftonsspektakel i en enda akt, men detta fordrar undersökningar först.

(*Samlade Verk*, 27: 109-10)

As for the technical aspects of composition, I have experimented with eliminating act divisions. The reason is that I believe our dwindling capacity for accepting illusion is possibly further disturbed by intermissions, during which the spectator has time to reflect and thereby escape the suggestive influence of the author-hypnotist. . . . My hope for the future is to so educate audiences that they can sit through a one-act play that lasts an entire evening. But this will require experimentation.

(*Five Plays*, 72-3)

The quotation suggests that Strindberg's interest in the one-act play is directly related to his ambition, as a naturalist playwright, to create maximal illusion.

In "Om modernt drama och modern teater," he notes that the "new"—i.e. naturalist—drama pays more attention to character description than to plot, that the unities of time and place are observed, and that in "det betydelsefulla motivets uppsökande," ["searching for the significant motif"], the playwrights focus on,

livets två poler, liv och död . . . kampen om makan, om existensmedlen, om äran, alla dessa strider, med deras slagfält, jämmerskri, sårade och döde, varunder man hörde den nya världsåskådningen om livet såsom kamp blåsa sina befruktande sunnanvindar.

Det var tragedier, sådana man icke sett förr; men de unga författarne . . . tycktes själva rygga för att påtruga sina lidanden på andra mera än nödigt var, och därför göra de pinan så kort som möjligt, låta smärtan rasa ut i en akt, stundom i en enda scen.

(*Samlade skrifter*, 17: 298-9)

life's two poles, life and death . . . the fight for the spouse, for the means of subsistence, for honor, all these struggles—with their battlefield cries of woe, wounded and dead during which one heard a new philosophy of life conceived as a struggle, blow its fertile winds from the south.

These were tragedies such as had not been seen before. The young authors . . . seemed reluctant to impose their suffering on others more than was absolutely necessary. Therefore, they made the suffering as brief as possible, let the pain pour forth in one act, sometimes in a single scene.

(Cole, 18-9)

Strindberg then sketches the history of the short one-act play, the *quart d'heure*, which he sees as the paradigmatic form for the presentation of modern man. At the same time, he regards "den utförda enaktaren" ["the fully executed one-act play"] as "det kommande dramats formule" ["the formula of the drama to come"]. Using Musset's proverbs as a model, one might, he declares, "[m]ed hjälp av ett bord och två stolar . . . få framställda de starkaste konflikter livet bjuder" ["by means of a table and two chairs . . . present the most powerful conflicts of life"], and this by resorting to "den moderna psykologiens upptäcter" (*Samlade skrifter,* 17: 301) ["the discoveries of modern psychology"] (Cole, 20-1).

At the time, Strindberg was strongly influenced by the so-called psychology of suggestion and was extremely anxious to be staged in Paris, where Zolaesque naturalism was *en vogue*. At the same time, he was trying to establish his Scandinavian Experimental Theater. These three facts explain why Strindberg precisely at this moment was so concerned with psychological, naturalistic one-act drama. As always, he desired to be abreast of the most recent developments, especially when they related to scientific achievements.

The demand of naturalism that staged events should mirror real ones is eminently fulfilled in the one-act play in the sense that unity of time and place are usually observed—so much so that the playing time (Germ. *Spielzeit*) often precisely corresponds with the scenic time (Germ. *gespielte Zeit,* the time assumed to pass between the raising and lowering of the curtain), a circumstance that does not occur in plays of more than one act.

Although Strindberg never became an out-and-out naturalist and definitely rejects what he calls petty naturalism, the eleven one-act plays he wrote between 1888 and 1892 may for want of a better label be considered naturalistic dramas. A congruence of playing time and scenic time characterizes *Den starkare, Paria,* and *Första varningen:* in all three the unity of place is also strictly observed. In *Första varningen,* Strindberg even alludes to this synchronism when, in the beginning, he has the Gentleman state that he is to leave in half an hour. The reason for observing these unities may well be a naturalist endeavor on Strindberg's part to heighten the slice-of-life character of these plays. Contrary to what is often assumed, *Fröken Julie* is in this respect less faithful to the requirements of naturalist verisimilitude. The drama is marked by a certain discrepancy between the playing time (around an hour and a half) and the scenic time (around twelve hours). But significantly the playwright disguises this discrepancy by having dancing peasants invade the kitchen midway through the play. The time seems extended, and there is no need for a curtain which means that the illusion of the spectator is never broken.

Given its brevity, the one-act play offers little possibility for varied description of characters and environment. The naturalistic emphasis on inherited traits and environment as determining factors is in many respects better suited to the narrative, as for example novel cycles like Zola's *Les Rougon-Macquart,* than to the concise and stylized form that the one-act play exemplifies. Here even the main characters tend to be types rather than individuals, and the limited scenic time prevents or at least obstructs the depiction of decisive mental changes. On the other hand, the fact that drama-in-performance by definition is a sensuous form presenting not by way of narration but in flesh and blood means that the drama in this sense concords better with the demands of naturalism than the epic. Yet this is more true of the play in several acts than of the one-act play. And in principle even more true of the modern equivalent of the nineteenth-century serial, the television soap opera. The one-act play, by contrast, lends itself to depicting parabolic situations. Here we deal not so much with people in conflict with each other as with man in conflict with an outward or inward fate. Existential and universal problems reign supreme.

It is hardly surprising, therefore, that in the studies devoted to the one-act play as genre, the naturalist one-act play has received only modest attention. While Schnetz focuses on the absurdist one-act play, Rudolf Halbritter discusses what he sees as the three main categories of the (Anglo-American) short play—the symbolist (Yeats), the epic-didactic (Wilder), and the grotesque (Pinter), and there are "vergleichweise wenige naturalistische und impressionistische Kurzdramen" (Halbritter, 28) [relatively few naturalistic and impressionistic short plays].

The question arises whether naturalism is inimical to the one-act form. If so, are Strindberg's "naturalist" one-act plays less faithful to naturalism than one generally assumes? Or, if we maintain that Strindberg's one-act plays are indeed naturalistic, do they represent a blind alley avoided by later playwrights? I believe there is something to be said for both. On one hand, Strindberg's one-act plays are more stylized and less naturalistic than usually thought. On the other, since the general trend in modern drama has been away from naturalism, we cannot expect any flourishing of this type of drama in plays intended for the stage, but rather in other media—radio, television. . . .

[I]n the lists of *dramatis personae,* Strindberg sometimes designates his characters by name, sometimes only by blood or other relationship (father, daughter, son-in-law), sometimes by profession, and sometimes by abstraction (Mr. X, Miss Y). The unavoidable conclusion is that the naturalistic Strindbergian one-act play is a protean phenomenon. Its homogeneity depends not so much on formal characteristics, as on thematic coherence—not surprisingly considering the author's own situation at the time, matrimonial relations stand central—coupled with an exceedingly dense dialogue, rich in subtext, and an almost cynical tone associated with the *comédie rosse.*

Strindberg's pioneering contribution is perhaps most noticeable in the shortest of his one-act plays, the monodrama ***Den starkare*** [***The Stronger***],[4] where the author dramatizes the coincidental meeting between two actresses in a cafe on Christmas Eve. At the end of Mrs. X's long monologue—Miss Y does not say a word—it is clear that Miss Y has been, and perhaps still is, the mistress of Mrs. X's husband.

Den starkare can be classified as a combination of monologue and duo-drama. Miss Y's reactions are extremely important, since they both motivate and qualify Mrs. X's statements. But the monodrama form is not unproblematic. While the exposition in a normal play usually is handled by secondary characters, whose "objective" information often ironically contrasts with the versions of the main characters, in ***Den starkare*** the protagonist, Mrs. X, must provide the exposition herself. As a result she presents both factual information and subjective interpretation of this information. Indeed part of the play's suggestive power lies in the fact that it is so hard to separate the one from the other.

Impressed by the French *quart d'heure* plays, Strindberg wrote ***Den starkare*** for the Scandinavian Experimental Theater he had founded in November 1888. It is likely that he wrote both parts in the play for his wife Siri von Essen; in performances in Sweden Siri, who was a Swedish-speaking Finn, could do the speaking part; in performances in Denmark she could do the silent one. The fact that the little theater group consisted of both Swedish- and Danish-speaking actors may, in fact, have contributed to Strindberg's choice of the monodrama form. According to another hypothesis, Strindberg wrote ***Den starkare*** to demonstrate that the monologue need not be banished from naturalist drama (*Strindbergs dramer,* 4:7). In the preface to ***Fröken Julie*** he notes: "Monologen är nu av våra realister bannlyst såsom osannolik, men om jag motiverar den, får jag den sannolik, och kan således begagna den med fördel" (*Samlade Verk,* 27:110) ["Our realists today condemn the monologue as implausible, but if I motivate it, I can make it plausible and use it to advantage"] (*Five Plays,* 72). By including Miss Y in the play, Strindberg could motivate Mrs. X's long monologue from a naturalist *tranche-de-vie* point of view, despite the fact that Mrs. X at times seems to be thinking aloud rather than addressing Miss Y. Far from a shortcoming, these fluctuations between soliloquy and monologue add to the suggestiveness and psychological depth of the playlet.

What is the relationship between Strindberg's one-act play and those in more than one act? In his influential *Theorie des modernen Dramas,* Peter Szondi devotes a short chapter to the one-act play under the telling title "Rettungsversuche" ["Rescue Attempts"]. When a number of leading playwrights began to write one-act plays in the 1880s, it was, according to Szondi, a symptom that the traditional form of drama had by that time become so undramatic that it had become problematic. The one-act play is an attempt to replace the tension based on diluted interhuman conflicts with a tension outside human relations. Instead of a conflict between the characters, the one-act play offers an existential or metaphysical conflict between man and some force outside him which he cannot master: fate, providence, or, to use Strindberg's expression, the Powers.

The most obvious example of this transition from one type of conflict to another Szondi finds precisely in Strindberg's work. Both in the three-act ***Fadren*** [***The Father***] and the one-act ***Inför döden,*** he points out, the protagonist is haunted by satanic women. But while the Captain in ***Fadren*** has an obvious antagonist in his wife Laura, Durand in ***Inför döden,*** being a widower, no longer has an antagonist,

> [. . .] *was Strindbergs Absage an die Intrige ausdrückt, zugleich die Annäherung des Einakters, der kein Geschehen mehr kennt, an die "analytische Technik". Die "weibliche Hölle" bilden Herrn Durands Töchter, die ihre Mutter gegen ihn erzog. Sein Untergang droht aber nicht von ihnen, sondern von außen her: die Pension, die er leitet, steht vor dem Bankrott. Daraus spricht die Ersetzung des Zwischenmenschlichen durchs Objektive, die Umbergründung der dramatischen Spannung, die nun von der Situation und nicht mehr von der Auseinandersetzung zwischen Mensch und Mensch geschaffen wird. Freilich schildert Strindberg seinen Helden nicht in völliger Ohnmacht. Er entgeht dem Bankrott, indem er sein Haus anzündet und Gift nimmt, um seinen Töchtern mit der Versicherungssumme zum Wohlstand zu verhelfen. Aber die "Handlung" des Einakters ist keine Folge von Ereignissen, die in den Entschluß zum Selbstmord münden, auch nicht die seelische Entwicklung, die diesem vorausgeht, sondern die Exposition eines von Haß und Zwist unterhöhlten Familienlebens, die ibsensche Analyse einer unglücklichen Ehe, die im gespannten Raum der nahenden Katastrophe, auch ohne daß ihnen eine neue Handlung beigegeben würde, zu "dramatischer" Wirkung gelangen.*
>
> (Szondi, 94-5)

[. . .] a sign indicating Strindberg's renunciation of intrigue and, at the same time, the movement of the one-act, which no longer inscribes an event, toward the "analytical technique." The "female hell" is created by Durand's daughters, who oppose him because their mother has raised them to do so. The threat of destruction does not come from them, however, but from outside his family: the pension that he manages is on the verge of bankruptcy. This shift corresponds to a displacement of the interpersonal by the objective, the refounding of dramatic tension, which will now be guaranteed by the situation rather than by a conflict between individuals. To be sure, Strindberg does not make his hero completely helpless. Durand escapes bankruptcy by setting fire to his house and taking poison so that his daughters can live comfortably from his insurance benefits. But the "action" of this one-act is not a series of incidents leading to his decision to kill himself or a portrayal of the psychological development that precedes this decision. Instead it is an exposition of family life undermined by hate and discord—an Ibsenesque analysis of an unhappy marriage, which, in the taut space of approaching catastrophe, achieves "dramatic" efficacy despite the absence of any additional new action.

(57)

Using *Inför döden* as a paradigm, Szondi sees the one-act play as one of many indications of the dedramatization and interiorization that is characteristic of modern drama and that constitutes its crisis. It is obvious that this view strongly contrasts with that of Strindberg. To him the one-act play, far from being dedramatized, is highly dramatic, since here everything unessential and distracting has been removed so that the fundamental opposition, what Strindberg terms the meaningful motif, is enacted. Szondi's and Strindberg's contrasting views represent two very different opinions of what dramatic tension or suspense actually means. While Strindberg is certainly anxious to demonstrate that the one-act play is a viable form within the framework of the naturalist aesthetic, Szondi is equally anxious to prove that it fits his overall idea that modern drama has become increasingly dedramatized and epic in nature.

An important question, in this context, is whether Szondi's description of *Inför döden*—this *King Lear* in miniature—is valid. The threat comes from outside, he writes; interhuman relations have been replaced by something extraneous. Such a characterization is, to put it mildly, a singular way of interpreting the play, determined, no doubt, by Szondi's need to make it fit his thesis about the problematic displacement of conflict in modern drama.

It is true that the bankruptcy of the pension fund constitutes an impending threat in the play, but two questions are of central importance: How did the bankruptcy come about and can the danger be avoided? In both cases, we deal with inter-human questions of guilt and responsibility. "Herr Durand," Smedmark says, "står inför valet att leva och se döttrarna gå under eller att offra livet och låta brandförsäkringen ge dem en ny start" (*Strindbergs dramer,* 4: 242) [has the choice between staying alive and seeing his daughters perish or sacrificing his life and letting the fire insurance give them a new start]. Such an interpretation is correct except for the verb form: Durand does not have a choice, Szondi here could protest, he had a choice. When the play opens he has already decided to sacrifice himself.

The play is structured in such a way that in the first eight scenes the audience sees the daughters' accusations against Durand, partly based on the dead wife's will. Durand is said to have been a deserter during the Franco-Prussian war, to have left his job with the railway, and to have squandered his means on the house. Not until the ninth and final scene is the audience informed about the true state of affairs by Durand himself. Far from having

deserted, he had on the contrary, volunteered to fight for his country, and his prodigal wife had squandered his means and forced him to leave his position with the railroad. Why then does Durand not protest against the unjust accusations? Strindberg provides a psychological explanation toward the end of the play when he has Durand, whose very name suggests his ability to endure, tell his eldest daughter:

> *Jag ville icke kasta in ofrid i era unga sinnen och komma er att tvivla på er mors förträfflighet, därför teg jag. Jag hade varit hennes korsdragare ett helt äkta samliv; bar alla hennes fel på min rygg, tog alla följderna av hennes misstag på mig, tills jag slutligen trodde mig vara den skyldige. Och hon var icke sen att tro sig först vara oförvitlig, sedan offret! "Skyll på mig", brukade jag säga när hon riktigt invecklat sig i något trassel. Och hon skyllde! Och jag bar! Men ju mer hon kom i skuld till mig, dess mer hatade hon mig med hela tacksamskyldighetens gränslösa hat, och slutligen föraktade hon mig, för att stärka sig av inbillningen att hon narrat mig! Och sist lärde hon er förakta mig också, för hon behövde ett stöd i sin svaghet! . . . Och för er blev jag en stackare, när jag var god, ett kräk när jag var finkänslig, en usling när ni fick er vilja fram och ni ruinerat huset.*

(Samlade Verk, 33: 178)

I didn't want to inflict anxiety and uneasiness on you young ones and cause you to doubt your mother's good character. . . . That is why I kept quiet! I had carried the cross for her throughout our whole married life. . . . I bore all the shortcomings and defects on my back, took upon me all the consequences of her mistakes—until, at last, I began to feel and believe that I was the guilty one. And it didn't take her long to come to the conclusion, first, that she was without blame, and, finally, that she was the victim! I used to say to her, whenever she had enmeshed herself in some serious muddle, "Blame it on me!" And she did! And I carried the brunt of the load and suffered for it! But, the more deeply she became indebted to me, the more she hated me with all the boundless hate of a debtor! And at last she began to nourish a contempt for me in order to strengthen the delusion within her that she had outwitted me! And, to top it all, she taught you to have contempt for me, too—for she needed support in her weakness! . . . And so I became nothing but a poor fool in your eyes whenever I did anything good, a miserable creature when I showed any sensibility, a base villain after you had managed to get the upper hand and finally ruined us all!

(*One-Act Plays,* 239)

We here get the picture of a man who was once active, but whose will was broken by his wife and daughters. Durand is, in fact, rather similar to the Captain in the closing scene of *Fadren.* In his sado-masochistic relation to his wife, he has come to play the role of scapegoat and martyr. After her death, this pattern has merely been strengthened for, as Durand himself points out, "Jag kan icke kära mot döda" (*Samlade Verk,* 33:177) ["I can't be the plaintiff against the dead"] (*Strindberg's One-Act Plays,* 238). And yet he plays precisely this role in an attempt to justify himself to his children before he dies.

From Durand's apology "in the face of death," it appears that the question of guilt plays a decisive role. When his wife slipped, he took the blame. As a consequence, his wife came to be indebted to her husband. To free herself from this indebtedness, she projected her own faults onto him and persuaded herself and her daughters that he possessed qualities which, in fact, were her own.

Ironically, Durand's apology functions in a similar way. Intended to justify himself, it becomes an accusation against his wife. What Durand does not perceive is that he has himself been part of the game, that his masochistic leanings have nourished her sadistic tendencies and that the guilt therefore is reciprocal.

While this psychological web is consistent with naturalism, the symbolic overtones and the grotesque depiction of both characters and situation point forward to Strindberg's post-Inferno plays. The symbolic and anticipatory element is particularly important when Durand says, "husets ställning är så grundligt undergrävd sedan flera år tillbaka att jag hellre ser det ramla än jag dag och natt skall sväva i oro för vad som måste komma!" (*Samlade Verk,* 33: 160) [the position of the house has been so undermined that I would rather see it collapse than constantly worry about what is to happen]. The subtle nuances may seem slight but they are important since they alone provide a clear link with the end of the play when the house catches fire. The symbolism anticipates that of *Ett drömspel* [*A Dream Play*] and the Chamber Plays, which constantly present rotting, burning, collapsing houses. In *Spöksonaten* [*The Ghost Sonata*], we journey from the House of Life to the Isle of the Dead, *Toteninsel.* In *Pelikanen* [*The Pelican*], the House of Life burns and makes room for a paradisiac vision of death. The heat from the fire that is to annihilate brother and sister brings about the final ecstatic line: "Nu börjar sommarlovet!" (*Samlade Verk,* 58: 297) [Now summer vacation begins!].

In the opening of *Inför döden,* the stage directions indicate that Durand "står med kikare i handen och ser utåt sjön" ["stands looking out across the lake through a pair of binoculars."] Over "topparne av kyrkogårdens cypresser" ["the tops of the churchyard cypresses"], he can see "Lac Leman med Savoyer-Alperna och franska badorten Évian" (*Samlade Verk,* 33, 154-5) ["Lake Leman with the Savoyard Alps and the French bathing resort Évian"] (*One-Act Plays,* 225). Durand here finds himself in a borderland. On the other side of the lake, he can see the country he has left: France—his own past. On this side of the lake he can see the churchyard, where he will soon be resting. With death close at hand, the landscape becomes richly symbolic. If the churchyard represents death, the cleansing—purging—Évian and above and beyond it, we may assume, the white, snow-covered mountains are actually a naturalistic version of the paradisiac "Isle of the Dead" appearing at the end of *Spöksonaten.* There he stands, Durand, searching the wind that will soon help demolish his house. Here, as in the late plays, we ultimately experience the House of Life that must be destroyed to make room for another, better existence. And Durand is, in the last instance, a representative of Man, "född till världen mitt i ett konkursbo" (*Samlade Verk,* 58: 167) [born into the world in the midst of a bankruptcy] as is said of the Student in *Spöksonaten.*

As my examination of this one-act play demonstrates, Szondi's thesis that the interaction in *Fadren,* in *Inför döden* has been replaced by a suspense based on an outward threat is dubious. The outward threat, the bankruptcy, is the result of a web of guilt that cannot be untangled and, therefore, takes on metaphysical proportions. Szondi is certainly right in noting that most of the decisive events in the one-act play belong to the prescenic action—to what has already happened when the curtain is raised—while in the three-act play some of the decisive events belong also to the staged action. But this difference is merely gradual, motivated largely by the shorter length of the one-act play. More striking than the differences between *Fadren* and *Inför döden* are the similarities. Thematically both plays anticipate the post-Inferno dramas.

With his eleven naturalist one-act plays, Strindberg created the basis for a genre that has proved exceedingly vital ever since. Not only have one-act plays for various reasons, not least economic ones, been relished by small theater groups, but new media—radio and television—also have meant an increasing demand for short plays. If Strindberg's kind of one-act play has been somewhat out of tune with the development of modern *stage* drama, it has certainly proved exceedingly suitable for the new media.

Next to *Fröken Julie, Den starkare* appears to have been the most important of Strindberg's one-act plays.[5] It inspired Eugene O'Neill to an early monodrama, *Before Breakfast;* Ingmar Bergman to one of his most important films, *Persona;*[6] Per Olov Enquist to his "counterdrama" *Tribadernas natt* [*The Night of the Tribades*], the most successful Swedish play after Strindberg; and Ljoedmila Petroesjevskaja to her recent *A Glass of Water.* Its reverberations can be sensed also in Herman Heijermans's Dutch piece *Verveling* [*Boredom*], in Jean Cocteau's *La Voix humaine,* and in Samuel Beckett's *Krapp's Last Tape.* Rarely, if ever, has such a short play had such an impact.

Notes

1. All translations, unless otherwise noted, are by the author.

2. The exception is, of course, *Fröken Julie,* which has been rather thoroughly researched. Apart from Martin Lamm's basic survey in *Strindbergs dramer,* Børge

Gedsø Madsen's dissertation, *Strindberg's Naturalistic Theatre: Its Relation to French Naturalism* may be mentioned. Barry Jacobs is responsible for a suggestive introduction in *Strindberg's One-Act Plays*. *Första varningen* [*The First Warning*] and *Den starkare* [*The Stronger*] are analyzed by Egil Törnqvist in his *Strindbergian Drama: Themes and Structure*, and *Paria* [*Pariah*] in his "The Modern(ist) One-Act Play," in *Facets of European Modernism: Essays in Honour of James McFarlane. Leka med elden* [*Playing with Fire*], finally, is dealt with in Hans-Göran Ekman's "Strindberg's *Leka med elden* as Comedy," in *Strindbergs Dramen im Lichte neuerer Methoden-diskussionen.*

3. The article is reprinted in August Strindberg, *Samlade skrifter,* vols. 17, 281-305.

4. For an examination of the monodrama form, see Törnqvist, "Monodrama: Term and Reality," and Paul.

5. For the impact of *Fröken Julie,* see Egil Törnqvist and Barry Jacobs, *Strindberg's 'Miss Julie': A Play and its Transpositions.* Norwich: Norvik Press, 1988: 114-35.

6. To date Bergman has produced four of Strindberg's one-act plays: *Leka med elden* (twice), *Första varningen, Moderskärlek,* and *Fröken Julie* (twice). There is a striking resemblance between *Leka med elden* and Bergman's film *Sommarnattens leende* [*Smiles of a Summer Night*]. The similarity between *Den starkare* and Bergman's film *Persona* has often been pointed out.

Works Cited

Cole, Toby, ed, *Playwrights on Playwriting.* New York: Hill and Wang, 1960.

Ekman, Hans-Göran. *"Leka med elden* as Comedy," *Strindbergs Dramen im Lichte neuerer Methoden-diskussionen.* Beiträge zur nordischen Philologie 2. Basel: Helbing und Lichtenhahn, 1981.

Halbritter, Rudolf. *Konzeptionsformen des modernen anglo-amerikanischen Kurzdramas.* Palaestra 263. Göttingen: Vandenhoeck und Ruprecht, 1975.

Jacobs, Barry. "Introduction" to *Strindberg's One-Act Plays.* Trans. Arvid Paulson. New York: Simon and Schuster, 1969.

Lamm, Martin. *Strindbergs dramer.* Stockholm: Bonnier, 1924.

Madsen, Børge Gedsø. *Strindberg's Naturalistic Theater: Its Relation to French Naturalism.* Seattle: U Washington P, 1962.

Paul, Fritz. "Strindberg og monodramaet." *Edda,* 5, 1976.

Schnetz, Diemut. *Der moderne Einakter: Eine poetologische Untersuchung.* Bern: Francke, 1967.

Strindberg, August. *August Strindbergs dramer.* 4 vols. Ed. Carl Reinhold Smedmark. Stockholm: Bonniers, 1970.

———. *August Strindbergs Samlade Verk.* 68 vols. Ed. Gunnar Ollén. Stockholm: Almqvist och Wiksell Förlag, 1984.

———. *Samlade skrifter av August Strindberg.* 55 vols. Ed. John Landquist. Stockholm: Bonniers Förlag, 1913.

———. *Strindberg: Five Plays.* Trans. Harry Carlson. Berkeley: U California P, 1981.

Szondi, Peter. *Theorie des modenen Dramas.* Frankfurt am Main: Suhrkamp Verlag, 1956.

———. *Theory of the Modern Drama.* Trans. and ed. Michael Hays. Theory and History of Literature 29. Minneapolis: U Minnesota P, 1987.

Törnqvist, Egil. "Monodrama: Term and Reality," *Essays on Drama and Theatre: Liber Amicorum Benjamin Hunningher.* Amsterdam: Baarn, Mousault, 1973.

———. *Strindbergian Drama: Themes and Structures.* Stockholm: Almqvist och Wiksell; Atlantic Heights, NJ: International Humanities P, 1982.

———. "The Modern(ist) One-Act Play" in *Facets of European Modernism: Essays in Honor of James McFarland.* Ed. Janet Garton. Norwich: U East Anglia P, 1985.

Marilyn Johns Blackwell (essay date fall 1999)

SOURCE: Blackwell, Marilyn Johns. "Strindberg's Early Dramas and Lacan's 'Law of the Father.'" *Scandinavian Studies* 71, no. 3 (fall 1999): 311-24.

[*In the following essay, Blackwell discusses contemporary attitudes toward sex roles and how Strindberg expressed them in his plays.*]

As the erosion of European patriarchal structures accelerated through the late nineteenth and twentieth centuries, many distinguished and important (largely but not exclusively) male readers and producers of culture responded to this development with varying degrees of horror, outrage, and counterattack. As two such pivotal figures, both August Strindberg and Jacques Lacan are central to the cultural conversation this development engendered and have been critiqued in light of the gender issues implicit and explicit in their respective representational systems. Ross Shideler notes, for instance, that

> seizing on his century's rapid changes in cultural and scientific knowledge, Strindberg fictionalized what Foucault might call the "discontinuities" of his age. . . . Supported by much of the Victorian thought and post-

Darwinian science of his day, Strindberg consistently
. . . portrays and defends in both his earlier Naturalistic
and his later so-called Expressionistic works the male
dominance that he sees as biological fact. . . . [He]
portrays both the challenge to the Victorian patriarchy
and family and the response to that challenge.

(226, 229)

Lacan's centrality to this discussion is likewise evident in
the keen and sustained attention he and his thought on
patriarchal systems as well as on much else have received
for many decades.

Interestingly these two authors represent certain patriarchy-
and gender-related issues in strikingly similar ways, even
as Strindberg's views are often seen as subjective aberration and Lacan's, just as often, as abiding "human"
psychological truth. An investigation of two early Strindberg dramas, *Fadren* [*The Father*] and *Fröken Julie* [*Miss
Julie*] in light of Lacan's thought on the Symbolic phase
of human development and the Law or Name of the Father
can serve to reveal some of the ideological connections
between these two ostensibly extremely strange bedfel-
lows.

A brief summary of some of Lacan's theories on this
subject might be helpful or appropriate here. Those ideas
which are most pertinent to this enterprise concern his notion of the Symbolic stage, that period in human development that Freud called the "Oedipal." This stage of life is
especially important because, as Sarup notes, "it is through
the Symbolic order that the subject is constituted" (85).
This period for Lacan is distinguished by all naming and
symbolic identification which are, for him, a function of
the Law of the Father, as well as by the child's learning
the lessons necessary for "normal" human development to
take place. The force that teaches these lessons is
designated by a number of interchangeable terms: the phallic signifier, the phallus, the name of the father, the law of
the father, the paternal metaphor, and the master signifier,
to name but a few.

The primary goal of the Symbolic stage of development is
a separation from the mother and an identification with the
name or law of the father. For Lacan, the father is
equivalent to the principle of law. Thus, the paternal
metaphor, the Name of the Father, the Phallus, and the
Law of the Father function to sever the close ties between
mother and child. As Ragland-Sullivan explains, "the
Father's Name(s) offer the mediation of language as a
means of flight or escape from, mastery of, a fusion too
profound to fathom" (86). But Bergoffen takes issue with
Lacan (and implicitly Ragland-Sullivan who is by and
large an apologist for the ramifications of Lacan's thought
for feminist issues) on this point contending that here aggression becomes "a subtle war of men against women. . . . Woman is given a place in the Symbolic only
so long as she assumes the name of the mother. In assum-

ing this name, however, she consents to her murder. Her
role in the family romance is to recognize the Name of the
Father. As mother, woman authorizes the phallic order"
(287). Woman continues to be permitted a place in the
Symboic only as the mother and only if she represses her
need for a relationship with her child in favor of supporting and sanctioning the phallic order.

If the child is to escape the suffocating bond with the
mother and achieve full subjectivity, it is essential for him
(the use of the masculine pronoun is required by the
linguistic gender system of French) to acquire the "name
of the father." Grosz points out:

> The child becomes a subject only with reference to the
> name-of-the-father and the sacrificed, absent body of
> the mother. . . . In introjecting the name-of-the-father,
> the child . . . is positioned with reference to the
> father's name. He is now bound to the law, . . . given
> a name, and an authorized speaking position. . . . The
> symbolic father is the (ideal) embodiment of paternal
> authority, the locus from which patriarchal law and
> language come.
>
> (71-2)

Lacan asserts that culture is always patriarchal: "C'est
dans le *nom du père* qu'il nous faut reconnaître le support
de la fonction symbolique qui, depuis l'orée des temps
historiques, identifie sa personne à la figure de la loi"
(*Écrits* 278) ["It is in the *name of the father* that we must
recognize the support of this symbolic function which,
from the dawn of history, has identified his person with
the figure of the law" (67)]. For Lacan, the law represented
by the father encompasses all psychological and social
structures. "The Name-of-the-Father was the symbol of an
authority at once legislative and punitive" (Bowie 108).
The Symbolic order, then, is synonymous with learning
language and the lessons of patriarchal law; it "lays out
the social hierarchy determined by the Name-of-the-Father.
It decides what the relationship of all the beings of the
society is according to socially sanctioned codes" (Lorraine
67).

The Symbolic stage is first and foremost the phase during
which the child achieves language. This accession to
language, in Lacan's view, occurs under the law of the
father. For him, the Law of the Father *is* the law of
language (Muller 402). Language is the symbolic system,
with its rules and structure, which the child has to negotiate if it is to situate itself in the social order, that is to say
in patriarchal society. Or as Grosz notes, "The paternal
metaphor names the child and thus positions it so that it
can be replaced discursively by the 'I', in order to enter
language as a speaking being" (Grosz 104). Lacan also asserts that it is the paternal that provides the child with
"l'authentification du néant de l'existence" (*Écrits* 433)
["the authentification of the nothingness of existence"
(143)]. While this claim might seem to fly in the face of

the common sense, empirical observation that, since the mother is almost always the caregiver, she rather than the father usually teaches the child what lessons it learns at this stage of life, in fact Lacan tries to circumvent this problem by positing that the mother, operating in the Symbolic and upholding the Law of the Father, transmits the latter as effectively as the father himself.

The phallus, Lacan's "signifier of signifiers," his "transcendent symbol," that defines each subject's access to the Symbolic order, is central to his system. Thus, the phallus embodies the primacy of the Law of the Father.

> The subject perceives the Phallus as the transcendental signifier that will restore coherence and unity, for it acts as the source of meaning. . . . Culture assumes the role of the Name-of-the-Father and performs as the holder of the Phallus. The Phallus is the source of meaning which promises the satisfaction of desire in the Symbolic world. The desire for control through possession of the Phallus becomes the primary motivating force of the subject. . . . [All of which] sets in motion a nexus of desire and control that is used to sustain social hierarchization. In attempting to centre the Self, the subject displaces its desires onto a control of the Other, the site which allows the subject to delineate itself through a series of distinguishing "differences."
>
> (Walton 7)

But Lacan went to some pains to argue that the phallus is not a male-specific symbol, contending that it applied equally to men and women and stating repeatedly that the phallus has nothing whatsoever to do with the penis.

The problems with using the phallus as a gender-neutral and "universal" signifier should be obvious. Despite Lacan's strong contention that the phallus is a gender-neutral term, he is suggesting that only one sexual organ has the power and force to be a candidate for his "transcendental signifier" or, as Bowie puts it, that "only one organ [can] *mean*" (128). Given the extensive historical association in our culture between the phallus and the penis, we cannot simply dismiss this association as irrelevant; for us, if not for Lacan, the phallus is the penis. Thus there is considerable slippage between his thought and the demands empirical experience places upon his late twentieth-century reader:

> As the word suggests, it is a term privileging masculinity. . . . The valorization of the penis and the relegation of female sexual organs to the castrated category are effects of a socio-political system that also enables the phallus to function as the "signifier of signifiers". . . . The symbolic function of the phallus envelops the penis as the tangible sign of privileged masculinity, thus in effect naturalizing male dominance. . . . By means of the phallus, the subject comes to occupy the position of "I" in discourse.
>
> (Grosz 122-3, 125)

Or, to quote Bowie, the phallus is the "male genital transcendentalized" (142). Lacan's thought is, then, undeniably phallocentric, surely in large part because he comes out of Freud, especially early Freud. His notions about the Symbolic and the Law of the Father were first developed in the 1930s, in the heyday of a certain kind of Freudianism which was itself a response to the erosion of European patriarchal structures.

Notably, Kress can argue that "once he identifies the phallus as the signifier, as the basis of our signification system, Lacan reconceives the relationship between femininity and the phallus, arguing not just that the phallus fails to encompass femininity adequately, but that it actually seeks to limit femininity" (1-2). He continues maintaining that "Lacanian psychoanalysis both identifies and critiques the phallus as signifier. . . . If that signifier fails to 'portray the truth of the subject,' then Lacan's rereading not only allows the concept of femininity itself to examine that signifier, but also enables us to ask different questions and to discover ways other than the phallus . . . to reconceive . . . subject positions" (13). But the fact that Lacan perceives these issues in terms of "femininity" and "masculinity," that subjecthood is defined in terms of its relationship, however negotiated, to the phallus suggests that this system of thought is still deeply imbued with conventional notions of gender difference.

Because embracing the Name and Law of the Father is so pivotal, for Lacan, to "normal" human development, the rejection of them leads to an anarchy of the self. He claims in many places that non-acceptance of the Father leads to psychosis; to reject the Father is literally insanity. Thus he asserts in "Du traitement possible de la psychose" that the psychotic has *foreclosed* the paternal metaphor and has thus been unable to find a subject position for himself within the Symbolic order. "Foreclosure" refers here to the exclusion of the Name of the Father from the Symbolic order, entailing a failure of the paternal metaphor and a concomitant reassertion of the connection with the mother (*Écrits* 558, 577).

Strindberg's **Fadren,** as Margareta Fahlgren has argued, is deeply informed by patriarchal values (85-109). One of the first visual clues in **Fadren** as to what kind of world we are entering comes in the initial stage directions. There are, we are told, "vapen på väggarne: gevär och jaktväskor" (11) [weapons on the walls, guns and hunting bags], and the captain is dressed in "släpuniform och ridstövlar med sporrar" (11) [fatigues with riding boots and spurs]. This specifically masculine space and costume are elaborated upon as we discover that the captain is a scientist as well as a military leader (32-3). Indeed Strindberg's letters emphasize the masculinity of this character (*Brev* VI, 282). Thus the father and his maleness are directly associated with the acquisition of knowledge and the perpetuation of culture, as he is in Lacan. That this individual, who is given a number of conventional masculine attributes, aligns himself with the Law is not surprising. After bragging that he can take care of the Nöjd problem, he fails quite badly and then commands that "Då får saken gå till tinget" (15) [Then the case will have to go to court].

Shortly hereafter the whole issue of paternity and the law is developed more fully. In a singular twist of logic, the captain argues that although we can not know if Nöjd is guilty, we certainly can and do know that the girl is guilty. Such logic of course allows him to sidestep the culpability of the male in this situation, leaving the female to take all responsibility. The role of the law in sexual relations is expanded when the captain, who might be directly espousing Lacan's Law of the Father, claims that "Barnen skola uppfostras i fadrens bekännelse, enligt gällandt lag" (24) [Children are to be raised in the faith of their father, according to current law]. Continuing this judicial metaphor, already on the next page, the captain asks Laura, "Och har domen redan färdig?" [Has the judgment already been handed down?] to which she responds, "Den är skriven i lagen" [It's written in the law], and he rejoins, "Det står icke i lagen vem som är barnets fader. . . . Klokt folk påstår att sådant kan man aldrig veta" [The law doesn't say who is the child's father. Intelligent people maintain that one can never know such things], to which finally Laura argues "Det var märkvärdigt! Kan man inte veta vem som är fadren till ett barn. . . . Hur kan fadren då ha sådana rättigheter över hennes barn?" (25-6) [That's strange! Can't one know who the father of a child is? . . . Then how can the father have such rights over her child?]. And here Laura has articulated the problem in its most essential form. It is precisely because a man can never know absolutely whether or not a child is his that masculine culture must create so many repressive mechanisms for women, to control their fidelity and their freedom, must create laws and customs that elevate the authority of the father and diminish the role of the mother. One suspects that it may be precisely this kind of masculine thinking that lies behind Lacan's persistent need to ennoble the father in order to delineate the mother and her values as that which must be abandoned. In a statement resonant of the Lacanian father, the captain shouts "Nej! Jag låter ingen inkräkta på mina rättigheter" (43) [No! I won't let anyone encroach on my rights]. We note that, as in Lacan's model, neither the child nor the mother have any rights in Strindberg's male world. Or in Adolf's words, "[Modren] har sålt sin förstfödslorätt i laga köp, och avträtt sina rättigheter mot att mannen drager försorg om henne och hennes barn" (24) [(The mother) has sold her birthright and given up her rights in return for her husband's assuming responsibility for her and her children]. Such rights must be sacrificed for the "healthy" development of the child.

The centrality of paternity and of absolute knowledge about paternity reflects the drama's overarching parallel between God the Father and the father in a family

(Ambjörnson 12-27). These issues culminate as the play progresses. The captain desperately cries "Laura, rädda mig och mitt förstånd. . . . Om barnet icke är mitt så har jag inga rättigheter och vill inga ha över det" (67) [Laura, save me and my sanity. . . . If the child isn't mine, I have no rights and don't want any over her]. Here it is clear that this struggle is about control of the child, but also about patrilineage, as we also see in the captain's statement shortly hereafter: "For mig som icke tror på ett kommande liv var barnet mitt liv efter detta. Det var min evighetstanke. . . . Tar du bort den, så är mitt liv avklippt" (67) [Since I don't believe in immortality, the child was my afterlife. She was my concept of eternity. . . . If you take that away, my life is severed].

What the two parents want for their child is telling; the father wants her to become a teacher since with that profession she can support herself and yet if she marries these skills would stand her in good stead with her own children. The mother, of course, wants her to be a painter, because she has shown an inclination in that direction and would appear to be good at it. We note that Adolf's choice for her is one of the "helping" professions to which women have been relegated since virtually time immemorial. The only real objection the captain lodges to Bertha's becoming an artist is that she was complimented on her work by a young man who was infatuated with her. One can, however, wonder how reliable he is on this point given how unreliable he is on so many others. It is pure speculation, of course, but one might wonder if his real objection is that painting is not a "womanly" profession and instead is one in which the authentic self (which, in Strindberg's thought, women do not have) is expressed. Lacan, of course, suggested that in the Symblic, the most important period of human development, the child must break with the mother and become aligned instead with the father. The woman's role during this phase is to support the paternal, to promote the will, the "Law" of the father, just as Adolf is asking Laura to do.

Of how Strindberg sees Adolf, we know a bit from his letters where he praises his character, his nobility, and his temperament. But as a reader or spectator, it is difficult to see him in the purely positive light Strindberg casts over him. He barks orders at his underlings (11), deals with his wife contemptuously when she turns in the household accounts (22), and treats her rudely and imperiously on several occasions before the conflict between them develops (22-3, 25, 43). He further rejects the notion of compromise with Laura as to Bertha's future, arguing quite condescendingly that compromise is completely impossible, whereas it is, of course, nothing of the sort.

As much as the captain likes to identify himself with strength, will, and law, the play implies that such identifications are wishful thinking on his part. Already at the beginning of the drama, he fails completely at solving the Nöjd problem, defeated by someone who is characterized as his military inferior. Too, for a self-avowed man of strength and will, he is remarkably self-pitying (69, 87, 93). Alternating with the self-pity is the posturing that is evident in his character development; imperiously he proclaims to Laura: "jag är en soldat, som med ett ord kan tämja människor och kreatur; jag begär endast medlidande som em sjuk, jag nedlägger min makts tecken och jag anropar om nåd för mitt liv" (69) [I am a soldier who with a single word can tame people and animals; I request only compassion as someone who is ill, I lay down the symbols of my power and I call for mercy for my life]. Yet it is clear that this man is no more capable of taming animals than he is of controling himself; his claim to the contrary is so much vainglory (perhaps it is this manifest weakness that leads Lagercrantz to claim that the captain's tragic flaw lies in the conflict between male and female in his character [194]). Finally he elevates himself to veritably transcendent, mythological status (Lacan might say an embracing of the paternal metaphor) when, toward the end of the play, he draws several parallels between himself and Hercules, both male figures robbed of their masculinity.

In keeping with Lacan's perception of women and their role it human development, Strindberg's women are defined in terms of their biology. The captain's statement "När kvinnor bli gamla [har de] upphört vara kvinnor" (71) [when women get old, they've stopped being women] suggests clearly that women cease to be women when they are no longer sexually attractive or capable of bearing children. Likewise, Lacan sees women in terms of their biology, specifically their ability to bear and bond with children. Once the Symbolic phase sets in, the mother's role becomes to support and sustain the Law of the Father. Any departure from those activities constitutes a deviation from her "right" role.

This "natural essence" of woman appears several times in *Fadren*. Laura explains that she loved Adolf as a child, but that when his feelings changed her blood felt shame: "Modern var din vän, ser du, men kvinnan var din fiende" (70) [the mother was your friend, you see, but the woman was your enemy]. Of course this notion is congruent with Lacau's system in which woman is biology and man represents the law; indeed woman must be cast aside for the child to learn the law. But not only is woman biology, she is also outside of the law and poses a threat to it. Laura's own brother describes her as not even having a conscience, her crime "ett omedvetet brott; omedvetet" (80) [an unconscious crime, unconscious]. But Strindberg goes on to characterize women as a sex as essentially immoral. Thus, Ollén is not so far off the mark when he describes Laura as a "helveteskvinna" (65) [hell woman]. Describing two similar women of his experience, the captain says of all women: "Det är just detta som är faran, att de äro omedvetna om sin instinktiva skurkaktighet" (62) [That's just the danger, that they're unconscious of their instinctive depravity].

Virtually all the women in the play are characterized as irrational. Laura's "irrationality" is clear, but the nurse too is a rabid Baptist, the mother-in-law wants Bertha to be a spritist, the maids try to convert her to the Salvation Army, and the grandmother makes her do "automatic writing" at night. Women are, then, consistently associated with forces of anti-reason. Thus, Adolf wants to get rid of his mother-in-law and his old nurse, a desire that we can again see in light of the threat that femininity poses to the masculine order once it can no longer serve through sexuality or child bearing.

Ultimately this male hostility to women is described as out and out warfare: "Det är mannen och kvinnan mot varandra oupphörlight" (20) [It's man against woman constantly]. Ultimately, the captain describes their relationship: "Det är som ras-hat detta" (72) [This is like racial hatred], for as his prose writings from the late 1880s demonstrate, Strindberg equates female inferiority with the ostensible inferiority of people of color, in the process making some of the most offensive racist and mysogynist remarks in the annals of Western literature. As the play draws to a close, the captain spews forth a litany naming all the women who have been his enemies. In this respect, Strindberg goes beyond even Lacan's misogyny; while the psychologist posits the beneficial necessity of women both as mother (primarily before the Symbolic stage) and as Other to man's subject, Strindberg sees *all* women as failing men, as fundamentally defective.

Fröken Julie conforms to the same Lacanian framework as *Fadren* but in an even more overt way. Prominently located on the set are the speaking tube and servant's bell for the count to call and command his servants. There are also continuing references to his boots which Jean must clean before his return. These references that are peppered throughout the text (133, 138, 150, 188) serve as persistent aural and visual reminders of the count's constant absent presence, of who really holds the power in this household. The power the count wields is expanded to an equating of his person and the law when Julie and Jean clarify that they live within a system of patrilineage in which only the male transfers the title and the power pertaining thereto (158). This sense that Julie has transgressed against a powerful patriarchal dictum is clear also in her comment: "Tänker ni att jag kan se min far i ansiktet efter detta? Nej! För mig bort härifrån: från förnedringen, och vanäran!" (153) [Do you think I can look my father in the face after this? No! Take me away from here: from the humiliation and dishonor!].

The absence of the count is central to this play. Indeed Margareta Wirmark holds that the count and his role in the drama suggest the omnipresence of the late nineteenth-century patriarchy in the background of Strindberg's work (87). Not surprisingly, this figure is consistently equated with proper rule. Kristin's criticism of Jean for stealing the count's wheat specifically equates this act of breaking the law with disloyalty toward the count and his patriarchal system. Too, as Kristin makes clear, the count and the authority he represents, symbolize in this play rightly stratified society; Julie's fall is one of violating the laws of that patriarchal stratification: "jag [har] aldrig sänkt mig under mitt stånd. Kom och säg att grevens kokerska haft något med ryktarn eller svindrängen! Kom och säg det!" (183) [I've never sunk beneath my station. Just say that the count's cook has had anything to do with the stableboy or the swineherd! Just say that!].

The count's association with the Law of the Father is also apparent when Julie explains the story of her parents' marriage and recounts that before getting married her mother gave all her money to her lover so that it was not, as it should have been by law, under the control of her father. The lover stole the money as a result of which the father lost his rightful resources with which he might have better reestablished his proper rule. Jean, despite his low birth, also strives to wield the patriarchal authority represented by the count. Indeed, his highest life goal is to be to go to Rumania where he "kan—märk väl jag säger *kan*—sluta som greve!" (150) [can—note well that I say *can*—end up as a count]. Another manifestation of proper rule is that this father, like Lacan's, imparts the lessons of life to his children. Julie tells us that there is not a lesson she has learned that she has not received from her father and that, more specifically, "tack vare min fars lärdomar" [thanks to my father's teachings], she learned that she cannot "skjuta skulden på Jesus" (187) [put the blame on Jesus], an important lesson to the Strindberg who, at this point in his life, sees religion as an impediment to the search for and embracing of truth.

The great authority and the law and rule thereof that the count embodies appear also in the dread he inspires in those left behind while he is away. His power is so great that even his boots terrify Jean (150). All three of the major characters in the drama express fear and apprehension about the count's eventual return (168, 174f., 179). Indeed it is he whom Jean and Julie are trying to flee when they develop their travel plans, his disapproval and his wrath, an attempt doomed from the outset.

At the same time that the count is described in terms of metaphors of absolute power, proper rule, correct law, and beneficent teaching, Strindberg also represents him as a martyr. He is described as someone who has suffered "så mycket sorg" (173) [so much sorrow], as a man who wanted to commit suicide but could not (186). The reason behind this pain is (hardly surprisingly, for Strindberg) his relationship with a woman. Julie's mother was of "ofrälse härkomst, något mycket enkelt" (160) [common family, something very undistinguished], an indication for Strindberg of her essential inferiority. Her initial refusal to marry the count suggests her defiance of the law with all that that means to both Strindberg and Lacan. She furthermore did not want to bear a child, an even worse sin in their

eyes, for a woman who refuses to become a mother violates the very distinction between subject and other on which Lacan's and Strindberg's sexual ideologies are based. The mother furthermore inverts "natural" difference by setting the men on the estate to "women's work" and vice versa. With no explanation from Strindberg as to why or how, this inversion resulted in the property's almost going under. But as soon as the father revolts, takes over the management of the property, and forces Julie's mother to marry him, i.e. reestablishes proper rule, the mother (it is strongly hinted) sets fire to the entire estate at precisely that window of opportunity when it is not insured thereby taking her revenge.

The mother's misrule is, Strindberg suggests, also to blame for the psychological chaos of Julie's personality and character. She claims she has both loved and hated her father, that while all her thoughts come from him, all her passions come from her mother (187). Julie's psychological confusion can be seen as precisely the kind of Lacanian psychosis that arises when an individual rejects the name or law of the father and thus is unable to position *him*self as a subject. The base mother, who compels the father to borrow her money from her lover to fix up the estate, is also described as degraded earlier in the play when Jean claims she was most comfortable in the kitchen and barn and went about with dirty cuffs (122). Woman's rule, then, is mis-rule; the "natural" law is for the male to assert his authority, as in Lacan's Symbolic stage. Woman, for Strindberg and Lacan, is that which must be conquered or transcended. Interestingly the conflict between the sexes is also laid at the feet of women; Julie states that it was from her mother that she learned hatred for men (163) and claims that her having slept with Jean is her mother's revenge on her father. Blaming the mother is, of course, a rationalization, for both Strindberg and Lacan, for the conflict between men and women that arises primarily because patriarchal authority needs to keep women in the position of other in order to retain its position as subject.

Finally, as the play comes to an end, the count arrives and everyone present cringes in obedience to him. Tellingly, even after this arrival, the count remains both invisible and inaudible, retaining a veritably godlike authority, as Jean and Julie remain on stage overwhelmed with anxiety as to what will happen. As Julie nervously examines the few options left to her, she decides that what she must do is commit suicide, less as an escape for herself, than to "rädda hans namn" (188) [save his name], an action that aligns her with Lacan's powerful Name of the Father and suggests her reabsorption into the paternal metaphor and thus her redemption. After Jean commands her twice not to think (presumably so that she might follow her instinct towards self-sacrifice in the name of the father), the bell rings loudly twice. The demands of the father are asserted suggesting the re-establishment, after this night of misrule, of the "right" rule of the father.

Historically Strindberg found himself writing in a volatile period during which the nineteenth century patriarchy was being seriously eroded. Vacillating as always between deep-seated insecurities and an egomania of virtually unparalleled proportions, he confronted the problem of finding an adequate response to the threat posed to the Oscarian patriarchy by the increasing number of unattached, single women who were demanding certain legal rights that by contemporary standards seem tame indeed. Walton's comments on the same problem in Anthony Trollope's œuvre are, I think, pertinent to Strindberg's situation:

> The centered subjects of the discourse are not themselves whole or unified, but occupy a privileged position and work to maintain and justify that position through control of others. By controlling, these subjects indirectly lend themselves the illusion that they are acting as sources of coherence and stability. . . . Exerting power lends the subjects the illusion of holding power. . . . These [works] display . . . ideological attempts to legitimize the social order and to affirm the hierarchy it generates. . . . Certainly, his [works] detail the operation of the Phallic drive, and this operation must be understood if masculinist ideology is to be divested of its seductive rhetoric and appeal. . . . Without [woman], the "unity" [man] desires cannot be achieved, for he lacks the Other which would consolidate his subject position. Woman's role in this discourse is covertly highlighted as a result, since it is her subordination that enables the perpetuation of the order.
>
> (Walton 8, 162-3)

Of course one cannot deny the importance and value of either Strindberg's or Lacan's contributions to Western letters; the place of the totality of their oeuvres in our culture is (and certainly deservedly) assured. But by linking Strindberg's literary practice with Lacan's psychological theories, I am suggesting that both are responses to the erosion of European patriarchal structures. Shideler rightly points out that "what we see in **The Father** . . . is the disintegration of the patriarchal family, even as the play dramatizes the attempt of the family to determine its own rules in the absence of any absolute authority" (253f.). So too does **Fröken Julie** suggest the threat that newly independent women and female sexuality posed to these structures. The beginning of the dissolution of certain masculine systems prompted these two ostensibly extremely different figures to respond in strikingly similar ways, for androcentrism avails itself of many of the same methods and techniques to justify and perpetuate the "natural" superiority of the male whether that androcentrism plays itself out in a late nineteenth-century Swedish playwright or a mid-twentieth century French psychiatrist. The Law of the Father positions the male as subject, the female as other; the father's dominance as "proper rule," the mother's as "misrule; men as rational and women as "irrational;" women as restricted to the realms of biology and "instinctive depravity" and the mere "name" of the father as worth dying for. Although contemporary feminist criticism is careful (and justifiably so) not to embrace the notion of a monolithic patriarchy, it is perhaps worth remembering that patriarchies, however divided spatially and temporally, can and often do use the selfsame strategies to naturalize male dominance whether within the realm of "natural law" or within that of the supposedly inexorable laws of the human psyche.

Works Cited

Ambjörnson, Ronny and Johan Cullberg. "Strindbergs Fadren och *Fordringsägare*: En guide till manlighetens paradoxer." BLM 1 (1987): 12-27.

Bergoffen, Debra. "Queering the Phallus." *Disseminating Lacan*. Ed. David Pettigrew and Francois Raffoul. Albany: State U New York P, 1996. 278-87.

Bowie, Malcolm. *Lacan*. Cambridge: Harvard UP, 1991.

Fahlgren, Maragreta. *Kvinnans ekvation: Kön, makt och rationalitet i Strindbergs författarskap*. Stockholm: Carlssons, 1994.

Grosz, Elizabeth. *Jacques Lacan: A Feminist Introduction*. New York: Routledge, 1990.

Kress, R. Lee. "Femininity, Castration, and the Phallus." *Literature and Psychology* 42.3 (1996): 1-14.

Lacan, Jacques. *Écrits*. Paris: Éditions du Seuil, 1966.

———. *Écrits: A Selection*. Trans. Alan Sheridan. New York: Norton, 1977.

Lagercrantz, Olof. *August Strindberg*. Stockholm: Wahlström och Widstrand, 1979.

Lorraine, Tamsin. *Gender, Identity, and the Production of Meaning*. Boulder, CO: Westview, 1990.

Muller, John and William Richardson. *Lacan and Language*. International UP, 1982.

Ollén, Gunnar. *Strindbergs dramatik*. Stockholm: Prisma, 1961.

Ragland-Sullivan, Ellie. "Stealing Material: The Materiality of Language according to Freud and Lacan." *Lacan and the Human Sciences*. Ed. Alexandre Leupin. Lincoln, NE: U Nebraska P, 1991.

Sarup, Madan. *Jacques Lacan*. New York: Harvester, 1995.

Shideler, Ross. *Questioning the Father: From Darwin to Zola, Ibsen, Strindberg, and Hardy*. Ms. forthcoming. Stanford: Stanford UP, 1999.

Strindberg, August. *Brev*. Ed. Torsten Eklund. Stockholm: Bonniers, 1948.

———. *Samlade verk* XXVII. Stockholm: Almqvist & Wiksell, 1984.

Walton, Priscilla. *Patriarchal Desire and Victorian Discourse: A Lacanian Reading of Anthony Trollope's Palliser Novels.* Toronto: U Toronto P, 1995.

Wirmark, Margareta. *Den kluvna scenen: Kvinnor i Strindbergs dramatik.* Värnamo: Gidlunds, 1989.

FADREN (*THE FATHER*)

CRITICAL COMMENTARY

John Eric Bellquist (essay date December 1986)

SOURCE: Bellquist, John Eric. "Strindberg's *Father:* Symbolism, Nihilism, Myth." *Modern Drama* 29, no. 4 (December 1986): 532-43.

[*In the following essay, Bellquist presents a detailed examination of* Fadren.]

As part of the Strindberg Festival held in Stockholm during May, 1981, the Stockholm Stadsteater presented a putatively polemical version of the play *Fadren* with the slightly reconstructed title *Fadern* instead.[1] In the foyer of the theater the play's audiences encountered displays intended to reveal the socio-economic plight of women in Strindberg's day; during the performance they were faced with Laura cast as a harassed, hapless victim rather than an implacable vampire; and upon its conclusion they departed in contemplation of the final image of the daughter Bertha, who had stood at the edge of the stage in order to focus the director's entreaties: the scarred survivor of an unfortunate parental conflict, an innocent victim of yet another skirmish in the "battle of the sexes" in which the male (including by implication the author of the play) was primarily at fault. Neither Bertha nor her mother, nor apparently even her father, was meant to be aware of anything to do with that "psychic murder" ("själamord") which Strindberg thought could be brought about in what he called the "battle of the brains" (hjärnornas kamp") instead. Yet in fact *Fadern* left an impression overwhelmingly different from what the director Jan Håkanson desired. In the role of the captain Adolf, the actor Keve Hjelm had managed to transcend his director's peculiar intent, simply by conveying Strindberg's ineradicable subjectivity. At the Strindberg Symposium held as part of the Festival in Stockholm, Hjelm himself explained—much to Håkanson's apparent consternation—why this had happened: for him *The Father* was a philosophical expression of the existential plight of the human soul, not at all a mere excuse to issue ideological equivocations.

The Father is certainly one of Strindberg's best plays—perhaps even the best. Unlike many of Strindberg's works, whose structures frequently seem discontinuous or internally arbitrary (though often, of course, intentionally so), *The Father* moves relentlessly to its conclusion without respite. Every element of the play's action fits: plot, character, language, theme, and setting. This is one reason why it has been read by some as a proto-expressionistic drama, a single "Ausstrahlung des Ichs" ("irradiation of the I") analogous to a painting such as Edvard Munch's *The Scream*.[2] Yet just as it is possible to include Munch among the Symbolist painters rather than label him an expressionist, *The Father* can also be likened to the Symbolist poet's "paysage d'âme," to a kind of "landscape of the mind" in which the rest of the characters either reflect or impinge upon the captain Adolf, who moves in their midst as if everything in the play is important only in so far as it represents the contents of his own consciousness. These, together with Adolf himself, in turn suggest the contents of the playwright's consciousness, which in the play become an intersubjective, at times even dream-like, aesthetic expression of reality.

Strindberg was well aware that *The Father* could be read in this manner; on at least one occasion he did so himself. In November, 1887 (he had finished the play in February), he wrote the following remarks to the author and journalist Axel Lundegård:

> It seems to me as if I am walking in my sleep; as if poetry and life are mixed. I don't know if *The Father* is a poem or if my life has been one; but it appears to me as if this ought, in a given, soon approaching moment, to become clear to me, and then I shall collapse in madness and pangs of conscience or in suicide. Through much writing my life has become a life of shadows; I think I am no longer walking upon the earth but floating without weight in an atmosphere not of air but of darkness. Should light fall into this darkness I would sink down crushed!

> Strange it is that [in] an often recurring night dream I feel myself flying, without weight, find it completely natural, just as also all concepts of right, unright, true untrue in me are dissolved, and that everything that happens, regardless of how unusual it may be, appears as it should.

> Yes, but these are of course the just consequences of the new world view, indeterminism, and it is possible that my unaccustomedness to the new is what amazes and terrifies me[3]

Even at the height of his "naturalistic" period Strindberg could be possessed by the vision of life as a dream, here expressed in the symbolic imagery of flight and weightlessness, darkness and death (all of which in this instance suggest the iconography of Symbolist poetry and painting); these images had a strongly ethical significance too, suggesting either guilt or madness given the existential threat of life's meaninglessness. For Strindberg the true and the untrue, the just and the unjust had become so mixed by the spirit of the age that the consolatory determinism of the naturalist had made way for an indeterminate chaos— "the modern fate," as he put it, which he had presented in *The Father* only particularly in the "form of an erotic passion".[4] Of course the crumbling of Strindberg's own marriage had contributed to the view of life in the words quoted above, just as *The Father* is clearly grounded in a plot of marital conflict. But it is also, as Carl Reinhold Smedmark has written, "the tragedy of the atheistic determinist"; that this tragedy can be thought of as embodying a mental reality simply reflects Strindberg's sense that life itself might be only a dream.[5] Indeed the imagery in the letter suggests that in so far as one can argue that the world of *The Father* is similarly dream-like, one might also say that although the play deals with the problem of atheism, it still does so symbolically, in a mythopoeic manner.

That *The Father* will deal with the problem of atheism is implicitly established in the opening scene, where we are confronted with the Pastor and the Captain—a man of God and a man of secular authority, respectively. With reference to the sexual escapades of the lieutenant Nöjd, whose very name (as readers have noticed) suggests erotic satisfaction, the Captain has already done all he can in the interests of restraint; now he has found fit to turn to the pastor, who of course knows him well enough to realize the irony in the situation:

PASTOR:

> Well, so you want me to preach to him. What do you think God's word will do for a cavalryman?

CAPTAIN:

> Yes, brother-in-law, it does nothing for me, you're right . . .

PASTOR:

> I certainly am!

CAPTAIN:

> But for him! Try anyway.[6]

These words are perhaps only a hint, but they do introduce what is to become the play's tragically serious theme: confident though the Captain may be in his rejection of religious faith, and questionable though the ministrations of a Lutheran pastor may be in matters of sexual conduct, the Captain's atheism apparently has not been enough to enable him to settle this particular case regarding moral conflict. So too in the discussion that ensues in Scene 2, which centers upon whether or not Nöjd has fathered the child that one of the servant girls is going to bear, neither the Captain nor the Pastor is able to settle the question of paternity, just as ultimately the Captain will be unable to

resolve his doubts about his own daughter's paternity either. The Captain, a man of natural science, is helpless in his arguments against Nöjd, so that turning the matter over to a court becomes his only recourse; the Pastor's appeal, in the end not even to religion but simply to common decency and honor, is only incidental. Religion, science, and common social morality are helpless against Nöjd's arguments.

While these two opening scenes may thus seem merely to present a well-constructed foreshadowing or microcosm of subsequent events, a kind of dramatic "argument" of the play, their language suggests still more than that. Natural science, after all, is a branch of scentific knowledge, or "vetenskap." So the discussion proceeds in the interrogative mood, with the Captain, a man interested in researching the facts and in trying to arrive at scientific principles that might account for them, leading the investigation. "*What* have you done, Nöjd?" he asks, and after the pastor has asked Nöjd to "confess," which leads only to evasion, "*What* does Ludvig have to do with this matter? Stick to the truth.'"[7] Then, in answer to whether or not Nöjd really is the child's father, comes the following:

NÖJD:

> How could one know that?

CAPTAIN:

> What are you talking about? Can't you know it?

NÖJD:

> No—that one can never know.

CAPTAIN:

> Weren't you alone then?

NÖJD:

> Yes—that time, but one can't know if one is the only one just because of that?

CAPTAIN:

> Are you trying to blame Ludvig then? Is that your intent?

NÖJD:

> It's not easy to know whom one should blame.[8]

As the exchange here suggests, the Captain is looking for causes or origins, asking for the "whats" and "hows" of experience as he tries to affix the blame scientifically ("skylla" for him is less a moral than an empirical word). The answer given over and over to the Captain's repeatedly thwarted stabs at obtaining absolute knowledge is that though he may want to "know" what lies behind the measurable fact that the girl is pregnant, one simply cannot "know" anything about this at all. Were Nöjd to know that he indeed is the child's father, he declares he would gladly help the girl out, "men se det kan en aldrig veta" ("but you see, that one can never know"). Thus beyond their rejection of religious, scientific, or moral means of getting at the truth, the play's first two scenes have an unsettling effect: questions are raised without answers, then dismissed for arbitrary resolution by legally constituted authority, and what might have seemed the simple human capacity for ascertaining fundamental truths about experience is undermined. This occurs not by resorting to any pattern of imagery, but by a verbal pattern that repeatedly emphasizes the precariousness of abstract knowledge, so that in the dialogue with Nöjd the Captain discovers himself to be floating in an epistemological ambiguity analogous to the abyss of indeterminate chaos so vividly painted by Strindberg in the letter I have previously quoted. "Jag kan inte reda i det här," the Captain says, "och det roar mig verkligen inte heller". And while his use of "reda" ordinarily would signify getting things straight, which he here admits he cannot do, it also refers to "order" as opposed to "disorder"—a disorder with which he is now, as he says, displeasingly confronted.

What ultimately precipitates the Captain's tragic end is therefore primarily twofold (as I have said, simple social morality contributes little): doubt about the grounds or validity of natural science or naturalistic determinism, and an absolute disbelief in metaphysical consolation. Within this context whatever points of view one may adopt become arbitrary, like so many bundles of atomic energy colliding without a center; human characters become wills engaged in a struggle for the survival and dominance not of the species but of the individual in the present moment. In the well-known passage at the start of Scene 3, where the Captain, true to his character, tells the Pastor that he does not want to discuss Bertha's confirmation but rather her whole upbringing ("uppfostran"), the themes of religion, determinism, and chaotic indeterminacy or discontinuity are brought together:

> Here the house is full of women, who all want to educate my child. Mother-in-law wants to make her into a spiritist; Laura wants to have her an artist; the governess wants to make her into a methodist; old Margaret wants to have her a baptist; and the servant girls want her in the Salvation Army. Naturally it isn't possible to patch together a soul in that way . . .[9]

A standard reading of these assertions—that they represent the Captain's paranoid (or even darkly comic) fear of a horde of women, tigresses whom he must ward off to preserve his very life—obscures what the passage is really about. As a Darwinian naturalist, the Captain knows that Bertha, whose "själ" ("soul") is in the process of being "uppfostrad" ("brought up"), stands at the center of all those influences which determine human character; "patching together a soul" out of them yields what his science tells us we are made of. Strindberg himself wrote often of this "characterlessness" of the human character—indeed

he was to do so again in the introduction to *Fröken Julie* shortly thereafter. Without some sort of metaphysical anchor (which early in *The Father* the Captain imagines he possesses by virtue of his own unquestioned paternity), such characterlessness can dissolve the mind into an indeterminate sea of chaos—of too many determining impulses washing in too many directions at once. The Captain's very philosophy, which gives him his reasons for trying to tear Bertha away (he wants, quite simply, to save her from determining impulses) ought to show him this is impossible (for he too really wants to determine her character on his own).

The passage on the house full of women reveals several characteristics of *The Father* which I have been attempting to point out. On the one hand, *The Father* can be read as tracing—or, if one's ideological position is more hostile toward Strindberg, perhaps only inadvertently revealing—the implications of the Captain's polemic against women. On another level, it presents the Captain's world-view (naturalistic determinism), while at the same time constantly reminding us how unstable this world-view is. Yet it is again this very precariousness which accounts in large part for the sense that everything in the play is somehow mysterious or uncanny, that it represents not just a physical, but a mental, reality. In the present instance, for example, the Captain conceives himself as being surrounded not just by women but by warring psychological and spiritual forces, which reflect Strindberg's theories about the psychology of suggestion; he seems really to be fencing with demons and powers rather than human beings. It is no mere coincidence that nearly all of the influences that the Captain cites as vying for Bertha's soul are religious or spiritual: despite his rejection of the supernatural, occult forces are at work behind the scenes, embodied especially in the spiritist grandmother, who remains continually off stage though her voice can occasionally be heard, and who terrifies Bertha by compelling her to practice automatic writing under the guidance of "the spirits" ("andarne"). The grandmother claims to be able to see realms inaccessible to the Captain's empirical science; she suspects his astronomy, declaring that he "inte kan trolla" ("is not able to practice magic"), because she knows that his scientific investigations threaten to demystify her mythic world.[10] But his opposition to her only serves to spread doubt throughout all the relationships which focus upon the child Bertha (if he says the grandmother lies, then he is saying the mother Laura is lying, Bertha tells him; and then she herself will not believe him any more), so that once again what might under other circumstances be an apparently sensible skepticism vengefully is turned back upon itself—just as the grandmother says the spirits will take revenge if Bertha betrays her relationship with them. In this way the Captain's own viewpoint, with which he intends to counteract all the other influences that surround Bertha, simply becomes yet another point of view, so that once again it too lacks absolute authority.

I say "it too"—for by no means should the presence of occult, mythic elements in **The Father** suggest that in this
play the powers provide a happy metaphysic that can solve
the riddle of life, which the Captain's search for organic
life in inorganic matter or his initial belief in the biological immortality of the race unfortunately cannot. The play
takes its philosophical shape by confronting the spectre of
nihilism. One way to understand Strindberg is to view him
as a mythopoeic writer, for whom the age's chaotic swarm
of points of view constituted the reality which he expressed
and shaped through mythopoesis. Myth, as Ernst Cassirer
writes, comes into being when the mind, charged with
profound emotion, confronts reality and understands it as
having animate significance; what compelled Strindberg
more than anything else was the threat of chaos, of nihilism, of the abyss.[11] Out of such chaos his demons were
born: in this case they became the occult house of women
which encloses the Captain and his Nietzschean ethics.
The conflicting points of view that cage in the Captain are
not religious: they are mythopoeic expressions, first, of
those naturalistic forces and influences, whether heriditary
or environmental, that meet in the formation of the human
character and account for the course of daily events, and
second, of those negating impulses that deny all such influences any absolute status. Had **The Father** been written
during or after the Inferno period, the house of women
would be the Hotel Orfila with its demons and powers
(described in the novel *Inferno*), or the house of vampires
in *The Ghost Sonata;* but since **The Father** marks a
transitional phase in the development of Strindberg's mythopoesis, more traditional representatives of Christianity,
along with an occult spiritist, sufficed. The impulse is the
same: they are a symbolic, mythic expression of determinism and its negation, of the position of the human self
born mysteriously into a godless universe.

The second scene in Act II most clearly illustrates what I
am calling Strindberg's mythopoesis in **The Father;** it sets
the dominant tone of the play's mythic background and
again combines several of the elements I have thus far
traced. Here, late at night when Bertha ought to be sleeping (and hence at the time when one dreams), the old wet-
nurse Margret reads the first two verses of the 391st hymn
in the 1819 edition of *Den swenska psalm-boken.* Written
by J. O. Wallin, whose poem "Dödens engel" also took up
the same theme, this psalm derives from a tradition of
Christian pessimistic poetry that flourished in eighteenth-
century Sweden, a tradition which the mythologies of the
Swedish Romantics attempted to displace:

> A mournful and wretched thing
> is life, and soon it's done.
> Death's angel floats all about
> and over the world calls out:
> Vanity! Mutability!
>
> Everything on earth that has a soul
> falls to the earth beneath his sword
> and sorrow alone remains alive

> to carve upon the wide grave:
> Vanity! Mutability![12]

For a poet such as the Romantic Tegnér, such poetry led
ultimately to a need for pagan, non-Christian solutions,
though he could never completely shake off the underlying
melancholy which gave rise to them in the first place; for
severe Baptists such as old Margret, it merely meant that
life was vanity, and that everyone must thus turn in devotion toward the Christian God. The Captain, in his demonic
battle of intersubjective will with Laura, is already
discovering just how lamentable and miserable life in fact
is, and soon he will learn how swiftly it can come to an
end: the doubt that Laura, like the ghost of Old Hamlet,
has dripped into his ears is turning his life into a landscape
of ashes. For him too all is vanity, everything is mutable.
Yet seen from the point of view of the play, the Angel of
Death scarcely reflects a Christian metaphysic or a mere
borrowing of a familiar Christian motif; on the contrary, it
is a mythic expression of the fact that, given the unquench-
able doubt that consumes the Captain, death is the only
absolute left in his world. And although the Captain
himself is not present during the scene, its theme is linked
directly to him. Bertha's fearful entrance during the reading of the psalm underlines the occult mystery that surrounds it: she is terrified by the mournful songs of ghosts
in the attic, next to the cradle in which old Margret
presumably once rocked not only her but also the Captain
himself to sleep; so the Angel of Death has hovered over
the entire household from cradle to grave. While to Margret it may represent grounds for Christian faith, with
respect to the Captain and the world within which he
moves it suggests the awful spectre of nihilism. Yet this
does not make it any less a mythic spectre.

According to Cassirer, to the mythopoeic mind "reality" is
indistinguishable from "dream"—which in Strindberg's
case brings to mind his Inferno and post-Inferno work at
once. In the novel *Inferno* and in **A Dreamplay,** where
Strindberg's obvious affinity for myth led him to draw
upon a wide range of mythological sources ranging from
the world's great exoteric religious traditions to the
esoteric and the occult, there is also a Strindbergian way
of seeing things that suggests the manner in which the mythopoeic consciousness conceives reality. In other contexts
I have tried to outline how an anatomy of Strindberg's
mythopoesis might look; here I simply want to point out
those aspects of Strindberg's mythmaking, such as the
song of the Angel of Death or the envisioning of life as a
dream, which appear in **The Father** and which link it with
Symbolist literature and art.[13]

As I have already said, it is clear from the letter on **The
Father** that the indeterminacy of modern life provided the
vision of life as dream. Strindberg's psychology of suggestion, whereby physical reality including even human
nature becomes determined by the manipulation of psychic
forces, places life on a plane of consciousness where all

that transpires recalls the contents of dreams too. The war between the sexes in *The Father* is thus psychic: one need only drop the seed of doubt into a character's mind and it will take him over to the point of obsession. And lest one think that the ease with which Laura brings about the Captain's psychic murder simply reflects a weakness of will that derives from his supposed mental illness, one need only consider the like ease with which the Captain himself, in Act III Scene 5, is able to insinuate the same doubt into the mind of the Doctor. Here too the power of doubt, that mental state which engulfs the Captain's mind, results explicitly from the problem of indeterminacy that the Captain must face: "Vad kan man veta?" ("What can one know?") asks the Pastor, to which the Captain replies: "Nothing! One never knows anything, one only believes, isn't that true Jonas? One believes, so one is blessed! . . . No—I know that a man can be damned by his faith! That I know."[14] Indeterminism leads to doubt, then, and doubt merely feeds the persistence of chaos; all that remains is the myth of psychically warring wills, where characters "hypnotize" one another "waking," where, even when one wakes, one finds oneself in the land of dreams amidst sleep-walkers:

> . . . we and the other people lived forth our lives, unconscious as children, full of fancies, ideals and illusions, and then we awoke; it was possible, but we awakened with our feet at the head of the bed, and the one who woke us was himself a sleepwalker . . . when the sun was about to come up, thus we found ourselves sitting in complete moonlight amidst the ruins . . . It had merely been a little morning nap with wild dreams, and it wasn't any awakening.[15]

This passage directly foreshadows the closing scene of the play, where the Doctor answers the Pastor after the Captain has lost consciousness:

PASTOR:

Is he dead?

DOCTOR:

No, he can still awaken to life, but to what awakening we do not know.[16]

The Doctor's remarks here are purposely ambiguous. From the scientific point of view, the Captain might wake up only to be irreparably marred by a stroke; and of course old Margret thinks he will awaken to a Christian after-life. Or again, the Doctor is quite likely uttering the agnostic's opinion: there may be life after death, but we cannot know anything about it if indeed there even is any. The force of the play, however, suggests that we already live in the world of the dream, a dream from which we cannot escape, so that if the Captain does wake once more, he will probably find himself among sleep-walkers once again.

The Father, then, is about the tragic failure of the Darwinian naturalist's ideals, given the threat of nihilism that these ideals inevitably contain; the dream, presided over by the Angel of Death and the mental forces involved in psychic struggle, is the myth that encircles the tragedy. From determinism and evolutionism to nihilism, and from nihilism to dream and myth—thus one can trace the concentric spheres of the play's thematic cosmos. In conceiving his myth thus, Strindberg was scarcely alone; the imagery and myth of *The Father* suggest his place in literary and aesthetic history. In the opening of this essay I likened the world of *The Father* to the "paysage d'âme" of the Symbolist poet, a landscape of pure subjectivity in which the Captain walks, as it were, within his own hallucinatory dream. This is a structure which Strindberg elaborated upon in his later dreamplays, which contain the dreamers who dream them (*To Damascus, A Dreamplay*); it can be found in his work still earlier, in the hallucinatory poem "The Fifth Night," composed in 1889 as a sequel to *Sleepwalker Nights* (1884), and even in the latter poem itself. What distinguishes these works from the Symbolist poem as such is just this concrete presence of the dreamer: in Symbolist poems, the "I" of the poet tends to be removed, and by means of a kind of "indirect discourse" the poetic image is made to express or reflect reality, both internal and external, as the contents of consciousness, while in Strindberg the dreaming consciousness is always concretely embodied, playing out its role upon reality's dreamed stage. Otherwise, however, the similarities are striking.[17] The mysterious suggestivity of the language of Symbolist poetry, for example, involves an intellectually sophisticated kind of mythopoesis; as Baudelaire wrote, nature is a temple of living pillars, a forest of symbols which familiarly regard the man who passes there. Yet the Symbolist poets also display an obsession with the *gouffre,* the inner abyss, which has led some critics to refer to their attempt not at spiritual, but at negative, or even material transcendence.[18] And this should bring to mind Strindberg's peculiar use of myth: in *The Father* he achieves more a mythopoeic apotheosis of that which negates metaphysical meaning, rather than that which might provide it. The same is true of Symbolist painting, with its darkly mythic iconography of the dream, of the fatal woman, of the mythic borderlines between the human and the bestial, between life and death.[19] Of the Strindberg who wrote *The Father* one can say, as did Maurice Denis of Odilon Redon, that he was powerless "to paint anything which is not representative of a state of soul, which does not express some depth of emotion, which does not translate an interior vision."[20] And just as Strindberg in his November letter defined his own interior vision as he had expressed it in *The Father,* so did Redon himself write of his own lithography that he used it "with the sole aim of producing in the spectator a sort of diffuse and dominating attraction in the dark world of the *indeterminate*."[21]

Notes

1. "Fadern" is simply the currently accepted spelling of the inflected definite form, which in Strindberg's day was written "fadren." For the 1981 production, Lars Bjurman and Jan Håkanson altered the play's text by

exchanging some of its mythological references for allusions to the time's feminism, drawn from Strindberg's letters and polemical articles. See the program written and compiled for *Fadern* (Stockholm, 1980-81).

2. Carl E. W. L. Dahlström, *Strindberg's Dramatic Expressionism,* 2d ed. (New York, 1965). See also Robert Brustein, *The Theatre of Revolt* (Boston, 1962), p. 104.

3. "Det förefaller mig som om jag går i sömnen; som om dikt och lif blandats. Jag vet inte om Fadren är en dikt eller om mitt lif varit det; men det tyckes mig som om detta i ett gifvet snart stundande ögonblick skulle komma att gå upp för mig, och då ramlar jag ihop antingen i vansinne med samvetsqval eller i sjelfmord. Genom mycken diktning har mitt lif blifvit ett skugglif; jag tycker mig icke längre gå på jorden utan sväfva utan tyngd i en atmosfer icke af luft utan af mörker. Faller ljus in i detta mörker så dimper jag ned krossad!

Eget är i att [*sic*] en ofta återkommande nattlig dröm jag känner mig flygande, utan tyngd, finner det helt naturligt, liksom också alla begrepp om rätt, orätt, sant osant hos mig äro upplösta, och att allt som sker huru ovanligt det än är, synes mig som det ska vara.

Ja, men det är ju rätta konseqvenserna af den nya verldsåskådningen, indeterminismen, och möjligt är att det är af ovana vid det nya jag häpnar och fruktar." August Strindberg, *Brev,* ed. Torsten Eklund (Stockholm, 1948-), 6:298. The translations are my own.

4. *Brev,* 6:282.

5. August Strindberg, *Samlade dramer,* ed. Carl Reinhold Smedmark (Stockholm, 1962-70), 3:194.

6. PASTORN:

Nå, så vill du jag ska läsa över honom. Vad tror du Guds ord tar på en kavallerist.

RYTTMÄSTARN:

Ja, svåger, inte biter det på mig, det vet du . . .

PASTORN:

Det vet jag nog!

RYTTMÄSTARN:

Men på honom!

Försök i alla fall.

Samlade dramer, 3:214.

7. *Samlade dramer,* 3:214; italics mine.

8. NÖJD:

Hur ska en kunna veta det?

RYTTMÄSTARN:

Vad för slag? Kan du inte veta det?

NÖJD:

Nej si det kan en då aldrig veta.

RYTTMÄSTARN:

Var du inte ensam då?

NÖJD:

Jo den gången, men inte kan en veta om en är ensam för det?

RYTTMÄSTARN:

Vill du skylla på Ludvig då? Är det din mening?

NÖJD:

Det är inte gott att veta vem en ska skylla på.

Samlade dramer, 3:215.

9. "Här är huset fullt med kvinnor, som alla vilja uppfostra mitt barn. Svärmor vill göra henne till spiritist; Laura vill ha henne till artist; guvernanten vill göra henne till metodist; gamla Margret vill ha henne till baptist; och pigorna, till frälsningsarmén. Det går naturligtvis inte an att lappa ihop en själ på det sättet . . ."

Samlade dramer, 3:217.

10. *Samlade dramer,* 3:234.

11. See Cassirer, *Language and Myth,* trans. Susanne Langer (New York, 1946), pp. 17-23 and 32-34.

12. En jämmerlig och usel ting
är livet, och tar snarligt slut.
Dödsängeln svävar alltomkring
och över världen ropar ut:
Fåfänglighet! Förgänglighet!

Allt som på jorden anda har
till jorden faller för hans glav
och sorgen ensam lever kvar
att rista på den vida grav:
Fåfänglighet! Förgänglighet!

Samlade dramer, 3:244.

13. See John E. Bellquist, "On Myth and Myth-making in Strindberg," *Scandinavica,* 23 (1984), 51-52, and "Strindberg's Mythmaking," paper presented at an annual meeting of the Midwest Modern Language Association, Bloomington, Indiana, Nov. 1984.

14. "Ingenting! Man vet aldrig någonting, man tror bara, inte sant Jonas? Man tror, så blir man salig! . . . Nej jag vet att en man kan bli osalig på sin tro! Det vet jag."

    Samlade dramer, 3:266.

15. . . . vi och de andra människorna levde fram vårt liv, omedvetna som barn, fulla av inbillningar, ideal och illusioner, och så vaknade vi; det gick an, men vi vaknade med fötterna på huvudgärden, och den som väckte oss var själv en sömngångare . . . när solen skulle gå upp, sa befunno vi oss sittande i fullt månsken med ruiner . . . Det hade bara varit en liten morgonlur med vilda drömmar, och det var icke något uppvaknande." *Samlade dramer,* 3:256.

16.   PASTORN:

      Ar han död?

      DOKTORN:

      Nej, han kan ännu vakna till liv, men till vilket uppvaknande veta vi ej.

      Samlade dramer, 3:274.

17. On the indirect discourse of the image in Symbolist poetry, see Anna Balakian, *The Symbolist Movement: A Critical Appraisal* (New York, 1977), p. 38.

18. See Balakian, pp. 32-37 and 51; cf. Hugo Friedrich, *The Structure of Modern Poetry: From the Mid-Nineteenth to the Mid-Twentieth Century,* trans. Joachim Neugroschel (Evanston, 1974), pp. 29-31, on the "empty ideality" of Baudelaire's poetry.

19. To take but one example, Symbolist painting is obsessed with representations of dark angels, including the Angel of Death. That Strindberg himself was interested in the iconography of Symbolism even at the height of his "naturalistic" period is most simply evidenced at the conclusion of *Miss Julie* where the beheading of the bird, which foreshadows Julie's suicide, is linked with the sermon on the beheading of John the Baptist, which the cook Kristin attends.

20. Quoted in Edward Lucie-Smith, *Symbolist Art* (New York, 1972), p. 71.

21. Quoted in Lucie-Smith, p. 78.

Arnold Weinstein (essay date summer 1994)

SOURCE: Weinstein, Arnold. "Child's Play: The Cradle Song in Strindberg's *Fadren.*" *Scandinavian Studies* 66, no. 3 (summer 1994): 336-60.

[*In the following essay, Weinstein highlights the child's voice in* Fadren.]

1

Fadren has long been seen as predominantly a war between the sexes, and it is hard not to view the role of the child, Bertha, as something of a pawn. As is well known, the play revolves around the power struggle as to who will finally control the fate of the child, and this nineteenth century custody battle finishes with Laura's triumphal cry, "Mitt Barn! Mitt eget Barn!" (98) ["My child! My own child!" (49)], leaving little doubt as to the central issues of the text: ownership, control.

But does the child herself have a voice?

This question is not irrelevant. The first time we meet her, she bursts into the room where the Captain and the Pastor are speaking, and she cries for protection against the spirits, spirits who turn out to be disturbingly (and invasively) lingual in nature. The child's seances with the Grandmother, we understand, turn crucially on issues of language and voice, or—more pointedly—the very origins of language and voice. The human child holds the pen over the paper, but the spirits are to do the writing; and they corral speech as well, since even to mention them orally is to invite revenge: "för mormor säger att andarne hämnas om man talar om" (39) ["Grandma says the spirits get revenge if you tell" (17)].[1] This night Grandmother is furious, however, because the child's writing turns out to be suspiciously recognizable, "cribbed" from elsewhere: "Och i kväll, så tror jag att jag skrev bra, men så sa mormor att det var un Stagnelius, och att jag narrat henne" (39) ["And tonight I thought I was writing well, but then Grandma said I got it out of a book, and that I had tricked her" (17)]. Strindberg is already hinting, here, at the scandal of textuality, the impossibility of being original in an always/already discursive world, a preformed network that precedes the human subject and governs both utterance and gesture. We shall see the full force of this view again, at the end of the play, when the Captain cites chapter and verse on the key topic of cuckoldry and the enigma of paternity, enlisting himself in a sort of serial parade of undone fathers. But what most strikes us in this initial scene is the riddling of the child's "own" voice, the presentation of the child as a mute stage for warring, alien voices, be they from Stagnelius or other spirits.

Later, in the second act, we encounter again the issue of a child's voice, only this time the spirits have taken over entirely:

BERTHA:

Jag törs inte sitta ensam däruppe, för jag tror att det spökar.

AMMAN:

Se där, vad sa jag! Ja, ni ska få sanna mina ord, i det här huset är ingen god tomte. Vad hörde Bertha för slag?

BERTHA:

Ah, vet du jag hörde en som sjöng uppe på vind.

AMMAN:

På vind! Så här dags!

BERTHA:

Ja det var en så sorglig, så sorglig sång, som jag aldrig hört. Och den lät som om den kom från vindskontoret, där vaggan står, du vet till vänster.

(56)

(BERTHA:

I don't dare sit up there alone. I think it's haunted.

MARGRET:

I knew it! I knew it! Yes, take my word for it, it's not Christmas elves that are watching over this house. What happened? Did you see something?

BERTHA:

No, but I heard someone singing up in the attic.

MARGRET:

In the attic? At this time of night?

BERTHA:

Yes, and it was so sad, the saddest song I ever heard. It sounded like it came from the store room, you know, to the left, where the cradle is.)

[25]

This sad song from the cradle—unlike any lullaby or *vaggsång*—may be understood as the very voice of the disenfranchised child, a kind of originary language of infancy that precedes the work of culture or the designs of the grandmother.[2] Coming to us as primitive music, it may be thought of as the *Ursprache* of Strindberg's play, a disembodied plaint that speaks of its severance and noises its hurt in ways that are hard to decipher and hard to ignore. For *Fadren* is child's play, and the cradle song represents a kind of pure rival discourse to the ongoing verbal exchanges of the play, as if Strindberg had wished to challenge the notion of *infans* as "speechless," and hence set out both to graph the silencing of the child's voice and strangely to recreate that voice in cradle song and theatrical play. It will be objected that we never even hear this cradle song, but my argument goes the other way: we are attending, every minute of the performance, to its compelling music, in the unfurling logic and displacements of the play itself. This is hardly to suggest that Bertha is the occulted center of the play, but rather to establish the *child's voice* as the figurative core of Strindberg's scheme. It is a peculiarly free-floating voice, and we are not to find it lodged securely in Bertha or even in the cradle in the attic; we shall see that its primary locus,

its genuine hiding place *därinne,* is in the Captain himself. The burden of the play is to broadcast that voice, to *telefonera* it to all the precincts of the stage, to bruit that voice with such power and pathos that all parties—not least the putative owner of the voice, the Captain—are subjected to its imperious governing authority.[3]

2

To read *Fadren* as the emergence of the child's voice may seem drastically reductive and univocal, but it should ultimately help us toward a view of the play's strange economy and poetry. The great Sophoclean dilemma of origins—can a man know where he comes from?—is given an apparent turn of the screw in Strindberg's heatedly gendered version: can a male know his child? A considerable amount of fanfare surrounds this riddle, peaking in the Captain's outcry that his connection with the child is tantamount to a secular afterlife: "För mig som icke tror på ett kommande liv, var barnet mitt liv efter detta. Det var min evighetstanke, och kanske den enda som har någon motsvarighet i verkligheten. Tar du bort den, så är mitt liv avklippt" (67) ["The child was my life to come. She was my immortality—the only kind that's valid, perhaps. If you take that away, you've cut off my life" (32)].[4] This severance imagery recurs more than once, entailing cut off arms and a full scale botanical fantasia of grafted limbs and branches, and a psychoanalytic criticism would have no difficulty discerning a castration scenario in these utterances. Strindberg very likely saw the play's central *agon* in these colors: a strong but dignified man is cast into a cage of women/tigers, and is ultimately destroyed by them. Laura as antagonist wages a brutal Darwinian battle against her more refined husband, and her chief weapon is the corrosive power of doubt regarding paternity. Take this away, and the father's life is cut off at the roots.

Blockage, severance and mutilation are hence sounded as the central dynamics of the play, but underneath this curbing/chopping scenario something radically different is coming to life: a new circuitry, a finally released flow, a creatural itinerary that is at last completed and brought to light. The father is slated to lose his connection to the child, yes, but his deeper fate is to return to infancy. Nay, not return, but discover that he has never left. Fathering is exposed as a fiction in *Fadren,* and only when all the sound and fury of foiled paternity are past does the actual condition of the Strindberg male stand exposed. This new male comes outfitted with a special voice: he has been dispossessed of the confident and independent patriarchal discourse he thought was his, but speaks, instead and increasingly, what may be thought of as cradle song, a poetic language of willlessness and metamorphosis, a language of pure theater.

To appreciate fully this transformation, let us recall the Captain's initial proud posture. Free and impenetrable, he brags to the Pastor that "God's word" has no "bite" on him, and in this play of competing ultimacies and isms—closing emblematically with a doctor and a pastor disputing a dead man's exit—the Captain's integrity bespeaks a freedom of belief and self that Strindberg found at once admirable and illusory. Man of science and dignity, he prides himself on his intactness, his composure, his ability to decipher external signs such as meteors and heavenly bodies, his confidence in logical processes, such as cause and effect, by which the world is to be known and named.[5] Just as receipts are to be kept, so the household economy can be assessed, so too does "recent research" indicate that there is only one kind of woman. This man professes to despise others who vacillate, and he understands his role in the social order to be one of authorized governance. About his daughter, he claims with utmost sincerity that he "äger första rätten att leda hennes naturell" (16) ["Should be making the decisions" (4)], it being naturally also the case that his wife "har sålt sin förstfödslorätt i laga köp, och avträtt sina rättigheter mot att mannen drager försorg om henne och hennes barn" (24) ["she sells her rights when she marries. In return her husband supports her and her children" (9)]. Exemplar of the Cartesian scientific legacy, confident in his prowess as thinker and his station as owner and ruler over those entrusted to his care, Strindberg's genteel and *sympathique* Captain represents no less than Patriarchy itself, and the burden of the play is to chronicle and to choreograph his spectacular fall.

At first, this fall rings Sophoclean and Shakespearean. Placed before the riddle of paternity, the Captain seems to be a nineteenth-century descendant of Oedipus, a proud man learning the dreadful limits of his knowledge, slated for an undoing of comparably massive proportions. The exiting of the blind Oedipus, led out by his daughter, broadcasts the same kind of grim news about male pretensions and power that will be exhibited at the end of *Fadren.* But the intrigue of Strindberg's play is also reminiscent of *Othello,* with Laura playing the double role of Desdemona and Iago, the wife whose virtue can never be known and the what-if? monster who can drive an honest man mad with consummate ease. Like Shakespeare, Strindberg has significantly reversed the Cartesian *cogito,* shown that *doubt* is at once corrosive and generative, that it dismantles what is given and goes on to build fantasies and "monomanier" of its own devising. At the height of his pain, the Captain exclaims to his brother-in-law that knowledge and belief are locked in a crazy dance:

> *Man vet aldrig någonting, man tror bara, inte sant Jonas? Man tror så blir man salig! Jo det blev man! Nej jag vet att man kan bli osalig på sin tro. Det vet jag.*
>
> (85)

> (You're never sure of anything. The only thing you can do is have faith, isn't that right, Jonas? Have faith and you'll be saved! Oh, yes! But I know that faith can damn you! That I know!
>
> [41])[6]

The nineteenth-century tug-of-war between scientific knowledge and religious belief is reconceived here, as belief becomes bottomless private obsession, resulting not in grace but in misery. We know that Strindberg regarded *Fadren* as an exemplary naturalist text, worthy of Zola's consideration. But, one also feels that Strindberg had a kind of large-souled allegorical drama in mind, that he endeavored to stage a nineteenth-century marriage in such a way as to mirror the great world forces at play in his time, not only the sweeping historical forces adumbrated by Hegel, but even more particularly the newer optics of Darwin, Nietzsche, and Marx. Hence the play treats us to disquisitions on genetic inheritance, on the exercise of will as power, on modern marriage as a business transaction with joint bank account. We feel Strindberg's cultural agenda here, his desire to write a play that keeps covenant with what is most unsettling and explosive in the burgeoning intellectual world around him.

3

But the play that emerges keeps covenant as well with what is most explosive *within* the Captain, and this non-programmed drama is ultimately what is most riveting about *Fadren.* The *plan* doubtless entailed writing a play in which the Father is overcome by the brutal forces he contends with, but the actual result is a dismantling rather than a collision, a disrobing of sorts by which Fatherhood—in all its guises: social, sexual, legal, epistemological—is shown to be a façade, a fraud. "Dismantling" and "disrobing" are themselves deeply theatrical gestures, because they hint at a kind of natural scheme behind our costumes and manners, while also acknowledging the power—indeed the magic power—of our robes and mantles. Just as Freud was to see the human psyche as a dramatic place, a *Spielraum,* so did Strindberg sense that the theater is a privileged locus for displaying these momentous "alterations," the donning and removing of garments that make up our cultural and libidinal dance. The play charts, at its deepest and most engaging level, neither the plight of the child nor the war between the sexes, but the song and dance of the Father, a performance that effectively renders Bertha and Laura unnecessary—redundant—since the Father-amalgram is to be imploded and then revealed as precisely child/woman. Ultimately this transformation displays, as we shall see, astonishing parallels with Lacanian thinking, especially regarding Strindberg's representation of the itineraries of the Mother and the Father—she from pre-Oedipal to Oedipal, he from law-giver to infant—in strikingly lingual terms, as both a take-over of language and a weaning from language, expressible only in a new theatrical code, as cradle song.

Let us consider first the traditional prerogative of Fathers: the bestowal of a name, the certitude of origin, the authority of decision-making, the generative and ordering principle of Logos itself. This is all going awry in Strindberg's play. The Captain will lose control of his child because he will lose connection to his child: propriety and property are in trouble here, and "his child" comes to be understood as a kind of linguistic joke. If one imagines Fatherhood as a kind of vital center, an energy-producing sun in the social and familial solar scheme, then the play stages something of an eclipse, a power failure. Not only is Bertha lost, but all his "outreach" efforts come to nought: communication with other scientists nullified, management of household affairs exposed as chaotic. Above all, the male as producer-origin is to be pronounced obsolete; Laura gives him the news: "Nu har du uppfyllt din bestämmelse som en tyvärr nödvändig far och som försörjare. Du behövs inte mer, och du får gå" (74) ["Now that you've fulfilled your unfortunately necessary function as father and breadwinner, you're not needed any more, so you can go" (36)]. Darwin couldn't have said it better.

No reader or spectator of the play has ever been much in doubt about the fundamental cashiering of the father. But to view this struggle as essentially a clash of wills, a survival of the fittest—which is how Laura herself sees it, how Strindberg wants it to be seen—is to miss the darker and richer wellsprings of the father's collapse. His props are taken out from under him, yes, but the heart of the matter is to expose him, to expose the father, patriarchy in general, as an affair of props. The deeper pathos of the play revolves around a man coming to understand that he is a construct, an assemblage, a mask. Thus, alongside the splendid agon—Laura battling the Captain, Laura systematically taking over his prerogatives, using his own principles and propositions against him, even to the tune of controlling the writing and examining the accounts—we also have the spectacle of an inside job, a creature being undone from within.

Of course, we have been seeing this all along. The role of Margret in the play is crucial because it incessantly highlights the child in the Captain. Ranging from "Hör nu herr Adolf lilla" (35) ["Mastor Adolf, I want you to listen to your old Margret" (15)] to the chastising and altogether more fateful "Han skulle skämmas! Men gamla Margret hon hiller andock mest av sin stora, stora gosse, och han kommer nog igen, som det snälla barnet, när det blir ur-väder" (38) ["Shame on you! But old Margret is still fond of her great big boy. He'll return to her, like a good child, when a storm comes up" (16)], Margret's motherly solicitude tells us about a Captain who has never grown up, tells us that "growing up" is a cultural fiction, one that will fall apart "när det blir urväder."[7]

And so the storm comes, and with it the sad song from the cradle, the new discourse of a man who can be both sick and up (for a while) before going permanently mute and down. It starts with irony and learned condescension. The Captain suavely explains to the doctor how new research has demonstrated the "instinktiva skurkaktighet" (62) ["instinctively wicked" [nature] (28)] of women, and with considerable dispatch ushers in his eavesdropping wife, so

as to have it out at last. It is here that the play moves from confrontation to infantilization. With frightening lucidity, the Captain urges Laura to leave him intact, out of her own self-interest, but his words betray a creatural vulnerability that nothing can assuage:

> *Nu förhåller det sig med min sjukdom på detta sätt: mitt förstånd är orubbat, som du vet, så att jag både kan sköta min tjänst och mina åligganden som far, mina känslor har jag ännu något i min makt så länge viljan är tämligen oskadad; men du har gnagt och gnagt på den att den snart släpper kuggarne och då surrar hela urverket opp baklänges.*
>
> (64)

(Since you're so interested in my condition, here it is. My reason, as you know, is undisturbed, so I can handle my responsibilities both as a soldier and a father. As for my feelings, I can control them as long as my will is intact. But you've gnawed and gnawed away at my will until it's ready to slip its gears and spin out of control.

[30])

This somewhat eighteenth-century mechanistic view of the person represents the peak of the scientific tradition to which the Captain aspires, but the animalism of human relationships, the "gnawing" of one's will by one's mate, bespeaks another regime, one closer to vampires and parasites than to formidable but delicate machines. This speech may be thought of as a high moment in European drama, a moment where the dark savagery of Iago's torture of Othello is brought utterly into the light, yielding a clairvoyant warrior, one who sees exactly what is being done to him and how he is responding. There is dignity and pathos in the Captain's recognition, but that does not reduce his victimization one whit. Arguably the most mature line in the play in the Captain's request—request!—that he *be allowed* to stay sane: "Att jag får be-hålla mitt förnuft" (65) ["That I can keep my reason" (31)]. There is a startling recognition here about coming apart, and we shall see that this collapse of reason is like a curtain going up, a revelation of a prior self that has no cover any longer. Hence when the Captain laments the loss of his child as the removal of his afterlife, his "evighetstanke," he signals the crucial directional shift of the play: from the future to the past.

4

In a striking intertextual reference, the Doctor mentions, at one point, Ibsen's Captain Alving from *Ghosts:* "när jag hörde fru Alving liktala sin döda man så tänkte jag för mig själv: förbannat synd att karlen ska vara död" (63) ["when I sat in the theatre the other night and heard Mrs. Alving in *Ghosts* talking about her dead husband, I thought to myself: what a damn shame the man isn't alive to speak for himself" (29)]. As Strindberg's Captain begins his descent into dementia, we are entitled to consider his plaint as the occulted material of Ibsen's text, as the generic discourse of fathers run amok, turned inside-out. Well before Freud unveiled his reading of Oedipus, Strindberg saw that the poise, prowess, and knowledge of *homo sapiens* were dreadfully two-tiered, that the male's secure station rested on an abyss, and that genuine scientific discovery—far from the realm of meteors and heavenly bodies—must consist in self-exploration, in turning the spectroscope "in," turning it precisely into the microscope, as the play's little joke will have it. Just as the information we can receive of Jupiter is located in the past—"inte vad som händer, utan vad som hänt" (33) ["Not what's happening, but what has happened" (14)]—so too the scrutiny of the Captain's life must now proceed thither. When one can no longer "keep one's reason," "då surrar hela urverket opp baklänges" and one simply *unwinds,* winds up backwards, where it all began. Discredited as origin and originator, cut off from progeny, the Captain begins his journey inward, to his own origins, and we now begin to see what he is, as the cradle song and the child's play commence.

This action begins conventionally enough, as the Captain trots out fragmentary memories surrounding Laura's pregnancy: his severe illness and feverish condition, overheard counsel between Laura and the lawyer, the crucial revelation that there must be a child if Laura is to inherit, and the cliff-hanging mystery as to whether Laura was or was not pregnant. With these elements of the *comédie du boulevard,* Strindberg makes the case for a putative hidden crime, an illegitimate child for purposes of inheritance, but as if he knew that the issue of inheritance itself—as Ibsen had so powerfully shown—is more an affair of genes than money, more a creatural than a financial legacy, Strindberg pushes his *grand guignol* scenario right to the limits: Laura crying in her sleep, and then, night before last: "Klockan var mellan två och tre på morgonen och jag satt uppe och läste. Du skrek som om någon ville kväva dig: 'kom inte, kom inte!' Jag bultade i väggen för att—jag inte ville höra mer" (69) ["It was between two and three in the morning and I was sitting up reading. You screamed as if someone was trying to smother you: 'Don't touch me, don't touch me!' I pounded on the wall because—I didn't want to hear any more" (32-3)]. Here is the direction the play *could* have gone: the Captain as calm, poised sleuth ("jag satt uppe och läste") and Laura as tortured libidinal outlaw.

But the Captain's control and decorum are not maintainable, and the sexual violence cargoed in this scene—"kom inte, kom inte!"—can no longer be kept at a distance. "Jag ville inte höra mer" says the Captain, but the text shows him pounding on the wall, much as he is to batter the walls and break through the door later, as if the pounding on the wall were an ambivalent poetic code, announcing its desire for silence while expressing an urgency all its own. It is here that the roles change. The libidinal turmoil ascribed to Laura's nightmare quite simply moves into the

Captain, and she will increasingly acquire his former control and mastery.

As for the father, he is gone. "Ser du icke att jag är hjälplös som ett barn" (69) ["Can't you see that I'm as helpless as a child" (33)]. And with this, the paternity plot disappears, along with its custody drama, and we see that the only child that counts, the one whose story must "out," is the child hidden inside the father, the child whose pretensions to manhood—husband, military career, scientific program—are placed front and center on the stage, exposed as specious, and blown sky high.

> [V]ill du icke glömma att jag är en man, att jag är en soldat, som med ett ord kan tämja människor och kreatur; jag begär endast medlidande som en sjuk, jag nedlägger min makts tecken och jag anropar om nåd för mitt liv.
>
> (69)

> (Won't you forget that I'm a man, that I'm a soldier who gives orders? I ask only the pity you'd show a sick person. I surrender my weapon and beg for mercy.)
>
> [33]

The male burdens are too heavy; the male charade is over; the masquerade—"min makts tecken"—can be at last put aside. Maleness is shown to be an inhuman construct, and Strindberg, (rather shamelessly) echoing Shakespeare's apology for Shylock, posits creatural vulnerability as the first and last truth[8]:

> Ja jag gråter, fastän jag är en man. Men har icke en man ögon? Har icke en man händer, lemmar, sinnen, tycken, passioner? Lever han icke ar samma föda, såras han icke av samma vapen, värmes han icke och kyles ar samma vinter och sommar som en kvinna? Om ni sticker oss blöda vi icke? Om ni kittlar oss, kikna vi icke? Om ni förgiftar oss dö vi icke? Varför skulle icke en man få klaga, en soldat få gråta? Därför att det är omanligt! Varför är det omanligt?
>
> (69)

> (Yes, I'm crying, although I'm a man. Doesn't a man have eyes? Doesn't a man have hands, limbs, senses, opinions, passions? Isn't he nourished by the same food as a woman, wounded by the same weapons, warmed and cooled by the same winter and summer? If you prick us, do we not bleed? If you tickle us, do we not laugh? If you poison us, do we not die? Why shouldn't a man be able to complain, a soldier be able to cry? Because it's unmanly? Why is it unmanly?
>
> [33])

Here is the first open breach in the male armor, and through it still more devastating libidinal material is to emerge. The Captain and Laura finally set the record straight about their sexual arrangements, and there is something almost obscene, in the nature of violated taboo or transgression, in these revelations, as if we were sharing, along with the central parties themselves, the fierce affective truths of their sexual make-up, home truths they are only now truly confronting. We are not dealing with closely guarded secrets, with a concealed past that is finally exposed; instead, we are discovering only now how it has always been, and one feels that both the Captain and Laura are as astonished at these eruptive tidings—each one's own as well as that of the other—as the spectator is.

In the eyes of Laura, the Captain, with his "stora starka kropp" ("big strong body"), has ever been "ett jättebarn" ("a huge baby"), and the male agrees, tells us that he came unwanted into the world, and hence came deprived of will. His connection with Laura has always been, at heart, that of child to mother; their sexual congress is and always was transgressive:

> varje gång dina känslor ändrade natur och du stod
> fram som min älskare, så blygdes jag, och din omfamn-
> ing var mig en fröjd som följdes av samvetsagg såsom
> om blodet känt skam. Modren blev älskarinna, hu!
>
> (70)

(each time your feelings changed and you came to me as a lover, I felt strage. Our lovemaking was a joy, but it was followed by the sense that my very blood was ashamed. The mother became the mistress—ugh!

[33-4])

These revelations are dreadful but neither deniable nor denied. Not unlike the Emperor's new clothes, the Captain's prowess goes up in smoke, as if it had been an optical illusion all along; she has given him his true colors, and he agrees: "Jag såg det, men förstod det ej. Och när jag trodde mig läsa ditt förakt över min omanlighet ville jag vinna dig som kvinna genom att vara man" (70) ["I saw but misunderstood. I thought you despised my lack of virility, and so I wanted to win you as a woman by proving myself as a man" (34)]. One feels that the very terms of the play are becoming increasingly specious and histrionic, that "omanlighet" and "vara man" are postures, perhaps impostures, that the elemental being is—trapped? fluid?—somewhere behind them, prior to gender markings, gradually coming into view. Childlike, will-less, extensionless, being systematically disempowered before our eyes, the *figure* of the Father emerges as a pure figure, a mannikin, a construct.[9] That is why Strindberg's text may be regarded as "child's play," as the spectacle of impotence and infantilization, of a man coming to understand his fictive status, of an undoing.

We are far, here, from battle cries and "hjärnornas kamp" ("battle of brains"). Not the war between the sexes, but the dismantling of the male, the going-out-of-business of the patriarchy is what Strindberg is, perhaps unwittingly, dramatizing. In the richest, most astonishing passage in the play, he transforms this drama of de-masculinization, of unmanning, into a well-nigh cosmic landscape that darkly expresses the true ramifications of the bloody business at hand. Women, the Captain realizes, contain the life principle; what, then, is man's fate?

> *Ja, ty hon har sina barn, men det har inte han.—Men
> vi och de andra människorna levde fram vårt liv, omed-
> vetna som barn, fulla av inbillningar, ideal och illu-
> sioner, och så vaknade vi; det gick an, men vi vaknade
> med fötterna på huvudgärden, och den som väckte oss
> var själv en sömngångare. När kvinnor bli gamla och
> upphört vara kvinnor, få de skägg på hakan, jag un-
> drar vad män få när de bli gamla och upphört vara
> män? De som gåvo hanegället voro icke längre hanar
> utan kapuner, och poularderna svarade på locket, så
> att när solen skulle gå upp, så befunno vi oss sittande i
> fullt månsken med ruiner, alldeles som i den gamla
> goda tiden. Det hade bara varit en liten morgonlur
> med vilda drömmar, och det var icke något upp-
> vaknande.*
>
> (71)

(Yes, because she has her children, and he has none.—And so we lived our lives like everyone else, as unconsciously as children—filled with fantasies, ideals, and illusions. Then we woke up. We woke up, all right, but with our feet on the pillow, and the one who woke us was himself a sleepwalker. When women grow old and stop being women, they get beards on their chins. I wonder what men get when they grow old and stop being men. And so, the dawn was sounded not by roosters but capons, and the hens that answered didn't know the difference. When the sun should have been rising, we found ourselves in full moonlight, among the ruins, just like in the good old days. So, it wasn't an awakening after all—just a little morning nap, with wild dreams.

[34-5])

This remarkable outburst takes Strindberg's ostensibly naturalist play into an arena of figurative activity that constitutes a bold poetic landscape of surpassing eloquence. Laura speaks for the commonsensical reader who has lost his bearings, as she brands the Captain "författare" and refers to his words as "fantasier" and "visioner" (71-3).

But this *tour-de-force* declaration, however unrelated it may seem to the play's nitty-gritty custody battle, adumbrates the new Strindbergian dispensation, shows us what the world looks like when the male principle is quashed. It is a place that is turned inside-out, a time of slippage and transformation operating on the solid real world, a prodigious metamorphosis into dream and fantasy.[10] Ordinary life, the life the Captain has led until now, was unconscious, and its goals, we now know, were based on "inbillningar, ideal och illusioner." One remembers Schiller's famous treatise "Über naive und sentimentalische Dichtung," with its special distinctions between subject and object, between innocent, seemingly direct renderings of the classics and the tortured, self-conscious mediated work of the (coming) romantics. Closer to our time, one thinks of Benjamin's influential notion of the aura, the indwelling radiance of an earlier art and culture versus the lusterless and spiritless artifacts and facsimiles of the modern era. To be sure, Benjamin was contrasting the authenticity and uniqueness of the material historical artifact with the reproductions made available by photography and film, whereas Strindberg is drawn to the crisis engendered by representation itself. Strindberg's Captain negotiates a fateful itinerary from vital integrity to facticity, facsimile, and fragmentation. His central trope is that of *awakening,* but it is deeply elegiac, an awakening to emptiness and decenteredness, an awakening that is ultimately a *wake.*

Here is what happens when "hela urverket [surrar] opp baklänges": the creatural rhythms, the forward march of time ("vi levde fram vårt liv"), are radically altered, put into reverse. One wakes up, but feet-first, with "fötterna på huvudgärden"; and one is awakened into deeper reaches of irreality, rather than by the clear light of day, and the agent of awakening "var själv en sömngångare." No less than one's connection with natural process is being sundered here, and we are issued into a world of barrenness and sterility, a post-sexual regime deprived of all vitality, condemned to imitation and histrionics. This new non-man is the partner for bearded women, and this reveille is sounded by capons, not roosters, is answered by "poularderna" rather than hens, so that we understand the new dawning to be an entry into facticity rather than truth, reflection rather than radiance, *Schein* rather than *Sein.* "Fantasier," "visioner," Laura has said, and she is dead right: her husband now understands his world to be, to have always been, a dream-world. This dream-world, untouched by the rays of the life-giving sun, is a place of ruins illuminated by the moon, and from this spectral artificial universe there can be no awakening, even though it is animated by wild dreams.

Strindberg's play charts the collapse of the fathering principle: no siring, no vital origin, no full presence, no immediacy, no innocence. Three quarters of a century before Derrida, he has prepared for us a portrait of *différance* and of the disinheritance that attends such a world view. "Ja det är rätt sjukligt här på orten för tillfället" (28) ["there's a lot of illness in the district just now" (11)], Laura has told the Doctor, and the reader has doubtless interpreted her words as mendacious and strategic, but there is indeed a sickness spreading out over this area, and—not unlike the plague that beset Sophocles's Thebes—the disease is perceptual and epistemological, as much as it is physical. An entire metaphysics is entering its death throes.

5

The Captain awakens to a world of facsimiles. And that is the news he brings, when he bursts through the tapestry door. The violence of breaking through the wall may seem

grotesquely inappropriate to the book-bearing, reference-citing scholar who emerges, but Strindberg knows what he is doing. With its heavy overlay of Darwin, caged tigers, crossed horses and zebras, the play appears to trumpet animality as its dark secret, the hidden truth about human beings, the occulted violence *därinne* that must come out into the open and be seen. But the man who crashes through the door with books in his hand actually betokens the ultimate trauma and threat of this play. Citing the prior words of Homer, Ezekiel, and Pushkin on the riddle of paternity, Strindberg's Captain announces the regime of textuality itself, a regime of models and precedents, an always/already scheme in which the pretense of origin or originality is doomed from the outset. Those books indeed signal an epistemological Reign of Terror, because the aura of all things is gone, and there is no route back to genuineness and integrity. There are only copies, only appearances. The fierce comedy of generalized cuckoldry, of world history as the antics of gullible men, covers a still fiercer view of life as fascimile, of perception as groundless, of doubt itself as plague.

With crudeness and pungency, the papier-maché Captain drags his fellows into the carnival, exposes their ponderous complacency. The man of the cloth and the man of science each profess ultimacies, but their professions and beliefs are no less illusory and inflammable than anyone else's.

RYTTMÄSTERN:

> *Hör du Jonas, tror du att du är far till dina barn? Jag minns at ni hade en informator i huset som var fager under ögonbrynen och som folket pratade om.*

PASTORN:

> *Adolf! Akta dig!*

RYTTMÄSTERN:

> *Känn efter under perucken får du känna om inte det sitter två knölar där. Min själ tror jag inte han bleknar! Ja-ja, de prata bara, men herre gud, de prata ju så mycket. Men vi ä allt ena löljliga kanaljer ändå vi äkta män. Inte sant herr doktor? Hur stod det till med er äkta soffa? Hade ni inte en löjtnant i huset, vad? Vänta nu ska jag gissa? Han hette—(viskar Doktron i örat)—! Se ni, han blekna också! Bli inte ledsen nu. Hon är ju död och begraven, och det som är gjort kan inte göras om! Jag kände honom emellertid och han är nu—se på mig doktor!—Nej, mitt i ögona—major på dragonerna! Vid gud tror jag inte att han har horn också!*

(86)

CAPTAIN:

> Listen, Jonas, do you believe you're the father of your children? I seem to remember you had a tutor in your house—a handsome devil everybody talked about.

PASTOR:

> Adolf! Take care!

CAPTAIN:

> Feel around under your wig and see if you don't find two little bumps there. Look at him—he's turning pale! Yes, yes, it was only talk, but how they talked! Well, we're all targets for that kind of ridicule, we husbands. Isn't that right, Doctor? By the way, how was your marriage bed? Wasn't there a certain lieutenant staying with you? Wait, let me guess. Wasn't he (*whispers in the Doctor's ear*)—Look, he's getting pale, too! Well, don't feel bad. She's dead and buried, so whatever she did can't be done again. Though as a matter of fact, I know the man and he's now—look at me, Doctor!—No look me right in the eye!—he's now a major in the dragoons! By God, I think you have horns, too!

[41-2]

Strindberg is pushing the comic givens of this situation in the direction that Ionesco will take, as he transforms men into rhinoceroses. Cuckoldry is generative drama, par excellence, and this passage emphasizes transformation, emphasizes the monstrously active and shaping character of belief—fantasies and visions, as Laura called them—that has no truck whatsoever with facts. "Hon är ju begraven, och det som är gjort kan inte göras om," but suspicion and doubt, like some radioactive materials, live forever.

To move from fact to facsimile, from truth to appearances, is at once comic and tragic. "Men vi ä allt ena löljliga kanaljer ändå vi äkta män" is arguably the very kernel of Strindberg's play. The rough-and-tumble of the line is in keeping with the species that began on four feet before standing upon two, and what it does in between, supine, is simply not amenable to the proprieties of bourgeois discourse. But the Swedish term for "husbands"—"äkta män"—is richly overdetermined here, since the play is about the utter collapse of "genuine men." And it is fair to say that the spectacle of a man uncovering his "ungenuineness," his "oäkt" reality, is like waking up with your feet on the pillow: you can still see, but what you see is ruins, and the artificial light comes from the moon.

At the end of the play, nearing total collapse, the Captain reports on the peculiar warfare he has waged, a combat all the more lethal for being imaginary:

> *Nu är det bara skuggor, som gömma sig i buskarna och sticka fram huvudet för att skratta, nu är det som att slås med luft, att göra simulaker med löst krut. En fatal verklighet skulle ha framkallat motstånd, spänt liv och själ till handling, men nu . . . tankarne upplösa sig i dunster, och hjärnan mal tomning tills den tar eld.*

(94)

> (Now there are only shadows, hiding in the bushes and sticking out their heads to laugh. It's like grappling with thin air, fighting with blank cartridges. A painful truth would have been a challenge, rousing body and soul to action, but now . . . my thoughts dissolve into mist, and my brain grinds emptiness until it catches fire.)

[47]

A new dramatic formula emerges here, a recognition of the energies that can be liberated by the struggle with shadows and effigies, and one feels that the fierce explosion noted here—the brain grinding emptiness until it catches fire—is a clear stand-in for the missing sun, a way of saying that psychic disarray is a form of internal combustion, a generator that will fuel the antics on the moonlit stage.[11] This stage, this place of artifice, this arena of false awakening, hosts, we remember, "vilda drömmar," and those wild dreams may be thought of as precisely the passions of sleep-walkers, the sound and fury ("inbillningar, ideal och illusioner") of the people at the wake. And, as we saw in the farce of the Pastor and the Doctor turning pale and feeling for horns, the power and energy of these "dreams" is irresistible, turns the most regulated beings into puppets. And this place with reflected light, wild dreams, and careening figures is, of course, the theater.

6

I have been arguing that Strindberg's gambit, in *Fadren,* consists in moving beyond the war of the sexes in order to disassemble patriarchy itself, to expose the phallocentric world view as a fictive construct, to depict a new regime of representation, textuality and facsimile where there had been presence, origin, and aura. He can hardly have intended to do any of this. He must, indeed, have thought his play to be a vital blow against the encroaching feminist movement, indeed a last gasp of virulent male assertion.[12] But what he wrought tells a different story. It may be that paranoia got the upper hand in writing *Fadren,* that once he began to imagine a strong man's fall, he found himself mining rich ore, that he had only to consult his own fears and anxieties to imagine Laura's take-over. After all, the triumph of the matriarch is hardly a mystery for the patriarch: it is his intolerably precise nightmare.

The point of this is not to psychoanalyze Strindberg; it is merely to indicate the obvious: *Fadren* decimates its male protagonist. No wonder that feminist criticism has found Strindberg to be fertile ground: their concern with gender dynamics is surely no more urgent than his own concern, and the play is astonishingly fair-minded in its findings, underscoring the Captain's fatuous complacency, his legalistic bullying, and his serene sense of the centrality of his function within the world order. Strindberg has not balked at any of this, and he has drained the cup of male humiliation to the dregs, as he takes this man apart, all the while thinking he's waging war against women.

Paranoia? Masochism? Perhaps it is wiser to look at the text itself for answers, rather than inside Strindberg. What we cannot fail to see is that this initially agonistic play turns, at a certain moment, inside-out, as it seems to discover its deeper quarry: the exposure and undoing of the Father, as part of a general metaphysical collapse of staggering proportions. I would like to suggest that that

235

course of action, that turn of events, struck Strindberg first and foremost as *theater,* as the kind of story that theater was uniquely equipped to tell. The drama of the Father turns out to be a crisis of representation, a devastating discovery that there is only representation. To move from original to facsimile, from sunlight to moonlight, is to discover that reality is nothing but theater. Theater is the realm where belief has become cancerous—where *veta* becomes *tro*—and in the hands of Strindberg these convictions move back and forth with lightning rapidity. We remember the Captain taunting the Pastor and the Doctor, yielding a putative on-the-spot metamorphosis. Horns? Or no horns? Strindberg's "truth" is of this kinetic order: not whether paternity can be proven or not, but the spectacle of doubt, belief, and transformation to which it gives rise. And at their best, these carnival scenes express something profound about psychic mobility and precariousness, about the roller-coaster world that lives inside of humans, waiting to be activated; when it is triggered, "då surrar hela urverket opp baklänges."

Nothing expresses more cleanly this shape-shifting than the Captain's simple tribute to Laura: "du kunde ge mig en rå potatis och inbilla mig att det var en persika" (71) ["You could have given me a raw potato and made me believe it was a peach" (34)]. Potatoes becoming peaches is what theater is all about. This troubling world can be entered only when things are divested of their surface unity, exploded into replicas, made to shimmer in their multiplicity. Toward the end of this play a doll, a christening cap, and a child's rattle are removed from a drawer and brought into the light, and we can measure their meaning, their immense human and emotional reach, only when we go beyond their apparent contours. Things and gestures echo, resonate, have dimensions. When a man throws a burning lamp at his wife, an entire life is illuminated.

That larger illumination entails bringing the full spectrum of psyche and temperament to light, and the "moonlight" of the theater outperforms the natural sun in this area. Theater is make-believe, the place where actors, clad in costumes, give speeches, and pretend to be what they are not. The spectator in the theater knows this, is constantly aware that they are *playing* on stage, that he is witnessing a spectacle, a performance, an act of representation. Strindberg has understood that role-playing, far from being limited to theater, constitutes the *modus operandi* of the human subject, that shape-shifting is nothing less than business as usual in the cultural and libidinal arrangements meted out to the human species.

So it is that *Fadren* closes with a crescendo of metamorphic activity, as if it wanted to expose, once and for all, that the central psychic dynamic in human life is an affair of potatoes becoming peaches, and that the theater is a privileged arena for such exposures and such transformations. Old Margret has the place of honor here, because she has always known that make-believe governs human

action; it is so with small children, and now she is to show us that it is so with grown-up children as well.

AMMAN:

> *Ack ja, men han ska höra på då! Minns han hur han en gång hade tagit stora köksk niven och ville tälja båtar, och hur jag kom in och måste narra kniven av honom. Han var ett oförståndligt barn och därför måste man narra honom, för han trodde inte att man ville honom väl.—Ge mig den där ormen, sa jag, annars bits han! Och se så släppte han kniven! (Tar revolvern ur Ryttmästarns hand.) Och så då när han skulle klä sig och inte ville. Då måste jag lirka med honom och säga att han skulle få en guldrock och bli klädd som en prins. Och då tog jag lilla livstycket, som bara var av grönt ylle, och så höll jag fram det för bröstet och sa: buss i med båda armarne! och så sa jag: sitt nu vackert stilla, medan jag knäpper det på ryggen! (Hon har fått tröjan på honom.) Och så sa jag: stig nu upp, och gå vackert på golvet får jag se hur den sitter. . . . (Hon leder honom till soffan.) Och så sa jag: nu ska han gå och lägga sig.*

> (90-1)

(MARGRET:

> All right, but you have to listen! Do you remember once how you took the big kitchen knife and wanted to carve wooden boats and how I came in and had to play a trick to get it away from you? You were such a silly boy, and we had to trick you because you didn't understand that we only wanted what was best for you. And so I said, "Give me that snake, or it'll bite you!" And then you dropped the knife. (*Takes the revolver out of his hand.*) And then there were the times you didn't want to get dressed. And I had to coax you by saying you were getting a golden coat and would look like a prince. And then I'd take your little green jacket, which was just ordinary wool, and hold it out in front of you like this and say: "In with your arms, both of them!" And then I'd say: "Sit nice and still now, while I button up the back." (*He is in the straitjacket.*) And then I'd say: "Stand up now, like a good boy, and walk across the floor so I can see how it fits. . . ." (*She guides him to the sofa.*) And then I'd say: "Now it's time for bed!")

> [44-5]

It is arguable that Strindberg never surpassed this beautiful sequence, even though his later work is technically more innovative, as it moves toward the surreal. Pure ballet of tumbling forms and shifting shapes, the evoked knife turns into a snake, so that Margret can remove its latter-day stand-in, the revolver. The choreography of displacement has become living theater. Sovereignly completing the snake-dance is the central metamorphosis of the piece, the rhythmic waltz that caps the play, brings into the open, at last, the flowing current and libidinal circuitry of Strindberg's scheme: the rich mantle of the past is at last figured forth in the green wool jacket that became the golden coat of the prince, and in this shimmering mantle of childhood, this coat of many colors, the Captain will, at last and definitively, cloak himself. Ensconced in his straight jacket, nearing the permanent silence of *infans,* completing his trek "baklänges" into the past, the Captain makes good on his voyage home, achieves his final identity, as Mallarmé said of Poe, "tel qu'en lui même enfin l'éternité le change." An entire figurative odyssey comes into view once we measure the avatars of that mantle. The itinerary we can sight moves at once from and towards childhood, and the theatrical language is at once exquisitely eloquent and dense, and also heading toward speechlessness, to the ultimate regressive state, a total eclipse of consciousness. This is the true homing action of the play, and it can be termed child's play, for there is no other play imaginable for the psyche that has been center stage here. And this rich metaphoric plaint of displacement and hypnotism, with its gamut of snakes and gold, with its magic capacity to *move* the human subject—could this play avoid outright violence any other way?—is what I have called "cradle song," is the theatrical, spectacular equivalent of that "sorglig sång" that Bertha heard in the attic.

The beauty of **Fadren** lies, at least in part, in the strange fullness of its theatrical language, a fullness beyond the ken of any single character. The Captain himself, to be sure, sees his downfall as a result of female wiles, and he reaches all the way into classical mythology in order to give its true measure: "Omfale! Omfale! Nu leker du med klubban medan Herkules spinner din ull!" (93) ["Omphale! It's Queen Omphale herself! Now you play with Hercules's club while he spins your wool!" (46)]. The sexual humiliation in this role reversal could hardly seem clearer. But little remains fixed in this swirling scheme. Hence Omphale reappears in the Captain's request for cover; Laura's shawl is spread out over him, and it occasions the softest, most lyrical outpouring of the play: warm, smooth flesh, vanilla-scented hair, birch woods, primroses and thrushes. But this shawl is transformed into a "cat," and the Captain orders it removed, to be replaced by his "vapenrock" ("tunic"), occasioning the last and most extended reference to Omphale:

> *Ack min hårda lejonhud, som du ville ta från mig. Omfale! Omfale! Du listiga kvinna som var fredsvän och uppfann avväpning. Vakna Herkules innan de ta klubban från dig! Du vill narra av oss rustningen också och låtsades tro att det var grannlåt. Nej det var järn, du, innan det blev grannlåt. Det var smeden som förr gjorde vapenrocken, men nu är det brodösen. Omfale! Omfale! Den råa styrkan har fallit för den lömska svagheten, tvi vare dig satans kvinna och förbannelse över ditt kön!*

(95-6)

(Ah, my tough lion's skin you wanted to take from me. Omphale! Omphale! You cunning woman who so loved peace you invented disarmament. Wake up, Hercules, before they take away your club! You wanted to lure us

out of our armor, calling it nothing but decoration. But it was iron, iron, before it was decoration! That was when the blacksmith made the battle dress; now it's the seamstress! Omphale! Omphale! Brute strength brought down by treacherous weakness. Curse you, damned woman, and your whole sex!)

[47]

Reaching back into myth for the appropriate parallels and models, Strindberg's Captain once more reveals his emplacement in a textualized scheme, but what most strikes us here is the interpretation that is given to the Omphale story.[13] The disarming of Hercules turns out to be a fable about disarmament proper, and Omphale is presented as "fredsvän," the founder of "avväpning." How does one un-weapon a powerful male? By calling "armor" mere "decoration," "grannlåt." Female cunning is enlisted, once again, in a project of dismantling, and the strategy consists in claiming that such protection is *merely* symbolic; Hercules's club and the Captain's armor are removable to the extent that Omphale can derealize them, deprive them of essence, transform them into "grannlåt," into mere representation. The Captain's plaint is an effort to undo the damage, roll back the deception, return to the raw power that preceded the symbol, retrieve presence itself. Hence he speaks of iron and of blacksmiths, of substance rather than sign: "Det var smeden som förr gjorde vapenrocken, nu är det brodösen." Something very grand is compressed into these strange lines, something virtually anthropological, entailing a shifting of cultures, a Kuhnian paradigm shift, a sighting of the fateful itinerary of power and belief, the moment they leave matter and move into effigy, leave the blacksmith to become the work of the seamstress.[14] Yes, this is a war between the sexes, but it is also an evolutionary fable, a passing of power from a primitive, integral material scheme to a culture of representation, based on difference and displacement.

This yearning for a return to substance and presence is mouthed by a man in a straitjacket on the edge of silence, and it is not going too far afield to see in it a nostalgia for the phallocentric order that the play has been smashing for some time now. But the beauty of the play lies in its multiple tongues, and its modernity lies in its vertiginous semiotic spectacle that converts "grannlåt" back into "vapenrock," showing that "mere" decoration, "mere" effigy, has a rich potency of its own.

Dismantling the father has been posited as the ultimate agenda of the play, but it is high time to recognize that the theater works in the opposite direction, that it discloses its truths through *mantling,* through the covers and decorations by which we code our lives and show what we are. The theater begins with the exit from the garden, and it has no interest in nakedness, since its gambit is "grannlåt," since it knows we are all clothed by culture. **Fadren** is a play about mantles, about the astounding semiotic power they have, about the theater as a co-player in this war of isms, this competition between clergyman and doctor. The central icon of the play is the Captain's coat of many colors, the garment that accommodates both the green wool jacket and the golden coat of the past, that is mirrored again, reflected over in the lion's skin and the shawl, the armor made of iron that becomes mere decoration. This mantle itself—not what is under it—is the text's truest "article of belief." Strindberg's dramaturgy consists in pirouetting this mantle, releasing its remarkable semiotic energies, showing how it broadcasts the life of its "occupant" in a theatrical code he himself cannot fathom. Longing for a return to origin and presence, the Captain is stranded in this new world of simulacras and signs, and it is for us—readers and spectators—to see that his actual life is written in these mantles.

Hercules himself thought that womenly chores were a humiliation, a threat to his manhood, but the tale of Omphale can be read otherwise, as a revelation of what Hercules could never say, as the index of a womanly side that is no less real for being unavowable. *Fadren* speaks of many mantles—of green wool and of gold, of shawls and of lion skin, of iron and of "grannlåt"—but it shows us only two: a Captain's uniform and a straitjacket. We are accustomed to thinking that the second *undoes, destroys,* the first, that the soldier/scholar is crushed back into madness and silence; but we are free, here as well, to read it otherwise, to grant the theatrical language its full due, to recognize that the uniform *is* the straitjacket. We then realize that that is what Strindberg has been telling us in his way, not openly in the ongoing warfare of the play, but surreptitiously, hauntingly, in that cradle song of displacement that Bertha heard, that music of children whom culture mantles and then moves about, as long as they live, in child's play.[15]

Notes

1. Harry Carlson suggestively links the mysterious script here to the "languages of the dead and of the dark world of unconscious impulses" (52). The burden of this essay is to show how remarkably *living* this language turns out to be.

2. John Eric Bellquist sees in the song to the presence of death, death as the immovable certainty that obtrudes in the Captain's nihilist scheme (538).

3. I am referring, of course, to the well known late passage where the Captain angrily confronts the Doctor: "Tyst! Jag vill inte tala med er; jag vill inte höra er telefonera vad man pratar därinne!" (85) ["Shut up! I'm not talking to you! I don't want to listen to you mouthing what they say in there!" (41)]. Barry Jacobs (113-121) has remarked that both telephones and spectroscopes were brand new to Sweden at the time of Strindberg's play, and that Strindberg's interest in perception and communication, clothed here in bold technological language, is notoriously difficult to render in translation (as Carlson's English shows).

4. Bellquist (536) refers to the child as an anchor that serves as a ballast against the free-floating "characterlessness" that Strindberg saw as the essentially modern condition.

5. Gail Finney argues astutely that the female sense-bound world proves to be more powerful than the male conceptual scheme (214-6); my argument for a kind of paradigm shift in the play has its parallels with Finney's gender analysis, but I ultimately think that Strindberg is moving beyond gender altogether in his mapping of power.

6. Carlson's translation misses the balletistic interaction of knowing and believing—*veta* and *tro*—that Strindberg achieves here.

7. Barry Jacobs (passim) passes in review the (sometimes insuperable) obstacles that hound English translators of Strindberg, and the menial use of the Swedish third person in these exchanges between the Captain and Margret ranks high on the list.

8. Shylock is doubtless the most conspicuous and conscious Shakespearean shadow in Strindberg's scheme, but, as the earlier parallels with Othello and Iago suggest, he does not stand alone. Still another Shakespearean candidate for inclusion would be Lady Macbeth, and Gail Finney has made a very persuasive case for the parallelisms between her famous "unsexing" (and the resultant feminization of her husband) and the gender/power arrangements between the Captain and Laura (223-5).

9. Once again one is reminded of Strindbergian "characterlessness" (as it is, for example, articulated in the preface to *Fröken Julie*), and it becomes clear that these views of the subject, of the cultural construction (and destruction) of identity, are astonishingly close to much current thinking about subjectivity.

10. Arthur Miller, himself a vital heir to the Strindberg legacy, reviewing the English translation of Olof Lagercrantz's magisterial Strindberg biography, has captured something of the irony and modernity of these strange cosmic landscapes: "the hallucinatory world Strindberg saw seems much closer now to being real. We really walk the moon, and with the press of a button can really crack the planet, and if we have mastered the physics of this magical power, the morals of it are, if anything, father from us than from Strindberg." Strindberg himself experienced a comparable giddiness and precariousness upon completion of *Fadren,* as we know from a letter written to Lundegård on November 12, 1887, two days before the premiere in Copenhagen: "Det förefaller mig som om jag går i sömnen; som om dikt och lif blandats. Jag vet inte om Fadren är en dikt eller om mitt lif varit det; men det tyckes mig som om detta i ett gifvet snart stundande ögonblick skulle komma

att gå upp för mig, och då ramlar jag ihop antingen i vansinne med samvetsqval eller i sjelfmord. Genom mycken diktning har mitt lif blifvit ett skugglif; jag tycker mig icke längre gå på jorden utan sväfva utan tyngd i en atmosfer icke af luft utan af mörker (298) ["It seems to me that I walk in my sleep—as though reality and imagination are one. I don't know if *The Father* is a work of the imagination or if my life has been; but I feel that at a given moment, possibly soon, it will cease, and then I will shrivel up, either in madness and agony, or in suicide. Through much writing my life has become a shadow-play; it is as though I no longer walk the earth, but hover weight-less in a space that is filled not with air but with darkness" (Meyer, 182)]. Rarely have the trade-offs between life and art, the ontological tug-of-war that governs the artist's life and work, been presented with more clarity.

11. The image of the mind as generator is at the heart of Strindberg's city poem, "Gatubilder, III" (*Ordalek och småkonst,* 52), which is worth citing as further evidence of the Kuhnian or technological dimension of Strindberg's view of power. Note especially the metaphor of "mal ljus" ("grinds light") which perfectly captures the shifting registers (from agrarian to hi-tech) that define the human brain's status as energy source:

> *Mork är backen, mörkt är huset—*
>
> *Mörkast dock dess källarvåning—*
>
> *Underjordisk, inga gluggar—*
>
> *Källarhalsen är båd dörr och fönster—*
>
> *Och därnere längst i mörkret*
>
> *Syns en dynamo som surrar,*
>
> *Så det gnistrar omkring hjulen;*
>
> *Svart och hemsk, i det fördolda*
>
> *Mal han ljus åt hela trakten.*

> (Dark is the hill, dark the house—
>
> but darkest is its cellar—
>
> subterranean, windowless—
>
> and the staircase serves a door and window—
>
> and down there deepest in the darkness
>
> stands a humming dynamo,
>
> sparks flying around its wheels:
>
> black and horrifying, hidden,
>
> it grinds light for the entire neighborhood.)
>
> (trans. Rovinsky, 21)

12. Strindberg's views on this subject at this time have been amply documented; see Lagercrantz (191-208) and Meyer (168-78).

13. It goes without saying that Omphale has received various critical commentaries. Carlson (55-60) has seen her in terms of the Good Mother vs. the Terrible Mother, whereas Lagercrantz (193-96), following psychoanalytic studies of the play, has delved into the Oedipal dimensions of the twin stories: Hercules "serving" Omphale, and the Captain's son/lover relation to Laura. Granting the validity of these models, I would nonetheless like to see this episode in a more anthropological light, as a meditation on power and its shifting modalities.

14. Carlson (54-5) has drawn attention to the extended imagery of nets, webs and shawls in this play, and Jacobs (115) has made some very suggestive links between male and female lines, "spear side" and "distaff side," or, as the Swedish significantly has it, "svärdsida" and "spinnsida."

15. See Lagercrantz (194-6) for a similar reading of the uniform/straitjacket. Such a view fits perfectly into Lagercrantz's image of Strindberg as vacillating between the masculine and feminine components of his make-up; but the metamorphic, anthropological, and theatrical dimensions of this "child's play" have not been sufficiently recognized.

Works Cited

Bellquist, John Eric. "Strindberg's *Father:* Symbolism, Nihilism, Myth." *Modern Drama* 17 (1986): 532-43.

Carlson, Harry, trans. *Strindberg: Five Plays.* New York: New American Library, 1984.

———. *Strindberg and the Poetry of Myth.* Berkeley: U of California P: 1982.

Eklund, Torsten, ed. *Strindbergs Brev.* Vol. 6. Stockholm: Bonniers, 1958.

Finney, Gail. *Women in Modern Drama.* Ithaca: Cornell UP, 1989.

Jacobs, Barry. "Strindberg's *Fadren* ("The Father") in English Translation." *Yearbook of Comparative and General Literature* 35 (1986): 113-21.

Lagercrantz, Olof. *Strindberg.* Stockholm: Wahlström & Widstrand, 1979.

Meyer, Michael. *Strindberg: A Biography.* New York: Random House, 1985.

Miller, Arthur. "The Mad Inventor of Modern Drama." *New York Times* 6 January 1985.

Rovinsky, Robert T., trans. *Forays into Swedish Poetry.* By Lars Gustafsson. Austin: U of Texas P, 1978.

Strindberg, August. *Fadren, Fröken Julie, Fordringsägare.* Stockholm: Almqvist & Wiksell, 1984. Vol. 27 of *August Strindbergs Samlade Verk.*

———. *Ordalek och småkonst och annan 1900-talslyrik.* Stockholm: Almqvist & Wiksell, 1989. Vol. 51 of *August Strindbergs Samlade Verk.*

FRÖKEN JULIE (*MISS JULIE*)

PRODUCTION REVIEW

Charles Spencer (review date 2 March 2000)

SOURCE: Spencer, Charles. "The Arts: Turn up the Heat." *The Daily Telegraph* (March 2, 2000): 26.

[*Below, Spencer offers a review of the production of* Miss Julie *at the Theatre Royal in Haymarket, London, directed by Michael Boyd.*]

It is de rigueur these days to mock those bewhiskered Victorians who took such exception to the scandalous Scandinavian plays of Ibsen and Strindberg. But though Ibsen now seems more like an earnest moralist than a shock merchant, Strindberg still comes over as a thoroughly disconcerting writer.

Few of us would now describe *Miss Julie* (1888) as "a heap of ordure", still less ban it from the stage, as happened in England as late as 1925 on the grounds that this "sordid" and "disgusting" work undermined the relationship between masters and servants.

Nevertheless, there is an edge of hysteria about Strindberg, an imaginative nastiness not far removed from mental unbalance, which ensures that his best plays retain an unwholesome fascination. In *Miss Julie,* for instance, there's an extraordinary passage in which the valet, Jean, recalls spying on his young aristocratic mistress from the stinking cesspit beneath an outside lavatory, a conjunction of sex and filth that tells us much about Strindberg's attitude to women. And when Miss Julie turns on Jean, by whom she has been ruined, and declares that she could "drink out of your skull . . . I could roast your heart and eat it", you realise that she would make an outstanding contributor to the Hannibal Lecter Celebrity Cookbook.

It's a brave play to stage in the West End, and Michael Boyd's production, in a new translation by Frank McGuinness, has a great deal going for it. In my view, however, it fails to penetrate to the play's dark heart. The problem is sex, or rather the lack of it.

The action is set on midsummer's night and the haughty Miss Julie, her engagement recently broken and her hormones running amok, has chosen to spend it dancing with her father's servants in the barn. There she has become fascinated by Jean, whom she pursues to the subterranean kitchen, which in Tom Piper's impressive, not-quite-naturalistic design is the size of a small factory, with a tall, red, spiral staircase climbing up to the master's quarters.

The willowy Aisling O'Sullivan, a vision in white, with rosebud lips and strawberry-blonde hair, superbly captures Miss Julie's patrician tones and quivering hysteria. Christopher Eccleston, he of the remarkably long nose, also effectively suggests Jean's uneasy mix of edgy impudence and fawning subservience. Yet apart from the moment when Miss Julie extends an elegant foot and commands the valet to kiss it, there is little sense of burning desire between the two characters.

It is always a matter of luck and chemistry whether two actors will ignite on stage, and here the vital spark is missing. Eccleston has acquired an excitable female following thanks to his intense performances on screen, but here he gives his admirers little to drool over, apart from one spectacular vault over the kitchen table.

Boyd might usefully have learnt from Polly Teale's fine production at the Young Vic a couple of years ago, which featured a brilliantly stylised, intensely erotic sex scene on the kitchen table. Instead he follows the convention of keeping sex safely off stage.

But if passionate desire goes AWOL, anger certainly doesn't. The rows and recriminations between Jean and Miss Julie, both burning with class hatred as they ponder their shattered lives, have a blazing intensity, with O'Sullivan in particular magnificently racked between snobbish hauteur and raw vulnerability.

The scene in which the other revelling servants take over the stage has exactly the right sinister, dreamlike quality, and there is touching support from Maxine Peake as Jean's down-to-earth fiancee.

This is an intelligent, notably well-acted production of a fascinatingly unpleasant play. Turn up the heat a couple of notches and it could prove sensational.

CRITICAL COMMENTARY

John L. Greenway (essay date May 1986)

SOURCE: Greenway, John L. "Strindberg and Suggestion in *Miss Julie*." *South Atlantic Review* 51, no. 2 (May 1986): 21-34.

[*In the following essay, Greenway explains how contemporary psychology influenced Strindberg's characters in* Miss Julie.]

Listing naturalistic elements in *Miss Julie* and reviewing Strindberg's preface to point out the many influences on the play would be tantamount to announcing the discovery of the wheel. Such work has been done thoroughly by Madsen, Lindström and Sprinchorn. While it is not our intent to reduce *Miss Julie* to a gloss of the history of physiology, one aspect of the drama and, more generally, Strindberg's knowledge of men and women can be freshly understood by discussing the play in the context of hypnotic suggestion. Banned for a century from scientific respectability as Mesmerism and animal magnetism, suggestion became a new area for legitimate research in the 1870s as part of the new theories of the unseen world of energy. Strindberg not only was aware of these theories, he considered his conclusions part of them and incorporated them into his naturalistic technique, particularly in his stage directions.

Strindberg took science seriously, although the converse has not been true. In 1889, shortly after writing *Miss Julie,* he wrote to his friend Ola Hansson that he intended to "transfer little by little to science" and to continue to explore nature with methods superior to those of the drama (Eklund 7: 348). He performed most of his actual experiments in the 1890s and described them in the *Blue Books* (1907-1912); but his library had always held a considerable number of scientific texts (Lindström, "Strindberg och böckerna"). Strindberg's scientific opinions—and particularly those concerning women—have not fared well, offending feminists and amusing scientists, who consider him harmlessly mad. The physiologist Hjalmar Öhrvall calls Strindberg's science "irresponsible" (*ovederhäftiga*), while Theodor Svedberg, winner of the Nobel Prize in 1926, calls his chemical experiments "little masterpieces of plausible idiocy" (Mörner 190; Johnson 86). Steene is being charitable when she says that "our feminist indignation can easily turn into bitter amusement and ridicule" (30). Literary critics dismiss the scientific views informing Strindberg's naturalism as a combination of pseudoscience and paranoia, agreeing with Madsen that, although Strindberg had absorbed a good bit of naturalistic doctrine and had read quite a bit in psychology in the 1870s and 1880s, his "so-called naturalistic theatre exhibits the characteristic Strindbergian subjectivity" (157).

In retrospect, Strindberg perhaps warrants these dismissals, but when discussing science and naturalism one needs to recall that science does not exist apart from the scientists who define the questions separating legitimate research from mere speculation. In the late nineteenth century scientists involved with what we now call field theory had to cope with unprecedented questions about the reality of the invisible world, and Strindberg believed himself part of a legitimate attempt to understand this invisible world of energy. If we acknowledge the conceptual challenge to the scientific imagination in the 1880s and 1890s that stemmed from experiments in the unseen world of electricity, magnetism, and radiation—wireless telegraphy, radio,

X-rays, to name but a few—we can begin to understand the openness of the field. James Clerk Maxwell, who developed the equations for electromagnetic fields in the 1860s, sensed the shift in scientific imagery; in 1870 he declared that it is "impossible to predict the general tone of the science of the future," but given the "new features of natural processes" scientists are "thus compelled to search for new forms of thought appropriate to these features" (2: 227). Before dismissing Strindberg's scientific pretensions completely, then, we need to recognize that Strindberg's theories of the relationship between men and women, based as they were upon theories of neural energy, would seem far more plausible to a physician attending the 1889 première of *Miss Julie* at the *Studentersamfund* in Copenhagen than they would to us today. In a new field the distinction between legitimate science and pseudoscience is by no means immediately obvious.

Indeed, a different picture of Strindberg's scientific interests emerges if one scans the memoirs of Carl Ludwig Schleich, a respected biologist, physician, and friend of Strindberg's, who was performing experiments in 1891. His work with the anesthetic effects of subcutaneous cocaine was probably a social asset with their bohemian friends at the Berlin cafe "Zum schwarzen Ferkel." Schleich characterizes Strindberg's science as "distorted and obscure," but notes his "astonishing knowledge of chemistry, botany, and astronomy" (245). He describes a radical experiment by Strindberg on plant physiology, dealing with the "electrical-molecular vibration of the protoplasm," in which he hypothesized that plants have no nerves but use the cell as a conductor. He was right, says Schleich; odd Strindberg was, but no dilettante (254-55). Schleich provides a corrective to the condescension of our later era by writing about Strindberg's alchemy that "he was not looking for gold, but for a new law of nature" and, in fact, anticipated the later discoveries of Madame Curie (247-48). While we do not suggest that Strindberg had the discipline to undertake a rigorous research program in the conventional sense, it does appear that he sensed the limitations of existing scientific theories and attempted to transform the scientific base of naturalism by incorporating current theories of neural energy.

Strindberg seems to have been aware that something unusual was going on in the scientific community. In the preface to *Miss Julie* he describes his characters as "modern," living in a "period of transition" (*övergangstid*). In "Psychic Murder" ("Själamord"), one of his "Vivisections" written in 1887, he notes that each age has "its binding pattern of thinking. . . . So it is dangerous to call anything crazy offhand, particularly in our time, when everything changes so quickly . . ." (*SS* 22: 188-201). While it is tempting to read this as self-justification, Strindberg was correct and used this thesis to modernize naturalism's scientific pretensions. "In these times of hypnotism and suggestibility," he continues in the essay, "new theses" for drama become plausible. He then began to write *Miss Julie.*

Let us dwell for a moment upon Strindberg's interest in hypnotism and suggestion that he demonstrates in the above-mentioned essay, "Psychic Murder." He developed his theories in another "Vivisection," "The Battle of the Brains" ("Hjärnornas kamp") (*SS* 22: 123-57).[2] In "The Battle of the Brains," Strindberg describes a battle of wills between his narrator and a "Herr Schilf." Initially, the protagonist feels himself hypnotized by the light reflecting from Schilf's glasses and crosses himself as a "hysteric" would. Later, he dominates Schilf mentally, destroying his opponent's neural energy, his "nervkraft." After the narrator has demolished Schilf by pounding his thoughts into Schilf's weakened brain, he recalls "magnetizers" and wonders if a transfer of "nervkraft" might be possible (151).

Bizarre as this hypothesis sounds, scientists had known that nervous tissue conducted electricity since the experiments of Galvani and Volta in the 1790s, and some had suspected that living tissue exerted a magnetic field and could itself then be magnetized (Walker 4). Scientists generally discredited "animal magnetism" in the eighteenth century, but Schopenhauer and Hartmann had reasserted its legitimacy. Strindberg greatly admired Hartmann's *Philosophy of the Unconscious;* he also had a copy of Broberg's 1866 survey of animal magnetism in his library. If rightly understood, he believed, there was a sound basis for the theory of animal magnetism: "nothing other than the neural impulse that gives a reading on a galvanometer" (*SS* 54:91). Many physicians would have agreed. For example, Joseph Ennemoser, in his *Anleitung zur mesmerischen Praxis* (Tübingen: Cotta, 1852), saw the process as demystified and completely intelligible.

Strindberg believed he had learned from Balzac and from Max Nordau (to be discussed below) that the will is itself a form of energy, so the idea of a magnetic "battle of the brains," that came to dominate Strindberg's perception of the relationships between people, appeared as an objective principle of biophysics. In a draft to the preface for *Miss Julie,* Strindberg described the battle of the brains as a form of Mesmerism, but his publisher Seligmann deleted the term (Lindström, *Hjärnornas kamp* 271). As peculiar as Strindberg's idea may appear today, its examination in the context of legitimate science reveals that he understood thought-transference as part of the clinical objectivity claimed by naturalism.

Mesmerism had fallen into disrepute as lascivious chicanery by the eighteenth century, but its sometimes startling successes in treating illness still could not be explained. By 1843, James Braid, whose book, *Neurypnology, or The Rationale of Nervous Sleep,* Strindberg also had in his library, had renamed it "hypnotism," and Jean-

Martin Charcot turned hypnotism into an accepted research program in his experiments at the Salpêtrière Hospital in the 1870s (Hillman 170). Charcot assumed, however, that the hypnotic state was a form of neurosis, with suggestion only possible when the subject was asleep: precisely the view Jean advances toward the end of *Miss Julie.* Such a restricted view of suggestion as a premise for realistic drama limited the applicability of the concept, but Strindberg drew upon the additional, more current research of Hyppolyte Bernheim.

Bernheim finally stripped hypnotism of Mesmerism's occult trappings in the 1870s, although the technique remained controversial. His work *De la suggestion et de ses applications à la therapeutique* (1886) was in Strindberg's library by 1892, along with many other works on psychology. Strindberg read many theories of psychology and suggestion during this time, but the view of suggestion he employs in *Miss Julie* seems closest to that of Bernheim. While Bernheim explicitly rejects the Mesmerists' view of conduction through a magnetic fluid, ascribing the hypnotic state to suggestion alone (26), his discovery in Chapter 5 that suggestion can be achieved in a waking state opened new dramatic possibilities for Strindberg's naturalism Furthermore, as Charcot had stated, hypnotism was not abnormal behavior that was brought about by mechanical manipulation. Bernheim notes that the states of lethargy, catalepsy, and somnambulism that Charcot had observed could all be induced by suggestion rather than by touching or other manipulation. Furthermore, "hypnotized naturally, we are all susceptible to suggestions and hallucinations by our own impressions or by impressions coming from others" (184).

In his clinic Bernheim observed that the subject was hypnotized through fixation—a method Herr Schilf employs in "The Battle of the Brains." All one had to say was "Wake up!" to revive the subject. Bernheim seemed aware of a new problem for the scientific imagination here, for "no interpretation exists in the present condition of science" as to how suggestion works. He was particularly concerned that "the experimental study of hypnotic phenomena could throw some light on the field of moral responsibility, still so obscure" (181, 185). Strindberg must have found this idea interesting while working on the play.[3]

We tend to think of hypnotism in *Miss Julie* in relation to the passage toward the end of the play when she says to Jean, "Haven't you ever been to the theatre and seen a magnetizer?" (*SS* 23: 186).[4] Her trance at the end seems a consequence of suggestion. A physician familiar with Bernheim's radically new work, however, would understand the dialogue and stage actions almost from the beginning as a series of suggestions and responses between the two characters that subtly underscore the play's more easily recognized actions and symbols.

First, while it is technically necessary for Strindberg to take the cook Kristin offstage, he does so in a peculiar manner. Both characters notice that she stumbles off in a quasi-somnambulistic state. While Kristin has not been subject to suggestion, Bernheim would observe that both characters now have the idea in their minds. He might also note that the early consumption of alcohol is not just symbolic: it could induce lethargy, the first stage of hypnosis. Strindberg uses the Swedish translation of Bernheim's term when Julie "fixes [*ruvar*] him with her eyes" after commanding "Come!" (132). Jean here could well be in a state of light hypnosis. His tone does change suddenly in the next lines when he says to her, "Do you know, you're strange" ("underlig" has a secondary, older, sense of "wonderful), and when he recalls his dream of being in a high tree. Next, telling him to "obey," she gives him a series of commands—"Kiss my hands!" but when he does try to kiss her, she slaps him. Bernheim used this technique to awaken patients: Jean immediately turns to polish the Count's boots (126).

Now Julie begins to respond to Jean's suggestions. To fix Julie's attention, Strindberg states in a stage direction that he "breaks a flower from the lilac and holds it under her nose" (138), while Jean tells her of his childhood encounter with her. The speech has an effect upon Julie, for she "lets the branch fall on the table," speaking "elegiacally" (*elegisk*) (138). Just prior to the Interlude, Julie shows her vulnerability to suggestion, and Jean (whose gaze is described as "fixating") obliges by first suggesting that she is vulnerable, then by giving her a command:

JULIE:

  Am I to obey you?

JEAN:

  For once. For your own sake, I beg you! It's late, drowsiness makes one drunk, one's head grows dizzy. Go to bed.

                                                                         (142)

After the Interlude, Julie takes two more drinks, which would certainly induce a lethargic state, and again asks for commands: "Just tell me what to do. Where shall I go? . . . I can't go. I can't stay. Help me! I'm so tired, so dreadfully tired. Order me! Make me do something! I can't think, can't act . . ." (166). Zola might interpret this as physical fatigue, but not Bernheim: she is exhibiting symptoms of acute susceptibility to suggestion and, ultimately, to somnambulism. Jean then tells her: "Go up to the house, get dressed, get some money for the journey and come back here." She obeys.

Scientifically speaking, could suggestion lead to a suicide such as Julie's? Bernheim considers the ethical aspects of suggestion crucial, and in Chapter 9 recounts case histories where suggestion resulted in immoral acts. He calls these apparently intelligent persons "instinctive imbeciles":

They are mentally-clear imbeciles; they talk well, reason correctly, are sensible, and sometimes brilliant in conversation; they can use finesse and intelligence in accomplishing projects they have conceived; but the instinctive sentimental part of the moral being which directs the every-day acts is as if atrophied. They have no moral spontaneity; they do not know how to behave, and, like somnambulists from a psychical point of view, obey all suggestions, submitting readily to all outside influences. This psychical condition exists in variable degrees, from simple instinctive weakness to absolute instictive idiocy. Under good guidance, these beings, deprived of moral sense, may fulfil a happy and useful career. Others are stranded in the mud, or before tribunals.

                                                                         (180)

As we will see, Julie's warped childhood (her feminist mother reversed gender roles on the estate and reared her as a male) would physiologically render her particularly susceptible to suggestion such as Jean's "guidance" at the end of the play when he gives her the razor.

Bernheim agreed with Charcot that the cataleptic state could be brought on by a nervous shock, usually triggered by light and noise. Bernheim would have found some details of the ending a bit dated, since Julie, startled by the sunrise ("Oh—the sun's rising!"), is shocked by Jean's bringing down the ax on her little bird (174). As incipient somnambulism can be "primarily induced by fixation or other methods," Bernheim would have noticed with approval the stage direction that "she goes toward the chopping block, as though drawn against her will" (175). While she listens to the carriage outside, she "keeps her eyes fixed all the while on the chopping block and the ax."

Jean's views also appear a little dated at the end; that is, he echoes Charcot when he replies to Julie's comment about the "magnetizer" that "the subject has to be asleep." Strindberg has Julie describe her state in a manner that Bernheim would have found more subtle. Strindberg has her exclaim "ecstatically" that "I'm already asleep, the whole room is hazy before me" (186). Strindberg emphasized this distinction between current and obsolete theories several times. In a letter to Edvard Brandes (4 October 1888), he described the play as "completely modern, with waking hypnotism (battle of the brains)" (Eklund 7: 130). In his novel *Shortcuts* (*Schleichwege;* 1887), his protagonist is aware of the difference between Charcot and Bernheim as his following statement reveals: "[when] the hypnotist says 'sleep,' and the person sleeps, . . . it's no more remarkable than when the recruit salutes when the corporal orders" (*SS* 54: 92).

Julie delivers her last lines in a "dull" voice, so Strindberg seems to prepare her for the final suggestion. Details of the last scene hint at hypnotic techniques. Audible cues such as the "two sharp rings on the bell" when the Count returns could induce a trance in somebody as vulnerable as Julie. In a deeper trance, according to Bernheim, "the subject is capable of manifesting the phenomena of catalepsy or somnambulism without the necessity of subjecting him to any manipulation" (89).

Bernheim states that all hypnotic states come from suggestion; as long as the idea is put in the brain, anything is possible. The idea of suicide comes to her with the sight of the razor. Julie initially says about the suicide: "I want to do it, but I can't"; when she is in her somnambulistic state, the state in which she is most susceptible to suggestion, and Jean, recently illuminated by the rising sun, "whispers in her ear," she can act. She "wakes" and exits to carry out what Bernheim called "post-hypnotic suggestion," a phenomenon he treated at length in his chapter on the ethical aspects of hypnotism.

Bernheim offered no hypotheses about the mechanism of suggestion; he stated only that "[t]he degree of hypnotic suggestibility has always seemed to us to depend upon individual temperament and the psychical influence exercised; not in the least upon the manipulation employed" (90). But Strindberg thought he had the answer, and here his science became pseudoscience. While the data constituting the explanation of suggestion were empirical, it is obvious from a later point of view that the explanations were regulated by social theory—to which Strindberg was susceptible. These explanations are curious indeed, and it is here that Strindberg's alleged misogyny had its ostensibly scientific base.

When Jean says that Julie should commit suicide but that he would not be able to do it if he were in her place, he notes that "there's a difference between us." Julie responds, "Because you're a man and I a woman? What difference does that make?" Jean replies, "The same difference between a man and a woman." This statement does not just reflect Jean's sexist arrogance (or that of Strindberg), but also a genuine program of research in the biology of the 1880s (Mosedale). It would appear as a quite lucid statement to a physician of the time, and would explain why Jean has the "stronger brain" at the end of the play.

Julie's "temperament" is important. Strindberg gives a stage direction that she is "extremely nervous" (*ytterligt nervöst*) at the end (172). Although this description says little today, it would have been of great significance to a physician in the 1880s. "Nervousness" had been an accepted research program in biology for several years. Letourneau, whose *Physiologie des Passions* (1868) was in Strindberg's library, typifies the medical interest in nervous energy when he asserts that "we have seen that man . . . is only an aggregate of histological elements, fibers and cells . . . governed . . . by . . . the nervous system" (219).

In his essay, "Psychic Murder," Strindberg describes all moderns as "neuropaths," and in his preface characterizes his age as "hysterical." While suggestion was an excitingly new area of research for the scientific community, "nervousness" had been a respectable disease for years. As had been the case with Mesmerism, neural disorders, known as "the vapors," had been on the fringes of medical science. Renamed "Neurasthenia" by G. M. Beard in 1871, the disease became part of medicine. Neurasthenia was essentially nervous exhaustion, brought on, Beard says, by our peculiar age, one facet of which is "the mental activity of women" (96).[5] Neurasthenia may result from any causes that exhaust the nervous system, "dephosphorizing" it, such as sexual excesses and abuse of stimulants. Through Jean, Strindberg emphasizes Julie's consumption of alcohol, which could partially explain her nervousness at the end.

The metaphors used in scientific inquiry to some degree regulate the kinds of research attempted and condition the results obtained (Kuhn 409-19). Theories of neural energy were governed largely by the metaphor of the battery; Strindberg described himself as an "overcharged Leyden jar."[6] As Beard (a friend of Edison) put it, "Men, like batteries, need a reserve force, and men, like batteries, need to be measured by the amount of the reserve, and not by what they are compelled to expend in ordinary daily life" (11). Lesions of the nerves come from "unusual drains," continued Beard, and cause "overload" (22). Doctors described patients as "run down."[7]

Neurasthenia, then, resulted from an excess expenditure of nervous energy. When combined with extensions of the battery metaphor it came to be of considerable importance in regulating gynecological theory. Strindberg's view of women and the phenomenon of the "semiwoman" (*halvkvinnan*), of which Julie is described as being typical, stemmed from this direction of research. The argument went as follows:

Physicians believed women to be particularly vulnerable to neurasthenia, sometimes called "hysteria," in that their frames were smaller than those of the male, and their neural reserves consequently less. Margaret Cleaves, M.D., in her *Autobiography of a Neurasthene* (1910), describes herself as just such a "halvkvinnan"; as a "mannish maiden" she was brought up to aspire to a man's role and ended up with a "sprained brain." Such aspirations are scientifically impossible, she writes, in that women do not have the quantity of nervous energy that a man has; hence, the drain on the nervous system when the woman is active is proportionally greater than upon that of the man. Cleaves mentions that for women "neurotic wires are down and the higher vibrations fail to reach us" through "a fundamental nutritive lack of the nerve centres" (109, 208).

The history of science has been kind to Charcot and Bernheim, seeing their research as forerunners to legitimate psychotherapy. On the frontier of science, however, the borderline between sound research and pseudoscientific speculation is easily traced only in retrospect. Such was the case with Strindberg, who thought he found a plausible electrical explanation for the phenomenon of suggestion in the works of Max Nordau. In *Paradoxes* (1885), translated into Swedish the same year, Nordau in an article on suggestion employs the battery metaphor to explain that suggestion consists of a transference of one brain's molecular motion to another. The activity of the will is then simply a neural current, which is Strindberg's reason for accepting animal magnetism. The molecular activity of a person in a hypnotic state, Nordau continues, is minimal, so that the person becomes more susceptible to suggestion (185-87). Strindberg explicitly employed this theory in his character's battle with "Herr Schilf," and does so more subtly with Julie and Jean.

If will is a form of energy, Jean's domination of Julie at the end of the play becomes more plausible yet. As a "nervous person," Strindberg's character in "Above the Clouds" (*Över molnen*) senses magnetic currents in the presence of a stronger person (*SS* 15: 156). In "Newlyminted" (*Nybyggnad*), the emancipated physician Blanche Chappuis is warned that hysterics (*övernervösa*) become so through the sensing of others' electricity (*SS* 15: 80).

As proof of the neural peril awaiting the "new woman," a physician could cite statistics, such as those of comparative cranial capacities. Alexander Sutherland, for instance, found that the male has. 73 ounces of brain per inch of height, while the woman has but 70.[8] As Otto Juettner put it in the *Bulletin* of the American Academy of Medicine (1908), "We, therefore, conclude that woman must degenerate structurally and functionally in proportion to her deviation from her fixed psychological standard" or "she becomes a sexless substitute for man" (351), that is, Strindberg's "semiwoman."

Now we can reconsider the effect of Juliet's unnatural upbringing: she could not escape the legacy of her feminist mother, who insisted on reversing gender roles and, plausibly enough, went insane. Juettner says that the man-woman "descends from a higher to a lower physiological level and soon shows the evidence of biologic regression" (351). Thus the effects of Julie's mother's training were not just behavioral, as Zola would argue, but physiological.

Generally, physicians advised passivity in sexual relations to avoid draining "vital energies" (Acton 135; Haller and Haller 96-102). Our physician would note that the sexual act during the interlude of *Miss Julie* would have two effects. First, there would be an enormous drain on the male's neural reserves that explained Jean's lethargy after the interlude; second, the effect on Julie would be more complicated. According to William Acton, the leading physician in sexuality of the 1870s, "the majority of women (happily for society) are not very much troubled with sexual feeling of any kind" (163)—hence there is not much danger of neural drain for the normal woman. But

Julie is different. Strindberg makes a point of her being aroused; so from a medical point of view if she were neurally involved in coitus, the drain on her system in the interlude must have been cataclysmic. In addition to the abnormal aspects of her psychology, she had fewer ganglia and reserves relative to Jean in the first place. Her sensuality would certainly appear unnatural to our physician-spectator, perhaps perverse, but physiologically it explains her acute nervousness in the last act and her vulnerability to suggestion at the end. One should remember, too, that Julie's natural womanhood had already been thrown out of balance by her mother.

In the preface Strindberg mentions her "time of the month" as a reason for her peculiar behavior. Medically, insofar as Victorian scientists talked about menstruation (and they did not do so very often), scientists accepted that women were unnaturally susceptible to shocks and incapacitation because of the drain upon their reproductive energy at this time and, of course, their already limited neural resources (Showalter and Showalter 83-89). James MacGrigor Allan declared to the Anthropological Society of London in 1869 that women are, during this "crisis," temporarily insane and "unfit for any great mental or physical labor" (cxcviii-cxix)—a point that went unchallenged. Strindberg and Jean describe Julie as "crazy" twice; as Madsen notes, "galen" in this context refers to the behavior of an animal in heat (79). While Strindberg balances the action in the play to create the possibility for a plausible struggle on stage, a nineteenth-century spectator would have seen that Julie has little chance in the "battle of the brains."

We have not attempted here to outline an interpretation of the play but merely to suggest how Strindberg's knowledge of contemporary science gave a subtle structure to his dialogue and stage directions consistent with then-current physiological theories. In a more general sense, we have suggested that some of the extreme extrapolations Strindberg drew from these theories stemmed from the social assumptions of the biology of his time, not just his own psychological quirks.

In "Misogyny and Gynecolatry" (*Kvinnohat och Kvinnodyrkan*) Strindberg states that he does not hate women at all, but hates their "intrusion into the male working-place"; in view of the above observations his opinions should not be dismissed as mere "subjectivity." Such intrusion creates, Strindberg claims, a class of "androgynes" (*SS* 27: 642). Although the theories of evolution and Social Darwinism were of great importance to Strindberg, it is not necessary to refer to them since the theories of neurology offer sufficient evidence for his notion that a woman would be incapable of achieving a man's mental output and would destroy herself in departing from her evolutionary niche. Hence Strindberg was not just feeling paranoid or even misogynistic when he criticized aggressive women; his arguments were, considering the state of research at the time, well-founded: as a naturalist he outlined what he conceived of as an unnatural, potentially catastrophic biological aberration. Physicians watching *Miss Julie* would have seen the "realistic" details not as physical, but as clinical and quite subtle: they would have agreed that Julie was typical of the deviant, modern, nervous woman, with a high vulnerability to suggestion.

Notes

1. The research for this article has been supported by a grant from the National Endowment for the Humanities program in Humanities, Science and Technology.

2. Words such as "experiment," "nervous," and "vivisection" had a special meaning in the medical literature of the time, "vivisection" implying Claude Bernard's radical anatomical and surgical methodology. While Mill used the term to mean "hygiene" in the 1860s, by Strindberg's time the term had a controversial connotation of "hard hearted" (Stevenson 17-31). Strindberg's insistence in the preface that we should feel no emotion at Julie's fate sounds peculiar, but Emmanuel Klein scandalized the Vivisection Committee in 1875 by testifying that the experimenter does not take the suffering of his subject into account (Klein 2677-79; 3534-49).

3. The question of moral responsibility for acts under hypnosis attracted much attention in legal and medical journals, but opinion was divided, according to Hillman. According to Swedish law, if Julie submitted to the trance at the end voluntarily, she would be responsible for the consequences. According to Björnström, however, Head Physician of the Stockholm Hospital in the 1880s, Jean would bear the guilt, in that "it is fully decided that the one most to blame for the suggested crime is the hypnotizer, or the one who has given the suggestion" (113).

4. The text of *Miss Julie* appears in *SS* 23: 97-187; in translating, I have been particularly concerned with Strindberg's use of medical terms in his stage directions.

5. On neurasthenia as a cultural phenomenon, see Gosling and Haller and Haller, Ch. 1: "The Nervous Century." Erb outlines the international nature of the malady, calling neurasthenia "the fashionable neurosis of the present time" (290). The scientific status of "nervousness" exerted an appeal to the literary as well as to the scientific imagination (Drinka).

6. Kärnell traces the pervasiveness of electrical metaphors in Strindberg's conception of character (193-200).

7. For more on the battery metaphor, see Haller and Haller 9-24. In the 1900 Sears catalog one could buy an electric belt to recharge one's neural supply. Sears describes the device as able to cure any form of debility, including "female weakness," the male pouch evidently being detachable. As an index of this metaphor's coming obsolescence, by 1909 Sears no longer carried the Heidelberg belt.

8. On the role of measurement in sex-differences, see Haller and Haller 47-87, and Gould 103-107.

Works Cited

Acton, William. *The Functions and Disorders of the Reproductive Organs in Childhood, Youth, Adult Age and Advanced Life Considered in Their Physiological, Social and Moral Relations*. 3rd ed. Philadelphia: Blakiston, 1871.

Allan, James McGrigor. "On the Real Differences in the Minds of Men and Women." *Anthropological Review* 7 (1869): cxcv-ccxix.

Beard, George Miller. *American Nervousness, Its Causes and Consequences, A Supplement to Nervous Exhaustion (Neurasthenia)*. New York: Putnam's, 1881.

Bernheim, Hyppolyte. *Suggestive Therapeutics: A Treatise on the Nature and Uses of Hypnotism*. Trans. Chr. Herter. New York: Brole, 1947.

Björnström, Frederik. *Hypnotism: Its History and Development*. Trans. Baron Nils Posse. 2nd ed. Humboldt Library of Popular Science Literature, Vol. 11. New York: Humboldt, [1889].

Cleaves, Margaret. *The Autobiography of a Neurasthene as Told by One of Them and Recorded by Margaret Cleaves, MD*. Boston: Badger, 1910.

Eklund, Torsten. *August Strindbergs brev*. 7 vols. Stockholm: Bonniers, 1948-.

Drinka, George Frederick. *The Birth of Neurosis: Myth, Malady and the Victorians*. New York: Simon and Schuster, 1984.

Ennemoser, Joseph. *Anleitung zur mesmerischen Praxis*. Stuttgart: Cotta, 1852.

Erb, Wilhelm. *Handbook of Electro-Therapeutics*. Trans. L. Putzel. Wood's Library of Standard Medical Authors. New York: Wm. Wood, 1883.

Gosling, Francis G. *American Nervousness: A Study in Medicine and Social Values in the Gilded Age, 1870-1900*. Norman, OK: Oklahoma Medical College, 1976.

Gould, Stephen Jay. *The Mismeasure of Man*. New York: Norton, 1981.

Haller, John S. and Robin M. *The Physician and Sexuality in Victorian America*. New York: Norton, 1977.

Hillman, Robert. "A Scientific Study of Mystery: The Role of Medical and Popular Press in the Nancy-Salpêtrière Controversy on Hypnotism." *Bulletin of the History of Medicine* 39 (1965): 163-82.

Juettner, Otto. "The Place of Women in the Modern Business World as Affecting the Future of the Race." *Bulletin, American Academy of Medicine* 9 (1908): 20-34.

Kärnell, Karl-Åke "Strindbergs bildkretsar." *Synpunkter på Strindberg*. Ed. Gunnar Brandell. Stockholm: Aldus/ Bonniers, 1964. 182-208.

Klein, Emmanuel. Testimony. *Report of the Royal Commission on the Practice of Subjecting Live Animals to Experiments for Scientific Purposes*. London, 1876. Sects. 2677-79, 3534-49.

Kahn, Thomas S. "Metaphor in Science." *Metaphor and Thought*. Ed. Andrew Ortony. Cambridge: Cambridge UP, 1979. 409-19.

Letourneau, Charles. *Physiologie des passions*. Paris: Baillière, 1868.

Lindström, Hans. *Hjärnornas kamp: psykologiska idéer och motiv i Strindbergs åttiotalsdiktning*. Uppsala: Appelberg, 1952.

————. "Strindberg och böckerna. 1. Biblioteken 1883, 1892 och 1912. Företeckningar och kommentarer." Skrifter utg. av Svenska Litteratursällskapet, 36. Stockholm: Almkvist and Wiksell, 1977.

Madsen, Börge Gedso. *Strindberg's Naturalistic Theatre: Its Relationship to French Naturalism*. Seattle: U of Washington P, 1962.

Maxwell, James Clerk. *Scientific Papers of James Clerk Maxwell*. Ed. W. D. Niven. 1890. 2 vols. New York: Dover, 1952.

Mörner, Birger. *Den Strindberg jag känt*. Stockholm: Bonniers, 1924.

Mosedale, Susan Sleeth. "Science Corrupted: Victorian Biologists Consider 'The Woman Question.'" *Journal of the History of Biology* 11 (1978): 1-55.

Nordau, Max. *Paradoxe*. Leipzig: Elischer, 1885.

Rosenberg, Charles E. "The Place of George M. Beard in Nineteenth-Century Psychiatry." *Bulletin of the History of Medicine* 36 (1962): 245-59.

Schleich, Carl Ludwig. "Strindberg-Erinnerungen." *Besonnte Vergangenheit*. Berline Rowohlt, 1924. 239-65.

Showalter, Elaine and English. "Victorian Women and Menstruation." *Victorian Studies* 14 (1970): 83-89.

Sprinchorn, Evert. *Strindberg as Dramatist*. New Haven: Yale UP, 1982.

Steene, Birgitta. "The Ambiguous Feminist." *Scandinavian Review* 64.3 (1970): 27-31.

Stevenson, Lloyd G. "Physiology, General Education and the Antivivisection Movement." *Clio Medica* 12 (1977): 17-31.

Strindberg, August. *Samlade Skrifter*. Ed. John Landquist. 55 Vols. in 35. Stockholm: Bonniers, 1912-1921. Abbreviated as *SS*.

Walker, W. C. "Animal Electricity before Galvani." *Annals of Science* 2 (1937): 84-113.

Edward S. Franchuk (essay date 1993)

SOURCE: Franchuk, Edward S. "Symbolism in *Miss Julie*." *Theatre Research International* 18, supplementary issue (1993): 11-15.

[*In the following essay, Franchuck explores the symbolism in* Miss Julie.]

The theme of Strindberg's **Miss Julie** (**Fröken Julie,** 1888), the struggle for sexual ascendancy between a liberated young woman and an ambitious young man who is her social inferior, continues to hold fascination even in times such as our own, which purport to be sexually liberated, socially egalitarian, and feminist. Perhaps, one might speculate, fascination with the play, its characters, and its situation is especially intense in such times. Certainly awareness of an interest in sexual politics have not lessened in the century since the play appeared. Since it has been a century dominated to a large extent by the theories of Dr. Sigmund Freud, this is hardly surprising.

Indeed, Freud has influenced not only the way we, as a late twentieth-century audience, see the play, but also to a considerable degree how directors and producers stage it. Alf Sjoberg's acclaimed film version (1950) perhaps laid the groundwork for a growing tradition of lading the play with as much Freudian symbolism as it can be made to bear. Who can forget the orgiastic dance around a very phallic maypole that Sjoberg substituted for the indoor peasant's dance that takes place while Jean is making physical love to Julie off-stage? More recently, the BBC version of the play, directed by Michael Simpson in 1987, used suggestively arranged phallic-shaped loaves of bread in the same scene (now transferred back indoors, as Strindberg intended) to the same purpose.

It is perhaps worth recalling, then, that *The Interpretation of Dreams* was not published until 1900, and that there is no evidence that Strindberg ever had any knowledge of either it or its author. It may be inevitable that we now view the play through Freud-tinted glasses; but a more useful way of viewing the play, and of staging it, might be with reference to Strindberg's own highly developed and consistent system of symbols, rather than to symbols which achieved popularity and significance only after the play had already done so.

Indeed **Miss Julie,** although the more naturalistic of Strindberg's plays, makes extensive use of symbolism. The problem—and the challenge—for the director is to find ways in which the play's symbols can be brought to the attention of the audience, particularly an audience which is not Scandinavian and which is not particularly familiar with either Strindberg or his times. Solutions are not always easily come by but, if successful, should permit the audience to enter more fully into the world of the play and into its meaning.

Unfortunately, some of the symbolism seems destined to remain inaccessible to the non-Scandinavian general audience: those associated with the fact that the action of *Miss Julie* occurs on Midsummer Eve. There are references to the dancing associated with the festival, to the custom of decorating with birch branches in leaf, to the folk belief that if unmarried girls collect nine midsummer flowers and sleep with them under their pillows they will dream of their future husbands, and to the very early sunrise, the light from which illuminates Jean in the final moments of the play. These elements, which are cultural, are perhaps best dealt with through programme notes.

Midsummer Day is the Feast of St John the Baptist (24 June), which explains the reference to the lesson to be read in church that day, concerning his beheading. The contrast between the sober respectability of the Feast and the pagan revelry of the Eve, a contrast pointed by the church-going Kristin, parallels the contrast between Julie's world of ideals and Jean's world of physical reality. The birch twigs in leaf which decorate the scene are traditional Swedish Midsummer accoutrements and symbolize all kinds of good things, such as life, joy, celebration, and the life force. At another time of year, however, birch twigs, not yet in leaf, have another significance: during Lent they symbolize penance and punishment for sin. Is there, perhaps, significance in Strindberg's placing his leafed birch twigs around Kristin's kitchen stove, another of his favourite symbols for suffering and punishment?

Strindberg admits that the Midsummer sunrise which closes the play is not a naturalistic device (it has symbolic significance: Jean has reached the place in the sun after which he strives in his recurring dream; he has exercised the power of life and death over another human being; something completely outside the scope of a mere lackey when he writes to publisher Karl Otto Bonnier (whose firm eventually refused the play) on 21 August 1888, concerning his next *The Creditors (Fordringsägare):*

> [. . .] in a week I shall send you a new naturalistic tragedy, better even than *Miss Julie,* with three characters, a table and two chairs, and no sunrise![1]

Also in the category of symbols which cannot easily be made accessible to the theatre audience is much of the rich imagery employed by Jean, the instrument through whom Strindberg, who only two years previously had written an autobiographical novel in which he characterized himself as *The Son of the Servant (Tjänstekvinnans son,* 1886),

avenged his feelings of inferiority towards (Baroness) Siri von Essen his first wife (to whom he was married from 1877 to 1891; it was Siri who premièred the Julie, in Copenhagen in 1889). Flower imagery forms an important part of this. Strindberg's comment in his preface to the play should be looked at in this connection:

> I think it must be the same with love as it is with the hyacinth, which must establish roots in the dark *before* it can produce a strong flower. Here, it shoots up and produces flower and seed all at once, and that is why the plant dies so quickly.[2]

This and examples of flower symbolism in the text of the play itself (Strindberg was very interested in and made habitual use of a fin-de-siècle enthusiasm known as the 'language of flowers', which assigned very specific meanings to most flowers and herbs and many other plants) are interesting, and unravelling the mysteries they conceal has its own pleasures: in the 'language of flowers' lilacs signified the, for instance, 'first emotions of love'.[3]

Other symbols, of course, are much more important and should be brought to an audience's attention *theatrically.* The earliest example of such symbolism in the play, and one which recurs throughout, is that of dogs. Julie has made her fiancé jump over her riding crop like a trained dog before the play opens; her pedigreed lapdog, significantly named Diana (the goddess known to the Greeks as Artemis, patroness of chastity and coincidentally, associated with dogs: witness the fate of hapless Actaeon), has mated with the gatekeeper's pug, with foreseeable consequences (later Kristin will draw the parallel to Julie's indiscretion with Jean, and Julie herself speculates on the possibility of bearing children to her former servant); Julie refers to Jean as 'you dog, who wear my collar';[4] and finally it is Julie who is the trained dog, jumping at Jean's command.

The choice of animal in these symbols is significant as well as appropriate: dogs were an animal Strindberg is known to have loathed. Indeed, he once observed that the only thing he despised more than dogs was people who kept dogs! This would seem to indicate that Strindberg had little sympathy for Julie, her former fiancé, or, indeed, Jean. It further indicates that at the beginning of the play it is Julie, mistress of both the performing fiancé and the unfortunate Diana, who has least sympathy, while when the tables are turned and Julie must jump over Jean's riding crop, it is he who has become the bigger villain. At any rate, there would seem to be ample suggestion here of the nature of Julie and Jean's love-making—raw unmitigated animal passion at the very least—without resorting to Freud-inspired phallic fantasies! Strindberg affords the director ample opportunity to underscore this and other symbolism in the unscripted peasant-dance interlude: to show their awareness of what is going on in Jean's bedroom, for instance, the peasants might very well howl, growl, bark, and even pantomime canine copulation (similarly, they might begin to beat each other with the Midsummer birch branches to emphasize the dual nature of this symbol: the passage from joy to sorrow).

A particularly effective example of animal symbolism, and one which has direct bearing on the nature of the relationship between Julie and Jean, occurs in a passage restored to the play only as recently as 1984.[5] As Julie gradually realizes that her affair with Jean can lead nowhere, her class consciousness returns to her and the sexual encounter suddenly appears monstrous to her. Jean's retort to her comments, quoting the punishment for bestiality prescribed by the Swedish Criminal Code, indicates that he knows exactly what she is thinking. After exposure to the passages mentioned above, the audience has no doubt about just what kind of animal is involved here:

MISS JULIE:

> . . . I'd like to have you put to death, like an animal . . .

JEAN:

> 'The guilty party is condemned to two years of hard labour and the animal is put to death!' Isn't that it?

MISS JULIE:

> Precisely![6]

The stark realism (not to say coarseness) of Jean's retort was too much for the original publisher of the play, Joseph Seligmann, who softened it considerably to the version which then stood for almost a century: 'As one hastens to shoot a mad dog. Isn't that it?' Not only is Strindberg's version much stronger, but it places the blame for what happened squarely on Julie rather than on the ambitious Jean, as the censored version does! With this piece of dialogue restored, Julie's reaction to her moment of sexual weakness is very similar to that exhibited by the hero of Strindberg's novella 'Chandala' ('Tschandala', written the same year as *Miss Julie,* 1888) after he has consumated his lust for the gypsy's sister. Like *Miss Julie,* that story also deals with a sexual liaison between social unequals, and it also makes particularly effective use of Strindberg's aversion to dogs.

By the end of *Miss Julie,* the heroine's fate is linked to that of another animal: the pet bird which is killed by Jean. Although its death fore-shadows Julie's own, making it clear that while her death is technically a suicide, it is Jean who wields the knife in both cases, it also symbolizes her fall from grace and innocence in the act of union with Jean. 'There is blood between us!' Julie exclaims after the bird has been killed, 'I curse the moment I saw you . . . !'[8] Symbolically, the blood is that of her virginity, which Jean has just taken as coldly and matter-of-factly as he has taken the bird's life!

Another symbolic pattern is central to the meaning of the play and runs through all of Strindberg's works, particularly those concerned with the struggle between the sexes or between classes, or as in the present instance, both)[9]: rising and falling. As Jean's star rises, Julie's falls. The pattern is first brought out in the recurring dreams Julie and Jean relate to each other. Julie's is:

> I've climbed a pillar and am sitting on top of it and I see no way of getting down. I get dizzy when I look down, and I must get down, but don't have the courage to throw myself down, but I can't stay where I am and I yearn to fall, but don't fall; and still I will have no peace until I come down! no rest until I come down, down to the ground, and were I to come down to the ground, I'd want to go down into the earth . . .[10]

and Jean's:

> I'm lying under a tall tree in a dark forest. I want to climb up, up to the top, to look out over the bright landscape where the sun shines, to rob the bird's nest up there, where the golden eggs lie. And I climb and climb, but the trunk is so thick and so smooth, and it's such a long way to the first branch! But I know that if only I reach the first branch I'll get to the top, as if on a ladder. I haven't reached it yet, but I will reach it . . .[11]

As she falls under the spell of Jean, Julie has a sensation of physically falling[12] (having first let the lilac she holds fall to the table):

MISS JULIE:

> . . . I'm, falling, I'm falling!

JEAN:

> Fall down to me, and I'll lift you up again!

MISS JULIE:

> What dreadful power drew me to you? the attraction of the weak to the strong? Of the falling to the rising![13]

This pattern is a variation on the mediaeval Wheel of Fortune motif: we are all situated on the rim of a huge wheel, and as it spins, the fortunes of those on one side rise while the fortunes of those on the other fall: there is no gain except at another's cost, there is no defeat except to the profit of another (this is one reason Strindberg opposed the women's emancipation movement: he believed that woman could raise herself only at the cost of man). The earliest appearance of the symbol in Strindberg's work is in the form of an illustration[14] to his popular history, *The Swedish People* (*Svenska folket,* 1881-2), in a chapter dealing with mediaeval art, which shows an allegorical wall painting. Although the text does not comment on the content of this painting, it is nevertheless a splendid illustration of the Wheel of Fortune (*Lyckans hjul*), a symbol which Strindberg was to use frequently and effectively in his subsequent works. The illustration shows four figures on the rim of a wooden wheel, which is apparently spinning in a clockwise direction. Straddling the top of the wheel is a wealthy and successful man; lying at the bottom is a corpse. Hanging on to the rim are two men, the one on the left rising and the one on the right falling headlong. Behind the rising man is the figure of a fool, who blows his noise-maker in his ear; beside the falling figure and pulling him downwards is a devil, preparing to dig his grave. The Wheel of Fortune symbol, and the associated symbolism of rising and falling, is significant as early as *Herr Bengt's Wife* (*Herr Bengts hustru,* written the same year as *Svenska folket* was completed) and remains important throughout Strindberg's career. The pattern, which is central to *Miss Julie,* might be reinforced by having this or a similar painting reproduced on one of the walls of the set: it would not be out of place even in the kitchen of the kind of dwelling which Julie may be imagined to inhabit. Alternately, a framed reproduction of the painting, which might be a possession of the pious Kristin, might Hang in a prominent position. The rising-and-falling/Wheel of fortune symbolism might be further emphasized through the judicious use of a multi-level stage with appropriate blocking.

Curiously, a recent production of the play for French television in an adaption by Boris Vian,[15] omits not only the peasant's dance, but also the two rising-and-falling dreams. The production, which is remarkable in many respects, is the worse for these omissions, apparently made to tailor the play to a one and one half hour time slot (the BBC version runs one hour and forty minutes).

Strindberg has given a fairly extensive commentary on the play, the characters, and their motivations in his preface. In 1908 he added to these comments in a note to Manda Björling, who was playing Julie on the stage of Strindberg's own Intimate Theatre (Intima teatern).[16] There he brought another of his symbols to bear on the character: the sleepwalker, whose world of dream and illusion prevents him from seeing the realities of the world around him and who often dies of shock, so the story goes, when suddenly awakened:

> Make the exit in the final scene like a sleepwalker: slowly, with your arms stretched out in front of you, inching out, as if searching the air for support in order to avoid tripping over stones and so forth; irresistibly out towards the last great darkness.[17]

Certainly staging the scene in this way provides a dramatic reason for Jean's earlier warnings, when Julie is about to arouse the sleeping Kristin: 'Don't disturb a person who is sleeping!' and '. . . sleep should be respected . . .'[18]

The off-stage suicide with which the play ends is, like the death of the hero of *The Father* (*Fadren,* 1887) an example of the power of suggestion, whereby an inferior

individual can gain ascendancy over a superior one (in this case a member of the lower classes over an aristocrat; in *Fadren* a woman over a man), a theme which always had great fascination for Strindberg. Julie's exit to embrance her fate, thus has two aspects: that of sleepwalking (the world of illusion from which it is disastrous to awaken) and that of the hypnotic trance (submission to the will of another).

It is, of course, possible to go more deeply into symbolism in *Miss Julie.* What have been examined here are the main streams of symbolism in the play, however, and those which might, perhaps, most readily and /or most profitably be given emphasis in production.

Notes

1. Quoted i *Samlade verk,* XXVII, 323: 'Om åtta dagar sänder jag Er ett nytt naturalistiskt sorgespel, bättre ändå än Fröken Julie, med tre personer, ett bord och två stolar, och utan soluppgång! Gunnar Ollén suggests that Strindberg is here referring not only to the sunrise at the end of *Miss Julie,* but also to that at the end of Ibsen's *Ghosts* (*Gengangere,* 1881). All translations are my own.

2. Ibid., 108: 'Jag tänker det är väl med kärleken som med hyacinten, som skall slå rötter i mörkret innan den kan skjuta en stark blomma. Här ränner den upp och går i blom och frö med en gång, och därför dör växten så fort.'

3. *The Language of Flowers.*

4. *Samlade verk,* XXVII, 178: '. . . du hund som bär mitt halsband.'

5. With the publication of *Samlade verk* XXVII.

6. *Samlade verk,* XXVII, 164: 'FRÖKEN: . . . Jag skulle vilja låta döda er som ett djur . . . / JEAN: "Den brottslige dömes till två års straffarbete och djuret dödas!" Inte så? / FRÖKEN: Just så!'

7. *Samlade skrifter,* XXIII, 161: 'Som man skyndar sig att skjuta en galen hund. Inte så?'

8. *Samlade verk* XXVII, 178: '. . . det är blod emellan oss! Jag förbannar den stund jag såg er . . . !'

9. Another particularly potent example of this pattern is found in *Herr Bengt's Wife* (*Herr Bengts hustru,* 1882).

10. *Samlade verk,* XXVII, 135: . . .

11. Ibid., 135: . . .

12. Freud, who can always help us to interpret a symbol, even if he should perhaps not always be allowed to suggest one, assures us (*The Interpretation of Dreams,* 235) that 'if a woman dreams of falling, it almost invariably has a sexual sense: she is imagining herself as a "fallen woman"'.

13. *Samlade verk,* XXVII, 153: 'FRÖKEN: . . . jag
faller, jag faller! / JEAN: Fall ner till mig, så skall
jag lyfta er sedan! / FRÖKEN: Vilken förfärlig makt
drog mig till er? Den svages till den starke? Den fal-
landes till den stigandes!'

14. Illustration 65 in *Samlade skrifter,* VII (294).

15. This version was seen in Canada on Radio France
Internationale in (I think) 1992. There is no mention
in the credits of the distributor's name, nor of the
year in which the version was made.

16. The performance in question was rather special. The
audience was to consist of only four people: Mr and
Mrs George Bernhard Shaw, the Swedish artist
Anders Zorn, and Strindberg. Shaw is reported to
have been so moved that he wept copiously, despite
the fact that he understood not a word of Swedish
(Ollén, 135)!

17. *Brev,* 241 (July 16, 1908): 'Gör slutscenens sortie
som en sömngångerska, långsamt, med armarne
sträckta framför Er, skridande ut, liksom sökande
stöd i luften att icke falla på stenar eller så; ut oc-
motståndligt mot det sista stora mörkret.'

18. *Samlade verk,* XXVII, 133: 'Inte störa den som
sovert!' and '. . . sömnen skall man respektera . . .'

Erik Näslund (essay date 1993)

SOURCE: Näslund, Erik. "*Miss Julie*—The Ballet, 1950-
1." *Theatre Research International* 18, supplementary issue (1993): 16-23.

[*In the following essay, Näslund presents a history of the
ballet version of* Miss Julie.]

If by a classic one means a work of art which has the ability to remain alive through various epochs and continue to
engage people's attention, then the word is suitable to
describe Birgit Cullberg's ballet *Miss Julie.* Perhaps one
ought to adjust the notion slightly and describe the ballet
as a 'modern classic', because we do not know how it will
have endured in, let us say, fifty or a hundred years.

But as the ballet, since its première on 7 March 1950, has
been staged in a further 35 productions all over the world
(to 31 December 1992), so it can without doubt be said to
bode well for the future. Taste changes from decade to
decade and Cullberg's ballet has survived a series of
changes in fashion within the area of dance: from the
neoclassical wave following George Balanchine, via the
breakthrough of the modern ballet with Glen Tetley and
Hans van Manen, up to a renewed interest in dramatic ballet, which undeniably favoured Cullberg's work in general
and especially *Miss Julie.* It can further be said that the

fusion of classical and modern technique achieved by Tetley and van Manen was anticipated by Cullberg in *Miss
Julie,* where the choreographer sets the classical and free
techniques against each other to distinguish between two
classes in society. Cullberg would after *Miss Julie* work
with an alloy of both schools.

In 1949 Cullberg was to work with the Swedish touring
theatre organization Riksteatern (Swedish National Theatre
Centre), with which she had carried out several tours during the 1940s. The tour was to take place in 1950 with the
young Swedish dancer Elsa Marianne von Rosen as 'star'
and her husband Allan Fridericia as director. In the summer of 1949 the trio found themselves in Paris and managed to see Roland Petit's *Carmen,* which led to the idea
of producing a ballet based on a Strindbergian theme. The
choice fell to *Miss Julie,* because the drama offered an
explicit female 'star' role for von Rosen, and because
Cullberg was attracted by the erotic and social conflict.
Petit's *Carmen* showed that it was possible even within
the bounds of the classical school to depict a psychological process. The drama's class differences could also
provide a worthwhile break in styles in purely choreographic terms. Behind Strindberg's dialogue, Cullberg also
very soon found a relationship of purely physical tension
which stimulated her choreographic imagination. But
dance itself also fulfilled a theme in the drama. It is as a
dancer in the barn scene that Jean is discovered by Julie.
Fiddler music is heard all the time in the distance during
the first half of the play and lies as a rhythmically stimulating foundation to the lively dialogue. The farmers'
encroachment on the palace kitchen during the dance and
song is even captioned by Strindberg as 'Ballet'.

To translate the drama into a new medium, Cullberg was
forced to violate content and form. Aristotle's principle of
unity which Strindberg had followed was shattered in the
ballet. Spatial units were broken up. Scenes which in the
drama were described only through dialogue were depicted
visually. New roles were created. The emphasis in the plot
came to lie to a large degree on the erotic plane, while for
example discussion of sexual roles was not able to be
depicted in choreographic terms. On the other hand those
events which build up the background to Julie's conflict—
such as the broken engagement, the midsummer dance in
the barn and something of the influence of the noble family—were able to be portrayed on the stage. The greatest
problem involved the final scene. Strindberg allowed Julie
to go behind scene and commit suicide. Cullberg leaves no
opening as to what actually happens at the end. She was
forced to write her own end to the drama. Cullberg's Julie
dies on stage, her suicide aided by Jean. Cullberg wanted
to show that Julie is a victim of the power of tradition.
Honour and family demand a victim for those mistakes
Julie had made. The ballet therefore emphasized the family tragedy in a different way than the drama.

The two leading roles were worked out in a way which
made them sought-after parts by many eminent dancers.

But the roles' inherent dramatic base has also the ability to draw out new sides of many artists and therefore Julie and Jean have come to mean the turning points in the careers of a long list of dancers. The Danish stardancer Erik Bruhn, for example, was already known as an excellent *danseur noble* when he was given the chance in 1938 to perform Jean at the American Ballet Theatre. Suddenly Bruhn showed himself to be a fully fledged character dancer and his already successful dance career took a new direction. Similar 'revolutions' have happened to other interpreters of the two roles and have naturally done much for the ballet's popularity even in dance circles. That the ballet has been staged successfully in so many parts of the world—even in Chile, Iran and Japan—could be a sign of its timelessness and that the drama between Julie and Jean in dance form has the power to move even in the most varying cultures.

The following concerns the reception the ballet received in Sweden after the première of 1950 and the impression it made on Swedish dance.

From the moment Miss Julie (Elsa Marianne von Rosen) made her stage entrance in the Västerås Theatre right up to the moment when Julie falls down dead, a state of acute tension reigned in the auditorium.[1] The ballet made such a strong impression that there was complete silence after the curtain had fallen. At first the dancers did not know how they should interpret the silence, and it was not until the lights went on in the auditorium that the tension and emotion in the audience were released, and cheers and applause broke loose.

The première of **Miss Julie** was a success without precedent in the history of Swedish dance. The tour—the ballet was performed 30 times in 21 localities from Östersund in the north to Växjö in the south—played to full houses, enthusiastic audiences and attracted eye-catching headlines. The public success was so great that the 'Julie' programme became one of few Swedish National Theatre Centre performances to make a profit.[2]

Press criticism was overwhelmingly enthusiastic. At the first performance on 1 March in Västerås (a small town in the interior of Sweden), the ballet was hailed as an indisputable critical success.

> Everybody felt, Stockholm reviewers as well as season ticket holders of the theatre in Västerås, that they had seen a ballet composition capable of shaking the audience just as intensely as a spoken drama. Cullberg's **Miss Julie** gave to many—and continued to give during the tour—an even stronger, more primitive direct experience of the innermost meaning of the drama than the other two versions just then on offer, the one at Dramaten and Alf Sjöberg's film with Anita Björk in the main role. Everybody agreed that any misgivings expressed before the première as to whether a ballet of **Miss Julie** implies a violation of Strindberg, 'a plunder-

ing of the dead', or a 'crime against a respected writer', had been groundless. Previously, insinuations of that kind had dominated everything written about **Miss Julie.** After the première they stopped abruptly.[3]

Most reviewers asked the question: How is it possible to transform a drama; based to such a large degree on 'the winning effectiveness of the repartee', into a ballet?[4] When Julie had sunk to the floor with a dagger in her heart, 'one was completely convinced of what excellent material had been treated with impressive choreographic ability, artistic temperament and personal insight. Let us say it at once: **Miss Julie** is the best Birgit Cullberg has accomplished as choreographer, the first time she has in earnest reached the level of the master Jooss.'[5]

The difficult and bold undertaking of converting Strindberg's drama to ballet was also, according to Anna Greta Ståhle in *Dagens Nyheter* one of the best Cullberg had achieved:

> She has succeeded in expressing the essential psychological developments of the drama through choreography. The characters of the main roles are packed with meaning, and because she presents the whole drama, even that which is just narrated in the play, the ballet has a definite form.[6]

The ballet's explicit erotic expressiveness attracted much attention and some reviewers, like Bengt Häger, compared it to Roland Petit's *Carmen.* One of the most brilliant scenes in Cullberg's ballet was, according to Häger, just when 'Julie seduces Jean, a sexual game of fearlessness and intensity, never seen before in ballet'.[7] Even Cullberg's arch-enemy Robin Hood (Bengt Idestam-Almquist) was forced to admit that taking on Strindberg was a bold undertaking: 'Miss Julie's art of seduction and sexual experience with the servant Jean is given an excellent interpretation in dance—just about the best we have seen in this manner here at home.'[8]

Other critics pointed to Cullberg's use of the classical traditions. 'I know that I myself have seldom seen the classical school so exceptionally smoothly incorporated in a dramatic, entirely informal pattern of movements, only as a means of achieving the dramatic expression of feelings, never as a technical end in itself', stated 'Lill' in *Svenska Dagbladet,* which also spoke of 'entirely sensual but at the same time aesthetically refined steps—and patterns of movement'.[9] Anna Greta Ståhle emphasized the way the ballet's two choreographic styles are dramatically utilized to emphasize the class differences between the aristocratic Julie and her servants.[10]

While on the whole reviews were quite brief regarding the ballet's content and form, all reviewers lavished space and praise on Elsa Marianne von Rosen, for whom the Julie-role was her great breakthrough. Her ability to convey dramatic insight and frenzy presumably took most by surprise, although it must be remembered that von Rosen had been seen almost exclusively in the years before 'Julie' in operettas at the Oscar Theatre. She was known for her sure, strong technique but 'she shows here a dramatic talent, which has not been seen previously. Her Miss Julie is a temperamental study in the contention between aristocratic pride and erotic constriction, which is first expressed in her disposition to torment and dominate and then explodes in primitive lust' (Robin Hood).[11] Margareta Sjögren also emphasized how von Rosen succeeded in gaining instant contact with the audience. Her surprisingly young, precocious and half-perverted upper-class girl gave a completely different impression of shameless but conscious eroticism and candidness than had been conveyed in the conventional understanding and interpretation of the role: 'there Julie is usually a mature, already disappointed woman right from the start'.[12]

Von Rosen's strong identification with her role was the reason for the deep impression she made on audiences and critics. Allan Fridericia mentions that the dancer's breasts carried obvious bloody signs of that mixture of symbolism and realism 'which was in fact the whole ballet, every time the cadet dagger had buried itself too deeply in the flesh in the suicide scene'. It had proved impossible to procure a theatrical dagger and the dancer had instead borrowed an authentic dagger from the von Rosen weapon collection. In the climactic moment the dancer had difficulty calculating the distance between breast and the tip of the dagger and she stabbed herself repeatedly. But, writes Friderica, 'later versions did not achieve the same effect as when the trembling dagger remained stuck in the stage floor after Julie's suicide, while the curtain slowly fell.'[13] Just as congenial was the relationship of role/interpretation in the question of Julius Mengarelli's Jean. He was a dancer of virile, almost primitive ower, characteristics which fitted the role perfectly. The animal energy mingled with underlying terror all shrouded in a cloud of vulgarity (Bengt Häger).[14] Margereta Sjögren found that Mengarelli's valet 'had the tom-cattish smoothness present in a son of the people who could bow deeply, but not so low that he could not look his lover in the eyes and desire her.'[15]

Reviewers were aware of the historical fervor surrounding this première and Bengt Häger was of the opinion that the ballet qualified Cullberg for the Stockholm Royal Opera House, Operan, 'which has lacked a Swedish choreographer so long. Now she has shown herself capable of the classical style there is no reason not to engage her as guest choreographer.'[16]

When the ballet was performed in Eskilstuna on 21-22 March, the press was informed that an impressive collection of Stockholm theatre experts were present: the director of the Royal Opera House, Joel Berglund, the Royal Opera House ballet master, Julian Algo, Agne Beijer, professor of theatre history, as well as the directors Anders

Sandrew and Nils Perne.[17] Berglund went back stage after the performance. The conversation between him and von Rosen was short. The director of the Royal Opera House introduced himself as 'Berglund'. The dancer not knowing what to say, replied: 'von Rosen'. With that the conversation was over.[18] By 26 March it was announced that the Royal Opera House had decided to include the ballet in its repertoire, choreographed by Cullberg and with Elsa Marianne von Rosen in the title role.[19] Thus two of Sweden's foremost dance artists working outside the royal institution entered the stronghold of classical ballet together.

Birgit Cullberg had achieved her goal: to show that she could 'make use of the classical technique' because 'otherwise I can never have any firm job as ballet master'.[20]

Miss Julie had its première in September 1950, in a design due to Sven Erixon (1899-1970), known as 'The X', whom Cullberg knew from Alf Sjöberg's production of Lorca's *Blood Wedding* at Dramaten in 1944, for which The X did the stage design and Cullberg the choreography. With *Blood Wedding* The X had become a celebrated scenepainter and it is not surprising that the choice fell to him, his art had the reputation of being deeply-rooted in 'the Swedish'.

The X gave the ballet an unmistakable Swedish local colour, especially successful in the barn scene. When it came to costumes he followed Fridericia's design almost exactly. *Miss Julie* was The X's stage designer début at the Royal Opera House, followed up by among others, *Carmen, Wozzeck* and *Aniara*.

Now, that the ballet was to be performed at the Royal Opera House, Ture Rangström's music which during the tour had been performed on piano, required orchestrating. This task was carried out by Hans Grossman.[21] When the music was magnified and performed by the Royal Opera House Orchestra (under Bertil Bokstedt's direction) it attracted more attention, 'so superbly apt that it gives the impression of being specially composed for the ballet'.[22] The pseudonymous 'Lill' in *Svenska Dagbladet,* was the only one who mentioned the connection between Strindberg and Rangström and said that this fully motivated the choice of this composer but that Cullberg however had not made it easy for herself: 'Rangström's music, with its Swedish tone and passionate mood, decidedly does not belong to the easily-danced. It is metrical and quite compact in tone range, but only in exceptional cases is it rhythmic. This gives even greater honour to the choreographer in that she has succeeded so well . . .'[23]

Birgit Cullberg also made minor adjustments to the choreography, due to the larger stage and a larger ensemble. The original company consisted of eight dancers. Because Cullberg now had several more dancers at her disposal, the barn scene dances were more strict and the steps more complicated and expressive. The foundation of the farmers' dance was in purely classical steps and hops but a little distorted with feet pointing upwards and crooked knees: 'primitive bodies' in a classical spirit.[24] Three gossipy old women were added and the ancestors' dance in the final scene made more elaborate.

The Royal Opera Houses première on 7 September 1950 was an historical occasion. The most modern ballet style which had developed on the continent was introduced to the Royal Opera; the Royal Ballet's repertoire received the addition of a ballet which was exceptionally strong and harmonious and which could hold its own on an international level. *Miss Julie*'s success was not confined to Sweden but became international. The seduction scene's daring expressiveness which had created something of a scandal in the spring tour of 1950 was further heightened in the opera première. For the audience, used to seeing glittering Hollywood spectacles or harmless fairy idylls on the ballet stage, the strong suffering and sensual passion on the stage came as something absolutely new and daring. Many spectators were either shocked or profoundly moved. Cullberg had, as Anna Greta Ståhle pointed out, broken the ballet's bounds of propriety. 'Eroticism had never been seen so openly portrayed and this gave a certain pornographic shimmer to the ballet, which seemed to act as a public drawcard.'[25] This taste of pornography was naturally given an extra push in the press and the large illustrated feature in the weekly magazine *Se,* where Julius is seen to rip von Rosen's skirt, became celebrated that autumn. The magazine announced on the cover that, 'A new love passion shook the venerable Royal Opera . . .' Many magazine covers were devoted to the beautiful 'authentic' count's daughter and the ballet received the attention of the press to an extent unparalleled in Swedish ballet history.

Miss Julie gave new life to Swedish ballet in general and to the Royal Opera ballet in particular. The renaissance of the Royal Opera Ballet since the fifties dates from *Miss Julie.* The 1950-1 season opened with the première of *Miss Julie* along with *Giselle. Miss Julie* was performed thirty-seven times in its first season to extremely large audiences: sixteen performances reached almost maximum capacity, with more than a thousand tickets sold, for a total of 1177 seats. At most other performances attendance figures hovered between 800 and 1000, but when 'Miss Julie' was not dancing, the attendance figures sank markedly. Therefore the opera management requested further appearance from von Rosen although, originally, she was offered a contract for only ten performances. Another dancer, Gun Skoogberg, was also given the chance to try the role, without great success. It was von Rosen the public came to see.

Thanks to the success of *Miss Julie* Cullberg was offered to choreograph the *Oscar Ball* based on Gustaf Fröding's poem *The Ball.* This premièred on 3 December 1950 with *Les Sylphides* and the 'Grand pas de deux classique' from

the *Nutcracker,* rehearsed by Maurice Béjart. This was the first time the Opera inserted a free-standing brilliant 'pas de deux' in a programme. Bengt Häger summed up the general atmosphere of success which now surrounded the theatre: 'With this pace of development the Royal Opera Ballet will soon be able to export guest ballet perfomances.'[26]

After *Miss Julie* had danced its first season at the Royal Theatre, the ballet went on tour in the summer of 1951 in folk parks with Mascagni's, opera *In Sicily.* The folk park tour began on 27 June in Södertälje, 40 kilometres south of Stockholm, and finished on 27 July in Kramfors, further to the north. *Miss Julie* created a public record in the parks in the summer of 1951.

At the very beginning of the tour *Miss Julie* celebrated its hundredth performance: a record in Swedish dance history. Previously only two Swedish dance works had been performed so many times in such a short time, namely Jean Börlin's *Midsummer Vigil* and *The Foolish Virgins* which were danced during the Swedish Ballet's first season in Paris in 1920-21, respectively 134 and 140 times, but outside Sweden.

The performance in Malmö of *Miss Julie* was seen by two young dancers with the Stadsteater there, engaged at the Stora Teatern in Gothenburg: Holger Reenberg and Marianne Fröijdh. They were both shaken by Cullberg's creation and resolved that they ought to try to bring Cullberg and the ballet to Gothenburg.[27]

And so it happened that *Miss Julie* premièred in Gothenburg in April 1952. The ballet was given a completely new stage design by the Gothenburg artist Nils Wedel (1897-1967), making his debut as a stage designer. Wedel had developed, inspired by Léger's cubism, a half-abstract style with a touch of surrealism, a surprising choice considering the subject's 'Swedishness': 'The touch of abstract austerity in the style of the scenery, where the horizon was strongly emphasized, and the lively southern colours in the costumes lent an international touch, which was not expected in a drama which centres on the Swedish midsummer. But this underlined the universal nature of the drama's conflict.'[28]

When Cullberg went to Gothenburg for rehearsals, she visited the ballet's morning school to audition dancers. She was captivated by a young blond dancer whom she thought was just the type for the title role, Marianne Fröijdh. Holger Reenberg informed Cullgerg that this was not possible because Fröijdh was not a première soloist. 'You must take Nina Gabay', Reenberg said. Gabay, who came to Stora Teatern in 1937 from the Monte Carlo ballet, was the theatre's ballerina, but Cullberg did not find her right for Julie. In the meantime both dancers rehearsed the role, with the conflict coming to a head before the première. The ballet did not make the same strong impression in Gothenburg as elswhere. Criticism was directed not only at Nina Gabay but also at the ballet itself. The production had not previously encountered such harsh judgements as these in Gothenberg. The critics objected to 'the cheek' of transforming Strinsberg's drama into a ballet accusing Cullberg of 'sacrilege' or of 'plundering of the dead'. 'Strindberg's drama has been stripped right down to the bones', wrote 'E.P.' in Gothenberg's daily newspaper. 'Only a naked plot remains; nothing is left of the work's spirit or the writer's pupose. But the choreographer is doing very well, living nicely off a sensational and popular title.'[29]

But some reviewers who were critical of making ballet from drama, conceded that Cullberg's choreography was 'in itself very captivating and gifted'.[30] Some of the most critical partly changed their minds when a few days later Marianne Fröijdh danced Julie, making the audience go wild with enthusiasm. 'Her dance . . . was performed with a frenzy which shattered every doubt in her ability to deal with this difficult role in terms of theatre and dance' stated Olle Halling, and the otherwise critical 'E.P.' wrote that here 'a human tragedy was brought to life, honestly, unadorned and consistently. Swedish dance art has gained a new star. It is always heartening to witness how a young star, who in earlier roles has made fine efforts, ultimately succeeds completely in making a breakthrough.'[31]

The role of Julie became a significant step in the career and development of the young Marianne Fröijdh. Cullberg and Julie 'opened many doors for me. During rehearsals Birgit gave fantastic guidance not only for the role, but also in introducing me to literature in general and especially to Strindberg, and so on. In short, Birgit and Julie gave me a lift, so that I could fly.'[32] Many dancers all over the world could say the same for the two leading roles of Julie and Jean. The *Miss Julie* programme (which consisted further of Benjamin Britten's cantata *Saint Nicholas* under Cullberg's direction) became a great success in Gothenburg and was played ten times during the spring of 1952 and the winter of 1952-3.

In Malmö, at the Stadsteatern, *Miss Julie* entered the repertoire in February 1955. Ingmar Bergman had perhaps a hand in this, as artistic advisor to the theatre director, Lars-Levi Læstadius.[33] These performances were the last in Sweden for a decade. After 1956 Cullberg was active above all internationally. But the ballet has since been staged anew in Gothenburg (1966 and 1992), in Malmö (1977) and for the Cullberg ballet (1968). But in the 1950s the work was performed by the Royal Opera Ballet once again in the folk parks on a month-long tour in the summer of 1955. Having been performed some 200 times in Sweden to an average of 500 spectators 100,000 Swedes saw *Miss Julie* in its ballet version in five years.

By means of summary it can be said that *Miss Julie* certainly did not inspire any direct followers in the psychological/realistic genre, but that the ballet marked a

turning point in the development of Swedish dance: it opened the door to a domestic ballet creation, above all at the Royal Theatre, it generated a markedly increased interest for ballet in general and in particular at the Stockholm Royal Opera House and for many Swedes it initiated their first contact with ballet as a form of art.

Notes

1. Allan Fridericia, *Elsa Marianne von Rosen. En svensk ballerina* (A Swedish ballerina), Stockholm 1953, p. 118.

2. Riksteatern: Management protocol 1 July 1947.

3. Margareta Sjögren, *Biljett till balett* (Ticket to the ballet), Stockholm 1957, p. 165.

4. Signed Lill., *Svenska Dagbladet,* 2 March 1950.

5. Ibid.

6. *Dagens Nyheter,* 2 March 1950.

7. *Morgon-Tidningen,* 2 March 1950.

8. *Stockholms-Tidningen,* 2 March 1950.

9. *Svenska Dagbladet,* 2 March 1950.

10. *Dagens Nyheter,* 2 March 1950.

11. *Stockholms-Tidningen,* 2 March 1950.

12. Sjögren, op. cit.

13. Fridericia, op. cit., p. 122-3.

14. *Stockholms-Tidningen,* 2 March 1950.

15. Sjögren, op. cit., p. 166.

16. *Svenska Dagbladet* and *Stockholms-Tidningen,* 2 March 1950.

17. *Aftonbladet,* 26 March 1950.

18. Fridericia, op. cit., p. 121-2.

19. Kungliga Teaterns Arkiv (Royal Theatre's Archives): K. Teatern's Protocol for the years 1946-52.

20. The Swedish Press Council Appendix 14, letter from Cullberg to Fridericia, 11 December 1949.

21. Bengt Häger in *Morgon-Tidningen,* 2 March 1950.

22. Ibid., 8 April 1950.

23. *Svenska Dagbladet,* 8 September 1950.

24. Interview with Birgit Cullberg, 29 August 1991.

25. Anna Greta Ståhle 'Birgit Cullberg's *Miss Julie*' in *Perspektiv på Fröken Julie* (Perspectives on *Miss Julie*), Stockholm 1972, p. 192.

26. *Morgon-Tidningen,* op. cit.

27. Interview with Marianne Fröijdh, 18 December 1991.

28. Carl Cramér in *Ny Tid,* 17 April 1952.

29. *Göteborgs-Tidningen,* 17 April 1952.

30. *Göteborgs Handels- och Sjöfarts-tidning,* 17 April 1952.

31. *Afton-Tidningen* resp. *Göteborgs-Tidningen,* 18 April 1952.

32. Interview with Fröijdh.

33. Henrik Sjögren, *Ingmar Bergman på teater* (Ingmar Bergman at the theatre), Stockholm 1968, p. 124.

Lorelei Lingard (essay date 1997)

SOURCE: Lingard, Lorelei. "The Daughter's Double Bind: The Single-parent Family as Cultural Analogue in Two Turn-of-the-Century Dramas." *Modern Drama* 40 (1997): 123-38.

[*In the following essay, Lingard examines the relationship between Julie and her father in* Miss Julie *in light of contemporary ideas of parental and sex roles.*]

It may seem surprising how frequently single-parent families are found in plays written at the turn of the twentieth century. The number of plays by Ibsen Chekhov, Brecht, Strindberg, and Shaw that involve single-parent families is remarkable, particularly as the issue of single parenthood itself rarely surfaces in the action. But upon examination, we can see how these fictional families often reflect the social dynamic of their era. As we encounter Nora Helmer, Hedda Gabler, Peer Gynt, the Prozorov sisters, the children of Mother Courage, Grusha's son, Miss Julie, and the daughters of Heartbreak House, the effect of the single-parent family is an important but implicit part of the action. These plays are not "about" the particular dynamics and politics of the single-parent family; indeed, the family make up seems almost accidental, not essential to the plot. It is, however, a critical part of the symbolic structure of the play.[1]

In these plays, the single-parent family symbolizes dysfunction and reflects a dysfunction in the culture as a whole. They focus not only on the symbolic meaning of one part of the parental unit but also on the absence of the other part. This imbalance in the dramatic family creates a gap or lack in the social analogy that, as the play unfolds, symbolizes a lack in the culture itself.

The single-parent family, as a dramatic tool, necessarily partakes of the conventional symbolism of the mother-father-child unit. The normative family system, which has its foundations in the sexual division of power and knowledge, becomes an increasingly critical and complex component in drama written and produced at the turn of the century. This emphasis is largely a result of two

phenomena: "the immense upheavals in the condition of women at the turn of the century";[2] and the theories of sexuality developed at this time by Sigmund Freud, especially in his work on the repressed unconscious (particularly in women) in *Studies in Hysteria* (1895) and on the significance of infantile sexuality in *Three Essays on the Theory of Sexuality* (1905).[3] Today, feminist theorists working with psychoanalysis

> [attempt to decenter] the reigning phallus from its dominant position in the symbolic order. They refuse ritual acts of obedience to the phallus, they refuse to accept the inevitable oppression of women described by Freud and Lévi-Strauss as the sine qua non of human culture: the obligatory journey from clitoris to vagina; the inevitable exchange of women.[4]

At the turn of the twentieth century, however, Freud's impact on the collective consciousness of the culture was unmediated by feminist rebuttal and his constructions of sexuality were readily absorbed into the educated person's understanding of the family unit.

Thus, because of these influences, the situation of women in the family enjoyed a particular emphasis in turn-of-the-century drama. As Finney points out,

> [r]ather than being confronted with the standard heroines of nineteenth-century farce and melodrama, turn-of-the-century theatergoers were treated to Shaw's Major Barbara and Candida, Synge's Pegeen Mike, Strindberg's Laura and Miss Julie, Wilde's Salomé, Ibsen's Nora Helmer and Hedda Gabler, Wedekind's Lulu, and a wealth of other individualized and memorable female characters.[5]

In this period, the dramatist turns his unrelenting eye to the burgeoning issues of gender and power. In the two plays this article focuses on, *Hedda Gabler* and **Miss Julie,** Ibsen and Strindberg situate themselves differently in relation to the social and psychological debates; nevertheless, both are engaged in a formative cultural conversation.

This article examines the diverse social commentaries enacted through a dramatic focus on a particular type of single-parent family, the father/daughter unit, in two turn-of-the-century plays.[6] In Ibsen's tragic *Hedda Gabler* (1890)[7] and Strindberg's naturalistic **Miss Julie** (1888),[8] the single-parent family creates a forum for social commentary through the inter-relations among the presence of the father, the absence of the mother, and the confusion, desperation, and choices of the tragic heroine, the daughter. While Ibsen and Strindberg have distinct visions of modern society, and Strindberg uses the issue of class to enhance his depiction of gender, the similarity in the role of the father and the fate of the daughter links these plays.

The daughter in these dramas finds herself at a social and sexual impasse, the fate of the individual woman representing symbolically the fate of the culture which shapes her.

Grasping for a power and autonomy her society will never grant her, she paradoxically denies and represses her inherent female power, thus participating in her own submission. The daughter is reduced to paralysis by the culture's construction of her sexuality, and her state of mind represents vividly the horror of this Foucauldian situation:

HEDDA:

> [. . .] I often think there is only one thing in the world I have any turn for.

BRACK:

> [*drawing near to her*]
>
> And what is that, if I may ask?

HEDDA:

> [*stands looking out*]
>
> Boring myself to death. Now you know it.
>
> (57)

JULIE:

> I can't go. I can't stay. Help me. I am so desperately tired. Order me to go. Set me in motion, because I don't know how to think or act any more.
>
> (35)

One recognizes in these outbursts the phenomenon that Simone de Beauvoir addresses with her assertion that

> what peculiarly signalizes the situation of woman is that she—a free and autonomous being like all human creatures—nevertheless finds herself living in a world where men compel her to assume the status of the Other. They propose to stabilize her as object and to doom her to immanence since her transcendence is to be overshadowed and forever transcended by another ego (*conscience*) which is essential and sovereign. The drama of woman lies in this conflict between the fundamental aspirations of every subject (ego)—who always regards the self as the essential—and the compulsions of a situation in which she is the inessential. How can a human being in woman's situation attain fulfillment? What roads are open to her? Which are blocked? How can independence be recovered in a state of dependency? What circumstances limit woman's liberty and how can they be overcome?[9]

These plays approach de Beauvoir's questions through their use of the single-parent family theme, and issues that will be raised by de Beauvoir and other feminists are climactically exposed in the final scenes of *Hedda Gabler* and *Miss Julie.* The deadly paralysis which causes the daughter's desperate cry places her in each play in a double bind from which suicide is perceived as the only escape.[10] Although Ibsen and Strindberg were differently affected by the upheavals of the "woman question" at the turn of the century (Strindberg decidedly not sharing Ibsen's feminist

sympathies), the final scene of each play serves as a grave condemnation of the position of women in the culture and the nature of human relationships between the sexes.

THE FATHER

As the primary parental figure in these two plays, the father assumes a particular importance in the family unit. His is the only parental influence enacted on the daughter during the drama (although, as we shall consider later, the mother's absence exerts its own influence on the family and, in particular, on the daughter). Because of the centrality of the father figure in the life of the daughter, what the father signifies in the play becomes a thematic focus in the action.

In both plays, the symbolic presence of the father is highlighted by the fact that, as a character, he never appears. In *Hedda Gabler,* he is dead before the play commences. His palpable presence despite his physical absence indicates the singular influence he must have had on his daughter while alive, to remain such a force in her life even after his death. . . .

General Gabler both begins and ends this play, in the opening focus on the portrait and in the critical role of the pistols in Act Four. His influence on his daughter, and his role in her eventual demise, is inescapable throughout the play, and suggests the importance of the father/daughter relationship in this tragedy. The father in Strindberg's *Miss Julie* similarly pervades the play even in his absence, suggesting his influential role in all of Julie's actions, but, in particular, in her choice of suicide.

Strindberg's Count is, however, a more complicated figure than Ibsen's General, and Julie's relationship with him is therefore more multifaceted than Hedda's unabashed identification with her father's power. General Gabler symbolizes power, law, and patriarchal control; the Count symbolizes these concepts and the loss of them through his unsuccessful suicide attempt, his cuckolding by his wife, and his servant Jean's trespasses. Despite these flaws in the stronghold of the father, Julie retains a sense of male power which she attributes both to her father and to Jean, as a surrogate, begging him in the last scene to "pretend that you are the Count and I am you" (45). The issue of class enhances the gendered division of power in the play, as Jean wields the power of the father over Julie despite her class advantage[11] but does not wield it over the Count, whose double advantage garners the respect of both Julie and Jean.

The Count's absence in the action of the play is balanced by his symbolic presence, evidenced by such items as the boots which Jean "places conspicuously on the floor" (12) at the play's opening and the servant's bell which precipitates Julie's desperate exit in the final scene.

Jean illustrates the Count's power, even in his absence, as he admits,

I feel insignificant if I just see his gloves lying in a chair! If I hear that bell up there I shy like a frightened horse; and look at those boots, standing there, stiff, arrogant—I feel my back beginning to bend at the very sight of them!

(26)

The relationship among gender, class, and power is further revealed in the coat of arms that represents the patriarchal line of inheritance in Julie's ancestry. Julie recognizes both the significance of the symbol and her own alienation from it in her exclamation that

God, it will be a relief to be finished with it all, all! If only it is finished. He'll have a stroke, he'll die, and we'll all be finished, every one of us, and I can have some peace . . . calm . . . eternal rest. The coat-of-arms will be smashed across the coffin, the Count's line at an end.

(40)

Julie's identification with her father and the power signified by his coat of arms is revealed by the title of the drama, *Miss Julie,* and this identification causes her to see his death as the end of everything, even her own existence. Simultaneously, however, she understands that such a breach in the father/daughter connection would be liberating for her, affording her "some peace . . . calm . . . eternal rest." Her strange speech illustrates the paradox of her position: she identifies with, and even tries unsuccessfully to wield over Jean the father's power; however, she also recognizes that this power is a repressive force in her life.

Unfortunately, this revelation does not extend to her actions, for she involves herself as a participant in that repression each time she threatens Jean with the symbols of the father's power. Jean is unconcerned by her threat that "My father will get home, find his desk ransacked, his money gone—and he'll ring the bell—*that* bell!—twice—for his manservant!" (40) for he knows that Julie has no access to this power herself. Like Hedda, Julie fails to see the potential power of her own, female influence, and, confused, she allows that natural source of power to be degraded into a victimized sexuality, in contrast with the natural force of the peasant dancers "with flowers in their hats" (25) who invade the kitchen exuding a powerful sensuality that even Jean respects.

In both plays, the physical absence of the father not only highlights his symbolic presence but also focuses attention on the dilemma of the daughter in relation to that symbolism. While the physical absence of both parents contributes to the foregrounded development of the daughter in each play, the father becomes, as we have seen, a symbolic presence through his absence, while the mother remains a symbolic absence as well as a physical absence. This parental presence/absence parallels the psychological development of self/other in the family and suggests a possible basis for the daughter's gender confusion in each play. The self/other dynamic is a key factor in the power relations of the family, for, as de Beauvoir recognizes, "[i]t amounts to this just as for the ancients there was an absolute vertical with reference to which the oblique was defined, so there is an absolute human type, the masculine."[12] She continues, explaining that woman

is defined and differentiated with reference to man and not he with reference to her, she is the incidental, the inessential as opposed to the essential. He is the Subject, he is the Absolute—she is the Other.[13]

Thus, in patriarchal society, woman is denied full selfhood; she cannot appropriate the male as Other to define herself, so "'[s]he' is indefinitely other in herself,"[14] alienating her from her own subjectivity.

In these plays, the daughter perceives her "self" in relation to her father as "other," because of their sexual and social differences; however, she relates the father with herself, as he is her sole parent during the action of the play and she aspires to his power and thus perceives her mother, and the female principle in general, as "other." This psychological contradiction, resulting from both identification with the father and recognition of difference from him, forms the foundation for both Hedda's and Julie's torment about and dissatisfaction with their place in the restrictive gender system of turn-of-the-century society.

THE MOTHER

The fathers in these plays have much in common. At first glance, the mothers do not seem to, particularly as Hedda's mother is not even mentioned and Julie's mother acts outside the conventional boundaries of her gender role, both in Strindberg's preface and in Julie's memories. But the mother's symbolism is similar in each play, and this symbolism reveals the thematic importance of the mother's absence to the daughters' development.

The symbolism of the mother figure can be gleaned from the action of the drama despite—perhaps even because of—the mother's physical absence.[15]. . . .

[The] absence of the mother in *Miss Julie* creates a similar confusion in the daughter between self and other. As Strindberg has given Julie's mother a particular role in the drama, her impact on the daughter is more complex than in Ibsen's play. Once again, though, the daughter's struggle is for power, as others struggle for power over her. While Strindberg claims a number of fantastic influences on Julie's behaviour in the drama, including

the festive atmosphere of Midsummer's Eve, her father's absence, her monthly period, her contact with animals, the inflaming influence of the dance, the cover of night, [and] the strongly aphrodisiac influence of the flowers,

(4)

many of these elements act as symbols of sexuality, in particular, female sexuality. Even the father's absence can be seen in terms of a break in the daughter's identification with him, allowing her hitherto suppressed, female sexuality to surface. Much can be understood about Julie's state of mind and her final exit by studying the effect on her sexuality of her relationship to her father and her mother's absence.

In his essay "Psychic Murder," Strindberg explains that "the struggle for power is no longer purely physical . . . but has developed to become psychic, though no less cruel."[16] Julie, like Hedda, struggles with her own preconceptions of power, and invests her faith in the power of the father, ignoring and even denying the power inherent in her female sexuality. Albeit less potent than the power of the Count, the power of natural sexuality exhibited by the dancers is at least accessible to Julie; in denying it, she acts as agent of her own repression.[17]

The struggles among gender, class, and power provide the basis for Julie's final, desperate choice, beginning in the struggles between her parents for control of the child's belief system.[18] Julie remembers of her mother that

> [a]s far as I can tell, she never wanted me. I was left to myself, except that I had to learn everything a boy normally learns, just to show that a woman can be as good as a man. I wore boy's clothes, learned to tend horses instead of dairy work. I groomed them, and I was made to go hunting. I even had to learn to plough.
>
> (31)

Through Julie's speeches and actions it becomes evident that neither the conventional system nor this inversion of it can solve her dilemma, which evolves from the binary opposition between male and female, not from her position on either pole. For Julie recognizes that her "mother has [her revenge on Julie's father]—through me" (44) by teaching her daughter "to distrust men and to hate them" (32), but she also admits that "it was my father who gave me my contempt for my own sex, he made me half woman and half man" (44).

Having stated her confusion, her entangled identifications with both her mother and her father, and her learned perception of both as the hated Other, Julie surveys her present situation, crying

> Whose fault is all this? My father's, my mother's, or my own? My own? Blame myself, when I have no self left? I don't have an idea except from my father, I don't have a passion except those given to me by my mother. . . . Whose fault? What does it matter to us whose fault it is? I am the one who has to bear the guilt and the consequences.
>
> (44)

Even as she realizes her dilemma, however, she remains caught in the system of binaries, associating intellect with

the father and passion with the mother. It is not surprising, then, that she cannot begin to accept and integrate the two poles of her own being.

Julie's recognition of the influence of both her father and her mother on her present state aids our understanding of her confusion, torn between self and other. But although Julie, unlike Hedda, remembers her mother and can articulate her influence, the physical absence of the mother in this play retains a certain thematic importance. The absence of Julie's mother represents the mother's absorption (as other) into the father and the daughter's consequent identification with the father. This identification is enhanced by the opening parallel between Julie's ability to command Jean and the Count's ability to do so. It is only as Julie succumbs to her sexuality, unavoidably female, that she begins to lose the identification with the father (as Hedda does through pregnancy) and lose her power to control Jean. Strindberg's stage directions describe her, after intercourse with Jean, as "shy, very feminine"(26), no longer the commanding aristocrat of previous scenes. As Julie's actions illustrate, her attempt to repress her own female sexuality results in its overcoming her. The situation in which Julie finds herself with Jean is one that Hedda would rather die than experience with Judge Brack; and, eventually, Julie makes a similar choice rather than face the "consequences" (35) of this new, weakened position.

The final act of these two, tragic daughters results from their entrapment in a double bind created by turn-of-the-century society. Doubly alienated from both self and other, and from both mother (a learned alienation) and father (a biological and social alienation), both heroines choose death as the only perceivable method of transcending the double bind. Succumbing to her female sexuality and the social restrictions that accompany it is not a viable response to the double bind for either woman, hypnotized as she is by the power of the father. Hedda cannot bear the domestic burden of pregnancy and motherhood and the consequent damage to her identification with the father, and she articulates this position clearly:

BRACK:

> [. . .] But suppose now that what people call—in elegant language—a solemn responsibility were to come upon you? [*Smiling.*] A new responsibility, Mrs Hedda?

HEDDA:

> [*angrily*]
>
> Be quiet! Nothing of that sort will ever happen!

BRACK:

> [*warily*]
>
> We will speak of this again a year hence—at the very outside.

HEDDA:

> [*curtly*]
>
> I have no turn for anything of the sort, Judge Brack.
> No responsibilities for me!
>
> (57)

Similarly, Julie experiences and rebels against the new position that her sexuality has placed her in, interrupting her "shy, very feminine" (26) interlude to rage at Jean:

> By God, I'd like to wade knee-deep through your guts, and drink your blood from your skull, I'd like to see your heart burned and roasted like mutton! You think I'm helpless; you think I love you, because my womb called for your seed—you think I'll carry your children under my heart, feed them with my blood, and give them *your* name!
>
> (40)

Julie fears not her father's wrath; in fact, she presumes that the news of her escapade would kill him (40). What terrifies her and contributes to her decision to kill herself is the possibility that her female sexuality might overwhelm her, that "it could happen again. . . . And there could be—consequences . . ." (35).

As with Hedda, Julie's fear is partly of scandal, and this fear is also connected to her relationship with the father. As Julia Kristeva contends,

> because of the privileged relationship between father and daughter, a woman takes social constraints even more seriously, has fewer tendencies toward anarchism, and is more mindful of ethics.[19]

In both dramas, death is preferred to scandal; more importantly though, it is preferred to sustained, female sexuality and the powerlessness that accompanies an identification with the mother. What does this say about the position of women in turn-of-the-century society?

Interestingly, although Strindberg's drama is based on a "real-life incident [which] . . . made a powerful impression on [him]" (3), in his preface to **Miss Julie** he considers the issue as one of "nature" rather than of the political and social conflict Ibsen's dramas reveal. He sees characters such as Julie and Hedda as aberrations of the natural order, not as products of an unsound social system. He claims

> Miss Julie is a modern character, not because the half-woman, the man-hater, would not have been found at all times, but because she has now been recognized, has pushed herself forward and made a fuss. The half-woman is a self-assertive type, who sells herself for power, decorations, distinctions, and diplomas, just as she once sold herself for money, and she betrays her primitive origin. Hers is not a sound species, for it has no endurance. . . . Fortunately they are destroyed,

> either by a lack of harmony with reality, the unchecked eruption of suppressed instincts, or failure to obtain a man. The type is tragic, offering as it does the drama of a confused struggle against nature, but it is a relic of romanticism now being dispersed by the Naturalists, who wish for nothing but happiness—and happiness demands a stronger and a better species.
>
> (5-6)

Strindberg is right on one point: happiness does indeed demand a stronger and a better species. And his statement that "[t]he heroine only arouses our pity because we are frail enough to fear that her fate might overtake us" (3) is especially true for women readers. However, these plays are tragic not only in terms of the daughter's demise, but also in terms of their stark depiction of human relationships. Both Ibsen and Strindberg, the latter quite accidentally, demonstrate through their portrayal of the father/daughter relationship a crippling double bind of the sort more easily recognized in the master/slave relationship. For despite the advantages of the father/master position in these binary partnerships, the dominant and the subordinate partners in these power dances are equally trapped within the static binary opposition. Until one or other breaks the silence and communicates about the double bind, it cannot be transcended: until it is transcended, social evolution is at a dangerous standstill.

Hedda's murder of her unborn child illustrates acutely this sterility that results from a paralysis in the evolutionary process, and Julie's suicide is at least in part an attempt to avoid the "consequences" of her sexuality, a child. That both women exit the stage with determination, "MISS JULIE *walk*[ing] firmly out through the doorway" (45) and Hedda speaking her final lines "*loud and clear*" (110), has been mistaken for a positive sign, a sign that these suicides are powerful acts, acts of liberation. But to see the suicides as liberating is to miss the tragic point of these two plays. That this is the best alternative for these women is a pathetic reflection of their situations; that dying is their most powerful act comments on their powerlessness in life, a powerlessness made more poignant by their participation in their own repression. In opposition to the revoking of closure which in feminist texts represents liberation and possibility, the undeniably harsh closure of these two dramas constitutes a bleak imprisonment, with no hope for any significant liberation. As a comment on turn-of-the-century society, these final scenes indicate a need for change in the social codes, not only so that women survive and emerge as "a stronger and better species" but also so that human relationships as a whole evolve and flourish.

Notes

1. By symbolic here I intend a traditional use of the term, following such theorists as Northrop Frye in his discussion of the "archetypal phase" of symbols in *Anatomy of Criticism: Four Essays* (Princeton,

NJ, 1957) and Claude Lévi-Strauss in his method of revealing analogies between very different aspects of life and society by seeing each as a structural system of symbols (*Introduction to a Science of Mythology*, trans., John and Doreen Weightman, 4 vols. ([New York, 1966], 9-81). In this article, I use the terms symbolic and symbol to describe the capacity of particular textual objects, images, and characters to represent and reveal social and psychological constructs. In each case, as Cleanth Brooks has insisted, the context lends significance to the particular image, word, or statement. For instance, General Gabler's pistols are, as a signifier, related to their ritual significance and serve the symbolic purpose of representing masculine power as Hedda perceives it.

2. Gail Finney, *Women in Modern Drama: Freud, Feminism, and European Theater at the Turn of the Century* (New York, 1989), 1.

3. Sigmund Freud and Joseph Breuer, *Studies in Hysteria,* trans. A. A. Brill (Boston, 1950); Sigmund Freud, *Three Essays on the Theory of Sexuality,* trans. James Strachey, rev. ed. (New York, 1962).

4. Elaine Marks and Isabelle de Courtivron, "Introduction III: Contexts of the New French Feminism," in *New French Feminisms: An Anthology,* ed. Elaine Marks and Isabelle de Courtivron (New York,1980), 36.

5. Finney, 1. See note 2

6. The subject of the father/daughter unit in literature is receiving more critical attention in recent years. The study *Daughters and Fathers* (Baltimore, 1989), a collection of essays edited by Lynda E. Boose and Betty S. Flowers, addresses the subject from a cultural/historical perspective, but concentrates primarily on fiction and poetry by and about women. The dynamic of the father/daughter unit in drama has yet to be examined in sufficient detail by critical scholarship.

7. Henrik Ibsen, *Hedda Gabler,* in *Three Plays by Ibsen* (New York, 1959). Subsequent references are from this edition and appear parenthetically in the text.

8. Johan August Strindberg, *Miss Julie,* in *Strindberg: Three Experimental Plays,* trans. F. R. Southerington. (Charlottesville, 1975). Subsequent references to Strindberg's Preface and the play are from this edition and appear parenthetically in the text.

9. Simone de Beauvoir, *The Second Sex,* trans. H. M. Parshley (New York, 1957).

10. A double bind is more than a mere contradiction because it cannot be resolved by a choice. According to Gregory Bateson, a double bind involves a genuine paradox: it is a situation that involves two equally correct but equally insufficient alternatives, each of which seems to be invalidated by the other (Jurgen Ruesch and Gregory Bateson, *Communication, The Social Matrix of Psychiatry* [New York, 1951]). In order to enjoy even marginal power in their social situations, Hedda and Julie would have to succumb to the construction of their gender that allows them access to power only through their sexual subordination to men. Faced with the paradox of desiring male power but only being able to access it through an acceptance and affirmation of her femaleness, her lack, the daughter has three options. She "may illogically deny the paradox and make a dogmatic choice, oscillate between the two contradictory positions within the paradox, or communicate *about* the paradox (thereby transcending it)." Richard M. Coe, "Logic, Paradox and Pinter's Homecoming," *Educational Theatre Journal,* 27:4 (December 1975), 491.

11. John Ward explains that "[Julie] is declassé as a result of her sexuality" (58), demonstrating the important interrelationship between sex and class in Julie's environment. John Ward, *The Social and Religious Plays of Strindberg* (London, 1980), 58.

12. de Beauvoir, xv. See note 9.

13. Ibid., xvi.

14. Luce Irigary, *This Sex Which Is Not One,* trans. Catherine Porter with Carolyn Burke (Ithaca, NY, 1985), 28.

15. Many feminist studies of the family, in history, religion, and literature, recognize the symbolic importance of the mother's absence in relation to the father's presence. Lynda E. Boose, in her essay "The Father's House and the Daughter in It: The Structures of Western Culture's Daughter-Father Relationship," observes that in the paradigm that the religious texts of Judeo-Christianity set up, father and son are made first analogous and then, in Christianity, synonymous. By the time the creation-fall narrative in the Hebrew text concludes, the story will have accomplished its father-to-son transmission, and Adam, the acknowledged son, will have graduated to the role of father. At this point the absent mother also will appear, emerging into designation out of the unnamed and unassigned female transgressor of the Father's garden. Within this narrative, what is conspicuously absent is the figure that lurks beneath the text, the figure who is also the one repeatedly subjected to erasure, extrusion, and transformation.

In Boose and Flowers, *Daughters and Fathers,* 48. See note 6.

16. Quoted by F. R. Southerington, in introduction to *Strindberg: Three Experimental Plays,* xv. See note 8.

17. Many critics have recognized the role of Julie's sexuality in the play; however, some have miscon-

strued its meaning, interpreting Julie's "strong sexuality" (Ward 59) as symbolic of female sexuality per se. It is, rather, a perverted version of the sexuality of the peasants, and as such it serves to weaken Julie's position rather than strengthen it. It is her distorted understanding of her sexuality that gives Jean the opportunity to exploit and manipulate her. This distinction, between female sexuality and the perversion of that sexuality, is essential to understanding the complexity of Julie's position in her father's house. However, as Strindberg provides only the character of Kristin against whom we could judge Julie's distorted sexuality, Julie's actions are easily mistaken for the symbol of female sexuality in general, rather than a particular perversion of it.

18. This struggle is violently played out in Strindberg's earlier drama, *The Father* (1887). The mother plays a focal role in this play, and Strindberg draws our attention to the particular combination of maternal power and social powerlessness embodied in Laura as she struggles violently with the Captain for control of their daughter's future. Gail Finney points out "the close and yet ambivalent relationship between Laura and Bertha" (216) in the play, observing that "Strindberg's recognition that the mother-daughter link is in part a reaction against the authority of the father unwittingly prefigures a central tenet of contemporary feminist theory" (217). This mother-daughter link is further problematized through Julie as she struggles with her identification with the omnipresent father.

19. Julia Kristeva, "Woman Can Never Be Defined," *Tel Quel* (Autumn 1974), 135-40.

BROTT OCH BROTT (CRIMES AND CRIMES)

CRITICAL COMMENTARY

Daniel Davy (essay date 1997)

SOURCE: Davy, Daniel. "Strindberg's Unknown Comedy." *Modern Drama* 15, no. 3 (1997): 305-24.

[*In the following essay, Davy analyzes* Crimes and Crimes *as a tragicomedy.*]

> How could a play entitled *Crime and Crime* and obviously preoccupied with a conflict between forces of good and evil be devoid of moral content?
>
> —James L. Allen, Jr.[1]

> Don't you know this is the witching hour? That's when you hear things—and see things sometimes. Staying up all night has the same sort of magic as crime. Puts you over and above the laws of nature.
>
> —*Crimes and Crimes*[2]

August Strindberg's comedy *Crimes and Crimes* is not "unknown" because of Strindberg—the play is clearly designated "A Comedy" on the title page—but because of the virtual unanimity of critical response to the play which totally ignores this classification. Although a considerable degree of variability exists between individual shadings of interpretation, the vast majority of criticism is of one mind in taking the "dark" or "serious" manifest content of the play at face value.

As Burry Jacobs observes, "The generic subtitle of *Brott och brott* has caused readers problems from the very start. . . . when he produced the play in 1902, Max Reinhardt relabelled it 'tragicomedy'."[3] As is evident from the following representative sampling of critical opinion, this "relabelling" has continued virtually all the way to the present day:

> The contest . . . comes to be reminiscent of the struggle between good and evil forces for the protagonist's soul in the typical morality drama. . . .
>
> . . . the battle of the sexes in *Crime and Crime* is representative of another battle in human experience, the battle between good and evil.[4]
>
> [T]he play is substantially a study of guilt and retribution . . . (and) a demonstration of the workings of sin. . . .[5]
>
> Though Strindberg attacks the evil will, the secret crime, he defends it . . . with characteristic ambivalence. . . . The result of this line of thought is, obviously, that a crime is something good . . . that it is a grace bestowed from on high, provided it is followed by pangs of conscience and purification through suffering.[6]
>
> Both the literary and theatrical value of the play depend upon the skill with which Strindberg and his producers create a dark mood that suggests moral license and depravity.[7]
>
> *There Are Crimes and Crime* [*sic*] may, then, be considered a study of guilt in dramatic form.[8]
>
> [*Crimes and Crimes* is] a play dealing with success, arrogance, and the power of secret desires. . . . The subject is the guilt felt by the hero for imagined crimes.[9]

One possible clue that the majority view of the play has been misdirected lies in a remark of F. L. Lucas, who dismisses the play in a single comment contained in a note: "I have not thought it worthwhile to deal with *Crime and Crime* . . . Though intense in certain scenes, it seems a rather foolish play.[10] This verdict on *Crimes and Crimes* is consistent with the relatively sparse body of commentary surrounding the work. Two major Strindberg studies of relatively recent origin—Egil Tornqvist's *Strindbergian Drama: Themes and Structure* (1982), and Harry Carlson's *Strindberg and the Poetry of Myth* (1982)—do not deal with it at all, a silence that clearly speaks an opinion inharmony with Lucas's appraisal of the play as "foolish" and unworthy of analysis. But is it not possible that Strindberg himself was well aware of the apparent discrepancy between comedy and his own play, and that the foolishness in question does not pertain to *Crimes and Crimes* but to a body of criticism which superimposes its own dramatic objective upon the play and then damns the play for failing to achieve it? Is it not also possible that the same cluster of characteristics—crime and the guilty conscience, "thought crime," the wanton abandonment of family and friends, the death of a child, and so on—which fails to cohere as a serious drama might well succeed if viewed from another, "comic," perspective? What might such a perspective be?

In an essay entitled "Strindberg: The Absence of Irony," R. J. Kaufmann takes issue with George Steiner's frequently cited view that Strindberg's dramatic work is the product of personal obsession and is lacking in unity and coherence.[11] Kaufmann agrees with the former view but argues that the obsessive character of Strindberg's writing leads to drama that is "overunified," and to dramatic "characters [that] are not free to choose, they cannot release their obsessive grip long enough to change, to choose or learn, they lack the illuminating irony and self-humor which is the emotional expression of this missing freedom."[12] Kaufmann then turns his attention to Strindberg's own views on "humor," citing a passage in *The Son of a Servant,* and then commenting:

> Humor reflects the double reaction of man to conventional morality. . . . Humor speaks with two tongues— one of the satyr, and the other of the monk. The humorist lets the maenad loose, but for old unsound reasons thinks that he ought to flog her with rods. . . . The greatest modern writers have thrown away the rod, and play the hypocrite no longer, but speak their minds plainly out.

> As always, Strindberg unquestioningly assumes that sincerity is the same as single-mindedness. . . . The doubleness of vision necessary to comic writing, from Aristophanes to Shaw, he sees as hypocritical compromise. The freedom of an irony which says one thing and means another, which lets folly be spoken and then measures it, he will not consider. . . . There is here as elsewhere a disastrous separation between the intellect and the feelings.[13]

In my view Kaufmann's identification of obsessive "single-mindedness" and the absence of self-irony as a dominant characteristic of Strindbergian drama is generally an accurate observation, with, however, *Crimes and Crimes* standing out as a single and notable exception. I would argue that "self-irony" is not only evident throughout the play but is indeed the controlling characteristic that defines the arena in which the comedy of *Crimes and Crimes* occurs. In being thus "self" oriented the play is typical of Strindberg, but singular and atypical in its quality of ironic self-reflection[14] spun out in dramatic form. In a sense, Strindberg has taken both his own advice and Kaufmann's; he has "let the maenad—or satyr—loose," but has sent the monk stalking after (comic spyslass in hand), and in doing so has achieved that "doubleness of vision" which Kaufmann accurately identifies as essential to comedic writing.

A clue to what I mean here occurs in the passage cited in the epigraph to this essay. The passage occurs near the middle of Act Two; Maurice is nervously reflecting upon his initial transgressions, and Henriette impatiently responds: "Don't you know this is the witching hour? That's when you hear things—and see things sometimes. Staying up all night has the same sort of magic as crime. Pats you over and above the laws of nature" (511). The key ideas here are "magic" and "over and above the laws of nature." I would argue that in this deceptively "naturalistic" play, Strindberg has created a consciously *artificial world* operating under subtly altered "laws of nature" wherein the sense of being circumscribed by irreconcilable psychic conflict has been "magically" transformed. The playwright has taken his own habitual psychic frown and placed it, as it were, in front of a fun-house mirror: the "serious themes" remain but are now addressed in a context where they can be quite consciously *played* with. Indeed, this sense of conscious *play* seems to me the operative law governing the world of *Crimes and Crimes.*

Such a dramatic strategy is clearly at a far remove from Kaufmann's charge of an absent self-irony in the playwright's work but just as clearly consistent, as previously noted, with artistic "self" absorption. The most prominent feature of the play that illustrates this point is the central motif of "thought crime" itself. The morbidly introspective artist who created a domestic and naturalistic world of sexual paranoia in *The Father* (but where the true dramatic arena is the psychology of the protagonist and the playwright) and the overtly "expressionistic" dramatist of *The Ghost Sonata* (whose Mummy exclaims: "Out Crimes and our secrets and our guilt bind us together! We have split up and gone our separate ways an infinite number of times. But we're always drawn back together again. . . ."[15]) is invariably "drawn back again" to his own obsessive psychology. The play, therefore, like so much of his other work, is very much "about" Strindberg but about us as well. The comic logic of *Crimes and Crimes* is in a sense the converse, in dramatic form, of the old joke, "Everything I like is either illegal, immoral or fattening." The (self-ironic) humor of this observation is derived from its underlying "dark" content: the too frequent gulf in human experience between what we perceive as "good" or morally *good* on the one hand, and what we spontaneously *desire* on the other, The "joke" neutralizes the psychological tension, usually trivial but at times profound, between the "maenad and the monk" (or between the Freudian "id" and "superego") that are so deeply embedded in human nature.

The terrain of this conflict is of course the mind or psychology, and so also the playing field of *Crimes and Crimes.* The dramatic converse of the above joke is an overtly serious action that covertly or strategically plays with the absurdity of this unresolvable predicament of the human condition.

Thought Crime! Is it not possible that this pivotal concept around which the entire play is based is intended as a *joke*? Is the soldier under fire who thinks and even speaks of running away but nevertheless holds his ground guilty of a "coward crime"? Is a partner in a marriage who entertains erotic thoughts of another guilty of adultery? Are we morally, or spiritually, responsible for our thoughts or our deeds; and are not our deeds, including our "non-sins of omission," all the more meritorious when maintained against strong, "bad," impulses to the contrary? The point seems too obvious to be in need of any real argument.

The concept of play, particularly the special category of "mind play" discussed above, goes to the very heart of the idea and function of dramatic comedy. Johan Huizinga says of play that,

> [I]t is a *significant* function—that is to say, there is some sense to it. In play there is something "at play" which transcends the immediate needs of life and imparts meaning to the action. . . . However we may regard it, the very fact that play has a meaning implies a non-materialistic quality in the nature of the thing itself.[16]

(original emphasis)

One key component of this "other-worldly" quality, says Huizinga, is play's powerful capacity to absorb our attention progressively: "This intensity of, and absorption in, play finds no explanation in biological analysis. Yet in this intensity, this absorption . . . lies the very essence, the primordial quality of play."[17] Hans-Georg Gadamer expands on the significance of play's power to "absorb" the mind:

> It is part of play that [its] movement is . . . without effort. It happens, as it were, by itself. The ease of play, which naturally does not mean that there is any real absence of effort, but phenomenologically refers only to the absence of strain, is experienced subjectively as relaxation. The structure of play absorbs the player into itself, and thus takes from him the burden of the initiative, which constitutes the actual strain of existence.[18]

If we were to summarize the respective points of Huizinga and Gadamer above, we would arrive at something like the following formula: play is a significant and "meaning-

ful" function that can totally absorb the mind, transcend the demands and problems of the "real" or material world as it does so, and simultaneously "relax" and *release* the mind via this very process of "transcendent" absorption. Whatever else it might be, therefore, play carries a deeply inherent quality of *affirmation* of self and the world, and the relationship between the two, a spirit which is of course closely associated with dramatic comedy. It is therefore astonishing, with reference to the "comedy" of *Crimes and Crimes* and the negation of that label by critical consensus, that the influence of Fredrich Nietzsche, particularly Nietzsche's concept of "eternal return," has been entirely overlooked.

That Strindberg was influenced by the ideas of Nietzsche is hardly in doubt: "My spirit has received in its uterus a tremendous outpouring of seed from Frederick Nietzsche, so that I feel as full as a pregnant bitch. He was my husband,"[19] Nietzsche's concept of the "eternal return" was first mentioned in *The Gay Science* (1882) and was first fully articulated as the central idea of what is probably his most famous work, *Thus Spoke Zarathustra* (1883-1885).[20] Strindberg, as the self-proclaimed "pregnant bitch" of his philosophical husband, carried on an extensive correspondence with Nietzsche which establishes that he had enthusiastically consumed *Zarathustra* by 1888.[21]

What exactly does the "eternal return" mean, how does it appear in *Crimes and Crimes,* and what is its significance to the play of "comedy" in the work. There are five more or less explicit references in the play, and without reference to the connection with Nietzsche, they might well appear as the very immature around which the "dark" thematic significance of the play is wound. The first overt reference occurs in Act Two when Maurice, at Henriette's urging, anticipates and "rehearse[s] the scene" of Adolphe's arrival at the café to confront the trio's changed relationship; Henriette enthusiastically responds: "Wonderful! Right on the nose! You must have been in this situation before," (510-11). The second reference occurs later in Act Two, immediately after the issue of Marion has been raised; Henriette exclaims, "Your child will kill our love!" and Maurice responds: "Never! Don't you see, our love will kill every thing that stands in its way, but it cannot be killed!" Henriette then consults the fates by "*cut-*⌈ting⌉ *a deck of cards"* (conveniently at hand), with the following result: "You see! The five of diamonds! The guillotine!—Is it really possible that everything is all worked out in advance? That our thoughts are led like water through pipes, and that there's nothing we can do about it?" (517). The third reference occurs near the end of Act Three where we find that time has confirmed the oracle of the deck of cards: Marion has died, the couple have been arrested, Maurice's theatrical success has collapsed, and now Adolphe has been abruptly elevated to the category of successful artist, as he and Henriette ruminate at the same table in the same café where Maurice and Henriette had celebrated earlier. Henriette says, "Strange how everything comes again, everything repeats itself. Exactly the same situation, the same words, as yesterday when we were waiting for you. . . ." (534-35). The last two references occur in Act Four, the first shortly after the now reunited Maurice and Henriette have failed to commit suicide and have exhausted themselves with a long round of recriminations and accusations: "Oh, Maurice! We're running around in circles, like slaves on a treadmill whipping each other. Let's stop before we drive each other crazy" (543). The final reference occurs in the play's final scene, where the threat of "craziness" seems possibly confirmed as Emile "returns" to Maurice a package from his sister. Maurice opens it: "The tie and the gloves that Jeanne gave me for the opening night of my play, I let Henriette throw them into the fire. . . . How did they get here? Everything is dug again, everything comes back!" (554).

The continual return of this motif (and there are additional implied instances) is so persistent as at least to imply its presence as a significant component in the fabric of Strindberg's play, as it is indeed in Nietzsche's philosophy Nietzsche asserts that a world lacking a transcendental dimension would be of necessity finite; in a finite creation, given enough time and despite—or *because* of—the continual flux of birth, death, and the mutability of all things, every possible "instant" of creation—with all things as they once were—would at length reformulate itself, or "return."[22] The eternal return thus turns any *meta*physical notion of "eternity" on its head, as it assigns a new kind of "immortal" status to each instant of this life and this world even as it passes away.

What are the consequences of this perspective for the human psychology that contemplates it? At the conclusion of *The Gay Science,* Nietzsche expresses the significance of this idea via an aphorism in which a "demon" whispers the eternal return into the ear of a human and then asks rhetorically if this would not be perceived as appalling and monstrous, with "nothing [ever] new" and every "pain . . . joy . . . thought and sigh . . . small or great" doomed to eternally come again, exactly as before. *Or,* and the aphorism concludes with this question:

> The question in each and every thing, "Do you desire this once more and innumerable times more?" would lie upon your actions as the greatest weight. *Or how well disposed would you have to become to yourself and to life to crave nothing more fervently than this ultimate eternal confirmation and seal?*[23]

(emphasis added)

If "everything comes back," where does "everything" begin? Are we *re-experiencing*—trapped!—what has already occurred, implying that the "world creates us," or experiencing what *will* return for the first time in the "now" of the present moment even as it passes, implying "we create the world"? The question is irrelevant because the

conception is not linear but circular: all "returning pasts," "waiting futures," and "lived experiences" are folded together in the eternal now of the present moment. And it is the very finitude and "materialism" of the conception that leads to the powerful and extraordinary impetus to *affirmation* implied in the concluding statement from *The Gay Science* quoted above. The huge "deck of cards" is not infinitely huge; some cards are present; others are absent: the deck is created only in the eternal now of lived experience. We create eternity right now. And the realization (or indeed, Aristotelian *anagnorisis*) of this point leads to the (incredulous!) smile of comedy rather than the frown of tragedy, for surely we would "crave nothing more fervently" than to "act" forever in the one archetype rather than the other. Nietzsche reflects upon his own initial "realization" of the concept in *Ecce Home* (1888; 1908): ". . . the *idea of the eternal recurrence* [original emphasis], *the extremest formula of affirmation that can ever be attained* [emphasis added]—belongs to the August of the year 1881: it was scribbled down on a piece of paper, with the postscript: '6,000 feet beyond man and time.'"[24]

Nietzsche, at "6,000 feet beyond," was clearly living in his own world at the moment of conceiving the eternal return, and so, I have argued, is Strindberg/Maurice in *Crimes and Crimes.* It is indeed a world full of "woe," but one cauted at an odd, "funhouse" angle so as to enable Strindberg to join Nietzsche, in Daniel Chapelle's words, "in unbridled and life-affirming experimentation and playfullness."[25] "Playfulness" is explicitly rendered in the first of the play's "return" instances cited above, as Henriette's calls for Maurice to "rehearse the scene" (510) of Adolphe's impending arrival. Strindberg, as "play"-wright Maurice, here metatheatrically "plays a scene" within his own play, a sequence of self reference whose artifice is only additionally enhanced via its construction within the growing "dark" scenario of a typical "Strindbergian drama." But is not this "darkness" rendered simply ridiculous upon consideration that its centerpiece of the grand and destructive passion of the two lovers is nothing more than "water [flowing] through pipes," (517) an assemblage, indeed, constructed by Strindberg himself, grinning in the wings? As Adolphe earnestly recounts to Madame Catherine in Act Three after briefly reviewing the tragic history of the pair: "It was as if an invisible being had woven the plot and driven them into each other's arms" (521). But the tragic couple, by Act Four seemingly trapped like Paolo and Francesca to blow around forever in the second circle of hell[26] ("Oh, Maurice! We're running around in circles, like slaves on a treadmill whipping each other" [543]), are perhaps comically redeemed shortly thereafter by Maurice's cry, "For God's sake, let's get off this merry-go-round," (546) shortly before the close of the first scene of the Act. Circling still, the pair have at least removed from slave's quarters to the carnival, where the gaudy, painted mounts (horses, dragons, etc.) on the spinning wheel bob merrily up and down like the respective fortunes of playwright and painter in *Crimes and Crimes.* And the weird "laws of nature" of the spooky fun house located next door are clearly in evidence as Jeanne's gifts to Maurice, burned up by Henriette in Act Two, are "dug up" and come round again shortly before the play's climax (MAURICE "How did they get here? . . . [E]verything comes back!" [554]).

But is there anything else? Strindberg called the play a comedy, and the reiterated comic affirmation of the eternal return would seem to confirm the playwright's stated intention, and yet there is much else in the play that remains still shrouded, apparently, in the gloom of psychic darkness. Let us return to the play and see what additional light might be shed upon it.

The first scene of **Crimes and Crimes** is set *"in the Montparnasse Cemetery,"* where Jeanne is waiting anxiously for Maurice to appear. Our attention is quickly drawn to the image of the cross with the somber Latin inscription, *"O Crux! Ave Spes Unica! [Hail the Cross! Our only hope!]"* (485). Critics have made much of this image as one of the obviously "serious" opening motifs in the play, and Strindberg's use of it does indeed seem significant but in quite another sense. Why, we must ask, is Jeanne meeting Maurice in a *cemetery* in the first place? There is no logical reason in the circumstances of the play for choosing such an ostentatiously gloomy rendezvous, and this aura of incongruity is only enhanced by the spectacle of little Marion, who accompanies her mother, "playing" amidst the tombstones and the dead and dying flowers of the departed.[27] The cemetery functions as a visual metaphor for the "oppressive" thematic material of the play, and yet when we consider it in the context of the logical circumstances of the plot, its use seems highly artificial and thus tends to highlight precisely *this* characteristic—as opposed to the grimly "realistic" interpretation—of the play's overall "crime" motif. The wages of sin may indeed be death and the grave, but the symbolic embracing of this "end" before the "cause" has even appeared seems slyly calculated to evoke at least a faint sense of the absurd from the very outset of the play.

The next event in the play is the appearance of Jeanne's brother Emile, and the discussion between the two carries an obvious expository function. However, Emile's appearance in this context provides the occasion for an additional infusion of the aura of absurdity that colors the entire scene. He enters with the line: "Hello, Sis! What are you doing here?" (487). This question—which we were just asking ourselves—might well be turned upon its author: what is *Emile* doing there? Is he simply out taking the air, strolling through the graveyard, when he stumbles upon his sister of all people? Thus far in the play the characters seem to be functioning in the manner of carrier pigeons, all homing in upon the cemetery with a pre-ordained "inevitability" that would appear distinctly ominous, were it not even more distinctly ridiculous.

This aura of the absurd and even surreal reappears immediately in scene two, of the scene shifts to *"The Crêmerie,"* the modest café operated by Madame Catherine (493). It is here that we—and Maurice—first encounter Henriette, whose initial appearance in the play is as strikingly exotic and sensational as was Jeanne's conversely "dark" appearance in the gloom of the cemetery, and equally as exaggerated and artificial. Maurice is already seated in the restaurant when Henriette abruptly enters, asks for Adolphe, and immediately exits; she spins in and out of the scene as a kind of glittering erotic cyclone, instantly bedazzling the fatally attracted Maurice. "Who in blue blazes was that?!" he exclaims (494),[28] and continues shortly afterward: "You saw, didn't you? She didn't walk through the door: she vanished, and a little whirlwind sprang up which pulled me after her.—Go ahead and laugh!—But why is that palm tree on the sideboard still shaking? What a diabolic woman!" (495). Henriette's "diabolic" presence sends Maurice into an erotic swoon that will continue until the end of the play, despite the fact that he has seen her for all of about fifteen seconds. This quality of giddy unreality generated by the initial contact between the lovers only intensifies as the scene continues. Madame Catherine's response to the seismic event of the sighting of Henriette is almost as hyper-accentuated as that of Maurice, as she at once sets about her series of frantic "warnings" that continue throughout the scene: "Well, then, get out, get out!" (495). After Henriette re-enters the scene somewhat later, Madame Catherine will twice gesture *"warning[s]"* to Maurice (496) and *"[knock]* over . . . glasses and bottles" in her efforts to intervene (501), and the scene will conclude with the following burst of near hysteria:

MADAME CATHERINE:

   Don't do it! Don't do it!

MAURICE:

   Do what?

MADAME CATHERINE:

   Just don't do it!

MAURICE:

   Fear not!

                                                        (502)

Given the instantaneous zeal with which she takes up her role as "blocking agent," Madame Catherine's function in the scene is as incongruous and artificial as the earlier initial appearances of Jeanne, Emile, and Henriette—particularly so when we consider the context of the sophisticated and casually amoral Parisian milieu in which the scene occurs.

During the course of this action Maurice attempts to flee the café through the rear entrance but is comically "blocked" in this direction as well, literally *"bump[ing]* into" (495) none other than Emile, who has expediently only just returned from his excursion through the cemetery. Maurice spins about only to confront Henriette, who just at that instant re-enters the café. At this point in the action one must check the instinct to return to the title page to see that it is indeed Strindberg and not Feydeau who is the author of the play.

When the two lovers finally begin to interact in the scene, an additional comedic element is generated, but one functioning on an altogether different plane. During the following exchange, the topic of "crime" occurs for the first time in the play:

HENRIETTE:

Who knows what goes on in our heads?

MAURICE:

Yes, imagine being held responsible for our thoughts. Life would be impossible.

HENRIETTE

Don't tell me you have evil thoughts?

MAURICE:

Of course I do. And in my dreams I commit the grimmest crimes . . .

HENRIETTE:

In dreams, oh, well—!

(498)

It seems to me quite relevant to the overall scheme of the play that Strindberg first introduces the idea of "crime" in the context of the purely subjective domain of "dreams" and "thoughts," a plane of existence where the objective "laws of nature" no longer operate. The mind's potential for release or freedom, its capacity for intellectual and artistic play with the forms, images, and ideational content of the mind on the level of thought, is far greater than that afforded by the limitations of objective reality, the grim "reality principle" of Strindberg's contemporary Freud. One can restructure one's "thoughts," accomplish literally anything in "dreams," and, very significantly, re-order the constituents of existence—both objective and subjective—in the *imagined* world, the artifact, of a "play."

This descent into the psyche and its inherently expanded potential for freedom and play continues and accelerates in Act Two, as the scene shifts to *"The Auberge des Adrets,"* yet another café but *"decorated in a flamboyantly theatrical, baroque style"* (503), a sensuous upgrade in decor expressionistically parallel to Maurice's increased intimacy with Henriette, and to the fulfillment of desire on all levels.[29] And it is precisely this pure note of "desire and fulfillment" that is sounded so emphatically in the scene, as Maurice exclaims: "What a night, what a wonderful day! I still can't believe it. A new life has begun for me! The producer thinks I'll make a hundred thousand francs out of this play. . . . [. . .] I'm buying a villa outside the city—and I'll still have eighty thousand left! I won't be able to take this all in until tomorrow. [. . .] (*Sinking down in his chair.*) Have you ever been really and truly happy?" (503). We are presented here with a kind of archetypal fantasy of the dream come true but consciously articulated, as the playwright descends into his own "primary process" and there aesthetically—and playfully—reconstructs the eternal conflict between "reality" and "pleasure" principles. As Maurice/Strindberg will shortly exclaim, remembering the "reality" of Jeanne's injunction that Marion needs new clothes: "But I don't get any fun out of it! And I want to get some fun out of life before it all disappears down the drain!"[30] (505). This outburst is almost immediately followed by the stage direction *"The clock strikes twelve,"* an obvious comic punctuation of the declaration just past. One thinks of Dr. Faustus poised on the brink in Act Five, "Therefore never send to know for whom the bell tolls," and any number of additional "fated" moments of literature and drama.

But it is not only the seizing of all that is instinctually "good" in the scene that calls attention to itself but also the striking levels of equally "instinctual" *aggression* in the scene as well. Henriette reminds Maurice of the many old friends waiting to congratulate him at Madame Catherine's, and Maurice responds with the first of a whole series of gratuitous bursts of aggression that will continue throughout the scene: "Let them wait! They made me promise, and now I take back my promise" (505). And a few moments later: "I can hear what they're saying. 'He'll come. Good guy. Doesn't forget his friends. Doesn't go back on his word. He'll come, take my word.'—Now they'll have to eat their words" (506). As for the former boyfriend and best friend Adolphe, he is symbolically smashed as a champagne glass and assailed in absentia with the following (in a series of exchanges with Henriette): "As I crush this glass under my feet, so shall I grind into dust that image of yourself which you have built in a little temple that shall be yours no longer!"; "I want to wipe him from the living, erase even the thought of him, render him unborn, unmade, nonexistent"; and "We'll drive his ghost into the wild woods, bury our memories of him, and let the days we spend with each other pile up like rocks on top of him" (507-08). If interpreted "seriously," this type of aggression might well be viewed as an overreaction against feelings of guilt; however, the extravagant imagery and hyperbole of the various denunciations (including friends with whom there is no intrinsic "guilt" relationship), coupled with the earlier expressions of jubilation over success and sensuality, all lend themselves to the notion that the entire scene is consciously and artificially designed as a kind of "dream of the id," a celebration of "me!" on all levels.[31]

This intense, "subjective" focus of the scene is additionally enhanced by the "voiceover" of the Beethoven sonata practice which begins offstage in the middle of the passionate colloquy between Maurice and Henriette.[32] The use of this device is significant in a number of ways. First, the nervous, hectic, semi-obsessed quality of the principal theme in this movement of the sonata is strongly evocative of the psychological rhythms of Maurice himself as he plunges every more deeply into Strindberg's weird world of dreamscape bliss and criminality. The music is a kind of aesthetic electroencephalogram, a parallel artistic expression of Maurice's melodic "movement" through the play.

Second, the element of repetition inherent in the pattern of sonata form in the music replicates the larger aesthetic motif in the play of eternal return. This pattern is not only inherent within the music but is itself repeated throughout the scene, as Strindberg indicates in a stage direction immediately before the scene's conclusion: *"During the whole of this scene, the pianist in the next room has been practicing the Beethoven Sonata, sometimes pianissimo, sometimes madly fortissimo"* (511). The repetitive, intensely "obsessive" quality of this piece, constantly repeated, functions as a kind of comic underlining, and undermining, of the "dark" theme of psychological crime and conflict in the play. Here are Maurice and Henriette on the topic of guilt:

MAURICE:

> We were driven together, like wild game by the baying hounds. Who's guilty in all this? Your friend, my friend [. . . .]

HENRIETTE:

> Guilty or not guilty—what's that got to do with it? And what's guilt?

(507)

"Guilty or not guilty [. . . .] what's guilt?" Once again we see the quality of a kind of hallucinatory giddiness evoked by the playwright; cause and effect are beginning to blur and run together; the "serious" guilt theme begins to spin as on a carnival merry-go-round, while the "serious" Beethoven theme plays madly in the background, its own "laws" altered so as to become but a zany, hurdy-gurdy accompaniment.[33]

One of the most prominent comic devices Strindberg employs in Acts Three and Four is the use of the "police"—obvious symbols of "crime" and "guilt"—whose initially "ominous" appearance in the action soon gives way to absurdity. Here is the Inspector early in Act Three presenting the case against Maurice:

> Last night Maurice was seen at the Auberge des Adrets with an unidentified lady. Their conversation [. . .] dealt with crime. Words like Place de Roquette and

guillotine were spoken [. . . .] More damaging is the testimony of the headwaiter who served them a champagne breakfast [. . .] this morning. He testifies to having heard them wish for the death of a child. The man is reported to have said, "Better if it never existed." To which the woman replied, "Absolutely. But it does exist." And later in the conversation someone said, "The one will kill the other," to which the reply was: "Kill. That's no word to use," and "Our love will kill anything that stands in its way"! And also: "The five of diamonds" . . . "the guillotine" . . . "Place de Roquette."—Now as you can see, all this builds quite a case against the man [. . . .] There you have the hard facts.

(523-24)

This overheated narrative, which establishes no coherent context and which consists entirely of a series of impressionistic fragments "overheard" by waiters rushing back and forth from the kitchen, constitutes the "hard facts" of the case against Maurice. One might indeed convict on such evidence in a courtroom of dreams or nightmares, but in the light of day this "evidence of crime," like so much else in the play, is more evocative of farce than fate.

By the end of Act Three the comedy inherent in the misadventures of Henriette and Maurice is increasingly apparent. Their "crimes" and subsequent "guilt" take on an obvious clown-like demeanor as they are evicted from the Auberge des Adrets as "tart" and deadbeat respectively,[34] then fall into a "despair" and opt for suicide, which results in the following exchange which opens Act Four:

HENRIETTE:

> You don't want to die?

MAURICE:

> I'm not up to it.

(540)

In the earlier scene the police are once again happily employed by Strindberg as they silently and auspiciously enter the action (*"Two Plainclothes Men have quietly seated themselves at one of the rear tables"* [536]) shortly after the entrance of Maurice, shadowing and "following" the accused in the style of the Boulevard crime thriller which had already been mockingly evoked by Strindberg. The police are of course the agents and icons of "morality" and "justice," wholly appropriate figures to be employed in a drama probing the high crimes of the spirit and the anguish which follows. It is therefore utterly ludicrous, and obviously comedic, that when at last the hand of justice falls on the shoulder of the fated pair, it is revealed in the following terms:

HENRIETTE:

> What do you want?

FIRST DETECTIVE:

> I'm with the vice squad. Yesterday you were here with
> one guy and today you're here with another. That looks
> like soliciting to me [. . . .]

> (538)[35]

Also notable is "*The Luxembourg Gardens. Near the statue
of Adam and Eve*" (540), as the setting for the initial scene
of Act Four. The obvious Garden of Eden symbolism, with
Maurice and Henriette as the innocents who sin and are
then cast out, has been stressed by numerous critics as one
of the more prominent of the dark symbols in the spiritually "dark" landscape of the play. But the serious purport
inherent in the symbolism does not necessarily imply its
serious dramatic function in the play. Adam and Eve are
created in the Garden of Eden, commit their crime within
the Divine sanctuary, and are then cast out; Maurice and
Henriette have played out their hapless melodrama of
"crime" in a wholly secular environment, fall into a
"despair" that leads to a clownish gesture at suicide, and
only then come blundering *into* this "Garden of Eden."
The somber "moral" implications of the symbolism are
neutralized and rendered comic by this deliberate switch-
ing around of the "cause and effect" relationships.

But having brought his protagonists into "Paradise,"
Strindberg cannot resist the opportunity of playing God
and casting them out again; what is notable is the particular
style of eviction He employs. The scene is set with the
following melodramatic stage direction: "*A roll of drums
is heard in the distance*" (546) Maurice and Henriette
respond with the following exchange:

MAURICE:

> They're closing the garden. . . . "Cursed is the ground
> for thy sake; . . . thorns and thistles shall it bring forth
> to thee."

HENRIETTE:

> "And the Lord said unto the woman. . . ."

> (546)

We can picture the contorted brows of Maurice and Henriette as they wrestle with biblical quotations in their efforts
to derive "meaning" from this pregnant moment. But who
appears as the Divine messenger to cast the hapless couple
forth?

A CARETAKER:

> (*in uniform. Politely*)

> Sorry, Madam, Monsieur; we have to close the garden.

> (546)

Maurice and Henriette thus make their way out of Eden
not with a tragic bang but with a comic whimper—
"politely"—and move into the play's final scene, perhaps
the most overtly comedic of the entire play.

The play's final scene is structured as a kind of great
"revolve" that brings Maurice back to his subjective origin
in the play of promise and great expectations, and thus
replicates in small the motif of eternal return that has
proved so significant throughout. The scene opens with
Maurice offstage; in quick succession Adolphe reveals that
Marion has died of natural causes, and Henriette enigmati-
cally announces, "Now I know what I have to do" (550)
before she exits the play as abruptly and portentously as
she had originally entered it. Maurice, ignorant of these
and other relevant events and still in the grip of sundry
"thought crimes," enters and is shortly followed by Emile,
who returns Jeanne's gifts which Henriette had earlier
thrown into the fire. "Reality" thus tilts on its axis: as
Henriette (and the "murder" of Marion) disappears, the
gifts reappear; the subjective apparitions of "pleasure" and
"crime" (subconscious id and super-ego, "Yes!" and "No!")
are now removed from the play, thus allowing Maurice to
"return" to a coherent order of being. This he attempts to
do via an exchange of moral courtesies with Emile, and a
vow to the Abbé to embrace the Church and turn away
from worldly pursuits forever. But the wheel continues to
turn—spinning Maurice giddily "through" the Church, as
it were; no sooner does Maurice utter his "serious" vow,
than he is interrupted by a comic phone call:

THE ABBÉ:

> Give me your hand. I don't want you looking back!

MAURICE:

> (*standing up and offering his hand*)

> Here is my hand, and all my heart!

THE WAITRESS:

> (*entering from the kitchen*)

> Telephone call for Monsieur Gérard!

MAURICE:

> From whom?

THE WAITRESS:

> From the theater.

> (555)

At this juncture the action is interrupted by the following
stage direction: "*Maurice tries to break away from The
Abbé, but The Abbé holds him fast by the hand.*" The
upshot of this farcical tug of war between this world and
the next is of course the climactic event of the play[36] and
also the single most prominent element of the drama to be
singled out for criticism. The ending, in which Maurice
spends a single night in the sanctuary and then returns to
his life in the theater, is generally regarded as weak and
anticlimatic given the dark and somber drama that has

gone before. This "logic of the serious"[37] is particularly procrustean when applied to this scene. Here is an example of a "serious" *defense* of the ending:

> The point of Maurice's choice is that although he decides to do both things, he chooses to do one *before* the other. Instead of rushing off to the renewed production of his play on it, opening night, he keeps his promise to go with the Abbé on that night and postpones attending the play until the following night. Instead of succumbing completely to his worldly interests, he puts first things first.
>
> (original emphasis)[38]

Yes indeed, Maurice offers his "penance," but it is so obviously a comic one! Twenty-four hours as a spiritual contemplative followed by a lifetime of worldly indulgence: one can imagine Groucho Marx devising such a solution to a "spiritual crisis."

Perhaps the Abbé can offer a more compelling rationale for the ending of the play, as he addresses Maurice moments before the final curtain: "I have nothing to give you except a good scolding and you can give yourself that.[. . . .] The fact that you've learned your lesson so fast indicates to me that you have suffered as much as if it had lasted an eternity. And if Providence has given you absolution, what more can I do?" (557). A "good scolding" is in fact all that is merited in this "dark" comedy of the mind, where "Providence" is the God of that domain and of the play—Strindberg, the "playwright" himself. And this comic climax, and "absolution," is indeed justified on a purely *subjective* level, where time does not exist, and two days will stand in quite nicely for eternity. For the Abbé invokes, not the logic of God, but of Nietzsche— the eternal now of the eternal return in the present moment. The climax of comedy is always the joyous grin of "yes!", and Nietzsche's question, "Do you desire this once more and innumerable times more?" is answered, in response to the "anticlimatic" ending, by the chorus of voices that end the play:

MADAME CATHERINE:

Maurice, I think you've got it!

ADOLPHE:

I know he's got it!

THE ABBÉ:

Why, I believe he has!

(557)

Notes

1. James L. Allen, Jr., "Symbol and Meaning in Strindberg's *Crime and Crime," Modern Drama* 9:1 (1966), 72.

2. August Strindberg, *Crimes and Crimes,* in *Selected Plays: August Strindberg,* trans. Evert Sprinchorn (Minneapolis, 1986), 511. Subsequent references appear parenthetically in the text.

3. Barry Jacobs, "Strindberg's *Advent* and *Brott och brott: Sagospel* and Comedy in a Higher Court," in *Strindberg and Genre,* ed. Michael Robinson (Norwich, England, 1991), 179.

4. Allen, Jr., 62-4. See note 1.

5. Maurice Valency, *The Flower and the Castle: An Introduction to Modern Drama* (New York, 1963), 309.

6. Gunnar Ollén, *August Strindberg,* World Dramatists (New York, 1972), 67-8.

7. John Ward, *The Social and Religious Plays of Strindberg* (London, 1980), 174.

8. Walter Johnson, introduction to *There Are Crimes and Crimes,* in *Dramas of Testimony: The Dance of Death I and II, Advent, Easter, There Are Crimes and Crimes,* by August Strindberg, trans. Walter Johnson (Seattle, 1975), 259.

9. Evert Sprinchorn, *Strindberg As Dramatist* (New Haven, 1982), 236, 238.

10. F. L. Lucas, *The Drama of Ibsen and Strindberg* (London, 1962), 387, n. 1.

11. "Strindberg's characters are emanations from his own tormented psyche and his harrowed life. Gradually, they lose all connection to a governing center and are like fragments scattered from some great burst of secret energy." George Steiner, *The Death of Tragedy* (New York, 1961), 298-99.

12. R. J. Kaufmann, "Strindberg: The Absence of Irony," in *Strindberg: A Collection of Critical Essays,* ed. Otto Reinert, Twentieth Century Views (Englewood Cliffs, NJ, 1971), 57-9.

13. Ibid., 59, quoting August Strindberg, *The Son of a Servant: The Story of the Evolution of a Human Being,* trans. Evert Sprinchorn (Garden City, NJ, 1966), 152-53.

14. The important notion here is *duality*—self reflecting on self—rather than the "single" mindedness so typical of Strindberg.

15. August Strindberg, *The Ghost Sonata,* in *Selected Plays: August Strindberg,* trans. Evert Sprinchorn (Minneapolis, 1986), 764.

16. Johan Huizinga, *Homo Ludens: A Study of the Play Element in Culture* (New York, 1970), 19.

17. Ibid., 21.

18. Hans-Georg Gadamer, *Truth and Method* (New York, 1985), 94.

19. August Strindberg, *Letters* [of Strindberg] to Harriet Bosse, trans. Arvid Paulson (New York: Nelson, 1959), 87, as quoted in Robert Brustein, *The Theatre of Revolt* (Boston, 1964), 102.

20. J. Hollingdale, *Nietzsche: The Man and His Philosophy* (Baton Rouge, LA, 1965), 167, 177.

21. "Without doubt you have given mankind the deepest book (*Thus Spake Zarathustra*) that it possesses, and what is more, you have had the courage and perhaps the urge, to spit these splendid sayings in the very face of the rabble.

   "I close all my letters to friends: Read Nietzsche! That is my *Carthago est delenda!*" Strindberg to Nietzsche, quoted in V. J. McGill, *August Strindberg: The Bedeviled Viking* (New York, 1965), 287. Only Parts 1 to 3 were included in the one-volume reissue of 1887; Strindberg would have had to read Part 4 in the private edition of 1885.

22. That is to say, the creation is rather like a deck of cards with a finite number of possible sequences of each card in the deck. However big the deck and however exponentially larger the possible number of combinations becomes, it is still a finite number. Keep "shuffling," and each sequence will eventually come round again.

23. Friedrich Nietzsche, *The Gay Science,* trans. Walter Kaufmann (New York, 1974), aphorism 341, quoted in Daniel Chapelle, *Nietzsche and Psychoanalysis* (Albany, NY, 1993), 1. For excellent elaborations of the concept and its significance, see Chapelle 1-14; and Walter Kaufmann, *Nietzsche: Philosopher, Psychologist, Antichrist* (Princeton, 1974), 316-33.

24. Friedrich Nietzsche, *Ecce Homo: How One Becomes What One Is,* sect. Z, quoted in Hollingdale, 177. The significance of eternal return is brought home even more powerfully in *Zarathustra:* "Pain, too, is a joy. . . . Have you ever said Yes to a single joy? . . . then you said Yes, too, to *all* woe. All things are entangled, ensnared, enamored. If ever you wanted one thing twice, if ever you said 'you please me, happiness! Abide, moment!' then you wanted back *all.* All anew, all eternally, all entangled, ensnared, enamored—oh, then you *loved* the world. Eternal ones, love it eternally and evermore: and to woe, too, you say: go, but return! *For all joy wants—eternity!*" *Thus Spoke Zarathustra,* vol. IV, sect. 19, quoted in Kaufmann, 320-21. See note 12.

25. Chapelle, 3. The quotation refers specifically to Nietzsche's conception of the human significance of eternal return. See note 24.

26. The famous lovers appear in Canto V of Dante's *Inferno.*

27. Although Strindberg has obviously created the setting of this initial scene to account for Marion's death (probably caused by arsenic poisoning contracted by close contact with these burial grounds), the very "planting" of this scenic environment calls attention to the self-conscious artfulness and playful nature of the play's construction and strategy. From a purely naturalistic perspective, the setting is entirely arbitrary and incongruous, particularly when one considers that Strindberg could easily have devised an alternative "realistic" explanation for Marion's death.

28. This "double" emphatic punctuation has apparently been added by Sprinchorn in his translation. Elizabeth Sprigge's translation is, however, equally emphatic in its own style:

   HENRIETTE:

   Thank you. But I would prefer to wait for him outside.

   (*Exit* HENRIETTE)

   MAURICE:

   Who . . . was . . . that?

   MME CATHÉRINE:

   That was Monsieur Adolphe's lady friend.

   MAURICE:

   Was . . . that . . . she?

   Elizabeth Sprigge, trans., *Crime and Crime: A Comedy,* by August Strindberg, in *Five Plays of Strindberg* (New York: Anchor, 1960), 65.

29. The setting serves another comedic function as well, as Evert Sprinchorn points out: "Strindberg had his tongue in his cheek when he let Henriette and Maurice have their rendezvous in a tavern called l'Auberge des Adrets. This aubere was the locale of a melodrama of the same name. In 1823 the actor Frédérick Lemaître achieved instant fame by playing this unbearably banal criminal drama for laughs." Sprinchorn, 241. Variations on a theme of "tongue in cheek" is of course the present argument for the entire play.

30. Strindberg has additional "fun" in the tongue-in-cheek mode with Henriette's and Adolphe's descriptions to Maurice of the play that has brought about this overwhelming success:

   HENRIETTE:

   [. . .] Don't you feel how the air caresses you today? It's filled with the good wishes of a thousand souls . . .

   [. . .]

   ADOLPHE:

   —a thousand souls thanking you for making them feel better. Everyone was writing such pes-

simistic stuff, saying people were bad, life hopeless, without meaning. Then you came along
with your play. Made everybody feel good. Felt
like lifting up their heads.

(515)

Strindberg's self-referential pun on his own typically
"dark" dramatic work seems obvious.

31. Maurice virtually confirms "Strindberg's" intent in a
later speech to Henriette:

No, it isn't a dream, but once upon a time it was!
You know, when I was a poor young man who
walked down there in the woods and looked up to
this pavilion, it seemed to me like a castle in a
fairy tale, and I'd dream that being up in this
room with its balcony and its thick curtains would
be absolute bliss! And to sit here with the woman
I love and watch the sun rise while the candelabra
were still burning—that was the wildest dream of
my youth. Now it's come true; I have nothing
more to live for!

(513)

We are thus presented with a continual self-
referential "flipping" of dream/fantasy and reality:
Maurice's boyhood "dream" which has now become
a "reality," but which is really only a "play," which
is Strindberg's own fantasy/dream, which is now
made real as a play, objectified on both page and
stage.

32. Strindberg's stage direction reads: "During this
speech someone in the next room has begun to play
Beethoven's Sonata No. 17 . . . the finale allegretto—at first very softly, then faster and faster,
passionately, stormily, and finally with complete
abandon" (506).

33. It is also worth noting that the Beethoven sonata
played here is frequently labeled "The Tempest," following a remark of Beethoven that the significance
of the piece could be found in Shakespeare's play of
that name (Jacobs, 187, n. 27). It is perhaps stretch-
ing a point but nevertheless strangely coincidental
that Shakespeare's famous play is also set in a special
"enchanted" world, and features a host of sinister
plots and "crimes" that are all effortlessly forestalled
by the powers of the protagonist/"playwright." The
"waving of the magic wand" to turn "darkness" to
light will of course also occur at the conclusion of
Crimes and Crimes.

34.   HENRIETTE:
       [. . .] I'm ready to throw myself in the river.
         How about you?

       MAURICE:

       (*taking her by the hand and walking out with her*)
       End it all? Sure. Why not?

(539)

These are the final lines of Act Three, which are
then immediately followed—or broken only by the
"dramatic pause" of the Act break, if so staged—by
the "change of heart" exchange that opens Act Four,
an obviously comic juxtaposition.

35. In the Luxembourg Gardens, the "plainclothesmen"
put in yet another appearance in this mode of
"pursuit" ("*Two Plainclothes men can be seen at the
rear*" [514]), but then simply hang about ineffectu-
ally in the background for the duration of the scene.
They appear but are ignored by the major characters;
they lack any genuine action in the scene, and the
absence of effective function cancels the "menace"
of their appearance and renders them ridiculous.

36. A "dramatic climax" which is comically undermined
via Madame Catherine's metatheatrical preamble:
"Well, playwright? How are you going to end this?"
(557). Madame Catherine had just a few seconds
earlier revealed her own "subjectivity"—actress!—in
the same metatheatrical style by responding to the
Abbé's injunction to "take this matter a little more
seriously": "I can't. I can't. I can't keep a straight
face any longer. (*She explodes into laughter, covering her mouth with her handkerchief.*)" (556).
Madame Catherine may be overly giddy, but the critics are not.

37. "A great deal of foreboding and psychological tension is built up throughout the first three acts, only to
be deflated gently in the fourth. Without pleading for
a theatre of catharsis, we can still require a climax,
which would make of the powerful evil we have had
preached at us for an hour and a half something more
than a slight case of extramarital adventure," Ward,
178. See note 7.

38. Allen, 72. See note 1. Evert Sprinchorn's comment
on the final scene is an interesting variation on Allen:

Though most readers feel that Strindberg provided
his drama with a false and happy end by letting
Maurice off too easily. . . . Maurice is being
denied the highest merit and is left in the limbo
of the unexceptional. . . . Since there is nothing
profound about him, neither his vastation nor his
regeneration, he can quickly slip back into his
normal mode of being.

(Sprinchorn, 239)

Once again, the criticism is of a "false and happy
end" of a play that is explicitly designated a comedy.
It seems to me that the strongest possible clue that
Sprinchorn is on the wrong track is once again the
logic employed to make sense of the play as a "serious" drama in this context: why would a playwright
as self-absorbed and with as great a propensity for
self-dramatization as Strindberg create a protagonist
as obviously autobiographical as Maurice, and yet

render him "unexceptional," as "average" and as mundane as the picture that emerges from the above quotation?

DÖDSDANSEN (THE DANCE OF DEATH)

PRODUCTION REVIEWS

Ben Brantley (review date 2001)

SOURCE: Brantley, Ben. "To Stay Alive, Snipe, Snipe." *The New York Times* (October 12, 2001): section E, page 1.

[*Below, Brantley presents a review of the production of* The Dance of Death *at the Broadhurst Theater, New York, directed by Sean Mathias.*]

Before the dance, there is the walk.

It is not a graceful walk, at least not by conventional standards, that is being practiced by Ian McKellen in the revival of Strindberg's *Dance of Death* that opened on Broadway last night. His legs stiffen and stray; his basic navigational instincts betray him. But his posture is as arrogantly erect as pain allows. And when a footstool intrudes itself into his path, as it will keep doing, Mr. McKellen kicks it away as if it were some importunate, helpless little animal. And he keeps walking. That's the important thing: he keeps walking.

Lumbering across the long stage of the Broadhurst Theater, Mr. McKellen brings something frightening and majestic to the act of putting one wayward foot before the other. As Edgar, the infirm army captain living in spiteful and isolated wedlock in a dank island outpost, Mr. McKellen projects an aggressive arrogance that doesn't so much conquer decay as ignore it. Every willed gesture, no matter how sloppy, becomes a death-defying act.

Watching Mr. McKellen's captain shooting sparks in the dark mouth of mortality is about as thrilling as theater gets. Too long absent from New York's stages, this English actor, much celebrated here for his Tony-winning performance in *Amadeus* 20 years ago, returns to Broadway to serve up an Elysian concoction we get to sample too little these days: a mixture of heroic stage presence, actorly intelligence and rarefied theatrical technique.

Those who know Mr. McKellen only from his recent eccentric film roles (he's the Hobbit-advising wizard in the forthcoming *Lord of the Rings*) can't begin to appreciate

his reputation as the greatest living actor of the English-speaking stage. Mr. McKellen needs the space, the amplitude that theater allows. Even playing small and inward, as he did in the title role of *Uncle Vanya* a decade ago, he projects big.

Too big, some critics have argued. But in an age dominated by the pocket Adonises of the screen, there's rich satisfaction in seeing a performer who combines intellectual integrity with an emotional reach that hugs the very last rows in the balcony. And when you have an actress of comparable fire power, the throaty siren known as Helen Mirren, playing the captain's adversarial helpmate, Alice . . . well, your only choice is to join the line for tickets.

That said, it must be admitted that this *Dance of Death,* which has been directed by Sean Mathias, doesn't entirely live up to its leading man. There is for starters the crucial question of the third member of the play's triangle of shifting power. That's Alice's cousin, Kurt, who is portrayed by David Strathairn, an excellent American actor, who here takes his character's passivity well past the vanishing point.

There are also chafing discrepancies in tone. In its portrait of marriage as a torture chamber, Strindberg's turn-of-the-century masterpiece presents an obvious temptation to go Gothic, with vampire versus vampire squaring off in the marital ring. To some degree, this product cultivates an aura of Transylvanian kitsch.

Don't forget that Mr. Mathias's last Broadway success was his rollicking production of Cocteau's *Indiscretions* (*Les Parents Terribles*), which was staged as an outlandish Symbolist romp. Here, Santo Loquasto's set exudes a similar, if more cluttered, look of diabolical whimsy, turning the captain's island fortress into a haunted house jointly designed by Dali and Disney.

And the music and sound design by Dan Moses Schreier sometimes seems borrowed from *Dark Shadows,* the vampire soap opera. Ditto Natasha Katz's artful but lurid lighting. When the two combine to underscore the ominous visit of a beggar woman (Anne Pitoniak), you feel you've wandered into an old Christopher Lee movie.

This is all, in truth, kind of a hoot. But what Ms. Mirren and especially Mr. McKellen are doing is much more devious and ultimately far more interesting. Working from the playwright Richard Greenberg's astutely loosened up adaptation and benefiting from Mr. Mathias's obviously affectionate direction, these performers elicit the Every Marriage aspect in the captain and Alice's relationship, especially in the first act.

This marriage may be a sort of hell on earth, yes. But is it really so different from that of many couples who have lived long and claustrophobically in each other's presence, the tics and habits of each tattooed into the mind of the other? What's shocking about the opening scenes of this *Dance* isn't the eye-popping open-walled castle of a set; it's the feeling that you've dropped in on a couple that you usually take pains to avoid visiting.

For there is Ms. Mirren, hunkered into her shawl on one side, her voice aquiver with fretfulness and a resentment of such long standing that it has worn at the edges. And there, oh so homey on the opposite side of the stage, is Mr. McKellen's captain, with an almost pleasant, rectangular smile revealing teeth to watch out for.

As they bicker and snipe, momentarily falling into nasty collusion over the failings of their distant neighbors, you know this is their everyday fare. They must long ago have settled into this acrimonious ritual, from which they clearly draw at least minor pleasure. Their defense of their respective (and hefty) egos is what keeps their blood circulating.

"I suppose you're attractive . . . to other people, when it suits you," he says to her, savoring each pause like old brandy. After a minor dispute on how to handle the servant question (a serious one in their case, since no one stays for long), she tells him, "You are a despot with the character of a slave."

How's that for a description for an actor to live up to? Yet Mr. McKellen miraculously does, giving credence to the idea that one may smile and smile, however humbly, and still be a tyrant. He is unfailingly polite, jocular and often soft-spoken. Yet there is a demure threat poised behind every courteous gesture.

Notice the captain's ostensibly loving physical contacts with Alice's cousin Kurt, who reappears in their lives after a long absence. Edgar clutches Kurt to his chest while pressing a cane or rifle horizontally against Kurt's back. When Mr. McKellen places his hands on Kurt's shoulders, you understand the look of slight, panicked nausea on Mr. Strathairn's face.

It is Kurt's mere presence, of course, that alters the routine chemistry between Alice and the captain. Now they have an audience and potentially an accomplice. Or is it a victim? In any case, their litany of reciprocal grievances turns into an operatic war that may be either the real thing or merely another diverting military exercise. Kurt may not altogether appreciate their vitriolic performance, but we sure do.

For this is when Ms. Mirren bursts into glorious artificial flower. This actress, known to Americans as the sublimely weary crime solver of "Prime Suspect," takes her cues from our knowledge that Alice was herself an actress. She has been waiting for a comeback as eagerly and as long as Norma Desmond.

With Kurt to observe her, Alice's face floods with light; her voice acquires ringing bell tones; anticipating her husband's imminent death, she sheds her at-home drudgery clothes in two witty variations on dressing to kill. Alice's seduction of her cousin, as she rocks fervidly from foot to foot, is scary, funny and sexual at once. And just wait till she (literally) lets her hair down.

This is also, unfortunately, where Mr. Strathairn's performance runs aground. In the earlier scenes with the couple, the actor's air of quiet uneasiness works fine, as he becomes both target and confessor to the ailing captain. The role is partly a stand-in for Strindberg, and it's tough to pull off. But at some point, Kurt has to be transformed into a monster on the level of his hosts, and Mr. Strathairn is unwilling to make that leap. He disappears when he should be most visible.

This sense of a vacuum detracts from *Dance* as a study of a marriage. We need that third point in the temporary triangle to make full sense of the dynamic that keeps Alice and the captain together. The emphasis instead shifts to another relationship, that of the captain with death. And if this makes the play a tad lopsided, it also allows Mr. McKellen to give a performance that will become a touchstone for anyone else playing the part.

I can't think of a more profound or unsettling study in denial from my theater-going experience. The first thing you have to know about Mr. McKellen's captain is that he is indeed dying; the second thing is that he intends to treat death as he has all things that contradict his wishes and beliefs, by pretending it doesn't exist.

There's fierceness in his decrepitude. If he can't manage the stairs, he'll slide down the banister. Though his head falls regularly to one side and his eyes will sometimes go dead and absent, he insists on ordering chateaubriand for breakfast in a voice that suggests God as a gourmand. There are also the cruel moments of recognition: of fear and acceptance, when he wraps his arms around himself and suddenly looks small and very cold. By the end, these accumulate into something like an epiphany.

Yet these scenes don't erase the memory of the dance of the boyars that the captain performs for Kurt, as Alice plays the piano. It's a furious, flustered performance, both heroic and pathetic, in which the captain seems to kick and punch at every dismal phantom in pursuit of him. These are not rehearsed steps. He's making it up as he goes along, with all the vitality that's left him. He is, to put it simply, staying alive.

Charles Spencer (review date 21 November 2001)

SOURCE: Spencer, Charles. "A Marrowing Odyssey to the Heart of Marital Hell." *Daily Telegraph* (November 21, 2001): 21.

[*Below, Spencer offers a review of the production of* The Dance of Death *at the Mercury Theatre, Colchester, directed by David Hunt.*]

What a tremendous terrifying play *The Dance of Death* (1900) is. And how terrific to see a regional theatre staging Strindberg—a dramatist usually regarded as box-office poison—with such passion, commitment and shockingly black humour.

Strindberg discovered long before Jean-Paul Sartre that hell is other people. On the evidence of this play—one of his most autobiographical—he was also a nightmare houseguest. After one of his periodic bouts of insanity, Strindberg sought refuge with his sister, Anna, who had given up her career as a violinist to marry Hugo Philp, a teacher. Strindberg being Strindberg, he naturally fancied his sister, and before long developed an intense hatred for her unexceptionable husband. He responded to his relations' hospitality by storming out of the house and writing *The Dance of Death* in a state of boiling rage. When the traduced Philp began to read it, he threw the manuscript on the fire.

At least Strindberg had the grace to disguise the characters. The married couple here are Edgar, captain of a remote artillery battery on a Swedish island, and his wife, Alice, who abandoned her career as an actress to marry him. They cordially loathe each other, and have sent their children to boarding school for fear they will be infected by the poisonous rancour of the household.

We discover them one evening, sitting yards apart, attempting to fill the yawning hours of yet another miserable night at home. Then Alice's poor sap of a cousin arrives as the island's newly appointed quarantine officer, and becomes disastrously involved in the couple's marital slugfest.

It's like watching two snakes trying to devour the same rabbit—horrible but absolutely fascinating.

Mike Poulton's sparky, four-lettered new version, which often seems like a forerunner of Edward Albee's *Who's Afraid of Virginia Woolf?*, wisely offers only the first part of the play. Part two was almost certainly an afterthought, and is a pale and sentimental shadow of its vicious predecessor. In this initial salvo you get Strindberg at his most intemperate, burning with rancid rancour and illicit desire.

In David Hunt's magnificent production, the autumn wind never stops howling and the couple's marital quarters, imaginatively designed by Michael Vale, seem to occupy a warzone, complete with fractured reinforced concrete and a gaping hole in the back wall.

Watching the battling couple, I longed to know where a woman's sympathies would lie. Gregory Floy's Captain may be a coldly calculating brute, but he is also a brute with style. He copes with a possibly terminal sickness with fortitude, and the sheer audacity of his wickedness in the second half is breathtaking (and Poulton has added a devastating final twist of his own).

In contrast, Christine Absalom's Alice is hideously and unforgettably repellent. Plain and overweight, she carps constantly, treats the servant abominably, rejoices in her husband's illness, and deploys her vilely manipulative sexuality like an offensive weapon. As she comes on strong to Ignatius Anthony's hilariously embarrassed and bewildered Gustav, you feel a great shudder of revulsion. No wonder Strindberg is so often perceived as a misogynist.

But what makes both play and production great, as well as vastly entertaining in the nastiest possible way, is the revelation that Edgar and Alice don't just hate each other. Somewhere, deep down, they love each other too, and that love is even more frightening than their hatred.

D. J. R. Bruckner (review date 15 March 2002)

SOURCE: Bruckner, D. J. R. "More of Strindberg's Peace amid Misery." *New York Times* (March 15, 2002): E.

[*In the following review, Bruckner comments on the production of* The Dance of Death *at the Bouwerie Lane Theater, New York, directed by Karen Lordi.*]

The Jean Cocteau Repertory company certainly has its mettle tested this year. Its production of Strindberg's *Dance of Death* recently entered its 2001-2 roster less than six weeks after the closing of a Broadway adaptation with the vastly admired British stars Ian McKellen and Helen Mirren in the leading roles. It's good to see that the Cocteau, using a translation that Strindberg signed off on, was not intimidated by the uptown competition. We can never see too many versions; each reveals something new about how much of 20th-century theater was created in those two hours, first onstage a century ago.

In the shabby elegance of the little Bouwerie Lane Theater, Edgar and Alice, who have dueled to the death through 25 years of marriage, are so close to the seats that audiences must often fear that they will be wiped out by their conflict, just as completely as Alice's cousin and Edgar's old buddy Curt is. He is demolished when he drops into the dungeon of the old castle that is the couple's home on an island that the locals call "little hell." In this atmosphere every wheeze and whisper burrow into the ear, and Strindberg's mastery of cliche becomes nearly unbearable as Edgar and Alice strip each other of emotional defense and individuality. This was surely the playwright's intention, pursued with intense concentration here by the director, Karen Lordi: the comedy is sophisticated; its characters are not.

But neither are they vulgar. Craig Smith and Elise Stone (members of this company who really are husband and wife) make the uncommonly acute intelligence of Edgar and Alice at once amusing and menacing, and they let us see how that very quickness of wit makes them vulnerable not only to each other but also to the society they loathe and avoid.

Our only glimpse of the world outside is Curt. Jason Crowl makes this crucial but enigmatic character strong enough to play Edgar and Alice off each other briefly, until they gang up on him before he realizes what is happening. And when Curt pities them even as they destroy him, his emotion feels genuine. That is not an easy trick for an actor.

Mr. Smith uses Edgar's histrionics—in everything from his heart seizures to his stuffing all his humiliations into a garbage bag to his attack on the family piano—to unmask gradually a sorrow this old soldier cannot speak of as he discovers, facing death, that life has no more joy than he found, and no purpose he can understand. (The cast list gives no credit to the luxurious black cat with a white muzzle that elicits, for only a moment, a hint of affection from this Edgar. I hope it was Hector, the cat for which this company's occasional late-night comic romps—Club Hector—are named.)

Ms. Stone's Alice can be confident in her scorn only as long as she can ignore the truth. When Curt, made playful by lust, merely suggests that her youthful acting career may have been of no importance, her voice in reply goes guttural; she growls at him. And after an evening of singing hallelujah at the thought of Edgar's dropping dead, when she finally realizes that he is dying, the despair that turns her face blank and freezes her shoulders into a hunch is painful to look at.

The great poet Rilke famously found a profound affirmation of humanity at the end of **The Dance of Death,** although he could not account for it. At the end of this performance, you cannot deny that a strange peace has settled on you. But the source of this odd sensation remains a mystery, as always. A number of Strindberg's remarks suggest that it mystified him, too.

ETT DRÖMSPEL (A DREAM PLAY)

CRITICAL COMMENTARY

Simon Grabowski (essay date winter 1970)

SOURCE: Grabowski, Simon. "Unreality in Plays of Ibsen, Strindberg and Hamsun." *Mosaic: A Journal for the Comparative Study of Literature and Ideas* 4, no. 2 (winter 1970): 63-8.

[*In the following essay, Grabowski explores Strindberg's innovative departure from realism in* A Dream Play.]

I

Towards and around the turn of the century, three leading Scandinavian authors were venturing, each in his own way, into a kind of drama which has traditionally been referred to as one of symbolism. The two older of the three, Ibsen and Strindberg, had already become established as dramatists of the foremost rank, while the third, Knut Hamsun, had only recently won fame as the author of three intensely lyrical novels, *Hunger* (1890), *Mysteries* (1892), and *Pan* (1894). Between the two latter works, Hamsun had published two straightforwardly realistic novels, *Editor Lynge* and *Shallow Soil,* and with *At the Gates of the Kingdom* (*Ved Rikets Port,* 1895), the introductory play in his trilogy about the philosopher Kareno, he was back again into what can best be described as a rather gross and wooden realism. But the second play in the trilogy, *The Game of Life* (*Livets Spil,* 1896), was realistic only in the most formal way; actually, it was farther away from realism than anything Hamsun had written or would ever write again. 1896 was also the year in which Ibsen published *John Gabriel Borkman,* which was followed three years later by his last play, *When We Dead Awaken.* At this very time, Strindberg had embarked on his trilogy **To Damascus** (1898-1904), and with that, on the last phase of his dramatic career—the high point of which was reached with **A Dream Play** in 1902.

For a conceptual frame of reference, the present discussion will bypass the concept of symbolism and rely in its stead on what I have termed the concept of unreality. This means that, in looking at the works to be discussed here, I will be concerned with the immediate dramatic texture and effect of the specific departure from "realistic" everyday experience made by each of these works, rather than with the conceptual "meaning" of their non-realistic contents. Thus the question "What does it mean?" is superseded by the two questions "How does it feel?" (i.e. from the point of view of the reader/spectator) and "How is it done?" (i.e. from the point of view of the author); in other words, the analytic effort is shifted from the interpretative to the strictly aesthetic level. Consider, as an example, *The Master Builder.* In this play, everything pertaining to Solness' previous career and current endeavour as a tower-builder comes across in a matter-of-fact way once one accepts the slightly unusual premise; furthermore, everything, including Solness' fall from the tower at the end of the play, is conveyed indirectly, i.e. not through immediate, visual stage action. Thus while the tower symbolism can be said to be, in a certain degree, "fantastic" (in that it embodies an extent of spiritual striving far beyond the average, materialistically bounded scope of human aspiration), it is never translated into action before our eyes with the kind of captivating immediacy which would create a true moment of "unreality" on the stage. By contrast, Hilde Wangel can be said to be an "unreal" figure inasmuch as she presents herself as an alter ego projection of Solness' own mind; but one never escapes the uncomfortable feeling that Ibsen is at the same time trying to get her accepted as a flesh-and-blood character and never really makes up his mind about what he thinks she is. Strindberg, in his fashioning of the characters surrounding the hero of *To Damascus,* is far more clear and bold. In this trilogy (as well as in such a work as *The Great Highway,* his last play), the reality of everything that goes on around the hero is formal to the point of transparency: through it we perceive, as through a two-way mirror suddenly lighted from behind, a second, "sub-real," authentic texture of reality underneath the seeming reality layer of flesh and blood, and we realize that the latter is an illusion—that, indeed, the external world around the hero is a mental shadow world projected, as it were, before our eyes as living, objective reality.

Mental contents—thoughts and feelings at the conscious level, secret hopes and fears at the level of the personal unconscious—projected as *immediate, objective reality:* this, then, would serve as a possible definition of unreality. It would certainly be a valid definition, as one realizes immediately when applying it to such works as Strindberg's later dramas or the novels of Kafka. On the other hand, these highlights of unreality writing are so uncompromisingly transfused with unreality that even a fairly general definition such as this one will fit. But when it comes to more hybrid creations, i.e. works of a fairly realistic framework with sudden, more or less isolated flashes or passages of unreality—works such as a number of Chesterton's detective stories, or the plays by Ibsen that we are going to discuss here—a more thorough-going clarification of the concept of unreality will be needed in order to grasp in depth the aesthetics of each particular moment of unreality. I will devote the following section to an attempt at such a clarification.

II

From a conceptual point of view, the most orthodoxyl classical example of unreality in Ibsen is furnished, paradoxically enough, not by one of his later plays, but by a play from his middle, so-called realistic period, the tragedy *Ghosts* (1881). The play[1] is patterned on a classical A_a-B-A_b structure, where A_a represents the originally known presence of some fateful circumstance relating to the life of the person/persons involved; B the stage at which this circumstance has been repressed or spontaneously forgotten to the point where the situation can be experienced as being totally divorced from it—i.e. reality B defined as the diametrical opposite of the original A; and A_b, the final, cataclysmic point at which A re-emerges and reveals itself as having always been present, secretly built into the situation all along, i.e. $B=A$.[2] It is this sudden, simultaneous presence of two seemingly totally opposite definitions of the reality, of matter and anti-matter, as it were, at one and the same time (they can't possibly

both be present at once, yet they are!) which creates the great abysmal moment of unreality: the moment at which the mirror suddenly becomes transparent, and a new, old truth—which at this very instant you realize that you somehow knew all along—imposes itself on the long-standing, accustomed reality from behind it, appearing together with it in the mirror for one frozen, ghostlike second before destroying it and dissolving everything into infinite disaster. (It should be added that the same structure can be used as a basis for comedy, with a happy surprise ending in the place of catastrophe.)

It may be said that, in terms of dramatic structure, Ibsen's most celebrated contribution to world drama was his development of a technique through which an originally concealed dimension, the buried past, was made to penetrate gradually into a surface dimension, the everyday present, so that eventually it shatters the picture of reality represented by the latter. The actual "unreality," as I have already pointed out, consists in the emerging awareness of not one but two layers of truth, and the seemingly abysmal contradiction between them. The evidence of the second layer may have been there all the time, but we perceive it only gradually. It should be noted that although the conclusive revelation always comes as a shock the recognition may actually have been emerging for quite a while, i.e. the formal reality of the surface situation may have started dissolving, more or less perceptibly, into unreality perhaps even before the middle of the plot. The great art of this double-level technique is to make us potentially aware of the truth at a relatively early stage, yet on the other hand to get us so involved in the goings-on at the surface level as simultaneously to make us continue our subscription to the illusion of the latter's claim to truth being the only valid one. Face to face with the final revelation, then, we are able to experience a shock which is doubly cataclysmic because we "never knew", yet "always knew." It should be pointed out that, in addition to its other functions, the chorus in the classical Greek tragedy contributes towards exactly this effect: the maintenance in the spectator of the awareness that hidden forces are operating underneath the surface, steering events towards an outcome which may seem negated in terms of the present, yet which will itself in time negate the present conclusively, transforming it back into the all-engulfing past.[3] Given this last formulation, we are now in a position to recognize the true cosmic foundation of the A-B-A structure. If for the A-quantity, "the allengulfing past," we substitute the quantity "eternity" (or "timelessness"), and for the B-quantity, "the present," the quantity "earthly life" (or "time"/"temporalness"), the resulting A-B-A structure now describes that journey from an eternity realm into a temporal life realm and back into eternity which not only organic life on this planet, but everything in the cosmos including the stars themselves, completes. As far as individual human existence is concerned, the idea of a so-called "rediscovery of eternity" refers to the fact that, having spent the first nine months of our lives in a most definite realm of timelessness, the womb, we carry the memory of this experience around with us, imprinted on our unconscious as an a priori experiential attitude: i.e. the built-in possibility of emerging, at some later point of our temporal existence, into a re-experiencing of the dimension of eternity: of merging totally into a vision of temporal things *sub specie aeternitatis,* as well as of the cosmic void beyond all temporal life. Whether or not the potential for these total unreality experiences is actually fulfilled depends, of course, entirely on what course an individual's personal existence takes, what kind of experiences he encounters in life, and so on. But it is undoubtedly part of a truly fulfilled existence that at some stage the individual will be entering into a new mode of experiencing his life and everything around him—as if from then on the temporal vision of the temporal is slowly receding, slowly blending with and giving way to the timeless version of itself. The increasing double-level quality of experience during this later phase—roughly speaking the second half of life—parallels, of course, the increasing unreality in the second half of the dramatic A-B-A structure, as the awareness of A is re-emerging into the present. It is this A-B polarity, then, which contains the key to the entire aesthetics of unreality. B as the temporal, A as the timeless—i.e. that which, throughout the vicissitudes of temporal reality, has been ever present in some secret, hidden form and suddenly starts re-emerging, totally redefining the reality of B—: behind what we were seeing as B there was A the authentic, eternal version of our reality, all along. Or, more schematically: A_a as the thesis, B as the antithesis, A_b as the synthesis of A and the presumed B, the climactic moment of unreality. On the basis of this fundamental polarity, we can designate a number of specific polarities contained by it: Earth vs. Cosmos/the spiritual realm, the Conscious vs. the Unconscious, Light vs. Darkness, Present vs. Past (and Future), Objective reality vs. Subjective imagination, Free agency vs. Fate—or, on an even more specific psychological level, Conscious awareness vs. Unconsciously (or half-consciously) registered (but not consciously embraced) information.[4] Out of all these individual polarities emerges a synthesizing definition of unreality as the timeless version of the temporal, or the emergence of a timeless realm into the realm of time-bound reality.

This second general definition is one of more far-reaching applicability, for it allows us to orient our aesthetic compass in terms of single, isolated moments of unreality, i.e. the scattered, but decisive veins of unreality in such works as may not actually exhibit a solid texture of unreality (in the manner of Kafka's later novels), nor have been structured on the basis of complete rediscovery models (in the way of Kafka's *Amerika* or Ibsen's *Ghosts*). I shall deal with four of Ibsen's later plays on this more fragment-oriented basis of analysis; however, before turning to this concluding task, I will attempt a brief delineation of the respective textures of unreality of two outstanding dramatic unreality creations from this period, Strindberg's **Dream Play** and Hamsun's *Game of Life.*

If *A Dream Play* must have seemed strikingly advanced at the time of its appearance, it still blooms today, almost seventy years later, with the same profound cosmic gaiety, the same priceless artistic freedom and sophistication. There is no doubt that this technique of seeking to reproduce, as Strindberg himself stated, "the disconnected, yet apparently logical, form of the dream" vastly influenced the technique of Kafka in his two last novels, *The Trial* and *The Castle.* In contradistinction from these two works, *A Dream Play* does not even exhibit a tenuously paraphrasable story line; its only forward movement rests on the play's formal design as a "Visitor's progress," i.e. the increasing degree to which Indra's daughter becomes personally involved as she proceeds on her sightseeing tour through life on the planet Earth, and the way in which the quality of her experiences changes in the process. But the basic "meaning" of the play's structure, i.e. the fundamental planetary anchorage of its aesthetic reality, is the "dream" itself: i.e. our planetary world as seen through the Hindu doctrine of material life as a dream Thus in addition to the consistent dissolution of time and space, the majority of scenes combine, with the absurd logic of the dream, elements of an extrinsically contradictory nature, thus creating a succession of intrinsically meaningful, "unreal" visions of human reality. Scene follows upon scene in a manner which seems totally arbitrary, yet in most cases each scene is subtly linked with the previous and following one through hidden associative devices of motif and language. Thus at the formal level this double-quality effect of fluidity and firmness reflects the vast flux and order of the cosmos—while at the ideational level all the play's scenes remain tightly bound together by the cardinal constructs—disillusionment, attrition, suffering—through which these beautifully bleeding, smiling vistas of earthly life are seen as they pass kaleidoscopically before our eyes. The play's texture is one of total, exquisite unreality, at a supreme level of integration. One feels that all basic aspects of human existence have been absorbed into it; indeed, the gatekeeper's star-quilt becomes a perfect metaphor of the totality of the play itself. Never has Strindberg's basic subjective negative construct on life translated itself into such an all-encompassing vision of life in general. Thus the play's central consciousness—"the consciousness of the dreamer" as he calls it—is not the expression of some limited subjectivity (the way it is so often felt in **To Damascus,** not to speak of the major part of that whole school of expressionism which was later to arise in Germany in the wake of Strindberg), but rather a supra-personal, super-objective eye with a claim to total planetary awareness. The play then becomes a journey from cosmic reality into a material earth-dream (which threatens to trap the central figure in a fake, i.e. pseudo-objective, temporal 'reality'), and back into the eternal cosmic realm from which she came.

Notes

1. In the following, a thorough familiarity with the plot of *Ghosts* is assumed on the part of the reader.

2. To be more mathematically precise, this can be more properly formulated as B=BCA), where the bracket indicates the realization of the hitherto unrealized presence of the A factor in the B process: this is the realization that B never stood alone but was always multiplied by A. This multiplication has now become a conscious act.

3. The awareness of the "tragedy" is then born in us through two realization: 1) That the hero's striving has been in vain from the beginning; 2) the realization of his *blidness* (It is characteristic that a traditional, conceptually oriented, view of tragedy will tend to center on the former factor, while an aesthetically oriented view will center on the latter. It is certainly the second one which is the more fascinating, since the sudden realization that this abyss had been existing all along, and that you had even somehow known it, produces that explosion of terror which is commonly known by the Aristotelian term *catharsis*.)

4. On the explicitly aesthetic level, corresponding polarities can be perceived in each individual sense field. Thus in music, a number of major-minor combinations will produce a mood of cosmic timelessness, and similar effects can be combinationally achieved in the field of colour. The feeling of coldness as a simultaneous response to a very hot stimulus is an unreality experience. Moving beyond individual sense fields into *combined* sense of experiences, we recognize the phenomenon of *synesthesia* as an exemplary unreality experience.

KRISTINA (QUEEN CHRISTINA)

CRITICAL COMMENTARY

Margareta Wirmark (essay date winter 1990)

SOURCE: Wirmark, Margareta. "Strindberg's *Queen Christina*: Eve and Pandora." *Scandinavian Studies* 62, no. 1 (winter 1990): 116-22.

[*In the following essay, Wirmark considers the relevance of the play-within-a-play in* Queen Christina.]

In the fourth act of Strindberg's drama *Queen Christina* (*Kristina*, 1901), there is a play within the play that draws upon Greek mythology. Let us call this play *Pandora*. It

takes place at a private party given by Christina for Klas Tott. The two lovers are the only actors. This drama is of great interest from different aspects, also from a dramaturgical point of view. The *Pandora* play is composed of two different and contrasting parts, as will be shown later, and both actors play several parts.

The queen herself is the producer of the play. It starts when Klas Tott arrives at the party, in all probability costumed as Prometheus. At the same moment a rain of flowers falls from above, sweet music is heard, and the light shines brighter. This is the triumphant beginning of the play. Klas Tott/Prometheus greets his beloved Kristina/Pandora with the following words:

KLAS TOTT:

> Pandora, "Allbegåvade" Eva; första kvinna och enda. Du, som skänker människobarnen livet, sedan du givit livet åt en man!

> [Strindberg, *SS* 39:242]

KLAS TOTT:

> Pandora with all the gifts, Eve, the first and only woman! You, who give life to children of men, when you have given life to a man!)

> [Johnson 70]

Christina is characterized as the breeder of life; she gives new life to a man as well as to children.

In the beginning of the play Christina and Klas Tott fully identify with their parts. As the play proceeds, this identification becomes less visible, and the actors' private identity comes to light. To begin with, the spectator is confronted with what seems to be a drama written beforehand, probably the ballet planned to take place the same night, but canceled. The initial lines have a very dignified tone. Further on, the dialogue changes into what can be characterized as common language; these late lines seem to grow out of improvisation.

The story told in the first part of the *Pandora* play is a mixed one. In part it stems from the Greek myth, in part it belongs to the private world of the lovers. The myth fuses with commonplace reality: the result is odd and rather confusing. The myth adds an extra dimension to the love story between Christina and Klas Tott: this is a saga about Man and Woman, not a story about two individuals.

The duo Pandora and Prometheus is a striking one. As Örjan Lindberger (249 f.) and Ola Kindstedt (189-206) have shown, the combination does not originate with Strindberg, however. It can be traced back to the classical works of Hesiod and Aischylus. Josephin Péladan—highly admired by Strindberg—also uses this couple in his *La Prométhéide,* which appeared in 1895. His is a translation of Aischylus's drama *Prometheus Bound* into French.

Furthermore Péladan adds the two missing parts of the trilogy. Strindberg uses the story told by Péladan in the fourth act of **Queen Christina.** He writes in *Ockulta dagboken* (1977; *The Occult Diary*):

> I Péladans Prométhéide skildras Pandora, Grekernas Eva, först såsom sänd av Zeus, (hvilken skrattade när han släppte ner henne) för att plåga menniskorna; men Prometheus förvandlade henne till menniskornas välsignelse i modren, makan . . .
>
> [Strindberg, *OD* 135]

> (In Péladan's *Prométhéide* Pandora, Eve of the Greeks, first is portrayed as being sent by Zeus (who laughed in letting her go) in order to torment mankind. Prometheus, however, transformed her into the blessing of mankind as mother and wife . . .)
>
> [My translation]

This story is told in *Prométhée, porteur du feu* (1895), the first part of the Péladan trilogy. Pandora has been sent down to earth by Zeus, who wants to punish Prometheus for the theft of fire, and she seems to be without conscience when she arrives. She is escorted by Hermes, who offers her to Epimetheus, Prometheus's less clever brother, as a wife. Epimetheus is tempted by Pandora's beauty and by her domestic skills and accepts the offer. In so doing, he breaks his promise to his brother not to accept any gift from the gods.

When Prometheus returns, he finds that Pandora has opened the lid of the golden box. The revenge of the gods seems to have succeeded. Prometheus manages to change the situation, however, by teaching Pandora how to love mankind. Pandora is transformed into a being like himself. For the second time mankind is saved; thanks to Prometheus's presence of mind the wrath of the gods is transformed into their blessing. This is the version of the Greek myth told by Josephin Péladan in his *Prométhéide*.

It is this story Christina selects for her drama. She invites Klas Tott to play the Prometheus part, and she herself takes the part of Pandora. Strindberg takes great care in describing her dress:

> en enda urringad vit tättfallande klädning som slutar vid anklarne med en bård. På fötterna vita sandaler. Hon har utslaget hängande hår, en rosenkrans på huvudet och är strålande skön
>
> [Strindberg, *SS* 39:235]

> (a one-piece, low-necked white, tight-fitting dress which ends in a border at the ankles; she has a garland of roses on her head.)
>
> [Johnson 66]

Her loose hanging hair, the white dress as well as the garland of roses are a sign of innocence. By her dress Christina stresses her strong decision to put an end to her former life and leave the past behind her. For the first time Christina has fallen in love; her new capacity is a gift from Prometheus. The white dress underlines that, as a loving creature, she is newborn.

Christina/Pandora carries in her hands the unopened engraved golden box, containing the royal crown. In the play the regalia is placed in the box as the equivalent of evil. Christina wants to get rid of the crown, the symbol of her former life. The only thing she intends to keep is Hope, which lies at the bottom of the box. What she is longing for is a life married to Klas Tott, a common life like anybody else's:

KLAS TOTT (*PÅ KNÄ*):

> Härska över mig, Zeus; jag böjer mig för din makt under kvinnan! d i n kvinna!

KRISTINA:

> Råd över min vilja, Zeus, att jag endast må vilja det goda.
>
> [Strindberg, *SS* 39:243 f.]

(TOTT (*ON HIS KNEES*):

> Rule over me, Zeus; I bow before your power, under woman! Your woman!

CHRISTINA (*ON HER KNEES*):

> Rule over my will, Zeus, so that I may will only what is good.)
>
> [Johnson 70]

Christina and Klas Tott kneel and make a solemn vow, asking Zeus for assistance. Once again Strindberg underlines that this is the starting point of something new.

A wedding follows this solemn invocation. Klas Tott takes Christina's hand, and she asks him to keep it in marriage. For the first time he is called Epimetheus, the name of Pandora's husband according to the Greek myth. Christina uses the myth to emphasize that a wedding has just taken place. A third ceremony follows, Christina's abdication from the throne. She takes out the royal crown and burns it. After that, a new king is proclaimed. Christina leads her husband up to a throne, the throne in her private kingdom:

KRISTINA:

> En krona ger jag dig icke, min härskare, men en tron, en tron i mitt lilla rike . . . mitt rike där ingen skillnad är på människa och människa! Hell dig konung!
>
> [Strindberg, *SS* 39:246]

(CHRISTINA:

> I don't give you a crown, my master, but a throne, a throne in my little kingdom . . . my kingdom in which there is no difference between people! Hail to thee, my king!)
>
> [Johnson 72]

The four ceremonies take place within a few minutes only. The Pandora play is a short one, and its tempo very fast. A grand finale is expected, a climax carefully planned by the director. At this very moment the front wall is meant to disintegrate to make room for the new paradise. Christina makes the sign as agreed upon and awaits the space to grow into endlessness. Nothing that she expects comes through, however.

> Man ser i stället för den väntade tablån—en skara underligt folk, alla oröriga, tysta, bleka i ansiktet.
>
> [Strindberg, *SS* 39:247]

> (One sees instead of the expected tableau a crowd of strange people, all of them motionless, silent, pale-faced.)
>
> [Johnson 72]

A wall of white faces hinders her entry into the new paradise. Numerous pairs of eyes are staring at her from the very place where she expects her new future to appear. These are the eyes of the past. These are the eyes of the Swedish people, eyes filled with accusation.

In this scene the names Prometheus, Epimetheus, and Pandora are not appropriate, and from this moment they are not used. These names were selected by the Queen as director. Up until now the story has followed Christina's intentions, but suddenly a new director—invisible, unknown—takes over the floor. The play chosen by Christina stops abruptly, and she loses the part she has chosen for herself. A new drama is immediately introduced, the drama about Eve, the myth from the Old Testament. Christina is forced to play a part she knows nothing about, a part she has never devised or selected.

Christina is confronted with her guilt very abruptly, but to the spectator is does not arrive unexpectedly. Her guilt has been hinted at earlier. Again and again during the act strange roars have been heard from the outside. They come from the crowd in the street protesting the Messeniuses being taken to their execution. Those roars prepare for the moment when Christina is confronted with the wall of white faces, and her guilt becomes visible even to herself.

The day of judgement has come. In the scene just analyzed Christina's trial has begun, and the Swedish people act as a jury. It examines the Queen, and sentence is passed. Christina is found guilty of having failed to do right by her own people.

The judgement on her reign is followed by another; this time her sexual past is focused upon. In this part of the trial Klas Tott acts as a judge; her former lovers Bourdellot and Pimentelli are witnesses. After having had to read a love letter delivered by Pimentelli, Klas Tott comes to know Christina's past, a past he cannot accept.

KRISTINA (*ANAR INNEHÅLLET OCH VILL RYCKA DET FRÅN* TOTT):

> Läs det inte, det är gift! Läs inte!

KLAS TOTT:

> Gift? (*läser, bleknar, ser på* PIMENTELLI, *raglar baklänges och faller.*)
>
> [Strindberg, *SS* 39:250]

(CHRISTINA [*SENSES THE CONTENTS OF THE LETTER AND WANTS TO SNATCH IT AWAY FROM* TOTT]:

> Don't read it! It's poison! Don't read it!

TOTT:

> Poison? [*Reads, becomes pale, looks at* PIMENTELLI, *staggers backwards and falls.*])
>
> [Johnson 74]

At the day of judgement Christina/Eve is the only one who is sentenced. Klas Tott never has to accept the Adam part. His role is to act as judge, to pronounce her conviction: "Sköka!" ("Whore!"). After that Tott leaves the stage.

The borderline between the two plays—the Pandora play and the play about Eve—is marked by the wall of white faces. When Christina/Eve is confronted with this wall she screams out, shrilly and piercingly. As she hears the sentence pronounced by Klas Tott, she puts her hand over her heart and falls to her knees. Defenseless and unmasked, she lies on the floor. She is forced to take on the role of Eve, to enact the drama from the Old Testament. She makes the same movements as Eve and pronounces almost the same words.

KRISTINA:

> Å! Giv mig min kappa! Jag är ju naken! Min kappa! (*Hon söker liksom svepa om sig det långa hängande håret.*)
>
> [Strindberg, *SS* 39:252]

(CHRISTINA:

> Give me my coat! . . . Why, I am naked! My coat! [*She tries to cover herself with her long, loose hair.*])
>
> [Johnson 75]

Her new role is strongly underlined with the help of costume. Up until now Christina has hidden herself behind the white Pandora costume. Now the royal coat is placed over her shoulders, and at the same time the past returns with all its accusations. Strindberg does not mention the color of the royal coat; in all probability it is red as blood.

To sum up: the first part of the play within the play has the innocent Pandora as its center. That play abruptly stops and is transformed into its opposite. The new play centers around Eve, the woman who brought sin into the world. In the first part Christina acts as a kind of savior; in the second part she is transformed into a whore. After the spiritual elevation follows the physical degradation. The curve of the play goes from triumph to defeat.

Strindberg's drama has yet another ending, however. Christina has the capacity to learn, and she manages to rise from her degradation. When the play within the play has come to an end, Christina has learned something about herself. The sacrifice she has made she does not undo. She remains an ex-monarch, just as planned. It is true that her future turns out to be other than her plans for it. The husband she hoped for has disappeared, and the wedding journey must be canceled. In spite of this she has the courage to leave her native country and exchange a secure life for something she knows very little about. The braveness of this behavior is striking and culminates in her farewell speech, in which she stands up for the right of the individual to follow her conscience. She pays homage to religious liberty and tolerance, and at this very moment she turns out to be a real ruler, the true daughter of the great Gustavus Adolphus. Thus Strindberg's drama ends in triumph for Queen Christina.

Works Cited

Johnson, Walter. *Strindberg's Queen Christina, Charles XII, Gustav III.* See Strindberg.

Kindstedt, Ola. *Strindbergs Kristina. Historiegestaltning och kärleksstrategier. Studier i dramats skapelseprocess.* Stockholm: Almqvist & Wiksell, 1988.

Lindberger, Örjan. "Some notes on Strindberg and Péladan." *Structures of Influence: A Comparative Approach to August Strindberg.* Ed. Marilyn Johns Blackwell. Chapel Hill: U of North Carolina P, 1981.

Péladan, (Sar) Josephin. *La Prométhéide: Trilogie d'Eschyle en quatre tableaux.* Paris, 1985.

Strindberg, August. [*OD*] *Ockulta dagboken.* Stockholm: Gidlunds, 1977.

———. [*SS*] *Samlade skrifter.* Vol. 39. Stockholm: Bonniers, 1916. 55 vols. 1912-20.

———. *Strindberg's Queen Christina, Charles XII, Gustav III.* Trans. and introd. Walter Johnson. Seattle: U of Washington P, 1955.

PÅSK (EASTER)

CRITICAL COMMENTARY

Harry G. Carlson (essay date 1982)

SOURCE: Carlson, Harry G. "*Easter:* Persephone's Return." In *Strindberg and the Poetry of Myth*, pp. 124-36. Bekerley: University of California Press, 1982.

[*In the following essay, Carlson provides an in-depth view of the play* Easter.]

One might argue that *Easter* only narrowly deserves to be included among Strindberg's major plays. Although audiences have been attracted to what was for Strindberg an unusually serene and reconciliatory tone, there is an awkwardness about the play. The playwright's effort to inform his drama with the solemnity of religious ritual observance by hanging the act structure on the temporal divisions of the Easter Passion—Maundy Thursday, Good Friday, and Easter Eve—led to uneven results. References to Christ are so numerous, analogies to the Passion so obviously drawn, that the effect produced is embarrassingly close to religiosity. Despite these weaknesses, however, the play is redeemed by an elemental power centered around one of Strindberg's most captivating and mythopoeically expressive characters: Eleonora.

The setting is realistic-naturalistic, at least on the surface: the Heyst home, located in a university town identified by scholars as Lund in southern Sweden.[1] The family is a troubled one. Mr. Heyst is away in prison serving time for embezzling trust funds, and his wife stubbornly says she believes him innocent, hoping his sentence will be overturned on a technicality. The present breadwinner is Elis, her son, a young teacher of Latin, who, like the Stranger in *To Damascus*, is profoundly alienated from the world and from himself. For a number of reasons he has become bitter and frustrated: because his mother refuses to accept that his father was guilty; because his friend and pupil/disciple Petrus has not only stolen ideas from his unfinished dissertation but appears to be trying to steal his fiancée Kristina as well; because Kristina offers him help and love, which he cannot accept; because he is obliged to provide a home and tutoring for a young orphan, Benjamin, whose trust funds were among those embezzled by Mr. Heyst; because another of his father's victims, Mr. Lindkvist, seems to have moved to town as a creditor come to claim his due; and finally, because he was compelled to have his mentally disturbed sister Eleonora institutionalized. Elis sees himself suffering as Christ did, and among the more blatant references to the Passion in the play is his reaction to the news that Petrus has befriended someone whose politics Elis abhors, the local governor: "and [Petrus] denied his teacher and said: 'I know not the man.' And the cock crowed again! Wasn't there a governor once called Pontius, surnamed Pilate?" (*33*, 85). This and lines like Mrs. Heyst's exclamation: "Oh God, why hast Thou forsaken me?" turn the family ordeal into perhaps too direct a parallel to the Passion (86). Because the Imitation of Christ becomes too palpable, its ability to set off poetic resonances is blunted, and other, perhaps more important mythic images are obscured in the process.

As in *The Father,* with which *Easter* seems at first to have nothing in common, the energy core is a group of characters who constitute an archetypal configuration: the eternal feminine. It is the task of the respective protagonists to integrate this configuration into their lives, but whereas the Captain succumbs in this effort and is lost, Elis is reborn and saved. The reason for the difference is a shift in focus; each play is dominated by a different phase of the archetype. In the first the phase is the maternal, that of the Great Goddess, who knows nothing but the secret of her womb. In the second it is a reunion of mother and daughter—*beuresis*[2]—a context of enormous creative potential for spiritual transformation. Whether consciously or unconsciously, Strindberg drew attention to one of the most eloquent examples in myth of heuresis: the story of Demeter, goddess of agriculture, and her daughter Persephone.

Persephone—or Prosperine as she is known in Ovid's *Metamorphoses,* a Strindberg favorite—while picking flowers is tricked by Hades, lord of the underworld, into reaching for a particularly lovely narcissus. The moment she touches the flower, the earth opens up and Hades spirits her away to his realm. Demeter becomes distraught over her daughter's disappearance. The result of her anguish is that all vegetation ceases to grow, and mankind is threatened with famine. Zeus is forced to intervene and negotiates an agreement with his brother Hades: Persephone may return for eight months of every year to her mother, but she must spend the winter with her husband in the underworld. And so, once a year, after mother and daughter are reunited, the earth becomes green again.

In *Easter,* details of the myth have been changed and the sequence of events has been rearranged, but the essential elements are present. The time is spring and Eleonora/Persephone returns from the mental institution. The vague but evocative outlines of her description of the place put one in mind of the sterile home of anguished shades in the dark regions of the underworld.

ELEONORA:

> . . . there, where I came from, where the sun never shines, where the walls are white and bare as in a bathroom, where only weeping and wailing is heard, where I sat away a year of my life!

BENJAMIN:

> What do you mean?

ELEONORA:

> Where people are tortured, worse than in a prison, where the damned live, where unrest has its home, where despair keeps watch night and day. A place from which no one ever returns.

BENJAMIN:

> Do you mean worse than a prison?

ELEONORA:

> In prison you are condemned, but there, you are damned! In prison they question you and listen to you. There, no one hears you!

> (102-103)

Like Persephone, Eleonora is a blend of innocence, sadness, and joy. In Greek mythology Persephone was referred to as "the maiden whose name may not be spoken."[3] When Eleonora appears and announces that she is a member of the family, Benjamin is surprised.

BENJAMIN:

> How strange that no one has ever talked about you.

ELEONORA:

> People don't talk about the dead!

> (59)

Both Persephone and Eleonora suffer terribly as the consequence of a momentary, pitifully innocent temptation: the desire to possess a flower. Eleonora, on her way home from the institution, takes a daffodil from an unattended florist's shop. Although she leaves payment for it, she later comes to fear that the money may go astray and that she will be accused of theft.

Strindberg could not have chosen a more appropriate flower, and, with his deep interest in botany, could not have been ignorant of the various meanings associated with it. The daffodil's genus is *Narcissus,* Persephone's flower. The Swedish name for it is *påsklilja,* which translated literally would be "Easter lily," and the lily, like the rose, is a traditional attribute of the Virgin Mary. As he did in *To Damascus,* Strindberg uses a flower as an ambivalent symbol of both the bond that joins and the tension that divides mother from daughter in the eternal-feminine configuration.

The basic rhythm of the play as of the myth—separation and reunion—is the counterbalancing movement of life itself, the diastole and the systole. For most of the play Mrs. Heyst does not fully and warmly acknowledge her daughter and in fact has been distant with her for some time. When Eleonora presses her mother's hand to her lips, Mrs. Heyst "restrains her emotion," according to the stage directions (80). But then comes Easter Eve and the end of alienation:

ELEONORA:

> You kissed me, Mother. You haven't done that for years.

> (110)

Mrs. Heyst has come to understand the sacrificial role her daughter plays as the messenger of vernal hope:

MRS. HEYST:

> This child of sorrow has come with joy, though not of this world. Her troubled feelings have been transformed into peace, and she shares it with everyone. Sane or not, for me she is wise because she understands how to bear life's burdens better than I do, than we do.

> (105)

A complication interrupts. The arrival of the newspaper confirms Mrs. Heyst's fear that Eleonora will be charged with theft of the flower and once again incarcerated. Like Demeter, she laments that her daughter must return to the darkness.

MRS. HEYST:

She's lost . . . found again and lost.

(108)

But like the final emergence of a spring whose return has been prolonged, the eventual establishment of Eleonora's innocence is certain. The triumph of Persephone is as inexorable as was her tragedy in the lengthening shadows of the preceding autumn. The florist finds the money the girl left behind; mother and daughter can once again be reunited.

The realization of the significance of her daughter's redemptive suffering has an enormously liberating effect upon Mrs. Heyst. She can now see through the veil of self-deception that clouded her vision. "Was I sane, Elis, was I sane when I believed your father was innocent? I was certainly aware that he was convicted on tangible, material evidence and that he had confessed!" She is free of the suffocating power of the past and can see that Elis is still trapped in delusion, that he cannot yet accept one of life's most demanding, but vital challenges.

MRS. HEYST:

And you, Elis, are you in your right mind when you can't see that Kristina loves you . . . and believe instead that she hates you?

ELIS:

It's a strange way to love!

MRS. HEYST:

No! Inwardly, she's been frozen by your coldness, and you're the one who hates. But you're unjust, and so you have to suffer.

(105)

The reunion of mother and daughter is not the climax of the play. Elis has more lessons to learn before the lost harmony he misses, both in himself and in his family, can be completely restored. What the heuresis, the vernal miracle, does is to set the stage for this restoration, and Strindberg enhances and amplifies the reunion by enveloping it in vegetation imagery.

Scholars have speculated that the source for the family name was a Belgian spa Strindberg visited for a fortnight in 1898: Heist-op-den-Berg.[4] This may be, but *heister* is the German word for sapling or young tree. And there are other surnames in the play associated with trees. Petrus'

last name is Holmblad, or Islet-leaf, and Benjamin's feared tutor is Algren, or Alderbranch. The creditor Lindkvist's name could be translated as Linden-switch, and switch reinforces the recurrent theme in the play of chastisement and punishment. Elis receives an anonymous gift of a bundle of birch twigs, which leads to the idea that he is in need of a "birching." But he senses that there may be a positive side to the gift: chastisement can lead to repentance, and repentance to reconciliation. Elis himself says the twig might carry the promise of an Aaron's rod, the stave of Moses's brother, which bloomed miraculously as a sign that God had chosen him (51).

In addition to the surnames and numerous mentions of Eleonora's daffodil, there are other tree, flower, plant, herb, and fruit references scattered throughout the play. A bird dropped a twig at Elis's feet as he walked past the cathedral, and he wishes it had been an olive branch; he remembers the willows and linden trees in bloom by the family's summer cottage as well as a student song in which birches and lindens were mentioned. Mrs. Heyst peels apples for applesauce. Eleonora says she heard starlings talking in a walnut tree, and she speaks with authority about the psychic effects produced by consuming henbane and belladonna; furthermore, she is conversant in "the silent language of the flowers" (67). As Elis reads the painful proceedings of his father's trial, a word catches like a thorn in his eye (77). A rumor says that a tulip was stolen and not a daffodil (84). Eleonora identifies with flowers that have blossomed prematurely and must endure a late spring frost—anemones and snowdrops—and she looks forward to the coming of violets.

The repetition of vegetation images is as pervasive as similar details in the background of a medieval tapestry, and the cumulative effect reinforces the Demeter-Persephone leitmotif. Even the order of associations has a natural rhythm: Eleonora and the daffodil, Mrs. Heyst and the apple—virgin with flower, mother with fruit.[5]

There are other mythic resonances in the play in addition to those connected with vegetation. The bird that dropped the twig at Elis's feet was a dove, and although the twig was not an olive branch, Elis took it as a token of peace. The Heysts await the coming of spring as Noah awaited the waters of the Deluge to recede. The day before *Easter* was to premiere, Strindberg wrote to Harriet Bosse, who was playing Eleonora: "I . . . thank God He sent you, the little dove with olive branch, not the birch. The Deluge has ended, the old has drowned, and the earth shall again be green."[6]

Elis complains that everything is obscured by a "black veil," which suggests the material, earthly prison of profane space and concrete time. To penetrate this veil, according to Mircea Eliade, it is necessary to return to a decisive cosmic moment in which profane space is transformed into transcendent space, and concrete time into mythic time.[7] Eleonora is the catalyst of this transformation. Her very presence turns the realistic moment into the magic of "once upon a time." "For me," she tells Benjamin, "time and space do not exist" (61). Her mission is to bring important messages, as Mrs. Heyst says, which cannot be adequately defined in terms like *rational* or *irrational*. Benjamin admits to Eleonora, "I really don't understand the words you're saying, but I think I understand what you mean" (62); and "It seems that everything you say, I've already thought myself" (69).

The feeling of "once upon a time" is established quickly in the moments immediately prior to and following Elonora's first entrance. A solemn mood is set as objects are handled almost ceremoniously, and allusions are made to punishment, spring, and hope.

ELIS:

> [*taking the birch bough from the dining room table and placing it behind the mirror*]

> It wasn't an olive branch the dove brought . . . it was a birch! [*He exits. Eleonora enters from upstage, a sixteen-year-old girl who wears a pigtail down her back. She is carrying a yellow daffodil in a pot. Without seeing, or seeming to see Benjamin, she takes the water carafe from the sideboard, waters the flower, and places it on the table, where she then sits opposite Benjamin, watching him and imitating his gestures. Benjamin reacts in surprise.*]

ELEONORA:

> [*pointing at the daffodil*]

> Do you know what *this* is?

BENJAMIN:

> [*childishly, simply*]

> Of course I know—it's a daffodil! . . . But who are you?

ELEONORA:

> [*friendly, but sadly*]

> Yes, who are you?

(58)

What a splendid entrance! Our attention is riveted upon the girl and the flower through a sweep of scenic action that is at once simple and concrete, strange and evocative. When Eleonora imitates Benjamin's gestures and repeats his question, an interesting effect is achieved: on the one hand, we are witnessing a meeting between troubled adolescents—an insecure boy and an emotionally disturbed girl; on the other hand, we are watching Benjamin on the brink of an archetypal confrontation, face to face with a counterpart, or double, whose purpose, at least in part, is

to introduce him to the mystery of the eternal feminine, to bring warmth and encouragement to someone who up till now has seen the world as cold and inhospitable.

But if Eleonora brings a hopeful message of vernal renewal and rebirth to the Heyst home, the message is tinged with melancholy. The return of spring can only partly mitigate the painful knowledge that the earthly passage remains a vale of tears. If Eleonora is Persephone, she is also, in the manner of Strindberg's polyphonic mythology, Sophia, the Gnostic figure of divine wisdom, fated to "suffer every possible kind of suffering."[8] Eleonora even suffers with distant loved ones: with her father in prison and her sister in America. Her illness, she says, is "not a sickness unto death, but to the glory of God." In her brother's life she is not just his mentally ill sister, she is also, as Strindberg himself described her in a letter, "Christ in Man."[9] Elis, in his reluctance to deal with her, becomes a variation of the Ahasuerus motif: the man who tries to deny the calling from the Christ within.

Elis's name is close to Elisa, the Swedish name for the Biblical Elisha, to whom Elijah passed his mantle, the symbol of the prophet's calling and mission, but also, in the language of Gnosticism, of the body, the earthly garment of flesh and blood, which must some day be exchanged and transcended. That Strindberg was aware of this twofold meaning is attested in a letter he wrote to Torsten Hedlund in 1896: "Cf.: Elijah's mantle! Nessus's shirt!"[10] In *Easter* the symbolic values of the mantle as calling and the garment as burden are made manifest in Elis's overcoat. In the opening scene he is seen removing the coat and hanging it up. "You know", says Elis to Kristina, "it's so heavy—[*hefting the coat with his hand*]—as if it had soaked up all the troubles of winter, the sweat of anguish and the dust of school"(39). When Eleonora passes the coat, she pats it sympathetically, and says "Poor Elis!"(70). Mrs. Heyst points to it and scolds her son: "I told you, that coat is not to hang there!"(71). For her, it represents unpleasant truths she would rather not be reminded of.

If Elis's name leads one to think of Elisha and Elijah, Helios, the Greek god of the sun also comes to mind. And if the coming of spring suggests the return of Persephone, it also suggests the return of Helios.

ELIS:

> Look, the sun has come back again . . . He went away in November. I remember the day he disappeared behind the brewery across the street. Oh, this winter! This long winter!

(40)

Later, the presence of the moon is felt.

ELEONORA:

> Go and draw the curtain, Benjamin. I want God to see
> us.
>
> [*Benjamin rises and obeys. Moonlight falls into the
> room.*]

ELEONORA:

> Do you see the full moon? It's the Easter moon! And
> now you know that the sun is still there, though it's the
> moon that gives us the light!

(97)

In some mythologies a brother-sister kinship exists
between the sun and moon, and in alchemy, the arcane science with which Strindberg was so preoccupied during
and after the Inferno years, there is the androgyne, or "Re-
bis," a being signifying the merging of opposites and the
end of the agony resulting from the separation of the sexes.
Strindberg's attitude toward the concept of the androgyne
is revealed implicitly and explicitly in letters in which he
identified two of the models he used for Eleonora. The
real-life model was his mentally ill sister, Elisabeth, whose
life seemed mystically bound with his own. "She was like
my twin," he wrote in a letter to Harriet Bosse in
December 1904.[11] The fictional model for the Easter girl
was the androgynous central character of Balzac's
Séraphita, whose parents were disciples of Swedenborg.
Explaining **Easter** to Harriet in a letter in 1901, he refers
to "Eleonora's kin, Balzac's *Séraphita-Séraphitus,* the
Angel, for whom earthly love does not exist because he-
she is *l'époux et l'épouse de l'humanité.* Symbol of the
highest, most perfect type of human being, which haunts
much of the very latest modern literature and which some
people feel is on its way down to us."[12]

The androgynous aspect of the relationship between Elis
and Eleonora helps to explain the different ways the
characters complement each other. Beyond the balancings
of male-female, brother-sister, sun-moon we have Elis, as
a teacher, associated with the life of the intellect, and Eleonora, poor, mad Eleonora, associated with the irrational
and the dark world of the unconscious. Elis dreads her
return from the institution, but she is a part of him that he
cannot repudiate. Their closeness is revealed in the girl's
description of her brother as her "only friend on earth"
(69).

Mother, beloved, and sister/androgyne: Elis must settle accounts with each of the faces of the eternal feminine, but,
as in **To Damascus,** the ultimate, superior creditor, the one
to whom the hero must eventually answer is a masculine,
paternal force. Just as the Stranger and the Lady are
haunted on their pilgrimage by reminders of the Doctor, so
the Heysts are constantly made aware that Lindkvist is approaching, frighteningly: in act two he stands by the street
lamp outside, and his shadow on the curtains expands
enormously—expressionistically—as he starts toward the
house.

Again, as in **To Damascus,** it is the maternal confrontation
that prepares the protagonist for the paternal confrontation.
Mrs. Heyst serves two functions in this regard. First, by
finally accepting the fact of her husband's guilt and reunit-
ing with her daughter, she dissipates much of the tension
in the house. Second, she provides an important answer to
Elis's question of whether the family ordeal has come to
an end.

ELIS:

> Now can we throw the birch on the fire?

MRS. HEYST:

> Not yet! There's something else.

ELIS:

> Lindkvist?

MRS. HEYST:

> He's standing outside.

ELIS:

> Now that I've seen a ray of sunshine I'm not afraid to
> meet the giant. Let him come!

Elis is confident to the point of cockiness, and Mrs. Heyst
warns him, "You know what happens to those who are
proud" (111). We are reminded of the Mother's warning in
To Damascus: "Pride must be cut down" (*29, 74*).

Lindkvist, a wonderfully grotesque invention, is a bogey-
man out of Dickens, and his entrance is a combination of
the terrifying and the absurd. Strindberg realized that the
character would present problems, that his presence could
spill a performance over into farce; Lindkvist, he insisted,
must not be played by a comic actor.[13]

> [*Lindkvist enters from the right. He is an earnest,
> elderly man of weird appearance. His gray hair is ar-
> ranged in an upswept forelock and trimmed at the
> temples in the manner of a hussar. Big, black bushy
> eyebrows. Short, close-clipped black sideburns. Round,
> black hornrimmed eyeglasses. Large carnelian charms
> on his watchchain; a Spanish cane in his hand. He is
> dressed in black with a fur coat; top boots with leather
> galoshes that squeak. When he enters, his eyes are
> riveted probingly on Elis. . . .*]

(*33,* 112)

The "upswept forelock" and earnest mien are reminiscent
of the stern God of Strindberg's creation play, who has
"horns like the Moses of Michelangelo." But as with the
Doctor in **To Damascus,** this godlike figure has given up
throwing thunderbolts. Much of his bite has gone, and
even his bark is more jovial than frightening: "Do you
know who I am? . . . [*disguising his voice*] I am the giant
of Skinflint Mountain, who scares little children!" (*124-
125*). And as in many fairy tales, the protagonist's fear of

the confrontation is worse than the confrontation itself. Lindkvist has good reason to want vengeance, but he does not seek it. On the contrary, he points a way for the hero to break out of the circle of guilt and anguish that torments him. To be sure, Elis still has a hard lesson to learn: he must recognize that he needs the saving grace of love, which he has lost, and that he has tendencies toward hubris that must be curbed.

ELIS:

> Why don't we just hand his paper over to the hangman? That way we can at least be spared this lengthy and painful execution.

LINDKVIST:

> I see.

ELIS:

> Young or not, I ask for no mercy, only justice!

LINDKVIST:

> Is that right? No mercy, no mercy!

(113)

Elis sounds like the Stranger refusing charity from the Abbess. But Lindkvist's arguments—now persuasive, now coercive—melt Elis's defiance and cause him to agree to resolve his differences with Petrus and Kristina. Lindkvist points out that his own family has suffered much because of Heyst's embezzlement and that Elis in his stubborness risks sacrificing his mother and sister on the altar of pride. What finally wins the day is the fact that Lindkvist has come not with a destructive claim but a healing gift. Although he has been wronged by Heyst, forty years earlier Elis's father was the only one in town to befriend him in a time of trouble. Because of that act of generosity, Lindkvist can now cancel his claim; the gift he brings is forgiveness, and with it, reconciliation. "You see," he says, "there is a charity which goes against justice and transcends it! . . . That is mercy!" (115).

If the analogies in *Easter* to the Passion seem too obvious or facile, one cannot deny the naive power of the ending effected by the gifts brought by the two angels, Eleonora and Lindkvist. As Lindkvist brings forgiveness, Eleonora brings an infinite capacity for bearing suffering so as to lighten the burdens of others; she is Sophia: victim and redeemer in one. Strindberg indicated the archetypal dimension of the reconciliation in a letter to Harriet Bosse on the day *Easter* was premiered (April 4, 1901): "The Lost Father wants to be introduced to his children—you have been given the honor of reestablishing the relationship."[14]

The message of the Passion, the return of Persephone, the wisdom of the melancholy Sophia, the creditor's forgiveness, and Elis's new-found capacity to accept love and mercy all coincide with the vernal promise of the Easter season. However forced some of the details in the play may seem, the resolution is no moment of simplistic mawkishness. The Heysts, all of them, have earned the right to turn their backs on the darkness and walk toward the light.

Notes

1. Martin Lamm, *August Strindberg,* trans. and ed. Harry G. Carlson (New York: Benjamin Blom, 1971), p. 367.

2. Erich Neumann, *The Great Mother,* trans. Ralph Manheim (Princeton: Princeton University Press, 1972), pp. 318-319.

3. Edith Hamilton, *Mythology* (New York: The New American Library, 1953), p. 54.

4. See Aage Kabell, "Påsk og det mystiske teater," *Edda* 54 (1954):164.

5. See Neumann, *The Great Mother,* p. 307.

6. *Brev* 14:57.

7. Mircea Eliade, *Patterns in Comparative Religion* (New York: Meridian, 1963), p. 296.

8. See Hans Jonas, *The Gnostic Religion,* 2d ed. (Boston: Beacon Press, 1963), pp. 301-303, on the passion of Sophia.

9. *Brev* 14:16.

10. Ibid., 11:253.

11. Ibid., 15:88.

12. Ibid., 14:34.

13. Ibid., 13:329.

14. Ibid., 14:58.

Jeffrey B. Loomis (essay date spring 1983)

SOURCE: Loomis, Jeffrey B. "The Intertestamental Dispensation of Strindberg's *Easter.*" *Renascence: Essays on Values in Literature* 35, no. 3 (spring 1983): 196-202.

[In the following essay, Loomis describes the religious and Biblical references in the play Easter.*]*

August Strindberg's *Easter* has been called a "Passion Play,"[1] and in a special way it is. But we must clarify the contextual meaning of that statement. The play dramatizes *imitations* of Christ's Passion within individual Swedish Christians at the turn of the twentieth century; yet Christ's own Passion also seems strongly present within the on-stage events. The play is set during the first three days of Easter weekend, with conscious back-reference to the

Lenten season. Thus, Strindberg suggests that Christ's sacrificial death is being seasonally repeated in the lives dramatized. He also hints that the Holy Spirit—the legacy of Christ to man announced on Maundy Thursday—will guide these souls through the Pentecostal season ahead.

Coupled with allusions to the archetypal church seasons is more explicit emphasis on the characters' need to join together the archetypal Old and New Testaments. To Strindberg's characters, this Easter weekend is felt like an intertestamental hiatus between two spiritual dispensations; however, the play eventually makes us feel that such a period of doubt, during which one searches the two testaments for their unity, may be a *special* dispensation of grace.

Three special features of the play's textual structure upon which I will focus are: Strindberg's realist-symbolist methods of characterization, his unique use of the *deus ex machina* device, and his selection of specific music as proper to the play's staging, in which he reveals special values in that somber self-examination proper to Easter weekend.

Eric Bentley has found *Easter* (1900) a work not easy to categorize among Strindberg's traditional groupings of dramas.[2] It is not clearly naturalistic, like *Miss Julie* (1888), nor clearly expressionistic, like *A Dream Play* (1901); in both tone and technique, it is a transitional work. *Easter* contains a naturalistic plot situation, as multiple disgraces visit a family after their father is imprisoned for theft. It also contains such expressionistic devices as the correlation in the script of weather-changes with modifications among characters' attitudes—mistrust in others bringing dark clouds, and open-hearted love bringing sunshine. This interrelation between weather and characters' personality changes is called the expressionistic *Ausstrahlungen des Ichs.*[3] Another expressionistic device, more marked in *Easter,* is Strindberg's use of symbolic names.

Strindberg consciously announces this importance of symbolic names in the play when the young girl Eleanora Heyst tells the student Benjamin that he will become her spiritual pupil, and that he is thus properly called Benjamin, because he is "the youngest of [her] friends."[4] The Hebrew meaning of the name Benjamin is "son of my right hand."[5] But the key symbolic name in this drama is that of the central protagonist—Eleanora's brother and Benjamin's teacher, Elis. His name derives either from the appellation of the prophet Elijah ("God is Jehova") or from that of Elijah's disciple-prophet Elisha ("God is generous").[6] The modern Swedish form of Elijah is Elia, the modern Swedish form of Elisha is Elisa; it is obvious that the name of Elis has a spelling midway between those of the two prophets.[7]

In the play, Elis, as "Elijah" figure, fears, with great starkness of spirit, a "Jehovah" god of wrath; he fears that his father's business associate Lindkvist, justly indignant at the Heyst family for the father's long-ago theft from him, is a modern incarnation of the angry Jehovah. Yet Elis also wishes, like Elisha, to trust God as his "generous" source of New Testament salvation, believing that he has "fallen from grace" (*Easter,* Act I), and not that grace is an impossibility. Importantly, too, when he quotes the words of Jesus, "Birds have nests and foxes have holes" (Act II), he seems ready to accept his own privation as a mark of his personal identification with Jesus. Still, Elis never reaches a fully quiescent New Testament faith, because he cannot fully accept his need to suffer the guilt and alienation from others caused by his father's crime. He wants the now-impossible: Edenic innocence and tranquility.

Elis's sister Eleanora provides more resolute religious attitudes. She is "in the prison with Father," she says, and also "in the classroom with [her] brother" (Act I)—suffering along with them, but without that bitterness which Elis and her mother feel toward suffering. Instead, she says, "God has been so good" to her (Act I), even though she evidently has endured a long bout with mental illness. When she tells the student Benjamin that she "embezzled some trust funds" and that her father "was blamed for it and put in prison" (Act I), we should not accept her words literally; she simply, like an expiatory mystic, is taking upon herself the blame for Mr. Heyst's crime, so that *she* believes those words literally.

Like "Elis," the name Eleanora also has symbolic value. If derived from its Greek root, "Helen," the name means "light." We notice that Eleanora almost always feels the sun or moon shining, even behind very cloudy skies. Yet there also exists a hebrew name "Elinoar," which means "God is my youth" (Kolatch, pp. 197-98). Eleanora Heyst becomes the "little child" who can "lead" her family toward the spiritual quiescence of a sensed unity between Old and New Testament messages about God (see *Isaiah* 11:6). In the several scenes in which Eleanora explains the mystical meaning of earthly travail to Benjamin, Eleanora voices a theology of cosmic sorrow and relief which explicates the sufferings of her family meaningfully. Yet the average theatergoer or play-reader will more likely identify with Elis's sweetheart Kristina than with Eleanora. Her name, after all, means "Christian," or "the anointed one" (Withycombe, p. 65; Kolatch, p. 184). Although she is humanly weak and given to her own fearful tremblings and sometimes a bit like Shakespeare's Polonius with her taste for clichéd slogans, Kristina strives to "anoint" Elis with realization of love's power to make human atonement (at-one-ment) possible. She dares (Act II) to visit Peter, a traitorous student who has plagiarized Elis's academic thesis, and to effect a reconciliation between the two men, convincing Peter to aid Elis in defending the Heysts from further community punishment for their father's crime. She visits Peter even though she knows that it may ruin her relationship with Elis.

The creditor, Lindkvist, eventually joins Kristina in this anointing function, and by doing so, creates for all the characters a sense of wholeness to the Christian experience, so that they can meaningfully unite Old Testament fear of God with New Testament capturing of grace. At first, however, Lindkvist exists as an ominous offstage presence whose very being tests the religious maturity of each character. Mrs. Heyst and Elis usually see him as a vicious symbol of their shame, while Kristina and Eleanora already feel that his impending threat can teach them suffering's value. Lindkvist, after all, is a *deus ex machina* figure, and his action in the play especially makes clear its thematic bridging of the Biblical testaments. Though at first he appears a godlike condemner bringing "Justice rather than mercy" (Act I), he mentions a "charity that contradicts the law and supersedes it" far earlier in his Act III encounter with Elis than the point at which Elis can sense that "charity" as Lindkvist's own. Lindkvist, indeed, progressively reveals the God of Easter and Pentecost. Even his name means "linden branch," a leafy summer tree, and thus partly dissociates him from that barren birch branch which he mails Elis early in the play as a symbol of Lenten contrition (Harlock, I, 1193; II, 1292).

In addition to the symbolic names and the *deux ex machina* figure, *Easter* contains music which contributes to the play's intertestamental religious atmosphere. Strindberg chooses as preludes to his three acts excerpts from Haydn's Good Friday oratorio *The Seven Last Words of Christ.* In Haydn's overture to his oratorio, which became the prelude to Strindberg's first act, the mood of ominous foreboding predominates. Throughout the movement, we seem to hear a dominant Jehovah's cry of anger from Mount Ebal. There punitive Israelites, whom Elis in Act I compares to his scornful neighbors, worked Jehovah's wrathful will against the wicked (*Deuteronomy* 27:13). Haydn's opening A-theme is immediately repeated twice, with little respite from a semi-orchestral interlude of lyricism; on the second repetition, the theme is developed with particular fury. A quieter B-theme later comes to several near-resolutions, but is always broken by reiterations of the A-theme. Then the key opening theme of thunder-notes repeats itself again, before a lengthy developmental section finally quiets the sense of threatening. A balance, at least, is now being achieved between ominousness and peace. Listeners can now sense, over the horizon, that Hebrew mountain of hope for which Elis in Act I longs—Mount Gerizim, the peak from which obedient Israelites received blessing. The light streaming from such an Old Testament mountain surely foreshadows the light of New Testament grace; but, for the Elis whose fears this Haydn music still proclaims, it appears that the clouds of God's wrath will not yet break.

As prelude to the second act of *Easter,* Strindberg chose Haydn's first choral movement in his oratorio: "Father, forgive them." Strindberg found Haydn's setting of these words markedly appropriate for the message in this play. Haydn did not give the words of Jesus's plea for man's atonement to a solo voice, but rather to a quartet, suggest-

ing that Jesus's sufferings are shared by all men and women. In the next choral section, he provided the Golgotha watchers' recognition of this truth: "thine only-begotten one, he pleas for sinners." Thus these transgressors' voices ask mercy for themselves (much as Elis Heyst is doing in this act of Strindberg's drama), and their *fortissimo,* at the end of the movement, is just as desperate as is Elis's basic mood. Even Eleanora, in this act of the play, begins to lose some of her calm confidence that God is directing her sufferings; she begins to fear destruction with almost as much trepidation as does any earthbound mortal. She had taken a daffodil from an open florist's shop and left money for it, but the money was misplaced and police had traced the flower to her home. As she hears that they have a suspect for the theft, near the end of Act II, she grows fearful, but in the next act the money is found and she is cleared of criminal accusation. But if Eleanora were to participate truly in a Good Friday which culminated the Old Testament, she at least always *knew* that she needed to share mankind's Old Testament despair at its sin, and to know the resultant suffering. Her serene moments of faith make both her brother and mother question their own bitterness all through the play, but they wait until almost the final curtain before they accept suffering as a necessary part of their own redemption.

As the final act begins, we hear Haydn's setting of Jesus's fifth word from the Cross: "Jesus calls: 'I thirst!'" Here New Testament light clearly begins to shine, especially as this is the one musical movement (both for Haydn and for Strindberg) in which a solo voice (a gentle tenor) represents Jesus. The symbolic result for Strindberg's drama is the sudden dominance of a single Atoning One, the Jesus of the Cross. Haydn and Strindberg affirm Him as the key to New Testamental (and all subsequent) history. Yet they also suggest that men and women are asked to respond to Jesus's suffering with "wine, which one mixes with gall." In the play *Easter,* pity is extended by one man (Lindkvist) to another man (Elis) in the scenes following this Act III prelude. We learn in the Strindberg act which this Haydn music launches that persons like Lindkvist, who are willing to embody in themselves the power of love and to see not only the evil but also the good in their fellows, can help redeem the spirit of hatred in the world. When Lindkvist finally appears onstage, he does not take long before revealing that he is a very real human being, a man who has only temporarily played with the guise of wrathful deity. And he withdraws his claim of a massive debt against the Heyst family, because, as he announces, Mr. Heyst, who later robbed him, had once— long, long ago—befriended him when he was a young and frightened newcomer to the city.

The sort of release from hatred which Lindkvist here illustrates can only begin, we now sense, when individual men and women recognize that they themselves are selfish and others not so bad as they seem. Such insight may, as it drives them to contemplate the culminating event of intertestamental history, force their own pride to a crucifixion. The active expression of that insight into love will fulfill the maundies, or mandates, of Maundy Thursday, the day which begins the one *continuous* day of Easter Weekend.[8] Those maundies—which also require the Pentecostal Spirit as their inner teacher—demand that men "love one another" (*John* 13:34). Through the aid of the Spirit, said the Jesus of Maundy Thursday, men can imitate the love which He showed to His disciples through the foot-washing in the upper room and to all men through the next afternoon's agony on Golgotha. Lent, Easter, and Pentecost—the seasons bridging the two Biblical Testaments—can then become part of inner experience. Love's Pentecostal maundies will unite the Decalogue with Grace, as "a new commandment"—*caritas*—is born (*John* 13:34).

On that Holy Saturday when Lindkvist comes to visit him, Elis Heyst must still come to understand those maundies which command Christian love of him. It is his pride, his self-righteousness, which has kept Elis from completing such understanding before, as Lindkvist tells him: "I would force out your pride and your malice" (Act III). Lindkvist's previous threatening letters to Elis, and his dour poses of doom-saying in the Act III confrontation scene, have both been tactics used to awaken Elis from his useless bitterness towards the neighbors who scorned the Heysts. Lindkvist realizes that Elis will not admit that a father's "iniquity" will be "visit[ed] upon the children to the third and the fourth generation" (*Exodus* 20:5)—that all are guilty, originally sinful, whether they become actual robbers, as Mr. Heyst did, or not. Lindkvist particularly deplores Elis's bitterness toward the traitorous Peter—a bitterness which, albeit explicable, has led him to avoid all attempts at reconciliation, forcing Kristina to make those attempts. We see Elis start to turn away from his foolish pride as the play's curtain falls, when he comes onstage, holding Kristina's hand in a gesture of tender gratitude. But Easter Day comes offstage, and we know that Elis's continued transformation must bring it to its fulfillment in Pentecostal love.

After those years of religious crisis which he had called his Inferno period, Strindberg by 1900 had conquered his earlier fear (much like Elis Heyst's) that Christ never made Atonement for human sins.[9] Hence August Strindberg had become able, much like Eleanora (and like Elis at those moments when he senses divine guidance), to acknowledge that God used his own sufferings and even let him expiate others' sins through his pains.

Thus, despite melodramatic touches (Lindvist's repeated stealthy walks past the Heyst home, and his wordless telephone call to them in Act II), and despite a finale scene where Lindkvist may seem a bit like a fairy tale genie, *Easter* conveys a deep understanding of the necessary Christian tension between penitential works and free grace, resembling that great religious drama of Judaism, *The Book of Job.* Elis Heyst's neighbors chastise him as merci-

lessly as did Job's companions, and his God—through the human voices of Eleanora, Kristina, and Lindkvist—tells him, just as resolutely as did Job's God, that self-pity is a folly. But Elis comes to remember that same hope which Job held staunchly even when his ordeal was quite new: "I know that my Redeemer lives, and at last he will stand upon the earth" (*Job* 19:25).

Notes

1. Brita M. E. Mortensen and Brian W. Downs, *Strindberg: An Introduction to His Life and Works* (Cambridge, England: Cambridge University Press, 1965), p. 135.

2. Eric Bentley, "On Strindberg," in *Six Plays of Strindberg,* ed. Elizabeth Sprigge (Garden City, N.Y.: Doubleday, 1955), p. v.

3. Carl Enoch William Leonard Dahlström, *Strindberg's Dramatic Expressionism* (New York: Benjamin Blom, 1965; originally published 1930), p. 172.

4. All quotations from *Easter* are taken from August Strindberg, *Three Plays,* trans. Peter Watts (New York: Penguin, 1958).

5. Alfred J. Kolatch, *Modern English and Hebrew Names* (New York: Jonathan David, 1967), p. 22.

6. E. G. Withycombe, *The Oxford Dictionary of English Names* (Oxford: Oxford University Press, 1977), pp. 98-99.

7. Walter Harlock, *Svensk-Engelsk Ordbok* (Stockholm: Svenska Bokförlaget. 1964), I, 783.

8. *The Schaff-Herzog Encyclopedia of Religious Knowledge,* ed. S. M. Jackson and G. W. Gilmore (Grand Rapids, Mich.: Baker Book House, 1959), p. 257. My first source for this centrally important knowledge about the Easter season was the Rev. Robert Duncan, Chapel of the Cross, Chapel Hill, North Carolina.

9. Martin Lamm, *August Strindberg,* trans. and ed. Harry G. Carlson (New York: Benjamin Blom, 1971), p. 299.

Stephen A. Mitchell (essay date June 1986)

SOURCE: Mitchell, Stephen A. "The Path from *Inferno* to the Chamber Plays: *Easter* and Swedenborg." *Modern Drama* 29, no. 2 (June 1986): 157-68.

[*In the following essay, Mitchell discusses the influence of Emmanuel Swedenborg's philosophy on Strindberg while he was writing* Easter.]

Response to the 1901 Swedish première of *Easter,* Strindberg's modern passion play, was sharply critical. Tor Hedberg, for example, complained: "The entire [play] is superficial and sentimental and concludes in a childish moral. . . . Those who are edified by such may be so, but for my part, I decline."[1] Yet despite this strong negative reaction, the play has been staged many times in the past eighty years, a fact which surely reflects the delight of audiences in seeing a drama in which Strindberg has, as Walter Johnson says, made the "interpretation of the Easter message believably human and comfortingly warm."[2] Clearly, the resolution of the various moral and economic dilemmas faced by the members of the guilt-ridden Heyst family provides the play with a satisfying conclusion and an overall structure which underscores the play's concern with basic Christological tenets. Especially prominent among these concerns is what Strindberg, in reference to *Easter*, later calls *satisfactio vicaria*, the soteriological concept which is present in much of Strindberg's post-Inferno production.[3]

The fact persists, however, that although audiences and performers have been drawn to this drama, the work has remained notoriously resistant to interpretation beyond the most superficial level, as Aage Kabell and Martin Lamm lament;[4] in their frustration, some have even gone so far as to dismiss it as "muddled" and "childish."[5] Recently, Harry G. Carlson suggested that we have failed to appreciate fully the allusions Strindberg had in mind in *Easter*, and thus missed much of the play's meaning.[6] His fascinating examination of the play's various classical and biblical dimensions places the work into an interesting mythological context. The present study seeks to expand this mythico-religious background somewhat and to identify elements of the play with a further late Strindbergian wellspring, namely, the writings of Emmanuel Swedenborg.[7] It is in essence a defense of *Easter*, for if the play appears wanting in dramatic tension and clear action, I contend that this fact resides in the failure of audiences to interpret fully what they see on stage, rather than in any deficiency in the structure or content of the work itself.

The highly complex nature of the play can be demonstrated, for example, by examining the figure of Eleonora, the Easter girl (*påskflicka*). She is a character Strindberg had long been developing: according to his own testimony some ten years after writing the play, she had already been "prepared" in *Inferno* and *Advent*.[8] He also makes it clear in a letter written to Harriet Bosse that Eleonora has had at least one other model: "She is . . . related to Balzac's Séraphita, Swedenborg's niece."[9] Furthermore, critics and students of Strindberg have also been quick to point out the similarities between Eleonora and Strindberg's sister Elisabeth, who spent her last years in an asylum in Uppsala, a sister to whom Strindberg felt so close that he writes of her in another letter to Harriet Bosse: "She was like my twin."[10] Thus, three elements typical of Strindberg's authorship shape the role of Eleonora in *Easter*, namely, his habit of reworking the "same" character time and again in his literary production, his heavy reliance on Swedenborg and Swedenborg-influenced works for his

own post-Inferno writings,[11] and the consistent incorporation of autobiographical events into his works. This concentration of influences in Strindberg's writing forms the basis for the following examination of *Easter*, specifically the thematic relationship this play bears to such earlier works as *Inferno* on the one hand and to later works such as *The Ghost Sonata* on the other.

The content and structure of *Easter* provide the audience with a drama which traces a classical comic curve, if in several truncated fashion. The isolated family, held up to public ridicule in its glass veranda, is threatened with becoming even further cut off from society in the small university town; but in the end, Elis and the rest of the Heyst household are spared by Lindkvist's kindness, and the play concludes in the hope of the family's eventual reintegration into society. This theme of redemption and hope is underscored on the temporal level by Strindberg's use of the divisions of the Christian Holy Week to label the play's three acts Maundy Thursday, Good Friday, and Easter Eve. The progression through the holiday is further emphasized by the successive uses of Haydn's *Sieben Worte des Erlösers* ("The Seven Words of the Redeemer") as overtures to each act. Likewise, Strindberg's use of lighting and atmospheric detail parallels this same descending and then rising thematic curve. In Act I, a sole shaft of light illuminates the stage, but even this small beam disappears by the last scene of the act. Act II begins with the drapes of the living room drawn and all natural light thus cut off; instead of hoped-for spring weather, there is nothing but cold and snow. Act III opens with this same gray weather, but concludes with the clouds parting and revealing the sun, "with the return of light and the joy of summertime," as Strindberg later described it.[12] These staging details serve initially to emphasize the mounting difficulties of the inhabitants of the Heyst household (their fears about Lindkvist, their debtor; Benjamin's failure to pass the Latin exam; the possibility that Mrs. Heyst will also be prosecuted; Elis's worries about Petrus's relationship with Kristina; and everyone's concern about Eleonora's "theft" and the likelihood that she will be returned to the asylum), but they also underscore the eventual resolution of the problems, as Lindkvist proves to be generous and merciful, as Eleonora's crime is cleared up, as Kristina's reasons for seeing Petrus are explained, and as the family finds renewed hope of leaving the city and getting to the country.

The Heysts' desire to leave Lund and go north to Lake Mälare significantly foreshadows the same urge in Elis as he asks, "shall I get away from this dreadful city, from Ebal, the mount of curses, and behold Garizim again?"[13] Ebal is, of course, the mountain from which the Israelites took possession of the Promised Land, but it is also the location on which they were cursed for their violations of God's commandments. Garizim, across the valley from Ebal, was a site of worship. "Understand that this day I offer you the choice of a blessing and a curse," Moses tells the Children of Israel. "The blessing will come if you listen to the commandments of the Lord your God which I give you this day, and the curse if you do notlisten to the commandments of the Lord your God but turn aside from the way that I command you this day and follow other gods whom you do not know. When the Lord your God brings you into the land which you are entering to occupy, there *on Mount Garizim you shall pronounce the blessing and on Mount Ebal the curse*" (Deuteronomy 11:26-29; emphasis added).[14] The significance of the two mountains is important for understanding the quest Elis is on, albeit unconsciously, in *Easter*—to move from Ebal to Garizim, from Lund to the country, from a cursed condition to a state of worshipfulness and religious perfection. The family's escape to the countryside thus represents far more than the possibility of their removing themselves from the critical society of a small town and Elis's dreams of marriage; the family's move will correspond to its spiritual purification.

That the university city of Lund is used as a symbol for the Heysts' woeful and cursed condition is hardly surprising, given the attitude Strindberg expresses towards it during his post-Inferno recovery.[15] He continued to hold this negative opinion for many years, as he demonstrates in a letter to Nils Andersson only a few months after *Easter* was completed. In it, Strindberg discusses the plans he and Harriet Bosse are making for their honeymoon: "she wants very badly to see *Lund, the Purgatory city,* in passing" (emphasis added).[16] That the family will leave Lund-Ebal and go to Lake Mälare-Garizim is the joyous final note on which the play concludes: "Now you must thank God, who has helped us come to the country!" exclaims Eleonora.[17] Thus, the journey, if not yet complete, has at the least a projected happy conclusion. And as the family moves from Lund-Ebal to the country-Garizim, so too they move forward morally, emotionally and spiritually, from the darkness of winter to the sunlight of summer.

Given the almost uniquely happy ending of *Easter* among Strindberg's dramas, the question naturally arises as to *how* the family is spiritually cleansed. This dimension of the play becomes more understandable when placed in the context of other later works by Strindberg. The argument has often been advanced that such post-Inferno plays as *The Ghost Sonata,* for example, can be best understood in terms of Swedenborg's concepts of Purgatory and Hell.[18] Key to this view are the comments Strindberg makes in *A Blue Book,* especially in those sections in which he discusses the concept of the "disrobing room" in Swedenborg's spiritual scheme:

> Swedenborg has a disrobing room in his hell, where the dead are taken immediately after death. There they are stripped of the garb they have been forced to don in society and family, and the angels see right away who they have before them.[19]

How appropriate then that in the opening scene of *Easter,* Elis enters the glassed-in veranda with its ray of sunlight, remarks about the various preparations for the coming of

spring, removes his overcoat and says: "yes, it's spring. . . . And I can hang up my winter overcoat . . . you know, it's as heavy—*weighs the coat in his hand*—as if it had soaked up all the pains of winter, the sweat of anguish, and the dust of the school. . . ."[20] Thus, just as *The Ghost Sonata* opens with a ship's bell to signal that we are on a journey, so *Easter* opens with a signal to those initiated in Swedenborgian theology that a journey is also under way in this play: we are witnessing Elis's arrival in the disrobing room, where he will be stripped, inspected and ultimately edified by celestial beings.

Swedenborg's Purgatory is, however, no mere post-mortem waiting room. It is primarily a *period* of instruction, and as Strindberg conceives of it, this spiritual dimension is not necessarily a geographical destination of the afterlife. "It is possible," Strindberg writes in *A Blue Book,* "that he [i.e., Swedenborg] means not a location, but rather a condition of the mind."[21] It is into this state of mind, as well as into this "Purgatory City," that Elis enters as the play opens, and it is here that he will receive his moral training during the course of the drama. Both the play and its author are quite explicit about the nature of this lesson. In a letter to his German translator, Emil Schering, from March 1901, some five months after completing *Easter,* Strindberg indicates the dread that weighed heavily on his mind: "My bride [i.e., Harriet Bosse] is now just as afraid of hubris (ὕβρις) as I am."[22] That this great fear of the one sin the gods will not forgive preyed on his mind lends weight to the appearance of the problem in the play and credence to the possibility that it plays a dominant role in *Easter.* Soon after the opening curtain the topic is broached in *Easter,* Benjamin, the student, comes home utterly dejected after having failed his Latin exam. Strindberg goes to great lengths to make the audience understand that Benjamin did not pass the exam precisely because of his overweening pride:[23]

ELEONORA

What setback have you experienced?

BENJAMIN

I failed a Latin test—although I was completely confident.

ELEONORA

Aha, you were certain, so certain, that you could bet on passing.

BENJAMIN

I did!

ELEONORA

I can believe it! Don't you see, it happened this way because you were so confident.

BENJAMIN

Do you think that was the reason?

ELEONORA

Certainly it was! Pride goes before a fall!

Nor in this context should the scholarly error Benjamin makes on the exam be overlooked: "I wrote *ut* with the indicative, although I knew it ought to have been the subjunctive."[24] Thus, Benjamin fails the exam because he is overconfident, too proud to be careful, so certain of his knowledge that he writes *the indicative* rather than *the subjunctive,* that is, he expresses an idea as an actual fact rather than as a possibility. Then, as Eleonora indicates, his pride goes before the fall. Likewise, Elis is guilty of this pride when he refuses to ask for, or accept, mercy: "I do not ask for mercy, only justice!" he proudly declares when Lindkvist confronts him.[25] Brought around to a more humble position by the possibility that his mother too will be imprisoned on account of his father's embezzlement, Elis is forced to listen to Lindkvist's summary of the situation: "there is a compassion which goes against the law, and over it! . . . it is mercy!"[26] Yet Elis misunderstands the full import of these words. When he finally shows greater understanding for Lindkvist's point of view and less concern for his own feelings—"I will think of your children and not complain!"[27]—Lindkvist continues on his course, which is to take Elis through humility and powerlessness to understanding and the acceptance of mercy. Thus, he barks out his approval of Elis's "confession" and declares his intention to continue Elis's instruction: "Good! . . . Now we'll go a step further!"[28]

This next step consists of forcing Elis to agree to visit the county administrator (*landshövding*), something to which Elis is at first utterly opposed. Lindkvist, it should be noted, is not concerned with whether or not Elis actually sees the governor; he only wants to bend Elis to his will and to have him agree to it, as he makes clear by the demand that Elis repeat his consent: "Say it again, and louder!"[29] With this stage of Elis's instruction complete, Lindkvist proceeds to one final, painful lesson: Elis must now thank his erstwhile friend Petrus, whom Elis suspects of being involved with Kristina. When Elis angrily refuses to have anything to do with Petrus, Lindkvist replies, "I'll have to squeeze you again, then,"[30] and he subsequently proceeds to maneuver Elis into a position where he will have to subjugate himself to his debtor's will.

At this juncture, Elis exhibits the wealth and depth of his ignorance: when he discovers that Petrus is now engaged to another woman, and that Kristina has acted as the go-between, he arrogantly asks: "And for their happiness I must endure this agony?"[31] His reponse is one of complete irritation, yet with this question, Elis helps focus our attention on one of the main theological and philosophical precepts of *Easter,* what Strindberg refers to as *satisfactio vicaria,* when "the one . . . suffers in place of the other."[32] This soteriological foundation is, of course, the very reason the play revolves around the Easter Passion: salvation comes through grace accumulated by a god's or hero's suffering or achievements.[33] The notion that sin can be expiated by proxy forms the thematic core around which the play is constructed and together with Lindkvist's

instruction of Elis in the disrobing room provides the play with its message.

Thus, Lindkvist replies to Elis's uninformed query as to why he must suffer for others by saying: "Yes! Those who suffered to prepare your happiness! . . . Your mother, your father, your fiancée, your sister."[34] The extent to which human beings must depend on the good deeds of others for their fortunes is underscored as Lindkvist relates the tale of how Elis's father had once helped him by acting out the part of the Good Samaritan. This narrative has a typically Strindbergian moral, but with a new twist: "everything repeats itself, even what is good."[35] As a result, the Heysts' crises are resolved, their moral and financial debts to Lindkvist annulled, facts which are emphasized scenically by the stage direction that, during Lindkvist's dialogue, "the weather clears up outside."[36] Within the experimental laboratory he makes of the glass veranda *qua* disrobing room, Strindberg thus examines the effects of hubris and the function of *satisfactio vicaria.* The family falters on the former, but is saved through the latter. Although it has become common to see in Eleonora the figure of the suffering innocent, it should be noted that both she *and* her brother Elis undergo the process of suffering, and learning, for the rest of the family.

Thus, the two central characters of *Easter,* Eleonora and Elis, are signs of the "new Strindberg," in the sense that the two of them together represent a composite of Strindberg's alter ego in the play. The similarity of the two names immediately suggests a relationship between them; further examination of the roles strengthens this impression. Surely Elis, the well-educated, domineering male who is forced into understanding by powers far beyond his control, presents us with one side of Strindberg, yet Strindberg himself speaks of Eleonora having been prepared in *Inferno,* in which the protagonist is clearly his alter ego.[37] His remarks in a letter written in 1904 on the relationship between Elizabeth, his sister, with whom he felt an especially strong bond, and Eleonora indicate that Elizabeth was indeed a conscious model for the role: "She was like my twin and when she died, we were grateful for her sake. I only want to show you 'the Easter girl,' who suffered for others, and because she took on their evils as her own, was unable to be really good."[38] But Eleonora is also patterned on Balzac's Séraphita-Séraphitus, "she-he," and "Eleonora's relative," as Strindberg calls her,[39] a reference which suggests that Strindberg may have been aware of his recent capacity for accepting both the feminine and masculine aspects of his personality. This view is taken by Robert Brustein, who argues that the ability to accept the dual quality of human nature is one of the main characteristics of the post-Inferno Strindberg.[40] The problem of the male-female split, of masculinity in women and femininity in men, is an old one in Strindberg's works; one senses the heavy presence of this same struggle already in many of the pre-Inferno works, such as *Son of a Servant.* In discussing his spiritual and intellectual relationship with the landlord's daughter, a woman twice the age of the fictionalized autobiography's fifteen-year-old protagonist, "Johann," Strindberg describes himself as an adolescent with "chubby little hands with long, well-manicured fingernails, small feet, slim legs and strong thighs" and "a fresh complexion"; the woman, on the other hand, he calls "tall and manlike."[41] The tendency towards such protagonists is typical of writers working under Swedenborg's influence, the pattern for such creations being his asexual angels; one thinks, for example, of Séraphita in Balzac's novel and Tintomara in Almquist's *The Queen's Jewel.*[42] Only four months after completing *Easter,* that is, on February 25, 1901, Strindberg writes to Harriet Bosse of Séraphita, that she-he is the "Symbol of the highest, most perfect type of humanity,"[43] to which he adds—quite significantly when one considers that the première of the drama was only little more than a month away (April 4, 1901) and that Bosse was to appear as Eleonora—that this sort of character "much haunts the most modern literature and is assumed by some to find itself on its way down here to us. Ask for no explanation, but keep this in mind."[44] Two related concepts thus converge in the post-Inferno Strindberg: the one, his long held view of sexual duality; the other, the literary and theological portrayal of the same issue in works connected with Swedenborg.

In my view, neither Eleonora nor Elis can be thought of as individually representing either Strindberg's alter ego or the protagonist of this play. The standard view of *Easter* has been that Eleonora is clearly the most important role in the drama, but only when she and Elis are taken together as the representatives of man's dualistic nature in a functional relationship do they represent a fully rounded figure. This aspect of the play has been overlooked because *Easter* can appear remarkably realistic, especially in comparison with such works as *To Damascus* and *A Dream-Play.* Yet it too has many dream-play qualities, such as the use of the *Ausstrahlungen des Ichs* ("Projections of Self") device suggested here with regard to Elis and Eleonora as projections of Strindberg's ego, a device which in *To Damascus I* typifies the ancillary figures in relation to The Stranger.[45]

Gunnar Ollén remarked some time ago that one of the remarkable things about *Easter* is that Strindberg could write a play about an Easter weekend in a small Swedish town and have something happen.[46] What happens in the play is, however, of considerably more complexity and much greater importance than what some viewers, such as Tor Hedberg, have seen on stage. *Easter* discusses more than the morality one customarily finds in the nursery: it represents several of the major themes of Strindberg's post-Inferno period, although in a somewhat embryonic and underarticulated state. Among other innovative aspects of this play, one shows Strindberg beginning to explore the idea of portraying Swedenborgian concepts on stage—movement into the spiritual plane and instruction in this otherwordly existence. It is a device he perfects most

notably in *The Ghost Sonata. Easter* is thus transitional in certain respects: it mirrors much of the Strindberg we know from *Inferno, Legends,* and *Advent;* and it foreshadows much of what will be found in the twentieth-century Strindberg, especially the disrobing and demasking themes so strongly associated with *The Burned House* and *The Ghost Sonata,* and the use of the suffering innocent found again in *The Crown-Bride* and *A Dream-Play.*

In *Easter,* we see the refinement of a new concept of characterization, a harmony of maleness and femaleness, the influence of Swedenborgian theology, and the belief in representative suffering (*satisfactio vicaria*). These elements lead the post-Inferno Strindberg to a joyous and sunlit conclusion in *Easter,* in contrast to suicide in deepest darkness, so typical of his other works, as Strindberg himself later commented.[47] While *Easter* may not be one of the most satisfying of Strindberg's dramas, it is a fascinating workshop for many of the modern elements we associate with him in the post-Naturalistic period. What is perhaps the play's most fascinating aspect is its ability to take the outward form of the medieval Passion play, but to reflect the inward shapes of Strindberg's eclectic new brand of Christianity and to incorporate into it elements of his new dramatic technique.

Notes

1. Quoted in Gunnar Ollén, *Strindbergs dramatik* (1961; rpt. Stockholm, 1966), p. 170. "Det hela blir flackt och pjåskigt och löper ut i en barnkammarmoral. . . . Den som blir uppbyggd av detta må bliva det—för min del betackar jag mig." All translations from Swedish are my own.

2. Walter Johnson, *August Strindberg* (Boston, 1976), p. 162.

3. See Strindberg's essay "Mitt och Ditt," in August Strindberg, *Samlade skrifter,* ed. John Landquist (Stockholm, 1919), hereafter cited as *SS;* LIII, 467-470; originally published in *Aftonbladet* in 1910.

4. Aage Kabell, "Påsk og det mystiske teater," *Edda,* 44 (1954), 161; Martin Lamm, *Strindbergs dramer* (Stockholm, 1926), II, 204, considers *Easter* to be one of the most difficult of Strindberg's plays to analyze.

5. C. E. W. L. Dahlström remarks in his classic *Strindberg's Dramatic Expressionism,* University of Michigan Publications in Languages and Literatures, VII (Ann Arbor, 1930), 170, that the action of *Easter* is muddled. Early in his Strindberg scholarship, that is, a decade before his *Strindberg och makterna* with its new appreciation for Swedenborg's influence on Strindberg, Lamm, *Strindbergs dramer,* II, 204, says of the play: "this childish drama is essentially a hymn to suffering: 'happiness makes everything banal'" ("detta barnsliga drama är innerst en hymn till lidandet: 'glädjen gör allting banalt'").

6. Harry G. Carlson, *Strindberg and the Poetry of Myth* (Berkeley and Los Angeles, 1982), pp. 124-136. Carlson suggests, for example, that the daffodil Eleonora feels compelled to take can be interpreted as referring to the flower Persephone picks in Greek myth, and that the play therefore is further connected with the seasonal cycle of death and rebirth.

7. Nils Erdmann, *August Strindberg. En kämpande och lidande själshistoria. II. Genom skärselden till korset* (Stockholm, 1920), 338-339, suggests that symbolism, Hinduism, archaic Christianity, Maeterlinck and Schopenhauer were the influences which contributed to the writing of *Easter.* With regard to the inspirational sources of the play, it is worth noting that a little pamphlet appeared two years before *Easter* was composed which bears the highly suggestive title *Emmanuel Swedenborg, August Strindberg och det ondas problem: Ett föredrag,* by Pastor (of Nya Kyrkans svenska församling) Albert Björck (Stockholm, 1898). This published lecture contains a statement that could well serve as the Stanislavskian summary of *Easter:* "The abuse of life is evil, but the suffering which accompanies this abuse is good" ("Missbruket af lifvet är det onda, men lidandet som missbruket för med sig är ett godt" [p. 39]).

8. "Mitt och Ditt," *SS,* LIII, 468.

9. *August Strindbergs brev,* ed. Torsten Eklund, Strindbergssällskapets skrifter (Stockholm, 1974), hereafter cited as *Brev;* XIV, 21. "Hon är . . . slägt med Balzacs Séraphita, Swedenborgs Nièce."

10. *Brev,* XV, 88. See n. 38.

11. The influence of Swedenborg on Strindberg has been a much discussed topic in recent years. On this issue, see especially Göran Stockenström, *Ismael i öknen: Strindberg som mystiker,* Acta Universitatis Upsaliensis. Historia Litteratum, V (Uppsala, 1972), and "The Symbiosis of 'Spirits' in *Inferno:* Strindberg and Swedenborg," transl. Matthew Dion, in M. J. Blackwell, ed., *Structures of Influence: A Comparative Approach to August Strindberg,* University of North Carolina Studies in the Germanic Languages and Literatures, XCVIII (Chapel Hill, 1981), 3-37; Evert Sprinchorn, "Hell and Purgatory in Strindberg," *Scandinavian Studies,* 50 (1978), 371-380, and "The Zola of the Occult: Strindberg's Experimental Method," *Modern Drama,* 17 (1974), 251-266. See also Martin Lamm, *Strindberg och makterna* (Stockholm, 1936). Nathan Söderblom, Professor at Uppsala, but formerly Swedish Pastor in Paris during Strindberg's time there, was one of the first to delve into this issue; in an article published just months after Strindberg's death, "Till frågan om Strindberg och religionen," *Bonniers månadshäften,* 6 (1912), 435-441, Söderblom discusses the impact of Swedenborg on Strindberg. Among other fascinating bits of information, one points out that on Strindberg's night stand at the time of his death were to be found Swedenborg's *Apocalypsis revelata* and Stroh's biography of the Swedish mystic.

12. "Mitt och Ditt," *SS,* LIII, 468.

13. *SS,* XXXIII, 46. "skall jag komma ifrån denna rysliga stad, från Ebal, förbannelsens berg och skåda Garizim åter?"

14. On the important role of Old Testament materials for Strindberg during the Inferno crisis, see Gunnar Brandell, *Strindberg in Inferno,* transl. Barry Jacobs (Cambridge, Mass., 1974), pp. 102-104. Spelled "Gerizim" in the English tradition, the mountain is respelled with an "a" here to conform to Strindberg's usage.

15. This is a view expressed publicly in *Inferno, Legends,* and *Jakob Wrestles.* A particularly vivid description of Strindberg's time in the town is given in Elizabeth Sprigge, *The Strange Life of August Strindberg* (New York, 1949), pp. 173-179.

16. *Brev,* XIV, 89. "Och hon vill gerna se Lund, Purgatoriostaden, i förbifarten." This view of Lund was one Strindberg held for a long time: in 1905 he wrote of "Philipot from Inferno-Lund" (*Brev.* XV, 126).

17. *SS,* XXXIII, 127. "Nu skall du tacka Gud, som hjälpte oss att få komma till landet!"

18. Göran Stockenström, "'The Journey from the Isle of Life to the Isle of Death': The Idea of Reconciliation in *The Ghost Sonata,*" *Scandinavian Studies,* 50 (1978), 133-149; Sprinchorn, "Hell and Purgatory in Strindberg"; Stephen A. Mitchell, "'Kama-Loka' and 'Correspondences': A New Look at *Spöksonaten,*" *Meddelanden från Strindbergssällskapet,* 61-62 (1979), 49-51.

19. *SS,* XLVI, 49-50. See also 114-115. "Swedenborg har i sitt helvete ett avklädningsrum, där de avlidne införas genast efter döden. Där avklädas de denna skrud, som de tvingats anlägga i samhället, umgänget och familjen; och änglarne se straxt vilka de ha för sig."

20. *SS,* XXXIII, 39. "ja, det är vår. . . . Och jag får hänga upp vinterrocken . . . vet du, den är så tung— *Väger rocken i handen.*—som om den supit in alla vinterns mödor, ångestens svett och skolans dam. . . ."

21. *SS,* XLVI, 26. "det är möjligt att han icke menar någon ort, utan ett sinnets tillstånd."

22. *Brev,* XIV, 50. . . .

23. *SS,* XXXIII, 60-61. "ELEONORA Vilken motgång har du haft? BENJAMIN Jag har blivit underkänd i latinskrivningen - fastän jag var alldeles säker. ELEONORA

Jasä, du var alldeles säker, så säker, att du kunde
hålla vad på att gå igenom. BENJAMIN Det gjorde jag
också! ELEONORA Jag kunde tro det! Ser du, så gick
det för att du var så säker. BENJAMIN Tror du det var
orsaken? ELEONORA Visst var det! Övermond går före
fall!"

24. *SS,* XXXIII, 53. "Jag har satt *ut* med indikativus,
fastän jag visste att det skulle vara konjunktivus."
While Benjamin's error plays specifically on the
theme with which the entire play resonates, there is
no doubt a secondary ironic edge to this mistake:
Elis's panicked resonse ("Then you're lost!" ["Då är
du förlorad!"]) is all out of proportion to the error
and is clearly a gibe at the small-mindedness of the
academic world.

25. *SS,* XXXIII, 113. "så begär jag ingen nåd, endast rät-
tvisa!"

26. *SS,* XXXIII, 115. "det finns en barmhärtighet, som
går emot rätten och över den! . . . Det är nåden!"

27. *SS,* XXXIII, 115. "Jag skall tänka på era barn och
icke klaga!"

28. *SS,* XXXIII, 115. "Bra! . . . Nu gå vi ett steg vidare!"

29. *SS,* XXXIII, 117. "Säg om det en gång till, och
högre!"

30. *SS,* XXXIII, 120. "Jag skall väl krama er igen, då."

31. *SS,* XXXIII, 123. "Och för deras lycka skulle jag
lida dessa kval?"

32. "Mitt och Ditt," *SS,* LIII, 468. "den ena . . . lider i
stället för den andra."

33. On the concept of soteriology, see, for example, "So-
teriology and Types of Salvation," in Max Weber,
The Sociology of Religion, trans. Ephraim Fischoff
(Boston, 1963), pp. 184-206.

34. *SS,* XXXIII, 123. "Ja! De, som lidit för att bereda er
lycka! . . . Er mor, er far, er fästmö, er syster."

35. *SS,* XXXIII, 124. "Så går allting igen, även det
goda."

36. *SS,* XXXIII, 123. "klarnar det utanför."

37. "Mitt och Ditt," *SS,* LIII, 468.

38. *Brev,* XV, 88. "Hon var liksom min tvilling, och när
hon dog lyckönskade vi henne. Jag vill bara visa Dig
'Påskflickan,' som led för andra, men tog upp andras
ondska i sig, så att hon ej kunde vara snäll rigtigt."

39. *Brev,* XIV, 34. "hon-han," "Eleonoras slägtning." See
also *Brev,* XIV, 16, 21.

40. Robert Brustein, *The Theatre of Revolt: An Approach
to the Modern Drama* (1962; rpt. Boston and Toronto, 1964), p. 122.

41. *SS,* XVIII, 137. "små knubbiga händer med långa,
väl skötta naglar, små fotter och smäckra ben med
starka vador"; "ett friskt hull"; "lång och karlavulen."

42. C. J. L. Almquist, one of Sweden's greatest literary
figures, was, like Strindberg, much influenced by
Swedenborg. Tintomara, the protagonist of his *Drott-
ningens juvelsmycke,* published in 1834, was conceived of as an *animal coeleste,* to use his terminology. As such, she is both male and female, beast and
human, and so forth.

43. *Brev,* XIV, 34. "Symbol af den högsta, fullkomligaste
menniskotyp."

44. *Brev,* XIV, 34. "hvilken spökar mycket i den modern-
aste literaturen och antages av några befinna sig på
vägen hit ner till oss. Begär nu ingen förklaring men
behåll ordet i minnet."

45. The extent to which *Easter* should be regarded as
part of Strindberg's "mystical theatre," as distinct
from the dream plays, is discussed in Vagn Børge,
*Strindbergs mystiske teater. Æstetiskdramaturgiske
analyser med særlig hensyntagen til Drömspelet*
(Copenhagen, 1942), pp. 160-162. See also his *Der
unbekannte Strindberg. Studie in nordischer Märch-
endichtung,* transl. Emil Schering (Copenhagen,
1935), and Kabell, "Påsk og det mystiske teater." On
the concept of *Ausstrahlungen des Ichs* and its function in other Strindbergian works, see, for example,
Walter Sokel, *The Writer in Extremis: Expressionism
in Twentieth-Century German Literature* (Stanford,
1959), pp. 34-37.

46. Ollén, *Strindbergs dramatik,* p. 166.

47. "Mitt och Ditt," *SS,* LIII, 468.

SVANEVIT (SWANWHITE)

PRODUCTION REVIEW

Jeremy Kingston (review date 3 December 1996)

SOURCE: Kingston, Jeremy. "Fairytale Love Among the
Archetypes." *The Times* London (December 3, 1996).

[*Below, Kingston presents a review of the production of*
Swanwhite *directed by Timothy Walker.*]

This charmingly peculiar fairytale [*Swanwhite*] shows how much there is of Strindberg that most of us know absolutely nothing about. The wife-taming Strindberg, yes, or rather the would-be wife-tamer; the dramatist of terrible family life, of lives unconvincingly redeemed by suffering, and plenty of lives not so redeemed; of strife under the Vasa kings (not that we are given many opportunities to see these).

Now that Timothy Walker has directed what is thought to be the British premiere of this full-length 1901 play written by, you might think, Hans Christian Strindberg, its characters of stern father, cruel stepmother, trusting maiden and loving prince obviously emerge from the same brain-box. But even if the simple starkness of the tale is what might be expected, the fact that he is telling it at all remains a surprise. I first became aware of Walker when he played an unforgettably fawning and grubby clerk in Cheek by Jowl's sublimely funny *A Family Affair* eight years ago. Though I ought to know better, this is the image that has unfairly hung about him in my mind and can now be replaced, or at least joined, by that of someone who has managed to create, on his directorial debut, a passionate tale of redemptive love among the archetypes that, against so many odds, holds the stage.

More than simply offering a fascinating glimpse of *fin de siècle* drama as written at the end of the last siècle, the play provides its cast with vivid characters to create and a language to do so that is certainly flowery but reminiscent of meadows and medieval gardens rather than the hothouse. Gregory Motton's translation serves his author well.

Young Swanwhite's father must set off for battle—"Farewell, my great war hero!"—and she is left to the mercy of the stepmother (Richenda Carey, wicked in rustling black velvet). A prince comes courting on behalf of a sottish king, and true love blossoms. The Green Gardener sows discord, horrid things happen in the Blue Tower; fire rages, seas pound, a brace of dead mothers bring blessings. It could all be perfectly absurd but isn't, because of the cast's convincing habitation of their roles.

Jules Melvin projects gravity and innocence without being mawkish; her wobbly gait at the start is like a bird, of course, but also suggests an enthusiastic, two-legged, newborn lamb. Her young prince, Jason Morell, declares his feelings in a most expressive, gently passionate voice, and they play their love scenes (and their show of discord) with stirring conviction.

On Gemma Fripp's set, with its sense that menace lurks in the shadows, the three candle-holding servants look as if they have stepped from an 1890s children's book. Apt image for Strindberg's dip into the pools of myth.

CARL XII (CHARLES XII)

CRITICAL COMMENTARY

Susan Brantly (essay date winter 1990)

SOURCE: Brantly, Susan. "The Formal Tension in Strindberg's *Carl XII*. *Scandinavian Studies* 62, no. 1 (winter 1990): 92-107.

[*In the following essay, Brantly examines* Carl XII *and considers its place in Strindberg's oeuvre.*]

In the cycle of twelve historical plays written after *Inferno* (1897), Strindberg is constantly aware of the Conscious Will in history and seeks to interpret the logic of its tendencies.[1] A central wish of the Conscious Will in Strindberg's historical cycle appears to be the rise of democracy and the abolishment of absolutism. Strindberg stresses this theme even at the expense of historical accuracy.

Among Sweden's rulers, Charles XII represents for Strindberg the acme of the abuse of absolutism. In Strindberg's vocabulary, Charles XII was synonymous with a lust for power and domination, at the expense of the Swedish people. No doubt Strindberg felt that Sweden's greatest tyrant deserved special treatment, and in 1901, he added *Carl XII* to his cycle of historical dramas, within which the play has come to enjoy a singular status. As Walter Johnson writes, "Remarkable as all the eleven other plays are in their variety of structure and characterization, none of them is as decidedly different from all other historical dramas as Charles XII" (289). The nature of this singularity is certainly worth exploring. The dramatic treatment of Charles XII prompted Strindberg to indulge in a daring formal experiment.

In *Öppna brev till Intima Teatern* (1909; *Open Letters to the Intimate Theater*), Strindberg refers to *Carl XII* as a drama of character and catastrophe, a fairly traditional type of historical drama (*SS* 50:251). One should perhaps bear in mind that at the time Strindberg was defending himself from an anonymous review of the premiere of *Carl XII,* which claimed: "ett virrvarr af lösligt samman-flätade delvis barocka scener få utgöra ett surrogat för en förnuftig, dramatisk handling [Brs.]"[2] ("a confusion of loosely woven, partially baroque scenes must serve as a surrogate for reasonable dramatic action"). In order to deny the charge of disorganization, Strindberg—in his characterization of his own work—emphasized *Carl XII*'s relation to more traditional forms of drama and de-emphasized the dramatic innovations of the piece. In any event, Strindberg was quite proud of the dramaturgy of

Carl XII. In a letter to Lars Nilsson written before the premier of *Carl XII*—and the ensuing flood of criticism—Strindberg writes: "Sjelf sätter jag CXII högst, i tekniskt dramatiskt hänseende, af mina historiska [*Strindbergs brev* #4592]" ("Myself I value Charles XII most highly of my historical dramas, from a technical, dramatic point of view").

After its premiere at the Dramatic Theater on February 1, 1902, the reactions of the earliest critics to *Carl XII* were primarily patriotic. Many took issue with Strindberg's treatment of Sweden's hero king and compared Strindberg's efforts unfavorably to Verner von Heidenstam's treatment of the same in *Karolinerna* (1897-98; *The Charles Men*). With regard to the artistic merits of Strindberg's play, however, the earliest critics were often disturbed by the "mystiska och symboliska interkaleringar [S.S-n]" ("mystical and symbolic interpolations") in this purportedly historical drama. Strindberg's notorious flexibility with historical details caused most of his historical dramas to be counted as failures when they appeared. In the 1920s, however, Martin Lamm was able to appreciate the uniqueness of Carl XII: "Med sin abrupta dialog, sina fantastiska situationer, sin underliga blandning av historisk verklighet och symbolistik är dramat tvivelsutan ett av de originellaste försöken inom det historiska skådespelet i modern tid [294]" ("With its abrupt dialogue, its fantastic situations, its peculiar mixture of historical reality and symbolism, the drama is without a doubt one of the most original attempts within the historical drama in modern times"). In later years, once expressionism became an official concept in Germany during the 1910s and 1920s, the dramaturgy of *Carl XII* became easier to discuss. Walter Johnson wrote in 1963 that "Strindberg's approach to his tragedy about Charles XII was primarily expressionistic, only secondarily realistic" (157). Birgitta Steene wrote in 1973 that King Charles is "an expressionistic character in an otherwise Naturalist drama. The power of Charles XII lies, in fact, in this formal tension within the play" (132).

Carl XII does indeed manifest dynamic formal tension, but in sorting out the source of this, it seems necessary to set aside the term "expressionistic" for the present, in order to emphasize the metaphysical and supernatural dimensions of the play. Expressionist interpretations of Strindberg's post-Inferno plays quite often provide a means of secularizing and psychologizing the pervasive metaphysical themes.[3] In this way, Strindberg's plays maintain their relevance to a modern audience, which has grown less interested in religious questions. Strindberg's belief in the Eternal One and a Conscious Will in history, however, differentiates him markedly from the later German Expressionists.

Carl XII is different from all of Strindberg's other historical plays precisely because it is the most metaphysical, the most Swedenborgian. As has been amply documented by Göran Stockenström, among others, Strindberg's acquain-

tance with Swedenborg's writings had a profound effect on his dramaturgy.[4] Swedenborg worked out an elaborate system of correspondences in which elements of the physical world correspond to counterparts in the spiritual world, so that, as Swedenborg puts it, "One would swear that the physical world was purely symbolical of the spiritual world" (Ward 118). In traditional historical drama, the stage is set with artifacts designed to create an appropriate historical flavor. In Strindbergian drama, scenic elements become pointers to the world beyond, clues to the workings of the Conscious Will in history. This religiously inspired utilization of scenic elements lies at the root of Strindberg's so-called "dramatic expressionism" (Dahlström). In fact, many of the techniques used by Strindberg in *Carl XII* prefigure his later "expressionistic" chamber plays.

The figure of Charles XII uniquely combined Strindberg's historical, political, and metaphysical interests. Politically, Strindberg found Charles XII abhorrent, and, consequently, the Conscious Will in history surely had to disapprove of such a tyrant. This judgement of Charles XII was confirmed by no less an authority than Emanuel Swedenborg himself, who held the monarch to be the most obstinate, egocentric, power-hungry man on earth. Swedenborg knew Charles XII personally, not only in actual life, but also in the spirit world. In Swedenborg's *Spiritual Diary* (*Diarium Spirituale,* 1843) which is a chronicle of his experiences (1747-55) as a guest in the spirit world, he gives an extensive characterization of Charles XII before and after his death.

With the support of Swedenborg's *Spiritual Diary,* Strindberg did not have to guess at what the powers thought of Charles XII. That relative certainty encouraged Strindberg to emphasize the metaphysical aspects of Charles XII's reign. Some of Strindberg's notes about *Carl XII* indicate that he toyed with the idea of incorporating nonrealistic moments into the play in the form of visions and dreams. For example, in one sketch, Strindberg considered a fifth act comprised of "Swedenborgs syner"[5] ("Swedenborg's visions"). Elsewhere, Strindberg considers "Skräck-synerna om natten vid Fredrikshall" and "Konungens onda drömmar [Ms. 2:6/12]" ("Horrible visions at night at Fredrikshall"; "The king's evil dreams"). According to Göran Stockenström, Strindberg meant for a parade of eerie figures to pass before Charles XII in a life review on stage ("*Charles XII* as Dream Play" 223).[6] Such a scene would have constituted a complete departure from a real and reasonable world. Instead of openly indulging in supernatural dream sequences, Strindberg chose to experiment with ambiguity in *Carl XII.*

The formal tension of *Carl XII* lies in the author's hesitation between giving a natural or a supernatural explanation of events. The resulting effect is not unlike the fantastic, as described by Tzvetan Todorov.[7] Strictly speaking, nowhere does Strindberg leave the realm of plausibility in his historical play. All events can be explained away naturally, and most have some support in the history books. Yet, at work behind this facade of reality is the "mysticism of history." Although the mystical explanation of events is strongly suggested, it is never insisted upon. The public must decide for itself.

In *Carl XII,* the boundary between the worlds of the dead and the living has become blurred, and the dead and living mix freely. The cause of this ambiguity is Charles XII himself, a dead man who refuses to accept his own death. Emanuel Swedenborg tells us in his *Spiritual Diary* and elsewhere that the newly dead often do not recognize that they no longer belong the world of the living. They may encounter old friends and, more importantly, old enemies in this stage of limbo. The dead undergo a process of vastation, or unmasking, orchestrated by the spirits that confront them. Strindberg referred to this first stage after death as "Sheol" and "Kama Loka." Barbro Ståhle Sjönell has documented the frequency with which this concept appeared in Strindberg's post-Inferno literary thinking (35-45). Evert Sprinchorn has illustrated that Strindberg appreciated the dramatic potential of Swedenborgian vastation and used it in many of his chamber plays. In Strindberg's play, Charles XII is a very reluctant spirit who clings to his worldly ambitions and resists the agents of his vastation. The result is disastrous, for as the supreme monarch of Sweden, Charles has dragged the entire country into limbo with him.

Carl XII is a play in five tableaux. As is so often the case in Strindberg's plays, the first tableau is one of exposition. The events leading up to the drama are alluded to, and the stage is set for the unfolding of subsequent events. Charles XII appears in the first tableau, but he does not speak audibly. We learn of him through the discourse of the people whose lives he has affected: the soldier who has returned from Siberia, the representatives of the four estates, the soon-to-be-executed captain of the Snapp-Opp, and the court dwarf.

The stage is set very carefully. The opening scene of *Carl XII* takes place in a ghost town on the coast of Skåne. On the stage, the audience sees the burnt ruins of a church and surrounding dwellings, including the crumbling, sooty structure of an abandoned house. Outside the house is a leafless appletree with one lone apple clinging to its branches. This tree has been interpreted as a symbol for Sweden, whose monarch, despite having drained away its vitality, clings to his dessicated country in defiance (Johnson 171). Almost as soon as the play begins, the returned soldier, who is simply called "Mannen" ("the Man"), begins, by means of his discourse, to recreate the town as it was 15 years earlier: "Här stod min stuga, här var mitt hem, här satt min hustru och mina två barn! Vid denna spis kokades min gröt, vid detta fönster lekte mina barn, på denna tröskel satt min hustru och väntade . . . [Strindberg, *SS* 35:117]" ("Here stood my house, here was

my home, here sat my wife and two children. On this stove, my porridge was cooked; by this window my children played; on this threshold my wife sat and waited"). The Man conjures up these deceased figures from the past, and through his discourse he enables the past and the present to occupy the same space simultaneously, with the more pleasant image of the past showing the ruin of the present in sharp relief. The topos of revealing ruins will be expanded later by Strindberg into a Chamber Play, *Brända tomten* (1907; *The Burned House*). In *Carl XII,* the conjuring up of the past over the ruins of the present creates a spacial and temporal ambiguity. Among these phantom buildings walk ghosts, figures from the past invading the present. The little town of the first tableau is located in a region where life and death intersect (cf. "*Charles XII* as Dream Play" 231). Moreover, this little town is referred to as representative of Sweden: as the Man says, "Så här ser väl hela riket ut [Strindberg, *SS* 35:117]!" ("The whole kingdom surely looks like this!").

Charles XII's landing on the coast of Skåne is a historical fact, but for Strindberg this reference to an actual past event and place is infused with metaphysical significance. When we first hear of Charles XII, he is at sea. In one of his visions in the *Spritual Diary,* Swedenborg beholds a great sea roaring with enormous waves: "It was said that this was representative of the phantasies of those who desire to be great in the world, and who wish to change all things into new, and thus acquire glory for themselves [1: #277]." Of Charles XII specifically, Swedenborg writes: "Nor did he aspire to the greatest name in his kingdom only, but in the universal globe, which also he wished to govern [4: #4748]." According to Swedenborg, Charles XII wanted to rule the world. Thus, Charles's historical arrival in Sweden upon stormy seas can also be viewed as a divine judgement on his ambition.

Charles's actual coming ashore is not seen by the audience; it is described by the Man and the Coast Guard. Just at the point at which Charles XII is apparently stepping onto Swedish soil, the stage directions state without explanation or elaboration: "Ett skot höres i fjärran [Strindberg, *SS* 35:122]" ("A shot is heard in the distance"). Perhaps this is the shot that will reach its mark in the final tableau.[8] Indeed, in the second tableau, Gyllenborg makes the ominous observation that a button is already missing from Charles's uniform. This detail is striking since legend has it that Charles is shot by a silver uniform button. In addition, the missing button suggests that Charles is already dead, since a button is the traditional fee paid to Charon, the ferryman to the underworld.[9]

The coming ashore of Charles XII represents a change of status. The image of the shore has often been used in literature to suggest the region where the world of the living touches the world of the dead. The shore of the Styx, for example, serves this function. A similar opposition of land/sea, life/death is used by Strindberg in *Dödsdansen*

(1900; *The Dance of Death*), completed in the same year as *Carl XII* (Törnqvist 4). In *Carl XII,* as the Coast Guard and the Man are watching the ships at sea, the Man makes a comment about the world of the living that implies the close proximity of its neighboring realm as well: "Tror du inte, att om man tände en fyr här, just här, både briganten och brigantinen skulle avlängsnas ur de levandes värld och riket därmed räddas [Strindberg, *SS* 35:120]?" ("Don't you think that if one lit a fire here, just here, both the brigand and the brigantine would be removed from the world of the living and the realm thereby be saved?"). There are two particularly significant aspects to this line. Firstly, the salvation of Sweden depends upon Charles XII entering the realm of the dead, and, secondly, fire is the means or the portal through which this transition should occur (cf. Stockenström, "*Charles XII* as Dream Play" 232).

In Ovid's *Metamorphosis,* fire is the highest element since it soars upward and constitutes a transition to the heavenly bodies. Furthermore, fire is capable of converting lower elements into high elements. This is indeed what takes place in the final scene of *Ett drömspel* (1901; *A Dream Play*) as all the characters throw the symbols of their earthly ties onto the bonfire.[10] In *Carl XII,* fire becomes a significant scenic element that functions as a portal to the next world. There are fires blazing onstage in three of the tableaux, and Charles shows a tendency to stare fixedly into these flames. Charles stares at the portal that will lead him from his worldly obsessions into the realm of the dead, but he makes no move to cross the threshold until the final scene. Also in this initial tableau, the Dwarf plays the saraband for the first time. Throughout the play, the tune accompanies Charles XII's dance with death, another favorite Strindbergian motif in his post-Inferno plays.

Thus, in the first tableau, through scenic elements and discourse, it is suggested that Charles XII is already dead, but like many Swedenborgian spirits he does not realize it, or at least refuses to acknowledge it. In the ensuing tableaux, Charles will undergo his vastation. He will be visited by a series of spirits who will confront and tempt him and try to make him acknowledge his circumstances. This will not be an easy task, since, as Swedenborg tells us, one of Charles XII's character traits was a stubbornness that did not allow him to admit error, "though he should suffer either the cruellest death or the most atrocious hell" (4:#4741).

The second tableau of *Carl XII* takes place in the king's audience room in Lund. Visually, there is nothing unusual presented to the audience, yet quickly, through discourse, the spacial and temporal tensions of the previous scene are reestablished. We learn that Lund burned some years ago, which connects Lund with the burned town on the coast. There is a reprise of the saraband, "infernalisk musik" ("infernal music"), which Gyllenborg says sounds like "gråtande barn.—Vet du, att det dött sextio tusen små barn i sista barnpesten [Strindberg, *SS* 35:133]?" ("crying children.—Do you know that 60,000 small children die in the last children's plague?"). The saraband emanate from the realm of the dead. Furthermore, Horn remark "Folk ser ut som spöken här i stan [*SS* 35:134]" ("People look like ghosts here in town"). The king himself, of course, is described as "En död man, vars hydda ga omkring och spökar [*SS* 35:133]" ("A dead man, whose shape walks about and haunts"). In his letter to the Intima Theater, Strindberg himself described Charles XII as "e gengångare, ett spöke [*SS* 50:251]" ("one who walks agair a ghost").[11]

The king enters the stage to begin receiving audiences o rather, the agents of his vastation. He is described as having a face that is "sjukligt askgrått [Strindberg, *SS* 35:137] ("sickly ashen gray"). In this description, one finds no only the suggestion that the king is a corpse, but also a allusion to the fire imagery. The king's first audience i with Arvid Horn, who, when asked what he thinks c Görtz, falls into a sort of trance and begins to give, poir for point, Swedenborg's assessment of Charles XII in hi *Spiritual Diary.*[12] Ostensibly speaking about Görtz, Horn i unaware that he is unmasking the king. During the speech the king suffers acute physical discomfort. When he i finished, Horn "liksom vaknande ur en dröm och inseend hela det infernaliska i situationen, blir stum av fasa [Strind berg *SS* 35:141]." ("as though waking from a dream an grasping the whole infernal situation, becomes mute wit horror"). Strindberg's own notes sum up this scene as fol lows: "Görtz karakteristik liknar på ett hår konungen, at denne fasar [Ms. 2:6,19]" ("The characterization of Gört. resembles the king to a hair, so that he is horrified").

Horn and Gyllenborg are dismissed, and Görtz enters fo an audience. The previous scene established the parallel between Charles XII and Görtz. Appropriately, the mai whom the king commissions with the task that will only prolong his own and Sweden's limbo is a man who "se dött ut i profil [Strindberg *SS* [35:144]" ("looks dead ir profile"). Görtz is half-living and half-dead, like the figure of Hel who presides over the underworld in Nordic mythol ogy. Swedenborg wrote that Charles XII, after his death "sought hells which should obey him, and in heaven such things as might also assist him in his purpose of reducing all of subjection and of making himself the supreme God— whom he had believed not to exist" [4:#4746]. Before Görtz's entrance, Horn had just made the point that "on Görtz [read Charles XII] doge i dag, skulle han i morgor resa dödsriket mot the himmelska makterna [Strindberg *SS* 35:139]" ("if Görtz died tomorrow, he would raise up the realm of the dead against the heavenly powers"). Gört. is a spirit from hell, with whom Charles XII conspires to bring himself greater glory. Swedenborg is a spirit from heaven, of whom Charles later makes use to further his own causes [cf. Stockenström, "*Charles XII* as Dream Play" 232].

The king's audience room is equipped, of course, with a fire, that ominous portal to the other world. The mystifying figure of the Professor stirs up the flames twice during the second tableau.[13] The first time, he warns that the fire might get out of control. The second time, the Professor pokes about in the fire while accompanied by the strains of the saraband just before the appearance of the Man in the king's chamber. While Charles is trying to rest, the Man appears to him like a spirit called forth from the flames, although a quite reasonable explanation is given as to how he could sneak into the king's chamber. After the audience, the Man disappears just as easily without being detected by guards. There is indeed something peculiar about the character. In this scene, the Man identifies himself as number 58 Svält, or Starvation, from Taube's dragoons. In the first tableau, however, the Man called himself number 73, from the Southern Scania regiment. The Man represents the spector of all of the soldiers who have fought and died for Charles XII.

The king suspects he is being visited by a spirit, but he shows none of the surprise that might be expected from someone who believes he is being confronted by a ghost. He shows no surprise, because he is beset by spirits constantly, both visible and invisible. His reaction to the vision is to rub his eyes, a gesture that he repeats elsewhere in the play [cf. Stockenström, "*Charles XII* as Dream Play" 230-31]. For example, the king rubs his eyes after he informs Feif, "Jag är icke ensam, Feif, jag är aldrig ensam [Strindberg SS 35:144]" ("I am not alone, Feif, I am never alone"). Among Strindberg's papers is the following notation about Charles XII: "Han var mörkrädd, rädd att sofva ensam om nätterna, sannolikt ej för synliga fiender (men osynliga) [Ms. 2:6,3]" ("He was afraid of the dark, afraid to sleep alone at night, most probably not because of visible enemies (but invisible)") Swedenborg reveals in his diary that Charles XII had spoken with chastising spirits for years before his death (4:#4763).

Yet, when the Man has vanished, the king convinces himself that he has been dreaming, since he can find no record of a #58 Svält from Taube's dragoons. He is therefore able to deny this supernatural experience. Charles then says of his people, "De äro onda på mig för att jag inte är död! . . . Och den här uppståndelsen har korsat många planer [Strindberg, SS 35:161]!" ("They are angry at me because I am not dead . . . And this resurrection has dashed many plans!"). Charles is still stubborn in his resolve not to acknowledge his death, and, in order to make plans for his resurrection, he sends again for Görtz.

In the third tableau, our attention is turned from Charles's struggles with the spirits, to the state of the country surrounding him. We are able to see the Lund that was described in the second tableau. Once again, the ruins of burned houses loom in the background. Having made his pact with Görtz, the king is sequestered in Görtz's house in an effort to close out the ghosts that walk the streets of Lund. As Swedenborg says of those who have led a wicked life, "They are much more frightened & terrified at the judgment of truth than others . . . nor do they know where to conceal themselves" (1:#149). The Dwarf again plays his saraband, which comes from "Sorgenland och Smärtarike" (The Land of Sorrow and the Realm of Pain") and which he used to play for Charles, "då han var bedrövad intill döden [Strindberg, SS 35:167]" ("when he was troubled unto death").

The ambiguity between the living and the dead is maintained. When the women in mourning approach Görtz's door, the Man asks his comrade, who is named Misnöjd ("Malcontent"), to describe them, "Du skall förtälja, ty jag har varit i dödsriket och känner icke mer de levande [Strindberg, SS 35:168]" ("You shall narrate, for I have been in the realm of the dead and know no longer the living"). The women in mourning are the "widows" of "those who are buried alive," that is to say, the wives of the men whom the king has left unransomed in Russia. One of the supplicants at the door appears to be the dead wife of the Man:

MANNEN:

Jag tror min själs salighet det är Karoline!

MISSNOJD:

Men hon är ju död!

MANNEN:

Fan vet

[Strindberg, SS 35:175]!

(THE MAN:

I'll be blessed, I believe it is Karoline!

MALCONTENT:

But she is dead!

THE MAN:

The devil knows!)

In this play, expressions like "I'll be blessed," "The devil knows," "Damn it" appear fairly frequently, but they are never uttered casually. The Man's suspicion—that Karoline, the daughter of the executed ship's captain, is his dead wife—is voiced four times and rings like a refrain as various people are turned away from the king's door. Charles refuses to be exposed to the litany of his wrongdoing, which would advance his vastation.

But another death is proclaimed in this tableau: the death of Louis XIV is announced: "Suveräniteten är död [Strindberg, SS 35:175]!" ("Absolutism is dead!").[14] This is perhaps the most celebrated anachronism of the play, since Louis XIV had died three years earlier. Strindberg felt the need to manipulate this point of history to emphasize that

Charles XII is struggling not only with his personal death, but the death of supreme monarchy.[15] The Conscious Will in history at that time clearly meant to abolish absolutism on earth.

The fourth tableau returns our attention to the vastation of the king. The tableau is set in a garden where the king has isolated himself. In one respect, the garden, complete with a statue of Venus, ought to remind the audience of the Garden of Eden and the Fall of Mankind—in Strindberg's view the ultimate source of all human suffering (cf. Stockenström "*Charles XII* as Dream Play"). The Professor, who drew the audience's attention to the spiritual element of fire in the second tableau, is present in this scene in a different capacity. At the beginning of the tableau the Professor busies himself with flowerpots, identifies himself as a medical doctor, and discusses with Hultman Charles XII's relationships with women. This time, the Professor draws the audience's attention to the physical, earthly side of mankind's existence. In the second tableau, before the fire, Charles XII's spiritual sins were exposed: egocentricity, cruelty, and his will to dominate. In the fourth tableau, Charles XII is confronted by earthly cares, and in the process, he displays a more positive side to his character than we have hitherto been able to glimpse.

The king's encounters with women, Ulrika Eleonora, Katarina Leczinska, and Emerentia Polhem, underscore the struggle between the sexes that has continued since the Fall. We may admire Charles XII for avoiding Emerentia's romantic snares, and we may feel pity for the man whose sister seems to long for his demise. Charles displays his political savvy to Katharina, in explaining why her husband, Stanislaus, was deposed from the throne of Poland. In this context, it is interesting to take note of the only praise Strindberg ever gave Charles XII. In a letter to his young daughter Kerstin, he wrote, "Und der König war ein frommer Mann, der nie Weiber, Wein und Gesang liebte" (*Strindbergs brev* 12:#3465).[16] From Strindberg's point of view, Charles's immunity to women was one of his most admirable qualities.

Also in this scene, Charles enlists the services of Emanuel Swedenborg. It is curious that in this Swedenborgian play, Swedenborg's usual penetrating vision seems to be obscured. To begin with, Swedenborg is blinded by his love for Emerentia until he is disabused by Charles. Moreover, Swedenborg is taken in by the seductive powers of Charles XII, a circumstance indicative of Strindberg's attention to historical detail. When Swedenborg was in the service of Charles XII, he had not yet begun to have visions and was one of the many who fell under the sway of Charles's compelling personality. The characterization of Charles XII in the *Spiritual Diary* was written years after Charles's death. So, since Swedenborg himself is bewitched by Charles XII in the play, Strindberg has Arvid Horn become the mouthpiece for much of the Swedenborgian commentary. Perhaps Strindberg made Horn in league

with the spirits because of his clever negotiations with Ulrika Eleonora after Charles's death, negotiations that prevented Sweden from ever having another absolute monarch. In contributing to the abolition of absolute monarchy, Horn was acting, according to Strindberg, in concert with the Conscious Will in history.

In one respect, the garden in the fourth tableau also represents the king's Garden of Gethsemane, where he finally contemplates the inevitability of his own death and exclaims, "Å min Gud! Gånge denna kalken ifrån mig [Strindberg, *SS* 35:186]!" ("Oh my God, let this cup pass from me!"). During the course of the scene, the king begins to realize that his life continues to hold Sweden in its infernal limbo. Worn down by his battles with the spirits, Charles finally expresses a wish to die. At the end of the scene, Görtz arrives with his bad tidings and announces "Landet i lågor [*SS* 35:206]!" ("The country in flames!"). Purging flames have begun racing through Sweden, flames which will usher Charles XII into the realm of the dead. By hastening off to Norway, Charles XII is rushing to meet death. In a letter to the Intimate Theater, Strindberg calls Charles's campaign in Norway "ett hederligt självmord [*SS* 50:253]" ("an honorable suicide"). When the king departs, his sanctum is invaded by "ruskiga figurer" ("horrid figures") that "smyga in tysta, spöklika, nyfikna, och fingrar på allt [*SS* 35:209] ("creep in quietly, ghostlike, curious, and touch everything"). There no longer exists a sanctuary where the king can shut himself off from his own mortality.

One may begin to perceive that there is a clear structure to *Carl XII*. Tableaux 1, 3, and 5 present external views of the king, in which he is discussed and evaluated by onlookers. In Tableaux 1, Charles enters into his state of limbo. In Tableau 3, he hides from the truth that knocks upon his door. In Tableau 5, he exits from his limbo. In Tableaux 2 and 4, Charles's internal struggles become apparent. After confronting the series of spirits participating in his vastation, Charles makes a decision. In Tableau 2, enlisting the service of Görtz, a spirit from hell, he plans on his resurrection. In Tableau 4, Charles successfully confronts worldly cares, and, enlisting the service of Swedenborg, a spirit from heaven, he runs off to meet death.

In the fifth tableau, all of Charles XII's forces are directed against Fredriksten fortress in Norway, the roof of which is said to resemble a large black sarcophagus. In other words, the king is still fighting against death, though perhaps more out of habit than real resistance. He is surrounded on all sides by fire. The stage directions call for three campfires on stage, one of which is by the king's blue and yellow campbed. The bed is also surrounded by burning torches. This campbed is a scenic element that is present in Tableaux 2, 4, and 5, or all of the scenes in which the king speaks. Its colors make it a rather obvious symbol for Sweden, or—more specifically—for the power of the monarchy with which Sweden has invested Charles

XII. This bed of power, then, he uses as his support and as a refuge in which he attempts to escape the consequences of his actions. When he goes forth to meet death, however, he cannot bring his rank with him, the democracy of death being another element reminiscent of the Medieval dance of death motif.

The fortress is catapulting balls of fire at the camp. All are waiting for the shot fired in the first tableau to reach its mark. The king sits on his campbed and stares into the fire watching his life slip away: "Ett stort rikt liv drar förbi . . . [*SS* 35:211]" ("A great rich life passes by . . ."). Horn, the drama's Swedenborgian oracle, gives a speech about "Denna man, som nu ligger där, väntande på sin griftefärd, ty han är död [*SS* 35:214]" ("That man, who now lies there waiting for his own funeral procession, for he is dead"). The king receives a dispatch describing various political intrigues, which he rolls disgustedly into a ball saying, "Hela livet är som denna boll, en väv av lögner, misstag, missförstånd [*SS* 35:217]!" ("All of life is like this ball, a web of lies, mistakes, misunderstanding"). The Web of Life is a symbol that appears often in Strindberg's works. The theme is best described in a speech from ***Brända tomten:***

> När man är ung ser man väven sättas opp: föräldrar, släkt, kamrater, umgänge, tjänare är ränningen: längre fram i livet ser man inslaget; och nu går ödets skyttel fram och tillbaks med tråden; den brister ibland, men knyts tillsammans, och så fortsätter det; bommen slår, garnet tvingas ihop till krumelurer och så ligger väven där. På ålderdomen när ögat blir seende, upptäcker man att all krumelurerna bilda ett mönster, ett namnchiffer, ett ornament, en hieroglyf, som man nu först kan tyda: det är livet! Världsväverskan har vävt det!
>
> [Strindberg, *SS* 45:96]

> (When one's young, one sees the web set up: parents, relatives, friends, acquaintances, servants are the warp; later on in life one sees the weft; and the shuttle of fate carries the thread back and forth; and sometimes it breaks but is tied together again, and then it goes on; the beam falls, the yarn's forced into twists and turns, and the web's done. In old age when one's eyes can really see, one discovers that all the twists and turns form a pattern, a cipher, an ornament, a hieroglyphic, which one can now interpret for the first time: That is life! The world weaveress has woven it!)

Charles casts the crumpled paper, which represents the web of his earthly life, into the fire. In doing so, Charles resembles the characters of ***Ett drömspel*** who cast their earthly ties onto the bonfire in the final scene. The saraband is played as background music to this dance with death.

Charles permits himself a final inquiry of Swedenborg: "Sådant är livet; hurudan är döden?" ("Such is life; how is death?"), to which Swedenborg answers, "Naturen gör inga språng [Strindberg, *SS* 35:218]" ("Nature makes no leaps"). At last, the king goes to meet the shot that all have been waiting for, with the parting line "Nu går jag till stormningen [*SS* 35:219]!" ("Off to the assault.") Charles is always the aggressor, even in death. When the shot is fired, the dead man belongs at last to the realm of the dead; the fires are immediately quenched; and Sweden is released from its limbo between the living and the dead. The stage is in darkness, but in the darkness a light can be seen.

The final lines of the play present the audience with a choice:

SWEDENBORG:

> . . . Men var kom den kulan ifrån?

FEIF:

> (*pekar uppåt fästningen*) Där uppifrån!

SWEDENBORG:

> (*pekar uppåt himlen*) Där uppifrån!
>
>   [Strindberg, SS 35:223]

(SWEDENBORG:

> . . . But where did the bullet come from?

FEIF:

> (*points toward the fortress*) From up there!

SWEDENBORG:

> (*points toward heaven*) From up there!)

The audience may choose a natural or supernatural explanation: the bullet came from the fortress or it came from the Eternal One. Strindberg lets his own preference be known when he allows Swedenborg to add, "Och kom den inte därifrån, så borde den ha kommit därifrån [Strindberg, *SS* 35:223]" ("And if it didn't come from up there, it should have come from up there"). Strindberg felt that the Conscious Will in history had intervened directly in the case of Charles XII's mysterious demise. The audience, however, is still left with a choice.

Nowhere else in Strindberg's historical dramas do the spirits take as active an interest in human history as they do in ***Carl XII.*** The dramatist's careful balancing act between the natural and the supernatural is ingenious. One can see Strindberg's brilliant associative imagination at work, finding symbolic and metaphysical import in the given facts of history. However, the metaphysical dimension of ***Carl XII,*** which provides the play with a potentially powerful dramatic tension, was seen as a serious flaw by the earliest critics. ***Carl XII*** became a formal experiment that Strindberg did not repeat in his subsequent historical plays.

Notes

1. For Strindberg, history was a story written by the Eternal One, a position that he expanded in his 1903 essay, "Världhistoriens mystik" (*SS,* 54:330-401). All quotations of Strindberg's works have been taken from Landquist's edition of *Samlade skrifter,* abbreviated in this essay as SS. I am responsible for all Swedish translations, but I admit to drawing heavily upon Walter Johnson's translations for inspiration.

2. Compare Strindberg's comment in *Öppna brev till Intima Teatern:* "En ganska kunning man upplyste mig häromdagen om att min Carl XXI icke var något drama, utan bara scener. Därpå skall jag nu svara skriftligen [SS 50:251]" ("a rather knowledgeable man informed me the other day that my Charles XII was not a drama, but rather scenes. To this, I shall now respond in writing").

3. The term "expressionism" is commonplace in treatments of Strindberg's post-Inferno dramas. The major work in this line is Carl Dahlström's. Walter Sokel, an authority on German expressionism, gives Strindberg credit for creating in *To Damascus* "the first fully Expressionist drama every written" (34).

4. See, for example, Stockenström's *Ismael i öknen* and Sprinchorn. Stockenström's most recent essay, "Charles XII as Dream Play," appeared after this paper was written and accepted for publication. Throughout my text I have indicated certain parallel points, arrived at independently, between Stockenström's essay and my own. In the endnotes, I have addressed some issues upon which we differ.

5. Manuscript (2:6/12) in the so-called "Green Sack." Further references to manuscripts in this collection will be abbreviated "Ms."

6. Stockenström's essay places its emphasis on the nonrealistic "dream-play" aspects of *Charles XII.* In my essay, I seek to explore the ambiguity between a realistic and a supernatural explanation of events in the play.

7. Todorov describes the fantastic as follows:

   In a world which is indeed our world, the one we know, a world without devils, sylphides, or vampires, there occurs an event which cannot be explained by the laws of this same familiar world. The person who experiences the event must opt for one of two possible solutions: either he is the victim of an illusion of the senses, of a product of the imagination—and laws of the world then remain what they are; or else the event has indeed taken place, it is an integral part of reality—but then this reality is controlled by laws unknown to us . . . The fantastic occupies the duration of this uncertainty. Once we choose one answer or the other, we leave the fantastic for a neighboring genre, the uncanny or the marvelous. The fantastic is the hesitation experienced by a person who knows only the laws of nature, confronting an apparently supernatural event.

   [25].

8. I first heard this suggested by Debora Regula in a paper read in a graduate seminar on August Strindberg's drama, given by Göran Stockenström at the University of Minnesota, Fall 1982. Further, Regula pointed out that the shot that fells Charles XII in the last act is never heard.

9. See, for example, Carl Michael Bellman's "Vila vid denna källa," in which we hear of Fredman, "Kloto re'n ur syrtuten avklippt en knapp vid Karons bud [*Svensk dikt* 156]" ("Kloto has already clipped a button from his coat at Charon's request").

10. See Delblanc for Strindberg's use of the four elements in *Ett drömspel.*

11. Despite all of the differences that have been seen between Strindberg's portrait of Charles XII and Verner von Heidenstam's in *Karolinerna,* the suggestion that Charles was a ghost was made first by Heidenstam. Heidenstam has Mazeppa say, "De svenskes unge furste stupade i segertumlet vid Narven, men hans skugga rider alltjämt vidare framför tropparna [119-20]" ("The young prince of the Swedes fell in the tumult of victory at Narva, but his shade rides ever before his troups."). One can even find in *Karolinerna* a juxtaposition of the worlds of the living and the dead in the case of the Black Battalion, a battalion of the ghosts of fallen soldiers that is said to follow the surviving troups.

12. This has been pointed out by Göran Stockenström in "Kring tillkomsten av Karl XII." The pertinent paragraphs in Swedenborg's diary are #4748 and #4741.

13. Stockenström claims that the Professor's "sole function in the play is to make the audience repeatedly aware of the symbolic meaning of the fire" ("*Charles XII* as Dream Play" 231). In the fourth tableau, however, the Professor serves another function, which I explain in my treatment of that scene.

14. Birgitta Steene has pointed out to me that the Swedish "Suveräniteten är död!" contains a triple-entendre. "Suveräniteten" can refer to His Supreme Highness Louis XIV, the office of the supreme monarch, or His Supreme Highness Charles XII.

15. In his letter to the Intimate Theatre, Strindberg writes of this: "Därpå sker något världshistoriskt, allegoriserat av flaggenshissande på halv stång: Ludvig XIV är död. Detta betyder ju Envåldets fall—och Carl XII:s stundande slut. Att denna akt uteslöts på Dra-

matiska teatern var ett stort misstag, som förtunnade min pjäs . . . [*SS* 50:252]" ("Thereupon, something world-historical happens, allegorized by the flying of the flag at half-mast: Louis XIV is dead. This means, of course, the fall of Absolutism—and Charles XII's approaching end. That this was excluded at the Dramatic Theatre was a great mistake, which weakened my play").

16. Stockenström cites this line in "Kring tillkomsten av Karl XII" 21.

Works Cited

Brs. "Karl XII på Dramatiska teatern." *Vårt Land* 14 February 1902.

Dahlström, Carl. *Strindberg's Dramatic Expressionism.* Ann Arbor: U of Michigan, 1930.

Delblanc, Sven. *Stormhatten. Tre Strindbergsstudier.* Stockholm: Alba, 1979.

Heidenstam, Verner von. *Karolinerna.* Ed. Kate Bang and Fredrik Böök. Vol. 7 of *Samlade verk.* Stockholm: Bonniers, 1944. 28 vols. 1943-44.

Johnson, Walter, *Strindberg and the Historical Drama.* Seattle. U of Washington P, 1963.

Lamm, Martin. *Strindbergs dramer.* Vol. 2. Stockholm: Bonnier, 1926.

S. S-n. "August Strindbergs Karl XII på Dramatiska teatern." *Helsingborgs dagblad* 24 February 1902.

Sokel, Walter. *The Writer in Extremis.* Stanford: Stanford U P, 1968.

Sprinchorn, Evert. "Hell and Purgatory in Strindberg." *Scandinavian Studies* 50.4 (1978): 371-80.

Steene, Birgitta. *The Greatest Fire.* Carbondale: Southern Illinois U P, 1973.

Stockenström, Göran. "Charles XII as Dream Play." *Strindberg's Dramaturgy.* Ed. Göran Stockenström. Minneapolis: U of Minnesota P, 1988. 223-44.

———. *Ismael i öknen. Strindberg som mystiker.* Diss. Uppsala U, 1972. Acta Universitatis Upsaliensis: Historia litterarum 5.

———. "Kring tillkomsten av Karl XII." *Meddelanden från Strindbergssällskapet* 45(1970): 20-43.

Strindberg, August. *August Strindbergs brev.* Ed. Torsten Eklund. Vols. 12 and 14. Stockholm: Bonnier, 1970 and 1974. 15 vols. 1948-76.

———. [Ms.] Manuscripts in the so-called "Green Sack." Kungliga Biblioteket. Stockholm. 2:6/3,8,12,13,19.

———. *Samlade skrifter.* Ed. John Landquist. Vols. 35, 45, 50, 54. Stockholm: Bonnier, 1916, 1917, 1919, 1919. 55 vols. 1912-20.

Ståhle Sjönell, Barbro. *Strindbergs Taklagsöl—ett prosaexperiment.* Stockholm: Almqvist & Wiksell International, 1986.

Svensk Dikt. Ed. Lars Gustafsson. Stockholm: Wahlström & Widstrand, 1980.

Swedenborg, Emanuel. *The Spiritual Diary.* Trans. George Bush and John H. Smithson. Vols. 1 and 4. London: James Speirs, 1883, 1889. 5 vols. 1883-1902.

Todorov, Tzvetan. *The Fantastic: A Structural Approach to a Literary Genre.* Trans. Richard Howard. Cleveland: Case Western Reserve U P, 1973.

Törnqvist, Egil. "Första turen i Dödsdansen." *Svensk litteraturtidskrift* 41.3 (1978): 3-20.

Ward, John. *The Social and Religious Plays of Strindberg.* London: Athlone P, 1980.

Egil Törnqvist (essay date winter 1990)

SOURCE: Törnqvist, Egil. "Verbal and Visual Scenery in Strindberg's Historical Plays: The Opening of *Carl XII* as Paradigmatic Example." *Scandinavian Studies* 62, no. 1 (winter 1990): 76-84.

[*In the following essay, Törnqvist breaks down* Carl XII *into its dramatic elements.*]

The double status of drama as verbal text and visual presentation gives rise to a number of fundamental questions, the consequences of which we only now begin to discover. Keeping in mind that a (Strindbergian) drama may be experienced either by a reader or a spectator, the significance of this circumstance will in the following be discussed with regard to the stage and acting directions, viewed in relation to the dialogue.

Consider, for example, the consequence of the fact that

(1) the drama text is experienced verbally (by means of linguistic signs), whereas the performance text (seen as an abstraction of the play produced) is experienced audiovisually;

(2) the stage/acting directions are "objective" (authorial), whereas the dialogue is "subjective" (figural);

(3) the reader (also) in this area receives information that partly differs from that received by the spectator;

(4) the three possible relationships between stage/acting directions and dialogue (identity, supplement, discrepancy) are different for readers and spectators;

(5) the (possible symbolic meaning of the stage/acting directions is decoded differently by readers and spectators;

(6) stage directions/scenery is first experienced in succession by reader/spectator (i.e., as process), then in retrospect (i.e., as system), so that we may distinguish between first-time readers/spectators (R1, S1) and re-readers/re-viewers (R2, S2).

In addition to this, we may consider the significance of the fact that

(7) some recipients (natives) partake of the original texts, whereas others (foreigners) partake of translations;

(8) some recipients (natives) are more familiar with the area where the action takes place than are others (foreigners);

(9) some recipients (natives) are familiar with the historical events described, whereas others (foreigners) are not.

The first eight points obviously apply to all plays experienced by both readers and spectators; only the last point—and to some extent the one preceding it—may be said to have special relevance for the subspecies "historical drama."

By relating the nine points to one paradigmatic example, the opening of *Carl XII,* I hope to be able to indicate the problems involved and the need for distinctions in this area of drama research—irrespective of which subspecies is examined.

The opening of the play reads:

> *Det är en blåsig morgon i december 1715, på skånska kusten. En stuga, förfallen och övergiven under pesten 1710, står med grunden nerbäddad i flygsanden. Fönsterna äro utslagna, takpannorna avrivna, dörren avlyftad. Spisen och skorstenen synas sotiga genom den nerramlade framsidan. Utanför stugan står ett avlövat, utblåst äppelträd med ett enda kvarsittande äpple, som skakas av vinden. Därinvid är en skräphög med vissna kardborrar. Till höger om stugan synas brända tometer av en kyrka och flera boningshus. Utanför ligger havet mörkt; i horisonten synes en ljusgrå strimma av dagningen.*
>
> *EN MAN klädd i trasor går och letar i ruinerna.*
>
> *EN KUSTBEVAKARE kommer in.*
>
> [Strindberg, *SS* 35:115]

> *(It is a windy morning on the Scanian coast in December 1715. At the center is a cottage, beyond repair; deserted in the plague of 1710; its foundation imbedded in the drifting sand. The windows are broken; the roofing tiles ripped off; the door is gone. The sooty stove and the chimney can be seen through the collapsed front of the house. Outside the cottage is a leafless wind-ravaged apple tree with one lone apple, which is being shaken in the wind. Next to the tree is a scrap pile with withered burdocks on it. To the right of the cottage can be seen the burned remains of a church and several houses. Beyond, the sea lies dark; on the horizon can be seen a pale gray ray of dawn.*

> *A MAN dressed in rags is walking about searching among the ruins.*
>
> *A COASTGUARD comes in.*
>
> [Johnson, *Charles XII* 107])

Here the reader is informed about the time (*"December 1715"*) and place ("on the Scanian coast")—and even about an event affecting it in the past (*"deserted in the plague of 1710"*). The spectator with a theatre program is informed vaguely about the season (*"a leafless . . . apple tree"*) and about the place, since the program would no doubt list—as does the play text: "Act I: *On the coast of Scania.*" The spectator without a theatre program is merely informed vaguely about the season.

By the term "spoken scenery" (*Wortkulisse*) is usually meant scenery that is not visualized on the stage but merely evoked in the dialogue. The bare Elizabethan stage often caused dramatists of that period to resort to this device. Thus, instead of visualizing a castle, Shakespeare in Macbeth merely has Duncan "report" to the audience what he sees:

> This castle hath a pleasant seat; the air
> Nimbly and sweetly recommends itself
> Unto our gentle senses.
>
> [I.vi. 1-3]

But spoken scenery can also be taken in a wider sense to mean those parts of the dialogue referring to the visualized scenery, as in the following speech from *Carl XII:*

KUSTBEVAKAREN:

> Tala högre, vinden bär undan dina ord!
>
> [Strindberg *SS* 35:116]

(COASTGUARD:

> Talk louder! The wind's blowing your words away!)
>
> [Johnson, *Charles XII* 107]

Although the stage directions have not informed us that it is windy, the words of the Coastguard indicate that it is. Indicate—because this figural piece of information, as we have earlier noted, cannot claim as high a degree of objectivity (reliability) as an authorial one. Similarly, the Coastguard's assurance that "the plague killed all the people" may be an exaggeration or even a lie as far as the spectator goes. But to the reader it seems a reliable statement, since it is supported by the authorial comment: *"a cottage . . . deserted in the plague of 1710."* The plague example pinpoints the difference between the two types of recipients: not only is the reader informed more objectively than the spectator but he is also informed at an earlier point.

Compare, for contrast, the opening of *Erik XIV:*

KARIN:

[*till* MAX]

Kom inte så nära! Kungen sitter oppe i fönstret där och spejar.

[Strindberg, *SS* 31:281]

(KARIN:

[*to* MAX]

Don't come any closer! The king's at the window up there spying on us.)

[Johnson, *The Vasa Trilogy* 263]

Since the king has not been mentioned in the initial stage directions, the reader here knows no more than the spectator. Both may wonder: is Karin a reliable observer?

If the reader is more informed than the spectator in some respects (as in the case of the plague of 1710), the spectator, on the other hand, receives more information than the reader in others. While the reader, for example, is never told about the color of the cottage, the spectator of a production of *Carl XII* will inevitably receive this type of information.

Let us now consider the three possible relationships between stage/acting directions and dialogue, referred to as "identity," "supplement," and "discrepancy." Of these the first (identity) is rare, since it would be completely redundant. The second (supplement) is the most common type. While the third (discrepancy) is again rare and, as far as drama texts go, seems to have been introduced by the absurdists.

To the reader the three alternatives might be construed as follows:

. . . *a cottage . . . deserted in the plague of 1710.* . . .

(a) * COASTGUARD: This cottage was deserted in the plague of 1710. [Identity]

(b) * COASTGUARD: This cottage, which used to be so cozy, was deserted in the plague. [Supplement]

(c) * COASTGUARD: This cottage was deserted in the plague four years ago.

However, to the (knowledgeable) reader of *Carl XII,* the reference to the plague of 1710 in a sense exemplifies discrepancy, since the plague indeed infested Stockholm in 1710, but not Scania until the spring of 1711 (Holm and Lindström 112). Is it a misprint? Has Strindberg been ignorant? Careless? Or does he deliberately refer to a date that would be generally connected with the arrival of the plague in Sweden in the minds of the recipients?

To the spectator the three alternatives might be construed as follows.

* *a red, dilapidated cottage*

(d) * COASTGUARD: This is a red, dilapidated cottage [Identity]

(e) * COASTGUARD: This cottage was deserted in the plague of 1710. [Supplement]

(f) * COASTGUARD: This is a cozy little cottage.

Note that if the present tense in (f) is replaced by past tense (was), the statement becomes supplementary.

While the cottage to the reader, as we have noted, is colorless (or has whatever color he chooses to give it), the spectator will be governed by the choice of director and scene designer. The staged cottage may, for example, be

(a) red—this color may seem highly authentic, yet it is not, since red would suggest mid-Sweden rather than Scania;

(b) black—this color is symbolically relevant but is not ethnically authentic;

(c) gray—this color seems both authentic and symbolically relevant: it harmonizes with the *"pale gray ray of down"* and with the general grayness of the opening.

With the last example we have entered the territory of symbolism and imagery. When concerned with stage representation, we must here be aware of a very trivial circumstance: the visibility of the stage properties. Assuming, for example, that the burdocks mentioned in the stage directions have symbolic relevance, can they be seen by the spectator? And what about the rottenness of the apple?

It does not say in the stage directions whether the tree is dead or not, whether the apple is rotten or not. What we get is,

MANNEN:

. . . Så här ser väl hela riket ut! . . . En ruin, en skräphög—och ett ruttet äpple i toppen . . .

KUSTBEVAKAREN:

Som borde skakas ner!

[Strindberg, *SS* 35:117]

(MAN:

. . . I suppose the whole country looks like this! . . . A ruin, a scrap heap . . . with a rotten apple on top . . .

COASTGUARD:

That ought to be shaken down!)

[Johnson, *Charles XII* 108]

A director can here choose between visualizing (a) * *a rotten apple* (identity) or (b) * *a fresh apple* (discrepancy). The fact that the apple does not fall when the tree is shaken may indicate that it is not as rotten as the men claim it is. The apple clearly signifies the king; the Swedish original significantly speaks of *"ett enda kvarsittande äpple,"* i.e., the king remains sitting (on the throne); the verb *"sitta"* (sit) is part of a positional cluster in the play: we see the king standing, walking, lying (on bed/in the trench), kneeling, and so forth. It should be clear that the way in which the apple is visualized is an oblique statement on whether Charles XII is or is not a rotten king. Fortunately, the apple is too small to give any clear indication to the spectator concerning its "health." The point is precisely that, just as in the case of the reader, the spectator must be puzzled rather than informed about the apple (the king).

Commenting on the apple tree, Walter Johnson writes:

> The single rotten apple on top that hangs stubbornly on but that his people feel ought to be shaken down represents Charles himself. The wind that cannot dislodge the rotten apple represents in turn the ineffective spoken protests and complaints of a people kept from the plucking of the apple directly because of the crippling effects of absolutism.
>
> [Johnson, ***Charles XII*** 97]

In his 1963 study of the historical plays, Johnson elaborates:

> The ruined Sweden that looks like a wasteland is symbolized, of course, by the wind-ravaged apple tree in Act I; the lone apple that clings stubbornly to its top and that should be shaken down represents Charles XII himself. But the tree itself is not dead in the cold gray December beside the dark sea; the tree itself may sprout new leaves and bear sound fruit when light and warmth return. The pale gray ray of dawn on the eastern horizon represents no doubt the hope of a long-suffering people that a brighter day will dawn when the crippling effects of absolutism need no longer deter them from getting rid of the rotten fruit. In concrete human terms, the hope is given form in Horn and Gyllenborg, the men who are waiting only for the apple to fall.
>
> [Johnson, *Strindberg and the Historical Drama* 171]

Although this interpretation—including the implication that the Man and the Coastguard are preparative substitutes for Horn and Gyllenborg—certainly makes sense, it is obvious that Johnson does not make any distinctions between authorial and figural comments, between objective and subjective information. To him, as to the two characters, the apple *is* rotten. But as we have seen, the point is precisely that we cannot be certain of this, neither in the beginning of the play nor at the end of it (where, in fact, the Man seems to reverse his initial opinion of the king by referring to him as "a devil of a fellow all the same").

When we experience the opening of the play as R1/S1, the information provided by the scenery is limited compared to when we experience it in retrospect, having partaken of the whole play, or when we re-experience it as R2/S2. Consider especially the following stage/acting directions in the final act:

> *Vid Fredrikstens fästning i Norge. Längst upp i fonden synes en del av fästningen. Taket liknar en stor, svart sarkofag. . . . Till höger i förgrunden sekreteraren Feifs bord—belyst av en stor lykta.*
>
> . . .
>
> *Nu synes Konungen uppe i löpgraven, vinkande med sin gula handske nedåt.*
>
> . . .
>
> *En fyrboll upplyser scenen och slocknar med en knall.*
>
> . . .
>
> *Det blir mörkt på scenen. Men nu synes en stor lykta uppe i löpgraven.*
>
> [Strindberg, *SS* 35:210-23]

> (*Before Fredriksten Fortress in Norway. Towards the top of the background can be seen a part of the fortress. The roof resembles a large black sarcophagus. . . . To the right in the foreground is Secretary* FEIF's *table—lighted by a large lantern.*
>
> . . .
>
> *The* KING *can be seen up in the trench signaling downwards with his yellow glove.*
>
> . . .
>
> *A flare lights up the stage and expires with a report.*
>
> . . .
>
> *The stage becomes dark. Finally a large lantern can be seen up in the trench.*)
>
> [Johnson, ***Charles XII*** 158-66]

We now realize that the little dilapidated cottage in the beginning, signifying Sweden, contrasts with the mighty fortress at the end, representing Denmark-Norway. Moreover, the hierarchy of the tree at the beginning has its counterpart in the hierarchy of the trench system at the end: the first trench, where we find the king, is not only closest to the enemy but also highest up; officers of higher and lower rank are walking below it; furthest down/away from the enemy we find representatives of the common people. In the beginning the king passes quickly by the church ruin; at the end we see him kneeling (praying).[1] The untranslatable word *"löpgraven"* (*grav* 'tomb') repeated three times, relates to the comparison of the enemy fortress to a black sarcophagus. The last we see of the king is his *"signaling* [vinkande] downwards with his yellow glove" To the enemy this almost suicidal gesture makes him an easy target. To the spectator the mobile yellow glove is replaced first by the flare of light (the fatal shot), then by Feif's *"large lantern"* next to the dying or dead king. The (rotten?) apple in the beginning has been, as it were, transformed into resplendent light—in accordance with the Man's revaluation of the king.²

Since we are dealing with a historical drama, another question especially related to this subgenre is of importance. Traditionally, it is formulated as follows: does the playwright stick to historical reality? To those who cherish the idea that he should do so as much as his dramaturgy allows him, it may be consoling to learn that "Stavstorp was one of the Scanian coastal villages destroyed by the invading Danes in 1709" (Johnson, *Charles XII* 172) and that Charles went ashore at four o'clock in the morning of December 13. It was then still dark, and raining (Fryxell 257). Strindberg is obviously well attuned to the historical data in his initial stage directions.

However, the question seems more relevant if it is reformulated: is the recipient aware of the extent to which the playwright adheres to historical reality? If he is not aware of it, he may run the risk of over-interpreting passages that merely reflect historical accuracy—though the opposite danger seems to me the greater one, at least in Strindberg's case: that the knowledgeable recipient rests content with a "nothing but" interpretation.

With a dwindling knowledge about national history, there is little doubt that the historical background information usually presented in translations of *historical* plays, Strindberg's included, is needed also in editions of original texts—as the Holm/Lindström school edition of *Carl XII* bears witness.

Our paradigmatic example has demonstrated that there is a close interaction between the stage directions/the visualized scenery on the one hand and the dialogue on the other. Both for the reader and for the spectator—but especially for the latter—the dialogue not only influences our way of experiencing the scenery, but the choice of scenery also influences the way in which we experience the dialogue. There is, in short, reciprocity between the verbal and visual elements. As we have seen, the stage directions evoke one kind of scenery for the reader and a somewhat different kind for he spectator. Finally, there is the obligatory difference between first-time experiencers and re-experiencers.

When dealing with the hybrid genre called drama—and with its subspecies historical drama—we should bear these circumstances, as well as the consequences flowing from them, in mind.

Notes

1. As Göran Stockenström points out, the King's kneeling at the end contrasts with his turning "his back to the kneeling representatives of the Swedish people" in the beginning. See Stockenström "Charles XII as Dream Play" 243.

2. The "flare" and the "lantern" are the culminating examples of the fire motif, which, as Stockenström has demonstrated, permeates the play.

Works Cited

Fryxell, Anders. *Berättelser ur svenska historien, i urval av Axel Strindberg*. Vol. 4. Stockholm: Gidlunds, 1983.

Holm, Ingvar, and Göran Lindström, eds. *August Strindberg: Carl XII*. Lund: Uniskol, 1964.

Johnson, Walter. *August Strindberg: Queen Christina, Charles XII, Gustav III*. Seattle: U of Washington P, 1955.

———. *August Strindberg: The Vasa Trilogy*. Seattle: U of Washington P, 1959.

———. *Strindberg and the Historical Drama*. Seattle: U of Washington P, 1963.

Stockenström, Göran. "Charles XII as Dream Play." In *Strindberg's Dramaturgy*. Ed. Göran Stockenström, Minneapolis: U of Minnesota P, 1988. 223-44.

Strindberg, August. [55] *Samlade skrifter*. Ed. by John Landquist. Vols. 31 and 35. Stockholm: Bonniers, 1915, 1916. 55 vols. 1912-20.

GUSTAV III

CRITICAL COMMENTARY

Matthew H. Wikander (essay date March 1987)

SOURCE: Wikander, Matthew H. "Strindberg's *Gustav III*: The Player King on the Stage of History." *Modern Drama* 30 no. 1 (March 1987): 80-9.

[*In the following essay, Wilkander critiques* Gustav III.]

Strindberg's interest in Sweden's Gustav III, founder of the Swedish Academy and both the Royal Opera and the Royal Theatre, began in 1882 with the Royal Theatre's plans to celebrate its centenary by presenting two of Gustav's plays. "Since Herr Josephson altered the program for the festival in September so that it became an ovation for instead of a protest against Gustav III and his so-called creation," he wrote in a letter to Josephson, "I am prevented in every way from participating, since I have, in two special forthcoming works, made a fool of both this king I despise and his 'Creation.'"¹ The young playwright's hostile portraits of Gustav III in *The Swedish People* and of the Royal Theatre in *The New Kingdom* did indeed soon follow. Twenty years later, Strindberg presented his *Gustav III* to the Royal Theatre; "It cannot be right," declared the censor, Nils Bonde, "to slander on this stage the great patron and progenitor of the Royal Theatre," and the play was rejected.[2] The rejection of *Gustav III* was more a response to Strindberg's notorious baiting of the Swedish Academy than an objection to the play itself. For in the intervening years, Strindberg's attitude towards Gustav III had become considerably more complex. What the play presents is not the derision and anger of the young Strindberg, but rather an attempt on the part of the mature Strindberg to see Gustav III and his theatre from a perspective governed by the researches into history which he would soon publish as "The Mysticism of World History" in 1903. Far from being a satirical attack upon Sweden's player-king, *Gustav III* offers a serious critique of the problems of acting and action in the theatre and in the world.

The play is set in 1789, on the days leading up to Gustav III's royalist seizure of power. With his usual delight in ironic coincidence, Strindberg emphasizes the parallelism between this event and the fall of the Bastille. From first to last, Gustav's absolutist *coup d'état* is presented against its historical background as an inappropriate *coup de théâtre;* over the course of the play the king's role shifts from that of playwright, managing events and news, to that of actor, forced to perform the role of assassin's victim in a script he neither controls nor understands.

As the play opens, the king's enemies gather at Holmberg's bookstore, welcoming the news of unrest in Paris and of Washington's election. "Can something new be happening in the world?" wonders Holmberg.[3] The hopes of the group seem to have been answered by accounts of Gustav's deposition; "The comedy is ended!" Holmberg exclaims (p. 246) in a line that will become a refrain for the whole play. But the accounts of Gustav's defeats are false; he lands victorious, and the act ends with news of the executions of the officers who conspired against him. The bookstore is closed. The unseen king masterfully reestablishes his power, although there is a latent threat in the act's last moment, as the revolutionary poet Thorild is left alone on stage, contemplating the bust of Rousseau.

In the second act, we are given our first look at the king himself, in his audience-room at the palace at Haga. The room is decorated with a mirror and a bust of Voltaire: under the watchful eyes of himself and of the philosopher, Gustav rehearses his appearance. He greets each of his visitors in a different manner. "Elis," he says to State Secretary Schröderheim, "do you believe that a person of high station could or should remain in a marriage which brings him only dishonor and ridicule?" (p. 256). Thinking that the king is referring to his own unhappy marriage, Schröderheim recommends a divorce, only to discover that he has been tricked into agreeing to divorce Lady Schröderheim. "He's written a new play," says the king

later to Lady Schröderheim, "with a leading role for you!" (p. 261). Eagerly she runs off to discover that the playwright is the king, not her husband, and that her role will be disgrace. The king's solution for his other political problems will be theatrical as well; he plans to dress in Dalecarlian costume and rally the Dalesmen to his support, just as his ancestor Gustav Vasa had done. "Not badly constructed," says his favorite, Armfelt, of the stratagem, "considered as a play." "Who knows?" replies the king, "maybe it is a play, all of it." "The last act, have you got that yet?" asks Armfelt. "That will come of itself," answers the player-king (p. 263).

Thus both the first and second acts present the king's duplicitous role-playing as a kind of improvisatory playwriting by means of which he manipulates opinion and controls events. But there are notes of foreboding: Thorild's revolutionary fervor and Armfelt's misgivings hint that events may have an impetus of their own. The play's third act, set at the home of Clas Horn, dramatizes a meeting of the conspirators; making an appropriately theatrical gesture, the king interrupts the conclave. "Soyons amis, Cinna, c'est moi qui t'en convie," he declaims, quoting from the scene in Corneille's *Cinna* in which Auguste confronts his would-be assassin. "Pour être plus qu'un roi, tu te crois quelque chose," replies Baron Pechlin, not to be outdone. But Gustav is unaware that Jakob Anckarström (who in history assassinated Gustav III with a pistol loaded with rusty nails at a masked ball in 1792) is hiding on the veranda. He feels some discomfiture, and asks if there is a cat in the room. The conspirators suggest that it might be the ghost of Göran Persson, advisor to Erik XIV, king of Sweden who went mad and was forcibly deposed in the sixteenth century. Gustav departs: "The exit was not so impressive as the entrance," jokes Baron Pechlin, "but that happens to even the best of actors" (p. 266).

In the final act, at Gustav's *fête champêtre* at Drottningholm, the king's loss of control becomes apparent. The troops whom he has expected to arrest the conspirators disband, the guests publicly rejoice at the news of the fall of the Bastille, scurrilous pamphlets questioning the paternity of the crown prince appear in the king's own room. The play's last scene is ironic not only in historical but also in explicitly theatrical terms. As the play ends, the king is shadowed in his movements by Anckarström, who lurks outside and takes aim at him with a pistol. This time he cannot get off a good shot, as the queen keeps stepping into the line of fire. "The queen is the most powerful piece in the game," quips Gustav, unaware of the assassin's presence, "and her function is protecting the king" (p. 276).

The reduction of Gustav from manipulator of events in the early acts of the play to the status of king in a chess-game reaches out to Strindberg's "Mysticism of World History," in which history appears as "a colossal chess-game, with a solitary player moving both black and white."[4] In these essays, Strindberg delineates a view of history which is thoroughly providential: a conscious will directs events; human freedom and agency are merely illusory. The introduction of the metaphor of the chess-game into the final stage-picture of *Gustav III* vividly presents an image of Gustav's entrapment in history. Anckarström will ultimately succeed; the king's establishment of absolutism, incongruous and inappropriate in the historical context of the fall of the Bastille, will ultimately fail.

The play's last lines enhance Strindberg's historical vision with a metatheatrical dimension. "Wasn't there someone named Brutus?" quips the queen in response to the king's assertion that he has been born with "Caesar's luck" (p. 276). These lines grow out of a complex system of reference in the play to two Renaissance tragedies of assassination, Corneille's *Cinna* and Shakespeare's *Julius Caesar.* As an actor and playwright himself, the historical Gustav relied upon the traditional language of the world as theatre, and one of his favorite roles was Cinna in Corneille's play. Thus when Strindberg calls upon the trope of *theatrum mundi* in his play, he does so against a specific background of allusion. Gustav's quotations from *Cinna* in the third act put him in the role of Auguste, who in Corneille's play overwhelms the would-be assassin with masterful clemency. But Baron Pechlin, cast by Gustav as Cinna in that scene, generates a reference to Shakespeare's tragedy: "Brutus, brutal Brutus," he cries when Anckarström reveals his plan to kill the king (p. 267). Strindberg's reading of *Julius Caesar* was highly individual: the play showed him that "Shakespeare is a providentialist just as the ancient writers of tragedy were," he wrote in his *Letters to the Intimate Theatre,* "so he does not depart from history without making sure that divine justice has been distributed even to the point of pettiness."[5] Thinking himself to be playing the part of the heroic, self-mastering emperor in Corneille's play, Strindberg's Gustav will find himself trapped in a world that Strindberg sees as Shakespearean, in which individuals are the playthings of an inscrutable Providence. He will be a Julius Caesar, the assassin's victim, not an embodiment, like Corneille's Auguste, of prudent enlightened rule.

The idea of miscasting is of special interest here because of the substantial body of plays written and acted in by the historical Gustav III. The plays of Gustav III featured monarchs who were heroic lovers, sacrificing all to deliver their people from bondage, national liberators like Gustav Vasa and Gustav Adolf. Determined to create a national drama independent of the French, Gustav wrote Swedish historical dramas with the help of various court poets. *Gustav Adolf's Magnanimity,* his first Swedish play, was performed by the lords and ladies of the court in 1783. The title makes clear the play's connection to the tradition of ideal rulers like Corneille's Auguste. In 1785, Gustav returned to this subject in *Gustav Adolf and Ebba Brahe;* here the king loses the woman he loves as his return to court is delayed while he rescues a peasant from drown-

ing. It is the peasant's wedding day; it should have been the king's as well, but Ebba Brahe misinterprets his letters and his absence and consents to a loveless marriage. *Gustav Vasa,* versified by the poet Kellgren who makes a brief appearance in Strindberg's play, was performed in 1786 as the first Swedish language opera; it played twenty-three performances to full houses. Forced to choose between liberating his country and his love for his mother, Gustav frees Sweden and also manages to save her life. Despite the patriotic subject-matter of these plays, French models lurk behind all of them. Voltaire's *Charlot* provided the plot of *Gustav Adolf's Magnanimity;* Collé's *Parti de Chasse de Henri IV* offered the scenes with the peasantry in *Gustav Adolf and Ebba Brahe;* echoes of Corneille's *Le Cid* and *Cinna* abound in *Gustav Vasa.*[6]

This is not surprising in light of the thorough immersion in French culture of Gustav III's court. Oskar Levertin's *Theatre and Drama under Gustav III,* first published in 1889, characterized Gustavian tragedy as "slavish imitation of Voltaire";[7] Strindberg, who thought of Levertin as a member of the Swedish literary establishment and thus an enemy, may nonetheless have consulted this book in his work on the play. Particularly well-documented and of special interest in relation to Strindberg's *Gustav III* are the amateur dramatic performances that occupied the court's attention over the Christmas and New Year's holidays of 1775-76 at Gripsholm. "At the end of a performance," grumbled Axel Fersen, one member of the nobility reluctant to share in the Gustavian reforms which ceded much of the aristocrats' power to the monarchy, "the king, together with the whole court, comes out for supper dressed in costume. Thus we have seen him dressed as Rhadamiste, Cinna, and the high priest of the temple of Jerusalem, presenting himself as an object of ridicule at his own table."[8] Strindberg's Gustav imagines himself to be Corneille's Auguste in *Cinna;* from Levertin or from Fersen's *Memoirs,* which he mentions needing to consult for his story on Gustav III in *Swedish Destinies and Adventures,* Strindberg might have learned that the historical Gustav played the title role.[9]

The alteration in casting may be accidental on Strindberg's part or it may be deliberate. In either case, what is striking is Strindberg's insistence upon role-reversal and miscasting as the dominant rhetorical figure in his play. "Full of contradictions," is how Strindberg summed up Gustav III in his *Letters to the Intimate Theatre,* "a tragedian who played comedy in his life; a hero and a dancing-master; an absolutist who loved freedom; a fighter for human rights; a disciple of Frederick the Great, Joseph II, and Voltaire."[10] The description is a *précis* of the characterization of Gustav III in "A Royal Revolution," the short story devoted to Gustav in Strindberg's *Swedish Destinies and Adventures;* there, too, the king is "above all, a comedian and declaimer."[11] In his prose summaries of Gustav, Strindberg emphasizes the paradoxical incompatibility between role and player on the historical stage. Gustav's aims and reforms are out of step with his times. "The Bastille has fallen," exclaims Armfelt, the king's favorite, in the last act of the play, "and Gustav the third establishes absolutism! . . . What a paradox!" (p. 271). Strindberg himself might have delighted in the fact, reported by Levertin, that a professional performance of Gustav's *Gustav Vasa* in Norrköping in 1795 inspired the audience to sing "La Marseillaise."[12] In *Gustav III,* the king's garden party in the final act is interrupted by an outburst of rejoicing: Louis XVI has been taken prisoner; "And that's why my guests are celebrating? In my Versailles?" asks Gustav. Outside, the voices are raised in "La Carmagnole."

Strindberg's whole play explores the idea of acting, blurring distinctions between acting as performance and acting as historical action. Martin Lamm was the first of the play's critics to sense in it a high degree of artificiality; *Gustav III* he pronounced to be "historical comedy in the style of Scribe," and he did not mean this characterization as praise. Walter Johnson, later, also noticed structural similarities between *Gustav III* and the historical comedies of Scribe, but for Johnson these could be understood as functional rather than as artistic weaknesses, "conveying the artificiality of a highly formalized court and the artificiality of the king's behavior."[13] Neither Lamm nor Johnson had looked to Gustav III's own dramas, with their misplaced letters, secret hiding places, and manufactured misunderstandings. But to Agne Beijer, an expert in Gustavian theatre, these "comedies of intrigue in historical costume" clearly anticipated the work of Scribe, and one of the standard histories of Swedish literature notices multiple affinities between Gustav's plays and mid-nineteenth-century French theatre.[14] Drawing upon the same models, Voltairean tragedy and the bourgeois *comédie larmoyante,* Gustav created a remarkably Scribean drama. Strindberg's quotations from *Cinna* in *Gustav III* and the decision of Gustav III to imitate Gustav Vasa by dressing in Dalecarlian costume to rally the Dalesmen in his support appear to have clear sources in the dramatic activities of the historical Gustav. So, too, the play's Scribean overtones may be better understood as Gustavian.

The play is framed by the operatic refrain "The comedy is ended"; this response to the false rumors of Gustav's deposition in the first act is echoed by Countess Schröderheim in the last act. "I'm not anywhere," she says to her husband, "but I'm standing here—standing on my own grave—like a cross on my grave—with the mask in my hand—unmasked—oh, the comedy is ended; and no one applauds" (p. 273). The mask she carries is real enough: she has just appeared before the king as Megaera, accompanied by the three Graces in a rather jarring moment of amateur acting. As a court Fury she is also a Shakespearean soothsayer; the line with which she has greeted Gustav is "Beware the Ides of March, Caesar!" (p. 269). But the part she gives up in this later scene is her whole role as a lady of the court. Schröderheim, who was tricked into divorcing her by Gustav, can only pity her loss of

social identity and status: "There's nothing left of Lady Schröderheim," he says; "now begins Lady Stapelmohr, the extension of Miss Stapelmohr." Her married life has been an illusory *entr'acte,* symbolized by the putting on and taking off of a name.

This identification of social role or name as mask and life as a play is stressed by Fersen, who in Strindberg's play shares the anti-theatrical bias of the historical Axel Fersen. "It's masquerade here all year round, apparently," says Fersen later in the fourth act, as Halldin passes by wearing a mask. "And the king—he was taught to lie when he was a child, particularly during the court's unsuccessful grabs for power. I was there then. And ever since he's lied himself away, so that he doesn't know who he is himself; because he makes a joke out of everything, he can't tell the difference between what's serious and what's a joke" (p. 274). Like Lady Schröderheim, the king without a mask is no one; her performance as the Fury, warning Gustav of the Ides of March, circumscribes both actors in a masque of Caesar and Brutus in which both are reluctant players. The two, linked by the refrain "The comedy is ended," both figure the finality of that end.

The refrain also has connections with Strindberg's attitude towards Gustav's period in history, the eighteenth century. "La comedia e finita!" exclaims Voltaire in "The Seven Fat Years," Strindberg's account of his last days at the court of Frederick the Great in the *Historical Miniatures.*[15] Voltaire's activities as a spy have been found out, and he has just been forced to leave. "Sic transit gloria mundi," says Doctor de la Mettrie. Many years later, the story resumes; in his house at Ferney, Voltaire receives a letter from Frederick. The seven fat years have been supplanted by the Seven Years' War; Frederick's ideals of enlightened despotism are in ruins. "This century, which saw all of Europe's monarchs marching at the head of revolutionary movements, is the strangest of all," Frederick writes. "We despots, who forced enlightenment and freedom upon our people, we were demagogues, and the people have rewarded us with ingratitude" (p. 306). Frederick the Great and Gustav III, as we have seen, were always linked in Strindberg's thought. "I dare not draw conclusions from these experiences," he continues, "for that would be to choose Barabbas and crucify Christ . . . Great men, small weaknesses; or better yet: great weaknesses. We, monsieur, have not been angels, but Providence has called us to great things" (p. 308). Frederick's apparent loss of faith after seven lean years of defeat and disillusion illuminates the cynicism of his nephew and disciple, Gustav III.

Unlike Gustav, Frederick for Strindberg was a world-historical individual, a man of providence; late in 1903, as he was preparing a second edition of *Gustav III* for the press, Strindberg was also enthusiastically planning a drama on Frederick the Great. This was to be one of his cycle of three trilogies of five-act plays on world-historical figures; the cycle was never concluded, although Strindberg did complete for it plays on Moses, Socrates, Christ, and Luther. Requesting of Emil Schering biographies and other materials to help in the project ("I've already read Voltaire's bitchy letters," he volunteers), Strindberg delineates the kind of project it would be: "His life is an Odyssey and an Iliad, so a long dramatic epic—which I will model on Götz for Shakespeare-Bühne'n" (his enthusiasm for the idea leads Strindberg to continue the letter in German).[16] "Strindberg was a great man," said John Landquist, his first editor, in an article about the hostile reception given the first performances of *Gustav III* by its critics, "and so he loved great men: especially really great men, like Gustav Vasa or Luther, but he also understood fragile men, who like Gustav III struggled passionately against greatness."[17]

Strindberg's ideas about "great men" as they are presented in "The Mysticism of World History" are highly dependent upon Hegel's theory of world-historical individuals, who, like Caesar "acted instinctively to bring to pass that which the times required." "The source of their actions is the inner spirit," Hegel continues, "still hidden beneath the surface but already knocking against the outer world as against a shell . . .".[18] Like a Hegelian hero, Strindberg's Frederick the Great finishes his career unhappy, but in tune with a higher plan: "History progresses like an avalanche," he writes to Voltaire, "the species is improved, the conditions of life become better, but mankind remains the same: faithless, ungrateful, depraved, and the righteous and the unrighteous can both go to hell" (p. 307). The sense of history's plan working out despite human agency and through the instinctive responses of great men—men of providence in Strindberg's language—infuses both "The Mysticism of World History" and "The Seven Fat Years."

The artificiality and theatricality of Gustav III (his responses are clearly not instinctive) are represented before a backdrop of significant human change and progress of which the audience is forcibly made aware throughout the play. The bust of Rousseau in Holmberg's bookstore and the bust of Voltaire in Gustav's audience-chamber direct our attention, like the references to France and America, to the period's most important individuals and ideas. "I'm the rabble-rouser," Gustav announces to Ole Olsson in the second act:

> . . . the democrat, the hater of the nobility, the first citizen of a free land! A man of the people, defender of the oppressed. I'm Rousseau's disciple . . . and Voltaire's. The social contract—*Le Contrat Social*—is my gospel, I keep it on my night-table! George Washington is my friend, Franklin my ideal. There you have me!

As Strindberg pointed out in all of his writings on Gustav III, this self-image is a paradoxical and willful miscasting: as absolutist revolutionary, Gustav turns his back on the course of history as the rest of Europe struggles towards liberty. Strindberg found in Gustav's period an extraordi-

nary harmony of ideas—"the spirit of the times, all-powerful," he writes of the eighteenth century in "The Mysticism of World History," "takes hold of all the senses, compels all ideas into harmony; and the human race awakens again" (p. 377). The news reports that Washington has been elected and that the Bastille has fallen—true accounts which are confused with the false reports of Gustav's deposition by the conspirators in the first act—reflect this universal drive for liberty. "Can't you see that he's playing Mirabeau and throwing dust in our eyes?" exclaims Anckarström in the second act; "he's performing the French Revolution on stage, he is, the king! It's totally perverse, just like him!" (p. 264). The king's surprise entrance is well-timed: his voice is heard off-stage, joining in the on-stage "Bravo!" as Horn reads to the others from "The Rights of Man" (pp. 265-66).

In addition to Mirabeau, the king arrogates to himself a more perversely revolutionary role in the language of the play. He recalls to the queen the success of his revolution of 1772, in which he restored the monarchy to a share in the government: "I remember that you wept when I sent my chamberlain to Ekolsund to tell you about my successful revolution—when I played Brutus to those homespun Caesars" (p. 262). As Gustav's roles mount, their incompatibility with their times and with each other becomes dazzling. "It was just recently that a court poet compared me with Gustav Vasa, our liberator from foreign powers," he tells the queen; "there may be a grain of truth in the flattery." At the end of the scene he looks over his Dalesman's costume, but whether he will be playing Gustav Vasa, Brutus, Corneille's Auguste or Cinna, or Shakespeare's Caesar for the rest of the play is in doubt. "But the last act," Armfelt asks, "have you got that yet?" "That will come of itself," replies the king; "That will come of itself," repeats Armfelt (p. 263). The player-king resigns himself to the status of actor in a script that will "come of itself." Metaphorically, the script is history, and Gustav's role in history is under scrutiny.

All the stage-sets of *Gustav III* invite scrutiny; they are glass houses, open to view. Holmberg's bookstore is characterized by a constant rush of activity as news from abroad arrives, both false and true. "At the back are windows and open glass doors overlooking the harbor; there masts and sails can be seen," reads the stage direction (p. 245). Gustav's audience-room in the palace at Haga is the scene of the second act: "the whole back wall consists of open glass doors, through which can be seen the park and Brunnviken" (p. 251). Even the conspirators' meeting in the third act takes place in a large room with "open glass doors leading out to a large wooden veranda"—this is where Anckarström lurks during the king's appearance—"overlooking the garden" (p. 263). The last act takes place in the Chinese pavilion at Drottningholm: "the doors at the back stand open overlooking the park"

(p. 267). The overall effect is one of openness and fresh air; yet again in the fourth act Anckarström lurks unseen outside the open doors.

Liberty and *freedom* transform themselves thus from words bandied about by the enlightened king and his opponents into metaphors in the stage set itself and into major issues in the play's dramatic representation of history. The play begins with discussion of the king's new restrictions of freedom of the press; his highsounding promises in 1772 are contrasted with current repressions. But the play ends with disturbing reference to such freedoms: just before Anckarström appears at the back, the king finds a scurrilous pamphlet distributed by Halldin questioning the paternity of his son. "This is horrible," he exclaims, "but there's nothing anyone can do about it!" "No," agrees Armfelt, leaving, "nothing" (p. 276). All the king's reforms seem to beget abuses; his establishment of absolutism on the next day will appear itself to be an abuse of power rather than a liberal reform. What action is possible to him is ironic in the deepest sense, out of step with the great movements of his age.

In his use of theatrical metaphor and revival of the world-as-stage image in **Gustav III** Strindberg then engages in a serious critique of the Renaissance idea of the theater as a center of a court, center of a culture, center of a world, as well as in a critique of the conservative Royal Theatre, Gustav's "creation." For the heroic images promulgated by the historical Gustav III, Strindberg substitutes a pattern of ironic miscasting and gratuitous role-playing that stresses Gustav's incompatibility with his historical context: the European Enlightenment. Acting becomes, on the glass-house stage of Gustav's artificial world, not the world-historical individual's performance of meaningful acts but the playerking's engagement in meaningless performance, circumscribed by the ruling metaphor of the game of chess. The king Strindberg denounced as a fraud early in his career becomes a universal token of humanity's entrapment in history.

Notes

1. August Strindberg, *Brev,* ed. Torsten Eklund, vol. 3 (Stockholm, 1952), pp. 73-74. Except where otherwise indicated, all translations are mine.

2. Quoted and translated by Michael Meyer, in *Strindberg* (New York, 1985), p. 434.

3. August Strindberg, *Gustav III,* in *Samlade Skrifter,* ed. Gunnar Brandell, vol. 10 (Stockholm, 1946), p. 247. All quotations are from this edition, and subsequent references are in the text.

4. August Strindberg, "Världshistoriens mystik," in *Samlade Skrifter,* ed. John Landquist, vol. 54 (Stockholm, 1920), p. 353. Subsequent references are in the text.

5. August Strindberg, *Öppna Brev till Intima Teatern,* in *Samlade Skrifter,* ed. John Landquist, vol. 50 (Stockholm, 1919), p. 114.

6. Swedish prose versions of Gustav's plays (which he often first wrote in French) are in Gustav III, *Skrifter* (Stockholm, 1807) vols. 2 and 3. For the production of *Gustav Vasa,* see Georg Nordensvän, *Svensk Teater och Svensk Skådespelare,* vol. 1 (Stockholm, 1917), p. 16. Oskar Levertin, in *Teater och Drama under Gustaf III,* 2nd ed. (Stockholm, 1911), discusses French source material, p. 106; see also detailed descriptions of individual plays in Levertin's *Gustaf III som dramatisk författare* (Stockholm, 1894).

7. Levertin, *Teater,* p. 101.

8. Levertin, *Teater,* p. 71.

9. August Strindberg, *Brev,* ed. Torsten Eklund, vol. 8 (Stockholm, 1964), pp. 187, 210.

10. Strindberg, *Öppna Brev,* p. 250.

11. August Strindberg, *Svenska Öden och Äfventyr,* vol. 3 (Stockholm, 1907), p. 535.

12. Levertin, *Teater,* p. 192.

13. Martin Lamm, *Strindbergs Dramer,* vol. 2 (Stockholm, 1926), p. 341. Walter Johnson, *Strindberg and the Historical Drama* (Seattle, 1963), p. 215.

14. Agne Beijer, "Gustaviansk teaterliv på Gripsholm," in *Gripsholm: Slottet och dess samlingar* (Stockholm, 1937), p. 100. Henrik Schück and Karl Warburg, *Illustrerad Svensk Litteraturhistoria,* 3rd ed., vol. 4, *Gustaviansk Tiden* (Stockholm, 1928), p. 497.

15. August Strindberg, *Samlade Skrifter,* ed. John Landquist, vol. 42, *Historiska Miniatyrer* (Stockholm, 1917), p. 303. Subsequent page references are in the text.

16. August Strindberg, *Brev,* ed. Torsten Eklund, vol. 14 (Stockholm, 1974), p. 322.

17. John Landquist, "Gustav III och kritiker," *Dagens Nyheter,* 9 May 1916. Despite plans to put the play on in Strindberg's lifetime, *Gustav III* was first performed at the Intimate Theatre in 1916.

18. G. W. F. Hegel, *Reason in History,* translated with an introduction by Robert S. Hartman (Indianapolis, 1953), pp. 39-40.

Matthew H. Wikander (essay date 1990)

SOURCE: Wikander, Matthew H. "Historical Vision and Dramatic Historiography: Strindberg's *Gustav III* in Light of Shakespeare's *Julius Caesar* and Corneille's *Cinna*." *Scandinavian Studies* 62, no. 1 (winter 1990): 123-29.

[*In the following essay, Wilander compares the way that three history plays, including Strindberg's* Gustav III, *treat their subjects.*]

Shakespeare är providentialist som antikens tragödier voro," Strindberg declared in *Öppna brev till Intima Teatern* (1909; *Letters to the Intimate Theater*), "därför försummar han icke det historiska, utan låter den högsta rätten skipas ända till småaktighet [114]" ("Shakespeare is a Providentialist, just as the ancient writers of tragedy were, so he does not leave history without making sure that divine justice has been distributed even to the point of pettiness"). Here Strindberg seems to speak more of his own vision of Shakespeare than of a Shakespearean's, but in opening the question of meting out justice "even to the point of pettiness," he raises an issue central to the criticism of both playwrights. The context of the remark is a discussion of *Julius Caesar* (1599), a play in which Shakespeare forces an audience to question the supernatural dimension of history. The omens that charge the air in the play's third scene; the nightmares that warn Caesar, as does the soothsayer, from the Capitol; the visit of Caesar's ghost to Phillippi—all these suggest to us, as to Casca, a possibility of divine intervention in the human sphere. "Either there is a civil strife in heaven, /" Casca proposes, "Or else the world, too saucy with the gods, / Incenses them to send destruction" (I.iii.10-12). For Casca, the portents of the night before the planned assassination of Caesar demand a religious explanation. The problem, as it so often is in Shakespeare's Roman plays, is that the pagan religion itself offers no answer: either the pagan heavens are another Rome, torn by civil war, and the portents a sign of that disturbance, or the gods are indeed offering to punish the "saucy" world. Whatever is the case, "I believe they are portentous things," Casca continues. His companion, the cool and sceptical Cicero, fails to follow along: "Indeed it is a strange disposed time," he agrees, "But men may construe things after their fashion, / Clean from the purpose of the things themselves" (31.34-35). Shakespeare's play pursues this observation, as Brutus's and Cassius's construction of the thing—the phenomenon of Caesar—collides with the thing itself.

The metaphor that informs *Julius Caesar's* scrutiny of "Providentialism" is the conventional one of the *theatrum mundi:* the role Cassius casts Brutus in, the role Brutus envisions himself playing in history, the part the conspirators see Marc Antony as playing at Caesar's funeral are all miscast and misconceived. Strindberg, in ***Gustav III*** (1902), employs the same image and to much the same effect. For both playwrights, the theater of the world provides a double perspective from which to regard human action in history. The image provides a way in which history can become charged with meaning, as man the actor plays out his role before the all-seeing eye of God. No detail is missed, for divine justice watches every aspect of every performance. Such an argument informs eighteenth-century defenses of the theater, where representations of "poetic justice," embodying the judgments of Providence, could be said to be more "accurate" (as Thomas Rymer put it) than representations of the actual events of history, which would be morally less clear (22). Yet the image of the theater of the world cuts another way as well: the Platonic antitheatrical tradition, rejecting all representation as dangerously false, sees man the actor as self-deluded, his actions trivialized and made meaningless by their analogy to the world of the stage.

Explanation of portents and omens with reference to the divine, as Cicero makes clear, involves the imaginative determination that strange weather must contain some sort of meaning; it is easy to reject Casca's response as superstitious. And because Casca himself cannot decide if the omens portend the action of divine retribution or merely indicate a random spill-over of divine "civil strife," we can easily be skeptical of his construction. Less easy to dismiss is the conspirators' vision of themselves as actors: "How many ages hence / Shall this our lofty scene be acted over / In states unborn and accents yet unknown!" exclaims Cassius as he stoops to wash his hands in Caesar's blood (III.i.111-13). The statement is prophetic, yet utterly misconstrued, for these men would never "be called / The men that gave their country liberty" (117-18), at least not on the English stage, in the specific state unborn that Shakespeare's audience would inhabit.

But the audience's relationship to the characters' interpretations of the events they participate in is not simply one of anachronistic superiority. "I think it is the weakness of my eyes," Brutus declares when he sees the ghost of Caesar, "That shapes this monstrous apparition" (IV.iii.276-77). The audience would agree, but that we see it, too. "You know I held Epicurus strong / And his opinion," Cassius confesses to Messala at the end; "Now I change my mind / And partly credit things that do presage" (V.i.77-78). "Partly credit": there's the rub. Only history—in the ironic fulfillments of the prophecies staged here—lends meaning to the "things themselves." But history itself is an imaginatively constructed narrative, conveying meaning as it simultaneously conveys artificiality.

Julius Caesar brings the issue of historical imagination to the forefront. The question of whether Caesar's assassination is just is absorbed into the larger question of whether Rome exists in a context in which divine retribution can take place or whether Rome's civil wars are merely a reflection of a random universe. Strindberg's profound attraction to *Julius Caesar* is an acknowledgement of a shared recognition of the urgency with which Providentialism leads to this larger question. The system of reference to *Julius Caesar* and to Corneille's *Cinna* (1640) in ***Gustav III*** places Strindberg's play solidly within the tradition of *theatrum mundi;* the play's vision of history privileges a Shakespearean Providentialism over a Corneillian glorification of the individual will. Gustav's actions are thus seen as deluded, his prophecies ironically fulfilled; but his humiliations lead to the corollary recognition, for an audience, that the world is not random. History is a meaningful progression; by moving in the wrong direction, Gustav confirms for us that a direction does exist.

Like Shakespeare, Strindberg charges his dramatized history with meaning through the use of prophetic omens and through invocation of the *theatrum mundi* image. They fuse in a densely allusive passage in the third act, when Gustav interrupts the meeting of the conspirators at the home of Clas Horn. "Soyons ami, Cinna, c'est moi qui t'en convie," he declaims upon his entrance (39:353). The quotation from Corneille's *Cinna* (V.i. 1701) is both metatheatrical and charged with historical irony. Gustav quotes from the scene in which Auguste confronts Cinna with his knowledge that Cinna has conspired to assassinate him: in Corneille's play, the emperor overcomes the conspirator with his clemency and persuades him to yield. Playing Auguste in this scene, Gustav thus informs the would-be assassins of his knowledge of their schemes and suggests that clemency would greet confession. "Pour être plus qu'un roi, tu te crois quelque chose," responds Baron Pechlin. Pechlin quotes from a different scene altogether (III.iv.990). His line is spoken by Émilie to Cinna; she showers him with scorn after his decision, earlier in the play, not to kill Auguste. Cinna's claim that a mere Roman citizen is greater than a king wins her contempt. There is a gender shift here, too. Pechlin, by speaking the lines of Cinna's lover, challenges his Roman, antimonarchical values, and—by extension—his manhood. "Prends un siège, Cinna," continues Gustav, reverting to Corneille's fifth act (V.i.1425). If we recall, as Strindberg must have, that the role Gustav III played in court performances of *Cinna* was the title role, not the role of the emperor Auguste, the ironies multiply (Levertin 71).

The struggle for mastery in this scene is a struggle to control the range of allusion. Strindberg's Gustav, casting himself in the role of the clement and wise Auguste, attributes to himself a Corneillian ethic of self-mastery. Through the first two acts of the play, Gustav has been presented as controlling events through masquerade and imposture. The men at Holmberg's bookstore have been duped by false reports of the king's defeats; in the second act, when we first see Gustav, he skillfully adapts his behavior to each of his visitors with the aid of a mirror. He sets out at the end of that act to solve his political problems by dressing in traditional costume and rallying the Dalesmen to his support, as his ancestor Gustav Vasa had done.

The rivalry in the third act between Gustav and Pechlin for control over Corneille's text ends in Gustav's confusion and discomfiture, which mark the turning point of the play. Gustav suddenly feels a disturbing presence and asks if there might be a cat in the room. Anckarström, who left the scene to hide on the veranda when Gustav entered, intrudes upon the king's consciousness as a vague sense of foreboding. The conspirators make explicit the threat he represents by suggesting that what Gustav senses might be the ghost of Göran Persson, advisor to the ill-fated Erik XIV. For an audience, the shudder of Gustav here is accompanied by a double irony, historical and metatheatrical. We recognize in Anckarström the assassin who will be successful—but not within the play itself—and so catch a glimpse of the historical future to which the play alludes. We also hear a reference to Strindberg's earlier historical play, *Erik XIV* (1899), with its powerful portrayal of another self-deluded monarch's fall. Finally, we must bear in mind Pechlin's characterization of Anckarström as "Brutus, brutal Brutus" (39:356), with its evocation of Shakespeare's *Julius Caesar.*

But the Brutus of *Julius Caesar* is himself encircled by the same multiple ironies of reference, historical and theatrical. "There was a Brutus once," Cassius reminds him, "that would have brooked / Th'eternal devil to keep his state in Rome / As easily as a king" (I.ii.159-61). Shakespeare's Brutus takes on the role of his great ancestor, the liberator of Rome from Tarquin's tyranny, only to find himself cast by Marc Antony's oration in the role of "honorable man," traitor to his benefactor. Civil war and parricide are the fruits of this assassination, not liberty. Corneille's Cinna, too, finds himself confronted with the historical irony of the two Brutuses—Lucius Junius the liberator and Marcus the parricide. Émilie insists that Cinna finish the work of Brutus and Cassius; Cinna recalls Brutus's hesitation on the brink of murder.

Behind the perplexity of models for Brutus in both plays lies a further confusion of models for Cinna. His problem in Corneille's play is one of choosing either to imitate Brutus or to serve Auguste. Strindberg, in linking Gustav with Corneille's Cinna, alludes to this choice. The error of casting, since Strindberg's Gustav takes the role of Auguste, while the historical Gustav is known to have taken the role of Cinna, compounds the perplexity. Pechlin, playing Émilie and shifting scenes, tries to manipulate Gustav into playing Cinna, a role that he rejects. Confusion about who is Cinna, furthermore, appears again to be a reference to Shakespeare's *Julius Caesar.* In a notorious case of mistaken identity, Cinna the poet is mistaken for Cinna the conspirator by the Roman mob and torn to pieces. Gustav's models extend beyond the two Brutuses to Cinna the poet and Cinna the conspirator. In Strindberg's play, Gustav is both a poet himself and a sponsor of poets, both a conspirator himself and the victim of conspirators.

Gustav, sticking to his goal of liberty and to his models, insists that he is a Brutus. But he does not recognize, as Strindberg does, the doubleness that this identification, like the identification with Cinna, implies. Gustav reminds his queen of his successful revolution, when he "spelade Brutus och störtade vadmals-Caesarna [Strindberg, 39:336]" ("played Brutus to those homespun Caesars"). Role reversal figures here as it does throughout Strindberg's characterization of Gustav, "full av motsägelser, en tragiker som spelar komedi i livet, en hjälte och en dansmästare, en envälde frihetsvän, en humanitetssträvare, en Frekrik den Stores, Josef II:s och Voltaires lärling [50:250]" ("full of contradictions, a tragedian who played comedy with his life; a hero and a dancing master; an absolutist who loved freedom; a fighter for human rights; a disciple of Frederick the Great, Joseph II, and Voltaire"). Gustav echoes Strindberg's paradoxical formulations in the second act of the play. "Jag är ju rabulisten, demokraten, den förste medborgaren i ett fritt land! Folkets man ock de förtrycktas försvarare! Jag är Rousseaus lärjunge . . . och Voltaires! Samhällsfördraget le Contrat Social är mitt evangelium, jag har det på mitt nattduksbord. Georg Washington är min vän! Franklin mitt ideal! Där har du mig! [39:314]" ("I'm the rabblerouser," he declares, "the democrat, the hater of the nobility, the first citizen of a free land! A man of the people, defender of the oppressed, I'm Rousseau's disciple . . . and Voltaire's. The social contract—*Le contrat social*—is my gospel, I keep it on my night table! George Washington is my friend, Franklin my ideal. There you have me!"). Like Shakespeare's Brutus, Strindberg's Gustav has cast himself in a role that history will not permit him to play. His self-proclamation here is of the same order as "I am Cinna the poet!"

The play concentrates on Gustav's self-contradictory policy of achieving liberal reform by re-establishing absolutism. Envisioning himself to be a Frederick the Great, the eighteenth century's perfect specimen of the enlightened despot, Gustav resents the free press that he himself liberated earlier and cruelly engineers the Schröderheim's divorce. Against a backdrop of an international drive towards liberation (Washington is elected, and the Bastille falls during the period of the play), Gustav institutes absolutist rule ("Vilken paradox! [39:376]" ["What a paradox"], his favorite, Armfelt, exclaims in the fourth act). Imagining himself to be an ideal of absolutist politics—Frederick or Corneille's Auguste—Strindberg's Gustav is lost in a hall of historically ironic mirrors.

"O, store Caesar, akta dig för Idus Martii [366]" ("Beware the Ides of March, Caesar"), Lady Schröderheim greets Gustav, when she appears costumed as the Fury Megaera in the *fête champêtre* of the final act. By quoting directly from Shakespeare's play, Strindberg adds a further dimension to the Soothsayer's line, even as he assigns the line to one of Gustav's victims, who now appears in vengeful guise. What Lady Schröderheim speaks is not merely prophecy, but one of the most famous prophecies in all of historical drama. Thus the line carries with it the full implications of Caesar's perilous blindness and reminds us of Shakespeare's urgent questioning of the nature of omens and prophecies. Like Caesar—Shakespeare's Caesar, not Corneille's Auguste, who with forethought and persuasion avoids assassination—Gustav believes what he chooses to believe and remains blind to the self-contradictory historical roles he asserts the freedom to play.

"Caesars lycka" ("Caesar's luck"), Gustav claims in the play's final moment, protects him; "Var det inte någon some hette Brutus? [Strindberg, 39:398]" ("Wasn't there

someone named Brutus?") asks the queen. Gustav's failure in historical understanding is highlighted by his failure to grasp the full context of his allusion. The scene both presages and postpones Gustav's doom, as the queen inadvertently blocks Anckarström's line of fire. Unaware of the assassin's presence, Gustav correctly envisions his situation as that of a king in a chess game, with the queen blocking the threat of checkmate: "Drottningen är den starkaste pjäsen i spelet," he jokes, "och har till uppgift att skydda kungen [398]" ("The queen is the most powerful piece in the game, and her function is protecting the king"). The reference to Strindberg's image of history in "Världshistoriens mystik" ("The Mysticism of World History") as "ett kolossalt schakparti av en ensam spelare som leder både witt och svart [54:353]" ("a colossal chess-game, with a solitary player moving both black and white") is clear. Gustav's absolutist goals are at odds with the current of history and will be wiped out, just as his assassin will eventually succeed. The only significant thing that can happen to a king in chess is that it can be checkmated.

But the image of the chess game, like the dense texture of self-fulfilling prophecy and omen in both *Gustav III* and *Julius Caesar*, points in two directions. In it, as in the image of *theatrum mundi*, human agency is belittled by analogy to the game, but there remains the further dimension of the solitary chessplayer. Like God in the *theatrum mundi*, this player is audience, playwright, and historian all in one. For both Strindberg and Shakespeare, human activity takes place in a grand arena. Nothing could be less like their vision than that of Corneille, whose Rome is haunted by no omens and whose Cinna and Émilie, learning their self-mastery from Auguste, master their vengeful passions at the end. "Men at some times are masters of their fates," Cassius urges; "The fault, dear Brutus, is not in our stars / But in ourselves that we are underlings" (I.ii.139-41). But the faults that are in Brutus and Cassius are most clearly marked by their illusion that they can master fate. Likewise, Strindberg's Gustav fails to recognize that the roles he adopts, like his policies, are self-contradictory. "Liberty," "freedom," the concepts to which Gustav pays lip-service as he engineers his absolutist coup, will prevail, although Anckarström's act, like Gustav's reforms, will be disastrous in the short run. The "conscious will" that directs Strindberg's history pushes towards individual rights and freedom from prejudice, ends that Gustav dimly intuits but cannot achieve. This Hegelian paradox—that of a deterministic universal movement of history towards individual human liberation—is at the heart of Strindberg's vision of history. The techniques of Shakespeare's dramatic historiography—misinterpreted omens, self-fulfilling prophecies, the image of the "world as stage"—permit Strindberg to examine not only the paradoxes of Gustav's personality and policies, but also the paradox of history itself.

Works Cited

Corneille, Pierre. Cinna, in *Théâtre Complet.*, Ed. Maurice Rat. Vol. 1. Paris: Garnier, 1966.

Levertin, Oskar. *Teater och drama under Gustaf III.* 2nd ed. Stockholm: Bonnier, 1911.

Rymer, Thomas. *The Critical Works of Thomas Rymer.* Ed. Curt A. Zimansky. New Haven: Yale UP, 1959.

Shakespeare, William. *Julius Caesar.* In *The Complete Works.* General ed. Alfred Harbage. Baltimore: Penguin, 1969.

Strindberg, August. *Samlade skrifter.* Ed. John Landquist. Vols. 39 (for *Gustav III*), 50 (for *Öppna brev till Intime Teatern*), and 54 (for "Världshistoriens mystik"). Stockholm: Bonnier, 1916, 1919, 1920. 55 vols. 1912-20.

SPÖKSONATEN (*THE GHOST SONATA*)

PRODUCTION REVIEW

Ron Jenkins (review date 17 June 2001)

SOURCE: Jenkins, Ron. "Letting Silence Speak of Anguish in Strindberg." *New York Times* (June 17, 2001): sec. 2, p. 5.

[*Below, Jenkins reviews a production of* The Ghost Sonata *performed at the National Theater in Oslo by the Royal Dramatic Theater of Sweden and directed by Ingmar Bergman.*]

"We are bound to each other by crimes and secrets and guilt," confesses one of the tormented characters in August Strindberg's *Ghost Sonata.* This web of anguish is a constant invisible presence throughout Ingmar Bergman's stark production of the Swedish play that opens on Wednesday at the Brooklyn Academy of Music. Although the characters often inhabit isolated areas of a mostly empty stage, their aching silences make it clear that they will never free themselves from the painful threads of memory that link them to one another's fates.

Seen at the National Theater in Oslo during a recent visit by the Royal Dramatic Theater of Sweden, *The Ghost Sonata* offers audiences a glimpse of Mr. Bergman's cinematic imagination grappling with the dramatic complexities of a Swedish playwright who was often viewed as mad: characters watch one another from odd angles of the stage, like voyeurs screening one another's most intimate actions through the distorted lenses of their longings. The five performances at the Harvey Theater at the academy—in Swedish with simultaneous translation through headsets—are part of an arrangement between the academy and the Royal Dramatic Theater of Sweden, known as Dramaten, which has already brought eight other Bergman productions to Brooklyn. The most recent was *The Image Makers* in 1999.

The central figure in Strindberg's story is Jacob Hummel, a bald, ghoulish old man who scurries across the stage on crutches like a four-legged insect stalking its prey. Even when he sits in his wheelchair at the center of the stage, Hummel's words are punctuated with audible intakes of breath that seem to suck the people around him closer to his venemous sphere of influence.

As interpreted by Mr. Bergman, Strindberg's plot unfolds according to an intricate geometry of pain. The fiancee who was jilted by Hummel when he was young sits knitting in a corner of the stage under the shadow of a relentlessly ticking grandfather clock. Time and sadness have left their marks on her wrinkled face, but she still waves like a flirtatious teenager whenever Hummel looks in her direction. In another corner, a gray-haired Colonel stares forlornly at a bare-breasted statue of his wife, Amelia, which captures her youthful beauty before she was seduced by Hummel (in revenge for the Colonel's illicit liaison with Hummel's fiancee) and gave birth to his child, a daughter that the Colonel has raised as if she were his own.

To underscore the poisoned feelings that connect all these characters, Mr. Bergman adds an ironic piece of stage business. A cleaning woman empties a chamber pot into a trap door below the stage, suggesting the presence of an underground sewer running beneath everyone's feet that feeds the subterranean fountain (beneath another trap door on the opposite side of the stage) from which a young student, whose father had been bankrupted by Hummel, took a drink in the play's opening moments. A beautiful milkmaid, who turns out to be the ghost of a girl murdered by Hummel, rinsed the student's eyes with water from the fountain, a prelude to his deeper involvement in Hummel's filthy affairs.

This is the fourth time that Mr. Bergman, who is 82, has directed *The Ghost Sonata,* a text that has often been criticized as unstageable. In 1924, when Eugene O'Neill chose the play as the inaugural production for his now legendary Provincetown Playhouse on Macdougal Street in Greenwich Village, the New York Times critic Alexander Woollcott dismissed its characters as "sickly phantasies" in "strange garb." For years after the play's premiere in 1907, even Strindberg's countrymen had a difficult time digesting a play in which metaphysical and physical realities coexist without regard for the rules of naturalism that prevailed in an era when the work of Henrik Ibsen dominated Europe's stages.

In 1941 Mr. Bergman's amateur staging of *The Ghost Sonata* marked the first time the play had been produced in Stockholm since its debut 34 years earlier.

While Mr. Bergman's reputation in America is based primarily on his films, he has enjoyed a distinguished career as a stage director throughout Europe, and the two playwrights he returns to most often are his fellow Scandinavians, Strindberg and Ibsen. He explained why in an interview quoted by the Bergman scholars Frederick J. Marker and Lisa Lone-Marker in their book *Ingmar Bergman: Four Decades in the Theater*. Speaking about his landmark 1982 production of Strindberg's *Miss Julie,* Mr. Bergman said: "To me, the most fascinating thing about Strindberg is that enormous awareness that everything in life, at every moment, is completely amoral, completely open. . . . With Ibsen you always have the feeling of limits, because Ibsen places them there himself. . . . He points the audience in the direction he wants it to go, closing doors, leaving no other alternatives. With Strindberg, as with Shakespeare, you always have the feeling that there are no such limits."

The director's admiration for Strindberg's free-spirited dramaturgy is linked to his affinity for the musicality of the playwright's language. "With Strindberg, you never run into difficulties," Mr. Bergman has noted, "because you can hear his way of breathing—you can feel his pulse rate—you know exactly how it's meant to work. Then all you have to do is recreate that rhythm."

Mr. Bergman's actors respond to the music of Strindberg's language not only with words but also with silences, gestures and extra-textual vocalizations. The most startling sounds come from the mouth of Gunnel Lindblom, an actress who has worked with Mr. Bergman over many years and who appeared in his films *The Seventh Seal* (1956), *The Virgin Spring* (1960) and *The Silence* (1963).

In *The Ghost Sonata,* Ms. Lindblom plays the aging Amelia, who has lived for 20 years in the dining room closet, wasting away into a caricature of the beauty her husband and Hummel still worship when they gaze at her statue. When she is in the closet, Amelia emits comic squawks and cackles like the family's oversized pet parrot—at one point she whistles a tune that sounds like an aria from "Carmen"—but her true nature is revealed when she emerges from behind the closet door to interrupt Hummel's romantic reverie with her statue. She wears a tattered gown the color of dried blood that seems to have deteriorated into a shroud of graying spider webs. At first her high-pitched squeals mock the amorous ravings of Hummel, who is caressing her statue unaware that the woman who was once the flesh and blood object of his desire is behind him. Then Amelia begins to coo, nestling her head against Hummel's chest like an attention-starved pigeon. But ultimately, overwhelmed by her anger at his betrayal, she shrieks and flails at him like a wild harpy.

The shifting tones in the battles between the sexes are matched by equally polyphonic and grotesque depictions of class warfare. Strindberg, who died in 1912, was obsessed with class distinctions and spoke often of the "slave blood" of his mother, an exaggerated reference to her lower-class background.

Orjan Ramberg's portrayal of Hummel's servant Johansson seems to be a model of slinky subservience in which he literally bends to every whim of his master, but in the end it is Johansson who straightens his spine and throws Hummel into the closet from which Amelia has escaped. Hummel's path to destruction is paved by the Colonel's butler, Bengtsson, another servant who shifts from a pretense of obedience to outright defiance. In one of Mr. Bergman's minor alterations of Strindberg's text, the director accentuates the theme of class warfare by having Bengtsson join the cook in laughing derisively at the daughter of their mistress and the student who is wooing her. "You sup on us while we sup on you," they jeer.

The family cook is the embodiment of what Strindberg called "psychic murder," a crime that recurs throughout the play as the leitmotif of Strindberg's theatrical sonata. A sort of culinary vampire, the cook sucks out the nourishment from the family's food before she feeds it to them, a variation on the technique by which the other characters suck the life out of one another by verbally stripping others of their identities. The most comical demonstration of this occurs when Hummel removes the Colonel's wig, false teeth and military jacket, reducing him to a shriveled-up babbling fraud. The opera buffo is repeated again in a tragic key when Hummel himself has the life sucked out of him after Amelia and Bengtsson reveal the truth about his past.

The Expressionistic techniques pioneered in Strindberg's *Ghost Sonata* helped set the stage for many 20th-century avant-garde theatrical movements, from the theater of the absurd to the theater of cruelty. Like *A Dream Play* (seen at the academy last November in a production by the Stockholm Stadsteater, directed, designed and lighted by Robert Wilson) and Strindberg's other so-called post-Inferno plays, *The Ghost Sonata* was written in 1907 after the author had suffered a series of psychotic incidents that left him unwilling to return to writing the naturalistic dramas that had made his reputation.

Instead, Strindberg wrote hallucinatory plays that offered a mix of psychological insight and mystical philosophy. (The working title for *The Ghost Sonata* was *Loka Kama*, a term used in Buddhist teachings to refer to an illusory "place of desire.") Strindberg believed that his metaphysical approach could reveal aspects of human nature that were more real than the ostensibly realistic plays championed by his contemporaries. In the program notes for the play's Provincetown Playhouse production, O'Neill called Strindberg's technique "hyper-naturalism" and hailed him as "the precursor of all modernity in our present theater."

Ibsen, sometimes viewed as the father of modern naturalistic drama, was obsessed with Strindberg, whose new style posed a challenge to his own. When Mr. Bergman's *Ghost Sonata* was in Oslo, the theater turned out to be only a few blocks from Ibsen's home. The Swedish actors went to visit the room where the Norwegian author wrote his last play in 1905 and told their guide that Mr. Bergman's next production would be a play by Ibsen. Hanging on the wall behind Ibsen's desk was a huge portrait of Strindberg that inspired Ibsen's famous assessment of his Swedish rival: "I can't write a word without that madman staring down at me with his insane eyes," a sentiment that would be shared by modern playwrights for decades.

PELIKANEN (*THE PELICAN*)

CRITICAL COMMENTARY

Paul Walsh (essay date 1988)

SOURCE: Walsh, Paul. "Textual Clues to Performance Strategies in *The Pelican.*" In *Strindberg's Dramaturgy,* edited by Göran Stockenström, pp. 330-41. Minneapolis: University of Minnesota Press, 1988.

[*In the following essay, Walsh remarks on the mixture of dramatic styles Strindberg used in* The Pelican.]

Despite its popularity in Scandinavia, *The Pelican* has been performed only rarely in the United States, and it has not attracted the kind of close critical attention given Strindberg's better known works. At first glance, the dramaturgical innovations in *The Pelican* strike one as slight compared, for example, with those in *The Ghost Sonata,* and the tone and tenor of the language, the catalog of mundane concerns, and the tangled skein of domestic relationships seem to reduce the play to a pathological melodrama about an unfortunately peculiar family. This was the reaction of the Stockholm critics to the premiere performance of *The Pelican* at the Intimate Theater. August Brunius, for example, wrote that although "the opening note of the play was interesting and, had it been carried out with energy, would have had a beautiful result," the play lacked "real conflicts, dramatic drive and power. The author foregrounds trivialities, an unending squabble over food and fuel." Sven Söderman found the play a depressing witness "to its author's inner brokenness" and "exclusively pathological" even in its strong scenes. Vera von Kraemer considered the question of food "the essential tragedy of the piece which functioned as incessantly pure parody."[1]

The critics of Strindberg's day were more intent on preserving distinct levels of representational style than are critics today. Consequently, they were baffled by the deliberate mixing of stylistic levels employed in the drama and chose to view its hyperbolic and symbolic domestic situations in relation to daily life—the referent usually postulated in realistic drama—rather than to the stylized and often exaggerated psychological states postulated as the referent in poetic tragedy. Thus, when judged by the standards of the conventional domestic *drame,* which had served as the basic organizing principle of the play, it was considered a pathological and grotesque testament to the author's obsession with trivialities. This initial assessment blinded critics to the dramaturgical innovations in the play—the deliberate mixing of stylistic levels, the conscious intensification of verbal and visual metaphors capable of intimating deeper significance, and the dual perspective achieved by the intentionally ambiguous parallel development of two carefully linked dramatic structures.

In the dramas of his naturalistic period, Strindberg had experimented with a dramaturgy based on surface action and psychological subtext. In the Chamber Plays he extended this experiment, focusing attention on the moments when surface and subtext change positions, while at the same time extending the subtext of the drama to include metaphysical resonances. In so doing, he shifted the weight of the drama away from the surface action to a second parallel action that intimates the presence of a metaphysical order operating beyond the physical action of the drama, although communicating and communicated through the same entanglements of domestic, mundane concerns.

The surface action of *The Pelican* moves forward with calculated precision, adhering as Ingvar Holm has demonstrated to Freytag's model of a "rising and falling action," which reaches its high point when Fredrick finds the posthumous letter from his father. The scenes that follow show the Mother humiliated as the children take their revenge, leading to a moment of recognition and the final catastrophe.[2] Parallel to this, however, is also a latent action in which the Mother is first tested and then punished by a power outside the realm of human control, which employs naturally explicable phenomena as agents. The compounding of two stories—the one a story of crime and retribution carried out by characters physically embodied by actors on the stage, and the other a story of guilt and punishment carried out not by physically embodied characters but by absent "powers" whose presence is made manifest in the stage properties and *mise en scène*—leads to inevitable and intentional ambiguities for actors and audience alike. The first story turns on the uncovering of a consciously concealed crime leading to externally motivated retribution; the second, on the internal recognition of unconscious guilt leading to a moment of reconciliation. That moment follows the catastrophe when Fredrick and Gerda are transported from the realistic scene onto a higher plane of spiritual enlightenment dramatized in the reverie of light and the talk of "summer holidays" beginning.[3]

The psychologically ambiguous motivations of the Mother are central to this parallel development and allow for the dramatic elaboration of the post-Inferno perspective in which "there are crimes and crimes." Without the surface action, and the suspense it affords, the more subtle structure would lose its dramatic intensity and theatrical viability, devolving into the florid poetic fantasies associated with the French symbolists of the 1890s and evident in the fragment *Toten-Insel,* which Strindberg set aside to write *The Pelican*.[4] It was to avoid such undramatic, overly significant flights of poetic fancy that Strindberg developed his theory of "new naturalism," elaborating in the Chamber Plays a new form to communicate his new perspectives on life.

Today we are better prepared to appreciate the deliberate mixing of representational levels in a play like *The Pelican* and the parallel development such mixing facilitates. On close examination, we see that the seemingly obsessional concern with mundane trivialities simultaneously serves as pivotal marker both to objectify the metaphysical dimension of this new perspective on life in concrete and familiar terms that can be realized on stage and to dematerialize these familiar and concrete objects into metaphoric vehicles for the metaphysical intimations associated with them in the text. Modern scholars generally agree that *The Pelican* shares central themes and motifs with the other Chamber Plays, among them the perception of the world as a "web of illusions and lies," the motif of sleepwalking in which psychological motivations are compounded by a reverie of escape into an idealized past, and a latent concern for the Swedenborgian settling of accounts.[5] As yet, however, the particular strategies for integrating these concerns and motifs into the drama and communicating them on the stage have not been examined, nor have the dramaturgical consequences of these strategies been appreciated.

Like the other Chamber Plays, *The Pelican* demands the audience divide its attention between plot and character on the one hand and the thematic development and tonal motifs on the other. To aid this shift in attention and to intensify the ambiguity generated by the parallel development of conflicting stories, both turning on the central character of the Mother, Strindberg has employed a number of textual markers to actors and audience alike, which can be read as deliberate clues to performance strategies.

Strindberg's own attention to stagecraft and the art of acting in the *Open Letters to the Intimate Theater* suggests that close critical attention to the markers and clues written into the text can prove valuable. Although it is perhaps premature to speak of a deliberate vocabulary of textual clues based predominantly on the evidence of a single text, the particular textual clues I examine here proved

valuable to the actors I worked with in a production of *The Pelican* at the University of Toronto in October 1982. Furthermore, they point with self-verifying consistency toward the explicit elucidation and elaboration of the dual movement in the drama outlined above and the dual perspective generated by it in the audience.

In his *Open Letters to the Intimate Theater,* Strindberg writes about the actor penetrating and "mastering the role."[6] He speculates that the actor becomes entranced, enters the role, and in fact becomes it, filling it from within with his own personality.[7] In the "Third Letter" he writes: "*Being* the character portrayed [*rollen*] intensively is to act well, but not so intensively that he forgets the 'punctuation'; then his acting becomes flat as a musical composition without nuances."[8] In the "First Letter" Strindberg cautioned the actors of the Intimate Theater not to slur over consonants and to pay particular attention to the internal rhythms of a speech, whether *legato* or *staccato*. Above all, the actors must remember they are "talking to an audience of many people whether . . . [they] want to or not."[9] The *legato* that Strindberg asks his actors to observe "means that all the words in the phrase steal after each other in rhythmic movement in keeping with one's breathing"; *staccato,* he says, "has its justified effect, as we know, when one is excited or angry and is gasping for breath."[10] It is my contention that the phrasing, rhythms, and stylistic alterations in *The Pelican* not only mark emotional nuances but also serve to underscore thematic transitions and juxtapositions that facilitate the shift of attention from plot and character to tonal and thematic development and back, while at the same time facilitating the elaboration of the parallel structure.

To illustrate the particular use Strindberg makes of textual markers in *The Pelican* and the integrating function they serve, I would like to examine closely a few selected segments in the drama, beginning with the opening of the third scene, which strikes me as particularly complex. In this brief exchange between mother and daughter, several themes from the first scene are compounded and reiterated in light of the expanded context supplied in the second scene. The segment is composed of nine elliptical sentences constituting three exchanges. In the first, the Mother asks if Gerda recognizes the music that is being played:

MOTHER:

> Do you recognize it?

GERDA:

> The waltz? Yes![11]

In the second exchange the Mother expands upon Gerda's curt answer, compounding her memory of the wedding and her hidden desires for Axel, which were exposed in the last part of scene 1 and in scene 2. The tone here suggests that of a dream as the Mother passes with unself-conscious ease from direct address to private reverie: "Your wedding waltz, which I danced right through to morning!" Gerda's response is again terse—"I?—where is Axel?"—but the elliptical progression of thought, marked in the text by the dash that separates the first and second sentence, is readily supplied by the audience from the information gleaned from the preceding scene. Knowing that Gerda has become aware of her mother's hidden desire for Axel, the audience follows Gerda's progression from the ambiguous personal pronoun to the accusatory, possibly cynical, and certainly direct question. The Mother's response—"How should I know?"—is psychologically ambiguous. It is either a direct evasion or a self-conscious denial that Gerda has penetrated the secret desire concealed in her momentary reverie. In Swedish the interrogative is contracted "Vaᵈ rör det mig?" (How should I know?), facilitating a *staccato* delivery that marks the heightened emotion of agitation or bewilderment. The ambiguity is partially resolved in Gerda's final response—"So! Quarrelled already?"—and the exchange of glances that fill the pause that follows it. Again this line is marked in Swedish by a contraction and ellision: "*Seså! Han I grälat redan?.*"

Recalling Strindberg's insistence that such contractions be avoided on stage, we can assume that here they are employed to mark a moment of particular intensity and significance. The final unanswered question reverberating in the pause is in fact a direct echo of the Mother's question to Axel in scene 1 where the audience learned from Axel that the wedding was "particularly successful," and that the Mother first cried and then "danced every dance" so that Gerda was "almost jealous" (229):

MOTHER:

What? Aren't you happy?

SON-IN-LAW:

Happy? Sure, what's that?

MOTHER:

So? Have you quarrelled already?

In Swedish, the moment is again introduced by a contracted interrogative (*Va?*) and intensified by Axel's dejected slang response. Axel then goes on to say that he and Gerda have done nothing but fight since the engagement began, calling into question his peculiarly truncated statement that the wedding was "particularly successful. Particularly" (229).

On further reflection, it is not only the line "Have you quarrelled already?" but the whole scene between Axel and the Mother that is echoed in the pause following the elliptical opening exchange of scene 3: the reverie called up in the Mother by mention of the wedding waltz; the question, "Where is Gerda?" (228), echoed in Gerda's question, "Where is Axel?"; Axel's dejected denunciation

of the possibility of happiness so carefully amplified and extended, revealed in the dialogue between Frederick and Gerda in scene 2 (244-47); and the Mother's dawning realization of her own entrapment. On a deeper level, the sense of déjà vu recorded in the exchange of glances during the pause reinforces the dramatic reversal of roles in the closing of scene 2 when Gerda invited Frederick and Axel into her kitchen for steak and sandwiches (257-58). Linking this reversal with the revelations of scene 1 compounds the pause with a sense of the settling of accounts as past moments and perceptions return to haunt the present.

On stage, I would suggest, this last sense is further intimated by the book Gerda is holding, which can be treated as a multivalent sign conjuring up the metaphysical themes associated with the inventory and the settling of accounts. In this way, the pause and the exchange of glances serve as a transitional marker into the subsequent dialogue about the cookbook, at which point the actors' and audience's associations with the book change. We know that Strindberg used such transformational strategies in *A Dream Play* and *The Ghost Sonata,* in which both stage properties and characters split, double, and multiply. Whereas there is no direct textual evidence or specific stage direction to suggest that the book be treated one moment as inventory ledger and the next as cookbook, or that Gerda one moment can embody the presence of the testing powers and the next the ethos of the revenging daughter such an interpretation underscores the implicit connection between the real inventory discussed in the opening scene, the inventory of crimes and recriminations dramatized in the surface action of the play, and the inventory of a soul's progress intimated in the latent structure. By writing into the drama text specific clues that mark segments where the surface and latent actions change positions, Strindberg allows the audience to follow the parallel development and encourages the dual perspective in which a thing is both itself and something else. At the same time, he draws the audience into an experience of the duality of human motivation and the multivalent nature of physical phenomena.

What is most surprising is that the subsequent dialogue about the cookbook proceeds as if the earlier exchange had not taken place. It is of course up to the actors to treat this earlier segment in such a way as to call its reality into question, marking the transition from one stylistic level to another, but Strindberg has given the actors sufficient clues for this and, in the transitional pause, has given the audience time to absorb the moment, catch its echoes, and carry the necessary associations into the subsequent dialogue.

In the Toronto production I chose to heighten the sense of dislocation in this segment and bring the metaphysical action deliberately to the surface by allowing the realistic tenor of the action to recede momentarily. This was marked in the *mise en scène* by increasing the intensity of the lighting. As the Mother danced the hypnotic wedding waltz, the actor playing the part of Gerda entered with book and pen, indicating gesturally the action of taking inventory of the contents of the room. When the Mother tried to extend her moment of internal reverie, she was confronted by a series of testing questions and accusations emanating not so much from the character Gerda as from the situation of inventory-taking. The truncated and abbreviated exchanges were deliberately phrased to echo the earlier moments in the drama to which they refer. At the end of the segment, the "powers" relinquished control of both Gerda and the Mother, with a demonic laugh emanating from the actor playing Gerda, after which the lighting changed back to what had been established as normal and the actor resumed her previous role. The pause served as a transitional marker between stylistically distinct levels of representation and as a pivotal point on which the actor playing the Mother could turn from internal reverie to characteristics associated with the Mother in the surface action, while the actor playing Gerda could turn from the embodiment of the testing powers to the character identified by the audience as Gerda.

The recapitulatory exchange at the beginning of scene 3 plays almost like a false start, ending with a showdown of unanswered questions. A similar exchange begins the play when Margret enters the sitting room already occupied by the Mother. Three times the Mother asks Margret to "Close the door please" (215). There is no indication in the text that Margret does. Instead she asks, "Is Madam alone?" to which the Mother responds by drawing attention to the "dreadful weather," and the Mother repeats her command. Only after the third repetition do the characters make contact and let the dialogue get under way.

As with the opening of scene 3, and throughout the play, the dialogue here can be psychologically explained and motivated, but the unsettling effect on the audience of the triple repetition and the disjointed *staccato* of unanswered questions cannot be denied. The ambiguity of dual perspectives is both deliberate and essential here as well. If the beginning of scene 3 serves as recapitulation, the opening of scene 1 serves as premonition, establishing the mood of enclosure, isolation, and nervous agitation that permeates the play. The abrupt shift from the repeated command to "Who is that playing?"—marked in the text by a dash—and Margret's apparently unconnected reference to the weather establish an unconscious link between the music, which only later we learn Fredrick plays to keep warm (216, 218), and the wind that invades the room twice, endowing both music and wind with an inexplicable sense of mystery while subtly and succinctly establishing the parameters of the room by the sounds that both surround and permeate it. The brief exchange serves further to indicate, and alert the audience to, the disjointed form of exposition employed in the play, which proceeds by intimation and the gathering of associations.

When a few lines later Margret asks why the Mother remains in the apartment where her husband died, she answers that the landlord will not let them move, nor can they so much as stir (216).[12] Here again a pause is used to indicate a transition in thought as the Mother's attention is drawn to the sofa: "Why did you take the cover off the red sofa?" On the surface the pause marks a change of focus; on a deeper level, however, it serves to underscore the preceding line, linking it with the subsequent one. The disjunction draws attention to the psychological thought process whereby the Mother associates her entrapment with the death of her husband. On the surface level of crime and retribution, the sofa, which later the Mother says "looks like a bloody butcher's block" (238), becomes a concrete symbolic reminder of her own part in her husband's death *and* of the possibility that she will be found out. On the metaphysical level, the sofa is not only a reminder but a scourge. The terrifying prospects of imprisonment that motivate the mother's hysterical denial of responsibility for the death of her husband later in the scene (239) are presaged here with the added ironic intimation that the Mother's fear of unjust imprisonment—that is, imprisonment outside the letter of the law—itself constitutes a prison for an act outside the letter of the law. While the Mother may be able to cover up her past actions, she cannot escape from their consequences. On the metaphysical level, both past actions and consequences are objectified in the room itself and its furnishings as items to be counted in the inventory. Again, the author's close attention to indicating within the rhythms and pauses of the text both surface motivations and latent metaphysical intimations, and the careful clues to actors and audience, establish implicit connections and associations without overweighing the realistic tenor of the scene. The room that the Mother had thought to take possession of at the death of her husband has in fact taken possession of her and holds her captive.

The mystical implications of this are subtly suggested in Margret's response, the naturalness of which is intruded upon by the pause that follows it: "I had to send it to be cleaned. (*Pause.*) Madam knows that, well, he drew his last breath on that sofa; but take it away then." (210). Margret, the chattering maid, functions on the metaphysical level as an agent of the testing "powers" that strive throughout the play to wake the Mother to consciousness. Here, as at the beginning of scene 3, the pause serves as a pivotal point on which the actor can turn from the embodiment of the testing "powers" to the realistically portrayed maid. It is Margret who has uncovered the sofa, the first in a long series of uncoverings; it is she, moreover, who has sent the cover to be cleaned. Her tasks as maid are at once realistic and endowed with metaphysical resonances.

The skill with which this opening scene is crafted ensures that, if the actors are conscious of the multiple levels of development, effect, and association here, these can be directly conjured up in the mind of the audience through only the most subtle accents on the part of the actors. The ambiguity of multiple messages is essential. The pauses and phrasing intimate the deeper significance and mark moments of stylistic transition, freeing the actors to respond naturally to the realistic flow of the scene. The pauses thus serve a dual function as pivotal points for the actors, marking the interchange of surface and latent actions, and as clues to the audience, indicating the psychological and metaphysical significance of the dialogue.

If we turn briefly to the other pauses in the opening dialogue, we see this strategy repeated. The pause that precedes Margret's suggestion that she light a fire echoes the unspoken accusation contained in her interjectory "Yes, yes . . . ," which had likewise prefaced her previous speech about the underdeveloped Gerda (217-18). Again the pause intensifies the transition, connecting the children's weakness and the money that cannot be accounted for with the unlit fire. The cold stove becomes another objectified accusation. At the same time, Margret's repeated interjection turns on and magnifies the psychological ambiguity of Margret's motivation, suggesting both that she has heard this all before and that she chooses to set aside the Mother's excuse for a more appropriate time and place.

On the metaphysical level, the repeated interjections mark the actual process of the inventory being taken while imputing into the scene a sense of testing as the unseen "powers," through the agency of Margret, offer the Mother the opportunity to recognize and acknowledge her guilt and its consequences. This last sense is further amplified in the next pause, following the Mother's admonition, "Watch yourself, Margret." (218). In the intervening lines Margret has stated her accusations more directly; the Mother responds first with nonchalance, then with a sense of dismissal, and last with agitation. At this point the progression is disrupted by a significantly ambiguous pause in which the Mother tries to locate a sound she has apparently heard from outside the room: "Is there someone out there?" Margret denies anyone is there, compounding the audience's momentary confusion and marking the haunting presence of the unidentified "power" hovering around the parameters of the room, presaged in the opening scene. This haunting presence, which gradually materializes out of the Mother's fear of punishment and her unacknowledged guilt, will remain ambiguously identified with both the dead husband and the benevolent "powers," aiding the simultaneous development of the surface action of crime and retribution and the parallel structure of testing and punishment, while subtly integrating the two.

The first pause after Fredrick's entrance, like those in the scene with the maid, is naturalistically motivated, as the stage direction indicates: Fredrick "pretends to read" (221). However, it follows the Son's verification of the chill in the room, calling up Margret's attempts to light a fire,

which had been similarly marked. Again the pause serves as a transitional pivot from the chill to the inventory and on the metaphysical level from "the death-like cold," which, Brian Rothwell writes, is "literally the past,"[13] to the settling of accounts. The precision with which the scene not only conjures up the chill in the room but links it with the metaphysical structure of the play, making both reverberate in the pause, identifies the cold not only as the past but as the haunting presence of the past in the present. Also prevalent is the chilling terror that, because palpably present in the furnishings and atmosphere of the room, the past will be found out. Here as elsewhere, the pause serves both to mark a transition and to draw connections on a level beneath the surface of the action.

The tone of profound exhaustion and the escape into a private reverie of dreams and memories, identified in the text with metaphors of sleepwalking, is marked by a similar series of textual clues, and connected implicitly with the profound sadness over the impossibility of happiness. This minor tonal motif, introduced in the initial exchange between the Mother and Axel, is amplified in the second scene between Gerda and Fredrick. "Are *you* happy?" (244), Fredrick asks, pausing after his declaration that he will never get married. "*Jaha!*" (Oh yes!) Gerda answers; "When one finally has what one has always wanted one is happy." A few lines later, after Fredrick has prompted Gerda to examine the facts of her situation—that Axel has gone off to a restaurant on their first evening home and that the honeymoon was cut short because Axel missed their Mother—he asks if Gerda "had a nice trip." "*Jaha!*" (245) she answers again, this time with less conviction, prompting Fredrick's compassionate "Poor Gerda." Later we learn that Axel struck her on their wedding night (254), a fact which Gerda tries both to cover up and to forget. On the psychological level, the revelation of that slap (Fredrick has apparently learned about it from the Mother, "who can use the telephone better than anyone" [245]), is intimated in the pauses that precede Fredrick's questions. On the metaphysical level, this discovery of Gerda's innermost secret intimates the eventual uncovering of all secrets, whether acknowledged or not. The complexity of this segment and its entangled exposition serve to implicate all the members of the household in the web of lies and illusions that is the world of the play. At the same time, Fredrick's simple statement of compassion—"Poor Gerda"—remains as a strikingly real moment of connection between brother and sister. This formula is repeated with growing intensity and frequency toward the end of the play; the phrase "poor mamma" appears four times in the closing reverie of the play after the Mother's death.

The mood of profound sadness and the compassion it generates is heightened and tied to the motif of sleepwalking when Gerda acknowledges that "the greatest pain" is to discover the emptiness of one's fondest happiness ("*den högsta lyckans intighet*") (247). Here too the statement is preceded by Fredrick's repetition of the phrase of compassion and interrupted by a signifying pause, and further marked by the substantive *lyckan* (happiness). This devastating admission follows Gerda's attempt to escape into a reverie of past memories: "Let me sleep!" The transition is marked in the text by a decelerating tempo and a three-part movement from direct address, through transitional impersonal pronoun, to a first-person present-tense recreation of a past moment: "Do you remember as a child . . . people called one evil if one spoke the truth. . . . You are so evil, they always said to me . . ." (246). Here as elsewhere in the drama, the escape into reverie is exposed by the presence of the other. Like the accusations physicalized in the furnishings of the room and in the intrusion of the outside power as wind and warning knocks, the moment of reverie brings the past palpably into the room as the actor physicalizes the moment recreated by the character from her memory.

In the foregoing analysis I have shown how Strindberg employs particular textual clues to mark important transitional segments in the drama where subtext surfaces and surface action recedes, or where past actions and motivations become palpably present on the stage, momentarily compounding the fictional present tense of the drama with the fictional past-made-present. I have shown how the interchange of surface and subtextual actions results in an alteration of stylistic levels of representation that integrates the tonal and thematic concerns of the drama into the surface action while intimating their deeper metaphysical resonances.

The most significant dramaturgical consequence of this experiment resides in the freedom it gives the dramatist to develop two contrary although parallel actions in the drama. The latent structure of testing and reconciliating can be seen to encircle the surface action of discovery and retribution; at the points where the surface action decelerates, the metaphysical process intensifies. Aware of the dramaturgical power of the suspense generated in the surface action, Strindberg carefully paces the intrusions into the room by the unseen "powers," whether represented scenographically (lights, sound, wind) or through the agency of one of the characters, so as not to interfere with the "rising and falling" pattern of the surface action. The deliberate ambiguity of contrary movements, like the deliberate mixing of stylistic levels and referents, enhances the peculiar sense of dislocation in the drama while allowing the latent metaphysical parallel action to change places with the surface action at carefully marked moments, enhancing the duality and otherworldliness of the dramatic experience.

I trust these few illustrations sufficiently suggest the parallel structure I have identified and confirm the internal integrity of the play and the function of the intentional mixing of representational styles. Further I hope these illustrations demonstrate the function of such textual clues as contractions, repetitions and pauses that serve as directives to both actors and audience, underscoring and amplifying the dynamic vision and shifting the perspective that informs the drama. Once these textual clues have been identified and explored, it remains for the actors and director to make them physically present on the stage. But without a doubt, the particular decisions and strategies that director and actors choose should not seek to resolve intentional ambiguities or ignore deliberate markers necessary for the shifting perspective demanded by the drama.

Notes

1. Quoted in Gunnar Ollén, *Strindbergs dramatik* (Stockholm: Radiotjänst, 1949), 33.

2. Ingvar Holm, *Drama på scen* (Stockholm: Bonniers, 1969), 180-81.

3. Brian Rothwell, "The Chamber Plays," in *Essays on Strindberg,* ed. Carl Reinhold Smedmark (Stockholm: Beckmans, 1966), 31, draws attention to the section "The Examination and Summer Holidays" in *En blå bok I* in which the fictional teacher describes how "the dissonances of life increase with the years" until one comes to live "more in memory than in the moment." This section of *En blå bok* elucidates both the psychological and the metaphysical processes explored in *The Pelican* and deserves fuller attention. Of particular importance here, however, is the metaphysical connection between testing and release, and the suggestion that this pattern of testing and release is a vital process of old age, when one has faith in an afterlife. This connection, indicated in the title of the section, is intensified in the closing line in which the "and" of the title is replaced by the stronger conjunction "with": "Examen med sommar lovet!" (Examination with summer holidays!). See *Samlade skrifter av August Strindberg,* 46, John Landquist (Stockholm: Bonniers, 1912-21), 247-48.

4. See Ollén, *Strindbergs dramatik,* 226-28. Ollén considers the discarded fragment, printed in *Samlade otryckta skrifter av August Strindberg* (Stockholm: Bonniers, 1918), 1:293-310, as "an introduction" to *The Pelican,* which, he suggests, traces the events on Earth following the burial of the main character in *Toten-Insel.* Martin Lamm, *Strindbergs dramer* (Stockholm: Bonniers 1926), 2:404, suggests that *The Pelican* represents an attempt by the author to rework in a new form the autobiographical material that had inspired *Toten-Insel.* Lamm does not, however, go on to examine how this new form allows the author to express the metaphysical convictions of *Toten-Insel* in a dramatic form that communicates both to the converted symbolist and to a wider public.

5. See, for example, Rothwell, "The Chamber Plays," 30-33; Evert Sprinchorn, *Strindberg as Dramatist* (New Haven: Yale University Press, 1982), 273; and

Egil Törnqvist's illuminating study "The Structure of *Pelikanen*" in *Strindbergs Dramen in Lichte neuerer Methodendiskussionen* (Basel: Helbing and Lichten-hahn, 1981), 69-81.

6. August Strindberg, *Open Letters to the Intimate Theater,* trans. Walter Johnson (Seattle: University of Washington Press, 1966), 26-27.

7. Ibid., 23.

8. Ibid., 132.

9. Ibid., 25.

10. Ibid., 27.

11. Strindberg, *Samlade skrifter* 45:259. All parenthetical page references in the text refer to this volume.

12. See Törnqvist, "The Structure of *Pelikanen*," 77, for a reading of the psychological and metaphysical connotations of this exchange. Törnqvist points out the existential character of the situation, which, he says, suggests "man's imprisonment in life, his awareness of his shortcomings and his concomitant fear of death." To this I would add the metaphysical intuitions of the link between testing and release suggested by the previously cited passage from *En blå bok I.*

13. Rothwell, "The Chamber Plays," 32.

ABU CASEMS TOFFLOR (*ABU CASEM'S SLIPPERS*)

CRITICAL COMMENTARY

Hans-Göran Ekman (essay date 1991)

SOURCE: Ekman, Hans-Göran. "*Abu Casems tofflor*: Strindberg's Worst Play?" In *Strindberg and Genre,* edited by Michael Robinson, pp. 188-99. Norvik Press, 1991.

[*In the following essay, Ekman critiques* Abu Casems tofflor.]

Strindberg criticism seems to agree on at least one point: that his 1908 *sagospel* (fairy tale) in five acts, *Abu Casems tofflor,* is the weakest of his published dramas.[1] In the final volume of his biography of Strindberg, Gunnar Brandell goes so far as to claim that it is the only one of Strindberg's plays that could have been written by someone else.[2]

My purpose here is not to proclaim *Abu Casems tofflor* a masterpiece out of sheer contrariness. However, I believe that it is unmistakably Strindbergian and as such of great interest to those who are also interested in Strindberg's personality.

Strindberg has for once generously recounted both the origins of this drama and the source of its theme. According to a letter of 8 September 1908 to Knut Michaelson at the Royal Theatre in Stockholm, he received the impulse to write a five-act *sagospel* when he attended a production of his *sagospel* from 1882, *Lycko-Pers resa,* at the Östermalm Theatre in spring 1907 with his daughter, Anne-Marie. As for the theme of the mean Abu Casem, the upright boy Soliman, and Suleika, the girl who hated men, Strindberg refers on the title page to *A Thousand and One Nights* and an unnamed French fairy tale.

This information should afford full knowledge of the genesis of the drama, and permit its interpretation according to the author's wishes, as a simple fairy tale inspired by simple fairy tales, with its prime objective the preaching of love and generosity. This doesn't sound very Strindbergian; nor is it the whole truth about the play.

In other words, there is a case for reacting with suspicion to the author's unusual readiness to account for the play's birth and its literary impulses. One naturally wonders if some personal conflict is once again involved, and if he is leading us astray.

The oriental setting provides a clue, so long as it is not associated exclusively with *A Thousand and One Nights*. It was not the first time that Strindberg had recourse to such a setting. In *Lycko-Pers resa* a wedding is celebrated in an oriental setting; the one-acter *Samum* with its decadent eroticism is set in an Arabian burial chamber; and the novel *Inferno* describes Strindberg's meeting with a woman at a masquerade, whose Eastern attire heightened her beauty and nearly drove him mad (SS 28, p. 29). We also know that a large part of Harriet Bosse's attraction for him was her Eastern looks, and when he wrote *Abu Casems tofflor,* his interest in the Orient was reflected in the rugs, fabrics and other materials with Eastern designs, with which he surrounded himself. A journalist from *Dagens Nyheter,* who visited him on 3 October 1908, reported that his room looked like a rajah's secret apartment. For some reason this setting suited his current frame of mind.

Abu Casems tofflor was written during the first days of September 1908,[3] hence shortly after Strindberg moved into Blå Tornet on 11 July 1908, after Harriet Bosse had exited from his private life and the even younger Fanny Falkner had made her entrance. The first time Strindberg saw the latter was at a rehearsal of *Herr Bengts hustru,* in which she was dressed in a page's costume.[4] Female clothes made a strong impression on Strindberg, who had a clear visual memory of how his three wives were dressed when he first saw them. Harriet Bosse was dressed as Puck in *A Midsummer Night's Dream,*[5] Frida Uhl was wearing a fatal green dress,[6] and he would recall Siri von Essen's blue veil[7] just as Dante remembered Beatrice's crimson dress in the *Vita nuova.*

Strindberg's interest in Fanny Falkner increased when they came to live in the same house, and the innocent relationship resulted in September 1909 in a short-lived engagement. Thus Strindberg was preoccupied with his love for this considerably younger woman at the time he was writing *Abu Casems tofflor,* and if the play is seen in this light, it is possible to discover a pattern that transforms the piece into something other than a simple fairy tale, and to see that no one but Strindberg could have written it.

Abu Casems tofflor was thus written by an adorer with a new faith in love but with his old reservations about sexuality intact. Fanny Falkner has affirmed that Strindberg's behaviour towards her was very gentlemanly: 'Han hade ju gått ett helt år och mer och tyckt om mig hela tiden . . . utan att på minsta sätt lägga sina känslor i dagen genom några intimiteter' (He had gone around liking me for a whole year and more without expressing his feelings at all in any kind of intimacy).[8] However, an attentive reading of *Abu Casems tofflor* reveals that Strindberg was in fact struggling with his sexual impulses in the play. He may have concealed them from Fanny Falkner, but they surface in his drama—in the form of a pair of troublesome slippers.

In my paper to the last Strindberg symposium in Seattle, I sought to demonstrate how Strindberg was clearly inclined to shoe and foot fetishism.[9] My point then was not to reveal another side of Strindberg's sexuality but rather to shed light on a characteristic that he made great use of as a dramatist. J. A. Uppvall pursues a similar line in his *August Strindberg. A Psychoanalytic Study* of 1920. Uppval's observations are made with reference to *En dåres försvarstal,*[10] but he fails to develop his theory by relating his observations to other texts, particularly the plays.

If we proceed from the assumption that shoes in Strindberg's work represent sexual impulses, and as such symbolize the 'low' side of life which he increasingly wishes to avoid, then Indra's Daughter's action at the end of *Ett drömspel* acquires great significance. She places her shoes on a fire, and this does not only mean that she is leaving the 'earthly'. Her gesture also symbolically expresses Strindberg's farewell to eroticism, the eroticism that played such a fatal part in his marriage to Harriet Bosse. And giving her this gesture to perform naturally means that Strindberg also wishes to see and hear Bosse take leave of eroticism in the same way, just as in the play *Kristina* from the same period, where the title role was also expressly written for his wife, Strindberg shows that he wishes her to renounce her ambitions. He makes Christina burn her crown, just as Indra's Daughter burns her shoes.

Eroticism does not, however, entirely vanish from Strindberg's life with the shoe-burning in *Ett drömspel.* Nor do shoes disappear from his works. The story *Taklagsöl,* which harks back to memories from a later period of his life with Harriet Bosse, ends with a man fleeing from an island where he is spending his summer holiday, having first thrown his wife's red slippers into a tree. The following summer the man returns, this time alone, only to see the slippers hanging obscenely in the tree-top: 'en flygande häxa med fötterna i vädret, tårna inåt; vinterns snö, regn och sol hade blekt dem, vridit dem vinda, fasliga att se på' ([it looked like] a witch in flight with her feet in the wind, her toes pointing inwards; the winter's snow, rain and sun had bleached them, twisted them, made them frightful to behold—SV 55, p. 49). And having been burnt in *Ett drömspel* and thrown into the air in *Taklagsöl,* shoes now resurface in *Abu Casems tofflor* where the principal character attempts to get rid of them in the same way as Strindberg, firstly by throwing them into a lake, then by burying them, and finally by burning them.

The curtain rises on the oriental setting of a Baghdad bazaar. On the left is Casem's perfume boutique, on the right the shoemaker's. Upstage is the entrance to the baths, in the centre a fountain. This looks like the simple setting for a fairy tale, but slightly more can be perceived if it is regarded in terms of Strindberg's erotic code. The shoemaker's is, of course, linked to sexuality, as is the perfume boutique. Casem sells rose oil, and roses and their scent play an important role in Strindberg's erotic associations. In his diary for 1908 until his first meeting with Fanny Falkner, roses often figure in connection with his telepathic relationship with Harriet Bosse: 'Hon söker mig nu med rosor i munnen, då jag står emot hennes eros' (Harriet seeks me now with roses in her mouth, when I resist her eros), he maintains on 13 June 1908, and there is a wealth of similar examples. Roses were the attribute of the steadfast cavalier in *Ett drömspel,* and it is clear from *Svanevit* that the rose, in contrast to the shoe, stands for an aesthetic and moral element in love which ennobles mankind: 'Rosen på bordet reser sig och öppnas. Styvmodrens och tärnornas ansikten belysas och få alla ett uttryck av skönhet, godhet och lycka' (The rose on the table rises and opens. The faces of the step-mother and the maidens are illuminated with an expression of beauty, goodness and joy—SS 36, p. 157).

In scenic terms, therefore, the shoemaker's represents the low side of love and the perfume boutique its nobility. I do not intend to read a sexual meaning into every object on stage, but naturally it is impossible not to interpret the fountain as a phallic symbol and the entrance to the baths as a symbol of the female sexual organ.

On the surface, what happens in the play is that Caliph Harun tests the mean Abu Casem by placing his tattered slippers outside his shop. Casem takes the bait, picks up the slippers, and immediately becomes a laughing stock. Street urchins run after him shouting 'Casems tofflor! Kom och se' (Casem's slippers, come and see!—SS 51, p. 112). Then the police chief appears and enters the baths, having taken off his slippers, as does Casem. The street urchins appear and kick away his slippers so that when Casem comes out of the baths, he sees only one pair of slippers, the police chief's, which he believes are a gift from his beautiful daughter, Suleika. Meanwhile Soliman, the shoemaker Hassan's son, returns after winning Casem's old slippers back from the street urchins. Casem is caught wearing the police chief's slippers and is led off stage. At the end of Act One, he realises that the slippers he has acquired only bring bad luck:

> Fördömda gåva, olycksgåva, tofflor I, som bringat mig oskyldige betala böter; nu kastar jag er ut i floden.

> (You damned slippers are an accursed gift, you caused me to be fined although I'm innocent; I'll throw you in the rive)

—p. 126

He cannot, however, get rid of them that easily. Two fishermen appear, unseen by Casem, with ripped nets and the slippers. They throw the slippers into his shop. The sound of breaking glass is heard as Casem's bottles of rose oil shatter. As the scene demonstrates, shoes and roses do not mix, just as twenty-five years earlier, in **Herr Bengts hustru,** Strindberg had employed another dualism to illustrate the discrepancy between realism and idealism: roast veal and roses.

In Act Two we meet the Prince, who is pining with love for Suleika. Due to a misunderstanding, however, she entertains suspicions about the opposite sex. The character of love in this act is platonic, and its symbolism requires some comment, though not before I have outlined the remainder of the action of a play that is generally ignored by even the most informed of Strindberg's critics. In Act Three we encounter Suleika and her father Abu Casem, who still believes that his slippers are lying at the bottom of the lake. They discuss Suleika's distrust of men. The Caliph enters and in a conversation with young Soliman he speaks highly of the elevated side of love as represented by Suleika. The lovesick Prince also appears. Towards the end of the act an ominous note is introduced when the fountain ceases to flow, for the fountain is associated with the ability to love. Casem says: 'Vad är det här? Fontänen stannat! Har källan sinat, eller drives spel av andra makter som förbannat när du välsignad älskog slog ihjäl!' (What is this? The fountain has stopped! Has the source dried up, or is it driven by other powers that have cursed when you killed blessed love!—p. 159). But he is at once presented with a more logical explanation: all the fountains in the town have run dry, and he believes that this is because his slippers have blocked a water pipe. (He is of course unaware that the fishermen have dragged them up.) The audience, on the other hand, is once again reminded of this at the end of the act when 'Apan synes ute på gatan med Casems tofflor' (The Monkey can be seen out in the street with Casem's slippers—p. 160).

Act Four begins with Casem burying the slippers, which he seems to have got back from the Monkey. No sooner has he done this, however, than the Monkey appears, digs them up again, and puts a coin in their place, causing Casem to be accused of burying treasure on illegal ground in the final act. The act ends when the Monkey takes the slippers and leaves (p. 168).

In the final act, Casem achieves redemption. We discover that his meanness stemmed from a desire to give his daughter a large dowry. He comes downstage and explains that he has now burnt the slippers: 'De äro brända ibland stadens sopor' (They are burnt amongst the refuse of the town—p. 175). However, the Monkey reappears, this time on Casem's roof, from where he throws the slippers at the Nurse, though without hitting her. The Caliph gets his slippers back and the Prince marries Suleika. Abu Casem's soul is set at rest and he arranges a feast for his daughter and her bridegroom. In the eyes of the audience, he has been transformed from a miserly slipper thief into a generous father.

Thus the slippers can be seen as a symbol of the sexual urge, and what is characteristic for them in the play is the obstinacy with which they keep reappearing, despite several attempts to get rid of them in water, earth and fire: just as in **Ett drömspel,** Strindberg seems consciously to have worked here with elemental symbolism.[11] To draw a parallel with the present, it could be maintained that Strindberg's use of these recalcitrant objects anticipates something that becomes a convention in the drama of the absurd.

The important thing about the slippers is to a great extent the way in which they are linked to the Monkey. In the list of characters the Monkey is unambiguously described as an 'evil spirit', and Soliman declares in Act Five: 'apan är ej något djur, det är en djävul!' (the monkey's no animal, it's a devil!—p. 172). In *En blå bok* it is easy to find evidence for Strindberg's dislike of monkeys. For example, in the article 'Tass eller hand' (Paw or Hand), they are called 'de sämsta av alla djur, bara gjorda av laster och brott' (the worst of all animals, consisting only of vices and crimes—SS 46, p. 301). Strindberg's dislike of monkeys stems, of course, from his distrust of Darwinism. Or it may be the other way round: the thought that the monkey could be his ancestor makes him reject Darwinism. In the play, the Monkey is made to symbolize the animal side of man. Its interest in the slippers therefore appears entirely logical.

It has been argued that *Abu Casems tofflor* is about two kinds of love: the sublime, as represented by the Prince and Suleika, and the physical, as represented by the Monkey, and it is into the latter sphere that Abu Casem is drawn when he becomes interested in slippers instead of rose oil. And it is the Monkey who is the real schemer in the play: this is clear from a stage direction where the Vizier gets the fatal idea of placing his slippers outside Casem's shop: 'Apan synes här och spelar som om han ingav de andra tankarna' (The Monkey can be seen here acting as if he inspired the others' thoughts—p. 107).

During the Prince's languishing soliloquy on love in Act Two, the Monkey is occasionally visible, but outside the window. In Act Three, set in Suleika's rooms, it is clearly present and turns off the tap to stop the water in the fountain. When the shoemaker Hassan enters, the Monkey hides and listens, grimacing. The shoemaker measures Suleika's feet, and an awareness of Strindberg's particular view of feet, his erotic code, is undoubtedly necessary for this scene to be meaningful:

> Se här min fot, tag måttet nätt,
> din marockin den ger sig ut i fukten—
> *Hassan kittlar henne under foten . . . Apan härmar*
> *Hassan; tar*
> *mått på Ali, Slavinnan och slutligen på Hassan.*

> (Here is my foot, measure it neatly,
> your moccasin will be going out in the wet—
> *Hassan tickles the soles of her feet . . . The Monkey*
> *imitates*
> *Hassan; measures Ali, the Slave Girl, and finally*
> *Hassan)*

—p. 150

In the same act, Soliman comes upon the Monkey in a scene in which the two kinds of love confront each other:

> *Apan härmar en kärlekssjuk.*
> SOLIMAN (*slår honom en örfil och sätter käringknep för*
> *honom*):
> Respekt, din hund! Där mänskohjärtat talar,
> där tige djuret!

> *The Monkey imitates a lovesick man.*
> SOLIMAN (*boxes him on the ear and trips him up*):
> Respect, you dog! When the human heart speaks,
> the animal remains silent!

—p. 156

In Act Four, it is the Monkey that digs up the slippers and then informs on Casem in sign language. Being a monkey he has to mime, but we also know that Strindberg's key scenes in his post-Inferno dramas (for example in *Till Damaskus, Ett drömspel, Dödsdansen,* and *Svarta handsken*) are often dumb shows.

Strindberg has thus given the Monkey a substantial if silent role in the play. It is clear from the original manuscript that this role became increasingly important:

on several occasions Strindberg enlarged the Monkey's part, inserting additions in the margin.[12] The Monkey directs people's destinies not as fate but as an evil power. It seems to embody the lower side of man and largely acts in a world of instinct; it is hardly evil in a metaphysical sense. It is clearly coupled in the play with footwear, which in Strindberg's works is generally a symbol of sexuality. On its final appearance, the Monkey is seated on the roof, throwing the slippers at the Nurse:

VEZIREN:

> Se där, se apan, mördarn, och se tofflorna!

CASEM:

> O ve! Den olycksgåvan lever än?

(THE VIZIER:

> Look, there's the monkey, the murderer, and the slippers!

CASEM:

> Alas! The gift of ill-omen lives on?)

—p. 177

The gift of ill-omen (the slippers, or sexuality) is regained at the end of the play by the Caliph, which is a prerequisite for its happy ending.

One further passage may be quoted in support of the theory that shoes and slippers articulate the secret desires of the subconscious. In Act Two the Nurse comes to the Prince with a letter she claims has been written by Suleika. The Prince is not completely awake and associates freely around the object that he, half-asleep, sees, and which is in fact a large white letter with a red and green seal:

> Vad ser jag nu i mörkret, vad?
> En ruta vit som golvets marmor,
> där liten fot i röda skor, nej gröna,
> det är båd rött och grönt,
> och det betyder kärlek, hopp!

> (What is it I see in the darkness? A white square, like
> a
> marble floor, there a little foot in red shoes, no, green,
> both
> red and green, and that means love and hope!)

—p. 131

The Prince's first and slightly far-fetched association (if one is unaware of Strindberg's erotic code) is a pair of shoes. Before he finally recognizes the letter as a letter he has two further associations: 'en duk, en vit, nej, det är ingen duk . . . *Reser sig* . . . att torka tårar med, en svetteduk det är, att hölja likets anlet när som den döde dödens ångest har bestått—den är för mig, ty jag är visserligen död!' (A handkerchief, a white, no, it's not a handkerchief

. . . He gets up . . . with which to dry tears, it's a shroud to cover a corpse's face when the agony of death remains, like the dead—it's for me, since I am surely dead!—p. 132)

These associations are also interesting. Following the shoes, he sees things that recall the symbols of suffering in *Ett drömspel* and *Påsk.* Both Elis' winter coat in *Påsk* and the Concierge's shawl in *Ett drömspel* function as a shroud.[13] In a sketch for the staging of *Till Damaskus* in 1908, Strindberg expressly related the Lady's embroidery to Veronica's shroud.[14] This is one of the motifs that preoccupied him in the early years of the century, and is coupled with the idea of a '*satisfactio vicaria*'. In the dream sequence in *Abu Casems tofflor,* in which Strindberg probably gave his own associations free rein, the shoe is confronted with the shroud, love with sorrow, in images of great relevance, at least for Strindberg himself. The problem with this private symbolism is that it generally fails to find its way over the footlights. In other words, it is inaccessible to semiotic analysis, and requires some sort of psychological analysis.

In no other Strindberg play is footwear given such a clearly defined role as in *Abu Casems tofflor;* it is, after all, named in the title. Strindberg could afford to do this since he was able to maintain that the plot was borrowed from a given source, and had not risen spontaneously out of his own, inner self. It is in fact a case of a story which Strindberg had known for a long time. Amongst the books that he left behind in Sweden in 1883 was S. A. Hägg's *Fotbeklädnadens, skomakeriets och namnkunniga skomakares historia från äldsta till närvarande tid* (The History of Footwear, Shoemaking and Celebrated Shoemakers, Past and Present, 1873).[15] This lavishly illustrated history of shoes relates the story of Abu Casem from *A Thousand and One Nights,* as does a German grammar with which Strindberg was also familiar,[16] but in retelling it, he alters and adds to it. In the original version, Abu Casem owns the slippers from the beginning; the action does not have the character of a test, nor does he have to return the slippers to anyone. In the story, Abu Casem also twice throws the slippers into water. The first time, as in Strindberg's play, the fishermen emerge with their damaged nets, but the second time the slippers get stuck in a pipe, causing the town's water supply to be cut off. Strindberg only retains the latter, as something ominous and associated with the ability to love. The Monkey is almost totally Strindberg's invention. A dog makes a brief appearance in the story, dropping the slippers from a roof as does the Monkey in the play, but Strindberg not only changes the dog into a monkey, he also substantially increases its role while the story of Suleika, the Prince and Soliman is taken from other sources. Nevertheless, it is the history of a pair of slippers that inspires him to write this play about the way in which base, animal love is vanquished by sublime love.

The play was sent to the Royal Theatre on 8 September 1908. The theatre took time replying so on the 16th Strindberg promised it to August Falck and the Intimate Theatre if the Royal Theatre would release it, which eventually they did. Towards the end of the month he showered Falck with letters, which indicated his eagerness to get the play staged. He told Falck that he had purchased some expensive oriental fabrics and wished to be present at its casting, and recommended several shops in Stockholm, such as the Oriental Shop and the Indian Bazaar, for the purchase of properties.

It is clear from Falck's account that opinions differed as to the play's quality: 'Jag tyckte aldrig att Abu Casems tofflor var lämplig för Intiman. Trots Strindbergs olika uppsättningsförslag var den svår att sätta i scen; var gång jag kom med en invändning gjorde han ivrigt ett nytt förslag, men när jag till slut i svaga ögonblick var på väg att ge med mig, var det han som ångrade sig' (I never thought that *Abu Casems tofflor* was suitable for the Intimate Theatre. Despite Strindberg's various suggestions about staging, it was difficult to put on; every time I made an objection, he eagerly made a new proposal, but when I finally weakened and was on the point of giving in, it was he who had misgivings).[18] But Strindberg was also in two minds about the play. 'Lägg undan Casem! Jag är rädd för den!' (Put Casem aside! I'm afraid of it), he wrote, on 4 January 1909 while after rereading it he observed, on the 17th: 'Då jag läste Casem om i kväll, fann jag ingen sak mot den!' (When I reread Casem this evening, I could find nothing against it). The play was never performed at the Intimate Theatre. The fact that Falck regarded it coolly and that Strindberg was in two minds was a poor starting point for a successful production, though towards the end of 1909, Strindberg did renew his efforts, though again to no avail. In any case, by then Karin Swanström had given the play its Swedish première at Gävle, on 28 December 1908.[19] It toured the country under her direction and earned its author 2,000 kronor, which he spent (if Falck may be believed) on a new decor for Blå Tornet.[20] The oriental adventure was over.

But as with all stories, we are bound to ask: 'What happened next?' Are shoes finished with in Strindberg's works? The answer is that they surface one last time, but with a new function, in *Svarta handsken.* Strindberg initially gave this play the appropriate subtitle 'Lyrisk fantasi (för scenen)' (Lyrical Fantasy (for the stage)—SS 45, p. 281) but then made it Opus 5 of the Chamber Plays, where it certainly does not belong. *Oväder, Brända tomten, Spöksonaten* and *Pelikanen* form a single unit due to their having been written in rapid succession. They also have a deeply misanthropic tone in common: this begins as melancholy in *Oväder* and ascends to a crescendo of total pessimism in *Pelikanen. Svarta handsken,* however, is more a morality play, ending happily on Christmas Eve itself, with a 'Tomte' blowing kisses to the mother and child. The first four plays were published in one volume in

1907 by Ljus. *Svarta handsken* was written a year and a half later, by which time Strindberg had written several other plays of a different nature, like *Bjälbojarlen* and *Siste riddaren*. He also undertook in his contract with Ljus to let them have the rights to any new chamber plays, and received an advance of 1,000 kronor.[21] It seems, therefore, that Strindberg's rechristening of his lyrical fantasy as Opus 5 was largely a result of his already having spent the advance. Both textual and factual criteria show that the play should not be counted one of the chamber plays. Strindberg's relationship to genres is complex and fascinating.

However designated, *Svarta handsken* is a play about redemption. It demonstrates that, in Strindberg's eyes, redemption can only occur once a woman has ceased to be a wife and lover and become solely a mother and/or daughter. Similarly, the woman must be brought to submission, and this can only happen once she has experienced loss. Perhaps Strindberg's grandest portrayal of this motif is to be found in the poem 'Chrysaëtos' (1902), which describes how a man loses his mind at the sight of his wife's coat in a cloakroom. A pair of galosches also figures in a draft of the poem.[22] This draft could, however, do equally well for *Svarta handsken* in which both items, coat and galosches, are to be found. The great difference is that in the play it is no longer a woman's garment but a little girl's. Strindberg has resolutely placed the woman in the man's role of the bereaved. She expresses her loss in the short second act in a long soliloquy but is otherwise silent in the presence of the lost child's garment; 'faller ner på knä vid stolen, och döljer ansiktet i den lilla barnkappan som hon smeker och kramar' (She falls to her knees by the chair and hides her face in the little child's coat which she caresses and embraces—p. 298). She also touches the child's galosches. Here, Strindberg gives the woman a taste of her own medicine. At the same time the old curator is sitting in an attic surrounded by mementos of his wedding. Strindberg himself preserved similar mementos.[23] What is happening here, if we compare it with his previous plays, is that clothes have ceased to be the objects of fetishism and become souvenirs. At this point, in Strindberg's penultimate play, the atmosphere becomes less dramatic and the tone more elegiac.

The theme of redemption can only resound fully once the woman has been given a new role, and it emerges as wholly appropriate that the woman in this play is the Curator's daughter. She is punished like a child. The Curator and the 'Tomte' act firstly as punishers, and then as forgiving fates. The demonic Monkey in *Abu Casems tofflor* has been replaced by kind old men. The function of shoes and other garments has been reworked, and their demonic power is past.

After completing both these plays, Strindberg proposed to Fanny Falkner in September 1909. The engagement was short-lived and the nature of their relationship remains mysterious. Fanny Falkner herself was most mystified by his strange engagement present. Strindberg gave her, to her great surprise, a pair of coarse, brown-striped sports socks, which he wished her to wear so that she would not freeze.

Notes

1. See for instance Martin Lamm, *Strindbergs dramer*, II (Stockholm, 1926), p. 422, and Sven Rinman, 'August Strindberg', in *Ny illustrerad svensk litteraturhistoria*, IV (Stockholm, 1967), pp. 136-137.

2. Gunnar Brandell, *Strindberg—ett författarliv*, IV (Stockholm, 1989), p. 360.

3. He had completed it by 7 September. See Gunnar Ollén, *Strindbergs dramatik* (Stockholm, 1982), p. 564.

4. Fanny Falkner, *August Strindberg i Blå Tornet* (Stockholm, 1921), p. 9.

5. Brandell, *Strindberg—ett författarliv*, IV, p. 144.

6. See August Strindberg, *Klostret*, ed. C.G. Bjurström (Stockholm, 1966), pp. 39-42, and Frida Strindberg, *Strindberg och hans andra hustru*, I (Stockholm, 1933), p. 117.

7. See the poem 'Segling' in *Dikter*, SS 13, p. 107.

8. Fanny Falkner, *Strindberg in Blå Tornet*, p. 101.

9. Hans-Göran Ekman, 'Strindberg's Use of Costume in *Carl XII* and *Christina*', manuscript. See also *Klädernas magi. En Strindbergsstudie* (Stockholm, 1991).

10. Axel Johan Uppvall, *August Strindberg. A Psychoanalytic Study with Special Reference to the Oedipus Complex* (Boston, 1920), pp. 71-72.

11. See Sven Delblanc, 'Ett drömspel', in *Stormhatten. Tre Strindbergsstudier (Stockholm, 1979)*, pp. 63-109.

12. Manuscript of *Abu Casems tofflor*, in Kungliga Biblioteket, Stockholm, pp. 4, 38, 40, 74.

13. SS 33, p. 39. Cf. Göran Stockenström, *Ismael i öknen. Strindberg som mystiker*, Acta Universitatis Upsaliensis: Historia Litterarum 5, (Uppsala, 1972) p. 532, n.109.

14. In a letter to August Falck, 26 September 1909. Kungliga Biblioteket, T 36:8.

15. See Hans Lindström, *Strindberg och böckerna*, Skrifter utgivna av Svenska litteratursällskapet 36 (Uppsala, 1977), p. 34.

16. See Gunnar Ollén's introduction to his edition of the play in Samlade Verk, forthcoming. Ollén points out that Strindberg's library contained both the German grammar, J. E. Lyth, *Tysk språklära*, 3rd ed, and an edition of *A Thousand and One Nights*.

17. Extracts from the letters are in August Falck, *Fem år med Strindberg* (Stockholm, 1935), pp. 187-189.

18. Falck, *Fem år med Strindberg,* p. 185.

19. Ollén, *Strindbergs dramatik,* p. 565.

20. Falck, *Fem år med Strindberg,* p. 187.

21. See Johan Svedjedal, 'Henrik Koppel, Ljus förlag och enkronasböckerna', *Samlaren,* 1988, pp. 21-22.

22. Kungliga Biblioteket, SgNM 8:9, 17.

23. See Strindberg's letter to Harriet Bosse, 3 May 1908, XVI, p. 289ff.

SVARTA HANDSKEN (THE BLACK GLOVE)

PRODUCTION REVIEW

Freddie Rokem (essay date 1993)

SOURCE: Rokem, Freddie. "*The Black Glove*: Wilhelm Carlsson's Production at the Dramaten, 1988." *Theatre Research International* 18, supplementary issue (1993): 24-36.

[*In the following essay, Rokem follows a production of* The Black Glove, *directed by Wilhem Carlsson and performed by the Royal Dramatic Theatre of Sweden, through rehearsals, noting changes and additions made by the director and cast to better frame the staging.*]

On 1 December 1987, the production team for Strindberg's last and least performed chamber play, **The Black Glove** (*Svarta Handsken*) written in 1909, had gathered in one of the rehearsal rooms at the Royal Dramatic Theatre (Dramaten) in Stockholm. Wilhelm Carlsson, the director of the performance, started by explaining to the producer, the scenographer, the dramaturg, the composer, the actors and the other members of the team who were present, as well as myself who was going to follow the rehearsals, all in all about twenty people,[2] that he had never directed Strindberg before, except for an exercise with **Miss Julie** during his training as a director at Dramatiska Institutet in Stockholm. His plan was then to present this much more frequently performed piece with an on-stage double bed and to have Kristin leave the room when the relations between Jean and Julie become intimate.

The Black Glove is a very different kind of play from **Miss Julie.** It has the quality of a fairy tale depicting the mysterious and seemingly disconnected events in a modern block of flats just before Christmas. At the centre of the play stands the trivial disappearance of a glove. But when a woman living in the house accuses one of her servants of theft, because one of her rings has also disappeared, supernatural forces in the shape of two figures, an angel and a puck-like spirit, what in Swedish is called a 'tomte', who can help the inhabitants in the house, but who also can, if they wish, disrupt their lives, are activated and take away her child as a form of retribution. The old man living on the top floor of the house, collector and naturalist, who in the end of the play turns out to be the woman's father, and another man, the janitor of the house, living in the cellar, help her to find the glove. And in the glove the lost ring is also found. When the woman regrets her unjust accusations, her child is returned again and they can all, except the old man who has passed away without being reunited to his lost child, celebrate Christmas in the right frame of mind.

The disappearance of the glove and the child, as well as several other seemingly trivial details, like the constant electricity failures in the house, are the scattered fragments of one single, almost cosmic, event, the fragments of which the characters themselves are not able to connect, but which the reader/spectator is supposed to see as one single whole. The play is written in verse and has a distinct lyrical quality, yet it is also firmly anchored in everyday realities. In its poetization of the technical modernities, like the elevator, it has an almost futuristic quality. There have been very few stagings of **The Black Glove** and Carlsson's production was the first at the Royal Dramatic Theatre in Stockholm.

Strindberg termed **The Black Glove,** 'Opus 5' among the chamber plays, but it is quite different from the other dramas belonging to this group, which express a much more sombre mood of recollection and in which death has almost completely taken over. In **Storm** (Opus 1) and **The Ghost Sonata** (Opus 3) old men, as in **The Black Glove,** also fail to be reunited with their daughters, but in these two plays the bitterness of the old men as a reaction to their loss is much stronger. In these plays there is no reconciliation as in the final outburst of Christian forgiveness which sets the final chord in **The Black Glove.** What this play has in common with the other chamber plays, though, is Strindberg's fascination with the modern block of flats as a microcosm where the modern technological forces are mysteriously united with different forms of mythic or supernatural forces which supposedly ruled the universe prior to these technical inventions and through them continue to do so.

In his presentation of **The Black Glove** for the members of the production team Carlsson stressed that the play presents a society where people are not able to meet or to confront each other. In such a world the supernatural forces simply take over and change the lives of the inhabitants in the house. What he wanted to show in the performance was the suddenness with which these changes take place. One moment there is anger, loss or mourning; the next, thanks to some magic intervention, everything is put in place again. His aim was to present and develop a theatrical form which concretized the apparent ease with which these changes took place through the intervention of the 'tomte' and the angel. This, he added, is a way to give expression to the inherent magic of the theatre where technology and transformation also have to be brought together into one single whole. Carlsson wanted to use the major theme of the play, the sudden transformations of everyday realities by the intevention of supernatural forces, to make a statement about the aesthetics of the theatre and the potentials of this art form to transform realities through some form of artistic magic and inspiration.

After exactly two months of rehearsals, on 30 January 1988, the performance premièred at Målarsalen, one of the smaller performance spaces at the theatre with a seating capacity of 150 spectators. The imagined bed from **Miss Julie** had now been replaced by an iron cradle placed at the very centre of the circular stage. This is where the young child sleeps and from which it is kidnapped by the Angel. During the rehearsals Carlsson's general intention 'to illuminate' the lives of the inhabitants in the modern block of flats was gradually given a concrete theatrical form. Most of the details of these intentions had been planned at the pre-production stage, but several significant ones were added during different stages of the rehcarsals. In this article, which is written a little more than four years after the production itself, I shall only present a few examples from the complex rehearsal process and their role in the finished performance. I shall, however, try to place these examples in the larger context of the director's work with the text, with the actors and with the production as a whole.

When Carlsson agreed to let me be present at the rehearsals of this production I had hoped not only to be able to make a detailed analysis of the performance, but also to examine more closely some of the principles informing the creative processes in an established theatrical institution. Several factors had led my interest in this direction. Most important was probably Wilhelm Carlsson's own background as the founder and director of the experimental group called Theatre Schahrazad which began in 1976, as part of the general rise of small independent or 'free' avant-garde theatres at that time, but which was forced to close due to lack of funds during the 1985-6 season. The work of this group, which in different ways had tried to develop and explore the basic principles of the theatrical process not only during the rehearsals but also in the communication with the spectators during the performance itself, had set a very high and sophisticated standard of theatre. The fact that Carlsson had started to work inside an institutional theatre like Dramaten, this being his second production there, raised a number of questions about the flow of ideas and aesthetic concepts between different kinds of institutions, about different kinds of working methods and above all about the place and role of these interactions in the theatrical and cultural milieux of Sweden in the late 1980s.

During the same year, 1987-8, I also followed the work of another Swedish director, Suzanne Osten, the founder of Unga Klara, a theatre, or, rather, a stage affiliated to the municipal theatre in Stockholm, as she directed a children's play called *The Aquarium of Toads* (*Paddakvariet*) written by the Swedish poet Eva Ström. Her whole working method with a losely defined group within the larger institution served as an additional and somewhat different example of the difficult balancing act between artistic experimentation and the relatively generous economic and technical resources of an established theatrical institution, compared at least, to the meagre flow of money allocated to the so-called 'free' theatres in Sweden during that time.

It is not yet possible to draw any definite conclusions with regard to how, in the long run, Carlsson and Osten have managed to balance their respective avant-garde temperaments and the 'necessities' of the free market economy to which the theatres in Sweden had to adjust during the late 1980s. I want to emphasize though that my examination and understanding of the work in the rehearsal room as well as on the stage when the productions were ready, was no doubt influenced by the general research questions I had raised concerning the complex interaction between experimentation and institutionalization. What I saw was that Osten continued to experiment and research during the rehearsals. She was able to guard the independent status of Unga Klara within the framework of the larger institution and her work with the actors on the text can in many ways be described as a continuing collective investigating process, still very much in the spirit of the group theatres.[3]

Carlsson, on the other hand, had no doubt adopted what could be considered as an experimental concept of how to play Strindberg, but the rehearsals themselves were primarily devoted to the application of this concept to working methods which were dictated by the institution, the Swedish National Theatre, and the way things have 'always' been done there. When a certain actor or actress had problems understanding or integrating the approach adopted by Carlsson, no real attempts to develop the artistic tools of their acting were made, and when such misunderstandings or conflicts arose, the rehearsals were mainly devoted to finding an acceptable compromise which was usually based on the initial concept of the director. This preliminary conclusion, drawn from my own observations and impressions during the rehearsals, does not imply that one of the productions was more interesting, or more experimental than the other, but relates directly to the application of experimental concepts within different kinds of established theatrical institutions.

The 'official' rehearsals of *The Black Glove* took place five days a week from 10.30 a.m. to 3 p.m. during the two winter months except for the Christmas and New Year's holidays. The 'work', in the larger sense of the word, was however not limited to these hours, and occupied much of the lunch and coffee breaks as well as other, more unconventional hours. But even if these discussions and consultations solved specific problems, the rehearsals themselves were mostly directed towards the minute realization of the fairly well planned conception of the finished performance.

Carlsson and the scenographer, Charles Koroly, had decided that the whole play was to be performed on a circular stage surrounded on all sides, except for the main entrance and two narrow stairways leading to the emergency exits, by two rows of benches for some 120 spectators. The stage and the seats were to be covered by a transparent roof turning the whole arena into a kind of compressed tower or light house, a cross between a circus and a greenhouse. This basic spatial arangement created what could be called a total setting which closed off the performance space completely from the somewhat larger room of Målarsalen.

According to the stage directions of Strindberg, who had basically written a play within the conventions of the realistic theatre, the first act of *The Black Glove* takes place in the staircase of a block of flats focusing on a door with a letterbox and a name plate in the background. The second act takes place in the hallway inside the door, the third in the Janitor's room in the basement, the fourth in a room in the loft where the Old Man lives and the fifth in the room of the child who was kidnapped from her mother and is returned at the end of the play. The play was written for a traditional proscenium stage where all the spectators view the stage frontally, with an end-on view of the stage. Carlsson/Koroly, however, had planned a production with only one setting for the whole performance. Because of the arena-shaped stage and auditorium, almost every spectator was going to see the performance from a different angle and the actors were going to be very close to the spectators at any given moment.

The metaphorical description of the block of flats as a 'Tower of Babel', repeated several times in Strindberg's play, was the notion which served as the point of departure for this transformation of the basic structure of the stage space. The educated Dramaten audience would no doubt also associate the tower on the stage with the house at Drottninggatan in Stockholm called 'The Blue Tower' where the Strindberg Museum is presently situated, and where Strindberg spent the last years of his life and wrote *The Black Glove*. The circular playing area was also intended to present the block of flats with its basically vertical organization of space, as it appears in the text and in reality, with one floor on top of the other, on a horizontal circular plane. This rearrangement of the 'lived-in' space

of separate units on top of each other, as in Strindberg's stage directions, to one single circular arena including both actors and spectators was basic to the concept which Carlsson wished to realize with his production of *The Black Glove*. When the conventional patterns of communication and privacy are disrupted by beaking down the walls as well as the floors/ceilings separating the different flats in the house a kind of chaos erupts which the characters have to cope with. As spectators we are perceiving the events from the point of view of the supernatural characters for whom no barriers exist when they enter the house.

Furthermore, the circular space where the actors are often present on the stage without playing an active part in the ongoing dialogue or action, which is usually not possible in realistic performance, creates many interesting possibilities for building up and structuring the mise en scene. The colour schemes chosen for the performance, ranging from yellow and brown used by the Old Man, the Janitor and the 'Tomte', black for the Woman and her two servants and white for the Angel added a dimension of variety to the constant movement on the stage. The idea behind the costumes was that each of the characters was to carry his 'home' with him or her in the clothes thus compensating for the fact that there is nothing in the fixed scenery to indicate where their home is. The Old Man also carried a box with his 'research' and the woman was always connected somehow with the cradle and these objects also helped to establish their respective homes in the otherwise neutral space.

In terms of the theatrical ideas guiding Wilhelm Carlsson in his work, as he explained during the first meeting with the production team, this spatial concept served as 'a challenge, a kind of additional resistance, which everyone has to pass through in order to elevate and emphasize the aesthetic dimension of the performance'. In his production of *The Black Glove,* he thus in many ways wanted to create a 'group' work based on the ideas he had developed during the Schahrazad years in productions like *Dr Dappertutto* (1981) and *Faustus* (1984), where important parts of the theatrical action were based on minutely directed 'mass-scenes' where all the actors participate even if the characters they represent are not directly involved in the stage action but are transformed into some kind of human backdrop which filled the stage with a constantly ongoing, sometimes even 'mechanical', movement. This concept of human movement on stage, which has been inspired by Meyerhold and perhaps also by the Bauhaus also influenced Carlsson's direction of *The Black Glove*.

The first day of rehearsals was devoted to finding concrete solutions or rather concrete ways of behaviour which would make it possible to confront the inherent contradictions between the circular scenic space where the performance would take place and the fictional space where the action of the play takes place, the block of flats. Carlsson explained that there would be a strong tension between most of the things the characters say and what the spectators see. This was one of the basic conventions which the performance wished to establish. When the Janitor is talking to the Old Man in the opening scene saying that he is going to climb the stairs to the attic in order to fix the electricity, we woud evidently see him moving horizontally, not climbing a staircase. 'This tension must not be shown with mimic illustrations of climbing', Carlsson emphasized several times, 'but rather with a kind of suggestion which totally ignores the contradiction and actually uses or employs the kind of "resistance" it gives rise to.'

Several times during the rehearsals, in the beginning as well as towards the very end, some of the actors doubted their capacity to cope with this tension. For others it was a challenge which they enthusiastically accepted. From the point of view of the director this way of working is connected with a theatrical aesthetics where the actor/actress is asked to 'pass through resistances' with his/her artistic instruments, the body and the mind. This 'resistance', in the positive as well as the negative sense of the word, was from the point of view of the actors most clearly felt when the supernatural creatures, the Angel and the Tomte, entered or were present on the stage. 'How is it possible not to see the "Tomte" when he is present in the room?' or 'How does an invisible creature move around in an apartment-house?' were some of the questions which had to be solved. Since the play tells a story about the intervention of supernatural creatures, their retribution and the grace they finally give the inhabitants of the house, the physical and psychological relations created between the two worlds, the natural/human world and the supernatural one, was of central importance to the inner life and meaning of the performance.

What was actually shown in the performance was that on the theatrical stage these two worlds can still interact even if the actors as well as the spectators no doubt believe that they are totally separated in the 'real' world outside of the theatre, if the supernatural world has any bearing at all on our lives. On the stage it is possible to 'play' with metaphysical belief systems to an extent which is probably unacceptable in any other context, except perhaps in a theological one. The supernatural figures in *The Black Glove* influence the lives of the inhabitants of the house directly, just like the Ghost of Hamlet's father, as well as a host of similar figures in Western drama, intervene in the material world. The meeting between two worlds, the natural/human and some form of supernaturality, seems to be a central aspect of theatrical fictionality and representation which I shall not analyse in detail here. It is necessary, however, to draw the attention to this aspect in connection with the performance I am analysing here.

In order to clarify these problems of theatrical representation from a more practical point of view Carlsson explained that he regarded *The Black Glove* as a mystery play where there is a heightened presence of each individual character, a kind of intensity, which also influences the power struggle which takes place in the house. This struggle leads to a total crisis in the social texture which in turn results in chaos, madness and death; the disappearance of the child, the despair of the young mother and the grief at the loss of her unknown and unrecognized father, the old naturalist living in the attic. Only when these forces have been totally integrated is it possible to create a new life and to find grace. All the characters, including the supernatural creatures, are drawn into this chaotic situation, and they all have to relate to each other in different ways at the same time as they must play the role which, in terms of the play, they have been assigned by fate. This conception of the play was realized by having many or even all of the characters present in the scenic room during most sequences even though some of them did not necessarily have an active role to play at that particular moment. This, of course, was a violation of the realistic conventions of the play as it was written where the intimacy of the drawing room supposedly protects those present on the stage from the threats of the outside world.

In order to make the description of the mise en scene as clear as possible I shall relate to the circular stage as the face of a clock. The audience entered the arena through a corrid or at 6 o'clock and this was also the point where the human characters made their entrances. This was the entrance floor. The top floor of the house, where the Old Man lived is situated at 12 o'clock. The 'Tomte' and the Angel made their first entrances through one of the staircases for the emergency exit, at 11 o'clock, which according to the spacial conventions developed in the performance, was from 'above'. When I place someone at a specific hour in my analysis I usually mean that this person is situated approximately one meter from the circumference of the circular stage.

The very first scene creates a problem. According to Strindberg's stage directions a glove is lying on the staircase floor. The Old Man sees the glove when he enters and picks it up with his stick. The spoken text starts when the Old Man asks a simple question directly relating to this glove, to which he provides his own answer:

> What is this?—A glove? Black, for a lady, size 6: it belongs to the woman in there, I can see that from the marks of the rings; left hand, two straight fingers and one with a diamond ring; a beautiful hand, but with a hard grip, a silky paw with sharp nails; I'll put it on the icebox so that the rightful owner can find it.[4]

> (SS 45, 283)

When this line is finished the Janitor, according to Strindberg's text, enters and when he has fixed the electricity he sees the glove on the icebox, takes care of it in order to put it in a place where it can be found.

In Strindberg's text the only two characters present in the opening scene are the Old Man and the Janitor, but Carlsson wanted to create a situation through which already before the Old Man started to say the words quoted above, we should get a sense of the complexity of the life in the house. Thus in the script for the production at Dramaten the first stage direction was changed so that immediately after the entrance, at 6 o'clock, of the Old Man, who was carrying a big box containing his papers and research materials, the Woman and her servant Kristin, carrying a large cradle, entered the circular arena in the same place. Thus, through the pantomimes of these entrances, the spectators were given a basic sense of how the house was organized. The two women quickly walked in front of the old man and arrived in the centre of the arena, where the mistress impatiently ordered her servant to put down the cradle in different places, where a bluish light suddenly lit up the floor for a short moment. This action was repeated three times until she was apparently satisfied and put down the cradle. She had found her home, which on the stage was situated slightly off-centre in the direction of 9 o'clock.

From the very beginning of the rehearsals the two women were told to follow the lights on the floor in order to find their home, signifying that they were in fact led by a force outside themselves which in some mysterious way was in charge of the lighting equipment in the theatre. This device, which emphasized the theatrical dimension of the world in which they lived, was also reinforced thematically by the play itself where the 'Tomte' has the ability to cause electricity failures, and as the rehearsals developed, so gradually was his relationship with the theatre lighting and this became an important aspect of the finished performance.

Carlsson's aim was to establish a sense of the 'life' in the house and he asked the Woman to show aggression towards the servant by her impatience and by making an aggressive movement with her hand when the servant wishes to kneel by the cradle, while the Old Man who passes by the apartment in the staircase supposedly hears the noises from behind the door. Only when this short pantomime between the two women had been completed was he supposed to find the glove on the floor and ask the question from the first lines of the text. When the rehearsals started the glove was placed at 4 o'clock, approximately one meter from the periphery of the circular arena. But this created a few problems which had to be solved. The glove had to be placed on the floor before the performance started, when the spectators entered the arena at 6 o'clock. But Carlsson was afraid that someone would pick it up thinking that a spectator had lost it.

When the solution to this problem was found the opening sequence of the performance, preceeding the entrance of the Old Man, had the following design: as the spectators entered the arena from the corridor leading to 6 o'cock the black glove was situated in the centre of the stage and it was illuminated by a spotlight. This would prevent us from thinking that it had been placed there by chance, and since it referred directly to the name of the performance it would even serve as a kind of trademark or emblem.

The performance itself started gradually. When all the spectators were seated a few indistinct clicking noises signifying the different activities in and of the house could be vaguely heard. Sometimes the spectators perceived that something was happening and became quiet, but mainly the usual pre-performance mumble continued. The stage action itself started very suddenly by having the 'Tomte' jump into the circular arena from the stairs at 11 o'clock. After inspecting the whole arena briefly he discovered the glove in the centre of the stage, picked it up and, made a movement with his hand through which the houselights were put out and placed the glove where the Old Man was very soon going to find it. By this brief introductory mime the 'Tomte' immediately became the ruler over the electricity, in the theatre as well as in the block of flats, and the machinery of the house and the theatre could start to revolve.

This was also the principle according to which the performance ended. After the enigmas had been solved and the child had been returned, the 'Tomte' appeared with a theatre spotlight in his hand, which had nothing to do with the stylized elements of the stage props, and directed it on the cradle in the centre of the stage. Where the lost glove was found by the 'Tomte' at the beginning of the performance, the returned child could now be found by its mother as it became magically illuminated by the theatre light. On the more general level this reflects how the whole performance, and perhaps even the theatre as an art, had illuminated the lives of the inhabitants of the house and the conflicts between them for a few short moments.

From the very beginning of the performance Carlsson wanted to establish the convention that there are connections between the different events in the house without having to point out the direct casual relationships between them. The 'failures' of the electricity, the appearance of the 'Tomte', as well as the aggression of the woman towards her servant and the glove with the ring which is lost and then found are two different aspects of the 'workings of the house'. We were supposed gradually to understand from the performance that the appearance of the supernatural creatures as well as the discovery of the family connections between the Woman and the Old Man, which they themselves were not even aware of until the very end, also belong to this machinery.

In the Dramaten production the opening speech of the Old Man, from which the last sentence, indicating that he would put the glove on the icebox, was cut out, emphasizing the convention of interconnectedness. The glove which, as he says, 'belongs to the Woman in there' (*därinne*) was now not directed towards the door of her flat, as Strindberg's text indicates, but pointed directly to her presence in the centre of the arena. And his comment, upon looking at the glove that the beautiful hand to which it belongs has 'a hard grip' and is 'a silky paw with sharp nails' had, in the performance, just been demonstrated by the woman's aggressive behaviour and by raising her hand as if to hit the servant. In a 'realistic' production we have to take his word for it; here, even before the old man comments on her behaviour, we have seen her 'hard grip' with our own eyes. The Old Man's comment created an additional interdependence between language, on the one hand, and behaviour and objects, on the other, which was developed on many levels of the production. One could even say that Wilhelm Carlsson brought out on the stage some of the things Strindberg had hidden behind the doors, just as he had wanted to bring out the bed on the stage in *Miss Julie*. The woman's aggressiveness was further emphasized when she discovered that she has lost her ring and actually slapped Kristin or when Ellen, the second servant, entered and she very forcefully searched her clothes and body for the lost ring without uttering a single word, very clearly humiliating her.

It is worth noting, however, how a director like Carlsson who started his directorial career with a firm belief in the autonomy of the human body as an artistic sign liberated from the linguistic features of communication in his production of *The Black Glove* takes a clear step in the direction of presenting a logocentric theatrical universe in which language points at the surrounding world through deixis. Deictic language or deixis, as Keir Elam observes, serves as a 'bridge' between gesture and speech, and it is perhaps the most direct and concrete way to establish a theatrical situation, a basic relationship between the actor and the space he is situated in as well as the concrete objects surrounding him through gesture and language. The semiotic polarity and division between language and gesture, which in certain aesthetic conceptions of the theatre, which Carlsson also had previously subscribed to, is made almost completely impossible by the opening words of this play. Strindberg's plays are very dense in terms of their use of deictic language. It is of course virtually impossible to find a drama without deictic language, but Strindberg's plays definitely deserve special attention in this respect. In *The Black Glove* every scene or sequence begins with some form of emphasized deixis which quickly establishes the dramatic situation and explains what is happening.

Except for the opening line of the play some other randomly chosen examples are the first line of the 'Tomte': 'Now I am sweeping'; or the first words of the woman in the play, towards the end of the third act, after her child has been kidnapped by the Angel: 'Where have I come? / And where am I? / Where did I come from? / Who am I?' The words of the 'Tomte' are very concrete and refer directly to the action he is engaged in and Carlsson decided that he should not be doing his sweeping with a brush. The words of the Woman are more complex because they show that as a result of the loss of her child she has lost contact with reality and, at this point in the performance, the stage was transformed into a dream landscape with cloud formations projected on the floor. Through this device, by literally placing the sky under the Woman, the directions in the fictional universe are further upset. In this upside-down landscape the behaviour of the Woman was clearly understood as a state of madness. The aesthetic-theatrical conception of the deictic situations in Carlsson's production served as a connecting link between the scenic and the fictional spaces which it was so important to create on the basis of the scenery used in this production.

Carlsson's choice of a non-realistic space, with no specific referentiality, made it possible radically to rearrange the scenic patterns of exits, entrances, and character presence on the stage in relation to Strindberg's own text. Instead of having the Woman briefly appear for the first time in the second act, immediately after she supposedly learns that her child has been taken away, she entered the stage at the very beginning of the Dramaten performance and remained on stage until the very end. The Old Man also remained on stage throughout the whole performance, while all the other characters were absent from the arena at certain points. In this manner Carlsson radically changed the sequence pattern of Strindberg's play through which the presence and/or absence of the characters on stage is regulated.

Strindberg sets the short second act in the hallway. The 'Tomte' is responsible for shutting down the electricity creating the darkness under the cover of which the child disappears. According to the original stage directions neither the characters in the play nor the spectators are supposed to see the actual disappearence of the child. While a piano from a neighbouring flat, according to the text can be heard playing 'Beethoven's Sonata 31, op. 110', which gradually changes into his funeral march, we see the Woman, who, as Strindberg indicates,

> listens and is caught by fear. There is a rattle in the icebox as when ice falls down. The cry of a child can be heard. The woman is struck by fear, but stops, petrified. There are bangings in a wall, the elevator shrieks, the surge of water in the waterpipe can be heard; human voices through the walls. Kristin enters. She is pale, her arms are uplifted, her hands folded together. She speaks unintelligible words to the Woman and rushes out. The Woman wants to run after her but she cannot—she falls to her knees and covers her face in a small children's coat which she pats and hugs.

(SS 45, 298)

After this dramatic series of events the curtain briefly falls. According to Strindberg we are only supposed to see the silent, pantomimic reaction to the disappearence of the child, while the event itself takes place, or rather has already taken place, somewhere else. In his version Carlsson radically changed this realistically oriented action and situated the kidnapping of the child in the very centre of the arena where the cradle had been for most of the time since the performance began.

According to Strindberg's text the Angel orders the 'Tomte' to punish the Woman for her pride with a short and sharp lesson which will make her behave with more compassion and understanding towards her servants (SS 45, 293). After that the Angel disappears and does not return until the very end of the play when everything has been put in order again. Carlsson kept the speech where the angel gives her orders (DT, 11),[6] and turned her into an active accomplice in carrying out the deed itself. The electricity failure initiated by the 'Tomte' which in the text is only mentioned as the cover for the disappearance of the child was for Carlsson the beginning of a series of events taking place on stage which led to the kidnapping as it was actually presented.

The third act, which follows directly after the Woman's dramatic reaction, presents a meeting between the Janitor and the Old Man in the basement. They are discussing various everyday matters without knowing anything about the tragic event which has just taken place. In the Dramaten performance the two men were seated at each end of the arena, the Janitor in the basement, at 6 o'clock, and the Old Man in the attic, at 12 o'clock, each one in his respective 'home' according to the conventions which had at this point been firmly established in the performance. After the short blackout signifying the electricity failure they light their lanterns and hold their discussion about their lives and about the wonders of the technology of modern housing—the elevator, the cold and warm water— over which the Janitor supposedly rules. He is of course not aware of the fact that the supreme rulers are actually the supernatural powers.

While this discussion took place the central area of the stage where the cradle had been placed was in darkness while the 'Tomte' was sneaking around it preparing for the kidnapping. Twice during the ongoing discussion, accompanied by strengthened sound effects which represented the gradual breakdown of the different 'machineries' of the house, he rocked the cradle and the Woman and her servants became very upset because they had no idea about the intervention of the supernatural powers to what to them seemed to be a regular electricity failure. While the atmosphere became more threatening the Woman suddenly took up her child, a piece of folded cloth in the performance, in order to give it and herself a sense of security, and when she felt more calm she put it back in the cradle.

There is a clear connection between the electricity of the house and the supernatural forces in Strindberg's text, but it was reinforced in the performance by the fact that while

we see how the 'Tomte' was performing his pranks the Old Man was at the same time praising the Janitor for his control over, what he calls the 'elements' of the house. And when the Janitor answered by saying that 'you honour me too much' (DT, 16) the 'Tomte' quickly blew out the candle of the old man, showing that it was he who was in charge, turned over the cradle and quickly spread out the cloth showing us, like a magician that the cloth is empty.

As this piece of magic was performed the Angel came running in from 6 o'clock with two burning swords. She placed one of the swords in a hole in the floor and she stuck the other into the first one so that they formed a burning cross. After she had made her 'signature' in this way she took the cloth from the 'Tomte' and ran triumphantly out again. The general pattern of this scene was worked out by Carlsson before the rehearsals started. During the rehearsals he made some minor cuts and rearrangements of Strindberg's text in order to emphasize the tensions between the more poetic or tranquil passages and the short intense sequences of almost hysterical panic.

When the Angel had disappeared with the child Kristin shouted: 'God help us!' (DT 16), a sentence which Carlsson added in his playtext, and immediately after that the Woman screamed 'My child!'. Her short exclamation does neither appear in Strindberg's text nor in Carlsson's original playtext and he added it during the rehearsals because it was felt that it was impossible for the Woman, if she is present, not to say anything as a reaction to her loss. This exclamation thus was her first verbal expression in the play. It was also basically deictic, since she had been guarding her child's cradle since the very beginning of the performance, but ironically she only said it when the child was no longer there.

This central scene in the performance emphasized the complex workings on all levels of the house, the human, the supernatural as well as the technological, and how intimately they are actually connected. This sense of interdependence and organic unity between the different worlds was probably the most significant aspect of Carlsson's production of *The Black Glove,* and it was the direct result of his decision to locate the performance in the arena-shaped structure. The circular stage was graudally transformed into a mechanism where the lost glove, the lost ring, the lost child and even a 'lost' father/daughter relationship were all recovered. The performance showed how these, as well as several other more local mysteries, like the disappearance of the keys, the appearance of the little shoe of a child, and so on, were created by the interference of the supernatural powers and how they were eventually solved. There are many hidden secrets in the house and the supernatural creatures activate the whole process, in fact the whole performance, through which almost all of these enigmas are solved.

One mystery, however, the secret of the world itself, remains unsolved in *The Black Glove.* It may perhaps sound pretentious to introduce the all-encompassing mystery of creation in the context of a lost glove and other seemingly trivial matters, but Strindberg has fashioned the Old Man as a philosopher-scientist who all his life, with almost Faustian intensity, has tried to solve the mysteries of life. In an argument with the 'Tomte', and this is the only time in the play when there is a direct dialogue between representatives from the two worlds, the Old Man realizes that all his efforts to find an answer have been in vain and he wants to die. The 'Tomte' even offers the Old Man renewed youth but he refuses. In a last effort to give the Old Man some meaning to his life the 'Tomte', who functions as a life-giving force in the play, shows him the black glove, and now the Old Man understands that because of this seemingly insignificant object the life in the house has been totally upset and he returns it to the servant who finds the ring hidden in it. When the reason for the false accusations with which the play started has been discovered the child is returned, the Woman realizes that she has found her father who has just died and the play can end on a note of reconciliation. The 'machinery' of the play where the trivial details of the everyday realities and the large metaphysical questions are brought together, has turned full circle.

It is clear that Carlsson started the rehearsals with quite a clear concept of how the finished performance was going look, primarily based on the spatial concept which made major changes in Strindberg's own dramaturgy necessary. Instead of a realistic performance where the characters enter and exit through doors and where the scenery changes several times according to the place of action, Carlsson's performance created an almost symbolic space where the life of the house, as a whole, was contained. This led to some problems on the part of the actors which were solved instrumentally, but were usually not dealt with on a more psychological level. Carlsson explained that his approach was based on his view that the actor possesses in-built resources of experience, that his body has a kind of trans-personal memory, which makes it possible for him/her to work with the role without asking psychological questions concerning the specific motivation of a certain moment of the character he/she is playing. These questions will answer themselves when the mise en scene has been solved, and for this the director is primarily responsible and which is based on his aesthetic concept of the whole performance. According to Carlsson, the physical or even psychological totality which the actors as a group build up has a potential power to create an aesthetic elevation which is realized by their energies and by choosing the circular arena for the production he believed that these energies would be intensified.

The actors participating in the performance have never seen this totality from the point of view of the director or the spectators and it took a long time for Wilhelm Carls-son fully to convince them that this kind of 'charging' of energies was possible in the very intimate space which was used. This insecurity, however, led to a kind of vulnerability which paradoxically gave the performance an added tension and deepened the sensitivity of the actors to each other's presence. They gave the spectators the impression that each actor was constantly trying to become more tuned to or aware of the presence of the others and this process did not stop when the rehearsals were completed. In the presence of spectators, at least during the beginning of the run, it was even intensified. It was, however, difficult to say how conscious the actors were of this process, but it seems to me that it created something very interesting and vital in each performance.

This way of working also, in some way, brought out the thematic kernel of the performance as it was formulated by Carlsson. Just as the power struggle between the characters in the Tower of Babel in the play affected their fate negatively, the actors had to watch over what all the others were doing in a different kind of power struggle which he wanted to affect them creatively. This added a metatheatrical dimension to the performance emphasizing the thematic aspects of the theatrical machinery. At the same time though it always left the performers in a situation of which they were only partially aware and which they did not totally master, while the spectators saw a totality, or at least had a feeling they did, because they had seen the 'Tomte' moving the glove at the very beginning of the performance, and viewed the performance from the priviliged point of view of the supernatural creatures.

It is difficult fully to reconstruct the totality of my perceptions a few years after the research itself was carried out, but even though it was necessary to 'leave' the material for a long time in order to approach it as analytically as possible my final impression was and still remains that the performance of *The Black Glove* succeeded in creating the kind of aesthetic elevation Carlsson had hoped to achieve. It also revealed some of the more difficult problems that a basically avant-garde director like Wilhelm Carlsson runs into at an institutional theatre like Dramaten, where he is not able to investigate the theoretical issues of his theatrical practice as thoroughly as he was used to during the Schahrazad years. It is almost as if the spirits of Dramaten itself with its established traditions, are always present and can start to pull unexpected strings behind the scenes at any moment. From this perspective the production of *The Black Glove* can, at least indirectly, be interpreted as an allegory for the attempts of the theatre to try to establish a kind of unity where all the theatrical elements can function as a machinery through which the mysteries of the stage in its meeting with the spectators can be revealed, at least for a short and passing moment.

Notes

1. This article is based on research carried out during 1987-8 when I was a research fellow at the Depart-

ment of Theatre Studies at the University of Stockholm funded by the Swedish Institute in Stockholm. Besides the extensive notes made during the rehearsals of *The Black Glove* I have consulted the video documentation done during one of the live performances, photographs and newspaper reviews. I want to thank all the members of the production team at Dramaten, and especially Wilhelm Carlsson, for their cooperation and encouragement, and Professor Kirsten Gram Holmstrom and Professor Willmar Sauter from the Department of Theatre at the University of Stockholm for their hospitality and support.

2. The production was given the following credits in the programme: Director: Wilhelm Carlsson, Scenography and Costume: Charles Koroly, Producer: Agneta Pauli, Dramaturg: Magnus Florin, Music: Thomas Jennefelt, Lighting: Bjorn Magnusson, Production Assistant: Mait Angberg, Props: Stefan Lundgren, Wigs: Sofia Ranow; The Old Man: Per Myrberg, The Tomte: Per Morberg, The Woman: Lil Terselius, The Janitor: Christian Berling, The Angel: Katarina Gustafsson, Kristin: Marie Richardson, Ellen: Lena Endre. In my description of the rehearsals for the production I shall for reasons of convenience only refer to the names of the characters.

3. For a short description and analysis of this production see my article 'Hur tvättar man ylle i varmt vatten utan att det krymper', *Nya Teatertidningen,* 42, October 1988, pp. 34-7. (Swedish)

4. All quotations from Strindberg's text are from *Samlade Skrifter,* vol. 45, Stockholm 1917. The translations are my own and the references in the text are to SS 45 and page number.

5. Keir Elam, *The Semiotics of Theatre and Drama,* Methuen, London, 1980, p. 73. For further discussions and bibliography on the topic see also Peter van Stapele, 'Analysis of Deixis', in *Performance Theory: Reception and Audience Research,* ed. Henri Schoenmakers, Amsterdam, 1992, pp. 189-204.

6. The quotations from the performance itself are from the production manuscript prepared by Wilhelm Carlsson which can be found at the archives of the Royal Dramatic Theatre in Stockholm. The translations are my own and the references are to DT and page number.

FURTHER READING

Criticism

Brater, Enoch. "*Play Strindberg* and the Theater of Adaptation." *Comparative Drama* 16, no. 1 (spring 1982): 12-25.

Describes a creative theatrical adaptation of *The Dance of Death* originally produced in Germany by Friedrich Dürrenmatt.

Bryant-Bertail, Sarah. "The Tower of Babel: Space and Movement in *The Ghost Sonata.*" In *Strindberg's Dramaturgy,* edited by Göran Stockenström, pp. 303-15. Minneapolis: University of Minnesota Press, 1988.

Explores the use of space as written into *The Ghost Sonata.*

Dahlbäback, Kerstin. "*Kristina* and Strindberg's Letters and Diary." *Scandinavian Studies* 62, no. 1 (winter 1990): 108-15.

Parallels Strindberg's writing of *Kristina* with events in his personal life as evidenced by letters written to his third wife, Harriet Bosse, and entries in his diary made during that time.

Erickson, Jon. "The *Mise en Scène* of the Non-Euclidean Character: Wellman, Jenkin and Strindberg." *Modern Drama* 16, no. 3 (fall 1998): 355-70.

Examines the evolution of character development and mise en scène according to the theory of Mac Wellman as exhibited in the work of Len Jenkin with the assertion that Strindberg was the formal precursor of this theory.

Luyat-Moore, Anne. "The Swedish Connection to *Victory* and *Chance.*" *Conradiana: A Journal of Joseph Conrad Studies* 18, no. 3 (1986): 219-23.

Considers the relationship between the two characters named Heyst in Strindberg's play *Påsk* and Joseph Conrad's novel *Victory.*

Meidal, Bjön. "A Strindberg Forgery: Carl Öhman's *August Strindberg and the Origin of Scenic Expressionism.*" *Scandinavica: An International Journal of Scandinavian Studies* 34, no. 1 (May 1995): 61-9.

Refutes Carl Öhman's work on Strindberg, claiming that it is based on documents that never existed or are forgeries.

Ofrat, Gideon. "The Structure of Ritual and Mythos in the Naturalistic Plays of August Strindberg." *Theatre Research International* 4, no. 2 (February 1979): 102-17.

Traces the mythological and ritualistic structure in Strindberg's naturalistic plays.

Robinson, Michael. "Finding a New Language: Strindberg and Symbolism." *Scandinavica: An International Journal of Scandinavian Studies* 33, no. 2 (November 1994): 201-15.

Examines Strindberg's thoughts about and use of symbolism.

———. "'Tror Ni, att någon annan kan stryka ut, vad Ni skriver?': Strindberg Old and New." *Scandinavica: An International Journal of Scandinavian Studies* 34, no. 1 (May 1995): 97-118.

Discusses the difference between criticism of Strindberg's works based on his own interpretations and that of the work as it is actually documented.

Roken, Freddie. "The Significance of the Screen-scenes in Strindberg's *Fordringsägare*." *Scandinavica: An International Journal of Scandinavian Studies* 34, no. 1 (May 1995): 37-60.

Dissects *Fordringsägare* into its scenic structure.

Additional coverage of Strindberg's life and career is contained in the following sources published by the Gale Group: *Contemporary Authors,* Vols. 104, 135; *Dictionary of Literary Biography,* Vol. 259; *DISCovering Authors; DISCovering Authors: British Edition; DISCovering Authors: Canadian Edition; DISCovering Authors Modules: Dramatists* **and** *Most-studied Authors; DISCovering Authors 3.0; Drama for Students,* Vols. 4, 9; *European Writers,* Vol. 7; *International Dictionary of Theatre: Playwrights; Literature Resource Center; Major 20th-Century Writers,* Ed. 2; *Reference Guide to World Literature,* Ed. 2; *Twentieth-Century Literary Criticism,* Vols. 1, 8, 21, 47; **and** *World Literature Criticism.***

How to Use This Index

Literary Criticism Series
Cumulative Author Index

33, 249; DLBY 1987; EXPS; LAIT 5;
MTCW 1, 2; NFS 4; RGAL 4; RGSF 2;
SATA 9; SATA-Obit 54; SSFS 2

Bale, John 1495-1563 .... **LC 62**
See also DLB 132; RGEL 2

Ball, Hugo 1886-1927 .... **TCLC 104**

Ballard, J(ames) G(raham) 1930- . **CLC 3, 6,
14, 36, 137; SSC 1, 53**
See also AAYA 3; BRWS 5; CA 5-8R;
CANR 15, 39, 65, 107; CN 7; DA3; DAM
NOV, POP; DLB 14, 207, 261; HGG;
MTCW 1, 2; NFS 8; RGEL 2; RGSF 2;
SATA 93; SFW 4

Balmont, Konstantin (Dmitriyevich)
1867-1943 .... **TCLC 11**
See also CA 109; 155

Baltausis, Vincas 1847-1910
See Mikszath, Kalman

Balzac, Honore de 1799-1850 ... **NCLC 5, 35,
53; SSC 5; WLC**
See also DA; DA3; DAB; DAC; DAM
MST, NOV; DLB 119; EW 5; GFL 1789
to the Present; RGSF 2; RGWL 2; SSFS
10; SUFW

Bambara, Toni Cade 1939-1995 ...... **CLC 19,
88; BLC 1; SSC 35; WLCS**
See also AAYA 5; AFAW 2; BW 2, 3; BYA
12, 14; CA 29-32R; 150; CANR 24, 49,
81; CDALBS; DA; DA3; DAC; DAM
MST, MULT; DLB 38, 218; EXPS;
MTCW 1, 2; RGAL 4; RGSF 2; SATA
112; SSFS 4, 7, 12; TCLC 116

Bamdad, A.
See Shamlu, Ahmad

Banat, D. R.
See Bradbury, Ray (Douglas)

Bancroft, Laura
See Baum, L(yman) Frank

Banim, John 1798-1842 .... **NCLC 13**
See also DLB 116, 158, 159; RGEL 2

Banim, Michael 1796-1874 .... **NCLC 13**
See also DLB 158, 159

Banjo, The
See Paterson, A(ndrew) B(arton)

Banks, Iain
See Banks, Iain M(enzies)

Banks, Iain M(enzies) 1954- .... **CLC 34**
See also CA 123; 128; CANR 61, 106; DLB
194, 261; HGG; INT 128; SFW 4

Banks, Lynne Reid .... **CLC 23**
See also Reid Banks, Lynne
See also AAYA 6; BYA 7

Banks, Russell 1940- .... **CLC 37, 72; SSC 42**
See also AMWS 5; CA 65-68; CAAS 15;
CANR 19, 52, 73; CN 7; DLB 130; NFS
13

Banville, John 1945- .... **CLC 46, 118**
See also CA 117; 128; CANR 104; CN 7;
DLB 14; INT 128

Banville, Theodore (Faullain) de
1832-1891 .... **NCLC 9**
See also DLB 217; GFL 1789 to the Present

Baraka, Amiri 1934- . **CLC 1, 2, 3, 5, 10, 14,
33, 115; BLC 1; DC 6; PC 4; WLCS**
See also Jones, LeRoi
See also AFAW 1, 2; AMWS 2; BW 2, 3;
CA 21-24R; CABS 3; CAD; CANR 27,
38, 61; CD 5; CDALB 1941-1968; CP 7;
CPW; DA; DA3; DAC; DAM MST,
MULT, POET, POP; DFS 3, 11; DLB 5,
7, 16, 38; DLBD 8; MTCW 1, 2; PFS 9;
RGAL 4; WP

Baratynsky, Evgenii Abramovich
1800-1844 .... **NCLC 103**
See also DLB 205

Barbauld, Anna Laetitia
1743-1825 .... **NCLC 50**
See also DLB 107, 109, 142, 158; RGEL 2

Barbellion, W. N. P. .... **TCLC 24**
See also Cummings, Bruce F(rederick)

Barber, Benjamin R. 1939- .... **CLC 141**
See also CA 29-32R; CANR 12, 32, 64

Barbera, Jack (Vincent) 1945- .... **CLC 44**
See also CA 110; CANR 45

Barbey d'Aurevilly, Jules-Amedee
1808-1889 .... **NCLC 1; SSC 17**
See also DLB 119; GFL 1789 to the Present

Barbour, John c. 1316-1395 .... **CMLC 33**
See also DLB 146

Barbusse, Henri 1873-1935 .... **TCLC 5**
See also CA 105; 154; DLB 65; RGWL 2

Barclay, Bill
See Moorcock, Michael (John)

Barclay, William Ewert
See Moorcock, Michael (John)

Barea, Arturo 1897-1957 .... **TCLC 14**
See also CA 111; 201

Barfoot, Joan 1946- .... **CLC 18**
See also CA 105

Barham, Richard Harris
1788-1845 .... **NCLC 77**
See also DLB 159

Baring, Maurice 1874-1945 .... **TCLC 8**
See also CA 105; 168; DLB 34; HGG

Baring-Gould, Sabine 1834-1924 ... **TCLC 88**
See also DLB 156, 190

Barker, Clive 1952- .... **CLC 52; SSC 53**
See also AAYA 10; BEST 90:3; BPFB 1;
CA 121; 129; CANR 71; CPW; DA3;
DAM POP; DLB 261; HGG; INT 129;
MTCW 1, 2

Barker, George Granville
1913-1991 .... **CLC 8, 48**
See also CA 9-12R; 135; CANR 7, 38;
DAM POET; DLB 20; MTCW 1

Barker, Harley Granville
See Granville-Barker, Harley
See also DLB 10

Barker, Howard 1946- .... **CLC 37**
See also CA 102; CBD; CD 5; DLB 13,
233

Barker, Jane 1652-1732 .... **LC 42**
See also DLB 39, 131

Barker, Pat(ricia) 1943- ...... **CLC 32, 94, 146**
See also BRWS 4; CA 117; 122; CANR 50,
101; CN 7; INT 122

Barlach, Ernst (Heinrich)
1870-1938 .... **TCLC 84**
See also CA 178; DLB 56, 118

Barlow, Joel 1754-1812 .... **NCLC 23**
See also AMWS 2; DLB 37; RGAL 4

Barnard, Mary (Ethel) 1909- .... **CLC 48**
See also CA 21-22; CAP 2

Barnes, Djuna 1892-1982 .... **CLC 3, 4, 8, 11,
29, 127; SSC 3**
See also Steptoe, Lydia
See also AMWS 3; CA 9-12R; 107; CAD;
CANR 16, 55; CWD; DLB 4, 9, 45; GLL
1; MTCW 1, 2; RGAL 4; TUS

Barnes, Julian (Patrick) 1946- . **CLC 42, 141**
See also BRWS 4; CA 102; CANR 19, 54;
CN 7; DAB; DLB 194; DLBY 1993;
MTCW 1

Barnes, Peter 1931- .... **CLC 5, 56**
See also CA 65-68; CAAS 12; CANR 33,
34, 64; CBD; CD 5; DFS 6; DLB 13, 233;
MTCW 1

Barnes, William 1801-1886 .... **NCLC 75**
See also DLB 32

Baroja (y Nessi), Pio 1872-1956 ..... **TCLC 8;
HLC 1**
See also CA 104; EW 9

Baron, David
See Pinter, Harold

Baron Corvo
See Rolfe, Frederick (William Serafino
Austin Lewis Mary)

Barondess, Sue K(aufman)
1926-1977 .... **CLC 8**
See also Kaufman, Sue
See also CA 1-4R; 69-72; CANR 1

Baron de Teive
See Pessoa, Fernando (Antonio Nogueira)

Baroness Von S.
See Zangwill, Israel

Barres, (Auguste-)Maurice
1862-1923 .... **TCLC 47**
See also CA 164; DLB 123; GFL 1789 to
the Present

Barreto, Afonso Henrique de Lima
See Lima Barreto, Afonso Henrique de

Barrett, Andrea 1954- .... **CLC 150**
See also CA 156; CANR 92

Barrett, Michele .... **CLC 65**

Barrett, (Roger) Syd 1946- .... **CLC 35**

Barrett, William (Christopher)
1913-1992 .... **CLC 27**
See also CA 13-16R; 139; CANR 11, 67;
INT CANR-11

Barrie, J(ames) M(atthew)
1860-1937 .... **TCLC 2**
See also BRWS 3; BYA 4, 5; CA 104; 136;
CANR 77; CDBLB 1890-1914; CLR 16;
CWRI 5; DA3; DAB; DAM DRAM; DFS
7; DLB 10, 141, 156; FANT; MAICYA 1,
2; MTCW 1; SATA 100; SUFW; WCH;
WLIT 4; YABC 1

Barrington, Michael
See Moorcock, Michael (John)

Barrol, Grady
See Bograd, Larry

Barry, Mike
See Malzberg, Barry N(athaniel)

Barry, Philip 1896-1949 .... **TCLC 11**
See also CA 109; 199; DFS 9; DLB 7, 228;
RGAL 4

Bart, Andre Schwarz
See Schwarz-Bart, Andre

Barth, John (Simmons) 1930- ... **CLC 1, 2, 3,
5, 7, 9, 10, 14, 27, 51, 89; SSC 10**
See also AITN 1, 2; AMW; BPFB 1; CA
1-4R; CABS 1; CANR 5, 23, 49, 64; CN
7; DAM NOV; DLB 2, 227; FANT;
MTCW 1; RGAL 4; RGSF 2; RHW;
SSFS 6

Barthelme, Donald 1931-1989 ... **CLC 1, 2, 3,
5, 6, 8, 13, 23, 46, 59, 115; SSC 2**
See also AMWS 4; BPFB 1; CA 21-24R;
129; CANR 20, 58; DA3; DAM NOV;
DLB 2, 234; DLBY 1980, 1989; FANT;
MTCW 1, 2; RGAL 4; RGSF 2; SATA 7;
SATA-Obit 62; SSFS 3

Barthelme, Frederick 1943- ...... **CLC 36, 117**
See also CA 114; 122; CANR 77; CN 7;
CSW; DLB 244; DLBY 1985; INT CA-
122

Barthes, Roland (Gerard)
1915-1980 .... **CLC 24, 83**
See also CA 130; 97-100; CANR 66; EW
13; GFL 1789 to the Present; MTCW 1, 2

Barzun, Jacques (Martin) 1907- ..... **CLC 51,
145**
See also CA 61-64; CANR 22, 95

Bashevis, Isaac
See Singer, Isaac Bashevis

Bashkirtseff, Marie 1859-1884 .... **NCLC 27**

Basho, Matsuo
See Matsuo Basho
See also RGWL 2; WP

Basil of Caesaria c. 330-379 .... **CMLC 35**

Bass, Kingsley B., Jr.
See Bullins, Ed

Bass, Rick 1958- .... **CLC 79, 143**
See also ANW; CA 126; CANR 53, 93;
CSW; DLB 212

Bassani, Giorgio 1916-2000 .... **CLC 9**
See also CA 65-68; 190; CANR 33; CWW
2; DLB 128, 177; MTCW 1; RGWL 2

Bastian, Ann .... **CLC 70**

Bastos, Augusto (Antonio) Roa
See Roa Bastos, Augusto (Antonio)

Bataille, Georges 1897-1962 .... **CLC 29**
See also CA 101; 89-92

Bates, H(erbert) E(rnest)
1905-1974 .... **CLC 46; SSC 10**
See also CA 93-96; 45-48; CANR 34; DA3;
DAB; DAM POP; DLB 162, 191; EXPS;
MTCW 1, 2; RGSF 2; SSFS 7

Bauchart
See Camus, Albert

Baudelaire, Charles 1821-1867 . **NCLC 6, 29,
55; PC 1; SSC 18; WLC**
See also DA; DA3; DAB; DAC; DAM
MST, POET; DLB 217; EW 7; GFL 1789
to the Present; RGWL 2

Baudouin, Marcel
See Peguy, Charles (Pierre)

Baudouin, Pierre
See Peguy, Charles (Pierre)

Baudrillard, Jean 1929- .... **CLC 60**

Baum, L(yman) Frank 1856-1919 ... **TCLC 7**
See also CA 108; 133; CLR 15; CWRI 5;
DLB 22; FANT; JRDA; MAICYA 1, 2;
MTCW 1, 2; NFS 13; RGAL 4; SATA 18,
100; WCH

Baum, Louis F.
See Baum, L(yman) Frank

Baumbach, Jonathan 1933- .... **CLC 6, 23**
See also CA 13-16R; CAAS 5; CANR 12,
66; CN 7; DLBY 1980; INT CANR-12;
MTCW 1

Bausch, Richard (Carl) 1945- .... **CLC 51**
See also AMWS 7; CA 101; CAAS 14;
CANR 43, 61, 87; CSW; DLB 130

Baxter, Charles (Morley) 1947- . **CLC 45, 78**
See also CA 57-60; CANR 40, 64, 104;
CPW; DAM POP; DLB 130; MTCW 2

Baxter, George Owen
See Faust, Frederick (Schiller)

Baxter, James K(eir) 1926-1972 .... **CLC 14**
See also CA 77-80

Baxter, John
See Hunt, E(verette) Howard, (Jr.)

Bayer, Sylvia
See Glassco, John

Baynton, Barbara 1857-1929 .... **TCLC 57**
See also DLB 230; RGSF 2

Beagle, Peter S(oyer) 1939- .... **CLC 7, 104**
See also BPFB 1; BYA 9, 10; CA 9-12R;
CANR 4, 51, 73; DA3; DLBY 1980;
FANT; INT CANR-4; MTCW 1; SATA
60, 130; SUFW; YAW

Bean, Normal
See Burroughs, Edgar Rice

Beard, Charles A(ustin)
1874-1948 .... **TCLC 15**
See also CA 115; 189; DLB 17; SATA 18

Beardsley, Aubrey 1872-1898 .... **NCLC 6**

Beattie, Ann 1947- ..... **CLC 8, 13, 18, 40, 63,
146; SSC 11**
See also AMWS 5; BEST 90:2; BPFB 1;
CA 81-84; CANR 53, 73; CN 7; CPW;
DA3; DAM NOV, POP; DLB 218; DLBY
1982; MTCW 1, 2; RGAL 4; RGSF 2;
SSFS 9

Beattie, James 1735-1803 .... **NCLC 25**
See also DLB 109

Beauchamp, Kathleen Mansfield 1888-1923
See Mansfield, Katherine
See also CA 104; 134; DA; DA3; DAC;
DAM MST; MTCW 2; TEA

Beaumarchais, Pierre-Augustin Caron de
1732-1799 .... **LC 61; DC 4**
See also DAM DRAM; DFS 14; EW 4;
GFL Beginnings to 1789; RGWL 2

Beaumont, Francis 1584(?)-1616 .... **LC 33;
DC 6**
See also BRW 2; CDBLB Before 1660;
DLB 58

**Beauvoir, Simone (Lucie Ernestine Marie
Bertrand) de** 1908-1986 .... **CLC 1, 2, 4,
8, 14, 31, 44, 50, 71, 124; SSC 35;
WLC**
See also BPFB 1; CA 9-12R; 118; CANR
28, 61; DA; DA3; DAB; DAC; DAM
MST, NOV; DLB 72; DLBY 1986; EW
12; FW; GFL 1789 to the Present; MTCW
1, 2; RGSF 2; RGWL 2

Becker, Carl (Lotus) 1873-1945 ..... **TCLC 63**
See also CA 157; DLB 17

Becker, Jurek 1937-1997 .... **CLC 7, 19**
See also CA 85-88; 157; CANR 60; CWW
2; DLB 75

Becker, Walter 1950- .... **CLC 26**

Beckett, Samuel (Barclay)
1906-1989 .. **CLC 1, 2, 3, 4, 6, 9, 10, 11,
14, 18, 29, 57, 59, 83; SSC 16; WLC**
See also BRWR 1; BRWS 1; CA 5-8R; 130;
CANR 33, 61; CBD; CDBLB 1945-1960;
DA; DA3; DAB; DAC; DAM DRAM,
MST, NOV; DFS 2, 7; DLB 13, 15, 233;
DLBY 1990; GFL 1789 to the Present;
MTCW 1, 2; RGSF 2; RGWL 2; SSFS
15; WLIT 4

Beckford, William 1760-1844 .... **NCLC 16**
See also BRW 3; DLB 39, 213; HGG;
SUFW

Beckman, Gunnel 1910- .... **CLC 26**
See also CA 33-36R; CANR 15; CLR 25;
MAICYA 1, 2; SAAS 9; SATA 6

Becque, Henri 1837-1899 .... **NCLC 3**
See also DLB 192; GFL 1789 to the Present

Becquer, Gustavo Adolfo
1836-1870 .... **NCLC 106; HLCS 1**
See also DAM MULT

Beddoes, Thomas Lovell
1803-1849 .... **NCLC 3; DC 15**
See also DLB 96

Bede c. 673-735 .... **CMLC 20**
See also DLB 146

Bedford, Donald F.
See Fearing, Kenneth (Flexner)

Beecher, Catharine Esther
1800-1878 .... **NCLC 30**
See also DLB 1, 243

Beecher, John 1904-1980 .... **CLC 6**
See also AITN 1; CA 5-8R; 105; CANR 8

Beer, Johann 1655-1700 .... **LC 5**
See also DLB 168

Beer, Patricia 1924- .... **CLC 58**
See also CA 61-64; 183; CANR 13, 46; CP
7; CWP; DLB 40; FW

Beerbohm, Max
See Beerbohm, (Henry) Max(imilian)

Beerbohm, (Henry) Max(imilian)
1872-1956 .... **TCLC 1, 24**
See also BRWS 2; CA 104; 154; CANR 79;
DLB 34, 100; FANT

Beer-Hofmann, Richard
1866-1945 .... **TCLC 60**
See also CA 160; DLB 81

Beg, Shemus
See Stephens, James

Begiebing, Robert J(ohn) 1946- .... **CLC 70**
See also CA 122; CANR 40, 88

Behan, Brendan 1923-1964 ...... **CLC 1, 8, 11,
15, 79**
See also BRWS 2; CA 73-76; CANR 33;
CBD; CDBLB 1945-1960; DAM DRAM;
DFS 7; DLB 13, 233; MTCW 1, 2

Behn, Aphra 1640(?)-1689 .... **LC 1, 30, 42;
DC 4; PC 13; WLC**
See also BRWS 3; DA; DA3; DAB; DAC;
DAM DRAM, MST, NOV, POET; DLB
39, 80, 131; FW; WLIT 3

Behrman, S(amuel) N(athaniel)
1893-1973 .... **CLC 40**
See also CA 13-16; 45-48; CAD; CAP 1;
DLB 7, 44; IDFW 3; RGAL 4

Belasco, David 1853-1931 .... **TCLC 3**
See also CA 104; 168; DLB 7; RGAL 4

Belcheva, Elisaveta Lyubomirova
1893-1991 .... **CLC 10**
See also Bagryana, Elisaveta

Beldone, Phil ''Cheech''
See Ellison, Harlan (Jay)

Beleno
See Azuela, Mariano

Belinski, Vissarion Grigoryevich
1811-1848 .... **NCLC 5**
See also DLB 198

Belitt, Ben 1911- .... **CLC 22**
See also CA 13-16R; CAAS 4; CANR 7,
77; CP 7; DLB 5

Bell, Gertrude (Margaret Lowthian)
1868-1926 .... **TCLC 67**
See also CA 167; DLB 174

Bell, J. Freeman
See Zangwill, Israel

Bell, James Madison 1826-1902 ... **TCLC 43;
BLC 1**
See also BW 1; CA 122; 124; DAM MULT;
DLB 50

Bell, Madison Smartt 1957- ...... **CLC 41, 102**
See also AMWS 10; BPFB 1; CA 111, 183;
CAAE 183; CANR 28, 54, 73; CN 7;
CSW; DLB 218; MTCW 1

Bell, Marvin (Hartley) 1937- .... **CLC 8, 31**
See also CA 21-24R; CAAS 14; CANR 59,
102; CP 7; DAM POET; DLB 5; MTCW
1

Bell, W. L. D.
See Mencken, H(enry) L(ouis)

Bellamy, Atwood C.
See Mencken, H(enry) L(ouis)

Bellamy, Edward 1850-1898 ...... **NCLC 4, 86**
See also DLB 12; NFS 15; RGAL 4; SFW
4

Belli, Gioconda 1949-
See also CA 152; CWW 2; HLCS 1

Bellin, Edward J.
See Kuttner, Henry

**Belloc, (Joseph) Hilaire (Pierre Sebastien
Rene Swanton)** 1870-1953 ...... **TCLC 7,
18; PC 24**
See also CA 106; 152; CWRI 5; DAM
POET; DLB 19, 100, 141, 174; MTCW 1;
SATA 112; WCH; YABC 1

Belloc, Joseph Peter Rene Hilaire
See Belloc, (Joseph) Hilaire (Pierre Sebastien Rene Swanton)

Belloc, Joseph Pierre Hilaire
See Belloc, (Joseph) Hilaire (Pierre Sebastien Rene Swanton)

Belloc, M. A.
See Lowndes, Marie Adelaide (Belloc)

Bellow, Saul 1915- . **CLC 1, 2, 3, 6, 8, 10, 13,
15, 25, 33, 34, 63, 79; SSC 14; WLC**
See also AITN 2; AMW; BEST 89:3; BPFB
1; CA 5-8R; CABS 1; CANR 29, 53, 95;
CDALB 1941-1968; CN 7; DA; DA3;
DAB; DAC; DAM MST, NOV, POP;
DLB 2, 28; DLBD 3; DLBY 1982;
MTCW 1, 2; NFS 4, 14; RGAL 4; RGSF
2; SSFS 12

Belser, Reimond Karel Maria de 1929-
See Ruyslinck, Ward
See also CA 152

Boccaccio, Giovanni 1313-1375 ... **CMLC 13;
SSC 10**
See also EW 2; RGSF 2; RGWL 2

Bochco, Steven 1943- .... **CLC 35**
See also AAYA 11; CA 124; 138

Bode, Sigmund
See O'Doherty, Brian

Bodel, Jean 1167(?)-1210 .... **CMLC 28**

Bodenheim, Maxwell 1892-1954 .... **TCLC 44**
See also CA 110; 187; DLB 9, 45; RGAL 4

Bodker, Cecil 1927- .... **CLC 21**
See also CA 73-76; CANR 13, 44; CLR 23;
MAICYA 1, 2; SATA 14, 133

Bodker, Cecil 1927-
See Bodker, Cecil

Boell, Heinrich (Theodor)
1917-1985 ..... **CLC 2, 3, 6, 9, 11, 15, 27,
32, 72; SSC 23; WLC**
See also Boll, Heinrich
See also CA 21-24R; 116; CANR 24; DA;
DA3; DAB; DAC; DAM MST, NOV;
DLB 69; DLBY 1985; MTCW 1, 2

Boerne, Alfred
See Doeblin, Alfred

Boethius c. 480-c. 524 .... **CMLC 15**
See also DLB 115; RGWL 2

Boff, Leonardo (Genezio Darci)
1938- .... **CLC 70; HLC 1**
See also CA 150; DAM MULT; HW 2

Bogan, Louise 1897-1970 .... **CLC 4, 39, 46,
93; PC 12**
See also AMWS 3; CA 73-76; 25-28R;
CANR 33, 82; DAM POET; DLB 45, 169;
MAWW; MTCW 1, 2; RGAL 4

Bogarde, Dirk
See Van Den Bogarde, Derek Jules Gaspard
Ulric Niven
See also DLB 14

Bogosian, Eric 1953- .... **CLC 45, 141**
See also CA 138; CAD; CANR 102; CD 5

Bograd, Larry 1953- .... **CLC 35**
See also CA 93-96; CANR 57; SAAS 21;
SATA 33, 89; WYA

Boiardo, Matteo Maria 1441-1494 .... **LC 6**

Boileau-Despreaux, Nicolas 1636-1711 . **LC 3**
See also EW 3; GFL Beginnings to 1789;
RGWL 2

Bojer, Johan 1872-1959 .... **TCLC 64**
See also CA 189

Bok, Edward W. 1863-1930 .... **TCLC 101**
See also DLB 91; DLBD 16

Boland, Eavan (Aisling) 1944- .. **CLC 40, 67,
113**
See also BRWS 5; CA 143; CANR 61; CP
7; CWP; DAM POET; DLB 40; FW;
MTCW 2; PFS 12

Boll, Heinrich
See Boell, Heinrich (Theodor)
See also BPFB 1; CDWLB 2; EW 13;
RGSF 2; RGWL 2

Bolt, Lee
See Faust, Frederick (Schiller)

Bolt, Robert (Oxton) 1924-1995 .... **CLC 14**
See also CA 17-20R; 147; CANR 35, 67;
CBD; DAM DRAM; DFS 2; DLB 13,
233; LAIT 1; MTCW 1

Bombal, Maria Luisa 1910-1980 ...... **SSC 37;
HLCS 1**
See also CA 127; CANR 72; HW 1; LAW;
RGSF 2

Bombet, Louis-Alexandre-Cesar
See Stendhal

Bomkauf
See Kaufman, Bob (Garnell)

Bonaventura .... **NCLC 35**
See also DLB 90

Bond, Edward 1934- .... **CLC 4, 6, 13, 23**
See also BRWS 1; CA 25-28R; CANR 38,
67, 106; CBD; CD 5; DAM DRAM; DFS
3,8; DLB 13; MTCW 1

Bonham, Frank 1914-1989 .... **CLC 12**
See also AAYA 1; BYA 1, 3; CA 9-12R;
CANR 4, 36; JRDA; MAICYA 1, 2;
SAAS 3; SATA 1, 49; SATA-Obit 62;
TCWW 2; YAW

Bonnefoy, Yves 1923- .... **CLC 9, 15, 58**
See also CA 85-88; CANR 33, 75, 97;
CWW 2; DAM MST, POET; DLB 258;
GFL 1789 to the Present; MTCW 1, 2

Bontemps, Arna(ud Wendell)
1902-1973 .... **CLC 1, 18; BLC 1**
See also BW 1; CA 1-4R; 41-44R; CANR
4, 35; CLR 6; CWRI 5; DA3; DAM
MULT, NOV, POET; DLB 48, 51; JRDA;
MAICYA 1, 2; MTCW 1, 2; SATA 2, 44;
SATA-Obit 24; WCH; WP

Booth, Martin 1944- .... **CLC 13**
See also CA 93-96; CAAE 188; CAAS 2;
CANR 92

Booth, Philip 1925- .... **CLC 23**
See also CA 5-8R; CANR 5, 88; CP 7;
DLBY 1982

Booth, Wayne C(layson) 1921- .... **CLC 24**
See also CA 1-4R; CAAS 5; CANR 3, 43;
DLB 67

Borchert, Wolfgang 1921-1947 .... **TCLC 5**
See also CA 104; 188; DLB 69, 124

Borel, Petrus 1809-1859 .... **NCLC 41**
See also DLB 119; GFL 1789 to the Present

Borges, Jorge Luis 1899-1986 ... **CLC 1, 2, 3,
4, 6, 8, 9, 10, 13, 19, 44, 48, 83; HLC 1;
PC 22, 32; SSC 4, 41; WLC**
See also AAYA 26; BPFB 1; CA 21-24R;
CANR 19, 33, 75, 105; CDWLB 3; DA;
DA3; DAB; DAC; DAM MST, MULT;
DLB 113; DLBY 1986; DNFS 1, 2; HW
1, 2; LAW; MSW; MTCW 1, 2; RGSF 2;
RGWL 2; SFW 4; SSFS 4, 9; TCLC 109;
WLIT 1

Borowski, Tadeusz 1922-1951 .... **TCLC 9;
SSC 48**
See also CA 106; 154; CDWLB 4, 4; DLB
215; RGSF 2; SSFS 13

Borrow, George (Henry)
1803-1881 .... **NCLC 9**
See also DLB 21, 55, 166

Bosch (Gavino), Juan 1909-2001
See also CA 151; DAM MST, MULT; DLB
145; HLCS 1; HW 1, 2

Bosman, Herman Charles
1905-1951 .... **TCLC 49**
See also Malan, Herman
See also CA 160; DLB 225; RGSF 2

Bosschere, Jean de 1878(?)-1953 ... **TCLC 19**
See also CA 115; 186

Boswell, James 1740-1795 ... **LC 4, 50; WLC**
See also BRW 3; CDBLB 1660-1789; DA;
DAB; DAC; DAM MST; DLB 104, 142;
WLIT 3

Bottomley, Gordon 1874-1948 ..... **TCLC 107**
See also CA 120; 192; DLB 10

Bottoms, David 1949- .... **CLC 53**
See also CA 105; CANR 22; CSW; DLB
120; DLBY 1983

Boucicault, Dion 1820-1890 .... **NCLC 41**

Boucolon, Maryse
See Conde, Maryse

Bourget, Paul (Charles Joseph)
1852-1935 .... **TCLC 12**
See also CA 107; 196; DLB 123; GFL 1789
to the Present

Bourjaily, Vance (Nye) 1922- .... **CLC 8, 62**
See also CA 1-4R; CAAS 1; CANR 2, 72;
CN 7; DLB 2, 143

Bourne, Randolph S(illiman)
1886-1918 .... **TCLC 16**
See also AMW; CA 117; 155; DLB 63

Bova, Ben(jamin William) 1932- ...... **CLC 45**
See also AAYA 16; CA 5-8R; CAAS 18;
CANR 11, 56, 94; CLR 3; DLBY 1981;
INT CANR-11; MAICYA 1, 2; MTCW 1;
SATA 6, 68, 133; SFW 4

Bowen, Elizabeth (Dorothea Cole)
1899-1973 . **CLC 1, 3, 6, 11, 15, 22, 118;
SSC 3, 28**
See also BRWS 2; CA 17-18; 41-44R;
CANR 35, 105; CAP 2; CDBLB 1945-
1960; DA3; DAM NOV; DLB 15, 162;
EXPS; FW; HGG; MTCW 1, 2; NFS 13;
RGSF 2; SSFS 5; SUFW; WLIT 4

Bowering, George 1935- .... **CLC 15, 47**
See also CA 21-24R; CAAS 16; CANR 10;
CP 7; DLB 53

Bowering, Marilyn R(uthe) 1949- .... **CLC 32**
See also CA 101; CANR 49; CP 7; CWP

Bowers, Edgar 1924-2000 .... **CLC 9**
See also CA 5-8R; 188; CANR 24; CP 7;
CSW; DLB 5

Bowie, David .... **CLC 17**
See also Jones, David Robert

Bowles, Jane (Sydney) 1917-1973 ..... **CLC 3,
68**
See also CA 19-20; 41-44R; CAP 2

Bowles, Paul (Frederick) 1910-1999 . **CLC 1,
2, 19, 53; SSC 3**
See also AMWS 4; CA 1-4R; 186; CAAS
1; CANR 1, 19, 50, 75; CN 7; DA3; DLB
5, 6, 218; MTCW 1, 2; RGAL 4

Bowles, William Lisle 1762-1850 . **NCLC 103**
See also DLB 93

Box, Edgar
See Vidal, Gore
See also GLL 1

Boyd, James 1888-1944 .... **TCLC 115**
See also CA 186; DLB 9; DLBD 16; RGAL
4; RHW

Boyd, Nancy
See Millay, Edna St. Vincent
See also GLL 1

Boyd, Thomas (Alexander)
1898-1935 .... **TCLC 111**
See also CA 111; 183; DLB 9; DLBD 16

Boyd, William 1952- .... **CLC 28, 53, 70**
See also CA 114; 120; CANR 51, 71; CN
7; DLB 231

Boyle, Kay 1902-1992 .... **CLC 1, 5, 19, 58,
121; SSC 5**
See also CA 13-16R; 140; CAAS 1; CANR
29, 61; DLB 4, 9, 48, 86; DLBY 1993;
MTCW 1, 2; RGAL 4; RGSF 2; SSFS 10,
13, 14

Boyle, Mark
See Kienzle, William X(avier)

Boyle, Patrick 1905-1982 .... **CLC 19**
See also CA 127

Boyle, T. C.
See Boyle, T(homas) Coraghessan
See also AMWS 8

Boyle, T(homas) Coraghessan
1948- .... **CLC 36, 55, 90; SSC 16**
See also Boyle, T. C.
See also BEST 90:4; BPFB 1; CA 120;
CANR 44, 76, 89; CN 7; CPW; DA3;
DAM POP; DLB 218; DLBY 1986;
MTCW 2; SSFS 13

Boz
See Dickens, Charles (John Huffam)

Brackenridge, Hugh Henry
1748-1816 .... **NCLC 7**
See also DLB 11, 37; RGAL 4

Bradbury, Edward P.
See Moorcock, Michael (John)
See also MTCW 2

Bradbury, Malcolm (Stanley)
1932-2000 .... **CLC 32, 61**
See also CA 1-4R; CANR 1, 33, 91, 98;
CN 7; DA3; DAM NOV; DLB 14, 207;
MTCW 1, 2

Bradbury, Ray (Douglas) 1920- ... **CLC 1, 3, 10, 15, 42, 98; SSC 29, 53; WLC**
See also AAYA 15; AITN 1, 2; AMWS 4;
BPFB 1; BYA 4, 5, 11; CA 1-4R; CANR
2, 30, 75; CDALB 1968-1988; CN 7;
CPW; DA; DA3; DAB; DAC; DAM MST,
NOV, POP; DLB 2, 8; EXPN; EXPS;
HGG; LAIT 3, 5; MTCW 1, 2; NFS 1;
RGAL 4; RGSF 2; SATA 11, 64, 123;
SCFW 2; SFW 4; SSFS 1; SUFW; YAW

Braddon, Mary Elizabeth
1837-1915 .... **TCLC 111**
See also Aunt Belinda
See also CA 108; 179; CMW 4; DLB 18,
70, 156; HGG

Bradford, Gamaliel 1863-1932 .... **TCLC 36**
See also CA 160; DLB 17

Bradford, William 1590-1657 .... **LC 64**
See also DLB 24, 30; RGAL 4

Bradley, David (Henry), Jr. 1950- ... **CLC 23, 118; BLC 1**
See also BW 1, 3; CA 104; CANR 26, 81;
CN 7; DAM MULT; DLB 33

Bradley, John Ed(mund, Jr.) 1958- . **CLC 55**
See also CA 139; CANR 99; CN 7; CSW

Bradley, Marion Zimmer
1930-1999 .... **CLC 30**
See also Chapman, Lee; Dexter, John; Gard-
ner, Miriam; Ives, Morgan; Rivers, Elfrida
See also AAYA 40; BPFB 1; CA 57-60; 185;
CAAS 10; CANR 7, 31, 51, 75, 107;
CPW; DA3; DAM POP; DLB 8; FANT;
FW; MTCW 1, 2; SATA 90; SATA-Obit
116; SFW 4; YAW

Bradshaw, John 1933- .... **CLC 70**
See also CA 138; CANR 61

Bradstreet, Anne 1612(?)-1672 ...... **LC 4, 30; PC 10**
See also AMWS 1; CDALB 1640-1865;
DA; DA3; DAC; DAM MST, POET; DLB
24; EXPP; FW; PFS 6; RGAL 4; WP

Brady, Joan 1939- .... **CLC 86**
See also CA 141

Bragg, Melvyn 1939- .... **CLC 10**
See also BEST 89:3; CA 57-60; CANR 10,
48, 89; CN 7; DLB 14; RHW

Brahe, Tycho 1546-1601 .... **LC 45**

Braine, John (Gerard) 1922-1986 . **CLC 1, 3, 41**
See also CA 1-4R; 120; CANR 1, 33; CD-
BLB 1945-1960; DLB 15; DLBY 1986;
MTCW 1

Bramah, Ernest 1868-1942 .... **TCLC 72**
See also CA 156; CMW 4; DLB 70; FANT

Brammer, William 1930(?)-1978 ...... **CLC 31**
See also CA 77-80

Brancati, Vitaliano 1907-1954 .... **TCLC 12**
See also CA 109

Brancato, Robin F(idler) 1936- .... **CLC 35**
See also AAYA 9; BYA 6; CA 69-72; CANR
11, 45; CLR 32; JRDA; MAICYA 2;
MAICYAS 1; SAAS 9; SATA 97; WYA;
YAW

Brand, Max
See Faust, Frederick (Schiller)
See also BPFB 1; TCWW 2

Brand, Millen 1906-1980 .... **CLC 7**
See also CA 21-24R; 97-100; CANR 72

Branden, Barbara .... **CLC 44**
See also CA 148

Brandes, Georg (Morris Cohen)
1842-1927 .... **TCLC 10**
See also CA 105; 189

Brandys, Kazimierz 1916-2000 .... **CLC 62**

Branley, Franklyn M(ansfield)
1915- .... **CLC 21**
See also CA 33-36R; CANR 14, 39; CLR
13; MAICYA 1, 2; SAAS 16; SATA 4, 68

Brathwaite, Edward Kamau 1930- . **CLC 11; BLCS**
See also BW 2, 3; CA 25-28R; CANR 11,
26, 47, 107; CDWLB 3; CP 7; DAM
POET; DLB 125

Brathwaite, Kamau
See Brathwaite, Edward Kamau

Brautigan, Richard (Gary)
1935-1984 ..... **CLC 1, 3, 5, 9, 12, 34, 42**
See also BPFB 1; CA 53-56; 113; CANR
34; DA3; DAM NOV; DLB 2, 5, 206;
DLBY 1980, 1984; FANT; MTCW 1;
RGAL 4; SATA 56

Brave Bird, Mary
See Crow Dog, Mary (Ellen)
See also NNAL

Braverman, Kate 1950- .... **CLC 67**
See also CA 89-92

Brecht, (Eugen) Bertolt (Friedrich)
1898-1956 ..... **TCLC 1, 6, 13, 35; DC 3; WLC**
See also CA 104; 133; CANR 62; CDWLB
2; DA; DA3; DAB; DAC; DAM DRAM,
MST; DFS 4, 5, 9; DLB 56, 124; EW 11;
IDTP; MTCW 1, 2; RGWL 2

Brecht, Eugen Berthold Friedrich
See Brecht, (Eugen) Bertolt (Friedrich)

Bremer, Fredrika 1801-1865 .... **NCLC 11**
See also DLB 254

Brennan, Christopher John
1870-1932 .... **TCLC 17**
See also CA 117; 188; DLB 230

Brennan, Maeve 1917-1993 ... **CLC 5; TCLC 124**
See also CA 81-84; CANR 72, 100

Brent, Linda
See Jacobs, Harriet A(nn)

Brentano, Clemens (Maria)
1778-1842 .... **NCLC 1**
See also DLB 90; RGWL 2

Brent of Bin Bin
See Franklin, (Stella Maria Sarah) Miles
(Lampe)

Brenton, Howard 1942- .... **CLC 31**
See also CA 69-72; CANR 33, 67; CBD;
CD 5; DLB 13; MTCW 1

Breslin, James 1930-
See Breslin, Jimmy
See also CA 73-76; CANR 31, 75; DAM
NOV; MTCW 1, 2

Breslin, Jimmy .... **CLC 4, 43**
See also Breslin, James
See also AITN 1; DLB 185; MTCW 2

Bresson, Robert 1901(?)-1999 .... **CLC 16**
See also CA 110; 187; CANR 49

Breton, Andre 1896-1966 .. **CLC 2, 9, 15, 54; PC 15**
See also CA 19-20; 25-28R; CANR 40, 60;
CAP 2; DLB 65, 258; EW 11; GFL 1789
to the Present; MTCW 1, 2; RGWL 2; WP

Breytenbach, Breyten 1939(?)- .. **CLC 23, 37, 126**
See also CA 113; 129; CANR 61; CWW 2;
DAM POET; DLB 225

Bridgers, Sue Ellen 1942- .... **CLC 26**
See also AAYA 8; BYA 7, 8; CA 65-68;
CANR 11, 36; CLR 18; DLB 52; JRDA;
MAICYA 1, 2; SAAS 1; SATA 22, 90;
SATA-Essay 109; WYA; YAW

Bridges, Robert (Seymour)
1844-1930 .... **TCLC 1; PC 28**
See also BRW 6; CA 104; 152; CDBLB
1890-1914; DAM POET; DLB 19, 98

Bridie, James .... **TCLC 3**
See also Mavor, Osborne Henry
See also DLB 10

Brin, David 1950- .... **CLC 34**
See also AAYA 21; CA 102; CANR 24, 70;
INT CANR-24; SATA 65; SCFW 2; SFW
4

Brink, Andre (Philippus) 1935- . **CLC 18, 36, 106**
See also AFW; BRWS 6; CA 104; CANR
39, 62, 109; CN 7; DLB 225; INT CA-
103; MTCW 1, 2; WLIT 2

Brinsmead, H. F(ay)
See Brinsmead, H(esba) F(ay)

Brinsmead, H. F.
See Brinsmead, H(esba) F(ay)

Brinsmead, H(esba) F(ay) 1922- ...... **CLC 21**
See also CA 21-24R; CANR 10; CLR 47;
CWRI 5; MAICYA 1, 2; SAAS 5; SATA
18, 78

Brittain, Vera (Mary) 1893(?)-1970 . **CLC 23**
See also CA 13-16; 25-28R; CANR 58;
CAP 1; DLB 191; FW; MTCW 1, 2

Broch, Hermann 1886-1951 .... **TCLC 20**
See also CA 117; CDWLB 2; DLB 85, 124;
EW 10; RGWL 2

Brock, Rose
See Hansen, Joseph
See also GLL 1

Brod, Max 1884-1968 .... **TCLC 115**
See also CA 5-8R; 25-28R; CANR 7; DLB
81

Brodkey, Harold (Roy) 1930-1996 ... **CLC 56**
See also CA 111; 151; CANR 71; CN 7;
DLB 130; TCLC 123

Brodskii, Iosif
See Brodsky, Joseph
See also RGWL 2

Brodsky, Iosif Alexandrovich 1940-1996
See Brodsky, Joseph
See also AITN 1; CA 41-44R; 151; CANR
37, 106; DA3; DAM POET; MTCW 1, 2

Brodsky, Joseph . **CLC 4, 6, 13, 36, 100; PC 9**
See also Brodsky, Iosif Alexandrovich
See also AMWS 8; CWW 2; MTCW 1

Brodsky, Michael (Mark) 1948- .... **CLC 19**
See also CA 102; CANR 18, 41, 58; DLB
244

Brodzki, Bella ed. .... **CLC 65**

Brome, Richard 1590(?)-1652 .... **LC 61**
See also DLB 58

Bromell, Henry 1947- .... **CLC 5**
See also CA 53-56; CANR 9

Bromfield, Louis (Brucker)
1896-1956 .... **TCLC 11**
See also CA 107; 155; DLB 4, 9, 86; RGAL
4; RHW

Broner, E(sther) M(asserman)
1930- .... **CLC 19**
See also CA 17-20R; CANR 8, 25, 72; CN
7; DLB 28

Bronk, William (M.) 1918-1999 .... **CLC 10**
See also CA 89-92; 177; CANR 23; CP 7;
DLB 165

Bronstein, Lev Davidovich
See Trotsky, Leon

Bronte, Anne 1820-1849 ..... **NCLC 4, 71, 102**
See also BRW 5; BRWR 1; DA3; DLB 21,
199

Bronte, (Patrick) Branwell
1817-1848 .... **NCLC 109**

Bronte, Charlotte 1816-1855 ...... **NCLC 3, 8, 33, 58, 105; WLC**
See also AAYA 17; BRW 5; BRWR 1; BYA
2; CDBLB 1832-1890; DA; DA3; DAB;
DAC; DAM MST, NOV; DLB 21, 159,
199; EXPN; LAIT 2; NFS 4; WLIT 4

Chambers, Robert W(illiam)
1865-1933 .... **TCLC 41**
See also CA 165; DLB 202; HGG; SATA
107; SUFW

Chamisso, Adelbert von
1781-1838 .... **NCLC 82**
See also DLB 90; RGWL 2; SUFW

Chance, John T.
See Carpenter, John (Howard)

Chandler, Raymond (Thornton)
1888-1959 .... **TCLC 1, 7; SSC 23**
See also AAYA 25; AMWS 4; BPFB 1; CA
104; 129; CANR 60, 107; CDALB 1929-
1941; CMW 4; DA3; DLB 226, 253;
DLBD 6; MSW; MTCW 1, 2; RGAL 4

Chang, Eileen 1921-1995 .... **SSC 28**
See also CA 166; CWW 2

Chang, Jung 1952- .... **CLC 71**
See also CA 142

Chang Ai-Ling
See Chang, Eileen

Channing, William Ellery
1780-1842 .... **NCLC 17**
See also DLB 1, 59, 235; RGAL 4

Chao, Patricia 1955- .... **CLC 119**
See also CA 163

Chaplin, Charles Spencer
1889-1977 .... **CLC 16**
See also Chaplin, Charlie
See also CA 81-84; 73-76

Chaplin, Charlie
See Chaplin, Charles Spencer
See also DLB 44

Chapman, George 1559(?)-1634 .... **LC 22**
See also BRW 1; DAM DRAM; DLB 62,
121; RGEL 2

Chapman, Graham 1941-1989 .... **CLC 21**
See also Monty Python
See also CA 116; 129; CANR 35, 95

Chapman, John Jay 1862-1933 .... **TCLC 7**
See also CA 104; 191

Chapman, Lee
See Bradley, Marion Zimmer
See also GLL 1

Chapman, Walker
See Silverberg, Robert

Chappell, Fred (Davis) 1936- ..... **CLC 40, 78**
See also CA 5-8R; CAAE 198; CAAS 4;
CANR 8, 33, 67; CN 7; CP 7; CSW; DLB
6, 105; HGG

Char, Rene(-Emile) 1907-1988 .... **CLC 9, 11,
14, 55**
See also CA 13-16R; 124; CANR 32; DAM
POET; DLB 258; GFL 1789 to the
Present; MTCW 1, 2; RGWL 2

Charby, Jay
See Ellison, Harlan (Jay)

Chardin, Pierre Teilhard de
See Teilhard de Chardin, (Marie Joseph)
Pierre

Chariton fl. 1st cent. (?)- .... **CMLC 49**

Charlemagne 742-814 .... **CMLC 37**

Charles I 1600-1649 .... **LC 13**

Charriere, Isabelle de 1740-1805 .. **NCLC 66**

Chartier, Emile-Auguste
See Alain

Charyn, Jerome 1937- .... **CLC 5, 8, 18**
See also CA 5-8R; CAAS 1; CANR 7, 61,
101; CMW 4; CN 7; DLBY 1983; MTCW
1

Chase, Adam
See Marlowe, Stephen

Chase, Mary (Coyle) 1907-1981 .... **DC 1**
See also CA 77-80; 105; CAD; CWD; DFS
11; DLB 228; SATA 17; SATA-Obit 29

Chase, Mary Ellen 1887-1973 .... **CLC 2;
TCLC 124**
See also CA 13-16; 41-44R; CAP 1; SATA
10

Chase, Nicholas
See Hyde, Anthony
See also CCA 1

Chateaubriand, Francois Rene de
1768-1848 .... **NCLC 3**
See also DLB 119; EW 5; GFL 1789 to the
Present; RGWL 2

Chatterje, Sarat Chandra 1876-1936(?)
See Chatterji, Saratchandra
See also CA 109

Chatterji, Bankim Chandra
1838-1894 .... **NCLC 19**

Chatterji, Saratchandra .... **TCLC 13**
See also Chatterje, Sarat Chandra
See also CA 186

Chatterton, Thomas 1752-1770 .... **LC 3, 54**
See also DAM POET; DLB 109; RGEL 2

Chatwin, (Charles) Bruce
1940-1989 .... **CLC 28, 57, 59**
See also AAYA 4; BEST 90:1; BRWS 4;
CA 85-88; 127; CPW; DAM POP; DLB
194, 204

Chaucer, Daniel
See Ford, Ford Madox
See also RHW

Chaucer, Geoffrey 1340(?)-1400 .. **LC 17, 56;
PC 19; WLCS**
See also BRW 1; BRWR 2; CDBLB Before
1660; DA; DA3; DAB; DAC; DAM MST,
POET; DLB 146; LAIT 1; PAB; PFS 14;
RGEL 2; WLIT 3; WP

Chavez, Denise (Elia) 1948-
See also CA 131; CANR 56, 81; DAM
MULT; DLB 122; FW; HLC 1; HW 1, 2;
MTCW 2

Chaviaras, Strates 1935-
See Haviaras, Stratis
See also CA 105

Chayefsky, Paddy .... **CLC 23**
See also Chayefsky, Sidney
See also CAD; DLB 7, 44; DLBY 1981;
RGAL 4

Chayefsky, Sidney 1923-1981
See Chayefsky, Paddy
See also CA 9-12R; 104; CANR 18; DAM
DRAM

Chedid, Andree 1920- .... **CLC 47**
See also CA 145; CANR 95

Cheever, John 1912-1982 ..... **CLC 3, 7, 8, 11,
15, 25, 64; SSC 1, 38; WLC**
See also AMWS 1; BPFB 1; CA 5-8R; 106;
CABS 1; CANR 5, 27, 76; CDALB 1941-
1968; CPW; DA; DA3; DAB; DAC;
DAM MST, NOV, POP; DLB 2, 102, 227;
DLBY 1980, 1982; EXPS; INT CANR-5;
MTCW 1, 2; RGAL 4; RGSF 2; SSFS 2,
14

Cheever, Susan 1943- .... **CLC 18, 48**
See also CA 103; CANR 27, 51, 92; DLBY
1982; INT CANR-27

Chekhonte, Antosha
See Chekhov, Anton (Pavlovich)

Chekhov, Anton (Pavlovich)
1860-1904 . **TCLC 3, 10, 31, 55, 96; DC
9; SSC 2, 28, 41, 51; WLC**
See also BYA 14; CA 104; 124; DA; DA3;
DAB; DAC; DAM DRAM, MST; DFS 1,
5, 10, 12; EW 7; EXPS; LAIT 3; RGSF
2; RGWL 2; SATA 90; SSFS 5, 13, 14

Cheney, Lynne V. 1941- .... **CLC 70**
See also CA 89-92; CANR 58

Chernyshevsky, Nikolai Gavrilovich
See Chernyshevsky, Nikolay Gavrilovich
See also DLB 238

Chernyshevsky, Nikolay Gavrilovich
1828-1889 .... **NCLC 1**
See also Chernyshevsky, Nikolai Gavrilov-
ich

Cherry, Carolyn Janice 1942-
See Cherryh, C. J.
See also CA 65-68; CANR 10

Cherryh, C. J. .... **CLC 35**
See also Cherry, Carolyn Janice
See also AAYA 24; BPFB 1; DLBY 1980;
FANT; SATA 93; SCFW 2; SFW 4; YAW

Chesnutt, Charles W(addell)
1858-1932 .... **TCLC 5, 39; BLC 1; SSC
7, 54**
See also AFAW 1, 2; BW 1, 3; CA 106;
125; CANR 76; DAM MULT; DLB 12,
50, 78; MTCW 1, 2; RGAL 4; RGSF 2;
SSFS 11

Chester, Alfred 1929(?)-1971 .... **CLC 49**
See also CA 196; 33-36R; DLB 130

Chesterton, G(ilbert) K(eith)
1874-1936 . **TCLC 1, 6, 64; PC 28; SSC
1, 46**
See also BRW 6; CA 104; 132; CANR 73;
CDBLB 1914-1945; CMW 4; DAM NOV,
POET; DLB 10, 19, 34, 70, 98, 149, 178;
FANT; MSW; MTCW 1, 2; RGEL 2;
RGSF 2; SATA 27; SUFW

Chiang, Pin-chin 1904-1986
See Ding Ling
See also CA 118

Ch'ien, Chung-shu 1910-1998 .... **CLC 22**
See also CA 130; CANR 73; MTCW 1, 2

Chikamatsu Monzaemon 1653-1724 ... **LC 66**
See also RGWL 2

Child, L. Maria
See Child, Lydia Maria

Child, Lydia Maria 1802-1880 .. **NCLC 6, 73**
See also DLB 1, 74, 243; RGAL 4; SATA
67

Child, Mrs.
See Child, Lydia Maria

Child, Philip 1898-1978 .... **CLC 19, 68**
See also CA 13-14; CAP 1; DLB 68; RHW;
SATA 47

Childers, (Robert) Erskine
1870-1922 .... **TCLC 65**
See also CA 113; 153; DLB 70

Childress, Alice 1920-1994 .. **CLC 12, 15, 86,
96; BLC 1; DC 4**
See also AAYA 8; BW 2, 3; BYA 2; CA 45-
48; 146; CAD; CANR 3, 27, 50, 74; CLR
14; CWD; DA3; DAM DRAM, MULT,
NOV; DFS 2, 8, 14; DLB 7, 38, 249;
JRDA; LAIT 5; MAICYA 1, 2; MAIC-
YAS 1; MTCW 1, 2; RGAL 4; SATA 7,
48, 81; TCLC 116; WYA; YAW

Chin, Frank (Chew, Jr.) 1940- ...... **CLC 135;
DC 7**
See also CA 33-36R; CANR 71; CD 5;
DAM MULT; DLB 206; LAIT 5; RGAL
4

Chin, Marilyn (Mei Ling) 1955- .... **PC 40**
See also CA 129; CANR 70; CWP

Chislett, (Margaret) Anne 1943- ...... **CLC 34**
See also CA 151

Chitty, Thomas Willes 1926- .... **CLC 11**
See also Hinde, Thomas
See also CA 5-8R; CN 7

Chivers, Thomas Holley
1809-1858 .... **NCLC 49**
See also DLB 3, 248; RGAL 4

Choi, Susan .... **CLC 119**

Chomette, Rene Lucien 1898-1981
See Clair, Rene
See also CA 103

Chomsky, (Avram) Noam 1928- ..... **CLC 132**
See also CA 17-20R; CANR 28, 62; DA3;
DLB 246; MTCW 1, 2

Cooper, James Fenimore
  1789-1851 .... **NCLC 1, 27, 54**
  See also AAYA 22; AMW; BPFB 1;
  CDALB 1640-1865; DA3; DLB 3, 183,
  250, 254; LAIT 1; NFS 9; RGAL 4; SATA
  19; WCH
Coover, Robert (Lowell) 1932- ...... **CLC 3, 7,**
  15, 32, 46, 87, 161; SSC 15
  See also AMWS 5; BPFB 1; CA 45-48;
  CANR 3, 37, 58; CN 7; DAM NOV; DLB
  2, 227; DLBY 1981; MTCW 1, 2; RGAL
  4; RGSF 2
Copeland, Stewart (Armstrong)
  1952- .... **CLC 26**
Copernicus, Nicolaus 1473-1543 .... **LC 45**
Coppard, A(lfred) E(dgar)
  1878-1957 .... **TCLC 5; SSC 21**
  See also CA 114; 167; DLB 162; HGG;
  RGEL 2; RGSF 2; SUFW; YABC 1
Coppee, Francois 1842-1908 .... **TCLC 25**
  See also CA 170; DLB 217
Coppola, Francis Ford 1939- ... **CLC 16, 126**
  See also AAYA 39; CA 77-80; CANR 40,
  78; DLB 44
Corbiere, Tristan 1845-1875 .... **NCLC 43**
  See also DLB 217; GFL 1789 to the Present
Corcoran, Barbara (Asenath)
  1911- .... **CLC 17**
  See also AAYA 14; CA 21-24R; CAAE 191;
  CAAS 2; CANR 11, 28, 48; CLR 50;
  DLB 52; JRDA; MAICYA 2; MAICYAS
  1; RHW; SAAS 20; SATA 3, 77, 125
Cordelier, Maurice
  See Giraudoux, Jean(-Hippolyte)
Corelli, Marie .... **TCLC 51**
  See also Mackay, Mary
  See also DLB 34, 156; RGEL 2; SUFW
Corman, Cid .... **CLC 9**
  See also Corman, Sidney
  See also CAAS 2; DLB 5, 193
Corman, Sidney 1924-
  See Corman, Cid
  See also CA 85-88; CANR 44; CP 7; DAM
  POET
Cormier, Robert (Edmund)
  1925-2000 .... **CLC 12, 30**
  See also AAYA 3, 19; BYA 1, 2, 6, 8, 9;
  CA 1-4R; CANR 5, 23, 76, 93; CDALB
  1968-1988; CLR 12, 55; DA; DAB; DAC;
  DAM MST, NOV; DLB 52; EXPN; INT
  CANR-23; JRDA; LAIT 5; MAICYA 1,
  2; MTCW 1, 2; NFS 2; SATA 10, 45, 83;
  SATA-Obit 122; WYA; YAW
Corn, Alfred (DeWitt III) 1943- .... **CLC 33**
  See also CA 179; CAAE 179; CAAS 25;
  CANR 44; CP 7; CSW; DLB 120; DLBY
  1980
Corneille, Pierre 1606-1684 .... **LC 28**
  See also DAB; DAM MST; EW 3; GFL
  Beginnings to 1789; RGWL 2
Cornwell, David (John Moore)
  1931- .... **CLC 9, 15**
  See also le Carre, John
  See also CA 5-8R; CANR 13, 33, 59, 107;
  DA3; DAM POP; MTCW 1, 2
Cornwell, Patricia (Daniels) 1956- . **CLC 155**
  See also AAYA 16; BPFB 1; CA 134;
  CANR 53; CMW 4; CPW; CSW; DAM
  POP; MSW; MTCW 1
Corso, (Nunzio) Gregory 1930-2001 . **CLC 1,**
  11; PC 33
  See also CA 5-8R; 193; CANR 41, 76; CP
  7; DA3; DLB 5, 16, 237; MTCW 1, 2;
  WP
Cortazar, Julio 1914-1984 ... **CLC 2, 3, 5, 10,**
  13, 15, 33, 34, 92; HLC 1; SSC 7
  See also BPFB 1; CA 21-24R; CANR 12,
  32, 81; CDWLB 3; DA3; DAM MULT,
  NOV; DLB 113; EXPS; HW 1, 2; LAW;
  MTCW 1, 2; RGSF 2; RGWL 2; SSFS 3;
  WLIT 1

Cortes, Hernan 1485-1547 .... **LC 31**
Corvinus, Jakob
  See Raabe, Wilhelm (Karl)
Corvo, Baron
  See Rolfe, Frederick (William Serafino
  Austin Lewis Mary)
  See also GLL 1; RGEL 2
Corwin, Cecil
  See Kornbluth, C(yril) M.
Cosic, Dobrica 1921- .... **CLC 14**
  See also CA 122; 138; CDWLB 4; CWW
  2; DLB 181
Costain, Thomas B(ertram)
  1885-1965 .... **CLC 30**
  See also BYA 3; CA 5-8R; 25-28R; DLB 9;
  RHW
Costantini, Humberto 1924(?)-1987 . **CLC 49**
  See also CA 131; 122; HW 1
Costello, Elvis 1955- .... **CLC 21**
Costenoble, Philostene 1898-1962
  See Ghelderode, Michel de
Costenoble, Philostene 1898-1962
  See Ghelderode, Michel de
Cotes, Cecil V.
  See Duncan, Sara Jeannette
Cotter, Joseph Seamon Sr.
  1861-1949 .... **TCLC 28; BLC 1**
  See also BW 1; CA 124; DAM MULT; DLB
  50
Couch, Arthur Thomas Quiller
  See Quiller-Couch, Sir Arthur (Thomas)
Coulton, James
  See Hansen, Joseph
Couperus, Louis (Marie Anne)
  1863-1923 .... **TCLC 15**
  See also CA 115; RGWL 2
Coupland, Douglas 1961- .... **CLC 85, 133**
  See also AAYA 34; CA 142; CANR 57, 90;
  CCA 1; CPW; DAC; DAM POP
Court, Wesli
  See Turco, Lewis (Putnam)
Courtenay, Bryce 1933- .... **CLC 59**
  See also CA 138; CPW
Courtney, Robert
  See Ellison, Harlan (Jay)
Cousteau, Jacques-Yves 1910-1997 .. **CLC 30**
  See also CA 65-68; 159; CANR 15, 67;
  MTCW 1; SATA 38, 98
Coventry, Francis 1725-1754 .... **LC 46**
Coverdale, Miles c. 1487-1569 .... **LC 77**
  See also DLB 167
Cowan, Peter (Walkinshaw) 1914- .... **SSC 28**
  See also CA 21-24R; CANR 9, 25, 50, 83;
  CN 7; DLB 260; RGSF 2
Coward, Noel (Peirce) 1899-1973 . **CLC 1, 9,**
  29, 51
  See also AITN 1; BRWS 2; CA 17-18; 41-
  44R; CANR 35; CAP 2; CDBLB 1914-
  1945; DA3; DAM DRAM; DFS 3, 6;
  DLB 10, 245; IDFW 3, 4; MTCW 1, 2;
  RGEL 2
Cowley, Abraham 1618-1667 .... **LC 43**
  See also BRW 2; DLB 131, 151; PAB;
  RGEL 2
Cowley, Malcolm 1898-1989 .... **CLC 39**
  See also AMWS 2; CA 5-8R; 128; CANR
  3, 55; DLB 4, 48; DLBY 1981, 1989;
  MTCW 1, 2
Cowper, William 1731-1800 ..... **NCLC 8, 94;**
  PC 40
  See also BRW 3; DA3; DAM POET; DLB
  104, 109; RGEL 2
Cox, William Trevor 1928-
  See Trevor, William
  See also CA 9-12R; CANR 4, 37, 55, 76,
  102; DAM NOV; INT CANR-37; MTCW
  1, 2
Coyne, P. J.
  See Masters, Hilary

Cozzens, James Gould 1903-1978 . **CLC 1, 4,**
  11, 92
  See also AMW; BPFB 1; CA 9-12R; 81-84;
  CANR 19; CDALB 1941-1968; DLB 9;
  DLBD 2; DLBY 1984, 1997; MTCW 1,
  2; RGAL 4
Crabbe, George 1754-1832 .... **NCLC 26**
  See also BRW 3; DLB 93; RGEL 2
Crace, Jim 1946- .... **CLC 157**
  See also CA 128; 135; CANR 55, 70; CN
  7; DLB 231; INT CA-135
Craddock, Charles Egbert
  See Murfree, Mary Noailles
Craig, A. A.
  See Anderson, Poul (William)
Craik, Mrs.
  See Craik, Dinah Maria (Mulock)
  See also RGEL 2
Craik, Dinah Maria (Mulock)
  1826-1887 .... **NCLC 38**
  See also Craik, Mrs.; Mulock, Dinah Maria
  See also DLB 35, 163; MAICYA 1, 2;
  SATA 34
Cram, Ralph Adams 1863-1942 ..... **TCLC 45**
  See also CA 160
Cranch, Christopher Pearse
  1813-1892 .... **NCLC 115**
  See also DLB 1, 42, 243
Crane, (Harold) Hart 1899-1932 .... **TCLC 2,**
  5, 80; PC 3; WLC
  See also AMW; CA 104; 127; CDALB
  1917-1929; DA; DA3; DAB; DAC; DAM
  MST, POET; DLB 4, 48; MTCW 1, 2;
  RGAL 4
Crane, R(onald) S(almon)
  1886-1967 .... **CLC 27**
  See also CA 85-88, DLB 63
Crane, Stephen (Townley)
  1871-1900 ...... **TCLC 11, 17, 32; SSC 7;**
  WLC
  See also AAYA 21; AMW; BPFB 1; BYA 3;
  CA 109; 140; CANR 84; CDALB 1865-
  1917; DA; DA3; DAB; DAC; DAM MST,
  NOV, POET; DLB 12, 54, 78; EXPN;
  EXPS; LAIT 2; NFS 4; PFS 9; RGAL 4;
  RGSF 2; SSFS 4; WYA; YABC 2
Cranshaw, Stanley
  See Fisher, Dorothy (Frances) Canfield
Crase, Douglas 1944- .... **CLC 58**
  See also CA 106
Crashaw, Richard 1612(?)-1649 .... **LC 24**
  See also BRW 2; DLB 126; PAB; RGEL 2
Craven, Margaret 1901-1980 .... **CLC 17**
  See also BYA 2; CA 103; CCA 1; DAC;
  LAIT 5
Crawford, F(rancis) Marion
  1854-1909 .... **TCLC 10**
  See also CA 107; 168; DLB 71; HGG;
  RGAL 4; SUFW
Crawford, Isabella Valancy
  1850-1887 .... **NCLC 12**
  See also DLB 92; RGEL 2
Crayon, Geoffrey
  See Irving, Washington
Creasey, John 1908-1973 .... **CLC 11**
  See also Marric, J. J.
  See also CA 5-8R; 41-44R; CANR 8, 59;
  CMW 4; DLB 77; MTCW 1
Crebillon, Claude Prosper Jolyot de (fils)
  1707-1777 .... **LC 1, 28**
  See also GFL Beginnings to 1789
Credo
  See Creasey, John
Credo, Alvaro J. de
  See Prado (Calvo), Pedro

Diderot, Denis 1713-1784 .... **LC 26**
See also EW 4; GFL Beginnings to 1789; RGWL 2

Didion, Joan 1934- . **CLC 1, 3, 8, 14, 32, 129**
See also AITN 1; AMWS 4; CA 5-8R; CANR 14, 52, 76; CDALB 1968-1988; CN 7; DA3; DAM NOV; DLB 2, 173, 185; DLBY 1981, 1986; MAWW; MTCW 1, 2; NFS 3; RGAL 4; TCWW 2

Dietrich, Robert
See Hunt, E(verette) Howard, (Jr.)

Difusa, Pati
See Almodovar, Pedro

Dillard, Annie 1945- .... **CLC 9, 60, 115**
See also AAYA 6, 43; AMWS 6; ANW; CA 49-52; CANR 3, 43, 62, 90; DA3; DAM NOV; DLBY 1980; LAIT 4, 5; MTCW 1, 2; NCFS 1; RGAL 4; SATA 10

Dillard, R(ichard) H(enry) W(ilde)
1937- .... **CLC 5**
See also CA 21-24R; CAAS 7; CANR 10; CP 7; CSW; DLB 5, 244

Dillon, Eilis 1920-1994 .... **CLC 17**
See also CA 9-12R, 182; 147; CAAE 182; CAAS 3; CANR 4, 38, 78; CLR 26; MAICYA 1, 2; MAICYAS 1; SATA 2, 74; SATA-Essay 105; SATA-Obit 83; YAW

Dimont, Penelope
See Mortimer, Penelope (Ruth)

Dinesen, Isak .... **CLC 10, 29, 95; SSC 7**
See also Blixen, Karen (Christentze Dinesen)
See also EW 10; EXPS; FW; HGG; LAIT 3; MTCW 1; NCFS 2; NFS 9; RGSF 2; RGWL 2; SSFS 3, 6, 13; WLIT 2

Ding Ling .... **CLC 68**
See also Chiang, Pin-chin

Diphusa, Patty
See Almodovar, Pedro

Disch, Thomas M(ichael) 1940- ... **CLC 7, 36**
See also AAYA 17; BPFB 1; CA 21-24R; CAAS 4; CANR 17, 36, 54, 89; CLR 18; CP 7; DA3; DLB 8; HGG; MAICYA 1, 2; MTCW 1, 2; SAAS 15; SATA 92; SCFW; SFW 4

Disch, Tom
See Disch, Thomas M(ichael)

d'Isly, Georges
See Simenon, Georges (Jacques Christian)

Disraeli, Benjamin 1804-1881 ... **NCLC 2, 39, 79**
See also BRW 4; DLB 21, 55; RGEL 2

Ditcum, Steve
See Crumb, R(obert)

Dixon, Paige
See Corcoran, Barbara (Asenath)

Dixon, Stephen 1936- .... **CLC 52; SSC 16**
See also CA 89-92; CANR 17, 40, 54, 91; CN 7; DLB 130

Doak, Annie
See Dillard, Annie

Dobell, Sydney Thompson
1824-1874 .... **NCLC 43**
See also DLB 32; RGEL 2

Doblin, Alfred .... **TCLC 13**
See also Doeblin, Alfred
See also CDWLB 2; RGWL 2

Dobrolyubov, Nikolai Alexandrovich
1836-1861 .... **NCLC 5**

Dobson, Austin 1840-1921 .... **TCLC 79**
See also DLB 35, 144

Dobyns, Stephen 1941- .... **CLC 37**
See also CA 45-48; CANR 2, 18, 99; CMW 4; CP 7

Doctorow, E(dgar) L(aurence)
1931- .... **CLC 6, 11, 15, 18, 37, 44, 65, 113**
See also AAYA 22; AITN 2; AMWS 4; BEST 89:3; BPFB 1; CA 45-48; CANR 2, 33, 51, 76, 97; CDALB 1968-1988; CN 7; CPW; DA3; DAM NOV, POP; DLB 2, 28, 173; DLBY 1980; LAIT 3; MTCW 1, 2; NFS 6; RGAL 4; RHW

Dodgson, Charles L(utwidge) 1832-1898
See Carroll, Lewis
See also CLR 2; DA; DA3; DAB; DAC; DAM MST, NOV, POET; MAICYA 1, 2; SATA 100; YABC 2

Dodson, Owen (Vincent)
1914-1983 .... **CLC 79; BLC 1**
See also BW 1; CA 65-68; 110; CANR 24; DAM MULT; DLB 76

Doeblin, Alfred 1878-1957 .... **TCLC 13**
See also Doblin, Alfred
See also CA 110; 141; DLB 66

Doerr, Harriet 1910- .... **CLC 34**
See also CA 117; 122; CANR 47; INT 122

Domecq, H(onorio Bustos)
See Bioy Casares, Adolfo

Domecq, H(onorio) Bustos
See Bioy Casares, Adolfo; Borges, Jorge Luis

Domini, Rey
See Lorde, Audre (Geraldine)
See also GLL 1

Dominique
See Proust, (Valentin-Louis-George-Eugene-)Marcel

Don, A
See Stephen, Sir Leslie

Donaldson, Stephen R(eeder)
1947- .... **CLC 46, 138**
See also AAYA 36; BPFB 1; CA 89-92; CANR 13, 55, 99; CPW; DAM POP; FANT; INT CANR-13; SATA 121; SFW 4; SUFW

Donleavy, J(ames) P(atrick) 1926- .... **CLC 1, 4, 6, 10, 45**
See also AITN 2; BPFB 1; CA 9-12R; CANR 24, 49, 62, 80; CBD; CD 5; CN 7; DLB 6, 173; INT CANR-24; MTCW 1, 2; RGAL 4

Donne, John 1572-1631 ..... **LC 10, 24; PC 1; WLC**
See also BRW 1; BRWR 2; CDBLB Before 1660; DA; DAB; DAC; DAM MST, POET; DLB 121, 151; EXPP; PAB; PFS 2, 11; RGEL 2; WLIT 3; WP

Donnell, David 1939(?)- .... **CLC 34**
See also CA 197

Donoghue, P. S.
See Hunt, E(verette) Howard, (Jr.)

Donoso (Yanez), Jose 1924-1996 .... **CLC 4, 8, 11, 32, 99; HLC 1; SSC 34**
See also CA 81-84; 155; CANR 32, 73; CDWLB 3; DAM MULT; DLB 113; HW 1, 2; LAW; LAWS 1; MTCW 1, 2; RGSF 2; WLIT 1

Donovan, John 1928-1992 .... **CLC 35**
See also AAYA 20; CA 97-100; 137; CLR 3; MAICYA 1, 2; SATA 72; SATA-Brief 29; YAW

Don Roberto
See Cunninghame Graham, Robert (Gallnigad) Bontine

Doolittle, Hilda 1886-1961 . **CLC 3, 8, 14, 31, 34, 73; PC 5; WLC**
See also H. D.
See also AMWS 1; CA 97-100; CANR 35; DA; DAC; DAM MST, POET; DLB 4, 45; FW; GLL 1; MAWW; MTCW 1, 2; PFS 6; RGAL 4

Doppo, Kunikida .... **TCLC 99**
See also Kunikida Doppo

Dorfman, Ariel 1942- .... **CLC 48, 77; HLC 1**
See also CA 124; 130; CANR 67, 70; CWW 2; DAM MULT; DFS 4; HW 1, 2; INT CA-130; WLIT 1

Dorn, Edward (Merton)
1929-1999 .... **CLC 10, 18**
See also CA 93-96; 187; CANR 42, 79; CP 7; DLB 5; INT 93-96; WP

Dor-Ner, Zvi .... **CLC 70**

Dorris, Michael (Anthony)
1945-1997 .... **CLC 109**
See also AAYA 20; BEST 90:1; BYA 12; CA 102; 157; CANR 19, 46, 75; CLR 58; DA3; DAM MULT, NOV; DLB 175; LAIT 5; MTCW 2; NFS 3; NNAL; RGAL 4; SATA 75; SATA-Obit 94; TCWW 2; YAW

Dorris, Michael A.
See Dorris, Michael (Anthony)

Dorsan, Luc
See Simenon, Georges (Jacques Christian)

Dorsange, Jean
See Simenon, Georges (Jacques Christian)

Dos Passos, John (Roderigo)
1896-1970 ... **CLC 1, 4, 8, 11, 15, 25, 34, 82; WLC**
See also AMW; BPFB 1; CA 1-4R; 29-32R; CANR 3; CDALB 1929-1941; DA; DA3; DAB; DAC; DAM MST, NOV; DLB 4, 9; DLBD 1, 15; DLBY 1996; MTCW 1, 2; NFS 14; RGAL 4

Dossage, Jean
See Simenon, Georges (Jacques Christian)

Dostoevsky, Fedor Mikhailovich
1821-1881 . **NCLC 2, 7, 21, 33, 43; SSC 2, 33, 44; WLC**
See also Dostoevsky, Fyodor
See also AAYA 40; DA; DA3; DAB; DAC; DAM MST, NOV; EW 7; EXPN; NFS 3, 8; RGSF 2; RGWL 2; SSFS 8

Dostoevsky, Fyodor
See Dostoevsky, Fedor Mikhailovich
See also DLB 238

Doughty, Charles M(ontagu)
1843-1926 .... **TCLC 27**
See also CA 115; 178; DLB 19, 57, 174

Douglas, Ellen .... **CLC 73**
See also Haxton, Josephine Ayres; Williamson, Ellen Douglas
See also CN 7; CSW

Douglas, Gavin 1475(?)-1522 .... **LC 20**
See also DLB 132; RGEL 2

Douglas, George
See Brown, George Douglas
See also RGEL 2

Douglas, Keith (Castellain)
1920-1944 .... **TCLC 40**
See also BRW 7; CA 160; DLB 27; PAB; RGEL 2

Douglas, Leonard
See Bradbury, Ray (Douglas)

Douglas, Michael
See Crichton, (John) Michael

Douglas, (George) Norman
1868-1952 .... **TCLC 68**
See also BRW 6; CA 119; 157; DLB 34, 195; RGEL 2

Douglas, William
See Brown, George Douglas

Douglass, Frederick 1817(?)-1895 .. **NCLC 7, 55; BLC 1; WLC**
See also AFAW 1, 2; AMWS 3; CDALB 1640-1865; DA; DA3; DAC; DAM MST, MULT; DLB 1, 43, 50, 79, 243; FW; LAIT 2; NCFS 2; RGAL 4; SATA 29

Dourado, (Waldomiro Freitas) Autran
1926- .... **CLC 23, 60**
See also CA 25-28R; 179; CANR 34, 81; DLB 145; HW 2

Estleman, Loren D. 1952- .... **CLC 48**
See also AAYA 27; CA 85-88; CANR 27, 74; CMW 4; CPW; DA3; DAM NOV, POP; DLB 226; INT CANR-27; MTCW 1, 2

Etherege, Sir George 1636-1692 .... **LC 78**
See also BRW 2; DAM DRAM; DLB 80; PAB; RGEL 2

Euclid 306B.C.-283B.C. .... **CMLC 25**

Eugenides, Jeffrey 1960(?)- .... **CLC 81**
See also CA 144

Euripides c. 484B.C.-406B.C. .... **CMLC 23, 51; DC 4; WLCS**
See also AW 1; CDWLB 1; DA; DA3; DAB; DAC; DAM DRAM, MST; DFS 1, 4, 6; DLB 176; LAIT 1; RGWL 2

Evan, Evin
See Faust, Frederick (Schiller)

Evans, Caradoc 1878-1945 ... **TCLC 85; SSC 43**
See also DLB 162

Evans, Evan
See Faust, Frederick (Schiller)
See also TCWW 2

Evans, Marian
See Eliot, George

Evans, Mary Ann
See Eliot, George

Evarts, Esther
See Benson, Sally

Everett, Percival
See Everett, Percival L.
See also CSW

Everett, Percival L. 1956- .... **CLC 57**
See also Everett, Percival
See also BW 2; CA 129; CANR 94

Everson, R(onald) G(ilmour)
1903-1992 .... **CLC 27**
See also CA 17-20R; DLB 88

Everson, William (Oliver)
1912-1994 .... **CLC 1, 5, 14**
See also CA 9-12R; 145; CANR 20; DLB 5, 16, 212; MTCW 1

Evtushenko, Evgenii Aleksandrovich
See Yevtushenko, Yevgeny (Alexandrovich)
See also RGWL 2

Ewart, Gavin (Buchanan)
1916-1995 .... **CLC 13, 46**
See also BRWS 7; CA 89-92; 150; CANR 17, 46; CP 7; DLB 40; MTCW 1

Ewers, Hanns Heinz 1871-1943 ..... **TCLC 12**
See also CA 109; 149

Ewing, Frederick R.
See Sturgeon, Theodore (Hamilton)

Exley, Frederick (Earl) 1929-1992 .... **CLC 6, 11**
See also AITN 2; BPFB 1; CA 81-84; 138; DLB 143; DLBY 1981

Eynhardt, Guillermo
See Quiroga, Horacio (Sylvestre)

Ezekiel, Nissim 1924- .... **CLC 61**
See also CA 61-64; CP 7

Ezekiel, Tish O'Dowd 1943- .... **CLC 34**
See also CA 129

Fadeyev, A.
See Bulgya, Alexander Alexandrovich

Fadeyev, Alexander .... **TCLC 53**
See also Bulgya, Alexander Alexandrovich

Fagen, Donald 1948- .... **CLC 26**

Fainzilberg, Ilya Arnoldovich 1897-1937
See Ilf, Ilya
See also CA 120; 165

Fair, Ronald L. 1932- .... **CLC 18**
See also BW 1; CA 69-72; CANR 25; DLB 33

Fairbairn, Roger
See Carr, John Dickson

Fairbairns, Zoe (Ann) 1948- .... **CLC 32**
See also CA 103; CANR 21, 85; CN 7

Fairfield, Flora
See Alcott, Louisa May

Fairman, Paul W. 1916-1977
See Queen, Ellery
See also CA 114; SFW 4

Falco, Gian
See Papini, Giovanni

Falconer, James
See Kirkup, James

Falconer, Kenneth
See Kornbluth, C(yril) M.

Falkland, Samuel
See Heijermans, Herman

Fallaci, Oriana 1930- .... **CLC 11, 110**
See also CA 77-80; CANR 15, 58; FW; MTCW 1

Faludi, Susan 1959- .... **CLC 140**
See also CA 138; FW; MTCW 1; NCFS 3

Faludy, George 1913- .... **CLC 42**
See also CA 21-24R

Faludy, Gyoergy
See Faludy, George

Fanon, Frantz 1925-1961 .... **CLC 74; BLC 2**
See also BW 1; CA 116; 89-92; DAM MULT; WLIT 2

Fanshawe, Ann 1625-1680 .... **LC 11**

Fante, John (Thomas) 1911-1983 ..... **CLC 60**
See also CA 69-72; 109; CANR 23, 104; DLB 130; DLBY 1983

Farah, Nuruddin 1945- .. **CLC 53, 137; BLC 2**
See also AFW; BW 2, 3; CA 106; CANR 81; CDWLB 3; CN 7; DAM MULT; DLB 125; WLIT 2

Fargue, Leon-Paul 1876(?)-1947 .... **TCLC 11**
See also CA 109; CANR 107; DLB 258

Farigoule, Louis
See Romains, Jules

Farina, Richard 1936(?)-1966 .... **CLC 9**
See also CA 81-84; 25-28R

Farley, Walter (Lorimer)
1915-1989 .... **CLC 17**
See also BYA 14; CA 17-20R; CANR 8, 29, 84; DLB 22; JRDA; MAICYA 1, 2; SATA 2, 43, 132; YAW

Farmer, Philip Jose 1918- .... **CLC 1, 19**
See also AAYA 28; BPFB 1; CA 1-4R; CANR 4, 35; DLB 8; MTCW 1; SATA 93; SCFW 2; SFW 4

Farquhar, George 1677-1707 .... **LC 21**
See also BRW 2; DAM DRAM; DLB 84; RGEL 2

Farrell, J(ames) G(ordon)
1935-1979 .... **CLC 6**
See also CA 73-76; 89-92; CANR 36; DLB 14; MTCW 1; RGEL 2; RHW; WLIT 4

Farrell, James T(homas) 1904-1979 . **CLC 1, 4, 8, 11, 66; SSC 28**
See also AMW; BPFB 1; CA 5-8R; 89-92; CANR 9, 61; DLB 4, 9, 86; DLBD 2; MTCW 1, 2; RGAL 4

Farrell, Warren (Thomas) 1943- ...... **CLC 70**
See also CA 146

Farren, Richard J.
See Betjeman, John

Farren, Richard M.
See Betjeman, John

Fassbinder, Rainer Werner
1946-1982 .... **CLC 20**
See also CA 93-96; 106; CANR 31

Fast, Howard (Melvin) 1914- ... **CLC 23, 131**
See also AAYA 16; BPFB 1; CA 1-4R, 181; CAAE 181; CAAS 18; CANR 1, 33, 54, 75, 98; CMW 4; CN 7; CPW; DAM NOV; DLB 9; INT CANR-33; MTCW 1; RHW; SATA 7; SATA-Essay 107; TCWW 2; YAW

Faulcon, Robert
See Holdstock, Robert P.

Faulkner, William (Cuthbert)
1897-1962 .... **CLC 1, 3, 6, 8, 9, 11, 14, 18, 28, 52, 68; SSC 1, 35, 42; WLC**
See also AAYA 7; AMW; AMWR 1; BPFB 1; BYA 5; CA 81-84; CANR 33; CDALB 1929-1941; DA; DA3; DAB; DAC; DAM MST, NOV; DLB 9, 11, 44, 102; DLBD 2; DLBY 1986, 1997; EXPN; EXPS; LAIT 2; MTCW 1, 2; NFS 4, 8, 13; RGAL 4; RGSF 2; SSFS 2, 5, 6, 12

Fauset, Jessie Redmon
1882(?)-1961 .... **CLC 19, 54; BLC 2**
See also AFAW 2; BW 1; CA 109; CANR 83; DAM MULT; DLB 51; FW; MAWW

Faust, Frederick (Schiller)
1892-1944(?) .... **TCLC 49**
See also Austin, Frank; Brand, Max; Challis, George; Dawson, Peter; Dexter, Martin; Evans, Evan; Frederick, John; Frost, Frederick; Manning, David; Silver, Nicholas
See also CA 108; 152; DAM POP; DLB 256

Fawkes, Guy
See Benchley, Robert (Charles)

Fearing, Kenneth (Flexner)
1902-1961 .... **CLC 51**
See also CA 93-96; CANR 59; CMW 4; DLB 9; RGAL 4

Fecamps, Elise
See Creasey, John

Federman, Raymond 1928- .... **CLC 6, 47**
See also CA 17-20R; CAAS 8; CANR 10, 43, 83, 108; CN 7; DLBY 1980

Federspiel, J(uerg) F. 1931- .... **CLC 42**
See also CA 146

Feiffer, Jules (Ralph) 1929- ... **CLC 2, 8, 64**
See also AAYA 3; CA 17-20R; CAD; CANR 30, 59; CD 5; DAM DRAM; DLB 7, 44; INT CANR-30; MTCW 1; SATA 8, 61, 111

Feige, Hermann Albert Otto Maximilian
See Traven, B.

Feinberg, David B. 1956-1994 .... **CLC 59**
See also CA 135; 147

Feinstein, Elaine 1930- .... **CLC 36**
See also CA 69-72; CAAS 1; CANR 31, 68; CN 7; CP 7; CWP; DLB 14, 40; MTCW 1

Feke, Gilbert David .... **CLC 65**

Feldman, Irving (Mordecai) 1928- ..... **CLC 7**
See also CA 1-4R; CANR 1; CP 7; DLB 169

Felix-Tchicaya, Gerald
See Tchicaya, Gerald Felix

Fellini, Federico 1920-1993 .... **CLC 16, 85**
See also CA 65-68; 143; CANR 33

Felsen, Henry Gregor 1916-1995 ..... **CLC 17**
See also CA 1-4R; 180; CANR 1; SAAS 2; SATA 1

Felski, Rita .... **CLC 65**

Fenno, Jack
See Calisher, Hortense

Fenollosa, Ernest (Francisco)
1853-1908 .... **TCLC 91**

Fenton, James Martin 1949- .... **CLC 32**
See also CA 102; CANR 108; CP 7; DLB 40; PFS 11

Ferber, Edna 1887-1968 .... **CLC 18, 93**
See also AITN 1; CA 5-8R; 25-28R; CANR 68, 105; DLB 9, 28, 86; MTCW 1, 2; RGAL 4; RHW; SATA 7; TCWW 2

Ferdowsi, Abu'l Qasem 940-1020 . **CMLC 43**
See also RGWL 2

Ferguson, Helen
See Kavan, Anna

Goldman, William (W.) 1931- ...... **CLC 1, 48**
See also BPFB 2; CA 9-12R; CANR 29, 69, 106; CN 7; DLB 44; FANT; IDFW 3, 4

Goldmann, Lucien 1913-1970 .... **CLC 24**
See also CA 25-28; CAP 2

Goldoni, Carlo 1707-1793 .... **LC 4**
See also DAM DRAM; EW 4; RGWL 2

Goldsberry, Steven 1949- .... **CLC 34**
See also CA 131

Goldsmith, Oliver 1730-1774 .. **LC 2, 48; DC 8; WLC**
See also BRW 3; CDBLB 1660-1789; DA; DAB; DAC; DAM DRAM, MST, NOV, POET; DFS 1; DLB 39, 89, 104, 109, 142; IDTP; RGEL 2; SATA 26; TEA; WLIT 3

Goldsmith, Peter
See Priestley, J(ohn) B(oynton)

Gombrowicz, Witold 1904-1969 .... **CLC 4, 7, 11, 49**
See also CA 19-20; 25-28R; CANR 105; CAP 2; CDWLB 4; DAM DRAM; DLB 215; EW 12; RGWL 2

Gomez de Avellaneda, Gertrudis
1814-1873 .... **NCLC 111**
See also LAW

Gomez de la Serna, Ramon
1888-1963 .... **CLC 9**
See also CA 153; 116; CANR 79; HW 1, 2

Goncharov, Ivan Alexandrovich
1812-1891 .... **NCLC 1, 63**
See also DLB 238; EW 6; RGWL 2

Goncourt, Edmond (Louis Antoine Huot) de
1822-1896 .... **NCLC 7**
See also DLB 123; EW 7; GFL 1789 to the Present; RGWL 2

Goncourt, Jules (Alfred Huot) de
1830-1870 .... **NCLC 7**
See also DLB 123; EW 7; GFL 1789 to the Present; RGWL 2

Gongora (y Argote), Luis de
1561-1627 .... **LC 72**
See also RGWL 2

Gontier, Fernande 19(?)- .... **CLC 50**

Gonzalez Martinez, Enrique
1871-1952 .... **TCLC 72**
See also CA 166; CANR 81; HW 1, 2

Goodison, Lorna 1947- .... **PC 36**
See also CA 142; CANR 88; CP 7; CWP; DLB 157

Goodman, Paul 1911-1972 ..... **CLC 1, 2, 4, 7**
See also CA 19-20; 37-40R; CAD; CANR 34; CAP 2; DLB 130, 246; MTCW 1; RGAL 4

Gordimer, Nadine 1923- ...... **CLC 3, 5, 7, 10, 18, 33, 51, 70, 123, 160, 161; SSC 17; WLCS**
See also AAYA 39; AFW; BRWS 2; CA 5-8R; CANR 3, 28, 56, 88; CN 7; DA; DA3; DAB; DAC; DAM MST, NOV; DLB 225; EXPS; INT CANR-28; MTCW 1, 2; NFS 4; RGEL 2; RGSF 2; SSFS 2, 14; WLIT 2; YAW

Gordon, Adam Lindsay
1833-1870 .... **NCLC 21**
See also DLB 230

Gordon, Caroline 1895-1981 . **CLC 6, 13, 29, 83; SSC 15**
See also AMW; CA 11-12; 103; CANR 36; CAP 1; DLB 4, 9, 102; DLBD 17; DLBY 1981; MTCW 1, 2; RGAL 4; RGSF 2

Gordon, Charles William 1860-1937
See Connor, Ralph
See also CA 109

Gordon, Mary (Catherine) 1949- .... **CLC 13, 22, 128**
See also AMWS 4; BPFB 2; CA 102; CANR 44, 92; CN 7; DLB 6; DLBY 1981; FW; INT CA-102; MTCW 1

Gordon, N. J.
See Bosman, Herman Charles

Gordon, Sol 1923- .... **CLC 26**
See also CA 53-56; CANR 4; SATA 11

Gordone, Charles 1925-1995 .. **CLC 1, 4; DC 8**
See also BW 1, 3; CA 93-96; 180; 150; CAAE 180; CAD; CANR 55; DAM DRAM; DLB 7; INT 93-96; MTCW 1

Gore, Catherine 1800-1861 .... **NCLC 65**
See also DLB 116; RGEL 2

Gorenko, Anna Andreevna
See Akhmatova, Anna

Gorky, Maxim .... **TCLC 8; SSC 28; WLC**
See also Peshkov, Alexei Maximovich
See also DAB; DFS 9; EW 8; MTCW 2

Goryan, Sirak
See Saroyan, William

Gosse, Edmund (William)
1849-1928 .... **TCLC 28**
See also CA 117; DLB 57, 144, 184; RGEL 2

Gotlieb, Phyllis Fay (Bloom) 1926- .. **CLC 18**
See also CA 13-16R; CANR 7; DLB 88, 251; SFW 4

Gottesman, S. D.
See Kornbluth, C(yril) M.; Pohl, Frederik

Gottfried von Strassburg fl. c.
1170-1215 .... **CMLC 10**
See also CDWLB 2; DLB 138; EW 1; RGWL 2

Gould, Lois 1932(?)-2002 .... **CLC 4, 10**
See also CA 77-80; CANR 29; MTCW 1

Gourmont, Remy(-Marie-Charles) de
1858-1915 .... **TCLC 17**
See also CA 109; 150; GFL 1789 to the Present; MTCW 2

Govier, Katherine 1948- .... **CLC 51**
See also CA 101; CANR 18, 40; CCA 1

Gower, John c. 1330-1408 .... **LC 76**
See also BRW 1; DLB 146; RGEL 2

Goyen, (Charles) William
1915-1983 .... **CLC 5, 8, 14, 40**
See also AITN 2; CA 5-8R; 110; CANR 6, 71; DLB 2, 218; DLBY 1983; INT CANR-6

Goytisolo, Juan 1931- .... **CLC 5, 10, 23, 133; HLC 1**
See also CA 85-88; CANR 32, 61; CWW 2; DAM MULT; GLL 2; HW 1, 2; MTCW 1, 2

Gozzano, Guido 1883-1916 .... **PC 10**
See also CA 154; DLB 114

Gozzi, (Conte) Carlo 1720-1806 .... **NCLC 23**

Grabbe, Christian Dietrich
1801-1836 .... **NCLC 2**
See also DLB 133; RGWL 2

Grace, Patricia Frances 1937- .... **CLC 56**
See also CA 176; CN 7; RGSF 2

Gracian y Morales, Baltasar
1601-1658 .... **LC 15**

Gracq, Julien .... **CLC 11, 48**
See also Poirier, Louis
See also CWW 2; DLB 83; GFL 1789 to the Present

Grade, Chaim 1910-1982 .... **CLC 10**
See also CA 93-96; 107

Graduate of Oxford, A
See Ruskin, John

Grafton, Garth
See Duncan, Sara Jeannette

Graham, John
See Phillips, David Graham

Graham, Jorie 1951- .... **CLC 48, 118**
See also CA 111; CANR 63; CP 7; CWP; DLB 120; PFS 10

Graham, R(obert) B(ontine) Cunninghame
See Cunninghame Graham, Robert (Gallnigad) Bontine
See also DLB 98, 135, 174; RGEL 2; RGSF 2

Graham, Robert
See Haldeman, Joe (William)

Graham, Tom
See Lewis, (Harry) Sinclair

Graham, W(illiam) S(idney)
1918-1986 .... **CLC 29**
See also BRWS 7; CA 73-76; 118; DLB 20; RGEL 2

Graham, Winston (Mawdsley)
1910- .... **CLC 23**
See also CA 49-52; CANR 2, 22, 45, 66; CMW 4; CN 7; DLB 77; RHW

Grahame, Kenneth 1859-1932 .... **TCLC 64**
See also BYA 5; CA 108; 136; CANR 80; CLR 5; CWRI 5; DA3; DAB; DLB 34, 141, 178; FANT; MAICYA 1, 2; MTCW 2; RGEL 2; SATA 100; WCH; YABC 1

Granger, Darius John
See Marlowe, Stephen

Granin, Daniil .... **CLC 59**

Granovsky, Timofei Nikolaevich
1813-1855 .... **NCLC 75**
See also DLB 198

Grant, Skeeter
See Spiegelman, Art

Granville-Barker, Harley
1877-1946 .... **TCLC 2**
See also Barker, Harley Granville
See also CA 104; DAM DRAM; RGEL 2

Granzotto, Gianni
See Granzotto, Giovanni Battista

Granzotto, Giovanni Battista
1914-1985 .... **CLC 70**
See also CA 166

Grass, Guenter (Wilhelm) 1927- ... **CLC 1, 2, 4, 6, 11, 15, 22, 32, 49, 88; WLC**
See also BPFB 2; CA 13-16R; CANR 20, 75, 93; CDWLB 2; DA; DA3; DAB; DAC; DAM MST, NOV; DLB 75, 124; EW 13; MTCW 1, 2; RGWL 2

Gratton, Thomas
See Hulme, T(homas) E(rnest)

Grau, Shirley Ann 1929- .... **CLC 4, 9, 146; SSC 15**
See also CA 89-92; CANR 22, 69; CN 7; CSW; DLB 2, 218; INT CA-89-92, CANR-22; MTCW 1

Gravel, Fern
See Hall, James Norman

Graver, Elizabeth 1964- .... **CLC 70**
See also CA 135; CANR 71

Graves, Richard Perceval
1895-1985 .... **CLC 44**
See also CA 65-68; CANR 9, 26, 51

Graves, Robert (von Ranke)
1895-1985 .. **CLC 1, 2, 6, 11, 39, 44, 45; PC 6**
See also BPFB 2; BRW 7; BYA 4; CA 5-8R; 117; CANR 5, 36; CDBLB 1914-1945; DA3; DAB; DAC; DAM MST, POET; DLB 20, 100, 191; DLBD 18; DLBY 1985; MTCW 1, 2; NCFS 2; RGEL 2; RHW; SATA 45

Graves, Valerie
See Bradley, Marion Zimmer

Gray, Alasdair (James) 1934- .... **CLC 41**
See also CA 126; CANR 47, 69, 106; CN 7; DLB 194, 261; HGG; INT CA-126; MTCW 1, 2; RGSF 2

Gray, Amlin 1946- .... **CLC 29**
See also CA 138

Gray, Francine du Plessix 1930- ..... **CLC 22, 153**
See also BEST 90:3; CA 61-64; CAAS 2; CANR 11, 33, 75, 81; DAM NOV; INT CANR-11; MTCW 1, 2

Gray, John (Henry) 1866-1934 ...... **TCLC 19**
See also CA 119; 162; RGEL 2

Gray, Simon (James Holliday) 1936- .... **CLC 9, 14, 36**
See also AITN 1; CA 21-24R; CAAS 3; CANR 32, 69; CD 5; DLB 13; MTCW 1; RGEL 2

Gray, Spalding 1941- ..... **CLC 49, 112; DC 7**
See also CA 128; CAD; CANR 74; CD 5; CPW; DAM POP; MTCW 2

Gray, Thomas 1716-1771 .... **LC 4, 40; PC 2; WLC**
See also BRW 3; CDBLB 1660-1789; DA; DA3; DAB; DAC; DAM MST; DLB 109; EXPP; PAB; PFS 9; RGEL 2; WP

Grayson, David
See Baker, Ray Stannard

Grayson, Richard (A.) 1951- .... **CLC 38**
See also CA 85-88; CANR 14, 31, 57; DLB 234

Greeley, Andrew M(oran) 1928- ...... **CLC 28**
See also BPFB 2; CA 5-8R; CAAS 7; CANR 7, 43, 69, 104; CMW 4; CPW; DA3; DAM POP; MTCW 1, 2

Green, Anna Katharine
1846-1935 .... **TCLC 63**
See also CA 112; 159; CMW 4; DLB 202, 221; MSW

Green, Brian
See Card, Orson Scott

Green, Hannah
See Greenberg, Joanne (Goldenberg)

Green, Hannah 1927(?)-1996 .... **CLC 3**
See also CA 73-76; CANR 59, 93; NFS 10

Green, Henry .... **CLC 2, 13, 97**
See also Yorke, Henry Vincent
See also BRWS 2; CA 175; DLB 15; RGEL 2

Green, Julian (Hartridge) 1900-1998
See Green, Julien
See also CA 21-24R; 169; CANR 33, 87; DLB 4, 72; MTCW 1

Green, Julien .... **CLC 3, 11, 77**
See also Green, Julian (Hartridge)
See also GFL 1789 to the Present; MTCW 2

Green, Paul (Eliot) 1894-1981 .... **CLC 25**
See also AITN 1; CA 5-8R; 103; CANR 3; DAM DRAM; DLB 7, 9, 249; DLBY 1981; RGAL 4

Greenaway, Peter 1942- .... **CLC 159**
See also CA 127

Greenberg, Ivan 1908-1973
See Rahv, Philip
See also CA 85-88

Greenberg, Joanne (Goldenberg)
1932- .... **CLC 7, 30**
See also AAYA 12; CA 5-8R; CANR 14, 32, 69; CN 7; SATA 25; YAW

Greenberg, Richard 1959(?)- .... **CLC 57**
See also CA 138; CAD; CD 5

Greenblatt, Stephen J(ay) 1943- ...... **CLC 70**
See also CA 49-52

Greene, Bette 1934- .... **CLC 30**
See also AAYA 7; BYA 3; CA 53-56; CANR 4; CLR 2; CWRI 5; JRDA; LAIT 4; MAICYA 1, 2; NFS 10; SAAS 16; SATA 8, 102; WYA; YAW

Greene, Gael .... **CLC 8**
See also CA 13-16R; CANR 10

Greene, Graham (Henry)
1904-1991 .... **CLC 1, 3, 6, 9, 14, 18, 27, 37, 70, 72, 125; SSC 29; WLC**
See also AITN 2; BPFB 2; BRWR 2; BRWS 1; BYA 3; CA 13-16R; 133; CANR 35, 61; CBD; CDBLB 1945-1960; CMW 4; DA; DA3; DAB; DAC; DAM MST, NOV; DLB 13, 15, 77, 100, 162, 201, 204; DLBY 1991; MSW; MTCW 1, 2; RGEL 2; SATA 20; SSFS 14; WLIT 4

Greene, Robert 1558-1592 .... **LC 41**
See also DLB 62, 167; IDTP; RGEL 2; TEA

Greer, Germaine 1939- .... **CLC 131**
See also AITN 1; CA 81-84; CANR 33, 70; FW; MTCW 1, 2

Greer, Richard
See Silverberg, Robert

Gregor, Arthur 1923- .... **CLC 9**
See also CA 25-28R; CAAS 10; CANR 11; CP 7; SATA 36

Gregor, Lee
See Pohl, Frederik

Gregory, Lady Isabella Augusta (Persse)
1852-1932 .... **TCLC 1**
See also BRW 6; CA 104; 184; DLB 10; IDTP; RGEL 2

Gregory, J. Dennis
See Williams, John A(lfred)

Grekova, I. .... **CLC 59**

Grendon, Stephen
See Derleth, August (William)

Grenville, Kate 1950- .... **CLC 61**
See also CA 118; CANR 53, 93

Grenville, Pelham
See Wodehouse, P(elham) G(renville)

Greve, Felix Paul (Berthold Friedrich)
1879-1948
See Grove, Frederick Philip
See also CA 104; 141, 175; CANR 79; DAC; DAM MST

Greville, Fulke 1554-1628 .... **LC 79**
See also DLB 62, 172; RGEL 2

Grey, Zane 1872-1939 .... **TCLC 6**
See also BPFB 2; CA 104; 132; DA3; DAM POP; DLB 9, 212; MTCW 1, 2; RGAL 4; TCWW 2

Grieg, (Johan) Nordahl (Brun)
1902-1943 .... **TCLC 10**
See also CA 107; 189

Grieve, C(hristopher) M(urray)
1892-1978 .... **CLC 11, 19**
See also MacDiarmid, Hugh; Pteleon
See also CA 5-8R; 85-88; CANR 33, 107; DAM POET; MTCW 1; RGEL 2

Griffin, Gerald 1803-1840 .... **NCLC 7**
See also DLB 159; RGEL 2

Griffin, John Howard 1920-1980 ..... **CLC 68**
See also AITN 1; CA 1-4R; 101; CANR 2

Griffin, Peter 1942- .... **CLC 39**
See also CA 136

Griffith, D(avid Lewelyn) W(ark)
1875(?)-1948 .... **TCLC 68**
See also CA 119; 150; CANR 80

Griffith, Lawrence
See Griffith, D(avid Lewelyn) W(ark)

Griffiths, Trevor 1935- .... **CLC 13, 52**
See also CA 97-100; CANR 45; CBD; CD 5; DLB 13, 245

Griggs, Sutton (Elbert)
1872-1930 .... **TCLC 77**
See also CA 123; 186; DLB 50

Grigson, Geoffrey (Edward Harvey)
1905-1985 .... **CLC 7, 39**
See also CA 25-28R; 118; CANR 20, 33; DLB 27; MTCW 1, 2

Grillparzer, Franz 1791-1872 . **NCLC 1, 102; DC 14; SSC 37**
See also CDWLB 2; DLB 133; EW 5; RGWL 2

Grimble, Reverend Charles James
See Eliot, T(homas) S(tearns)

Grimke, Charlotte L(ottie) Forten
1837(?)-1914
See Forten, Charlotte L.
See also BW 1; CA 117; 124; DAM MULT, POET

Grimm, Jacob Ludwig Karl
1785-1863 .... **NCLC 3, 77; SSC 36**
See also DLB 90; MAICYA 1, 2; RGSF 2; RGWL 2; SATA 22; WCH

Grimm, Wilhelm Karl 1786-1859 .. **NCLC 3, 77; SSC 36**
See also CDWLB 2; DLB 90; MAICYA 1, 2; RGSF 2; RGWL 2; SATA 22; WCH

Grimmelshausen, Hans Jakob Christoffel von
See Grimmelshausen, Johann Jakob Christoffel von
See also RGWL 2

Grimmelshausen, Johann Jakob Christoffel von 1621-1676 .... **LC 6**
See also Grimmelshausen, Hans Jakob Christoffel von
See also CDWLB 2; DLB 168

Grindel, Eugene 1895-1952
See Eluard, Paul
See also CA 104; 193

Grisham, John 1955- .... **CLC 84**
See also AAYA 14; BPFB 2; CA 138; CANR 47, 69; CMW 4; CN 7; CPW; CSW; DA3; DAM POP; MSW; MTCW 2

Grossman, David 1954- .... **CLC 67**
See also CA 138; CWW 2

Grossman, Vasily (Semenovich)
1905-1964 .... **CLC 41**
See also CA 124; 130; MTCW 1

Grove, Frederick Philip .... **TCLC 4**
See also Greve, Felix Paul (Berthold Friedrich)
See also DLB 92; RGEL 2

Grubb
See Crumb, R(obert)

Grumbach, Doris (Isaac) 1918- . **CLC 13, 22, 64**
See also CA 5-8R; CAAS 2; CANR 9, 42, 70; CN 7; INT CANR-9; MTCW 2

Grundtvig, Nicolai Frederik Severin
1783-1872 .... **NCLC 1**

Grunge
See Crumb, R(obert)

Grunwald, Lisa 1959- .... **CLC 44**
See also CA 120

Guare, John 1938- .... **CLC 8, 14, 29, 67**
See also CA 73-76; CAD; CANR 21, 69; CD 5; DAM DRAM; DFS 8, 13; DLB 7, 249; MTCW 1, 2; RGAL 4

Gubar, Susan (David) 1944- .... **CLC 145**
See also CA 108; CANR 45, 70; FW; MTCW 1; RGAL 4

Gudjonsson, Halldor Kiljan 1902-1998
See Laxness, Halldor
See also CA 103; 164; CWW 2

Guenter, Erich
See Eich, Guenter

Guest, Barbara 1920- .... **CLC 34**
See also CA 25-28R; CANR 11, 44, 84; CP 7; CWP; DLB 5, 193

Guest, Edgar A(lbert) 1881-1959 ... **TCLC 95**
See also CA 112; 168

Guest, Judith (Ann) 1936- .... **CLC 8, 30**
See also AAYA 7; CA 77-80; CANR 15, 75; DA3; DAM NOV, POP; EXPN; INT CANR-15; LAIT 5; MTCW 1, 2; NFS 1

Guevara, Che .... **CLC 87; HLC 1**
See also Guevara (Serna), Ernesto

Guevara (Serna), Ernesto
    1928-1967 .... **CLC 87; HLC 1**
    See also Guevara, Che
    See also CA 127; 111; CANR 56; DAM
    MULT; HW 1
Guicciardini, Francesco 1483-1540 ..... **LC 49**
Guild, Nicholas M. 1944- .... **CLC 33**
    See also CA 93-96
Guillemin, Jacques
    See Sartre, Jean-Paul
Guillen, Jorge 1893-1984 . **CLC 11; HLCS 1;
    PC 35**
    See also CA 89-92; 112; DAM MULT,
    POET; DLB 108; HW 1; RGWL 2
Guillen, Nicolas (Cristobal)
    1902-1989 .... **CLC 48, 79; BLC 2; HLC
    1; PC 23**
    See also BW 2; CA 116; 125; 129; CANR
    84; DAM MST, MULT, POET; HW 1;
    LAW; RGWL 2; WP
Guillen y Alavarez, Jorge
    See Guillen, Jorge
Guillevic, (Eugene) 1907-1997 .... **CLC 33**
    See also CA 93-96; CWW 2
Guillois
    See Desnos, Robert
Guillois, Valentin
    See Desnos, Robert
Guimaraes Rosa, Joao
    See Rosa, Joao Guimaraes
    See also LAW
Guimaraes Rosa, Joao 1908-1967
    See also CA 175; HLCS 2; LAW; RGSF 2;
    RGWL 2
Guiney, Louise Imogen
    1861-1920 .... **TCLC 41**
    See also CA 160; DLB 54; RGAL 4
Guinizelli, Guido c. 1230-1276 ...... **CMLC 49**
Guiraldes, Ricardo (Guillermo)
    1886-1927 .... **TCLC 39**
    See also CA 131; HW 1; LAW; MTCW 1
Gumilev, Nikolai (Stepanovich)
    1886-1921 .... **TCLC 60**
    See also CA 165
Gunesekera, Romesh 1954- .... **CLC 91**
    See also CA 159; CN 7
Gunn, Bill .... **CLC 5**
    See also Gunn, William Harrison
    See also DLB 38
Gunn, Thom(son William) 1929- .. **CLC 3, 6,
    18, 32, 81; PC 26**
    See also BRWS 4; CA 17-20R; CANR 9,
    33; CDBLB 1960 to Present; CP 7; DAM
    POET; DLB 27; INT CANR-33; MTCW
    1; PFS 9; RGEL 2
Gunn, William Harrison 1934(?)-1989
    See Gunn, Bill
    See also AITN 1; BW 1, 3; CA 13-16R;
    128; CANR 12, 25, 76
Gunn Allen, Paula
    See Allen, Paula Gunn
Gunnars, Kristjana 1948- .... **CLC 69**
    See also CA 113; CCA 1; CP 7; CWP; DLB
    60
Gurdjieff, G(eorgei) I(vanovich)
    1877(?)-1949 .... **TCLC 71**
    See also CA 157
Gurganus, Allan 1947- .... **CLC 70**
    See also BEST 90:1; CA 135; CN 7; CPW;
    CSW; DAM POP; GLL 1
Gurney, A(lbert) R(amsdell), Jr.
    1930- .... **CLC 32, 50, 54**
    See also AMWS 5; CA 77-80; CAD; CANR
    32, 64; CD 5; DAM DRAM
Gurney, Ivor (Bertie) 1890-1937 ... **TCLC 33**
    See also BRW 6; CA 167; PAB; RGEL 2
Gurney, Peter
    See Gurney, A(lbert) R(amsdell), Jr.

Guro, Elena 1877-1913 .... **TCLC 56**
Gustafson, James M(oody) 1925- ... **CLC 100**
    See also CA 25-28R; CANR 37
Gustafson, Ralph (Barker)
    1909-1995 .... **CLC 36**
    See also CA 21-24R; CANR 8, 45, 84; CP
    7; DLB 88; RGEL 2
Gut, Gom
    See Simenon, Georges (Jacques Christian)
Guterson, David 1956- .... **CLC 91**
    See also CA 132; CANR 73; MTCW 2;
    NFS 13
Guthrie, A(lfred) B(ertram), Jr.
    1901-1991 .... **CLC 23**
    See also CA 57-60; 134; CANR 24; DLB 6,
    212; SATA 62; SATA-Obit 67
Guthrie, Isobel
    See Grieve, C(hristopher) M(urray)
Guthrie, Woodrow Wilson 1912-1967
    See Guthrie, Woody
    See also CA 113; 93-96
Guthrie, Woody .... **CLC 35**
    See also Guthrie, Woodrow Wilson
    See also LAIT 3
Gutierrez Najera, Manuel 1859-1895
    See also HLCS 2; LAW
Guy, Rosa (Cuthbert) 1925- .... **CLC 26**
    See also AAYA 4, 37; BW 2; CA 17-20R;
    CANR 14, 34, 83; CLR 13; DLB 33;
    DNFS 1; JRDA; MAICYA 1, 2; SATA 14,
    62, 122; YAW
Gwendolyn
    See Bennett, (Enoch) Arnold
H. D. .... **CLC 3, 8, 14, 31, 34, 73; PC 5**
    See also Doolittle, Hilda
H. de V.
    See Buchan, John
Haavikko, Paavo Juhani 1931- .. **CLC 18, 34**
    See also CA 106
Habbema, Koos
    See Heijermans, Herman
Habermas, Juergen 1929- .... **CLC 104**
    See also CA 109; CANR 85; DLB 242
Habermas, Jurgen
    See Habermas, Juergen
Hacker, Marilyn 1942- **CLC 5, 9, 23, 72, 91**
    See also CA 77-80; CANR 68; CP 7; CWP;
    DAM POET; DLB 120; FW; GLL 2
Hadrian 76-138 .... **CMLC 52**
Haeckel, Ernst Heinrich (Philipp August)
    1834-1919 .... **TCLC 83**
    See also CA 157
Hafiz c. 1326-1389(?) .... **CMLC 34**
    See also RGWL 2
Haggard, H(enry) Rider
    1856-1925 .... **TCLC 11**
    See also BRWS 3; BYA 4, 5; CA 108; 148;
    DLB 70, 156, 174, 178; FANT; MTCW
    2; RGEL 2; RHW; SATA 16; SCFW; SFW
    4; SUFW; WLIT 4
Hagiosy, L.
    See Larbaud, Valery (Nicolas)
Hagiwara, Sakutaro 1886-1942 .... **TCLC 60;
    PC 18**
    See also CA 154
Haig, Fenil
    See Ford, Ford Madox
Haig-Brown, Roderick (Langmere)
    1908-1976 .... **CLC 21**
    See also CA 5-8R; 69-72; CANR 4, 38, 83;
    CLR 31; CWRI 5; DLB 88; MAICYA 1,
    2; SATA 12
Hailey, Arthur 1920- .... **CLC 5**
    See also AITN 2; BEST 90:3; BPFB 2; CA
    1-4R; CANR 2, 36, 75; CCA 1; CN 7;
    CPW; DAM NOV, POP; DLB 88; DLBY
    1982; MTCW 1, 2

Hailey, Elizabeth Forsythe 1938- ..... **CLC 40**
    See also CA 93-96; CAAE 188; CAAS 1;
    CANR 15, 48; INT CANR-15
Haines, John (Meade) 1924- .... **CLC 58**
    See also CA 17-20R; CANR 13, 34; CSW;
    DLB 5, 212
Hakluyt, Richard 1552-1616 .... **LC 31**
    See also DLB 136; RGEL 2
Haldeman, Joe (William) 1943- .... **CLC 61**
    See also Graham, Robert
    See also AAYA 38; CA 53-56, 179; CAAE
    179; CAAS 25; CANR 6, 70, 72; DLB 8;
    INT CANR-6; SCFW 2; SFW 4
Hale, Sarah Josepha (Buell)
    1788-1879 .... **NCLC 75**
    See also DLB 1, 42, 73, 243
Halevy, Elie 1870-1937 .... **TCLC 104**
Haley, Alex(ander Murray Palmer)
    1921-1992 .... **CLC 8, 12, 76; BLC 2**
    See also AAYA 26; BPFB 2; BW 2, 3; CA
    77-80; 136; CANR 61; CDALBS; CPW;
    CSW; DA; DA3; DAB; DAC; DAM MST,
    MULT, POP; DLB 38; LAIT 5; MTCW
    1, 2; NFS 9
Haliburton, Thomas Chandler
    1796-1865 .... **NCLC 15**
    See also DLB 11, 99; RGEL 2; RGSF 2
Hall, Donald (Andrew, Jr.) 1928- ..... **CLC 1,
    13, 37, 59, 151**
    See also CA 5-8R; CAAS 7; CANR 2, 44,
    64, 106; CP 7; DAM POET; DLB 5;
    MTCW 1; RGAL 4; SATA 23, 97
Hall, Frederic Sauser
    See Sauser-Hall, Frederic
Hall, James
    See Kuttner, Henry
Hall, James Norman 1887-1951 ..... **TCLC 23**
    See also CA 123; 173; LAIT 1; RHW 1;
    SATA 21
Hall, (Marguerite) Radclyffe
    1880-1943 .... **TCLC 12**
    See also BRWS 6; CA 110; 150; CANR 83;
    DLB 191; MTCW 2; RGEL 2; RHW
Hall, Rodney 1935- .... **CLC 51**
    See also CA 109; CANR 69; CN 7; CP 7
Hallam, Arthur Henry
    1811-1833 .... **NCLC 110**
    See also DLB 32
Halleck, Fitz-Greene 1790-1867 .... **NCLC 47**
    See also DLB 3, 250; RGAL 4
Halliday, Michael
    See Creasey, John
Halpern, Daniel 1945- .... **CLC 14**
    See also CA 33-36R; CANR 93; CP 7
Hamburger, Michael (Peter Leopold)
    1924- .... **CLC 5, 14**
    See also CA 5-8R; CAAE 196; CAAS 4;
    CANR 2, 47; CP 7; DLB 27
Hamill, Pete 1935- .... **CLC 10**
    See also CA 25-28R; CANR 18, 71
Hamilton, Alexander
    1755(?)-1804 .... **NCLC 49**
    See also DLB 37
Hamilton, Clive
    See Lewis, C(live) S(taples)
Hamilton, Edmond 1904-1977 .... **CLC 1**
    See also CA 1-4R; CANR 3, 84; DLB 8;
    SATA 118; SFW 4
Hamilton, Eugene (Jacob) Lee
    See Lee-Hamilton, Eugene (Jacob)
Hamilton, Franklin
    See Silverberg, Robert
Hamilton, Gail
    See Corcoran, Barbara (Asenath)
Hamilton, Mollie
    See Kaye, M(ary) M(argaret)
Hamilton, (Anthony Walter) Patrick
    1904-1962 .... **CLC 51**
    See also CA 176; 113; DLB 10, 191

Hiraoka, Kimitake 1925-1970
　　See Mishima, Yukio
　　See also CA 97-100; 29-32R; DA3; DAM
　　DRAM; MTCW 1, 2
Hirsch, E(ric) D(onald), Jr. 1928- .... **CLC 79**
　　See also CA 25-28R; CANR 27, 51; DLB
　　67; INT CANR-27; MTCW 1
Hirsch, Edward 1950- .... **CLC 31, 50**
　　See also CA 104; CANR 20, 42, 102; CP 7;
　　DLB 120
Hitchcock, Alfred (Joseph)
　　1899-1980 .... **CLC 16**
　　See also AAYA 22; CA 159; 97-100; SATA
　　27; SATA-Obit 24
Hitchens, Christopher (Eric)
　　1949- .... **CLC 157**
　　See also CA 149; CANR 89
Hitler, Adolf 1889-1945 .... **TCLC 53**
　　See also CA 117; 147
Hoagland, Edward 1932- .... **CLC 28**
　　See also ANW; CA 1-4R; CANR 2, 31, 57,
　　107; CN 7; DLB 6; SATA 51; TCWW 2
Hoban, Russell (Conwell) 1925- ... **CLC 7, 25**
　　See also BPFB 2; CA 5-8R; CANR 23, 37,
　　66; CLR 3, 69; CN 7; CWRI 5; DAM
　　NOV; DLB 52; FANT; MAICYA 1, 2;
　　MTCW 1, 2; SATA 1, 40, 78; SFW 4
Hobbes, Thomas 1588-1679 .... **LC 36**
　　See also DLB 151, 252; RGEL 2
Hobbs, Perry
　　See Blackmur, R(ichard) P(almer)
Hobson, Laura Z(ametkin)
　　1900-1986 .... **CLC 7, 25**
　　See also Field, Peter
　　See also BPFB 2; CA 17-20R; 118; CANR
　　55; DLB 28; SATA 52
Hoccleve, Thomas c. 1368-c. 1437 ...... **LC 75**
　　See also DLB 146; RGEL 2
Hoch, Edward D(entinger) 1930-
　　See Queen, Ellery
　　See also CA 29-32R; CANR 11, 27, 51, 97;
　　CMW 4; SFW 4
Hochhuth, Rolf 1931- .... **CLC 4, 11, 18**
　　See also CA 5-8R; CANR 33, 75; CWW 2;
　　DAM DRAM; DLB 124; MTCW 1, 2
Hochman, Sandra 1936- .... **CLC 3, 8**
　　See also CA 5-8R; DLB 5
Hochwaelder, Fritz 1911-1986 .... **CLC 36**
　　See also Hochwalder, Fritz
　　See also CA 29-32R; 120; CANR 42; DAM
　　DRAM; MTCW 1
Hochwalder, Fritz
　　See Hochwaelder, Fritz
　　See also RGWL 2
Hocking, Mary (Eunice) 1921- .... **CLC 13**
　　See also CA 101; CANR 18, 40
Hodgins, Jack 1938- .... **CLC 23**
　　See also CA 93-96; CN 7; DLB 60
Hodgson, William Hope
　　1877(?)-1918 .... **TCLC 13**
　　See also CA 111; 164; CMW 4; DLB 70,
　　153, 156, 178; HGG; MTCW 2; SFW 4;
　　SUFW
Hoeg, Peter 1957- .... **CLC 95, 156**
　　See also CA 151; CANR 75; CMW 4; DA3;
　　DLB 214; MTCW 2
Hoffman, Alice 1952- .... **CLC 51**
　　See also AAYA 37; AMWS 10; CA 77-80;
　　CANR 34, 66, 100; CN 7; CPW; DAM
　　NOV; MTCW 1, 2
Hoffman, Daniel (Gerard) 1923- . **CLC 6, 13, 23**
　　See also CA 1-4R; CANR 4; CP 7; DLB 5
Hoffman, Stanley 1944- .... **CLC 5**
　　See also CA 77-80
Hoffman, William 1925- .... **CLC 141**
　　See also CA 21-24R; CANR 9, 103; CSW;
　　DLB 234

Hoffman, William M(oses) 1939- ..... **CLC 40**
　　See also CA 57-60; CANR 11, 71
Hoffmann, E(rnst) T(heodor) A(madeus)
　　1776-1822 .... **NCLC 2; SSC 13**
　　See also CDWLB 2; DLB 90; EW 5; RGSF
　　2; RGWL 2; SATA 27; SUFW; WCH
Hofmann, Gert 1931- .... **CLC 54**
　　See also CA 128
Hofmannsthal, Hugo von
　　1874-1929 .... **TCLC 11; DC 4**
　　See also CA 106; 153; CDWLB 2; DAM
　　DRAM; DFS 12; DLB 81, 118; EW 9;
　　RGWL 2
Hogan, Linda 1947- .... **CLC 73; PC 35**
　　See also AMWS 4; ANW; BYA 12; CA 120;
　　CANR 45, 73; CWP; DAM MULT; DLB
　　175; NNAL; SATA 132; TCWW 2
Hogarth, Charles
　　See Creasey, John
Hogarth, Emmett
　　See Polonsky, Abraham (Lincoln)
Hogg, James 1770-1835 .... **NCLC 4, 109**
　　See also DLB 93, 116, 159; HGG; RGEL 2;
　　SUFW
Holbach, Paul Henri Thiry Baron
　　1723-1789 .... **LC 14**
Holberg, Ludvig 1684-1754 .... **LC 6**
　　See also RGWL 2
Holcroft, Thomas 1745-1809 .... **NCLC 85**
　　See also DLB 39, 89, 158; RGEL 2
Holden, Ursula 1921- .... **CLC 18**
　　See also CA 101; CAAS 8; CANR 22
Holderlin, (Johann Christian) Friedrich
　　1770-1843 .... **NCLC 16; PC 4**
　　See also CDWLB 2; DLB 90; EW 5; RGWL
　　2
Holdstock, Robert
　　See Holdstock, Robert P.
Holdstock, Robert P. 1948- .... **CLC 39**
　　See also CA 131; CANR 81; DLB 261;
　　FANT; HGG; SFW 4
Holinshed, Raphael fl. 1580- .... **LC 69**
　　See also DLB 167; RGEL 2
Holland, Isabelle (Christian)
　　1920-2002 .... **CLC 21**
　　See also AAYA 11; CA 21-24R; CAAE
　　181; CANR 10, 25, 47; CLR 57; CWRI
　　5; JRDA; LAIT 4; MAICYA 1, 2; SATA
　　8, 70; SATA-Essay 103; SATA-Obit 132;
　　WYA
Holland, Marcus
　　See Caldwell, (Janet Miriam) Taylor
　　(Holland)
Hollander, John 1929- .... **CLC 2, 5, 8, 14**
　　See also CA 1-4R; CANR 1, 52; CP 7; DLB
　　5; SATA 13
Hollander, Paul
　　See Silverberg, Robert
Holleran, Andrew 1943(?)- .... **CLC 38**
　　See also Garber, Eric
　　See also CA 144; GLL 1
Holley, Marietta 1836(?)-1926 .... **TCLC 99**
　　See also CA 118; DLB 11
Hollinghurst, Alan 1954- .... **CLC 55, 91**
　　See also CA 114; CN 7; DLB 207; GLL 1
Hollis, Jim
　　See Summers, Hollis (Spurgeon, Jr.)
Holly, Buddy 1936-1959 .... **TCLC 65**
Holmes, Gordon
　　See Shiel, M(atthew) P(hipps)
Holmes, John
　　See Souster, (Holmes) Raymond
Holmes, John Clellon 1926-1988 ...... **CLC 56**
　　See also CA 9-12R; 125; CANR 4; DLB
　　16, 237
Holmes, Oliver Wendell, Jr.
　　1841-1935 .... **TCLC 77**
　　See also CA 114; 186

Holmes, Oliver Wendell
　　1809-1894 .... **NCLC 14, 81**
　　See also AMWS 1; CDALB 1640-1865;
　　DLB 1, 189, 235; EXPP; RGAL 4; SATA
　　34
Holmes, Raymond
　　See Souster, (Holmes) Raymond
Holt, Victoria
　　See Hibbert, Eleanor Alice Burford
　　See also BPFB 2
Holub, Miroslav 1923-1998 .... **CLC 4**
　　See also CA 21-24R; 169; CANR 10; CD-
　　WLB 4; CWW 2; DLB 232
Homer c. 8th cent. B.C.- .... **CMLC 1, 16; PC 23; WLCS**
　　See also AW 1; CDWLB 1; DA; DA3;
　　DAB; DAC; DAM MST, POET; DLB
　　176; EFS 1; LAIT 1; RGWL 2; TWA; WP
Hongo, Garrett Kaoru 1951- .... **PC 23**
　　See also CA 133; CAAS 22; CP 7; DLB
　　120; EXPP; RGAL 4
Honig, Edwin 1919- .... **CLC 33**
　　See also CA 5-8R; CAAS 8; CANR 4, 45;
　　CP 7; DLB 5
Hood, Hugh (John Blagdon) 1928- . **CLC 15, 28; SSC 42**
　　See also CA 49-52; CAAS 17; CANR 1,
　　33, 87; CN 7; DLB 53; RGSF 2
Hood, Thomas 1799-1845 .... **NCLC 16**
　　See also BRW 4; DLB 96; RGEL 2
Hooker, (Peter) Jeremy 1941- .... **CLC 43**
　　See also CA 77-80; CANR 22; CP 7; DLB
　　40
hooks, bell .... **CLC 94**
　　See also Watkins, Gloria Jean
　　See also DLB 246
Hope, A(lec) D(erwent) 1907-2000 .... **CLC 3, 51**
　　See also BRWS 7; CA 21-24R; 188; CANR
　　33, 74; MTCW 1, 2; PFS 8; RGEL 2
Hope, Anthony 1863-1933 .... **TCLC 83**
　　See also CA 157; DLB 153, 156; RGEL 2;
　　RHW
Hope, Brian
　　See Creasey, John
Hope, Christopher (David Tully)
　　1944- .... **CLC 52**
　　See also AFW; CA 106; CANR 47, 101;
　　CN 7; DLB 225; SATA 62
Hopkins, Gerard Manley
　　1844-1889 .... **NCLC 17; PC 15; WLC**
　　See also BRW 5; BRWR 2; CDBLB 1890-
　　1914; DA; DA3; DAB; DAC; DAM MST,
　　POET; DLB 35, 57; EXPP; PAB; RGEL
　　2; WP
Hopkins, John (Richard) 1931-1998 .. **CLC 4**
　　See also CA 85-88; 169; CBD; CD 5
Hopkins, Pauline Elizabeth
　　1859-1930 .... **TCLC 28; BLC 2**
　　See also AFAW 2; BW 2, 3; CA 141; CANR
　　82; DAM MULT; DLB 50
Hopkinson, Francis 1737-1791 .... **LC 25**
　　See also DLB 31; RGAL 4
Hopley-Woolrich, Cornell George 1903-1968
　　See Woolrich, Cornell
　　See also CA 13-14; CANR 58; CAP 1;
　　CMW 4; DLB 226; MTCW 2
Horace 65B.C.-8B.C. .... **CMLC 39**
　　See also AW 2; CDWLB 1; DLB 211;
　　RGWL 2
Horatio
　　See Proust, (Valentin-Louis-George-Eugene-
　　)Marcel
Horgan, Paul (George Vincent
　　O'Shaughnessy) 1903-1995 .. **CLC 9, 53**
　　See also BPFB 2; CA 13-16R; 147; CANR
　　9, 35; DAM NOV; DLB 102, 212; DLBY
　　1985; INT CANR-9; MTCW 1, 2; SATA
　　13; SATA-Obit 84; TCWW 2

Hunter, Mary
See Austin, Mary (Hunter)
Hunter, Mollie 1922- .... **CLC 21**
See also McIlwraith, Maureen Mollie
Hunter
See also AAYA 13; BYA 6; CANR 37, 78;
CLR 25; DLB 161; JRDA; MAICYA 1,
2; SAAS 7; SATA 54, 106; WYA; YAW
Hunter, Robert (?)-1734 .... **LC 7**
Hurston, Zora Neale 1891-1960 .. **CLC 7, 30,**
61; BLC 2; DC 12; SSC 4; WLCS
See also AAYA 15; AFAW 1, 2; AMWS 6;
BW 1, 3; BYA 12; CA 85-88; CANR 61;
CDALBS; DA; DA3; DAC; DAM MST,
MULT, NOV; DFS 6; DLB 51, 86; EXPN;
EXPS; FW; LAIT 3; MAWW; MTCW 1,
2; NFS 3; RGAL 4; RGSF 2; SSFS 1, 6,
11; TCLC 121; YAW
Husserl, E. G.
See Husserl, Edmund (Gustav Albrecht)
Husserl, Edmund (Gustav Albrecht)
1859-1938 .... **TCLC 100**
See also CA 116; 133
Huston, John (Marcellus)
1906-1987 .... **CLC 20**
See also CA 73-76; 123; CANR 34; DLB
26
Hustvedt, Siri 1955- .... **CLC 76**
See also CA 137
Hutten, Ulrich von 1488-1523 .... **LC 16**
See also DLB 179
Huxley, Aldous (Leonard)
1894-1963 .... **CLC 1, 3, 4, 5, 8, 11, 18,**
35, 79; SSC 39; WLC
See also AAYA 11; BPFB 2; BRW 7; CA
85-88; CANR 44, 99; CDBLB 1914-1945;
DA; DA3; DAB; DAC; DAM MST, NOV;
DLB 36, 100, 162, 195, 255; EXPN;
LAIT 5; MTCW 1, 2; NFS 6; RGEL 2;
SATA 63; SCFW 2; SFW 4; YAW
Huxley, T(homas) H(enry)
1825-1895 .... **NCLC 67**
See also DLB 57
Huysmans, Joris-Karl 1848-1907 ... **TCLC 7,**
69
See also CA 104; 165; DLB 123; EW 7;
GFL 1789 to the Present; RGWL 2
Hwang, David Henry 1957- .. **CLC 55; DC 4**
See also CA 127; 132; CAD; CANR 76;
CD 5; DA3; DAM DRAM; DFS 11; DLB
212, 228; INT CA-132; MTCW 2; RGAL
4
Hyde, Anthony 1946- .... **CLC 42**
See also Chase, Nicholas
See also CA 136; CCA 1
Hyde, Margaret O(ldroyd) 1917- ..... **CLC 21**
See also CA 1-4R; CANR 1, 36; CLR 23;
JRDA; MAICYA 1, 2; SAAS 8; SATA 1,
42, 76
Hynes, James 1956(?)- .... **CLC 65**
See also CA 164; CANR 105
Hypatia c. 370-415 .... **CMLC 35**
Ian, Janis 1951- .... **CLC 21**
See also CA 105; 187
Ibanez, Vicente Blasco
See Blasco Ibanez, Vicente
Ibarbourou, Juana de 1895-1979
See also HLCS 2; HW 1; LAW
Ibarguengoitia, Jorge 1928-1983 ...... **CLC 37**
See also CA 124; 113; HW 1
Ibsen, Henrik (Johan) 1828-1906 ... **TCLC 2,**
8, 16, 37, 52; DC 2; WLC
See also CA 104; 141; DA; DA3; DAB;
DAC; DAM DRAM, MST; DFS 15; EW
7; LAIT 2; RGWL 2
Ibuse, Masuji 1898-1993 .... **CLC 22**
See also Ibuse Masuji
See also CA 127; 141; MJW

Ibuse Masuji
See Ibuse, Masuji
See also DLB 180
Ichikawa, Kon 1915- .... **CLC 20**
See also CA 121
Ichiyo, Higuchi 1872-1896 .... **NCLC 49**
See also MJW
Idle, Eric 1943-2000 .... **CLC 21**
See also Monty Python
See also CA 116; CANR 35, 91
Ignatow, David 1914-1997 .... **CLC 4, 7, 14,**
40; PC 34
See also CA 9-12R; 162; CAAS 3; CANR
31, 57, 96; CP 7; DLB 5
Ignotus
See Strachey, (Giles) Lytton
Ihimaera, Witi 1944- .... **CLC 46**
See also CA 77-80; CN 7; RGSF 2
Ilf, Ilya .... **TCLC 21**
See also Fainzilberg, Ilya Arnoldovich
Illyes, Gyula 1902-1983 .... **PC 16**
See also CA 114; 109; CDWLB 4; DLB
215; RGWL 2
Immermann, Karl (Lebrecht)
1796-1840 .... **NCLC 4, 49**
See also DLB 133
Ince, Thomas H. 1882-1924 .... **TCLC 89**
See also IDFW 3, 4
Inchbald, Elizabeth 1753-1821 ...... **NCLC 62**
See also DLB 39, 89; RGEL 2
Inclan, Ramon (Maria) del Valle
See Valle-Inclan, Ramon (Maria) del
Infante, G(uillermo) Cabrera
See Cabrera Infante, G(uillermo)
Ingalls, Rachel (Holmes) 1940- .... **CLC 42**
See also CA 123; 127
Ingamells, Reginald Charles
See Ingamells, Rex
Ingamells, Rex 1913-1955 .... **TCLC 35**
See also CA 167; DLB 260
Inge, William (Motter) 1913-1973 ..... **CLC 1,**
8, 19
See also CA 9-12R; CDALB 1941-1968;
DA3; DAM DRAM; DFS 1, 5, 8; DLB 7,
249; MTCW 1, 2; RGAL 4
Ingelow, Jean 1820-1897 .... **NCLC 39, 107**
See also DLB 35, 163; FANT; SATA 33
Ingram, Willis J.
See Harris, Mark
Innaurato, Albert (F.) 1948(?)- ... **CLC 21, 60**
See also CA 115; 122; CAD; CANR 78;
CD 5; INT CA-122
Innes, Michael
See Stewart, J(ohn) I(nnes) M(ackintosh)
See also MSW
Innis, Harold Adams 1894-1952 .... **TCLC 77**
See also CA 181; DLB 88
Insluis, Alanus de
See Alain de Lille
Ionesco, Eugene 1912-1994 ... **CLC 1, 4, 6, 9,**
11, 15, 41, 86; DC 12; WLC
See also CA 9-12R; 144; CANR 55; CWW
2; DA; DA3; DAB; DAC; DAM DRAM,
MST; DFS 4, 9; EW 13; GFL 1789 to the
Present; MTCW 1, 2; RGWL 2; SATA 7;
SATA-Obit 79
Iqbal, Muhammad 1877-1938 .... **TCLC 28**
Ireland, Patrick
See O'Doherty, Brian
Irenaeus St. 130- .... **CMLC 42**
Iron, Ralph
See Schreiner, Olive (Emilie Albertina)

Irving, John (Winslow) 1942- ... **CLC 13, 23,**
38, 112
See also AAYA 8; AMWS 6; BEST 89:3;
BPFB 2; CA 25-28R; CANR 28, 73; CN
7; CPW; DA3; DAM NOV, POP; DLB 6;
DLBY 1982; MTCW 1, 2; NFS 12, 14;
RGAL 4
Irving, Washington 1783-1859 . **NCLC 2, 19,**
95; SSC 2, 37; WLC
See also AMW; CDALB 1640-1865; DA;
DA3; DAB; DAC; DAM MST; DLB 3,
11, 30, 59, 73, 74, 183, 186, 250, 254;
EXPS; LAIT 1; RGAL 4; RGSF 2; SSFS
1, 8; SUFW; WCH; YABC 2
Irwin, P. K.
See Page, P(atricia) K(athleen)
Isaacs, Jorge Ricardo 1837-1895 ... **NCLC 70**
See also LAW
Isaacs, Susan 1943- .... **CLC 32**
See also BEST 89:1; BPFB 2; CA 89-92;
CANR 20, 41, 65; CPW; DA3; DAM
POP; INT CANR-20; MTCW 1, 2
Isherwood, Christopher (William Bradshaw)
1904-1986 .... **CLC 1, 9, 11, 14, 44**
See also BRW 7; CA 13-16R; 117; CANR
35, 97; DA3; DAM DRAM, NOV; DLB
15, 195; DLBY 1986; IDTP; MTCW 1, 2;
RGAL 4; RGEL 2; WLIT 4
Ishiguro, Kazuo 1954- .. **CLC 27, 56, 59, 110**
See also BEST 90:2; BPFB 2; BRWS 4;
CA 120; CANR 49, 95; CN 7; DA3;
DAM NOV; DLB 194; MTCW 1, 2; NFS
13; WLIT 4
Ishikawa, Hakuhin
See Ishikawa, Takuboku
Ishikawa, Takuboku
1886(?)-1912 .... **TCLC 15; PC 10**
See also CA 113; 153; DAM POET
Iskander, Fazil 1929- .... **CLC 47**
See also CA 102
Isler, Alan (David) 1934- .... **CLC 91**
See also CA 156; CANR 105
Ivan IV 1530-1584 .... **LC 17**
Ivanov, Vyacheslav Ivanovich
1866-1949 .... **TCLC 33**
See also CA 122
Ivask, Ivar Vidrik 1927-1992 .... **CLC 14**
See also CA 37-40R; 139; CANR 24
Ives, Morgan
See Bradley, Marion Zimmer
See also GLL 1
Izumi Shikibu c. 973-c. 1034 .... **CMLC 33**
J .... **CLC 8**
See also CA 33-36R; CANR 28, 67; CN 7;
DLB 2, 28, 218; DLBY 1980
J .... **TCLC 123**
See also DLB 98
J. R. S.
See Gogarty, Oliver St. John
Jabran, Kahlil
See Gibran, Kahlil
Jabran, Khalil
See Gibran, Kahlil
Jackson, Daniel
See Wingrove, David (John)
Jackson, Helen Hunt 1830-1885 .... **NCLC 90**
See also DLB 42, 47, 186, 189; RGAL 4
Jackson, Jesse 1908-1983 .... **CLC 12**
See also BW 1; CA 25-28R; 109; CANR
27; CLR 28; CWRI 5; MAICYA 1, 2;
SATA 2, 29; SATA-Obit 48
Jackson, Laura (Riding) 1901-1991
See Riding, Laura
See also CA 65-68; 135; CANR 28, 89;
DLB 48
Jackson, Sam
See Trumbo, Dalton
Jackson, Sara
See Wingrove, David (John)

Kerouac, Jack 1922-1969 ...... **CLC 1, 2, 3, 5, 14, 29, 61; WLC**
See also Kerouac, Jean-Louis Lebris de
See also AAYA 25; AMWS 3; BPFB 2; CDALB 1941-1968; CPW; DLB 2, 16, 237; DLBD 3; DLBY 1995; GLL 1; MTCW 2; NFS 8; RGAL 4; TCLC 117; WP

Kerouac, Jean-Louis Lebris de 1922-1969
See Kerouac, Jack
See also AITN 1; CA 5-8R; 25-28R; CANR 26, 54, 95; DA; DA3; DAB; DAC; DAM MST, NOV, POET, POP; MTCW 1, 2

Kerr, Jean 1923- .... **CLC 22**
See also CA 5-8R; CANR 7; INT CANR-7

Kerr, M. E. .... **CLC 12, 35**
See also Meaker, Marijane (Agnes)
See also AAYA 2, 23; BYA 1, 7, 8; CLR 29; SAAS 1; WYA

Kerr, Robert .... **CLC 55**

Kerrigan, (Thomas) Anthony 1918- .. **CLC 4, 6**
See also CA 49-52; CAAS 11; CANR 4

Kerry, Lois
See Duncan, Lois

Kesey, Ken (Elton) 1935-2001 ... **CLC 1, 3, 6, 11, 46, 64; WLC**
See also AAYA 25; BPFB 2; CA 1-4R; CANR 22, 38, 66; CDALB 1968-1988; CN 7; CPW; DA; DA3; DAB; DAC; DAM MST, NOV, POP; DLB 2, 16, 206; EXPN; LAIT 4; MTCW 1, 2; NFS 2; RGAL 4; SATA 66; SATA-Obit 131; YAW

Kesselring, Joseph (Otto) 1902-1967 .... **CLC 45**
See also CA 150; DAM DRAM, MST

Kessler, Jascha (Frederick) 1929- ...... **CLC 4**
See also CA 17-20R; CANR 8, 48

Kettelkamp, Larry (Dale) 1933- ...... **CLC 12**
See also CA 29-32R; CANR 16; SAAS 3; SATA 2

Key, Ellen (Karolina Sofia) 1849-1926 .... **TCLC 65**
See also DLB 259

Keyber, Conny
See Fielding, Henry

Keyes, Daniel 1927- .... **CLC 80**
See also AAYA 23; BYA 11; CA 17-20R, 181; CAAE 181; CANR 10, 26, 54, 74; DA; DA3; DAC; DAM MST, NOV; EXPN; LAIT 4; MTCW 2; NFS 2; SATA 37; SFW 4

Keynes, John Maynard 1883-1946 .... **TCLC 64**
See also CA 114; 162, 163; DLBD 10; MTCW 2

Khanshendel, Chiron
See Rose, Wendy

Khayyam, Omar 1048-1131 ... **CMLC 11; PC 8**
See also Omar Khayyam
See also DA3; DAM POET

Kherdian, David 1931- .... **CLC 6, 9**
See also AAYA 42; CA 21-24R; CAAE 192; CAAS 2; CANR 39, 78; CLR 24; JRDA; LAIT 3; MAICYA 1, 2; SATA 16, 74; SATA-Essay 125

Khlebnikov, Velimir .... **TCLC 20**
See also Khlebnikov, Viktor Vladimirovich
See also EW 10; RGWL 2

Khlebnikov, Viktor Vladimirovich 1885-1922
See Khlebnikov, Velimir
See also CA 117

Khodasevich, Vladislav (Felitsianovich) 1886-1939 .... **TCLC 15**
See also CA 115

Kielland, Alexander Lange 1849-1906 .... **TCLC 5**
See also CA 104

Kiely, Benedict 1919- .... **CLC 23, 43**
See also CA 1-4R; CANR 2, 84; CN 7; DLB 15

Kienzle, William X(avier) 1928-2001 .... **CLC 25**
See also CA 93-96; CAAS 1; CANR 9, 31, 59; CMW 4; DA3; DAM POP; INT CANR-31; MSW; MTCW 1, 2

Kierkegaard, Soren 1813-1855 ...... **NCLC 34, 78**
See also EW 6

Kieslowski, Krzysztof 1941-1996 .... **CLC 120**
See also CA 147; 151

Killens, John Oliver 1916-1987 .... **CLC 10**
See also BW 2; CA 77-80; 123; CAAS 2; CANR 26; DLB 33

Killigrew, Anne 1660-1685 .... **LC 4, 73**
See also DLB 131

Killigrew, Thomas 1612-1683 .... **LC 57**
See also DLB 58; RGEL 2

Kim
See Simenon, Georges (Jacques Christian)

Kincaid, Jamaica 1949- ..... **CLC 43, 68, 137; BLC 2**
See also AAYA 13; AFAW 2; AMWS 7; BRWS 7; BW 2, 3; CA 125; CANR 47, 59, 95; CDALBS; CDWLB 3; CLR 63; CN 7; DA3; DAM MULT, NOV; DLB 157, 227; DNFS 1; EXPS; FW; MTCW 2; NCFS 1; NFS 3; SSFS 5, 7; YAW

King, Francis (Henry) 1923- .... **CLC 8, 53, 145**
See also CA 1-4R; CANR 1, 33, 86; CN 7; DAM NOV; DLB 15, 139; MTCW 1

King, Kennedy
See Brown, George Douglas

King, Martin Luther, Jr. 1929-1968 .... **CLC 83; BLC 2; WLCS**
See also BW 2, 3; CA 25-28; CANR 27, 44; CAP 2; DA; DA3; DAB; DAC; DAM MST, MULT; LAIT 5; MTCW 1, 2; SATA 14

King, Stephen (Edwin) 1947- .... **CLC 12, 26, 37, 61, 113; SSC 17**
See also AAYA 1, 17; AMWS 5; BEST 90:1; BPFB 2; CA 61-64; CANR 1, 30, 52, 76; CPW; DA3; DAM NOV, POP; DLB 143; DLBY 1980; HGG; JRDA; LAIT 5; MTCW 1, 2; RGAL 4; SATA 9, 55; SUFW; WYAS 1; YAW

King, Steve
See King, Stephen (Edwin)

King, Thomas 1943- .... **CLC 89**
See also CA 144; CANR 95; CCA 1; CN 7; DAC; DAM MULT; DLB 175; NNAL; SATA 96

Kingman, Lee .... **CLC 17**
See also Natti, (Mary) Lee
See also CWRI 5; SAAS 3; SATA 1, 67

Kingsley, Charles 1819-1875 .... **NCLC 35**
See also CLR 77; DLB 21, 32, 163, 178, 190; FANT; MAICYA 2; MAICYAS 1; RGEL 2; WCH; YABC 2

Kingsley, Henry 1830-1876 .... **NCLC 107**
See also DLB 21, 230; RGEL 2

Kingsley, Sidney 1906-1995 .... **CLC 44**
See also CA 85-88; 147; CAD; DFS 14; DLB 7; RGAL 4

Kingsolver, Barbara 1955- . **CLC 55, 81, 130**
See also AAYA 15; AMWS 7; CA 129; 134; CANR 60, 96; CDALBS; CPW; CSW; DA3; DAM POP; DLB 206; INT CA-134; LAIT 5; MTCW 2; NFS 5, 10, 12; RGAL 4

Kingston, Maxine (Ting Ting) Hong 1940- .... **CLC 12, 19, 58, 121; AAL; WLCS**
See also AAYA 8; AMWS 5; BPFB 2; CA 69-72; CANR 13, 38, 74, 87; CDALBS; CN 7; DA3; DAM MULT, NOV; DLB 173, 212; DLBY 1980; FW; INT CANR-13; LAIT 5; MAWW; MTCW 1, 2; NFS 6; RGAL 4; SATA 53; SSFS 3

Kinnell, Galway 1927- ..... **CLC 1, 2, 3, 5, 13, 29, 129; PC 26**
See also AMWS 3; CA 9-12R; CANR 10, 34, 66; CP 7; DLB 5; DLBY 1987; INT CANR-34; MTCW 1, 2; PAB; PFS 9; RGAL 4; WP

Kinsella, Thomas 1928- .... **CLC 4, 19, 138**
See also BRWS 5; CA 17-20R; CANR 15; CP 7; DLB 27; MTCW 1, 2; RGEL 2

Kinsella, W(illiam) P(atrick) 1935- . **CLC 27, 43**
See also AAYA 7; BPFB 2; CA 97-100; CAAS 7; CANR 21, 35, 66, 75; CN 7; CPW; DAC; DAM NOV, POP; FANT; INT CANR-21; LAIT 5; MTCW 1, 2; NFS 15; RGSF 2

Kinsey, Alfred C(harles) 1894-1956 .... **TCLC 91**
See also CA 115; 170; MTCW 2

Kipling, (Joseph) Rudyard 1865-1936 ... **TCLC 8, 17; PC 3; SSC 5, 54; WLC**
See also AAYA 32; BRW 6; BYA 4; CA 105; 120; CANR 33; CDBLB 1890-1914; CLR 39, 65; CWRI 5; DA; DA3; DAB; DAC; DAM MST, POET; DLB 19, 34, 141, 156; EXPS; FANT; LAIT 3; MAICYA 1, 2; MTCW 1, 2; RGEL 2; RGSF 2; SATA 100; SFW 4; SSFS 8; SUFW; WCH; WLIT 4; YABC 2

Kirk, Russell (Amos) 1918-1994 .. **TCLC 119**
See also AITN 1; CA 1-4R; 145; CAAS 9; CANR 1, 20, 60; HGG; INT CANR-20; MTCW 1, 2

Kirkland, Caroline M. 1801-1864 . **NCLC 85**
See also DLB 3, 73, 74, 250, 254; DLBD 13

Kirkup, James 1918- .... **CLC 1**
See also CA 1-4R; CAAS 4; CANR 2; CP 7; DLB 27; SATA 12

Kirkwood, James 1930(?)-1989 .... **CLC 9**
See also AITN 2; CA 1-4R; 128; CANR 6, 40; GLL 2

Kirshner, Sidney
See Kingsley, Sidney

Kis, Danilo 1935-1989 .... **CLC 57**
See also CA 109; 118; 129; CANR 61; CDWLB 4; DLB 181; MTCW 1; RGSF 2; RGWL 2

Kissinger, Henry A(lfred) 1923- ..... **CLC 137**
See also CA 1-4R; CANR 2, 33, 66, 109; MTCW 1

Kivi, Aleksis 1834-1872 .... **NCLC 30**

Kizer, Carolyn (Ashley) 1925- ... **CLC 15, 39, 80**
See also CA 65-68; CAAS 5; CANR 24, 70; CP 7; CWP; DAM POET; DLB 5, 169; MTCW 2

Klabund 1890-1928 .... **TCLC 44**
See also CA 162; DLB 66

Klappert, Peter 1942- .... **CLC 57**
See also CA 33-36R; CSW; DLB 5

Klein, A(braham) M(oses) 1909-1972 .... **CLC 19**
See also CA 101; 37-40R; DAB; DAC; DAM MST; DLB 68; RGEL 2

Klein, Joe
See Klein, Joseph

Klein, Joseph 1946- .... **CLC 154**
See also CA 85-88; CANR 55

Klein, Norma 1938-1989 .... **CLC 30**
See also AAYA 2, 35; BPFB 2; BYA 6, 7, 8; CA 41-44R; 128; CANR 15, 37; CLR 2, 19; INT CANR-15; JRDA; MAICYA 1, 2; SAAS 1; SATA 7, 57; WYA; YAW

Leffland, Ella 1931- .... **CLC 19**
  See also CA 29-32R; CANR 35, 78, 82;
  DLBY 1984; INT CANR-35; SATA 65
Leger, Alexis
  See Leger, (Marie-Rene Auguste) Alexis
  Saint-Leger
**Leger, (Marie-Rene Auguste) Alexis
  Saint-Leger** 1887-1975 .. **CLC 4, 11, 46;
  PC 23**
  See also Perse, Saint-John; Saint-John Perse
  See also CA 13-16R; 61-64; CANR 43;
  DAM POET; MTCW 1
Leger, Saintleger
  See Leger, (Marie-Rene Auguste) Alexis
  Saint-Leger
Le Guin, Ursula K(roeber) 1929- ..... **CLC 8,
  13, 22, 45, 71, 136; SSC 12**
  See also AAYA 9, 27; AITN 1; BPFB 2;
  BYA 5, 8, 11, 14; CA 21-24R; CANR 9,
  32, 52, 74; CDALB 1968-1988; CLR 3,
  28; CN 7; CPW; DA3; DAB; DAC; DAM
  MST, POP; DLB 8, 52, 256; EXPS;
  FANT; FW; INT CANR-32; JRDA; LAIT
  5; MAICYA 1, 2; MTCW 1, 2; NFS 6, 9;
  SATA 4, 52, 99; SCFW; SFW 4; SSFS 2;
  SUFW; WYA; YAW
Lehmann, Rosamond (Nina)
  1901-1990 .... **CLC 5**
  See also CA 77-80; 131; CANR 8, 73; DLB
  15; MTCW 2; RGEL 2; RHW
Leiber, Fritz (Reuter, Jr.)
  1910-1992 .... **CLC 25**
  See also BPFB 2; CA 45-48; 139; CANR 2,
  40, 86; DLB 8; FANT; HGG; MTCW 1,
  2; SATA 45; SATA-Obit 73; SCFW 2;
  SFW 4; SUFW
Leibniz, Gottfried Wilhelm von
  1646-1716 .... **LC 35**
  See also DLB 168
Leimbach, Martha 1963-
  See Leimbach, Marti
  See also CA 130
Leimbach, Marti .... **CLC 65**
  See also Leimbach, Martha
Leino, Eino .... **TCLC 24**
  See also Loennbohm, Armas Eino Leopold
Leiris, Michel (Julien) 1901-1990 ... **CLC 61**
  See also CA 119; 128; 132; GFL 1789 to
  the Present
Leithauser, Brad 1953- .... **CLC 27**
  See also CA 107; CANR 27, 81; CP 7; DLB
  120
Lelchuk, Alan 1938- .... **CLC 5**
  See also CA 45-48; CAAS 20; CANR 1,
  70; CN 7
Lem, Stanislaw 1921- ...... **CLC 8, 15, 40, 149**
  See also CA 105; CAAS 1; CANR 32;
  CWW 2; MTCW 1; SCFW 2; SFW 4
Lemann, Nancy 1956- .... **CLC 39**
  See also CA 118; 136
Lemonnier, (Antoine Louis) Camille
  1844-1913 .... **TCLC 22**
  See also CA 121
Lenau, Nikolaus 1802-1850 .... **NCLC 16**
L'Engle, Madeleine (Camp Franklin)
  1918- .... **CLC 12**
  See also AAYA 28; AITN 2; BPFB 2; BYA
  2, 4, 5, 7; CA 1-4R; CANR 3, 21, 39, 66,
  107; CLR 1, 14, 57; CPW; CWRI 5; DA3;
  DAM POP; DLB 52; JRDA; MAICYA 1,
  2; MTCW 1, 2; SAAS 15; SATA 1, 27,
  75, 128; SFW 4; WYA; YAW
Lengyel, Jozsef 1896-1975 .... **CLC 7**
  See also CA 85-88; 57-60; CANR 71;
  RGSF 2
Lenin 1870-1924
  See Lenin, V. I.
  See also CA 121; 168

Lenin, V. I. .... **TCLC 67**
  See also Lenin
Lennon, John (Ono) 1940-1980 .. **CLC 12, 35**
  See also CA 102; SATA 114
Lennox, Charlotte Ramsay
  1729(?)-1804 .... **NCLC 23**
  See also DLB 39; RGEL 2
Lentricchia, Frank, (Jr.) 1940- .... **CLC 34**
  See also CA 25-28R; CANR 19, 106; DLB
  246
Lenz, Gunter .... **CLC 65**
Lenz, Siegfried 1926- .... **CLC 27; SSC 33**
  See also CA 89-92; CANR 80; CWW 2;
  DLB 75; RGSF 2; RGWL 2
Leon, David
  See Jacob, (Cyprien-)Max
Leonard, Elmore (John, Jr.) 1925- . **CLC 28,
  34, 71, 120**
  See also AAYA 22; AITN 1; BEST 89:1,
  90:4; BPFB 2; CA 81-84; CANR 12, 28,
  53, 76, 96; CMW 4; CN 7; CPW; DA3;
  DAM POP; DLB 173, 226; INT CANR-
  28; MSW; MTCW 1, 2; RGAL 4; TCWW
  2
Leonard, Hugh .... **CLC 19**
  See also Byrne, John Keyes
  See also CBD; CD 5; DFS 13; DLB 13
Leonov, Leonid (Maximovich)
  1899-1994 .... **CLC 92**
  See also CA 129; CANR 74, 76; DAM
  NOV; MTCW 1, 2
Leopardi, (Conte) Giacomo
  1798-1837 .... **NCLC 22; PC 37**
  See also EW 5; RGWL 2; WP
Le Reveler
  See Artaud, Antonin (Marie Joseph)
Lerman, Eleanor 1952- .... **CLC 9**
  See also CA 85-88; CANR 69
Lerman, Rhoda 1936- .... **CLC 56**
  See also CA 49-52; CANR 70
Lermontov, Mikhail Iur'evich
  See Lermontov, Mikhail Yuryevich
  See also DLB 205
Lermontov, Mikhail Yuryevich
  1814-1841 .... **NCLC 5, 47; PC 18**
  See also Lermontov, Mikhail Iur'evich
  See also EW 6; RGWL 2
Leroux, Gaston 1868-1927 .... **TCLC 25**
  See also CA 108; 136; CANR 69; CMW 4;
  SATA 65
Lesage, Alain-Rene 1668-1747 .... **LC 2, 28**
  See also EW 3; GFL Beginnings to 1789;
  RGWL 2
Leskov, N(ikolai) S(emenovich) 1831-1895
  See Leskov, Nikolai (Semyonovich)
Leskov, Nikolai (Semyonovich)
  1831-1895 .... **NCLC 25; SSC 34**
  See also Leskov, Nikolai Semenovich
Leskov, Nikolai Semenovich
  See Leskov, Nikolai (Semyonovich)
  See also DLB 238
Lesser, Milton
  See Marlowe, Stephen
Lessing, Doris (May) 1919- ... **CLC 1, 2, 3, 6,
  10, 15, 22, 40, 94; SSC 6; WLCS**
  See also AFW; BRWS 1; CA 9-12R; CAAS
  14; CANR 33, 54, 76; CD 5; CDBLB
  1960 to Present; CN 7; DA; DA3; DAB;
  DAC; DAM MST, NOV; DLB 15, 139;
  DLBY 1985; EXPS; FW; LAIT 4; MTCW
  1, 2; RGEL 2; RGSF 2; SFW 4; SSFS 1,
  12; WLIT 2, 4
Lessing, Gotthold Ephraim 1729-1781 . **LC 8**
  See also CDWLB 2; DLB 97; EW 4;
  RGWL 2

Lester, Richard 1932- .... **CLC 20**
Levenson, Jay .... **CLC 70**
Lever, Charles (James)
  1806-1872 .... **NCLC 23**
  See also DLB 21; RGEL 2
Leverson, Ada 1865(?)-1936(?) .... **TCLC 18**
  See also Elaine
  See also CA 117; DLB 153; RGEL 2
Levertov, Denise 1923-1997 .. **CLC 1, 2, 3, 5,
  8, 15, 28, 66; PC 11**
  See also AMWS 3; CA 1-4R; 178; 163;
  CAAE 178; CAAS 19; CANR 3, 29, 50,
  108; CDALBS; CP 7; CWP; DAM POET;
  DLB 5, 165; EXPP; FW; INT CANR-29;
  MTCW 1, 2; PAB; PFS 7; RGAL 4; WP
Levi, Jonathan .... **CLC 76**
  See also CA 197
Levi, Peter (Chad Tigar)
  1931-2000 .... **CLC 41**
  See also CA 5-8R; 187; CANR 34, 80; CP
  7; DLB 40
Levi, Primo 1919-1987 . **CLC 37, 50; SSC 12**
  See also CA 13-16R; 122; CANR 12, 33,
  61, 70; DLB 177; MTCW 1, 2; RGWL 2;
  TCLC 109
Levin, Ira 1929- .... **CLC 3, 6**
  See also CA 21-24R; CANR 17, 44, 74;
  CMW 4; CN 7; CPW; DA3; DAM POP;
  HGG; MTCW 1, 2; SATA 66; SFW 4
Levin, Meyer 1905-1981 .... **CLC 7**
  See also AITN 1; CA 9-12R; 104; CANR
  15; DAM POP; DLB 9, 28; DLBY 1981;
  SATA 21; SATA-Obit 27
Levine, Norman 1924- .... **CLC 54**
  See also CA 73-76; CAAS 23; CANR 14,
  70; DLB 88
Levine, Philip 1928- .. **CLC 2, 4, 5, 9, 14, 33,
  118; PC 22**
  See also AMWS 5; CA 9-12R; CANR 9,
  37, 52; CP 7; DAM POET; DLB 5; PFS 8
Levinson, Deirdre 1931- .... **CLC 49**
  See also CA 73-76; CANR 70
Levi-Strauss, Claude 1908- .... **CLC 38**
  See also CA 1-4R; CANR 6, 32, 57; DLB
  242; GFL 1789 to the Present; MTCW 1,
  2
Levitin, Sonia (Wolff) 1934- .... **CLC 17**
  See also AAYA 13; CA 29-32R; CANR 14,
  32, 79; CLR 53; JRDA; MAICYA 1, 2;
  SAAS 2; SATA 4, 68, 119; SATA-Essay
  131; YAW
Levon, O. U.
  See Kesey, Ken (Elton)
Levy, Amy 1861-1889 .... **NCLC 59**
  See also DLB 156, 240
Lewes, George Henry 1817-1878 ... **NCLC 25**
  See also DLB 55, 144
Lewis, Alun 1915-1944 .... **TCLC 3; SSC 40**
  See also BRW 7; CA 104; 188; DLB 20,
  162; PAB; RGEL 2
Lewis, C. Day
  See Day Lewis, C(ecil)
Lewis, C(live) S(taples) 1898-1963 .... **CLC 1,
  3, 6, 14, 27, 124; WLC**
  See also AAYA 3, 39; BPFB 2; BRWS 3;
  CA 81-84; CANR 33, 71; CDBLB 1945-
  1960; CLR 3, 27; CWRI 5; DA; DA3;
  DAB; DAC; DAM MST, NOV, POP;
  DLB 15, 100, 160, 255; FANT; JRDA;
  MAICYA 1, 2; MTCW 1, 2; RGEL 2;
  SATA 13, 100; SCFW; SFW 4; SUFW;
  WCH; WYA; YAW
Lewis, Cecil Day
  See Day Lewis, C(ecil)
Lewis, Janet 1899-1998 .... **CLC 41**
  See also Winters, Janet Lewis
  See also CA 9-12R; 172; CANR 29, 63;
  CAP 1; CN 7; DLBY 1987; RHW;
  TCWW 2

MacCarthy, Sir (Charles Otto) Desmond
1877-1952 .... TCLC 36
See also CA 167

MacDiarmid, Hugh .... CLC 2, 4, 11, 19, 63;
PC 9
See also Grieve, C(hristopher) M(urray)
See also CDBLB 1945-1960; DLB 20;
RGEL 2

MacDonald, Anson
See Heinlein, Robert A(nson)

Macdonald, Cynthia 1928- .... CLC 13, 19
See also CA 49-52; CANR 4, 44; DLB 105

MacDonald, George 1824-1905 .... TCLC 9,
113
See also BYA 5; CA 106; 137; CANR 80;
CLR 67; DLB 18, 163, 178; FANT; MAI-
CYA 1, 2; RGEL 2; SATA 33, 100; SFW
4; SUFW; WCH

Macdonald, John
See Millar, Kenneth

MacDonald, John D(ann)
1916-1986 .... CLC 3, 27, 44
See also BPFB 2; CA 1-4R; 121; CANR 1,
19, 60; CMW 4; CPW; DAM NOV, POP;
DLB 8; DLBY 1986; MSW; MTCW 1, 2;
SFW 4

Macdonald, John Ross
See Millar, Kenneth

Macdonald, Ross ..... CLC 1, 2, 3, 14, 34, 41
See also Millar, Kenneth
See also AMWS 4; BPFB 2; DLBD 6;
MSW; RGAL 4

MacDougal, John
See Blish, James (Benjamin)

MacDougal, John
See Blish, James (Benjamin)

MacDowell, John
See Parks, Tim(othy Harold)

MacEwen, Gwendolyn (Margaret)
1941-1987 .... CLC 13, 55
See also CA 9-12R; 124; CANR 7, 22; DLB
53, 251; SATA 50; SATA-Obit 55

Macha, Karel Hynek 1810-1846 .... NCLC 46

Machado (y Ruiz), Antonio
1875-1939 .... TCLC 3
See also CA 104; 174; DLB 108; EW 9;
HW 2; RGWL 2

Machado de Assis, Joaquim Maria
1839-1908 ..... TCLC 10; BLC 2; HLCS
2; SSC 24
See also CA 107; 153; CANR 91; LAW;
RGSF 2; RGWL 2; WLIT 1

Machen, Arthur .... TCLC 4; SSC 20
See also Jones, Arthur Llewellyn
See also CA 179; DLB 156, 178; RGEL 2;
SUFW

Machiavelli, Niccolo 1469-1527 ..... LC 8, 36;
DC 16; WLCS
See also DA; DAB; DAC; DAM MST; EW
2; LAIT 1; NFS 9; RGWL 2

MacInnes, Colin 1914-1976 .... CLC 4, 23
See also CA 69-72; 65-68; CANR 21; DLB
14; MTCW 1, 2; RGEL 2; RHW

MacInnes, Helen (Clark)
1907-1985 .... CLC 27, 39
See also BPFB 2; CA 1-4R; 117; CANR 1,
28, 58; CMW 4; CPW; DAM POP; DLB
87; MSW; MTCW 1, 2; SATA 22; SATA-
Obit 44

Mackay, Mary 1855-1924
See Corelli, Marie
See also CA 118; 177; FANT; RHW

Mackenzie, Compton (Edward Montague)
1883-1972 .... CLC 18
See also CA 21-22; 37-40R; CAP 2; DLB
34, 100; RGEL 2; TCLC 116

Mackenzie, Henry 1745-1831 .... NCLC 41
See also DLB 39; RGEL 2

Mackintosh, Elizabeth 1896(?)-1952
See Tey, Josephine
See also CA 110; CMW 4

MacLaren, James
See Grieve, C(hristopher) M(urray)

Mac Laverty, Bernard 1942- .... CLC 31
See also CA 116; 118; CANR 43, 88; CN
7; INT CA-118; RGSF 2

MacLean, Alistair (Stuart)
1922(?)-1987 .... CLC 3, 13, 50, 63
See also CA 57-60; 121; CANR 28, 61;
CMW 4; CPW; DAM POP; MTCW 1;
SATA 23; SATA-Obit 50; TCWW 2

Maclean, Norman (Fitzroy)
1902-1990 .... CLC 78; SSC 13
See also CA 102; 132; CANR 49; CPW;
DAM POP; DLB 206; TCWW 2

MacLeish, Archibald 1892-1982 ... CLC 3, 8,
14, 68
See also AMW; CA 9-12R; 106; CAD;
CANR 33, 63; CDALBS; DAM POET;
DFS 15; DLB 4, 7, 45; DLBY 1982;
EXPP; MTCW 1, 2; PAB; PFS 5; RGAL
4

MacLennan, (John) Hugh
1907-1990 .... CLC 2, 14, 92
See also CA 5-8R; 142; CANR 33; DAC;
DAM MST; DLB 68; MTCW 1, 2; RGEL
2

MacLeod, Alistair 1936- .... CLC 56
See also CA 123; CCA 1; DAC; DAM
MST; DLB 60; MTCW 1; RGSF 2

Macleod, Fiona
See Sharp, William
See also RGEL 2; SUFW

MacNeice, (Frederick) Louis
1907-1963 .... CLC 1, 4, 10, 53
See also BRW 7; CA 85-88; CANR 61;
DAB; DAM POET; DLB 10, 20; MTCW
1, 2; RGEL 2

MacNeill, Dand
See Fraser, George MacDonald

Macpherson, James 1736-1796 .... LC 29
See also Ossian
See also DLB 109; RGEL 2

Macpherson, (Jean) Jay 1931- .... CLC 14
See also CA 5-8R; CANR 90; CP 7; CWP;
DLB 53

Macrobius fl. 430- .... CMLC 48

MacShane, Frank 1927-1999 .... CLC 39
See also CA 9-12R; 186; CANR 3, 33; DLB
111

Macumber, Mari
See Sandoz, Mari(e Susette)

Madach, Imre 1823-1864 .... NCLC 19

Madden, (Jerry) David 1933- ...... CLC 5, 15
See also CA 1-4R; CAAS 3; CANR 4, 45;
CN 7; CSW; DLB 6; MTCW 1

Maddern, Al(an)
See Ellison, Harlan (Jay)

Madhubuti, Haki R. 1942- . CLC 6, 73; BLC
2; PC 5
See also Lee, Don L.
See also BW 2, 3; CA 73-76; CANR 24,
51, 73; CP 7; CSW; DAM MULT, POET;
DLB 5, 41; DLBD 8; MTCW 2; RGAL 4

Maepenn, Hugh
See Kuttner, Henry

Maepenn, K. H.
See Kuttner, Henry

Maeterlinck, Maurice 1862-1949 ..... TCLC 3
See also CA 104; 136; CANR 80; DAM
DRAM; DLB 192; EW 8; GFL 1789 to
the Present; RGWL 2; SATA 66

Maginn, William 1794-1842 .... NCLC 8
See also DLB 110, 159

Mahapatra, Jayanta 1928- .... CLC 33
See also CA 73-76; CAAS 9; CANR 15,
33, 66, 87; CP 7; DAM MULT

Mahfouz, Naguib (Abdel Aziz Al-Sabilgi)
1911(?)- .... CLC 153
See also Mahfuz, Najib (Abdel Aziz al-
Sabilgi)
See also BEST 89:2; CA 128; CANR 55,
101; CWW 2; DA3; DAM NOV; MTCW
1, 2; RGWL 2; SSFS 9

Mahfuz, Najib (Abdel Aziz al-Sabilgi)
.... CLC 52, 55
See also Mahfouz, Naguib (Abdel Aziz Al-
Sabilgi)
See also AFW; DLBY 1988; RGSF 2;
WLIT 2

Mahon, Derek 1941- .... CLC 27
See also BRWS 6; CA 113; 128; CANR 88;
CP 7; DLB 40

Maiakovskii, Vladimir
See Mayakovski, Vladimir (Vladimirovich)
See also IDTP; RGWL 2

Mailer, Norman 1923- ... CLC 1, 2, 3, 4, 5, 8,
11, 14, 28, 39, 74, 111
See also AAYA 31; AITN 2; AMW; BPFB
2; CA 9-12R; CABS 1; CANR 28, 74, 77;
CDALB 1968-1988; CN 7; CPW; DA;
DA3; DAB; DAC; DAM MST, NOV,
POP; DLB 2, 16, 28, 185; DLBD 3;
DLBY 1980, 1983; MTCW 1, 2; NFS 10;
RGAL 4

Maillet, Antonine 1929- .... CLC 54, 118
See also CA 115; 120; CANR 46, 74, 77;
CCA 1; CWW 2; DAC; DLB 60; INT
120; MTCW 2

Mais, Roger 1905-1955 .... TCLC 8
See also BW 1, 3; CA 105; 124; CANR 82;
CDWLB 3; DLB 125; MTCW 1; RGEL 2

Maistre, Joseph 1753-1821 .... NCLC 37
See also GFL 1789 to the Present

Maitland, Frederic William
1850-1906 .... TCLC 65

Maitland, Sara (Louise) 1950- .... CLC 49
See also CA 69-72; CANR 13, 59; FW

Major, Clarence 1936- . CLC 3, 19, 48; BLC
2
See also AFAW 2; BW 2, 3; CA 21-24R;
CAAS 6; CANR 13, 25, 53, 82; CN 7;
CP 7; CSW; DAM MULT; DLB 33; MSW

Major, Kevin (Gerald) 1949- .... CLC 26
See also AAYA 16; CA 97-100; CANR 21,
38; CLR 11; DAC; DLB 60; INT CANR-
21; JRDA; MAICYA 1, 2; MAICYAS 1;
SATA 32, 82; WYA; YAW

Maki, James
See Ozu, Yasujiro

Malabaila, Damiano
See Levi, Primo

Malamud, Bernard 1914-1986 .. CLC 1, 2, 3,
5, 8, 9, 11, 18, 27, 44, 78, 85; SSC 15;
WLC
See also AAYA 16; AMWS 1; BPFB 2; CA
5-8R; 118; CABS 1; CANR 28, 62;
CDALB 1941-1968; CPW; DA; DA3;
DAB; DAC; DAM MST, NOV, POP;
DLB 2, 28, 152; DLBY 1980, 1986;
EXPS; LAIT 4; MTCW 1, 2; NFS 4, 9;
RGAL 4; RGSF 2; SSFS 8, 13

Malan, Herman
See Bosman, Herman Charles; Bosman,
Herman Charles

Malaparte, Curzio 1898-1957 .... TCLC 52

Malcolm, Dan
See Silverberg, Robert

Malcolm X .... CLC 82, 117; BLC 2; WLCS
See also Little, Malcolm
See also LAIT 5

Malherbe, Francois de 1555-1628 .... LC 5
See also GFL Beginnings to 1789

Mallarme, Stephane 1842-1898 ...... NCLC 4,
41; PC 4
See also DAM POET; DLB 217; EW 7;
GFL 1789 to the Present; RGWL 2

Mayo, Jim
See L'Amour, Louis (Dearborn)
See also TCWW 2
Maysles, Albert 1926- .... **CLC 16**
See also CA 29-32R
Maysles, David 1932-1987 .... **CLC 16**
See also CA 191
Mazer, Norma Fox 1931- .... **CLC 26**
See also AAYA 5, 36; BYA 1, 8; CA 69-72;
CANR 12, 32, 66; CLR 23; JRDA; MAI-
CYA 1, 2; SAAS 1; SATA 24, 67, 105;
WYA; YAW
Mazzini, Guiseppe 1805-1872 .... **NCLC 34**
McAlmon, Robert (Menzies)
1895-1956 .... **TCLC 97**
See also CA 107; 168; DLB 4, 45; DLBD
15; GLL 1
McAuley, James Phillip 1917-1976 .. **CLC 45**
See also CA 97-100; DLB 260; RGEL 2
McBain, Ed
See Hunter, Evan
See also MSW
McBrien, William (Augustine)
1930- .... **CLC 44**
See also CA 107; CANR 90
McCabe, Patrick 1955- .... **CLC 133**
See also CA 130; CANR 50, 90; CN 7;
DLB 194
McCaffrey, Anne (Inez) 1926- .... **CLC 17**
See also AAYA 6, 34; AITN 2; BEST 89:2;
BPFB 2; BYA 5; CA 25-28R; CANR 15,
35, 55, 96; CLR 49; CPW; DA3; DAM
NOV, POP; DLB 8; JRDA; MAICYA 1,
2; MTCW 1, 2; SAAS 11; SATA 8, 70,
116; SFW 4; WYA; YAW
McCall, Nathan 1955(?)- .... **CLC 86**
See also BW 3; CA 146; CANR 88
McCann, Arthur
See Campbell, John W(ood, Jr.)
McCann, Edson
See Pohl, Frederik
McCarthy, Charles, Jr. 1933-
See McCarthy, Cormac
See also CANR 42, 69, 101; CN 7; CPW;
CSW; DA3; DAM POP; MTCW 2
McCarthy, Cormac .... **CLC 4, 57, 59, 101**
See also McCarthy, Charles, Jr.
See also AAYA 41; AMWS 8; BPFB 2; CA
13-16R; CANR 10; DLB 6, 143, 256;
TCWW 2
McCarthy, Mary (Therese)
1912-1989 .. **CLC 1, 3, 5, 14, 24, 39, 59;
SSC 24**
See also AMW; BPFB 2; CA 5-8R; 129;
CANR 16, 50, 64; DA3; DLB 2; DLBY
1981; FW; INT CANR-16; MAWW;
MTCW 1, 2; RGAL 4
McCartney, (James) Paul 1942- . **CLC 12, 35**
See also CA 146
McCauley, Stephen (D.) 1955- .... **CLC 50**
See also CA 141
McClaren, Peter .... **CLC 70**
McClure, Michael (Thomas) 1932- ... **CLC 6,
10**
See also CA 21-24R; CAD; CANR 17, 46,
77; CD 5; CP 7; DLB 16; WP
McCorkle, Jill (Collins) 1958- .... **CLC 51**
See also CA 121; CSW; DLB 234; DLBY
1987
McCourt, Frank 1930- .... **CLC 109**
See also CA 157; CANR 97; NCFS 1
McCourt, James 1941- .... **CLC 5**
See also CA 57-60; CANR 98
McCourt, Malachy 1932- .... **CLC 119**
See also SATA 126
McCoy, Horace (Stanley)
1897-1955 .... **TCLC 28**
See also CA 108; 155; CMW 4; DLB 9

McCrae, John 1872-1918 .... **TCLC 12**
See also CA 109; DLB 92; PFS 5
McCreigh, James
See Pohl, Frederik
McCullers, (Lula) Carson (Smith)
1917-1967 .... **CLC 1, 4, 10, 12, 48, 100;
SSC 9, 24; WLC**
See also AAYA 21; AMW; BPFB 2; CA
5-8R; 25-28R; CABS 1, 3; CANR 18;
CDALB 1941-1968; DA; DA3; DAB;
DAC; DAM MST, NOV; DFS 5; DLB 2,
7, 173, 228; EXPS; FW; GLL 1; LAIT 3,
4; MAWW; MTCW 1, 2; NFS 6, 13;
RGAL 4; RGSF 2; SATA 27; SSFS 5;
YAW
McCulloch, John Tyler
See Burroughs, Edgar Rice
McCullough, Colleen 1938(?)- .. **CLC 27, 107**
See also AAYA 36; BPFB 2; CA 81-84;
CANR 17, 46, 67, 98; CPW; DA3; DAM
NOV, POP; MTCW 1, 2; RHW
McDermott, Alice 1953- .... **CLC 90**
See also CA 109; CANR 40, 90
McElroy, Joseph 1930- .... **CLC 5, 47**
See also CA 17-20R; CN 7
McEwan, Ian (Russell) 1948- ..... **CLC 13, 66**
See also BEST 90:4; BRWS 4; CA 61-64;
CANR 14, 41, 69, 87; CN 7; DAM NOV;
DLB 14, 194; HGG; MTCW 1, 2; RGSF
2
McFadden, David 1940- .... **CLC 48**
See also CA 104; CP 7; DLB 60; INT 104
McFarland, Dennis 1950- .... **CLC 65**
See also CA 165
McGahern, John 1934- ... **CLC 5, 9, 48, 156;
SSC 17**
See also CA 17-20R; CANR 29, 68; CN 7;
DLB 14, 231; MTCW 1
McGinley, Patrick (Anthony) 1937- . **CLC 41**
See also CA 120; 127; CANR 56; INT 127
McGinley, Phyllis 1905-1978 .... **CLC 14**
See also CA 9-12R; 77-80; CANR 19;
CWRI 5; DLB 11, 48; PFS 9, 13; SATA
2, 44; SATA-Obit 24
McGinniss, Joe 1942- .... **CLC 32**
See also AITN 2; BEST 89:2; CA 25-28R;
CANR 26, 70; CPW; DLB 185; INT
CANR-26
McGivern, Maureen Daly
See Daly, Maureen
McGrath, Patrick 1950- .... **CLC 55**
See also CA 136; CANR 65; CN 7; DLB
231; HGG
McGrath, Thomas (Matthew)
1916-1990 .... **CLC 28, 59**
See also AMWS 10; CA 9-12R; 132; CANR
6, 33, 95; DAM POET; MTCW 1; SATA
41; SATA-Obit 66
McGuane, Thomas (Francis III)
1939- .... **CLC 3, 7, 18, 45, 127**
See also AITN 2; BPFB 2; CA 49-52;
CANR 5, 24, 49, 94; CN 7; DLB 2, 212;
DLBY 1980; INT CANR-24; MTCW 1;
TCWW 2
McGuckian, Medbh 1950- ... **CLC 48; PC 27**
See also BRWS 5; CA 143; CP 7; CWP;
DAM POET; DLB 40
McHale, Tom 1942(?)-1982 .... **CLC 3, 5**
See also AITN 1; CA 77-80; 106
McIlvanney, William 1936- .... **CLC 42**
See also CA 25-28R; CANR 61; CMW 4;
DLB 14, 207
McIlwraith, Maureen Mollie Hunter
See Hunter, Mollie
See also SATA 2
McInerney, Jay 1955- .... **CLC 34, 112**
See also AAYA 18; BPFB 2; CA 116; 123;
CANR 45, 68; CN 7; CPW; DA3; DAM
POP; INT 123; MTCW 2

McIntyre, Vonda N(eel) 1948- .... **CLC 18**
See also CA 81-84; CANR 17, 34, 69;
MTCW 1; SFW 4; YAW
McKay, Claude .... **TCLC 7, 41; BLC 3; PC
2; WLC**
See also McKay, Festus Claudius
See also AFAW 1, 2; AMWS 10; DAB;
DLB 4, 45, 51, 117; EXPP; GLL 2; LAIT
3; PAB; PFS 4; RGAL 4; WP
McKay, Festus Claudius 1889-1948
See McKay, Claude
See also BW 1, 3; CA 104; 124; CANR 73;
DA; DAC; DAM MST, MULT, NOV,
POET; MTCW 1, 2
McKuen, Rod 1933- .... **CLC 1, 3**
See also AITN 1; CA 41-44R; CANR 40
McLoughlin, R. B.
See Mencken, H(enry) L(ouis)
McLuhan, (Herbert) Marshall
1911-1980 .... **CLC 37, 83**
See also CA 9-12R; 102; CANR 12, 34, 61;
DLB 88; INT CANR-12; MTCW 1, 2
McMillan, Terry (L.) 1951- .... **CLC 50, 61,
112; BLCS**
See also AAYA 21; BPFB 2; BW 2, 3; CA
140; CANR 60, 104; CPW; DA3; DAM
MULT, NOV, POP; MTCW 2; RGAL 4;
YAW
McMurtry, Larry (Jeff) 1936- .. **CLC 2, 3, 7,
11, 27, 44, 127**
See also AAYA 15; AITN 2; AMWS 5;
BEST 89:2; BPFB 2; CA 5-8R; CANR
19, 43, 64, 103; CDALB 1968-1988; CN
7; CPW; CSW; DA3; DAM NOV, POP;
DLB 2, 143, 256; DLBY 1980, 1987;
MTCW 1, 2; RGAL 4; TCWW 2
McNally, T. M. 1961- .... **CLC 82**
McNally, Terrence 1939- .... **CLC 4, 7, 41, 91**
See also CA 45-48; CAD; CANR 2, 56; CD
5; DA3; DAM DRAM; DLB 7, 249; GLL
1; MTCW 2
McNamer, Deirdre 1950- .... **CLC 70**
McNeal, Tom .... **CLC 119**
McNeile, Herman Cyril 1888-1937
See Sapper
See also CA 184; CMW 4; DLB 77
McNickle, (William) D'Arcy
1904-1977 .... **CLC 89**
See also CA 9-12R; 85-88; CANR 5, 45;
DAM MULT; DLB 175, 212; NNAL;
RGAL 4; SATA-Obit 22
McPhee, John (Angus) 1931- .... **CLC 36**
See also AMWS 3; ANW; BEST 90:1; CA
65-68; CANR 20, 46, 64, 69; CPW; DLB
185; MTCW 1, 2
McPherson, James Alan 1943- .. **CLC 19, 77;
BLCS**
See also BW 1, 3; CA 25-28R; CAAS 17;
CANR 24, 74; CN 7; CSW; DLB 38, 244;
MTCW 1, 2; RGAL 4; RGSF 2
McPherson, William (Alexander)
1933- .... **CLC 34**
See also CA 69-72; CANR 28; INT
CANR-28
McTaggart, J. McT. Ellis
See McTaggart, John McTaggart Ellis
McTaggart, John McTaggart Ellis
1866-1925 .... **TCLC 105**
See also CA 120; DLB 262
Mead, George Herbert 1873-1958 . **TCLC 89**
Mead, Margaret 1901-1978 .... **CLC 37**
See also AITN 1; CA 1-4R; 81-84; CANR
4; DA3; FW; MTCW 1, 2; SATA-Obit 20
Meaker, Marijane (Agnes) 1927-
See Kerr, M. E.
See also CA 107; CANR 37, 63; INT 107;
JRDA; MAICYA 1, 2; MAICYAS 1;
MTCW 1; SATA 20, 61, 99; SATA-Essay
111; YAW

Millhauser, Steven (Lewis) 1943- .... **CLC 21, 54, 109**
See also CA 110; 111; CANR 63; CN 7; DA3; DLB 2; FANT; INT CA-111; MTCW 2

Millin, Sarah Gertrude 1889-1968 ... **CLC 49**
See also CA 102; 93-96; DLB 225

Milne, A(lan) A(lexander)
1882-1956 .... **TCLC 6, 88**
See also BRWS 5; CA 104; 133; CLR 1, 26; CMW 4; CWRI 5; DA3; DAB; DAC; DAM MST; DLB 10, 77, 100, 160; FANT; MAICYA 1, 2; MTCW 1, 2; RGEL 2; SATA 100; WCH; YABC 1

Milner, Ron(ald) 1938- .... **CLC 56; BLC 3**
See also AITN 1; BW 1; CA 73-76; CAD; CANR 24, 81; CD 5; DAM MULT; DLB 38; MTCW 1

Milnes, Richard Monckton
1809-1885 .... **NCLC 61**
See also DLB 32, 184

Milosz, Czeslaw 1911- ...... **CLC 5, 11, 22, 31, 56, 82; PC 8; WLCS**
See also CA 81-84; CANR 23, 51, 91; CD-WLB 4; CWW 2; DA3; DAM MST, POET; DLB 215; EW 13; MTCW 1, 2; RGWL 2

Milton, John 1608-1674 ..... **LC 9, 43; PC 19, 29; WLC**
See also BRW 2; BRWR 2; CDBLB 1660-1789; DA; DA3; DAB; DAC; DAM MST, POET; DLB 131, 151; EFS 1; EXPP; LAIT 1; PAB; PFS 3; RGEL 2; TEA; WLIT 3; WP

Min, Anchee 1957- .... **CLC 86**
See also CA 146; CANR 94

Minehaha, Cornelius
See Wedekind, (Benjamin) Frank(lin)

Miner, Valerie 1947- .... **CLC 40**
See also CA 97-100; CANR 59; FW; GLL 2

Minimo, Duca
See D'Annunzio, Gabriele

Minot, Susan 1956- .... **CLC 44, 159**
See also AMWS 6; CA 134; CN 7

Minus, Ed 1938- .... **CLC 39**
See also CA 185

Miranda, Javier
See Bioy Casares, Adolfo
See also CWW 2

Mirbeau, Octave 1848-1917 .... **TCLC 55**
See also DLB 123, 192; GFL 1789 to the Present

Miro (Ferrer), Gabriel (Francisco Victor)
1879-1930 .... **TCLC 5**
See also CA 104; 185

Misharin, Alexandr .... **CLC 59**

Mishima, Yukio ... **CLC 2, 4, 6, 9, 27; DC 1; SSC 4**
See also Hiraoka, Kimitake
See also BPFB 2; DLB 182; GLL 1; MJW; MTCW 2; RGSF 2; RGWL 2; SSFS 5, 12

Mistral, Frederic 1830-1914 .... **TCLC 51**
See also CA 122; GFL 1789 to the Present

Mistral, Gabriela
See Godoy Alcayaga, Lucila
See also DNFS 1; LAW; RGWL 2; WP

Mistry, Rohinton 1952- .... **CLC 71**
See also CA 141; CANR 86; CCA 1; CN 7; DAC; SSFS 6

Mitchell, Clyde
See Ellison, Harlan (Jay); Silverberg, Robert

Mitchell, James Leslie 1901-1935
See Gibbon, Lewis Grassic
See also CA 104; 188; DLB 15

Mitchell, Joni 1943- .... **CLC 12**
See also CA 112; CCA 1

Mitchell, Joseph (Quincy)
1908-1996 .... **CLC 98**
See also CA 77-80; 152; CANR 69; CN 7; CSW; DLB 185; DLBY 1996

Mitchell, Margaret (Munnerlyn)
1900-1949 .... **TCLC 11**
See also AAYA 23; BPFB 2; BYA 1; CA 109; 125; CANR 55, 94; CDALBS; DA3; DAM NOV, POP; DLB 9; LAIT 2; MTCW 1, 2; NFS 9; RGAL 4; RHW; WYAS 1; YAW

Mitchell, Peggy
See Mitchell, Margaret (Munnerlyn)

Mitchell, S(ilas) Weir 1829-1914 .... **TCLC 36**
See also CA 165; DLB 202; RGAL 4

Mitchell, W(illiam) O(rmond)
1914-1998 .... **CLC 25**
See also CA 77-80; 165; CANR 15, 43; CN 7; DAC; DAM MST; DLB 88

Mitchell, William 1879-1936 ...... **TCLC 81**

Mitford, Mary Russell 1787-1855 ... **NCLC 4**
See also DLB 110, 116; RGEL 2

Mitford, Nancy 1904-1973 .... **CLC 44**
See also CA 9-12R; DLB 191; RGEL 2

Miyamoto, (Chujo) Yuriko
1899-1951 .... **TCLC 37**
See also Miyamoto Yuriko
See also CA 170, 174

Miyamoto Yuriko
See Miyamoto, (Chujo) Yuriko
See also DLB 180

Miyazawa, Kenji 1896-1933 .... **TCLC 76**
See also CA 157

Mizoguchi, Kenji 1898-1956 .... **TCLC 72**
See also CA 167

Mo, Timothy (Peter) 1950(?)- ... **CLC 46, 134**
See also CA 117; CN 7; DLB 194; MTCW 1; WLIT 4

Modarressi, Taghi (M.) 1931-1997 ... **CLC 44**
See also CA 121; 134; INT 134

Modiano, Patrick (Jean) 1945- .... **CLC 18**
See also CA 85-88; CANR 17, 40; CWW 2; DLB 83

Mofolo, Thomas (Mokopu)
1875(?) 1948 .... **TCLC 22; BLC 3**
See also AFW; CA 121; 153; CANR 83; DAM MULT; DLB 225; MTCW 2; WLIT 2

Mohr, Nicholasa 1938- .... **CLC 12; HLC 2**
See also AAYA 8; CA 49-52; CANR 1, 32, 64; CLR 22; DAM MULT; DLB 145; HW 1, 2; JRDA; LAIT 5; MAICYA 2; MAIC-YAS 1; RGAL 4; SAAS 8; SATA 8, 97; SATA-Essay 113; WYA; YAW

Mojtabai, A(nn) G(race) 1938- ..... **CLC 5, 9, 15, 29**
See also CA 85-88; CANR 88

Moliere 1622-1673 ..... **LC 10, 28, 64; DC 13; WLC**
See also DA; DA3; DAB; DAC; DAM DRAM, MST; DFS 13; EW 3; GFL Beginnings to 1789; RGWL 2

Molin, Charles
See Mayne, William (James Carter)

Molnar, Ferenc 1878-1952 .... **TCLC 20**
See also CA 109; 153; CANR 83; CDWLB 4; DAM DRAM; DLB 215; RGWL 2

Momaday, N(avarre) Scott 1934- ...... **CLC 2, 19, 85, 95, 160; PC 25; WLCS**
See also AAYA 11; AMWS 4; ANW; BPFB 2; CA 25-28R; CANR 14, 34, 68; CDALBS; CN 7; CPW; DA; DA3; DAB; DAC; DAM MST, MULT, NOV, POP; DLB 143, 175, 256; EXPP; INT CANR-14; LAIT 4; MTCW 1, 2; NFS 10; NNAL; PFS 2, 11; RGAL 4; SATA 48; SATA-Brief 30; WP; YAW

Monette, Paul 1945-1995 .... **CLC 82**
See also AMWS 10; CA 139; 147; CN 7; GLL 1

Monroe, Harriet 1860-1936 .... **TCLC 12**
See also CA 109; DLB 54, 91

Monroe, Lyle
See Heinlein, Robert A(nson)

Montagu, Elizabeth 1720-1800 .... **NCLC 7**
See also FW

Montagu, Mary (Pierrepont) Wortley
1689-1762 .... **LC 9, 57; PC 16**
See also DLB 95, 101; RGEL 2

Montagu, W. H.
See Coleridge, Samuel Taylor

Montague, John (Patrick) 1929- ..... **CLC 13, 46**
See also CA 9-12R; CANR 9, 69; CP 7; DLB 40; MTCW 1; PFS 12; RGEL 2

Montaigne, Michel (Eyquem) de
1533-1592 .... **LC 8; WLC**
See also DA; DAB; DAC; DAM MST; EW 2; GFL Beginnings to 1789; RGWL 2

Montale, Eugenio 1896-1981 ... **CLC 7, 9, 18; PC 13**
See also CA 17-20R; 104; CANR 30; DLB 114; EW 11; MTCW 1; RGWL 2

Montesquieu, Charles-Louis de Secondat
1689-1755 .... **LC 7, 69**
See also EW 3; GFL Beginnings to 1789

Montessori, Maria 1870-1952 ...... **TCLC 103**
See also CA 115; 147

Montgomery, (Robert) Bruce 1921(?)-1978
See Crispin, Edmund
See also CA 179; 104; CMW 4

Montgomery, L(ucy) M(aud)
1874-1942 .... **TCLC 51**
See also AAYA 12; BYA 1; CA 108; 137; CLR 8; DA3; DAC; DAM MST; DLB 92; DLBD 14; JRDA; MAICYA 1, 2; MTCW 2; RGEL 2; SATA 100; WCH; WYA; YABC 1

Montgomery, Marion H., Jr. 1925- .... **CLC 7**
See also AITN 1; CA 1-4R; CANR 3, 48; CSW; DLB 6

Montgomery, Max
See Davenport, Guy (Mattison, Jr.)

Montherlant, Henry (Milon) de
1896-1972 .... **CLC 8, 19**
See also CA 85-88; 37-40R; DAM DRAM; DLB 72; EW 11; GFL 1789 to the Present; MTCW 1

Monty Python
See Chapman, Graham; Cleese, John (Marwood); Gilliam, Terry (Vance); Idle, Eric; Jones, Terence Graham Parry; Palin, Michael (Edward)
See also AAYA 7

Moodie, Susanna (Strickland)
1803-1885 .... **NCLC 14, 113**
See also DLB 99

Moody, Hiram F. III 1961-
See Moody, Rick
See also CA 138; CANR 64

Moody, Minerva
See Alcott, Louisa May

Moody, Rick .... **CLC 147**
See also Moody, Hiram F. III

Moody, William Vaughan
1869-1910 .... **TCLC 105**
See also CA 110; 178; DLB 7, 54; RGAL 4

Mooney, Edward 1951-
See Mooney, Ted
See also CA 130

Mooney, Ted .... **CLC 25**
See also Mooney, Edward

Mrs. Belloc-Lowndes
See Lowndes, Marie Adelaide (Belloc)
M'Taggart, John M'Taggart Ellis
See McTaggart, John McTaggart Ellis
Mtwa, Percy (?)- .... **CLC 47**
Mueller, Lisel 1924- .... **CLC 13, 51; PC 33**
See also CA 93-96; CP 7; DLB 105; PFS 9, 13
Muggeridge, Malcolm (Thomas)
1903-1990 .... **TCLC 120**
See also AITN 1; CA 101; CANR 33, 63; MTCW 1, 2
Muir, Edwin 1887-1959 .... **TCLC 2, 87**
See also Moore, Edward
See also BRWS 6; CA 104; 193; DLB 20, 100, 191; RGEL 2
Muir, John 1838-1914 .... **TCLC 28**
See also AMWS 9; ANW; CA 165; DLB 186
Mujica Lainez, Manuel 1910-1984 ... **CLC 31**
See also Lainez, Manuel Mujica
See also CA 81-84; 112; CANR 32; HW 1
Mukherjee, Bharati 1940- .... **CLC 53, 115; AAL; SSC 38**
See also BEST 89:2; CA 107; CANR 45, 72; CN 7; DAM NOV; DLB 60, 218; DNFS 1, 2; FW; MTCW 1, 2; RGAL 4; RGSF 2; SSFS 7
Muldoon, Paul 1951- .... **CLC 32, 72**
See also BRWS 4; CA 113; 129; CANR 52, 91; CP 7; DAM POET; DLB 40; INT 129; PFS 7
Mulisch, Harry 1927- .... **CLC 42**
See also CA 9-12R; CANR 6, 26, 56
Mull, Martin 1943- .... **CLC 17**
See also CA 105
Muller, Wilhelm .... **NCLC 73**
Mulock, Dinah Maria
See Craik, Dinah Maria (Mulock)
See also RGEL 2
Munford, Robert 1737(?)-1783 .... **LC 5**
See also DLB 31
Mungo, Raymond 1946- .... **CLC 72**
See also CA 49-52; CANR 2
Munro, Alice 1931- .... **CLC 6, 10, 19, 50, 95; SSC 3; WLCS**
See also AITN 2; BPFB 2; CA 33-36R; CANR 33, 53, 75; CCA 1; CN 7; DA3; DAC; DAM MST, NOV; DLB 53; MTCW 1, 2; RGEL 2; RGSF 2; SATA 29; SSFS 5, 13
Munro, H(ector) H(ugh) 1870-1916
See Saki
See also CA 104; 130; CANR 104; CDBLB 1890-1914; DA; DA3; DAB; DAC; DAM MST, NOV; DLB 34, 162; EXPS; MTCW 1, 2; RGEL 2; SSFS 15; WLC
Murakami, Haruki 1949- .... **CLC 150**
See also Murakami Haruki
See also CA 165; CANR 102; MJW; SFW 4
Murakami Haruki
See Murakami, Haruki
See also DLB 182
Murasaki, Lady
See Murasaki Shikibu
Murasaki Shikibu 978(?)-1026(?) ... **CMLC 1**
See also EFS 2; RGWL 2
Murdoch, (Jean) Iris 1919-1999 ... **CLC 1, 2, 3, 4, 6, 8, 11, 15, 22, 31, 51**
See also BRWS 1; CA 13-16R; 179; CANR 8, 43, 68, 103; CDBLB 1960 to Present; CN 7; DA3; DAB; DAC; DAM MST, NOV; DLB 14, 194, 233; INT CANR-8; MTCW 1, 2; RGEL 2; TEA; WLIT 4
Murfree, Mary Noailles 1850-1922 ... **SSC 22**
See also CA 122; 176; DLB 12, 74; RGAL 4
Murnau, Friedrich Wilhelm
See Plumpe, Friedrich Wilhelm

Murphy, Richard 1927- .... **CLC 41**
See also BRWS 5; CA 29-32R; CP 7; DLB 40
Murphy, Sylvia 1937- .... **CLC 34**
See also CA 121
Murphy, Thomas (Bernard) 1935- ... **CLC 51**
See also CA 101
Murray, Albert L. 1916- .... **CLC 73**
See also BW 2; CA 49-52; CANR 26, 52, 78; CSW; DLB 38
Murray, James Augustus Henry
1837-1915 .... **TCLC 117**
Murray, Judith Sargent
1751-1820 .... **NCLC 63**
See also DLB 37, 200
Murray, Les(lie Allan) 1938- .... **CLC 40**
See also BRWS 7; CA 21-24R; CANR 11, 27, 56, 103; CP 7; DAM POET; DLBY 01; RGEL 2
Murry, J. Middleton
See Murry, John Middleton
Murry, John Middleton
1889-1957 .... **TCLC 16**
See also CA 118; DLB 149
Musgrave, Susan 1951- .... **CLC 13, 54**
See also CA 69-72; CANR 45, 84; CCA 1; CP 7; CWP
Musil, Robert (Edler von)
1880-1942 .... **TCLC 12, 68; SSC 18**
See also CA 109; CANR 55, 84; CDWLB 2; DLB 81, 124; EW 9; MTCW 2; RGSF 2; RGWL 2
Muske, Carol .... **CLC 90**
See also Muske-Dukes, Carol (Anne)
Muske-Dukes, Carol (Anne) 1945-
See Muske, Carol
See also CA 65-68; CANR 32, 70; CWP
Musset, (Louis Charles) Alfred de
1810-1857 .... **NCLC 7**
See also DLB 192, 217; EW 6; GFL 1789 to the Present; RGWL 2; TWA
Mussolini, Benito (Amilcare Andrea)
1883-1945 .... **TCLC 96**
See also CA 116
My Brother's Brother
See Chekhov, Anton (Pavlovich)
Myers, L(eopold) H(amilton)
1881-1944 .... **TCLC 59**
See also CA 157; DLB 15; RGEL 2
Myers, Walter Dean 1937- .. **CLC 35; BLC 3**
See also AAYA 4, 23; BW 2; BYA 6, 8, 11; CA 33-36R; CANR 20, 42, 67, 108; CLR 4, 16, 35; DAM MULT, NOV; DLB 33; INT CANR-20; JRDA; LAIT 5; MAICYA 1, 2; MAICYAS 1; MTCW 2; SAAS 2; SATA 41, 71, 109; SATA-Brief 27; WYA; YAW
Myers, Walter M.
See Myers, Walter Dean
Myles, Symon
See Follett, Ken(neth Martin)
Nabokov, Vladimir (Vladimirovich)
1899-1977 .... **CLC 1, 2, 3, 6, 8, 11, 15, 23, 44, 46, 64; SSC 11; WLC**
See also AMW; AMWR 1; BPFB 2; CA 5-8R; 69-72; CANR 20, 102; CDALB 1941-1968; DA; DA3; DAB; DAC; DAM MST, NOV; DLB 2, 244; DLBD 3; DLBY 1980, 1991; EXPS; MTCW 1, 2; NFS 9; RGAL 4; RGSF 2; SSFS 6, 15; TCLC 108
Naevius c. 265B.C.-201B.C. .... **CMLC 37**
See also DLB 211
Nagai, Kafu .... **TCLC 51**
See also Nagai, Sokichi
See also DLB 180
Nagai, Sokichi 1879-1959
See Nagai, Kafu
See also CA 117

Nagy, Laszlo 1925-1978 .... **CLC 7**
See also CA 129; 112
Naidu, Sarojini 1879-1949 .... **TCLC 80**
See also RGEL 2
Naipaul, Shiva(dhar Srinivasa)
1945-1985 .... **CLC 32, 39**
See also CA 110; 112; 116; CANR 33; DA3; DAM NOV; DLB 157; DLBY 1985; MTCW 1, 2
Naipaul, V(idiadhar) S(urajprasad)
1932- .... **CLC 4, 7, 9, 13, 18, 37, 105; SSC 38**
See also BPFB 2; BRWS 1; CA 1-4R; CANR 1, 33, 51, 91; CDBLB 1960 to Present; CDWLB 3; CN 7; DA3; DAB; DAC; DAM MST, NOV; DLB 125, 204, 207; DLBY 1985, 2001; MTCW 1, 2; RGEL 2; RGSF 2; WLIT 4
Nakos, Lilika 1899(?)- .... **CLC 29**
Narayan, R(asipuram) K(rishnaswami)
1906-2001 . **CLC 7, 28, 47, 121; SSC 25**
See also BPFB 2; CA 81-84; 196; CANR 33, 61; CN 7; DA3; DAM NOV; DNFS 1; MTCW 1, 2; RGEL 2; RGSF 2; SATA 62; SSFS 5
Nash, (Frederic) Ogden 1902-1971 . **CLC 23; PC 21**
See also CA 13-14; 29-32R; CANR 34, 61; CAP 1; DAM POET; DLB 11; MAICYA 1, 2; MTCW 1, 2; RGAL 4; SATA 2, 46; TCLC 109; WP
Nashe, Thomas 1567-1601(?) .... **LC 41**
See also DLB 167; RGEL 2
Nathan, Daniel
See Dannay, Frederic
Nathan, George Jean 1882-1958 .... **TCLC 18**
See also Hatteras, Owen
See also CA 114; 169; DLB 137
Natsume, Kinnosuke
See Natsume, Soseki
Natsume, Soseki 1867-1916 .... **TCLC 2, 10**
See also Natsume Soseki; Soseki
See also CA 104; 195; RGWL 2
Natsume Soseki
See Natsume, Soseki
See also DLB 180
Natti, (Mary) Lee 1919-
See Kingman, Lee
See also CA 5-8R; CANR 2
Navarre, Marguerite de
See de Navarre, Marguerite
Naylor, Gloria 1950- . **CLC 28, 52, 156; BLC 3; WLCS**
See also AAYA 6, 39; AFAW 1, 2; AMWS 8; BW 2, 3; CA 107; CANR 27, 51, 74; CN 7; CPW; DA; DA3; DAC; DAM MST, MULT, NOV, POP; DLB 173; FW; MTCW 1, 2; NFS 4, 7; RGAL 4
Neff, Debra .... **CLC 59**
Neihardt, John Gneisenau
1881-1973 .... **CLC 32**
See also CA 13-14; CANR 65; CAP 1; DLB 9, 54, 256; LAIT 2
Nekrasov, Nikolai Alekseevich
1821-1878 .... **NCLC 11**
Nelligan, Emile 1879-1941 .... **TCLC 14**
See also CA 114; DLB 92
Nelson, Willie 1933- .... **CLC 17**
See also CA 107
Nemerov, Howard (Stanley)
1920-1991 .... **CLC 2, 6, 9, 36; PC 24; TCLC 124**
See also AMW; CA 1-4R; 134; CABS 2; CANR 1, 27, 53; DAM POET; DLB 5, 6; DLBY 1983; INT CANR-27; MTCW 1, 2; PFS 10, 14; RGAL 4

Planche, James Robinson
    1796-1880 .... NCLC 42
    See also RGEL 2
Plant, Robert 1948- .... CLC 12
Plante, David (Robert) 1940- . CLC 7, 23, 38
    See also CA 37-40R; CANR 12, 36, 58, 82;
    CN 7; DAM NOV; DLBY 1983; INT
    CANR-12; MTCW 1
Plath, Sylvia 1932-1963 ..... CLC 1, 2, 3, 5, 9,
    11, 14, 17, 50, 51, 62, 111; PC 1, 37;
    WLC
    See also AAYA 13; AMWS 1; BPFB 3; CA
    19-20; CANR 34, 101; CAP 2; CDALB
    1941-1968; DA; DA3; DAB; DAC; DAM
    MST, POET; DLB 5, 6, 152; EXPN;
    EXPP; FW; LAIT 4; MAWW; MTCW 1,
    2; NFS 1; PAB; PFS 1, 15; RGAL 4;
    SATA 96; WP; YAW
Plato c. 428B.C.-347B.C. ... CMLC 8; WLCS
    See also AW 1; CDWLB 1; DA; DA3;
    DAB; DAC; DAM MST; DLB 176; LAIT
    1; RGWL 2
Platonov, Andrei
    See Klimentov, Andrei Platonovich
Platt, Kin 1911- .... CLC 26
    See also AAYA 11; CA 17-20R; CANR 11;
    JRDA; SAAS 17; SATA 21, 86; WYA
Plautus c. 254B.C.-c. 184B.C. ...... CMLC 24;
    DC 6
    See also AW 1; CDWLB 1; DLB 211;
    RGWL 2
Plick et Plock
    See Simenon, Georges (Jacques Christian)
Plieksans, Janis
    See Rainis, Janis
Plimpton, George (Ames) 1927- .... CLC 36
    See also AITN 1; CA 21-24R; CANR 32,
    70, 103; DLB 185, 241; MTCW 1, 2;
    SATA 10
Pliny the Elder c. 23-79 .... CMLC 23
    See also DLB 211
Plomer, William Charles Franklin
    1903-1973 .... CLC 4, 8
    See also AFW; CA 21-22; CANR 34; CAP
    2; DLB 20, 162, 191, 225; MTCW 1;
    RGEL 2; RGSF 2; SATA 24
Plotinus 204-270 .... CMLC 46
    See also CDWLB 1; DLB 176
Plowman, Piers
    See Kavanagh, Patrick (Joseph)
Plum, J.
    See Wodehouse, P(elham) G(renville)
Plumly, Stanley (Ross) 1939- .... CLC 33
    See also CA 108; 110; CANR 97; CP 7;
    DLB 5, 193; INT 110
Plumpe, Friedrich Wilhelm
    1888-1931 .... TCLC 53
    See also CA 112
Po Chu-i 772-846 .... CMLC 24
Poe, Edgar Allan 1809-1849 ..... NCLC 1, 16,
    55, 78, 94, 97; PC 1; SSC 1, 22, 34, 35,
    54; WLC
    See also AAYA 14; AMW; BPFB 3; BYA 5,
    11; CDALB 1640-1865; CMW 4; DA;
    DA3; DAB; DAC; DAM MST, POET;
    DLB 3, 59, 73, 74, 248, 254; EXPP;
    EXPS; HGG; LAIT 2; MSW; PAB; PFS
    1, 3, 9; RGAL 4; RGSF 2; SATA 23;
    SCFW 4; SFW 4; SSFS 2, 4, 7, 8; SUFW;
    WP; WYA
Poet of Titchfield Street, The
    See Pound, Ezra (Weston Loomis)
Pohl, Frederik 1919- .... CLC 18; SSC 25
    See also AAYA 24; CA 61-64; CAAE 188;
    CAAS 1; CANR 11, 37, 81; CN 7; DLB
    8; INT CANR-11; MTCW 1, 2; SATA 24;
    SCFW 2; SFW 4

Poirier, Louis 1910-
    See Gracq, Julien
    See also CA 122; 126; CWW 2
Poitier, Sidney 1927- .... CLC 26
    See also BW 1; CA 117; CANR 94
Polanski, Roman 1933- .... CLC 16
    See also CA 77-80
Poliakoff, Stephen 1952- .... CLC 38
    See also CA 106; CBD; CD 5; DLB 13
Police, The
    See Copeland, Stewart (Armstrong); Sum-
    mers, Andrew James; Sumner, Gordon
    Matthew
Polidori, John William 1795-1821 . NCLC 51
    See also DLB 116; HGG
Pollitt, Katha 1949- .... CLC 28, 122
    See also CA 120; 122; CANR 66, 108;
    MTCW 1, 2
Pollock, (Mary) Sharon 1936- .... CLC 50
    See also CA 141; CD 5; CWD; DAC; DAM
    DRAM, MST; DFS 3; DLB 60; FW
Polo, Marco 1254-1324 .... CMLC 15
Polonsky, Abraham (Lincoln)
    1910-1999 .... CLC 92
    See also CA 104; 187; DLB 26; INT 104
Polybius c. 200B.C.-c. 118B.C. ...... CMLC 17
    See also AW 1; DLB 176; RGWL 2
Pomerance, Bernard 1940- .... CLC 13
    See also CA 101; CAD; CANR 49; CD 5;
    DAM DRAM; DFS 9; LAIT 2
Ponge, Francis 1899-1988 .... CLC 6, 18
    See also CA 85-88; 126; CANR 40, 86;
    DAM POET; GFL 1789 to the Present;
    RGWL 2
Poniatowska, Elena 1933- . CLC 140; HLC 2
    See also CA 101; CANR 32, 66, 107; CD-
    WLB 3; DAM MULT; DLB 113; HW 1,
    2; LAWS 1; WLIT 1
Pontoppidan, Henrik 1857-1943 .... TCLC 29
    See also CA 170
Poole, Josephine .... CLC 17
    See also Helyar, Jane Penelope Josephine
    See also SAAS 2; SATA 5
Popa, Vasko 1922-1991 .... CLC 19
    See also CA 112; 148; CDWLB 4; DLB
    181; RGWL 2
Pope, Alexander 1688-1744 ...... LC 3, 58, 60,
    64; PC 26; WLC
    See also BRW 3; BRWR 1; CDBLB 1660-
    1789; DA; DA3; DAB; DAC; DAM MST,
    POET; DLB 95, 101, 213; EXPP; PAB;
    PFS 12; RGEL 2; WLIT 3; WP
Popov, Yevgeny .... CLC 59
Porter, Connie (Rose) 1959(?)- .... CLC 70
    See also BW 2, 3; CA 142; CANR 90, 109;
    SATA 81, 129
Porter, Gene(va Grace) Stratton .. TCLC 21
    See also Stratton-Porter, Gene(va Grace)
    See also BPFB 3; CA 112; CWRI 5; RHW
Porter, Katherine Anne 1890-1980 ... CLC 1,
    3, 7, 10, 13, 15, 27, 101; SSC 4, 31, 43
    See also AAYA 42; AITN 2; AMW; BPFB
    3; CA 1-4R; 101; CANR 1, 65; CDALBS;
    DA; DA3; DAB; DAC; DAM MST, NOV;
    DLB 4, 9, 102; DLBD 12; DLBY 1980;
    EXPS; LAIT 3; MAWW; MTCW 1, 2;
    NFS 14; RGAL 4; RGSF 2; SATA 39;
    SATA-Obit 23; SSFS 1, 8, 11
Porter, Peter (Neville Frederick)
    1929- .... CLC 5, 13, 33
    See also CA 85-88; CP 7; DLB 40
Porter, William Sydney 1862-1910
    See Henry, O.
    See also CA 104; 131; CDALB 1865-1917;
    DA; DA3; DAB; DAC; DAM MST; DLB
    12, 78, 79; MTCW 1, 2; YABC 2
Portillo (y Pacheco), Jose Lopez
    See Lopez Portillo (y Pacheco), Jose

Portillo Trambley, Estela 1927-1998
    See Trambley, Estela Portillo
    See also CANR 32; DAM MULT; DLB
    209; HLC 2; HW 1
Posse, Abel .... CLC 70
Post, Melville Davisson
    1869-1930 .... TCLC 39
    See also CA 110; 202; CMW 4
Potok, Chaim 1929-2002 ... CLC 2, 7, 14, 26,
    112
    See also AAYA 15; AITN 1, 2; BPFB 3;
    BYA 1; CA 17-20R; CANR 19, 35, 64,
    98; CN 7; DA3; DAM NOV; DLB 28,
    152; EXPN; INT CANR-19; LAIT 4;
    MTCW 1, 2; NFS 4; SATA 33, 106; YAW
Potter, Dennis (Christopher George)
    1935-1994 .... CLC 58, 86, 123
    See also CA 107; 145; CANR 33, 61; CBD;
    DLB 233; MTCW 1
Pound, Ezra (Weston Loomis)
    1885-1972 .. CLC 1, 2, 3, 4, 5, 7, 10, 13,
    18, 34, 48, 50, 112; PC 4; WLC
    See also AMW; AMWR 1; CA 5-8R; 37-
    40R; CANR 40; CDALB 1917-1929; DA;
    DA3; DAB; DAC; DAM MST, POET;
    DLB 4, 45, 63; DLBD 15; EFS 2; EXPP;
    MTCW 1, 2; PAB; PFS 2, 8; RGAL 4;
    WP
Povod, Reinaldo 1959-1994 .... CLC 44
    See also CA 136; 146; CANR 83
Powell, Adam Clayton, Jr.
    1908-1972 .... CLC 89; BLC 3
    See also BW 1, 3; CA 102; 33-36R; CANR
    86; DAM MULT
Powell, Anthony (Dymoke)
    1905-2000 ...... CLC 1, 3, 7, 9, 10, 31
    See also BRW 7; CA 1-4R; 189; CANR 1,
    32, 62, 107; CDBLB 1945-1960; CN 7;
    DLB 15; MTCW 1, 2; RGEL 2; TEA
Powell, Dawn 1896(?)-1965 .... CLC 66
    See also CA 5-8R; DLBY 1997
Powell, Padgett 1952- .... CLC 34
    See also CA 126; CANR 63, 101; CSW;
    DLB 234; DLBY 01
Powell, (Oval) Talmage 1920-2000
    See Queen, Ellery
    See also CA 5-8R; CANR 2, 80
Power, Susan 1961- .... CLC 91
    See also BYA 14; CA 160; NFS 11
Powers, J(ames) F(arl) 1917-1999 ..... CLC 1,
    4, 8, 57; SSC 4
    See also CA 1-4R; 181; CANR 2, 61; CN
    7; DLB 130; MTCW 1; RGAL 4; RGSF
    2
Powers, John J(ames) 1945-
    See Powers, John R.
    See also CA 69-72
Powers, John R. .... CLC 66
    See also Powers, John J(ames)
Powers, Richard (S.) 1957- .... CLC 93
    See also AMWS 9; BPFB 3; CA 148;
    CANR 80; CN 7
Pownall, David 1938- .... CLC 10
    See also CA 89-92, 180; CAAS 18; CANR
    49, 101; CBD; CD 5; CN 7; DLB 14
Powys, John Cowper 1872-1963 ... CLC 7, 9,
    15, 46, 125
    See also CA 85-88; CANR 106; DLB 15,
    255; FANT; MTCW 1, 2; RGEL 2; SUFW
Powys, T(heodore) F(rancis)
    1875-1953 .... TCLC 9
    See also CA 106; 189; DLB 36, 162; FANT;
    RGEL 2; SUFW
Prado (Calvo), Pedro 1886-1952 ... TCLC 75
    See also CA 131; HW 1; LAW
Prager, Emily 1952- .... CLC 56
Pratolini, Vasco 1913-1991 .... TCLC 124
    See also DLB 177; RGWL 2

Rabe, David (William) 1940- .. **CLC 4, 8, 33; DC 16**
See also CA 85-88; CABS 3; CAD; CANR 59; CD 5; DAM DRAM; DFS 3, 8, 13; DLB 7, 228

Rabelais, Francois 1494-1553 .... **LC 5, 60; WLC**
See also DA; DAB; DAC; DAM MST; EW 2; GFL Beginnings to 1789; RGWL 2

Rabinovitch, Sholem 1859-1916
See Aleichem, Sholem
See also CA 104

Rabinyan, Dorit 1972- .... **CLC 119**
See also CA 170

Rachilde
See Vallette, Marguerite Eymery

Racine, Jean 1639-1699 .... **LC 28**
See also DA3; DAB; DAM MST; EW 3; GFL Beginnings to 1789; RGWL 2

Radcliffe, Ann (Ward) 1764-1823 ... **NCLC 6, 55, 106**
See also DLB 39, 178; HGG; RGEL 2; SUFW; WLIT 3

Radclyffe-Hall, Marguerite
See Hall, (Marguerite) Radclyffe

Radiguet, Raymond 1903-1923 ...... **TCLC 29**
See also CA 162; DLB 65; GFL 1789 to the Present; RGWL 2

Radnoti, Miklos 1909-1944 .... **TCLC 16**
See also CA 118; CDWLB 4; DLB 215; RGWL 2

Rado, James 1939- .... **CLC 17**
See also CA 105

Radvanyi, Netty 1900-1983
See Seghers, Anna
See also CA 85-88; 110; CANR 82

Rae, Ben
See Griffiths, Trevor

Raeburn, John (Hay) 1941- .... **CLC 34**
See also CA 57-60

Ragni, Gerome 1942-1991 .... **CLC 17**
See also CA 105; 134

Rahv, Philip .... **CLC 24**
See also Greenberg, Ivan
See also DLB 137

Raimund, Ferdinand Jakob
1790-1836 .... **NCLC 69**
See also DLB 90

Raine, Craig (Anthony) 1944- .. **CLC 32, 103**
See also CA 108; CANR 29, 51, 103; CP 7; DLB 40; PFS 7

Raine, Kathleen (Jessie) 1908- ..... **CLC 7, 45**
See also CA 85-88; CANR 46, 109; CP 7; DLB 20; MTCW 1; RGEL 2

Rainis, Janis 1865-1929 .... **TCLC 29**
See also CA 170; CDWLB 4; DLB 220

Rakosi, Carl .... **CLC 47**
See also Rawley, Callman
See also CAAS 5; CP 7; DLB 193

Ralegh, Sir Walter
See Raleigh, Sir Walter
See also BRW 1; RGEL 2; WP

Raleigh, Richard
See Lovecraft, H(oward) P(hillips)

Raleigh, Sir Walter 1554(?)-1618 .... **LC 31, 39; PC 31**
See also Ralegh, Sir Walter
See also CDBLB Before 1660; DLB 172; EXPP; PFS 14; TEA

Rallentando, H. P.
See Sayers, Dorothy L(eigh)

Ramal, Walter
See de la Mare, Walter (John)

Ramana Maharshi 1879-1950 .... **TCLC 84**

Ramoacn y Cajal, Santiago
1852-1934 .... **TCLC 93**

Ramon, Juan
See Jimenez (Mantecon), Juan Ramon

Ramos, Graciliano 1892-1953 .... **TCLC 32**
See also CA 167; HW 2; LAW; WLIT 1

Rampersad, Arnold 1941- .... **CLC 44**
See also BW 2, 3; CA 127; 133; CANR 81; DLB 111; INT 133

Rampling, Anne
See Rice, Anne
See also GLL 2

Ramsay, Allan 1686(?)-1758 .... **LC 29**
See also DLB 95; RGEL 2

Ramsay, Jay
See Campbell, (John) Ramsey

Ramuz, Charles-Ferdinand
1878-1947 .... **TCLC 33**
See also CA 165

Rand, Ayn 1905-1982 ...... **CLC 3, 30, 44, 79; WLC**
See also AAYA 10; AMWS 4; BPFB 3; BYA 12; CA 13-16R; 105; CANR 27, 73; CDALBS; CPW; DA; DA3; DAC; DAM MST, NOV, POP; DLB 227; MTCW 1, 2; NFS 10; RGAL 4; SFW 4; YAW

Randall, Dudley (Felker) 1914-2000 . **CLC 1, 135; BLC 3**
See also BW 1, 3; CA 25-28R; 189; CANR 23, 82; DAM MULT; DLB 41; PFS 5

Randall, Robert
See Silverberg, Robert

Ranger, Ken
See Creasey, John

Rank, Otto 1884-1939 .... **TCLC 115**

Ransom, John Crowe 1888-1974 .. **CLC 2, 4, 5, 11, 24**
See also AMW; CA 5-8R; 49-52; CANR 6, 34; CDALBS; DA3; DAM POET; DLB 45, 63; EXPP; MTCW 1, 2; RGAL 4

Rao, Raja 1909- .... **CLC 25, 56**
See also CA 73-76; CANR 51; CN 7; DAM NOV; MTCW 1, 2; RGEL 2; RGSF 2

Raphael, Frederic (Michael) 1931- ... **CLC 2, 14**
See also CA 1-4R; CANR 1, 86; CN 7; DLB 14

Ratcliffe, James P.
See Mencken, H(enry) L(ouis)

Rathbone, Julian 1935- .... **CLC 41**
See also CA 101; CANR 34, 73

Rattigan, Terence (Mervyn)
1911-1977 .... **CLC 7; DC 18**
See also BRWS 7; CA 85-88; 73-76; CBD; CDBLB 1945-1960; DAM DRAM; DFS 8; DLB 13; IDFW 3, 4; MTCW 1, 2; RGEL 2

Ratushinskaya, Irina 1954- .... **CLC 54**
See also CA 129; CANR 68; CWW 2

Raven, Simon (Arthur Noel)
1927-2001 .... **CLC 14**
See also CA 81-84; 197; CANR 86; CN 7

Ravenna, Michael
See Welty, Eudora (Alice)

Rawley, Callman 1903-
See Rakosi, Carl
See also CA 21-24R; CANR 12, 32, 91

Rawlings, Marjorie Kinnan
1896-1953 .... **TCLC 4**
See also AAYA 20; AMWS 10; ANW; BPFB 3; BYA 3; CA 104; 137; CANR 74; CLR 63; DLB 9, 22, 102; DLBD 17; JRDA; MAICYA 1, 2; MTCW 2; RGAL 4; SATA 100; WCH; YABC 1; YAW

Ray, Satyajit 1921-1992 .... **CLC 16, 76**
See also CA 114; 137; DAM MULT

Read, Herbert Edward 1893-1968 ..... **CLC 4**
See also BRW 6; CA 85-88; 25-28R; DLB 20, 149; PAB; RGEL 2

Read, Piers Paul 1941- .... **CLC 4, 10, 25**
See also CA 21-24R; CANR 38, 86; CN 7; DLB 14; SATA 21

Reade, Charles 1814-1884 .... **NCLC 2, 74**
See also DLB 21; RGEL 2

Reade, Hamish
See Gray, Simon (James Holliday)

Reading, Peter 1946- .... **CLC 47**
See also CA 103; CANR 46, 96; CP 7; DLB 40

Reaney, James 1926- .... **CLC 13**
See also CA 41-44R; CAAS 15; CANR 42; CD 5; CP 7; DAC; DAM MST; DLB 68; RGEL 2; SATA 43

Rebreanu, Liviu 1885-1944 .... **TCLC 28**
See also CA 165; DLB 220

Rechy, John (Francisco) 1934- ...... **CLC 1, 7, 14, 18, 107; HLC 2**
See also CA 5-8R; CAAE 195; CAAS 4; CANR 6, 32, 64; CN 7; DAM MULT; DLB 122; DLBY 1982; HW 1, 2; INT CANR-6; RGAL 4

Redcam, Tom 1870-1933 .... **TCLC 25**

Reddin, Keith .... **CLC 67**
See also CAD

Redgrove, Peter (William) 1932- . **CLC 6, 41**
See also BRWS 6; CA 1-4R; CANR 3, 39, 77; CP 7; DLB 40

Redmon, Anne .... **CLC 22**
See also Nightingale, Anne Redmon
See also DLBY 1986

Reed, Eliot
See Ambler, Eric

Reed, Ishmael 1938- .. **CLC 2, 3, 5, 6, 13, 32, 60; BLC 3**
See also AFAW 1, 2; AMWS 10; BPFB 3; BW 2, 3; CA 21-24R; CANR 25, 48, 74; CN 7; CP 7; CSW; DA3; DAM MULT; DLB 2, 5, 33, 169, 227; DLBD 8; MSW; MTCW 1, 2; PFS 6; RGAL 4; TCWW 2

Reed, John (Silas) 1887-1920 .... **TCLC 9**
See also CA 106; 195

Reed, Lou .... **CLC 21**
See also Firbank, Louis

Reese, Lizette Woodworth 1856-1935 . **PC 29**
See also CA 180; DLB 54

Reeve, Clara 1729-1807 .... **NCLC 19**
See also DLB 39; RGEL 2

Reich, Wilhelm 1897-1957 .... **TCLC 57**
See also CA 199

Reid, Christopher (John) 1949- .... **CLC 33**
See also CA 140; CANR 89; CP 7; DLB 40

Reid, Desmond
See Moorcock, Michael (John)

Reid Banks, Lynne 1929-
See Banks, Lynne Reid
See also CA 1-4R; CANR 6, 22, 38, 87; CLR 24; CN 7; JRDA; MAICYA 1, 2; SATA 22, 75, 111; YAW

Reilly, William K.
See Creasey, John

Reiner, Max
See Caldwell, (Janet Miriam) Taylor (Holland)

Reis, Ricardo
See Pessoa, Fernando (Antonio Nogueira)

Remarque, Erich Maria 1898-1970 . **CLC 21**
See also AAYA 27; BPFB 3; CA 77-80; 29-32R; CDWLB 2; DA; DA3; DAB; DAC; DAM MST, NOV; DLB 56; EXPN; LAIT 3; MTCW 1, 2; NFS 4; RGWL 2

Remington, Frederic 1861-1909 ..... **TCLC 89**
See also CA 108; 169; DLB 12, 186, 188; SATA 41

Remizov, A.
See Remizov, Aleksei (Mikhailovich)

Remizov, A. M.
See Remizov, Aleksei (Mikhailovich)

Remizov, Aleksei (Mikhailovich)
1877-1957 .... **TCLC 27**
See also CA 125; 133

Robbins, Thomas Eugene 1936-
See Robbins, Tom
See also CA 81-84; CANR 29, 59, 95; CN 7; CPW; CSW; DA3; DAM NOV, POP; MTCW 1, 2

Robbins, Tom .... **CLC 9, 32, 64**
See also Robbins, Thomas Eugene
See also AAYA 32; AMWS 10; BEST 90:3; BPFB 3; DLBY 1980; MTCW 2

Robbins, Trina 1938- .... **CLC 21**
See also CA 128

Roberts, Charles G(eorge) D(ouglas)
1860-1943 .... **TCLC 8**
See also CA 105; 188; CLR 33; CWRI 5; DLB 92; RGEL 2; RGSF 2; SATA 88; SATA-Brief 29

Roberts, Elizabeth Madox
1886-1941 .... **TCLC 68**
See also CA 111; 166; CWRI 5; DLB 9, 54, 102; RGAL 4; RHW; SATA 33; SATA-Brief 27; WCH

Roberts, Kate 1891-1985 .... **CLC 15**
See also CA 107; 116

Roberts, Keith (John Kingston)
1935-2000 .... **CLC 14**
See also CA 25-28R; CANR 46; DLB 261; SFW 4

Roberts, Kenneth (Lewis)
1885-1957 .... **TCLC 23**
See also CA 109; 199; DLB 9; RGAL 4; RHW

Roberts, Michele (Brigitte) 1949- ..... **CLC 48**
See also CA 115; CANR 58; CN 7; DLB 231; FW

Robertson, Ellis
See Ellison, Harlan (Jay); Silverberg, Robert

Robertson, Thomas William
1829-1871 .... **NCLC 35**
See also Robertson, Tom
See also DAM DRAM

Robertson, Tom
See Robertson, Thomas William
See also RGEL 2

Robeson, Kenneth
See Dent, Lester

Robinson, Edwin Arlington
1869-1935 .... **TCLC 5, 101; PC 1, 35**
See also AMW; CA 104; 133; CDALB 1865-1917; DA; DAC; DAM MST, POET; DLB 54; EXPP; MTCW 1, 2; PAB; PFS 4; RGAL 4; WP

Robinson, Henry Crabb
1775-1867 .... **NCLC 15**
See also DLB 107

Robinson, Jill 1936- .... **CLC 10**
See also CA 102; INT 102

Robinson, Kim Stanley 1952- .... **CLC 34**
See also AAYA 26; CA 126; CN 7; SATA 109; SCFW 2; SFW 4

Robinson, Lloyd
See Silverberg, Robert

Robinson, Marilynne 1944- .... **CLC 25**
See also CA 116; CANR 80; CN 7; DLB 206

Robinson, Smokey .... **CLC 21**
See also Robinson, William, Jr.

Robinson, William, Jr. 1940-
See Robinson, Smokey
See also CA 116

Robison, Mary 1949- .... **CLC 42, 98**
See also CA 113; 116; CANR 87; CN 7; DLB 130; INT 116; RGSF 2

Rochester
See Wilmot, John
See also RGEL 2

Rod, Edouard 1857-1910 .... **TCLC 52**

Roddenberry, Eugene Wesley 1921-1991
See Roddenberry, Gene
See also CA 110; 135; CANR 37; SATA 45; SATA-Obit 69

Roddenberry, Gene .... **CLC 17**
See also Roddenberry, Eugene Wesley
See also AAYA 5; SATA-Obit 69

Rodgers, Mary 1931- .... **CLC 12**
See also BYA 5; CA 49-52; CANR 8, 55, 90; CLR 20; CWRI 5; INT CANR-8; JRDA; MAICYA 1, 2; SATA 8, 130

Rodgers, W(illiam) R(obert)
1909-1969 .... **CLC 7**
See also CA 85-88; DLB 20; RGEL 2

Rodman, Eric
See Silverberg, Robert

Rodman, Howard 1920(?)-1985 .... **CLC 65**
See also CA 118

Rodman, Maia
See Wojciechowska, Maia (Teresa)

Rodo, Jose Enrique 1871(?)-1917
See also CA 178; HLCS 2; HW 2; LAW

Rodolph, Utto
See Ouologuem, Yambo

Rodriguez, Claudio 1934-1999 .... **CLC 10**
See also CA 188; DLB 134

Rodriguez, Richard 1944- .... **CLC 155; HLC 2**
See also CA 110; CANR 66; DAM MULT; DLB 82, 256; HW 1, 2; LAIT 5; NCFS 3; WLIT 1

Roelvaag, O(le) E(dvart) 1876-1931
See Rolvaag, O(le) E(dvart)
See also CA 117; 171

Roethke, Theodore (Huebner)
1908-1963 .... **CLC 1, 3, 8, 11, 19, 46, 101; PC 15**
See also AMW; CA 81-84; CABS 2; CDALB 1941-1968; DA3; DAM POET; DLB 5, 206; EXPP; MTCW 1, 2; PAB; PFS 3; RGAL 4; WP

Rogers, Samuel 1763-1855 .... **NCLC 69**
See also DLB 93; RGEL 2

Rogers, Thomas Hunton 1927- .... **CLC 57**
See also CA 89-92; INT 89-92

Rogers, Will(iam Penn Adair)
1879-1935 .... **TCLC 8, 71**
See also CA 105; 144; DA3; DAM MULT; DLB 11; MTCW 2; NNAL

Rogin, Gilbert 1929- .... **CLC 18**
See also CA 65-68; CANR 15

Rohan, Koda
See Koda Shigeyuki

Rohlfs, Anna Katharine Green
See Green, Anna Katharine

Rohmer, Eric .... **CLC 16**
See also Scherer, Jean-Marie Maurice

Rohmer, Sax .... **TCLC 28**
See also Ward, Arthur Henry Sarsfield
See also DLB 70; MSW; SUFW

Roiphe, Anne (Richardson) 1935- .. **CLC 3, 9**
See also CA 89-92; CANR 45, 73; DLBY 1980; INT 89-92

Rojas, Fernando de 1475-1541 .... **LC 23; HLCS 1**
See also RGWL 2

Rojas, Gonzalo 1917-
See also CA 178; HLCS 2; HW 2; LAWS 1

Rolfe, Frederick (William Serafino Austin Lewis Mary) 1860-1913 .... **TCLC 12**
See also Corvo, Baron
See also CA 107; DLB 34, 156; RGEL 2

Rolland, Romain 1866-1944 .... **TCLC 23**
See also CA 118; 197; DLB 65; GFL 1789 to the Present; RGWL 2

Rolle, Richard c. 1300-c. 1349 ...... **CMLC 21**
See also DLB 146; RGEL 2

Rolvaag, O(le) E(dvart) .... **TCLC 17**
See also Roelvaag, O(le) E(dvart)
See also DLB 9, 212; NFS 5; RGAL 4

Romain Arnaud, Saint
See Aragon, Louis

Romains, Jules 1885-1972 .... **CLC 7**
See also CA 85-88; CANR 34; DLB 65; GFL 1789 to the Present; MTCW 1

Romero, Jose Ruben 1890-1952 .... **TCLC 14**
See also CA 114; 131; HW 1; LAW

Ronsard, Pierre de 1524-1585 . **LC 6, 54; PC 11**
See also EW 2; GFL Beginnings to 1789; RGWL 2

Rooke, Leon 1934- .... **CLC 25, 34**
See also CA 25-28R; CANR 23, 53; CCA 1; CPW; DAM POP

Roosevelt, Franklin Delano
1882-1945 .... **TCLC 93**
See also CA 116; 173; LAIT 3

Roosevelt, Theodore 1858-1919 ..... **TCLC 69**
See also CA 115; 170; DLB 47, 186

Roper, William 1498-1578 .... **LC 10**

Roquelaure, A. N.
See Rice, Anne

Rosa, Joao Guimaraes 1908-1967 ... **CLC 23; HLCS 1**
See also Guimaraes Rosa, Joao
See also CA 89-92; DLB 113; WLIT 1

Rose, Wendy 1948- .... **CLC 85; PC 13**
See also CA 53-56; CANR 5, 51; CWP; DAM MULT; DLB 175; NNAL; PFS 13; RGAL 4; SATA 12

Rosen, R. D.
See Rosen, Richard (Dean)

Rosen, Richard (Dean) 1949- .... **CLC 39**
See also CA 77-80; CANR 62; CMW 4; INT CANR-30

Rosenberg, Isaac 1890-1918 .... **TCLC 12**
See also BRW 6; CA 107; 188; DLB 20, 216; PAB; RGEL 2

Rosenblatt, Joe .... **CLC 15**
See also Rosenblatt, Joseph

Rosenblatt, Joseph 1933-
See Rosenblatt, Joe
See also CA 89-92; CP 7; INT 89-92

Rosenfeld, Samuel
See Tzara, Tristan

Rosenstock, Sami
See Tzara, Tristan

Rosenstock, Samuel
See Tzara, Tristan

Rosenthal, M(acha) L(ouis)
1917-1996 .... **CLC 28**
See also CA 1-4R; 152; CAAS 6; CANR 4, 51; CP 7; DLB 5; SATA 59

Ross, Barnaby
See Dannay, Frederic

Ross, Bernard L.
See Follett, Ken(neth Martin)

Ross, J. H.
See Lawrence, T(homas) E(dward)

Ross, John Hume
See Lawrence, T(homas) E(dward)

Ross, Martin 1862-1915
See Martin, Violet Florence
See also DLB 135; GLL 2; RGEL 2; RGSF 2

Ross, (James) Sinclair 1908-1996 ... **CLC 13; SSC 24**
See also CA 73-76; CANR 81; CN 7; DAC; DAM MST; DLB 88; RGEL 2; RGSF 2; TCWW 2

Sebestyen, Ouida 1924- .... **CLC 30**
See also AAYA 8; BYA 7; CA 107; CANR
40; CLR 17; JRDA; MAICYA 1, 2; SAAS
10; SATA 39; WYA; YAW

Secundus, H. Scriblerus
See Fielding, Henry

Sedges, John
See Buck, Pearl S(ydenstricker)

Sedgwick, Catharine Maria
1789-1867 .... **NCLC 19, 98**
See also DLB 1, 74, 183, 239, 243, 254;
RGAL 4

Seelye, John (Douglas) 1931- .... **CLC 7**
See also CA 97-100; CANR 70; INT 97-
100; TCWW 2

Seferiades, Giorgos Stylianou 1900-1971
See Seferis, George
See also CA 5-8R; 33-36R; CANR 5, 36;
MTCW 1

Seferis, George .... **CLC 5, 11**
See also Seferiades, Giorgos Stylianou
See also EW 12; RGWL 2

Segal, Erich (Wolf) 1937- .... **CLC 3, 10**
See also BEST 89:1; BPFB 3; CA 25-28R;
CANR 20, 36, 65; CPW; DAM POP;
DLBY 1986; INT CANR-20; MTCW 1

Seger, Bob 1945- .... **CLC 35**

Seghers, Anna -1983 .... **CLC 7**
See also Radvanyi, Netty
See also CDWLB 2; DLB 69

Seidel, Frederick (Lewis) 1936- .... **CLC 18**
See also CA 13-16R; CANR 8, 99; CP 7;
DLBY 1984

Seifert, Jaroslav 1901-1986 .. **CLC 34, 44, 93**
See also CA 127; CDWLB 4; DLB 215;
MTCW 1, 2

Sei Shonagon c. 966-1017(?) .... **CMLC 6**

Sejour, Victor 1817-1874 .... **DC 10**
See also DLB 50

Sejour Marcou et Ferrand, Juan Victor
See Sejour, Victor

Selby, Hubert, Jr. 1928- .... **CLC 1, 2, 4, 8;
SSC 20**
See also CA 13-16R; CANR 33, 85; CN 7;
DLB 2, 227

Selzer, Richard 1928- .... **CLC 74**
See also CA 65-68; CANR 14, 106

Sembene, Ousmane
See Ousmane, Sembene
See also AFW; CWW 2; WLIT 2

Senancour, Etienne Pivert de
1770-1846 .... **NCLC 16**
See also DLB 119; GFL 1789 to the Present

Sender, Ramon (Jose) 1902-1982 ...... **CLC 8;
HLC 2**
See also CA 5-8R; 105; CANR 8; DAM
MULT; HW 1; MTCW 1; RGWL 2

Seneca, Lucius Annaeus c. 4B.C.-c.
65 .... **CMLC 6; DC 5**
See also AW 2; CDWLB 1; DAM DRAM;
DLB 211; RGWL 2

Senghor, Leopold Sedar 1906-2001 . **CLC 54,
130; BLC 3; PC 25**
See also AFW; BW 2; CA 116; 125; CANR
47, 74; DAM MULT, POET; DNFS 2;
GFL 1789 to the Present; MTCW 1, 2;
TWA

Senna, Danzy 1970- .... **CLC 119**
See also CA 169

Serling, (Edward) Rod(man)
1924-1975 .... **CLC 30**
See also AAYA 14; AITN 1; CA 162; 57-
60; DLB 26; SFW 4

Serna, Ramon Gomez de la
See Gomez de la Serna, Ramon

Serpieres
See Guillevic, (Eugene)

Service, Robert
See Service, Robert W(illiam)
See also BYA 4; DAB; DLB 92

Service, Robert W(illiam)
1874(?)-1958 .... **TCLC 15; WLC**
See also Service, Robert
See also CA 115; 140; CANR 84; DA;
DAC; DAM MST, POET; PFS 10; RGEL
2; SATA 20

Seth, Vikram 1952- .... **CLC 43, 90**
See also CA 121; 127; CANR 50, 74; CN
7; CP 7; DA3; DAM MULT; DLB 120;
INT 127; MTCW 2

Seton, Cynthia Propper 1926-1982 .. **CLC 27**
See also CA 5-8R; 108; CANR 7

Seton, Ernest (Evan) Thompson
1860-1946 .... **TCLC 31**
See also ANW; BYA 3; CA 109; CLR 59;
DLB 92; DLBD 13; JRDA; SATA 18

Seton-Thompson, Ernest
See Seton, Ernest (Evan) Thompson

Settle, Mary Lee 1918- .... **CLC 19, 61**
See also BPFB 3; CA 89-92; CAAS 1;
CANR 44, 87; CN 7; CSW; DLB 6; INT
89-92

Seuphor, Michel
See Arp, Jean

Sevigne, Marie (de Rabutin-Chantal)
1626-1696 .... **LC 11**
See also GFL Beginnings to 1789

Sewall, Samuel 1652-1730 .... **LC 38**
See also DLB 24; RGAL 4

Sexton, Anne (Harvey) 1928-1974 ..... **CLC 2,
4, 6, 8, 10, 15, 53, 123; PC 2; WLC**
See also AMWS 2; CA 1-4R; 53-56; CABS
2; CANR 3, 36; CDALB 1941-1968; DA;
DA3; DAB; DAC; DAM MST, POET;
DLB 5, 169; EXPP; FW; MAWW;
MTCW 1, 2; PAB; PFS 4, 14; RGAL 4;
SATA 10

Shaara, Jeff 1952- .... **CLC 119**
See also CA 163; CANR 109

Shaara, Michael (Joseph, Jr.)
1929-1988 .... **CLC 15**
See also AITN 1; BPFB 3; CA 102; 125;
CANR 52, 85; DAM POP; DLBY 1983

Shackleton, C. C.
See Aldiss, Brian W(ilson)

Shacochis, Bob .... **CLC 39**
See also Shacochis, Robert G.

Shacochis, Robert G. 1951-
See Shacochis, Bob
See also CA 119; 124; CANR 100; INT 124

Shaffer, Anthony (Joshua)
1926-2001 .... **CLC 19**
See also CA 110; 116; 200; CBD; CD 5;
DAM DRAM; DFS 13; DLB 13

Shaffer, Peter (Levin) 1926- .. **CLC 5, 14, 18,
37, 60; DC 7**
See also BRWS 1; CA 25-28R; CANR 25,
47, 74; CBD; CD 5; CDBLB 1960 to
Present; DA3; DAB; DAM DRAM, MST;
DFS 5, 13; DLB 13, 233; MTCW 1, 2;
RGEL 2; TEA

Shakey, Bernard
See Young, Neil

Shalamov, Varlam (Tikhonovich)
1907(?)-1982 .... **CLC 18**
See also CA 129; 105; RGSF 2

Shamlu, Ahmad 1925-2000 .... **CLC 10**
See also CWW 2

Shammas, Anton 1951- .... **CLC 55**
See also CA 199

Shandling, Arline
See Berriault, Gina

Shange, Ntozake 1948- .... **CLC 8, 25, 38, 74,
126; BLC 3; DC 3**
See also AAYA 9; AFAW 1, 2; BW 2; CA
85-88; CABS 3; CAD; CANR 27, 48, 74;
CD 5; CP 7; CWD; CWP; DA3; DAM
DRAM, MULT; DFS 2, 11; DLB 38, 249;
FW; LAIT 5; MTCW 1, 2; NFS 11;
RGAL 4; YAW

Shanley, John Patrick 1950- .... **CLC 75**
See also CA 128; 133; CAD; CANR 83;
CD 5

Shapcott, Thomas W(illiam) 1935- .. **CLC 38**
See also CA 69-72; CANR 49, 83, 103; CP
7

Shapiro, Jane 1942- .... **CLC 76**
See also CA 196

Shapiro, Karl (Jay) 1913-2000 ...... **CLC 4, 8,
15, 53; PC 25**
See also AMWS 2; CA 1-4R; 188; CAAS
6; CANR 1, 36, 66; CP 7; DLB 48; EXPP;
MTCW 1, 2; PFS 3; RGAL 4

Sharp, William 1855-1905 .... **TCLC 39**
See also Macleod, Fiona
See also CA 160; DLB 156; RGEL 2

Sharpe, Thomas Ridley 1928-
See Sharpe, Tom
See also CA 114; 122; CANR 85; INT CA-
122

Sharpe, Tom .... **CLC 36**
See also Sharpe, Thomas Ridley
See also CN 7; DLB 14, 231

Shatrov, Mikhail .... **CLC 59**

Shaw, Bernard
See Shaw, George Bernard
See also DLB 190

Shaw, G. Bernard
See Shaw, George Bernard

Shaw, George Bernard 1856-1950 .. **TCLC 3,
9, 21, 45; WLC**
See also Shaw, Bernard
See also BRW 6; BRWR 2; CA 104; 128;
CDBLB 1914-1945; DA; DA3; DAB;
DAC; DAM DRAM, MST; DFS 1, 3, 6,
11; DLB 10, 57; LAIT 3; MTCW 1, 2;
RGEL 2; TEA; WLIT 4

Shaw, Henry Wheeler 1818-1885 .. **NCLC 15**
See also DLB 11; RGAL 4

Shaw, Irwin 1913-1984 .... **CLC 7, 23, 34**
See also AITN 1; BPFB 3; CA 13-16R; 112;
CANR 21; CDALB 1941-1968; CPW;
DAM DRAM, POP; DLB 6, 102; DLBY
1984; MTCW 1, 21

Shaw, Robert 1927-1978 .... **CLC 5**
See also AITN 1; CA 1-4R; 81-84; CANR
4; DLB 13, 14

Shaw, T. E.
See Lawrence, T(homas) E(dward)

Shawn, Wallace 1943- .... **CLC 41**
See also CA 112; CAD; CD 5

Shchedrin, N.
See Saltykov, Mikhail Evgrafovich

Shea, Lisa 1953- .... **CLC 86**
See also CA 147

Sheed, Wilfrid (John Joseph) 1930- . **CLC 2,
4, 10, 53**
See also CA 65-68; CANR 30, 66; CN 7;
DLB 6; MTCW 1, 2

Sheldon, Alice Hastings Bradley
1915(?)-1987
See Tiptree, James, Jr.
See also CA 108; 122; CANR 34; INT 108;
MTCW 1

Sheldon, John
See Bloch, Robert (Albert)

Sheldon, Walter J(ames) 1917-1996
See Queen, Ellery
See also AITN 1; CA 25-28R; CANR 10

Warung, Price .... **TCLC 45**
See also Astley, William
See also DLB 230; RGEL 2

Warwick, Jarvis
See Garner, Hugh
See also CCA 1

Washington, Alex
See Harris, Mark

Washington, Booker T(aliaferro)
1856-1915 .... **TCLC 10; BLC 3**
See also BW 1; CA 114; 125; DA3; DAM
MULT; LAIT 2; RGAL 4; SATA 28

Washington, George 1732-1799 .... **LC 25**
See also DLB 31

Wassermann, (Karl) Jakob
1873-1934 .... **TCLC 6**
See also CA 104; 163; DLB 66

Wasserstein, Wendy 1950- .. **CLC 32, 59, 90;
DC 4**
See also CA 121; 129; CABS 3; CAD;
CANR 53, 75; CD 5; CWD; DA3; DAM
DRAM; DFS 5; DLB 228; FW; INT CA-
129; MTCW 2; SATA 94

Waterhouse, Keith (Spencer) 1929- . **CLC 47**
See also CA 5-8R; CANR 38, 67, 109;
CBD; CN 7; DLB 13, 15; MTCW 1, 2

Waters, Frank (Joseph) 1902-1995 . **CLC 88**
See also CA 5-8R; 149; CAAS 13; CANR
3, 18, 63; DLB 212; DLBY 1986; RGAL
4; TCWW 2

Waters, Mary C. .... **CLC 70**

Waters, Roger 1944- .... **CLC 35**

Watkins, Frances Ellen
See Harper, Frances Ellen Watkins

Watkins, Gerrold
See Malzberg, Barry N(athaniel)

Watkins, Gloria Jean 1952(?)-
See hooks, bell
See also BW 2; CA 143; CANR 87; MTCW
2; SATA 115

Watkins, Paul 1964- .... **CLC 55**
See also CA 132; CANR 62, 98

Watkins, Vernon Phillips
1906-1967 .... **CLC 43**
See also CA 9-10; 25-28R; CAP 1; DLB
20; RGEL 2

Watson, Irving S.
See Mencken, H(enry) L(ouis)

Watson, John H.
See Farmer, Philip Jose

Watson, Richard F.
See Silverberg, Robert

Waugh, Auberon (Alexander)
1939-2001 .... **CLC 7**
See also CA 45-48; 192; CANR 6, 22, 92;
DLB 14, 194

Waugh, Evelyn (Arthur St. John)
1903-1966 .. **CLC 1, 3, 8, 13, 19, 27, 44,
107; SSC 41; WLC**
See also BPFB 3; BRW 7; CA 85-88; 25-
28R; CANR 22; CDBLB 1914-1945; DA;
DA3; DAB; DAC; DAM MST, NOV,
POP; DLB 15, 162, 195; MTCW 1, 2;
NFS 13; RGEL 2; RGSF 2; TEA; WLIT
4

Waugh, Harriet 1944- .... **CLC 6**
See also CA 85-88; CANR 22

Ways, C. R.
See Blount, Roy (Alton), Jr.

Waystaff, Simon
See Swift, Jonathan

Webb, Beatrice (Martha Potter)
1858-1943 .... **TCLC 22**
See also CA 117; 162; DLB 190; FW

Webb, Charles (Richard) 1939- .... **CLC 7**
See also CA 25-28R

Webb, James H(enry), Jr. 1946- ...... **CLC 22**
See also CA 81-84

Webb, Mary Gladys (Meredith)
1881-1927 .... **TCLC 24**
See also CA 182; 123; DLB 34; FW

Webb, Mrs. Sidney
See Webb, Beatrice (Martha Potter)

Webb, Phyllis 1927- .... **CLC 18**
See also CA 104; CANR 23; CCA 1; CP 7;
CWP; DLB 53

Webb, Sidney (James) 1859-1947 .. **TCLC 22**
See also CA 117; 163; DLB 190

Webber, Andrew Lloyd .... **CLC 21**
See Lloyd Webber, Andrew
See also DFS 7

Weber, Lenora Mattingly
1895-1971 .... **CLC 12**
See also CA 19-20; 29-32R; CAP 1; SATA
2; SATA-Obit 26

Weber, Max 1864-1920 .... **TCLC 69**
See also CA 109; 189

Webster, John 1580(?)-1634(?) .... **LC 33; DC
2; WLC**
See also BRW 2; CDBLB Before 1660; DA;
DAB; DAC; DAM DRAM, MST; DLB
58; IDTP; RGEL 2; WLIT 3

Webster, Noah 1758-1843 .... **NCLC 30**
See also DLB 1, 37, 42, 43, 73, 243

Wedekind, (Benjamin) Frank(lin)
1864-1918 .... **TCLC 7**
See also CA 104; 153; CDWLB 2; DAM
DRAM; DLB 118; EW 8; RGWL 2

Wehr, Demaris .... **CLC 65**

Weidman, Jerome 1913-1998 .... **CLC 7**
See also AITN 2; CA 1-4R; 171; CAD;
CANR 1; DLB 28

Weil, Simone (Adolphine)
1909-1943 .... **TCLC 23**
See also CA 117; 159; EW 12; FW; GFL
1789 to the Present; MTCW 2

Weininger, Otto 1880-1903 .... **TCLC 84**

Weinstein, Nathan
See West, Nathanael

Weinstein, Nathan von Wallenstein
See West, Nathanael

Weir, Peter (Lindsay) 1944- .... **CLC 20**
See also CA 113; 123

Weiss, Peter (Ulrich) 1916-1982 .. **CLC 3, 15,
51**
See also CA 45-48; 106; CANR 3; DAM
DRAM; DFS 3; DLB 69, 124; RGWL 2

Weiss, Theodore (Russell) 1916- ... **CLC 3, 8,
14**
See also CA 9-12R; CAAE 189; CAAS 2;
CANR 46, 94; CP 7; DLB 5

Welch, (Maurice) Denton
1915-1948 .... **TCLC 22**
See also CA 121; 148; RGEL 2

Welch, James 1940- .... **CLC 6, 14, 52**
See also CA 85-88; CANR 42, 66, 107; CN
7; CP 7; CPW; DAM MULT, POP; DLB
175, 256; NNAL; RGAL 4; TCWW 2

Weldon, Fay 1931- . **CLC 6, 9, 11, 19, 36, 59,
122**
See also BRWS 4; CA 21-24R; CANR 16,
46, 63, 97; CDBLB 1960 to Present; CN
7; CPW; DAM POP; DLB 14, 194; FW;
HGG; INT CANR-16; MTCW 1, 2; RGEL
2; RGSF 2

Wellek, Rene 1903-1995 .... **CLC 28**
See also CA 5-8R; 150; CAAS 7; CANR 8;
DLB 63; INT CANR-8

Weller, Michael 1942- .... **CLC 10, 53**
See also CA 85-88; CAD; CD 5

Weller, Paul 1958- .... **CLC 26**

Wellershoff, Dieter 1925- .... **CLC 46**
See also CA 89-92; CANR 16, 37

Welles, (George) Orson 1915-1985 .. **CLC 20,
80**
See also AAYA 40; CA 93-96; 117

Wellman, John McDowell 1945-
See Wellman, Mac
See also CA 166; CD 5

Wellman, Mac .... **CLC 65**
See also Wellman, John McDowell; Well-
man, John McDowell
See also CAD; RGAL 4

Wellman, Manly Wade 1903-1986 ... **CLC 49**
See also CA 1-4R; 118; CANR 6, 16, 44;
FANT; SATA 6; SATA-Obit 47; SFW 4;
SUFW

Wells, Carolyn 1869(?)-1942 .... **TCLC 35**
See also CA 113; 185; CMW 4; DLB 11

Wells, H(erbert) G(eorge)
1866-1946 .... **TCLC 6, 12, 19; SSC 6;
WLC**
See also AAYA 18; BPFB 3; BRW 6; CA
110; 121; CDBLB 1914-1945; CLR 64;
DA; DA3; DAB; DAC; DAM MST, NOV;
DLB 34, 70, 156, 178; EXPS; HGG;
LAIT 3; MTCW 1, 2; RGEL 2; RGSF 2;
SATA 20; SCFW; SFW 4; SSFS 3; SUFW;
WCH; WLIT 4; YAW

Wells, Rosemary 1943- .... **CLC 12**
See also AAYA 13; BYA 7, 8; CA 85-88;
CANR 48; CLR 16, 69; CWRI 5; MAI-
CYA 1, 2; SAAS 1; SATA 18, 69, 114;
YAW

Welsh, Irvine 1958- .... **CLC 144**
See also CA 173

Welty, Eudora (Alice) 1909-2001 .. **CLC 1, 2,
5, 14, 22, 33, 105; SSC 1, 27, 51; WLC**
See also AMW; AMWR 1; BPFB 3; CA
9-12R; 199; CABS 1; CANR 32, 65;
CDALB 1941-1968; CN 7; CSW; DA;
DA3; DAB; DAC; DAM MST, NOV;
DLB 2, 102, 143; DLBD 12; DLBY 1987,
2001; EXPS; HGG; LAIT 3; MAWW;
MTCW 1, 2; NFS 13, 15; RGAL 4; RGSF
2; RHW; SSFS 2, 10

Wen I-to 1899-1946 .... **TCLC 28**

Wentworth, Robert
See Hamilton, Edmond

Werfel, Franz (Viktor) 1890-1945 ... **TCLC 8**
See also CA 104; 161; DLB 81, 124;
RGWL 2

Wergeland, Henrik Arnold
1808-1845 .... **NCLC 5**

Wersba, Barbara 1932- .... **CLC 30**
See also AAYA 2, 30; BYA 6, 12, 13; CA
29-32R, 182; CAAE 182; CANR 16, 38;
CLR 3, 78; DLB 52; JRDA; MAICYA 1,
2; SAAS 2; SATA 1, 58; SATA-Essay 103;
WYA; YAW

Wertmueller, Lina 1928- .... **CLC 16**
See also CA 97-100; CANR 39, 78

Wescott, Glenway 1901-1987 .. **CLC 13; SSC
35**
See also CA 13-16R; 121; CANR 23, 70;
DLB 4, 9, 102; RGAL 4

Wesker, Arnold 1932- .... **CLC 3, 5, 42**
See also CA 1-4R; CAAS 7; CANR 1, 33;
CBD; CD 5; CDBLB 1960 to Present;
DAB; DAM DRAM; DLB 13; MTCW 1;
RGEL 2

Wesley, Richard (Errol) 1945- .... **CLC 7**
See also BW 1; CA 57-60; CAD; CANR
27; CD 5; DLB 38

Wessel, Johan Herman 1742-1785 .... **LC 7**

West, Anthony (Panther)
1914-1987 .... **CLC 50**
See also CA 45-48; 124; CANR 3, 19; DLB
15

West, C. P.
See Wodehouse, P(elham) G(renville)

West, Cornel (Ronald) 1953- .... **CLC 134;
BLCS**
See also CA 144; CANR 91; DLB 246

Wiley, Richard 1944- .... **CLC 44**
　　See also CA 121; 129; CANR 71
Wilhelm, Kate .... **CLC 7**
　　See also Wilhelm, Katie (Gertrude)
　　See also AAYA 20; CAAS 5; DLB 8; INT
　　CANR-17; SCFW 2
Wilhelm, Katie (Gertrude) 1928-
　　See Wilhelm, Kate
　　See also CA 37-40R; CANR 17, 36, 60, 94;
　　MTCW 1; SFW 4
Wilkins, Mary
　　See Freeman, Mary E(leanor) Wilkins
Willard, Nancy 1936- .... **CLC 7, 37**
　　See also BYA 5; CA 89-92; CANR 10, 39,
　　68, 107; CLR 5; CWP; CWRI 5; DLB 5,
　　52; FANT; MAICYA 1, 2; MTCW 1;
　　SATA 37, 71, 127; SATA-Brief 30
William of Ockham 1290-1349 ..... **CMLC 32**
Williams, Ben Ames 1889-1953 ..... **TCLC 89**
　　See also CA 183; DLB 102
Williams, C(harles) K(enneth)
　　1936- .... **CLC 33, 56, 148**
　　See also CA 37-40R; CAAS 26; CANR 57,
　　106; CP 7; DAM POET; DLB 5
Williams, Charles
　　See Collier, James Lincoln
Williams, Charles (Walter Stansby)
　　1886-1945 .... **TCLC 1, 11**
　　See also CA 104; 163; DLB 100, 153, 255;
　　FANT; RGEL 2; SUFW
Williams, (George) Emlyn
　　1905-1987 .... **CLC 15**
　　See also CA 104; 123; CANR 36; DAM
　　DRAM; DLB 10, 77; MTCW 1
Williams, Hank 1923-1953 .... **TCLC 81**
Williams, Hugo 1942- .... **CLC 42**
　　See also CA 17-20R; CANR 45; CP 7; DLB
　　40
Williams, J. Walker
　　See Wodehouse, P(elham) G(renville)
Williams, John A(lfred) 1925- ..... **CLC 5, 13;**
　　BLC 3
　　See also AFAW 2; BW 2, 3; CA 53-56;
　　CAAE 195; CAAS 3; CANR 6, 26, 51;
　　CN 7; CSW; DAM MULT; DLB 2, 33;
　　INT CANR-6; RGAL 4; SFW 4
Williams, Jonathan (Chamberlain)
　　1929- .... **CLC 13**
　　See also CA 9-12R; CAAS 12; CANR 8,
　　108; CP 7; DLB 5
Williams, Joy 1944- .... **CLC 31**
　　See also CA 41-44R; CANR 22, 48, 97
Williams, Norman 1952- .... **CLC 39**
　　See also CA 118
Williams, Sherley Anne 1944-1999 . **CLC 89;**
　　BLC 3
　　See also AFAW 2; BW 2, 3; CA 73-76; 185;
　　CANR 25, 82; DAM MULT, POET; DLB
　　41; INT CANR-25; SATA 78; SATA-Obit
　　116
Williams, Shirley
　　See Williams, Sherley Anne
Williams, Tennessee 1911-1983 . **CLC 1, 2, 5,**
　　7, 8, 11, 15, 19, 30, 39, 45, 71, 111; DC
　　4; WLC
　　See also AAYA 31; AITN 1, 2; AMW; CA
　　5-8R; 108; CABS 3; CAD; CANR 31;
　　CDALB 1941-1968; DA; DA3; DAB;
　　DAC; DAM DRAM, MST; DFS 1, 3, 7,
　　12; DLB 7; DLBD 4; DLBY 1983; GLL
　　1; LAIT 4; MTCW 1, 2; RGAL 4
Williams, Thomas (Alonzo)
　　1926-1990 .... **CLC 14**
　　See also CA 1-4R; 132; CANR 2
Williams, William C.
　　See Williams, William Carlos

Williams, William Carlos
　　1883-1963 .... **CLC 1, 2, 5, 9, 13, 22, 42,**
　　67; PC 7; SSC 31
　　See also AMW; AMWR 1; CA 89-92;
　　CANR 34; CDALB 1917-1929; DA;
　　DA3; DAB; DAC; DAM MST, POET;
　　DLB 4, 16, 54, 86; EXPP; MTCW 1, 2;
　　PAB; PFS 1, 6, 11; RGAL 4; RGSF 2;
　　WP
Williamson, David (Keith) 1942- ..... **CLC 56**
　　See also CA 103; CANR 41; CD 5
Williamson, Ellen Douglas 1905-1984
　　See Douglas, Ellen
　　See also CA 17-20R; 114; CANR 39
Williamson, Jack .... **CLC 29**
　　See also Williamson, John Stewart
　　See also CAAS 8; DLB 8; SCFW 2
Williamson, John Stewart 1908-
　　See Williamson, Jack
　　See also CA 17-20R; CANR 23, 70; SFW 4
Willie, Frederick
　　See Lovecraft, H(oward) P(hillips)
Willingham, Calder (Baynard, Jr.)
　　1922-1995 .... **CLC 5, 51**
　　See also CA 5-8R; 147; CANR 3; CSW;
　　DLB 2, 44; IDFW 3, 4; MTCW 1
Willis, Charles
　　See Clarke, Arthur C(harles)
Willy
　　See Colette, (Sidonie-Gabrielle)
Willy, Colette
　　See Colette, (Sidonie-Gabrielle)
　　See also GLL 1
Wilmot, John 1647-1680 .... **LC 75**
　　See also Rochester
　　See also BRW 2; DLB 131; PAB
Wilson, A(ndrew) N(orman) 1950- .. **CLC 33**
　　See also BRWS 6; CA 112; 122; CN 7;
　　DLB 14, 155, 194; MTCW 2
Wilson, Angus (Frank Johnstone)
　　1913-1991 .. **CLC 2, 3, 5, 25, 34; SSC 21**
　　See also BRWS 1; CA 5-8R; 134; CANR
　　21; DLB 15, 139, 155; MTCW 1, 2;
　　RGEL 2; RGSF 2
Wilson, August 1945- . **CLC 39, 50, 63, 118;**
　　BLC 3; DC 2; WLCS
　　See also AAYA 16; AFAW 2; AMWS 8; BW
　　2, 3; CA 115; 122; CAD; CANR 42, 54,
　　76; CD 5; DA; DA3; DAB; DAC; DAM
　　DRAM, MST, MULT; DFS 15; DLB 228;
　　LAIT 4; MTCW 1, 2; RGAL 4
Wilson, Brian 1942- .... **CLC 12**
Wilson, Colin 1931- .... **CLC 3, 14**
　　See also CA 1-4R; CAAS 5; CANR 1, 22,
　　33, 77; CMW 4; CN 7; DLB 14, 194;
　　HGG; MTCW 1; SFW 4
Wilson, Dirk
　　See Pohl, Frederik
Wilson, Edmund 1895-1972 .. **CLC 1, 2, 3, 8,**
　　24
　　See also AMW; CA 1-4R; 37-40R; CANR
　　1, 46; DLB 63; MTCW 1, 2; RGAL 4
Wilson, Ethel Davis (Bryant)
　　1888(?)-1980 .... **CLC 13**
　　See also CA 102; DAC; DAM POET; DLB
　　68; MTCW 1; RGEL 2
Wilson, Harriet
　　See Wilson, Harriet E. Adams
　　See also DLB 239
Wilson, Harriet E. Adams
　　1827(?)-1863(?) .... **NCLC 78; BLC 3**
　　See also Wilson, Harriet
　　See also DAM MULT; DLB 50, 243
Wilson, John 1785-1854 .... **NCLC 5**
Wilson, John (Anthony) Burgess 1917-1993
　　See Burgess, Anthony
　　See also CA 1-4R; 143; CANR 2, 46; DA3;
　　DAC; DAM NOV; MTCW 1, 2; NFS 15

Wilson, Lanford 1937- .... **CLC 7, 14, 36**
　　See also CA 17-20R; CABS 3; CAD; CANR
　　45, 96; CD 5; DAM DRAM; DFS 4, 9,
　　12; DLB 7; TUS
Wilson, Robert M. 1944- .... **CLC 7, 9**
　　See also CA 49-52; CAD; CANR 2, 41; CD
　　5; MTCW 1
Wilson, Robert McLiam 1964- .... **CLC 59**
　　See also CA 132
Wilson, Sloan 1920- .... **CLC 32**
　　See also CA 1-4R; CANR 1, 44; CN 7
Wilson, Snoo 1948- .... **CLC 33**
　　See also CA 69-72; CBD; CD 5
Wilson, William S(mith) 1932- .... **CLC 49**
　　See also CA 81-84
Wilson, (Thomas) Woodrow
　　1856-1924 .... **TCLC 79**
　　See also CA 166; DLB 47
Wilson and Warnke eds. .... **CLC 65**
Winchilsea, Anne (Kingsmill) Finch
　　1661-1720
　　See Finch, Anne
　　See also RGEL 2
Windham, Basil
　　See Wodehouse, P(elham) G(renville)
Wingrove, David (John) 1954- .... **CLC 68**
　　See also CA 133; SFW 4
Winnemucca, Sarah 1844-1891 ..... **NCLC 79**
　　See also DAM MULT; DLB 175; NNAL;
　　RGAL 4
Winstanley, Gerrard 1609-1676 .... **LC 52**
Wintergreen, Jane
　　See Duncan, Sara Jeannette
Winters, Janet Lewis .... **CLC 41**
　　See also Lewis, Janet
　　See also DLBY 1987
Winters, (Arthur) Yvor 1900-1968 .... **CLC 4,**
　　8, 32
　　See also AMWS 2; CA 11-12; 25-28R; CAP
　　1; DLB 48; MTCW 1; RGAL 4
Winterson, Jeanette 1959- .... **CLC 64, 158**
　　See also BRWS 4; CA 136; CANR 58; CN
　　7; CPW; DA3; DAM POP; DLB 207, 261;
　　FANT; FW; GLL 1; MTCW 2; RHW
Winthrop, John 1588-1649 .... **LC 31**
　　See also DLB 24, 30
Wirth, Louis 1897-1952 .... **TCLC 92**
Wiseman, Frederick 1930- .... **CLC 20**
　　See also CA 159
Wister, Owen 1860-1938 .... **TCLC 21**
　　See also BPFB 3; CA 108; 162; DLB 9, 78,
　　186; RGAL 4; SATA 62; TCWW 2
Witkacy
　　See Witkiewicz, Stanislaw Ignacy
Witkiewicz, Stanislaw Ignacy
　　1885-1939 .... **TCLC 8**
　　See also CA 105; 162; CDWLB 4; DLB
　　215; EW 10; RGWL 2; SFW 4
Wittgenstein, Ludwig (Josef Johann)
　　1889-1951 .... **TCLC 59**
　　See also CA 113; 164; DLB 262; MTCW 2
Wittig, Monique 1935(?)- .... **CLC 22**
　　See also CA 116; 135; CWW 2; DLB 83;
　　FW; GLL 1
Wittlin, Jozef 1896-1976 .... **CLC 25**
　　See also CA 49-52; 65-68; CANR 3
Wodehouse, P(elham) G(renville)
　　1881-1975 ... **CLC 1, 2, 5, 10, 22; SSC 2**
　　See also AITN 2; BRWS 3; CA 45-48; 57-
　　60; CANR 3, 33; CDBLB 1914-1945;
　　CPW 1; DA3; DAB; DAC; DAM NOV;
　　DLB 34, 162; MTCW 1, 2; RGEL 2;
　　RGSF 2; SATA 22; SSFS 10; TCLC 108
Woiwode, L.
　　See Woiwode, Larry (Alfred)
Woiwode, Larry (Alfred) 1941- ... **CLC 6, 10**
　　See also CA 73-76; CANR 16, 94; CN 7;
　　DLB 6; INT CANR-16

Author Index

Literary Criticism Series
Cumulative Topic Index

This index lists all topic entries in Gale's *Classical and Medieval Literature Criticism, Contemporary Literary Criticism, Drama Criticism, Literature Criticism from 1400 to 1800, Nineteenth-Century Literature Criticism,* and *Twentieth-Century Literary Criticism.*

LITERARY CRITICISM SERIES

Topic Index

DC Cumulative Nationality Index

DC-18 Title Index

ISBN 0-7876-5947-9

90000